A PEOPLE AND A NATION

Brief Edition

m

668 792 18

A PEOPLE

A

HOUGHTON MIFFLIN COMPANY   •   BOSTON
Dallas   Geneva, Illinois   Princeton, New Jersey   Palo Alto

AND A NATION
History of the United States

Brief Edition
Second Edition

MARY BETH NORTON
Cornell University

DAVID M. KATZMAN
University of Kansas

PAUL D. ESCOTT
University of North Carolina, Charlotte

HOWARD P. CHUDACOFF
Brown University

THOMAS G. PATERSON
University of Connecticut

WILLIAM M. TUTTLE, JR.
University of Kansas

and

WILLIAM J. BROPHY
Stephen F. Austin State University

Copyright © 1988 by Houghton Mifflin Company. All rights reserved. No
part of this work may be reproduced or transmitted in any form or by any
means, electronic or mechanical, including photocopying and recording, or
by any information storage or retrieval system without the prior written
permission of Houghton Mifflin Company unless such copying is expressly permitted by federal copyright law. Address inquiries to Permissions, Houghton Mifflin
Company, One Beacon Street, Boston, Massachusetts 02108.

Printed in the U.S.A.
Library of Congress Catalog Card Number: 87-80263
ISBN: 0-395-35952-X
     EFGHIJ-DOH-9543210-89

CONTENTS

Chapter 1

THE MEETING OF OLD WORLD AND NEW, 1492–1650

Chapter 2

AMERICAN SOCIETY TAKES SHAPE, 1650–1720

Chapter 3

GROWTH AND DIVERSITY, 1720–1770

Chapter 4

SEVERING THE BONDS OF EMPIRE, 1754–1774

Chapter 5

A REVOLUTION, INDEED, 1775–1783

Chapter 6

FORGING A NATIONAL REPUBLIC, 1776–1789

Chapter 7

POLITICS AND SOCIETY IN THE EARLY REPUBLIC, 1790–1800

Chapter 8

THE EMPIRE OF LIBERTY, 1801–1824

Chapter 9

A MARKET AND INDUSTRIAL ECONOMY, 1800–1860

Chapter 10

TOWARD GREATER DIVERSITY: THE AMERICAN PEOPLE, 1800–1860

Chapter 15

RECONSTRUCTION BY TRIAL AND ERROR, 1865–1877

Chapter 16

TRANSFORMATION OF THE WEST AND SOUTH, 1877–1892

Chapter 17

THE MACHINE AGE, 1877–1920

Chapter 31

REFORM, RADICALISM, AND DISAPPOINTED EXPECTATIONS, 1961–1973

Chapter 32

DISILLUSIONMENT AND ECONOMIC UNCERTAINTY, 1973–1981

Chapter 33

A TURN TO THE RIGHT: AMERICA SINCE 1981

APPENDIX

Maps/Charts

PREFACE
to the Brief Second Edition

This text is a condensation of the very successful Second Edition of *A People and a Nation*. It preserves all the strengths of that full-length edition—its readability, its comprehensiveness, and, most importantly, its blend of social, political, diplomatic, and economic history—in a form that is approximately half as long as the full-length edition. This condensation of the whole story of American history is ideally suited for short courses or courses in which additional readings are assigned.

This brief version is available in one-volume and two-volume formats. In the two-volume format, Volume A (Chapters 1–15) begins with a discussion of the three cultures—Native American, African, and European—that intersected during the exploration and colonization of the New World and ends with a discussion of the Reconstruction era. Volume B (Chapters 15–33) begins with Reconstruction and extends to the present. The chapter on Reconstruction appears in both volumes to provide greater flexibility in matching the appropriate volume with the beginning and closing dates of a course.

This brief edition is not a simple revision of the first brief edition: it reflects the changes in content and organization incorporated into the full-length Second Edition. William J. Brophy, who prepared the condensation, collaborated closely with the six authors of the full-length edition. Deletions were made with great care. Rather than simply cut entire sections, we

Creation of
the Brief
Edition

opted for a line-by-line approach to the removal of material. The objective was to eliminate detail. Where two examples were given in the full-length edition, we have deleted one; where many statistics were presented, we have used a few. We have deleted or abridged some of the longer quotations from diaries and letters and some of the longer stories of individuals but have retained many quotations and individual experiences of everyday life. We have also combined some of the chapters from the full-length edition: the chapter on the city from 1877 to 1920 has been combined with the chapter on everyday life during the same period, and the two chapters on the Depression and the New Deal have been combined.

Two aspects of this brief edition should be noted. We have used the opportunity of a new edition to update thoroughly the chapter that covers the Reagan years. And, in comparison with the previous brief edition, the numbers of maps and illustrations have been significantly increased.

As was the case for the full-length edition, a full set of ancillaries are available with the brief edition. These include a *Study Guide* (in two volumes), by George C. Warren and Cynthia L. Ricketson; *Microstudy Plus*, an interactive computer study guide; an *Instructor's Manual with Test Items*, by Richard B. Rowe and George C. Warren; *Microtest*, a computerized test item file; and *Map Transparencies*. Each volume of the *Study Guide* includes an introductory chapter on study techniques, as well as learning ob-

Ancillaries

jectives, a thematic guide, and various kinds of study questions for each chapter in the text. The *Instructor's Manual with Test Items* includes learning objectives, chapter outlines, lecture suggestions and topics, lists of audio-visual resources, and a variety of test questions for each chapter in the text.

Though each of us feels answerable for the whole of *A People and a Nation*, we take primary responsibility for particular chapters: Mary Beth Norton, Chapters 1–7; David M. Katzman, Chapters 8–10, 12; Paul D. Escott, Chapters 11, 13–15; Howard P. Chudacoff, Chapters 16–20, 23; Thomas G. Paterson, Chapters 21–22, 24–25, 28, 30, and part of 33; William M. Tuttle, Jr., Chapters 26–27, 29, 31–32, and part of 33.

Many people have contributed their thoughts and labors to this work. We are especially appreciative of the staff at Houghton Mifflin Company, and we thank the following reviewers, who provided detailed comments on the various drafts of our manuscript:

James Barrett, *University of Illinois, Urbana-Champaign*
Lorin Cary, *University of Toledo*
George Davis, *Wabash College*
Robert Fairbanks, *University of Texas, Arlington*
Thomas Frazier, *Baruch College, CUNY*
L. Ray Gunn, *University of Utah*
Martin Haas, *Adelphi University*
H. James Henderson, *Oklahoma State University*
Donald Higginbotham, *University of North Carolina, Chapel Hill*
Barbara Lindemann, *Santa Barbara City College*
Sally McMillen, *Middle Tennessee State University*
Millard Morgan, *College of Marin*
J. Murray Murdock, *Cedarville College*
David Rowe, *Middle Tennessee State University*
Terry Seip, *University of Southern California*
Nancy Unger, *San Francisco State University*
Peter Wallenstein, *Virginia Polytechnic University*

W.J.B.

PREFACE
to the Full-Length Second Edition

The generous reception given to the first edition of this volume by our colleagues in history, the encouragement and suggestions of the many instructors who used the book in their classrooms, and the appearance of new scholarship in the last few years have afforded us the opportunity to improve and update *A People and a Nation*. In this second edition we have retained and strengthened those characteristics of the first edition that students and faculty found attractive. As teachers and students we are always recreating our past, rediscovering the personalities and events that have shaped us, inspired us, and bedeviled us. This book is our rediscovery of America's past—its people and the nation they founded and sustained. Sometimes we find this history comforting, sometimes disturbing. As with our own personal experience, it is both triumphant and tragic, filled with injury as well as healing. As a mirror on our lives, it is always significant.

We draw on recent research as well as on seasoned, authoritative works to offer a comprehensive book that tells the whole story of American history. Presidential and party politics, congressional legislation, Supreme Court decisions, diplomacy and treaties, wars and foreign interventions, economic patterns, and state and local government have been the stuff of American history for generations. Into this traditional fabric we weave social history, broadly defined. We investigate the history of the majority of Americans—women—and of minorities. We study the history of social classes, and we

Characteristics
of the Book

illuminate the private, everyday life of the American people.

From the ordinary to the exceptional—the factory worker, the slave, the office secretary, the local merchant, the small farmer, the plantation owner, the ward politician, the president's wife, the film star, the scientist, the army general—Americans have had personal stories that have intersected with the public policies of their government. Whether victors or victims, all have been actors in their own right, with feelings, ideas, and aspirations that have fortified them in good times and bad. All are part of the American story; all speak here through excerpts from their letters, diaries, and other writings, and oral histories.

Several questions guided our telling of this narrative. On the official, or public, side of American history, we emphasize Americans' expectations of their governments and the everyday practice of those local, state, and federal institutions. We identify the mood and mentality of an era, in which Americans reveal what they think about themselves and their public officials. And in our discussion of foreign policy we particularly probe its domestic sources.

Major Themes

In the social and economic spheres, we emphasize patterns of change in the population, geographic mobility, and people's adaptation to new environments. We study the interactions of people of different races, ethnic backgrounds, religions, and genders, the social divisions that emerged, and the efforts made, often in reform movements, to heal them. As well, we focus on the effects of technological development on the economy, the worker and workplace, and lifestyles.

In the private, everyday life of the family and the home, we pay particular attention to sex roles, childbearing and childrearing, and diet and dress. We ask how Americans have chosen to entertain themselves, as participants or spectators, with sports, music, the graphic arts, reading, theater, film, and television. Throughout American history, of course, this private part of American life and public policy have interacted and influenced one another.

Students and instructors have liked our use of clear, concrete language, and have commented on how enjoyable the book is to read. They have also told us that we challenged them to think about the meaning of American history, not just to memorize it; to confront our own interpretations and at the same time to understand and respect the views of others; and to show how an historian's mind works to ask questions and to tease conclusions out of a mass of information.

For this revised edition, the authors met to discuss at length the themes and questions of the book. We reviewed numerous reports from instructors and worked to incorporate their suggestions. We also researched the most recent scholarship, alert to new evidence and new interpretations. As well, we examined every line of the text with an eye to conciseness, clarity, and readability. In the course of writing, the six of us read and reread one another's drafts and debated one another with a friendly spirit and mutual respect that strengthened us as scholars.

Several changes in this second edition stand out. First, that part of the book devoted to the post-1941 years has been substantially reorganized to match the

Changes in the Second Edition

way most instructors teach that period. All of the material on the Second World War—domestic and foreign—is now in Chapter 28. The Truman years are covered in Chapter 29 and the Eisenhower years in 30. They are followed by a chapter (31) on the social history of the postwar period. Chapter 32, a foreign policy segment, has been recast to emphasize the origins, experience, and aftermath

of the Vietnam War. Chapter 33 then treats the domestic effects of the war and political and economic events for 1961–1973, whereas Chapter 34 does so for 1973–1981. Finally, an altogether new Chapter 35 studies the Reagan years and the interaction among social, political, economic, and diplomatic currents in the 1980s.

Second, Chapter 1 has been significantly reworked to provide the stories of the three divergent cultures—Native American, African, and European—that intersected in the New World to mold the early history of the United States. Third, we have expanded our coverage of Asians and Hispanics, constitutional history, and the nuclear arms race. Fourth, throughout the book we have explained the significance of gender in employment—the sexual division of labor. Fifth, we have set out more prominently the themes of each chapter, following the opening vignette. And, finally, A People and a Nation has a new look. Not only have new illustrations and maps been added—they have also been improved through the use of full color. Full color makes the maps (all ninety of them) easier to read and understand and the illustrations (all historically accurate because they are contemporaneous with a chapter's period) truer prints of their originals.

As in the first edition, each chapter opens with the story of an American, ordinary or exceptional, whose experience was representative of the times or whose

Study Aids

commentary facilitates our understanding of the chapter themes, which immediately follow this vignette. To help students study and review, we use bold-typed notes—like the one here—to highlight key personalities, events, concepts, and trends. Significant concepts and words are defined and italicized; important events are listed in a chart near the end of most chapters; and suggested readings for further study close each chapter. The Appendix, updated and expanded, is a unique compendium providing a historical overview of the American people and their nation.

To make the book as useful as possible for students and instructors, several learning and teaching ancillaries are available, including a *Study Guide* and *Com-*

Ancillaries

puterized *Study Guide*, an *Instructor's Manual*, a *Test Items* file, a *Computerized Test Items* file, and *Map Transparencies*. The *Study Guide*, which was prepared by George Warren and Cynthia Ricketson of Central Piedmont Community College, includes an introductory chapter on study techniques for history students, as well as learning objectives and a thematic guide for each chapter in the text and exercises on evaluating and using information and on finding the main idea in passages from the text, as well as test questions on the content of each chapter. The *Study Guide* is also available in a computerized version that provides the student with tutorial instruction. The *Instructor's Manual*, by Richard Rowe of Golden West College, contains chapter outlines, suggestions for lectures and discussion, and lists of audiovisual resources. The accompanying *Test Items* file, also by Professor Rowe, offers more than 1,500 multiple-choice and essay questions and more than 700 identification terms. The test items are available to adoptors on computer tape and disk. In addition, there is a set of forty full-color map transparencies available on adoption.

Though each of us feels answerable for the whole, we take primary responsibility for particular chapters: Mary Beth Norton, Chapters 1–7, David M. Katzman, Chapters 8–10, 12; Paul D. Escott, Chapters 11, 13–15; Howard P. Chudacoff, Chapters 16–21, 24; Thomas G. Paterson, Chapters 22–23, 25, 27, 30, 32, and part of 35; William M. Tuttle, Jr., Chapters 26, 28–29, 31, 33–34, and part of 35. Thomas G. Paterson also served as the coordinating author and prepared the Appendix.

Acknowledgments

Many instructors have read and criticized the successive drafts of our manuscript. Their constructive suggestions have informed and improved this second edition. We heartily thank:

John K. Alexander, *University of Cincinnati*
Roberta Alexander, *University of Dayton*
John Borden Armstrong, *Boston University*
James Barrett, *University of Illinois*
John Britton, *Francis Marion College*

Richard Burns, *California State University, Los Angeles*
Ballard Campbell, *Northeastern University*
Ron Carden, *South Plains College*
Patricia Cohen, *University of California, Santa Barbara*
Frank Costigliola, *University of Rhode Island*
Jay Coughtry, *University of Nevada, Las Vegas*
William Fleming, *Pan American University*
James Gormly, *Pan American University*
Maurine Greenwald, *University of Pittsburgh*
Linda Guerrero, *Palomar College*
James Hijiya, *Southeastern Massachusetts University*
Richard J. Hopkins, *Ohio State University*
George Juergens, *Indiana University*
Harry Lupold, *Lakeland Community College*
Bart McCash, *Middle Tennessee State University*
John Muldowny, *University of Tennessee*
Leonard Murphy, *San Antonio College*
Paul L. Murphy, *University of Minnesota*
Philip Nicholson, *Nassau Community College*
Lawrence Powell, *Tulane University*
Howard Rabinowitz, *University of New Mexico*
Roy Rosenzweig, *George Mason University*
James H. Sasser, *Central Piedmont Community College*
Constance Schulz, *University of South Carolina*
Peter Shattuck, *California State University, Sacramento*
Rebecca Shoemaker, *Indiana State University*
Harvard Sitkoff, *University of New Hampshire*
William R. Swagerty, *University of Idaho*
Emory Thomas, *University of Georgia*
James Walter, *Sinclair Community College*
Nelson Woodard, *California State University, Fullerton*

We acknowledge with thanks as well the contributions of Ruth Alexander, Nancy Fisher Chudacoff, J. Garry Clifford, Christopher Collier, Mary Ellen Erickson, Elizabeth French, William Gienapp, James L. Gormly, Frederick Hoxie, Nathan Huggins, Jacqueline Jones, Sharyn A. Katzman, Freeman Meyer, William H. Moore, Holly Izard Paterson, Shirley Rice, Barney J. Rickman, III, Janice Riley, Daniel Usner, Deborah White, David Wyllie, and Thomas Zoumaras. We also appreciate the continued guidance and generous assistance of the staff of the Houghton Mifflin Company.

T.G.P.

A PEOPLE AND A NATION

Brief Edition

CHAPTER 1

THE MEETING OF
OLD WORLD AND NEW
1492–1650

"*It spread over* the people as great destruction," the old man told the priest. "Covered, mantled with pustules, very many people died of them. And very many starved; there was death from hunger. . . ."

By European reckoning, it was September 1520. Spanish troops led by Hernando Cortés abandoned the Aztec capital of Tenochtitlan after failing in their first attempt to gain control of the city. But they unknowingly left behind the smallpox germs that would ensure their eventual triumph. Three months later they returned to besiege the Aztec capital; the disease-weakened defenders finally surrendered in the Aztec year Three House, on the day One Serpent (August 1521). The Spaniards had conquered Mexico, and on the site of Tenochtitlan they constructed what is now Mexico City.

By the time Spanish troops occupied Tenochtitlan, the age of European expansion and colonization was already well under way. Over the next three hundred and fifty years, Europeans would spread their civilization across the globe. The history of the English colonies in North America that eventually became the United States must be seen in the broader context of worldwide exploration and exploitation.

That context is complex. After 1400, European nations sought to improve their positions relative to neighboring countries not only by fighting wars on their own continent but also by acquiring valuable colonies elsewhere in the world. Simultaneously, the warring tribes and nations of Asia, Africa, and the Americas attempted to use the alien intruders to their own advantage or, failing that, to adapt successfully to the Europeans' presence in their midst. All the participants in the resulting interaction of divergent cultures were indelibly affected. Although Europeans emerged politically dominant at the end of the long process of interaction among divergent cultures, they by no means controlled every aspect of it.

Nowhere is that lack of European control shown more clearly than in the early history of the English settlements in North America. England's first attempts to establish colonies on the mainland failed completely. Its second tries—in the early seventeenth century—succeeded only because neighboring Indians assisted the newcomers. The English colonists prospered by learning to grow such unfamiliar American crops as corn and tobacco and by developing extensive trading relationships with Native Americans. Eventually, as shall be seen in Chapter 2, they discovered a third source of prosperity—importing enslaved African laborers to work in their fields.

To achieve the first goal of providing food, they had to adopt agricultural techniques suited both to the new crops and to an alien environment. As for the second goal, maintaining the trade networks essential to their survival required them to deal regularly on a more or less equal basis with people who seemed very different from themselves and who were far more familiar with America than they were. The early history of the United States, in short, can best be understood as a series of complex interactions among different peoples and environments rather than as the simple story of a triumph by the English colonists.

SOCIETIES OF THE AMERICAS

AND AFRICA

In the Christian world, it was the year 1400; by the Muslim calendar, 802; and to the Maya, who had the most accurate calendar of all, the era started with the date 1 Ahau 18 Ceh. Regardless of the name or the reckoning system, the two-hundred-year period that followed changed the course of history. As European explorers and colonizers sought to exploit the resources of the rest of the globe, societies that had for thousands of years developed largely in isolation from each other came into regular contact for the first time.

The civilizations that had evolved separately had several basic characteristics in common. All had political structures governing their secular affairs, kinship systems regulating their social life, and one or more sets of indigenous religious beliefs. In addition, they all organized their work assignments on the basis of the sexual division of labor. Many, but not all, of the societies shared yet another characteristic: they relied on agriculture for their essential food supply. Agricultural civilizations, assured of steady supplies of food, did not have to devote all their energies to mere subsistence. They accumulated wealth, produced ornamental objects, and created elaborate rituals and ceremonies. In brief, they developed distinctive cultural traditions.

These cultural distinctions became the focal point for the interactions that occurred in the fifteenth century and thereafter. The basic similarities were obscured by the shock of discovering that not all people were the same color as oneself, that other folk worshipped other gods, or that some people defined the separate roles of men and women differently from the way one's own society did. Because Native Americans, Africans, and Europeans met and mingled on the soil of the Western Hemisphere during the age of European colonization, their relationships can be examined in that context.

Since the earliest known humanlike remains have been found in what is now Ethiopia, it is likely that human beings originated in Africa. During many millennia, people slowly dispersed to the other continents. Some crossed a now-submerged stretch of land that joined the Asian and North American continents at the site of the Bering Strait. These forerunners of the Native American population, known as Paleo-Indians, probably arrived in the Americas more than thirty thousand years ago. The Paleo-Indians were nomadic hunters of game and gatherers of wild plants. Over many centuries, they spread through North and South America, probably moving as extended families, or "bands." ("Tribes" were composed of groups of allied bands.)

Paleo-Indians

By approximately 5,500 years ago, Indians living in central Mexico had begun to cultivate food crops. As knowledge of agricultural techniques spread, most Indian groups started to live a more stationary existence. Some established permanent settlements; others moved two or three times a year among fixed sites. Over the centuries, groups of North American Indians adapted their once-similar ways of life to specific and very different geographical settings, thus creating the diversity of cultures that Europeans encountered when they first arrived (see map, page 4).

Those Indian bands that lived in environments not well suited to agriculture (for example, the Great Basin, now Nevada and Utah) continued the nomadic lifestyle of their ancestors. Bands of such hunter-gatherers were small, because of the difficulties of finding sufficient food for more than a few people. They were usually composed of one or more related families, with men hunting small animals and women gathering seeds and berries. Where large game was more plentiful and food supplies therefore more certain, as in present-day Canada or the Great Plains, bands of hunters could be somewhat larger.

In more favorable environments, Indians combined agriculture in varying degrees with gathering, hunting, and fishing. Those tribes that lived near the seacoasts, like the Chinook of present-day Washington and Oregon, consumed large quantities of fish and shellfish, in addition to growing crops and gathering seeds and berries. Tribes of the interior (for example, the Arikara of the Missouri River valley) hunted large game animals while also cultivating fields of corn, squash, and beans. That was true, too, of the Algonkian tribes that inhabited much of what is now eastern Canada and the northeastern United States. (Indians are often described by linguistic groups, since large numbers of tribes spoke related languages and shared similar cultures. For example, the most important linguistic groups east of the Mississippi River were the Algonkians and the Iroquoians, found primarily in the north, and the Muskogeans of the south.)

Agricultural Indians differed in how they assigned the task of cultivating crops to the sexes. In the Southwest, the Pueblo peoples defined agricultural labor as "men's work." In the East, by contrast, Algonkian, Iroquoian, and Muskogean peoples allocated agricultural chores to women. Among these eastern tribes, men's major assignments were hunting large animals and clearing the land. In all the cultures, women gathered wild foods, prepared the food for consumption or storage, and cared for the children.

Sexual Division of Labor in America

The southwestern and eastern agricultural Indians had similar social organizations. They lived in villages, sometimes sizable ones with a thousand or more inhabitants. Pueblo villages were large multistoried buildings, constructed on terraces along the sides of cliffs or other easily defended sites. Most of the eastern villages were also laid out defensively, often being surrounded by wood palisades and ditches. In these cultures, each dwelling housed an extended family defined *matrilineally* (that is, through the female line). The families in such dwellings were linked together into clans, again defined by matrilineal kinship ties.

In both southwestern and eastern cultures, the most important political structures were those of the village. Indeed, among Pueblo and Muskogean peoples the village council, composed of ten to thirty men, was the highest political authority; there was no government at the tribal level. The Iroquois, by contrast, had an elaborate political hierarchy linking villages into tribes, and tribes into a widespread confederation. In all the cultures, political power was divided between civil and war chiefs, who had authority only so long as they retained the confidence of the people.

Indian Politics and Religion

The political position of women varied from tribe to tribe. Women were more likely to assume leadership roles among the agricultural peoples than among nomadic hunters. For example, women could become chiefs of certain Algonkian bands, but they never

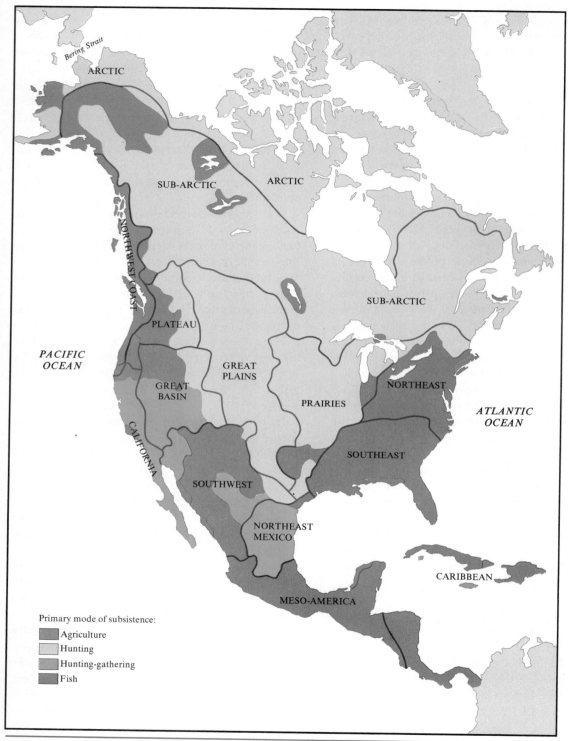

Bering Strait

ARCTIC

SUB-ARCTIC

ARCTIC

NORTHWEST COAST

SUB-ARCTIC

PACIFIC OCEAN

PLATEAU

GREAT PLAINS

GREAT BASIN

PRAIRIES

NORTHEAST

ATLANTIC OCEAN

CALIFORNIA

SOUTHWEST

SOUTHEAST

NORTHEAST MEXICO

CARIBBEAN

MESO-AMERICA

Primary mode of subsistence:

Agriculture
Hunting
Hunting-gathering
Fish

Indian Cultures of North America

held that position in the hunting tribes of the Great Plains. Probably the most powerful female chiefs were found in what is now the southeastern United States. In the mid-sixteenth century a female ruler known as the Lady of Cofitachique governed a large group of villages in present-day western South Carolina.

Indian religious beliefs varied even more than did their political systems. One common thread was that they were all *polytheistic*: that is, they all involved a multitude of gods. Another was the relationship of the most important rituals to the tribe's chief means of subsistence. That is, the major deities of agricultural Indians like Pueblos and Muskogeans were associated with cultivation, and their chief festivals centered on planting and harvest. The most important gods of hunting tribes, by contrast, were associated with animals, and their major festivals were related to hunting. The tribe's main source of food and women's role in its production helped to determine women's potential as religious leaders. Women held the most prominent positions in those agricultural societies (like the Iroquois) in which they were also the chief food producers.

The most advanced Indian civilizations on the North American continent were located in present-day Mexico and Guatemala (Mesoamerica). The major Indian societies encountered by the Spanish in the sixteenth century were the Aztec and the Maya. The Aztec, who entered central Mexico in the fourteenth century, were a warlike people who had consolidated their control over the entire region by the time of Cortés's arrival. The Maya, whose civilization was already in decline when the Spaniards came, had invented sophisticated systems of writing and mathematics.

Aztec and Maya

In the fifteenth century, then, a wide variety of Indian cultures, comprising perhaps 4 to 6 million people, inhabited North America. In modern Mexico, hereditary rulers presided over vast agricultural empires. Along the Atlantic coast of the present-day United States, Indians likewise cultivated crops, but their political systems differed greatly from those of Mesoamerica. To the north and west, in what is now

Canada and the Great Plains, lived nomadic and seminomadic societies primarily dependent on hunting large animals. Still farther west were the hunter-gatherer bands of the Great Basin and the agricultural Indians of the Southwest. Finally, on the Pacific coast lived tribes that based their subsistence chiefly on fish. All told, these diverse groups spoke well over one thousand different languages. They did not consider themselves to be one people.

Fifteenth-century Africa also housed a variety of cultures adapted to different geographical settings (see map, page 6). In the north, along the Mediterranean, lived the Berbers, a Muslim people of Middle Eastern origin. (Muslims are adherents of the Islamic religion, founded by the prophet Mohammed in the seventh century.) On the east coast of Africa, city-states dominated by Muslim merchants engaged in extensive trade with India, the Moluccas (part of modern Indonesia), and China. Through these ports passed a considerable share of the trade between the eastern Mediterranean and Far East; the rest followed the long land route across Central Asia known as the Silk Road.

Africa: Its Peoples

In the African interior, south of the Mediterranean coast, lie the great Sahara and the Libyan desert. Below the deserts, much of the continent is divided between tropical rain forests and grassy plains. Over the centuries, this fertile landscape came to be dominated by Bantu peoples, who left their homeland in modern Nigeria about two thousand years ago and slowly migrated southward across the continent, assimilating and conquering other ethnic groups as they went.

Most of the unwilling black migrants to the Americas came from West Africa, or Guinea, a land of tropical forests and small-scale agriculture. The northern region, or Upper Guinea, was heavily influenced by Islamic culture. As early as the eleventh century, many of its inhabitants had become Muslims; more important, the trans-Saharan trade between Upper Guinea and the Muslim Mediterranean was black Africa's major connec-

West Africa (Guinea)

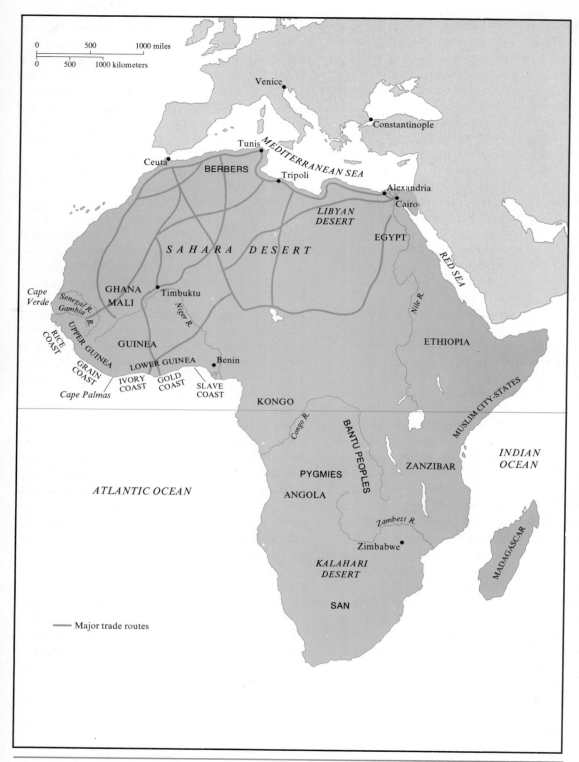

0   **500**   **1000 miles**

0   **500**   **1000 kilometers**

Venice

Constantinople

Tunis

MEDITERRANEAN SEA

Ceuta

BERBERS

Tripoli

Alexandria

Cairo

LIBYAN
DESERT

EGYPT

RED SEA

S A H A R A   D E S E R T

Cape
Verde

Senegal R.
Gambia R.

GHANA
MALI

Timbuktu

Niger R.

RICE
COAST

UPPER GUINEA

GUINEA

Nile R.

ETHIOPIA

GRAIN
COAST

LOWER GUINEA

Benin

IVORY
COAST

GOLD
COAST

SLAVE
COAST

Cape Palmas

KONGO

Congo R.

BANTU PEOPLES

MUSLIM CITY-STATES

ATLANTIC OCEAN

PYGMIES

ANGOLA

ZANZIBAR

INDIAN
OCEAN

Zambezi R.

Zimbabwe

MADAGASCAR

KALAHARI
DESERT

SAN

—— Major trade routes

Africa and Its Peoples, ca. 1400

tion to Europe and the Middle East. In return for salt, dates, and such manufactured goods as silk and cotton cloth, Africans exchanged ivory, gold, and slaves with the northern merchants. (Slaves, who were mostly captives of war, were in great demand as household servants in the homes of the Muslim Mediterranean elite.) This commerce was controlled first by the great kingdom of Ghana (ca. 900–1100), then by its successor, the empire of Mali. Black Africa and Islam intersected at the city that was the intellectual and commercial heart of the trade, the near-legendary Timbuktu. A cosmopolitan center, Timbuktu attracted merchants and scholars from all parts of North African and the Mediterranean.

Along the coast of West Africa and in the south, or Lower Guinea, most Africans continued to practice their indigenous religions, which revolved around rituals designed to ensure good harvests. The vast interior kingdoms of Mali and Ghana had no counterparts on the coast. Throughout Lower Guinea, individual villages composed of groups of kin were linked into small, often rigidly hierarchical kingdoms. At the time of initial contact with Europeans, the region was characterized by fragmented political and social authority.

Just as the political structures varied, so too did the means of subsistence pursued by the different peoples of Guinea. People living on the Rice Coast in Upper Guinea fished and cultivated rice in coastal swamplands. The inhabitants of the thinly populated Grain Coast concentrated on farming and animal husbandry. The Ivory Coast and the Gold Coast, in Lower Guinea, were each named by Europeans for the major trade goods they obtained there. The Gold Coast, comprising thirty little kingdoms known as the Akan States, later formed the basis of the great Asante kingdom. Initially many of the slaves destined for sale in the Americas came from the Akan States. By the eighteenth century, though, it was the next section of Lower Guinea, which became known as the Slave Coast, that supplied most of the Africans sold in the English colonies. The Adja kings of the region encouraged the founding of slave trading posts and served as middlemen in the trade.

The ancient kingdom of Benin (modern Nigeria), which lay east of the Slave Coast, was the strongest and most centralized coastal state in Guinea. Long before Europeans arrived it was, like Mali, a center of trade for West and North Africa. Those who lived in Benin along the delta of the Niger River made much of their living from the water. They fished, made salt, and used skillfully constructed dugout canoes to carry on a wide-ranging commerce.

The societies of West Africa, like those of the Americas, assigned different tasks to men and women. In general, the sexes shared agricultural duties, but in some Guinean cultures women bore the primary responsibility for growing crops, whereas in others men assumed that chore. In addition, men hunted, managed livestock, and did most of the fishing. Women were responsible for childcare, food preparation, and cloth manufacture. Everywhere in West Africa women were the primary local traders.

Sexual Division of Labor in West Africa

Despite their different modes of subsistence and deep political divisions, the peoples of West Africa had largely similar social systems. In the societies of West Africa, each sex handled its own affairs: just as male political and religious leaders governed the men, so females ruled the women. Moreover, indigenous religious beliefs likewise stressed the complementary nature of male and female roles. Both women and men served as heads of the cults and secret societies that directed the spiritual life of the villages. Although African women rarely held formal power over men, they did govern other females.

The West Africans brought to the Americas, then, were agricultural peoples, skilled at tending livestock, hunting, fishing, and manufacturing cloth from plant fibers and animal skins. Both men and women were accustomed to working communally, alongside other members of their own sex. They were also accustomed to a relatively egalitarian relationship between the sexes. In the New World, they entered societies that used their labor but had little respect for their cultural traditions. Of the three peoples whose experience intersected in the Americas, their lives were the most disrupted.

EUROPE AND ITS EXPLORATIONS

After 1400, Europe had begun to recover from centuries of decline. Northern Europe had long been an intellectual and economic backwater, far outstripped in importance by the states of the Mediterranean, especially the great Italian city-states like Venice and Florence. The cultural flowering known as the Renaissance began in those city-states in the fourteenth century and spread northward. At the same time, the pace of economic activity quickened and near-constant warfare promoted feelings of nationalism. All these developments helped to set the stage for extraordinary political and technological change after the middle of the fifteenth century.

Yet in the midst of that change the life of Europe's common people remained basically untouched for at least another century. European societies were hierarchical, with a few wealthy aristocratic families wielding arbitrary power over the majority of the people. Most Europeans, like most Africans or Native Americans, lived in small agricultural villages. Such farmers, or peasants, had separate landholdings, but worked their fields communally, like most Africans and Native Americans. That was because fields had to lie fallow every second or third year to regain their fertility after having been planted with wheat or rye, the most common European food grains. A family could not have ensured its own food supply in alternate years had not the work and the crop been shared annually by all the villagers.

In European cultures, men did most of the field work, with women helping out chiefly at planting and harvest. At other times, women's duties consisted primarily of childcare and household tasks (including food preservation, milking cows, and caring for poultry). Since Europeans usually kept domesticated animals (especially pigs, sheep, and cattle) to use for meat, hunting had little economic importance in their cultures.

Sexual Division of Labor in Europe

Whereas in African or Native American societies women often played major roles in politics and religion, in Europe men were dominant in all areas of life. A few women from noble families—for example, Queen Elizabeth I of England—achieved status or power, but the vast majority of European women were excluded from positions of political authority. In the Catholic church, leadership roles were reserved for men. At the familial level, husbands and fathers expected to control the lives of their wives, children, and servants (a *patriarchal* system of family governance). In short, European women held inferior positions in both public and private realms.

The traditional hierarchical social structure of Europe changed little in the fifteenth century, but the opposite was true of politics. The century witnessed rapid and dynamic political change, as ruthless monarchs expanded their territories through conquest and marriage and centralized previously diffuse political power in their own hands. In England, Henry VII in 1485 founded the Tudor dynasty and began uniting a previously divided land. In France, the successors of Charles VII unified the kingdom and established new, more secure sources of revenue. Most successful of all, at least in the short run, were Ferdinand of Aragon and Isabella of Castile. In 1469 they married and combined their kingdoms, thus creating the foundation of a strongly Catholic Spain.

Political and Technological Change

The fifteenth century also brought significant technological changes to Europe. The development and refinement of navigational instruments enabled mariners to estimate their positions on the high seas. The widespread dissemination of Marco Polo's *Travels*, published in 1477, convinced many Europeans that they could trade directly with China via ocean-going vessels. (Publication of the book was made possible by the invention in the 1450s of movable type and the printing press.) A sea route to China would allow Europeans to acquire Asian goods without depending upon either the Silk Road or the Muslim merchants of East Africa.

Thus the European explorations of the fifteenth and sixteenth centuries were made possible by technological advances and by the financial might of newly powerful national rulers. But the primary motivation for the exploratory voyages was a desire for direct access to the wealth of the East. That motive was supported by a secondary concern to spread Christianity around the world. The linking of materialist and spiritual goals might seem contradictory today, but fifteenth-century Europeans saw no necessary conflict between the two.

Motives for Exploration

The seafaring Portuguese people began the age of European expansion in 1415 when they seized control of Ceuta, a Muslim city in North Africa (see map, page 6). Prince Henry the Navigator, son of King John I, realized that vast wealth awaited the first European nation to tap the riches of Africa and Asia directly. Each year he dispatched ships southward along the coast of Africa, attempting to discover a passage to the East. Not until after Prince Henry's death did Bartholomew Dias round the southern tip of Africa (1488) and Vasco da Gama finally reach India (1498). Long before that, the Portuguese had established trading posts in Guinea. They earned immense profits by transporting African goods swiftly to Europe. Among their most valuable cargoes were slaves. Thus the Portuguese introduced the custom of black slavery into Europe.

Spain, with its reinvigorated monarchy, was the next country to sponsor exploratory voyages, chiefly those of Christopher Columbus, a Genoese sea captain. Like other experienced sailors, Columbus believed the world to be round. Where he differed from his contemporaries was in his estimate of its size. He believed that Japan lay only 3,000 miles from the southern European coast and therefore that it would be easier to reach the East by

Christopher Columbus

sailing west than by making the difficult voyage around the southern tip of Africa.

After being rejected as a crackpot by the monarchs of France, Portugal, and England, Columbus sought and received financial backing from Queen Isabella. On August 3, 1492, with three ships under his command—the *Pinta*, the *Niña*, and the *Santa Maria*—Columbus sailed west from the port of Palos in Spain. On October 12, he landed in the Bahamas, on an island that he named San Salvador and claimed for the king and queen of Spain. Because he thought he had reached the Indies, he called the inhabitants of the region Indians. Columbus made three more voyages to the west, during which he explored most of the major Caribbean islands and sailed along the coasts of Central and South America. Until the day he died in 1506, Columbus continued to believe that he had reached Asia. Even before his death, others knew better. Because the Florentine Amerigo Vespucci (who explored the South American coast in 1499) was the first to publish the idea that a new continent had been discovered, a mapmaker in 1507 labeled the land *America*.

More than five hundred years earlier, Norse explorers had briefly colonized present-day Newfoundland, but it was the voyages of Columbus and his successors that finally brought the Old and New Worlds together. John Cabot (1497), Giovanni da Verrazano (1524), Jacques Cartier (1534), and Henry Hudson (1609 and 1610) all explored the North American coast (see map, page 10). Although they were primarily searching for the nonexistent "Northwest Passage" through the Americas, hoping to find an easy route to the riches of the East, their discoveries interested European nations in colonizing the New World.

Only Spain immediately moved to take advantage of the discoveries. On his first voyage, Columbus had established a base on the island of Hispaniola. From there, Spanish explorers fanned out around the Caribbean basin. In the 1520s Spain's dreams of wealth were realized when Cortés conquered the Aztec empire, killing its ruler, Moctezuma, and seizing a fab-

Conquistadores

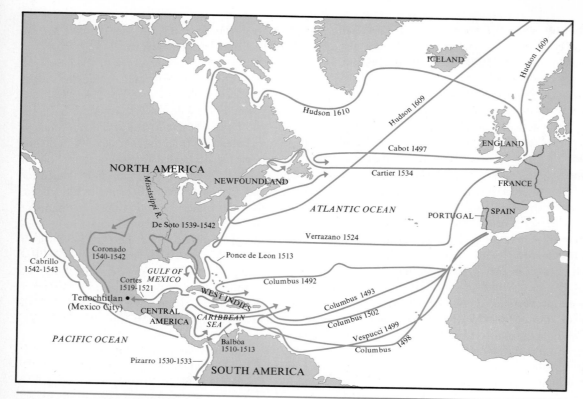

European Explorations in America

ulous treasure of gold and silver. Moreover, Francisco Pizarro, who explored the western coast of South America, conquered and enslaved the Inca in 1535, thus acquiring the richest silver mines in the world. Just half a century after Columbus's first voyage, the Spanish monarchs controlled the richest, most extensive empire Europe had known since ancient Rome.

Spain established the model of colonization that other countries later attempted to imitate, a model with three major elements. First, the Crown maintained tight control over the colonies, establishing a rigidly hierarchical government that allowed little autonomy to New World jurisdictions. Second, the colonies' wealth was based on the exploitation of both the native population and slaves imported from Africa. Third, the colonists sent from Spain were al-

most wholly male. They married Indian—and later black—women, thereby creating the racially mixed population that characterizes Latin America to the present day.

American civilizations suffered from the Spanish presence. The Spaniards deliberately leveled Indian cities, building cathedrals and monasteries on sites once occupied by Aztec, Incan, and Mayan temples. Despite the protests of some priests, they sought to erase all vestiges of the great Indian cultures by burning whatever written records they found. As a result, present-day knowledge of the Aztec, Maya, and Inca civilizations rests almost entirely on architectural remains, pottery artifacts, and a few records left by priests who sympathized with the Indians.

The native peoples to the north initially fared somewhat better because the English, French, and

Dutch did not immediately start to colonize the coast their sailors had explored. Instead, they left the region to European mariners, who came to fish in the rich waters off Newfoundland. Eventually, these fishermen learned that they could supplement their profits by exchanging cloth and metal goods (like pots and knives) for the Indians' beaver pelts. At first the Europeans conducted their trading from ships sailing along the coast, but later they established permanent outposts on the mainland to centralize and control the traffic in furs. Among the most successful of these were the French trading posts at Quebec (1608) and Montreal (1642) on the St. Lawrence River; the Swedish settlement at Fort Christina (1638) on the Delaware River; and the Dutch forts of New Amsterdam and Fort Orange on the Hudson River, both founded in 1624. All were inhabited chiefly by male adventurers, whose sole aim was to send as many pelts as possible home to Europe.

Even though the northern Europeans did not conquer the Indians, as the Spanish had, their trading activities had a significant effect on the native societies. The Europeans' insatiable demand for furs was matched by the Indians' desire for European goods that could make their lives easier and establish their superiority over neighboring tribes. The Indians changed their traditional ways of life to take advantage of the new opportunities. Some tribes specialized in producing pelts for the market, others in supplying foodstuffs to the fur hunters. Indeed, the fur hunters, rather than the Europeans themselves, became the agriculturalists' major source of European trade goods.

The Europeans' greatest impact on the Americas was, however, unintended. Diseases carried from the Old World to the New killed millions of Native Americans who had no immunity to germs that had infested Europe, Asia, and Africa for centuries. The greatest killer was smallpox. The reason why Pizarro conquered the Incas so easily was that their society had been devastated by a smallpox epidemic shortly before his arrival. Smallpox was not the only villain; influenza, measles, and other diseases added to the destruction.

The statistics are staggering. When Columbus landed on Hispaniola in 1492, about one million Indians resided there. Fifty years later, only five hundred were still alive. Several million Indians inhabited central Mexico before Cortés's invasion. By the end of the century, fewer than one million remained. Even in the north, where smaller Indian populations encountered only a few European explorers, traders, and fishermen, disease ravaged the countryside.

The Americans, though, took a revenge of sorts. They gave the Europeans a virulent form of syphilis. The first recorded case of the new disease in Europe occurred in Barcelona, Spain, in 1493, shortly after Columbus's return from the Caribbean. Although less deadly than smallpox, syphilis was a dangerous and debilitating disease.

The exchange of diseases was only part of a broader mutual transfer of plants and animals that resulted directly from Columbus's voyages. Europeans introduced large domesticated mammals to the Americas, and they obtained from the New World a variety of vegetables (corn, beans, squash, and potatoes) that were more nutritious than the Old World's wheat and rye. Thus, the diets of both peoples were enriched.

The exchange of two other commodities significantly influenced the two civilizations. In America the Europeans discovered tobacco, and smoking and chewing the "Indian weed" quickly became a fad in the Old World. But more important than tobacco's influence on Europe was the impact of horses on certain Native American cultures. The conquistadores brought with them the first horses Americans had ever seen. Inevitably, some escaped or were stolen by the natives; such horses were traded north through Mexico into the Great Plains, where they eventually changed the lifestyles of tribes like the Apache, Comanche, Sioux, and Blackfeet, who made the horse the focal point of their existence.

ENGLAND COLONIZES THE NEW WORLD

When Englishmen began to think about planting colonies in the Western Hemisphere, they took Spain's possessions in the New World as both a model and a challenge. New Spain's existence posed a threat to England, Spain's greatest rival, not only because of the wealth Spain derived from the colonies, but also because of their strategic importance. By establishing its own settlements, England could prevent Spain from dominating the Western Hemisphere and could also gain direct access to valuable American commodities.

England's first colonial planners thus hoped to reproduce Spanish successes. In the 1580s, a group that included Sir Humphrey Gilbert and his younger half-brother Sir Walter Raleigh promoted a scheme to establish outposts that could trade with the Indians and provide bases for attacks on New Spain. Approving the idea, Queen Elizabeth I authorized Raleigh and Gilbert to colonize North America. Gilbert failed to plant a colony in Newfoundland, and Raleigh was only briefly more successful. In 1587 he sent 117 colonists to the territory he named Virginia (for Elizabeth, the "Virgin Queen"). They established a settlement on Roanoke Island, in what is now North Carolina, but in 1590 a supply ship could not find them. The colonists had vanished, leaving only the word "Croatoan" (the name of a nearby island) carved on a tree.

Raleigh's Roanoke Colony

The failure of Raleigh's attempt to colonize Virginia ended English efforts at settlement in North America for nearly two decades. When, in 1606, Englishmen decided to try once more, they again planned colonies that imitated the Spanish model. Success came only when they abandoned that model and founded settlements very different from those of other European powers. Unlike Spain, France, or the Netherlands, England eventually sent large numbers of men *and women* to set up *agriculturally based* colonies in the New World. Before the history of those colonies is discussed, it is important to examine the two major developments that prompted approximately two hundred thousand ordinary English men and women to move to North America in the seventeenth century and that led their government to encourage them.

The first development was a significant change in English religious practice, a transformation that eventually led large numbers of English dissenters to leave their homeland. In 1533, Henry VIII, wanting a male heir and infatuated with Anne Boleyn, sought to annul his marriage to his Spanish-born queen, Catherine of Aragon, despite nearly twenty years of marriage. When the pope refused to approve the annulment, Henry left the Roman Catholic church, founded the Church of England, and—with Parliament's concurrence—proclaimed himself its head. At first the reformed Church of England differed little from Catholicism in its practices, but under Henry's daughter Elizabeth I (child of his marriage to Anne Boleyn), new currents of religious belief that had originated on the European continent early in the sixteenth century dramatically affected the English church.

English Reformation

The leaders of the continental Protestant Reformation were Martin Luther, a German monk, and John Calvin, a French cleric and lawyer. Combating the Catholic doctrine that priests had to serve as intermediaries between lay people and God, they both insisted that each person could interpret the Bible for him- or herself. Both Luther and Calvin rejected Catholic rituals and denied the need for an elaborate church hierarchy. They also asserted that salvation came through faith alone, rather than—as Catholic teaching had it—through a combination of faith and good works. Calvin, though, went further than Luther in stressing God's absolute omnipotence and emphasizing the need for people to submit totally to His will.

Elizabeth I tolerated religious diversity among her subjects as long as they generally acknowledged her authority as head of the Church of England. Accordingly, during her long reign (1558–1603) Calvin's ideas gained influence within the English church. By the early seventeenth century, many English Calvinists believed that the Reformation had not gone far enough. Because these seventeenth-century English Calvinists said they wanted to *purify* the church, they became known as Puritans.

Puritans

Elizabeth I's Stuart successors, her cousin James I (1603–1625) and his son Charles I (1625–1649) were less tolerant of Puritans than she. As Scots, they also had little respect for the traditions of representative government that had developed in England under the Tudors and their predecessors. The Stuarts insisted that a monarch's power came directly from God and that his subjects had no alternative but to obey him. A king's authority, they argued, was absolute. Both James I and Charles I believed that their authority included the power to enforce religious conformity among their subjects and so they authorized the persecution of Puritans, who were challenging many of the most important precepts of the English church. Consequently, in the 1620s and 1630s a number of English Puritans decided to move to America, where they hoped to put their religious beliefs into practice unmolested by the Stuarts or the church hierarchy.

The second major development that led English people to move to North America was the onset of dramatic social and economic change caused by the doubling of the English population in the 150-year period after 1530. All those additional people needed food, clothing, and other goods. The competition for goods led to high inflation, coupled with a fall in real wages as the number of workers increased. In these new economic and demographic circumstances, those with sizable landholdings frequently prospered. Others, particularly landless laborers, tenant farmers who had been forced off the land, and those with small amounts of land, fell into unremitting poverty.

Social Change in England

Well-to-do English people reacted with alarm to what they saw as the disappearance of traditional ways of life. The streets and highways were filled with steady streams of the landless and the homeless. Officials became obsessed with the problem of maintaining order and came to believe that England was overcrowded. They concluded that colonies established in the New World could siphon off England's "surplus population," thus easing the social strains at home. For similar reasons, many English people decided that they could improve their circumstances by migrating from a small, land-scarce, apparently overpopulated island to a large, land-rich continent.

The initial impetus for the establishment of what was to become England's first permanent colony in the Western Hemisphere came from a group of merchants and wealthy gentry. In 1606, envisioning the possibility of earning great profits from a New World settlement, they set up a joint-stock company, the Virginia Company, to plant colonies in America.

Joint-stock companies had been developed in England during the sixteenth century as a mechanism for pooling the resources of a large number of small investors. These forerunners of modern corporations were funded through the sale of stock. Until the founding of the Virginia Company, they had been used primarily to finance trading voyages; for that purpose they worked well. No one person risked too much money, and investors usually received quick returns. But joint-stock companies turned out to be a poor way to finance colonies, because the early settlements required enormous amounts of capital and with rare exceptions failed to return much immediate profit. The colonies founded by joint-stock companies accordingly suffered from a chronic lack of capital.

Joint-Stock Companies

The Virginia Company was no exception to this rule. Chartered by King James I in 1606, the company tried but failed to start a colony in Maine, and barely succeeded in planting one in Virginia. In 1607 it dispatched 144 men and boys to North America. Ominously, only 104 of them sur-

Founding of Virginia

vived the voyage. In May of that year, they established the settlement called Jamestown. Many of the first migrants were gentlemen unaccustomed to working with their hands and artisans with irrelevant skills like glassmaking. They resisted living "like savages," retaining English dress and casual work habits despite their desperate circumstances. Such attitudes, combined with the effects of chronic malnutrition and epidemic disease, took a terrible toll. Only when Captain John Smith, one of the colony's founders, imposed military discipline on the colonists in 1608 was Jamestown saved from collapse. Still, after Smith's departure, some colonists resorted to cannibalism during the notorious "starving time," the winter of 1609 to 1610. Although conditions later improved somewhat, as late as 1624 only 1,300 of approximately 8,000 English migrants to Virginia remained alive.

That the colony survived at all was a tribute not to the English but rather to the Indians within whose territories they settled. The Powhatan Confederacy

Powhatan Confederacy

was led by Powhatan, a powerful figure, who was consolidating his authority over some twenty-five other small tribes in the area at the time the Europeans arrived. Fortunately for the Englishmen, Powhatan viewed them as potential allies instead of threats to his control of the region. And, indeed, Powhatan found the English colony a reliable source of such items as steel knives and guns, which gave him a technological advantage over his Indian neighbors. In return, Powhatan's tribes traded their excess corn and other foodstuffs to the starving colonists. In 1614, Powhatan signed a formal treaty with the settlers and sealed the deal in traditional fashion by marrying his daughter Pocahontas to John Rolfe, one of the English colony's most prominent residents.

Yet the relationship between the Jamestown colony and the coastal tribes was an uneasy one. English and Algonkian peoples had much in common (deep religious beliefs, a lifestyle oriented around agriculture, clear political and social hierarchies, and sharply defined sex roles), but the English and Indians themselves usually focused on their cultural dif-

ferences, not their similarities. English men thought that Indian men were lazy because they hunted (a sport in English eyes) and did not work in the fields, whereas Indian men thought English men effeminate because they did "women's work" of cultivation. In the same vein, the whites believed that Indian women were oppressed since they did heavy field labor.

Other differences between the two cultures caused serious misunderstandings. Although both societies were hierarchical, the nature of the hierarchies

Algonkian and English Cultural Differences

differed considerably. Among the east-coast Algonkian tribes, people were not born to automatic positions of leadership, nor were political power and social status necessarily inherited through the male line. The English gentry did inherit their position from their fathers. English leaders tended to rule autocratically, whereas the authority of Indian leaders rested largely on the consent of their fellow tribesmen. Accustomed to the European concept of powerful kings, the English sought such figures within the tribes. Often (for example, when negotiating treaties) they willfully overestimated the ability of chiefs to make independent decisions for their people.

Furthermore, the Indians and the English had very different notions of property ownership. In most eastern tribes, land was held communally by the entire group. It could not be bought or sold absolutely, although certain rights to use the land (for example, for hunting or fishing) could be transferred. The English, on the other hand, were accustomed to individual farms and to buying and selling land. In addition, the English refused to accept the validity of Indian claims to traditional hunting territories, insisting that only land intensively cultivated could be regarded as owned or occupied by a tribe.

An aspect of the cultural clash that needs particular emphasis is the English settlers' unwavering belief in the superiority of their civilization. They expected the Indians to adopt English customs and to convert to Christianity. They showed little respect for traditional Indian ways of life, especially when

Chapter 1: THE MEETING OF OLD WORLD AND NEW, 1492–1650

John White, an artist who accompanied the exploratory mission Sir Walter Raleigh sent to America in 1585, sketched Pomeioc, a typical Algonkian village composed of houses made from woven mats stretched over poles, and surrounded by a defensive wooden palisade.   Library of Congress.

they believed their own interests were at stake. That attitude was clearly revealed in the Virginia colony's treatment of the Powhatan Confederacy in the years following the treaty of 1614.

What upset the previous balance between the English and the Indians was the spread of tobacco cultivation. In tobacco the settlers and the Virginia Company found the salable commodity for which they had been searching. John Rolfe planted the first crop in 1611. Within twenty years, 1.5 million pounds were being exported annually—tobacco had become the foundation of Virginia's prosperity.

Tobacco: The Basis of Virginia's Success

Successful tobacco cultivation required abundant land, since the crop quickly drained soil of nutrients. Planters soon learned that a field could produce only about three satisfactory crops before it had to lie fallow for several years to regain its fertility. Thus the once small English settlements began to expand rapidly: eager planters applied to the Virginia Company for large land grants on both sides of the James River and its tributary streams.

Opechancanough, Powhatan's brother and successor, watched the English colonists steadily encroaching on Indian lands and attempting to convert members of the tribes to Christianity. He recognized the danger his brother had overlooked. On March 22 (Good Friday), 1622, under his leadership, the confederacy launched coordinated attacks all along the river. By the end of the day, 347 colonists (about one-third of the total) lay dead. The colony survived both this

Opechancanough's Attack

war and the one waged by Opechancanough in 1644. His defeat in the latter war cost him his life and ended the Powhatan Confederacy's efforts to resist the spread of white settlement.

Life in the Chesapeake: Virginia and Maryland

After the 1622 massacre, James I revoked the company's charter and made Virginia a royal colony. But he allowed the company's headright system and a representative assembly to survive. The headright granted each colonist fifty acres of land, with a proportional number of headrights allotted to those financing the passage of others. The assembly, called the House of Burgesses, had been created in 1619. It gave the settlers a representative system of government with considerable local autonomy.

In 1634, Virginia acquired a neighbor: the proprietorship of Maryland was founded in the area north of the Potomac River. The Calvert family, who founded Maryland, intended the colony to serve as a haven for their fellow Roman Catholics, who were being persecuted in England. Cecilius Calvert, second Lord Baltimore, became the first colonizer to offer prospective settlers freedom of religion, as long as they were practicing Christians. In that respect Maryland differed from Virginia, where the Church of England was the only officially recognized religion. In other ways, however, the two Chesapeake colonies resembled each other. In Maryland as in Virginia, tobacco planters spread out along the riverbanks, establishing isolated farms instead of towns.

Founding of Maryland

The planting, cultivation, and harvesting of tobacco had to be done by hand; these tasks did not take much skill, but they were repetitive and time-consuming. When the headright system was adopted in Maryland in 1640, a prospective tobacco planter anywhere in the Chesapeake could simultaneously obtain both land and the labor to work it. Through good management a planter could use his profits to pay for the passage of more workers, gain title to more land, and accumulate substantial wealth rapidly.

There were two possible sources of laborers for the growing tobacco farms of the Chesapeake: Africa and England. In 1619, a Dutch privateer brought more than twenty blacks from the Spanish Caribbean islands to Virginia; they were the first known black inhabitants of the English colonies in North America. Over the next few decades, small numbers of blacks were carried to the Chesapeake, but even as late as 1670 the black population of Virginia was at most 2,000. Chesapeake planters looked to England, not Africa or the West Indies, to supply their labor needs. Workers migrated from England as indentured servants: that is, in return for their passage they contracted to work for planters for periods ranging from four to seven years.

Indentured servants accounted for 75 to 85 percent of the approximately 130,000 English migrants to Virginia and Maryland during the seventeenth century. Roughly three-quarters of them were men between the ages of fifteen and twenty-four. Most had been farmers and laborers. (Because men did the agricultural work in England, the colonists preferred males as field laborers.) They were what their contemporaries called the "common" or "middling" sort. Judging by their youth, though, most had probably not yet established themselves in England.

Migrants to the Chesapeake

What motivated the servants to leave their homeland? Many came from areas of England that were experiencing severe economic disruption. For such people the Chesapeake appeared to offer good prospects. Once they had fulfilled the terms of their indentures, servants were promised "freedom dues," consisting of clothes, tools, livestock, casks of corn and tobacco, and sometimes even land.

Chapter 1: The Meeting of Old World and New, 1492–1650

Their lives as servants were difficult. They typically worked six days a week, ten to fourteen hours a day, in a climate much warmer than they were accustomed to. Their masters could discipline or sell them, and they faced severe penalties for running away. Even so, the laws did offer them some protection. For example, their masters had to supply them with sufficient food, clothing, and shelter, and they could not be beaten excessively.

Conditions of Servitude

On occasion, servants turned to the courts with complaints of mistreatment. Judges clearly favored masters, yet tried to prevent the worst atrocities. A 1655 case illustrated the way the Maryland courts balanced the financial interests of masters against the physical well-being of servants. A runaway maidservant, who complained of "Extream Usage" and was known to have been beaten by her mistress for "two hours by the clock," was ordered freed from her indenture. Yet the court insisted that she compensate her master for the loss of her time.

Servants and planters alike had to contend with epidemic disease; death rates in the Chesapeake were higher than England's. After surviving a process called "seasoning"—a bout with disease (probably malaria)—immigrants were confronted with dysentery, influenza, typhoid, and recurrences of malaria. As a result, approximately 40 percent of the male servants did not survive long enough to become freedmen.

For those who survived the term of their indentures, however, the opportunities for advancement were real. Until the last decades of the century, former servants were usually able to become independent planters ("freeholders") and to live a modest but comfortable existence. Some even became prominent. But after 1670 tobacco prices fell, land became expensive, and Maryland dropped its requirement that freed servants receive land as part of their freedom dues. By 1700 the Chesapeake was no longer the land of opportunity it had once been.

Life in the Chesapeake was hard for everyone. Prior to being cultivated, fields had to be cleared of trees. Most settlers lived in houses that were little more than shacks, had few material possessions, and consumed a diet based upon pork and corn. Indeed, the lack of a nutritious diet magnified the health problems caused by epidemic disease.

Family Life in the Chesapeake

The predominance of males, the incidence of servitude, and the high mortality rates combined to produce unusual patterns of family life. Female servants normally were not allowed to marry during their terms of indenture, since masters did not want pregnancies to deprive them of workers. Many male ex-servants could not marry at all, because there were so few women. On the other hand, nearly every adult free woman in the Chesapeake married, and the many widows commonly remarried within a few months of a husband's death. Yet because their marriages were delayed by servitude or broken by death, Chesapeake women bore only one to three children, in contrast to English women, who normally had at least five.

As a result of the demographic patterns that led to a low rate of natural increase, recent migrants made up a majority of the Chesapeake population throughout the seventeenth century. That fact had important implications for politics in Maryland and Virginia. Since migrants dominated the population, they also composed the vast majority of the membership of both Virginia's House of Burgesses and Maryland's House of Delegates (established in 1635). So too they dominated the governors' councils in both colonies. (The council acted in three important capacities: as part of the legislature, as the colony's highest court, and as executive advisor to the governor.)

Chesapeake Politics

English-born colonists naturally tended to look to England for solutions to their problems, and migrants frequently relied on English allies to advance their cause. The seventeenth-century leaders of the Chesapeake colonies engaged in bitter and prolonged struggles for power and personal economic advantage; these struggles often thwarted the colonial governments' ability to function effectively. As a result, the existence of representative institutions failed to lead to political stability. Thus, the people of the Chesapeake paid a high price for the area's unusual population patterns.

The Chesapeake was not, however, representative of all the English settlements in North America. In New England, immigrants seeking freedom of religion established a very different society.

THE FOUNDING OF NEW ENGLAND

The economic motives that prompted English people to move to the Chesapeake colonies also drew men and women to New England. But because Puritans organized the New England colonies, and because the northern landscape and climate were more conducive to diversified small farms than to large production units producing staple crops, the northern settlements turned out very differently from those in the South.

Religion was a constant presence in the lives of pious Puritans. As followers of John Calvin, they believed that an omnipotent God predestined souls to heaven or hell before birth. One of their primary duties as Christians, though, was to assess the state of their own souls. They thus devoted themselves to self-examination and Bible study. Yet even the most pious could never be absolutely certain that they were numbered among the saved. Consequently, devout Puritans were filled with anxiety about their spiritual state.

Puritan Beliefs

Some Puritans (called Congregationalists) wanted to reform the Church of England rather than abandon it. Another group, known as Separatists, believed that church to be so corrupt it could not be salvaged. The only way to purify it, they believed, was to start anew, establishing their own religious bodies, with membership restricted to the saved (as nearly as they could be identified).

Founding of Plymouth

In 1620 some Separatists, many of whom had earlier migrated to Holland in quest of the right to practice their religion freely, obtained permission to settle in part of the territory controlled by the Virginia Company. A total of 101 men and women, some of them "strangers" (non-Separatists), set sail in September on the aged, crowded *Mayflower*. Two months later they sighted land—the tip of Cape Cod, which was outside the northern boundary of the company's territory. But by then it was too late in the fall to go elsewhere. The Pilgrims located their settlement on a fine harbor that had been occupied by an Indian village destroyed in a great epidemic in 1616–1618. While everyone was still on board the ship, the Pilgrims drafted the Mayflower Compact, through which they established a "Civil Body Politic" and a rudimentary legal authority for the colony.

Survival was the major challenge facing the Pilgrims in 1620 and 1621. Like the Jamestown settlers before them, they were poorly prepared to survive in the new environment. Their difficulties were compounded by the season of their arrival, for they barely had time to build shelters before winter descended on them. Only half of the *Mayflower*'s passengers were still alive by spring. But, again like the Virginians, the Pilgrims benefited from the political circumstances of their Indian neighbors.

The Pokanoket (also known as the Wampanoag) controlled the area in which the Pilgrims had settled, yet their villages had suffered terrible losses in the epidemic. In order to protect themselves from the powerful Narragansett Indians of the southern New England coast, the Pokanoket decided to ally themselves with the newcomers. In the spring of 1621, their leader, Massasoit, signed a treaty with the Pilgrims, and during the colony's first difficult years the Pokanoket supplied the English with essential foodstuffs. The settlers were also assisted by what one of them termed "a special instrument sent of God" in the person of Squanto, a friendly Indian. Squanto, an escaped kidnap victim of an English sea captain, spoke good English and served as the Pilgrims' interpreter. He also showed them how to plant corn Indian-style and where to fish.

Before the 1620s had ended, a group of Congregationalists launched the colonial enterprise that would come to dominate New England. When Charles I, who was more hostile to Puritan beliefs than his father, James I, became king in 1625, some non-Separatists began to think about settling in America. A group of Congregationalist merchants sent out a body of settlers to Cape Ann, north of Cape Cod, in 1628. The following year the merchants obtained a royal charter, constituting themselves as the Massachusetts Bay Company. They boldly decided to transfer the headquarters of the Massachusetts Bay Company to New England. The settlers would then be answerable to no one in the mother country and would be able to handle their affairs, secular and religious, as they pleased

Founding of Massachusetts Bay Company

The most important recruit to the new venture was John Winthrop, a pious gentleman from Suffolk and a justice of the peace. In October 1629, the members of the Massachusetts Bay Company elected the forty-one-year-old Winthrop as their governor. It thus fell to Winthrop to organize the initial segment of the great Puritan migration to America. In 1630 more than one thousand English men and women came to Massachusetts—most of them to Boston, which soon became the largest town in North America. By 1643 nearly twenty thousand compatriots had followed them.

Governor John Winthrop

Winthrop's was a transcendent vision. The society he foresaw in Puritan America was a true commonwealth, a community in which each person put the good of the whole ahead of his or her private concerns. In America, he asserted, "we shall build a city upon a hill, the eyes of all people are upon us." People in this "city upon a hill" were to live according to the precepts of Christian charity, loving friends and enemies alike. The creation of an ideal society was a special mission to Puritans.

The Puritans' communal ideal was expressed chiefly in the doctrine of the covenant. They believed God had made a covenant—that is, an agreement or contract—with them when He chose them for the special mission to America. In turn they covenanted with each other, promising to work together toward their goals. The founders of churches and towns in the new land often drafted formal documents setting forth the principles on which such institutions would be based. The same was true of the colonial governments of New England.

Ideal of the Covenant

The leaders of Massachusetts Bay likewise transformed their original joint-stock company charter into the basis for a covenanted community based on mutual consent. Under pressure from the settlers, they gradually changed the General Court, officially merely the company's governing body, into a colonial legislature and opened the status of freeman, or voting member of the company, to all adult male church members resident in Massachusetts. Less than two decades after the first large group of Puritans had arrived in Massachusetts Bay, the colony had a functioning system of self-government composed of a governor and a two-house legislature.

The colony's method of distributing land helped to further the communal ideal. Groups of families—often from the same region of England—applied together to the General Court for grants of land on which to establish towns. The men who received the original town grant determined how the land would be distributed. Understandably, they copied the villages from which they came. First they laid out town lots for houses and a church. Then they gave each family parcels of land scattered around the town center: pasture here, a woodlot there, an arable field elsewhere. They also reserved the best

New England Towns

and largest plots for the most distinguished among them (usually including the minister); people who had been low on the social scale in England were given much smaller and less desirable allotments. Even when migrants began to move beyond the territorial limits of the Bay Colony into Connecticut (1636), New Haven (1638), and New Hampshire (1638), the same pattern of town land grants was maintained.

Thus New England settlements initially tended to be more compact than those of the Chesapeake. Town centers grew up quickly, developing in three distinctly different ways. Some, chiefly isolated agricultural settlements in the interior, tried to sustain Winthrop's vision of harmonious community life based on diversified family farms. A second group, the coastal towns like Boston and Salem, became bustling seaports, serving as the places of entry for thousands of new migrants and as focal points for trade. The third category, commercialized agricultural towns, grew up in the Connecticut River valley. There the easy water transportation made it possible for farmers to sell surplus goods readily.

The migration to the Connecticut valley ended the Puritans' relative freedom from clashes with neighboring Indians. The first English settlers in the valley moved there from Newtown (Cambridge), under the direction of their minister, Thomas Hooker. Connecticut was fertile, though remote from the other English towns, and the wide river promised ready access to the ocean. The site had just one problem: it fell within the territory controlled by the Pequot Indians.

Pequot dominance was based on their role as primary middlemen in the trade between New England Indians and the Dutch in New Netherland. The arrival of English settlers signaled the end of Pequot power over the regional trading networks, for their tributary bands could now trade directly with Europeans. Clashes between the Pequot and the English began even before the Connecticut valley settlements were established, but their founding tipped the balance toward war. After trying without success to en-

Pequot War

list other Indians to resist English expansion into the interior, the Pequot (after an English raid on their villages) attacked the new town of Wethersfield in April 1637, killing nine and capturing two of the colonists. In retaliation, a Massachusetts Bay expedition the following month attacked and burned the main Pequot town on the Mystic River. The Englishmen and their Narragansett Indian allies slaughtered at least four hundred people, many of them women and children. The few surviving Pequots were captured and enslaved.

Just five years later the Narragansett leader Miantonomi realized that the Pequot had been correct in assessing the danger posed by the Puritan settlements. He tried but failed to forge a pan-Indian alliance, and he was killed in 1643 by other Indians acting at the English colonists' behest.

For the next thirty years, the New England Indians tried to accommodate themselves to the spread of white settlement. They traded with the whites and sometimes worked for them, but for the most part they resisted acculturation or incorporation into English society. Indeed, most whites showed little interest in the Indians except as laborers or producers of valuable trade goods. Only a few Puritan clerics (most notably John Eliot) seriously attempted to convert the Massachusetts Bay Indians to Christianity and they met with relatively little success.

LIFE IN NEW ENGLAND

Two sets of comparisons will help to illuminate the lives of early New Englanders: first, with the Indians of the region, and second, with the Chesapeake colonists.

The major contrast between the lifestyles of Indian and white residents of New England was the mobility of the former and the stability of the latter. The agricultural Algonkians of New England commonly moved four or five times a year to take full advantage

Indian and English Lifestyles Compared

of their environment. In the spring, women would plant the fields, but once the crops were well established they would not need regular attention for several months. Accordingly, villages then broke into small mobile bands; women occupied themselves with gathering, men with hunting and fishing. The village would reassemble for harvest, then once again disperse for the fall hunting season. Finally, the people would spend the harsh winter months together, probably in some protected valley, before returning to their fields again in the spring.

The English settlers, by contrast, lived year-round in the same location. Unlike the Indians or the Chesapeake colonists, New Englanders constructed sturdy, permanent dwellings intended to last for many years. They used the same fields again and again. Although they hunted and fished, their chief source of meat was the livestock they bred on their farms. Farmers had to fence their croplands to keep hogs, sheep, and cattle from eating the growing plants; many disputes between neighbors or even entire towns had their origins in one side's livestock having invaded the other side's fields. When New Englanders began to spread out over the countryside, the reason was not so much human crowding as it was animal crowding.

In their heavy reliance on cattle and hogs, white New Englanders resembled their Chesapeake counterparts. But in other ways they differed sharply from them.

Unlike migrants to the Chesapeake, Puritans commonly moved to America in family groups. Thus, the age range of New Englanders was wide and the sexes more balanced numerically, so that the population could immediately begin to reproduce itself. Moreover, New England's climate was much healthier than that of the Chesapeake. Once Puritan settlements had survived the difficult first two or three years and established self-sufficiency in foodstuffs, New England proved to be even healthier than the mother country.

Consequently, although Chesapeake population patterns made for families that were few in number, small in size, and transitory, the demographic characteristics of New England made families there numerous, large, and long-lived. In New England most men were able to marry; migrant women married young (at twenty, on the average); and marriages lasted longer and produced more children, who were more likely to live to maturity.

Family Life in New England

The nature of the population had other major implications for family life. New England in effect created grandparents, since in England people rarely lived long enough to know their children's children. And whereas seventeenth-century southern parents normally died before their children married, northern parents exercised a good deal of control over their adult children. Young men could not marry without acreage to cultivate, and because of the communal land-grant system they were dependent on their fathers to supply them with that land. Daughters, too, needed the dowry of household goods their parents would give them when they married. Yet parents needed their children's labor and were often reluctant to see them marry and start their own households. That at times led to considerable conflict between the generations. On the whole, though, children seem to have obeyed their parents' wishes, for they had few alternatives.

Another important difference lay in the influence of religion on New Englanders' lives. The governments of Massachusetts Bay, Plymouth, Connecticut, and the other early northern colonies were all controlled by Puritans. Congregationalism was the only officially recognized religion; members of other sects had no freedom of worship except in Rhode Island. In most of the colonies only male church members could vote. All households were taxed to build meetinghouses and pay ministers' salaries. Massachusetts' *Body of Laws and Liberties* incorporated regulations drawn from Old Testament scriptures into the legal code of the colony.

In the New England colonies, church and state were intertwined. Puritans objected to secular interference in religious affairs, but at the same time expected the church to influence the conduct of poli-

IMPORTANT EVENTS

1492	Christopher Columbus reaches Bahama Islands		1619	First blacks arrive in Virginia
1518–30	Smallpox pandemic decimates Indian population of Central and South America		1620	Plymouth Colony founded
			1622	Powhatan Confederacy attacks Virginia colony
1521	Tenochtitlan surrenders to Cortés; Aztec empire falls to Spaniards		1624	Dutch settle on Manhattan Island
			1625	Charles I becomes king
1533	Henry VIII divorces Catherine of Aragon; English reformation begins		1630	Massachusetts Bay Colony founded
			1634	Maryland founded
1535	Francisco Pizarro conquers the Incas		1635	Roger Williams expelled from Massachusetts Bay; founds Providence, Rhode Island
1558	Elizabeth I becomes queen			
1587–90	Sir Walter Raleigh's Roanoke colony fails		1636	Connecticut founded
1603	James I becomes king		1637	Pequot War
1607	Jamestown founded			Anne Hutchinson expelled from Massachusetts Bay Colony
1611	First Virginia tobacco crop			

tics. They also believed that the state had an obligation to support and protect the one true church—theirs. As a result, though they came to America seeking freedom to worship as they wished, they saw no contradiction in their refusal to grant that freedom to others. Indeed, the two most significant divisions in early Massachusetts were caused by religious disputes and by Massachusetts Bay's unwillingness to tolerate dissent.

Roger Williams, a Separatist, migrated to Massachusetts Bay in 1631 and became assistant pastor at Salem. Williams soon began to express the eccentric

Roger Williams

ideas that the king had no right to give away land belonging to the Indians, that church and state should be kept entirely separate, and that Puritans should

not impose their religious beliefs on others. Banished from Massachusetts in 1635, Williams founded the town of Providence on Narragansett Bay. Because of his beliefs, Providence and other towns in what became the colony of Rhode Island adopted a policy of tolerating all religions, including Judaism.

The other dissenter, and an even greater challenge to Massachusetts Bay orthodoxy, was Anne Marbury Hutchinson. She was a follower of John Cotton, a

Anne Hutchinson

minister who stressed God's free gift of salvation to unworthy humans (the covenant of grace). In 1636 Hutchinson began holding meetings in her home. At first, her gatherings included only women, but later men attended as well. She talked about the covenant of grace, going beyond the views of John Cotton. Indeed, Hutchinson embraced the Antinomian heresy—the belief that the elect can communicate directly with God and be assured of salvation. She thus offered Puritans relief from the tension associated with the uncertainty of salvation.

Anne Hutchinson posed a dual threat, one theological and one social, to the Puritan world. She was charged by the General Court with having libeled the colony's clerics by claiming that they preached salvation through works. Her banishment to Rhode Island was assured when she stated that God had spoken directly to her. Equally significant was her challenge to traditional gender roles. Her judges were almost as outraged by her "masculine" behavior as by her heretical beliefs. As one of them told her, "You have stept out of your place, you have rather bine a Husband than a Wife and a preacher than a Hearer; and a Magistrate than a Subject."

The New England authorities' reaction to Anne Hutchinson reveals the depth of their adherence to European gender-role concepts. To them, an orderly society required the submission of wives to husbands as well as the obedience of subjects to rulers. Indeed, one reason why they perceived Indian societies as disorderly was because Indian women seemed to be largely independent of male authority. English people intended to change many aspects of their lives by colonizing North America, but not the sexual division of labor or the assumption of male superiority.

In 1630 John Winthrop wrote to his wife Margaret, who was still in England, "my deare wife, we are heer in a paradise." Yet even though America was not a paradise, it was a place where English men and women could free themselves from Stuart persecution or attempt to better their economic circumstances. Many died, but those who lived laid the foundation for subsequent colonial prosperity. That they did so by dispossessing the Indians bothered few besides Roger Williams. By the middle of the seventeenth century, English people had unquestionably come to North America to stay.

The permanent presence of Europeans on the soil of the Americas signaled major changes for the peoples of both Old and New Worlds. European political rivalries, once confined to their own continent, now spread around the globe, as the competing nations of England, Spain, Portugal, France, and the Netherlands vied for control of the peoples and resources of Asia, Africa, and the Americas. In the years to come, the European rivalries would grow even fiercer, and residents of the Americas—whites, Indians, and blacks alike—would inevitably be drawn into them. Not until after France and England in the mid-eighteenth century had fought the greatest war yet known, and until the thirteen American colonies had won their independence, would those rivalries cease to affect Americans of all races.

SUGGESTIONS FOR FURTHER READING

General

Charles M. Andrews, *The Colonial Period of American History: The Settlements*, 3 vols. (1934–1937); Gary B. Nash, *Red, White, and Black: The Peoples of Early America*, 2nd ed. (1982); Robert V. Wells, *Revolutions in Americans' Lives: A Demographic Perspective on the History of Americans, Their Families, and Their Society* (1982).

Indians

Harold E. Driver, *Indians of North America*, 2nd ed. (1969); Alvin Josephy, Jr., *The Indian Heritage of America* (1968); Alice B. Kehoe, *North American Indians: A Comprehensive Account* (1981); Robert F. Spencer, Jesse D. Jennings, *et al., The Native Americans*, 2nd ed. (1977).

Africa

Richard Olaniyan, *African History and Culture* (1982); Roland Oliver and J. D. Fage, *A Short History of Africa* (1975).

England

Peter Laslett, *The World We Have Lost* (1965); Wallace

Notestein, *The English People on the Eve of Colonization 1603–1630* (1954); Michael Walzer, *The Revolution of the Saints* (1965); Keith Wrightson, *English Society 1580–1680* (1982).

Exploration and Discovery

Alfred W. Crosby, Jr., *The Columbian Exchange: Biological and Cultural Consequences of 1492* (1972); Samuel Eliot Morison, *The European Discovery of America: The Northern Voyages, A.D. 1500–1600* (1971), *The Southern Voyages, A.D. 1492–1616* (1974); J. H. Parry, *The Age of Reconnaissance* (1963); David B. Quinn, *North America from Earliest Discovery to First Settlements* (1977).

Early Contact Between Whites and Indians

James Axtell, *The Invasion Within* (1985); William Cronon, *Changes in the Land* (1983); Francis Jennings, *The Invasion of America* (1975); Karen O. Kupperman, *Roanoke: The Abandoned Colony* (1984); Neal Salisbury, *Manitou and Providence* (1982); Alden T. Vaughan, *American Genesis: Captain John Smith and the Founding of Virginia* (1975).

New England

Ben Barker-Benfield, "Anne Hutchinson and the Puritan Attitude Toward Women," *Feminist Studies,* I (1972), 65–96; John Demos, *A Little Commonwealth* (1970); Philip J. Greven, Jr., *Four Generations* (1970); Stephen Innes, *Labor in a New Land* (1983); Lyle Koehler, *A Search for Power: The "Weaker Sex" in Seventeenth-Century New England* (1980); Kenneth A. Lockridge, *A New England Town: The First Hundred Years* (1970); Edmund S. Morgan, *The Puritan Dilemma: The Story of John Winthrop* (1958); Edmund S. Morgan, *The Puritan Family* (1966); Alan Simpson, *Puritanism in Old and New England* (1955).

Chesapeake

Lois Green Carr and Lorena Walsh, "The Planter's Wife: The Experience of White Women in Seventeenth-Century Maryland," *William and Mary Quarterly,* 3rd ser., 34 (1977), 542–571; Wesley Frank Craven, *The Southern Colonies in the Seventeenth Century, 1607–1689* (1949); David Galenson, *White Servitude in Colonial America* (1981); Ivor Noel Hume, *Martin's Hundred* (1979); Gloria L. Main, *Tobacco Colony* (1983); Edmund S. Morgan, *American Slavery, American Freedom* (1975); Darrett Rutman and Anita Rutman, *A Place in Time* (1984); Abbot E. Smith, *Colonists in Bondage* (1947); Thad W. Tate and David L. Ammerman, eds., *The Chesapeake in the Seventeenth Century* (1979).

CHAPTER 2

AMERICAN SOCIETY TAKES SHAPE 1650–1720

Olaudah Equiano was eleven years old in 1756 when black raiders in search of slaves kidnapped him from his village in what is now Nigeria. As a captive, Equiano passed from master to master, finally arriving at the coast, where an English slave ship lay at anchor. Terrified by the light complexions, long hair, and strange language of the sailors, he was afraid that "I had gotten into a world of bad spirits and that they were going to kill me." Equiano was placed below decks, where "with the loathsomeness of the stench and crying together, I became so sick and low that I was not able to eat, nor had I the least desire to taste anything."

The youthful Equiano was carried to Virginia, where he was separated from the other Africans and put to work weeding and clearing rocks from the fields. "I was now exceedingly miserable and thought myself worse off than any of the rest of my companions," Equiano recalled in a narrative of his life, "for they could talk to each other, but I had no person to speak to that I could understand. In this state I was constantly grieving and pining and wishing for death rather than anything else."

Equiano's story illustrates one of the major developments in colonial life during the century after 1650: the importation of more than two hundred thousand unwilling, captive Africans into North America. The introduction of the institution of slavery and the arrival of large numbers of West African peoples dramatically reshaped colonial society. Indeed, the geographic patterns of that migration continue to influence the United States to the present day.

The other important trends in colonial life between 1650 and 1720 involved the English colonists' relationships with their mother country and their American neighbors. Dramatic events in England during this period affected its New World colonies, and by the end of the seventeenth century they were no longer isolated outposts but an integral part of a far-flung mercantile empire. Further, as the Anglo-American settlements expanded, they came into violent conflict not only with powerful Indian tribes but also with the Dutch, French, and Spanish. By 1720, war was an all too frequent feature of American life.

THE ENGLISH CIVIL WAR, THE STUART RESTORATION, AND THE AMERICAN COLONIES

By the time Charles I became king in 1625, members of the Puritan sect dominated Parliament. For eleven years (1629–1640) Charles, who wanted to suppress Puritanism, refused to call Parliament into session. When Parliament finally met, it passed laws limiting the monarch's authority. In 1642 civil war broke out. Four years later, Parliament triumphed; Charles I was executed in 1649.

Oliver Cromwell, the leader of the parliamentary army, controlled the government until his death in 1658. Parliament decided to restore the monarchy if Charles I's son and heir would agree to certain restrictions on his authority. In 1660, Charles II assumed the throne, having promised to seek Parliament's consent for any new taxes and to support the Church of England. Thus ended the tumultuous chapter in English history known as the Interregnum (Latin for "between reigns").

The Civil War and Interregnum had important consequences for England's American colonies. Political disruption in the mother country fostered similar disruption in America. For several years both Virginia and Maryland were wracked by disputes over the structure of political and religious authority. In New England the effects were long-term. Because the Puritan triumph in England removed dissenters' major incentive for moving to America, migration to Massachusetts Bay largely ceased after 1640. This had a profound impact on the colony's economy and its subsequent development. The Stuart Restoration, which again placed Anglicans (members of the Church of England) in power, effectively isolated the New England Puritans within the empire. By the last quarter of the century, friction between the northern colonies and the mother country had increased substantially.

The reign of Charles II (1660–1685) had enormous significance for the future United States. Six of the colonies that eventually would form the nation were either founded or came under English rule during that period: New York, New Jersey, Pennsylvania (including Delaware), and North and South Carolina. All were proprietorships: that is, like Maryland they were granted in their entirety to one man or a group of men, who both held title to the soil and controlled the government. Charles II gave these vast American holdings as rewards to the men who had supported him during his years of exile.

One of the first to benefit was Charles's younger brother James, the Duke of York. In March 1664, acting as though the Dutch colony of New Netherland did not exist, Charles II gave James the region between the Connecticut and Delaware rivers, including the Hudson Valley and Long Island. James immediately organized an invasion fleet. In late August the vessels anchored off Manhattan Island and demanded New Netherland's surrender. The Dutch complied without firing a shot.

Thus England acquired a tiny but heterogeneous possession. New Netherland had been founded in 1624, but had remained small in comparison to its English neighbors. As a trading outpost of the Dutch West India Company, whose chief economic interests lay elsewhere, New Netherland was neglected. And because the Dutch were not afflicted by the economic and religious pressures that caused English people to move to the New World, migration was sparse. Even a company policy of 1629 that offered a large land grant, or patroonship, to anyone who would bring fifty settlers to the province failed to attract takers. In the mid-1660s, when the Duke of

New Netherland Becomes New York

t' Fort nieúw Amsterdam op de Manhatans

New Amsterdam in 1651. Appropriately, given their importance to the survival of the colony, fur-trading Indians and vessels of the Dutch West India Company figure prominently in the earliest known view of the Dutch outpost on Manhattan Island.   Library of Congress.

York assumed control, New Netherland had only about five thousand inhabitants.

Logically enough, the Dutch made up the largest proportion of the population. New York, as it was now called, also included within its population Puritans who had left New England, migrants from several areas of Europe, and Africans. Because the Dutch West India Company actively imported slaves into the colony, almost one-fifth of New York City's approximately 1,500 inhabitants were black. Slaves thus constituted a higher proportion of New York's urban population than of the Chesapeake's at the same time.

Recognizing the diversity of the population, the Duke of York's representatives moved cautiously in their efforts to establish English authority. Dutch forms of local government were maintained and Dutch land titles confirmed. Religious toleration was guaranteed: each town was permitted to decide which church to support with its tax revenues. Furthermore, the Dutch were allowed to maintain their customary legal practices. Much to the chagrin of English residents of the colony, the duke made no provision for a representative assembly. James was suspicious of legislative bodies, and so not until 1683 did he agree to the colonists' requests for an elected legislature.

The English takeover thus had little immediate effect on the colony. Its population grew slowly, barely reaching eighteen thousand by the time of the first English census in 1698. One of the chief reasons why the English conquest brought so little change to New York was that the Duke of York quickly regranted the land between the Hudson

Founding of New Jersey

and Delaware rivers—New Jersey—to his friends Sir George Carteret and John Lord Berkeley. That left his own colony confined between Connecticut to the east and New Jersey to the west, depriving it of much fertile land and hindering its economic growth. He also failed to promote migration. Meanwhile the New Jersey proprietors acted rapidly to attract settlers, promising generous land grants, freedom of religion, and—without authorization from the Crown—a representative assembly.

Within twenty years, Berkeley and Carteret sold their interests in New Jersey to Quakers, who were seeking a refuge from persecution in England. The Quakers, formally known as the Society of Friends, denied the need for an intermediary between the individual and God. Anyone, they believed, could receive the "inner light" and be saved, and all were equal in God's sight. They had no formally trained clergy; any Quaker, male or female, who felt the call could become a "public Friend" and travel from meeting to meeting to discuss God's word. Moreover, any member of the Society could speak in meeting if he or she desired. In short, the Quakers were true religious radicals in the mold of Anne Hutchinson.

The Quakers obtained a colony of their own in 1681, when Charles II granted the region between Maryland and New York to William Penn, one of the sect's most prominent members. **Pennsylvania, a Quaker Haven** Penn's father, Admiral William Penn, had originally served Oliver Cromwell, but later joined forces with Charles II and even loaned the monarch a substantial sum of money. The younger Penn became a Quaker in the mid-1660s, much to his father's dismay. But despite Penn's radical political and religious beliefs, he and Charles II were close personal friends. The publicly stated reason for the grant—repayment of the loan from Penn's father—was a public rationalization for a private act.

William Penn held the colony as a personal proprietorship, and the vast property holdings earned profits for his descendants until the American Revolution. Even so, Penn saw the province not merely as a source of revenue but also as a haven for his persecuted coreligionists. Penn offered land to all comers on liberal terms, promised toleration for all religions (though only Christians were given the right to vote), guaranteed such English liberties as the right to bail and trial by jury, and pledged to establish a representative assembly.

Penn's activities and the natural attraction of his lands for Quakers gave rise to a migration whose magnitude was equaled only by the Puritan exodus to New England in the 1630s. By mid-1683, over three thousand people—among them Welsh, Irish, Dutch, and Germans—had already moved to Pennsylvania, and within five years the population had reached twelve thousand. Philadelphia, carefully planned to be the major city in the province, drew merchants and artisans from throughout the English-speaking world. Pennsylvania's lands were both plentiful and fertile, and the colony soon began exporting flour and other foodstuffs to the West Indies. Practically overnight Philadelphia acquired more than two thousand citizens and began to challenge Boston's commercial pre-eminence.

A pacifist with egalitarian principles, Penn was determined to treat the Indians of Pennsylvania fairly. He purchased tracts of land from the Delaware (or Lenni Lenape), the dominant tribe in the region, before selling them to settlers. Penn also established strict regulations for the Indian trade and forbade the sale of alcohol to tribesmen. Penn's Indian policy prompted several tribes to move to Pennsylvania. By a supreme irony, however, the same toleration that attracted Indians to Penn's domains also brought non-Quaker Europeans who showed little respect for Indian claims to the soil. In effect, Penn's policy was so successful that it caused its own downfall. The Scotch, Irish, Palatine Germans, and Swiss who settled in Pennsylvania in the first half of the eighteenth century clashed repeatedly over land with tribes that had also recently migrated to the colony.

The other proprietary colony, granted by Charles II in 1663, encompassed a huge tract of land stretching from the southern boundary of Virginia to Span-

Founding of
Carolina

ish Florida. The proprietors named their new province Carolina in Charles's honor (in Latin his name was Carolus). The "Fundamental Constitutions of Carolina," which they asked the political philosopher John Locke to draft for them, set forth an elaborate plan for a colony governed by a hierarchy of landholding aristocrats and characterized by a carefully structured distribution of political and economic power. But Carolina failed to follow the course the proprietors laid out. Instead it quickly developed two distinct population centers, which in 1729 permanently split into two separate colonies.

The Albemarle region that became North Carolina was first settled by Virginians. They established a society much like their own, with an economy based on tobacco cultivation and the export of such forest products as pitch, tar, and timber. South Carolina developed quite differently. Its first settlers—who founded Charleston in 1670—came from Barbados with their slaves. Perhaps one-quarter to one-third of the first residents of South Carolina were black, and of those three-fourths were male. The high proportion of Africans and Caribbean-born blacks in South Carolina's population from the very beginning inexorably shaped the colony's early history.

THE FORCED MIGRATION

OF AFRICANS

During the first six decades of English settlement in America few blacks were imported into the mainland colonies. After 1670 that pattern changed dramatically. Why did the change occur, in the Chesapeake as well as in South Carolina? And, more important, since England itself had no tradition of slavery, why did English settlers in the New World begin to enslave Africans at all? The answers to both

questions lie in the combined effects of economics and racial attitudes.

The English were an ethnocentric people who believed firmly in the superiority of their values and civilization. Furthermore, they believed that fair-skinned peoples like themselves were superior to the darker-skinned races. Those beliefs alone did not cause them to enslave Indians and Africans, but the idea that other races were inferior to whites helped to justify slavery.

Although the English had not previously practiced slavery, the Spanish and Portuguese had; moreover, Christian doctrine allowed the enslavement of heathen peoples as a means of converting them. Yet the Indians' familiarity with the American environment made them difficult to enslave, and Indian captives were often able to escape from their white masters. But Africans were a different story. Transported far from home and set down in alien surroundings, they were frequently unable to communicate with their fellow workers. They were also the darkest (and thus, to European eyes, the most inferior) of all peoples. Black Africans therefore seemed to be ideal candidates for perpetual servitude.

Slavery
Established

Nevertheless, a fully developed system of lifelong slavery did not emerge immediately in the English colonies. Lack of historical evidence makes it difficult to determine the legal status of blacks during the first two or three decades of English settlement, but many of them seem to have been indentured, like whites, which meant that they eventually became free. (Massachusetts, in 1641, was the first to mention slavery in its legal code.) After 1640, some blacks were being permanently enslaved in each of the English colonies. By the end of the century, the blacks' status was fixed. Barbados adopted a comprehensive slave code as early as 1661, and the mainland provinces soon did the same.

But why did Chesapeake tobacco planters, who had long relied on indentured English servants, begin to purchase blacks in ever-increasing numbers near the end of the seventeenth century? The answer was simple: After about 1675 they could no longer obtain an adequate supply of white workers. A falling birth rate and improved economic conditions in England decreased the number of possible migrants to the colonies. When the shortage of servants became acute in the mid-1670s, the importation of Africans increased dramatically. By 1690, the Chesapeake colonies contained more black slaves than white indentured servants.

Yet not all white planters could afford to devote so much money to purchasing workers. Accordingly, the transition from indentured to enslaved labor increased the social and economic distance between richer and poorer planters. Whites with enough money could acquire slaves and accumulate greater wealth, while less affluent whites could not. As time passed, white Chesapeake society thus became more and more stratified; that is, the gap between rich and poor steadily widened.

Blacks in South Carolina

In South Carolina the first slaves arrived with the first white settlers. Indeed, one-quarter to one-third of South Carolina's early population was black. Whites quickly discovered that Africans had a variety of skills well suited to the semitropical environment of South Carolina. African-style dugout canoes became the chief means of transportation in the colony, which was crisscrossed by rivers. Fishing nets copied from African models proved to be more efficient than those of English origin. And slaves adapted African techniques of cattleherding for use in the American context. Since meat and hides were the colony's chief exports in its earliest years, blacks obviously contributed significantly to South Carolina's prosperity.

The similarity of South Carolina's environment to West Africa, coupled with the large number of blacks in the population, ensured that more aspects of West African culture survived in that colony than elsewhere on the mainland of North America. Only in South Carolina did black parents continue to give their children African names; only there did a dialect develop that combined English words with African terms. (Known as Gullah, it was used in certain areas until the twentieth century.) African skills remained useful, and so techniques that in other regions were lost when the migrant generation died were instead passed down to their children. And in South Carolina, as in West Africa, black women were the primary traders, dominating the markets of Charleston as they did those of Gambia or Benin.

Blacks' central position in the colony's economy was firmly established near the end of the seventeenth century, when South Carolinians began to cultivate a new staple crop: rice. English people knew little about the techniques of growing and processing rice, but slaves from Africa's so-called Rice Coast (present-day Ghana and Sierra Leone) had spent their lives working in the rice fields. It may well have been their expertise that enabled their English masters to grow rice successfully. As the colony's commitment to rice cultivation grew, so did the demand for African workers.

South Carolina later developed a second staple crop, and it too made use of blacks' special skills. The crop was indigo, much prized in Europe as a blue dye for clothing. In the 1740s, Eliza Lucas, a young white West Indian woman who was managing her father's South Carolina plantations, began to experiment with indigo cultivation. Drawing on the knowledge of white and black West Indians, she developed the planting and processing techniques later adopted throughout the colony. Indigo was grown on high ground, and rice was planted in low-lying swampy areas; rice and indigo also had opposite growing seasons. Thus the two crops complemented each other perfectly.

Slavery in the North

After 1700 white southerners were irrevocably committed to black slavery as their chief source of labor. The same was not true of white northerners, for small-scale northern agriculture did not require slave labor. Still, wealthy northerners wanted domestic servants, and slaves could fill that need. By the 1740s, blacks constituted more than 10 percent of the population of New York City, Newport, Rhode Island, and other cities.

The introduction of large-scale slavery in the

South, coupled with its near-absence in the North, accentuated regional differences that had already begun to develop in England's American colonies. To the distinction between diversified agriculture and staple-crop production was now added a difference in the race and status of most laborers. That difference was one of degree, but it was nonetheless crucial.

Between 1492 and 1770 more Africans than Europeans came to the New World. But only about 275,000 of the millions of enslaved Africans were taken to the English mainland colonies in the eighteenth century. By contrast, approximately nine million enslaved blacks were transported to the Caribbean and South America. The magnitude of this trade raises three important and related questions. First, what was its impact on West Africa? Second, how was the trade organized and conducted? Third, what was its effect on the blacks it carried?

The West African coast was one of the most fertile and densely inhabited regions of the continent. Despite the extent of forced migration to the Western Hemisphere, the area was not noticeably depopulated by the trade in human beings. In Guinea, the primary consequences of the trade were political. The coastal kings who served as middlemen in the trade used it as a vehicle to consolidate their power and extend their rule over larger territories. They controlled European traders' access to slaves and at the same time controlled inland peoples' access to desirable European trade goods. The trade thus helped in the formation of such powerful eighteenth-century kingdoms as Dahomey and Asante.

West Africa and the Slave Trade

These West African kings played a crucial role in the functioning of the slave trade. Europeans set up permanent slave-trading posts in Lower Guinea under the protection of local rulers, who then supplied the resident Europeans with slaves to fill the ships that stopped regularly at the coastal forts. Most persons thereby sold into American slavery were wartime captives, criminals sentenced to enslavement, or persons seized for nonpayment of debts. A smaller proportion had been kidnapped, like Olaudah Equiano.

At first, most of the slaves imported into the English colonies went to the Caribbean islands. As mainland planters began to purchase slaves in greater numbers, some blacks were re-exported from the West Indies to meet the demand. Even before the end of the seventeenth century, though, most blacks brought to the future United States came directly from Africa. And although Chesapeake and South Carolina planters initially bought approximately equal numbers of slaves, by the middle of the eighteenth century Carolinians were purchasing three times as many blacks each year as Virginians and Marylanders combined. One result was that blacks made up a majority of the population of South Carolina even before midcentury.

The experience of the Middle Passage (thus named because it was the middle section of the so-called triangular trade among England, Africa, and the Americas) was always traumatic and sometimes fatal for the Africans who made up the ship's cargo. An average of 10 to 20 percent of the slaves died en route, but on voyages that were particularly long or were hard hit by epidemic diseases, the mortality rates were much higher. In addition, some slaves usually died either before the ships left Africa or shortly after their arrival in the New World. Their white captors died at the same, if not higher, rates, chiefly through exposure to alien African germs.

The Middle Passage

On shipboard, men were usually kept shackled in pairs, while women and children were released from any bonds once the ship was well out to sea. In good weather, they were normally allowed on deck for fresh air, because only healthy slaves commanded high prices. Many ships also carried a doctor whose primary role was to treat the slaves' illnesses. The average size of a cargo was about 250 slaves, although since the size of ships varied greatly, so too did the number of slaves carried.

Records of slave traders reveal numerous instances of Africans' resistance to captivity. Some committed suicide; others participated in shipboard revolts. Yet most of the Africans who embarked on the slave vessels arrived in the Americas alive and still in captiv-

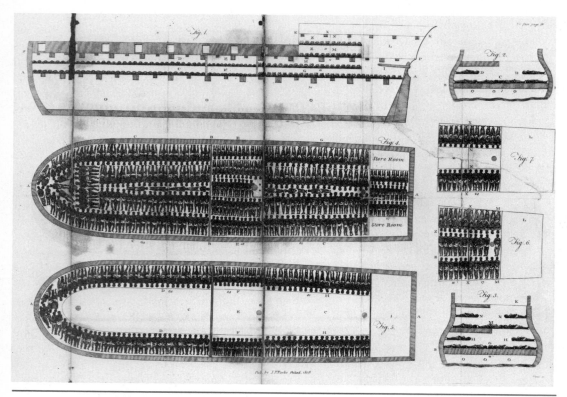

Eighteenth-century diagram of a slave ship, with its human cargo stowed according to British regulations. Many captains did not give slaves even this much room. On the assumption that a large number of Africans would die en route, shipmasters packed as many slaves as possible into the hold to increase their profit.   Library of Congress.

ity; the whites saw to that, for only thus could they make a profit.

RELATIONS BETWEEN WHITES AND INDIANS

Everywhere in North America, European colonizers depended heavily on the labor of native peoples. But their reliance on the Indians took varying forms in different parts of the continent. In the Northeast, France, England, and the Netherlands competed for the pelts supplied by Indian hunters. In the Southeast, England, Spain, and later France each tried to control a thriving trade with the tribes in deerskins and Indian slaves. Finally, in the Southwest, Spain attempted to exploit the agricultural and artisan skills of the Pueblo peoples.

Spanish colonizers first settled in the present-day United States during the last half of the sixteenth century. In 1565, Pedro Menéndez de Avilés, a Spanish noble, along with a group of soldiers, settlers, and priests, established the first permanent settlement in the United States: St. Augustine, Florida. Just over thirty years later (1598) a similar group led by Juan de Oñate, a Mexican-born adventurer, colonized New Mexico. By the late eighteenth century Spain claimed a vast territory that stretched from California (initially colonized in 1769) through Texas (chiefly settled after 1700) to the Gulf Coast.

But Spain's ability to control such an immense area was questionable, to say the least. Nowhere was that more clear than in New Mexico, the heartland of northern New Spain. During the

Popé and the Pueblo Revolt

seventeenth century, Spanish settlers and missionaries based at Santa Fé ruthlessly forced Indian laborers to work their fields and care for their livestock. The Franciscans also adopted brutal tactics as they tried to wipe out all vestiges of the native religion. Finally, in 1680 the Pueblos revolted under the leadership of Popé, a respected medicine man, and successfully drove the Spaniards out of New Mexico. Although Spanish authority was nominally restored in 1692, Spain had learned its lesson. From that time on Spanish governors stressed cooperation, rather than confrontation, with the Pueblos and no longer attempted to reduce them to bondage or to violate their cultural integrity. The Pueblo revolt was the most successful and longest sustained Indian resistance movement in colonial North America.

Along the eastern seaboard Europeans valued the Indians as hunters rather than as agricultural workers, but they were no less dependent on Indian labor than were the Spanish in the west. South Carolina provides a case in point. The Barbadians who colonized the region moved quickly to establish a vigorous trade in deerskins with nearby tribes. The trade gave rise to other exchanges that reveal the complexity of the economic relationships among Indians and Europeans. For example, the horses white Carolinians needed to carry the deerskins came from the Creek Indians, who had in turn obtained them from the Spaniards through trade and capture.

Another important component of the Carolina trade was traffic in Indian slaves. The warring tribes of South Carolina (especially the Creek) profited from selling their captive enemies to the whites. There are no reliable statistics on the extent of the trade in Indian slaves, but in 1708 they made up 14 percent of the population of South Carolina. Many were Christians converted by the Spanish missions in northern Florida, then captured by Englishmen and their Indian allies.

Indian Slave Trade

A major conflict between white Carolinians and neighboring tribes also added to the supply of Indian slaves. In 1711, the Tuscarora, an Iroquoian people who had migrated southward many years earlier, attacked the Swiss-German settlement of New Bern, which had expropriated their lands without payment. The Tuscarora had been avid slavers and had sold many captives from weaker Algonkian tribes to the whites. Those tribes seized the opportunity to settle old scores, joining with the English colonists to defeat their enemy. In the end, more than a thousand Tuscarora were themselves sold into slavery, and the remnants of the tribe drifted northward, returning to their ancient homeland in northern Pennsylvania and southern New York.

The abuses of the slave trade led to the most destructive Indian war in Carolina. White traders were notorious for cheating the Indians, physically abusing them (including raping the women), and selling friendly tribesmen into slavery when no enemy captives came readily to hand. In the spring of 1715 the Yamasee, aided by the Creek and a number of other tribes, retaliated by attacking the English colonists. At times the Creek-Yamasee offensive came close to driving the intruders from the mainland altogether. But then colonial reinforcements arrived from the north, and the Cherokee joined the whites against their ancient enemies, the Creek. Their cause lost, the Yamasee moved south to seek Spanish protection, and the Creek retreated to their villages in the west.

That the Yamasee could escape by migrating southward exposed the one remaining gap in the line of English coastal settlements, the area between the southern border of South Carolina and Spanish Florida. The gap was plugged in 1732 with the chartering

Founding of Georgia

of Georgia, the last of the colonies that would become part of the United States. Intended as a haven for debtors by its founder James Oglethorpe, Georgia was specifically designed as a garrison province. Since all its landholders were expected to serve as militiamen to defend English settlements, the charter prohibited women from inheriting or purchasing land in the colony. The charter also prohibited the use of alcoholic beverages and forbade the introduction of slavery. Such provisions reveal the founders' intention that Georgia should be peopled by sturdy, sober yeoman farmers who could take up their weapons against the Indians or Spaniards at a moment's notice. None of the conditions could be enforced, however, and all had been abandoned by 1752, when Georgia became a royal colony.

In the Northeast, the Iroquois decided to become the major supplier of pelts to the Europeans. They achieved their goal in the 1640s by practically exterminating the rival Hurons. By defeating the Hurons, the Iroquois made themselves a force in the region that the Europeans could not ignore.

The Iroquois nation was not one tribe, but five: the Mohawk, Oneida, Onondaga, Cayuga, and Seneca. (In 1722 the Tuscarora became the sixth.) Un-

Iroquois Confederacy

der the terms of a defensive alliance forged early in the sixteenth century, key decisions of war and peace for the entire Iroquois Confederacy were made by a council composed of tribal representatives. Each tribe retained some autonomy, and no tribe could be forced to comply with a council directive against its will. The Iroquois were unique among Indians not only because of the strength and persistence of their alliance but also because of the role played by their tribal matrons. The older women of each village chose its chief and could either start wars (by calling for the capture of prisoners to replace dead relatives) or stop them (by refusing to supply warriors with necessary foodstuffs).

Before the arrival of the Europeans, the Iroquois had waged wars primarily for the purpose of acquiring

A French settler in Canada made this drawing of an Iroquois about 1700. The artist's fascination with his subject's mode of dress and patterned tattoos is evident. Such pictorial representations of "otherness" help to suggest the cultural gulf that divided the European and Indian residents of North America. Library of Congress.

captives to replenish their population. Contact with white traders, however, created an economic motive for warfare: the desire to control the fur trade and gain unimpeded access to European goods. The war with the Huron was but the first of a series of conflicts with other tribes known as the Beaver Wars, in which the Iroquois fought desperately to maintain a preeminent position in the trade. In the mid-1670s, the French stepped in to prevent an Iroquois triumph (which would have destroyed France's plans to trade directly with the Indians of the Great Lakes and Mississippi Valley regions). Over the next twenty years the French launched repeated attacks on Iroquois villages. The English offered little assistance other than weapons to their trading partners and nominal allies. Their people and resources depleted by constant warfare, the Iroquois in 1701 negotiated neutrality treaties with France, England, and their tribal neighbors. For the next half-century they maintained their power through diplomacy and trade.

In the Carolinas and the middle colonies, then, friction arising from trade relationships produced the major conflicts between whites and Indians. But in Virginia, the cause of a renewed outbreak of violence was the white colonists' hunger for land on which to grow still more tobacco.

In the 1670s, white Virginians who coveted the rich lands north of the York River started a war by attacking the villages of the Doeg and Susquehannock Indians. After the attacks, the Susquehannock tribe began to raid plantations in the winter of 1676. The land-hungry whites rallied behind the leadership of Nathaniel Bacon, a planter who had arrived in the colony only two years before. Governor William Berkeley, however, hoped to avoid setting off a major war like that raging in New England.

Berkeley and Bacon soon clashed. After Bacon forced the House of Burgesses to authorize him to attack the Indians, Berkeley declared Bacon and his men to be in rebellion. As the cha-

Bacon's Rebellion
otic summer of 1676 wore on, Bacon alternately pursued Indians and battled with the governor's supporters. In September he marched on Jamestown itself and burned the capital to the ground. But after Bacon died of dysentery the following month, the rebellion collapsed. Still, a new treaty signed in 1677 opened most of the disputed territory to whites.

It was more than coincidence that New England, which had also been settled more than fifty years earlier, was wracked by conflict with Indians at precisely the same time. In both areas the whites' original accommodation with the tribes no longer satisfied both parties. In New England, though, it was the Indians, rather than the whites, who felt aggrieved.

In the mid-1670s, Metacomet—known to the English as King Philip—set out to expel the whites from New England. Metacomet, whose father, Massasoit, had signed a treaty with the Pilgrims in 1621, was concerned because his lands on Narragansett Bay were being surrounded by white settlements. He was further concerned over the impact of European culture on his people. In late June 1675, Metacomet and his Pokanoket warriors began to attack nearby white communities.

King Philip's War

Soon two other local tribes, the Nipmucs and the Narragansetts, joined Metacomet's forces. In the fall, the three tribes jointly attacked settlements in the northern Connecticut River valley; in the winter and spring of 1676, they totally destroyed twelve of the ninety Puritan towns and attacked forty others. New England's very survival seemed at stake, but after Metacomet was killed the alliance crumbled. Surviving members of the tribes were captured and enslaved. The power of New England's coastal tribes was broken. Thereafter, they lived in small clusters, working as servants or sailors.

NEW ENGLAND AND THE WEB OF IMPERIAL TRADE

The New England settlements that Metacomet attacked had changed in three major ways since the early years of colonization. The population had grown dramatically; the nature of the residents' religious commitment had altered; and the economy had developed in unanticipated ways.

By 1700, New England's population, which increased mainly because of the birthrate and not continued migration, had quadrupled to reach approximately 100,000. That placed great pressure on the available land, and many members of the third and fourth generations of New Englanders had to migrate—north to New Hampshire or

Population Pressures

Maine, south to New York, west beyond the Connecticut River—to find sufficient farm land for themselves and their children. Others abandoned agriculture and learned skills like blacksmithing or carpentry so that they could support themselves in the growing number of towns that dotted the countryside in that area.

In addition, American-born Puritans did not display the same religious fervor that had prompted their ancestors to cross the Atlantic. Many of them had not experienced the gift of God's grace, or "saving faith," which was required for full membership in the Congregational church. Yet they had been baptized as children, attended church services regularly, and wanted their own infants to be baptized, even though that sacrament was supposed to be available only to the children of church members. A synod of Massachusetts ministers, convened in 1662 to consider the problem, responded by establishing the Halfway Covenant. The clergymen declared that adults who had been baptized as children but were not full church members could have their children baptized. In return, such parents had to acknowledge the authority of the church and live according to moral precepts. They were not allowed to vote in church affairs or take communion.

Halfway Covenant

By the 1660s another change in church membership was evident: the proportion of females in the typical congregation was increasing. Indeed, at the end of the century women constituted a majority in many churches. In response, Cotton Mather—the most prominent member of a family of distinguished ministers—began to deliver sermons outlining women's proper role in church and society. His sermons were the first formal examination of that theme in American history. Mather urged women to be submissive to their husbands, watchful of their children, and attentive to religious duty.

The differential rate of church membership in late-seventeenth-century New England suggests a growing division between pious women and their more worldly husbands. That split reflected significant economic changes, which constitute the third major way in which the Puritan colonies were being transformed.

New England's first economic system had been based on two pillars: the fur trade and the constant flow of migrants. Together those had allowed New Englanders to acquire the manufactured goods they needed: the fur trade gave them valuable pelts to sell in England, and the migrants were always willing to exchange clothing and other items for the earlier settlers' surplus seed grains and livestock. But New England's supply of furs was limited, and the migrants stopped coming with the outbreak of civil war in England. Thus in 1640 that first economic system collapsed.

The Puritans then began a search for new salable crops and markets. They found such crops in the waters off the coast—fish—and on their own land—grain and wood products. By 1643 they had also found the necessary markets: first the Wine Islands (the Azores and Canaries) in the Atlantic, and then the new English colonies in the Caribbean, which were beginning to cultivate sugar intensively and to invest heavily in slaves. The islands lacked precisely the goods New England could produce in abundance: cheap food (corn and salted fish) to feed the slaves, and wood for barrels to transport wine (from the Atlantic islands) and molasses (from the Caribbean colonies).

New England's Trading System

Thus developed the series of transactions that has become known, inaccurately, as the triangular trade. Since New England's products duplicated England's, the northern colonists sold their goods in the West Indies and elsewhere to earn the money with which to purchase English products. There soon grew up in New England's ports a cadre of merchants who acquired—usually through barter—cargoes of timber and foodstuffs, which they then dispatched to the West Indies for sale. In the Caribbean the ships sailed from island to island, exchanging fish, barrel staves, and grains for molasses, fruit, spices, and slaves. Then they would return to Boston, Newport, or New

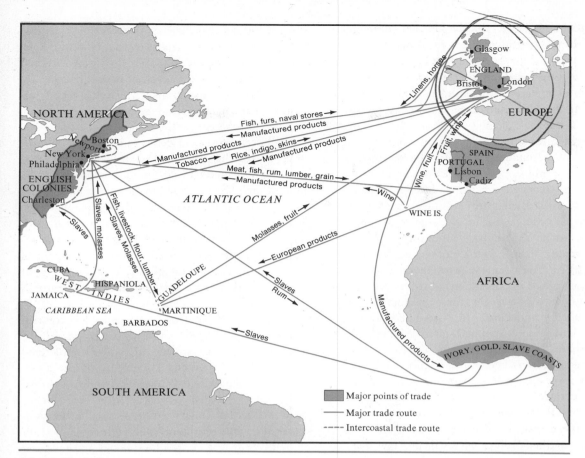

Labels on the map:

Glasgow
ENGLAND
Bristol · London
EUROPE
Linens, horses
Fish, furs, naval stores →
← Manufactured products
NORTH AMERICA
Newport
Boston
New York
Philadelphia
← Manufactured products
Tobacco
Rice, indigo, skins →
← Manufactured products
ENGLISH COLONIES
Charleston
Meat, fish, rum, lumber, grain →
← Manufactured products
Wine, fruit
Fruit, wine
SPAIN
PORTUGAL
Lisbon · Cadiz
← Wine
WINE IS.
ATLANTIC OCEAN
Slaves
Fish, livestock, flour, lumber
Slaves, Molasses
Slaves, molasses
Molasses, fruit
← European products
CUBA
WEST INDIES
HISPANIOLA
JAMAICA
GUADELOUPE
CARIBBEAN SEA
MARTINIQUE
BARBADOS
← Slaves
← Slaves
Rum
AFRICA
Manufactured products
IVORY, GOLD, SLAVE COASTS
SOUTH AMERICA

Major points of trade
Major trade route
Intercoastal trade route

Atlantic Trade Routes

Haven to dispose of their cargoes. Thus the trading pattern was not a neat triangle but a shifting set of irregular polygons (see map). Its sole constant was uncertainty, due to the weather, rapid changes of supply and demand in the small island markets, and the delicate system of credit on which the entire structure depended.

The Puritan New Englanders who ventured into commerce were soon differentiated from their rural counterparts by their ties to a wider transatlantic world and by their preoccupation with material endeavors. The gulf between commercial and farming interests widened after 1660, when Anglican mer-

chants began to migrate to New England. Such men had little stake in the survival of Massachusetts Bay and Connecticut in their original form, and some were openly antagonistic to Puritan traditions. As non-Congregationalists they were denied the vote, and they resented their exclusion from the governing elite. Congregationalist clergymen returned their hostility in full measure and preached sermons called jeremiads lamenting New England's new commercial orientation. The Reverend Increase Mather (Cotton Mather's father) reminded his congregation in 1676 that "*Religion and not the World*" was that which our Fathers came hither for." But Mather spoke for the past, not the future or even for his own contemporaries, because New England and the other American colonies were by the 1670s deeply enmeshed in an intricate international trading network.

American commerce thus attracted the attention of English officials seeking a new source of revenue after the disruptions of the Civil War. They realized that the colonies could make important contributions to England's economic well-being. The king needed tax revenues, and English merchants wanted to ensure that they reaped the benefits of trading with the English colonies. Parliament and the restored Stuart monarchs accordingly began to design a system of laws that would, they hoped, confine the profits of colonial trade primarily to the mother country.

They based their commercial policy on a series of assumptions about the operations of the world's economic system. Collectively, these assumptions are usually called *mercantilism.* The economic world was seen as a collection of national states, each competing for shares of a finite amount of wealth. Each nation's goal was to become as economically self-sufficient as possible while maintaining a favorable balance of trade with other countries (that is, exporting more than it imported). Colonies had an important role to play in such a scheme. They could supply the mother country with valuable raw materials to be consumed at home or sent abroad, and they could serve as a market for the mother country's manufactured goods.

Parliament applied that mercantilist theory to the American colonies in a series of laws known as the Navigation Acts. The major acts—passed in 1651, 1660, 1663, and 1673—established **Navigation Acts** three main principles. First, only English or colonial merchants and ships could engage in trade in the colonies. Second, certain valuable American products (called enumerated goods) could be sold only in the mother country. Third, all foreign goods destined for sale in the colonies had to be shipped via England and pay English import duties. Some years later, a new series of laws declared a fourth principle: the colonies could not make or export items that competed with English products (such as wool clothing, hats, and iron). The intention of the Navigation Acts was clear: American trade was to center on England.

The English authorities soon learned that it was easier to write mercantilist legislation than to enforce it. The many harbors of the American coast provided ready havens for smugglers, and colonial officials often looked the other way when illegally imported goods were offered for sale. In ports such as Curaçao in the Dutch West Indies, American merchants could easily dispose of enumerated goods and purchase foreign items on which duty had not been paid. Consequently, Parliament in 1696 enacted another Navigation Act, designed to strengthen enforcement of the first four. This law established in America a number of vice-admiralty courts, which operated without juries.

England took another major step in colonial administration in 1696 by creating the Board of Trade and Plantations to replace the loosely structured standing committee of the Privy **Board of Trade** Council that had handled colonial affairs since 1675. The fifteen-member Board of Trade thereafter served as the chief organ of government concerned with the American colonies. Still, the Board of Trade did not have any direct powers of enforcement. Furthermore, it shared jurisdiction over American affairs not only with the customs service and the navy but also with the secretary of state for the southern department (the member of the ministry responsible for the colonies). In short, supervision of the American provinces remained decentralized and haphazard.

Even inefficient enforcement of the Navigation Acts was too much for many colonists, and they resisted the laws in various ways—not only by attempting to circumvent them but also by formally protesting to the government in London. But protests had little effect, chiefly because policymakers in England were more concerned about preserving the revenues obtained from colonial trade than about any adverse impact the acts might have on the colonies.

Colonial Political Development and Imperial Reorganization

nglish officials who dealt with colonial administration in the 1670s and 1680s were confronted not only by resistance to the Navigation Acts but also by a bewildering array of colonial governments. Massachusetts Bay still functioned under its original corporate charter, and its New England neighbors Connecticut and Rhode Island had been granted similar corporate status by Charles II in 1662 and 1663, respectively. Virginia was a royal colony, and New York became one when its proprietor ascended the throne in 1685 as James II, but all the other mainland settlements were proprietorships.

Still, the political structures of the colonies shared certain characteristics. Most were ruled by a governor and a two-house legislature. In New England, the governors were elected by the people or the legislature; in the Chesapeake, they were appointed by the king or the proprietor. A council, elected in some colonies and appointed in others, advised the governor on matters of policy and sometimes served as the province's highest court. The council also had a legislative function: initially its members met jointly with representatives elected by their districts to debate and vote on laws affecting the colony. But as time passed, the fundamental differences between the two legislative groups' purposes and constituencies led them to separate into two distinct houses. Thus developed the bicameral legislature still used in almost all of the United States.

Colonial Political Structures

While provincial governments were taking shape, so too were local political institutions. In New England, elected selectmen governed the towns at first, but by the end of the century the town meeting, held at least annually and attended by most adult white townsmen, handled most matters of local concern. In the Chesapeake the same function was performed by the judges of the county court and by the parish vestry, a group of laymen charged with overseeing church affairs, whose power also encompassed secular concerns.

By late in the seventeenth century, therefore, the American colonists were accustomed to exercising a considerable degree of local political autonomy. The tradition of consent was especially firmly established in New England. Everywhere in the English colonies, white males owning more property than a stated minimum (which varied from province to province) expected to have an influential voice in how they were governed, and especially how they were taxed.

After James II became king, these expectations clashed with those of their monarch. The new king and his successors sought to bring order to the apparently chaotic state of colonial administration by tightening the reins of government and reducing the colonies' political autonomy. They began to chip away at the privileges granted in colonial charters and to reclaim proprietorships for the Crown. New Hampshire (1679), its parent colony, Massachusetts (1691), New Jersey (1702), and the Carolinas (1729) all became royal colonies. The charters of Rhode Island, Connecticut, Maryland, and Pennsylvania were temporarily suspended as well, but were ultimately restored to their original status.

The most drastic reordering of colonial administration was attempted in 1686 through 1689, and its chief target was Puritan New England. Reports from America had convinced English officials that New England was a hotbed of smuggling. Moreover, the Puritans refused to allow freedom of religion and insisted on maintaining laws that often ran counter to English practice. New England thus seemed an appropriate place to exert English authority with greater vigor. The charters of all the colonies from New Jersey to Maine (then part of Mas-

Dominion of New England

sachusetts) were revoked and a Dominion of New England was established in 1686. Sir Edmund Andros, the governor, was given immense power: all the assemblies were dissolved, and he needed only the consent of an appointed council to make laws and levy taxes.

New Englanders endured Andros's autocratic rule for more than two years. Then came the dramatic news that James II had been overthrown in a bloodless rebellion (known as the Glorious Revolution) and had been replaced on the throne by his daughter Mary and her husband, the Dutch prince William of Orange. Seizing the opportunity to rid themselves of the hated Dominion, New Englanders jailed Andros and his associates, proclaimed their loyalty to William and Mary, and wrote to England for instructions as to the form of government they should adopt.

In other American colonies too, the Glorious Revolution proved to be a signal for revolt. In Maryland the Protestant Association overturned the government of the Catholic proprietor, and in New York Jacob Leisler, a militia officer of German origin, assumed control of the government. Like the New Englanders, the Maryland and New York rebels allied themselves with the supporters of William and Mary. They saw themselves as carrying out the colonial phase of the English revolt against Stuart absolutism. The problem was that the new monarchs and their colonial administrators did not view American events in the same light.

The Glorious Revolution occurred in the mother country because members of Parliament feared that once again, just as in Charles I's reign, a Stuart king was attempting to seize absolute power. The Glorious Revolution affirmed the supremacy of Parliament and of Protestantism when Parliament offered the throne to the Protestants William and Mary. But it did not directly affect English policies toward America. William and Mary, like James II, believed that the colonies were too independent and that England should exercise tighter control over its unruly American possessions.

Consequently, the only American rebellion that received royal sanction was that in Maryland, which was approved primarily because of its anti-Catholic thrust. Massachusetts, to the dismay of its Puritan leaders, became a royal colony, complete with an appointed governor. The province was allowed to retain its town meeting system of local government and to elect its council, but the new charter issued in 1691 removed the traditional Puritan religious test for voting. An Anglican parish was even established in the heart of Boston.

Compounding New England's difficulties in a time of political uncertainty and economic change was a war with the French and their Indian allies. In Europe, the conflict, which lasted from 1689 until 1697, was known as the War of the League of Augsburg, but the colonists called it King William's War. The American phase of the war was fought chiefly on the northern frontiers of New England and New York.

In this period of extreme stress there occurred the famous outbreak of witchcraft accusations in Salem Village (now Danvers), Massachusetts, a rural community adjoining the bustling port of Salem Town. Like their contemporaries elsewhere, seventeenth-century New Englanders believed in the existence of witches, whose evil powers came from the devil. If people could not find rational explanations for their troubles, they tended to suspect they were bewitched. Before 1689, 103 New Englanders, most of them middle-aged women, had been accused of practicing witchcraft. Although most such accusations occurred singly, on occasion a witchcraft panic could result when one charge set off a chain reaction of similar charges. But nothing else in New England's history ever came close to matching the Salem Village cataclysm.

The crisis began in early 1692 when a group of adolescent girls accused some older women of having bewitched them. Before the hysteria spent itself ten months later, nineteen people (including several men, most of them related to accused female witches) had been hanged, another pressed to death by heavy

Chapter 2: American Society Takes Shape, 1650–1720

stones, and more than one hundred persons jailed. Historians have proposed various explanations for this puzzling episode, but to be understood it must be seen in its proper context—one of political and legal disorder, of Indian war, and of religious and economic change. It must have seemed to Puritan New Englanders as though their entire world was collapsing. At the very least they could have had no sense of security about their future.

Nowhere was that more true than in Salem Village, a farming town torn between old and new styles of life because of its position on the edge of a commercial center. And for no residents of the village was a feeling of insecurity sharper than it was for the girls who issued the initial accusations. Many of them had been orphaned in the recent Indian attacks on Maine; some were living in Salem Village as domestic servants. Their involvement with witchcraft began when they experimented with fortunetelling as a means of foreseeing their futures. As the most powerless people in a town apparently powerless to affect its fate, they offered their fellow New Englanders a compelling explanation for the seemingly endless chain of troubles afflicting them: their province was under direct attack from the devil and his legion of witches. Interpreted thus, it is not the number of witchcraft accusations that seems surprising but rather their abrupt cessation in the fall of 1692.

There were two reasons for the rapid end to the crisis. First, the accusers had grown too bold. When they started to charge some of the colony's most distinguished and respected residents with being in league with the devil, members of the ruling elite began to doubt their veracity. Second, the new royal charter was fully implemented in late 1692, ending the worst period of political uncertainty and removing a major source of psychological stress. The war continued, and the Puritans were not entirely pleased with the charter, but at least order had formally been restored.

Over the course of the next three decades, Massachusetts and the rest of the English colonies in America accommodated themselves to the new imperial order. Most colonists did not like the class of alien

IMPORTANT EVENTS

1642–46	English Civil War
1649	Charles I executed
1660	Stuarts restored to throne; Charles II becomes king
1662	Halfway Covenant drafted
1663	Carolina chartered
1664	English conquer New Netherland; New York founded New Jersey established
1675–76	King Philip's (Metacomet's) War (New England)
1676	Bacon's Rebellion (Virginia)
1680–92	Pueblo revolt (New Mexico)
1681	Pennsylvania chartered
1685	James II becomes king
1686–89	Dominion of New England
1688–89	James II deposed in Glorious Revolution; William and Mary ascend throne
1689–97	King William's War
1692	Witchcraft outbreak in Salem Village
1696	Board of Trade and Plantations established
1701	Iroquois adopt neutrality policy
1702–13	Queen Anne's War
1711–13	Tuscarora War (North Carolina)
1715	Yamasee War (South Carolina)
1732	Georgia chartered

officials who arrived in America, but they adjusted to their demands and to the trade restrictions imposed by the Navigation Acts. They fought another imperial war—the War of the Spanish Succession, or Queen Anne's War—from 1702 to 1713. Colonists who allied themselves with royal governors received patronage in the form of offices and land grants and composed "court parties" that supported English officials. Others, who were perhaps less fortunate in their friends, or more principled in defense of colonial autonomy (opinions differ), made up the opposition, or "country" interest. By the end of the first quarter of the eighteenth century, most men in both groups were native-born Americans, members of elite families whose wealth derived from staple-crop production in the South and commerce in the North.

During the seventy years from 1650 to 1720, then, the English colonies in America had changed dramatically. In 1650, there were just two isolated centers of population, New England and the Chesapeake; in 1720, nearly the entire eastern coast of mainland North America was in English hands. What had been a migrant population was now mostly American-born; economies originally based on the fur trade had become far more complex and more closely linked with the mother country; and a wide variety of political structures had been reshaped into a more uniform pattern. Yet at the same time the introduction of large-scale slavery into the Chesapeake and the Carolinas had irrevocably differentiated their societies from those of the colonies to the north. Staple-crop production for the market was not the key distinguishing feature of the southern regional economies; rather, their uniqueness lay in their reliance on a racially based system of perpetual servitude.

By 1720, the essential elements of the imperial structure that would govern the colonies until 1775 were in place. And the regional economic systems originating in the late seventeenth and early eighteenth centuries continued to dominate American life for another century. This period, in other words, established the basic economic and political patterns that were to structure all subsequent change in colonial American society.

SUGGESTIONS FOR FURTHER READING

General

Charles M. Andrews, *The Colonial Period of American History*, vol. 4 (1938); Carl Bridenbaugh, *Cities in the Wilderness: The First Century of Urban Life in America, 1625–1742* (1938); Wesley Frank Craven, *The Colonies in Transition, 1660–1713* (1968); Gary Walton and James Shepherd, *The Economic Rise of Early America* (1979).

Africa and the Slave Trade

Philip D. Curtin, *The Atlantic Slave Trade* (1969); David B. Davis, *The Problem of Slavery in Western Culture* (1966); Herbert Klein, *The Middle Passage* (1978); James Rawley, *The Transatlantic Slave Trade: A History* (1981).

Blacks in Anglo-America

T. H. Breen and Stephen Innes, *"Myne Own Ground": Race and Freedom on Virginia's Eastern Shore, 1640–1676* (1980); Edgar J. McManus, *Black Bondage in the North* (1973); Edmund S. Morgan, *American Slavery, American Freedom* (1975); Peter H. Wood, *Black Majority* (1974).

Indian-White Relations

Henry Bowden, *American Indians and Christian Missions* (1981); Judith K. Brown, "Economic Organization and the Position of Women among the Iroquois," *Ethnohistory*, 17 (1970), 151–167; Verner W. Crane, *The Southern Frontier, 1670–1732* (1929); Francis Jennings, *The Ambiguous Iroquois Empire* (1984); Elizabeth A. H. John, *Storms Brewed in Other Men's Worlds* (1975); Douglas Leach, *Flintlock and Tomahawk: New England in King Philip's War* (1958); J. Leitch Wright, Jr., *The Only Land They Knew: The Tragic Story of the American Indians in the Old South* (1981).

New England

Bernard Bailyn, *The New England Merchants in the Seventeenth Century* (1955); Paul Boyer and Stephen Nissenbaum, *Salem Possessed* (1974); Richard Bushman, *From Puritan to Yankee* (1967); John Demos, *Entertaining Satan* (1982); Perry Miller, *The New England Mind: From Colony to Province* (1953); Robert G. Pope, *The Half-Way Covenant* (1969); Laurel Thatcher Ulrich, *Good Wives: Image and Reality in the Lives of Women in Northern New England 1650–1750* (1982).

New Netherland and the Restoration Colonies

Edwin B. Bronner, *William Penn's "Holy Experiment"* (1962); Thomas J. Condon, *New York Beginnings* (1968); Wesley Frank Craven, *New Jersey and the English Colonization of North America* (1964); Michael Kammen, *Colonial New York* (1975); Robert C. Ritchie, *The Duke's Province* (1977); Robert M. Weir, *Colonial South Carolina* (1983).

Colonial Politics

Lois Green Carr and David W. Jordan, *Maryland's Revolution of Government 1689–1692* (1974); Richard R. Johnson, *Adjustment to Empire: The New England Colonies, 1675–1715* (1981); David S. Lovejoy, *The Glorious Revolution in America* (1972); Jack M. Sosin, *English America and the Restoration Monarchy of Charles II* (1980).

Imperial Administration

Viola F. Barnes, *The Dominion of New England* (1923); Lawrence A. Harper, *The English Navigation Laws* (1939); Michael Kammen, *Empire and Interest* (1970); I. K. Steele, *Politics of Colonial Policy* (1968); Stephen Saunders Webb, *The Governors-General* (1979); Stephen Saunders Webb, *1676: The End of American Independence* (1984).

CHAPTER 3

GROWTH AND DIVERSITY
1720–1770

*I*n June 1744, Dr. Alexander Hamilton, a thirty-four-year-old Scottish-born physician living in Annapolis, Maryland, paid his first visit to Philadelphia. There he encountered two quite different worlds. One consisted of men of his own status, the merchants and professionals he called "the better sort." The other world he found at a tavern. Here Hamilton met men of different ethnic backgrounds and religious beliefs. He thought of these ordinary folk as "rabble" and "comicall grotesque phizzes." To Hamilton, the "better sort" engaged in entertaining and informed conversation; the "rabble," he thought, spoke "ignorantly," regardless of subject.

And what of the women in Philadelphia? Hamilton met few of them. "The ladies," he explained, "for the most part, keep att home and seldom appear in the streets, never in publick assemblies except att the churches or meetings." Hamilton was referring, of course, to women of "the better sort." He could hardly have walked the streets of the city without seeing many female domestic servants, market women, and wives of ordinary laborers going about their daily chores.

Despite his obvious biases, Dr. Hamilton was an astute observer of mid-eighteenth-century Philadelphia. The residents' chief employment, he wrote, "is traffick and mercantile business"; and the richest merchants of all were the Quakers. Members of that sect also controlled the government of Pennsylvania, but, Hamilton noted, "the standing or falling of the Quakers in the House of Assembly depends upon their making sure the interest of the Palatines [Germans] in this province, who of late have turned so numerous that they can sway the votes which way they please." And Hamilton deplored the impact on the city of the Great Awakening, a religious revival that was then sweeping the colonies. "I never was in a place so populous where the gout [taste] for publick gay diversions prevailed so little," he remarked.

Hamilton's observations about Philadelphia applied to other places as well. Non-English migrants were settling throughout the mainland colonies, especially in the cities. Their arrival increased the population, altered political balances worked out before 1720, and affected the religious climate by increasing the number of sects. Moreover, others shared Philadelphians' assessment of the importance of commerce. Indeed, by the middle of the eighteenth century, Americans of all descriptions were tied to an international commercial system.

As was true of other well-educated men, Dr. Hamilton was heavily influenced by the Enlightenment, the major European intellectual movement of the day. The Enlightenment stressed reason and empirical knowledge. Hamilton, like other enlightened thinkers, believed above all in rationality. From this perspective came his distaste for the Great Awakening, the hallmark of which was emotion, expressed in a single identifiable moment of conversion. To a believer in the primacy of reason, the passions of the newly converted were more than foolish—they were idiotic.

The Enlightenment affected Dr. Hamilton in another way as well, for it helped to create the elite world of which he was a part, a world that seemed so different from that of ordinary folk. Wealthy, well-read Americans participated in a transatlantic intellectual community, whereas most colonists of "the lesser sort" could neither read nor write. Hamilton and his peers lived in comfortable houses and entertained at lavish parties; most colonists struggled just to make ends meet. Hamilton could take a leisurely four-month journey for his health, but most Americans had to work daily from dawn to dark. The eighteenth century, then, brought an increasing gap between rich and poor. The colonies had always been composed of people of different ranks, but by the last half of the century the social and economic distance between those ranks had widened noticeably.

Above all, the eighteenth-century colonies present a picture of growth and diversity. Population increased dramatically, and the area settled by whites and blacks expanded until it filled almost all of the region between the Appalachian Mountains and the

Atlantic Ocean. At the same time, the colonies became more diverse; the two original regional economies (the Chesapeake and New England) became four (those two plus the middle colonies and the Lower South). By midcentury, many of the colonies were home to a variety of ethnic groups and religious sects. The urban population, though still tiny by today's standards, grew larger; and in the cities were found the greatest extremes of wealth and poverty. Such changes transformed the character of England's North American possessions. The colonies that revolted in unison against British rule after 1765 were very different from the colonies that revolted separately against Stuart absolutism in 1689.

POPULATION GROWTH AND ETHNIC DIVERSITY

One of the most striking characteristics of the mainland colonies in the eighteenth century was their rapid population growth. Only about 250,000 people (excluding Indians) resided in the colonies in 1700; by 1775 it had become 2.5 million. Although immigration accounted for a considerable share of the growth, most of it resulted from natural increase. By 1750 the sex ratio among both whites and blacks was approximately equal throughout the mainland colonies. Most white women married in their early twenties, most black women in their late teens. Women usually bore between five and eight children, becoming pregnant every two or three years throughout their fertile years, and a large proportion of their children survived to maturity. In 1775 about half the American population, white and black, was under sixteen years of age.

Such a dramatic phenomenon did not escape the attention of contemporaries. As early as the 1720s, Americans began to point with pride to their fertility, citing population growth as evidence of the advantages of living in the colonies. In 1755 Benjamin Franklin published his *Observations Concerning the Increase of Mankind,* which predicted that America's amazing growth rate would within a century make it more populous than Britain. Franklin's purpose in writing his *Observations* was to argue that Britain should prevent Germans from migrating to Pennsylvania. Since the English population in America was increasing so rapidly, he asked, "Why should Pennsylvania, founded by the English, become a Colony of *Aliens,* who will shortly be so numerous as to Germanize us instead of our Anglifying them, and will never adopt our Language or Customs?"

Whether Franklin's fears were shared by a majority of his American-born contemporaries is not known. But the eighteenth-century migration to the English colonies was massive; it comprised approximately 375,000 whites and 275,000 blacks. Because some of the whites (for example, convicts sentenced to exile by English courts) and all the blacks did not choose freely to come to the colonies, nearly half the eighteenth-century migrants moved to America against their will.

Africans made up the largest single racial or ethnic group that came to the colonies during the eighteenth century. Even so, in the first half of the century the black population of the mainland colonies began to grow faster through natural increase than through importation. In the slaveholding societies of South America and the Caribbean, a surplus of males over females and appallingly high mortality rates together produced very different slave population patterns. There, only massive and continuing importations from Africa were able to maintain the enslaved work force at adequate levels. South Carolina, where rice cultivation was difficult and unhealthy work, bore some resemblance to such colonies in that it too required a constant influx of Africans. But in the Chesapeake the black population grew primarily through natural increase after 1740.

The Germans who so worried Franklin numbered about 100,000. Most emigrated to Pennsylvania between 1730 and 1755; not all, however, stayed in

German Immigration

that colony. Some who landed at Philadelphia moved west and then south along the eastern slope of the Appalachian Mountains, eventually finding homes in western Maryland and Virginia. Others sailed first to Charleston or Savannah and settled in the interior of South Carolina or Georgia. The German immigrants belonged to a wide variety of Protestant sects—primarily Lutheran, German Reformed, and Moravian.

Many Germans arrived in America as redemptioners. Under that variant form of indentured servitude, immigrants paid as much as possible of the cost of their passage before sailing from Europe. After they landed in the colonies, the rest of the fare had to be "redeemed." If poor immigrants had no friends or relatives in America willing to take on the burden of payment, they were indentured for a term of service proportional to the amount they still owed. That term could be as brief as a year or two, but was more likely to be four.

The largest group of white non-English immigrants to America was the Scotch-Irish, chiefly descended from Presbyterian Scots who had settled in Protestant portions of Ireland during the seventeenth century. Perhaps as many as 250,000 Scotch-Irish people moved to the colonies. Fleeing economic distress and religious discrimination, they were lured as well by hopes of obtaining land in America. Like the Germans, many of the Scotch-Irish landed in Philadelphia. They also moved west and south from that city, settling chiefly in the western portions of Pennsylvania, Maryland, Virginia, and the Carolinas. Frequently unable to afford to buy any acreage, they squatted on land belonging to Indian tribes, land speculators, or colonial governments.

Scotch-Irish and Scottish Immigration

The more than 25,000 Scots who came directly to America from Scotland should not be confused with the Scotch-Irish. Many Scottish immigrants were supporters of Stuart claimants to the throne of England, or Jacobites. After the death of William and

Mary's successor Queen Anne in 1714, the British throne passed to the German house of Hanover, in the person of King George I. In 1715 and again in 1745, Jacobite rebels attempted unsuccessfully to capture the crown for the Stuart pretender, and many were exiled to America as punishment for their treason. Most of the Jacobites settled in North Carolina. Ironically, they tended to become loyalists during the Revolutionary War because of their strong commitment to monarchy. Another wave of Scottish immigration began in the 1760s and flowed mainly into northern New York.

Because of these migration patterns and the concentration of slaveholding in the South, half the colonial population south of New England was of non-English origin by 1775. Whether the migrants assimilated readily into Anglo-American culture depended largely on the patterns of settlement, the size of the group, and the strength of the migrants' ties to their common culture. The Huguenots, for instance, were French Protestants who settled in tiny enclaves in American cities but were unable to sustain their distinctive religious practices. The equally small group of colonial Jews, by contrast, largely maintained a separate identity. They established synagogues and worked actively to preserve their culture by opposing marriage with Christians. Members of the larger groups of migrants (the Germans, Scotch-Irish, and Scots) found it easier to sustain Old World ways if they wished. Countless local areas of the colonies were settled almost exclusively by one group or another.

Recognizing that it was to their benefit to keep other racial and ethnic groups divided, the dominant English on occasion deliberately fostered antagonisms. When the targets of their policies were European migrants, the goal was the maintenance of political and economic power. When the targets were Indians and blacks, as they were in South Carolina, the stakes were considerably higher. Whites, who composed a minority of the population of the colony, wanted to prevent Indians and blacks from making common cause against them. So that slaves would not try to run away to join the Indians, whites hired Indians as slave catchers. So that Indians would not trust blacks, whites used blacks as soldiers in Indian wars.

Although the dominant elites probably would have preferred to ignore the colonies' growing racial and ethnic diversity, they could not do so for long and still maintain their power. When such men decided to lead a revolution in the 1770s, they recognized that they needed the support of non-English Americans. Not by chance, then, did they begin to speak of "the rights of man," rather than "English liberties," when they sought recruits for their cause.

ECONOMIC GROWTH AND DEVELOPMENT

The eighteenth-century American economy was characterized by sharp fluctuations, which were caused by European wars and variations in the overseas demand for American products. The dramatic increase in colonial population was the only source of stability in the shifting economic climate.

Each year the rising population generated ever-greater demands for goods and services. As the area of settlement expanded, new roads, bridges, mills, and stores were built to serve the new communities. A lively coastal trade developed; by the late 1760s, 54 percent of the vessels leaving Boston harbor were sailing to other mainland colonies rather than to foreign ports. Such ships were not only collecting goods for export and distributing imports, but also selling items made in America. In the middle decades of the eighteenth century, the colonies finally began to move away from their earlier pattern of near-total dependence on Europe for manufactured goods.

The major energizing—yet destabilizing—influence on the colonial economy was foreign trade. Colonial prosperity still depended heavily on overseas demand for American products like tobacco, rice, and barrel staves, for it was through the sale of such items that the colonists earned the credit they needed to purchase English and European imports. If the demand for American exports slowed, the colonists' income dropped and so did their demand for imported goods. Accordingly, even small merchants could be affected by sudden economic downswings they had not anticipated.

Despite fluctuations, the economy grew slowly over the course of the eighteenth century, an increase that resulted in higher standards of living for all property-owning Americans. Diet im-

Rising Standard of Living

proved; estate inventories reveal larger quantities and wider varieties of stored foods. After 1750, luxury items like silver plate appeared in the homes of the wealthy, and the "middling sort" started to purchase imported English ceramics and teapots. Even the poorest property owners showed some improvement in the number and type of their household possessions.

Yet the benefits of economic growth were not evenly distributed: wealthy Americans improved their position relative to other colonists. The native-born elite families who dominated American political, economic, and social life by 1750 were those who had begun the century with sufficient capital to take advantage of the changes caused by population growth. The rise of a group of monied families comprising urban merchants, large landowners, slave traders, and the owners of rum distilleries helped to make the social and economic structure of mid-eighteenth-century America more rigid than it had been previously. The new non-English immigrants did not have the opportunities for advancement that had greeted their English predecessors.

At the very bottom of the social scale, poverty increased in colonial cities. Families of urban laborers lived on the edge of destitution. In Philadelphia, for instance, a male laborer's average

Urban Poverty

annual earnings fell short of the amount needed to supply his family

with the bare necessities. Even in a good year, then, other members of the family had to do wage work; in a bad year, the family could be reduced to beggary. By the 1760s, urban poor-relief systems were overwhelmed with applicants for assistance, and some cities began to build workhouses or almshouses to shelter the growing number of poor people. How could that have happened at a time when the lot of the average American family was improving?

A possible answer is that, although the living standard of property owners was rising, some colonists were being deprived of any access to property. Such people clustered in the cities, where they could more easily find work. Another explanation might be that poverty was a stage people passed through at particular points in their lives rather than a constant condition. A third answer points to the preponderance of women, mostly widows, among the urban poor. Since women in the eighteenth century, like women today, were paid about half the wages men earned for the same or comparable work, it may well be that urban poverty was primarily a sex-typed phenomenon, with poor *men* being the aberration rather than the rule.

Within this overall picture, it is important to distinguish among the various regions. In New England, three elements combined to exert a major influence on economic development: the nature of the landscape, New England's leadership in colonial shipping, and the impact of the imperial wars. New England's soil was rocky and thin, and farmers did not normally produce large surpluses to sell abroad. The region had the lowest average wealth per freeholder in the colonies. New England's wealthy men were the merchants and professionals whose income was drawn from overseas trade, primarily with the West Indies.

Boston's central position in the New England economy and its role as a shipbuilding center ensured that it would be directly affected by any resumption of warfare. Thus when England de-

New England and King George's War

clared war on Spain in 1739, setting off the conflict that was known in Europe as the War of the Austrian Succession and in America as

King George's War, the first impact on Boston's economy was positive. Ships and sailors were in great demand, and wealthy merchants profited from contracts to supply military expeditions.

But Boston suffered heavy losses of manpower in the war. After France became Spain's ally, a Massachusetts force captured the French fortress of Louisbourg, at the mouth of the St. Lawrence River, but the colony had to levy heavy taxes on its residents to pay for the expensive effort. The town was left with unprecedented numbers of widows and children on its relief rolls, the boom in shipbuilding ended when the war did, and taxes remained high. As a final blow, Britain gave Louisbourg back to France in the treaty of Aix-la-Chapelle (1748).

Because of one key difference between the northernmost and the middle colonies, the latter were more positively affected by King George's War and its aftermath. That difference was the **Prosperity of the Middle Colonies** greater fertility of the soil in New York and Pennsylvania, where commercial farming was already the norm. With the outbreak of war, farmers in the middle colonies were able to profit from the increased demand for foodstuffs, especially in the West Indies. After the war a series of poor grain harvests in Europe caused flour prices to rise even more rapidly. Philadelphia and New York took the lead in the foodstuffs trade, while Boston found its economy stagnating.

The increased European demand for grain (and consequent higher prices) in the mid-eighteenth century also had a significant impact on the Chesapeake. After 1745, some Chesapeake planters began to convert tobacco fields to wheat and corn, because the price of grain was rising faster than that of tobacco. They saw the benefit of diversifying their crops. But tobacco still was the largest single export from the mainland colonies. Thus it is useful to focus briefly on tobacco's continuing impact on the Chesapeake.

Two major results of the region's concentration on tobacco growing can be discerned in the mid-eighteenth century. The first derived from the substitution of enslaved for indentured labor. The offspring of slaves were also slaves, whereas the children of servants were free. The consequences of that fact were **Natural Increase of Black Population** not clear until the black population of the Chesapeake began to grow through natural increase, which occurred between 1720 and 1740. It then became evident that a planter who began with only a few slave families could watch the size of his labor force increase steadily over the years without making additional major investments in workers. Not coincidentally, the first truly large Chesapeake plantations appeared in the 1740s.

The second effect of tobacco cultivation on the Chesapeake related to patterns of trade. In the first half of the eighteenth century, wealthy planters served as middlemen in the tobacco **Scots Factors** trade. They collected and shipped tobacco grown by their less prosperous neighbors, extended credit to them, and ordered the English imports they wanted. This system changed in the 1740s when Scottish merchants entered into the tobacco trade. The Scots organized their efforts differently from their London-based competitors. They stationed representatives (called factors) in the Chesapeake to purchase tobacco, arrange for shipments, and sell imports. The arrival of the Scots factors created genuine competition for the first time and thus pushed up tobacco prices. When the Chesapeake finally began to develop port towns later in the century, they grew up in centers of Scots mercantile activity or in regions that had largely converted to grain production.

The Lower South, like the Chesapeake, depended on staple crops and an enslaved labor force for its prosperity, but its pattern of economic growth was **Lower South Trade Patterns** distinctive. In contrast to tobacco prices, which rose slowly through the middle decades of the century, rice prices climbed steeply. The sharp rise was caused primarily by a heavy demand for rice in southern Europe. Because Parliament removed rice from the list of enumerated products in 1730, South Carolinians were able to trade directly with continental Europe. But dependence on European sales had its drawbacks, as rice growers discovered at the outbreak of King George's War in 1739. Trade with the continent was completely disrupted, rice prices plummeted, and South Carolina entered a depression. Still, by the 1760s prosperity had returned; indeed, in that period the Lower South experienced more rapid economic growth than the other regions of the colonies. Partly as a result, it had the highest average wealth per freeholder in Anglo-America by the time of the Revolution.

Each region of the colonies, then, had its own economic rhythm derived from the nature of its export trade. King George's War initially helped New England and hurt the Lower South, but in the long run those effects were reversed. In the Chesapeake and the middle colonies, the war initiated a long period of prosperity. The variety of these economic experiences points up a crucial fact about the eighteenth-century mainland colonies: they did not compose a unified whole. They were linked economically into regions, but they had few political or social ties beyond or even within those regions.

DAILY LIFE

The basic unit of colonial society was the household. Headed by a white male (or perhaps his widow), the household was the chief mechanism of production and consumption in the colonial economy. Its members—bound by ties of blood or servitude—worked together to produce goods for consumption or sale. The white male head of the household represented it to the outside world, serving in the militia or political posts, casting the household's sole vote in elections. He managed the finances and held legal authority over the rest of the family—his wife, his children, and his servants or slaves. (Eighteenth-century Americans used the word *family* for people who lived together in one house,

whether or not they were blood kin.) Such households were considerably larger than American families today; in 1790, the average home contained 5.7 whites. And most of those large families were nuclear—that is, they did not include extended kin like aunts, uncles, or grandparents.

The vast majority of eighteenth-century American families—more than 90 percent of them—lived in rural areas. Therefore nearly all adult white men were farmers and all adult white women farm wives. In colonial America, household tasks were allocated by gender. The master, his sons, and his male servants or slaves performed one set of chores; the mistress, her daughters, and her female servants or slaves, an entirely different set. So rigid were the gender classifications that when households for some reason lacked a master or mistress the appropriate jobs were often not done. Only in emergencies and for brief periods of time would women do "men's work" or men do women's.

Sexual Division of Labor among White Americans

The mistress of the rural household was responsible for what were termed indoor affairs. She and her female helpers prepared the food, kept the house clean and neat, did the laundry, and often made the clothing. The phrase "indoor affair" is somewhat deceptive. The preparation of food, an "indoor" function, involved planting and cultivating a garden, harvesting and preserving vegetables, salting and smoking meat, drying apples and pressing cider, milking cows and making butter and cheese, not to mention cooking and baking. Women's single most time-consuming task was making clothing, which required spinning and weaving as well as sewing.

The head of the household and his male helpers, responsible for outdoor affairs, also had heavy work loads. They had to plant and cultivate fields, build fences, chop wood for the fireplaces, harvest and market crops, and butcher cattle and hogs to provide the household with meat. Only in the plantation South and in northern cities could even a few adult white males lead lives free from arduous physical labor.

In 1775 a Connecticut woman, Prudence Punderson, created this needlework picture, which she entitled The First, Second, and Last Scene of Mortality. *At right she depicted a baby tended by a black servant; at center a mature woman doing needlework; and at left a coffin. Thus she summed up a woman's life from birth to the grave, with traditionally female work—like her picture itself—at its core.* The Connecticut Historical Society.

Farm households were governed by the seasons and by the hours of daylight. Men and boys had the most leisure in the winter, when there were no crops that needed care. Women and girls were freest in the summer, before embarking on autumn food preservation and winter spinning and weaving. Other activities, including education, had to be subordinated to seasonal work. Thus farm boys attended school in the winter, and their sisters went to classes in the summer. The seasons also affected

Rhythms of Rural Life

travel plans. Because the roads were muddy in spring and fall, most visiting took place in summer and, in the North, in winter, when sleighs could be used.

Because most farm families were relatively isolated from their neighbors and had these heavy seasonal work obligations, rural folk took advantage of every possible opportunity for socializing. Men taking grain to be milled would stop at a crossroads tavern for a drink and conversation with friends. Women gathering to assist at childbirth would drink tea and exchange news. And work itself provided opportunities for visiting. Harvest frolics, corn-husking bees, barn raisings, quilting parties, spinning bees, and other communal endeavors brought together neighbors from miles around, often for several days of work followed by feasting, dancing, and singing in the evenings.

The few eighteenth-century colonial cities were nothing but large towns by today's standards. (The largest, Boston, had just seventeen thousand inhabitants.) Still, city life differed considerably from rural life. City dwellers were not inextricably tied to the seasons. Year-round, they could purchase foodstuffs and wood at city markets and cloth at dry-goods stores. They could see friends any time they wished. Wealthy urbanites had plenty of leisure time to read, take walks around town or rides in the countryside, play cards, or attend dances, plays, and concerts, for by midcentury most colonial cities had theaters and assembly halls.

Rhythms of Urban Life

City people also had much more contact with the world beyond their own homes than did their rural compatriots. By the middle of the century, every major city had at least one weekly newspaper, and most had two or three. Newspapers printed the latest "advices from London" and news of events in other English colonies, as well as reports on matters of local interest. However, contact with the outside world also had drawbacks. Contagious diseases were sometimes brought into port cities by sailors, causing epidemics that the countryside largely escaped.

Cities attracted many migrants from rural areas. Young men seeking to become apprentices, laborers in need of work, and widows looking for a means of supporting their families often moved into the cities. Widows could sell their services as nurses, teachers, seamstresses, servants, or prostitutes, or (if they had some capital) open shops, inns, or boardinghouses. In rural areas, where the economy was based largely on subsistence agriculture and most families produced nearly all their own necessities, there was little demand for the services that landless women and men could perform. In the cities, though, someone always needed another servant, blacksmith, or laundress.

Only widows and the very few never-married women could legally run independent businesses. Under the common-law doctrine of coverture, a married woman became one person with her husband. She could not sue or be sued, make contracts, buy or sell property, or draft a will. Any property she owned prior to marriage became her husband's after the wedding; any wages she earned were legally his; and all children of the marriage fell under his absolute control.

Status of Women

Anglo-American men expected their wives to defer to their judgment. Most wives seem to have accepted secondary status without murmuring. When girls married, they were commonly advised to devote themselves to their husbands' interests. A Virginia woman remarked, for example, that it was the wives' responsibility "to give up to their husbands" whenever differences of opinion arose between them. Not until very late in the eighteenth century, during and after the American Revolution, would women begin to question these traditional notions.

The man's legal and customary authority extended to his children as well. Indeed, childrearing was the one task regularly undertaken by both men and women in colonial America. The father set the general standards by which children were raised and usually had the final word on such matters as their education or vocational training. White parents normally insisted on unquestioning obedience from their offspring, and many freely used physical punishment to break a child's will.

Not all families in the English colonies, of course, were white. And more than 95 percent of black families were held in perpetual bondage. In South Carolina, a majority of the population was black; in Georgia, about half; and in the Chesapeake, 40 percent. A trend toward consolidation of landholding and slave ownership after 1740 had a profound effect on the lives of Afro-Americans. In areas with high proportions of blacks in the population, most slaves resided on plantations with at least nine other bondspeople. Although many southern blacks lived on farms with only one or two other slaves, the majority

An Overseer Doing His Duty, *by Benjamin H. Latrobe.*
Most slave women were field hands like these, sketched in
1798 near Fredericksburg, Virginia. White women were be-
lieved to be unsuited for heavy outdoor labor. Maryland
Historical Society, Baltimore.

had the experience of living and working in a largely black setting.

The size of such plantation households allowed for the specialization of labor. Encouraged by planters whose goal was to create as self-sufficient a household as possible, Afro-American men and women became highly skilled at tasks whites believed appropriate to their sex. Each large plantation had its own male blacksmiths, carpenters, valets, shoemakers, and gardeners, and female dairymaids, seamstresses, cooks, and at least one midwife, who attended pregnant white and black women alike.

Sexual Division of Labor among Black Americans

These skilled slaves—between 10 and 20 percent of the black population—were essential to the smooth functioning of the plantation. But whites assigned most male and female slaves to work in the fields.

The typical Chesapeake tobacco plantation was divided into small "quarters" located at some distance from one another. White overseers supervised work on the distant quarters, while the planter personally took charge of the "home" quarter (which included the planter's house). Planters commonly assigned "outlandish" (African-born) slaves to do field labor in order to accustom them to plantation work routines and to enable them to learn some English.

Plantation Life

Artisans, on the other hand, were usually drawn from among the plantation's American-born blacks. In such families skills were passed down from father to son and from mother to daughter; such knowledge often constituted a slave family's most valuable possession.

Eighteenth-century planters were considerably less worried that their slaves might run away than were their counterparts seventy-five years later, and with good reason. All the English colonies legally permitted slavery, so blacks had few places to go to escape bondage. Sometimes recently arrived Africans tried to steal boats to return home or ran off in groups to the frontier. Occasionally slaves from South Carolina tried to reach Spanish Florida. But Afro-Americans usually recognized that they had few long-term alternatives to remaining on their plantations.

This is not to say that Afro-American slaves never ran away. They did, in large numbers. But they did so to visit friends or relatives, or simply to escape their normal work routines for a few days or months; they could have had little hope of remaining permanently at large.

Afro-Americans did try to improve the conditions of their bondage and gain some measure of control over their lives. Their chief vehicle for doing so was the family. Planters' records reveal how members of extended kin groups provided support, assistance, and comfort to each other. They asked to live on the same quarters, protested excessive punishment administered to relatives, and often requested special treatment for children or siblings. The extended-kin ties that developed among Afro-American families who had lived on the same plantation for several generations served as insurance against the uncertainties of existence under slavery. If a nuclear family was broken up by sale, there were always relatives around to help with childrearing and other tasks. Among colonial blacks, in other words, the extended family probably served a more important function than it did among whites.

Blacks were always subject to white intrusions into their lives, but most black families managed to carve out a small measure of autonomy. On many plantations, slaves were allowed to plant their own gardens, hunt, or fish in order to supplement the standard diet of corn and salt pork. Some Chesapeake mistresses permitted their female slaves to raise chickens, which they could then sell or exchange for such items as extra clothing or blankets.

In South Carolina, slaves were often able to accumulate personal property, because most rice and indigo plantations operated on a task system. Once slaves had completed their assigned tasks for the day, they were free to work for themselves. In Maryland and Virginia, where by the end of the century some whites had begun to hire out their slaves to others, blacks were sometimes allowed to keep a small part of the wages they earned. Such advances were slight, but against the bleak backdrop of slavery they deserve to be highlighted.

Relations between blacks and whites varied considerably from household to household. In some, masters and mistresses enforced their will chiefly through physical coercion. On other plantations, masters were more lenient and respectful of slaves' property and their desire to live with other members of their families. But even in households where whites and blacks displayed genuine affection for one another, there were inescapable tensions. Such tensions were caused not only by the whites' uneasiness about the slave system in general but also by the dynamics of day-to-day relationships when a small number of whites wielded absolute legal power over the lives of many blacks.

Thomas Jefferson was deeply concerned about that issue. In 1780 he observed, "The whole commerce between master and slave is a perpetual exercise of the most boisterous passions, the most unremitting despotism on the one part, and degrading submission on the other. Our children see this, and learn to imitate it." What troubled him most was the impact of the system on whites. Before the Revolution, only a tiny number of Quakers took a different approach,

Black Families

Black-White Relations

criticizing slavery out of sympathy for blacks. The few other white colonists who questioned slavery took Jefferson's approach.

In the third quarter of the eighteenth century, the daily work routines of most Americans had changed little from those of their Old World ancestors. Ordinary white folk lived in farm households, their lives governed by the sexual division of labor. Most Afro-Americans were held in perpetual bondage, but their work was performed as it had been in West Africa, communally in the fields. Even in colonial cities life differed little from European cities in previous centuries. Yet if the routines of daily life seemed unchanging, the wider context in which those routines occurred did not. In both Europe and America the eighteenth century was a time of great cultural and intellectual ferment. The movement known as the Enlightenment at first primarily influenced the educated elites. But since enlightened thinking played a major part in the ideology of the American Revolution, it was eventually to have an important impact on the lives of all Americans.

COLONIAL CULTURE

The older, traditional form of colonial culture was oral, communal, and—for at least the first half of the eighteenth century—intensely localized. The newer culture of the elite was print-oriented, more individualized, and self-consciously cosmopolitan. The two will be discussed separately, but they also mingled in a variety of ways, since people of both descriptions lived side by side in small communities.

A majority of the residents of British America could neither read nor write. That had important consequences for the transmission and development of American culture. In the

Oral Culture absence of literacy, the primary means of communication was face-to-face conversation. Informatio[n] slowly and within relatively confi[n]ent locales developed divergent and those differences were heigh[tened] ethnic variations.

When Europeans or Africans [migrated to the col]onies, they left familiar environments behind but brought with them sets of cultural assumptions about how society should work. In North America, those assumptions influenced the way they organized their lives. Yet Old World customs usually could not be recreated intact in the New World, because people from different origins now resided in the same communities. Accordingly, the colonists had to forge new cultural identities for themselves.

In New England, communal culture centered on the church and on religious observances in the civic sphere. Colonial governments proclaimed official

Religious Rituals days of thanksgiving or days of fasting and prayer. Everyone in the community was expected to participate in the public rituals held on such occasions. Attendance at church was perhaps the most important public ritual in New England. Church services publicly affirmed one's standing in the community. In Congregational (Puritan) churches, seating was assigned by church leaders: each family had its own pew, whose location at the front, back, or sides of the church depended on the family's wealth and social prominence. A similar statement about the local status hierarchy was conveyed at Anglican parishes in Virginia. Quite a different message came from the entirely egalitarian, but sex-segregated, seating system used in Quaker meetinghouses. Where one sat in colonial churches, in other words, symbolized one's place in society and the values of the local community.

Other aspects of the service also reflected communal values. In most colonial churches, trained clergymen delivered formal sermons, but in Quaker services members of the meeting spoke informally to each other. Communal singing in Congregational churches added an egalitarian element to an other-

...s-conscious experience. Not by accident ...e first book printed in the colonies *The Bay* ...m *Book* (1640), consisting of Old Testament ...salms recast in short, rhyming, metrical lines so they could be easily learned, remembered, and sung even by people who could not read. Communal singing helped to bring a kind of crude democracy into the church. Everyone participated in the singing on an equal basis and all had an equal voice in deciding which version of the psalms to use.

In the Chesapeake, some of the most important cultural rituals were civic in nature, in particular court and election days. When the county court was in session, men would come from miles around to sue one another for debt, appear as witnesses, serve as jurors, or simply observe the goings-on. Attendance at court functioned as a method of civic education; from watching the proceedings men learned what behavior their neighbors expected of them. Elections served the same purpose, for freeholders voted in public. An election official, often flanked by the candidates for the office in question, would call each man forward in turn to declare his preference. The voter would then be thanked politely by the gentleman for whom he had cast his oral ballot. Traditionally, the candidates also treated their supporters to rum at nearby taverns.

Civic Rituals

In such settings as church and courthouse, then, elite and ordinary folk alike participated in the oral, communal culture that served as the cement holding their communities together. But the genteel residents of the colonies also took part in a newer kind of culture, one organized through the world of print.

Literacy was certainly less essential in eighteenth-century America than it is today. People—especially women—could live their entire lives without ever being called upon to read a book or write a letter. Thus education beyond the bare rudiments of reading, writing, and "figuring" was usually regarded as a frill for either sex. Education accordingly was an accomplishment, a sign of status. Only parents who wanted their children to

Attitudes Toward Education

be distinguished from less fortunate peers were willing to forgo their children's valuable labor to allow them to attend school. And when parents did so, the education they gave their sons differed from that given their daughters. Girls ordinarily received little intellectual training beyond the rudiments, though they might learn music, dancing, or fancy needlework. Elite boys, on the other hand, studied with tutors or attended grammar schools that prepared them to enter college at age fourteen or fifteen.

Not surprisingly, therefore, the colonial system of higher education for males was more fully developed than was basic instruction for either sex. The first American colleges were chiefly designed to train young men for the ministry. But during the eighteenth century the curriculum and character of colleges changed considerably. Their students, the sons of the colonial elite, were now interested in careers in medicine, law, and business instead of the ministry. And the learned men who headed the colleges, though ministers themselves, were deeply affected by the Enlightenment.

In the seventeenth century, some European thinkers had begun to analyze nature in an effort to determine the laws that govern the universe. They and their successors in subsequent centuries employed experimentation and abstract reasoning to discover general principles behind such everyday phenomena as the motions of the planets and stars, the behavior of falling objects, and the characteristics of light and sound. Above all, the Enlightenment philosophers emphasized acquiring knowledge through reason, rather than through intuition and revelation.

The Enlightenment

The Enlightenment had an enormous impact on well-to-do, educated people in Europe and America. It supplied them with a common vocabulary and a unified view of the world, one that insisted that the enlightened eighteenth century was better than all previous ages. It joined them in a common endeavor, the effort to make sense of God's orderly creation. Thus American naturalists like John and William Bartram supplied European scientists with information about New World plants and animals, so that they could be fitted into newly formulated universal classification systems.

These intellectual currents had a dramatic effect on the curriculum of the colonial colleges. Whereas in the seventeenth century Harvard courses focused on the study of the ancient languages and theology, after the 1720s colleges began to introduce courses in mathematics (including algebra, geometry, and calculus), the natural sciences, law, and medicine (including anatomy and physiology). The young men educated in such colleges—and their sisters at home, with whom they occasionally shared their books and ideas—developed a rational outlook on life that differentiated them from their fellow colonists.

Well-to-do graduates of American colleges, along with others who had obtained their education in Great Britain, formed the core of genteel culture in the colonies. Men and women from these families wanted to set themselves apart from ordinary folk. Beginning in the 1720s they constructed grandiose residences, substantial houses furnished with imported carpets, silver plate, and furniture. They entertained their friends at elaborate dinner parties and balls, at which all present dressed in the height of fashion. They cultivated polite manners and saw themselves as part of a transatlantic and intercolonial network.

Elite Culture

In what ways did this genteel, enlightened culture affect the lives of the majority of colonists? Certainly no resident of the colonies could have avoided some contact with members of the elite. Some groups were directly affected; for example, the elite's demand for consumer goods of all kinds led to the growth of artisan industries (like silversmithing or fine furniture-making) in the colonies. But the Enlightenment's most immediate impact on all Americans was in the realm of medicine.

The key figure in the drama was the Reverend Cotton Mather, the Puritan clergyman, who was a member of England's Royal Society. In a Royal Society publication Mather read about the benefits of inoculation (deliberately infecting a person

Smallpox Inoculations

with a mild case of a disease) as a protection against the dreaded smallpox. In 1720 and 1721, when Boston suffered a major smallpox epidemic, Mather and a doctor ally urged people to be inoculated; there was fervent opposition, including that of Boston's leading physician. When the epidemic had ended, the statistics bore out Mather's opinion: of those inoculated, fewer than 3 percent died; of those who became ill without inoculation, nearly 15 percent perished.

If the lives of genteel and ordinary folk in the eighteenth-century colonies seemed to follow different patterns, there was one man who in his person appeared to combine their traits. That man was Benjamin Franklin. Born in Boston in 1706, he was the perfect example of a self-made, self-educated man. Apprenticed at an early age to his older brother James, a Boston printer and newspaper publisher, Franklin ran away to Philadelphia in 1723. There he worked as a printer and eventually started his own publishing business, printing the *Pennsylvania Gazette* and *Poor Richard's Almanack*. The business was so successful that Franklin was able to retire from active control in 1748. He thereafter devoted himself to intellectual endeavors and public service. Franklin's *Experiments and Observations on Electricity* (1751) was the most important scientific work by a colonial American; it established the terminology and basic theory of electricity still in use today.

Benjamin Franklin, the Symbolic American

Franklin proposed the establishment of a new educational institution in Pennsylvania. The purpose of Franklin's "English School" was not to produce clerics or scholars but to prepare young men "for learning any business, calling or profession, except such wherein languages are required." The College of Philadelphia, in other words, was intended to graduate youths who would resemble Franklin himself—talented, practical men of affairs competent in a number of different fields.

Franklin and the student he envisioned were perfect representatives of colonial culture. Like Franklin, he would rise from an ordinary family into the ranks of the genteel, thereby transcending the cultural boundaries that divided the colonists. The American would be a true child of the Enlightenment, knowledgeable about European culture yet not bound by its fetters, advancing through reason and talent alone. To him all things would be possible, all doors open.

The contrast with the original communal ideals of the early New England settlements could not have been sharper. Franklin's American was an individual, free to make choices about his future, able to contemplate a variety of possible careers. John Winthrop's American had been a component of a greater whole that required his unhesitating, unquestioning submission. But the two visions had one point in common: both described only white males. Neither blacks nor females played any part in them.

Not until many years later would America formally recognize what had been true all along: that females and nonwhites had participated in the creation of the nation's cultural traditions.

POLITICS AND RELIGION:
STABILITY AND CRISIS
AT MIDCENTURY

In the first decades of the eighteenth century, colonial political life developed a new stability. Despite the large migration from overseas, a majority of the residents of the mainland colonies were now native-born. Men from genteel families dominated the political structures in each province, for voters (white men who met property-holding requirements) tended to defer to their well-educated "betters" on election days.

Logically enough, colonial political leaders sought to increase the powers of the elected assemblies relative to those of the governors and other appointed officials. Colonial assemblies began to claim privi-

leges associated with the British House of Commons, such as the right to initiate all tax legislation and to control the militia. The assemblies also developed effective ways of influencing British appointees, especially by threatening to withhold their salaries. In some colonies (like Virginia and South Carolina), the elite members of the assemblies most often presented a united front to royal officials, but in others (like New York), they fought with each other long and bitterly.

Rise of the Assemblies

Yet eighteenth-century assemblies bore little resemblance to twentieth-century state legislatures. In the first place, much of their business was what today would be termed administrative; only on rare occasions did they formulate new policies or pass laws of major importance. Second, members of the assemblies conceived of their role differently from modern legislators. Instead of believing that they should act *positively* to improve the lives of their constituents, eighteenth-century assemblymen saw themselves as acting *negatively* to prevent encroachments on the people's rights. In their minds their primary function was to stop the governors or councils from enacting (for example) oppressive taxes; it was not to pass laws that would actively benefit their constituents.

By the middle of the century, politically aware colonists commonly drew analogies between their governments and the balance among king, lords, and commoners found in Great Britain—a combination that was thought to produce a stable polity. Although the analogy was not exact, the colonists equated their governors with the monarch, their councils with the aristocracy, and their assemblies with the House of Commons. All three were thought essential to good government, but Americans did not regard them with the same degree of approval. They saw the governors and appointed councils as representatives of England rather than America, who posed a potential threat to colonial freedoms and customary ways of life. Colonists saw the assemblies, on the other hand, as the people's protectors. And for their part, the assemblies regarded themselves as representatives of the people.

But again, such beliefs should not be equated with

modern practice. The assemblies, firmly controlled by dominant families whose members were re-elected year after year, rarely responded to the concerns of their poorer constituents. Although settlement continually spread westward, assemblies failed to reapportion themselves to provide adequate representation for newer communities. Moreover, the assemblies occasionally acted in a manner that appears oppressive to modern eyes. Thus it is important to distinguish between the colonial *ideal*, which placed the assembly to the forefront in the protection of people's liberties, and the *reality*, in which the people protected tended chiefly to be the wealthy and wellborn.

At midcentury, the political structures that had stabilized in a period of relative calm confronted a series of crises. None affected all the mainland provinces, but on the other hand no colony escaped wholly untouched by at least one. The crises foreshadowed the greater disorder of the revolutionary era. Most important, they demonstrated that the political accommodations arrived at in the aftermath of the Glorious Revolution were no longer adequate to govern Britain's American empire.

One of the first—and greatest—of the crises occurred in South Carolina. Early one morning in September 1739, about twenty South Carolina slaves gathered near the Stono River south of Charleston. After seizing guns and ammunition from a store, they killed the storekeepers and some nearby planter families. Then, joined by other slaves from the area, they headed south toward Spanish Florida. Later that day the militia caught up with the fugitives (about one hundred) and killed a number of them. Within a week most of the remaining conspirators were captured. Those not killed on the spot were later executed.

The Stono Rebellion shocked white South Carolinians and residents of other colonies as well. Laws governing the behavior of blacks were stiffened throughout British America. But the most immediate response came in New York, which itself had suffered a slave revolt in 1712. There the news from the South, coupled with fears of Spain generated by the outbreak of King George's War, set off a reign of terror in the summer of 1741. Hysterical whites transformed a biracial gang of thieves and arsonists into malevolent conspirators who wanted to foment a slave uprising under the guidance of a supposed priest in the pay of Spain. By summer's end, thirty-one blacks and four whites had been executed for participating in the "plot." Not only did the Stono Rebellion and the New York Conspiracy expose and confirm whites' deepest fears about the dangers of slaveholding, they also revealed the assemblies' inability to prevent serious internal disorder. Events of the next two decades confirmed that pattern.

By midcentury, most of the fertile land east of the Appalachians had been purchased or occupied. As a result, conflicts over land titles and conditions of landholding grew in number and frequency as colonists competed for control of land good for farming. In 1746, for example, New Jersey farmers holding land under grants from the governor of New York (dating from the brief period when both provinces were owned by the Duke of York) clashed violently with agents of the East Jersey proprietors. The proprietors claimed the land as theirs and demanded annual payments, called quitrents, for the use of the property. Similar violence occurred in the 1760s in the region that later became Vermont.

The most serious land riots of the period took place along the Hudson River in 1765 and 1766. Late in the seventeenth century, Governor Benjamin Fletcher of New York had granted several huge tracts in the lower Hudson Valley to prominent colonial families. The proprietors in turn divided these estates into small farms, which they rented chiefly to poor Dutch and German migrants. After 1740, though, increasing migration from New England brought conflict to the great New York estates. The New Englanders squatted on vacant portions of the manors and resisted all attempts to evict them. In the mid-1760s, the Philipse family brought suit against the New Englanders, some of whom had lived on Philipse land for twenty or thirty years. New York courts up-

Stono Rebellion

Land Riots

held the Philipse claim and ordered the squatters to make way for tenants with valid leases. Instead of complying, the farmers organized a rebellion against the proprietors. For nearly a year the insurgent farmers terrorized proprietors and loyal tenants, freed their friends from jail, and on one occasion battled a county sheriff and his posse. The rebellion was put down only after British troops dispatched from New York City captured its most important leaders.

Violent conflicts of a different sort erupted just a few years later in the Carolinas. The "Regulator" movements of the late 1760s (South Carolina) and early 1770s (North Carolina) pitted backcountry farmers against the eastern planters who controlled their provinces' governments. The frontier dwellers protested their lack of an adequate voice in colonial political affairs. The South Carolinians for months policed the countryside in vigilante bands, contending that law enforcement in the region was too lax. The North Carolinians, many of whose grievances had their origin in heavy taxation, fought a battle with eastern militiamen at Alamance in 1771.

The Regulators

The most widespread of all midcentury crises occurred not in politics but in religion. From the late 1730s through the 1760s, waves of religious revivalism—known collectively as the Great Awakening—swept over various parts of the colonies, primarily New England (1735–1745) and Virginia (1750s and 1760s). Eighteenth-century America was ripe for religious renewal, because orthodox Calvinists were troubled by the influence on religion of Enlightenment rationalism (which denied innate human depravity).

First Great Awakening

The first indications of what was to become the Great Awakening occurred in western Massachusetts, in the Northampton congregation of the Reverend Jonathan Edwards, a noted preacher and theologian. During 1734 and 1735, Edwards noticed a remarkable response in his flock (and especially its more youthful members) to a message based squarely on Calvinist principles. Individuals, Edwards argued, could attain salvation only through recognition of their own de-

George Whitefield (1714–1770), an English evangelist who made frequent tours of the American colonies. This portrait, painted in England, shows the effects his powerful preaching had on his listeners.   National Portrait Gallery, London.

praved natures and the need to surrender completely to God's will. People in Edwards's congregation began to experience that surrender as a single identifiable moment of conversion.

The effects of such conversions remained isolated until 1739, when George Whitefield, an English adherent of the Methodist branch of Anglicanism, arrived in America. For fifteen months Whitefield toured the colonies, preaching to large audiences, and he became the chief generating force behind the Great Awakening. Regular clerics at first welcomed Whitefield, as well as other evangelist preachers. But many churchmen soon realized that the revived religion ran counter to their own more rationalistic faith.

Opposition to the Awakening heightened rapidly, and large numbers of churches splintered in its wake.

"Old Lights"—traditional clerics and their followers—engaged in bitter disputes with the "New Light" evangelicals. American religion, already characterized by numerous sects, became further divided as the major denominations split into Old Light and New Light factions, and as new evangelical sects—Methodists and Baptists—quickly gained adherents. Paradoxically, the rise in the number of distinct denominations eventually led to an American willingness to tolerate religious diversity. No one sect could make an unequivocal claim to orthodoxy and so they all had to coexist if they were to exist at all.

The most important effect of the Awakening was its impact on American modes of thought. Common folk had long been expected to accept unhesitatingly the authority of their "betters." The message of the Great Awakening directly challenged that tradition of deference. The revivalists, many of whom were not ordained clergymen, claimed they understood the word of God far better than orthodox clerics. The Awakening's emphasis on emotion rather than learning as the road to salvation further undermined the validity of received wisdom. Supported by the belief that God was with them, New Lights began to question not only religious but also social and political orthodoxy.

At midcentury the Great Awakening injected an egalitarian strain into American life. Although primarily a religious movement, the Awakening also had important social and political consequences, calling into question habitual modes of behavior in the secular as well as the religious realm. In combination with the other changes occurring in the colonies—the increasing ethnic and racial diversity, the expanding economy, the introduction of new lifestyles and forms of thought—the Great Awakening helped to break Americans' ties to their limited seventeenth-century origins. A century and a half after English people had first settled in North America, the colonies were only nominally English. Rather, they mixed diverse European, American, and African traditions into a novel cultural blend. That culture owed much to the Old World, but just as much, if not more, to the New. In the 1760s Americans began to

IMPORTANT EVENTS

1720–21	Smallpox inoculation controversy, Boston
1720–40	Black population of Chesapeake begins to grow by natural increase
1739	Stono Rebellion George Whitefield arrives in America; Great Awakening broadens
1739–48	King George's War
1741	Slave revolt scare, New York City
1765–66	Hudson River land riots
1767–69	Regulator movement (South Carolina)
1771	North Carolina Regulators defeated at Battle of Alamance

recognize that fact. They realized that their interests were not necessarily those of Great Britain.

SUGGESTIONS FOR FURTHER READING

General

James A. Henretta, *The Evolution of American Society, 1700–1815* (1973); Richard Hofstadter, *America at 1750: A Social Portrait* (1971).

Rural Society

Carl Bridenbaugh, *Myths and Realities: Societies of the*

Colonial South (1963); Rhys Isaac, *The Transformation of Virginia 1740–1790* (1982); Sung Bok Kim, *Landlord and Tenant in Colonial New York* (1978); James T. Lemon, *The Best Poor Man's Country* (1972); Michael Zuckerman, *Peaceable Kingdoms* (1970).

Urban Society

Carl Bridenbaugh, *Cities in Revolt* (1955); Gary B. Nash, *The Urban Crucible* (1979); Frederick B. Tolles, *Meeting House and Counting House* (1948).

Economic Development

Paul G. E. Clemens, *The Atlantic Economy and Colonial Maryland's Eastern Shore* (1980); Alice Hanson Jones, *Wealth of a Nation to Be* (1980); Edwin J. Perkins, *The Economy of Colonial America* (1980); Gary M. Walton and James F. Shepherd, *The Economic Rise of Early America* (1979).

Politics

Bernard Bailyn, *The Origins of American Politics* (1968); Patricia U. Bonomi, *A Factious People* (1971); Edward M. Cook, Jr., *The Fathers of the Towns* (1976); Jack P. Greene, *The Quest for Power* (1963).

Immigration

Jon Butler, *The Huguenots in America* (1983); R. J. Dickson, *Ulster Immigration to Colonial America, 1718–1775* (1966); Ned C. Landsman, *Scotland and Its First American Colony, 1683–1765* (1985).

Blacks

Ira Berlin, "Time, Space, and the Evolution of Afro-American Society in British Mainland America," *American Historical Review*, 85 (1980), 44–78; Herbert Gutman, *The Black Family in Slavery and Freedom 1750–1925* (1976); Allan Kulikoff, *Tobacco and Slaves* (1986); Gerald W. Mullin, *Flight and Rebellion* (1972).

Women and Family

J. William Frost, *The Quaker Family in Colonial America* (1972); Philip J. Greven, *The Protestant Temperament* (1977); Mary Beth Norton, *Liberty's Daughters* (1980); Daniel Blake Smith, *Inside the Great House* (1980).

Colonial Culture and the Enlightenment

Daniel J. Boorstin, *The Americans: The Colonial Experience* (1958); Richard Beale Davis, *Intellectual Life in the Colonial South, 1585–1763*, 2 vols. (1978); Brooke Hindle, *The Pursuit of Science in Revolutionary America* (1956); Henry F. May, *The Enlightenment in America* (1976); Louis B. Wright, *The Cultural Life of the American Colonies, 1607–1763* (1957).

Education

James Axtell, *The School upon a Hill* (1974); Bernard Bailyn, *Education in the Forming of American Society* (1960); Patricia Cline Cohen, *A Calculating People* (1982); Lawrence A. Cremin, *American Education: The Colonial Experience 1607–1783* (1970); Kenneth A. Lockridge, *Literacy in Colonial New England* (1974).

Religion and the Great Awakening

Carl Bridenbaugh, *Mitre and Sceptre* (1962); J. M. Bumsted and John E. Van de Wetering, *What Must I Do to Be Saved?* (1976); Edwin S. Gaustad, *The Great Awakening in New England* (1957); Alan E. Heimert, *Religion and the American Mind* (1966); Patricia Tracy, *Jonathan Edwards, Pastor* (1980).

CHAPTER 4

SEVERING THE BONDS
OF EMPIRE
1754–1774

*I*n *late October* 1769, the young Boston shopkeeper Betsy Cuming was visiting a sick friend when outside the house she heard "a voilint Skreeming Kill him Kill him." Betsy ran to the window and saw John Mein, a bookseller and newspaper publisher, being chased by "a larg Croud of those who Call themselves Gentelman." She learned the next day that Mein had taken shelter in a British Army guardhouse. That same night, he fled to a vessel anchored in the harbor. Mein later sailed to England and never returned to the city.

What had John Mein done? He published a newspaper that generally supported the British side in the current disputes with the colonies. The offense that led to the mobbing, though, was more specific: he had printed several lists of names of local merchants who had recently cleared imports through the Boston customs house. But why was the information Mein revealed so explosive? Because in the fall of 1769 many American merchants had signed an agreement

not to import goods from Great Britain; Mein's lists indicated that some of the most vocal supporters of nonimportation (including John Hancock) had been violating the agreement. That was why the "gentlemen" of Boston had to silence the outspoken publisher.

John Mein was not the first, and he would be far from the last, resident of the colonies who found his life wholly disrupted by the growing political antagonism between England and her American possessions. Long afterwards, John Adams identified the years between 1760 and 1775 as the period in which the true American Revolution had occurred. The Revolution, Adams declared, was "in the Minds of the people," involving not the actual winning of independence but rather a shift of allegiance from England to America.

The story of the 1760s and early 1770s is one of an ever-widening split between England and America. In the long history of British settlement in the

A LIST of the Names of *those* who AUDACIOUSLY continue to counteract the UNITED SENTIMENTS of the BODY of Merchants thro'out NORTH-AMERICA ; by importing British Goods contrary to the Agreement.

John Bernard,
    (In King-Street, almost opposite Vernon'sHead.

James McMasters,
    (On Treat's Wharf.

Patrick McMasters,
    (Opposite the Sign of the Lamb.

John Mein,
    (Opposite the White-Horse, and in King-Street.

Nathaniel Rogers,
    (Opposite Mr. Henderson Inches Store lower End King-Street.

William Jackson,
    At the BrazenHead, Cornhill, near the Town-House.

Theophilus Lillie,
    (Near Mr. Pemberton's Meeting-House, North-End.

John Taylor,
    (Nearly opposite the Heart and Crown in Cornhill.

Ame & Elizabeth Cummings,
    (Opposite the Old Brick Meeting House, all of Boston.

Israel Williams, Esq; & Son,
    (Traders in the Town of Hatfield.

And, Henry Barnes,
    (Trader in the Town of Marlboro'.

The following Names should have been inserted in the List of Justices.

County of Middlesex.	County of Lincoln.
Samuel Hendley	
John Borland	John Kingsbury
Henry Barnes	
Richard Cary	County of Berkshire.
County of Bristol.	Mark Hopkins
George Brightman	Elijah Dwight
County of Worcester.	Israel Stoddard
Daniel Bliss	

A blacklist printed in the North American Almanac for 1770 identified those Boston merchants who had ignored the nonimportation agreement. Among their number were both John Mein, the object of the mob's wrath the previous October, and Betsy (Elizabeth) Cuming, the narrator of the story, who—with her sister Anne—ran a small dry-goods store. *Library of Congress.*

Western Hemisphere, there had at times been considerable tension in the relationship between individual provinces and mother country. Still, that tension had rarely been sustained for long, nor had it been widespread, except in 1688 and 1689. In the 1750s, however, a series of events began to change that. It all started with the French and Indian War (1754–1763).

Britain's overwhelming victory in that war forever altered the balance of power in North America. France was ousted from the continent, an event with major consequences for both the Indian tribes of the interior and the residents of the British colonies. Northern Indians could no longer play European powers off against one another. Anglo-Americans, for their part, no longer had to fear a French threat on their borders. The British colonies would never have dared to break with their mother country, some historians have argued, if an enemy nation and its Indian allies had controlled the interior of the continent.

The British victory in 1763 also had a significant impact on Great Britain, one that soon affected the colonies as well. To win the war, Britain had gone heavily into debt. To reduce the debt, Parliament for the first time laid revenue-raising taxes on the colonies. That decision exposed differences in the political thinking of Americans and Britons.

During the 1760s, a broad coalition of white Americans, men and women alike, resisted new tax levies and attempts by British officials to tighten controls over the provincial governments. America's elected leaders became even more suspicious of Britain's motives as the years passed. They laid aside traditional intercolonial antagonisms to coordinate their response to the new measures, and they slowly began to reorient their political thinking. As late as the summer of 1774, though, most were still seeking a solution within the framework of the empire; few harbored thoughts of independence. When independence, as opposed to loyal resistance, did become the issue, the coalition of the 1760s broke down. That, however, did not happen until after the battles of Lexington and Concord in April 1775. Before then, only a few Americans, most of them closely connected to colonial administration or the Church of England, opposed the trend of resistance.

Renewed Warfare among Europeans and Indians

While the English colonists had been consolidating control of the Atlantic seaboard, the French and Spanish had been extending their influence into the interior of North America around the edges of English settlement. The Spanish outposts in Florida and along the coast of the Gulf of Mexico posed little threat to the English, for Spain's days as a major power had passed. The French, though, were another matter. In the late seventeenth and early eighteenth centuries France had explored the Great Lakes and Mississippi valley regions, establishing a long chain of forts and settlements stretching from New Orleans at the mouth of the Mississippi to the junction of Lakes Huron and Michigan. In none of the three wars fought between 1689 and 1748 was England able to shake France's domination of the North American interior. Under the Peace of Utrecht, which ended Queen Anne's War in 1713, the English won control of such peripheral northern areas as Newfoundland, Hudson's Bay, and Nova Scotia (Acadia). But Britain made no other territorial gains in King George's War (see map, page 66).

During both Queen Anne's War and King George's War, the Iroquois Confederacy took no formal role. Instead, the Iroquois council skillfully played the Europeans off against one another, refusing to commit its warriors fully to either side. When the Iroquois went to war in those years, it was against a traditional southern enemy, the Catawba. Since the French repeatedly urged them to attack the Catawba (a tribe allied with the English), the Iroquois thereby achieved two desirable goals. They kept the French happy and simultaneously consolidated their control over the entire interior region north of Virginia. In addition, these southern wars (by identifying a common enemy) enabled the confederacy to

Iroquois Neutrality

cement its alliance with its weaker tributaries, the Shawnee and Delaware.

But even the careful Iroquois diplomats could not prevent the region inhabited by the Shawnee and Delaware (now western Pennsylvania and eastern Ohio) from providing the spark that set off a major war. That conflict spread from America to Europe and proved decisive in the contest for North America. Trouble began in 1752 when English fur traders ventured into the area, known as the Ohio country, for the French could not permit their English rivals to dominate the region. A permanent English presence in the Ohio country could challenge France's control of the western fur trade and even threaten its prominence in the Mississippi valley. Accordingly, in 1753 the French pushed southward from Lake Erie into the Ohio country.

In response to the threat posed by the French, delegates from seven northern and middle colonies gathered in Albany, New York, in June 1754. With the backing of administrators in London, they sought two goals: to persuade the Iroquois to abandon their traditional neutrality, and to coordinate the defenses of the colonies. In neither aim were they successful. The Iroquois, while listening politely to the colonists' arguments, saw no reason to change a policy that had served them well for half a century. And although the Albany Congress delegates adopted a Plan of Union (which would have established an elected intercolonial legislature with the power to tax), the plan was uniformly rejected by their provincial governments—primarily because those governments feared a loss of autonomy.

Albany Congress

The delegates to the Congress did not know that, while they deliberated, the war they sought to prepare for was already beginning. The governor of Virginia, which claimed the region that is now western Pennsylvania, had sent a small militia force westward to counter the French moves. But the Virginia militiamen arrived too late. The French had already taken possession of the strategic point—now Pittsburgh—where the Al-

Beginning of the French and Indian War

Quebec

NEW FRANCE

Lake Superior

CHIPPEWA

Montreal

Ft. Western
(Augusta)

St. Lawrence R.

MAINE
(Part of Mass.)

Falmouth
(Portland)

Lake Huron

Lake Michigan

CHIPPEWA

Lake Ontario

MOHAWK

OTTAWA

Ft. Niagara

ONEIDA
TUSCARORA
ONONDAGA
CAYUGA

Ft. Stanwix
Albany

N.H.

Portsmouth

Boston

MASS.

POTAWATOMI
MIAMI

Ft. Detroit

SENECA

Lake Erie

Allegheny R.

NEW YORK

Hartford

CONN.

Providence
R.I.

WYANDOT

1720-1760

PENNSYLVANIA

New York

ILLINOIS CONFEDERATION

DELAWARE

Ft. Duquesne
(Pitt)

Monongahela R.

Philadelphia

N.J.

OHIO COUNTRY

Ft.
Necessity

Tuscarora Migration

New Castle

WEA

Baltimore

SHAWNEE

MD.

DEL.

Ohio R.

Line of 1763

Richmond

VIRGINIA

Williamsburg

ATLANTIC OCEAN

Mississippi R.

Proclamation

CHEROKEE

Salem

Hillsboro

NORTH CAROLINA

New Bern

CATAWBA

Camden

Wilmington

CHICKASAW

SOUTH CAROLINA

Ft. Augusta
(Augusta)

Charleston

GEORGIA

CREEK

Savannah

CHOCTAW

NEW SPAIN

St. Augustine

Total population of
English colonies: c.1.5 million

Extent of settlement

0   100   200 miles

0   100   200   300 kilometers

European Settlements and Indian Tribes, 1750

legheny and Monongahela rivers meet to form the Ohio, and they were constructing Fort Duquesne there. The foolhardy and inexperienced young colonel who commanded the Virginians allowed himself to be trapped by the French in his crudely built Fort Necessity at Great Meadows, Pennsylvania. After the twenty-two-year-old George Washington surrendered, he and his men were allowed to return to Virginia.

Washington had blundered grievously. He had sparked a war that would eventually encompass nearly the entire world. In 1755, General Edward Braddock, two regiments of regulars, and some colonial troops suffered a disastrous defeat a few miles south of Fort Duquesne. For the next three years, the French were consistently victorious.

Finally, under the leadership of William Pitt, who was named secretary of state in 1757, the British mounted the effort that won them the war in North America. They captured the fortress at Louisbourg in 1758, Quebec in 1759, and Montreal—the last French stronghold—in 1760. The war in America was over, but it continued elsewhere for three more years. When the Treaty of Paris was finally signed in 1763, France ceded its major North American holdings to Britain. Spain, an ally of France toward the end of the war, gave Florida to the victorious English. And since Britain feared the presence of France in Louisiana, it forced the French to cede that region to Spain, a weaker power. No longer would the English seacoast colonies have to worry about the threat to their existence posed by France's extensive North American territories.

Pitt achieved this stunning victory by encouraging cooperation between the colonists and Great Britain. In the early years of the war, British army and navy officers had adopted coercive recruiting techniques. They arbitrarily commandeered supplies from American farmers and merchants and ordered the quartering of royal troops in private homes. All these actions aroused the colonists' ire. Pitt, by contrast, agreed to reimburse the colonies for their military expenditures and placed troop recruitment wholly in local hands.

Consequently, Americans (especially New Englanders) began to support the war effort more fully.

Yet British commanders denigrated the American contributions to the winning campaigns. For one thing, most of the actual fighting was carried on by British regulars, with colonial troops being relegated to support roles (a practice the Americans resented). For another, the British army leaders alleged that American merchants were prolonging the conflict by continuing to trade with the French West Indies. (The Americans responded that their economies would collapse without the West Indian trade.) And, finally, redcoat officers and enlisted men alike looked down on their American counterparts as undisciplined and ignorant of military procedures.

Anglo-American Tensions

Over the decade and a half following the close of the American phase of the war in 1760, each drew on impressions of the other gained during the French and Indian War. The British dismissed any suggestion of American military prowess. The Americans, meanwhile, remembered the threat of arbitrary military power, the British officers' arrogance, and their own wounded pride. In other words, the victorious alliance had done nothing to dispel—and possibly much to promote—the gathering clouds of disagreement.

1763: A TURNING POINT

The overwhelming British victory over France had an irreversible impact on North America. Its effects were felt first by the Indian tribes that had used the competition among European powers to maintain their autonomy. With France excluded from the continent, the diplomatic strategy that had served the tribes well for so long could no longer be employed. The consequences were immediate and devastating.

Even before the Treaty of Paris, southern Indians had to adjust to the new circumstances. After the British gained the upper hand in the American war in 1758, the Creek and Cherokee lost their ability to force concessions from the British by threatening to turn instead to the French or the Spanish. In desperation and in retaliation for British atrocities, the Cherokee attacked the Carolina and Virginia frontiers in 1760. Although initially victorious, the tribesmen were defeated the following year. Late in 1761 the two sides concluded a treaty under which the Cherokee allowed the construction of English forts in tribal territories and also opened a large tract of land to white settlement.

In the Northwest the tribes—Ottawa, Chippewa, and Potawatomi—became angry when Great Britain, no longer facing French competition, raised the price of trade goods, ended the practice of paying rent for forts, and allowed settlers to move into the Monongahela and Susquehanna valleys.

Pontiac, the war chief of an Ottawa village near Detroit, understood the implications of such British actions. Only unity among the western tribes, he realized, could possibly prevent total dependence on and subordination to the victorious British. In the spring of 1763 he forged an unprecedented alliance among the Huron, Chippewa, Potawatomi, Delaware, and Shawnee tribes, even gaining the participation of some Mingoes (Pennsylvania Iroquois). Pontiac then laid siege to the fort at Detroit while his war parties attacked and took possession of most of the other British outposts in the Great Lakes region.

Pontiac's Uprising

That was the high point of the uprising. The tribes raided the Virginia and Pennsylvania frontiers at will throughout the summer, killing at least two thousand whites. But they could not take the strongholds of Niagara, Fort Pitt, or Detroit. In early August, a combined force of Delawares, Shawnees, Hurons, and Mingoes was soundly defeated at Bushy Run, Pennsylvania, by troops sent from the coast. Conflict

ceased when Pontiac broke off the siege of Detroit in late October, after most of his warriors had returned to their villages. A formal treaty ending the war was finally negotiated in 1766.

In the aftermath of the bloody summer of 1763, Scotch-Irish frontiersmen from Paxton Township, Pennsylvania, sought revenge on the only Indians within reach, a peaceful band of Christian converts living at Conestoga. In December the whites raided the Indian village twice, killing twenty people. Two months later hundreds of frontier dwellers known to history as the Paxton Boys marched on Philadelphia to demand military protection against future Indian attacks. City officials feared violence and mustered the militia to repel the westerners, but the protesters presented their request in an orderly fashion and returned home.

Pontiac's uprising and the march of the Paxton Boys showed that Great Britain would not find it easy to govern the huge territory it had just acquired from France. In October, in a futile attempt to assert control over the interior, the ministry issued the Proclamation of 1763, which declared the headwaters of rivers flowing into the Atlantic from the Appalachian Mountains to be the temporary western boundary for colonial settlement. The proclamation was intended to prevent future clashes between Indians and colonists by forbidding whites to move onto Indian lands until the tribes had given up their land by treaty. But many whites had already established farms west of the proclamation line, and the policy was doomed to failure from its outset.

Proclamation of 1763

The proclamation directly affected only frontier families; other decisions made in London had a much broader impact in British North America. The problems and opportunities confronting Great Britain in the 1760s required leadership that was both skilled and flexible. The twenty-two-year-old king, George III, who had assumed the throne in 1760, possessed neither of these qualities. He was instead an immature man of mediocre intellect who was an erratic judge of character. Furthermore, he regarded adherence to the status quo as the hallmark of patriotism.

In 1764 Colonel Henry Bouquet, the victor the preceding year at the battle of Bushy Run, negotiated with representatives of the Seneca, Shawnee, and Delaware at a council held on the Muskingum River in the Ohio Country. The agreement reached there opened part of the region to white settlement. Library of Congress.

In 1763, the king selected George Grenville as his prime minister. Grenville confronted a financial crisis: England's burden of indebtedness had nearly doubled since 1754, from £73 million to £137 million. Obviously, Grenville's ministry had to find new sources of funds, and the English people themselves were already heavily taxed. Since the colonists had been major beneficiaries of the wartime expenditures, Grenville concluded that the Americans should be asked to pay a greater share of the cost of running the empire.

Grenville did not question Great Britain's right to levy taxes on the colonies. Like all his countrymen, he believed that the government's legitimacy derived ultimately from the consent of the people, but he defined consent far more loosely than did the colonists.

Americans had come to believe that they could be represented only by men for whom they or their property-holding neighbors had actually voted. To Grenville and his English contemporaries, Parliament represented all English subjects, wherever they resided. According to this theory of government, called *virtual representation,* the colonists were said to be virtually, if not actually, represented in Parliament. Thus their consent to acts of Parliament could be presumed.

The colonists, on the other hand, had become accustomed to a government that wielded only limited authority over them and affected their daily lives very little. In consequence, they believed that a good government was one that largely left them alone, a view

Theories of Representation

in keeping with the theories of a group of British writers known as the Real Whigs. These writers stressed the dangers inherent in a powerful government, particularly one headed by a monarch. They warned that rulers would try to corrupt and oppress the people, that government was always to be feared, and that only the perpetual vigilance of the people and their elected representatives could preserve freedom.

Britain's attempts to tighten the reins of colonial government in the 1760s and early 1770s convinced many Americans that the Real Whigs' reasoning applied to their circumstances. They began to see evil designs behind the actions of Grenville and his successors. In the mid-1760s, the colonists did not, however, immediately accuse Grenville of an intent to oppress them. They at first simply questioned the utility of the new laws.

The first such measures, the Sugar and Currency Acts, were passed by Parliament in 1764. The Sugar Act revised the existing system of customs regulations; laid new duties on certain

Sugar and Currency Acts

foreign imports into the colonies; established a vice-admiralty court at Halifax, Nova Scotia; and included special provisions aimed at stopping the widespread smuggling of molasses, one of the chief commodities in American trade. Although the Sugar Act appeared to resemble the Navigation Acts (see page 38), it broke with tradition because it was explicitly designed to raise revenue, not to channel American trade through Britain. The Currency Act in effect outlawed colonial issues of paper money. Americans could accumulate little hard cash, since they imported more than they exported; thus the act seemed to the colonists to deprive them of a useful medium of exchange.

Since the American economy was suffering a severe postwar depression, it is not surprising that both individual colonists and colonial governments decided to protest the new policies. But, lacking any precedent for a united campaign against acts of Parliament, Americans in 1764 took only hesitant and uncoordinated steps. Eight colonial legislatures sent separate petitions to Parliament requesting repeal of the Sugar Act. They argued that the act placed severe restrictions on their commerce and that they had not consented to its passage. The protests had no effect. The law remained in force and Grenville proceeded with another revenue plan.

THE STAMP ACT CRISIS

The Stamp Act, Grenville's most important proposal, was modeled on a law that had been in effect in England for nearly a century. It touched nearly every colonist by requiring tax stamps on most printed materials. Anyone who purchased a newspaper or pamphlet, made a will, transferred land, bought dice or playing cards, needed a liquor license, accepted a government appointment, or borrowed money would have to pay the tax. Never before had a revenue measure of such scope been proposed for the colonies. The act would also require that tax stamps be paid for with hard money and that violators be tried in vice-admiralty courts, without juries. Finally, such a law would break decisively with the colonial tradition of self-imposed taxation.

The most important colonial pamphlet protesting the Sugar Act and the proposed Stamp Act was *The Rights of the British Colonies Asserted and Proved*, by

Otis's Rights of the British Colonies

James Otis, Jr., a brilliant young Massachusetts attorney. Otis starkly exposed the ideological dilemma that was to confound the colonists for the next decade. How could they justify their opposition to certain acts of Parliament without questioning Parliament's authority over them? On the one hand, Otis asserted that Americans were "entitled to all the natural, essential, inherent, and inseparable rights" of Britons, including the right not to be taxed without their consent. On the other hand, Otis was forced to admit that, under the British system, "the power of parliament is uncontroulable, but by themselves, and we must obey."

Otis thus implied that Parliament could not tax the colonies because Americans were not represented in its ranks. But he also accepted the prevailing British theory of parliamentary supremacy. In an effort to find a middle ground, Otis proposed colonial representation in Parliament; the idea was never seriously considered on either side of the Atlantic. The British believed that the colonists were already virtually represented in Parliament, and the Americans quickly realized that a handful of colonial delegates to London would simply be outvoted.

Otis wrote his pamphlet before the Stamp Act was passed. When Americans learned of its adoption in the spring of 1765, they did not at first know how to react. Few colonists publicly favored the law. But colonial petitions had already failed to prevent its adoption, and further lobbying appeared futile. Perhaps Otis was right, and the only course open to the Americans was to pay the stamp tax until Parliament saw its error and repealed the law.

Not all the colonists, however, were resigned to paying the new tax without a fight. Just such a man was a twenty-nine-year-old lawyer serving his first term as a member of the Virginia House of Burgesses. Patrick Henry later recalled that he was appalled by his fellow legislators' unwillingness to oppose the Stamp Act openly. Henry decided to act. "Alone, unadvised, and unassisted, on a blank leaf of an old law book," he wrote the Virginia Stamp Act Resolves.

Patrick Henry and the Virginia Stamp Act Resolves

Patrick Henry introduced his proposals in late May, near the end of the legislative session. Henry's fiery speech in support of his resolutions, led the Speaker of the House to accuse him of treason but Henry quickly denied the charge. The small number of burgesses remaining in Williamsburg adopted five of Henry's resolutions by a bare majority. Though they repealed the most radical resolution the next day, their action had far-reaching effects.

The four propositions adopted by the burgesses repeated the arguments James Otis had already advanced. The colonists had never forfeited the rights of British subjects, they declared, and consent to taxation was one of the most important of those rights. The other three resolutions went much further. The one that was repealed claimed for the burgesses "the only exclusive right" to tax Virginians. The final two asserted that residents of the colony did not have to obey tax laws passed by other legislative bodies (namely Parliament) and termed any opponent of that opinion "an Enemy to this his Majesty's Colony."

Over the course of the next ten years, America's political leaders searched for a formula that would enable them to control their internal affairs, especially taxation, but remain within the British Empire. The chief difficulty lay in British officials' inability to compromise on the issue of parliamentary power. The notion that Parliament could exercise absolute authority over all colonial possessions was basic to the British theory of government.

The ultimate effectiveness of Americans' opposition to the Stamp Act did not rest on ideological arguments over parliamentary power. What gave the resistance its primary force were the decisive and inventive actions of some colonists during the late summer and fall of 1765.

In August the Loyal Nine, a Boston social club of printers, distillers, and other artisans, organized a demonstration against the Stamp Act. Hoping to show that people of all social and economic ranks opposed the act, they approached the leaders of the city's rival laborers' associations, one based in the North End and one in the South End. The Loyal Nine convinced them to lay aside their differences and participate in the demonstration.

Loyal Nine

Early in the morning of August 14, the demonstrators hung an effigy of Andrew Oliver, the province's stamp distributor, from a tree on Boston Common. That night, after a peaceful parade, a crowd destroyed a building they assumed was going to be a tax office. The wood from the structure was used to build a bonfire near Oliver's house. In an unplanned act, members of the crowd broke most of Oliver's windows, and then Oliver publicly promised not to fulfill the duties of his office. Twelve nights later another mob, reportedly led by the South End leader, Ebenezer MacIntosh, attacked the homes of several customs officials. This time the violence was almost universally condemned, for the mob completely destroyed Lieutenant Governor Thomas Hutchinson's elaborately furnished townhouse.

The differences between the two Boston mobs of August 1765 exposed divisions that would continue to characterize colonial protests in the years that followed. The skilled craftsmen who composed the Loyal Nine and members of the educated elite like merchants and lawyers preferred orderly demonstrations confined to political issues. For the city's laborers, by contrast, economic grievances may well have been paramount.

Americans' Divergent Interests

The colonies, like the mother country, had a long tradition of crowd action, in which disfranchised people took to the streets to redress deeply felt local grievances. But the Stamp Act controversy drew ordinary urban folk into the vortex of imperial politics for the first time. Matters that had previously been of concern only to genteel folk, or to members of colonial legislatures, were now discussed on every street corner. Sally Franklin observed as much when she wrote to her father, Benjamin, who was then serving as a colonial agent in London, that "nothing else is talked of, the Dutch [Germans] talk of the stompt act the Negroes of the tamp, in short every body has something to say."

The entry of lower-class whites and blacks—both men and women—into the realm of imperial politics both threatened and afforded an opportunity to the well-to-do white men who wanted to mount effective opposition to British measures. On the one hand, crowd action could have a stunning impact. The demonstrations were so successful that by November 1, when the law was scheduled to take effect, not a single stamp distributor was willing to carry out the duties of his office. As a result, the act could not be enforced. But at the same time, members of the elite recognized that mobs composed of the formerly powerless could potentially endanger their own dominant position in society.

Therefore, they attempted to channel resistance into acceptable forms by creating an intercolonial association, the Sons of Liberty. The first such group was created in New York City in early November, and branches spread rapidly through the colonies. Largely composed of merchants, lawyers, prosperous tradesmen, and the like, the Sons of Liberty linked resistance leaders in cities from Charleston, South Carolina, to Portsmouth, New Hampshire, by early 1766.

Sons of Liberty

During the fall and winter of 1765 and 1766, opposition to the Stamp Act proceeded on three separate fronts. The colonial legislatures petitioned Parliament to repeal the hated law and sent delegates to an intercolonial congress, the first since 1754. In October the Stamp Act Congress met in New York to draft a unified but relatively conservative statement of protest. At the same time, the Sons of Liberty held mass meetings in an effort to win public support for the resistance movement. Finally, American merchants organized nonimportation associations to put economic pressure on British exporters. By the 1760s one-quarter of all British exports were being sent to the colonies, and American merchants reasoned that London merchants whose sales had suffered severely would lobby for repeal. (Nonimportation also enabled colonial merchants to reduce bloated inventories.)

In March 1766, Parliament repealed the Stamp Act. The nonimportation agreements had had the anticipated effect, creating allies within the powerful circle of wealthy London merchants. Success, however, was largely a result of Grenville's replacement by Lord Rockingham. The new prime minister, an opponent of the tax, pushed for repeal. But he linked repeal to the passage of the Declaratory Act, which asserted Parliament's ability to tax and legislate for Britain's American possessions "in all cases whatsoever." As they celebrated the Stamp Act's repeal, few Ameri-

Repeal of the Stamp Act

British Ministries and Their American Policies

Head of Ministry	Major Acts
George Grenville	Sugar Act (1764)
	Currency Act (1764)
	Stamp Act (1765)
Lord Rockingham	Stamp Act repeal (1766)
	Declaratory Act (1766)
William Pitt/Charles Townshend	Townshend Acts (1767)
Lord North	Townshend duties repealed (all but tea tax) (1770)
	Coercive Acts (1774)
	Quebec Act (1774)

cans recognized the Declaratory Act's ominous implications.

Resistance to the Townshend Acts

The colonists had accomplished their immediate aim, but the long-term prospects were unclear. Another change in the ministry, in the summer of 1766, revealed how fragile their victory had been. Charles Townshend, a Grenvillite, was named chancellor of the exchequer in a new administration headed by the ailing William Pitt, and he decided to renew the attempt to obtain additional funds from the colonies.

The taxes Townshend proposed in 1767 were to be levied on trade goods like paper, glass, and tea, and thus seemed on the surface to be nothing more than extensions of the existing Navigation Acts. But the Townshend duties differed from previous customs taxes in two ways. First, they were levied on items imported into the colonies from Britain, not from foreign countries. Second, they were designed to raise money to pay the salaries of royal officials in the colonies. That posed a direct challenge to the colonial assemblies, which derived considerable power from threatening to withhold officials' salaries. In addition, Townshend's scheme provided for the establishment of an American Board of Customs Commissioners and for the creation of vice-admiralty courts at Boston, Philadelphia, and Charleston. Lastly, Townshend proposed the appointment of a secretary of state for American affairs and the suspension of the New York legislature for its refusal to supply necessary items to British troops in that colony.

The Townshend Acts drew a quick response. One series of essays in particular, *Letters from a Farmer in Pennsylvania* by the prominent lawyer John Dickinson, expressed the consensus prevailing among his fellow colonists. Dickinson contended that Parliament could regulate colonial trade, but could not exercise that power for the purpose of raising revenues. He thus avoided the complicated question of colonial consent to parliamentary legislation. But his argument had another flaw: it was clearly unworkable for Americans to assess Parliament's motives for passing a trade law before deciding whether to obey it.

The Massachusetts assembly responded to the Townshend Acts by drafting a circular letter to the other colonial legislatures, calling for unity and suggesting a joint petition of protest.

Massachusetts Assembly Dissolved

It was less the letter itself than the ministry's reaction to it that united the colonies. When Lord Hillsborough, the first secretary of state for America, learned of the circular letter, he ordered Governor Francis Bernard of Massachusetts to insist that the assembly recall it. He also directed other governors to prevent their assemblies from discussing the letter. Hillsborough's order gave the colonial assemblies the incentive they needed to forget their differences and join forces to meet the new threat to their prerogatives. In late 1768 the Massachusetts legislature met, debated, and resoundingly rejected recall by a vote of 92 to 17. Bernard immediately dissolved the assembly, and other governors followed suit when their legislatures debated the circular letter.

During the two-year campaign against the Townshend duties, the Sons of Liberty and other American leaders made a deliberate effort to involve ordinary folk in the formal resistance movement. In a June 1769 Maryland nonimportation agreement, for instance, the signers (who were identified as "Merchants, Tradesmen, Freeholders, Mechanics [artisans], and other Inhabitants") agreed not to import or consume items of British origin. Such tactics helped to increase the number of colonists who were publicly aligned with the protest movement.

Just as the pamphlets by Otis, Dickinson, and others acquainted literate colonists with the issues raised by British actions, so public rituals taught illiterate

Rituals of Resistance

Americans about the reasons for resistance and familiarized them with the terms of the argument. When Boston's revived Sons of Liberty invited hundreds of the city's residents to dine with them each August 14 to commemorate the first

Stamp Act uprising, and the Charleston Sons of Liberty held their meetings in public, crowds gathered to watch and listen. The participants in such events were openly expressing their commitment to the cause of resistance and encouraging others to join them.

Women, who had previously regarded politics as outside their proper sphere, now took a part in resisting British policy. In towns throughout America, young women calling themselves Daughters of Liberty met to spin in public, in an effort to spur other women to make homespun and end the colonies' dependence on English cloth. These symbolic displays of patriotism served an important purpose. When young ladies from well-to-do families sat publicly at spinning wheels all day, eating only American food and drinking local herbal tea, and afterwards listening to patriotic sermons, they were acting as political instructors.

Daughters of Liberty

Women also took the lead in promoting nonconsumption of tea. In Boston more than three hundred matrons publicly promised not to drink tea, "Sickness excepted." Housewives throughout the colonies exchanged recipes for tea substitutes or drank coffee instead. The best known of the protests (because it was satirized by a British cartoonist), the so-called Edenton Ladies' Tea Party, actually had little to do with tea; it was a meeting of prominent North Carolina women who pledged formally to work for the public good and to support resistance to British measures.

But the colonists were by no means united in support of nonimportation. If the Stamp Act protests had occasionally revealed a division between artisans and merchants, on the one hand, and common laborers, on the other, resistance to the Townshend Acts exposed new splits in the American ranks. The most important divided the former allies of 1765 and 1766, the urban artisans and merchants, and it arose from a change in economic circumstances. The Stamp Act boycotts had helped to revive a depressed economy. In 1768 and 1769, by contrast, merchants were en-

Divided Opinion over Boycotts

joying boom times and had no financial incentive to support a boycott. As a result, merchants signed the agreements only reluctantly. However, artisans, who recognized that the absence of British goods would create a market for their own manufactures, used coercion to enforce nonimportation.

Coercion tactics were effective: colonial imports from England dropped dramatically in 1769, especially in New York, New England, and Pennsylvania. But they also aroused significant opposition. Some Americans who supported resistance to British measures began to question the use of violence to force others to join the boycott. In addition, wealthier and more conservative colonists were frightened by the threat to private property inherent in the campaign. Moreover, political activism on the part of ordinary colonists who had once deferred to the judgment of their superiors posed a threat to the local ruling classes.

Americans were relieved when the news arrived in April 1770 that a new prime minister, Lord North, had persuaded Parliament to repeal the Townshend

Repeal of the Townshend Duties

duties, except the tea tax, on the grounds that duties on trade within the empire were bad policy. Although some political leaders argued that nonimportation should be continued until the tea tax was repealed, merchants quickly resumed importing. The rest of the Townshend Acts remained in force, but repeal of the taxes made the other laws appear less objectionable.

GROWING RIFTS

At first the new ministry did nothing to antagonize the colonists. Yet on the very day Lord North proposed repeal of the Townshend duties, a clash between civilians and soldiers in Boston led to the death of five Americans. The origins of the event patriots called the Boston Massacre lay in repeated clashes between customs officers and the people of Massachusetts. One of these clashes, the *Liberty* riot of 1768 (caused by the seizure of John Hancock's sloop *Liberty* on suspicion of smuggling), led the British to station two regiments in Boston. This act confirmed Bostonians' worst fears; the redcoats were a constant reminder of the oppressive potential of British power.

Bostonians, accustomed to leading their lives with a minimum of interference from government, now found themselves hemmed in at every turn. Guards on Boston Neck, the entrance to the city, checked all travelers and their goods. Redcoat patrols roamed the city day and night, questioning and sometimes harassing passers-by. But the greatest potential for violence lay in the uneasy relationship between the soldiers and Boston laborers. Many redcoats sought employment in their off-duty hours, competing for unskilled jobs with the city's ordinary workingmen, and members of the two groups brawled repeatedly in taverns and on the streets.

On March 2, 1770, workers at a ropewalk (a ship-rigging factory) attacked some redcoats seeking jobs. Three days later, the tension exploded. Early on the

Boston Massacre

evening of March 5, a crowd began throwing hard-packed snowballs at sentries guarding the Customs House. Goaded beyond endurance, the sentries fired on the crowd against express orders to the contrary, killing four and wounding eight, one of whom died a few days later. Resistance leaders idealized the dead rioters as martyrs for the cause of liberty. The best-known engraving of the massacre, by Paul Revere, was itself a part of the propaganda campaign. It depicts a peaceful crowd, an officer ordering the soldiers to fire, and shots coming from the window of the Customs House.

The leading patriots wanted to make certain the soldiers did not become martyrs as well. Despite the political benefits the patriots derived from the massacre, it is unlikely that they approved of the crowd action that provoked it. Thus when the soldiers were tried for the killings in November, they were defended by John Adams and Josiah Quincy, Jr., both

The Bloody Massacre perpetrated in King Street Boston on March 5th 1770 by a party of the 29th Regt.

Paul Revere's engraving of the Boston Massacre, a masterful piece of propaganda. At right the British officer seems to be ordering the soldiers to fire on a peaceful, unresisting crowd. The Customs House has been labeled Butcher's Hall, and smoke drifts up from a gun barrel sticking out of the window.   Library of Congress.

newspapers, such as the *Boston Gazette*, the *Pennsylvania Journal*, and the *South Carolina Gazette*, published essays drawing on Real Whig ideology and accusing Great Britain of a deliberate plan to oppress America. Patriot writers played repeatedly on the word *enslavement*. Most white colonists had direct knowledge of slavery (either being slaveholders themselves or having slave-owning neighbors), and the threat of enslavement by Britain must have hit them with peculiar force.

Still, no one yet advocated complete independence from the mother country. Though the patriots were becoming increasingly convinced that they should seek freedom from parliamentary authority, they continued to acknowledge their British identity and to pledge their allegiance to George III. They began, therefore, to try to envision a system that would enable them to be ruled largely by their own elected legislatures while remaining loyal to the king. But any such scheme was totally alien to Britons' conception of the nature of their government. In the British mind, Parliament encompassed the king as well as the House of Lords and the Commons, and so separating the monarch from the legislature was impossible.

In the fall of 1772, the North ministry began to implement the portion of the Townshend Acts that provided for governors and judges to be paid from customs revenues. In early Novem-

Committees of Correspondence

ber, voters at a Boston town meeting established a Committee of Correspondence to publicize the decision by exchanging letters with other Massachusetts towns. Heading the committee was the man who had proposed its formation, Samuel Adams. Adams was fifty-one years old in 1772, thirteen years the senior of his distant cousin John and a decade older than most other leaders of American resistance. An experienced political organizer, Adams continually stressed the necessity of prudent collective action. His Committee of Correspondence thus undertook to create an informed consensus among all the citizens of Massachusetts.

unwavering patriots. All but two of the accused men were acquitted, and those convicted were released after having been branded on the thumb. Undoubtedly the favorable outcome of the trials prevented London officials from taking further steps against the city.

For more than two years after the Boston Massacre and the repeal of the Townshend duties, a superficial calm descended on the colonies. Local incidents, like the burning of the British customs vessel *Gaspée* in 1772 by Rhode Islanders, marred the relationship of individual colonies and the mother country, but nothing caused Americans to join in a unified protest. Even so, the resistance movement continued to gather momentum. The most outspoken colonial

Chapter 4: SEVERING THE BONDS OF EMPIRE, 1754–1774

Such committees, which were soon established throughout the colonies, represented the next logical step in the organization of American resistance. Until 1772, the protest movement was largely confined to the seacoast, and primarily to major cities and towns. Adams realized that the time had now come to widen the movement's geographic scope, to attempt to involve the residents of the interior in the struggle that had hitherto enlisted chiefly the residents of urban areas. Accordingly, the Boston town meeting directed the Committee of Correspondence "to state the Rights of the Colonists and of this Province in particular," to list "the Infringements and Violations thereof that have been, or from time to time may be made," and to send copies to the other towns in the province.

Samuel Adams, James Otis, Jr., and Josiah Quincy, Jr., prepared the statement of the colonists' rights. Declaring that Americans had absolute rights to life, liberty, and property, the committee asserted that the idea that "a British house of commons, should have a right, at pleasure, to give and grant the property of the colonists" was "irreconcileable" with "the first principles of natural law and Justice . . . and of the British Constitution in particular." The list of grievances, drafted by another group of prominent patriots, was similarly sweeping. It complained of taxation without representation, the presence of unnecessary troops and customs officers on American soil, the use of imperial revenues to pay colonial officials, the expanded jurisdiction of vice-admiralty courts, and even the nature of the instructions given to American governors by their superiors in London.

The response of the Massachusetts towns to the committee's pamphlet must have caused Samuel Adams to rejoice. Some towns disagreed with Boston's assessment of the state of affairs, but most aligned themselves with the city. From Braintree came the assertion that "all civil officers are or ought to be Servants to the people." The town of Holden declared that "the People of New England have never given the People of Britain any Right of Jurisdiction over us." The citizens of Petersham commented that resistance to tyranny was "the first and highest social Duty of this people." It was beliefs like these that made the next crisis in Anglo-American affairs the final one.

THE BOSTON TEA PARTY

The only one of the Townshend duties still in effect by 1773 was the tax on tea. Although a continuing tea boycott was less than fully effective, tea retained its explosive symbolic character. In May 1773, Parliament passed an act designed to save the East India Company from bankruptcy by changing the way British tea was sold in the colonies. Resistance leaders were immediately suspicious. Under the Tea Act, certain duties paid on tea were to be returned to the company. Furthermore, tea was to be sold only by designated agents, which would enable the East India Company to avoid colonial middlemen and undersell any competitors, even smugglers. The net result would be cheaper tea for American consumers. But many colonists interpreted the new measure as a pernicious device to make them admit Parliament's right to tax them, since the less expensive tea would still be taxed under the Townshend law. Others saw the Tea Act as the first step in the establishment of an East India Company monopoly of all colonial trade.

Tea Act

New York, Boston, Charleston, and Philadelphia were singled out to receive the first shipments of tea. Only Boston was the site of a dramatic confrontation. There both sides—the town meeting, joined by participants from nearby towns, and Governor Thomas Hutchinson—rejected compromise.

The first of three tea ships, the *Dartmouth*, entered Boston harbor on November 28. Under the customs laws, a cargo had to be landed and the appropriate duty paid within twenty days of a ship's arrival. If that was not done, the cargo would be seized by customs officers. After a series of mass meetings, Bostonians voted to prevent the tea from being unloaded and to post guards on the wharf. Hutchinson, for his part, refused to permit the vessels to leave the harbor.

On December 16, 1773, one day before the cargo would have to be confiscated, more than five thousand people (nearly a third of the city's population) crowded into Old South Church. The meeting, chaired by Samuel Adams, made a final attempt to persuade Hutchinson to send the tea back to England. But Hutchinson remained adamant. At about 6 p.m., Adams reportedly announced "that he could think of nothing further to be done—that they had now done all they could for the Salvation of their Country." As if his statement were a signal, cries rang out from the back of the crowd: "Boston harbor a teapot night! The Mohawks are come!" Small groups pushed their way out of the meeting. Within a few minutes, about sixty men crudely disguised as Indians assembled at the wharf, boarded the three ships, and dumped the cargo into the harbor. By 9 p.m. their work was done: 342 chests of tea worth approximately £10,000 floated in splinters on the ebbing tide.

The North administration reacted with considerably less enthusiasm when it learned of the Tea Party. In March 1774, the ministry proposed the first of the four laws that became known as the Coercive, or Intolerable, Acts. It called for closing the port of Boston until the tea was paid for and prohibiting all but coastal trade in food and firewood. Later in the spring, Parliament passed three further punitive measures. The Massachusetts Government Act altered the province's charter, substituting an appointed council for an elected one, increasing the powers of the governor, and forbidding special town meetings. The Justice Act provided that a person accused of committing murder in the course of suppressing a riot or enforcing the laws could be tried outside the colony where the incident had occurred. Finally,

Coercive and Quebec Acts

the Quartering Act gave broad authority to military commanders seeking to house their troops in private dwellings.

After passing the last of the Coercive Acts in early June, Parliament turned its attention to much-needed reforms in the government of Quebec. The Quebec Act, though unrelated to the Coercive Acts, thus became linked with them in the minds of the patriots. The law granted religious freedom to Catholics, reinstated French civil law, and established an appointed council (rather than an elected legislature) as the colony's governing body. To protect Indians from white settlement, the act annexed to Quebec the area east of the Mississippi River and north of the Ohio River. Thus that region, parts of which were claimed by individual seacoast colonies, was removed from the colonists' jurisdiction.

Members of Parliament who voted for the punitive legislation believed that the acts would be obeyed. But the patriots showed little inclination to bow to the wishes of Parliament. In their eyes, the Coercive Acts and the Quebec Act proved what they had feared since 1768: that Great Britain had embarked on a deliberate plan to oppress them. If the port of Boston could be closed, why not those of Philadelphia or New York? If the royal charter of Massachusetts could be changed, why not that of South Carolina? If the Roman Catholic church could receive favored status in Quebec, why not everywhere? It seemed as though the full dimensions of the plot against American rights and liberties had at last been revealed.

The Boston Committee of Correspondence urged all the colonies to join in an immediate boycott of British goods. But the other provinces were not yet ready to take such a drastic step. Instead, they suggested that another intercolonial congress be convened to consider an appropriate response to the Coercive Acts. Few people wanted to take hasty action; even the most ardent patriots still hoped for reconciliation with Great Britain. And so the colonies agreed to send delegates to Philadelphia in September.

IMPORTANT EVENTS

1754	Albany Congress French and Indian War begins
1760	American phase of war ends George III becomes king
1763	Treaty of Paris Pontiac's uprising Proclamation of 1763
1764	Sugar Act
1765	Stamp Act Sons of Liberty formed
1766	Repeal of Stamp Act Declaratory Act
1767	Townshend Acts
1770	Lord North becomes prime minister Repeal of Townshend duties except tea tax Boston Massacre
1772	Boston Committee of Correspondence formed
1773	Tea Act Boston Tea Party
1774	Coercive Acts

Over the preceding decade, momentous changes had occurred in the ways politically aware colonists thought about themselves and their allegiance. Once linked unquestioningly to Great Britain, they had begun to develop a sense of their own identity as Americans. During the next decade, they would forge the bonds of a new American nationality to replace rejected Anglo-American ties.

SUGGESTIONS FOR FURTHER READING

General

Ian R. Christie and Benjamin W. Labaree, *Empire or Independence, 1760–1776* (1976); Lawrence Henry Gipson, *The Coming of the Revolution 1763–1775* (1954); Merrill Jensen, *The Founding of a Nation: A History of the American Revolution, 1763–1776* (1968); Edmund S. Morgan, *The Birth of the Republic, 1763–1789* (1956).

Colonial Warfare and the British Empire

Fred Anderson, *A People's Army: Massachusetts Soldiers and Society in the Seven Years' War* (1984); Howard H. Peckham, *The Colonial Wars, 1689–1762* (1963); Alan Rogers, *Empire and Liberty: American Resistance to British Authority, 1755–1763* (1974).

British Politics and Policy

George L. Beer, *British Colonial Policy 1754–1765* (1907); John Brooke, *King George III* (1973); John L. Bullion, *A Great and Necessary Measure* (1981); Bernard Donoughue, *British Politics and the American Revolution* (1965); Lewis B. Namier, *England in the Age of the American Revolution*, 2nd ed. (1961).

Indians and the West

Thomas P. Abernethy, *Western Lands and the American Revolution* (1959); Richard Aquila, *The Iroquois Restoration* (1983); David H. Corkran, *The Cherokee Frontier* (1962); Howard H. Peckham, *Pontiac and the Indian Uprising* (1947); Jack M. Sosin, *Whitehall and the Wilderness* (1961).

Political Thought

Bernard Bailyn, *The Ideological Origins of the American Revolution* (1967); Jay Fliegelman, *Prodigals & Pilgrims: The American Revolution Against Patriarchal Authority 1750–1800* (1982); Caroline Robbins, *The Eighteenth-Century Com-*

monwealthman (1959); Clinton Rossiter, *Seedtime of the Republic* (1953).

American Resistance

David Ammerman, *In the Common Cause* (1974); Richard Beeman, *Patrick Henry* (1974); Richard D. Brown, *Revolutionary Politics in Massachusetts* (1970); Dirk Hoerder, *Crowd Action in Revolutionary Massachusetts, 1765–1780* (1977); Rhys Isaac, *The Transformation of Virginia, 1740–1790* (1982); Benjamin W. Labaree, *The Boston Tea Party* (1964); Pauline R. Maier, *From Resistance to Revolution* (1972); Pauline R. Maier, *The Old Revolutionaries* (1980); Edmund S. Morgan and Helen M. Morgan, *The Stamp Act Crisis* (1953); Gary B. Nash, *The Urban Crucible* (1979); Peter Shaw, *American Patriots and the Rituals of Revolution* (1981); John J. Waters, Jr., *The Otis Family in Provincial and Revolutionary Massachusetts* (1968); Hiller B. Zobel, *The Boston Massacre* (1970).

CHAPTER 5

A REVOLUTION, INDEED
1775–1783

One *April morning* in 1775, Hannah Winthrop awoke with a start to drumbeats, bells, and the continuous clang of the Cambridge fire alarm. She and her husband, a professor at Harvard, soon learned that redcoat troops had left Boston late the evening before, bound for Concord. A few hours later they watched British soldiers march through Cambridge to reinforce the first group. The Winthrops quickly decided to leave home and seek shelter elsewhere. They made their way to an isolated farmhouse, but it was no secure haven. They were, Mrs. Winthrop later wrote, "for some time in sight of the Battle, the glistening instruments of death proclaiming by an incessant fire that much blood must be shed, that many widowd and orphand ones be left as monuments of that persecuting Barbarity of British Tyranny."

Hannah Winthrop was convinced that nothing would be the same again. In that expectation she was wrong. The Winthrops returned to their Cambridge home and resumed their normal lives. But the Revolution did bring major changes. It uprooted thousands of civilian families, disrupted the economy, reshaped society by forcing many colonists into permanent exile, and led Americans to develop new conceptions of politics. Indeed, even before the shooting began the patriots had established functioning revolutionary governments throughout the colonies.

The struggle for independence required revolutionary leaders to accomplish three separate but closely related tasks. The first was political and ideological. They had to transform the 1760s consensus favoring loyal resistance into a coalition supporting independence. The second task was diplomatic. To win their independence, the patriot leaders knew they needed international recognition and aid, particularly assistance from France.

Only the third task directly involved the British. George Washington, commander-in-chief of the

American army, quickly realized that his primary goal should be not to win battles but rather to avoid losing them decisively. He understood that, as long as his army survived to fight another day, the outcome of any individual battle was more or less irrelevant. Accordingly, the story of the Revolutionary War reveals British action and American reaction, British attacks and American defenses. The American war effort was aided by British military planners' failure to analyze accurately the problem confronting them. Until it was too late, they treated the war against the colonists as they did wars against other Europeans; that is, they concentrated on winning battles and did not consider the difficulties inherent in achieving their main goal, retaining the colonies' allegiance. In the end, the Americans' triumph owed more to their own endurance and to Britain's mistakes than to their military prowess.

GOVERNMENT BY CONGRESS AND COMMITTEE

When the fifty-five delegates to the First Continental Congress convened in Philadelphia in September 1774, they knew that any measures they adopted were likely to enjoy support among many of their fellow countrymen and women. During the summer of 1774, open meetings held in towns, cities, and counties throughout the colonies had endorsed the idea of another nonimportation pact. The committees of correspondence that had been established in many communities publicized these popular meetings so effectively that Americans everywhere knew about them. Most of the congressional delegates were selected by extralegal provincial conventions whose members were chosen at such local gatherings, since the royal governors had forbidden the regular as-

First Continental Congress

semblies to conduct formal elections. Thus the very act of designating delegates to attend the congress involved Americans in open defiance of British authority.

The congressmen faced three tasks when they convened at Carpenters Hall on September 5, 1774. The first two were explicit: defining American grievances and developing a plan for resistance. The third was implicit—outlining a theory of their constitutional relationship with England—and proved troublesome. The delegates readily agreed on a list of the laws they wanted repealed (notably the Coercive Acts) and chose as their method of resistance an economic boycott coupled with petitions for relief. But they could not reach a consensus on the constitutional issue.

The most radical congressmen, like Richard Henry Lee of Virginia and Roger Sherman of Connecticut, agreed with the position published a few weeks earlier by Thomas Jefferson—who was not a delegate—in his *Summary View of the Rights of British America.* Jefferson argued that the colonists owed allegiance only to George III, and that Parliament was nothing more than "the legislature of one part of the empire" with no legitimate authority over the provinces.

Meanwhile the conservative Joseph Galloway of Pennsylvania and his ally James Duane of New York insisted that the congress should acknowledge Parliament's supremacy over the empire and its right to regulate American trade. Galloway embodied these ideas in a formal plan of union. His plan proposed the establishment of an American legislature, its members chosen by individual colonial assemblies, which would have to consent to laws pertaining to America. After a heated debate, the delegates rejected Galloway's proposal. But they were not prepared to go as far as Jefferson had.

Finally, they accepted a compromise position worked out by John Adams. The crucial clause Adams drafted in the congress's Declaration of Rights and Grievances read in part: "From the necessity of the case, and a regard to the mutual interest of both countries, we cheerfully consent to the operation of such acts of the

Declaration of Rights and Grievances

British parliament, as are bona fide, restrained to the regulation of our external commerce." Note the key phrases. "From the necessity of the case" indicated Americans' abandonment, once and for all, of their unquestioning loyalty to the mother country. "Bona fide, restrained to the regulation of our external commerce" resonated with overtones of the Stamp Act controversy and Dickinson's arguments in his *Farmer's Letters.* The delegates intended to make clear to Lord North that they would continue to resist taxes in disguise, like the Townshend duties. Most striking of all was that such language, which only a few years before would have been regarded as irredeemably radical, could be presented and accepted as a compromise in the fall of 1774.

Once the delegates had resolved the constitutional issue, they discussed the tactics by which to force another British retreat. They adopted an agreement known as the Continental Association, which called for nonimportation of all goods from Great Britain and Ireland, as well as tea and molasses from other British possessions and slaves from any source, effective December 1. An end to the consumption of British products was also readily accepted, to become effective on March 1, 1775. Nonexportation, on the other hand, generated considerable debate. The Virginia delegation adamantly refused to accept a ban on exports to England until after its planters had had a chance to market their 1774 tobacco crop. As a result, the congress provided that nonexportation would not begin until September 10, 1775.

More influential than the details of the Continental Association was the method the congress recommended for its enforcement: the election of committees of observation and inspection in every county, city, and town in America. Such committees were officially charged only with overseeing enforcement of the association, but over the next six months they became de facto governments. Since the congress specified that committee members be chosen by all persons qualified to vote for members of the lower house of the colonial legislatures, the committees were guaranteed a broad popular base.

Committees of Observation

Furthermore, their numbers ensured that many new men would be incorporated into the resistance movement.

At first the committees confined themselves to enforcing the nonimportation clause. But the Continental Association also promoted home manufactures and encouraged Americans to adopt simple modes of dress and behavior. Wearing homespun garments again became a sign of patriotism. Since expensive leisure-time activities were symbols of vice and corruption, the congress urged Americans to forgo dancing, gambling, horse racing, cockfighting, and other forms of "extravagance and dissipation." In enforcing these injunctions, the committees gradually extended their authority over nearly all aspects of American life.

The committees also attempted to identify opponents of American resistance. In their quest to protect American rights, the patriots denied freedom of speech to those who disagreed with them. They developed elaborate spy networks, circulated copies of the association for signatures, and investigated reports of dissident remarks and activities. Suspected dissenters were first urged to convert to the colonial cause; if that failed, the committees had them watched or restricted their movements. Sometimes people engaging in casual political exchanges with friends one day found themselves charged with "treasonable conversation" the next.

While the committees were expanding their power during the winter and early spring of 1775, the established governments of the colonies were collapsing. Only in Connecticut, Rhode Island, Delaware, and Pennsylvania did regular assemblies continue to meet without encountering patriot challenges to their authority. In every other colony, popularly elected provincial conventions took over the task of running the government, sometimes entirely replacing the legislatures and at other times holding concurrent sessions. In late 1774 and early 1775, these conventions approved the Continental Association, elected delegates to the Second Continental Congress (scheduled for May), organized mi-

Provincial Conventions

litia units, and gathered arms and ammunition. The British-appointed governors and councils, unable to stem the tide of resistance, watched helplessly as their authority crumbled. Courts were prevented from holding sessions; taxes were paid to agents of the conventions rather than provincial tax collectors; sheriffs' powers were questioned; and militiamen refused to muster except by order of the local committees. In short, during the six months preceding the battles at Lexington and Concord, independence was being won at the local level, but without formal acknowledgment and for the most part without shooting or bloodshed. Not many Americans fully realized what was happening. The vast majority of colonists still proclaimed their loyalty to Great Britain and denied that they sought to leave the empire. Among the few Americans who did recognize the trend toward independence were those who opposed it.

CHOOSING SIDES: LOYALISTS, BLACKS, AND INDIANS

The first protests against British measures, in the mid-1760s, had won the support of most colonists. Only in the late 1760s and early 1770s did a significant number of Americans begin to question both the aims and the tactics of the resistance movement. In 1774 and 1775 such people found themselves in a difficult position. Like their more radical counterparts, most of them objected to parliamentary policies and wanted some kind of constitutional reform. Nevertheless, if forced to a choice, these colonists sympathized with Great Britain rather than with an independent America.

In 1774 and 1775 some conservatives began to publish essays and pamphlets critical of the congress and its allied committees. In New York City, a group of Anglican clergymen jointly wrote pamphlets and essays arguing the importance of maintaining a cor-

dial connection between England and America. In Massachusetts, the young attorney Daniel Leonard, writing under the pseudonym Massachusettensis, engaged in a prolonged newspaper debate with Novanglus (John Adams). All the conservative authors stressed the point that Leonard put so well in his sixth essay in January 1775: "There is no possible medium between absolute independence and subjection to the authority of parliament." Leonard and his fellows realized that what had begun as a dispute over the extent of American subordination within the empire had now raised the question of whether the colonies would remain linked to Great Britain at all.

Some colonists heeded the conservative pamphleteers' warnings. About one-fifth of the white American population remained loyal to Great Britain, actively opposing independence. With

Loyalists, Patriots, and Neutrals

notable exceptions, most people of the following types remained loyal to the crown: British-appointed government officials; merchants whose trade depended on imperial connections; Anglican clergy everywhere and lay Anglicans in the North; former officers and enlisted men from the British army; non-English ethnic minorities, especially Scots; tenant farmers; members of persecuted religious sects; and many of the backcountry southerners who had rebelled against eastern rule in the 1760s and early 1770s. All these people had one thing in common: the patriot leaders were their longstanding enemies, though for different reasons. Local and provincial disputes thus helped to determine which side a person chose in the imperial conflict.

The active patriots, who accounted for about two-fifths of the population, came chiefly from the groups that had dominated colonial society, either numerically or politically. Among them were yeoman farmers, members of dominant Protestant sects (both Old and New Lights), Chesapeake gentry, merchants dealing mainly in American commodities, city artisans, elected officeholders, and people of English descent. Wives usually but not always adopted their husbands' political beliefs.

There remained the two-fifths of the population

> **RUN** away from *Hampton,* on *Sunday* laſt, a luſty Mulatto Fellow named ARGYLE, well known about the Country, has a Scar on one of his Wriſts, and has loſt one or more of his fore Teeth; he is a very handy Fellow by Water, or about the Houſe, &c. loves Drink, and is very bold in his Cups, but daſtardly when ſober. Whether he will go for a Man of War's Man, or not, I cannot ſay; but I will give 40 s. to have him brought to me. He can read and write.
> NOVEMBER 2, 1775. JACOB WRAY.

An advertisement for a runaway slave suspected of joining Lord Dunmore—a common sight in Virginia and Maryland newspapers during the fall and winter of 1775 and 1776. Virginia State Library.

that tried to avoid taking sides. Among them were pacifist Quakers and those colonists who simply wanted to be left alone. In the southern backcountry, many Scotch-Irish took a neutral position, for they had grievances against both the British and the patriot gentry.

To American patriots, that sort of apathy or neutrality was a crime as heinous as loyalism: those who were not for them were against them. By the winter of 1775–1776, the Continental Congress was recommending to the states that all "disaffected" persons be disarmed and arrested. The state legislatures quickly passed laws prescribing severe penalties for suspected loyalists. Many began to require all voters to take oaths of allegiance; the punishment for refusal was usually banishment or extra taxes. In 1778 and thereafter, many states formally confiscated the property of banished loyalists. Perhaps 100,000 white loyalists were forced into exile, but they were not the only Americans to concern the patriots.

The Blacks' Dilemma

Afro-American slaves faced a dilemma at the beginning of the Revolution: how could they best achieve their goal of escaping perpetual servitude? Should they fight with or against their white masters? The correct choice was not immediately apparent, and so blacks made different decisions. Some joined the revolutionaries, others the British. In the early days of the war, those who decided to join the American side were primarily free blacks from New England.

For blacks who were still enslaved, alliance with the British held out more promise. Not surprisingly, therefore, news of slave conspiracies surfaced in different parts of the colonies in late 1774 and early 1775. All shared a common element: a plan to assist the British in return for freedom. A group of blacks petitioned General Thomas Gage, the commander-in-chief of the British army in Boston, promising to fight for the redcoats if he would liberate them. The governor of Maryland authorized the issuance of extra guns to militiamen in four counties where slave uprisings were expected. The most serious incident occurred during the summer of 1775 in Charleston, where Thomas Jeremiah, a free black harbor pilot, was brutally executed after being convicted of attempting to foment a slave revolt.

Concern over the slave population affected the level of revolutionary sentiment in the colonies. In the North, where whites greatly outnumbered blacks, revolutionary fervor was at its height. But in South Carolina, which was over 60 percent black, and Georgia, where the racial balance was nearly even, whites were noticeably less enthusiastic about

Racial Composition and Patriotic Fervor

resistance. Georgia, in fact, sent no delegates to the First Continental Congress, and reminded its representatives at the Second Continental Congress to consider its circumstances, "with our blacks and tories within us," when voting on the question of independence.

The whites' worst fears were realized in November 1775, when Lord Dunmore, the governor of Virginia, offered to free any slaves and indentured servants who would leave their patriot masters to join the British forces. Dunmore hoped to use blacks in his fight against the revolutionaries, and to disrupt the economy by depriving white Americans of their labor force. But fewer blacks than expected rallied to the British standard in 1775 and 1776 (there were at most two thousand). Even so, Dunmore's proclamation led Congress in January 1776 to modify its previous policy prohibiting the enlistment of blacks in the Continental Army (the first New England black patriots served only in local militias). And the patriots turned rumors of slave uprisings to their own advantage. South Carolinians were told that whites needed the Continental Association to protect them from blacks. This appeal to white unity brought wavering Carolinians into the patriot camp.

A similar factor—the threat of Indian attacks—helped to persuade some reluctant westerners to support the struggle against Great Britain. In the years

Indian Neutrality

since the Proclamation of 1763, British officials had won the trust and respect of the interior tribes by attempting to protect them from land-hungry whites. In 1768 the British-appointed superintendents of Indian affairs, John Stuart in the South and Sir William Johnson in the North, negotiated two treaties—signed at Hard Labor Creek, South Carolina, and Fort Stanwix, New York—with the tribes. The treaties supposedly established permanent borders for the colonies. But just a few years later, the British pushed the southern boundary even

farther west to accommodate the demands of whites in western Georgia and the "overmountain" region known as Kentucky.

By the time of the Revolution, the Indians were impatient with the Americans' aggressive pressure on their lands. They also resented the whites' unwillingness to prosecute frontiersmen who wantonly killed innocent natives. In combination with the tribes' confidence in Stuart and Johnson, these grievances predisposed most Indians toward an alliance with the British. Even so, the British hesitated to make full and immediate use of their potential Indian allies. The superintendents were well aware that the tribes might prove a liability, since their aims and style of fighting were not necessarily compatible with those of the British. Accordingly, the superintendents sought only the neutrality of the tribes.

The patriots, recognizing that their standing with the tribes was poor, also sought the Indians' neutrality. In 1775 the Second Continental Congress sent a general message to the tribes describing the war as "a family quarrel between us and Old England" and requesting that they "not join on either side." A branch of the Cherokee tribe, led by Chief Dragging Canoe, nevertheless decided that the whites' "family quarrel" would allow them to settle some old scores. They attacked white settlements along the western borders of the Carolinas and Virginia in the summer of 1776. But a coordinated campaign by Carolina and Virginia militia destroyed many Cherokee towns, along with crops and large quantities of supplies. Dragging Canoe and his diehard followers fled west to the Tennessee River, while the rest of the Cherokee agreed to a treaty that ceded more of their land to the whites.

The fate of the Cherokee—forced to fight alone without other Indian allies—foreshadowed much of the history of Indian involvement in the American Revolution. During the eighteenth century the Iroquois had forcefully established their dominance over neighboring tribes. But the basis of their power had started to disintegrate with the British victory over France in 1763, and their subsequent friendship with Sir William Johnson could not prevent the erosion of their position during the years before 1775. Tribes long resentful of Iroquois power (and of the similar status of the Cherokee in the South) saw little reason to ally themselves with those from whose dominance they had just escaped, even to achieve the goal of preventing white encroachment on their lands. Consequently, during the Revolution most tribes pursued a course that aligned them with neither side, but which for the most part kept them out of active involvement in the war.

Thus, although the patriots could never completely ignore the threats posed by loyalists, blacks, neutrals, and Indians, only rarely did fear of these groups seriously hamper the revolutionary movement. Indeed, the practical impossibility of a large-scale slave revolt, coupled with tribal feuds and the patriots' successful campaign to disarm and neutralize loyalists, ensured that the revolutionaries would remain firmly in control as they fought for independence.

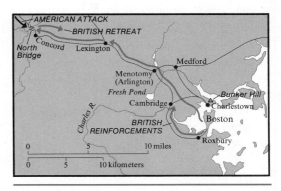

Lexington and Concord, April 19, 1775

War Begins

On January 27, 1775, the secretary of state for America, Lord Dartmouth, addressed a fateful letter to General Thomas Gage in Boston. Expressing his belief that American resistance was nothing more than the response of a "rude rabble without plan," Dartmouth ordered Gage to arrest "the principal actors and abettors in the provincial congress." If such a step were taken swiftly and silently, Dartmouth observed, no bloodshed need occur.

By the time Dartmouth's letter reached Gage on April 14, though, the major patriot leaders had already left Boston. Gage, spurred to action by the letter, decided to send a force to confiscate the provincial military supplies stockpiled at Concord. Bostonians dispatched two messengers, William Dawes and Paul Revere (later joined by a third, Dr. Samuel Prescott), to rouse the countryside. Thus when the British vanguard approached Lexington at dawn on April 19, they found a straggling group of seventy militiamen—approximately half the adult male population of the town—drawn up before them on the town common. The Americans' commander, Captain John Parker, ordered his men to withdraw, realizing that they were too few to halt the redcoat advance. But as they began to disperse, a shot rang out; the British soldiers then fired several volleys. When they stopped, eight Americans lay dead and another ten had been wounded. The British moved on to Concord, five miles away (see map).

At Concord, British troops suffered their first casualties of the war when they were attacked by patriot militia at the North Bridge. Before the day ended, thousands of colonial militiamen harassed the British on their march back to Boston. The redcoats suffered 272 casualties (70 dead) and inflicted but 93 casualties on the colonists.

By the evening of April 20, perhaps as many as twenty thousand American militiamen had gathered around Boston. Many did not stay long, since they were needed at home for spring planting, but those who remained dug in along siege lines encircling the city. For nearly a year the two armies sat and stared at each other. The only battle occurred on June 17 when the British attacked Breed's Hill. There, in the misnamed Battle of Bunker Hill, the British incurred

Battles of Lexington and Concord

over 1,000 casualties (228 dead). Elsewhere, in the first eleven months of the war the colonists captured Fort Ticonderoga, with its much needed cannon, and failed in a Canadian campaign. Most significantly, the lull of the first year gave both sides time to re-group, organize, and make plans.

Lord North and his new American secretary, Lord George Germain, made three major assumptions about the war they faced. First, they concluded that

British Strategy

patriot forces could not withstand the assaults of trained British regu-lars. Accordingly, they dispatched to America the largest single force Great Britain had ever assembled anywhere: 370 transport ships carrying 32,000 troops and tons of supplies, accompanied by 73 naval vessels and 13,000 sailors. Such an extraordinary effort would, they thought, ensure a quick victory. Second, British of-ficials and army officers persisted in comparing this war to wars they had fought successfully in Europe. Thus they adopted a conventional strategy of captur-ing major American cities. Third, they assumed that a clear-cut military victory would automatically bring about their goal of retaining the colonies' allegiance.

All these assumptions proved false. North and Germain vastly underestimated the Americans' com-mitment to armed resistance. Defeats on the battle-field did not lead the patriots to abandon their polit-ical aims and sue for peace. At one time or another the British captured all major American ports, but with 1,500 miles of coastline their actions did not halt essential commerce. And since less than 5 per-cent of the population lived in the cities, their loss meant little to the colonists.

Most of all, the British did not at first understand that a military victory would not necessarily bring about a political victory. Securing the colonies per-manently would require hundreds of thousands of Americans to return to their original allegiance. The conquest of America was thus a far more complicated task than the defeat of France twelve years earlier. The British needed not only to overpower the pa-triots, but also to convert them. They never fully re-

alized that they were not fighting a conventional Eu-ropean war at all, but rather an entirely new kind of conflict: the first modern war of national liberation.

The British at least had a bureaucracy ready to su-pervise the war effort. The Americans had only the Second Continental Congress, originally intended

Second Continental Congress

merely as a brief gathering of colo-nial representatives to consider the British response to the Continental Association. Instead, the delegates who convened in Philadelphia on May 10, 1775, found that they had to assume the mantle of intercolonial government. That summer the congress authorized the printing of money with which to purchase necessary goods, established a committee to supervise relations with foreign coun-tries, and took steps to strengthen the militia. Most important of all, it created the Continental Army and appointed its generals.

Until the congress met, the Massachusetts provin-cial congress had taken responsibility for organizing the massive army of militia encamped at Boston. Be-cause the cost of maintaining the army was too great, Massachusetts asked the Continental Congress to as-sume control of the army. Also, as the war was thus far largely a northern affair, congress, to ensure unity, selected a non-New Englander, George Washington of Virginia, to be the commander-in-chief.

Washington was no fiery radical, nor was he a re-flective political thinker. He had not played a prom-inent role in the prerevolutionary agitation, but his

George Washington: A Portrait of Leadership

devotion to the American cause was unquestioned. He was digni-fied, conservative, respectable, and a man of unimpeachable integrity. Though unmistakably an aristocrat, Washington was unswervingly com-mitted to representative government. Moreover, he both looked and acted like a leader. Other patriots praised his judgment, steadiness, and discretion, and even a loyalist admitted that Washington could "atone for many demerits by the extraordinary cool-ness and caution which distinguish his character."

Washington needed all the coolness and caution he could muster when he took command of the army outside Boston in July 1775. It took him months to impose hierarchy and discipline on the unruly troops and to bring order to the supply system. But by March 1776, the army was prepared to act. As it happened, an assault on Boston proved unnecessary. Sir William Howe, who had replaced Gage, wanted to transfer his troops to New York City. The patriots' bombardment of Boston, with cannon brought from Ticonderoga, early in the month decided the matter. On March 17, the British and more than a thousand of their loyalist allies abandoned Boston forever.

That spring of 1776, as the British fleet left Boston for the temporary haven of Halifax, Nova Scotia, the colonies were moving inexorably toward the unthinkable—a declaration of independence. One man in January 1776 not only thought the unthinkable but advocated it.

Thomas Paine's *Common Sense* exploded on the American scene like a bombshell. Within three months of publication, it sold 120,000 copies. The author, a radical English printer who had lived in America only since 1774, called stridently and stirringly for independence. More than that: Paine rejected the notion that a balance of monarchy, aristocracy, and democracy was necessary to preserve freedom and advocated the establishment of a republic. Instead of acknowledging the benefits of a connection with the mother country, Paine insisted that Britain had exploited the colonies unmercifully. In place of the frequent assertion that an independent America would be weak and divided, he substituted an unlimited confidence in America's strength when freed from European control.

Thomas Paine's Common Sense

There is no way of knowing how many people were converted to the cause of independence by reading *Common Sense*. But by late spring 1776 independence had clearly become inevitable. On May 10, the Second Continental Congress formally recommended that individual colonies "adopt such governments as shall, in the opinion of the representatives of the people, best conduce to the happiness and safety of their constituents in particular, and America in general." From that source grew the first state constitutions.

Then on June 7 came the confirmation of the movement toward independence. Richard Henry Lee of Virginia, seconded by John Adams of Massachusetts, introduced the crucial resolution: "That these United Colonies are, and of right ought to be, free and independent States, that they are absolved of all allegiance to the British Crown, and that all political connection between them and the State of Great Britain is, and ought to be, totally dissolved." The congress debated the resolution and named a committee composed of Thomas Jefferson, John Adams, Benjamin Franklin, Robert R. Livingston of New York, and Roger Sherman of Connecticut to draft a declaration of independence. The committee in turn assigned primary responsibility for writing the declaration to Jefferson, a Virginia lawyer widely read in history and political theory and with an acknowledged talent for felicitous expression.

Declaration of Independence

The draft of the declaration was laid before congress on June 28. The delegates officially voted for independence four days later, then debated the wording of the declaration for two more days, adopting it with some changes on July 4. Since Americans had long since ceased to see themselves as legitimate subjects of Parliament, the Declaration of Independence concentrated on George III (see Appendix). But the declaration's chief long-term importance did not lie in its lengthy catalogue of grievances against George III. It lay instead in the ringing statements of principle that have served ever since as the ideal to which Americans aspire. "We hold these truths to be self-evident: That all men are created equal; that they are endowed by their Creator with certain unalienable rights; that among these are life, liberty and the pursuit of happiness; that, to secure these rights, governments are instituted among men, deriving their just powers from the consent of the governed; that whenever any form of government becomes destructive of

After listening to the first formal reading of the Declaration of Independence in New York City on July 9, 1776, a crowd of soldiers and civilians spontaneously pulled down a statue of George III that stood on the Bowling Green in the heart of the city. Most of the statue was later melted down and made into bullets, but some pieces of it were found a few years ago in Connecticut.   Library of Congress.

these ends, it is the right of the people to alter or to abolish it, and to institute new government." These phrases have echoed down through American history like no others.

The delegates in Philadelphia who voted to accept the Declaration of Independence did not have the advantage of our two hundred years of hindsight. When they adopted the declaration, they risked their necks: they were committing treason. Thus when they concluded the declaration with the assertion that they "mutually pledge[d] to each other our lives, our fortunes, and our sacred honor," they spoke no less than the truth. The real struggle still lay before them.

THE LONG STRUGGLE

IN THE NORTH

On July 2, 1776, the first of Sir William Howe's troops from Halifax landed on Staten Island. But Howe delayed his attack on New York City until mid-August, when additional troops arrived from England. The delay gave Washington sufficient time to march his army south to

Battle for New York City

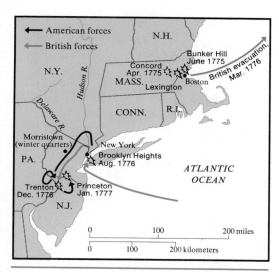

The War in the North, 1775–1777

meet the threat. To defend New York, Washington had approximately seventeen thousand soldiers. Neither he nor most of his men had ever fought a major battle against the British, and their lack of experience led to disastrous mistakes. The difficulty of defending New York City only compounded the errors.

Washington's problem was as simple as the geography of the region was complex (see map). To protect the city adequately, he would have to divide his forces among Long Island, Manhattan Island, and the mainland. But the British fleet under Admiral Lord Richard Howe, Sir William's brother, controlled the harbors and rivers that separated the American forces. The patriots thus constantly courted catastrophe, for swift action by the British navy could cut off the possibility of retreat and perhaps even communication. But despite these dangers, Washington could not afford to surrender New York to the Howes without a fight. Not only did the city occupy a strategic location, but the region that surrounded it was known to contain many loyalist sympathizers. A show of force was essential if the revolutionaries were to retain any hope of persuading waverers to join them.

On August 27, Sir William Howe's forces attacked the American positions on Brooklyn Heights, push-

ing the untried rebel troops back into their defensive entrenchments. But he failed to press his advantage, even neglecting to send his brother's ships into the East River to cut off a retreat. Consequently, the Americans were able to escape. Washington then moved north along the island, retreating onto the mainland. But 3,000 men he left behind on the west shore of Manhattan at Fort Washington had to surrender to Howe.

George Washington had defended New York, but he had done a bad job of it. He had repeatedly broken a basic rule of military strategy: never divide your force in the face of a superior enemy. In the end, though, the Howe brothers' failure to move quickly prevented a decisive defeat of the Americans. Although Washington's army had been seriously reduced, its core remained. Through November and December, Washington led his men in a retreat across New Jersey. Sir William Howe followed at a leisurely pace, setting up a string of outposts manned mostly by Hessian mercenaries. After Washington crossed the Delaware River into Pennsylvania, the British commander turned back and settled into comfortable winter quarters in New York City.

The British now controlled most of New Jersey. Hundreds of Americans accepted the pardons offered by the Howes. The occupying troops met with little opposition, and the revolutionary cause appeared to be in disarray. Thomas Paine's new pamphlet, *The Crisis*, declared, "These are the times that try men's souls."

In the aftermath of battle, as at its height, the British generals let their advantage slip away. The redcoats stationed in New Jersey went on a rampage of rape and plunder. Because loyalists and patriots were indistinguishable to the British and Hessian troops, families on both sides suffered nearly equally. Houses were looted and burned, churches and public buildings desecrated. But nothing was better calculated to rally doubtful Americans to the cause of independence than the wanton murder of innocent civilians and rape of women.

The soldiers' marauding alienated potentially loyal

New Jerseyites and Pennsylvanians whose allegiance the British could ill afford to lose. It also spurred Washington's determination to strike back. With enlistments of many troops scheduled to expire on December 31, Washington decided to strike quickly. He first struck the Hessian encampment at Trenton on December 26. A few days later he attacked Princeton. With these two victories the 1776 campaign ended.

Battle of Trenton

The campaign of 1776 established patterns that were to persist throughout much of the war. British forces, although numerically superior to the Americans, engaged in ponderous maneuvering, lacked familiarity with the terrain, and antagonized the populace. Washington always seemed to lack regular troops, but during critical moments he could usually depend on the militia. These men would not fight far from home and would leave the army to plant and harvest crops, but they were invaluable at times of crisis.

As the war dragged on, the Continental Army and the militia took on decidedly different characters. State militias attracted farmers with families, who preferred short-term duty, while members of the Continental Army tended to be young and single. Only they were willing to serve extended periods of time. In the North recruiters augmented white recruits with blacks, and many of the nearly five thousand blacks who served in the army secured their freedom as a result. Female camp followers also rendered service to the army. These women (usually the wives and widows of poor soldiers) worked as cooks, nurses, and launderers for partial rations and low pay. The American army was shapeless and difficult to manage, yet this shapelessness provided an almost unlimited supply of man and woman power.

In 1777, the chief British effort was planned by the flashy "Gentleman Johnny" Burgoyne, a playboy general who had gained the ear of Lord George Germain. Burgoyne convinced Germain that he could lead an invading force of redcoats and Indians down the Hudson River from Canada, cutting off New England

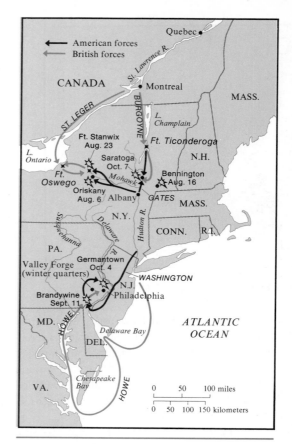

Campaign of 1777

from the rest of the states. He proposed to rendezvous near Albany with a similar force that would move east from Niagara along the Mohawk River valley. The combined force would then presumably link up with that of Sir William Howe in New York City.

That Burgoyne's scheme would give "Gentleman Johnny" all the glory and relegate Howe to a supporting role did not escape the latter's notice. While Burgoyne was plotting in London, Howe was laying his own plans to take Philadelphia. Howe achieved his objective in an inexplicable fashion. Instead of marching his forces from New

Howe Takes Philadelphia

Chapter 5: A Revolution, Indeed, 1775–1783

York, he waited for months and then transported them by sea. The six-week voyage brought him only forty miles closer to Philadelphia, debilitated his men, depleted his supplies, and gave Washington time to prepare a defense of the city. Washington encountered the enemy at Brandywine Creek and at Germantown. He lost both battles but the Americans handled themselves well. By the time Howe took Philadelphia in late September, the 1777 campaign was virtually over (see map).

Burgoyne and his men had set out from Montreal in mid-June, floating down Lake Champlain into New York. In early June they had easily taken Fort

Burgoyne's Campaign in New York

Ticonderoga from its outnumbered and outgunned defenders. But trouble began as Burgoyne started his overland march. Because of his clumsy artillery carriages and baggage wagons, Burgoyne took twenty-four days to travel twenty-three miles. Moreover, the 800 German mercenaries he sent into Vermont on a foraging expedition were soundly defeated at Bennington. Burgoyne's failure to recognize the seriousness of his situation cost the British dearly. He continued toward Albany and was surrounded by the Americans. On October 17, 1777, he surrendered 6,000 men to General Horatio Gates.

Long before, the 1,400 redcoats and Indians marching along the Mohawk River toward Albany had also been turned back. The troops, under the command of Colonel Barry St. Leger, fought the patriots at Oriskany on August 6. The British claimed victory in the battle, but they and their Indian allies lost their taste for further fighting.

The battle of Oriskany marked a split of the Iroquois Confederacy. In 1776 the Six Nations had formally pledged to remain neutral in the Anglo-American struggle. But two influ-

Split of the Iroquois Confederacy

ential Mohawk leaders, Joseph and Mary Brant, worked tirelessly to persuade their fellow Iroquois to join the British. Mary Brant, a powerful tribal matron, was also the widow of the re-

The Mohawk chief Joseph Brant (1742–1807), painted in London in 1786 by Gilbert Stuart.   New York State Historical Association, Cooperstown.

spected Indian superintendent Sir William Johnson. Her younger brother Joseph, a renowned warrior, was convinced that the Six Nations should ally themselves with the British in order to prevent American encroachment on their lands. The Brants won over to the British the Seneca, Cayuga, and Mohawk. But the Oneida preferred the American side, bringing the Tuscarora with them. At Oriskany, the three-hundred-year league of friendship among the Iroquois was torn apart, as confederation warriors fought on both sides.

The collapse of Iroquois unity and the confederacy's abandonment of neutrality had important consequences for both whites and Indians in subsequent years. In 1778, Iroquois warriors allied with the British raided the New York frontier villages of Wyoming and Cherry Valley; to retaliate, the whites dispatched an expedition to burn Iroquois crops, orchards, and settlements. The destruction was so thorough that many bands had to seek food and shelter with the British north of the Great Lakes. A large number of Iroquois people never returned to New York, but settled permanently in British Canada.

For the Indians, Oriskany was the most significant battle of the northern campaign; for the whites, it was Saratoga. Burgoyne's surrender prompted Lord North to authorize a peace commission to offer the Americans everything they had requested in 1774—in effect, a return to the imperial system of 1763. It was, of course, far too late for that: the patriots rejected the overture and the peace commission sailed back to England empty-handed in mid-1778.

Most important of all, the American victory at Saratoga drew France formally into the conflict. Ever since 1763, the French had sought to avenge their defeat in the French and Indian War, and the American Revolution provided them with that opportunity. Even before Benjamin Franklin arrived in Paris in late 1776, France was covertly supplying the revolutionaries with military necessities.

The Franco-American Alliance of 1778

Franklin's attempts to strengthen the ties between the two nations were aided by his style. By presenting himself as a representative of American simplicity, he played upon the French image of Americans as virtuous yeomen. His efforts culminated in February 1778 when the countries signed two treaties. In the first, France recognized American independence; the second provided for a formal alliance between the two nations until the war was won.

The French alliance had two major benefits for the patriot cause. First, France began to aid the Americans openly, sending troops and naval vessels in addition to supplies of arms, ammunition, clothing, and blankets. Second, the British could no longer focus their attention on the American mainland alone, for they had to fight the French in the West Indies and elsewhere. Spain's entry into the war in 1779 as an ally of France (but not the United States) further magnified Britain's problems.

THE LONG STRUGGLE IN THE SOUTH

In the aftermath of the Saratoga disaster, Lord George Germain and the military officials in London reassessed their strategy. Maneuvering in the North had done them little good; perhaps shifting the field of battle southward would bring success. The new British commander-in-chief, Sir Henry Clinton, became convinced that a southern strategy would work when Savannah and Augusta fell easily into British hands. Consequently, in late 1779, he sailed toward Charleston with an invasion force of 8,500 men (see map).

The Americans worked hard to bolster Charleston's defenses, but on May 12, 1780, General Benjamin Lincoln surrendered the city and the entire southern army of 5,500 troops.

Fall of Charleston

Clinton's forces then spread throughout South Carolina. As South Carolinians professed their loyalty to the crown, Clinton organized loyalist regiments in hopes of securing the countryside. Yet the British triumph was less complete and secure than it appeared. The widely dispersed British armies involved in the southern campaign depended on the navy to communicate with one another. But French naval power could possibly disrupt British communications and threaten the entire southern enterprise. The continuing presence of patriot guerrilla bands in the state also created problems for the Crown. Finally, the loss of Charleston failed to dishearten the patriots; instead it spurred them to greater exertions.

Still the war went badly for the Americans. In August 1780 the reorganized southern army under Horatio Gates was defeated by Lord Cornwallis at Camden, South Carolina. Moreover, the southern economy was disrupted when thousands of blacks joined the British. Many blacks served the British as scouts, guides, and laborers.

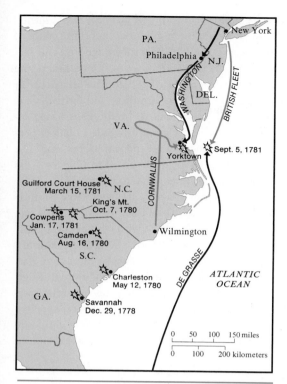

The War in the South

mountain men" from the settlements west of the Appalachians had defeated a large party of redcoats and loyalists. Then in January 1781 Greene's trusted aide, Brigadier General Daniel Morgan, brilliantly defeated the crack British regiment Tarleton's Legion at Cowpens, near the border between North and South Carolina. And in March Greene engaged the main body of British troops at Guilford Court House, North Carolina. Though the Americans lost, Lord Cornwallis's force was largely destroyed.

Then Cornwallis, in violation of his orders not to leave South Carolina unless it was safely in British hands, moved north into Virginia. With a new army of 7,200 men, Cornwallis withdrew to the tip of the peninsula between the York and James rivers. There he fortified Yorktown and in effect waited for the end. Seizing the opportunity, Washington quickly moved over 7,000 troops south from New York City. When a French fleet under the Comte de Grasse arrived from the West Indies to cut the Britons' vital sea supply line, Cornwallis was trapped. On October 19, 1781, Cornwallis surrendered to the combined American and French forces while his military band played "The World Turned Upside Down."

Surrender at Yorktown

When news of the surrender reached England, Lord North's ministry fell. Parliament voted to cease offensive operations in America and authorized peace negotiations. But guerrilla warfare between patriots and loyalists continued to ravage the Carolinas and Georgia for more than a year, and in the North, vicious retaliatory raids by Indians and whites kept the frontier aflame. The persistence of conflict between whites and Indians after Yorktown, all too often overlooked in accounts of the Revolution, serves to underline the degree to which the Indians were the real losers in the war initiated by whites.

The fighting finally ended when Americans and Britons learned of the signing of a preliminary peace treaty at Paris in November 1782. The American negotiators—Benjamin Franklin, John Jay, and John Adams— ignored their instructions to be

Treaty of Paris

After the defeat at Camden, Washington placed General Nathanael Greene in charge of the southern campaign. Greene adopted a plan calling for conciliation and stability. Loyalists were given the chance to secure pardons, and troops were ordered not to loot their property.

Greene also took a conciliatory approach to the southern Indians, a strategy dictated by his need for troops. When he took command, the southern army had but 1,600 regulars. Greene needed volunteers, and he could not secure them if the people's homes had to be defended against Indian attacks. Thus Greene negotiated treaties with the tribes. By the war's end only the Creeks remained allied with the redcoats.

Even before Greene took command of the southern army in December 1780, the tide had begun to turn. At King's Mountain in October, a force of "over-which the British had acquired in 1763, was returned to Spain. In ceding so much land unconditionally to the Americans, the British entirely ignored the territorial rights of their Indian allies. Once again, the tribes' interests were sacrificed to the demands of European power politics. Loyalists and British merchants were also poorly served by the British negotiators. The treaty's ambiguously worded clauses pertaining to the payment of prewar debts and the postwar treatment of loyalists caused trouble for years to come and proved impossible to enforce.

The long war finally over, the victorious Americans could look back on their achievement with satisfaction and awe. In 1775, with an inexperienced ragtag army, they had taken on the greatest military power in the world—and eight years later they had won. They had accomplished their goal more through persistence and commitment than through brilliance on the battlefield. Actual victories had been few, but their army had always survived defeat and stand-offs to fight again. Ultimately, the Americans had simply worn their enemy down.

guided by France and instead struck a separate agreement with Great Britain. Their instincts were sound: the French government was more an enemy to Britain than a friend to the United States. In fact, French ministers worked secretly behind the scenes to try to prevent the establishment of a strong, unified, independent government in America. The new British ministry, headed by Lord Shelburne, was weary of war and made numerous concessions.

Under the treaty, signed formally on September 3, 1783, the Americans were granted unconditional independence and unlimited fishing rights off Newfoundland. The boundaries of the new nation were generous: to the north, approximately the current boundary with Canada; to the south, the thirty-first parallel; to the west, the Mississippi River. Florida,

SUGGESTIONS FOR FURTHER READING

General

Edward Countryman, *The American Revolution* (1985); Stephen G. Kurtz and James H. Hutson, eds., *Essays on the American Revolution* (1973); Edmund S. Morgan, *The Challenge of the American Revolution* (1976); Alfred Young, ed., *The American Revolution* (1976).

Military

John Richard Alden, *The American Revolution 1775–1783* (1964); John C. Dann, ed., *The Revolution Remembered: Eyewitness Accounts of the War for Independence* (1980);

Don Higginbotham, *The War of American Independence* (1971); Piers Mackesy, *The War for America, 1775–1783* (1964); Charles Royster, *A Revolutionary People at War* (1980).

Local and Regional

Edward Countryman, *A People in Revolution: The American Revolution and Political Society in New York, 1760–1790* (1981); Robert A. Gross, *The Minutemen and Their World* (1976); Ronald Hoffman, Thad W. Tate, and Peter Albert, eds., *An Uncivil War: The Southern Backcountry During the American Revolution* (1985).

Indians, Blacks, and Women

Barbara Graymont, *The Iroquois in the American Revolution* (1972); Linda K. Kerber, *Women of the Republic* (1980); Duncan J. MacLeod, *Slavery, Race, and the American Revolution* (1974); Mary Beth Norton, *Liberty's Daughters* (1980); James H. O'Donnell, III, *Southern Indians in the American Revolution* (1973); Benjamin Quarles, *The Negro in the American Revolution* (1961).

Loyalists

Bernard Bailyn, *The Ordeal of Thomas Hutchinson* (1974); Robert Calhoon, *The Loyalists in Revolutionary America 1760–1781* (1973); William H. Nelson, *The American Tory* (1961); Mary Beth Norton, *The British-Americans* (1972); James W. Walker, *The Black Loyalists* (1976).

Foreign Policy

Felix Gilbert, *To the Farewell Address* (1961); Ronald Hoffman and Peter Albert, eds., *Diplomacy and Revolution* (1981); Richard B. Morris, *The Peacemakers* (1965); Richard W. Van Alstyne, *Empire and Independence* (1965).

Patriot Leaders

Fawn M. Brodie, *Thomas Jefferson* (1974); James T. Flexner, *George Washington*, 4 vols. (1965–1972); Eric Foner, *Tom Paine and Revolutionary America* (1976); Claude A. Lopez and Eugenia Herbert, *The Private Franklin* (1975); Dumas Malone, *Jefferson and His Time*, 6 vols. (1948–1981); Peter Shaw, *The Character of John Adams* (1976).

CHAPTER 6

FORGING A NATIONAL REPUBLIC 1776–1789

"*In the new* Code of Laws which I suppose it will be necessary for you to make I desire you would Remember the Ladies," Abigail Adams wrote her congressman husband John on March 31, 1776. "Remember all Men would be tyrants if they could," she continued. "If particular care and attention is not paid to the Laidies we are determined to foment a Rebelion, and will not hold ourselves bound by any Laws in which we have no voice, or Representation."

These famous words were a sign of the impact the Revolution and its ideology had had on American society. At the core of the changes lay new commitment to republicanism: the notion that the government should be based wholly on the consent of the people. When they left the British Empire, Americans abandoned the idea that the best system of government balanced monarchy, aristocracy, and democracy. Instead they substituted a belief in the superiority of republicanism, in which the people, not Parliament, were sovereign. Americans disagreed,

however, on such critical issues as how to define "the people" and how fully and frequently to obtain their consent. Although almost all white men agreed that women and blacks should be excluded from formal participation in politics, they found it difficult to reach a consensus on how many of their own number should be included. And when should consent be sought: semiannually? annually? at intervals of two or more years? Further, how should governments be structured so as to reflect the people's consent most accurately?

Republican political ideas carried with them a host of implications for other areas of American life. Because it was widely believed that the citizens of a republic had to be especially virtuous or the republic would not survive, America's political and intellectual leaders worked hard to inculcate virtue in their fellow countrymen and women. Women played a particularly important role in the preservation of virtue. As the mothers of the republic's children, they were

*In the mid-1780s Abigail Adams (1744–1818) and her hus-
band, John (1735–1826), sat for these portraits in London.
John Adams was then American ambassador to Great Britain.
Left: Boston Athenaeum; right: New York State Historical Association, Cooperstown.*

primarily responsible for ensuring their nation's future. For the first time America's leaders became concerned about the nature and content of women's education. If the United States was to endure, they
concluded, the mothers of the rising generation had
to be properly educated.

Other elements of republicanism had more troublesome connotations. Should a republic conduct its
dealings with Indian tribes, or with foreign countries,
any differently from other types of governments? Did
republics, in other words, have an obligation to negotiate fairly and honestly at all times? Even more
bothersome, how could white republicans justify
slavery?

The most important task facing Americans in these
years was the construction of a national government.

Forging a national republic was neither easy nor simple. America's first such government, the Articles of
Confederation, proved to be inadequate. But the nation's political leaders learned from their experiences
and tried another approach when they drafted the
Constitution in 1787. Some historians have argued
that the Articles of Confederation and the Constitution reflected opposing political philosophies,
the Constitution representing an "aristocratic" counterrevolution against the "democratic" Articles.
The two documents are more accurately viewed
as separate and successive attempts to solve the
same problems. Both in part applied theories of
republicanism to practical problems of governance;
neither was entirely successful in resolving those
difficulties.

CREATING A VIRTUOUS REPUBLIC

Many years after the Revolution, John Dickinson recalled that in 1776, when the colonies declared their independence from Great Britain, "there was no question concerning forms of Government. . . . We knew that the people of this country must unite themselves under . . . the Republican form." But what, precisely, was a republic?

Three different definitions of republicanism emerged in the new United States. The first, held chiefly by members of the educated elite, was based directly on ancient history and political theory. It insisted that republics were especially fragile forms of government that could succeed only if they were small in size and homogeneous in population. Furthermore, unless the citizens of a republic were willing to sacrifice their own private interests for the good of the whole, the government would inevitably collapse. In return for sacrifices, though, a republic offered its citizens equality of opportunity. Under such a government, rank would not be abolished but instead would be based on merit rather than inherited wealth and status.

Varieties of Republicanism

A second definition of republicanism, also advanced by members of the elite but in addition by some skilled craftsmen, drew more on economic than political thought. This version of republicanism emphasized individuals' pursuit of rational self-interest. When republican men sought to improve their own economic and social circumstances, the entire nation would benefit. Republican virtue would be achieved through the advancement of private interests, rather than through their subordination to some communal ideal.

The third notion of republicanism was less influential, because it was popular primarily with people who were illiterate or barely literate, and who thus wrote little to promote their beliefs. But it certainly involved a more egalitarian approach to governance than did either of the other two. Such late-eighteenth-century Americans can be termed democrats in more or less the modern sense. They emphasized the importance of widespread participation in political activities, wanted government to be responsive to their needs, and openly questioned the gentry's ability to speak for them.

Despite the differences, it is important to recognize that the three strands of republicanism shared many of the same assumptions. For example, all three contrasted a virtuous, industrious America to the corrupt luxury of England and Europe. In the first version, that virtue manifested itself in frugality and self-sacrifice; in the second, it would prevent self-interest from becoming vice; in the third, it was the justification for including even propertyless white men in the ranks of voters.

As the citizens of the United States set out to construct their republic, then, they believed they were embarking on an unprecedented enterprise. With great pride in their new nation, they wanted to exchange the vices of monarchical Europe for the virtues of republican America. They wanted to embody republican principles not only in their governments (see page 106) but also in their society and their culture. They looked to painting, literature, drama, and architecture to convey messages of nationalism and virtue to the public.

But Americans faced a crucial contradiction at the very outset of their efforts. To some republicans, the fine arts were themselves manifestations of vice.

Virtue and the Arts

What need did a frugal yeoman have for a painting—or, worse yet, a novel? Why should anyone spend hard-earned wages to see a play in a lavishly decorated theater? The first American artists, playwrights, and authors were thus trapped in a dilemma. They wanted to produce works embodying virtue, but those very works, regardless of their content, were viewed by many as corrupting.

Still, they tried. William Hill Brown's *Power of Sympathy* (1789), the first novel written in the United States, was a lurid tale of seduction intended as a warning to young women, who made up a large proportion of America's fiction readers. The most popular book of the era, Mason Locke Weems's *Life of Washington*, published in 1800 shortly after its subject's death, was, the author declared, designed to "hold up his great Virtues . . . to the imitation of Our Youth." Weems could hardly have been accused of being subtle. The famous tale he invented—six-year-old George bravely admitting cutting down his father's favorite cherry tree—ended with George's father exclaiming, "Run to my arms, you dearest boy. . . . Such an act of heroism in my son, is worth more than a thousand trees, though blossomed with silver, and their fruits of purest gold."

Painting, too, was expected to embody high moral standards. Gilbert Stuart, one of the era's most significant artists, painted portraits of outstanding republican citizens. Another major artist, John Trumbull, depicted in his paintings such milestones in American history as the Battle of Bunker Hill and Cornwallis's surrender at Yorktown. Both men attempted to arouse patriotic virtues in their viewers.

Architects likewise hoped to convey in their buildings a sense of the young republic's ideals, and most of them consciously rejected British models. When the Virginia government asked Thomas Jefferson, then ambassador to France, for advice on the design of a state capitol in Richmond, Jefferson unhesitatingly recommended copying a Roman building, the Maison Carrée at Nîmes. "It is very simple," he explained, "but it is noble beyond expression." Jefferson set forth ideals that would guide American neoclassical architecture for a generation to come: simplicity of line, harmonious proportions, a feeling of grandeur.

But republican theorists did not always have their way. By the mid-1780s, some Americans were beginning to detect signs of luxury and corruption all around them. The end of the war and resumption of European trade brought a return to fashionable clothing styles for both men and women and abandonment of the simpler homespun garments patriots had once worn with such pride. Balls and concerts resumed in the cities and were attended by well-dressed elite families. Parties no longer seemed complete without gambling and card-playing. Social clubs for young people multiplied. Especially alarming to fervent republicans was the establishment of the Society of the Cincinnati, a hereditary organization of Revolutionary War officers and their descendants. Many feared that the group would become the nucleus of a native-born aristocracy. All these developments directly challenged the United States's image as a virtuous, self-sacrificing republic.

Their deep-seated concern for the future of the infant republic focused Americans' attention on their children, the "rising generation." Education acquired new significance in the context of the republic. Formerly, education had been seen chiefly as a family matter. Now, though, it would serve a public purpose. If young people were to resist the temptation of vice, they would have to learn the lessons of virtue at home and at school. In fact, the very survival of the nation depended on it. The early republican period was thus a time of major educational reform.

Educational Reform

The 1780s and 1790s brought two significant changes in American educational practice. First, some states began to be willing to use tax money to support public elementary schools. Second, schooling for girls was improved. Americans' recognition of the importance of the rising generation led to the realization that mothers would have to be properly educated if they were to be able to instruct their children adequately. Therefore Massachusetts insisted in its 1789 law that town elementary schools be open to girls as well as boys. Throughout the United States, private academies were founded to give teenage girls from well-to-do families an opportunity for advanced schooling. No one yet proposed opening colleges to women, but a few fortunate girls could now study history, geography, rhetoric, and mathematics.

The chief theorist of women's education in the early republic was Judith Sargent Murray, of Gloucester, Massachusetts. In a series of essays pub-

Judith Sargent Murray on Education

lished in the 1780s and 1790s, Murray argued that women and men had equal intellectual capacities. Therefore, concluded Murray, boys and girls should be offered equivalent scholastic training. She further contended that girls should be taught to support themselves by their own efforts: "Independence should be placed within their grasp." Because she rejected the prevailing notion that a young woman's chief goal in life should be finding a husband, Judith Sargent Murray deserves the title of the first American feminist. (That distinction is usually accorded to better-known nineteenth-century women like Margaret Fuller or Sarah Grimké.)

Murray's direct challenge to the traditional colonial belief that (as one man put it) girls "knew quite enough if they could make a shirt and a pudding" was part of a general rethinking of women's position that occurred as a result of the Revolution. Male patriots who enlisted in the army or served in Congress were away from home for long periods of time. In their absence their wives, who had previously handled only the "indoor affairs" of the household, had to shoulder the responsibility for "outdoor affairs" as well.

In many households, the necessary shift of responsibilities during the war taught men and women that their notions of proper sex roles had to be rethought.

Women's Role in the Republic

Both John and Abigail Adams took great pride in Abigail's developing skills as a "farmeress." Abigail Adams, like her female contemporaries, stopped calling the farm "yours" in letters to her husband, and began referring to it as "ours"—a revealing change of pronoun. Both men and women realized that female patriots had made a vital contribution to winning the war through their work at home. Thus, in the years after the Revolution, Americans began to develop new ideas about the role women should play in a republican society.

Although most, including Abigail Adams, did not

Judith Sargent (1751–1820), later Mrs. John Murray, painted by John Singleton Copley when she was in her late teens. Although her steady gaze suggests clear-headed intelligence, there is little in the stylized portrait—typical of Copley's work at the time—to suggest her later emergence as the first notable American feminist theorist.   Frick Art Reference Library/Private Collection.

believe women should vote, a few women thought differently. In New Jersey the state constitution of 1776 had defined voters as "all free inhabitants" who met certain property qualifications. The vote was thus given to property-holding white spinsters and widows, as well as free black men. In the 1780s and 1790s women successfully claimed the right to vote in New Jersey's local and congressional elections. They continued to exercise that right until 1807, when women and blacks were disfranchised on the grounds that their votes could be easily manipulated.

Such episodes were unusual. On the whole the re-evaluation of women's position had its greatest impact on private life. The traditional colonial view of

Marriage and Motherhood

marriage had stressed the subordination of wife to husband. But in 1790 a female "Matrimonial Republican" asserted that "marriage ought never to be considered as a contract between a superior and an inferior. . . . The obedience between man and wife is, or ought to be mutual." This new understanding of the marital relationship seems to have contributed to a rising divorce rate after the war. Dissatisfied wives proved less willing to remain in unhappy marriages than they had been previously. At the same time, state judges became more sympathetic to women's desires to be freed from abusive or unfaithful husbands. Even so, divorces were still rare; most marriages were for life.

The republican decades witnessed an ever-increasing emphasis on the importance of mothers. In 1790 one woman even argued publicly for female superiority, resting her claim on woman's maternal role. Men, she said, had assumed primacy in the past "on the vain presumption of their being assigned the most important duties of life." But God had clearly intended otherwise, since to women He had "assigned the care of making the first impressions on the infant minds of the whole human race."

Other Americans did not go that far. They still viewed woman's role in traditional terms. Like Abigail Adams, they accepted the notion of equality, but within the context of men's and women's separate spheres. Whereas their forebears had seen women as inferior and subordinate to men, members of the revolutionary generation regarded the sexes and their roles as more nearly equal in importance. However, equality did not mean sameness.

Indeed, the differences they perceived between the male and female characters eventually enabled Americans to resolve the conflict between the two most influential strands of republican thought. Because married women could not own property or participate directly in economic life, women in general came to be seen as the embodiment of self-sacrificing, disinterested republicanism. Through female-run charitable and other social welfare groups, they assumed responsibility for the welfare of the community as a whole. Thus men were freed from any naggings of conscience as they pursued their economic self-interest (that other republican virtue), secure in the knowledge that their wives and daughters were fulfilling the family's obligation to the common good. The ideal republican man, therefore, was an individualist, seeking advancement for himself and his family; the ideal republican woman, by contrast, always put the wellbeing of others ahead of her own.

Together white men and women established the context for the creation of a virtuous republic. But nearly 20 percent of the American population was black. How did approximately 700,000 Afro-Americans fit into the developing national plan?

EMANCIPATION AND THE GROWTH OF RACISM

Revolutionary ideology exposed one of the primary contradictions in American society. Just as Abigail Adams pointed out to her husband his failure to apply revolutionary doctrines to the status of women, so too both blacks and whites recognized the irony of slaveholding Americans claiming that one of their aims in taking up arms was to prevent Britain from "enslaving" them.

As early as 1764, James Otis, Jr., had identified the basic problem in his pamphlet *The Rights of the British Colonies Asserted and Proved.* If according to natural law all people were born free and equal, that meant *all* humankind, black and white. "Does it follow that 'tis right to enslave a man because he is black?" Otis asked. In 1773 the Philadelphia doctor Benjamin Rush warned that "the plant of liberty is of so tender a nature that it cannot thrive long in the neighborhood of slavery."

Afro-Americans themselves were quick to recognize the implications of revolutionary ideology. In 1779 a group of slaves from Portsmouth, New Hampshire, asked the state legislature "from what authority [our masters] assume to dispose of our lives, freedom and property," and pleaded "that the name of slave may not more be heard in a land gloriously contending for the sweets of freedom." That same year several black residents of Fairfield, Connecticut, petitioned the legislature for their freedom.

Both legislatures responded negatively. But the postwar years did witness the gradual abolition of slavery in the North. Vermont abolished slavery in its 1777 constitution. Massachusetts courts decided in the 1780s that the clause in the state constitution declaring that "all men are born free and equal, and have certain natural, essential, and unalienable rights" prohibited slavery in the state. Pennsylvania passed an abolition law in 1780; four years later Rhode Island and Connecticut provided for gradual emancipation, followed by New York (1799) and New Jersey (1804).

Gradual Emancipation

No southern state adopted similar general emancipation laws, but the legislatures of Virginia (1782), Delaware (1787), and Maryland (1790 and 1796) did decide to change laws that had restricted masters' ability to free slaves. South Carolina and Georgia never considered adopting such acts, though, and North Carolina insisted that all manumissions (emancipations of individual slaves) be approved by county courts.

Thus revolutionary ideology had limited impact on the well-entrenched economic interests of large slaveholders. Only in the North, where there were few slaves and where little money was invested in human capital, could state legislatures vote to abolish slavery with relative ease. Even there, legislators' concern for property rights led them to favor gradual emancipation over immediate abolition.

Despite the slow progress of abolition, the free black population of the United States grew dramatically in the first years after the Revolution. Before the war there had been few free blacks in America. Most prewar free blacks were mulattoes, born of unions between white masters and enslaved black women. But wartime disruptions radically changed the size and composition of the free black population. Slaves who had escaped from plantations during the war, others who had served in the American army, and still others who had been emancipated by their owners or by state laws were now free. Because most of them were not mulattoes, dark skin was no longer an automatic sign of slave status. By 1790 there were nearly 60,000 free people of color in the United States; ten years later they numbered more than 108,000 and represented nearly 11 percent of the total black population. Most lived in the states of the upper South.

Growth of the Free Black Population

In the 1780s and thereafter, freed people often made their way, as had landless colonists decades before them, to the port cities of the North. They moved to Boston and Philadelphia in particular, where slavery was abolished sooner than it was in New York City. Women outnumbered men among the migrants by a margin of three to two. Like female whites, black women found more opportunities for employment, particularly as domestic servants, in the cities than in the countryside. Some black men also worked in domestic service, but larger numbers were employed as unskilled laborers or seamen. A few of the women and a sizable proportion of men (nearly a third of those in Philadelphia in 1795) were skilled workers or retailers. These freed people chose new names for themselves, exchanging the surnames of their former masters for names like Newman or Brown. They also began to cluster their residences in certain neighborhoods, probably as a result of both discrimination by whites and a desire for black solidarity.

Emancipation did not bring equality, though. Even whites who recognized Afro-Americans' right to freedom were unwilling to accept them as equals. Laws discriminated against emancipated blacks as they had against slaves—South Carolina, for example, did not permit free blacks to testify against whites in court. Public schools often refused to educate the children of free black parents. Freedmen found it difficult to purchase property and find good jobs. And whites rarely allowed them an equal voice in church affairs.

The Reverend Lemuel Haynes was one of the best-known black clergymen of the late eighteenth and early nineteenth centuries. He attacked the institution of slavery both in print and from the pulpit.   Museum of Art, Rhode Island School of Design; Gift of Miss Lucy T. Aldrich.

Gradually free blacks developed their own separate institutions. In Charleston, mulattoes formed the Brown Fellowship Society, which provided insurance coverage for its members, financed a school for free children, and helped to support black orphans. In 1787 blacks in Philadelphia and Baltimore founded churches that eventually became the African Methodist Episcopal (AME) denomination. AME churches later sponsored schools in a number of cities and, along with African Baptist and African Presbyterian churches, became cultural centers of the free black community.

Development of Black Institutions

Such endeavors were all the more important be-cause the postrevolutionary years ironically witnessed the development of a coherent racist theory in the United States. Whites had long regarded blacks as inferior, but the most influential writers on race had attributed that inferiority to environmental, rather than hereditary, factors. In the aftermath of the Revolution, white southerners needed to defend their holding other human beings in bondage against the notion that "*all* men are created equal." Consequently, they began to argue that blacks were less than fully human, that the principles of republican equality applied only to whites.

Development of Racist Theory

Their racism had several intertwined elements. First was the insistence that, as Thomas Jefferson suggested in 1781, blacks were "inferior to the whites in the endowments both of body and mind." Second came the belief that blacks were congenitally lazy, dishonest, and uncivilized (or uncivilizable). Third, and of crucial importance, was the notion that all blacks were sexually promiscuous and that black men lusted after white women. The specter of interracial sexual intercourse involving black men and white women haunted early American racist thought. The reverse situation, which occurred with far greater frequency (as white masters sexually exploited their female slaves), aroused little comment.

Afro-Americans did not allow these developing racist notions to pass unnoticed. Benjamin Banneker, a free black surveyor, astronomer, and mathematical genius, directly challenged Thomas Jefferson's belief in blacks' intellectual inferiority. In 1791 Banneker sent Jefferson a copy of his latest almanac (which included his astronomical calculations), as an example of blacks' mental powers. Jefferson's response admitted Banneker's capabilities but implied that he regarded Banneker as an exception.

At its birth, then, the republic was defined as an exclusively white enterprise. Indeed, some historians have argued that the subjection of blacks was a necessary precondition for equality **A Republic for** among whites. They have pointed **Whites Only** out that identifying a common racial antagonist helped to create white solidarity and to lessen the threat to gentry power posed by the enfranchisement of poorer whites. It was less dangerous to allow whites with little property to participate formally in politics than to open the possibility that they might combine with freed blacks to question the rule of the "better sort." That was one reason why, in the postrevolutionary years, the division of American society between slave and free was transformed into a division between black—some of whom were free—and white. The white male wielders of power ensured their continued dominance in part by making certain that race replaced enslavement as the primary determinant of Afro-Americans' status.

DESIGNING REPUBLICAN GOVERNMENTS

On May 10, 1776, the Continental Congress directed the states to devise new republican governments to replace the provincial congresses and committees that had met since **Drafting of** 1774. Thus Americans initially **State** concentrated on drafting state con- **Constitutions** stitutions. They immediately faced the problem of defining just what a constitution was. The British constitution could not serve as a model because it was an unwritten mixture of law and custom; Americans wanted tangible documents specifying the fundamental structures of government. They also wanted to make their documents special. Thus they began to call conventions for the sole purpose of drafting constitutions. The states sought direct authorization from the people—the theoretical sovereigns in a republic—before establishing new governments. After the new constitutions had been drawn up, delegates submitted them to the people for ratification.

Those who wrote the state constitutions concerned themselves primarily with outlining the distribution of and limitations on governmental power. As colonists, Americans had learned to fear the power of the governor—in most cases the appointed agent of the king or the proprietor—and to trust the legislature. Accordingly, the first state constitutions typically provided for the governor to be elected annually (usually by the legislature), limited the number of terms any one governor could serve, and gave him little independent authority. At the same time the constitutions expanded the powers of the legislature.

They redrew the lines of electoral districts to reflect population patterns more accurately and increased the number of members in both the upper and lower houses. Finally, most states lowered property qualifications for voting. Thus the revolutionary era witnessed the first deliberate attempt to broaden the base of American government.

But the authors of the state constitutions knew that governments designed to be responsive to the people would not necessarily provide sufficient protection should tyrants be elected to office. Consequently, they included limitations on governmental authority in the documents they composed. Seven of the constitutions contained formal bills of rights, and the others had similar clauses. Most of them guaranteed citizens freedom of the press and of religion, the right to a fair trial, the right of consent to taxation, and protection against general search warrants. An independent judiciary was charged with upholding such rights.

In sum, the constitution-makers put far greater emphasis on preventing state governments from becoming tyrannical than on making them effective wielders of political authority. But establishing such weak political units, especially in wartime, practically ensured that the constitutions would soon need revision. Invariably, the revised versions increased the powers of the governor and reduced the scope of the legislature's authority. Only in the 1780s did Americans start to develop a formal theory of checks and balances as the primary means of controlling governmental power.

The most heated constitutional debate took place in Pennsylvania. There the adherents of the third—or democratic—philosophy of republicanism dominated the Pennsylvania Assembly that drafted the state's first constitution. The document replaced the office of governor with an executive council, established a one-house (unicameral) legislature, and extended the vote to tax-paying (not property-holding) males. The constitution limited the number of terms that officials

Pennsylvania's Constitutional Debate

could serve and required a bill to be passed by two separate legislative sessions before it became law.

The Pennsylvania Constitution of 1776 represented such a break with the previous form of government that it immediately aroused intense opposition, chiefly among the educated elite. The Republicans (as the critics termed themselves) called for an effective governor and a two-house (bicameral) legislature. They also stressed the need for a balance of powers among governmental branches. In 1790, when Pennsylvania revised its constitution, the Republicans won the prolonged struggle. Pennsylvania's experiment in direct democracy had proved to be out of step with developing American notions of proper political structure.

The constitutional theories that Americans applied at the state level did not at first influence their conception of the nature of a national government. The powers and structure of the Continental Congress evolved by default early in the war, since Americans had little time to devote to legitimizing their de facto government while organizing the military struggle against Britain. Not until late 1777, after Burgoyne's defeat at Saratoga, did Congress send the Articles of Confederation to the states for ratification.

The chief organ of national government was a unicameral legislature in which each state had one vote. Its powers included the conduct of foreign relations, the settlement of disputes between states, control over maritime affairs, the regulation of Indian trade, and the valuation of state and national money. The articles did not give the national government the ability to tax effectively or to enforce a uniform commercial policy. The United States of America was described as "a firm league of friendship" in which each state "retains its sovereignty, freedom and independence."

Articles of Confederation

The articles required the unanimous consent of the state legislatures for ratification or amendment, and a clause concerning western lands turned out to be troublesome. The draft accepted by Congress allowed the states to retain all land claims derived from their original colonial charters. Because Maryland did not want to be overpowered by states with large land claims deriving from their colonial charters, the state absolutely refused to accept the articles until 1781. Only when Virginia and other states promised to surrender their holdings to national jurisdiction did Maryland accept the articles (see map).

The fact that a single state could delay ratification for three years was a portent of the fate of American government under the Articles of Confederation. The authors of the articles had not given adequate thought to the distribution of power within the national government or to the relationship between the Confederation and the states. The congress they created was simultaneously a legislative body and a collective executive, but it had no independent income and no authority to compel the states to accept its rulings. What is surprising, in other words, is not how poorly the Confederation functioned in the following years, but rather how much the government was able to accomplish.

TRIALS OF THE
CONFEDERATION

During and after the war the most persistent problem faced by the American governments, state and national, was finance. Because of a reluctance to

Monetary
Problems

levy taxes on their fellow countrymen, both Congress and the states tried to finance the war by simply printing currency. Even though the money was backed by nothing but good faith, it circulated freely and without excessive depreciation during 1775 and most of 1776. Late that year, though, as the American army suffered major battlefield reverses in New York and New Jersey, prices began to rise and inflation set in. The value of the currency rested on Americans' faith in their government, a

faith that was sorely tested in the years that followed. Both Congress and the states attempted to control inflation, but by 1780 it took forty paper dollars to purchase one in silver. A year later Continental currency was worthless.

Although many suffered from inflation, especially those on fixed incomes, some benefited from such economic conditions. Military contractors, large-scale farmers, and investors could make sizable profits. More risky, but potentially even more profitable, was privateering against enemy shipping—an enterprise that attracted venturesome sailors and wealthy merchants alike. Indeed, as a Nantucket, Massachusetts, mother wrote her son in early 1778, "it was Never better times here for Seamen then it is Now."

Such accumulations of private wealth did not help Congress with its financial problems. In 1781, faced with the total collapse of the monetary system, the delegates undertook major reforms. After establishing a department of finance under the wealthy Philadelphia merchant Robert Morris, they asked the states to amend the Articles of Confederation to allow Congress to levy a duty on imported goods. Morris put national finances on a solid footing, but the customs duty was never adopted.

Congress also faced major diplomatic problems at the close of the war. Chief among them were issues involving the peace treaty itself. Article 4, which

Failure to
Enforce the
Treaty of Paris

promised the repayment of prewar debts (most of them owed by Americans to British merchants), and Article 5, which recommended that states allow loyalists to recover their confiscated property, aroused considerable opposition. States passed laws denying British subjects the right to sue for recovery of debts or property in American courts, and town meetings decried the loyalists' return. As residents of Norwalk, Connecticut, put it, few Americans wanted to permit the "Tory Villains" to return "while filial Tears are fresh upon our Cheeks and our Murdered Brethren scarcely cold in their Graves." Because prominent patriots had purchased most of the confiscated loyalist property, state governments also did not want to enforce Article 5.

Chapter 6: FORGING A NATIONAL REPUBLIC, 1776–1789

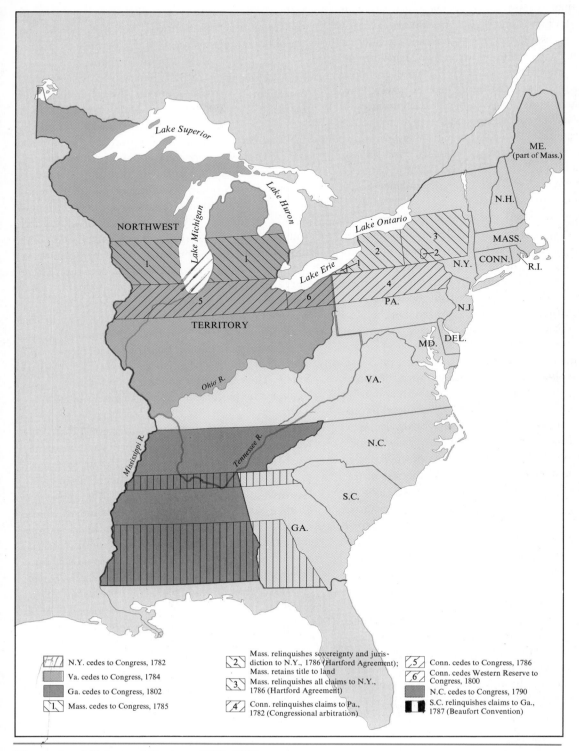

Lake Superior

Lake Michigan

Lake Huron

Lake Ontario

Lake Erie

NORTHWEST

TERRITORY

1   1

5   6

ME.
(part of Mass.)

N.H.

MASS.

CONN.

R.I.

N.Y.

2

3

(–2)

4

PA.

N.J.

MD.   DEL.

Ohio R.

VA.

Mississippi R.

Tennessee R.

N.C.

S.C.

GA.

N.Y. cedes to Congress, 1782

Va. cedes to Congress, 1784

Ga. cedes to Congress, 1802

1 Mass. cedes to Congress, 1785

2 Mass. relinquishes sovereignty and jurisdiction to N.Y., 1786 (Hartford Agreement);
Mass. retains title to land

3 Mass. relinquishes all claims to N.Y.,
1786 (Hartford Agreement)

4 Conn. relinquishes claims to Pa.,
1782 (Congressional arbitration)

5 Conn. cedes to Congress, 1786

6 Conn. cedes Western Reserve to
Congress, 1800

N.C. cedes to Congress, 1790

S.C. relinquishes claims to Ga.,
1787 (Beaufort Convention)

Western Land Claims and Cessions, 1782–1802

The failure of state and local governments to comply with Articles 4 and 5 gave Britain an excuse to maintain posts on the Great Lakes long after its troops were supposed to be withdrawn. Furthermore, Congress's inability to convince the states to implement the treaty pointed up its lack of power. Concerned nationalists argued publicly that enforcement of the treaty, however unpopular, was a crucial test for the republic. "Will foreign nations be willing to undertake anything with us or for us," asked Alexander Hamilton, "when they find that the nature of our governments will allow no dependence to be placed on our engagements?"

Congress's weakness was especially evident in the realm of trade, because the Articles of Confederation specifically denied it the power to establish a national commercial policy. Immediately following the war, Britain, France, and Spain restricted American trade with their colonies. When British goods began to flood the United States, an outraged but helpless Congress could do nothing. Though Americans opened a profitable trade with China in 1784, it was no substitute for access to closer and larger markets.

Congress also had difficulty dealing with the threat posed by Spain's presence on the southern and western borders of the United States. Determined to prevent the new nation's expansion, Spain in 1784 closed the Mississippi River to American navigation. It thus deprived the settlements west of the Appalachians of their major access route to the rest of the nation and the world. If Spain's policy were not reversed, westerners might have to accept Spanish sovereignty as the price for survival. Congress opened negotiations with Spain in 1785, but even John Jay, one of the nation's most experienced diplomats, could not win the necessary concessions on navigation.

Diplomatic problems of another sort confronted congressmen when they considered the status of the land on the United States's western borders. In 1783, Britain ceded all land east of the Mississippi (except for that held by Spain) to the United States. The major Indian tribes, however, had made no such cession. To eliminate this problem, American representatives signed treaties of questionable legality with the Iroquois at Fort Stanwix, New York (1784) and the Choctaw, Chickasaw, and Cherokee at Hopewell, South Carolina (1785 and 1786). When whites poured across the southern Appalachians, the Creek tribe, which had not signed at Hopewell, declared war. Only in 1790, when the Creek chief Alexander McGillivray traveled to New York to negotiate a treaty, did the tribe finally come to terms with the United States.

Encroachment on Indian Lands

In 1786 the Iroquois Confederacy formally repudiated the Fort Stanwix treaty and threatened new attacks on frontier settlements, but both whites and Indians knew the threat was an empty one. The flawed treaty was permitted to stand by default. At intervals during the remainder of the decade the state of New York purchased land from individual Iroquois tribes. By 1790 the once-proud Iroquois Confederacy was confined to a few scattered reservations. In the West tribes like the Shawnee, Chippewa, Ottawa, and Potawatomi formed their own confederacy and demanded direct negotiations with the United States. Their aim was to present a united front, so as to avoid the piecemeal surrender of land by individual tribes.

Congress, though, ignored the western Indian confederacy and organized the Northwest Territory, bounded by the Mississippi River, the Great Lakes, and the Ohio River. Ordinances passed in 1784, 1785, and 1787 outlined the process through which the land could be sold to settlers and formal governments organized. To ensure orderly development, Congress directed that the land be surveyed into townships six miles square, each divided into thirty-six sections of 640 acres (one square mile). Revenue from the sale of the sixteenth section of each township was to be reserved for the support of public schools—the first instance of federal aid to education in American history. The minimum price per acre was set at one dollar, and the minimum sale was to be 640 acres. Congress was not especially concerned about helping the small farmer: the minimum

Northwest Ordinances

outlay of $640 was beyond the reach of most Americans. The proceeds from the land sales were the first independent revenues available to the national government.

The most important ordinance was the third, passed in 1787. The Northwest Ordinance contained a bill of rights guaranteeing settlers in the territory freedom of religion and the right to a jury trial, prohibiting cruel and unusual punishments, and abolishing slavery. It also specified the process by which residents of the territory could eventually organize state governments and seek admission to the union "on an equal footing with the original States."

The Ordinance of 1787 was purely theoretical at the time it was passed. The Miami, Shawnee, and Delaware refused to acknowledge American sovereignty and insisted on their right to the land. They opposed white settlement violently, attacking unwary pioneers who ventured too far north of the Ohio River. In 1788 the Ohio Company established the town of Marietta at the juncture of the Ohio and Muskingum rivers. But the Indians prevented the company from extending settlement very far into the interior. After General Arthur St. Clair, the first governor of the Northwest Territory, failed to negotiate a meaningful treaty with the tribes in early 1789, it was apparent that the United States could not avoid a clash with a western confederacy, composed of eight tribes and led by the Miami.

Little Turtle, the war chief of the Miami confederacy, defeated first General Josiah Harmar (1790) and then St. Clair (1791) in major battles near the present border between Indiana and Ohio. More than six hundred of St. Clair's men were killed; it was the whites' worst defeat in the entire history of the American frontier. In 1793 the Miami confederacy declared that peace could be achieved only if the United States recognized the Ohio River as the boundary between white and Indian lands. But the national government refused to relinquish its claim to the Northwest Territory. A new army under the command of General Anthony Wayne, a Revolutionary War hero, attacked and de-

War in the Northwest

feated the tribesmen in August 1794, at the Battle of Fallen Timbers (near Toledo, Ohio). This victory made it possible for serious negotiations to begin.

The Treaty of Greenville (1795) gave each side a portion of what it wanted. The United States gained the right to settle much of what was to become the state of Ohio, the tribes retaining only the northwest corner of the region. The Indians received the acknowledgment they had long sought: American recognition of their rights to the soil. At Greenville, the United States formally accepted the principle of Indian sovereignty, by virtue of residence, over all lands the tribes had not yet ceded. Never again would the United States government claim that it had acquired Indian territory solely through negotiation with a European or American country.

The problems the United States encountered in ensuring safe settlement of the Northwest Territory pointed up, once again, the basic weakness of the Confederation government. Not until after the Articles of Confederation were replaced with a new constitution could the United States muster sufficient force to implement all the provisions of the Northwest Ordinance. Thus, although the ordinance is often viewed as one of the few major accomplishments of the Confederation Congress, it must be seen within a context of political impotence.

FROM CRISIS TO A CONSTITUTION

The most obvious deficiencies of the Articles of Confederation lay in the areas of trade and foreign relations. Congress could not impose its will on the states to establish a uniform commercial policy or to ensure the enforcement of treaties. The problems involving trade were particularly serious. Trade restrictions imposed by European powers adversely affected the American economy, which slid into a depression less than a year after the war's end. Although recovery had begun by 1786, the war's effects proved impossible to erase entirely.

The war had wrought permanent change in the American economy. The near-total cessation of commerce in nonmilitary items during the war years proved a great stimulus to domestic manufacturing. Consequently, despite the influx of European goods after 1783, the postwar period witnessed the stirrings of American industrial development—for example, the first American textile mill began production in Pawtucket, Rhode Island, in 1790. Moreover, foreign trade patterns shifted from Europe and toward the West Indies. Indeed, foodstuffs shipped to the French and Dutch Caribbean islands became America's largest single export.

Recognizing the Confederation Congress's inability to deal with commercial matters, Virginia invited the other states to a conference at Annapolis, Maryland, to discuss trade policy. Although eight states named representatives to the meeting in September 1786, only five delegations attended. Those present realized that they were too few in number to have any real impact on the political system. They issued a call for another convention, to be held in Philadelphia in nine months, "to devise such further provisions as shall . . . appear necessary to render the constitution of the federal government adequate to the exigencies of the Union."

That fall an incident in western Massachusetts helped to convince other Americans that broad changes were necessary in their national government. Crowds of farmers angered by high taxes and the low supply of money halted court proceedings in which the state was trying to seize property for nonpayment of taxes. The insurgents were led by Daniel Shays, a farmer who had risen to the rank of captain in the Revolutionary army; many of them were respected war veterans, described as "gentlemen" in contemporary accounts of the riots. Clearly the episode could not be dismissed as the work of an unruly rabble.

Shays' Rebellion

To residents of eastern Massachusetts and other citizens of the United States, the most frightening aspect of the uprising was the rebels' attempt to forge direct links with the earlier struggle for independence. Massachusetts officials in response asserted that the formation of the republic had narrowed the range of acceptable political alternatives. The crowd actions that had once been a justifiable response to British tyranny were no longer legitimate. In a republic, reform had to come about through the ballot box rather than by force. If the nation's citizens refused to submit to legitimate authority, the result would be chaos and collapse of the government.

Shays' Rebellion symbolically seemed to challenge the existence of the entire United States, though it never seriously threatened even the state of Massachusetts. (The rebels were easily dispersed by militia early in 1787.) Of the major American political thinkers, only Thomas Jefferson could view the Massachusetts incidents without alarm. "What country can preserve its liberties, if its rulers are not warned from time to time that their people preserve the spirit of resistance?" Jefferson wrote from Paris, where he was serving as American ambassador.

But Jefferson was clearly exceptional. Shays' Rebellion unquestionably hastened the movement toward comprehensive revision of the Articles of Confederation. In February 1787, after most of the states had already appointed delegates, the Confederation Congress belatedly endorsed the convention. In mid-May, fifty-five men, representing all the states but Rhode Island, assembled in Philadelphia to begin their deliberations.

Calling of the Constitutional Convention

The vast majority of the delegates were men of property and substance. Among their number were merchants, planters, physicians, generals, governors, and especially lawyers. Most had been born in America, and many came from families that had arrived in the seventeenth century. In an era when only a tiny proportion of the population had any advanced education, more than half had attended college. A few had been educated in Britain, but most were graduates of American institutions. The youngest delegate was twenty-six, the oldest—Benjamin Franklin—eighty-one. Like George Washington, whom they elected chairman, most were in their vigorous middle years. A dozen men did the bulk of the convention's work. Of the dozen, James Madison of Virginia was the most important; he truly deserves the title Father of the Constitution.

Madison was unique among the delegates in his systematic preparation for the Philadelphia meeting. Through Jefferson in Paris he bought more than two hundred books on history and government, and carefully analyzed their accounts of past confederacies and republics. In April 1787, a month before the convention began, he summed up the results of his research in a lengthy paper entitled "Vices of the Political System of the United States." After listing the eleven major flaws he perceived in the current structure of the government, Madison set forth the principle of checks and balances.

The government, he believed, had to be constructed in such a way that it could not become tyrannical or fall wholly under the influence of a particular interest group. He regarded the large size of a potential national republic as an advantage in that respect. Rejecting the common assertion that republics had to be small to survive, Madison argued that a large, diverse republic was in fact to be preferred. Because the nation would include many different interest groups, no one of them would be able to control the government. Political stability would result from compromises among the contending parties.

Madison's conception of national government was embodied in the so-called Virginia plan, introduced on May 29 by his colleague Edmund Randolph. The

Virginia and New Jersey Plans

plan provided for a two-house legislature with proportional representation in both houses, an executive elected by Congress, a national judiciary, and congressional veto over state laws. It gave Congress the broad power to legislate "in all cases to which the separate states are

incompetent." Had the Virginia plan been adopted intact, it would have created a government in which national authority reigned unchallenged and state power was greatly diminished.

But the convention included many delegates who, while recognizing the need for change, believed that the Virginians had gone too far in the direction of national consolidation. The disaffected delegates united under the leadership of William Paterson. On June 15 Paterson presented an alternative scheme, the New Jersey plan, calling for modifications in the Articles of Confederation rather than a complete overhaul of the government. Although the delegates rejected Paterson's narrow interpretation of their task, he and his allies won a number of major victories.

The delegates began their work by discussing the structure and functions of Congress. They readily concurred that the new national government should have a two-house legislature. But then they discovered that they differed widely in their answers to three key questions: Should there be representation proportional to population in both houses of Congress? How was that representation in either or both houses to be apportioned among the states? And, finally, how were the members of the two houses to be elected?

The last issue was the easiest to resolve. In the words of John Dickinson, the delegates thought it "essential" that members of one branch of Congress be elected directly by the people and "expedient" that members of the other be chosen by the state legislatures. Since the legislatures had selected delegates to the Confederation Congress, they would expect a similar privilege in the new government.

Considerably more difficult was the matter of proportional representation in the Senate. The delegates accepted without much debate the principle of proportional representation in the lower house. The Senate was another matter. Delegates from the large states favored proportional representation; those from the small states wanted equal representation. After weeks of debate and deadlock, a committee was appointed to work out a compromise. The committee recommended equal representation for states in the Senate, coupled with a proviso that all appropriation bills must originate in the lower house. The dispute continued and was finally resolved when the delegates agreed that the two senators from each state could vote as individuals rather than as a bloc.

One potentially divisive question remained unresolved: how was representation in the lower house to be apportioned among the states? Delegates from states with large numbers of slaves wanted all people, black and white, to be counted equally; delegates from states with few slaves wanted only free people to be counted. The issue was resolved by using a formula developed by the Confederation Congress in 1783 to allocate taxation among the states: three-fifths of the slaves would be included in the population totals. (The formula reflected the delegates' judgment that slaves were less efficient producers of wealth than free people, not that they were 60 percent human and 40 percent property.) After the three-fifths compromise was linked to a clause allowing Congress to stop the slave trade after twenty years, it was unanimously accepted.

Other issues proved to be less difficult to resolve. The delegates agreed to enumerate the powers of Congress but to allow it to pass all laws "necessary and proper" for carrying out its functions. Foreign policy was placed in the hands of the executive, who was also made the commander-in-chief of the armed forces. The idea of a legislative veto over state action was rejected, but an implied judicial veto was included. Moreover, the Constitution, national laws, and treaties were made the supreme law of the land. Finally, the delegates established the electoral college and a short term for the chief executive, who could seek re-election.

The key to the Constitution was the distribution of political authority—separation of powers among the executive, legislative, and judicial branches of the national government, and di-

Separation of Powers

vision of powers between states and nation. The system of checks and balances would made it difficult for

the government to become tyrannical, as Madison had intended. At the same time, though, the elaborate system would sometimes prevent the government from acting quickly and decisively. Finally, the line between state and national powers was ambiguously and vaguely drawn.

The convention held its last session on September 17, 1787. Of the forty-two delegates present, only three refused to sign the Constitution. (Two of the three, George Mason and Elbridge Gerry, declined because of the lack of a bill of rights.) Though the delegates had accepted the Constitution, the question remained as to whether or not the states would ratify it.

OPPOSITION AND RATIFICATION

The ratification clause of the Constitution provided for the new system to take effect once it was approved by special conventions in at least nine states. The delegates to each state convention were to be elected by the people. Thus the national constitution, unlike the Articles of Confederation, would rest directly on popular authority.

As the states began to elect delegates to the special conventions, pro- and anti-Constitution forces emerged. Critics of the Constitution, who became known as Antifederalists, em-

Antifederalists

phasized the threat to the states embodied in the new national government and stressed the dangers to individuals posed by the lack of a bill of rights. The Antifederalists saw the states as the chief protectors of individual rights. They also regarded Madison's argument that a large republic was preferable to a small one as heretical nonsense.

As the months passed and public debate continued, the Antifederalists focused more sharply on the

Constitution's lack of a bill of rights. Even if the states were weakened by the new system, they believed, the people could still be protected from tyranny if their rights were specifically guaranteed. *Letters of a Federal Farmer*, perhaps the most widely read Antifederalist pamphlet, listed the rights that should be protected: freedom of the press and of religion, the right to trial by jury, and guarantees against unreasonable search warrants.

As the state conventions met to consider ratification, the lack of a bill of rights loomed larger and larger as a flaw in the new form of government. Four

Ratification of the Constitution

of the first five states to ratify did so unanimously, but serious disagreements then began to surface. Massachusetts ratified by a majority of only 19 votes out of 355 cast; in New Hampshire the Federalists won by a majority of 57 to 47. When New Hampshire ratified, in June 1788, the requirement of nine states had been satisfied. But New York and Virginia had not yet voted, and everyone realized the new constitution could not succeed unless those key states accepted it. In Virginia, despite a valiant effort by the Antifederalist Patrick Henry, the pro-Constitution forces won 89 to 79. In New York James Madison, John Jay, and Alexander Hamilton campaigned for ratification by publishing *The Federalist*, a political tract that explained the theory behind the Constitution and masterfully answered its critics. Their reasoned arguments, coupled with the promise that a bill of rights would be added to the Constitution, helped win the battle. On July 26, 1788, New York ratified the Constitution by the slim margin of 3 votes. The new government was a reality, even though the last state (Rhode Island, which had not participated in the convention) did not formally join the union until 1790.

The experience of fighting a war and of struggling for survival as an independent nation in the 1780s had altered the political context of American life. Whereas at the outset of the war most politically aware Americans believed that "that government which governs best governs least," by the late 1780s many had changed their minds. These were the draft-

	IMPORTANT EVENTS
1776	Second Continental Congress directs states to draft constitutions
1777	Articles of Confederation sent to states for ratification
1781	Articles of Confederation ratified
1786	Annapolis Convention
1786–87	Shay's Rebellion
1787	Northwest Ordinance Constitutional Convention
1788	Hamilton, Jay, and Madison, *The Federalist* Constitution ratified
1794	Battle of Fallen Timbers
1795	Treaty of Greenville
1800	Weems, *Life of Washington*

ers and supporters of the Constitution, who won their point when the Constitution was adopted, however narrowly.

White males wholly dominated the new United States. The era that saw the formation of the union also witnessed the systematic formulation of American racist thought, and the two processes were intimately linked. One way to preserve the freedom of all whites was to ensure the continued subjection of all blacks, slave or free. Likewise, one way to preserve the unchallenged economic independence of white men was to ensure the economic and political dependence of white women on their husbands, fathers, and brothers. Even if the leaders of the United States were not consciously aware of adopting such strategies, their decisions ensured that only white males would hold political power in the new republic.

Suggestions for Further Reading

General

Staughton Lynd, *Class Conflict, Slavery, & the United States Constitution* (1967); Forrest McDonald, *E Pluribus Unum* (1965); Jackson Turner Main, *The Social Structure of Revolutionary America* (1965); Curtis P. Nettels, *The Emergence of a National Economy, 1775–1815* (1962); Gordon S. Wood, *The Creation of the American Republic, 1776–1787* (1969).

Continental Congress and Articles of Confederation

H. James Henderson, *Party Politics in the Continental Congress* (1974); Merrill Jensen, *The Articles of Confederation* (1959); Merrill Jensen, *The New Nation* (1950); Jack N. Rakove, *The Beginnings of National Politics* (1979).

State Politics

Willi Paul Adams, *The First American Constitutions* (1980); Ronald Hoffman and Peter Albert, eds., *Sovereign States in an Age of Uncertainty* (1981); Jackson Turner Main, *Political Parties Before the Constitution* (1973); Jackson Turner Main, *The Sovereign States, 1775–1783* (1973); J. R. Pole, *Political Representation in England and the Origins of the American Republic* (1966); David P. Szatmary, *Shays' Rebellion* (1980).

The Constitution

Charles A. Beard, *An Economic Interpretation of the Constitution of the United States* (1913); Michael Kammen, *A Machine That Would Go of Itself* (1986); Forrest McDonald,

Novus Ordo Seclorum (1985); Jackson Turner Main, *The Anti-Federalists* (1961); Frederick W. Marks III, *Independence on Trial* (1973); Clinton Rossiter, *1787: The Grand Convention* (1973); Robert A. Rutland, *The Ordeal of the Constitution* (1966); Garry Wills, *Explaining America* (1981).

Education and Culture

Lawrence A. Cremin, *American Education: The National Experience, 1783–1876* (1981); Joseph J. Ellis, *After the Revolution* (1979); Russel B. Nye, *The Cultural Life of the New Nation: 1776–1803* (1960); Kenneth Silverman, *A Cultural History of the American Revolution* (1976).

Women

Charles Akers, *Abigail Adams: An American Woman* (1980); Nancy F. Cott, *The Bonds of Womanhood* (1977); Linda K. Kerber, *Women of the Republic* (1980); Mary Beth Norton, *Liberty's Daughters* (1980); Lynn Withey, *Dearest Friend: A Life of Abigail Adams* (1980).

Blacks and Slavery

Ira Berlin and Ronald Hoffman, eds., *Slavery and Freedom in the Age of the American Revolution* (1983); David Brion Davis, *The Problem of Slavery in the Age of Revolution, 1770–1823* (1975); Carol V. R. George, *Segregated Sabbaths* (1973); Winthrop Jordan, *White over Black* (1968); Donald L. Robinson, *Slavery in the Structure of American Politics 1765–1820* (1971); Arthur Zilversmit, *The First Emancipation* (1967).

Indians

Dorothy Jones, *License for Empire* (1982); Francis Paul Prucha, *American Indian Policy in the Formative Years* (1962); Bernard Sheehan, *Seeds of Extinction* (1973); Anthony F. C. Wallace, *The Death and Rebirth of the Seneca* (1969).

CHAPTER 7

POLITICS AND SOCIETY IN THE EARLY REPUBLIC 1790–1800

*C*harles Thomson, *secretary* to Congress, arrived at Mount Vernon, Virginia, around noon on April 14, 1789. He brought momentous news: the first electoral college convened under the new Constitution had unanimously elected George Washington president of the United States, and Congress had confirmed the choice.

The United States formally honored its first president with an outpouring of affection and respect that has rarely been equaled since. Washington's inauguration allowed the people to express their pride in the Revolution, the new Constitution, and most of all in the nation itself. The struggle against Britain had nurtured in Americans an intense nationalism. They believed their republican experiment placed them in the vanguard of political reform, and they optimistically expected a future of prosperity, expansion, national unity, and independence from Europe.

Yet Americans were unsuccessful in their quest for unity and unqualified independence during the 1790s. Nowhere was their failure more evident than in the realm of national politics. The fierce battle over the Constitution foreshadowed an even wider division over the major political issues the republic had to confront. Americans believed that the Constitution would resolve the problems that had arisen during the Confederation period, and they expected the new government to rule largely by consensus. Accordingly, they found it difficult to understand and deal with partisan tensions that developed out of disputes over such fundamental questions as the extent to which authority should be centralized in the national government; the formulation of foreign policy in an era of continual warfare in Europe; and the limits of dissent within the republic.

Prosperity and expansion too were not easily attained. The United States economy still depended on the export trade, as it had throughout the colonial era. When warfare between England and France resumed in 1793, Americans found their commerce disrupted once again. Moreover, the strength of the Miami confederacy blocked the westward expansion of white settlement north of the Ohio River until after the Treaty of Greenville in 1795. South of the Ohio, settlements were established west of the mountains as early as the 1770s, but the geographical barrier of the Appalachians tended to isolate them from the eastern seaboard. Not until the last years of the century did the frontier settlements become more fully integrated into American life through the vehicle of the Second Great Awakening, a religious revival that swept both east and west.

BUILDING A WORKABLE GOVERNMENT

In 1788 Americans celebrated the ratification of the Constitution with a series of parades, held in many cities on the Fourth of July. The processions were carefully planned to symbolize the unity of the new nation and to recall its history to the minds of the watching throngs. The parades, like prerevolutionary protest meetings, served as political educators for literate and illiterate Americans alike. Men and women who could not read were thereby informed of the significance of the new Constitution in the life of the nation. They were also instructed about political leaders' hopes for industry and frugality on the part of a virtuous American public.

The ratification processions expressed a nationalistic spirit that carried over into the first session of Congress. In the congressional elections, held late in 1788, only a few Antifederalists had run or been elected to office.

First Congress

Thus the First Congress was composed chiefly of men who were considerably more inclined toward a strong national government than had been the delegates to the Constitutional Convention. Since the Constitution had deliberately left many key issues undecided, the nationalists' domi-

nation of Congress meant that their views on those points quickly prevailed.

Congress faced four immediate problems when it convened in April 1789: raising revenue to support the new government, responding to the state ratification conventions' calls for the addition of a bill of rights to the Constitution, setting up executive departments, and organizing the federal judiciary. The latter task was especially important. The Constitution established a Supreme Court but left it to Congress to decide whether to have other federal courts as well.

The Virginian James Madison, who had been elected to the House of Representatives, soon became as influential in Congress as he had been at the Philadelphia convention. Only a few months into the session, he persuaded Congress to impose a tariff on certain imported goods. The new government would have problems, but lack of revenue in its first years was not one of them.

Madison also took the lead on the issue of constitutional amendments, introducing nineteen proposed amendments, of which Congress accepted twelve and the states ten. These ten amendments officially became part of the Constitution on December 15, 1791. Not for many years, though, did they become known collectively as the Bill of Rights.

Bill of Rights

The first amendment specifically prohibited Congress from passing any law restricting the people's right to freedom of religion, speech, press, peaceable assembly, or petition. The next two arose directly from the former colonists' fear of standing armies as a threat to freedom. The second amendment guaranteed the people's right "to keep and bear arms" because of the need for a "well regulated Militia"; the third defined the circumstances in which troops could be quartered in private homes. The next five pertained to judicial procedures. The fourth amendment prohibited "unreasonable searches and seizures"; the fifth and sixth established the rights of accused persons; the seventh specified the conditions for jury trials in civil, as opposed to criminal, cases;

and the eighth forbade "cruel and unusual punishments." Finally, the ninth and tenth amendments reserved to the people and the states other unspecified rights and powers. In short, the authors of the amendments made clear that in listing some rights explicitly they did not mean to preclude the exercise of others.

While debating the proposed amendments, Congress also concerned itself with the organization of the executive branch. It readily agreed to continue the three administrative departments established under the Articles of Confederation: War, Foreign Affairs (renamed State), and Treasury. Congress also instituted two lesser posts: the attorney general—the nation's official lawyer—and the postmaster general, who would oversee the Post Office. The only serious controversy was whether the president alone could dismiss officials whom he had originally appointed with the consent of the Senate. After some debate, the House and Senate agreed that he had such authority. Thus was established the important principle that the heads of the executive departments are responsible solely to the president.

Aside from the constitutional amendments, the most far-reaching piece of legislation enacted by the First Congress was the Judiciary Act of 1789. The Judiciary Act provided for the Supreme Court to have six members: a chief justice and five associate justices. It also defined the jurisdiction of the federal judiciary and established thirteen district courts and three circuit courts of appeal. The act's most important provision may have been Section 25, which allowed appeals from state courts to the federal court system when certain types of constitutional issues were raised. This section was intended to implement Article VI of the Constitution, which stated that federal laws and treaties were to be considered "the supreme Law of the Land." If Article VI was to be enforced uniformly, the national judiciary clearly had to be able to overturn state court decisions in cases involving the Constitution, federal laws, or treaties.

Judiciary Act of 1789

During the first decade of its existence, the Supreme Court handled few cases of any importance. But in a significant 1796 decision, *Ware v. Hylton*, the Court for the first time declared a state law unconstitutional. That same year it also reviewed the constitutionality of an act of Congress, upholding its validity in the case of *Hylton v. United States*. The most important case of the decade, *Chisholm v. Georgia* (1793), established that states could be freely sued in federal courts by citizens of other states; this decision, unpopular with the states, was overruled five years later by the Eleventh Amendment to the Constitution.

DOMESTIC AND FOREIGN POLICY UNDER WASHINGTON AND HAMILTON

During his first months in office Washington acted cautiously, knowing that whatever he did would set precedents for the future. For example, he concluded that he should exercise his veto power over congressional legislation very sparingly—only, indeed, if he was convinced a bill was unconstitutional. His first major task as president was to choose the men who would head the executive departments. For the War Department he selected an old comrade-in-arms, Henry Knox, who had been his reliable general of artillery during much of the Revolution. His choice for the State Department was his fellow Virginian Thomas Jefferson, who had just returned to the United States from his post as ambassador to France. Finally, for the crucial position of secretary of the treasury, the president chose the brilliant, intensely ambitious Alexander Hamilton.

Two traits distinguished Hamilton from most of his contemporaries. First, he displayed an undivided, un-

Alexander Hamilton (1737–1804), painted by John Trumbull in 1792. Hamilton was then at the height of his influence as secretary of the treasury, and his haughty, serene expression reveals his supreme self-confidence. Trumbull, an American student of the English artist Benjamin West, painted the portrait at the request of John Jay.   National Gallery of Art, Gift of the Avalon Foundation.

liance on people's capacity for virtuous and self-sacrificing behavior. That outlook set him apart from those republicans who foresaw a rosy future in which public-spirited citizens would pursue the common good rather than their own private advantage.

In 1789 Congress ordered the new secretary of the treasury to study the state of the public debt and to submit recommendations for supporting the government's credit. Hamilton discovered that the country's remaining war debts fell into three categories: those owed by the United States to foreign governments and investors, mostly to France (about $11 million); those owed by the national government to merchants, former soldiers, holders of revolutionary bonds, and the like (about $27 million); and, finally, similar debts owed by state governments (roughly estimated at $25 million). With respect to the national debt, there was little disagreement: politically aware Americans recognized that if their new government was to succeed it would have to pay the obligations the nation had incurred while winning independence.

National Debt

The state debts were quite another matter. Some states had already paid off most of their war debts. They would oppose the national government's assumption of responsibility for other states' debts, since their citizens would be taxed to pay such obligations in addition to their own. Conversely, states with large debts favored assumption. The possible assumption of state debts also had political implications. Consolidation of the debt in the hands of the national government would unquestionably help to concentrate both economic and political power at the national level.

Hamilton's "Report on Public Credit," sent to Congress in January 1790, reflected both his national loyalty and his cynicism. It proposed that Congress assume outstanding state debts, combine them with national obligations, and issue new securities covering both principal and accumulated unpaid interest. Current holders of state or national debt certificates would

Hamilton's "Report on Public Credit"

questioning loyalty to the nation as a whole. Since he had been born in the West Indies, Hamilton had no ties to an individual state. He showed little sympathy for, or understanding of, demands for local autonomy. Thus his fiscal policies aimed always at consolidation of power at the national level. Furthermore, he never feared the exercise of centralized executive authority, as did his older counterparts who had clashed repeatedly with colonial governors.

Second, he regarded his fellow human beings with unvarnished cynicism. Perhaps because of the poverty of his early years and his own overriding ambition, Hamilton believed people to be motivated primarily, if not entirely, by self-interest—particularly economic self-interest. He placed absolutely no re-have the option of taking a portion of their payment in western lands. Hamilton's aims were clear: he wanted to expand the financial reach of the United States government and reduce the economic power of the states. He also wanted to ensure that the holders of public securities—many of them wealthy merchants and speculators—would have a significant financial stake in the survival of the national government.

Hamilton's plan stimulated lively debate in Congress. The opposition coalesced around his former ally James Madison. Believing with some reason that speculators had purchased large quantities of debt certificates at a small fraction of their face value, Madison proposed that the original holders of the debt also be compensated by the government. But Madison's plan was exceedingly complex and perhaps impossible to administer. The House of Representatives rejected it.

At first, however, the House also rejected the assumption of state debts. Since the Senate, by contrast, adopted Hamilton's plan largely intact, a series of compromises followed. The traditional story that Hamilton and Madison agreed over Jefferson's dinner table to exchange assumption of state debts for a southern site for the national capital is not supported by the surviving evidence, but a political deal was undoubtedly struck. The Potomac River was designated as the site for the capital. Simultaneously, the four congressmen from Maryland and Virginia whose districts contained the most likely locations for the new city switched from opposition to support for assumption. As a result, the first part of Hamilton's financial program became law in August 1790.

Four months later Hamilton submitted to Congress a second report on public credit, recommending the chartering of a national bank. Hamilton modeled his bank on the Bank of England. The

First Bank of the United States

Bank of the United States was to be capitalized at $10 million, with only $2 million coming from public funds. The rest would be supplied by private investors. Its charter was to run for twenty years, and one-fifth of its directors were to be named

by the government. Its bank notes would circulate as the nation's currency; it would also act as the collecting and disbursing agent for the treasury, and lend money to the government. Most people recognized that such an institution would benefit the country, especially because it would solve the problem of America's perpetual shortage of an acceptable medium of exchange. But there was another issue: did the Constitution give Congress the power to establish such a bank?

James Madison, for one, answered that question with a resounding no. He pointed out that the delegates at the Philadelphia convention had specifically rejected a clause authorizing Congress to issue corporate charters.

Washington, disturbed by Madison's contention, decided to request other opinions before signing the bill. Edmund Randolph, the attorney general, and Thomas Jefferson, the secretary of state, agreed with Madison that the bank was unconstitutional. Jefferson referred to Article I, Section 8, of the Constitution, which gave Congress the power "to make all Laws which shall be necessary and proper for carrying into Execution the foregoing Powers." *Necessary* was the key word, Jefferson argued: Congress could do what was needed but not what was merely desirable without specific constitutional authorization. Thus Jefferson formulated the strict-constructionist interpretation of the Constitution.

Washington asked Hamilton to reply to these negative assessments of his proposal. Hamilton's "Defense of the Constitutionality of the Bank," presented to Washington in February 1791, was a brilliant exposition of what has become known as the broad-constructionist view of the Constitution. Hamilton argued forcefully that Congress could choose any means not specifically prohibited by the Constitution to achieve a constitutional end. In short, if the end was constitutional and the means was not *unconstitutional*, then the means was also constitutional. Washington accepted Hamilton's logic and signed the bill.

In December 1791, Hamilton presented to Congress his "Report on Manufactures," the third and last

An American artist painted this view of President George Washington in army uniform once again, as he (on October 18, 1794) reviewed the troops that had been summoned to suppress the Whiskey Rebellion.   Metropolitan Museum of Art, Gift of Edgar William and Bernice Chrysler Garbisch, 1963. (63.201.2.)

of his prescriptions for the American economy. In it he outlined an ambitious plan for encouraging and protecting the United States's infant industries, like shoemaking and textile manufacturing. But because most congressmen were convinced that America's future was agrarian, they rejected Hamilton's report.

That same year Congress did accept the other part of Hamilton's financial program, an excise tax on whiskey, because of the need for additional government revenues and because of the congressmen's desire to reduce the nation's consumption of distilled spirits. The new tax most directly affected western farmers, who sold their grain crops in the form of distilled spirits as a means of avoiding the high costs of transporting wagonloads of bulky corn over the mountains. News of the excise law set off immediate protests in frontier areas of Pennsylvania and the Carolinas. But matters did not come to a head until the summer of 1794, when western Pennsylvania farmers tried to stop a federal marshal from arresting some men charged with violating the

Whiskey Rebellion

law. Washington, determined to prevent a recurrence of Shays' Rebellion, ordered the insurgents to disperse by September 1 and summoned more than 12,000 militiamen. But the troops arrived after the riots were over. Only two of those arrested were convicted of treason, and Washington pardoned them.

The chief importance of the Whiskey Rebellion lay in the message it forcefully conveyed to the American public. The national government, Washington had demonstrated, would not allow violent organized resistance to its laws. In the new republic, change would be effected peacefully, by legal means.

By 1794, a group of Americans had already begun to seek change systematically within the confines of electoral politics, even though traditional political theory regarded organized opposition—especially in a republic—as illegitimate. The leaders of the opposition, Jefferson and Madison, saw themselves as the true heirs of the revolution. To emphasize their support of republican principles, they and their followers called themselves Republicans and formed groups called Democratic-Republican societies. Hamilton and his supporters claimed to be the rightful interpreters of the Constitution and took the name Federalists. Each side contended the other was a faction bent upon subversion. (By traditional definition, a faction was opposed to the public good.)

PARTISAN POLITICS AND FOREIGN POLICY

The first years under the Constitution were blessed by international peace. Eventually, however, the French Revolution, which began in 1789, brought about the resumption of hostilities between France, America's wartime ally, and Great Britain, America's most important trading partner.

At first, Americans welcomed the news that France was turning toward republicanism. But by the early 1790s the reports from France were disquieting. Outbreaks of violence continued, ministries succeeded each other with bewildering rapidity, and executions were commonplace. The king himself was beheaded in early 1793. Although many Americans, including Jefferson and Madison, retained their sympathy for the French revolutionaries, others began to view France as a prime example of the perversion of republicanism. As might be expected, Alexander Hamilton fell into the latter group.

At that juncture, France declared war on Britain, Spain, and Holland. The Americans thus faced a dilemma. The 1778 treaty with France bound them to that nation "forever," and a mutual commitment to republicanism created ideological bonds. Yet the United States was connected to Great Britain as well. Aside from sharing a common history and language, America and England were economic partners.

The political and diplomatic climate was further complicated in April 1793, when Citizen Edmond Genêt, a representative of the French government, landed in Charleston. As Genêt made his leisurely way northward to New York City, he was wildly cheered and lavishly entertained at every stop. En route, he recruited Americans for expeditions against British and Spanish possessions in the Western Hemisphere and distributed privateering commissions with a generous hand. Genêt's arrival raised a series of key questions for President Washington. Should he receive Genêt, thus officially recognizing the French revolutionary government? Should he acknowledge an obligation to aid France under the terms of the 1778 treaty? Or should he proclaim American neutrality in the conflict?

For once, Hamilton and Jefferson saw eye to eye. Both told Washington that the United States could not afford to ally itself firmly with either side. Washington agreed; thus he received Genêt officially, but also issued a proclamation informing the world that the United States would adopt "a conduct friendly and impartial toward the belligerent powers." How-

Citizen Genêt

ever, the domestic divisions Genêt had helped to widen were perpetuated by the Democratic-Republican societies.

Americans sympathetic to the French Revolution and worried about trends in the Washington administration formed forty of these Democratic-Republican societies between 1793 and 1800. Their members saw themselves as the heirs of the Sons of Liberty, seeking the same goal as their predecessors: protection of the people's liberties against encroachment by corrupt and evil rulers. Like the Sons of Liberty, the Democratic-Republican societies were composed chiefly of artisans and craftsmen of various kinds, although professionals, farmers, and merchants also joined.

Democratic-Republican Societies

The rapid growth of criticism of the Washington administration deeply disturbed Hamilton and eventually Washington himself. Newspapers sympathetic to the Federalists charged that the societies were subversive agents of a foreign power. The climax of the attack came in the fall of 1794, when Washington accused the societies of having fomented the Whiskey Rebellion.

In retrospect, Washington's and Hamilton's reaction to the Democratic-Republican societies seems hysterical and overwrought. But it must be kept in mind that the Democratic-Republican societies were the first formally organized political dissenters in the United States. As such, they aroused the fear and suspicion of elected officials who had not yet accepted the idea that one component of a free government was an organized loyal opposition.

That same year George Washington decided to send Chief Justice John Jay to England to try to reach agreement on four major unresolved questions affecting Anglo-American affairs. After France declared war on England in 1793, the British had begun to seize American merchant ships trading in the French West Indies. The United States wanted to establish the principle of freedom of the seas and to assert its right, as a neutral nation, to trade freely with both sides. Second, Great Britain had not yet carried out its promise in the Treaty of Paris (1783) to evacuate its posts in the American Northwest. Third and fourth, the Americans hoped for a commercial treaty and sought compensation for the slaves who had left with the British army at the end of the war.

The negotiations in London proved difficult, since Jay had little to offer Britain in exchange for the concessions he wanted. In the end, Britain did agree to evacuate the western forts and ease the restrictions on American trade to England and the West Indies. No compensation for lost slaves was agreed to, but Jay accepted a provision establishing an arbitration commission to deal with the matter of prewar debts owed to British creditors. A similar commission was to handle the question of compensation for the seizures of American merchant ships. Under the circumstances, Jay had done remarkably well: the treaty averted war with England. Nevertheless, most Americans, including the president, were dissatisfied with at least some parts of the treaty.

Jay Treaty

At first, however, potential opposition was blunted, because the Senate debated and ratified the treaty in secret. Not until after it was formally approved in June 1795 was the public informed of its provisions. The Democratic-Republican societies led protests against the treaty.

In March 1796, opponents of the treaty tried in the House of Representatives to prevent approval of the appropriations needed to implement various treaty provisions. To that end, they called on Washington to submit to the House all documents pertinent to the negotiations. In successfully resisting the House's request, Washington established the doctrine of executive privilege—that is, the power of the president to withhold information from Congress if he believes circumstances warrant doing so. At first the treaty's opponents seemed to be in the majority. But the desires of frontier residents to have the British posts evacuated and of merchants to trade with the British Empire weakened their position. Finally, Federalist senators threatened to reject a treaty Thomas Pinckney had negotiated with Spain unless the funds for

Jay's Treaty were approved. Since Pinckney's Treaty had secured American navigation rights on the Mississippi, it was popular with southerners and westerners. For these reasons the House by a 51 to 48 margin voted the necessary funds.

Analysis of the vote reveals both the regional nature of the division and the growing cohesion of the Republican and Federalist factions in Congress. Voting in favor of the appropriations were 44 Federalists and 7 Republicans; voting against were 45 Republicans and 3 Federalists. The vast majority of votes against the bill were cast by southerners. The bill's supporters were largely from New England and the middle states, with the exception of two South Carolina Federalists.

Republicans and Federalists

The growing division cannot be accurately explained in the terms used by Jefferson and Madison (aristocrats versus the people) or by Hamilton and Washington (true patriots versus subversive rabble). Simple economic differences between agrarian and commercial interests do not provide the answer either, since more than 90 percent of Americans in the 1790s lived in rural areas. Yet certain distinctions can be made. Republicans tended to be self-assured, confident optimists who were not fearful of instability and who sought to widen the people's participation in government. Federalists, on the other hand, were insecure, uncertain of the future. They stressed the need for order, authority, and regularity in the political world. Unlike Republicans, they had no grassroots political organization and put little emphasis on involving ordinary people in government. The nation was, in their eyes, perpetually threatened by potential enemies, both internal and external, and best protected by a continuing alliance with Great Britain.

If the factions' respective attitudes are translated into economic and regional affiliations, the pattern is clear. Northern merchants and commercially oriented farmers, well aware of the uncertainties of international trade, tended to be Federalists. Since New England's soil was poor and agricultural production could not be expanded, northern subsistence farmers also gravitated toward the more conservative party, which wanted to preserve the present (and past) rather than look to the future.

Republican southern planters, on the other hand, firmly in control of their region and of a class of enslaved laborers, could anticipate unlimited westward expansion. Many planters had successfully shifted from the cultivation of soil-draining tobacco to grains and other foodstuffs. The invention of the cotton gin in 1793 allowed southerners to plant many more acres of cotton. For their part, small farmers in the South found the Republicans' democratic rhetoric (despite aristocratic leadership) more congenial than the Federalist viewpoint. So too urban artisans, who stressed their role as independent producers of necessary goods, supported the Republican position.

Finally, the two sides drew supporters from different ethnic groups. Americans of English stock tended to be Federalists, while those of Irish or Scots origin were more likely to be Republicans. Another large group, the Germans, was split fairly evenly at first but eventually moved into the Republican camp. To what degree ethnic antagonisms contributed to the growing political split is impossible to say. But it is conceivable that ethnicity was as important as other factors in determining political alignments.

In September 1796, at the end of his second term, Washington published his "Farewell Address," most of which was written by Hamilton. In it Washington outlined two principles that guided American foreign policy until the late 1940s: maintain commercial but not political ties to other nations and enter no permanent alliances. He also attacked the legitimacy of the Republican opposition to his presidency.

The presence of the two organized groups, not yet parties in the modern sense but nonetheless active contenders for office, made the presidential election of 1796 the first that was seriously contested. To succeed Washington, the Federalists put forward the candidacy of Vice President John Adams, with the diplomat Thomas Pinckney of South

Election of 1796

Carolina as his vice-presidential running mate. The Republicans in Congress chose Thomas Jefferson as their candidate; the lawyer, revolutionary war veteran, and active Republican politician Aaron Burr of New York agreed to run for vice president.

That the election was contested did not mean that its outcome was decided by the people. Under the Constitution, electors, not the people, voted. Though in most cases the people chose their electors, over 40 percent of the electors were selected by state legislatures. The system provided that each elector would cast two votes. The man receiving the highest vote total became the president; the second highest became vice president. Thus Adams, the Federalist with 71 votes, became the new president and Jefferson, the Republican with 68 votes, became vice president.

JOHN ADAMS AND POLITICAL DISSENT

John Adams took over the presidency peculiarly blind to the partisan developments of the previous four years. As president he never abandoned the outdated notion George Washington had discarded as early as 1794: that the president should be above politics, an independent and dignified figure who did not seek petty factional advantage. Thus Adams kept Washington's cabinet intact, despite its key members' allegiance to his chief rival, Alexander Hamilton. He often adopted a passive posture, letting others (usually Hamilton) take the lead, when he should have acted decisively. When Adams's term ended, the Federalists were severely divided and the Republicans had won the presidency. But at the same time Adams's detachment from Hamilton's maneuverings enabled him to weather the greatest international crisis

the republic had yet faced: the so-called Quasi-War with France.

The Jay Treaty improved America's relationship with England, but it provoked retaliation from France. When French vessels began seizing American ships carrying British goods, Adams sent three special commissioners to France to reach a settlement: Elbridge Gerry of Massachusetts, John Marshall of Virginia, and Charles Cotesworth Pinckney of South Carolina. At the same time Congress increased military spending. The negotiations never materialized, however, because of a French precondition that a $250,000 bribe had to be paid before talks could begin. Upon receiving word of the French demand, Adams informed Congress of the impasse and recommended further appropriations for the military.

XYZ Affair

Convinced that Adams had deliberately sabotaged the negotiations, congressional Republicans insisted that the dispatches be turned over to Congress. Aware that releasing the reports would work to his advantage, Adams complied. He withheld only the names of the French agents, referring to them as X, Y, and Z. The revelation that the Americans had been treated with utter contempt stimulated a wave of anti-French sentiment in the United States. Cries for war filled the air. Congress formally abrogated the 1778 treaty and authorized American ships to seize French vessels.

Thus began the United States's first undeclared war. The Quasi-War with France was fought in the West Indies, between French privateers seeking to capture American merchant vessels and warships of the United States Navy. Although initial American losses of merchant shipping were heavy, by early 1799 the navy had established its superiority in Caribbean waters. Its ships captured a total of eight French privateers and naval vessels, easing the threat to America's vital West Indian trade.

The Republicans, who opposed war and continued to sympathize with France, could do little to stem the tide of anti-French feelings. The Federalists saw this climate of opinion as an opportunity to deal a death blow to their Republican opponents. Now that the country seemed to see the truth of what they had been saying ever since the Whiskey Rebellion in 1794—that the Republicans were subversive foreign agents—the Federalists sought to codify that belief into law. In the spring and summer of 1798, the Federalist-controlled Congress adopted a set of four laws known as the Alien and Sedition Acts, intended to suppress dissent and prevent further growth of the Republican party.

Three of the acts were aimed at immigrants, whom the Federalists quite correctly suspected of being Republican in their sympathies. The Naturalization Act

Alien and Sedition Acts

lengthened the residency period required for citizenship from five to fourteen years and ordered all resident aliens to register with the federal government. The Alien Enemies Act provided for the detention of enemy aliens in time of war. The Alien Friends Act, which was to be in effect for only two years, gave the president almost unlimited authority to deport any alien he deemed dangerous to the nation's security. (Adams never used that authority. The Alien Enemies Act was not implemented either, since war was never formally declared.)

The fourth law, the Sedition Act, sought to control both citizens and aliens. It outlawed conspiracies to prevent the enforcement of federal laws and set the maximum punishment for such offenses at five years in prison and a $5,000 fine. The act also tried to control speech. Writing, printing, or uttering "false, scandalous and malicious" statements "against the government of the United States, or the President of the United States," became a crime punishable by as much as two years imprisonment and a fine of $2,000.

In all, there were fifteen indictments and ten convictions under the Sedition Act. Most of the accused were outspoken Republican newspaper editors who failed to mute their criticism of the administration in response to the law. But the first victim—whose story may serve as an example of the rest—was a Republican congressman from Vermont, Matthew Lyon. The

congressman received a $1,000 fine and a four-month prison sentence for declaring in print that John Adams had "an unbounded thirst for ridiculous pomp, foolish adulation, and selfish avarice."

Faced with the prosecutions of their major supporters, Jefferson and Madison sought an effective means of combating the Alien and Sedition Acts.

Virginia and Kentucky Resolutions

They turned to constitutional theory and the state legislatures. Carefully concealing their own role, Jefferson and Madison each drafted a set of resolutions. Introduced into the Kentucky and Virginia legislatures respectively in the fall of 1798, the resolutions differed somewhat but their import was the same. Since the Constitution was created by a compact among the states, they contended, the people speaking through their states had a legitimate right to judge the constitutionality of actions by the federal government. Both sets of resolutions pronounced the Alien and Sedition Acts null and void and asked other states to join in the protest.

Although no other state replied positively to the Virginia and Kentucky resolutions, they nevertheless had major significance. In the first place, they were superb political propaganda, rallying Republican opinion throughout the country. They placed the opposition party squarely in the revolutionary tradition of resistance to tyrannical authority. Second, the theory of union they proposed was expanded on by southern states'-rights advocates in the 1830s and thereafter.

Adams's decision not to seek a declaration of war against France had, in the meantime, split the Federalists, for Hamilton wanted a declared war. When the French government privately indicated that it regretted the earlier treatment of the three commissioners, Adams dispatched an envoy to Paris. The United States asked two things of France: nearly $20 million in compensation for ships the French had seized since 1793, and abrogation of the Treaty of 1778. The Convention of 1800, which ended the Quasi-War, included the latter but not the former. But the results of the negotiations were not known until after the

Matthew Lyon, the congressman convicted of violating the Sedition Act, had a fiery temper. In January 1798, before his arrest and trial, he engaged in this brawl with a congressman from Connecticut in the chamber of the House of Representatives.   Library of Congress.

election of 1800, and by then the split in the Federalist ranks had already cost Adams his re-election.

The Republicans entered the 1800 presidential race firmly united behind the Jefferson-Burr ticket. Though they won the election, their lack of foresight almost cost them dearly. The problem was caused by the system of voting in the electoral college. All Republican electors voted for both

Election of 1800

Jefferson and Burr, giving each of them 73 votes (Adams had 65). Because neither Republican had a plurality, the Constitution required that the contest be decided in the House of Representatives, with each state's congressmen voting as a unit. In the House, Federalist congressmen decided the election by selecting Jefferson on the thirty-fifth ballot. As a result of the tangle, the Twelfth Amendment to the Constitution (1804) changed the method of voting in the electoral college to allow for a party ticket.

WESTWARD EXPANSION, SOCIAL CHANGE, AND RELIGIOUS FERMENT

In the postrevolutionary years, the United States experienced a dramatic increase in internal migration. As much as 5 to 10 percent of the population moved each year, half of them relocating in another state. Young white men were the most mobile segment of the populace. The major population shifts were from east to west: from New England to upstate New York, from New Jersey to western Pennsylvania, from the Chesapeake to the new states of Kentucky and Tennessee, which entered the union in 1792 and 1796, respectively. Very few people moved north or south.

The first permanent white settlements beyond the mountains were established in western North Carolina in 1771. But not until after the American Revolution and the defeat of the Shaw-

White Settlement in the West

nee and the Cherokee in 1774 and 1776 did significant numbers of settlers move west of the mountains and south of the Ohio River. By 1790 more than 100,000 people lived in the future states of Tennessee and Kentucky. North of the Ohio River, white settlements grew more slowly because of the strength of the Miami confederacy. But once the Treaty of Greenville was signed in 1795, Ohio too grew rapidly.

The westward migration of slaveholding whites, first to Kentucky and Tennessee and then later into the rich lands of western Georgia and eventually the Gulf Coast, tore apart the web of

Blacks in the West

family connections blacks had built up over several generations of residence in the Chesapeake. Even those few large planters who moved their entire slave force west could not have owned all the members of

very family on their plantations. Far more commonly the white migrants were younger sons of eastern slaveholders, whose inheritance included only a portion of the family's slaves, or small farmers who owned just one or two blacks. In the early years of American settlement in the West, the population was widely dispersed; accordingly, Chesapeake blacks who had been raised in the midst of large numbers of kin had to adapt to lonely lives on isolated farms. The approximately 100,000 Afro-Americans forcibly moved west by 1810 had to begin to build new families there to replace those unwillingly left behind in the East.

The mobility of both blacks and whites created a volatile population mix in frontier areas. Since most of the migrants were young single men just starting to lead independent lives, western society was at first unstable. Like the seventeenth-century Chesapeake, the late-eighteenth-century American West was a society in which single women married quickly. The other side of the same coin was that the few women among the migrants lamented their lack of congenial female friends. Isolated, far from familiar surroundings, women and men both strove to create new communities to replace those they had left behind.

Perhaps the most meaningful of the new communities was that supplied by evangelical religion. Among the migrants to Kentucky and Tennessee were clergymen and committed lay

Second Great Awakening

members of the evangelical sects that arose in America after the First Great Awakening: Baptists, Presbyterians, and Methodists. At camp meetings, sometimes attended by thousands of people and usually lasting from three days to a week, clergymen exhorted their audiences to repent their sins and become genuine Christians. They stressed that salvation was open to all, downplaying the doctrine of predestination that had characterized orthodox colonial Protestantism. The emotional nature of the conversion experience was emphasized far more than the need for careful study and preparation. Such preachers thus brought the message of religion to the people in more ways than one. They were in effect "democratizing"

American religion, making it available to all rather than to a preselected and educated elite.

The sources of the Second Great Awakening, which revitalized Protestant Christianity in the United States during the nineteenth century, were embedded in late-eighteenth-century American society in the East as well as the West. From the 1760s through the 1780s, religious concerns had been subordinated to secular affairs. Indeed, clerics had created a kind of "civil religion" for the nation, in which the fervor of the veneration for the republic sometimes surpassed the fervor of religious worship. Moreover, the orthodox churches, showing the influence of Enlightenment thought, had for decades stressed reason more than revelation. Circumstances were thus ripe for a movement of spiritual renewal that would appeal to the emotional side of people's natures.

In addition, America's largest Protestant denominations had to find new sources of financial and membership support after the Revolution. In the colonial period, most of the provinces had had established, or state-supported, churches. Many states dissolved their ties to churches during or immediately after the war, and others vastly reduced state support for established denominations.

Disestablishment of Religion

These changes meant that congregations could no longer rely on tax revenues and that all churches were placed on the same footing with respect to the government. Church membership was now entirely voluntary, as were monetary contributions from members. If congregations were to survive, they had to generate new sources of support, by increasing their number of enthusiastic members; revivals proved a convenient means of doing so. The revivals represented genuine outpourings of religious sentiment, but their more mundane function must not be overlooked.

An analysis of secular society can help to explain the conversion patterns of the Second Awakening. Unlike the First Great Awakening, when con-

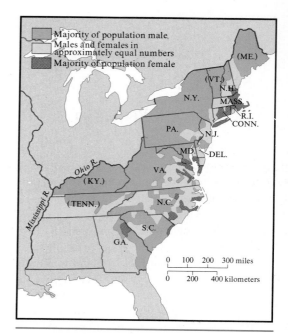

Sex Ratio of White Population, 1790

Women and the Second Awakening

verts were evenly divided by sex, more women than men—particularly young women—answered the call of Christianity during the Second Awakening. The increase in female converts seems to have been directly related to major changes in women's circumstances at the end of the eighteenth century. In some areas of the country, especially New England, women outnumbered men after 1790 (see map). Thus eastern girls could no longer count on finding marital partners. The uncertainty of their social and familial position seems to have led them to seek spiritual certainty in the church. And in these churches they formed innumerable female associations to dispense charity to widows and orphans or to support foreign missions.

The religious ferment among both blacks and whites in frontier regions of the Upper South contributed to racial ferment as well. People of both races attended the camp meetings, and sometimes black preachers exhorted whites in addition to

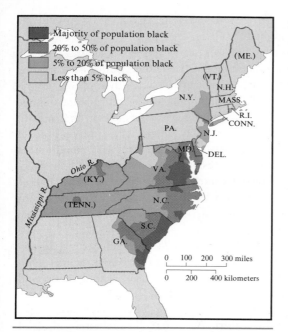

Black Population, 1790: Proportion of Total Population Source: Lester J. Cappon, et al., eds., *Atlas of Early American History: The Revolutionary Era 1760–1790.* Copyright © 1976 by Princeton University Press.

members of their own race. When revivals spread eastward into more heavily slaveholding areas (see map), white planters became fearful of the egalitarianism implied in the evangelical message of universal salvation and harmony. At the same time, revivals created a group of respected black leaders—preachers—and provided them with a ready audience.

Blacks and the Second Awakening

Recent events in the West Indies gave whites ample reason for apprehension. In the 1790s, mulattoes and blacks in the French colony of Saint Domingue (Haiti) overthrew European rule under the leadership of a mulatto, Toussaint L'Ouverture. In an attempt to prevent the spread of such unrest to their own slaves, southern state legislators passed laws forbidding white Haitian refugees from bringing their slaves with them. But North American blacks learned about the revolt anyway. Furthermore, the preconditions for racial upheaval already existed in the South.

In Virginia a revolt was planned by Gabriel Prosser, a blacksmith who argued that blacks should fight to obtain the same rights as whites, and who explicitly placed himself in the tradition not only of the French Revolution but also in that of the successful slave rebellion on Haiti. At revival meetings led by his brother Martin, a preacher, Gabriel recruited other blacks like himself—artisans who moved easily in both black and white circles and who lived in semifreedom under minimal white supervision. The artisan leaders then enlisted rural blacks in the cause. The conspirators planned to attack Richmond on the night of August 30, 1800, setting fire to the city, seizing the state capitol, and capturing the governor. Their plan showed considerable political sophistication, but heavy rain made it impossible to execute the plot as scheduled. Several whites then learned of the plan from their slaves and spread the alarm. Gabriel avoided capture for some weeks, but most of the other leaders of the rebellion were quickly arrested and interrogated. The major conspirators, including Prosser himself, were hanged, but in the months that followed, other insurrectionary scares continued to frighten Virginia slaveowners.

Gabriel's Rebellion

Significantly, the Iroquois were affected by a religious revival at the same time as American whites and blacks were experiencing the Second Great Awakening. Led by their prophet, Handsome Lake, the remaining American Iroquois, who were scattered on small reservations, embraced the traditional values of their culture and renounced such destructive white customs as drinking alcohol and playing cards. At the same time, though, they began abandoning their ancient way of life. With Handsome Lake's approval, Quaker missionaries taught the Iroquois Anglo-American styles of agricultural subsistence; men were now to be cultivators rather than hunters and women housekeepers rather than cultivators. Since the tribes had lost their hunting territories to

IMPORTANT EVENTS

1789	George Washington inaugurated
	Judiciary Act of 1789
	French Revolution begins
1790	Alexander Hamilton's first "Report on Public Credit"
1791	First ten amendments (Bill of Rights) ratified
1793	France declares war on Britain, Spain, and Holland
	Democratic-Republican societies founded
1794	Whiskey Rebellion
1795	Jay Treaty
1796	First contested presidential election: John Adams elected president, Thomas Jefferson vice president
1798	XYZ affair
	Alien and Sedition Acts
	Virginia and Kentucky resolutions
1798–99	Quasi-War with France
1800	Franco-American Convention
	Jefferson elected president, Aaron Burr vice president
	Second Great Awakening begins
	Gabriel's Rebellion

the changes too vigorously, and eventually he triumphed.

As the new century began, then, white, red, and black inhabitants of the United States were moving toward an accommodation to their new circumstances. The United States was starting to take shape as a free nation no longer dependent on England. In domestic politics, the Jeffersonian interpretation of republicanism had prevailed over the Hamiltonian approach. As a result, the country would be characterized by a decentralized economy, minimal government (especially at the national level), and maximum freedom of action and mobility for individual white males.

But that freedom would be purchased at the expense of white females and black men, women, and children. In the decades to come, both groups would be subject to further control. Within a few years after the establishment of the republic, women and blacks had little realistic hope that the egalitarian ideals of the Declaration of Independence would apply to them. And a pattern was set that would deny Indians not only their rights but also their land.

SUGGESTIONS FOR FURTHER READING

National Government and Administration

Ralph Adams Brown, *The Presidency of John Adams* (1975); Forrest McDonald, *Alexander Hamilton* (1979); Forrest McDonald, *The Presidency of George Washington* (1974); John C. Miller, *The Federalist Era, 1789–1801* (1960); Merrill D. Peterson, *Thomas Jefferson & The New Nation* (1970); Garry Wills, *Cincinnatus: George Washington and the Enlightenment* (1984).

Partisan Politics

Lance Banning, *The Jeffersonian Persuasion* (1978); Richard W. Buel, *Securing the Revolution* (1972); William Nisbet

white farmers, Iroquois men accepted the changes readily. But many women—especially the powerful tribal matrons—resisted the shift in the gender division of labor. They realized that when they surrendered control over food production they would jeopardize their status in the tribe. But Handsome Lake branded as "witches" any women who opposed

Chambers, *Political Parties in a New Nation* (1963); Joseph Charles, *The Origins of the American Party System* (1956); Richard Hofstadter, *The Idea of a Party System* (1970); Adrienne Koch, *Jefferson and Madison: The Great Collaboration* (1950); John R. Nelson, Jr., *Liberty and Property* (1987); Thomas J. Slaughter, *The Whiskey Rebellion* (1986); John Zvesper, *Political Philosophy and Rhetoric: A Study of the Origins of American Party Politics* (1977).

Foreign Policy

Jerald A. Combs, *The Jay Treaty* (1970); Alexander DeConde, *Entangling Alliance* (1958); Alexander DeConde, *The Quasi-War* (1966); Felix Gilbert, *To the Farewell Address* (1961); Reginald Horsman, *The Diplomacy of the New Republic, 1776–1815* (1985); William Stinchcombe, *The XYZ Affair* (1981); Paul A. Varg, *Foreign Policies of the Founding Fathers* (1963).

Civil Liberties

Leonard W. Levy, *Emergence of a Free Press* (1987); Leonard W. Levy, *Origins of the Fifth Amendment* (1968); Robert A. Rutland, *The Birth of the Bill of Rights, 1776–1791* (1955); James Morton Smith, *Freedom's Fetters* (1956).

Women and Blacks

Ira Berlin and Ronald Hoffman, eds., *Slavery and Freedom in the Age of the American Revolution* (1983); Mary H. Blewett, "Work, Gender, and the Artisan Tradition in New England Shoemaking, 1780–1860," *Journal of Social History*, 17 (1983), 221–248; Nancy F. Cott, *The Bonds of Womanhood* (1977); Gerald W. Mullin, *Flight and Rebellion: Slave Resistance in Eighteenth-Century Virginia* (1972).

Social Change and Westward Expansion

Howard Rock, *Artisans of the New Republic* (1979); Malcolm Rohrbough, *The Trans-Appalachian Frontier* (1979); W. J. Rorabaugh, *The Alcoholic Republic* (1979); Charles G. Steffen, *The Mechanics of Baltimore* (1984); Sean Wilentz, *Chants Democratic* (1984).

Religion

Catharine Albanese, *Sons of the Fathers* (1976); Fred J. Hood, *Reformed America 1783–1837* (1980); William McLoughlin, *Revivals, Awakenings, and Reform* (1978).

CHAPTER 8

THE EMPIRE OF LIBERTY
1801–1824

"*I have this* morning witnessed one of the most interesting scenes a free people can ever witness," Margaret B. Smith, a Philadelphian, wrote on March 4, 1801, to her sister-in-law. "The changes of administration, which in every government and in every age have most generally been epochs of confusion, villainy and bloodshed, in this our happy country take place without any species of distraction, or disorder." On that day, Thomas Jefferson strolled from his New Jersey Avenue boardinghouse in the new federal capital of Washington, D.C., to be sworn in as president at the Capitol building. The precedent of an orderly and peaceful change of government had been established.

Jefferson's inauguration marked a change of style in government. Almost overnight the formality of the Federalist presidencies of Washington and Adams was significantly altered as Jefferson set the tone for the Republican government. Jefferson abandoned the aristocratic garb of his predecessors, and ordinary folk converged on the federal district at Washington to celebrate the Republican victory.

The district, carved out of Maryland and Virginia, had been chosen because of its central location. Washington was thus beholden to neither the colonial past nor any single state. Few buildings were needed to house the government, which essentially collected tariffs, delivered mail, and defended the nation's borders. But a small government suited the republic. Even for the Federalists, the adoption of the Constitution had been more a result of dissatisfaction with the Articles of Confederation than a sign of their confidence in central government. The election of the Republican Thomas Jefferson in 1800 began the Virginia dynasty and a swing back to state authority that lasted until 1825. In an age when it took some congressmen more than a week to reach the capital, most Americans favored government closer to home.

The transfer of power to the Republicans from the

Federalists intensified political conflict and voter interest. Republican presidents sought to limit government and decentralize authority. Federalists prized a stronger national government with more order and authority in a centralized system. With both parties competing for adherents and popular support, the basis was laid for the evolution of democratic party politics. But factionalism and the partisanship of personal disputes within each party prevented the development of true political parties.

Events abroad both encouraged and threatened the expansionism of the young nation. Seizing one opportunity, the United States purchased the Louisiana Territory, pushing the frontier farther west. But then from the high seas came war. Caught between the British and the French, the United States found itself a victim of European conflict with its shipping rights as a neutral, independent nation ignored and violated. When the humiliation became too great, Americans took up arms in the War of 1812 both to defend their rights as a nation and to expand farther to the west and north.

The War of 1812 unleashed a wave of nationalism and self-confidence. The disruption of trade with Europe during the war promoted the development of manufacturing in the United States. The war also pointed up the need for better transportation within the country. Following the war, the government became the champion of business and promoted the building of roads and canals. The new spirit encouraged economic growth and western expansion at home and assertiveness throughout the hemisphere, as was evident in the Monroe Doctrine. By the 1820s the United States was no longer an experiment; a new nation had emerged.

Trumbull's formal portrait of Thomas Jefferson. Increasingly Jefferson preferred plainer garb. At his inaugural he was simply dressed as he spoke to his fellow citizens of republican virtue and reconciliation.   The Metropolitan Museum of Art, Bequest of Cornelia Cruger, 1923. (24.19.1.)

JEFFERSON IN POWER

Jefferson delivered his inaugural address in the Senate chamber, the only part of the Capitol that had been completed. "We are all Republicans, we are all Federalists," he told the assembly in an appeal for unity. Confidently addressing those with little faith in the people's ability to govern themselves, he called America's republican government "the world's best hope."

Jefferson's Inaugural Address

The new president went on to outline his own and his party's republican goals:

A wise and frugal government, which shall restrain men from injuring one another, which shall leave them otherwise free to regulate their own pursuits. . . .

Equal and exact justice to all men, of whatever state or persuasion, religious or political. . . .

The support of the state governments in all their rights, as the most competent administrators for our domestic concerns and the surest bulwarks against antirepublican tendencies.

At the same time, he assured Federalists that he shared some of their concerns as well:

The preservation of the general government in its whole constitutional vigor. . . .

The honest payment of our debts and sacred preservation of the public faith. . . .

Encouragement of agriculture and of commerce as its handmaid.

Yet Jefferson and his fellow Republicans distrusted the Federalists. They considered them to be antidemocratic and antirepublican at heart. One of Jefferson's first acts was to extend the grasp of Republicanism over the federal government. Virtually all appointed officials were loyal Federalists. To counteract Federalist power, Jefferson refused to recognize Adams's last-minute "midnight appointments" to local offices in the District of Columbia. Next he dismissed Federalist customs collectors from New England ports. Vacant treasury and judicial offices were awarded to Republicans, until by July 1803 only 130 of 316 presidentially controlled offices were held by Federalists. Jefferson, in restoring political balance in government, used patronage to reward his friends, to build a party organization, and to compete with the Federalists.

The Republican Congress similarly proceeded to affirm its republicanism. Guided by Secretary of the Treasury Albert Gallatin and John Randolph of Virginia, Jefferson's ally in the House, the federal government went on a diet. Congress repealed all internal taxes, even the whiskey tax. Gallatin cut the army budget in half, to just under $2 million, and reduced the navy budget from $3.5 to $1 million in 1802. Moreover, Gallatin laid plans to reduce the national debt—Alexander Hamilton's engine of economic growth—from $83 to $57 million, as part of a plan to retire it altogether by 1817.

More than frugality, however, separated Republicans from Federalists. Opposition to the Alien and Sedition laws of 1798 had helped united Republicans. Now Congress let them expire in 1801 and 1802 and repealed the Naturalization Act of 1798. The 1802 act that replaced it required only five years of residency, acceptance of the Constitution, and the forsaking of foreign allegiance and titles.

The Republicans turned next to the judiciary, the last stronghold of unchecked Federalist power. During the 1790s not a single Republican had been appointed to the federal bench. Moreover, the Judiciary Act of 1801, passed in the last days of the Adams administration, had created fifteen new judgeships (which Adams filled in his midnight appointments, made when his term was just hours away from expiring) and would reduce by attrition the number of justices on the Supreme Court from six to five. Since that reduction would have denied Jefferson any Supreme Court appointments until two vacancies had occurred, the new Republican-dominated Congress repealed the 1801 act as one of its first moves.

Attacks on the Judiciary

Republicans also targeted opposition judges for removal. At Jefferson's suggestion, the House impeached (indicted) Federal District Judge John Pickering of New Hampshire; in 1804 the Senate removed him from office. Although he was an alcoholic and emotionally disturbed, Pickering had not committed any crime.

The same day Pickering was convicted, the House impeached Supreme Court Justice Samuel Chase for judicial misconduct. Chase had repeatedly denounced Jefferson's administration from the bench. The Republicans, however, failed to muster the two-thirds majority necessary to convict him; they had gone too far. Their failure to remove Chase preserved the Court's independence and established a precedent for narrow interpretation of the grounds for impeachment (criminal rather than political). Time soon cured Republican grievances; by the year Jefferson left office, he had appointed three new Supreme Court justices. Nonetheless, under Chief Justice John Marshall, the Court remained a Federalist stronghold.

Marshall, a Virginia Federalist, was an astute lawyer with keen political sense. Under his domination, the Supreme Court retained a Federalist viewpoint even after Republican justices achieved a majority. From 1801 until 1835, the period of Marshall's tenure, the Court upheld federal supremacy over the states and protected the interests of commerce and capital. More important, Marshall made the Court an equal branch of government in practice as well as theory. First, he made a place on the Court a coveted honor. Second, he unified the Court, influencing the justices to issue single majority opinions rather than individual concurring judgments. Marshall himself became the voice of the majority. From 1801 through 1805 he wrote 24 of the Court's 26 decisions.

John Marshall

Finally, Marshall increased the Court's power. *Marbury* v. *Madison* (1803) was the landmark case that enabled Marshall to strengthen the Court. William Marbury had been designated a justice of the peace in the District of Columbia as part of Adams's midnight appointments. He now sued the new secretary of state, James Madison, for failing to certify his appointment so that Jefferson could appoint a Republican. In his suit Marbury requested a writ of mandamus (a court order compelling Madison to appoint him).

Marbury v. *Madison*

At first glance, the case presented a political dilemma. Even if the Supreme Court ruled in favor of Marbury and issued a writ of mandamus, the president might not comply. On the other hand, if the Court refused to issue the writ, it would be handing the Republicans a victory. Marshall avoided both alternatives. Speaking for the Court, he ruled that Marbury had a right to his commission but that the Court could not compel Madison to honor it, because the Constitution did not grant the Court power to issue a writ of mandamus. Thus Marshall declared unconstitutional Section 13 of the Judiciary Act of 1789, which authorized the Court to issue such writs. Marbury lost his job and the justices denied themselves the power to issue writs of mandamus, but the Supreme Court claimed its power to judge the constitutionality of laws passed by Congress.

In succeeding years Marshall fashioned the theory of judicial review. Since the Constitution was the supreme law, he reasoned, any act of Congress contrary to the Constitution must be null and void. And since the Supreme Court was responsible for upholding the law, it had a duty to decide whether or not a conflict existed between a legislative act and the Constitution. If such a conflict did indeed exist, the Court would declare the congressional act unconstitutional.

Marshall's decision rebuffed Republican criticism of the Court as a partisan instrument. He avoided a confrontation with the Republican-dominated Congress by not ruling on its repeal of the 1801 Judiciary Act. And he enhanced the Court's independence by claiming the power of judicial review.

While President Jefferson fought with the Federalist judiciary and struggled to reduce federal spending, Americans continued to trek into the Ohio and Mississippi valleys. Western settlers—and there were hundreds of thousands of them by 1800—were dependent upon the Ohio and Mississippi rivers to get their products to New Orleans for export. The port city, however, was part of Spain's Louisiana Territory. As long as Spain owned Louisiana, Americans did not fear. But in 1802 Napoleonic France acquired the vast territory in an ambitious bid to rebuild its empire in the New World. On the eve of ceding control to the French, Spain violated Pinckney's Treaty by denying Americans the privilege of storing their products at New Orleans prior to transshipment to foreign markets. Western farmers and eastern merchants thought a devious Napoleon had closed the port; they grumbled and talked war.

Louisiana Purchase

To relieve the pressure for war and to prevent westerners from joining Federalists in opposition to his administration, Jefferson simultaneously prepared for war and accelerated talks with the French. In January

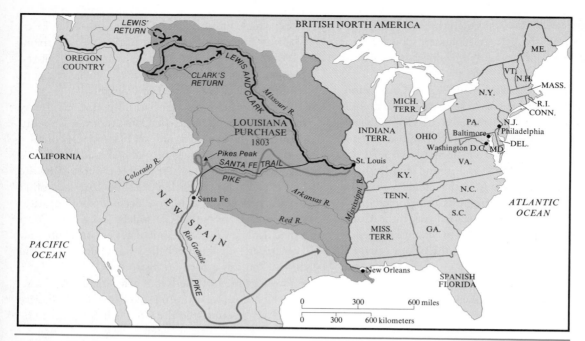

Louisiana Purchase

1803 he sent James Monroe to France to help the American minister Robert Livingston in negotiating to buy New Orleans. Meanwhile, Congress authorized a call-up of eighty thousand militia if it proved necessary. Arriving in Paris in April, Monroe was astonished to learn that France had already offered to sell all 827,000 square miles of Louisiana to the United States for $15 million. On April 30 Monroe and Livingston signed a treaty to purchase the vast territory, whose borders were left undefined at that time (see map).

The Louisiana Purchase doubled the size of the nation and opened the way for westward expansion across the continent. The acquisition was the single most popular achievement of Jefferson's presidency. But its legality was questionable. The Constitution gave him no clear authority to acquire new territory and incorporate it into the nation. Jefferson considered requesting a constitutional amendment to allow the purchase, but in the end he justified it on the grounds that it was part of the president's implied powers to protect the nation. The people, he knew, would accept or reject the purchase on election day in 1804.

The president had had a long-standing interest in Louisiana and the West. As secretary of state he had commissioned a French émigré, André Michaux, to explore the Missouri River. Allegations of Michaux's complicity in the Genêt Affair aborted this mission. In 1803 Jefferson renewed Michaux's instructions when he sent Meriwether Lewis and William Clark to the Pacific Ocean via the Missouri and Columbia rivers. Lewis and Clark, from 1804 to 1806, headed the nearly fifty-strong "Corps of Discovery," which was aided by trappers and American Indians along the way.

Lewis and Clark

The Lewis and Clark expedition, planned in secrecy before the Louisiana Purchase, reflected both Jefferson's scientific curiosity and his interest in western commercial development. Other explorers soon followed them, led in 1805 and 1806 by Lieutenant Zebulon Pike in search of the source of the Mississippi. A year later Pike attempted to find a navigable path to the Far West and sought the headwaters of the Arkansas River. He reached the Rocky Mountains in present-day Colorado and wandered into Spanish territory to the south, where he was arrested by the Spanish and held captive for several months in Santa Fe. After his release, Pike wrote an account of his experiences that set commercial minds spinning. He described a potential commercial market in southwestern Spanish cities as well as the bounty of furs and precious minerals to be had. The vision of the road to the Southwest became a reality with the opening of the Santa Fe Trail in the 1820s.

REPUBLICANS VERSUS FEDERALISTS

Campaigning for re-election in 1804, Jefferson claimed credit for western expansion and the restoration of republican values. He had removed the

1804 Election

Federalist threat to liberty by allowing the Alien and Sedition and Judiciary Acts to expire. At the same time he had reduced the size and cost of government by cutting spending. And despite his opponents' charges, he proved that Republicans supported commerce. Charles Cotesworth Pinckney, a wealthy South Carolina lawyer and former Revolutionary War aide to General George Washington, carried the opposition standard. Jefferson and his running mate, George Clinton of New York, swamped Pinckney and Rufus King in the electoral college by 162 votes to 14, carrying fifteen of the seventeen states.

Jefferson's re-election was both a personal and a party triumph. The political dissenters of the 1790s had turned their Democratic-Republican societies into a political party—an organization for the purpose of winning elections. More than anything else, opposition to the Federalists had molded and uni-

fied them. Indeed, it was where the Federalists were strongest that the Republicans had organized most effectively.

Until the Republican successes in 1800 and 1804, Federalists had disdained popular campaigning. They believed in government by the "best" people—those whose education, wealth, and experience marked them as leaders. For candidates to debate their qualifications before their inferiors—the voters—was unnecessary and undignified. The direct appeals of the Republicans therefore struck them as a subversion of the natural political order.

But after their resounding defeat in 1800, a younger generation of Federalists began to imitate the Republicans. They organized statewide and, led by

Younger Federalists

men like Josiah Quincy, a young congressman from Massachusetts, began to campaign for popular support. Quincy cleverly identified the Federalists as the people's party, attacking Republicans as autocratic planters. In attacking frugal government, the self-styled Younger Federalists played on fears of a weakened army and navy. Merchants depended on a strong navy to protect ocean trade while westerners, encroaching on Indian tribes, looked for federal support.

In the states where both parties organized and ran candidates, participation in elections increased markedly. People became more interested in politics generally, especially at the local level; and as participation in elections increased, the states expanded suffrage. Nevertheless, the popular base of the parties was still restricted. Property qualifications for voting and holding office remained common and in six states the legislatures still selected presidential electors in 1804.

In response to the new competition, the Republicans introduced the political barbecue, which became the symbol of grassroots campaigning. Soon both parties were using barbecues to appeal directly to voters. Holidays became occasions for partying and electioneering, a practice that helped to make the Fourth of July a day of national celebration and local oratory.

Citizens gather at the State House in Philadelphia to whip up support for their candidates and parties. This picture, drawn on Election Day in 1816, suggests the overwhelming white, exclusively male composition of the electorate.   Library of Congress.

Older Federalists still opposed such blatant campaigns. And although they were strong in a few states like Connecticut and Delaware, the Federalists never offered the Republicans sustained competition. Divisions between Older and Younger Federalists often hindered them, and the extremism of some Older Federalists tended to discredit the party. A case in point was Timothy Pickering, a Massachusetts congressman who urged the secession of New England in 1803 and 1804. Pickering won some support among the few Federalists in Congress, but others opposed his plan for a northern confederacy. When Vice Pres-

ident Burr lost his bid to become governor of New York in 1804, the plan collapsed. (Burr, more an opportunist than a loyal Republican, was to have led New York into secession, with the other states to follow.)

Both political parties suffered from factionalism. In 1804, for instance, the Federalist Alexander Hamilton backed a rival Republican faction against Burr in his race for the governorship of New York; Hamilton had caught wind of the Pickering-Burr conspiracy. Burr, his political career in

Hamilton-Burr Duel

ruins, turned his resentment on Hamilton and challenged him to a duel. Hamilton accepted the challenge and was killed.

The Burr-Hamilton conflict highlights some of the limitations of the early party system. Personal animosities often prompted the crossing of party lines and the appearance of new, temporary factions. Moreover, although politicians appealed for voter support and participation in politics broadened, the electoral base remained narrow. As the election of 1804 revealed, the Federalists could offer only weak competition at the national level. And where Federalists were too weak to be a threat, Republicans succumbed to the temptation to fight among themselves.

Thus, although this period is commonly called the era of the first party system, parties as such never fully developed. Competition encouraged party organization, but personal ambition, personality clashes, and local, state, and regional loyalties worked against it. Increasingly, external events intruded, and these would occupy most of Jefferson's time in his second administration.

PRESERVING AMERICAN NEUTRALITY IN A WORLD AT WAR

"Peace, commerce, and honest friendship with all nations, entangling alliance with none," President Jefferson had sensibly proclaimed in his first inaugural address. And Jefferson's efforts to stand clear of European conflict worked until 1805. Indeed, for two years after the renewal of the Napoleonic Wars in May 1803, American commerce actually benefited from the conflict. As the world's largest neutral carrier, the United States became the chief supplier of food to Europe. American merchants also gained control of most of the West Indian trade, which was often transshipped through American ports to Europe.

Meanwhile, the United States victory over Tripolitan pirates on the north coast of Africa (the Barbary states) provided Jefferson with his one clear success in protecting American trading rights. In 1801 Jefferson had refused the demands of the Sultan of Tripoli for payment of tribute. Instead he sent a naval squadron to the Mediterranean to protect American merchant ships from Barbary Coast pirates. The United States signed a peace treaty with Tripoli in 1805, but continued to pay tribute to other Barbary states.

That same year American merchants became victims of Anglo-French enmity. First Britain tightened its control over the high seas with its victory over the French and Spanish fleets at the Battle of Trafalgar in October 1805. Two months later Napoleon defeated the Russian and Austrian armies at Austerlitz. Stalemated, the two powers waged commercial war, blockading and counterblockading each other's trade. As a trading partner of both countries, the United States paid a high price.

The British navy at the same time stepped up impressments of American sailors. Britain, whose navy was the world's largest, was suffering a severe shortage of sailors. Few enlisted, and those already in service frequently deserted. The Royal Navy resorted to stopping American ships and forcibly removing British deserters, British-born naturalized American seamen, and other unlucky sailors mistakenly suspected of being British. Approximately six to eight thousand Americans were drafted in this manner between 1803 and 1812.

In February 1806 the Senate denounced British impressment as aggression and a violation of neutral rights. To protest the insult Congress passed the Non-Importation Act, prohibiting importation from Great Britain of a long list of cloth and metal articles. In November Jefferson suspended the act temporarily while William Pinckney, a leading Baltimore lawyer, joined James Monroe in London in an attempt to negotiate a settlement. But the treaty Monroe and

Pinckney carried home violated their instructions—it did not mention impressment—and Jefferson never submitted it to the Senate for ratification.

Less than a year later the *Chesapeake* Affair exposed American military weakness. In June 1807 the forty-gun frigate U.S.S. *Chesapeake* left Norfolk, Virginia.

Chesapeake Affair

About ten miles out, still inside American territorial waters, it met the fifty-gun British frigate *Leopard*. When the *Chesapeake* refused to be searched for deserters, the *Leopard* repeatedly emptied its guns broadside into the American ship. Three Americans were killed and eighteen wounded. Four sailors were impressed—three of them American citizens, all of them deserters from the Royal Navy. Damaged, the *Chesapeake* crept back into port. President Jefferson responded by strengthening the military and putting economic pressure on Great Britain: in July Jefferson closed American waters to British warships to prevent similar incidents and soon thereafter he increased military and naval expenditures. On December 14, 1807, Jefferson again invoked the Non-Importation Act, followed eight days later by a new measure, the Embargo Act.

Intended as a short-term measure, the Embargo Act forbade virtually all exports from the United States to any country. Imports came to a halt as well, since foreign ships delivering goods would have to leave American ports with empty holds. Smuggling blossomed overnight.

Embargo Act

Few American policies were as well intentioned but as unpopular and unsuccessful as Jefferson's embargo. The lucrative American merchant trade collapsed; exports fell by 80 percent from 1807 to 1808. Federalist New England felt the brunt of the depression. Ships rotted in harbors and grass grew on wharves; unemployment soared. In the winter of 1808 and 1809, talk of secession spread through New England port cities. Great Britain, in contrast, was only mildly affected by the embargo. Finally, the policy gave the French an excuse to privateer against American ships that had managed to escape the embargo by avoiding American ports. The French argued that such ships must be British ships in disguise, since the embargo barred American ships from the seas.

In the election of 1808, the Republicans faced the Federalists, the embargo, and factional dissent in their own party. Jefferson followed Washington's example, renouncing a third term and supporting James Madison, his secretary of state, as the Republican standard-bearer. Madison and his running mate, George Clinton, defeated the Federalist ticket of Charles C. Pinckney and Rufus King.

As for the embargo, it eventually collapsed under the weight of domestic opposition. Jefferson withdrew it in his last days in office, replacing it with the Non-Intercourse Act of 1809. The act reopened trade with all nations except Britain and France, and authorized the president to resume trade with either country if it ceased to violate neutral rights. But the new act solved only the problems that had been created by the embargo; it did not convince Britain and France to change their policies.

Non-Intercourse Act

When the Non-Intercourse Act expired in spring 1810, Congress created a variant, relabeled Macon's Bill Number 2. The bill reopened trade with both Great Britain and France, but provided that if either nation ceased to violate American rights, the president could shut down American commerce with the other. Madison, eager to use the bill rather than go to war, was tricked at his own game. When Napoleon declared that French edicts against United States shipping would be lifted, Madison declared nonintercourse against Great Britain in March 1811. But Napoleon did not keep his word. The French continued to seize American ships, and nonintercourse failed a second time.

Britain, not France, was the main target of American hostility, since the Royal Navy controlled the Atlantic. New York harbor was virtually blockaded by the British, so reopening trade with any nation had little practical effect. Angry American leaders tended to blame even Indian resistance in the West on British agitation, ignoring the Indians' legitimate protests against white encroachment and treaty violations. Frustrated and having exhausted all efforts to alter British policy, the United States in 1811 and 1812 drifted into war with Great Britain.

Meanwhile, unknown to the president and Congress, Great Britain was changing its policy. The Anglo-French conflict had ended much of British commerce with the European continent, and exports to the United States had fallen 80 percent. Depression had hit the British Isles. On June 16, 1812, Britain opened the seas to American shipping. But two days later, before word had crossed the Atlantic, Congress declared war.

The War of 1812 was the logical outcome of United States policy after the renewal of war in Europe in 1803. The grievances enumerated in President Madison's message to Congress on June 1, 1812, were old ones: impressment, interference with neutral commerce, and the British alliances with western Indians. Unmentioned was the resolve to defend American independence and honor—and the thirst of expansionists for British Canada. Yet Congress and the country were divided. Much of the sentiment for war came from the War Hawks, land-hungry southerners and westerners led by Henry Clay of Kentucky and John C. Calhoun of South Carolina. Most representatives from the coastal states opposed war, since armed conflict with the great naval power threatened to close down all American shipping. The vote for war—79 to 49 in the House, 19 to 13 in the Senate—reflected these sharp regional differences. The split would also be reflected in the way Americans fought the war.

THE WAR OF 1812

War was a foolish adventure for the United States in 1812; despite six months of preparation, American forces remained ill equipped. Because the army had neither an able staff nor an adequate force of enlisted men, the burden of fighting fell on the state militias—and not all the states cooperated. The navy did have a corps of well-trained, experienced officers but next to the Royal Navy, the ruler of the seas, the U.S. Navy was minuscule.

For the United States, the only readily available battlefront on which to confront Great Britain was Canada. The mighty Royal Navy was useless on the waters separating the United States and Canada, since no river afforded it access from the sea. Invasion of Canada, thousands of miles from British supply sources, therefore might give the United States an edge.

Invasion of Canada

Begun with high hopes, the invasion of Canada ended as a disaster. The American strategy was to concentrate on the West, splitting Canadian forces and isolating the Shawnee, Potawatomi, and other tribes that supported the British. General William Hull marched his troops into Lower Canada, near Detroit. But the British anticipated the invasion, moved troops into the area, and demanded Hull's surrender. When a pro-British, mostly Potawatomi, contingent captured Fort Dearborn, near Detroit, Hull capitulated (see map, page 144). Farther west, other American forts surrendered. By the winter of 1812 and 1813, the British controlled about half the Old Northwest (Ohio, Indiana, Illinois, Michigan, and Wisconsin).

The United States had no greater success on the Niagara front, where New York borders Canada. At the Battle of Queenstown, north of Niagara, the United States regular army met defeat because the New York state militia refused to leave the state. This scene was repeated near Lake Champlain, where American plans to attack Montreal were foiled when the militia declined to cross the border.

The navy provided the only bright note in the first year of the war: the U.S.S. *Constitution*, the U.S.S. *Wasp*, and the U.S.S. *United States* all bested British warships on the Atlantic. But their victories gave the United States only a brief advantage. In defeat the British lost just 1 percent of their strength; in victory the Americans lost 20 percent. The British admiralty

Map labels:

L. Superior

CANADA
(Great Britain)

St. Lawrence R.

Montreal

ME.
(part of Mass.)

L. Michigan

L. Huron

L. Champlain

L.
Champlain
VT.
N.H.

York
Ft. Niagara
L. Ontario
NEW YORK

MICHIGAN
TERR.

The Thames
Detroit
L. Erie

Queenstown
Buffalo

MASS.
Hartford
CONN. R.I.

Ft. Dearborn

Put-in-Bay
Erie

Long Island
Sound

ILLINOIS
TERR.

INDIANA
TERR.

OHIO

PENNSYLVANIA

N.J.

Baltimore
Washington
DEL.
MD.

Delaware Bay

VIRGINIA

Chesapeake Bay

KENTUCKY

ATLANTIC
OCEAN

Mississippi R.

TENNESSEE

NORTH CAROLINA

Huntsville

SOUTH
CAROLINA

BRITISH BLOCKADE

MISSISSIPPI
TERRITORY
Horseshoe Bend

GEORGIA

LOUISIANA
(admitted
in 1812)

Mobile
Pensacola

New Orleans

FLORIDA
(Spain)

GULF OF MEXICO

0   100   200   300 miles
0   200   400 kilometers

Major Campaigns of the War of 1812

simply shifted its fleet away from the American ships, and by 1813 the Royal Navy again commanded the seas.

In 1813 the two sides also vied for control of the Great Lakes, the key to the war in the Northwest.

Great Lakes Campaign

The contest was largely a shipbuilding race. Under Master Commandant Oliver Hazard Perry and shipbuilder Noah Brown, the United States outbuilt the British on Lake Erie and defeated them at the bloody Battle of Put-in-Bay on September 10. With this victory, the Americans gained control of Lake Erie.

General William Henry Harrison then began the march that proved to be America's most successful moment in the war. Harrison's 4,500-man force, mostly Kentucky volunteers, crossed Lake Erie and pursued the British, Shawnee, and Chippewa forces into Canada, defeating them at the Battle of the Thames on October 5. The great Shawnee chief Tecumseh died in that battle, ending the Indian confederacy he had formed to resist American expansion. Harrison's campaign gave the United States virtual control of the Old Northwest.

Outside the Old Northwest the British set Americans back. In December 1812 the Royal Navy blockaded the Chesapeake and Delaware bays. By 1814 the blockade extended southward from **British Naval Blockade** New England down the Atlantic coast and then westward along the Gulf of Mexico. The blockade was so effective that between 1811 and 1814 American trade declined by nearly 90 percent.

Following their defeat of Napoleon in April 1814, the British stepped up the land campaign against the United States, concentrating their efforts in the Chesapeake. In retaliation for the burning of York (now Toronto)—and to divert American troops from Lake Champlain, where the British planned a new offensive—royal troops occupied Washington and set it to the torch. The attack on the capital was, however, only a raid. The major battle occurred at Baltimore, where the Americans held firm. Although the British inflicted heavy damages both materially and psychologically, they achieved no more than a stalemate. The British offensive at Lake Champlain proved equally unsuccessful. An American fleet forced a British flotilla to turn back at Plattsburgh on Lake Champlain, and the offensive was discontinued.

The last campaign of the war was waged in the South, along the Gulf of Mexico. It began when Tennessee militia general Andrew Jackson defeated the Creek Indians at the Battle of Horseshoe Bend in March 1814. The battle ended the year-long Creek War. As a result, the Creek nation ceded two-thirds of its land and withdrew to southern and western Alabama. Jackson became a major general in the regular army and continued south toward the Gulf. To forestall a British invasion at Pensacola Bay, which provided an overland route to New Orleans, Jackson seized Pensacola—in Spanish Florida—on November 7, 1814. After securing Mobile, he marched on to New Orleans.

The Battle of New Orleans was the final military engagement. Early in December the British fleet landed 1,500 men east of New Orleans, hoping to gain control of the Mississippi **Battle of** River. They faced an American **New Orleans** force of regular army troops, plus a larger contingent of Tennessee and Kentucky frontiersmen and two companies of free black volunteers from New Orleans. Finally, on January 8, 1815, the two forces met head-on. Jackson and his mostly untrained army held their ground against two frontal assaults and a reinforced British contingent of 6,000. It was a massacre. More than 2,000 British soldiers lay dead or wounded at the day's end; the Americans suffered only 21 casualties. Andrew Jackson emerged a national hero. Ironically, the Battle of New Orleans was fought two weeks after the end of the war; unknown to Jackson, a treaty had been signed in Ghent, Belgium, on December 24, 1814.

The Ghent treaty made no mention of the issues that had led to war. The United States received no satisfaction on impressment, blockades, or other maritime rights for neutrals. Likewise, **Treaty of** British demands for an Indian **Ghent** buffer state in the Northwest and territorial cessions from Maine to Minnesota went unmet. Essentially, the Treaty of Ghent restored the prewar status quo. It provided for an end to hostilities, release of prisoners, restoration of conquered territory, and arbitration of boundary disputes. Other questions—notably compensation for losses and fishing rights—would be negotiated by joint commissions.

Why did the negotiators settle for so little? Events

in Europe had made peace and the status quo acceptable at the end of 1814, as they had not been in 1812. Napoleon's fall from power allowed the United States to abandon its demands, since peace in Europe made impressment and interference with American commerce moot questions. Similarly, war-weary Britain, its treasury nearly depleted, gave up pressing for a military victory.

The War of 1812 reaffirmed the independence of the young American republic. Although conflict with Great Britain continued, it never again led to war. The experience strengthened America's resolve to steer clear of European politics, for it had been the British-French conflict that had drawn the United States into war. It also convinced the government to maintain a standing army of 10,000 men—three times its size under Jefferson.

Effects of War of 1812

The war had disastrous results for most Indian tribes. With the death of Tecumseh, they lost their most powerful political and military leader; with the withdrawal of the British, they lost their strongest ally. Although in the peace treaty the United States agreed to return Indian lands seized after 1811, the collapse of Indian leadership and British withdrawal made this provision moot.

Possibly most important of all, the war stimulated economic change. The embargo, the Non-Importation and Non-Intercourse Acts, and the war itself had spurred the production of manufactured goods—cloth and metal—to replace banned imports. And in the absence of commercial opportunities abroad, New England capitalists had begun to invest in manufactures.

The war also sealed the fate of the Federalist party. Its presidential nominee in 1812, De Witt Clinton, lost by a wide margin to James Madison. But it was their extremism that was the Federalists' undoing. During the war Older Federalists had revived talk of secession, and from December 15, 1814, to January 5, 1815, Federalist delegates from New England met in Hartford, Connecticut, to take action. With the war in a stalemate and trade in

Hartford Convention

ruins, they planned to revise the national compact or pull out of the republic. Moderates prevented a resolution of secession, but convention members continued to call for radical changes in the Constitution. The changes sought would have limited presidents to one term and weakened the Republicans.

If nothing else, the timing of the Hartford Convention proved fatal. The victory at New Orleans and news of the peace treaty made the Hartford Convention, with its talk of secession and proposed constitutional amendments, look ridiculous, if not treasonous. Rather than harassing a beleaguered wartime administration, the Federalists now retreated before a rising tide of nationalism. Though it remained strong in a handful of states until the 1820s, the Federalist party began to dissolve.

POSTWAR NATIONALISM AND DIPLOMACY

With peace came a new sense of American nationalism. Self-confidently, the nation asserted itself at home and abroad as Republicans aped Federalists in encouraging economic development and commerce. In his last message to Congress in December 1815, President Madison embraced Federalist doctrine by recommending military expansion and a program to stimulate economic growth. Wartime experiences had, he said, demonstrated the need for a national bank (the first bank had expired) and for better transportation. To raise government revenues and perpetuate the wartime growth in manufacturing, Madison called for a protective tariff—a tax on imported goods. Yet in straying from Jeffersonian Republicanism, Madison did so within limits. Only a constitutional amendment, he argued, could give the federal government authority to build roads and canals that were less than national in scope.

The congressional leadership pushed Madison's nationalist program energetically. Congressman John C. Calhoun and Speaker of the House Henry Clay,

American System

who named the program the American System, believed it would unify the country. They looked to the tariff on imported goods to stimulate industry. New mills would purchase raw materials; new millworkers would buy food from the agricultural South and West. New roads would make possible the flow of produce and goods, and tariff revenues would provide the money to build them. Finally, a national bank would facilitate all these transactions.

In 1816 Congress enacted into law much of the nationalistic program. The Second Bank of the United States was chartered. Like its predecessor, the bank had a twenty-year charter, was a blend of public and private ownership, and had one-fifth of its directors appointed by the government. The nation's first protective tariff was also passed. Duties were placed on imported cottons and woolens and on iron, leather, hats, paper, and sugar.

Congress did not share Madison's reservations about the constitutionality of using federal funds to build local roads. "Let us, then, bind the republic together," Calhoun declared, "with a perfect system of roads and canals." But Madison vetoed Calhoun's internal improvements bill, which provided for the construction of roads of mostly local benefit, adamantly insisting that it was unconstitutional. Internal improvements were the province of the states and of private enterprise. (Madison did, however, approve funds for the continuation of the National Road to Ohio, on the grounds that it was a military necessity.)

James Monroe, Madison's successor as president, retained Madison's domestic program, supporting the bank and tariffs and vetoing internal improvements on constitutional grounds. After he had easily defeated Rufus King, the last Federalist nominee, Monroe optimistically declared that "discord does not belong to our system." The American people were, he said, "one great family with a common interest." A Boston newspaper dubbed the one-party period the "Era of Good Feelings." And for Monroe's first term that seemed true.

Under Chief Justice John Marshall, the Supreme Court during this period also became the bulwark of a nationalist point of view. In *McCulloch v.*

McCulloch v. Maryland

Maryland (1819), the Court struck down a Maryland law taxing the federally chartered Second Bank of the United States. Maryland had adopted the tax in an effort to destroy the bank's Baltimore branch. The issue was thus one of state versus federal power. Speaking for a unanimous Court, Marshall asserted the supremacy of the federal government over the states.

Having established federal supremacy, the Court in *McCulloch v. Maryland* went on to consider whether Congress could issue a bank charter. No such power was specified in the Constitution. But Marshall noted that Congress had the authority to pass "all laws which shall be necessary and proper for carrying into execution" the enumerated powers of the government (Article I, Section 8). Therefore Congress could legally exercise "those great powers on which the welfare of the nation essentially depends." If the ends were legitimate and the means were not prohibited, Marshall ruled, a law was constitutional. The bank charter was declared legal.

In *McCulloch v. Maryland* Marshall combined Federalist nationalism with Federalist economic views. By asserting federal supremacy he was protecting the commercial and industrial interests that favored a national bank. This was Federalism in the tradition of Alexander Hamilton. The decision was only one in a series. In *Fletcher v. Peck* (1810) the Court voided a Georgia law that violated individuals' right of contract. Similarly, in the famous *Dartmouth College v. Woodward* (1819), the Court nullified a New Hampshire act altering the charter of Dartmouth College, which Marshall ruled constituted a contract. In protecting such contracts, Marshall thwarted state interference in commerce and business.

John Quincy Adams, Monroe's secretary of state, matched the self-confident Marshall Court in nationalism and assertiveness. From 1817 to 1825 he

John Quincy Adams (1767–1848), secretary of state from 1817 to 1825 and architect of the Monroe Doctrine, in an early daguerreotype taken by Philip Haas shortly before his death. This famous photograph suggests Adams's bulldog tenacity.   The Metropolitan Museum of Art, Gift of I. N. Phelps Stokes, Edward S. Hawes, Alice Mary Hawes, Marion Augusta Hawes, 1937. (37.14.34.)

John Quincy Adams as Secretary of State

managed the nation's foreign policy brilliantly. Adams stubbornly pushed for expansion, fishing rights for Americans in Atlantic waters, political distance from the Old World, and peace. An ardent expansionist, he nonetheless placed limits on expansion: it must come through negotiations, not war, and newly acquired territories must not permit slavery. In appearance a small, austere man, once de-

scribed by a British official as a "bulldog among spaniels," Adams was a superb diplomat who knew six languages.

Adams's first step was to strengthen the peace with Great Britain. In April 1817 the two nations agreed to the Rush-Bagot Treaty. Through the treaty Great Britain and the United States agreed to limit their Great Lakes naval forces to one ship each on Lake Ontario and Lake Champlain and two vessels each on the other lakes. This first disarmament treaty of modern times began the process that led to demilitarization of the United States–Canadian border. Adams then pushed for the Convention of 1818, which fixed the United States–Canadian border from Lake of the Woods west to the Rockies. When agreement could not be reached on the territory west of the mountains, the two nations settled on joint occupation of Oregon for ten years.

Adams's next move was to settle long-term disputes with Spain. During the War of 1812 the United States seized Mobile and the remainder of West Florida. Afterward it took advantage of Spain's preoccupation with domestic and colonial troubles to negotiate for the purchase of East Florida. Talks took place in 1818, while General Andrew Jackson's troops occupied much of Florida on the pretext of suppressing Seminole raids against American settlements across the border. Adams was furious with Jackson, but defended his brazen act. The following year, on behalf of Spain, Don Luis de Onís, Spanish minister to the United States, agreed to cede Florida to the United States without payment. In this Transcontinental, or Adams-Onís, Treaty, the United States also defined the southern boundary of the Louisiana Purchase. In return, the United States government assumed $5 million worth of claims by American citizens against Spain and gave up its dubious claim to Texas. Expansion had thus been achieved at little cost and without war, and American territorial claims now stretched from the Atlantic to the Pacific.

While the Rush-Bagot Treaty, the Convention of 1818, and the Adams-Onís Treaty temporarily re-

Adams-Onís Treaty

solved conflict between the United States and European nations, events to the south still threatened United States interests. John Quincy Adams's desire to insulate the United States and the Western Hemisphere from European conflict led to his greatest achievement: the Monroe Doctrine.

Specifically, the thorny issue of the recognition of new governments in Latin America had to be confronted. The United Provinces of the Río de la Plata (present-day northern Argentina, Paraguay, and Uruguay), Chile, Peru, Colombia, and Mexico had all broken free from Spain between 1808 and 1822. Many Americans wanted to recognize the independence of these former colonies. But Monroe and Adams moved cautiously. They sought to avoid conflict with Spain and its allies and to assure themselves of the stability of the revolutionary regimes. But in 1822, shortly after the Adams-Onís Treaty with Spain was safely signed and ratified, the United States became the first nation outside Latin America to recognize the new states.

Later the same year, events in Europe again threatened the stability of the New World. Spain experienced a domestic revolt, and France occupied Spain in an attempt to bolster the weak monarchy against the rebels. The United States feared that France and its allies might also seek to overturn the new Latin American states and restore them to Spanish rule. Great Britain, which shared this concern, proposed joint United States–British protection of South America. But Adams rejected the British overture, fearing any European intervention in the New World. He insisted that the United States act independently and on its own initiative; action in concert with Britain would violate the principle of avoiding foreign entanglements.

The result was the Monroe Doctrine, a unilateral declaration against European interference in the New World. The president enunciated the famous doctrine in his last message to Congress on December 2, 1823. Monroe called for, first, *noncolonization* of the Western Hemisphere by European nations, a principle that expressed American anxiety not only about Latin America but also about Russian expansion in Alaska. Second, he demanded *nonintervention* by Europe in the affairs of independent New World nations. Finally, Monroe pledged *noninterference* by the United States in European affairs, including those of Europe's existing New World colonies.

Monroe
Doctrine

The Monroe Doctrine, however, had no force behind it. Indeed, the policy could not have succeeded without the support of the British, who were already committed to keeping other European nations out of the New World. Europeans ignored the doctrine; it was the Royal Navy they respected, not American policy.

THE PANIC OF 1819 AND RENEWED SECTIONALISM

Monroe's domestic achievements could not match the diplomatic success that John Quincy Adams brought to his administration. By 1819 postwar nationalism and confidence had eroded, and financial panic darkened the land. (Neither panic nor the resurgence of sectionalism hurt Monroe politically; without a rival political party to rally opposition, he won a second term in 1820 unopposed.)

But hard times spread. The postwar expansion had been built on loose money and widespread speculation. State banks extended credit and printed notes too freely, fueling a speculative western land boom. When it slowed, the manufacturing depression that had begun in 1818 deepened. The Second Bank of the United States, in order to protect its assets, reduced loans, thus accelerating the contraction in the economy. Distressed

Economic
Depression

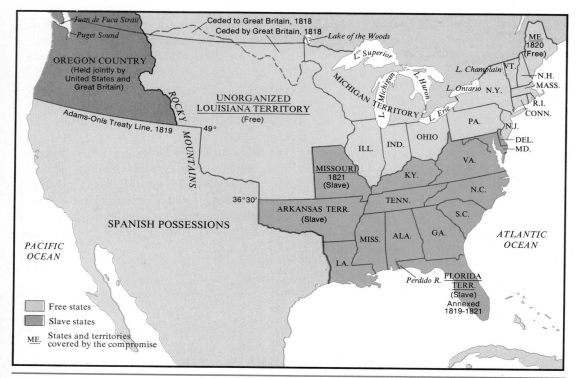

*The Missouri Compromise and the State of the
Union, 1820*

urban workers lobbied for relief and began to take a more active role in politics. Farmers, on the other hand, wanted lower tariffs. Southern planters, for example, railed at the protective Tariff of 1816, which had raised prices at the same time cotton prices were falling sharply.

Western farmers suffered too. Those who had purchased public land on credit could not repay their loans. To avoid mass bankruptcy, Congress delayed payment of the money, and western state legislatures passed "stay laws" restricting mortgage foreclosures. Many westerners blamed the panic on the Second Bank of the United States, which in self-protection had cut off loans it had issued in the previous three years.

Even more divisive was the question of slavery. Ever since the drafting of the Constitution, political

Slavery Question

leaders had largely avoided the issue. The one exception was the 1807 act closing the slave trade after January 1, 1808, which passed without much opposition. In February 1819, however, slavery finally crept onto the political agenda when Missouri residents petitioned Congress for admission to the Union as a slave state. For the next two-and-one-half years the issue dominated all congressional action.

The debate transcended slavery in Missouri. At stake was the undoing of the compromises that had kept the issue quarantined since the Constitutional Convention. Five new states had joined the Union since 1812—Louisiana (1812), Indiana (1816), Mississippi (1817), Illinois (1818), and Alabama (1819). Missouri was on the same latitude as free Illinois, In-

Chapter 8: THE EMPIRE OF LIBERTY, 1801–1824

diana, and Ohio, and its admission as a slave state would thus thrust slavery farther northward. It would also tilt the political balance toward the states committed to slavery. In 1819 the Union consisted of an uneasy balance of eleven slave and eleven free states. If Missouri entered as a slave state, the slave states would have a two-vote edge in the Senate.

But what made the issue so divisive was not the politics of admission to statehood, but white people's emotional attitudes toward slavery. Many northerners had come to the conclusion that it was evil. Thus when Representative James Tallmadge, Jr., of New York introduced an amendment providing for gradual emancipation in Missouri, it led to passionate and sometimes violent debate on moral grounds. The House, which had a northern majority, passed the Tallmadge amendment, but the Senate rejected it. The two sides were deadlocked.

A compromise emerged in 1820 under pressure from House Speaker Henry Clay: the admission of free Maine, carved out of Massachusetts, was linked with that of slave Missouri. In the

Missouri Compromise rest of the Louisiana Territory north of 36°30′ (Missouri's southern boundary), slavery was prohibited forever (see map). Though the compromise carried, the issue ultimately destroyed Republican unity and ended the reign of the Virginia dynasty.

Sectionalism and the question of slavery would ultimately threaten the Union itself. Still, the first decades of the nineteenth century were a time of nationalism and growth for the young republic. Political parties channeled and limited partisan divisions, and a tradition of peaceful transition of power through presidential elections was established. A second war with Britain—the War of 1812—had to be fought to reaffirm American independence; thereafter the nation was able to settle many disputes at the bargaining table. The foreign policy problems confronting the infant republic from the turn of the century through the mid-1820s strikingly resemble those faced today by the newly established nations of the Third World. The mother country often treated its former colony as if it had not won its independence. And like Third

IMPORTANT EVENTS	
1801	John Marshall becomes Chief Justice Jefferson inaugurated
1801–05	Tripoli War
1803	*Marbury v. Madison* Louisiana Purchase
1804	Jefferson re-elected
1804–06	Lewis and Clark expedition
1807	*Chesapeake* Affair Embargo Act
1808	Madison elected president
1812–15	War of 1812
1814	Treaty of Ghent
1814–15	Hartford Convention
1815	Battle of New Orleans
1816	Monroe elected president Second Bank of United States chartered
1817	Rush-Bagot Treaty
1819	*McCulloch v. Maryland* Adams-Onís Treaty
1819–23	Financial panic; depression
1820	Missouri Compromise Monroe re-elected
1823	Monroe Doctrine

World nations today, the young United States steered clear of alliances with superpowers, preferring neutrality and unilateralism.

After the war, all branches of the government,

responding to the popular mood, pursued a more vigorous national policy. The Supreme Court further advanced national unity by extending federal power over the states and encouraging commerce and economic growth. And disruption of trade during the war had promoted the manufacturing of goods in the United States. The development of faster transportation further promoted the economy, and old cities expanded in the market-oriented North as new ones sprouted up in the West on trade and transportation routes.

But along with the nationalism and growth of the country came the problem of sectionalism. While the manufacturers and commercial interests in the North were becoming increasingly connected with the agricultural producers in the West through transportation and trade, the South was developing its own economy and culture based on cotton crops, export markets, a plantation system, and slavery. Politicians kept the question of slavery off the national agenda as long as possible and worked out the Missouri Compromise as a stopgap measure. But new land acquisitions and further westward expansion in the 1840s and 1850s, combined with a rising tide of reform impulse, eventually made the question of slavery unavoidable.

Suggestions for Further Reading

General

George Dangerfield, *The Awakening of American Nationalism, 1815–1828* (1965); John Mayfield, *The New Nation, 1800–1845* (1981); Marshall Smelser, *The Democratic Republic, 1801–1815* (1968).

Party Politics

Noble E. Cunningham, Jr., *The Jeffersonian Republicans in Power: Party Operations, 1801–1809* (1963); David Hackett

Fischer, *The Revolution of American Conservatism: The Federalist Party in the Era of Jeffersonian Democracy* (1965); Linda K. Kerber, *Federalists in Dissent* (1970); Richard P. McCormick, *The Presidential Game. The Origins of American Presidential Politics* (1982); James Sterling Young, *The Washington Community, 1800–1828* (1966).

The Virginia Presidents

Harry Ammon, *James Monroe: The Quest for National Identity* (1971); Irving Brant, *The Fourth President: A Life of James Madison* (1970); Noble E. Cunningham, Jr., *The Process of Government Under Jefferson* (1978); James Ketcham, *James Madison* (1970); Forrest McDonald, *The Presidency of Thomas Jefferson* (1976); Merrill D. Peterson, *The Jefferson Image in the American Mind* (1960); Merrill D. Peterson, *Thomas Jefferson and the New Nation* (1970).

The Supreme Court and the Law

Richard E. Ellis, *The Jeffersonian Crisis: Courts and Politics in the Young Republic* (1971); Charles G. Haines, *The Role of the Supreme Court in American Government and Politics, 1789–1835* (1944); Morton J. Horowitz, *The Transformation of American Law, 1780–1860* (1977); R. Kent Newmyer, *The Supreme Court Under Marshall and Taney* (1968); Francis N. Stites, *John Marshall: Defender of the Constitution* (1981).

Expansion and the War of 1812

Roger H. Brown, *The Republic in Peril: 1812* (1964); Alexander De Conde, *This Affair of Louisiana* (1976); Clifford L. Egan, *Neither Peace nor War: Franco-American Relations, 1803–1812* (1983); Reginald Horsman, *The War of 1812* (1969); Burton Spivak, *Jefferson's English Crisis: Commerce, Embargo, and the Republican Revolution* (1974); J. C. A. Stagg, *Mr. Madison's War. Politics, Diplomacy, and Warfare in the Early Republic, 1783–1830* (1983).

The Monroe Doctrine

Samuel F. Bemis, *John Quincy Adams and the Foundations of American Foreign Policy* (1949); Walter LaFeber, ed., *John Quincy Adams and American Continental Empire* (1965); Ernest R. May, *The Making of the Monroe Doctrine* (1976); Dexter Perkins, *Hands Off: A History of the Monroe Doctrine* (1941).

CHAPTER 9

A MARKET AND INDUSTRIAL ECONOMY

1800–1860

John Jervis's life bridged the old and the new. His roots lay in the rural area of upstate New York. He had learned to read and write during occasional attendance at common school, and to farm and handle an axe from his father. But in 1817 he left behind much of that tradition and became involved in undertakings that would lead to a new, far different nation. Hired to clear a cedar swamp for the Erie Canal, Jervis had to acquire skills not used on the farm: the ability to follow construction plans and to work precisely in tandem with others. As he learned new skills, he advanced from axeman to surveyor to engineer to superintendent of a division.

When the Erie Canal was completed in 1825, Jervis moved on to become second-in-command of the Delaware and Hudson Canal project. Later, as a supervisor of an early rail experiment, he redesigned the locomotive's wheel assembly. Jervis spent two decades building the 98-mile Chenango Canal and the fresh-water supply system for New York City. In 1864, at age sixty-nine, he returned home to Rome, New York, and organized an iron mill.

The canals and railroads John Jervis helped build were the most visible signs of the evolution of the American economy from 1800 through 1860. The canal boat, the steamboat, the locomotive, and the telegraph were all agents of change and economic growth. They helped to open up the frontier and brought mostly self-sufficient farmers into the market economy. They made it profitable to manufacture cloth in New England and ship the finished goods to retail outlets in New Orleans or St. Louis or even, by the 1850s, San Francisco. They forged the beginnings of a national, capitalist economy.

The dramatic transformation of the United States between 1800 and 1860 was manifest nearly everywhere. In 1800 most of the 5.3 million Americans earned a living working the land and serving those who did. Except in Kentucky and Tennessee, settlement had not stretched far to the west. By 1860, 31.4

million Americans had spread across the continent. Though still primarily agricultural, the economy was being transformed by an enormous commercial and industrial expansion.

Promotion of economic growth became the hallmark of government, especially in the nationalist mood after the War of 1812. Government sought to encourage individual freedom and choice by furthering an environment in which farming and industry could flourish. New financial institutions amassed the capital for large-scale enterprises like factories and railroads. Mechanization took root; factories and precision-made machinery began to replace home workshops and handmade goods, while reapers and sowers revolutionized farming.

THE MARKET ECONOMY

Most farmers in the early nineteenth century geared production to family needs. They lived in interdependent communities and kept detailed account books of labor and goods exchanged with neighbors. Farm families tended to produce much of what they needed but traded agricultural surpluses for or purchased items they could not produce. On such farms, men selling cordwood and women selling eggs, butter, cheese, and poultry produced the family's only cash. By the Civil War, however, the United States had an industrializing economy in which an increasing number of men and women worked in factories or offices for a wage, and in which most citizens had become dependent on store-bought necessities.

In the market economy crops were grown and goods were produced for sale in the marketplace, at home or abroad. The money received in market transactions, whether from the sale of goods or of a person's labor, purchased items produced by other people. Such a system encouraged specialization. Formerly

Definition of a Market Economy

self-sufficient farmers, for example, began to grow just one or two crops. Farm women gave up spinning and weaving at home and purchased fabric produced by wage-earning farm girls in Massachusetts textile mills.

Sustained growth was the result of this economic evolution. Improvements in transportation and technology, the division of labor, and new methods of financing all fueled expansion of the economy—that is, the multiplication of goods and services. In turn, this growth prompted new improvements. The effect was cumulative; by the 1840s the economy was growing more rapidly than in the previous four decades. Per capita income doubled between 1800 and 1860.

The Ohio dairy industry illustrates this process. In the first decades of the century, Ohio farm women made whatever cheese they needed for their own tables. Some made cheese to sell elsewhere, but only because they had a surplus of milk. However, the development of canals and railroads in the 1830s and 1840s changed Ohio farming. Farmers began to specialize, finding it more profitable to invest in better tools and spend all their time on one product. Some chose to grow wheat or tobacco for market. Others, especially in northeastern Ohio, decided to devote themselves full time to dairy farming. Beginning in 1847, entrepreneurs built cheese factories in rural towns and contracted to buy curd from these local dairy farmers. In 1851 one such factory in Gustavus, Ohio, produced a daily average of 5,000 pounds of cheese from the milk of 2,500 cows. The cheese was shipped by canal and railroad to cities and eastern ports. In Boston and New York, some merchants turned to handling cheese and other dairy products exclusively, selling to consumers as far away as California, England, and China. By 1860 Ohio dairymen were producing 21.6 million pounds of cheese a year for market—a huge leap in production over the early 1800s.

The changes in Ohio dairy husbandry altered farm life. Traditionally the making of cheese was a family industry in which men fed and tended the cows, men or women milked them, and women made the cheese. As cheese production increased, women's work on family-run dairy farms intensified as they added cheese-making to their regular tasks. The work was physically arduous and continuous, requiring daily attention both to the new day's curds and to the previous days' cheese, which needed to be pressed and turned. The *Ohio Cultivator* in 1848 noted that "the condition of women in dairies is frequently little better than servitude." In large, commercial dairies, however, where making cheese was a male task, gender roles had shifted under the pressure of market demands.

Though economic change and growth were sustained, their pace was uneven. Prosperity reigned during two long periods, from 1823 to 1835 and from 1843 to 1857. But there were long stretches of economic contraction as well. During the time from Jefferson's 1807 embargo through 1815, the growth rate was negative—that is, fewer goods and services were produced. Contraction and deflation occurred again during the depressions of 1819 through 1823, 1839 through 1843, and 1857. These periods were characterized by the collapse of banks, business bankruptcies, and a decline in wages and prices. For workers, the down side meant lower wages and higher unemployment rates.

What caused the cycles of boom and bust? In general, they were a direct result of the new market economy. Prosperity inevitably stimulated greater demand for staples and finished goods. Increased demand led in turn to higher prices and still higher production, to speculation in land, and to the flow of foreign currency into the country. Eventually production surpassed demand, leading to lower prices and wages; and speculation outstripped the true value of land and stocks. The inflow of foreign money led first to easy credit and then to collapse when unhappy investors withdrew their funds.

Cause of Boom-and-Bust Cycles

Some economists considered this process beneficial—a self-adjusting cycle in which unprofitable economic ventures were eliminated. In theory, people concentrated on the activities they did best, and the economy as a whole became more efficient. Advocates of the system argued also that it furthered individual freedom, since ideally each seller, whether of goods or labor, was free to determine the conditions of the sale. But in fact the system put workers on a perpetual rollercoaster; they had become dependent on wages—and the availability of jobs—for their very existence.

GOVERNMENT PROMOTES ECONOMIC GROWTH

The eighteenth-century political ideas which had captured the imagination of the Revolutionary War generation and found expression in the ideal of republican virtue were paralleled in economic thought by the writings of Adam Smith, a Scottish political economist. Smith's *Wealth of Nations* first appeared in 1776, the year of the Declaration of Independence; both works emphasized individual liberty, one economic, the other political. Both were reactions against forceful government: Jefferson attacked monarchy and distant government, while Smith attacked mercantilism, government regulation of the economy to benefit the state (see page 38). They believed that virtue was lodged in individual freedom and that the entire community would benefit most from individuals pursuing their own self-interest.

Jefferson, however, recognized that government was nonetheless a necessary instrument in promoting individual freedom. Freedom, he believed, thrived where individuals had room for independence, creativity, and choices; individuals fettered by government, monopoly, or economic dependence could not be free. Committed to the idea that a republican democracy would flourish best in a nation of independent farmers and artisans and an atmosphere of widespread political participation, Jefferson worked to realize those ideals. Beginning with the purchase of

Louisiana in 1803, Republican party policy, no less than that of the Federalists, turned to using government as an active promoter of the economy.

Once Louisiana had been acquired, the federal government played an active role in promoting economic growth and in fulfilling the spirit of manifest destiny by encouraging westward expansion and settlement and by promoting agriculture. The Lewis and Clark expedition from 1804 to 1806 was the beginning of a continuing federal interest in geographic and geologic surveying and the first step in the opening of western lands to exploitation and settlement.

To encourage western agriculture, the federal government offered public lands for sale at reasonable prices and evicted Indian tribes from their traditional lands. And because transportation was crucial to development of the frontier, the government financed roads and subsidized railroad construction through land grants. Even the State Department aided agriculture: its consular offices overseas collected horticultural information, seeds, and cuttings and published technical reports in an effort to improve American farming.

The federal government played a key role in technological and industrial growth. Federal arsenals pioneered new manufacturing techniques and helped to develop the machine-tool industry. The United States Military Academy at West Point, founded in 1802, emphasized technical and scientific subjects in its curriculum. And the U.S. Post Office stimulated interregional trade and played a brief but crucial role in the development of the telegraph. Finally, to create an atmosphere conducive to economic growth and individual creativity, the government protected inventions and domestic industries. Patent laws gave inventors a seventeen-year monopoly on their inventions, and tariffs protected American industry from foreign competition.

The federal judiciary validated government promotion of the economy and encouraged business enterprise. In *Gibbons* v. *Ogden* (1824), the Supreme Court overturned a New York state law that had given Robert Fulton and Robert Livingston a monopoly on the New York–New Jersey steamboat trade.

Ogden, their successor, lost his monopoly when Chief Justice John Marshall ruled that the trade fell under the sway of the commerce clause of the Constitution. Thus Congress, not New York, had the controlling power. Since the federal government issued such licenses on a nonexclusive basis, the decision ended monopolies on waterways throughout the nation. In defining interstate commerce broadly, the Marshall Court expanded federal powers over the economy while limiting the ability of states to control economic activity within their borders.

Legal Foundations of Commerce

Federal and state courts, in conjunction with state legislatures, also encouraged the proliferation of corporations—groups of investors that could hold property and transact business as one person. In 1800 the United States had about 300 incorporated firms; in 1830 the New England states alone had issued 1,900 charters. At first each firm needed a special legislative act to incorporate, but after the 1830s applications became so numerous that incorporation was authorized by general state laws.

A further encouragement to economic development, corporate development, and free enterprise was the Supreme Court's ruling in *Charles River Bridge* v. *Warren Bridge* (1837). The case involved issues of great importance: should a new interest be able to compete against existing, older privileges, and should the state protect existing privilege or encourage innovation to benefit all? In 1785 the Massachusetts legislature chartered the Charles River Bridge Company, and in 1791 extended its charter to a seventy-year term. In return for the risk of building the bridge between Charlestown and Boston, the owners received the privilege of collecting tolls. In 1828 the legislature chartered another company to build the Warren Bridge across the Charles, with the right to collect tolls for six years, after which the bridge would be turned over to the state and be toll-free. With the terminus of the new bridge only ninety yards away from its own, the Charles River Bridge Company sued in 1829, claiming that the new bridge breached the earlier charter. Justice Roger Taney,

The Marshall Court encouraged business competition by ending the state-licensed monopolies on inland waterways. Gibbons v. Ogden (1824) opened up the New York–New Jersey trade to new lines, and within a short time dozens of steamboats ferried passengers and freight across the Hudson River. The New-York Historical Society.

speaking for the Court majority, noted that the original charter did not confer the privilege of monopoly and therefore exclusivity could not be implied. Focusing on the question of corporate privilege rather than the right of contracts, Taney ruled that charter grants should be interpreted narrowly and that ambiguities would be decided in favor of the public interest. New enterprises should not be restricted under old charters.

State governments far surpassed the federal government in promoting the economy. From 1815 through 1860, for example, 73 percent of the $135

State Promotion of the Economy

million invested in canals was government money, mostly from the states. In the 1830s the states shifted their investments to rail construction. Even though the federal government played a larger role in building railroads than canals, state and local governments provided more than half of southern rail capital. Overall, railroads received 131 million acres in land subsidies, 48 million of which were provided by the states. States actually equaled or surpassed private enterprise in their investments.

From the end of the War of 1812 until 1860 the United States experienced uneven but sustained economic growth largely as a result of these government efforts. Though political controversy raged over questions of state versus federal activity—especially with regard to internal improvements and banking—all parties agreed on the general goal of economic expansion. Indeed, the major restraint on government action during these years was not philosophical but financial: both the government and the public purse were small.

TRANSPORTATION AND REGIONALIZATION

From 1800 through 1860 the North, South, and West followed distinctly different paths economically. Everywhere agriculture remained the foundation of the American economy. Nevertheless, industry, commerce, and finance came to characterize the North, plantations and subsistence farms the South, and commercialized family farms, agricultural processing, and implement manufacturing the West. Paradoxically, this tendency toward regional specialization made the sections at once more different from and more dependent on each other.

The revolution in transportation and communications was probably the single most important cause of these changes. It was the North's heavy investment in canals and railroads that made it the center of American commerce. The South, with most of its capital invested in slave labor, built fewer canals, railroads, and factories and remained largely rural and undeveloped.

Before the canal and railroad fevers, it was by no means self-evident that New England and the Middle Atlantic states would dominate American economic life. In fact, the southward-flowing Ohio and Mississippi rivers oriented the frontier of 1800—Tennessee,

Kentucky, and Ohio—to the South. But the pattern changed in the 1820s and 1830s. New roads and turnpikes opened up east-west travel. The National Road, a stone-based gravel-topped highway beginning in Cumberland, Maryland, reached Columbus, Ohio, in 1833. More important, the Erie Canal, completed in 1825, forged an east-west axis from the Hudson River to Lake Erie, linking the Great Lakes with New York City and the Atlantic Ocean. Railroads and later the telegraph would solidify these east-west links. By contrast, only at one place—Bowling Green, Kentucky—did a northern railroad actually connect with a southern one. In 1850 the bulk of western trade flowed eastward. Thus, by the eve of the Civil War, the northern and Middle Atlantic states were closely tied to the former frontier of the Old Northwest.

Changes in Trade Routes

Construction of the 363-mile-long Erie Canal was a visionary enterprise. Vigorously promoted by Governor De Witt Clinton, the Erie cost $7 million. The canal shortened the journey between Buffalo and New York City from twenty to six days and reduced freight charges from $100 to $5 a ton.

Canals

The Erie triggered an explosion of canal building. Other states and cities, sensing the advantage New York had gained, rushed to follow suit. By 1840 canals crisscrossed the Northeast and Midwest, and canal mileage in the United States had reached 3,300—an increase of more than 2,000 miles in a single decade. Unfortunately for investors, none of these canals enjoyed the financial success achieved by the Erie. As a result, investment in canals began to slump in the 1830s. By 1850 more miles were being abandoned than built, and the canal era had ended.

Meanwhile, railroad construction was on the upswing, and visionaries like John Jervis left canals for railroads. The railroad era began in 1830 when Peter Cooper's locomotive, *Tom Thumb*, first steamed along 13 miles of track constructed by the Baltimore and Ohio Railroad. By 1850 the United States had nearly 9,000 miles of railroad; by 1860, roughly 31,000.

Railroads

The earliest railroads connected two cities or one city and its surrounding area. But in the 1850s technological improvements, competition, and economic recovery prompted the development of regional and later national rail networks. The West experienced a railroad boom. By 1853 rail lines linked New York to Chicago, and a year later track had reached the Mississippi River. By 1860 rails stretched as far west as St. Joseph, Missouri—the edge of the frontier. In that year the railroad network east of the Mississippi approximated its physical pattern for the next century, but the process of corporate integration had only begun. Most lines were still independently run, separated by gauge, scheduling, differences in car design, and a commitment to serve their home towns first and foremost.

Railroads did not completely replace water transportation. Steamboats, first introduced in 1807 when Robert Fulton's *Clermont* paddled up the Hudson from New York City, still plied the rivers. Until the 1850s, when western rail development blossomed, steamboats outdid railroads in carrying freight. Great Lakes steamers managed to hold their own even into the fifties, for the sealike lakes permitted the construction of giant ships and the widespread adoption of propellers in place of paddle wheels.

Steamboats

Gradually steamboats replaced sailing vessels on the high seas. In 1818 steam-powered packets made four round trips a year between New York and Liverpool, sailing on schedule rather than waiting for a full cargo as ships had done before then. The breakthrough came in 1848, though, when Samuel Cunard introduced regularly scheduled steamships to the Atlantic run between Liverpool and New York, reducing travel time from twenty-five days eastbound and forty-nine days westbound to ten to fourteen days each way. Sailing ships quickly lost first-class passengers and light cargo to these swift steamships.

By far the fastest spreading technological advance of the era was the magnetic telegraph. Samuel F. B. Morse's invention freed messages from the restraint of traveling no faster than the messenger; instantaneous communication became possible even over long distances. By 1853, only nine years after construction of the first experimental line, 23,000 miles of telegraph wire spread across the United States; by 1860, 50,000. In 1861 the telegraph bridged the continent, connecting the east and west coasts. The new invention revolutionized news-gathering, provided advance information for railroads and steamships, and altered patterns of business and finance. Rarely has innovation had so great an impact so quickly.

Telegraph

The changes in transportation and communications from 1800 to 1860 were revolutionary. Railroads reduced the number of loadings and unloadings, were cheap to build over difficult terrain, and remained in use all year. But time was the key. In 1800 it took four weeks to travel from New York City to Detroit. By 1857 Detroit was but an overnight trip. This reduced travel time saved money and facilitated commerce. During the first two decades of the century, wagon transportation cost 30 to 70 cents per ton per mile. By 1860, railroads in New York State carried freight at an average charge of 2.2 cents per ton per mile; wheat moved from Chicago to New York for 1.2 cents a ton-mile. In sum, the transportation revolution had transformed the economy—and with it the relationships of the North, West, and South.

THE RISE OF MANUFACTURING AND COMMERCE

In 1851 hundreds of American products made their international debut at the London Crystal Palace Exhibition, the first modern world's fair. There the design and quality of American machines and wares astonished observers. Most impressive to the Europeans were three simple machines: Alfred C. Hobbs's unpickable padlocks, Samuel Colt's revolvers, and Robbins and Lawrence's six rifles with completely interchangeable parts. All were machine- rather than hand-tooled, products of what the British called the American system of manufacturing.

The American system of manufacturing used precision machinery to produce interchangeable parts that needed no filing or fitting. In 1798 Eli Whitney had used a primitive system of interchangeable parts when he contracted with the federal government to make ten thousand rifles in twenty-eight months. By the 1820s the Connecticut manufacturer Simeon North, the Springfield, Massachusetts, Arsenal, and the Harpers Ferry, Virginia, Armory were all producing machine-made interchangeable parts for firearms. From the arsenals the American system spread, giving birth to the machine-tool industry—the mass manufacture of specialized machines for other industries. One by-product was an explosion in the production of inexpensive consumer goods whose quality was uniformly high.

American System of Manufacturing

Interchangeable parts and the machine-tool industry were uniquely American contributions to the industrial revolution. Both paved the way for America's swift industrialization following the Civil War. The process of industrialization began, however, in a simple and traditional way, not unlike that of other nations. In 1800 manufacturing was relatively unimportant to the American economy. What manufacturing there was took place mostly in small workshops or homes, where journeymen and apprentices worked with and under master craftsmen, or women spun thread and wove cloth alone at home. Tailors, shoemakers, and blacksmiths made articles by hand for a specific customer.

The clothing trades illustrate well the nineteenth-century changes in manufacturing and distribution. In the eighteenth century, most men wore clothes made by their mothers, wives, or daughters, or occasionally bought used clothing. Wealthy men had clothing made by tailors who cut and sewed unique garments to fit them. A tailor was a master craftsman whose journeymen and apprentices worked with him to produce goods made to or-

Clothing Trades

der. By the 1820s and 1830s, clothiers and clothing manufacturers had replaced most, though not all, of the old craftsmen and journeymen. In the 1820s clothiers appeared with stocks of ready-made clothes. T. S. Whitmarsh of Boston advertised in 1827 that "he keeps constantly for Sale, from 5 to 10,000 Fashionable ready-made Garments."

Upon entering Whitmarsh's emporium a customer found row after row of ready-made goods without a sign of tailors or a workshop. Unlike the eighteenth-century tailor, the nineteenth-century ready-to-wear clothier was exclusively a retailer. The merchant most likely bought the goods wholesale. Moreover, the goods were no longer produced through the master-journeyman-apprentice system. Instead, entrepreneurs employed cheap unskilled and semiskilled laborers to do most of the sewing on a piece-rate basis.

Essential to this change in the clothing industry was the development of the New England textile industry. The first American textile mill, built in Pawtucket, Rhode Island, in 1790, used water-powered spinning machines constructed by the English immigrant Samuel Slater. By 1800 the mill employed one hundred people. Soon other mills sprang up in New England, especially between 1807 and 1815, when there was an embargo placed on British imports.

Early mills also used the putting-out system. Traditionally women had spun their own thread and woven it into cloth for their own families; now many women received thread from the mills and returned finished cloth. The change was subtle but significant: although the work itself was familiar, women now operated their looms for piece-rate wages and produced cloth for the market, not for their own use.

Textile manufacturing was radically transformed in 1813 by the construction of the first American power loom and the chartering of the Boston Manufacturing Company. The corporation was capitalized at $400,000—ten times the amount behind the Rhode Island mills—by Francis Cabot Lowell and other Boston merchants. Its goal was to eliminate problems of timing, shipping, coordination, and quality control inherent

Waltham (Lowell) System

in the putting-out system. The owners erected their factories in Waltham, Massachusetts, combining all the manufacturing processes at a single location. They also employed a resident manager to run the mill, thus separating ownership from management. The company produced cloth suitable for the mass market.

In the rural setting of Waltham not enough hands could be found to staff the mill, so the managers recruited New England farm daughters, accepting responsibility for their living conditions and their virtue. To persuade young women to come, they offered cash wages, company-run boardinghouses, and such cultural events as evening lectures—none of which were available on the farm. This paternalistic approach, called the Waltham or Lowell system, was adopted in other mills erected alongside New England rivers. By the 1850s, though, another work force had entered the mills—Irish immigrants. With a surplus of cheap labor available, Lowell and other mill towns abandoned their model systems. Within a few years, the typical cotton mill had become a modern factory, and work relationships in American society had been radically altered.

Though textile mills were in the vanguard of industrialization, manufacturing grew in many areas. Woolen textiles, farm implements, machine tools, iron, glass, and finished consumer goods all became major industries. "White coal"—water power—was widely used to run the machines. Yet by 1860, the United States was still predominantly an agricultural nation; just over one-half of the work force was engaged in agriculture. Manufacturing accounted for only a third of total production, even though that percentage had doubled in twenty years.

Several factors, including the need for home manufactures created by the War of 1812, population growth, and government policy, stimulated industrialization. Essential to the process, however, was the growth of, and specialization in, commerce. Cotton, for instance, had once been traded by plantation agents who handled all the goods produced and bought by the owners, extending

Specialization of Commerce

credit where needed. As cotton became a great staple export following the invention of the cotton gin in 1793, exports rose. Gradually some agents came to specialize in finance alone: cotton brokers appeared, men who for a commission brought together buyers and sellers. Similarly, wheat and hog brokers sprang up in the West. The supply of finished goods also became more specialized. Wholesalers bought large quantities of a particular item from manufacturers, and jobbers broke down the wholesale lots for retail stores and country merchants.

Commercial specialization made some traders in the big cities, especially New York, virtual merchant princes. New York had emerged as the dominant port in the late 1790s. When the Erie Canal opened, the city became a standard stop on every major trade route—from Europe, the ports of the South, and the West. New York traders were the middlemen in southern cotton and western grain trading; in fact, New York was the nation's major cotton-exporting city. Merchants in other cities played a similar role within their own regions.

These newly rich traders invested their profits in processing and then manufacturing, further stimulating the growth of northern cities. Some cities became leaders in specific industries: Rochester became a milling center and Cincinnati—"Porkopolis"—the first meat-packing center.

Banking and other financial institutions also played a significant role in the expansion of commerce and manufacturing and were themselves an important industry. The new financial

Banking and Credit Systems

institutions (banks, insurance companies, and corporations) linked savers—those who put money in the bank—with producers or speculators—those who wished to borrow money for equipment. The expiration of the First Bank of the United States in 1811 after Congress refused to renew its charter acted as a stimulus to state-chartered banks, and in the next five years the number of banks more than doubled. Nonetheless, state banks proved inadequate to spur national growth, and in 1816 Congress chartered the Second Bank of the United States (see page 147).

From then until 1832, however, many farmers, local bankers, and politicians denounced the bank as a monster, and then finally succeeded in killing it.

The closing of the Second Bank in 1836 caused a nationwide credit shortage that, along with the Panic of 1837, stimulated major reforms in banking. Michigan and New York introduced charter laws promoting what was called *free banking*. Previously every new bank had required a special legislative charter, which made each bank incorporation a political decision. Under the new laws, any proposed bank that met certain minimum conditions—amount of money, notes issued, and types of loans to be made—would automatically receive a state charter. Although banks were thus freer to incorporate, more restrictions were placed on their practices, slightly reducing the risk of bank failure. Other states soon followed suit.

Free banking proved a significant stimulus to the economy in the late 1840s and 1850s. New banks sprang up everywhere, providing merchants and manufacturers with the credit they needed. The free banking laws also served as a precedent for general incorporation statutes, which allowed manufacturing firms to receive state charters without special acts. Investors in corporations, called shareholders, were granted *limited liability,* or freedom from responsibility for the company's debts. An attractive feature to potential investors, limited liability thus encouraged people to back new business ventures.

In the 1850s, with credit and capital both more easily obtainable, the pace of industrialization increased. In the North, industry began to rival agriculture and commerce in dollar volume. Meanwhile commercial farming, financed by the credit boom, integrated the early frontier into the northern economy. By 1860 six northern states—Massachusetts, New York, Pennsylvania, Connecticut, Rhode Island, and Ohio—were highly industrialized. The clothing, textile, and shoe industries employed more than 100,000 workers each, lumber 75,000, iron 65,000, and woolens and leather 50,000. Although agriculture still predominated even in these states, industrial employment would soon surpass it.

MILL GIRLS AND MECHANICS

Oh, sing me the song of the Factory Girl!
So merry and glad and free!
The bloom in her cheeks, of health how it speaks,
Oh! a happy creature is she!
She tends the loom, she watches the spindle,
And cheerfully toileth away,
Amid the din of wheels, how her bright eyes kindle,
And her bosom is ever gay.

This idyllic portrait of factory work was an anachronism when it appeared in 1850. But it was a fitting song for the teenage, single women who first left the villages and farms of New England to work in the mills. The mill owners, believing that the degradation of English factory workers arose from their living conditions and not from the work itself, designed a model community offering airy courtyards and river views, secure dormitories, prepared meals, and cultural activities.

Kinship ties, the promise of steady work, and good pay at first lured rural young women into the mills. Many pairs of sisters and cousins worked in the same mill and lived in the same boardinghouse. They helped each other adjust, and letters home brought other kin to the mills. Girls then had few opportunities for work outside their own homes and at the same time their families had less need for their labor. The commercial production of thread and cloth had reduced a good part of the work done in farm households by New England daughters, whereas sons were still needed to assist their fathers. Moreover, the mills paid better wages than did farm work, domestic service, or sewing.

By the 1840s, however, the paternalism of the Lowell system had been replaced by exploitation. In their race for profits, owners lengthened hours, cut wages, and tightened discipline. They also introduced the speed-up and the stretch-out to expand production. The speed-up increased the speed of the

This 1853 timetable from the Lowell Mills illustrates the regimentation workers had to submit to in the new environment of the factory. Note that workers frequently began before daylight, finished after sunset, and were given only half an hour for meals. Museum of American Textile History.

machines, and the stretch-out increased the number of machines a worker had to operate.

What happened in the New England mills occurred in less dramatic fashion throughout the nation. Workers experienced undesirable changes in their tasks and in their relationships with the employers. In the old journeyman-apprentice system that skilled workers had known for centuries, the master had worked alongside his employees, often living in the same household. Work relationships were intensely personal, and there was little social distance between master and journeyman. All

Changes in the Workplace

had an interest in the standards of their craft, and they made their finished goods to order and with pride.

But textile mills, shoe factories, insurance companies, wholesale stores, canals, and the railroads were the antithesis of the old master-journeyman tradition. Supervisors separated the workers from the owners. The division of labor and the use of machines reduced the skills required of workers. And the coming and going of the large work forces was governed by the bell, the steam whistle, or the clock.

New England mill workers responded to their deteriorating working conditions by organizing and striking. In 1834, in reaction to a 25-percent wage cut, they unsuccessfully "turned out" (struck) against the Lowell mills. Two years later, when boardinghouse rates were raised, they turned out again. As conditions worsened, workers changed their methods of resistance. By the 1850s strikes had given way to a concerted effort to shorten the workday. Massachusetts mill women joined forces with other workers to press for legislation mandating a ten-hour day and aired their complaints in worker-run newspapers.

Mill Girl Protests

Economic upheaval and divisions among the workers (native-born versus immigrant) tended to keep organized labor weak during this period. Labor unions tended to be local in nature; the strongest resembled medieval guilds. The first unions arose among urban journeymen in printing, woodworking, shoemaking, and tailoring. These craftsmen sought to protect themselves against the competition of inferior workmen by regulating apprenticeship and establishing minimum wages. In the 1820s and 1830s craft unions—unions organized by occupation—forged larger umbrella organizations in the cities, including the National Trades Union (1834). But in the depression of 1839 through 1843, the movement fell apart amidst wage reductions and unemployment. In the 1850s the deterioration of working conditions strengthened the labor movement again. Workers won a reduction in hours, and the ten-hour day be-

Women shoe workers strike for higher wages at Lynn, Massachusetts, in 1860.   Library of Congress.

came standard. Though the Panic of 1857 wiped out the umbrella organizations, some of the new national unions for specific trade groups survived.

Organized labor's greatest achievement during this period was in gaining recognition of its right to exist. When journeymen shoemakers organized in the first decade of the century, employers turned to the courts, charging criminal conspiracy. The cordwainers' conspiracy cases, which involved six trials from 1806 through 1815, left labor organizations in a tenuous position. Although the journeymen's right to organize was recognized, the courts ruled unlawful any

Right to Strike

coercive action that harmed other businesses or the public. In effect, therefore, strikes were unlawful. Eventually a Massachusetts case, *Commonwealth* v. *Hunt* (1842), effectively reversed the decision when Chief Justice Lemuel Shaw ruled that Boston journeymen bootmakers had a right to combine and strike "in such manner as best to subserve their own interests."

The impact of economic and technological change, however, fell more heavily on individual workers than on their organizations. As a group, the workers' share of the national wealth declined after the 1830s. Individual producers—craftsmen, factory workers,

Chapter 9: A Market and Industrial Economy, 1800–1860

and farmers—had less economic power than they had had a generation or two before. And workers were increasingly losing control over their own work.

COMMERCIAL FARMING

Beyond the town and city limits, agriculture remained the backbone of the economy. Although urban areas were growing quickly, so too were rural districts, and America was still overwhelmingly rural. Indeed, it was rural population growth that transformed so many farm villages into bustling small cities. And it was the ability of farmers to feed the growing town and village populations that made possible the concentration of population and the development of commerce and industry.

New England and Middle Atlantic farmers in 1800 worked as their fathers and mothers had. They tilled relatively small plots of land centered around a household economy in which the needs

Northeastern Agriculture of the family and the labor it supplied mostly determined what was produced and in what amounts. But then canals and railroads began transporting grains, especially wheat, eastward from the fertile Old Northwest. And at the same time, northeastern agriculture developed some serious problems. Northeastern farmers had already cultivated all the land they could; expansion was impossible. Moreover, these small New England farms with their uneven terrain did not lend themselves to the new labor-saving farm implements introduced in the 1830s. Many northeastern farms also suffered from soil exhaustion.

In response to these problems and to competition from the West, many northern farmers either went west or gave up farming for jobs in the merchant houses and factories. Those farmers who remained proved to be quite adaptable. By the 1850s New England and Middle Atlantic farmers were successfully adjusting to western competition. They abandoned commercial production of wheat and corn and stopped tilling poor land. Instead they improved their livestock, especially cattle, and specialized in vegetable and fruit production and dairy farming. They financed these changes through land sales or borrowing. In fact, their greatest profit was made from increasing land values, not from farming itself.

Even so, the Old Northwest gradually and inevitably replaced the northeastern states as the center of American family agriculture. Farms in the Old Northwest were much larger than

Mechanization of Agriculture northeastern ones and better suited to the new mechanized farming implements. The farmers of the region bought machines such as the McCormick reaper on credit and paid for them with the profits from their high yields. By 1847 Cyrus McCormick was selling a thousand reapers a year. Using interchangeable parts, he expanded production to five thousand a year, but still demand outstripped supply. Similarly, John Deere's steel plow, invented in 1837, replaced the inadequate iron plow; steel blades kept the soil from sticking and were tough enough to break the roots of prairie grass. By 1856, Deere's sixty-five employees were making 13,500 plows a year.

These machines eased the problem of scarce farm labor and permitted a 70-percent surge in wheat production in the 1850s alone. By that time the area that had been the western wilderness in 1800 had become one of the world's leading agricultural regions. Midwestern farmers fed an entire nation and a generation of immigrants, and had food to export.

THE WESTERN FRONTIER

Between 1800 and 1860 the frontier moved westward at an incredible pace. In 1800 the edge of settlement formed an arc from western New York through the new states of Kentucky and Tennessee, south to Georgia. Twenty years later it had shifted to

Ohio, Indiana, and Illinois in the North and Louisiana, Alabama, and Mississippi in the South. By 1860 settlement had reached the West Coast. Unsettled

Movement of the Frontier

land remained—mostly between the Mississippi River and the Sierra Nevada—but essentially the frontier and its native inhabitants, the Indians, had given way to white settlement. All that remained for whites was to people the plains and mountain territories.

The lore of the vanishing frontier forms part of the mythology of America. It includes fur trappers, explorers, and pioneers braving an unknown environment and hostile Indians; settlers crossing the arid plains and snow-covered Rockies by Conestoga wagon to bring civilization to the wilderness; Mormons finding Zion in the Great American Desert; forty-niners sailing on clipper ships to California in search of gold.

Americans have only recently come to recognize that there are other sides to these familiar stories. Women, Indians, and blacks as well as white men were pioneers. Explorers and pioneers did not discover North America by themselves, nor did the wagon trains fight their way across the plains—Indians guided them along traditional paths and led them to food and water. And rather than civilizing the frontier, settlers at first brought a rather primitive economy and society, which did not compare favorably with the well-ordered Indian civilizations. Moreover, all those who sought furs, gold, and lumber spoiled the natural landscape in the name of progress and development.

No figure has come to symbolize the frontier more aptly than the footloose, rugged fur trapper, who roamed thousands of unmapped miles in search of pelts. The trapper, with his

Fur Trade

backpack, rifle, and kegs of whiskey, spearheaded America's manifest destiny (see page 221), extending the United States presence to the Pacific Slope. Indeed, the history of trapping was in essence the history of the opening up of the frontier. Early fur traders exploited friendly Indian tribes; then pioneers—mountain trap-

The gold rush brought treasure seekers—men and women, white and black, native and foreign-born—to California. Few found their fortune in gold, but most stayed to settle the West Coast.   California State Library.

pers—monopolized the trade through the systematic organization and financial backing of trading companies. Soon settlements and towns sprang up along the trappers' routes. By the 1840s, with demand at a low ebb and the beaver nearing extinction, fur trading declined. The mining and cattle frontiers were to continue for another half-century, following the development of the fur-trading frontier.

But not all regions followed this pattern. By contrast, California was settled almost overnight. In January 1848 James Marshall, a carpenter, spotted a few gold-like particles in the millrace

California Gold Rush

at Sutter's Mill (now Coloma), California. Word of the discovery spread, and other Californians rushed to garner instant fortunes. By 1849 the news had spread eastward; hundreds of thousands of fortune-seekers flooded in. Most forty-niners never

Chapter 9: A Market and Industrial Economy, 1800–1860

found enough gold to pay their expenses. "The stories you hear frequently in the States," one gold-seeker wrote home, "are the most extravagant lies imaginable—the mines are a humbug. . . . the almost universal feeling is to get home." But many stayed, unable to afford the passage back home, or tempted by the growing labor shortage in California's cities and agricultural districts. San Francisco, the gateway from the coast to the interior, became an instant city, ballooning from 1,000 people in 1848 to 35,000 just two years later.

About one-seventh of the travelers on the overland trails were women, many of whom found their domestic skills in high demand. They received high fees for cooking, laundering, and sewing, and inevitably the boardinghouses and hotels were run by women, as men shunned domestic work. Not all women were entrepreneurs. Some found their domestic skills offered free by over-hospitable husbands. Abigail Scott Duniway, a leading western crusader for women's suffrage and a veteran of the Overland Trail to Oregon, wrote in 1859 of one woman's experience, "It was a hospitable neighborhood composed chiefly of bachelors, who found comfort in mobilizing at meal time at the homes of the few married men of the township, and seemed especially fond of congregating at the hospitable cabin home of my good husband, who was never quite so much in his glory as when entertaining men at this fireside, while I, if not washing, scrubbing, churning, or nursing the baby, was preparing their meals in our lean-to kitchen."

Frontier Women

Gold altered the pattern of settlement along the entire Pacific Coast. Before 1848 most overland traffic flowed north over the Oregon Trail; fewer pioneers turned south to California or used the Santa Fe Trail. But by 1849 a pioneer observed that the Oregon Trail "bore no evidence of having been much traveled this year." Traffic was instead flowing south, and California was becoming the new population center of the Pacific Slope. One measure of the shift was the overland mail routes. In the 1840s the Oregon Trail had been the major communications link between the Pacific and the Midwest. But the Post Office officials who organized mail routes in the 1850s terminated them in California; there was no route farther north than Sacramento.

By 1860 California, like the Great Plains and prairies farther east, had become a farmers' and merchants' frontier. What made farm settlement possible was the availability of land and credit. Some public lands were granted as a reward for military service: veterans of the War of 1812 received 160 acres; veterans of the Mexican War could purchase land at reduced prices. And until 1820, civilians could buy government land at $2 an acre (a relatively high price) on a liberal four-year payment plan. More important, from 1800 to 1817 the government successively reduced the minimum purchase from 640 to 80 acres. However, when the availability of land prompted a flurry of land speculation that ended in the Panic of 1819, the government discontinued credit sales. Instead it reduced the price further, to $1.25 an acre.

Land Grants and Sales

Some eager pioneers settled land before it had been surveyed and put up for sale. Such illegal settlers, or squatters, then had to buy the land they lived on at auction, and faced the risk of being unable to purchase it. In 1841, to facilitate settlement, simplify land sales, and end property disputes, Congress passed the Pre-emption Act, which legalized settlement prior to surveying.

Towns and cities were the lifelines of the agricultural West. Steamboats connected eastern markets and ports with river and lake cities like Louisville and Chicago, carrying grain east and returning with finished goods. These western cities eventually developed into manufacturing centers when merchants shifted their investments from commerce to industry.

For the nation as a whole, the period from 1800 through 1860 was one of sustained growth. Population increased sixfold. Settlement, once restricted to the Atlantic seaboard and the eastern rivers, extended more than a thousand miles inland by 1860 and was spreading east from the Pacific Ocean as well. Whereas agriculture had completely dominated

Important Events

1807	Fulton's steamboat, *Clermont*
1812–15	War of 1812
1813	Boston Manufacturing Company founded
1818	National Road reaches Wheeling, Virginia
1819–23	Depression
1820s	New England textile mills expand
1824	*Gibbons* v. *Ogden*
1825	Erie Canal completed
1830	Baltimore and Ohio Railroad begins operation
1831	McCormick invents the reaper
1834	Mill women strike at Lowell
1837	*Charles River Bridge* v. *Warren Bridge*
1839–43	Depression
1844	Baltimore-Washington telegraph line
1849	California gold rush
1853	British study of American system of manufacturing
1854	Railroad reaches the Mississippi
1857	Depression

gether economic activities hundreds and thousands of miles apart. The market economy brought both sustained growth and cycles of boom and bust. Hard times and unemployment became frequent occurrences.

At the same time, commercial and industrial growth altered production and consumption. Manufactured goods changed farm work as farmers began to purchase goods produced formerly by wives and daughters. Many New England farm daughters left the farms to become the first factory workers in the new textile industry. As factories grew larger and as factory production replaced the master-journeyman-apprentice system, workplace relations became more impersonal and conditions harsher. Immigrants began to form a new industrial group, and some workers organized labor unions.

The American people too were changing. Immigration and western expansion made the people and society more diverse. Urbanization, commerce, and industry produced significant divisions among Americans. And their reach extended deeply into the home as well as the workshop.

Suggestions for Further Reading

General

Stuart Bruchey, *The Roots of American Economic Growth, 1607–1861: An Essay in Social Causation* (1965); David Klingaman and Richard Vedder, eds., *Essays in 19th Century History* (1975); Otto Mayr and Robert C. Post, eds., *Yankee Enterprise. The Rise of the American System of Manufactures* (1981); Douglass C. North, *Economic Growth of the United States, 1790–1860* (1966).

Transportation

Robert G. Albion, *The Rise of New York Port, 1815–1860* (1939); Carter Goodrich, *Government Promotion of Ameri-*

the nation at the turn of the century, by midcentury farming was being challenged by a booming manufacturing sector. And agriculture itself was becoming mechanized.

Economic development changed the American landscape and the way people lived. Canals, railroads, steamboats, and telegraph lines linked tocan Canals and Railroads, 1800–1890 (1960); Harry N. Scheiber, *Ohio Canal Era: A Case Study of Government and the Economy, 1820–1861* (1969); Ronald E. Shaw, *Erie Water West: Erie Canal, 1797–1854* (1966); George R. Taylor, *The Transportation Revolution, 1815–1860* (1951).

Commerce and Manufacturing

Alfred D. Chandler, Jr., *The Visible Hand: Managerial Revolution in American Business* (1977); Thomas C. Cochran, *Frontiers of Change: Early Industrialization in America* (1981); Louis Hartz, *Economic Policy and Democratic Thought: Pennsylvania, 1776–1860* (1954); David J. Jeremy, *Transatlantic Industrial Revolution: The Diffusion of Textile Technologies Between Britain and America, 1790s–1830s* (1981); Stanley I. Kutler, *Privilege and Creative Destruction. The Charles River Bridge Case* (1971); Merritt Roe Smith, *Harpers Ferry Armory and the New Technology* (1977).

Agriculture

Allan G. Bogue, *From Prairie to Corn Belt: Farming on the Illinois and Iowa Prairies in the Nineteenth Century* (1963); Clarence Danhof, *Change in Agriculture: The Northern United States, 1820–1870* (1969); Paul W. Gates, *The Farmer's Age: Agriculture, 1815–1860* (1962); Benjamin H. Hibbard, *A History of Public Land Policies* (1939); Robert Leslie Jones, *History of Agriculture in Ohio to 1880* (1983).

The Western Frontier

Ray A. Billington and Martin Ridge, *Westward Expansion*, 5th ed. (1982); John Mack Faragher, *Women and Men on the Overland Trail* (1979); William H. Goetzmann, *Exploration and Empire: The Explorer and the Scientist in the Winning of the American West* (1966); Julie Roy Jeffrey, *Frontier Women. The Trans-Mississippi West 1840–1880* (1979); Theodore J. Karamanski, *Fur Trade and Exploration. Opening the Far Northwest 1821–1852* (1983); John D. Unruh, Jr., *The Overland Emigrants and the Trans-Mississippi West, 1840–1860* (1979); David J. Wishart, *The Fur Trade of the American West, 1807–1840* (1979).

Workers

Alan Dawley, *Class and Community: The Industrial Revolution in Lynn* (1977); Thomas Dublin, *Women at Work: The Transformation of Work and Community in Lowell, Massachusetts, 1826–1860* (1979); Alice Kessler-Harris, *Out to Work. A History of Wage-Earning Women in the United States* (1982); Norman Ware, *The Industrial Worker, 1840–1860* (1924); Sean Willentz, *Chants Democratic: New York City and the Rise of the American Working Class* (1984).

CHAPTER 10

TOWARD GREATER DIVERSITY: THE AMERICAN PEOPLE 1800–1860

*T*he *Englishwoman Frances* Trollope, in her *Domestic Manners of the Americans* (1832), described the audience at a Cincinnati theater: "The spitting was incessant," accompanied by "the mixed smell of onions and whiskey. . . . The noises, too, were perpetual, and of the most unpleasant kind." Indeed, theater regularly evoked the strongest of passions among Americans. "When a patriotic fit seized them, and 'Yankee Doodle' was called for," Trollope observed, "every man seemed to think his reputation as a citizen depended on the noise he made."

During the first half of the nineteenth century, the theater was both a pre-eminent institution and a mirror of American social life. Like society itself, theater audiences were divided by occupation, wealth, status, sex, and race. But as the gap between the classes yawned wider, different houses began to cater to different classes. In New York, the Park Theater enjoyed the patronage of the carriage trade, the Bowery drew the middle class, and the Chatham attracted workers. The opera house generally became the upper-class playhouse.

As the United States grew, its society became at once more diverse and more turbulent. More and more people lived in cities, where poverty, overcrowding, and crime set them against each other. Opulent mansions existed within sight of notorious slums, and both wealth and poverty reached extremes unknown in traditional agrarian America.

Private life changed too during these years. With increasing industrialization, the home began to lose its function as a workplace, especially among the middle and upper classes. It became woman's domain, a refuge from the jungle of a man's world. At the same time birth control was more widely practiced and families became smaller.

To a great degree, many Americans were uncomfortable with the new direction of American life. Antipathy toward immigrants was common among native-born Americans, who feared competition for jobs. Some blacks fought unceasingly for equality, and many Indians tried unsuccessfully to resist forced removal. And a minority of women began to raise their voices against the restrictions they faced. In a diverse and complex society, conflict became common.

COUNTRY LIFE, CITY LIFE

Communities, and life within them, changed significantly in the first half of the nineteenth century. Within a generation many frontier settlements became sources rather than recipients of migration. Villages in western New York State lured the sons and daughters of New England in the first two decades of the century. Yet in the 1820s and 1830s, young people moved from New York villages to the new frontier in the Old Northwest. Later, Ohio and Michigan towns and farms would send their young people farther west. Similarly, migrants from the Upper South went to Illinois and Ohio as people on the move farther south settled the Gulf states.

Throughout the United States the farm community dominated rural America. The farm village was the center of rural life. But rural social life was not limited to trips to the village; families gathered on each other's farms to do as a community what they could not do individually. Barn-raising was among the activities that regularly brought people together. In preparation for the event, the farmer and an itinerant carpenter built a platform and cut beams, posts, and joists. When the neighbors arrived by buggy and wagon, they put together the sides and raised them into position. After the roof was up, everyone celebrated with a communal meal, and perhaps with singing and dancing.

Farm Communities

Similar gatherings took place at harvest time and on special occasions.

Rural women met more formally than did men. Farm men had frequent opportunities to mix at general stores, markets, and taverns. Women had to prearrange their regular work and social gatherings: after-church dinners; sewing, quilting, and corn-husking bees; and preparations for marriages and baptisms. These were times to exchange experiences and thoughts, offer each other support, and swap letters, books, and news.

Concurrent to the movement of rural folk in a westerly direction was the growth of the nation's cities, especially in the North. The transportation revolution and the expansion of commerce and manufacturing, fed by immigration and internal migration, caused cities to burst their colonial boundaries. Between 1800 and 1860, the number of Americans increased sixfold to 31.4 million. As the population grew, the frontier receded, and rural settlements became towns. In 1800 the nation had only 33 towns with 2,500 or more people and only 3 with more than 25,000. By 1860, 392 towns exceeded 2,500 in population, 35 had more than 25,000, and 9 exceeded 100,000 (see maps, page 172).

On the eve of the Civil War, the nation had several great metropolitan cities. In 1860 New York City's population reached 1,174,779. Elsewhere in the nation certain communities came to dominate their geographic areas. In the South, Baltimore and New Orleans became the pre-eminent cities. San Francisco dominated the West Coast, and in the Midwest the new lake cities of Chicago, Detroit, and Cleveland began to overtake the older river cities of Cincinnati, Louisville, and Pittsburgh.

Rapid urban growth in turn brought about a radical change in American commerce and trade. In 1800 most merchants performed the functions of retailer, wholesaler, importer and exporter, and banker. But in New York and Philadelphia in the 1790s, and increasingly in all large cities after the War of 1812, the general merchant gave way to the specialist. As a result, the distribution of goods became more systematic. By the 1830s and 1840s, urban centers had been

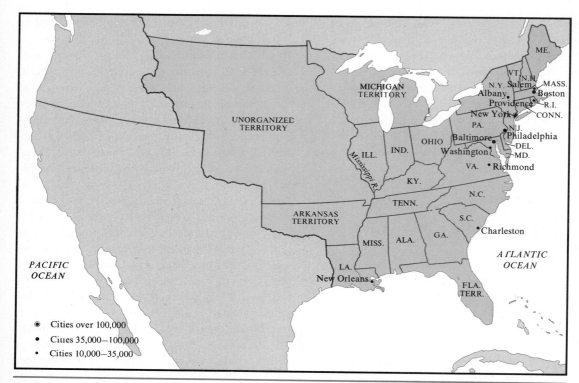

Major American Cities, 1820

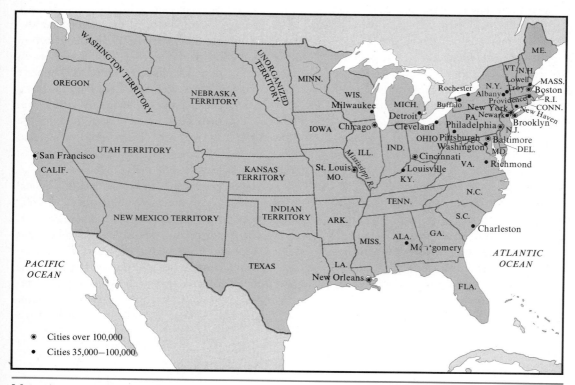

Major American Cities, 1860

transformed into a pattern we would recognize today: retail shops featured such specialized lines as shoes, wines and spirits, dry goods, and hardware. Within the downtown area importers and exporters, wholesalers, bankers, and insurance brokers clustered on particular streets, near transportation and the merchant exchanges that catered to specialized trades.

Other city institutions became more complex as well. As the workplace and home grew apart, there were fewer opportunities to turn work into festivals or family gatherings as rural folk did in barn-raisings and corn-shuckings.

City Life

In cities, amusements were more organized than in the country. Entertainment became part of specialized commerce; one purchased a ticket—to the theater, the circus, or P. T. Barnum's American Museum; or in the 1840s, to the racetrack; or a decade later, to the baseball park. The concentration of population in cities supported this diversity of activities.

By twentieth-century standards, early nineteenth-century cities were disorderly, unsafe, and unhealthy. Expansion occurred so suddenly and swiftly that few cities could handle the problems it brought. For example, migrants from rural areas were used to relieving themselves and throwing refuse in any vacant area. But in the city, waste spread disease, polluted wells, and gave off obnoxious smells. In some districts scavengers and refuse collectors carted away garbage and human waste, but in much of the city it just rotted.

Crime was another problem. To keep order and provide for public safety, Boston supplemented (1837) and New York replaced (1845) its colonial watchmen and constables with paid policemen. Nonetheless, middle-class men and women did not venture out alone at night, and during the day stayed clear of many city districts. And the influx of immigrants to the cities compounded social tensions by pitting people of different backgrounds against each other in the contest for jobs and housing. Ironically, in the midst of the dirt, the noise, the crime, and the conflict, rose the opulent residences of the very rich.

EXTREMES OF WEALTH

Some observers, notably the young French visitor Alexis de Tocqueville, saw the United States before the Civil War as a place of equality and opportunity. To Tocqueville, American equality—the relative fluidity of the United States social order—was the result of its citizens' geographic mobility. Migration offered people opportunities to start anew regardless of where they came from or who they were. Prior wealth or family or education mattered little; a person could be known by deeds alone. Talent and hard work, many Americans and Europeans believed, found their just reward in such an atmosphere. It was common advice that anyone could advance by working hard and saving money.

But other observers recorded the rise of a new aristocracy based on wealth and power, and growing class and ethnic divisions. Among those who disagreed with the egalitarian view of

Differences in Wealth

American life was *New York Sun* publisher Moses Yale Beach, author of twelve editions of *Wealth and Biography of the Wealthy Citizens of New York City*. In 1845 Beach listed a thousand New Yorkers with assets of $100,000 or more. Tocqueville himself, ever sensitive to the conflicting trends in American life, had described the growth of an American aristocracy based on industrial wealth. The rich and well educated "come forward to exploit industries," Tocqueville wrote, and become "more and more like the administrators of a huge empire. . . . What is this if not an aristocracy?"

Wealth throughout the United States was becoming concentrated in the hands of a relatively small number of people. In New York City between 1828 and 1845, the wealthiest 4 percent of the city's population increased their holdings from an estimated 63 percent to 80 percent of all individual wealth. By 1860 the top 5 percent of American families owned more than half the nation's wealth; the top tenth owned over 70 percent.

Inequality, urbanization, and immigration contributed to the renewal of urban conflict as rioting and sporadic incidents of violence became frequent. The colonial tradition of crowd action, in which disfranchised people took to the streets, had diminished in the first three decades of the nineteenth century. In the 1830s riots again became commonplace as professionals and merchants, skilled craftsmen, and ordinary laborers vented their rage against their opponents. "Gentlemen of property and standing," unnerved by the abolitionist attack on American society and traditional leadership, sacked abolitionist newspapers and offices and attacked antislavery advocates throughout the nation. In the 1840s "respectable" citizens waged war against the Mormons, driving them from Illinois and Missouri. Skilled workers raged against new migrants to the cities and other symbols of the new industrial order. These disturbances climaxed in the great riots of 1844, in which mostly Protestant skilled workers fought Irish Catholics. In the 1850s nativist riots peaked. By 1840 more than 125 people had died in urban riots, and by 1860 more than 1,000.

Urban Riots

A cloud of uncertainty hung over working men and women. Many were afraid that in periods of economic depression they would become part of the urban flotsam and jetsam of able-bodied men and women, white and black, who could not find steady work. They feared the competition of immigrant and slave labor. They feared the insecurities and indignities of poverty, chronic illness, disability, old age, widowhood, and desertion. And they had good reason.

Indeed, poverty and squalor stalked the urban working class as cities grew. Cities were notorious for the dilapidated districts where newly arrived immigrants, indigent blacks, working poor, and thieves, beggars, and prostitutes lived. Five Points in New York City's Sixth Ward became the worst slum

Urban Slums

in pre–Civil War America. The neighborhood was equally divided between Irish and blacks. Ill-suited to human habitation and lacking such amenities as running water and sewers, it exemplified the worst of urban life.

A world apart from Five Points and the people of the streets was the upper-class elite society of Philip Hone, one-time mayor of New York. Hone's diary, meticulously kept from 1826 until his death in 1851, records the activities of an American aristocrat. On February 28, 1840, for instance, Hone attended a masked ball at the Fifth Avenue mansion of Henry Breevoort, Jr., and Laura Carson Breevoort. The ball began at the fashionable hour of 10 P.M., and the five hundred ladies and gentlemen who filled the mansion wore costumes adorned with ermine and gold. Few balls attained such grandeur, but at one time or another similar parties were held in Boston, Philadelphia, Baltimore, and Charleston.

Urban Elite

The basis of this new wealth tended to be inherited. For every John Jacob Astor who made his millions in the western fur trade, or George Law who left a farm to become a millionaire contractor and investor in railroads and banks, there were ten who built additional wealth on money they inherited or married. Many of the wealthiest bore the names of the colonial commercial elite—Beekman, Breevoort, Roosevelt, Van Rensselaer, and Whitney. Yet these men were not an idle class; they devoted energy to increasing their fortunes and power. Hardly a major canal, railroad, bank, or mill venture lacked the names and investments of the fashionable elite. Wealth begat wealth, and family ties through inheritance and marriage were essential in that world.

More modest in wealth, though hard working, were those in the expanding middle class. The growth and specialization of trade had rapidly increased their numbers, and they were a distinct part of the urban scene. The men were businessmen or professionals, the women homemakers. They were mindful that the gulf between themselves and manual workers was narrow.

The infamous Five Points section of New York City's Sixth Ward, probably the worst slum in pre–Civil War America. Immodestly dressed prostitutes cruise the streets or gaze from windows, while a pig roots for garbage in their midst. Courtesy of the New-York Historical Society.

WOMEN AND THE FAMILY

Economic change transformed women and families too, and made them more diverse. What had been fairly similar backgrounds of native-born white women began to splinter and to show differences by class, life cycle, and place of residence. Families too varied greatly, and change affected them at different rates and in varying ways.

Increasingly, women's and men's work grew apart, as men left their homes to "go to work." On farms, there was still an overlap, but in the new shops, offices, and factories, tasks diverged. Specialization in business and production accompanied specialization in work tasks; men acquired new, narrower skills, which were applied in set ways with purposefully designed tools and systems. Authority within the work

While sensitive to the changing life cycles of women, the above lithograph emphasizes the domestic ideal to which most women aspired. But in depicting the roles of daughter, wife, and mother, it neglects woman's paid employment. Library of Congress.

environment, removed from the household, became more formal and impersonal.

Some women shared these experiences for brief periods in their lives. New England farm daughters who were the first textile-mill workers left home to perform new specialized work tasks. The new urban department stores hired young women as clerks and cash runners. Others worked in the expanding needle trades. Paid employment represented merely a stage in their life cycle, a brief period between their parental and marital households.

Working-class women—the poor, widows, free

Working Women

blacks—worked for wages most of their lives. Leaving their parental homes as early as twelve or thirteen, they took jobs, with only short respites for bearing children and rearing infants. Unlike men, however, most of these women did not work in the new shops and factories. Instead they worked as domestic servants in other women's homes and as laundresses, seamstresses, cooks, and boardinghouse keepers.

Increasingly work took on greater gender meaning and segregation. Most women's work centered, as it always had, on the home. As the family lost its importance in the production of goods, household upkeep and childbearing continued to magnify in importance, requiring women's full-time attention. Education, religion, morality, domestic arts, and culture began to overshadow the productive functions of the family. These roles became associated for many with ideal female characteristics, what has come to be called woman's sphere or the cult of domesticity of the nineteenth century.

Many American women and men placed great importance on the family. The role of the mother was to ensure the nation's future by rearing her children and providing her husband with a spiritual and virtuous environment. The family was to be a moral institution where selflessness and cooperation ruled. Thus women were idealized as the embodiment of self-sacrificing republicanism. Amidst a rapidly changing world in which single men and women left their parental homes and villages, in which factories and stores replaced traditional production and distribution, the family was supposed to be a rock of stability and traditional values.

The domestic ideal limited the paying jobs middle-class women could hold outside the home. Most paid work was viewed with disapproval since it conflicted with the ideal of domesticity. One occupation did come to be recognized as consistent with the genteel female nature: teaching. In 1823 Catharine Beecher established a female academy with her sister Mary. Their Hartford Female Seminary added philosophy, history, and science to the traditional women's curriculum of domestic arts and religious education. In the 1830s Catharine Beecher campaigned to establish schools for girls and training seminaries for female teachers. Viewing formal education as an extension of women's nurturing role, Beecher had great success in spreading her message. By the 1850s schoolteaching became a popular vocation for women, with women teachers in the majority in most large cities. Their pay, however, was often half that of male teachers.

While woman's work outside the home remained limited, family size was shrinking. A number of factors lowered the birth rate. For many people, family life became less important as migration loosened family bonds. Others came to believe that by having fewer children they could provide greater opportunities to their offspring. City life, by placing less pressure on young people to marry than did rural life, also contributed to the lower birth rate. Finally, marriage manuals stressed the harmful effects of too many births on a woman's health.

Decline in the Birth Rate

How did men and women limit their families in the early nineteenth century? Many married later, thus shortening the period of childbearing. More important, however, was the fairly widespread use of birth control. The popular marriage guide by the physician Charles Knowlton, *Fruits of Philosophy; or, the Private Companion of Young Married People* (1832), provides us with a glimpse of contemporary birth control methods. Probably the most widespread practice was *coitus interruptus,* or withdrawal of the male before completion of the sexual act. But medical devices were beginning to compete with this ancient folk practice. Cheap rubber condoms were widely adopted when they became available in the 1850s. And some couples used the rhythm method—attempting to confine intercourse to a woman's infertile periods. Knowledge of the "safe period," however, was uncertain even among physicians. Another method was abstinence, or less frequent sexual intercourse. For those desiring to terminate a pregnancy, surgical abortions became common after 1830. By 1860, however, twenty states had outlawed abortions.

Birth Control

Sarah Ripley of Massachusetts, an eighteenth-century young girl and a nineteenth-century adult, revealed in her diaries the changes American society was experiencing. Daughter of a Greenfield shopkeeper, she had a privileged childhood. After completing school she worked as a shop assistant in her father's store. In 1812, after a five-year courtship, she married Charles Stearns of Shelburn. "I have now acquitted the abode of my youth, left the protection of my parents and given up the name I have always borne," she recorded in her diary. "May the grace of God enable me to fulfill with pru-

Sarah Ripley Stearns

dence and piety the great and important duties which now evolve on me." Yet she missed the bustle of the shop, as she confessed in her diary.

Sarah Ripley Stearns's life was not a settled one; change was everywhere. During the six years following her marriage, she bore three children, moved three times, became a widow, and found an anchor in religion. For Stearns, as well as other middle-class women, social interaction within the church made it possible to extend the bounds of the ideal of domesticity. Stearns and her neighbors, for example, sponsored a school society and juvenile home. Such benevolent-society work both aided poor children and allowed the female participants to gain experience in raising funds, chairing meetings, and cultivating an extended network with other women.

At the same time, working women were pioneering new roles for women beyond the home. Many found teaching a rewarding profession and preferred it to marriage and domesticity. Mill girls forged new roles for women, as did the women who assembled at Seneca Falls, New York, in 1848. Modeling their protest on the Declaration of Independence, they called for political, social, and economic equality for women. Free black women, however, had little choice between paid employment and maintaining households and rearing children. Their different tasks had to be accomplished simultaneously. Immigrant women, too, often had to combine many roles at the same time.

IMMIGRANT LIVES IN AMERICA

No less than gender, ethnic and religious differences divided Americans. In numbers alone immigrants drastically altered the United States. The 5 million immigrants who settled in the states between 1820 and 1860 outnumbered the entire population of the country at the first census in 1790. They came from all continents, though Europeans made up the vast majority. The peak period of pre–Civil War immigration was from 1847 through 1857; in that eleven-year period, 3.3 million immigrants entered the United States, 1.3 million from Ireland and 1.1 million from the German states. By 1860, 15 percent of the white population was foreign-born.

This massive migration had been set in motion decades earlier when the Napoleonic wars initiated one of the greatest population shifts in history. One part of the movement, increasingly significant as time went on, was emigration of Europeans to the United States. War, revolution, famine, industrialization, and religious persecution oppressed weary Europeans. Meanwhile, the United States beckoned, offering them economic opportunity and religious freedom.

European Immigration

So they came, enduring the hardships of travel and of settling in a strange land. The journey was difficult. The average crossing took six weeks; in bad weather it could take three months. Disease spread unchecked among people huddled together like cattle in steerage. More than 17,000 immigrants, mostly Irish, died from "ship fever" in 1847. On disembarking, immigrants became fair game for the con artists and swindlers who worked the docks. In 1855, in response to the immigrants' plight, New York State's commissioners of emigration established Castle Garden as an immigrant center. There, at the tip of Manhattan Island, the major port of entry, immigrants were somewhat sheltered from fraud.

Most immigrants gravitated toward the cities, since only a minority had farming experience or the means to purchase land and equipment. Many stayed in New York itself. By 1845, 35 percent of the city's 371,000 people were of foreign birth. Ten years later 52 percent of its 623,000 inhabitants were immigrants. Boston, an important entry point for the Irish, took on a European tone. Throughout the 1850s the city was about 35 percent foreign-born, of whom more than two-thirds were Irish. In the South, too, major cities had large immigrant populations. In

1860 New Orleans was 44 percent foreign-born, Savannah 33 percent, and the border city of St. Louis, 61 percent. On the West Coast, San Francisco had a foreign-born majority.

Some immigrants, however, did settle in rural areas. In particular, German, Dutch, and Scandinavian farmers gravitated toward the Midwest. Greater percentages of Scandinavians and Netherlanders took up farming than other nationalities; both groups came mostly as religious dissenters and migrated in family units. The Dutch, under such leaders as Albertus C. Van Raalte, fled persecution in their native land to establish new and more pious communities—Holland and Zeeland, Michigan, among them.

Success in America bred further emigration. "I wish, and do often say that we wish you were all in this happy land," wrote shoemaker John West of Germantown, Pennsylvania, to his kin in Corsley, England, in 1831. "A man nor woman need not stay out of employment one hour here," he advised. "No war nor insurrection here. *But all is plenty and peace.*" Others wrote of the room still left in America.

Promotion of Immigration

American institutions, both public and private, actively recruited European emigrants. Western states lured potential settlers in the interest of promoting their economies. In the 1850s, for instance, Wisconsin appointed a commissioner of emigration, who advertised the state's advantages in American and European newspapers. Wisconsin also opened a New York office and hired European agents to compete with other states and with firms like the Illinois Central Railroad for immigrants' attention.

Before the potato blight hit Ireland, tens of thousands of Irish were lured to America by recruiters. They came to swing picks and shovels on American canals and railroads, to dig the foundations of mills and factories. Thousands of those who came, however, found bitter disappointment and returned to Ireland.

Immigrant Disenchantment

Among them was Michael Gaugin, who had the misfortune of arriving in New York City during the financial panic of 1837. Gaugin, an assistant engineer in the construction of the Ballinasloe Canal in Dublin, had been attracted to the states by the promise that "he should soon become a wealthy man." Within two months of arriving in the United States, Gaugin had become a pauper. In August 1837 he declared he was "now without means for the support of himself and his family, and has no employment, and has already suffered great deprivation since he arrived in this country; and is now soliciting means to enable him to return with his family home to Ireland." Many of those who had come with the Gaugins had already returned home.

Such experiences did not deter Irish men and women from coming to the United States. Ireland was the most densely populated European country, and among the most impoverished. From 1815 on, small harvests prompted a steady stream of Irish to emigrate to America. Then in 1845 and 1846 potatoes—the basic Irish food— rotted in the fields. From 1845 to 1849, death in the form of starvation, malnutrition, and typhus spread. In all, 1 million died and about 1.5 million fled, two-thirds of them to the United States.

Irish Immigrants

In the 1840s and 1850s a total of 1.7 million Irish men and women entered the United States. At the peak of Irish immigration, from 1847 to 1854, 1.2 million came. By the end of the century there would be more Irish in the United States than in Ireland.

The new Irish immigrants differed greatly from those who had left Ireland to settle in the American colonies. In the eighteenth century, the Scotch-Irish predominated, and their journey had involved moving from one part of the British Empire to another. The nineteenth-century Roman Catholic Irish travelers to America, however, moved from still-colonial Ireland to an independent republic, and the political and religious differences made their cultural adaptation that much more difficult. In comparison with the Scotch-Irish, the newer immigrants from Ireland tended to be younger, increasingly female, and mostly from the rural provinces.

In the urban areas, where they clustered in poverty, most Irish immigrants met growing anti-immigrant, anti-Catholic sentiment. Everywhere "No Irish Need Apply" signs appeared. During the colonial period, white Protestant settlers had feared "popery" as a system of tyranny and had discriminated against the few Catholics in America. Following the Revolution, anti-Catholicism receded. But in the 1830s the trend reversed, and anti-Catholicism appeared wherever the Irish did. Attacks on the papacy and the church circulated widely in the form of libelous texts like *The Awful Disclosures of Maria Monk* (1836), which alleged sexual orgies among priests and nuns. Nowhere was anti-Catholicism more open and nasty than in Boston, though such sentiments were widespread.

Anti-Catholicism

The native-born who embraced anti-Catholicism were motivated largely by anxiety. They feared that a militant Roman church would subvert American society, that unskilled Irish workers would displace American craftsmen, and that the slums inhabited in part by the Irish were undermining the nation's values. Every American problem from immorality and the evils of alcohol to poverty and economic upheaval was blamed on immigrant Irish Catholics. Friction increased as Irish-American men fought back against anti-Irish and anti-Catholic prejudice; in the 1850s they began to vote and to become active in politics.

Though potato blight also sent many Germans to the United States in the 1840s, other hardships contributed to the steady stream of German immigrants. Many came from areas where small landholdings made it hard to eke out a living and to pass on land to their sons. Others were craftsmen displaced by the industrial revolution. These refugees were joined by middle-class Germans who had sought to unify the three dozen or so German states in a

German Immigrants

liberal republic. Frustration with abortive revolutions like one that occurred in 1848 led them to emigrate to the United States. For some, the only other choice was jail.

Unlike the Irish, who tended to congregate in towns and cities, Germans settled everywhere. Many came on German cotton boats, disembarked at New Orleans, and traveled up the Mississippi. In the South they became peddlers and merchants; in the North and West they worked as farmers, urban laborers, and businessmen. Also unlike the Irish, they tended to migrate in families. A strong desire to maintain the German language and culture prompted them to colonize areas as a group.

In adhering to German traditions, German-Americans too met with antiforeign attitudes. More than half the German immigrants were Catholic, and their Sabbath practices were different from the Protestants'. On Sundays German families typically gathered at beer gardens to eat and drink beer, to dance, sing, and listen to band music, and sometimes to play cards. Protestants were outraged by such violations of the Lord's day.

Their persistence in using the German language and their different religious beliefs set them apart. Besides the Catholic majority, a significant number of German immigrants were Jewish. And even the Protestants—mostly Lutherans—founded their own churches and often educated their children in German-language schools. Not all Germans, however, were religious. The failure of the revolution of 1848 had sent to the United States a whole generation of liberals and freethinkers, some of whom were socialists, communists, and anarchists. The freethinkers entered politics with a loud voice, embracing abolitionism and the Republican party.

For immigrants, conflict centered around their desire to be part of American society, albeit for some on their own terms. Once here, they claimed their right to a fair economic and political share. Indians, on the other hand, had to defend what they conceived of as prior rights. Their land, their religion, their way of life came under constant attack as they were most often viewed as an obstacle to expansion and economic growth.

INDIAN RESISTANCE AND REMOVAL

The clash between Indians and the larger society had been inherited from the colonial past. Population growth, westward expansion, the transportation revolution, and invigorated capitalism underlay the designs and demands on Indian land. At best Indians could hope for mutual understanding, but when that rare event occurred, it was only on a personal level. Whatever good intentions motivated the leaders of the republic, they were subordinated to the desire for Indian land. Indian resistance proved incapable of protecting either their land or their traditional culture.

As the colonial powers in North America had done, the United States treated Indian tribes as sovereign nations until Congress ended the practice in 1871. In its relations with tribal leaders, the government followed the ritual of international protocol. Indian chiefs and delegations who visited Washington were received with the appropriate pomp and ceremony. Agreements between a tribe and the United States were signed, sealed, and ratified as was any international pact.

In practice, however, Indian sovereignty was a fiction. Though protocol seemed to acknowledge independence and mutual respect, treaty negotiations exposed the fiction. Essentially, treaty-making was a process used to acquire Indian land. Differences in power made it less than the bargaining of two equal nations. Treaties were often made between victors and vanquished. In a context of coercion, old treaties often gave way to new ones in which the Indians ceded their traditional holdings in return for different lands in the West.

The War of 1812 snuffed out whatever realistic hopes Indian leaders might have had of resisting American expansion by warfare. Armed resistance persisted, and it was bloody on both sides, as in the Seminole Wars, but only the revived idea of pan-Indian federation offered any hope to counter the military might of the United States. The Shawnee chiefs Prophet and Tecumseh attempted to build such a movement, taking advantage of Anglo-American friction in the decade before the War of 1812, but in the end it failed. And with it died the most significant resistance to the federal government's treaty-making tactics.

Prophet's early experiences mirror the fate that befell many frontier tribes. Born in 1775, a few months after his father had died in battle, Prophet was afterward abandoned by his mother, who rejoined her native tribe farther west. He was raised by his sister and called Lalawethika (noisemaker) as a young man. He was among the defeated Shawnee at the Battle of Fallen Timbers and among the Indians expelled under the 1795 Treaty of Greenville (see page 111). Within the shrunken territory granted in the treaty, game became scarce and Lalawethika found it difficult to feed his family. Disease among his people and encroachment by whites further discouraged him.

Prophet

In 1804 Lalawethika, who had earlier been befriended by a local shaman, became a medicine man. The following year he emerged from an illness as a new man, called Prophet. Claiming to have died and been resurrected, he told a visionary tale of this experience and warned of damnation for those who drank whiskey. In the following years, Prophet traveled widely in the Northwest as a holy man, attacking the decline of moral values among Indians, condemning intertribal battles, and stressing harmony and respect for elders. In essence he preached the re-

The Shawnee Chiefs Prophet (left) and Tecumseh (right).
The two brothers preached Indian federation against white en-
croachment. In the War of 1812 they allied themselves with
the British, but Tecumseh's death and British indifference there-
after caused Indian resistance to collapse. Prophet: National
Museum of American Art, Smithsonian Institution; Gift of
Mrs. Joseph Harrison, Jr. Tecumseh: Courtesy Field Museum
of Natural History, Chicago (#93851).

vitalization of traditional Shawnee culture. Return to
the old ways, he told the Indians of the Old Northwest, abandon white customs.

Prophet's message was a reassuring one to the
Shawnee, Potawatomi, and other Indians of the Old
Northwest who felt unsettled and threatened by
whites. Prophet won converts by performing mira-
cles—he darkened the sun by coinciding this act with
an eclipse—and used opposition to federal Indian
policy to draw others into his camp.

The government and white settlers were alarmed
by the religious revival led by Prophet. With his

brother, Tecumseh, he refused to leave lands claimed
by the government. In 1808 Proph-
et and his brother began to turn
from a message of spiritual renewal
to one of resistance to white aggression. In repudiat-
ing land sales to the government under the Treaty of
Fort Wayne (1809), Tecumseh told Indiana's Governor William Henry Harrison at Vincennes in 1810,
"The only way to check and stop this evil is, for all
the red men to unite in claiming a common and equal
right in the land." Tecumseh then warned that the
Indians would resist white occupation of the 2.5 mil-

Tecumseh

lion acres on the Wabash they had ceded to the United States in the Treaty of Fort Wayne.

A year later, using a Potawatomi raid on an Illinois settlement as an excuse, Harrison attacked and demolished Prophet's Town, Tecumseh's headquarters on Tippecanoe Creek in Indiana Territory. Losses on both sides were heavy. When the War of 1812 started, Tecumseh joined the British in return for a promise of an Indian country in the Great Lakes region. But he was killed in the Battle of the Thames in October 1813, and with his death Indian unity collapsed. (Prophet failed in his attempt to rally the remnants of the movement. He emigrated with the Shawnee to Kansas, where he died in 1836.)

By 1820 Indians in Ohio, southern Indiana and Illinois, southwestern Michigan, most of Missouri, central Alabama, and southern Mississippi had been forced to cede their lands. They **Indian Policy** had given up nearly 200 million acres for pennies an acre. But white settlers' appetites were insatiable; the expansion of commercial farming in the Midwest and of cotton plantations in the South increased demands for Indian land and for Indians to assimilate. One instrument that served both purposes was the Indian agency system, which monopolized trade with Indians in a designated locality and paid out the rations, supplies, and annuities that Indians received in exchange for abandoning their land. The tribes became dependent on these government payments—a dependency intended to make them more docile in treaty negotiations.

At the same time, reformers sought to assimilate Indians into American society by educating and Christianizing them. Motivated by a sincere concern for Indians and influenced by the Second Great Awakening, female missionary and benevolent societies assisted in founding four Christian schools for Indians by 1819. In that year, under missionary lobbying, Congress appropriated $10,000 annually for the "civilization of the tribes adjoining the frontier settlements." This "civilization act" was a means to teach Indians to live like white settlers.

To settlers eyeing Indian land, assimilation through education was too slow a process, and Indians themselves questioned the instruction. Some Indian tribes, for example, found the missionary message repugnant. The Creek nation permitted the schools only after being assured that there would be no preaching. Zealous missionaries violated the agreement, preaching to the Creek and their black slaves. With no other recourse available, a band of Creek sacked the school.

It became apparent in the 1820s that neither economic dependency nor education could force Indians to cede voluntarily much more land to meet the demands of expansionists. Attention focused on the Cherokee, Creek, Choctaw, Chickasaw, and Seminole tribes in the South because much of their land remained intact after the War of 1812 and because they aggressively resisted white encroachment.

In his last annual message in December 1824, President James Monroe suggested to Congress that all **Indian Removal** Indians settle beyond the Mississippi River. Monroe, in a subsequent special message to Congress, advocated the removal of the Indians. The southern tribes unanimously rejected Monroe's plan.

Pressure from Georgia had prompted Monroe's policy. Most Cherokee and some Creek lived in northwestern Georgia, and in the 1820s the state accused the federal government of not fulfilling its 1802 promise to remove the Indians in return for the state's renunciation of its claim to western lands. Georgia sought complete removal and was not satisfied by Monroe's removal messages. Meanwhile, the Cherokees in 1827 attempted to resist forced removal by adopting a written constitution modeled after the United States system and by organizing themselves officially as an independent nation. But in 1828 the Georgia legislature annulled the constitution, extended state sovereignty over the Cherokee, and ordered the seizure of tribal lands.

In 1829 the Cherokee turned to the federal courts to defend their treaty with the United States and prevent Georgia's seizure of their land. In *Cherokee Nation v. Georgia* (1831), Chief Justice John Marshall

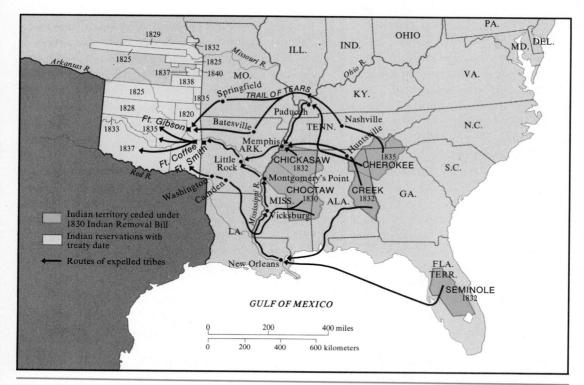

Removal of the Indians from the South,
1820–1840 Source: Redrawn by permission of Macmillan
Publishing Company, Inc. From American History Atlas *by*
Martin Gilbert, cartography by Peter Kingsland. Copyright ©
1968 by Martin Gilbert.

ruled that under the federal Constitution an Indian tribe was neither a foreign nation nor a state, and therefore had no standing in federal courts. Nonetheless, said Marshall, the Indians had an unquestioned right to their lands; they could lose title only by voluntarily giving it up. A year later, in *Worcester* v. *Georgia*, Marshall defined the Cherokee position more clearly. The Indian nation was, he declared, a distinct political community in which "the laws of Georgia can have no force" and into which Georgians could not enter without permission or treaty privilege.

Cherokee Nation v. Georgia

President Andrew Jackson had little sympathy for the Indians and ignored the Supreme Court's ruling. Keen to open up new lands for settlement, he was determined to remove the Cherokee at all costs. In the Removal Act of 1830 Congress provided Jackson the funds he needed to negotiate new treaties and resettle the resistant tribes west of the Mississippi. The Choctaw were the first to go (see map). Soon other tribes were forced west: the Creek in 1836 and the Chickasaw in 1837. The Cherokee, having fought through the courts to stay, found themselves divided. Some recognized the hopelessness of further

Trail of Tears

Chapter 10: TOWARD GREATER DIVERSITY: THE AMERICAN PEOPLE, 1800–1860

resistance and accepted removal as the only chance to preserve their civilization. The leaders of this minority signed a treaty in 1835 in which they agreed to exchange their southern home for western land. But when the time for evacuation came in 1838, most Cherokee refused to move. President Martin Van Buren then sent federal troops to round up the Indians. About twenty thousand Cherokee were evicted, held in detention camps, and marched to Oklahoma under military escort. Nearly one-quarter died of disease and exhaustion on the infamous Trail of Tears. When it was all over, the Indians had traded about 100 million acres of land east of the Mississippi for 32 million acres west of the river plus $68 million.

A small band of Seminole successfully resisted removal and remained in Florida. In the 1832 Treaty of Payne's Landing, tribal chiefs agreed to relocate to the West within three years. Under

Seminole War

Osceola, however, a minority refused to vacate their homes, and from 1835 on they waged a fierce guerrilla war against the United States. The army in turn attempted, ruthlessly but unsuccessfully, to exterminate the Seminole. In 1842 the United States finally abandoned the Seminole War; it had cost 1,500 soldiers' lives and $20 million. Osceola's followers remained in Florida.

A complex set of attitudes drove whites to force Indian removal. Most merely wanted Indian lands. Others were aware of the injustice, but believed the Indians must inevitably give way to white settlement. Some, like John Quincy Adams, believed the only way to preserve Indian civilization was to remove the tribes and establish a buffer zone between Indians and whites. Others, including Thomas Jefferson, hoped to "civilize" the Indians and assimilate them slowly into American culture. Whatever the source of white behavior, the outcome was the same: the devastation of Native American people and their culture.

Another minority experienced insecurity and struggled for recognition and legal rights. Like most Indians, they too were involuntarily a part of American society. Unlike Indians, however, they wished to be fully a part of the American people.

FREE PEOPLE OF COLOR

No black person was safe, wrote the abolitionist and former slave Frederick Douglass after the Philadelphia riot of 1849. "His life—his property—and all that he holds dear are in the hands of a mob. . . ." For free people of color, mobs could take many forms. They could come in the shape of slave hunters, seeking fugitive slaves but as likely to kidnap a free black as a slave. Or they could take the form of civil authority, as in Cincinnati in 1829, when city officials, frightened by the growing black population, drove one to two thousand blacks from the city by enforcing a law requiring cash bonds for good behavior. In whatever form, free blacks faced insecurity daily.

Under federal law, blacks held an uncertain position. The Bill of Rights seemed to apply to free blacks; the Fifth Amendment specified that "no person shall . . . be deprived of life, liberty, or property, without due process of law." Yet the racist theory of the eighteenth century that defined a republic as being only for whites seemed to exclude blacks. This exclusion was reflected in early federal legislation. In 1790 naturalization was limited to white aliens, and in 1792 the militia was limited to white male citizens. Moreover, Congress approved the admission to the Union of states whose constitutions restricted the rights of blacks. Following the admission of Missouri in 1821, every new state admitted until the Civil War banned blacks from voting. And when the Oregon and New Mexico territories were organized, public land grants were limited to whites.

In the North blacks faced legal restrictions nearly everywhere. Only in Massachusetts, New Hampshire, Vermont, and Maine could blacks vote on an equal basis with whites throughout the pre–Civil War period. Blacks gained the right to vote in Rhode Island in 1842, but they had lost it earlier in Pennsylvania and Connecticut. No state but Massachusetts permitted blacks to serve on juries; four midwestern

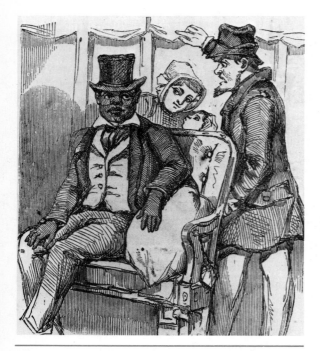

A free black man being expelled from a whites-only railway car in Philadelphia. Prior to the Civil War, blacks were commonly segregated or excluded from public places in the North. Library of Congress.

states and California did not allow blacks to testify against whites. In Oregon blacks could not own real estate, make contracts, or sue in court.

Legal status was important, but practice and custom were crucial. Although Ohio repealed its law barring black testimony against whites in 1849, the exclusion persisted as custom in southern Ohio counties. Throughout the North free people of color were either excluded from or segregated in public places. Abolitionist Frederick Douglass was repeatedly mèt by the phrase "We don't allow niggers in here," during a speaking tour of the North in 1844. Hotels and restaurants were closed to blacks, as were most theaters and churches. But probably no practice inflicted greater injury than the general discrimination in hiring. Fac-

Exclusion and Segregation of Blacks

tory and skilled work were virtually closed to northern blacks.

Free people of color faced more severe legal and social barriers in the southern slave states, where their presence was often viewed as an incentive to insurrection. There the state legislatures, with the dual intent of restricting free blacks and encouraging them to migrate north, adopted "black codes." Blacks were required to have licenses for certain occupations and were barred from others. Some states forbade blacks to assemble without a license; some prohibited blacks from being taught to read and write. All the slave states except Delaware barred blacks from testifying against whites. In the late 1830s, when these black codes were enforced with vigor for the first time, free blacks increasingly moved northward, even though northern states discouraged the migration.

Black Codes

In spite of these obstacles, the free black population rose dramatically in the first part of the nineteenth century, from 108,000 in 1800 to almost 500,000 in 1860 (see table). Nearly half lived in the North, occasionally in rural settlements like Hammond County, Indiana, but more often in cities like Philadelphia, New York, or Cincinnati. Baltimore had the largest free black community; sizable free black populations also existed in New Orleans, Charleston, and Mobile.

The ranks of free blacks were constantly increased by ex-slaves. Some, like Frederick Douglass and Harriet Tubman, were fugitives. Tubman, a slave on the eastern shore of Maryland, escaped to Philadelphia in 1849 when her master's death led to rumors that she would be sold out of the state. Within the next two years she returned twice to free her two children, her sister, her mother, and her brother and his family. Other slaves were voluntarily freed by their owners. Some, like a Virginia planter named Sanders who settled his slaves as freedmen in Michigan, sought to cleanse their souls by freeing their slaves in their wills. Some freed elderly slaves after a lifetime of service rather than support them in old age.

Fugitive Slaves

BLACK POPULATION OF THE UNITED STATES, 1800–1860

Year	Total Black Population	Percentage of Total U.S. Population	Free People of Color	Free Blacks as a Percentage of Black Population
1800	1,002,000	18.9	108,000	10.8
1810	1,378,000	19.0	186,000	13.5
1820	1,772,000	18.4	234,000	13.2
1830	2,329,000	18.1	320,000	13.7
1840	2,874,000	16.8	386,000	13.4
1850	3,639,000	15.7	435,000	11.9
1860	4,442,000	14.1	488,000	11.0

In response to their oppression, free blacks founded strong, independent self-help societies to meet their unique needs and fight their less-than-equal status.

Founding of Black Institutions In every black community there appeared black churches, fraternal and benevolent associations, literary societies, and schools. Many black leaders believed that these mutual aid societies would encourage thrift, industry, and morality, thus equipping their members to improve their lot. But no amount of effort could counteract white prejudice. Blacks remained second-class in status.

The network of societies among urban free black men and women provided a base for black protest. From 1830 to 1835, and thereafter irregularly, free blacks held national conventions with delegates drawn from ad hoc city and state organizations. Under the leadership of the small black middle class, which included the Philadelphia sail manufacturer James Forten and the orator Reverend Henry Highland Garnet, the convention movement served as a forum to attack slavery and agitate for equal rights.

The struggle was also joined by militant new black publications, such as *Freedom's Journal* (1827) and the *Weekly Advocate* (1837).

Although abolitionism and civil rights remained at the top of the blacks' agenda, the mood of free blacks began to shift in the late 1840s and 1850s. Some black leaders became more militant, and a few joined John Brown in his plans for rebellion. But many more were swept up in the tide of black nationalism, which stressed racial solidarity and unity, self-help, and a growing interest in Africa. Before this time, efforts to send Afro-Americans "back to Africa" had originated with whites seeking to solve racial problems by ridding the United States of blacks. But in the 1850s blacks held emigrationist conventions of their own under the leadership of Henry Bibb and Martin Delany. With the coming of the Civil War and emancipation, however, all but a few blacks lost interest in migrating to Africa.

Black Nationalism

The United States in 1860 was a far more diverse and complex society than it had been in 1800. Industrialization, specialization, urbanization, and im-

IMPORTANT EVENTS

1805	Prophet emerges as Shawnee leader
1810	New York surpasses Philadelphia in population
1813	Death of Tecumseh
1819	Indian "Civilization Act"
1823	Beechers' Hartford Female Seminary established
1824	Monroe proposes Indian removal
1827	*Freedom's Journal* first published
1830s– 1850s	Urban riots
1831	*Cherokee Nation v. Georgia*
1831–38	Trail of Tears
1835–42	Seminole War
1837	Boston employs paid policemen
1845	Start of Irish potato famine
1848	Abortive German revolution
1849	New York theater riot

promise of jobs and of political and religious toleration. Yet most found the going rough even though conditions were often better than in their native lands. Competition and diversity bred intolerance and prejudice. None were to feel that more painfully than Indians and free blacks, who were most often made to feel as aliens in their own land. Indians were expelled from their traditional lands while free people of color were second-class citizens.

SUGGESTIONS FOR FURTHER READING

Communities and Inequality

Stuart M. Blumin, *The Urban Threshold: Growth and Change in a Nineteenth-Century American Community* (1976); Don H. Doyle, *The Social Order of a Frontier Community: Jacksonville, Illinois, 1825–1870* (1978); Edward Pessen, *Riches, Class and Power Before the Civil War* (1973); Jonathan Prude, *The Coming of Industrial Order. Town and Factory Life in Rural Massachusetts, 1810–1860* (1983); Edward K. Spann, *The New Metropolis: New York City, 1840–1857* (1981); Stephan Thernstrom, *Poverty and Progress: Social Mobility in a Nineteenth Century City* (1964); Alexis de Tocqueville, *Democracy in America*, 2 vols. (1835–1840); Anthony F. C. Wallace, *Rockdale: The Growth of an American Village in the Early Industrial Revolution* (1978).

Women and the Family

Nancy F. Cott, *The Bonds of Womanhood: "Woman's Sphere" in New England, 1780–1835* (1977); Carl N. Degler, *At Odds: Women and the Family in America from the Revolution to the Present* (1980); Hasia R. Diner, *Erin's Daughters in America. Irish Immigrant Women in the Nineteenth Century* (1983); Linda Gordon, *Woman's Body, Woman's Rights: A Social History of Birth Control in America* (1976); Mary P. Ryan, *Cradle of the Middle Class: The Family in Oneida County, New York, 1790–1865* (1981); Kathryn

migration had altered the ways people lived and worked. Amidst these changes, middle-class families sought to insulate their homes from the competition of the market economy. Many women found fulfillment in the domestic ideal, although others found it confining. More and more, urban women became associated with nurturing roles, first in homes and schools, then in churches and reform societies.

In Europe, famine and religious and political oppression sent millions of people across the Atlantic. They were drawn to the United States by the

Kish Sklar, *Catharine Beecher: A Study in American Domesticity* (1973); Robert V. Wells, *Revolutions in Americans' Lives* (1982); Barbara Welter, "The Cult of True Womanhood, 1820–1860," *American Quarterly*, 18 (Summer 1966), 151–174.

Immigrants

Rowland Berthoff, *British Immigrants in Industrial America* (1953); Theodore C. Blegen, *Norwegian Migration to America, 1825–1860* (1931); Kathleen Neils Conzen, *Immigrant Milwaukee: 1836–1860* (1976); Charlotte Erickson, *Invisible Immigrants* (1972); Robert Ernst, *Immigrant Life in New York City, 1825–1863* (1949); Oscar Handlin, *Boston's Immigrants: A Study in Acculturation*, rev. ed. (1959); Philip Taylor, *The Distant Magnet: European Emigration to the United States of America* (1971); Mark Wyman, *Immigrants in the Valley: Irish, Germans and Americans in the Upper Mississippi, 1830–1860* (1984).

Native Americans

Robert F. Berkhofer, Jr., *The White Man's Indian* (1978); R. David Edmunds, *The Shawnee Prophet* (1983); Grant Foreman, *Indian Removal: The Emigration of the Five Civilized Tribes of Indians*, rev. ed. (1953); Michael D. Green, *The Politics of Indian Removal: Creek Government and Society in Crisis* (1982); Charles Hudson, *The Southeastern Indians* (1976); Francis P. Prucha, *American Indian Policy in the Formative Years* (1962); Herman J. Viola, *Thomas L. McKenney, Architect of America's Early Indian Policy: 1816–1830* (1974).

Free People of Color

Ira Berlin, *Slaves Without Masters: The Free Negro in the Antebellum South* (1974); Leonard P. Curry, *The Free Black in Urban America 1800–1850* (1981); Luther Porter Jackson, *Free Negro Labor and Property Holding in Virginia, 1830–1860* (1942); David M. Katzman, *Before the Ghetto: Black Detroit in the Nineteenth Century* (1973); Rudolph M. Lapp, *Blacks in Gold Rush California* (1977); Leon Litwack, *North of Slavery: The Negro in the Free States, 1790–1860* (1961); Juliet E. K. Walker, *Free Frank: A Black Pioneer on the Antebellum Frontier* (1983); Arthur Zilversmit, *The First Emancipation: The Abolition of Slavery in the North* (1967).

CHAPTER 11

SLAVERY AND THE GROWTH OF THE SOUTH 1800–1860

He was weeping, sobbing. In a humble voice he had begged his master not to give him to Mr. King, who was going away to Alabama, but it had done no good. Now his voice rose and he uttered "an absolute cry of despair." Raving and "almost in a state of frenzy," he declared that he would never leave the Georgia plantation that was home to his father, mother, wife, and children.

To Fanny Kemble, watching from the doorway, it was a horrifying and disorienting scene. One of the most famous British actresses ever to tour America, Fanny had grown up breathing England's antislavery tradition as naturally as the air. In New England she had become friends with enlightened antislavery thinkers. Then the man she married took her away from New England to a Georgia rice plantation.

Pierce Butler, Fanny's husband, was all that a cultured Philadelphia gentleman should be. He had lived all his life in the North, though part of his family's fortune had always sprung from southern slavery.

When Fanny chose him from dozens of suitors, he had seemed an attractive exemplar of American culture. Yet now he shattered his slave's hopes without hesitation. Only with tears and vehement pleas was she able to convince Butler to keep the slave family together. He finally agreed as a favor to her, not on principle or because she had a right to be consulted.

This incident, which occurred in 1839, illustrates both the similarities between South and North and the differences that were beginning to emerge. Though racism pervaded the North, its influence was far more visible on southern society. And though some northerners, like Pierce Butler, were undisturbed by the idea of human bondage, a growing number considered it shocking and backward, inappropriate to their thriving economy and contrary to natural rights.

In the South too, the years from 1800 to 1860 were a time of growth and prosperity; new lands were settled and new states peopled. But as the North grew and changed, economically the South merely grew; change there only reinforced existing economic patterns. Steadily the South emerged as the world's most extensive and vigorous slave economy. Its people were slaves, slaveholders, and nonslaveholders rather than farmers, merchants, mechanics, and manufacturers. Its well-being depended on agriculture alone, rather than agriculture plus commerce and manufacturing. Its population was almost wholly rural rather than rural and urban.

THE SOUTH REMAINS RURAL

The South in the early 1800s was the product of precisely the kind of resource-exploiting commercial agriculture that most of the early colonies had aspired to develop. Only there, nonmechanized agriculture remained highly profitable. Southern planters were not sentimentalists who held onto their slaves for noneconomic reasons even in the face of the industrial revolution. Like other Americans, they were profit-oriented. But circumstances allowed them to continue to profit from a plantation economy.

At the time of the Revolution, slave-based agriculture was not exceedingly lucrative. After the war, however, England's burgeoning textile industry required more and more cotton. Only one thing held back a major cotton explosion in the South: a device was needed to remove the sticky seeds from the fibers of the cotton. Eli Whitney solved the problem with the invention of the cotton gin (1793). By 1800 cotton and slavery were spreading rapidly westward from the seaboard states.

So the antebellum South, or Old South, became primarily a cotton South. Tobacco continued to be grown in Virginia and North Carolina, and rice and sugar were still very important in certain coastal areas, especially in South Carolina, Georgia, and Louisiana. But cotton was the largest crop, the most widespread, and the force behind the South's hunger for new territory. Ambitious cotton growers poured across the Appalachians into the West. The boom in the cotton economy came in the 1830s in Alabama and Mississippi. But not until the 1850s did the wave of cotton expansion cross Louisiana and pour into Texas (see maps, page 192).

Rise of the Cotton South

An unfortunate consequence of the cotton boom was the relative indifference of farmers to the long-term fertility of the soil. In an expanding economy, with cheap and superior land available farther west, most people preferred to exhaust the land and move on rather than invest heavily in preserving it. Only in the older states of the upper South, where the major landholders stayed behind, and where the cotton boom had less impact, did serious interest in diversified farming develop.

An even more important consequence of the boom was thin population distribution. Producers spread out over as large an area as possible in order to maximize production and income. Because farms were far apart, southern society remained predominantly rural. Population density, low even in the older plantation states, was especially so in the frontier areas being brought under cultivation. In 1860 there were only 2.3 people per square mile in Texas, 15.6 in Louisiana, and 18.0 in Georgia. By contrast, the Northeast had an average of 65.4 persons per square mile, and in some places the density was much higher. Massachusetts, for example, had 153.1 people per square mile.

Population Distribution

Society in such rural areas was characterized by relatively weak institutions, for it takes people to create and support organized activity. Where the concentration of people was low, it was difficult to finance and operate schools, churches, libraries, let alone hotels, restaurants, and other urban amenities. Southerners were strongly committed to their churches, and some believed in the importance of universities, but all such institutions were far less developed than those in the North.

The few southern cities were likewise smaller and less developed than those in the North. As exporters,

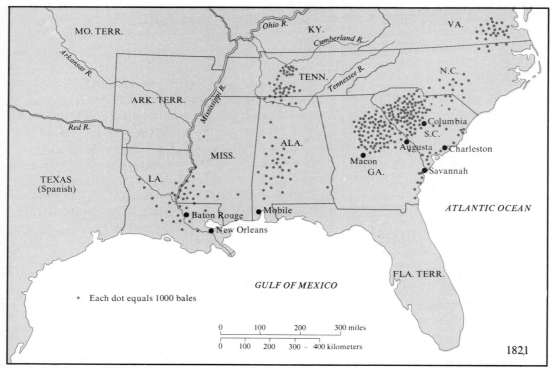

MO. TERR.

Ohio R.
KY.
Cumberland R.
VA.

Arkansas R.

ARK. TERR.

Mississippi R.

TENN.
Tennessee R.

N.C.

Red R.

MISS.

ALA.

S.C.
● Columbia
● Augusta
Macon ●
GA.
● Charleston
● Savannah

TEXAS
(Spanish)

LA.

● Baton Rouge
● Mobile
● New Orleans

ATLANTIC OCEAN

FLA. TERR.

● Each dot equals 1000 bales

GULF OF MEXICO

0   100   200   300 miles
0 100 200 300   400 kilometers

1821

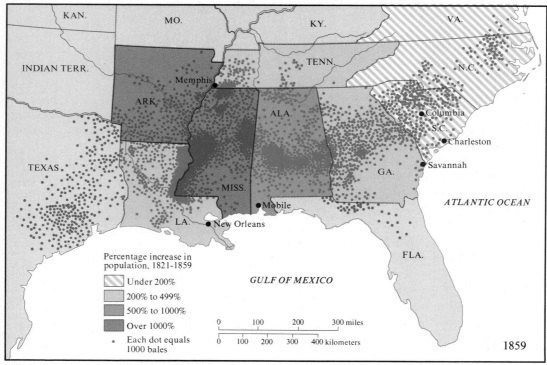

KAN.
MO.
KY.
VA.

INDIAN TERR.
TENN.
N.C.

ARK.
● Memphis

ALA.

● Columbia
S.C.
● Charleston

TEXAS

MISS.

GA.
● Savannah

● Mobile

LA.
● New Orleans

ATLANTIC OCEAN

FLA.

Percentage increase in
population, 1821-1859

GULF OF MEXICO

Under 200%
200% to 499%
500% to 1000%
Over 1000%

● Each dot equals
1000 bales

0   100   200   300 miles
0 100 200 300   400 kilometers

1859

Cotton Production in the South

southerners did not need large cities; a small group of merchants working in connection with northern brokers sufficed to ship their cotton overseas and to import necessary supplies and luxuries. As planters, southerners invested most of their capital in slaves; they had little money left to build factories—another source of urban growth. A few southerners did invest in iron or textiles on a small scale. But the largest southern "industry" was lumbering and the largest factories were cigar factories, where slaves finished tobacco products.

Weak Urban Sector

Moreover, the society that developed in this largely agrarian economy was one of extremes. The social distance between a wealthy planter and a small slaveholder was as great as the distance between a slaveholder and a nonslaveholder (to say nothing of the distance between whites and slaves). And, contrary to popular belief, planters were neither the most numerous nor the most typical group. The typical white southerner was a yeoman farmer.

YEOMEN FARMERS

More than two-thirds of white southern families owned no slaves. Some of them lived in towns and ran stores or businesses, but most were farmers who owned their own land and grew their own food. Independent and motivated by a hearty share of frontier individualism, these people lived a self-sufficient farming life. They had little connection with the market or its type of progress. Families might raise a small surplus to trade for needed items or spending cash, but they were far from major market networks and therefore not particularly concerned about a larger cash income. They valued instead their self-reliance and freedom from others' control.

Yeomen pioneered the southern wilderness as herders of livestock and then as farmers. In successive waves they moved down the southern Appalachians into new Gulf lands following the War of 1812. The herdsmen grazed their cattle and pigs on the abundant natural vegetation in the woods. Before long, however, the next wave of settlers arrived and broke ground for crops. These yeomen farmers forced many herdsmen farther west, and eventually across the Mississippi.

Some yeomen acquired large tracts of level land and became wealthy planters. Others clung to the beautiful mountainous areas they loved. As they moved, they tended to stick to the climate and soils they knew best. Yeomen could not afford the richest bottomlands, which were swampy and required expensive draining, but they owned land almost everywhere else.

Observers sometimes concluded that these people were poor and idle, especially the herdsmen who sat on their cabin porches while their stock foraged in the woods. It is more accurate to say that they were frontiersmen and farmers who did not manage to become rich. They worked hard, as farmers do everywhere, and enjoyed a folk culture based on family, church, and community. They spoke with a drawl and their inflections were reminiscent of their Scottish and Irish backgrounds. Once a year they flocked to religious revivals and in between they enjoyed events such as house-raisings, logrollings, quilting bees, and corn-shuckings. The men did most of the farming; though the women occasionally helped in the fields, they commonly spent their time preserving and preparing food, making clothes, blankets, and candles, and tending to household matters. Both sexes worked hard for the family economy, continuing the colonial tradition of outdoor work for men and indoor work for women.

Folk Culture of the Yeoman

Beyond these basic facts, historians know little about the yeomen. Because their means were modest, they did not generate the voluminous legal papers, such as contracts, wills, and inventories of estates, that document the activities of the rich. Only a few letters have found their way into libraries and archives. It is reasonable to suppose, though, that yeomen held a variety of opinions and pursued individual

Like the figures in George Caleb Bingham's painting The Squatters *(1850), southern yeomen were tough, independent people who tamed the frontier.   Courtesy Museum of Fine Arts, Boston. Bequest of Henry L. Shattuck in memory of the late Ralph W. Gray. 1971.154.*

goals. Some envied the planters and strove to be rich; others were content with their independence, recreation, family life, and religion.

Toil, with even less security, was the lot of two other groups of free southerners: landless whites and free blacks. From 25 to 40 percent of the white workers in the South were laborers who owned no land. Their property consisted of a few household items and some animals—usually pigs—that could feed themselves on the open range. In addition to unskilled laborers, the landless included some immi-

grants, especially Irish, who did heavy and dangerous work such as building railroads and digging ditches.

Conditions were worse for free blacks. In 1860 nearly a quarter million of them led lives that were often little better than the slaves'. The free blacks of

Free Blacks

the Upper South were usually descendants of men and women emancipated by their owners in the 1780s and 1790s, a period of postrevolutionary idealism that coincided with a decline in tobacco prices. Most did not own land and had to labor in

Chapter 11: SLAVERY AND THE GROWTH OF THE SOUTH, 1800–1860

someone else's field, frequently beside slaves. By law they could not own a gun or liquor, violate curfew, assemble except in church, testify in court, or (everywhere after 1835) vote. Despite these obstacles, a minority bought land, and others found jobs as artisans, draymen, boatmen, and fishermen. A few owned slaves, who were often their wives and children, purchased from bondage.

In the Lower South a large proportion of free blacks were mulattoes, the privileged offspring of wealthy planters. Some received good educations and financial backing from their fathers, who recognized a moral obligation to them. In a few cities such as New Orleans and Mobile, extensive interracial sex had produced a mulatto population that was recognized as a distinct class. These mulattoes formed a society of their own and sought a status above slaves and other freedmen, if not equal to planters. But outside New Orleans, Mobile, and Charleston such groups were rare, and most mulattoes encountered disadvantages more frequently than they enjoyed benefits from their light skin tone.

SLAVEHOLDING PLANTERS

At the opposite end of the spectrum from free blacks were the slaveholders. As a group slaveowners lived well, on incomes that enabled them to enjoy superior housing, food, clothing, and luxuries. But most did not live on the opulent scale that legend suggests. A few statistics tell the story: 88 percent of southern slaveholders had fewer than twenty slaves; 72 percent had fewer than ten; 50 percent had fewer than five. Thus the average slaveholder was not a man of great wealth but an aspiring farmer. Instead of being a polished aristocrat, he was usually a person of humble origins, with little formal education and many rough edges to his manner.

The wealth of the greatest planters gave ambitious

men something to aspire to. If most planters lived in spacious, comfortable farmhouses, some did live in mansions. If most slaveowners sat down at mealtimes to an abundance of tempting country foods, the sophisticated elite consumed such delights as "gumbo, ducks and olives, *suprême de volaille*, chickens in jelly, oysters, lettuce salad, chocolate cream, jelly cake, claret cup, etc."

Among the wealthiest and oldest families, slaveholding men dominated through a paternalistic ideology. Instead of stressing the acquisitive aspects of commercial agriculture, they focused on *noblesse oblige*. They saw themselves as custodians of the welfare of society as a whole and of the black families who depended on them. The paternalistic planter saw himself not as an oppressor but as the benevolent guardian of an inferior race. He developed affectionate feelings toward his slaves (as long as they kept in their place) and was genuinely shocked at outside criticism of his behavior.

Southern Paternalism

The letters of Paul Carrington Cameron, North Carolina's largest slaveholder, illustrate this mentality. After a period of sickness among his one thousand North Carolina slaves, Cameron wrote, "I fear the Negroes have suffered much from the want of proper attention and kindness under this late distemper . . . no love of lucre shall ever induce me to be cruel, or even to make or permit to be made any great exposure of their persons at inclement seasons."

There is no doubt that the richest southern planters saw themselves in this way. It was comforting to do so, and slaves, accommodating themselves to the realities of power, encouraged their masters to think their benevolence was appreciated. Paternalism also provided a welcome defense against abolitionist criticism. Still, for most planters, paternalism affected the manner and not the substance of their behavior. It was a matter of style. Its softness and warmth covered harsher assumptions: blacks were inferior; planters should make money.

Relations between men and women in the planter class were similarly paternalistic. An upper-class southern woman typically was raised and educated to

Woman's Role be a wife and subordinate companion of men. She was not to venture into politics and other worldly affairs. The education of elite women, for example, emphasized grammar, penmanship, composition, geography, literature, and languages. The sciences, which encouraged critical thinking, were largely ignored. In a social system based on the coercion of an entire race, no woman could be allowed to challenge society's rules. If she defied or questioned the status quo, she risked universal condemnation.

Within the domestic circle the husband reigned supreme. For the fortunate woman, like North Carolina diarist Catherine Devereux Edmondston, whose marriage joined two people of shared tastes and habits, the husband's authority weighed lightly or not at all. But other women were acutely conscious of that authority. "He is master of the house," wrote South Carolina's Mary Boykin Chesnut. "To hear is to obey . . . all the comfort of my life depends upon his being in a good humor." In a darker mood Chesnut once observed that "there is no slave . . . like a wife." Unquestionably there were satisfying relationships between men and women in the planter class, but many women were dissatisfied.

The upper-class southern woman had to clear several barriers in the way of happiness. Making the right choice of a husband was especially important. Once married, she lost most of her legal rights to her husband and became part of his family. On the plantation she was expected to oversee the cooking and preserving of food, manage the house, care for the children, and attend to sick slaves. As a woman she was forbidden to travel and visit unless accompanied by men. All the circumstances of her future life depended on the man she chose.

Childbearing brought grief and sickness as well as joy to southern women. In 1840 the birthrate for southern women in their fertile years was almost 20 percent higher than the national average. At the beginning of the nineteenth century, the average southern woman could expect to bear eight children; by 1860 the figure had decreased only to six, and a mis-

carriage was likely among so many pregnancies. The high birthrate took a toll on women's health, for complications of childbirth were a major cause of death. Moreover, a mother had to endure the loss of many of the children she bore. In the South in 1860 almost five out of ten children died before age five.

Slavery was another source of trouble for white women. "Violations of the moral law . . . made mulattoes as common as blackberries," protested a woman in Georgia, but wives had to play "the ostrich game." "A magnate who runs a hideous black harem," wrote Mrs. Chesnut, "under the same roof with his lovely white wife, and his beautiful accomplished daughters . . . poses as the model of all human virtues to these poor women whom God and the laws have given him. From the height of his awful majesty, he scolds and thunders at them, as if he never did wrong in his life."

In the early 1800s, some southern women, especially Quakers, had spoken out against slavery. Even when they did not criticize the "peculiar institution," white women approached it differently from men, seeing it less as a system and more as a series of relationships with individuals. Perhaps southern men sensed this, for they wanted no discussion by women of the slavery issue. In the 1840s and 1850s, as national and international criticism of slavery increased, southern men published a barrage of articles stressing that women should restrict their concerns to the home.

But southern women were beginning to chafe at their customary exclusion from financial matters. A study of women in Petersburg, Virginia, has revealed behavior that amounted to an implicit criticism of the institution of marriage and the loss of autonomy it entailed. During several decades before 1860 the proportion of women who had not married, or not remarried after the death of a spouse, grew to exceed 33 percent. Likewise the number of women who worked for wages, controlled their own property, or even ran businesses increased. In managing property these women benefited from legal reforms, beginning with Mississippi's Married Women's Property Act of

1839, a law that gave women some property rights in order to protect families from ruin caused by the husband's indebtedness.

Restrictions on freedom and the use of education were not limited to upper-class women. For a large category of southern men and women, freedom was wholly denied and education in any form was not allowed. Male or female, slaves were expected to accept bondage and ignorance as their condition.

SLAVES AND THE CONDITIONS
OF THEIR SERVITUDE

For Afro-Americans, slavery was a curse that brought no blessings other than the strengths they developed to survive it. Slaves knew a life of poverty, coercion, toil, heartbreak, and resentment. They had few hopes that were not denied; often they had to bear separation from their loved ones; and they were despised as an inferior race. That they endured and found loyalty and strength among themselves is a tribute to their courage, but it could not make up for a life without freedom or opportunity.

Southern slaves enjoyed few material comforts beyond the bare necessities. Their diet was plain, their clothing coarse, and their housing rudimentary. A slave's diet consisted of cornmeal, fat pork, molasses, and sometimes coffee. Despite occasional supplements of green vegetables and fish, their diet was nutritionally deficient; many slaves suffered from beriberi and pellagra. The few clothes issued to slaves were made either of light cotton or a coarse heavy material called osnaburg. Because shoes were normally not issued until the weather became cool, slaves frequently contracted parasitic diseases such as hookworm. Slave quarters were one-room cabins with dirt floors, few furnishings, and straw mattresses. One and sometimes two families had to share the small cabins, fostering the spread of infection and contagious diseases.

Slave Diet, Clothing, and Housing

Hard work was the central fact of the slaves' existence. In Gulf-coast cotton districts long hours and large work gangs suggested factories in the field rather than the small-scale, isolated work patterns of slaves in the eighteenth-century Chesapeake. Overseers rang the morning bell before dawn, making it possible for slaves to be in the fields and prepared to work at first light. Except in urban settings and on some rice plantations, where slaves were assigned daily tasks to complete at their own pace, working from "sun to sun" became universal in the South. These long hours and hard work were at the heart of the advantage of slave labor. As one planter put it, slaves were the best labor because "you could command them and *make* them do what was right." White workers, by contrast, were few and couldn't be *driven*; "they wouldn't stand it."

Slave Work Routines

Planters aimed to keep all their laborers busy all the time. Profit took precedence over paternalism's "protection" of women: slave women did heavy field work, often as much as the men and even during pregnancy. Old people—of whom there were few— were kept busy caring for young children, doing light chores, or carding, ginning, or spinning cotton. Children had to gather kindling for the fire, carry water to the fields, or sweep the yard. But slaves had a variety of ways to keep from being worked to death. It was impossible for the master to supervise every slave every minute, and slaves slacked off when they were not being watched.

Of course the slave could not slow his labor too much, because the owner enjoyed a monopoly on force and violence. Whites throughout the South believed that Negroes "can't be governed except with the whip." Evidence suggests that whippings were less frequent on small farms than on large plantations, but the reports of former slaves show that a large majority even of small

Physical and Mental Abuse of Slaves

farmers plied the lash. These beatings symbolized authority to the master and tyranny to the slaves, who made them a benchmark for evaluating a master. In the words of former slaves, a good owner was one who did not "whip too much," whereas a bad owner "whipped till he'd bloodied you and blistered you."[1]

As this testimony suggests, terrible abuses could and did occur. Courts did not recognize the word of a chattel. Pregnant women were whipped, and there were burnings, mutilations, tortures, and murders. Yet the physical cruelty of slavery may have been less in the United States than elsewhere in the New World. In sugar-growing or mining regions of the Western Hemisphere in the 1800s, slaves were regarded as an expendable resource to be replaced after seven years. Treatment was so poor and families so uncommon that death rates were high and the heavily male slave population did not replace itself, and rapidly shrank in size. In the United States, by contrast, the slave population showed a steady natural increase, as births exceeded deaths, and each generation grew larger.

The worst evil of American slavery was not its physical cruelty but the fact of slavery itself: coercion, loss of freedom, belonging to another person. American slaves hated their oppression, and contrary to some whites' perceptions, they were not grateful to their oppressors. Although they had to be subservient and speak honeyed words in the presence of their masters, they talked quite differently later on among themselves. The evidence of their resistant attitudes comes from their actions and from their own life stories.

Former slaves reported some kind feelings between masters and slaves, but the overwhelming picture was one of antagonism and resistance. Slaves mistrusted

Slaves'
Attitudes
Toward Whites

kindness from whites and suspected self-interest in their owners. A woman whose mistress "was good to us Niggers" said her owner was kind " 'cause she was raisin' us to work for her." Christmas presents of clothing from the master did not mean anything, observed another, " 'cause he was going to [buy] that anyhow."

Slaves were sensitive to the thousand daily signs of their degraded status. One man recalled the general rule that slaves ate cornbread and owners ate biscuits. If blacks did get biscuits, "the flour that we made the biscuits out of was the third-grade shorts." A woman reported that on her plantation "Old Master hunted a heap, but us never did get none of what he brought in." If the owner took slaves' garden produce to town and sold it for them, the slaves suspected him of pocketing part of the profits.

Suspicion and resentment often grew into hatred. According to a former slave from Virginia, "the white folks treated the nigger so mean that all the slaves prayed God to punish their cruel masters." When a yellow fever epidemic struck in 1852, many slaves saw it as God's retribution. A young slave girl who had suffered abuse as a house servant admitted that she took cruel advantage of her mistress when the woman had a stroke. Instead of fanning the mistress to keep flies away, the young slave struck her in the face with the fan whenever they were alone. "I done that woman bad," the slave confessed, but "she was so mean to me."

---

[1]Accounts by ex-slaves are quoted from *The American Slave: A Composite Autobiography,* edited by George P. Rawick (Westport, Conn.: Greenwood Press, First Reprint Edition 1972, Second Reprint Edition 1974), from materials assembled by the Library of Congress and originally published in 1941. The spelling in these accounts has been standardized.

SLAVE CULTURE AND

EVERYDAY LIFE

The force that helped slaves to maintain such defiance was their culture. They had their own view of the world, a body of beliefs and values born of both their past and their present, as well as the fellowship and support of their own community. With power overwhelmingly in the hands of whites, it was not possible for slaves to change their world. But drawing strength from their culture, they could resist their condition and struggle on against it.

Slave culture changed significantly after the turn of the century. Between 1790 and 1808, when Congress banned further importation of slaves, there was a rush to import Africans. After that the proportion of native-born blacks rose steadily, reaching 96 percent in 1840 and almost 100 percent in 1860. With time the old African culture faded further into memory as an Afro-American culture matured.

In one sense African influences remained primary. For African practices and beliefs reminded the slaves that they were and ought to be different from their oppressors, and thus encouraged them to resist. The most visible aspects of African culture were the slaves' dress and recreation. Some slave men plaited their hair into rows and fancy designs; slave women often wore their hair "in string"—tied in small bunches with a string or piece of cloth. A few men and many women wrapped their heads in kerchiefs following the styles and colors of West Africa. For entertainment slaves made musical instruments with carved motifs that resembled some African stringed instruments. Their drumming and dancing clearly followed African patterns.

Remnants of African Culture

Many slaves continued to see and believe in spirits. Whites also believed in ghosts, but the belief was more widespread among slaves. It closely resembled the African concept of the living dead—the idea that deceased relatives visited the earth for many years until the process of dying was complete. Slaves also practiced conjuration, voodoo, and quasi-magical root medicine. By 1860 the most notable conjurers and root doctors were reputed to live in South Carolina, Georgia, Louisiana, and other isolated coastal areas of heavy slave importation.

These cultural survivals provided slaves with a sense of their separate past. Black achievement in music and dance was so exceptional that whites felt entirely cut off from it; in this one area some whites became aware that they did not "know" their slaves and that the slave community was a different world. Conjuration and folklore also directly fed resistance; slaves could cast a spell or direct the power of a hand (a bag of articles belonging to the person to be conjured) against the master. Not all masters felt confident enough to dismiss such a threat.

In adopting Christianity, slaves fashioned it too into an instrument of support and resistance. Theirs was a religion of justice quite unlike that of the propaganda their masters pushed at them. Former slaves scorned the preaching arranged by their masters. "You ought to have heard that preachin'," said one man. " 'Obey your master and mistress . . . ,' but nary a word about havin' a soul to save." To the slaves, Jesus cared about their souls and their present plight. They rejected the idea that in heaven whites would have "the colored folks . . . there to wait on 'em." Instead, when God's justice came, the slaveholders would be "broilin' in hell for their sin."

Slave Religion

For slaves Christianity was a religion of personal and group salvation. Beyond seeking personal guidance, these worshippers prayed "for deliverance of the slaves." Some waited "until the overseer got behind a hill" and then laid down their hoes and called on God to free them. Others held fervent secret prayer meetings that lasted far into the night. From such activities many slaves gained the unshakable belief that God would end their bondage. As one man asserted, "it was the plans of God to free us niggers." This faith and the joy and emotional release that accompanied their worship sustained blacks.

Slaves also developed a sense of racial identity. The whole experience of southern blacks taught them that whites despised their race. Blacks naturally drew together, helping each other in danger, need, and resistance. "We never told on each other," one woman declared. Former slaves were virtually unanimous in denouncing those who betrayed the group or sought personal advantage through allegiance to whites. And because most slaves lived in small units, there was no overriding class system within the black community.

The main source of support was the family. Slave families faced severe dangers. At any moment the master could sell a husband or wife, give a slave child away as a wedding present, or die in debt, forcing a division of his property. Many families were broken in such ways. Others were uprooted in the trans-Appalachian expansion of the South, which caused a large interregional movement of the black population. Between 1810 and 1820 alone, 137,000 slaves were forced to move from North Carolina and the Chesapeake states to Alabama, Mississippi, and other western regions. An estimated 2 million persons were sold between 1820 and 1860. When the Union Army registered thousands of black marriages in Mississippi and Louisiana in 1864 and 1865, 25 percent of the men over forty reported that they had been forcibly separated from a previous wife. Probably a substantial minority of slave families suffered disruption of one kind or another.

But this did not mean that slave families could not exist. American slaves clung tenaciously to the personal relationships that gave meaning to life. For although American law did not protect slave families, masters permitted them. In fact, slaveowners expected slaves to form families and have children. As a result, there remained a normal ratio of men to women, young to old.

Following African kinship taboos, Afro-Americans avoided marriage between cousins (a frequent occurrence among aristocratic slaveowners). Adapting to the circumstances of their captivity, they did not condemn unwed mothers, although they did expect a young girl to form a stable marriage after one pregnancy, if not before. By naming their children after relatives of past generations, Afro-Americans emphasized their family histories. If they chose to bear the surname of a white slaveowner, it was often not their current master's but that of the owner under whom their family had begun.

Slaves abhorred interference in their family lives. Some of their strongest protests sought to prevent the breakup of a family. Rape was a horror for both men and women. Some husbands faced death rather than permit their wives to be sexually abused, and women sometimes fought back. In other cases slaves seethed with anger at the injustice but could do nothing except soothe each other with human sympathy and understanding. Significantly, blacks condemned the guilty party, not the victim.

Slave men did not dominate their wives in a manner similar to white husbands, but it is misleading to say that slave women enjoyed equality of power in sex roles and family life. Under the pressures of bondage, the responsibilities of parenthood had to be shared. Each might have to stand in for the other and assume extra duties. Similarly, uncles, aunts, and grandparents sometimes raised the children of those who had been sold away.

In two other respects, however, distinct gender roles remained very important. First, after work in the fields was done, men's activities focused on traditional "outdoor" tasks while women did "indoor" work. Second, the life cycle and pattern of work routines frequently placed slave women in close associations with each other that heightened their sense of sisterhood. Female slaves lived significant portions of their lives as part of a group of women, a fact that emphasized the gender-based element of their experience.

Slaves brought to their efforts at resistance the same common sense, determination, and practicality that characterized their family lives. American slavery produced some fearless and implacable revolutionaries. Gabriel Prosser's conspiracy (1800) apparently was known to more than a thousand slaves. A similar conspiracy in Charleston in 1822, headed by a free black named Denmark Vesey, involved many of the most trusted slaves of lead-

Slave Family Life

Sex Roles

Resistance to Slavery

Chapter 11: Slavery and the Growth of the South, 1800–1860

ing families. But the most famous rebel of all, Nat Turner, rose in violence in Southampton County, Virginia, in 1831.

The son of a runaway slave and an African woman who passionately hated her enslavement, Turner was a precocious child who learned to read very young. Encouraged by his first owner to study the Bible, he enjoyed some special privileges but also knew changes of masters and hard work. In time young Turner became a preacher. He also developed a tendency toward mysticism, and he became increasingly withdrawn. After nurturing his plan for several years, Turner led a band of rebels from house to house in the predawn darkness of August 22, 1831. The group severed limbs and crushed skulls with axes or killed their victims with guns. Before they were stopped, Nat Turner and his followers had slaughtered sixty whites of both sexes and all ages. About two hundred blacks, including Turner, lost their lives as a result of the rebellion.

But most slave resistance was not violent, for the odds against revolution were especially poor in North America. Consequently slaves directed their energies toward creating means of survival and resistance within slavery. A desperate slave could run away for good, but as often or probably more often slaves simply ran off temporarily to hide in the woods. Every day that a slave "lay out" in this way the master lost a day's labor. Most owners chose not to mount an exhaustive search and sent word instead that the slave's grievances would be redressed. The runaway would then return to bargain with the master. Most owners would let the matter pass, for, like the owner of a valuable cook, they were "glad to get her back."

Other modes of resistance had the same object: to resist but survive under bondage. Appropriating food (stealing, in the master's eyes) was so common that even whites sang humorous songs about it. Blacks were also alert to the attitudes of individual whites, and learned to ingratiate themselves or play off one white person against another. Field hands frequently tested a new overseer to intimidate him or win more favorable working conditions.

HARMONY AND TENSION IN A SLAVE SOCIETY

Not only for blacks but for whites too, slave labor stood at the heart of the South's social system. A host of consequences flowed from its existence, from the organization of society to an individual's personal values.

For blacks, the nineteenth century brought a strengthening and expansion of the legal restrictions of slavery. In all things, from their workaday movements to Sunday worship, slaves fell under the supervision of whites. Courts held that a slave "has no civil right" and could not even hold property "except at the will and pleasure of his master." When slaves revolted, legislators tightened the legal straitjacket. The year after the Nat Turner insurrection, for example, the Virginia legislature prohibited owners from teaching their slaves to read.

The weight of this legal and social framework fell on nonblacks as well. All white male citizens bore an obligation to ride in patrols to discourage slave movements at night. White southerners who criticized the slave system out of moral conviction or class resentment were intimidated, attacked, or legally prosecuted. Urban residents who did not supervise their domestic slaves as closely as planters found themselves subject to criticism. And the South's few manufacturers felt pressure to use slave rather than free labor.

Slavery had a deep effect on southern values because it was the main determinant of wealth in the South. Ownership of slaves guaranteed the labor to produce cotton and other crops on a large scale. Slaves were therefore vital to the acquisition of a fortune. Beyond that, slaves were a commodity and an investment; people bought them on speculation, hop-

Slavery as the Basis of Wealth and Social Standing

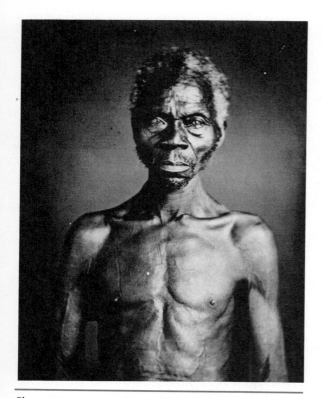

Slave property was tangible wealth to whites. Increasingly they tried to deny that slaves were people who suffered, as this rare photograph of Renty, an elderly "Congo" field hand, reminds us. Peabody Museum, Harvard University, N27432.

As slavery became entrenched, its influence spread throughout the social system until even the values and mores of nonslaveholders bore its imprint. For one thing, the availability of slave labor tended to devalue free labor. Nonslaveholders therefore preferred to work for themselves rather than to hire out. Whites who had to sell their labor tended to resent or reject tasks that seemed degrading. This kind of thinking engendered an aristocratic value system ill-suited to a newly established democracy.

In modified form the attitudes characteristic of the planter elite gained a considerable foothold among the masses. The ideal of the aristocrat emphasized lineage, privilege, power, pride, and refinement of person and manner. Some of those qualities were in short supply in the expanding cotton kingdom, however; they mingled with and were modified by the tradition of the frontier. In particular, independence, and defense of one's honor were highly valued by planter and frontier farmer alike. Thus, instead of gradually disappearing, as it did in the North, the code duello, which required men to defend their honor through the rituals of a duel, hung on in the South and gained an acceptance that spread throughout the society.

Aristocratic Values and Frontier Individualism

Other aristocratic values that marked the planters as a class were less acceptable to the average citizen. Simply put, planters believed they were better than other people. In their pride, they expected not only to wield power but to receive special treatment. By the 1850s, some planters openly rejected the democratic creed, vilifying Jefferson for his statement that all men were equal.

These ideas shaped the outlook of the southern elite for generations, but they were never acceptable to the individualistic members of the yeomen class. Independent and proud of their position, yeomen resisted any infringement of their rights. They believed that they were as good as anyone and knew that they lived in a nation in which democratic ideals were gaining strength. Thus there were occasional con-

ing for a steady rise in their value. Surplus capital was invested in slaves—not factories and railroads.

It was therefore natural that slaveholding should be the main determinant of a man's social position. Wealth in slaves was also the foundation on which the ambitious built their reputations. Ownership of slaves brought political power: a solid majority of political officeholders were slaveholders, and the most powerful of them were generally large slaveholders. Though lawyers and newspaper editors were sometimes influential, they did not hold independent positions in the economy or society. Dependent on the planters for business and support, they served planters' interests and reflected their outlook.

flicts between aristocratic pretensions and democratic zeal.

Yeomen farmers and citizens resented their under-representation in state legislatures, corruption in government, and undemocratic control over local government. After vigorous debate, the reformers won most of their battles. Five states—Alabama, Mississippi, Tennessee, Arkansas, and Texas—adopted what was for that time a thoroughly democratic system: popular election of governors, white manhood suffrage, legislative apportionment based on the white population, and locally chosen county government. Indeed, only South Carolina and Virginia effectively defended property qualifications for office, legislative malapportionment, appointment of county officials, and selection of the governor by the lawmakers. Democracy had expanded with the cotton kingdom.

Democratic Reform Movements

Even in Virginia, nonslaveholding westerners raised a basic challenge to the slave system. Following the Nat Turner rebellion, advocates of gradual abolition forced a two-week legislative debate on slavery, arguing that it was injurious to the state and inherently dangerous. When the House of Delegates finally voted, the motion favoring abolition lost by just 73 to 58. This was the last major debate on slavery in the antebellum South.

With such tension in evidence, it was perhaps remarkable that slaveholders and nonslaveholders did not experience frequent and serious conflict. Why were class confrontations among whites so infrequent? Historians who have considered this question have given many answers. In a rural society, family bonds and kinship ties are valued, and some of the poor nonslaveholding whites were related to the rich new planters. The experience of frontier living must also have created a relatively informal, egalitarian atmosphere. And there is no doubt that the South's racial ideology, which stressed whites' superiority to blacks and race, not class, as the social dividing line, tended to reduce conflict among whites. Moreover, the South was an expanding, mobile society in which yeomen and planters rarely depended on each other. Yeomen farmed mainly for themselves; planters farmed for themselves and for the market.

There were signs, however, that the relative lack of conflict between slaveholders and nonslaveholders was coming to an end. As the region grew older, non-slaveholders saw their opportunities beginning to narrow; meanwhile wealthy planters enjoyed an expanding horizon. The risks of cotton production were becoming too great and the cost of slaves too high for many yeomen to rise in society. Thus from 1830 to 1860 the percentage of white southern families holding slaves declined steadily from 36 to 25 percent. At the same time, the monetary gap between the classes was widening. Although nonslaveholders were becoming more prosperous, slaveowners' wealth was increasing much faster. And though slaveowners made up a smaller portion of the population in 1860, their share of the South's agricultural wealth remained at between 90 and 95 percent. In fact, the average slaveholder was almost fourteen times as rich as the average nonslaveholder.

Hardening of Class Lines

Urban artisans and mechanics felt the pinch acutely. Their numbers were few, their place in society was hardly recognized, and in bad times they were often the first to lose work. Moreover, they faced stiff competition from urban slaves, whose masters wanted them to hire their time and bring in money by practicing a trade. White workers demanded that economic competition from slaves be forbidden. This demand was always ignored—the powerful slaveowners would not tolerate interference with their property or the income they derived from it. But the angry protests of white workers often resulted in harsh restrictions on *free* black workers and craftsmen, who lacked any powerful allies to stand behind them.

Pre–Civil War politics reflected these tensions. Facing the prospect of a war to defend slavery, slaveowners expressed growing fear about the loyalty of nonslaveholders and discussed schemes to widen slave ownership. In North Carolina, a prolonged and increasingly bitter controversy over the combination of high taxes on land and low taxes on slaves erupted. A class-conscious nonslaveholder named Hinton R. Helper attacked slavery in his book *The Impending Crisis*, published in New York in 1857. Discerning planters knew that such fiery controversies lay close at hand in every southern state.

But for the moment slaveowners stood secure. They held from 50 to 85 percent of the seats in state legislatures and a similarly high percentage of the South's congressional seats. In addition to their near-monopoly on political office, they had established their point of view in all the other major social institutions. Professors who criticized slavery had been dismissed from colleges and universities; schoolbooks that contained "unsound" ideas had been replaced. And almost all the clergy had given up preaching against the institution. In fact, except for a few obscure persons of conscience, southern clergy had become its most vocal defenders. Society as southerners knew it seemed stable, if not unthreatened.

Elsewhere in the nation, however, society was anything but stable. Change had become one of the major characteristics of the northern economy and society, and social conflict was an increasingly common phenomenon. Throughout the North, in a variety of ways, people were trying to cope with change.

SUGGESTIONS FOR FURTHER READING

Southern Society

W. J. Cash, *The Mind of the South* (1941); Clement Eaton, *The Growth of Southern Civilization, 1790–1860* (1961); Clement Eaton, *Freedom of Thought in the Old South* (1940); William W. Freehling, *Prelude to Civil War* (1965); Eugene D. Genovese, "Yeoman Farmers in a Slaveholders' Democracy," *Agricultural History*, 49 (April 1975), 331–342; Wil-

liam Sumner Jenkins, *Pro-Slavery Thought in the Old South* (1935); Donald G. Mathews, *Religion in the Old South* (1977); Robert McColley, *Slavery and Jeffersonian Virginia* (1964); Frederick Law Olmsted, *The Slave States*, ed. Harvey Wish (1959); Charles S. Sydnor, *The Development of Southern Sectionalism, 1819–1848* (1948); Ralph A. Wooster, *Politicians, Planters, and Plain Folk* (1975); Ralph A. Wooster, *The People in Power* (1969); Gavin Wright, *The Political Economy of the Cotton South* (1978); Bertram Wyatt-Brown, *Southern Honor* (1982).

Slaveholders and Nonslaveholders

Bennet H. Barrow, *Plantation Life in the Florida Parishes of Louisiana, as Reflected in the Diary of Bennet H. Barrow*, ed. Edwin Adams Davis (1943); Ira Berlin, *Slaves Without Masters* (1974); William J. Cooper, *The South and the Politics of Slavery, 1828–1856* (1978); Everett Dick, *The Dixie Frontier* (1948); Clement Eaton, *The Mind of the Old South* (1967); Drew Faust, *James Henry Hammond and the Old South* (1982); Drew Faust, *A Sacred Circle: The Dilemma of the Intellectual in the Old South* (1977); John Hope Franklin, *The Free Negro in North Carolina, 1790–1860* (1943); Luther P. Jackson, *Free Negro Labor and Property Holding in Virginia, 1830–1860* (1942); Michael P. Johnson and James L. Roark, *Black Masters* (1984); Frances Anne Kemble, *Journal of a Residence on a Georgian Plantation in 1838–1839* (1863); Robert Manson Myers, ed., *The Children of Pride* (1972); James Oakes, *The Ruling Race* (1982); Frank L. Owsley, *Plain Folk of the Old South* (1949); J. Mills Thornton, III, *Politics and Power in a Slave Society* (1978).

Southern Women

Carol Bleser, *The Hammonds of Redcliffe* (1981); Jane Turner Censer, *North Carolina Planters and Their Children, 1800–1860* (1984); Catherine Clinton, *The Plantation Mistress* (1982); Jacqueline Jones, *Labor of Love, Labor of Sorrow* (1985); Suzanne Lebsock, *Free Women of Petersburg* (1983); Elisabeth Muhlenfeld, *Mary Boykin Chesnut* (1981); Mary D. Robertson, ed., *Lucy Breckinridge of Grove Hill* (1979); Ann Firor Scott, *The Southern Lady* (1970); Deborah G. White, *Arn'n't I a Woman?* (1985); C. Vann Woodward and Elisabeth Muhlenfeld, eds., *The Private Mary Chesnut* (1985).

Conditions of Slavery

Kenneth F. Kiple and Virginia H. Kiple, "Black Tongue and Black Men," *Journal of Southern History*, XLIII (August 1977), 411–428; Ronald L. Lewis, *Coal, Iron, and Slaves* (1979); Richard G. Lowe and Randolph B. Campbell, "The Slave Breeding Hypothesis," *Journal of Southern History*, XLII (August 1976), 400–412; Willie Lee Rose, ed., *A Documentary History of Slavery in North America* (1976); Todd L. Savitt, *Medicine and Slavery* (1978); Kenneth M. Stampp, *The Peculiar Institution* (1956); Robert S. Starobin, *Industrial Slavery in the Old South* (1970).

Slave Culture and Resistance

Herbert Aptheker, *American Negro Slave Revolts* (1943); John W. Blassingame, *The Slave Community* (1972); Judith Wragg Chase, *Afro-American Art and Craft* (1971); Paul D. Escott, *Slavery Remembered* (1979); Eric Foner, ed., *Nat Turner* (1971); Eugene D. Genovese, *From Rebellion to Revolution* (1979); Eugene D. Genovese, *Roll, Jordan, Roll* (1974); Herbert G. Gutman, *The Black Family in Slavery and Freedom, 1750–1925* (1976); Vincent Harding, *There Is a River* (1981); Charles Joyner, *Down by the Riverside* (1984); Lawrence W. Levine, *Black Culture and Black Consciousness* (1977); Stephen B. Oates, *The Fires of Jubilee* (1975); Albert J. Raboteau, *Slave Religion* (1978); Robert S. Starobin, *Denmark Vesey* (1970).

CHAPTER 12

REFORM, POLITICS, AND EXPANSION 1824–1844

The gaunt, bearded New Englander Henry David Thoreau was skeptical of the value of the artifacts of a changing economy and society: railroads, steamboats, the telegraph, factories, and cities. "There is an illusion about" such improvements, he wrote in *Walden, or Life in the Woods* (1854). "There is not always a positive advance. . . . Men think that it is essential that the *Nation* have commerce, and export ice, and talk through a telegraph, and ride thirty miles an hour . . . but whether we should live like baboons or like men, is a little uncertain."

Thoreau was seeking to escape the marketplace, to forgo the world of cities and factories, to live simply in the landscape that existed before the plow and the engine, when he retreated to the wilderness shores of Walden Pond in Concord, Massachusetts. Yet for all his idealization of the simple life, Thoreau did not withdraw from the world, much less from Concord. While at Walden he dined with townsfolk and joined the men congregating around the grocery-store stove.

In reality his everyday life was infused with all those modern improvements he seemed to spurn. Thoreau even raised a cash crop—beans—and sold it to support himself at Walden. As he said in his own journal, he loved "society as much as most." But he was caught up in a basic ambivalence toward industrialization and urbanization that he shared with millions of other Americans. They were lured on the one hand by the simplicity and beauty of pastoral days gone by, pulled on the other by their belief in progress and the promise of machine-generated prosperity and happiness.

In the early nineteenth century, reformers of all kinds sought to find or impose harmony on a society in which economic change and discord had reached a crescendo. Prompted by the evangelical ardor of the Second Great Awakening and convinced of the perfectibility of the human race, they crusaded for individual improvement. Some withdrew from the everyday competitive world to seek perfection in utopian communities. Others sought to improve themselves by renouncing alcohol. Inevitably the personal impulse to reform oneself led to the creation and reshaping of institutions. Schools, penitentiaries, and other institutions all underwent scrutiny and reform. Women were prominent in the reform movement, and the role of women in public life became an issue in itself.

Eventually one concern overrode all others: antislavery. No single issue evoked the depth of passion that slavery did. On a personal level it pitted neighbor against neighbor, settler against settler, section against section. Territorial expansion in the 1840s and 1850s would make it politically explosive as well.

Reform and Religious Revival

While the South was becoming more entrenched in a plantation system and slave society, the vast changes taking place in the rest of the country were having an unsettling effect. An apprentice tailor could find his trade obsolete by the time he became a journeyman; a student could find himself lacking sufficient arithmetic to enter a counting house when he graduated; a young rural woman could find her tasks unneeded on her family's farm.

Disturbed by change, yet convinced that the world could be improved, and confident that they could do something about it, various reformers and reform movements began to emerge and coalesce during the 1820s. Basically, reformers sought to restore order to a society made disorderly by economic, social, and cultural change. Thus it is not surprising that most reform movements originated in the dynamic North rather than in the socially and economically static South.

Reform was at its core an attempt to impose more direction on society. The movement encompassed both individual improvement (religion, temperance, health) and institutional reform (antislavery, women's rights, and education). Some reformers were motivated more by fear than by hope—Antimasonic, nativist, and anti-Catholic. Not all the problems that reformers addressed were new to the nineteenth century; some were generations old. Slavery had existed in the United States for two centuries, and alcohol had been a colonial problem; yet neither became a national issue until the 1820s and after, when the reformist ferment prompted action.

The prime motivating force behind organized reform was probably religion. Starting in the late 1790s, a tremendous religious revival, the Second Great Awakening, galvanized Protestants, especially women. The Awakening intensified in the 1820s in western New York, which experienced such continuous and heated waves of revivalism that it became known as the "burned-over" district. The opening of the Erie Canal and westward expansion carried the reform ferment to the Midwest.

Second Great Awakening

Evangelical Christianity was a religion of the heart, not the head. In 1821 Charles G. Finney, "the father of modern revivalism," experienced a soul-shaking conversion, which, he said, brought him "a retainer from the Lord Jesus Christ to plead his cause." In everyday language, he told his audiences that "God has made man a moral free agent." In other words, evil was avoidable; Christians were not doomed by original sin. Hence anyone could achieve salvation simply by choosing to do the right things.

The Second Great Awakening also raised people's hopes for the Second Coming of the Christian messiah and the establishment of the Kingdom of God on earth. Revivalists set out to speed the Second Coming by creating a heaven on earth. They joined the forces of good and light—reform—to combat those of evil and darkness. Some revivalists even believed that the United States had a special mission in God's design, and therefore a special role in eliminating evil.

Regardless of theology, all shared a belief in individual perfection as a moving force. In this way the

Second Great Awakening bred reform, and evangelical Protestants became missionaries for both religious and secular salvation. Wherever they preached, voluntary societies arose. Evangelists organized an association for each issue—temperance, education, Sabbath observance, antidueling, and later antislavery. They also organized grassroots political movements. In the 1830s and 1840s evangelicals rallied around the newly established Whig party to use government as an instrument of reform.

Women were the earliest converts, and they tended to sustain the Second Great Awakening. When Finney led daytime prayer meetings in Rochester, New York, for instance, pious middle-class women visited families while the men were away at work. Slowly they brought their families and husbands into the churches and under the influence of reform. Women more than men tended to feel personally responsible for the increasingly secular orientation of the expanding market economy. Many women felt guilty for neglecting their religious duties, and the emotionally charged conversion experience set them on the right path again.

At first, revival seemed to reinforce the cult of domesticity, since piety and religious values were associated with the domestic sphere. Yet the commitment

From Revival to Reform to spread the word, to become evangelicals, led to new, public roles for women. The organized prayer groups and female missionary societies that preceded and accompanied the Second Great Awakening were soon surpassed by greater organized reform and religious activity. Thus revival prompted and legitimized woman's public role, providing a path of certainty and stability amidst a rapidly changing economy and society.

The establishment and work of female reform societies were not merely responses to inner voices; they were reactions to the poverty and wretched urban conditions found in the growing cities. At the turn of the nineteenth century, most of the expanding cities had women's societies to help needy women and orphans. The spread of poverty and vice that accompanied urbanization increasingly affected women, especially those caught up in the fervor of revival.

An 1830 exposé of prostitution in New York City demonstrated the convergence of urban problems, revival, and reform. The Female Moral Reform Society led the crusade against prostitution. Over the next decade, the New York–based association expanded its activities and geographical scope as the American Female Moral Reform Society. By 1840, it had 555 affiliated female societies among the converted across the nation. These women not only fought the evils of prostitution but also assisted poor women and orphans and entered the political sphere. In New York State in the 1840s the movement fostered public morality by successfully crusading for criminal sanctions against seducers and prostitutes.

Another response to change was the interest in utopian communities. Such settlements offered an antidote to the market economy and to the untamed growth of large urban communities, and an opportunity to restore tradition and social cohesion. Whatever their particular philosophy, utopians sought order and regularity in their daily lives and a cooperative rather than competitive environment.

America's earliest utopian experiments were organized by the Shakers, who derived their name from the way they danced and swayed at worship services.

Shakers An offshoot of the Quakers, their sect was established in America in 1774 by the English Shaker Ann Lee. Shakers believed that the end of the world was near, and that sin entered the world through sexual intercourse. They regarded existing churches as too worldly and considered the Shaker family the instrument of salvation.

In 1787 the Shakers "gathered in" at New Lebanon, New York, to live, worship, and work communally. Other colonies soon followed. At its peak, between 1820 and 1860, the sect had about six thousand members in twenty settlements in eight states. Though economically conservative, the Shakers were social radicals. They abolished individual families, practiced celibacy, and made no distinction between the sexes in their government, economy, or

Etching of a Shaker dance during worship.   Library of Congress.

society. Each colony was one large family, with religious authority vested in elders and eldresses and economic leadership in deacons and deaconesses. The Shaker ministry was headed by a woman, Lucy Wright, during its period of greatest growth.

Not all utopian communities were founded by religious groups. Robert Owen's New Harmony was a short-lived attempt to found a socialist utopia in Indiana. A wealthy Scottish industrialist, Owen established the cooperative community in 1825. According to his plan, its nine hundred members were to exchange their labor for goods at a communal store. Handicrafts (hat- and boot-making) flourished at New Harmony. But the economic base of the community, its textile mill, failed after Owen gave it to the community to run. By 1827 the experiment had ended.

More successful were the New Englanders who lived and worked at the Brook Farm cooperative in West Roxbury, Massachusetts. Inspired by the

Brook Farm transcendental philosophy that the spiritual rises above the worldly, its members rejected materialism and sought satisfaction in a communal life combining spirituality, work, and play. Though short-lived, Brook Farm played a significant part in the Romantic movement. There Hawthorne, Emerson, and the editor of the *Dial* (the leading transcendentalist journal), Margaret Fuller, joined Thoreau, James Fenimore Cooper, Herman Melville, and others in helping to create what is known today as the American Renaissance—the flowering of a national literature. In poetry and prose these Romanticists praised individualism and intuition, rejecting or modifying the ordered world of the Enlightenment in favor of the mysteries of nature. Rebelling against convention, both social and literary, they probed and celebrated the American character and the American experience.

Far and away the most successful communitarians

were the Mormons. Organized by Joseph Smith in 1830 as the Church of Jesus Christ of Latter-day Saints, the church spread from its birthplace in New York and established communities dedicated to Christian cooperation. Fleeing persecution in Ohio, Illinois, and Missouri because of their claims of divine sanction and their newly adopted practice of polygamy, the Mormons trekked across the continent in 1846 and 1847 to found a New Zion in the Great Salt Lake Valley. There, under Brigham Young, head of the Twelve Apostles (their governing body), they established a cohesive community of Saints—a heaven on earth. The Mormons created agricultural settlements and distributed land according to family size. An extensive irrigation system, constructed by men who contributed their labor according to the quantity of land they received and the amount of water they expected to use, transformed the arid valley into a rich oasis. As the colony developed, its cooperative principles gradually gave way to benevolent corporate authority, and the church elders came to control water, trade, industry, and even the territorial government of Utah.

Mormon Community of Saints

TEMPERANCE, PUBLIC EDUCATION, AND FEMINISM

One of the most successful reform efforts was the campaign against the consumption of alcohol. As a group, American men liked to drink alcoholic spirits. They gathered in public houses, saloons, and rural inns to gossip, discuss politics, play cards, escape work and home pressures, and drink. And though respectable women did not drink in public, many regularly tippled alcohol-based patent medicines promoted as cure-alls.

Why then did temperance become such a vital issue? And why were women specially active in the movement? As with all reform, temperance had a strong religious base. To evangelicals, the selling of whiskey was a chronic symbol of Sabbath violation, for workers commonly labored six days a week, then spent Sunday at the public house drinking and socializing. Temperance leaders, who produced a body of literature laced with images of abandoned wives, prodigal sons, and drunken fathers, saw alcohol as a destroyer of families. Outside the home, the habit of drinking could not be tolerated in the new world of the factory. Employers complained that drinkers took "St. Monday" as a holiday to recover from Sunday.

Demon rum thus became a major target of reformers. As the movement gained momentum, they shifted their emphasis from temperate use of spirits to voluntary abstinence and finally to a crusade to prohibit the manufacture and sale of spirits. The American Society for the Promotion of Temperance, organized in 1826 to urge drinkers to sign a pledge of abstinence, shortly thereafter became a pressure group for state prohibition legislation. By the mid-1840s the annual per capita consumption of alcohol had fallen from more than five gallons to less than two gallons. Furthermore, many northern states, beginning with Maine in 1851, enacted laws prohibiting the manufacture and sale of alcohol.

Temperance Societies

Another important part of the reform impulse was the development of new institutions to meet the social needs of citizens. Public education was one of the more lasting results of the age of institution building. In 1800 there were no public schools outside New England; by 1860 every state had some public education. Massachusetts took the lead, especially under Horace Mann, secretary of the state board of education from 1837 to 1848. Under Mann, Massachusetts established a minimum school year of six months, increased the number of high schools, formalized the training of teachers, and emphasized secular subjects and applied skills rather than religious training. In the process, teaching became a woman's profession.

Horace Mann on Education

Horace Mann's preaching on behalf of free state education would eventually change schooling throughout the nation. "If we do not prepare children to become good citizens," Mann prophesied, ". . . then our republic must go down to destruction." The abolition of ignorance, Mann claimed, would end misery, crime, and suffering.

In laying the basis of free public schools, Mann also broadened the scope of education. Previously, education had focused exclusively on literacy, religious training, and discipline. Under Mann's leadership, the school curriculum became more secular and appropriate for future clerks, farmers, and workers. Students now studied geography, American history, arithmetic, and science. Moral education was retained, but direct religious indoctrination was dropped.

A more controversial reform movement was the rise of American feminism in the 1840s. Ironically, it was women's traditional image as pious and spiritual that brought them into the public sphere. Revivalism, with its emphasis on conversion through the heart, served to elevate women; they were thought to be more emotional than men, and emotion was the most important element in being reborn. Organized into groups like the American Female Moral Reform Society, women slowly entered the public arena.

Reaction to the growing involvement of women in reform movements led many women to re-examine their position in society. In 1837 two antislavery lecturers, Angelina and Sarah Grimké, became particular objects of controversy. Natives of Charleston, South Carolina, they moved north in the 1820s to speak and write more openly and forcefully against slavery. They received a hostile reception for speaking before mixed groups of men and women. This reaction turned the Grimkés' attention from slavery to women's condition. The two attacked the concept of "subordination to man."

Angelina and Sarah Grimké

In arguing against slavery, some women noticed the similarities between their own position and that of slaves. They saw parallels in their legal disabilities—inability to vote or control their own property, except in widowhood—and their social restrictions—exclusion from advanced schooling and from most occupations. "The investigation of the rights of the slave," Angelina Grimké confessed, "has led me to a better understanding of my own." Her *Letters to Catharine E. Beecher* and Sarah Grimké's *Letters on the Equality of the Sexes and the Condition of Women,* both published in 1838, were the opening volleys in the war against the legal and social inequality of women.

Unlike other reform movements, which succeeded in building a broad base of individual and organizational support, the movement for women's rights was limited. Some men joined the ranks, notably abolitionist William Lloyd Garrison and ex-slave Frederick Douglass, but most were actively opposed. Though the Seneca Falls Convention, led by Elizabeth Cady Stanton and Lucretia Mott, issued a much-published indictment of women's disabilities in 1848, it had little effect. By the 1850s feminists were focusing more and more on the single issue of suffrage. But their arguments for the right to vote fell on deaf ears. Another cause eclipsed the suffrage movement, at least for a time.

THE ANTISLAVERY MOVEMENT

Sparked by territorial expansion, the issue of slavery eventually became so overpowering that it consumed all other reforms. Passions would become so heated that they would threaten the nation itself. Above all else, those opposed to slavery saw it as a moral issue, evidence of the sinfulness of the American nation.

From colonial days to 1830 few whites, if any, advocated the immediate abolition of slavery. Some, most notably the Quakers, hoped that moral suasion would convince slaveholders to free their chattels. Others favored gradual abolition coupled with the resettling of blacks in Africa. The American Colonization Society had been founded in 1816 with this objective. Only free blacks pushed for an immediate end to slavery. By 1830 there were at least fifty black antislavery societies. These societies assisted fugitive slaves, attacked slavery at every turn, and reminded the nation that its mission as defined in the Declaration of Independence remained unfulfilled. A free black press helped to spread their word. When the climate of opinion changed and whites became more committed to antislavery, black abolitionists like Frederick Douglass, Sojourner Truth, and Harriet Tubman worked with white reformers in the American Anti-Slavery Society.

Black Antislavery Movement

In the 1830s a small minority of white reformers made antislavery their primary commitment and made abolitionism a crusade. The most prominent and uncompromising abolitionist, though clearly not the most representative, was William Lloyd Garrison, who demanded "immediate and complete emancipation." Recruited to the abolitionist cause in 1828 by Benjamin Lundy, a gradualist, Garrison made his break from the moderate abolitionists in 1831. In that year he published the first issue of the *Liberator*, which was to be his major weapon against slavery for thirty-five years. "I am in earnest—I will not equivocate—I will not excuse—I will not retreat a single inch—and *I will be heard*," he wrote in the first issue.

William Lloyd Garrison

Garrison alone could not have made antislavery a central issue. By the 1830s many northern reformers were recognizing the evils of slavery and preparing to act. Moral and religious ferment primed evangelists to enter the fray. And the reform activities of the 1820s, including antislavery, had built a network of interrelated organizations.

Ironically, it was in defense of the constitutional rights of abolitionists, not slaves, that many whites entered the struggle. Wherever they went, abolitionists found their civil rights in danger. Southern mobs, for example, seized and destroyed much of the propaganda mailed by the American Anti-Slavery Society, and the state of South Carolina intercepted and burned abolitionist propaganda coming into the state (with the approval of the postmaster general). Elijah Lovejoy, an abolitionist editor, was killed by an Alton, Illinois, mob that had come to sack his office. Such actions gained sympathy and support for the abolitionists.

Another civil rights confrontation developed in Congress. Exercising their constitutional right to petition Congress, abolitionists mounted a campaign to abolish slavery and the slave trade in the District of Columbia. But Congress responded in 1836 by adopting the so-called gag rule, which automatically tabled abolitionist petitions, effectively preventing debate on them. In a dramatic defense of the right of petition, ex-president John Quincy Adams, then a Massachusetts representative, took to the floor repeatedly to defy the gag rule and eventually succeeded in getting it repealed (1844).

Gag Rule

The effect of the unlawful, violent, and obstructionist tactics used by proslavery advocates cannot be overestimated. Antislavery was not at the outset a unified movement. It was splintered and factionalized, and its adherents fought each other as often as they fought the defenders of slavery. They were divided over Garrison's emphasis on "moral suasion" versus the more practical political approach of James G. Birney, the Liberty party's candidate for president in 1844. And they disagreed over the place of free black people in American society. Even so, abolitionists eventually managed to unify and make antislavery a major issue in the politics of the 1850s.

ANTIMASONRY

A ntimasonry did not have the lasting appeal that antislavery had, but for a brief time it matched the intensity of abolitionism. The Antimasonry movement appeared like a comet in 1826, and it stirred political activity before disappearing in the 1840s. The political arena quickly absorbed Antimasonry, but its short life illustrates the close tie between politics and reform from the 1820s through the 1840s.

Antimasonry was a reaction to Freemasonry, which had come to the United States from England in the eighteenth century. Freemasonry was a secret middle- and upper-class fraternity that emphasized the Deity as opposed to organized religion and brotherhood as opposed to one church. In the early nineteenth century it spread in the growing towns, attracting many commercial and political leaders.

The Morgan Affair was the catalyst for Antimasonry as an organized movement. In 1826, William Morgan, a disillusioned Mason, wrote an exposé of

Morgan Affair
Masonry, to which his printer, David Miller, had added a scathing attack on the order. On September 12, 1826, prior to the book's appearance, a group of Masons abducted Morgan outside the Canandaigua, New York, jail. It was widely believed that the Masons had murdered Morgan, whose body was never found.

What energized the Antimasonry crusade was that its worst fears and charges seemed to be confirmed. Many of the officeholders in western New York, especially prosecutors, were Masons and they appeared to obstruct the investigation of Morgan's abduction. Public outcry and opposing political factions pressed for justice, and a series of notorious trials from 1827 through 1831 led many to suspect a conspiracy at work. The cover-up became as much the issue as Masonry itself, and the movement spilled over to other states. In the Morgan Affair, Antimason claims of a secret conspiracy seemed to be justified. Opponents of Masonry charged that the order's secrecy was antidemocratic and antirepublican. As church leaders took up the moral crusade against Masonry, evangelicals labeled the order satanic.

As a moral crusade, however, Antimasonry crossed over into politics almost immediately. The issue itself

In this contemporary Antimason cut, Freemasonry is represented as a Hydra-headed monster, with its tail strangling the Tree of Liberty. William Morgan, at the far right with an open book, is unmasking the monster, assisted by Antimasons. The winged figures are the Angels of Light and Truth with a holy mandate to finish off the monster.   Library of Congress.

was a political one since obstruction of justice was a signal element. Antimasonry attracted the lower and middle classes, pitting them against higher-status Masons and exploiting the general public's distrust and envy of local political leaders.

Unwittingly the Masons stoked the fires of Antimasonry. The silence of the order seemed to condone the murder of Morgan, and the construction of monumental lodges advertised their determination to remain a public force. When editors who were Masons ignored the crusade against Masonry, the Antimasons started their own newspapers. The struggle, carried out within and without political parties, aroused public interest in politics.

Antimasonry spread as a popular movement and introduced the convention system for choosing political candidates. In defense of public morality and the

Convention System
republic, the Antimasons held conventions in 1827. In the following year the conventions supported the National Republican candidate and

opposed Andrew Jackson because he was a Mason. In 1831 the Antimasons held the first national political convention in Baltimore, and a year later nominated in convention William Wirt as their presidential candidate.

By the mid-1830s Antimasonry had lost force as a political movement. Most Antimasons found a comfortable anti-Jackson vehicle in the Whig party. Yet the movement left an indelible mark on the politics of the era. It inspired wider participation in the political process. Moreover, revivalist and reform impulses in movements like Antimasonry further stimulated and awakened disagreements over values and ideology that were reinforced by conflicts over wealth, religion, and status. These differences helped polarize politics and shape parties as organizations to express those differences. The Antimasons contributed specifically to party development by pioneering the convention system and by stimulating greater grassroots involvement.

JACKSONIANISM AND THE BEGINNINGS OF MODERN PARTY POLITICS

The distinction between reform and politics eroded in the 1820s and after as reform inched its way into politics. The Antimasons, and then the abolitionists, appealed directly to voters. Although their means often differed, party leaders too sought to deal with the problems created by an expanding, urbanizing, market-oriented nation. President John Quincy Adams advocated a nationalist program and an activist federal government; Andrew Jackson and his followers adhered to the Jeffersonian ideal of a more limited federal government.

The election of 1824, in which Adams and Jackson faced each other for the first time, signaled the beginning of a new, more open political system. From 1800 through 1820 a caucus in the House of Representatives had chosen the Republican presidential nominees. In 1824, the caucus chose William H. Crawford, secretary of the treasury. But by this date most electors were selected by the voters rather than by the state legislatures. Thus, several individuals decided to ignore the caucus and seek the presidency by going directly to the voters.

End of the Caucus System

John Quincy Adams drew support from New England, and westerners backed Speaker of the House Henry Clay of Kentucky. Secretary of War John C. Calhoun looked to the South for support, and hoped to win Pennsylvania as well. Andrew Jackson, a popular military hero whose political views were unknown, was nominated by resolution of the Tennessee legislature and won support everywhere. By boycotting the deliberations of the caucus and by attacking it as undemocratic, these men and their supporters ended the presidential nominating role of the congressional caucus.

Though Andrew Jackson led in both popular and electoral votes in the four-way presidential election of 1824, no one received a majority (see map). Adams finished second, and Clay and Crawford trailed far behind. (Calhoun dropped out of the race before the election.) Under the Constitution, the selection of a president in such circumstances fell to the House of Representatives. Clay, as Speaker of the House and leader of the Ohio Valley states, backed Adams, who received the votes of thirteen out of twenty-four state delegations. Clay was rewarded with the position of secretary of state in the Adams administration—the traditional stepping-stone to the presidency. Angry Jacksonians denounced the arrangement as a "corrupt bargain" that had stolen the office from the clear frontrunner.

As president, John Quincy Adams took a strong nationalist position emphasizing Henry Clay's American System of protective tariffs, a national bank, and internal improvements. Adams believed the federal

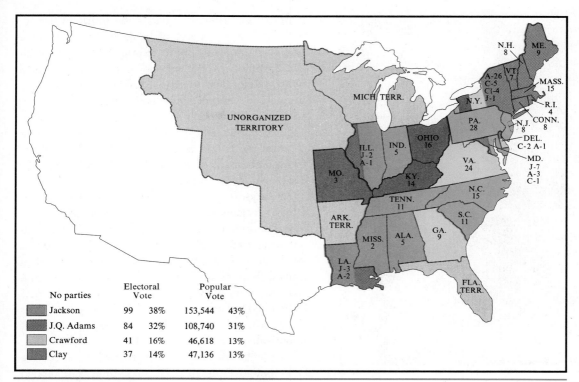

No parties	Electoral Vote		Popular Vote	
Jackson	99	38%	153,544	43%
J.Q. Adams	84	32%	108,740	31%
Crawford	41	16%	46,618	13%
Clay	37	14%	47,136	13%

Presidential Election, 1824

government should take an activist role not only in the economy but in education, science, and the arts; accordingly, he proposed a national university in Washington, D.C.

Brilliant as a diplomat and secretary of state, Adams was sadly inept as president. He underestimated the lingering effects of the Panic of 1819 and the ensuing bitter opposition to a national bank and protective tariffs. Meanwhile, supporters of Andrew Jackson sabotaged Adams's administration at every opportunity.

The 1828 campaign between Adams and Jackson was an intensely personal conflict. Whatever principles the two men stood for were obscured by the mudslinging of both sides.

Jackson polled 56 percent of the popular vote and won in the electoral college, 178 to 83. For him and

his supporters, the election of 1828 was the culmination of a long-fought, well-organized campaign based on party organization. An era had ended, and the Democratic party became the first truly modern political party in the United States. The future belonged to well-organized political parties and leaders who engaged in party politics.

Andrew Jackson was nicknamed "Old Hickory," after the toughest American hardwood. A rough-and-tumble, ambitious man, he rose from humble birth

Andrew Jackson to become a wealthy planter and slaveholder. Jackson was the first American president not born into comfortable circumstances, a self-made man at ease among both frontiersmen and southern planters.

Jackson and his supporters offered a distinct alter-

Andrew Jackson in 1832, at the peak of his success and power.   Library of Congress.

power of government—that is, he utilized the veto and cut federal support of banks and corporations. Democratic opposition to reform was tied to their perception of government and concern for individual rights. Reformers sought to achieve their goals through an interventionist government: Jacksonians advocated individual rights. Democrats, for example, opposed public education because it interfered with parental rights and responsibilities. Finally, neither Jackson nor many of his supporters shared the reformers' humanitarian concerns.

Yet Jackson and the Jacksonians considered themselves reformers in a different way. In following Jefferson's notion of restraint in government and in emphasizing individualism, Jackson and his followers sought to restore old republican virtues. Individual traits such as industriousness, prudence, sobriety, and economy were highly prized. No less than reformers he favored human goodness. He believed that his party was the best instrument to restore those traditional values.

Like Jefferson, Jackson strengthened the executive branch of government at the same time as he tended to weaken the federal role. Given his popularity and the strength of his personality, this concentration of power in the presidency was perhaps inevitable; but his deliberate policy of combining the roles of party leader and chief of state centralized even greater power in the White House. Invoking the principle that rotating officeholders would make government more responsive to the public will, Jackson used the spoils system to reward loyal Democrats with appointments to office. Though he removed fewer than one-quarter of federal officeholders in his two terms, his use of patronage nevertheless strengthened party organization and loyalty.

Jackson invigorated the philosophy of limited government. In 1830 he vetoed the Maysville Road bill, which would have provided a federal subsidy to construct a sixty-mile turnpike from Maysville to Lexington, Kentucky. Jackson insisted that an internal improvement confined to one state was unconstitutional, and that such projects were properly a state

native to the strong national government Adams had advocated. They and their party, the Democratic-Republicans (shortened to Democrats), represented a wide range of beliefs but shared some common ideals. Fundamentally, they sought to foster the Jeffersonian concept of an agrarian society, harkening back to the belief that a strong central government was the enemy of individual liberty, a tyranny to be feared. Thus, like Jefferson, they favored limited government and emphasized state sovereignty.

Democrats

Jacksonians were as fearful of the concentration of economic power as they were of political power. They saw government intervention in the economy as benefiting special-interest groups and the rich. To counter special privilege, Jackson used the negative responsibility. The veto undermined Henry Clay's American System and personally embarrassed Clay, since the project was in his home district.

THE NULLIFICATION AND BANK CONTROVERSIES

Jackson had to face more directly the question of the proper division of sovereignty between state and central government. The slave South, especially South Carolina, was fearful of federal power. To protect their interests, South Carolinian political leaders developed the doctrine of *nullification,* according to which a state had the right to overrule federal legislation. The act that directly inspired this doctrine was the passage in 1828 of the Tariff of Abominations. In his unsigned *Exposition and Protest,* John C. Calhoun argued that in any disagreement between the federal government and a state, a special state convention—like those called to ratify the Constitution—would decide the conflict by either nullifying or accepting the federal law. Only the power of nullification could protect the minority against the tyranny of the majority, Calhoun asserted.

In public, John C. Calhoun let others take the lead in advancing nullification. As Jackson's running mate in 1828, he avoided publicly identifying with nullification and thus embarrassing the ticket. And as vice president, he hoped to win Jackson's support as Democratic presidential nominee. Thus a silent Calhoun presided over the Senate and its packed galleries when Senators Daniel Webster (New Hampshire) and Robert Y. Hayne (South Carolina) debated nullification in January 1830. Though debating Hayne, Webster aimed his remarks at Calhoun as he depicted the nation as a compact of people, not merely states. In the climax of his career

Webster-Hayne Debate

as a debator, he invoked two images. One, which he hoped he would not see, was the outcome of nullification: "states dissevered, discordant, belligerent; on a land rent with civil feuds, or drenched . . . in fraternal blood!" The other was a patriotic vision of a great nation flourishing under the motto "Liberty *and* Union, now and forever, one and inseparable."

South Carolina first invoked its theory of nullification against the tariff of 1832. Though this tariff had the effect of reducing some duties, it retained high taxes on imported iron, cottons, and woolens. A majority of southern representatives supported the new tariff, but South Carolinians refused to go along. In their view, their constitutional right to control their own destiny had been sacrificed to the demands of northern industrialists. They feared the consequences of accepting such an act; it could set a precedent for congressional legislation on slavery. In November 1832 a South Carolina state convention nullified the tariff, making it unlawful for officials to collect duties in the state after February 1, 1833. Immediately recruiters began to organize a volunteer army to ensure nonenforcement of the tariff.

Nullification Crisis

"Old Hickory" responded with toughness. On December 10, 1832, Jackson issued his own proclamation nullifying nullification. He moved troops to federal forts in South Carolina and prepared United States marshals to collect the required duties. At Jackson's request, Congress passed the Force Act, which supposedly renewed Jackson's authority to call up troops; it was actually a scheme to avoid the use of force by collecting duties before ships reached South Carolina. At the same time, Jackson extended the olive branch by recommending tariff reductions. Calhoun, disturbed by South Carolina's drift toward separatism, resigned as vice president and became a South Carolina senator. In the Senate he worked with Henry Clay to draw up the compromise tariff of 1833. Quickly passed by Congress and signed by the president, the revision lengthened the list of duty-free items and reduced duties over the next nine years. Satisfied, South Carolina's convention repealed its nullification law, and in a final salvo nullified Jackson's Force Act. Jackson ignored the gesture.

The nullification controversy represented a genuine debate on the true nature and principles of the republic. Each side believed it was upholding the Constitution. Neither side won a clear victory. Another issue, that of a central bank, would define the powers of the federal government more clearly.

At stake was the rechartering of the Second Bank of the United States, whose twenty-year charter expired in 1836. One of the bank's functions was to act as a clearinghouse for state banks, keeping them honest by refusing to accept their notes if they had insufficient gold in reserve. Many state banks resented the central bank's police role; by presenting state bank notes for redemption all at once, the Second Bank could easily ruin a state bank. Moreover, state banks found themselves unable to compete on an equal footing with the Second Bank. And many state governments regarded the national bank as unresponsive to local needs. Finally, westerners and urban workers remembered with bitterness the bank's conservative credit policies during the Panic of 1819. To many westerners the bank's conservative, anti-Jacksonian president, Nicholas Biddle, symbolized all that was wrong with the Second Bank.

Although the bank's charter would not expire until 1836, Biddle, aware of Jackson's hostility and encouraged by the National Republican presidential candidate, Henry Clay, sought to make it an issue in the campaign of 1832. His strategy backfired. In July 1832 Jackson vetoed the rechartering bill, and the Senate failed to override the veto. Jackson's veto message was an emotional attack on the undemocratic nature of the bank. The bank was the major issue of the 1832 campaign, and Jackson used it to attack special privilege and economic power.

After his victory and second inauguration in 1833, Jackson moved not only to dismantle the Second Bank of the United States but to ensure that it would

not be resurrected. He deposited federal funds in favored state-chartered ("pet") banks; without federal money, the bank shriveled. When its federal charter expired in 1836, it became just another Pennsylvania-chartered private bank. In 1841 it closed its doors.

In the aftermath of the fight against the bank, Congress in 1836 passed the Deposit Act. One portion of the law provided that the federal surplus in excess of $5 million be distributed to the states in interest-free loans. The surplus had derived from speculation in public lands. At the heart of the speculation craze were the bank notes issued by state banks.

Following his hard-money instinct and his opposition to paper currency, President Jackson ordered Treasury Secretary Levi Woodbury to issue the Specie Circular. It provided that after August 15, 1836, only specie—gold or silver—or Virginia land scrip would be accepted as payment for federal lands. By ending credit sales, the circular reduced significantly public land purchases and forced a halt to the distribution of the surplus to the states; the final payments were never made since the surplus evaporated.

The policy was a disaster on many fronts. Although federal land sales were sharply reduced, speculation still continued as available land for sale became a scarce commodity. The ensuing increased demand for specie squeezed banks, and many suspended specie payment (the redemption of bank notes for specie). This led to further credit contraction, as banks issued fewer notes and gave less credit. In the waning days of Jackson's administration, Congress voted to repeal the circular. The president, however, pocket-vetoed the bill.

Jackson used the veto power more often than did all his predecessors combined. And he was the first to use the pocket veto—refusing to sign or veto a bill at the end of a congressional session, thus killing it. Previous presidents believed that vetoes were justified only on constitutional grounds, but Jackson negated bills merely because he disagreed with them. He made the veto an important weapon in controlling

Second Bank of the United States

Specie Circular

Congress, since representatives and senators had to consider the possibility of a presidential veto on any bill. In effect, he made the executive power equal to that of two-thirds of both houses of Congress.

THE WHIG CHALLENGE AND THE SECOND PARTY SYSTEM

Once historians described the 1830s and 1840s as the Age of Jackson, and the personalities of the leading political figures dominated history books. Increasingly, however, historians have viewed these years as an age of popularly based political parties and reformers. For it was only when the passionate concerns of evangelicals and reformers spilled into politics that party differences became important again and party loyalties solidified. For the first time grass-roots political groups, organized from the bottom up, set the tone of political life.

In the 1830s the Democrats' opponents found shelter under a common umbrella, the Whig party. Resentful of Jackson's domination of Congress, the Whigs borrowed their name from the British party that had opposed the tyranny of Hanoverian monarchs in the eighteenth century. From the congressional elections of 1834 through the 1840s, they and the Democrats competed nearly equally; only a few percentage points separated the two parties in national elections. They fought at every level—city, county, and state—and achieved a stability previously unknown in American politics. The two parties took different approaches to numerous fundamental issues during these years. Though both favored economic expansion, the Whigs sought it through an activist government, the Democrats through limited government. Thus the Whigs supported corporate charters, a national bank, and paper currency; the Democrats were opposed. The Whigs also favored

Whigs

more humanitarian reforms than did the Democrats—public schools, abolition of capital punishment, temperance, and prison and asylum reform.

In general, Whigs were simply more optimistic than Democrats, and more enterprising. They did not hesitate to help one group if doing so would promote the general welfare. The chartering of corporations, they argued, expanded economic opportunity for everyone. Meanwhile the Democrats, distrustful of the concentration of economic power and of moral and economic coercion, held fast to their Jeffersonian principle of limited government.

Ironically, the basic economic issues of the era were not the determinants of party affiliation. Although the Whigs attracted more of the upper and middle classes, both sides drew support from manufacturers, merchants, laborers, and farmers. Religion and ethnicity, however, were more strongly correlated with party allegiance. In the North, the Whigs' concern for energetic government and humanitarian and moral reform won the favor of native-born and British-American evangelical Protestants. Democrats, on the other hand, tended to be foreign-born Catholics and nonevangelical Protestants, both groups that preferred to keep religious and secular affairs separate.

The Whig party thus became the vehicle of evangelical Christianity. Indeed, Whigs practiced a kind of political revivalism. Their rallies resembled camp meetings; their speeches echoed evangelical rhetoric; their programs embodied the perfectionist beliefs of reformers. In unifying evangelicals, the Whigs alienated members of other faiths. Sabbath laws, temperance legislation, and Protestant-inspired public education threatened the religious freedom and individual liberty of these groups, which generally opposed state interference in moral and religious questions. As a result, more than 95 percent of Irish Catholics, 90 percent of Reformed Dutch, and 80 percent of German Catholics voted Democratic.

Whigs and Reformers

Jackson hand-picked Vice President Martin Van Buren to head the Democratic ticket in the presidential election of 1836. The Whigs, who had not yet coalesced into a national party, entered three sectional candidates: Daniel Webster of New England, Hugh White of the South, and William Henry Harrison of the West. By splintering the vote, they hoped to throw the election into the House, but Van Buren squeaked through with a 25,000-vote edge out of a total of 1.5 million.

Van Buren took office just weeks before the American credit system collapsed. Unfortunately, Van Buren followed Jackson's hard-money policies. He

Martin Van Buren and Hard Times

curtailed federal spending, thus accelerating deflation, and opposed the Whigs' advocacy of a national bank, which would have expanded credit. Even worse, Van Buren proposed a new treasury system under which the government would keep its funds in regional treasury offices rather than banks. The treasury branches would accept and pay out only gold and silver coin; they would not accept paper currency or checks drawn on state banks. Van Buren's independent treasury bill was passed in 1840. By creating a constant demand for hard coin, it deprived banks of gold and added to the general deflation.

With the nation in a depression, the Whigs confidently prepared for the election of 1840. The Democrats renominated President Van Buren in a somber

Election of 1840

convention. The Whigs rallied behind the military hero General William Henry Harrison and his running mate, John Tyler of Virginia. Eighty percent of the eligible voters cast ballots, and the Whigs won.

Unfortunately for the Whigs, Harrison died within a month of his inauguration. Tyler, a former Democrat who had left the party in opposition to Jackson's Nullification Proclamation, turned out to be more of a Democrat than a Whig. He consistently opposed the party's program, vetoing bills that provided for protective tariffs, internal improvements, and a revived Bank of the United States. Understandably, the Whigs virtually expelled him from the party.

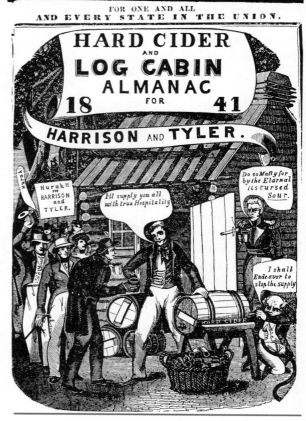

Using many of the techniques of twentieth-century politics, General William Henry Harrison ran a "log cabin and hard cider" campaign—a popular crusade—against Jackson heir, President Martin Van Buren. The almanac cover shows a victorious Harrison receiving the people's acclaim while Jackson's cider—popularity—has turned sour and Van Buren is unable to stem the Whig's appeal.   Library of Congress.

Tyler thus turned his attention to territorial questions. A major dispute with Great Britain emerged over the imprecisely defined boundary between Maine and New Brunswick. In the winter of 1838 and 1839, Canadian lumberjacks moved into the area. Shortly thereafter, Maine attempted to expel them. The Canadians captured the Maine land agent, both sides mobilized, and Congress authorized a call-up of fifty thousand men. Fortunately, war was avoided. Both sides compromised on their claims in the Webster-Ashburton Treaty (1842).

The border dispute with Great Britain prefigured an issue that became prominent in national politics in the mid- to late 1840s: the westward expansion of the United States. Tyler's succession to power in 1841 and a Democratic victory in the presidential election of 1844 ended activist, energetic government on the federal level for the rest of the decade. Meanwhile economic issues were eclipsed by debate over the nation's destiny to stretch from coast to coast.

MANIFEST DESTINY

Americans had been hungry for new lands ever since the colonists first turned their eyes westward. There lay fertile soil, valuable minerals, and the chance for a better life or a new beginning. Agrarian Democrats saw the West as an antidote to urbanization and industrialization. Enterprising Whigs looked to the new commercial opportunities the West offered. Equally important was both a fierce national pride and a desire to acquire western land to secure the nation from external enemies. Finally, Americans believed that westward expansion would extend American freedom and democracy to "less fortunate people." In the 1840s *manifest destiny*, the belief that American expansion westward was inevitable, divinely ordained, and just, served the nation's expansionists (see map, page 222).

Among the long-standing objectives of expansionists was the Republic of Texas. Originally part of Mexico, Texas attracted thousands of Americans in the 1820s and 1830s. The Mexican government's extremely generous land policy enticed settlers into the area. In return for the right to settle

Republic of Texas

in Texas, settlers were expected to become Mexican citizens, to obey Mexican law, and to adopt the Catholic faith.

By 1835, 35,000 Americans, including many slaveholders, lived in Texas. These new settlers ignored local laws and oppressed native Mexicans, and when the Mexican government attempted to tighten its control over the region, it stimulated a rebellion instead. The desires of Texans to avenge the defeat at the Alamo and to secure their independence were fulfilled in 1836 through Sam Houston's victory in the Battle of San Jacinto.

Americans were generally delighted with the revolution's result, but joy did not mean that the Texas request for annexation into the Union was welcomed. Texas was a slave republic and this made annexation a potentially explosive political issue. Jackson delayed recognition of Texas because of the political danger, and Van Buren ignored annexation altogether. Texans then talked about developing ties with Britain and expanding to the Pacific. President Tyler feared that a Texas alliance with the English might threaten American independence. He was also committed to expansion and hoped to build support in the South by enlarging the area of slavery. Tyler, therefore, pushed for annexation. But in a sectional vote, the Senate in April 1844 rejected a treaty of annexation.

Just as southerners sought expansion to the Southwest, northerners looked to the Northwest. In 1841 "Oregon fever" struck thousands. Lured by the glowing reports of missionaries, migrants organized hundreds of wagon trains and embarked on the Oregon Trail. The two-thousand-mile journey took six months or more, but within a few years five thousand settlers had arrived in the fertile Willamette Valley south of the Columbia River.

Oregon Fever

Since the Anglo-American convention of 1818, Britain and the United States had jointly occupied the disputed Oregon Territory. Beginning with the administration of President John Quincy Adams, the United States had tried to fix the boundary at the

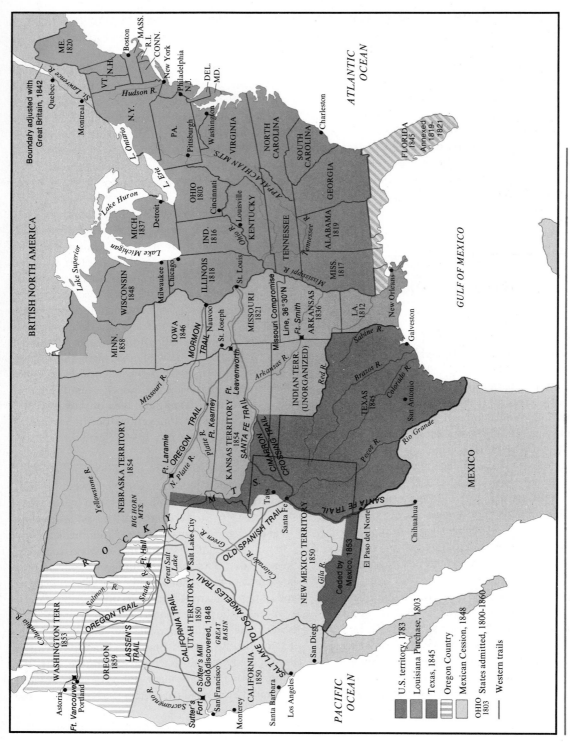

Westward Expansion, 1800–1860

IMPORTANT EVENTS

1790s–1840s	Second Great Awakening
1825	House of Representatives elects John Quincy Adams president
1826	American Society for the Promotion of Temperance founded Morgan Affair
1828	Tariff of Abominations Jackson elected president
1830	Webster-Hayne debate
1830s–1840s	Second party system
1831	*Liberator* begins publication First national Antimason Convention
1832	Veto of Second Bank of the United States recharter Jackson re-elected
1832–33	Nullification crisis
1836	Republic of Texas established Specie Circular Van Buren elected president
1837	Financial panic
1837–39	U.S.–Canada border tensions
1837–48	Horace Mann heads Massachusetts Board of Education
1839–43	Depression
1840	Whigs under Harrison win presidency
1841–47	Brook Farm
1841	Tyler assumes the presidency Oregon Fever
1844	Polk elected president
1845	Texas admitted to the Union
1846–47	Mormon trek to the Great Salt Lake
1848	Woman's Rights Convention, Seneca Falls, New York

49th parallel, but Britain refused. Time only increased the American appetite. In 1843 a Cincinnati convention demanded that the United States obtain the entire Oregon Territory, up to its northernmost border of 54°40′. Soon "Fifty-four Forty or Fight" had become the rallying cry of American expansionists.

The expansion into Oregon and the rejection of annexation of Texas, both favored by antislavery forces, heightened southern pessimism. Thus southern leaders became anxious about their diminishing ability to control the debate over slavery. Calhoun persuaded the 1844 Democratic convention to adopt a rule that the presidential nom-

Election of 1844

inee receive two-thirds of the convention votes. In effect, the southern states acquired a veto, and they used it to block Van Buren as the nominee. Instead, the party chose House Speaker James K. Polk, a hard-money Jacksonian and avid expansionist from Tennessee. Henry Clay, the Whig nominee, believed that the Democrats would provoke a war with Great Britain or Mexico. He favored expansion through negotiations.

The Democrats captured the White House by 170 electoral votes to 105 (they won the popular vote by just 38,000 out of 2.7 million). Polk carried New York's 36 electoral votes by just 6,000 votes; abolitionist James G. Birney, the Liberty party candidate, drew almost 16,000 votes away from Clay, handing the state and the election to Polk. Thus abolitionist forces had influenced the choice of a president.

Interpreting Polk's victory as a mandate for annexation, President Tyler proposed in his last days in office that Texas be admitted to statehood by joint resolution of Congress. Proslavery and antislavery congressmen debated the extension of slavery into the territory, and the resolution passed the House 120 to 98 and the Senate 27 to 25. Three days before leaving office, Tyler signed the measure. Mexico immediately broke relations with the United States; war loomed.

Politics, the reform spirit, and expansionism commingled in the 1830s and 1840s. Reform imbued with revivalism sought to bring order in a rapidly changing society. But reformers had no monopoly on claims of republican virtue; their opponents too claimed descent from the revolutionary values that held dear individual liberty. Once reform entered politics, it sparked a broader-based interest. Political organization and conflict stimulated even greater interest in campaigns and political issues. Eventually, however, one issue absorbed nearly all attention and created a crisis in the Union: slavery.

SUGGESTIONS FOR FURTHER · READING

Religion and Revivalism

Leonard J. Arrington and Davis Bitton, *The Mormon Experience. A History of the Latter-day Saints* (1979); Whitney R. Cross, *The Burned-Over District* (1950); Paul E. Johnson, *A Shopkeeper's Millennium: Society and Revivals in Rochester, New York, 1815–1837* (1978); William G. McLoughlin, *Revivals, Awakenings, and Reform: An Essay on Religion and Social Change in America, 1607–1977* (1978); Timothy L. Smith, *Revivalism and Social Reform in Mid-Nineteenth Century America* (1957).

Reform

Ray Allen Billington, *The Protestant Crusade, 1800–1860: A Study of the Origins of American Nativism* (1938); Lawrence Foster, *Religion and Sexuality: Three American Communal Experiments of the Nineteenth Century* (1981); Clifford S. Griffin, *The Ferment of Reform, 1830–1860* (1967); David J. Rothman, *The Discovery of the Asylum: Social Order and Disorder in the New Republic* (1971); Mary P. Ryan, *Cradle of the Middle Class. The Family in Oneida County, New York, 1790–1865* (1981); Alice Felt Tyler, *Freedom's Ferment* (1944); Ronald G. Walter, *American Reformers, 1815–1860* (1978).

Temperance, Education, and Feminism

Barbara J. Berg, *The Remembered Gate: Origins of American Feminism. The Woman and the City, 1800–1860* (1977); Lawrence A. Cremin, *American Education: The National Experience, 1783–1876* (1980); Ellen C. Du Bois, *Feminism and Suffrage: The Emergence of an Independent Woman's Movement in America 1848–1869* (1978); Carl Kaestle, *Pillars of the Republic: Common Schools and American Society, 1780–1860* (1982); W. J. Rorabaugh, *The Alcoholic Republic: An American Tradition* (1979); Ian R. Tyrrell, *Sobering Up: From Temperance to Prohibition in Antebellum America, 1800–1860* (1979).

Antislavery and Abolitionism

Frederick Douglass, *Life and Times of Frederick Douglass* (1881); Aileen S. Kraditor, *Means and Ends in American Abolitionism: Garrison and His Critics on Strategy and Tactics* (1967); Gerda Lerner, *The Grimké Sisters of South Carolina* (1967); Lewis Perry and Michael Fellman, eds., *Antislavery Reconsidered* (1979); Benjamin Quarles, *Black Abolitionists* (1969); Leonard L. Richards, *"Gentlemen of Property and Standing": Anti-Abolition Mobs in Jacksonian America* (1970); Ronald G. Walters, *The Antislavery Appeal: American Abolitionism After 1830* (1976).

Andrew Jackson and the Jacksonians

Lee Benson, *The Concept of Jacksonian Democracy: New York as a Test Case* (1964); Richard B. Latner, *The Presidency of Andrew Jackson* (1979); Marvin Meyers, *The Jacksonian Persuasion* (1960); John Niven, *Martin Van Buren* (1983); Edward Pessen, *Jacksonian America: Society, Person-*

ality, and Politics, rev. ed. (1979); Robert V. Remini, Andrew Jackson and the Course of American Democracy (1984); Robert V. Remini, Andrew Jackson and the Course of American Freedom, 1822–1832 (1981); John William Ward, Andrew Jackson: Symbol for an Age (1955); Harry L. Watson, Jacksonian Politics and Community Conflict. The Emergence of the Second American Party System in Cumberland County, North Carolina (1981).

Democrats and Whigs

Ronald P. Formisano, The Transformation of Political Culture. Massachusetts Parties, 1790s–1840s (1983); Daniel Walker Howe, The Political Culture of the American Whigs (1979); Kathleen Smith Kutolowski, "Antimasonry Reexamined: Social Bases of the Grass-Roots Party," Journal of American History, 71 (September 1984), 269–293; Richard P. McCormick, The Second American Party System: Party Formation in the Jacksonian Era (1966); William Preston Vaughn, The Antimasonic Party in the United States 1826–1843 (1983).

Manifest Destiny and Foreign Policy

Norman B. Graebner, ed., Manifest Destiny (1968); Reginald Horsman, Race and Manifest Destiny (1981); Frederick Merk, Manifest Destiny and Mission in American History (1963); David M. Pletcher, The Diplomacy of Annexation: Texas, Oregon, and the Mexican War (1973); Paul A. Varg, United States Foreign Relations, 1820–1860 (1979).

CHAPTER 13

TERRITORIAL EXPANSION
AND SLAVERY:
THE ROAD TO WAR
1845–1861

"*Our people have* filled the eastern valley of the Mississippi, adventurously ascended the Missouri to its headsprings, and are already engaged in establishing the blessings of self-government in valleys of which the rivers flow to the Pacific. Our title to the country of Oregon," continued James K. Polk, "is 'clear and unquestionable.'" With these words, spoken in 1845, a new president made territorial expansion the centerpiece of his administration's agenda and pledged his support for Americans' expansionist energies.

Fifteen years later the nation's territories figured prominently in another political gathering. In 1860 tense and angry Democrats gathered at Charleston for their party's nominating convention. Charging that southern rights in the territories were being denied, delegates from six deep-South states walked out of the meeting. That walkout destroyed the last remaining national party and began the destruction of the Union.

Some experienced politicians had foreseen just such a result, because slavery lay at the root of territorial controversies. Each time the nation expanded it confronted a thorny issue—whether new territories and states should be slave or free. Over this question there were disagreements too violent to compromise. A host of political leaders, including Henry Clay, Lewis Cass, Stephen A. Douglas, and Presidents Jackson and Van Buren, labored from the 1830s through the 1850s to postpone or compromise disagreements about slavery in the territories. But repeatedly these disputes injected the bitterness surrounding slavery into national politics.

As Americans fought over slavery in the territories, the conflict broadened to encompass many other issues. Northerners came to believe that their liberties, political rights, and economic interests were under attack by an aggressive South. Southerners began to fear that their safety, rights, and prosperity were in peril from a hostile North.

Battles over slavery in the territories broke the second party system apart and then shaped a realigned system that emphasized sectional enmity. Sectional parties replaced nationwide organizations. The belief that North and South were too different to thrive within the same country grew. A northern ideology advanced by the new Republican party suggested that progress depended on the free labor, civil liberties, and economic change that the South opposed. A southern ideology depicted northern society as unstable, lacking in respect for the Constitution, and prone to interfere with slavery.

Not all Americans were obsessed with these conflicts. In fact, the results of the 1860 presidential election strongly suggested that most voters wanted neither disunion nor civil war. Yet within six months they had both. By 1860 both sections felt threatened and anxious, and an area of disagreement that once had been limited to a small minority of extremists now engaged two powerful groups: the victorious Republican party and defensive southern slaveholders. On a collision course, these groups chose not to accept last-minute compromises offered to resolve their differences.

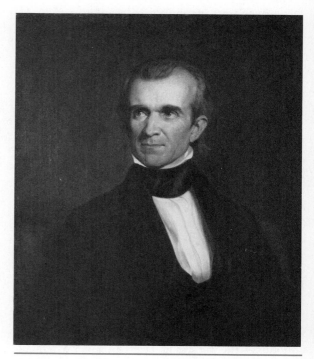

James K. Polk was an effective president who achieved his goals. But territorial expansion led to sectional conflict. Painting by George Peter Alexander Healy in the Collection of the Corcoran Gallery of Art, Museum Purchase, Gallery Fund, 1879.

CONFLICT BEGINS: THE MEXICAN WAR

James K. Polk, by stressing territorial expansion, pushed the nation in the direction of war. Despite his claim, the United States title to Oregon was not "clear and unquestionable." Since 1818 America and Britain had jointly occupied the disputed territory, and for over twenty years the British had refused to accept a boundary dividing the two nations' jurisdictions at the 49th parallel. But when he entered office, Polk found that Texas was the more pressing crisis. Congress's annexation of Texas had outraged Mexican leaders. They had severed relations with the United States, yet American ambitions in that region remained undiminished.

Faced with imminent war in the Southwest, President Polk decided to use diplomacy to avoid a second conflict with Great Britain in the Northwest. Dropping the demand for a boundary at 54°40′, he kept up pressure on the British to accept the 49th parallel. Eventually, in 1846 Great Britain agreed. In the Oregon Treaty, the United States gained all of present-day Oregon, Washington, and Idaho and parts of Wyoming and Montana.

Determined to acquire California and New Mexico in addition to all the land claimed by Texas, Polk charted a firm course in regard to Mexico. He ordered American troops to defend the border claimed by Texas but disputed by Mexico, and he attempted to buy a huge tract of land in the Southwest from the resentful Mexicans. After purchase failed Polk resolved to ask Congress for a declaration of war and set to work compiling a list of grievances. This task became unnecessary when word arrived that Mexican forces had engaged a body of American troops in disputed territory. American blood had been shed. Eagerly Polk declared that "war exists by the act of Mexico itself" and summoned the nation to arms.

Congress voted to recognize a state of war between Mexico and the United States in May 1846, but controversy rapidly grew. Public opinion about the war was sharply divided, with southwesterners enthusiastic and New Englanders strenuously opposed. In Congress Whigs charged that Polk had "literally provoked" an unnecessary war and "unsurped the power of Congress by making war upon Mexico." The aged John Quincy Adams passionately opposed the war, and a tall young Whig from Illinois named Abraham Lincoln questioned its justification. Moreover, a small minority of antislavery Whigs agreed with abolitionists—the war was no less than a plot to extend slavery.

These charges fed fear of the Slave Power. Abolitionists long had warned that there was a Slave Power—a slaveholding oligarchy in control of the South and intent on controlling the nation. The Slave Power's assault on northern liberties, abolitionists argued, had begun in 1836, when Congress passed the gag rule. Many white northerners, even those who saw nothing wrong with slavery, had viewed John Quincy Adams's stand against the rule as a defense of free speech and the right to petition. The fight over the gag rule increased the influence of the largely unpopular abolitionists. Anxieties about free speech and civil liberties first made the idea of a Slave Power credible.

Idea of a Slave Power

Now the Mexican War increased fears of this sinister power. Sectional acrimony took a marked turn for the worse as Congress debated the conduct of the war. A Democratic representative from Pennsylvania, David Wilmot, rose to offer an amendment to an

Wilmot Proviso

appropriations bill in support of the war. Wilmot's Proviso added a simple but fateful condition: "neither slavery nor involuntary servitude shall ever exist" in any territory gained from Mexico. The Wilmot Proviso failed but soon became a rallying cry for abolitionists and Free-Soilers (members of a party whose slogan was "Free Soil, Free Speech, Free Labor, and Free Men").

David Wilmot, like most northerners, was not an abolitionist. He explained that his goal was to defend "the rights of white freemen." Wilmot wanted California "for free white labor"; he was fighting for opportunity for "the sons of toil, of my own race and own color." His involvement in antislavery controversy showed the alarming ability of the slavery issue to broaden through territorial questions.

Despite this dissension at home, events on the battlefield went well for American troops, who as in previous wars were mainly volunteers furnished by the states. General Zachary Taylor's forces attacked and occupied Monterrey, securing northeastern Mexico (see map). Polk then ordered Colonel Stephen Kearney to invade the remote provinces of New Mexico and California. Once in California, Kearney joined forces with rebellious American settlers under Captain John C. Frémont and some naval units. Together they wrested control of California from Mexico with ease. General Winfield Scott's daring invasion of Mexico City brought the war to an end, and on February 2, 1848, representatives signed the Treaty of Guadalupe Hidalgo. The United States gained California and New Mexico (including present-day Nevada, Utah, and Arizona) and recognition of the Rio Grande as the southern boundary of Texas. In return, the American government agreed to settle the claims of its citizens against Mexico and to pay Mexico a mere $15 million for the new territory. The nation's manifest destiny had been achieved: the American flag waved on Atlantic and Pacific shores. The cost was thirteen thousand Americans and fifty thousand Mexicans dead, and Mexican-American enmity lasting into the twentieth century.

Treaty of Guadalupe Hidalgo

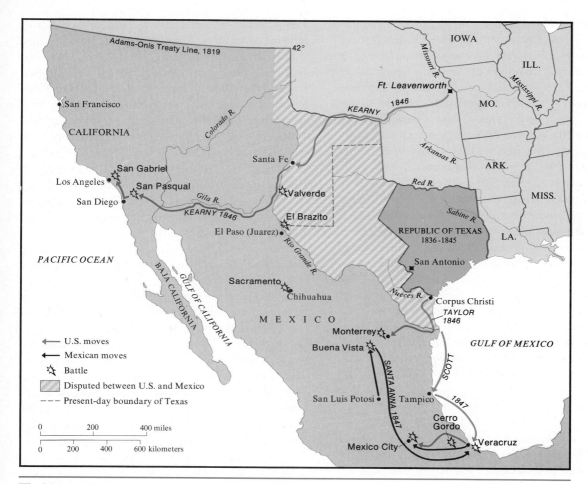

The Mexican War

But the acquisition of new territory fed sectional distrust and acrimony. Hoping to stem growing factionalism among Democrats, Polk had renounced a second term early in his administration. He also offered regular Democrats nearly all they could ask for in the way of traditional Jacksonian economic policy. He persuaded Congress to reinstitute the independent treasury system and to remove protectionist features from the tariff, and he vetoed internal improvements. But slavery in the territories was one issue beyond solution by him or anyone else. When Polk recommended that Oregon be a free territory, south-

erners felt anew the old fear that congressional power would be used against slavery. Some northern expansionists, on the other hand, thought that Texas had received priority over Oregon because of a Slave Power plot.

In the presidential election of 1848 slavery in the territories was the one overriding issue. Both parties tried to push this question into the background, but it dominated the conventions, the campaign, and the election. The Democrats tried to avoid sectional conflict by nominating General Lewis Cass of Michigan for president. Cass devised the idea of "popular sovereignty" for the territories—letting residents in the territories decide the question of slavery for themselves. His party's platform declared that Congress did not have the power to interfere with slavery and criticized those who pressed the question. Some Democrats broke with the party and nominated former President Van Buren. Also backed by members of the Liberty party and abolitionist Whigs, Van Buren became the Free-Soil candidate.

The regular Whigs nominated General Zachary Taylor, the military hero of the Mexican War and a slaveholding southerner, along with Millard Fillmore for vice president. Though the Whig convention refused to assert congressional power over slavery in the territories, its attempt to avoid the issue proved futile. Van Buren divided the Democratic vote, allowing Taylor to carry states he might not otherwise have won. Again New York, Van Buren's home state, provided the crucial marginal votes—enough to put Taylor in the White House. Antislavery crusaders had again influenced the outcome of an election.

The election of 1848 and the conflict over slavery in the territories shaped politics in the 1850s. At the national level, all issues would be seen through the prism of sectional conflict over slavery in the territories. The nation's uncertain attempts to deal with economic and social change would give way to more pressing questions about the nature of the Union itself. And the second party system would itself succumb to crisis.

TERRITORIAL PROBLEMS ARE COMPROMISED BUT RE-EMERGE

The first sectional battle of the decade involved the territory of California. More than eighty thousand Americans flooded into California in 1849.

President Taylor, seeing a simple solution to the challenge of governing lands acquired from Mexico, urged the settlers to apply for admission to the Union. The proposed state constitution submitted by California, however, prohibited slavery, and southerners objected. At a minimum southerners wanted the Missouri Compromise line extended through California.

Sensing that the Union was in peril, Henry Clay marshaled his energies. To hushed Senate galleries the "Great Pacificator" presented a series of compromise measures. Clay and Senator Stephen A. Douglas, an Illinois Democrat, moved through the Congress compromises balancing the issues of California and the nearby territories, the Texan boundary claim, runaway slaves, and the slave trade in the District of Columbia. The problems to be solved were thorny indeed, and made more so because of conflicting theories over settlers' rights in the territories. It was these theories that proved most troublesome in the continuing debate over the territories.

Clay and Douglas hoped to avoid a specific formula and preserve the ambiguity that existed about settlers' rights in the territories. In 1847 Lewis Cass had introduced the idea of popular sovereignty. Though Congress had to approve statehood for a territory, it should "in the meantime," Cass said, allow the people living there "to regulate their own concerns in their own way." But, what was the meaning of "meantime"?

When could settlers bar slavery? Southerners claimed that they had equal rights in the territories. Therefore neither Congress nor a territorial legislature could bar slavery. Only when settlers framed a state constitution could they take that step. Northerners, meanwhile, argued that Americans living in a territory were entitled to local self-government, and thus could outlaw slavery at any time, if they allowed it at all. To avoid dissension within their party, northern and southern Democrats had explained Cass's statement to their constituents in these two incompatible ways. Their conflicting interpretations caused strong disagreement in the debate on Clay's proposals.

After months of labor, Clay and Douglas finally

Holy Bible.
Thou shalt not deliver unto the master his servant which has escaped from his master unto thee. He shall dwell with thee. Even among you in that place which he shall choose in one of thy gates where it liketh him best. Thou shalt not oppress him. Deut XXIII 15, 16.

Effects of the Fugitive-Slave-Law.

Declaration of independence.
We hold that all men are created equal, that they are endowed by their Creator with certain unalienable rights, that among these are life, liberty and the pursuit of happiness.

Despite their racial prejudice, many northerners disapproved of slavery and viewed summary proceedings that could send a man into slavery as contrary to the Bill of Rights.   Library of Congress.

brought their package to a vote, and met defeat. But the determined Douglas had not given up. With Clay sick and absent from Washington, Douglas brought the compromise measures up again, one at a time. Congress lacked a majority to approve the package, but Douglas shrewdly realized that different majorities might be created for each of the measures. The strategy worked. The Compromise of 1850, as it was called, became law.

Under the terms of its various measures, California was admitted as a free state, and the Texan boundary was set at its present limits. The United States paid Texas $10 million in consideration of the boundary agreement. And the territories of New Mexico and Utah were organized with power to

Compromise of 1850

legislate on "all rightful subjects . . . consistent with the Constitution." A stronger fugitive slave law and an act to suppress the slave trade in the District of Columbia completed the compromise.

Jubilation greeted passage of the Compromise of 1850. There was in reality, however, less cause for celebration than citizens thought. The compromise was an artful evasion of the sectional disputes. It did not solve the problems; it postponed them. Furthermore, the compromise had two basic flaws. The first pertained to popular sovereignty. What were "rightful subjects of legislation, consistent with the Constitution"? During debate, southerners had defined them one way, northerners another. In one politician's words, the legislators seemed to have enacted a lawsuit instead of a law.

The second flaw lay in the Fugitive Slave Act, which stirred up controversy instead of laying it to rest. The new law empowered slaveowners to go into court in their own states and present evidence that a slave who owed them service had escaped. The transcript of such a proceeding, including a description of the fugitive, was to be taken as conclusive proof of a person's slave status, even in free states and territories. Legal authorities had to decide only whether the black person brought before them was the person described, not whether he or she was indeed a slave. The accused was denied the right to a trial by jury and the right to present evidence or to cross-examine witnesses. Fines and penalties encouraged U.S. marshals to assist in apprehending fugitives and discouraged citizens from harboring them. (Authorities were paid $10 if the alleged fugitive was turned over to the slaveowner, $5 if he was not.)

Fugitive Slave Act

At this point a relatively unknown writer dramatized the plight of the slave in a way that captured the sympathies of millions of northerners. Harriet Beecher Stowe, daughter of a religious New England family, wrote *Uncle Tom's Cabin* out of deep moral conviction. Her book, published in March 1852, showed how slavery brutalized the men and women who suffered under it. Stowe also portrayed slavery's evil effects on slaveholders. By mid-1853 the book had sold over a million copies. Stowe had brought the issue of slavery home to many who had never before given it much thought.

Uncle Tom's Cabin

The popularity of *Uncle Tom's Cabin* alarmed and appalled many southerners, who had long been sensitive about slavery. Southern leaders were intelligent men who were fully aware of the worldwide movement away from slavery and the forces gathering against it within the United States. They were also men who tended to see the world from the perspective of their plantations. Human bondage was so central to their world that life without slavery was almost unimaginable to them. Accordingly, they fought every battle in the sectional crisis with a white-hot intensity. In so doing, they developed a variety of proslavery arguments.

By the 1850s virtually all southern representatives were familiar with the latest arguments in proslavery theory. At a moment's notice they could discuss the anthropological evidence for the separate origin of the races, physicians' views on the inferiority of the black body, and sociological arguments for the superiority of the slave-labor system. But in private and in their hearts, most of these men fell back on two rationales: a belief that blacks were inferior and biblical accounts of slaveholding. Some, such as Jefferson Davis, reverted to the eighteenth-century argument that southerners were doing the best they could with a situation they had inherited.

Proslavery Theories

The South's defenders also developed a set of arguments to prove the necessity of expanding slavery into the territories. Expansion was essential to the welfare of the Negro, they declared, for prejudice lessened where the concentration of blacks decreased. They further argued that expansion was necessary to the prosperity of the South. But few slaveholders moved into the territories. A more likely cause of southern concern over the territories was the fear that if nearby areas became free soil, they would be used as a base from which to spread abolitionism into the slave states.

To try to control Congress, southern leaders relied on their chief tool in defending slavery: constitutional theory. Drawing on Thomas Jefferson's concept of strict construction, they emphasized that the nation arose from a compact among sovereign states; that the states were primary and the central government secondary; that the states retained all powers not expressly granted to the central government; and that the states were to be treated equally. Along with these theories went the philosophy that the power of the federal government should be kept to a minimum. By keeping government close to home, southerners hoped to maintain slavery.

Many of them hoped that slavery would be secure and allowed to expand under the administration of a new president. Franklin Pierce, a Democrat from New Hampshire, won a smashing victory in 1852 over the Whig presidential nominee, General Winfield Scott. Pierce's victory derived less from his strengths than from his opponents' weaknesses. The Whigs, while viable in Congress, lacked commanding presidents in an era of strong leaders. The deaths of President Taylor (1850), Webster (1852), and Clay (1852) and discord between the party's northern and southern wings dealt a lethal blow to the Whigs. The party ran its last presidential candidate in 1852.

Election of 1852

Americans, northerner and southerner alike, hoped that the election of Pierce would end sectional divisions. Because Pierce had given firm support to the Compromise of 1850, his victory seemed to confirm the public's endorsement of the compromise.

But Pierce did not seem able to avoid sectional conflict. His proposal for a transcontinental railroad ran into congressional dispute over where it should be built, North or South. His attempts to acquire foreign territory stirred up more trouble. An annexation treaty with Hawaii failed because southern senators would not vote for another free state, and Pierce's efforts to annex Cuba angered antislavery northerners. The shattering blow to sectional harmony, however, came from Congress rather than the White House.

TERRITORIAL PROBLEMS
SHATTER THE PARTY SYSTEM

In 1854 Senator Stephen Douglas, one of the architects of the Compromise of 1850 and a potential presidential candidate, introduced a bill to organize the Kansas and Nebraska territories. As a senator from Illinois, Douglas hoped for a midwestern trans-continental railroad to boost Chicago's economy and encourage settlement on the Great Plains. A necessary precondition for a railroad was the organization of the territory it would cross. Thus it was probably in the interest of building such a railroad that Douglas introduced a bill that inflamed sectional passions, completed the destruction of the Whig party, damaged the northern wing of the Democratic party, gave birth to the Republican party, and injured his own ambitions for national office.

The Kansas-Nebraska bill exposed the first flaw of the Compromise of 1850, and conflict over popular sovereignty erupted once more. Douglas's bill clearly left "all questions pertaining to slavery in the Territories . . . to the people residing therein," but northerners and southerners still disagreed violently over what territorial settlers could constitutionally do. The Kansas-Nebraska bill also opened a Pandora's box by explicitly repealing the Missouri Compromise. Douglas's bill, which became law in May 1854, threw land open to slavery where it had been prohibited (see map, page 234).

Kansas-Nebraska Bill

The Kansas-Nebraska Act inflamed fears and angers that had only simmered before. Abolitionists charged that the act was sinister aggression by the Slave Power. Between 1855 and 1859 seven northern states passed personal liberty laws designed to interfere with the swift action of the Fugitive Slave Act. These laws reflected northern fear of the Slave Power. Southerners saw the personal liberty laws as signs of bad faith. Finally, the Kansas-Nebraska Act had a devastating impact on political parties.

The act divided the Whig party's northern and southern wings so irrevocably that it fell apart shortly thereafter. The Democrats survived, but they suffered at the polls in 1854 for their role in the legislation. Moreover, anger over the territorial issue created a new political party. In the summer and fall of 1854, antislavery Whigs and Democrats, Free-Soilers, and other reformers throughout the Old Northwest met to form a new

The New Republican Party

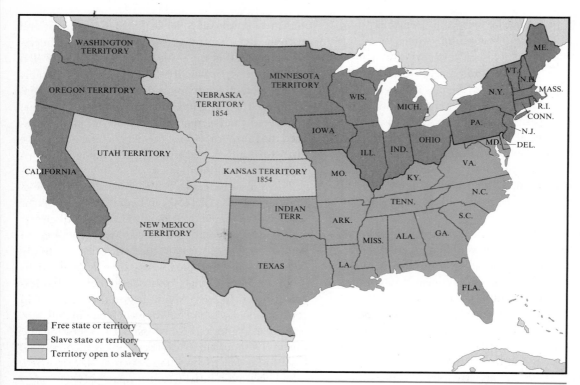

The Kansas-Nebraska Act, 1854

Republican party, dedicated to keeping slavery out of the territories. The Republicans' influence rapidly spread to the East, and they won a stunning victory in the 1854 elections by capturing a majority of House seats in the North.

For the first time, a sectional party based on a sectional issue had gained significant power in the political system. In the second party system, Whigs and Democrats had been strong in both the North and the South. The national base of support enjoyed by each had moderated sectional conflict, as party leaders compromised to achieve unity. But now the Whigs were gone, and politics in the 1850s would never be the same.

Nor were Republicans the only new party. An anti-immigrant organization, the American party, also seemed likely for a few years to replace the Whigs.

Know-Nothings

This party, popularly known as the Know-Nothings (because its members at first kept their purposes secret, answering all queries with the words "I know nothing"), exploited nativist fear of foreigners. By the mid-1850s the American party was powerful and growing; in 1854 so many new congressmen won office with anti-immigrant as well as anti-slavery support that Know-Nothings could claim they outnumbered Republicans. But like the Whigs, the Know-Nothings could not keep their northern and southern wings together, and they melted away after 1856. That left the field to the Republicans.

Know-Nothings, Republicans, and Democrats were all scrambling to attract former Whig voters. The death of that party insured a major realignment of the political system. For practical politicians the grand prize was the old Whig following. To woo these home-less Whigs, the remaining parties

Realignment of Political System

stressed a variety of issues, including immigration, temperance, the tariff, internal improvements, and the need for a homestead law. For many Americans these issues, not the controversy over slavery, were the real stuff of politics.

The Republicans appealed strongly to groups interested in the economic development of the West. Commercial agriculture was booming in the Ohio–Mississippi–Great Lakes area, but

Republican Appeals

residents of that region needed more canals, roads, and river and harbor improvements to reap the full benefit of their labors. Because credit was scarce, there was also widespread interest in a federal land-grant program: its proponents argued that western land should be made available free to those who would use it. After vetoes of internal improvement bills by the Democratic presidents Pierce and Buchanan (elected in 1856) and of an 1859 homestead bill by Buchanan, the Republicans added internal-improvements and land-grant planks to their platform. They also backed higher tariffs as an enticement to industrialists and businessmen.

Another major feature of the realigned political system was ideology. In the North, Republicans attracted many voters through effective use of ideology. They spoke to the image that northerners had of themselves, their society, and their future when they preached "Free Soil, Free Labor, Free Men." These phrases resonated with traditional ideals of equality, liberty, and opportunity under self-government—the heritage of republicanism.

"Free Soil, Free Labor, Free Men" seemed to fit with a northern economy that was energetic, expanding, and prosperous. Untold thousands of farmers had moved west to establish productive farms and growing communities. Midwestern farmers were using machines that multiplied their yields. Railroads were carrying their crops to market. And industry was beginning to perform wonders of production, making available goods that had hitherto been beyond the reach of the average person. As northerners surveyed the general growth and prosperity, they thought they saw a reason for it.

The key to progress seemed, in the eyes of many, to be free labor. People believed in the dignity of labor and the incentive of opportunity. Any hard-working, virtuous person, it was

Republican Ideology

thought, could improve his condition and gain economic independence by applying himself to opportunities that the country had to offer. Republicans pointed out that the South, which relied on slave labor rather than paid labor and industry, appeared backward and retrograde in comparison. Praising both laborers and opportunity, the Republican party projected an ideology that captured much of the spirit of the age in the North.

Thus the Republican party picked up support from a variety of sources. Opposition to the extension of slavery had brought the party together, but party members carefully broadened their appeal by adopting the causes of other groups. They were wise to do so. As the newspaper editor Horace Greeley wrote in 1860, "An Anti-Slavery man *per se* cannot be elected." But, he added, "a Tariff, River-and-Harbor, Pacific Railroad, Free Homestead man, *may* succeed *although* he is Anti-Slavery."

Greeley's last remark was insightful. The Republican party was an amalgam of many interests, but functionally it had only one stand in the North-South controversy. Since a high proportion of the original activist Republicans were strongly opposed to slavery, the party's position on slavery and the territories was immune to change. Thus southerners perceived Republican strength as antislavery strength.

A similar process was under way in the South. The disintegration of the Whig party had left many southerners at loose ends politically. Some of these people

Southern Democrats

gravitated to the American party, but not for long. By advocating states' rights, Democratic leaders managed to convert most of the

The Republicans had to appeal to various reformers and interests in order to build a winning coalition. This Democratic cartoon tries to ridicule the new party as a collection of dangerous and selfish cranks.   Library of Congress.

formerly Whig slaveholders. The party spoke to the class interests of slaveowners and the slaveowners responded.

In the South, however, yeomen rather than slaveholders were the heart of the party. Thus Democratic politicians, though often slaveowners themselves, had lauded the common man and appeared to champion his interests. The yeomen did not immediately object to the entry into the party of these ex-Whig slaveowners. Republican stands did not appeal to yeomen. Their party loyalties were strong, and as long as political issues were not posed in a class-conscious way, they did not become restive.

Slaveholding Democrats were careful to portray the sectional controversies as matters involving injustice to planter and yeoman alike. Their ultimate weapon was the appeal to race prejudice. They argued, as Jefferson Davis put it in 1851, that slavery elevated the status of the nonslaveholder and enabled the poor man to "stand upon the broad-level of equality with the rich man." Slaveholders warned that the overriding issue was "shall negroes govern white men, or white men govern negroes?"

The result of these arguments was a one-party system in the South that emphasized sectional issues. Racial fears and traditional political loyalties kept this political alliance between yeomen and planters intact through the 1850s. In the South as in the

North, political realignment obscured support for the Union and made sectional divisions seem sharper and deeper than they really were.

In both sections political leaders argued that opportunity was threatened. The *Montgomery* (Alabama) *Mail* blatantly claimed that the aim of the Republicans was "to free the negroes and force amalgamation between them and the children of the poor men of the South." Republicans likewise charged that if slavery entered the territories, the great reservoir of opportunity for decent people without means would be poisoned. These claims and counterclaims aroused anxieties and fears and made the gap between the sections even wider.

Like successive hammer blows, events also continued to drive North and South farther apart. Controversy over Kansas did not subside; it grew. For among the settlers in the territory were partisans of both sides, each determined to make Kansas free or slave. Abolitionists and religious groups sent Free-Soil settlers to save the territory from slavery; southerners sent their own reinforcements. Clashes between the two groups led to violence, and soon the whole nation was talking about "Bleeding Kansas."

When elections for a territorial legislature were held in 1855, thousands of proslavery Missourians invaded the polls and ran up a large but unlawful majority for slavery candidates. The legislature that resulted promptly legalized slavery, and in response Free-Soilers called an unauthorized convention and created their own government and constitution. A proslavery posse sent to arrest the Free-Soil leaders sacked the town of Lawrence; in revenge, John Brown, a fanatic who saw himself as God's instrument to destroy slavery, murdered five proslavery settlers. Soon armed bands of guerrillas roamed the territory.

Bleeding Kansas

The passion generated by this conflict erupted in the chamber of the United States Senate in May 1856, when Charles Sumner of Massachusetts denounced "the Crime against Kansas." Idealistic and radical in his antislavery views, Sumner censored the president, the South, and Senator Andrew P. Butler of South Carolina. Soon thereafter Butler's nephew, Representative Preston Brooks, approached Sumner at his Senate desk and beat him brutally with a cane. Voters in Massachusetts and South Carolina seethed; the country was becoming polarized.

The election of 1856 showed how far the polarization had gone. When Democrats met to select a nominee, they shied away from prominent leaders whose views on the territories were well known. Instead they chose James Buchanan of Pennsylvania, whose chief virtue was that he had been in Britain for four years, serving as ambassador, and thus had not been involved in territorial controversies. This anonymity and superior party organization helped Buchanan win 1.8 million votes and the election, but he owed his victory to southern support. The Republican candidate, John C. Frémont, won eleven of sixteen free states and 1.3 million votes; Republicans had become the dominant party in the North. The Know-Nothing candidate, Millard Fillmore, won almost 1 million votes, but this election was his party's last hurrah. The future battle was between a sectional Republican party and an increasingly divided Democratic party.

CONTROVERSY DEEPENS INTO CONFRONTATION

For years the issue of slavery in the territories had convulsed Congress, and for years the members of Congress had tried to settle the issue with vague formulas. In 1857 a different branch of government stepped onto the scene with a different approach. The Supreme Court addressed this emotion-charged subject and attempted to lay controversy to rest with a definitive verdict.

A Missouri slave named Dred Scott had sued his owner for his freedom. Dred Scott based his suit on the fact that his former owner, an army surgeon, had

Dred Scott Case

taken him for several years into Illinois, a free state, and into the Wisconsin Territory, from which slavery had been barred by the Missouri Compromise. Scott first won and then lost his case as it moved on appeal through the state courts, into the federal system, and finally after eleven years to the Supreme Court. Chief Justice Roger B. Taney wrote that Scott was not a citizen either of the United States or Missouri; that residence in free territory did not make Scott free; and most importantly, that Congress lacked the power to bar slavery from a territory, as it had done in the Missouri Compromise.

A storm of angry reaction broke in the North. The decision alarmed a wide variety of northerners—abolitionists, would-be settlers in the West, and those who hated black people but feared the influence of the South. Every charge against the aggressive Slave Power seemed now to be confirmed. "There is such a thing as THE SLAVE POWER," warned the *Cincinnati Daily Commercial;* the *Cincinnati Freeman* asked, "What security have the Germans and Irish that their children will not, within a hundred years, be reduced to slavery in this land of their adoption?"

Republican politicians, including Abraham Lincoln, capitalized on these fears of the Slave Power. At the crux of the matter was the self-interest of whites. Pointing to the southern obsession with the territories, Lincoln declared that they must be reserved "as an outlet for *free white people everywhere.*" After the Dred Scott decision, Lincoln charged that the next step in the unfolding Slave Power conspiracy would be a Supreme Court decision "declaring that the Constitution does not permit a State to exclude slavery from its limits. . . ."

Abraham Lincoln on the Slave Power

Lincoln's most eloquent statement against the Slave Power was his famous House Divided speech. In it Lincoln declared: "I do not expect the Union to be dissolved—I do not expect the House to fall—but I do expect it to cease to be divided. It will become all one thing or all the other. Either the opponents of slavery will arrest the further spread of it, and place

it where the public mind shall rest in the belief that it is the course of ultimate extinction; or its advocates will push it forward, till it shall become alike lawful in all the States, old as well as new, North as well as South. Have we no tendency to the latter condition?" The concluding question was the key element of the passage, for it drove home the idea that slaveholders were trying to extend bondage over the entire nation.

The brilliance of Republican tactics offset the difficulties the Dred Scott decision posed for them. By endorsing southern constitutional arguments, the Court had invalidated the central position of the Republican party: no extension of slavery. Republicans could only repudiate the decision, appealing to a "higher law," or hope to change the personnel of the Court.

A northern Democrat like Stephen Douglas, meanwhile, faced an awful dilemma. He had to find a way to ease the fears of northerners without losing the support of southerners. Douglas chose to stand by his principle of popular sovereignty, which encountered a second test in Kansas in 1857. There, after Free-Soil settlers boycotted an election, proslavery forces met at Lecompton and wrote a constitution that permitted slavery. New elections to the territorial legislature, however, returned an antislavery majority, and the legislature promptly called for a popular vote on the new constitution, which was defeated by more than ten thousand votes. Despite this overwhelming evidence that Kansans did not want slavery, President Buchanan tried to force the Lecompton constitution through Congress. Douglas threw his weight against a document the people had rejected; he gauged their feelings correctly, and in 1858 Kansas voters rejected the constitution a third time. But his action infuriated southern Democrats.

In his well-publicized debates with Abraham Lincoln, his challenger for the Illinois Senate seat in 1858, Douglas further alienated the southern wing of his party. Speaking at Freeport, Illinois, he attempted to revive the notion of popular sovereignty with some tortured extensions of his old arguments. Asserting that the Court had not ruled on the powers of a *ter-*

ritorial legislature, Douglas claimed that a territorial legislature could bar slavery either by passing a law against it or by doing nothing. Without the patrol laws and police regulations that support slavery, he reasoned, the institution could not exist. This argument, called the Freeport Doctrine, temporarily shored up Douglas's crumbling position in the North, but it alarmed southern Democrats. Some, like William L. Yancey of Alabama, concluded that southern rights would be safe only in a separate southern nation.

Stephen Douglas Proposes the Freeport Doctrine

The immediate problem, however, was that the Dred Scott decision had hardened the position of southerners dramatically. Most southerners, probably most slaveowners, were not ready to decide that slavery could be safe only in a southern nation. But after Dred Scott they *were* ready to demand what they saw as their rights. Through years of controversy southern political leaders had fought for the rights flowing from Calhoun's theory of the Constitution and the territories. Now the Supreme Court had affirmed those rights, and southern leaders determined to demand them, both from the nation and from their party. Thus the territorial issue continued to generate wider and more dangerous conflict.

THE BREAKUP OF THE UNION

Again, events gave the nation no rest from the growing sectional confrontation. One year before the 1860 presidential election, violence inflamed passions further when John Brown led a small band in an attack on Harpers Ferry, Virginia, hoping to trigger a slave rebellion. Brown failed miserably, and was quickly captured, tried, and executed. It came to light, however, that Brown had had the financial backing of several prominent abolitionists, and northern intellectuals such as Emerson and Thoreau praised him as a hero and a martyr. Since slave rebellion excited the deepest fears in the white South, these disclosures multiplied southerners' fear and anger many times over. The unity of the nation was now in peril.

Many observers feared that the election of 1860 would decide the fate of the Union. An ominous occurrence at the beginning of the campaign did nothing to reassure them. For several years, the Democratic party had been the only remaining organization that was truly national in scope. At its 1860 convention, however, the Democratic party broke in two.

Stephen A. Douglas wanted the party's presidential nomination, but could not afford to alienate northern opinion by accepting a strongly southern position on the territories. Southern Democrats like William L. Yancey, on the other hand, were determined to have their rights recognized, and they moved to block Douglas's nomination. When Douglas nevertheless marshaled a majority for his version of the platform, delegates from the five Gulf states plus South Carolina, Georgia, and Arkansas walked out of the convention hall in Charleston. Efforts at compromise failed, so the Democrats presented two nominees: Douglas for the northern wing, Vice President John C. Breckinridge of Kentucky for the southern. The Republicans nominated Abraham Lincoln. A Constitutional Union party, formed to preserve the nation but strong only in Virginia and the Upper South, nominated John Bell of Tennessee.

Splintering of the Democratic Party

The results of the balloting were sectional in character, but they indicated clearly that most voters were satisfied in the Union. Lincoln led in the North and Breckinridge in the South, but more votes were cast for Douglas and for Bell than for any single candidate. Moreover, many supporters of Lincoln or Breckinridge did not favor secession. Even in the states that remained loyal to the Union, Lincoln gained only a plurality (see table, page 240); his victory was won in the electoral college.

Election of 1860

Although a majority of voters had rejected the ex-

PRESIDENTIAL VOTE IN 1860

	Lincoln	Other Candidates
Entire United States	1,866,452	2,815,617
North plus border and southern states that rejected secession prior to war[1]	1,866,452	2,421,752
North plus border states that fought for union[2]	1,864,523	1,960,842

Note the large vote for other candidates in the righthand column.
[1]Kentucky, Missouri, Maryland, Delaware, Virginia, North Carolina, Tennessee, Arkansas
[2]Kentucky, Missouri, Maryland, Delaware

Source: David Potter, *Lincoln and His Party in the Secession Crisis* (New Haven and London: Yale University Press, 1942, 1967), p. 189.

treme choices and the opportunity for compromise existed, Lincoln decided not to soften his party's position on the territories. In his inaugural address he spoke of the necessity of maintaining the bond of faith between voter and candidate, of declining to set "the minority over the majority." But Lincoln's party was *not* the majority. His refusal to compromise probably had more to do with the unity of the Republican party than with the integrity of the democratic process. Many Republicans favored compromise, but the original and strongest party members—antislavery voters and "conscience Whigs"—would not back away from the platform. To preserve the unity of his party, then, Lincoln had to take a position that endangered the Union.

Southern leaders in the Senate were willing, conditionally, to accept a compromise formula drawn up by Senator John J. Crittenden of Kentucky. Crittenden, hoping to don the mantle of Henry Clay and avert disaster, had suggested that the two sections divide the territories between them at 36°30′. But the southerners would agree to this *only* if the Republicans did too. When Lincoln rejected the possibility

that Republicans would make concessions on the territorial issue, Crittenden's peacemaking effort collapsed. Virginians called for a special convention in Washington, to which several states sent representatives. But this gathering, too, failed to find a magical formula or to reach unanimity on disputed questions.

Furthermore, political leaders in the North and the South tragically misjudged each other. Lincoln and other prominent Republicans believed that southerners were bluffing when they threatened secession; they expected a pro-Union majority in the South to assert itself. On their side, southern leaders had become convinced that northerners were not taking them seriously, and that a posture of strength was necessary to win respect for their position. Thus, southern leaders who hoped to avert disaster did not offer compromise for fear of inviting aggression. Northern leaders who loved the Union believed compromise unnecessary and unwise. The misunderstanding was complete, the communication between the two groups nil.

Meanwhile the Union was being destroyed. On December 20, 1860, South Carolina passed an ordi-

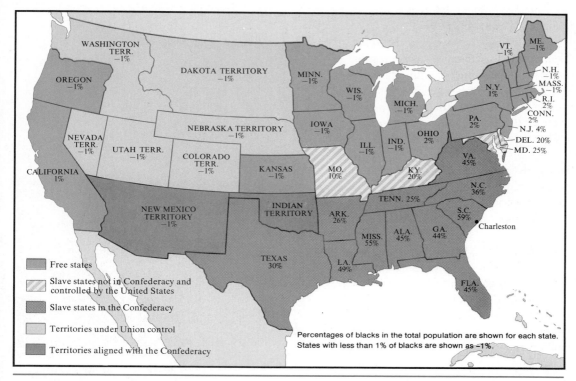

The Divided Nation—Slave and Free Areas, 1861

Map legend:
- Free states
- Slave states not in Confederacy and controlled by the United States
- Slave states in the Confederacy
- Territories under Union control
- Territories aligned with the Confederacy

Percentages of blacks in the total population are shown for each state. States with less than 1% of blacks are shown as –1%.

nance of secession amid jubilation and cheering. This step marked the inauguration of a strategy known as separate-state secession. Foes of the Union, despairing of persuading all the southern states to challenge the federal government simultaneously, had concentrated their hopes on the most extreme proslavery state. With South Carolina out of the Union, they hoped other states would follow suit and momentum would build toward disunion.

Secession of South Carolina

Southern extremists soon got their way. Overwhelming their opposition, they quickly called conventions and passed secession ordinances in six other states: Mississippi, Florida, Alabama, Georgia, Louisiana, and Texas. By February 1861 these states had joined with South Carolina to form a new government in Montgomery, Alabama: the Confederate States of America. Choosing Jefferson Davis as their president, they began to function independently of the United States.

Confederate States of America

Yet this apparent unanimity of action was deceiving. Confused and dissatisfied with the alternatives, many voters who had cast a ballot for president stayed home rather than vote for delegates who would consider secession. In some conventions the vote to secede had been close, the balance tipped by the overrepresentation of plantation districts. Furthermore, the conventions were noticeably reluctant to seek ratification of their acts by the people. Four states in the Upper South—Virginia, North Carolina, Tennessee, and Arkansas—flatly rejected secession, and did not join the Confederacy until after the fighting had started. In Kentucky and Missouri popular sentiment was too divided for decisive action;

these states remained under Union control, along with Maryland and Delaware (see map, page 241).

Misgivings about secession were not surprising, since it posed new and troubling issues for southerners, not the least of them the possibility of war and the question of who would be sacrificed. A careful look at election returns indicates that slaveholders and nonslaveholders were beginning to part company politically. Heavily slaveholding counties drew together in strong support of secession, but many counties with fewer slaves took an antisecession position or were staunchly Unionist. In other words, yeomen were beginning to act on class interests. Finally, there was still considerable love for the Union in the South.

The dilemma facing President Lincoln on inauguration day in March 1861 was how to maintain the authority of the federal government without provoking war in the states that had left the Union. He decided to proceed cautiously; by holding onto federal fortifications, he reasoned, he could assert federal sovereignty while waiting for a restoration of relations. But Jefferson Davis, who could not claim to lead a sovereign nation if its ports and military facilities were under foreign control, would not cooperate. A collision was inevitable.

It came in the early morning hours of April 12, 1861, at Fort Sumter in Charleston harbor. A federal garrison there was running low on food. Lincoln had

Attack on Fort Sumter

decided to send a supply ship and had notified the South Carolinians of his intention. For the Montgomery government, the only alternative to an attack on the fort was submission to Lincoln's authority. Accordingly, orders were sent to obtain surrender or attack the fort. Under heavy bombardment for two days, the federal garrison finally surrendered. The Confederates permitted the soldiers to sail away on unarmed vessels while the residents of Charleston celebrated. Thus the bloodiest war in the nation's history began in a deceptively gala spirit.

Throughout the 1840s and 1850s many able leaders had worked diligently to avert this outcome.

After a fierce bombardment, the Confederate flag replaced the Stars and Stripes over Fort Sumter. The nation's bloodiest war had begun. National Archives.

North and South, most had hoped to keep the nation together. As late as 1858 even Jefferson Davis had declared, "This great country will continue united." He had explained sincerely that the United States "is my country and to the innermost fibers of my heart I love it all, and every part." Why, then, did the war occur? Why did all the efforts to prevent it fail?

Slavery was an issue that could not be compromised. The conflict over slavery was fundamental and beyond adjustment. Too many powerful emotions were engaged in attacking or defending it. Too many important economic and social interests were involved in maintaining or destroying it. It was entwined with a host of other issues that mattered deeply to people. Ultimately each section regarded slavery as too important to the future to ignore.

Even after extreme views were put aside, the North

IMPORTANT EVENTS

1846	War with Mexico
	Wilmot Proviso
1847	Lewis Cass proposes idea of popular
	sovereignty
1848	Taylor elected president
1849	California applies for admission to
	Union as free state
1850	Compromise of 1850
1852	Harriet Beecher Stowe, *Uncle Tom's*
	Cabin
	Pierce elected president
1854	Kansas-Nebraska bill
	Republican party formed
	Democrats lose ground in
	congressional elections
1856	Preston Brooks attacks Charles
	Sumner in Senate chamber
	Bleeding Kansas
	Buchanan elected president
1857	*Dred Scott v. Sanford*
	Lecompton Constitution
1858	Voters reject Lecompton Constitution
	Lincoln-Douglas debates
	Freeport Doctrine
1859	John Brown raids Harpers Ferry
1860	Democratic party splits in half
	Lincoln elected president
	Crittenden Compromise fails
	South Carolina secedes from Union
1861	Six more southern states secede
	Confederacy established
	Attack on Fort Sumter

and the South had different approaches to the institution. The logic of Republican ideology tended in the direction of abolishing slavery, though Republicans denied any such intention. Similarly, the logic of arguments by southern leaders led toward establishing slavery everywhere, though southerners also denied that they sought any such thing. Lincoln put the problem succinctly. Soon after the 1860 election he assured his old friend Alexander Stephens of Georgia that the Republican party would not attack slavery in the states where it existed. But Lincoln continued, "You think slavery is *right* and ought to be extended; while we think it is *wrong* and ought to be restricted. That I suppose is the rub."

Concerns about slavery had driven all the other conflicts, but the fighting began with this, its central issue, shrouded in confusion. How would the Civil War affect slavery, its place in the law, and black people's place in society?

SUGGESTIONS FOR FURTHER READING

Politics: General

Thomas B. Alexander, *Sectional Stress and Party Strength* (1967); Ray Allen Billington, *The Protestant Crusade, 1800–1860* (1938 and 1964); Stanley W. Campbell, *The Slave Catchers* (1968); Avery O. Craven, *The Coming of the Civil War* (1942); Don E. Fehrenbacher, *The Dred Scott Case* (1978); Holman Hamilton, *Prologue to Conflict* (1964); Michael F. Holt, *The Political Crisis of the 1850s* (1978); Stephen E. Maizlish and John J. Kushma, eds., *Essays on American Antebellum Politics, 1840–1860* (1982); Roy F. Nichols, *The Disruption of American Democracy* (1948); Russell B. Nye, *Fettered Freedom* (1949); Stephen B. Oates, *To Purge This Land with Blood,* 2nd ed. (1984); David M. Potter, *The Impending Crisis, 1848–1861* (1976); Joel H. Silbey, *The Transformation of American Politics,*

1840–1860 (1967); Gerald W. Wolff, *The Kansas-Nebraska Bill* (1977).

The South and Slavery

William L. Barney, *The Secessionist Impulse* (1974); Drew G. Faust, *The Ideology of Slavery* (1981); Drew G. Faust, *A Sacred Circle: The Dilemma of the Intellectual in the Old South* (1978); Eugene D. Genovese, *The World the Slaveholders Made* (1969); Eugene D. Genovese, *The Political Economy of Slavery* (1967); William Sumner Jenkins, *Pro-Slavery Thought in the Old South* (1935); David M. Potter, *The South and the Sectional Conflict* (1968); William R. Stanton, *The Leopard's Spots* (1960); J. Mills Thornton III, *Politics and Power in a Slave Society* (1978).

The North and Antislavery

Eugene H. Berwanger, *The Frontier Against Slavery* (1967); Louis Filler, *The Crusade Against Slavery, 1830–1860* (1960); Eric Foner, *Free Soil, Free Labor, Free Men* (1970); William E. Gienapp, *The Origins of the Republican Party, 1852–1856* (1986); Henry V. Jaffa, *Crisis of the House Divided* (1959); Aileen S. Kraditor, *Means and Ends in American Abolitionism* (1969); Lewis Perry and Michael Fellman, eds., *Antislavery Reconsidered* (1979); Jeffrey Rossbach, *Ambivalent Conspirators* (1982); Alice Felt Tyler, *Freedom's Ferment* (1944); Ronald G. Walters, *American Reformers* (1978).

The Mexican War and Foreign Policy

Reginald Horsman, *Race and Manifest Destiny* (1981); Ernest M. Lander, Jr., *Reluctant Imperialists: Calhoun, the South Carolinians, and the Mexican War* (1980); Robert E. May, *The Southern Dream of a Caribbean Empire, 1854–1861* (1973); Frederick Merk, *The Oregon Question* (1967); David M. Pletcher, *The Diplomacy of Annexation: Texas, Oregon, and the Mexican War* (1973); John H. Schroeder, *Mr. Polk's War* (1973); Otis A. Singletary, *The Mexican War* (1960).

CHAPTER 14

TRANSFORMING FIRE:
THE CIVIL WAR
1861–1865

Moncure Conway, a Virginian who had converted to abolitionism and settled in New England, saw the Civil War as a momentous opportunity to bring justice to human affairs by abolishing slavery forever. In the words of one slave, it was God's "Holy War for the liberation of the poor African slave people." Union troops often took a different perspective. When a Yankee soldier ransacked a slave family's cabin and stole their best quilts, the mother exclaimed, "Why you nasty, stinkin' rascal. You say you come down here to fight for the niggers, and now you're stealin' from em." The soldier replied, "You're a G-- D--- liar, I'm fightin' for $14 a month and the Union."

White southerners too acted from limited and pragmatic motives, fighting in self-defense or out of regional loyalty. A Union officer interrogating Confederate prisoners noticed the poverty of one captive. Clearly the man was no slaveholder, so the officer asked him why he was fighting. "Because y'all are down here," replied the Confederate.

For each of these people and millions of others, the Civil War was a life-changing event. Armies numbering in the hundreds of thousands marched over the South, devastating once-peaceful countrysides. Families struggled to survive without their men; businesses tried to cope with the loss of workers. Women, North and South, faced added responsibilities in the home and moved into new jobs in the work force. Nothing seemed untouched.

Change was most drastic in the South, where the leaders of the secession movement had launched a revolution for the purpose of keeping things unchanged. Southern whites had feared that a peacetime government of Republicans would interfere with slavery and upset the routine of plantation life. Instead their own actions led to a war that turned southern life upside down and imperiled the very existence of slavery.

War altered the North as well, but not as deeply. Since the bulk of the fighting took place on southern soil, most northern farms and factories remained physically unscathed. The drafting of workers and the changing needs for products slowed the pace of industrialization somewhat, but factories and businesses remained busy. Though workers lost ground to inflation, the economy hummed. And a new probusiness atmosphere dominated Congress. To the discomfort of many, the powers of the federal government and the president increased during the war.

Ultimately, the Civil War forced new social and racial arrangements on the nation. Its greatest effect was to compel leaders and citizens to deal with an issue they had often tried to avoid: slavery. This issue had, in complex and indirect ways, given rise to the war; now the scope and demands of the war forced reluctant Americans to deal with it.

THE SOUTH GOES TO WAR

In the first bright days of the southern nation, few foresaw the changes that were in store. Lincoln's call for troops to put down the Confederate insurrection stimulated an outpouring of regional loyalty that unified the classes. And in the South a half-million men volunteered to fight; there were so many would-be soldiers that the government could not arm all of them.

This ground swell of popular support for the Confederacy generated a mood of optimism and gaiety. Confident recruits boasted of whipping the Yankees and returning home in time for dinner. And the first major battle of the war only increased such cockiness. On July 21, 1861, 30,000 federal troops attacked 22,000 southerners at a stream called Bull Run, near Manassas Junction, Virginia. Both armies were ill-trained, and confusion reigned on the battlefield. But nine thousand Confederate reinforcements and a timely stand by General Thomas Jackson (thereafter known as "Stonewall" Jackson) won the day for the South. Union troops fled back to

Battle of Bull Run

Washington in disarray, and shocked northern picnickers who had expected to witness a victory suddenly feared their capital would be taken.

As 1861 faded into 1862, however, the North undertook a massive buildup of troops in northern Virginia. In the wake of Bull Run, Lincoln had given command of the army to General George B. McClellan, an officer who had always been better at organization and training than at fighting. McClellan devoted the fall and winter to readying a formidable force of a quarter of a million men. The North also moved to blockade southern ports in order to choke off the Confederacy's avenues of commerce and supply. Initially, the Union blockade of the Confederacy was woefully inadequate. But the Union Navy gradually increased the blockade's effectiveness, though it never bottled up southern commerce completely.

In the fall of 1861 Union naval power came ashore in the South. Federal squadrons captured Cape Hatteras and Hilton Head, part of the Sea Islands off Port Royal, South Carolina. Of greater significance, in April 1862, ships commanded by Admiral David Farragut smashed through log booms on the Mississippi and fought their way upstream to capture New Orleans (see map).

Union Naval Campaign

With the approach of spring 1862, the military outlook for the Confederacy darkened again, this time in northern Tennessee. There General Ulysses S. Grant captured forts Henry and Donelson, securing two prime routes into the Confederacy's heartland. A path into Tennessee, Alabama, and Mississippi now lay open before the Union army.

Grant's Campaign in Tennessee

But on April 6, Confederate General Albert Sidney Johnston caught Grant's army at Pittsburg Landing in southern Tennessee. The Confederates inflicted heavy damage, but Johnston was killed. The next day a reinforced Union army forced the enemy to withdraw to Corinth, Mississippi. Though the Battle of Shiloh was a Union victory, destruction reigned. Northern troops lost 13,000 of 63,000 men; southerners sacrificed 11,000 out of 40,000.

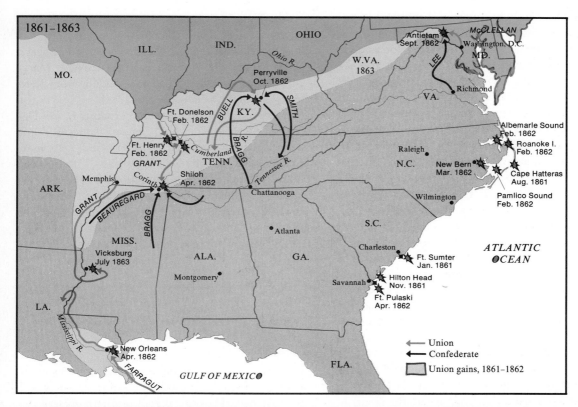

1861–1863

ILL. IND. OHIO

MO.

McCLELLAN

W.VA. 1863

Antietam Sept. 1862

Washington, D.C.

MD.

LEE

VA.

Richmond

Perryville Oct. 1862

Ohio R.

BUELL

KY.

SMITH

Ft. Donelson Feb. 1862

BRAGG

Ft. Henry Feb. 1862

Cumberland

TENN.

GRANT

Tennessee R.

Memphis

Corinth

Shiloh Apr. 1862

Chattanooga

GRANT

BEAUREGARD

BRAGG

ARK.

MISS.

Vicksburg July 1863

ALA.

Atlanta

GA.

Montgomery

Raleigh

N.C.

New Bern Mar. 1862

Wilmington

Albemarle Sound Feb. 1862

Roanoke I. Feb. 1862

Cape Hatteras Aug. 1861

Pamlico Sound Feb. 1862

S.C.

Charleston

Ft. Sumter Jan. 1861

Savannah

Hilton Head Nov. 1861

Ft. Pulaski Apr. 1862

ATLANTIC OCEAN

LA.

Mississippi R.

New Orleans Apr. 1862

FARRAGUT

GULF OF MEXICO

FLA.

→ Union
→ Confederate
▭ Union gains, 1861–1862

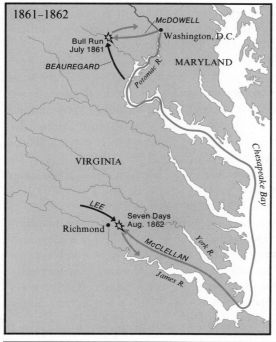

1861–1862

McDOWELL

Bull Run July 1861

Washington, D.C.

BEAUREGARD

Potomac R.

MARYLAND

VIRGINIA

Chesapeake Bay

LEE

Seven Days Aug. 1862

Richmond

McCLELLAN

York R.

James R.

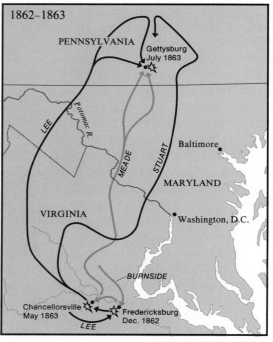

1862–1863

PENNSYLVANIA

Gettysburg July 1863

LEE

Potomac R.

MEADE

STUART

Baltimore

MARYLAND

VIRGINIA

Washington, D.C.

BURNSIDE

Chancellorsville May 1863

Fredericksburg Dec. 1862

LEE

The Civil War, 1861–1863

Both soldiers and civilians were beginning to recognize the enormous costs of this war. Never before in Europe or America had such massive forces pummeled each other with weapons of such destructive power. Yet the Civil War's armies seemed virtually indestructible. Even in the bloodiest engagements the losing army was never destroyed—only men died. The improved range of modern rifles multiplied casualties. Since medical knowledge was rudimentary, even minor wounds often led to death through infection.

The scope and duration of the conflict began to have unexpected effects. As the spring of 1862 approached, southern officials worried about the strength of their armies. The volunteer spirit had died out, and three states threatened or instituted a draft. Finally, the Confederate government enacted the first national conscription law in American history. The war had forced an unprecedented change on states that had seceded for fear of change.

Confederacy Resorts to a Draft

With their ranks reinforced, southern armies moved into heavier fighting. Early in 1862 most of the combat centered on Virginia, where the Confederacy had relocated its capital. General McClellan sailed his troops to the York peninsula and advanced on Richmond from the east. But when McClellan sent his legions into combat, Generals Jackson and Lee managed to stave off his attacks. First, Jackson drew some of the federal troops away from Richmond to protect their own capital. Then, in a series of engagements culminating in the Seven Days' battles, Lee held McClellan off. On August 3 McClellan withdrew to the Potomac, and Richmond was safe for almost two more years.

Buoyed by these results, Jefferson Davis conceived an ambitious plan to turn the tide of the war and compel the United States to recognize the Confederacy. He ordered a general offensive, sending Lee north to Maryland and Generals Kirby Smith and Braxton Bragg to Kentucky. The South would abandon the defensive and take the war

Davis Orders an Offensive

north. The plan was promising, but every part of the offensive failed. In the bloodiest single day of fighting, September 17, 1862, McClellan turned Lee back in the Battle of Antietam near Sharpsburg, Maryland. Smith and Bragg had to withdraw from Kentucky. The entire effort had collapsed.

But southern arms were not exhausted. On December 13, Lee decimated General Ambrose Burnside's soldiers as they charged his fortified positions at Fredericksburg, Virginia. Nevertheless, the Confederacy had marshaled all its strength for a breakthrough and had failed. Profoundly disappointed, Davis admitted to a committee of Confederate representatives that southerners had entered "the darkest and most dangerous period we have yet had."

WAR TRANSFORMS THE SOUTH

Even more than the fighting itself, changes in civilian life robbed southerners of their gaiety and nonchalance. The war altered southern society beyond all expectations and with astonishing speed. One of the first traditions to fall was the southern preference for local government.

The South had been an area of little government. States' rights had been its motto, but even the state governments were weak and sketchy affairs by modern standards. To withstand the massive power of the North, however, the South had to centralize; like the colonial revolutionaries, southerners faced a choice of join or die. No one saw the necessity of centralization more clearly than Jefferson Davis. If the states insisted on fighting separately, said Davis, "we had better make terms as soon as we can."

From the outset, Davis pressed to bring all arms, supplies, and troops under his control. He advocated conscription when the states failed to enroll enough new soldiers. And he took a strong leadership role toward the Confederate congress, which raised taxes and later passed a tax-in-kind—a levy not on money but on wheat, corn, oats, rye, cotton, peas, and other farm products. Almost three thousand agents dispersed to collect the tax, assisted by almost fifteen hundred appraisers. Where opposition arose, the government suspended the writ of habeas corpus and imposed martial law. In the face of a political opposition that cherished states' rights, Davis proved unyielding.

Centralization of Power in the South

Soon the Richmond administration was taking virtually complete direction of the southern economy. Because it controlled the supply of labor through conscription, the administration could regulate industry, compelling factories to work on government contracts to supply government needs. In addition, the Confederate congress passed laws giving the central government almost full control of the railroads; and later shipping, too, came under extensive regulation. New statutes even limited corporate profits and dividends. A large bureaucracy sprang up to administer these operations: over seventy thousand civilians were needed to run the Confederate war machine. By the war's end the southern bureaucracy was proportionally larger than its northern counterpart.

The mushrooming bureaucracy expanded the cities. Clerks and subordinate officials, many of them women, crowded the towns and cities where Confederate departments had their offices.

Effects of War on Southern Cities and Industry

These sudden population booms stretched the existing housing supply and stimulated new construction. The pressure was especially great in Richmond, whose population increased two-and-a-half times.

Another prime cause of urban growth was industrialization. Because of the Union blockade, the traditionally agricultural South became interested in industry. Davis exulted that southerners were manufacturing their own goods. And indeed, though the Confederacy started from scratch, it achieved tremendous feats of industrial development.

As a result of these changes southerners adopted new values. Women, sheltered in the patriarchal antebellum society, gained substantial new responsi-

Change in the Southern Woman's Role

bilities. The wives and mothers of soldiers became heads of households and undertook what had previously been considered men's work. In slaveowning families women assumed management roles. City women also found new and respectable roles and paying jobs in the workforce. "Government girls" who staffed the Confederate bureaucracy and female schoolteachers became a familiar sight. Such experiences undermined the image of the omnipotent male and gave thousands of women new confidence in their abilities.

The Confederate experience introduced and sustained many other new values. Legislative bodies yielded power to the executive branch of government, which could act more decisively in time of war. The traditional emphasis on aristocratic lineage gave way to respect for achievement and bravery under fire. Finally, sacrifice for the cause discouraged the pursuit of pleasure.

For some the sacrifice was symbolic, but for millions of southerners it was terrifyingly real. Mass poverty descended on the South, afflicting for the first

Human Suffering in the South

time a large minority of the white population. The crux of the problem was that many yeoman families had lost their breadwinners to the army. The poor sought help from relatives, neighbors, friends, anyone. Sometimes they took their cases to the Confederate government, as did an elderly Virginian who pleaded, "If you dount send [my son] home I am bound to louse my crop and cum to suffer."

Inflation became a major problem as prices rose by almost 7,000 percent. People of once-modest means looked around them and found abundant evidence

Inequities of the Confederate Draft

that all classes were not sacrificing equally. They saw that the wealthy curtailed only their luxuries, while many poor families went without necessities. They saw that the government contributed to these inequities through policies that favored the upper class.

The war separated many young lovers forever. Probably some girl treasured the photo on the left of Private Edwin Francis Jennison of Georgia, killed at Malvern Hill shortly after the picture was taken. The portrait on the right was found beside the body of a Confederate who fell on the battlefield at Chancellorsville. Left: Library of Congress; right: Museum of the Confederacy.

Until the last year of the war, for example, prosperous southerners could avoid military service by furnishing a hired substitute. Well over fifty thousand upper-class southerners purchased such substitutes.

Anger at such discrimination exploded when in October 1862 the Confederate congress exempted from military duty anyone who was supervising at least twenty slaves. This "twenty nigger law" became notorious. Immediately protests arose from every corner of the Confederacy, and North Carolina's legislators formally condemned the law. Its defenders ar-

gued, however, that the exemption preserved order and aided food production, and the statute remained on the books.

Dissension spread as growing numbers of citizens concluded that the struggle was "a rich man's war and a poor man's fight." Alert politicians and newspaper editors warned that class resentment was building to a dangerous level; letters to Confederate officials during this period contained a bitterness that suggested the depth of the people's anger. "If I and my little children suffer [and] die while there Father is in serv-

Chapter 14: TRANSFORMING FIRE: THE CIVIL WAR, 1861–1865

ice," threatened one woman, "I invoke God Almighty that our blood rest upon the South." Trouble was brewing in the Confederacy.

HARPER'S WEEKLY.

A
JOURNAL OF CIVILIZATION

Vol. V.—No. 238.]   NEW YORK, SATURDAY, JULY 20, 1861.   [SINGLE COPIES SIX CENTS.
[$2.50 PER YEAR IN ADVANCE.

THE NORTHERN ECONOMY COPES WITH WAR

With the onset of war, a tidal wave of change rolled over the North, just as it had over the South. Factories and citizens' associations geared up to support the war, and the federal government and its executive branch gained power they had never had before. Civil liberties were restricted; social values were influenced by both personal sacrifice and wartime riches. Idealism and greed flourished together.

Initially, the war was a shock to business. With the sudden closing of the southern market, firms could no longer predict the demand for their goods; many companies had to redirect their activities in order to remain open. And southern debts became uncollectible, jeopardizing not only merchants but many western banks. In farming regions, families struggled with an aggravated shortage of labor. For reasons such as these, the war initially caused an economic slump.

Initial Slump in Northern Business

Overall the war slowed industrialization in the North. But historians have shown that the war's economic impact was not all negative. Certain entrepreneurs, such as wool producers, benefited from shortages of competing products, and soaring demand for war-related goods swept some businesses to new heights of production. To feed the voracious war machine the federal government pumped unprecedented amounts of money into the economy. As a result, industries producing weapons, munitions, uniforms, boots, camp equipment, saddles, ships, food, and other war necessities prospered.

In both North and South women entered the factories to boost wartime production. This Harper's Weekly *cover shows women filling cartridges in the United States arsenal at Watertown, Massachusetts.   Library of Congress.*

War production also promoted the development of heavy industry in the North. The output of coal rose substantially. Iron makers improved the quality of their product while boosting the production of pig iron. And although new railroad construction slowed, the manufacture of rails increased. Of considerable significance for the future were the railroad industry's adoption of a standard gauge for track and foundries' development of new and less expensive ways to make steel.

Effects of War on Northern Industry and Agriculture

Another strength of the northern economy was the complementary relationship between agriculture and industry. The mechanization of agriculture had begun well before the war. Now, though, wartime recruitment and conscription gave western farmers an added incentive to purchase labor-saving machinery. This shift from human labor to machines had beneficial effects. New markets for industry were created and the food supply for the industrial work force was expanded. Finally, farm families whose breadwinners had gone to war did not suffer as they did in the South.

Northern industrial and urban workers did not fare as well. Though jobs were plentiful following the initial slump, inflation took much of a worker's paycheck. Studies of the cost of living indicate that between 1860 and 1864 consumer prices rose at least 76 percent; meanwhile daily wages rose only 42 percent. To make up the difference, workers' families had to do without.

As their real wages shrank, industrial workers also lost job security. To increase production, some employers replaced workers with labor-saving machines.

New Militancy among Northern Workers

Other employers urged the government to liberalize immigration procedures so they could import cheap labor. Workers responded by forming unions and sometimes by striking. Skilled craftsmen organized to combat the loss of their jobs and status to machines; women and unskilled workers, excluded by the craftsmen, formed their own unions. And in recognition of the increasingly national scope of business activity, thirteen occupational groups—including tailors, coal miners, and railway engineers—formed national unions during the Civil War. Because of the tight labor market, unions won many of their demands without striking; but still the number of strikes rose steadily.

Troublesome as unions were, they did not prevent many employers from making a profit. The highest profits were made in profiteering on government contracts. Unscrupulous businessmen took advantage of the sudden demand for goods for the army by selling clothing and blankets made of "shoddy"—wool fibers reclaimed from rags or worn cloth. The goods often came apart in the rain; most of the shoes purchased in the early months of the war were worthless too. Contractors sold inferior guns for double the usual price and tainted meat for the price of good. Corruption was so widespread that it led to a yearlong investigation by the House of Representatives.

Legitimate enterprises also turned a neat profit. The output of woolen mills increased so dramatically that dividends in the industry nearly tripled. Some

Wartime Benefits to Northern Business

cotton mills, though they reduced their output, made record profits on what they sold. And railroads carried immense quantities of freight and passengers, increasing their business to the point that railroad stocks doubled or even tripled.

In fact, railroads were a leading beneficiary of government largesse. Congress had failed in the 1850s to resolve the question of a northern versus a southern route for the first transcontinental railroad. But with the South out of Congress, the northern route quickly prevailed. In 1862 and 1864 Congress chartered two corporations, the Union Pacific Railroad and the Central Pacific Railroad, and assisted them financially in connecting Omaha, Nebraska, with Sacramento, California. For each mile of track laid, the railroads received a loan of $16,000 to $48,000 plus twenty square miles of land along a free four-hundred-foot-wide right of way. Overall, the two corporations gained approximately 20 million acres of land and nearly $60 million in loans.

Another measure that pleased the business community was the tariff. Northern businesses did not uniformly favor high import duties; some manufacturers desired cheap imported raw materials more than they feared foreign competition. But northeastern congressmen traditionally supported higher tariffs, and after southern lawmakers left Washington, they had their way: the Tariff Act of 1864 raised tariffs generously. And, as one would expect, some healthy industries made artificially high profits by raising their prices to a level just below that of the foreign

Chapter 14: TRANSFORMING FIRE: THE CIVIL WAR, 1861–1865

competition. By the end of the war, tariff rates averaged 47 percent, more than double the rates of 1857.

Wartime Society in the North start. 4th Dec.

The frantic wartime activity, the booming economy, and the Republican alliance with business combined to create a new atmosphere in Washington. The balance of opinion shifted against consumers and wage earners and toward large corporations; the notion spread that government should aid businessmen but not interfere with them. This was the golden hour of untrammeled capitalism, and railroad builders and industrialists took advantage of government loans, grants, and tariffs.

As long as the war lasted, the powers of the federal government and the president continued to grow. At the beginning of the conflict, Abraham Lincoln launched a major shipbuilding program without waiting for Congress to assemble. The lawmakers later approved his decision, and Lincoln continued to act in advance of Congress when he deemed it necessary. In one striking exercise of executive power, Lincoln suspended the writ of habeas corpus for all people living between Washington and Philadelphia. The justification for this action was practical rather than legal; Lincoln was ensuring the loyalty of Maryland. Lincoln also used his wartime authority to bolster his political power. He and his generals proved adept at arranging furloughs for soldiers who could vote in close elections. Needless to say, the citizens in arms whom Lincoln helped to vote usually voted Republican.

Wartime Powers of the U.S. Executive

Among the clearest examples of the wartime expansion of federal authority were the National Banking Acts of 1863, 1864, and 1865. Prior to the Civil War the nation did not have a uniform currency.

Banks operating under a variety of state charters issued no fewer than seven thousand different kinds of notes. Under the new laws, Congress established a national banking system empowered to issue a maximum number of national bank notes. At the close of the war in 1865, Congress laid a prohibitive tax on state bank notes and forced most major institutions to join the system.

The rapidly increasing scale of things may have been best sensed by soldiers, whose first experiences with large organizations were often unfortunate. Blankets, clothing, and arms were often inferior. Vermin were commonplace. Hospitals were badly managed at first. Rules of hygiene in large camps were badly written or unenforced; latrines were poorly made or carelessly used. Indeed, conditions were such that 224,000 Union troops died from disease or accidents, far more than the 140,000 who died in battle.

Such conditions would hardly have predisposed the soldier to sympathize with changing social attitudes on the home front. Amid the excitement of money-making, a gaudy culture of vulgar display flourished in the largest cities. A writer for the *New York Herald* observed, "This war has entirely changed the American character. . . . The individual who makes the most money—no matter how—and spends the most—no matter for what—is considered the greatest man. . . . The world has seen its iron age, its silver age, its golden age, and its brazen age. This is the age of shoddy."

Self-indulgence versus Sacrifice in the North

Yet strong elements of idealism coexisted with ostentation. Abolitionists, after initial uncertainty over whether to fight the South or allow division of the Union to separate the North from slavery, campaigned to turn the war into a war against slavery. Free black communities and churches both black and white responded to the needs of slaves who flocked to the Union lines. They sent clothing, ministers, and teachers in generous measure to aid the runaways.

Northern women, like their southern counter-

*[handwritten: women *]*

parts,' took on new roles. Those who stayed home organized over ten thousand soldiers' aid societies, rolled innumerable bandages, and raised $3 million. Thousands served as nurses in front-line hospitals, where they pressed for better care of the wounded. But the professionalization of medicine since the Revolution had created a medical system dominated by men; able female nurses had to fight both military regulations and professional hostility to win the chance to make their contribution. In the hospitals they quickly proved their worth, but only the wounded welcomed them. Even Clara Barton, the most famous female nurse, was ousted from her post during the winter of 1863.

Thus northern society embraced strangely contradictory tendencies. Materialism and greed flourished alongside idealism, religious conviction, and self-sacrifice. While wealthy men purchased 118,000 substitutes and almost 87,000 commutations at $300 each to avoid service in the Union army, other soldiers risked their lives out of a desire to preserve the Union or extend freedom. It was as if there were several different wars under way, each of them serving different motives.

[handwritten: fighting for different values.]

[handwritten left margin: men their help to own?]

THE STRANGE ADVENT OF EMANCIPATION

A t the very highest levels of government there was a similar lack of clarity about the purpose of the war. Through the first several months of the struggle, both Davis and Lincoln studiously avoided references to slavery, the crux of the matter. Davis told southerners that they were fighting for constitutional liberty. He feared that stressing slavery might alienate nonslaveholders. Lincoln, hoping that a pro-Union majority would assert itself in the South, recognized that mention of slavery would end any chance of coaxing the seceded states back into the

Union. Moreover, many Republicans were not vitally interested in the slavery issue. An early presidential stand making the abolition of slavery and not the preservation of the Union the war's objective could have split the party.

Lincoln first broached the subject of slavery in a major way in March 1862, when he proposed that the states consider emancipation on their own. He asked

Lincoln's Plan for Gradual Emancipation

Congress to pass a resolution promising aid to any state that decided to emancipate, and he appealed to border-state representatives to give the idea of emancipation serious consideration. What Lincoln was talking about was gradual emancipation, with compensation for slaveholders and colonization of the freed slaves outside the United States. Thus his was as conservative a scheme as could be devised. Moreover, since the states would make the decision voluntarily, no responsibility for it would attach to Lincoln.

But others wanted to go much farther. A group of congressional Republicans known as the Radicals had, from the early days of the war, concerned themselves with slavery. In August

Confiscation Acts

1861, at the Radicals' instigation, Congress passed its first confiscation act. Designed to punish the Confederate rebels, the law confiscated all property used for "insurrectionary purposes." That is, if the South used slaves in a hostile action, those slaves were declared seized and liberated from their owners' possession. A second confiscation act (July 1862) was much more drastic: it confiscated the property of all those who supported the rebellion, even those who merely resided in the South and paid Confederate taxes. Their slaves were "forever free of their servitude, and not again [to be] held as slaves."

When Lincoln refused to enforce the second confiscation act, Horace Greeley, editor of the *New York Tribune,* criticized him. Lincoln's reply was an explicit statement of his complex and calculated approach to the question. "I would save the Union," announced Lincoln. "If I could save the Union without freeing *any* slave I would do it, and if I could save

[handwritten vertical right margin: Stop support of confederate and free slaves.]

it be freeing *all* the slaves I would do it; and if I could save it by freeing some and leaving others alone I would also do that. What I do about slavery, and the colored race, I do because I believe it helps to save the Union."

When he wrote those words, Lincoln had already decided to issue the Emancipation Proclamation. He waited until the opportune time. On September 22, 1862, shortly after the Battle of Antietam, Lincoln issued the first part of his two-part proclamation. Invoking his powers as commander-in-chief of the armed forces, he announced that in a proclamation to be issued on January 1 he would emancipate the slaves in states whose people "shall then be in rebellion against the United States."

Emancipation Proclamations

Lincoln's designation of the areas in rebellion on January 1 is worth noting. He excepted from his list every Confederate county or city that had fallen under Union control. And in a telling omission, Lincoln neglected to liberate slaves in the border slave states that remained in the Union. "The President . . . has proclaimed emancipation only where he has notoriously no powers to execute it," complained the *New York World*. *Not satisfied w/ this*

As a moral document the <u>Emancipation Procla</u>mation, which in fact freed no slaves, was inadequate. As a political document it was nearly flawless. Because the proclamation defined the war as a war against slavery, liberals could applaud it. Yet at the same time it protected Lincoln's position with conservatives, leaving him room to retreat if he chose and forcing no immediate changes on the border slave states. The president had not gone as far as Congress had, and he had taken no position he could not change.

In June 1864, however, Lincoln gave his support to the constitutional end of slavery. On the eve of the Republican national convention, he called the party's chairman to the White House and instructed him to have the party "put into the platform as the keystone, the amendment of the Constitution abolishing and prohibiting slavery forever." It was done; the party called for a new constitutional amendment,

North wanted compromise. South did no.

the thirteenth. Lincoln showed his commitment by lobbying Congress for quick approval of the measure. He succeeded, and the proposed amendment went to the states for ratification or rejection. Lincoln's strong support for the Thirteenth Amendment—an unequivocal prohibition of slavery—constitutes his best claim to the title Great Emancipator.

Yet Lincoln soon clouded that clear stand, for in 1865 the newly re-elected president considered allowing the defeated southern states to re-enter the Union and delay or defeat the amendment. In February he and Secretary of State Seward met with three Confederate commissioners at Hampton Roads, Virginia. There, Seward talked of how re-entry into the Union would allow the southern states to block the pending amendment. Lincoln spoke of ratification with a five-year delay and of a promise to seek $400 million in compensation for slaveowners. The president was apparently motivated by a desire to create a new and broader Republican party based on an alliance with southern Whigs and moderates. The proposals were not discussed in the South because of Jefferson Davis's total commitment to independence.

Hampton Roads Conference

Before the war was over, the Confederacy too addressed the issue of emancipation. Ironically, a strong proposal in favor of liberation came from <u>Jefferson Davis, who was willing to sacrifice slavery to achieve independence.</u> After considering the alternatives, especially the need for manpower, Davis concluded in the fall of 1864 that it was necessary to act. He advocated the purchase and arming of slave soldiers and insisted that such soldiers, and later their wives and children, must be freed.

Davis's Plan for Emancipation

Confederate emancipation began too late to revive southern armies or win diplomatic advantages with antislavery Europeans. But Lincoln's Emancipation Proclamation stimulated a vital infusion of manpower into the Union armies. Beginning in 1863 blacks shouldered arms for the North. Before the war was over, 186,000 of them had fought for freedom and the Union. Their participation was crucial to northern victory, and it discouraged recognition of the Confederacy by foreign governments.

The Disintegration of Confederate Unity

During the final two years of fighting, both northern and southern governments waged the war in the face of increasing opposition at home. The unrest was connected to the military stalemate: neither side was close to victory in 1863. But protest also arose from fundamental stresses in the social structures of the North and the South.

One ominous development for the South was the increasing opposition of planters to their own government, whose actions often had a negative effect on them. Not only did the Richmond government impose high taxes and a tax-in-kind, Confederate military authorities also impressed slaves to build fortifications. And when Union forces advanced on plantation areas, Confederate commanders sent detachments through the countryside to burn stores of cotton that lay in the enemy's path. Such interference with plantation routines and financial interests was not what planters had expected of their government, and they resisted.

The Confederate constitution, drawn up by the leading political thinkers of the South, had in fact granted substantial powers to the central government, especially in time of war. But for many planters, states' rights had become virtually synonymous with complete state sovereignty. In effect, years of opposition to the federal government within the Union had frozen southerners in a defensive posture. Now they erected the barrier of states' rights as a defense against change. Planters sought a guarantee that their plantations and their lives would remain untouched; they were deeply committed neither to

building a southern nation nor to winning independence. Thus, when secession revolutionized their world, they could not or would not adjust to it.

Meanwhile, at the bottom of southern society, there were other difficulties. Food riots occurred in the spring of 1863 in several communities. On April 2, a crowd assembled in the Confederate capital of Richmond to demand relief. A passerby, noticing the excitement, asked a young girl, "Is there some celebration?" "There is," replied the girl. "We celebrate our right to live. We are starving. As soon as enough of us get together we are going to the bakeries and each of us will take a loaf of bread." Soon they did just that, sparking a riot that Davis himself had to quell at gunpoint.

Food Riots in Southern Cities

Throughout the rural South, ordinary people resisted more quietly—by refusing to cooperate with impressments of food, conscription, or tax collection. "In all the States impressments are evaded by every means which ingenuity can suggest, and in some openly resisted," wrote a high-ranking commissary officer. Farmers who did provide food refused to accept certificates of credit or government bonds in lieu of cash, as required by law. And conscription officers increasingly found no one to draft—men of draft age were hiding out in the forests.

Such civil discontent was certain to affect the Confederate armies. Spurred by concern for their loved ones and resentment of the rich man's war, large numbers of men did indeed leave the armies, supported by their friends and neighbors. The problem of desertion became so acute that by November 1863, Secretary of War James Seddon admitted that one-third of the army could not be accounted for. And the situation was to worsen.

The gallantry of those who stayed on in Lee's army and the daring of their commander made for a deceptively positive start to the 1863 campaign. On May 2 and 3 at Chancellorsville, Virginia, 130,000 members of the Union Army of the Potomac bore down on fewer than 60,000 Confederates. Lee and Stonewall Jack-

Battle of Chancellorsville

*A southern family flees its home as the battle lines draw near.
Photographed by Matthew Brady.   National Archives.*

son boldly divided their forces, ordering 30,000 men under Jackson on a day-long march westward and to the rear for a flank attack. Jackson arrived at his position late in the afternoon to witness unprepared Union troops "laughing, smoking," playing cards, and waiting for dinner. "Push right ahead," Jackson said, and his weary but excited corps swooped down on the Federals and drove their right wing back in confusion. The Union forces left Chancellorsville the next day defeated. Though Stonewall Jackson had been fatally wounded, it was a remarkable southern victory.

But two critical battles in July 1863 brought crushing defeats to the Confederacy. General Ulysses S. Grant, after finding an advantageous approach to Vicksburg, laid siege to that vital western fortifica-

tion. If Vicksburg fell, U.S. forces would control the Mississippi, cutting the Confederacy in half and gaining an open path into the interior. Meanwhile, Lee proposed a Confederate invasion of the North, to turn the tables on the Union and divert attention from Vicksburg. Both movements drew toward conclusion early in July.

In the North, Lee's troops streamed through western Maryland and into Pennsylvania, threatening both Washington and Baltimore. The possibility of a major victory before the Union capital became more and more likely. But along the Mississippi, Confederate prospects darkened. Davis and Secretary of War Seddon repeatedly wired General Joseph E. Johnston to concentrate his forces and attack Grant's army. Johnston, despite the prodding from his superiors, did nothing to relieve the garrison. In the meantime, Grant's men were supplying themselves by drawing on the agricultural riches of the Mississippi River valley. With ample provisions, they could continue their siege indefinitely. In such circumstances the fall of Vicksburg was inevitable, and on July 4, 1863, its commander surrendered.

That same day a battle that had been raging since July 1 concluded at Gettysburg, Pennsylvania. On July 1 and 2, the Union and Confederate forces had both made gains in furious fighting.

Battle of Gettysburg Then on July 3 Lee ordered a direct assault on Union fortifications atop Cemetery Ridge. Full of foreboding, General James Longstreet warned Lee that "no 15,000 men ever arrayed for battle can take that position." But Lee, hoping success might force the Union to accept peace with independence, stuck to his plan. His brave troops rushed the position, and a hundred momentarily breached the enemy's line. But most fell in heavy slaughter. On July 4 Lee had to withdraw, having suffered almost 4,000 killed and approximately 24,000 missing and wounded.

Though southern troops had displayed a courage and dedication that would never be forgotten, the results had been disastrous. Intelligent southerners knew that defeat lay ahead. Equally significant, the defeats quickened the pace of the Confederacy's internal disintegration. Southern leaders began to realize that they were losing the support of the common people. Moreover, a few newspapers and politicians began to call for peace or negotiations. These movements came to naught, but they attracted several prominent southern politicians, including Vice President Alexander Stephens.

By 1864 much of the opposition to the war had moved entirely outside politics. Southerners were simply giving up the struggle, withdrawing their cooperation from the government, and forming a sort of counter-society. Deserters joined with ordinary citizens who were sick of the war to dominate whole towns and counties. Secret societies dedicated to reunion, such as the Heroes of America, sprang up. Active dissent spread throughout the South but was particularly common in upland and mountain regions. The government was losing the support of its citizens.

ANTIWAR SENTIMENT IN THE NORTH

In the North opposition to the war was similar in many ways, but not as severe. There was concern over the growing centralization of government, and war-weariness was a frequent complaint. Discrimination and injustice in the draft sparked protest among poor citizens, just as they had in the South. But the Union was so much richer than the South in human resources that none of these problems ever threatened the stability of the government. Fresh recruits were always available, and food and other necessaries were not subject to severe shortages.

What was more, Lincoln possessed a talent that Davis lacked: he knew how to stay in touch with the ordinary citizen. Through letters to newspapers and to soldiers' families, he reached the common people and demonstrated that he had not forgotten them. Their grief was his also, for the war was his personal tragedy. His words helped to contain northern discontent, though they could not remove it.

Much wartime protest sprang from politics. The Democratic party, though nudged from its dominant position, was determined to regain power. Party leaders attacked the war, the expansion of federal powers, the high tariff, inflation, and the improved status of blacks. They also supported states' rights, called for reunion on the basis of "the Constitution as it is and the Union as it was," and charged that the Republicans were going to flood the North with blacks. In 1862 Democratic criticism of the war helped the party make a substantial comeback in the congressional elections.

Peace Democrats

Led by outspoken men like Clement L. Vallandigham of Ohio, the pro-peace Democrats were highly visible. Vallandigham criticized Lincoln as a dictator who had suspended the writ of habeas corpus without congressional authority and arrested thousands of innocent citizens. He stayed carefully within legal bounds, but his attacks were so damaging to the war effort that military authorities arrested him after Lincoln suspended habeas corpus. Fearing that Vallandigham might gain the stature of a martyr, the president decided against a jail term and exiled him to the Confederacy.

Lincoln believed that antiwar Democrats were linked to secret organizations that harbored traitorous ideas. Likening such groups to a poisonous snake striking at the government, Republicans sometimes branded them—and by extension the peace Democrats—as Copperheads. Though Democrats were connected with these organizations, most engaged in politics rather than treason.

Most violent opposition to the government came from ordinary citizens facing the draft, especially the urban poor and immigrants, who were called in disproportionate numbers. Northerners witnessed scores of disturbances and melees. Enrolling officers received rough treatment in many parts of the North, and riots occurred in Ohio, Indiana, Pennsylvania, Illinois, and Wisconsin, and in such cities as Troy, Albany, and Newark. By far the most serious outbreak of violence, however, occurred in New York City in July 1863, where three days of rioting left seventy-four people dead. The riot had heavy racist overtones, for many Irish immigrants resented competition from free black workers.

Once inducted, northern soldiers reacted to their loneliness and grievances in much the same way as their southern counterparts. Thousands of men slipped away from authorities. Indeed, the Union army had a desertion rate as high as the Confederates'. Those who did not desert were often discouraged at the lack of progress in defeating the South.

Discouragement and war-weariness neared their peak during the summer of 1864. At that point the Democratic party nominated the popular General George B. McClellan for president and put a qualified peace plank into its platform. The plank, written by Vallandigham, condemned "four years of failure to restore the Union by the experiment of war" and called for an armistice. Lincoln concluded that it was "exceedingly probable that this Administration will not be re-elected." The fortunes of war, however, soon changed the electoral situation.

NORTHERN PRESSURE AND SOUTHERN WILL

The year 1864 brought to fruition the North's long-term diplomatic strategy. From the outset the Union's paramount diplomatic goal had been to

Diplomatic Strategy

prevent European recognition of the Confederacy and the military and economic aid it would bring. Southerners had depended for recognition on England's need for southern cotton, but their strategy failed because England had a surplus of cotton on hand and developed new sources during the war. Britain watched the battlefield and refused to be stampeded into acknowledging the Confederacy.

More than once the Union strategy nearly broke down. A major crisis occurred in 1861 when the overzealous commander of an American frigate stopped the British steamer *Trent* and abducted two Confederate ambassadors. The British reacted strongly, but Lincoln and Seward were able to delay until a less-excited public opinion allowed them to back down and return the ambassadors. In a series of confrontations, the United States protested against the building and sale of warships to the Confederacy. A few ships built in Britain, notably the *Alabama,* reached open water to serve the Confederacy. But soon the British government began to bar delivery to the Confederacy of warships such as the Laird rams, formidable vessels whose pointed prows were designed to break the Union blockade.

Back on American battlefields, the northern victory was far from won. Most engagements had demonstrated the advantages enjoyed by the defense and the extreme difficulty of destroying an opposing army. As General William Tecumseh Sherman recognized, the North had to "keep the war South until they are not only ruined, exhausted, but humbled in pride and spirit." Yet the world's recognized military authorities agreed that deep invasion was extremely difficult and risky. The farther an army penetrated enemy territory, the more vulnerable its own communications and support became. Moreover, noted the Prussian expert Karl von Clausewitz, if the invader encountered a "truly national" resistance, his troops would be "everywhere exposed to attacks by an insurgent population."

General Grant decided to test these obstacles—and southern will—with an innovation of his own: the strategy of raids. Raids were not new, but what Grant had in mind was on a massive scale. He proposed to use whole armies, not just cavalry. Federal armies, abandoning their lines of support, would live off the land while they laid waste all resources useful to the Confederacy. After General George H. Thomas's troops won the Battle of Chattanooga in November 1863, the heartland of the South lay open. Moving to the Virginia theater, Grant entrusted General Sherman with 100,000 men for such a raid deep into the South, toward Atlanta.

Jefferson Davis countered by placing the army of General Johnston in Sherman's path. Davis's entire political strategy for 1864 depended on the demonstration of Confederate military strength and a successful defense of Atlanta. With the federal elections of 1864 approaching, Davis hoped that a display of strength and resolution by the South would defeat Lincoln and elect a president who would sue for peace.

When Johnston slowly but steadily fell back toward Atlanta, Davis grew anxious and pressed his commander for information and assurances that Atlanta would be held. From a purely military point of

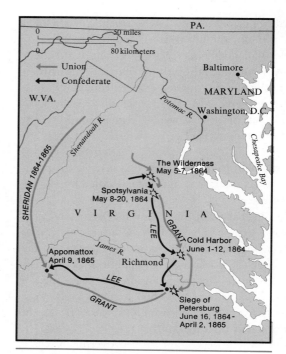

The War in Virginia, 1864–1865

view, Johnston was conducting the defense skillfully, but Jefferson Davis could not take a purely military point of view. When Johnston remained uninformative and continued to drop back, Davis replaced him with General John Hood, who knew his job was to fight. Hood attacked but was beaten, and Sherman's army occupied Atlanta on September 2, 1864. The victory buoyed northern spirits, assured Lincoln's reelection, and cleared the way for Sherman's march from Atlanta to the sea.

As he moved across Georgia Sherman cut a path fifty to sixty miles wide; the totality of the destruction was awesome. A Georgia woman described the "Burnt Country" this way: "The fields were trampled down and the road was lined with carcasses of horses, hogs, and cattle that the invaders, unable either to consume or to carry away with them, had wantonly shot down to starve our people and prevent them from making their crops. The stench in some places was unbearable." Such devastation diminished the

Chapter 14: Transforming Fire: The Civil War, 1861–1865

Abraham Lincoln's face betrays the strain of four years of war. Compare his youthful appearance in Springfield, Illinois, on August 13, 1860, left, with the photograph on the right, taken in Washington, April 10, 1865, four days before his assassination. Library of Congress.

South's material resources, but, more importantly, it was bound to impact on the faltering southern will to resist.

In Virginia the preliminaries to victory were protracted and ghastly. Throughout the spring and summer Grant hurled his troops at Lee's army and suffered appalling losses: almost 18,000 casualties in the Battle of the Wilderness, more than 8,000 at Spotsylvania, and 12,000 in the space of a few hours at Cold Harbor (see map). But the heavy fighting did prepare the way for eventual victory: Lee's army shrank to the point that offensive action was no longer possible, while the Union army kept replenishing its forces with new recruits.

The end finally came in the spring of 1865. Grant kept battering at Lee, who tried but failed to break through the federal line east of Petersburg on March 25. With the numerical superiority of Grant's army now upwards of two-to-one, Confederate defeat was inevitable. On April 2 Lee abandoned Richmond and Petersburg.

Heavy Losses Force Lee's Surrender

IMPORTANT EVENTS

1861	Four more southern states secede from Union
	Battle of Bull Run
	General McClellan organizes Union Army
	Union blockade begins
	First Confiscation Act
1862	Capture of Forts Henry and Donelson
	Capture of New Orleans
	Battle of Shiloh
	Confederacy adopts conscription
	McClellan attacks Virginia
	Second Confiscation Act
	Confederacy mounts offensive
	Battle of Antietam
1863	Emancipation Proclamation
	National Banking Act
	Union adopts conscription
	Black soldiers join Union Army
	Food riots in southern cities
	Battle of Chancellorsville
	Battle of Gettysburg and surrender of Vicksburg
	Draft riots in New York City
1864	Battle of Cold Harbor
	Lincoln requests party plank abolishing slavery
	General Sherman enters Atlanta
	Lincoln re-elected
	Jefferson Davis proposes Confederate emancipation
	Sherman marches through Georgia
1865	Sherman drives through Carolinas
	Congress approves Thirteenth Amendment
	Hampton Roads Conference
	Lee surrenders at Appomattox
	Lincoln assassinated

On April 9, hemmed in by federal troops, short of rations, and with fewer than 30,000 men left, Lee surrendered to Grant. At Appomattox Courthouse the Union general treated his rival with respect and paroled the defeated troops. Within weeks Jefferson Davis was captured, and the remaining Confederate forces laid down their arms and surrendered. The war was over at last.

Lincoln did not live to see the last surrenders. On the evening of Good Friday, April 14, he went to Ford's Theatre in Washington, where an assassin named John Wilkes Booth shot him at pointblank range. Lincoln died the next day. The Union had lost its wartime leader, and to many, relief at the war's end was tempered by uncertainty about the future.

COSTS AND EFFECTS

The costs of the Civil War were enormous. Approximately 364,222 federal soldiers died, 140,070 of them from wounds suffered in battle. Another 275,175 Union soldiers were wounded but survived. On the Confederate side, an estimated 258,000 lost their lives, and even a conservative estimate of Confederate wounded brought the total number of casualties on both sides to more than 1 million—a frightful toll for a nation of 31 million people.

Casualties

Property damage and financial costs were also enormous, though difficult to tally. Federal loans and taxes during the conflict totaled almost $3 billion, and interest on the war debt was $2.8 billion. The Confederacy borrowed over $2 billion but lost far more in the destruction of homes, fences, crops, livestock, and other property. Thoughtful scholars have noted that small farmers lost just as much, proportionally, as planters whose slaves were emancipated.

Financial Cost of the War

Estimates of the total cost of the war exceeded $20 billion—five times the total expenditure of the federal government from its creation to 1865. As late as the 1880s interest on the war debt constituted 40 percent of the federal budget and soldiers' pensions another 20 percent. Moreover, the war had brought an increase in both federal power and federal help to business. In political terms, too, national power increased. Extreme forms of states' rights were dead.

Yet despite all these changes, a crucial question remained unanswered: what was the place of black men and women in American life? They awaited an answer, which would have to be found during Reconstruction.

SUGGESTIONS FOR FURTHER READING

The War and the South

Thomas B. Alexander and Richard E. Beringer, *The Anatomy of the Confederate Congress* (1972); Robert F. Durden, *The Gray and the Black* (1972); Paul D. Escott, *Many Excellent People* (1985); Paul D. Escott, *After Secession* (1978); Paul D. Escott, " 'The Cry of the Sufferers': The Problem of Poverty in the Confederacy," *Civil War History*, XXIII (September 1977), 228–240; Archer Jones *et al.*, *Why the South Lost the Civil War* (1985); J. B. Jones, *A Rebel War Clerk's Diary*, 2 vols., ed. Howard Swiggett (1935); Stanley

Lebergott, "Why the South Lost," *Journal of American History*, 70 (June, 1983), 58–74; Ella Lonn, *Desertion During the Civil War* (1928); Larry E. Nelson, *Bullets, Ballots, and Rhetoric* (1980); Harry P. Owens and James J. Cooke, eds., *The Old South in the Crucible of War* (1983); Charles W. Ramsdell, *Behind the Lines in the Southern Confederacy*, ed. Wendell H. Stephenson (1944); James L. Roark, *Masters Without Slaves* (1977); Georgia Lee Tatum, *Disloyalty in the Confederacy* (1934); Emory M. Thomas, *The Confederate Nation* (1979); Emory M. Thomas, *The Confederacy as a Revolutionary Experience* (1971); Emory M. Thomas, *The Confederate State of Richmond* (1971); Bell Irvin Wiley, *The Life of Johnny Reb* (1943); Bell Irvin Wiley, *The Plain People of the Confederacy* (1943); W. Buck Yearns, ed., *The Confederate Governors* (1985).

The War and the North

Ralph Andreano, ed., *The Economic Impact of the American Civil War* (1962); Robert Cruden, *The War That Never Ended* (1973); Wood Gray, *The Hidden Civil War* (1942); Frank L. Klement, *The Copperheads in the Middle West* (1960); Susan Previant Lee and Peter Passell, *A New Economic View of American History* (1979); George Winston Smith and Charles Burnet Judah, *Life in the North During the Civil War* (1966); George Templeton Strong, *Diary*, 4 vols., ed. Allan Nevins and Milton Halsey Thomas (1952); Paul Studenski, *Financial History of the United States* (1952); Bell Irvin Wiley, *The Life of Billy Yank* (1952).

Women

John R. Brumgardt, ed., *Civil War Nurse: The Diary and Letters of Hannah Ropes* (1980); Beth Gilbert Crabtree and James W. Patton, eds., *"Journal of a Secesh Lady": The Diary of Catherine Ann Devereux Edmondston, 1860–1866* (1979); Jacqueline Jones, *Labor of Love, Labor of Sorrow* (1985); Mary D. Robertson, ed., *Lucy Breckinridge of Grove Hill: The Journal of a Virginia Girl, 1862–1864* (1979); C. Vann Woodward and Elisabeth Muhlenfeld, eds., *The Private Mary Chesnut* (1984); C. Vann Woodward, ed., *Mary Chesnut's Civil War* (1981).

Blacks

Ira Berlin, ed., *Freedom: A Documentary History of Emancipation, 1861–1867*, Series II, *The Black Military Experience* (1982); Dudley Cornish, *The Sable Arm* (1956); James M.

McPherson, *The Negro's Civil War* (1965); James M. McPherson, *The Struggle for Equality* (1964); Benjamin Quarles, *The Negro in the Civil War* (1953).

Military History

Bern Anderson, *By Sea and by River* (1962); Bruce Catton, *Grant Takes Command* (1969); Thomas L. Connelly and Archer Jones, *The Politics of Command* (1973); Burke Davis, *Sherman's March* (1980); William C. Davis, ed., *The Image of War*, multivolume (1983–1985); Shelby Foote, *The Civil War, a Narrative*, 3 vols. (1958–1974); William A. Frassanito, *Grant and Lee: The Virginia Campaigns, 1864–1865* (1983); Douglas Southall Freeman, *R. E. Lee*, 4 vols. (1934–1935); Herman Hattaway and Archer Jones, *How the North Won* (1983); Archer Jones *et al.*, *Why the South Lost the Civil War* (1986); Archer Jones, *Confederate Strategy from Shiloh to Vicksburg* (1961); James Lee McDonough, *Chattanooga* (1984); James Lee McDonough and Thomas L. Connelly, *Five Tragic Hours* (1984); Grady McWhiney and Perry D. Jamieson, *Attack and Die* (1982); J. B. Mitchell, *Decisive Battles of the Civil War* (1955).

Diplomatic History

Stuart L. Bernath, *Squall Across the Atlantic: American Civil War Prize Cases and Diplomacy* (1970); David P. Crook, *Diplomacy During the American Civil War* (1975); David P. Crook, *The North, the South, and the Powers, 1861–1865* (1974); Charles P. Cullop, *Confederate Propaganda in Europe* (1969); Frank J. Merli, *Great Britain and the Confederate Navy* (1970); Frank L. Owsley and Harriet Owsley, *King Cotton Diplomacy* (1959); Gordon H. Warren, *Fountain of Discontent: The Trent Affair and Freedom of the Seas* (1981).

Abraham Lincoln and the Union Government

LaWanda Cox, *Lincoln and Black Freedom* (1981); Richard N. Current, *The Lincoln Nobody Knows* (1958); David Donald, *Charles Sumner and the Rights of Man* (1970); Ludwell H. Johnson, "Lincoln's Solution to the Problem of Peace Terms, 1864–1865," *Journal of Southern History*, XXXIV (November 1968); 441–447; Peyton McCrary, *Abraham Lincoln and Reconstruction* (1978); Stephen B. Oates, *With Malice Toward None* (1977); James G. Randall, *Mr. Lincoln* (1957); Benjamin F. Thomas, *Abraham Lincoln* (1952); Hans L. Trefousse, *The Radical Republicans* (1969); Glyndon G. Van Deusen, *William Henry Seward* (1967); T. Harry Williams, *Lincoln and His Generals* (1952); T. Harry Williams, *Lincoln and the Radicals* (1941).

CHAPTER 15

RECONSTRUCTION BY TRIAL AND ERROR 1865–1877

It was a beautiful spring day in 1868. Sunlight and balmy weather bathed the nation's capital on Saturday, May 16, but few people paused to relax or enjoy their surroundings. Spectators packed the Senate galleries and thousands more milled about. Precisely at noon the Chief Justice of the United States entered the Senate. All principals of a solemn drama were present before the High Court of Impeachment except the accused: Andrew Johnson, President of the United States. Johnson, who never appeared to defend himself in person, waited anxiously at the White House as Chief Justice Salmon Chase ordered the calling of the roll. To each senator he put the questions, "How say you? Is the respondent, Andrew Johnson, President of the United States, guilty or not guilty of a high misdemeanor, as charged in this article?" Thirty-five senators answered, "Guilty," nineteen, "Not guilty." The total was one short of a two-thirds majority. The nation had come within one vote of removing its president from office.

How had this extraordinary event come about? What had brought the executive and legislative branches of government into such severe conflict? An unprecedented problem—the reconstruction of the Union—furnished the occasion, and deepening differences over the proper policy to pursue had led to the confrontation.

In 1865, at the end of the war, such a result seemed most unlikely. Although he was a southerner from Tennessee, Johnson had built his career upon criticizing the wealthy planters and championing the South's small farmers. Former slaveholders believed they had reason to fear Johnson, and when a northern Radical suggested the exile or execution of ten or twelve leading rebels, Johnson had vigorously replied, "How are you going to pick out so small a number? Robbery is a crime; rape is a crime; *treason* is a crime; and *crime* must be punished."

Moreover, fundamental change was already under way in the South. During his army's last campaign,

General William T. Sherman had issued Special Field Order No. 15, which set aside for Negro settlement the Sea Islands and all abandoned coastal lands thirty miles to the interior, from Charleston to the Saint John's River in northern Florida. Black refugees quickly poured into these lands; by the middle of 1865, forty thousand freed people were living in their new homes.

Before the end of 1865, however, these signs of change were reversed. Although Jefferson Davis was imprisoned for two years, no Confederate leaders were executed, and southern aristocrats soon came to view Andrew Johnson not as their enemy but as their friend and protector. Johnson pardoned rebel leaders liberally, allowed them to take high offices, and ordered government officials to reclaim the freedmen's land and give it back to the original owners.

The unexpected outcome of Johnson's program led Congress to examine his policies and design new plans for Reconstruction. Out of negotiations in Congress and clashes between the president and the legislators, there emerged first one, and then two, new plans for Reconstruction. Before the process was over, the nation had adopted the Fourteenth and Fifteenth Amendments and impeached its president.

For black people the benefits of freedom were most often practical and ordinary. They moved out of slave quarters and built cabins of their own; they worked together in family units and worshiped in their own churches without white supervision. Blacks also took the risk of political participation, voting in large numbers and gaining some offices. But they knew their political success depended on the determination and support of the North.

In the South, opposition to Reconstruction grew steadily. By 1869 the Ku Klux Klan had added organized violence to southern whites' repertoire of resistance. Despite federal efforts to protect them, black people were intimidated at the polls, robbed of their earnings, beaten, or murdered. By the early 1870s the failure of Reconstruction was apparent. The nation had proclaimed anew the principle of human equality but failed to secure it in fact.

EQUALITY:
THE UNRESOLVED ISSUE

For America's former slaves, Reconstruction had one paramount meaning: a chance to explore freedom. The slaves on one Texas plantation jumped up and down and clapped their hands as one man shouted, "We is free—no more whippings and beatings." One grandmother who had long resented her treatment "dropped her hoe" and ran to confront the mistress. "I'm free!" she yelled at her. "Yes, I'm free! Ain't got to work for you no more! You can't put me in your pocket [sell me] now!" Another man recalled that he and others "started on the move" and left the plantation, either to search for family members or just to exercise their new-found freedom of movement.

Most freedmen reacted more cautiously and shrewdly. As slaves they had learned to expect hostility from white people, and they did not presume it would instantly disappear. Life in freedom, they knew, might still be a matter of what was allowed, not what was right. One sign of this shrewd caution was the way freedmen evaluated potential employers. If a white person had been relatively considerate to blacks in bondage, blacks reasoned that he might prove a desirable employer in freedom. Other blacks left their plantation all at once, for, as one put it, "that master am sure mean."

Even more urgently than a fair employer, the freedmen wanted land of their own. Land represented a chance to farm for themselves, independence, and compensation for generations of bondage. A northern observer noted that freedmen made "plain, straight-forward" inquiries as they settled the land set aside for them by Sherman. They wanted to be sure the land "would be theirs after they had improved it."

Blacks' Desire for Land

Chapter 15: RECONSTRUCTION BY TRIAL AND ERROR, 1865–1877

But no one could say how much of a chance the whites, who were in power, would give to blacks. During the war the federal government had refused to arm black volunteers. Necessity, however, forced a change in policy. Because the war was going badly the administration authorized black enlistments. By spring 1863 black troops were proving their value. "They fight like fiends," said one observer.

Black people hoped that service to the nation would secure the rights of citizenship. The wartime experiences of black soldiers, however, seemed to indicate that equal rights would not be forthcoming. Uniformed blacks immediately encountered varying forms of discrimination, including inferior pay. The government paid white privates $13 per month plus a clothing allowance of $3.50. Black troops earned $10 per month less $3 deducted for clothing. Blacks resented this injustice so deeply that in protest two regiments refused to accept any pay, and eventually Congress remedied the discrimination.

Black Service in the Military

Whether soldier or civilian, blacks found that northerners had mixed attitudes on racial questions. On the one hand, wartime idealism had promoted equality and weakened discrimination. Many abolitionists had worked vigorously to extend equal rights to black Americans, and a powerful element in the Republican party had committed itself to fighting racism. In 1864 their efforts brought about the acceptance of black testimony in federal courts and the desegregation of New York City's streetcars. And one state, Massachusetts, enacted a comprehensive public accommodations law.

On the other hand, there were many more signs of resistance to racial equality. The Democratic party adopted an explicit and vociferous stand against blacks, charging that Republicans favored race-mixing and were undermining the status of the white worker. Moreover, voters in three states—Connecticut, Minnesota, and Wisconsin—rejected black suffrage in 1865. The racial attitudes of northerners seemed to be in flux, the outcome uncertain.

JOHNSON'S RECONSTRUCTION PLAN

Throughout 1865 the formation of Reconstruction policy rested solely with Andrew Johnson, for shortly before he became president Congress recessed and did not reconvene until December. Thus Johnson had almost eight months to design a plan of reconstruction on his own, unhindered by legislative suggestions.

Johnson had a few precedents to follow in Lincoln's wartime plans for Reconstruction. In December 1863 Lincoln had proposed a "10-percent" plan for a government being organized in captured portions of Louisiana. According to this plan, a state government could be established as soon as 10 percent of those who had voted in 1860 took an oath of future loyalty. Only high-ranking Confederate officials would be denied a chance to take the oath, and Lincoln urged that at least a few well-qualified blacks be given the ballot. At the time of his death, Lincoln had given general approval to a plan drafted by Secretary of War Stanton that would have imposed military authority and provisional governors as steps toward new state governments.

Lincoln's Reconstruction Plan

Johnson began with the plan Stanton had drafted for consideration by the cabinet. At a cabinet meeting on May 9, 1865, Johnson's advisors split evenly on the question of voting rights for freedmen in the South. Johnson said that he favored black suffrage, but only if the southern states adopted it voluntarily. A champion of states' rights, he regarded this decision as too important to be taken out of the hands of the states.

Such conservatism had an enduring effect on Johnson's policies, but at first it appeared that his old enmity toward the planters might produce a plan for radical changes in class relations among whites. As he appointed provisional governors in the South, Johnson also proposed rules that would keep the wealthy planter class out of power. He required every southern voter to swear an oath of loyalty as a condition of gaining amnesty or pardon. But some southerners would face special difficulties in regaining their rights.

Johnson barred certain classes of southerners from taking the oath and gaining amnesty. Former federal officials who had violated their oaths to support the United States and had aided the Confederacy could not take the oath. Nor could graduates of West Point or Annapolis who had resigned their commissions to fight for the South. The same was true for high-ranking Confederate officers and Confederate political leaders. Also barred were southerners whose taxable property was worth more than $20,000. All such individuals had to apply personally to the president for pardon and restoration of political rights, or risk legal penalties, including confiscation of land.

Oaths of Amnesty and New State Governments

Thus it appeared that the South's old leadership class would be removed from power, for virtually all the rich and powerful whites of prewar days needed Johnson's special pardon. Many observers, South and North, sensed that the president meant to take his revenge on the aristocrats and to raise up a new leadership of deserving yeomen.

Johnson's provisional governors began the Reconstruction process by calling constitutional conventions. The delegates chosen for these conventions had to draft new constitutions eliminating slavery and invalidating secession. After ratification of these constitutions, new governments could be elected, and the states would be restored to the Union with full congressional representation. But no southerners could participate in this process who had not taken the oath of amnesty or who had been ineligible to vote on the day the state seceded. Black southerners, being in the latter category, had no voice in the process.

But the plan did not work as Johnson had hoped. Ironically, Johnson himself had a hand in subverting his own plan. He pardoned first one and then another of the aristocrats and chief rebels. By the time the southern states had completed the process of constitution-making and elections, Confederate leaders had emerged in powerful positions. The president decided to stand by his new governments and declare Reconstruction completed. Thus in December 1865 many Confederate congressmen traveled to Washington to claim seats in the House of Representatives. And the vice president of the Confederacy, Alexander Stephens, returned to the capital as a senator.

Confederates Regain Power

The election of such prominent rebels was not the only result of Johnson's program that sparked negative comment in the North. Some of the state conventions were slow to repudiate secession; others only grudgingly admitted that slavery was dead. Of great concern to northern politicians was the enactment of the so-called black codes. In these laws southern state legislatures defined the status of freedmen. Some states merely revised sections of the old slave codes by substituting the word freedman for slave. Typical codes required blacks to carry passes and observe a curfew. In some cases restrictions kept blacks out of many desirable occupations and forced them to live in housing provided by a landowner. States also denied blacks access to public institutions such as schools and orphanages. To northerners, the South seemed intent on returning black people to a position of servility.

Black Codes

Thus it was not surprising that a majority of northern congressmen decided to take a close look at the results of Johnson's plan. On reconvening, they voted not to admit the newly elected southern representatives, whose credentials were subject under the Constitution to congressional scrutiny. The House and Senate established a joint committee to examine Johnson's policies and advise on new ones. Reconstruction had entered a second phase, one in which Congress would play a strong role.

THE CONGRESSIONAL RECONSTRUCTION PLAN

Northern congressmen disagreed on what to do, but they did not doubt their right to play a role in Reconstruction. The Constitution mentioned neither secession nor reunion, but it did assign to Congress a duty to guarantee to each state a republican government. Under this provision, the legislators thought they could devise policies for Reconstruction.

They soon found that other constitutional questions had a direct bearing on the policies they followed. What, for example, had the fact of rebellion done to the relationship between southern states and the Union? Lincoln had always insisted that the Union remained unbroken. But congressmen who favored vigorous Reconstruction measures tended to argue that war *had* broken the Union. The southern states had committed legal suicide and reverted to the status of territories, they argued, or the South was a conquered nation subject to the victor's will. Moderate congressmen held that the states had forfeited their rights through rebellion, and had thus come under congressional supervision.

These diverse theories mirrored the diversity of Congress itself. Northern legislators fell into four major categories: Democrats, conservative Republicans, moderate Republicans, and Radical Republicans. No one of these groups had decisive power. The Republican party had a majority, but there was considerable distance between conservative Republicans, who desired a limited federal role in Reconstruction and were fairly happy with Johnson's actions, and the Radicals. These men, led by Thaddeus Stevens, Charles Sumner, and George Julian, believed that it was essential to democratize the South, establish public education, and ensure the rights of freedmen. They favored black suffrage, often supported land

The Radicals

confiscation and redistribution, and were willing to exclude the South from the Union for several years if necessary to achieve their goals. Between these two factions lay the moderates, who held the balance of power.

Through their actions, Johnson and the Democrats forced these diverse Republican factions to come together. The president and the northern Democrats refused to cooperate with moderate and conservative Republicans, arguing that Reconstruction was over and calling for the seating of the southern delegates in Congress. Moreover, Johnson refused to support an apparent compromise on Reconstruction. Under its terms Johnson would have agreed to two modifications of his program. The life of the Freedmen's Bureau, which fed the hungry, negotiated labor contracts, and started schools, would be extended by one bill; and a civil rights bill would be passed to counteract the black codes. This bill, drawn up by a conservative Republican, gave federal judges the power to remove from southern courts cases in which blacks were treated unfairly.

Congress Struggles for a Compromise

But in spring 1866, Johnson destroyed the compromise by vetoing both bills (they were later repassed). Denouncing any change in his program, the president condemned Congress's action in inflammatory language. In so doing he questioned the legitimacy of congressional involvement in policymaking. All hope of working with the president was now gone. Instead of a compromise program, the various Republican factions developed a new Reconstruction plan. It took the form of a proposed amendment to the Constitution—the fourteenth—and it represented a compromise between radical and conservative elements of the party.

Of four points in the amendment, there was nearly universal agreement on one: the Confederate debt was declared null and void, the war debt of the United States guaranteed. There was also fairly general support for a section prohibiting prominent Confederates from holding any na-

Fourteenth Amendment

tional or state political office. Only at the discretion of Congress, by a two-thirds vote of each house, could these political penalties be removed.

The section of the Fourteenth Amendment that would have by far the greatest legal significance in later years was the first. On its face, this section was an effort to strike down the black codes and guarantee basic rights to freedmen. It conferred citizenship on freedmen and prohibited states from abridging their constitutional "privileges and immunities." Similarly, the amendment barred any state from taking a person's life, liberty, or property "without due process of law" and from denying "equal protection of the laws." These clauses were phrased broadly enough to become in time powerful guarantees of black Americans' civil rights.

The second section of the amendment clearly revealed the compromises and political motives that had produced the document. Northerners, in Congress and out, disagreed about whether black citizens should have the right to vote. What was more, Republicans feared that emancipation, which made every former slave five-fifths of a person instead of three-fifths for purposes of congressional representation, might increase the South's power in Congress. If it did, and if blacks were not allowed to vote, the former secessionists would gain seats in Congress.

What a strange result that would seem to most northerners! They had never planned to reward the South for rebellion, and Republicans in Congress were determined not to hand over power to their political enemies. So they offered the South a choice. According to the second section of the Fourteenth Amendment, states did not have to give black men the right to vote. But if they did not do so, their representation would be reduced proportionally. If they did, it would be increased proportionally—but Republicans would be able to appeal to the new black voters.

Though the Fourteenth Amendment dealt with the voting rights of black men, it ignored all female citizens and angered women's rights advocates. When legislators defined them as nonvoting citizens, prominent women's leaders such as Elizabeth Cady Stan-

ton and Susan B. Anthony decided that it was time to end their alliance with abolitionists. Thus the independent women's rights movement grew.

In 1866, however, the major question in Reconstruction politics was how the public would respond to the amendment. Would the northern public support Congress's plan or the president's? Johnson did his best to block the Fourteenth Amendment and to convince northerners to reject it. Condemning Congress's plan and its refusal to seat southern representatives, the president urged state legislatures in the South to vote against ratification. Every southern legislature except Tennessee's rejected the amendment. In the North, Johnson arranged a National Union convention to publicize his program. Then he boarded a special train for a "swing around the circle" that carried his message into the Midwest. Increasingly audiences hooted and jeered at him, however.

Southern Rejection of the Fourteenth Amendment

The 1866 elections were a resounding victory for Republicans in Congress. Men whom Johnson had denounced won re-election by large margins, and the Republican majority increased as some new candidates defeated incumbent Democrats. Everywhere Radical and moderate Republicans gained strength. Thus Republican congressional leaders received a mandate to continue with their Reconstruction plan.

Recognizing that nothing could be accomplished under the existing southern governments and with blacks excluded from the electorate, Congress decided to act. It passed the Military Reconstruction Act of 1867, which called for new governments in the South, with a return to military authority in the interim (see map). It barred from political office those Confederate leaders listed in the Fourteenth Amendment. It guaranteed freedmen the right to vote in elections for state constitutional conventions and for subsequent state governments. In addition, each southern state was required to ratify the Fourteenth Amendment; to ratify its new constitution; and to submit the new consti-

Military Reconstruction Act of 1867

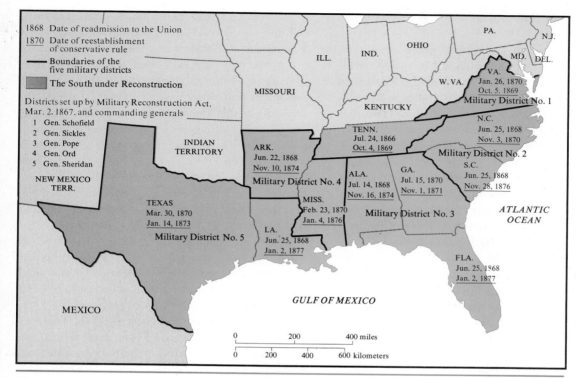

The Reconstruction

Map legend:

1868 Date of readmission to the Union
1870 Date of reestablishment of conservative rule
— Boundaries of the five military districts
The South under Reconstruction

Districts set up by Military Reconstruction Act, Mar. 2, 1867, and commanding generals
1 Gen. Schofield
2 Gen. Sickles
3 Gen. Pope
4 Gen. Ord
5 Gen. Sheridan

NEW MEXICO TERR.

INDIAN TERRITORY

MISSOURI

ILL. IND. OHIO PA. N.J.

KENTUCKY

W. VA. MD. DEL.

VA. Jan. 26, 1870 / Oct. 5, 1869
Military District No. 1

N.C. Jun. 25, 1868 / Nov. 3, 1870
Military District No. 2

TENN. Jul. 24, 1866 / Oct. 4, 1869

ARK. Jun. 22, 1868 / Nov. 10, 1874
Military District No. 4

S.C. Jun. 25, 1868 / Nov. 28, 1876

ALA. Jul. 14, 1868 / Nov. 16, 1874

GA. Jul. 15, 1870 / Nov. 1, 1871

Military District No. 3

TEXAS Mar. 30, 1870 / Jan. 14, 1873
Military District No. 5

MISS. Feb. 23, 1870 / Jan. 4, 1876

LA. Jun. 25, 1868 / Jan. 2, 1877

FLA. Jun. 25, 1868 / Jan. 2, 1877

ATLANTIC OCEAN

MEXICO

GULF OF MEXICO

0   200   400 miles
0   200   400   600 kilometers

tution to Congress for approval. Thus black people gained an opportunity to fight for a better life through the political process. The only weapon put into their hands was the ballot, however. The law required no redistribution of land and guaranteed no basic changes in southern social structure.

Congress's role as the architect of Reconstruction was not quite over. To restrict Johnson's influence and safeguard its plan, Congress passed a number of controversial laws. First it set the date for its own reconvening—an unprecedented act, since the president had traditionally summoned the legislature to Washington. Then it limited Johnson's power over the army by requiring the president to issue military orders through the General of the Army, Ulysses S. Grant, who could not be sent from Washington without the Senate's consent. Finally, Congress passed the Tenure of Office Act, which gave the Senate power to interfere with changes in the president's

cabinet. Designed to protect Secretary of War Stanton, who sympathized with the Radicals, this law violated the tradition that a president controlled his own cabinet.

Johnson took several belligerent steps of his own. He issued orders to military commanders in the South limiting their powers and increasing the powers of the civil governments he had created in 1865. Then he removed army officers who conscientiously enforced Congress's new law. Finally, in August 1867 he tried to remove Secretary of War Stanton. With this act the confrontation reached its climax.

The House Judiciary Committee, which had twice before considered impeaching the president, again initiated the removal process. The 1868 indictment

Impeachment and Trial

concentrated on Johnson's violation of the Tenure of Office Act. Modern scholars, however, regard his efforts to impede enforcement of the Military Reconstruction Act as a far more serious offense.

Johnson's trial in the Senate lasted more than three months. The prosecution, led by such Radicals as Thaddeus Stevens and Benjamin Butler, argued that Johnson was guilty of "high crimes and misdemeanors." But they also advanced the novel idea that impeachment was a political matter, not a judicial trial of guilt or innocence. The Senate ultimately rejected such reasoning, which would have transformed impeachment into a political weapon against any chief executive who disagreed with Congress. Though a majority of senators voted to convict Johnson, the prosecution fell one vote short of the necessary two-thirds majority. Johnson remained in office for the few months left in his term, and his acquittal established the precedent that only serious misdeeds merited removal from office.

In 1869, in an effort to write democratic principles and color-blindness into the Constitution, the Radicals succeeded in presenting the Fifteenth Amendment for ratification. This measure

Fifteenth Amendment forbade states to deny the right to vote "on account of race, color, or previous condition of servitude." Ironically, the votes of four uncooperative southern states—required by Congress to approve the amendment as an added condition to rejoining the Union—proved necessary to impose this principle on parts of the North. Although several states outside the South refused to ratify, the Fifteenth Amendment became law in 1870.

RECONSTRUCTION POLITICS
IN THE SOUTH

From the start, Reconstruction encountered the resistance of white southerners. Their opposition to change appeared in the black codes and other pol-

icies of the Johnson governments as well as in private attitudes. Many

White Resistance whites set their faces against emancipation, and the former planter class proved especially unbending. In 1866 a Georgia newspaper frankly declared, "Most of the white citizens believe that the institution of slavery was right, and . . . they will believe that the condition, which comes nearest to slavery, that can now be established will be the best."

Fearing the end of their control over slaves, some planters attempted to postpone freedom by denying or misrepresenting events. Former slaves reported that their owners "didn't tell them it was freedom" or "wouldn't let [them] go." To hold onto their workers some landowners claimed control over black children and used guardianship and apprentice laws to bind black families to the plantation. Whites also blocked blacks from acquiring land.

After President Johnson encouraged the South to resist congressional Reconstruction, many white conservatives worked hard to capture the new state governments. Elsewhere, large numbers of whites boycotted the polls in an attempt to defeat Congress's plans. Since the new constitutions had to be approved by a majority of registered voters, registered whites could defeat them by sitting out the elections. This tactic was tried in North Carolina and succeeded in Alabama, forcing Congress to readjust and base ratification on a majority of those voting.

Very few black men stayed away from the polls. Enthusiastically and hopefully they seized the opportunity to participate in politics, voting solidly Republican. Most agreed with one man who felt that he should "stick to the end with the party that freed me."

With a large black turnout, and with prominent Confederates barred from politics under the Fourteenth Amendment, a new southern Republican party came to power in the constitutional conventions. Some blacks won seats as delegates, along with northerners who had moved to the South and some native southern whites. Together they brought the South's fundamental law into line with progressive reforms that had been adopted in the rest of the nation. The new constitutions were more democratic— they eliminated property qualifications for voting and holding office, made more state and local offices elective, provided for public schools and institutions for the mentally ill, the blind, the deaf, the destitute, and the orphaned, and ended imprisonment for debt.

The conventions also broadened women's rights in possession of property and divorce. Usually, the main goal was not to make women equal but to provide relief to thousands of suffering debtors. In families left poverty-stricken by the war and weighed down by debts, the husband had usually contracted the debts. Thus, giving women legal control over their own property provided some protection to their families. There were some delegates, however, whose goal was to elevate women. Blacks in particular called for women's suffrage but were ignored by their white colleagues.

Under these new constitutions the southern states elected new governments. Again the Republican party triumphed, bringing new men into positions of power. The ranks of state legislators

Triumph of Republican Governments
in 1868 included black southerners for the first time in history. Congress's second plan for Reconstruction was well under way. It remained to be seen what these new governments would do and how much change they would bring to society.

There was one possibility of radical change through these new governments. That possibility depended on the disfranchisement of substantial numbers of Confederate leaders. If the Republican regimes used their new power to exclude many whites from politics, as punishment for rebellion, they would have a solid electoral majority based on black voters and their white allies. Land reform and the assurance of racial equality would be possible. But none of the Republican governments did this, or even gave it serious consideration.

Why did the new legislators shut the door on the possibility of deep and thoroughgoing reform? First, they appreciated the realities of power and the depth

of racial enmity. In most states whites were the majority, and former slaveowners controlled the best land and other sources of economic power. James Lynch, a leading black politician from Mississippi, candidly explained why Negroes shunned "the Folly of" disfranchisement. Unlike northerners, who "can leave when it becomes too uncomfortable," former slaves "must be in friendly relations with the great body of whites in the state." Second, blacks believed in the principle of universal suffrage and the Christian goal of reconciliation. Far from being vindictive toward the race that had enslaved them, they treated leading rebels with generosity and appealed to white southerners to adopt a spirit of fairness and cooperation.

Thus the South's Republican party committed itself to a strategy of winning white support. To put the matter another way, the Republican party condemned itself to defeat if white voters would not cooperate.

But for a time both Republicans and their opponents, who called themselves Conservatives or Democrats, moved to the center and appealed for support from a broad range of groups. Some propertied whites accepted congressional Reconstruction as a reality and declared that they would try to compete under the new rules. As these Democrats angled for some black votes, Republicans sought to attract more white voters. Both parties found an area of agreement in economic policies.

The Reconstruction governments devoted themselves to stimulating industry. This policy reflected northern ideals, of course, but it also sprang from a growing southern interest in industrialization. Accordingly, Reconstruction legislatures designed many tempting inducements to investment. Loans, subsidies, and exemptions from taxation for periods up to ten years helped to bring new industries into the region.

Policies appealing to black voters never went beyond equality before the law. In fact, the whites who controlled the southern Republican party were reluctant to allow blacks a share of offices proportionate to their electoral strength. Black leaders, aware of their weakness, did not push for revolutionary change. Recognizing the level of hostility in the South, black leaders, with the exception of some urban mulattoes, did not fight for civil rights. Nor did they advocate the confiscation and redistribution of land. Instead, they led the fight to establish public schools in the region. The schools established, however, were segregated, setting the precedent for segregated theaters, trains, and other public accommodations.

Other Republican Policies

Within a few years, as centrists in both parties met failure, the other side of white reaction to congressional Reconstruction began to dominate. Some conservatives had always favored fierce opposition to Reconstruction through pressure and racist propaganda. They put economic and social pressure on blacks. Charging that the South had been turned over to ignorant blacks, conservatives deplored "black domination." The cry of "Negro rule" now became constant.

Such attacks were gross distortions. Blacks were a minority in eight out of ten state conventions (northerners were a minority in nine out of ten). Of the state legislatures, only in the lower house in South Carolina did blacks ever constitute a majority; generally their numbers among officials were far inferior to their proportion in the population. Sixteen blacks won seats in Congress before Reconstruction was over, but none was ever elected governor. Although blacks participated in politics, they neither dominated nor controlled.

Conservatives also stepped up their propaganda against the allies of black Republicans. "Carpetbagger" was a derisive name for whites who had come from the North. It suggested an evil and greedy northern politician, recently arrived with a carpetbag into which he planned to stuff ill-gotten gains before fleeing. There were a few northerners who deserved this unsavory description. But of the thousands of northerners who settled in the South after the war, only a small portion entered politics. And most of them wanted to democratize the South

Carpetbaggers and Scalawags

and to introduce northern ways, such as industry, public education, and the spirit of enterprise.

Conservatives invented the term "scalawag" to stigmatize and discredit any native white southerner who cooperated with the Republicans. A substantial number of southerners did so. Most scalawags were men from mountain areas and small farming districts—average white southerners who saw that they could benefit from the education and opportunities promoted by Republicans. Banding together with the freedmen, they pursued common class interests and hoped to make headway against the power of the long-dominant planters. Both carpetbaggers and scalawags, however, shied away from support for racial equality.

Besides propaganda, the conservatives had other weapons to use against Reconstruction. Financially the Republican governments were doomed to be unpopular. Republicans wanted to continue prewar services, repair war's destruction, and support such important new ventures as public schools. But the Civil War had destroyed much of the South's tax base, so an increase in taxes was necessary even to maintain traditional services, and new ventures required much higher taxes.

Corruption was another powerful charge levied against the Republicans. Unfortunately, it was true. Many carpetbaggers and black politicians sold their votes, taking part in what scholars recognize was a nationwide surge of corruption. Although white Democrats often shared in the guilt, and despite the efforts of some Republicans to stop it, Democrats convinced many voters that scandal was the inevitable result of a foolish Reconstruction program based on blacks and carpetbaggers.

All these problems damaged the Republicans, but in many southern states the death blow came through violence: the murders, whippings, and intimidation of the Ku Klux Klan. Terrorism against blacks had occurred throughout Reconstruction, but after 1867 white violence became more organized and purposeful. The Ku Klux Klan rode to frustrate Reconstruction and keep the freedmen in subjection.

Ku Klux Klan

Nighttime visits, whippings, beatings, and murder became common, and in some areas virtually open warfare developed despite the authorities' efforts to keep the peace.

Although the Klan persecuted blacks who stood up for their rights as laborers or people, its main purpose was political. Lawless nightriders made active Republicans the target of their attacks. Prominent white Republicans and black leaders were killed in several states. After blacks who worked for a South Carolina scalawag started voting, terrorists visited the plantation and "whipped every nigger man they could lay their hands on." Klansmen also attacked Union League Clubs (Republican organizations that mobilized the black vote) and schoolteachers who were aiding blacks.

Klan violence was not simply spontaneous; certain social forces gave direction to racism. In North Carolina, for example, Alamance and Caswell counties were the sites of the worst Klan violence. They were in the Piedmont, where slim Republican majorities rested on cooperation between black voters and whites of the yeoman class.

In a successful effort to regain power, wealthy and influential men organized the campaign of terror. These men served as Klan leaders at the county and local levels, recruited members, and planned atrocities. They did what they deemed necessary to split the Republican coalition and restore a Democratic majority.

Thus a combination of difficult fiscal problems, Republican mistakes, racial hostility, and terror brought down the Republican regimes, and in most southern states so-called Radical **Failure of** Reconstruction was over after only **Reconstruction** a few years. But the most lasting failure of Reconstruction governments was not political—it was social. The new governments failed to alter the southern social structure or its distribution of wealth and power. Exploited as slaves, blacks remained vulnerable to exploitation during Reconstruction. Without land of their own, they were dependent on white landowners, who could use their economic power to compromise blacks' political freedom. Armed only with the ballot, southern blacks had little chance to effect major changes.

THE SOCIAL AND ECONOMIC MEANING OF FREEDOM

Black southerners entered upon life after slavery hopefully, determinedly, but not naively. They had too much experience with white people to assume that all would be easy. Expecting to meet with hostility, black people tried to gain as much as they could from their new circumstances. Often the most valued changes were personal ones—alterations in location, employer, or surroundings that could make an enormous difference to individuals or families.

One of the first decisions that many took was whether to leave the old plantation or remain. This meant making a judgment about where the chances of liberty and progress would be greatest. Former slaves drew upon their experiences in bondage to assess the whites with whom they had to deal. "Most all the Negroes that had good owners stayed with them," said one man. Not surprisingly, cruel slaveholders usually saw their former chattels walk off en masse.

On new farms or old the newly freed men and women reached out for valuable things in life that had been denied them. One of these was education. Whatever their age, blacks hun-**Education** gered for the knowledge in books **for Blacks** that had been permitted only to whites. With freedom they filled the schools both day and night. The federal government and northern reformers assisted this search for education. In its brief life the Freedmen's Bureau founded over four thousand schools, and idealistic men and women from the North established others and staffed them ably.

Blacks and their white allies also realized that higher education was essential. The American Missionary Association founded seven colleges, including Fisk and Atlanta universities, between 1866 and 1869. The Freedmen's Bureau helped to establish Howard University in Washington, D.C., and northern religious groups, such as Methodists, Baptists, and Congregationalists, supported dozens of seminaries, colleges, and teachers' colleges. By the late 1870s black churches had joined in the effort, founding numerous colleges despite their smaller financial resources. Though some of the new institutions did not survive, they brought knowledge to those who would educate others and laid a foundation for progress.

Even in Reconstruction, blacks were choosing many highly educated individuals as leaders. Many blacks who won public office during Reconstruction came from the prewar elite of free people of color. This group had benefited from its association with wealthy whites, who were often blood relatives. The two black senators from Mississippi, Blanche K. Bruce and Hiram Revels, for example, were both privileged in their educations. Bruce was the son of a planter who had provided tutoring on his plantation; Revels was the son of free North Carolina mulattoes who had sent him to Knox College in Illinois. These men and others brought experience as artisans, businessmen, lawyers, teachers, and preachers to political office.

While elected officials wrestled with the political tasks of Reconstruction, millions of former slaves concentrated on improving life at home, on their farms, and in their neighborhoods. Throughout the South they devoted themselves to reuniting their families, moving away from the slave quarters, and founding black churches. Given the eventual failure of Reconstruction, the practical gains that blacks made in their daily lives often proved the most enduring and significant changes of the period.

The search for long-lost family members was awe-inspiring. With only shreds of information to guide them, thousands of black people embarked on odysseys in search of a husband, wife, child, or parent. By relying on the black community for help and in-

Reunification of Black Families

formation, many succeeded in their quest. Others walked through several states and never found their loved ones.

For the thousands of husbands and wives who had belonged to different owners, freedom meant the opportunity to establish homes together for the first time. It also meant that wives would not be ordered to work in the fields. And it meant that parents finally would have the right to raise their children.

Black people frequently wanted to minimize contacts with whites. To avoid the influence of intrusive whites, blacks abandoned the slave quarters and fanned out into distant corners of the land they worked. Some moved away to build new homes in the woods. Others established small all-black settlements that still exist today along the backroads of the South.

The other side of this distance from whites was closer communion within the black community. The secret church of slavery, for instance, now came out into the open. Within a few years independent black branches of the Methodist and Baptist churches had attracted the great majority of black Christians in the South.

Founding of Black Churches

This desire to gain as much independence as possible carried over into the former slaves' economic arrangements. Since most lacked money to buy land, they preferred the next best thing—renting the land they worked. But many whites would not consider renting land to blacks; there was strong social pressure against it. And few blacks had the means to rent a farm. Therefore other alternatives had to be tried.

Northerners and officials of the Freedmen's Bureau favored contracts between owners and laborers. To northerners who believed in "free soil, free labor, free men," contracts and wages seemed the key to progress. For a few years the Freedmen's Bureau helped to draw up and enforce such contracts, but they proved unpopular with both blacks and whites. Owners often filled the contracts with detailed requirements that reminded blacks of their circumscribed lives under slavery. Disputes frequently arose over efficiency, lost time, and other matters. Besides, times were hard and the failure of Confederate banks left the South with a shortage of credit facilities.

Black farmers and white landowners therefore turned to a system of sharecropping: in return for use of the land and "furnishing" (tools, mules, seed, a cabin, and food to last until harvest), the farmer paid the landowner a share of his crop. The cost of food and clothing was deducted from the crop before the owner took his share. After such deductions, each party usually received one-half of the crop.

Rise of the Sharecropping System

The sharecropping system originated as a desirable compromise. It eased landowners' problems with cash and credit; blacks accepted it because it gave them a reasonable amount of freedom from daily supervision. Instead of working under a white overseer as in slavery, they were able to farm a plot of land on their own in family groups. But sharecropping later proved to be a disaster, both for blacks and for the South, because the region overspecialized in cotton just as worldwide demand for the crop began to grow more slowly.

THE END OF RECONSTRUCTION

The North's commitment to racial equality had never been total. And by the early 1870s it was evident that even its partial commitment was weakening. New issues were capturing people's attention, and soon voters began to look for reconciliation with southern whites. In the South Democrats won control of one state after another, and they threatened to defeat Republicans in the North as well. Before long the situation had returned to "normal" in the eyes of southern whites.

The Supreme Court, after first re-establishing its power, participated in the northern retreat from Reconstruction. During the Civil War the Court had been cautious and reluctant to assert itself. Reaction to the Dred Scott decision had been so violent, and the Union's wartime emergency so great, that the Court had refrained from blocking or interfering with government actions.

But in 1866 the landmark case *Ex parte Milligan* reached the Court. Lambdin P. Milligan of Indiana had participated in a plot to free Confederate prisoners of war and overthrow state governments; for these acts a military court had sentenced Milligan, a civilian, to death. In sweeping language the Court declared that military trials were illegal when civil courts were open and functioning, thus indicating that it intended to reassert itself as a major force in national affairs.

Supreme Court Decisions on Reconstruction

In 1873 the *Slaughter-House* cases tested the scope and meaning of the Fourteenth Amendment. In 1869 the Louisiana legislature had granted one company a monopoly on the slaughtering of livestock in New Orleans. Rival butchers in the city promptly sued. Their attorney, former Supreme Court justice John A. Campbell, argued that the Fourteenth Amendment had revolutionized the constitutional system by bringing individual rights under federal protection. Campbell expressed what had been a major Radical goal: to nationalize civil rights and guard them from state interference.

The Court, however, rejected Campbell's argument. Neither the "privileges and immunities" clause nor the "due process" clause of the amendment guaranteed the great basic rights of the Bill of Rights against state action, the justices said. National citizenship involved only such things as the right to travel freely from state to state and to use the navigable waters of the nation. Thus the Court limited severely the amendment's potential for securing the rights of black citizens.

In 1876 the Court regressed even further, emasculating the enforcement clause of the Fourteenth Amendment and interpreting the Fifteenth in a narrow and negative fashion. In *United States v. Cruikshank* the Court dealt with Louisiana whites who were indicted for attacking a meeting of blacks and conspiring to deprive them of their rights. The justices ruled that the Fourteenth Amendment did not extend federal power to cover the misdeeds of private individuals against other citizens; only flagrant state discrimination was covered. And in *United States* v. *Reese* the Court held that the Fifteenth Amendment did not guarantee a citizen's right to vote, but merely listed certain impermissible grounds for denying suffrage. Thus a path lay open for southern states to disfranchise blacks for supposedly nonracial reasons—lack of education, lack of property, or lack of descent from a grandfather qualified to vote before the Military Reconstruction Act. ("Grandfather clauses" became a way of excluding blacks from suffrage, since most blacks were slaves before Reconstruction and hence could not vote.)

The retreat from Reconstruction continued steadily in politics as well. In 1868 Ulysses S. Grant, a Republican, defeated a Democrat, Horatio Seymour, in a presidential campaign that revived sectional divisions. In office Grant sometimes used force to support Reconstruction, but only when he had to. He hoped to avoid confrontation with the South, to erase the image of dictatorship that his military background summoned up.

Election of 1868

In 1870 and 1871 the violent campaigns of the Ku Klux Klan moved Congress to pass two Force Acts and an anti-Klan law. These acts (important precedents for the modern enforcement of civil rights) permitted martial law and suspension of the writ of habeas corpus to combat murders, beatings, and threats by the Klan. Federal troops and prosecutors used them vigorously but unsuccessfully, for a conspiracy of silence frustrated many prosecutions.

In 1872 a revolt within the Republican ranks made Grant even more unwilling to coerce the South. A group calling itself the Liberal Republicans bolted the party and nominated Horace Greeley, the well-known editor of the *New York Tribune,* for president. The Liberal Republicans were a varied group, including civil-

Liberal Republicans Revolt

service reformers, foes of corruption, and advocates of a lower tariff; they often spoke of a more lenient policy toward the South. That year the Democrats too gave their nomination to Greeley. Though the combination was not enough to defeat Grant, it reinforced his desire to avoid confrontation with white southerners.

The Liberal Republican challenge revealed growing dissatisfaction with Grant's administration. Corruption within his administration had become widespread, and Grant foolishly defended some of the culprits. As a result, Grant's popularity, and that of his party, declined; the Democrats gained control of the House in the 1874 elections.

Congress's resolve on southern issues also weakened steadily. By joint resolution it had already removed the political disabilities of the Fourteenth Amendment from many former Confederates. Then in 1872 it adopted a sweeping Amnesty Act, which pardoned most of the remaining rebels and left only five hundred excluded from political participation. A Civil Rights Act passed in 1875 purported to guarantee black people equal accommodations in public places, like inns and theaters. But it was weak and contained no effective provisions for enforcement. Moreover, by 1876 the Democrats had regained control of or "redeemed" all but three of the southern states (South Carolina, Louisiana, and Florida).

Amnesty Act

Meanwhile, northerners were tiring of the same old issues, and the Panic of 1873, which threw 3 million people out of work, focused attention on economic and monetary problems. Businessmen were disturbed by the strikes and industrial violence that accompanied the panic; debtors and the unemployed sought easy-money policies to spur economic expansion. It was obvious to most political observers that the North was no longer willing to pursue the goals of Reconstruction. The results of a disputed presidential election confirmed this fact. Samuel J. Tilden, Democratic governor of New York, ran strongly in the South and took a commanding

Election of 1876

lead in both the popular vote and the electoral college over Rutherford B. Hayes, the Republican nominee. Tilden won 184 electoral votes and needed only one more for a majority. Nineteen votes from Louisiana, South Carolina, and Florida were disputed; both Democrats and Republicans claimed to have won in those states despite fraud on the part of their opponents. One vote from Oregon was undecided due to a technicality.

To resolve this unprecedented situation, on which the Constitution gave no guidance, Congress established a fifteen-member electoral commission. In the interest of impartiality, membership on the commission was to be balanced between Democrats and Republicans. But one independent Republican, Supreme Court Justice David Davis, refused appointment in order to accept his election as a senator. A regular Republican took his place, and the Republican party prevailed 8 to 7 on every decision, a strict party vote. Hayes would then become the winner if Congress accepted the commission's findings.

Congressional acceptance was not a certainty, and many Americans feared that the crisis might lead to another civil war. Democrats, however, acquiesced in the election of Hayes. Scholars have found that negotiations went on between some of Hayes's supporters and southerners who were interested in federal aid to railroads, internal improvements, federal patronage, and removal of troops from southern states. But the most recent studies suggest that these negotiations did not have a deciding effect on the outcome. Neither party was well enough organized to implement and enforce a bargain between the sections. Northern and southern Democrats decided they could not win and failed to contest the election. Thus Hayes became president, and southerners looked forward to the withdrawal of federal troops from the South. Reconstruction was unmistakably over.

Southern Democrats rejoiced, but black Americans grieved over the betrayal of their hopes for equality. After 1877 the hope for many southern blacks was "to go to a territory by ourselves." In South Carolina, Louisiana, Missis-

Black Exodusters

sippi, and other southern states, thousands gathered up their possessions and migrated to Kansas. They were known as Exodusters, disappointed people still searching for their share in the American dream.

Thus the nation ended over fifteen years of bloody civil war and controversial reconstruction without establishing full freedom for black Americans. Their status would continue to be one of the major issues facing the nation. As the nation turned away from the needs of black Americans, its people and government focused attention on the problems related to industrialism.

Suggestions for Further Reading

National Policy, Politics, and Constitutional Law

Richard H. Abbott, *The Republican Party and the South, 1855–1877* (1986); Herman Belz, *Emancipation and Equal Rights* (1978); Michael Les Benedict, *A Compromise of Principle* (1974); William S. McFeely, *Grant* (1981); Eric L. McKitrick, *Andrew Johnson and Reconstruction* (1966); James M. McPherson, *The Abolitionist Legacy* (1975); Kenneth M. Stampp, *Era of Reconstruction* (1965); Mark W. Summers, *Railroads, Reconstruction, and the Gospel of Prosperity* (1984).

The Freed Slaves

Roberta Sue Alexander, *North Carolina Faces the Freedmen* (1985); Edmund L. Drago, *Black Politicians and Reconstruction in Georgia* (1982); Paul D. Escott, *Slavery Remembered* (1979); Leon Litwack, *Been in the Storm So Long* (1979); Willie Lee Rose, *Rehearsal for Reconstruction* (1964); Clarence Walker, *A Rock in a Weary Land* (1982).

Politics and Reconstruction in the South

W. E. B. Du Bois, *Black Reconstruction* (1935); Paul D. Escott, *Many Excellent People* (1985); W. McKee Evans, *Ballots and Fence Rails* (1966); Eric Foner, *Nothing But Freedom* (1983); William C. Harris, *Day of the Carpetbagger* (1979); Michael Perman, *The Road to Redemption* (1984); Allen Trelease, *White Terror* (1967); Ted Tunnell, *Crucible of Reconstruction* (1984); Sarah Woolfolk Wiggins, *The Scalawag in Alabama Politics, 1865–1881* (1977).

Reconstruction's Legacy for the South

Robert G. Athearn, *In Search of Canaan* (1978); Jay R. Mandle, *The Roots of Black Poverty* (1978); Nell Irvin Painter, *Exodusters* (1976); Howard Rabinowitz, *Race Relations in the Urban South, 1865–1890* (1978); Roger L. Ransom and Richard Sutch, *One Kind of Freedom* (1977); C. Vann Woodward, *Origins of the New South* (1951).

CHAPTER 16

TRANSFORMATION OF THE WEST AND SOUTH 1877–1892

Though shaggy and dressed in buckskins, William F. "Buffalo Bill" Cody earned his nickname for his work, not his looks. Equipped with a powerful rifle, Cody had unequaled hunting skills. Buffalo Bill had such an illustrious reputation by the 1870s that the Kansas Pacific Railroad hired him to supply meat for the company's twelve hundred track layers. For $500 a month, Cody contracted to kill twelve buffalo a day, have them butchered, and deliver them for roasting the same night. In one eight-month stretch he killed over four thousand buffalo.

The millions of buffalo (bison) that roamed the American West helped to feed railroad workers, but they also were bothersome and dangerous. Foraging herds slowed construction, the bulky animals knocked over telegraph poles, and a stampede could derail a train. Railroad operators tried to remove the nuisance and raise money at the same time by sponsoring buffalo hunts for eastern sportsmen. These were hardly sporting events: rifle-toting men sat on slow-moving trains and shot away at the huge targets.

Some hunters collected the $1 to $3 offered by tanneries for hides, but others did not even stop to pick up their kill. As a result, by the 1880s only a few hundred remained of the estimated 13 million buffalo that had existed in the 1850s.

The destruction of the buffalo had a more important consequence than facilitating railroad construction: it undermined the culture of Plains Indians, who depended on the animals for almost every essential of life. For centuries natives had cooked and preserved buffalo meat; fashioned hides into clothing, shoes, and blankets; used sinew for thread and bowstrings; carved tools from bones; and made horns into implements. As buffalo became more scarce, the natives were forced to assume a different way of life, where they were more dependent on white traders and the government for their subsistence and where their hunting and territorial claims posed less of a threat to white ambitions for land and profit. Whites were fully aware of these consequences. As one army officer urged during the wars against Plains Indians,

"Kill every buffalo you can. Every buffalo dead is an Indian gone."

The buffalo were victims of expansion, and their fate, along with that of the Indians, exemplifies what happened when white Americans transformed the West and South in the late nineteenth century. Settlement of the West proceeded at a furious pace. Between 1870 and 1890 the population living between the Mississippi River and the Pacific Ocean swelled from 7 million to 17 million. By 1890 farms, ranches, mines, towns, and cities could be found in almost every region of what was to become the continental United States. That year, the superintendent of the census acknowledged that a frontier line of settlement no longer existed.

In popular American thought, the frontier—which has been defined as "the edge of the unused"—has represented the birthplace of American self-confidence and individualism. Taming the continent's vast wilderness and bringing forth foodstuffs and raw materials from it, not to mention building cities in a single generation, filled Americans with a consciousness of power and a belief that anyone eager and persistent enough could succeed. Yet that very self-confidence was easily transformed into an arrogant attitude that Americans were somehow special, and individualism often exerted itself at the expense of racial minorities and the propertyless.

Life in the newly won West was less romantic and comfortable than settlers might have anticipated. Hopeful settlers often had to contend with barren land where water, trees, and contacts with the outside world were scarce and the weather was fickle and often cruel. Moreover, farming expanded so rapidly that the impossible abruptly became a reality: productivity outstripped the nation's and the world's capacities to consume. As crop output and foreign competition increased in the 1880s, prices fell. Farmers' goals of wealth and comfort gave way to the necessity of producing more just to make ends meet. Thus the passing of the frontier and the accompanying agricultural transformation created social and economic problems that would plague the nation for several decades.

EXPLOITATION OF NATURAL RESOURCES

In the years just before the Civil War, eager prospectors began to comb remote forests and mountains looking for iron, coal, timber, oil, and copper. By 1900, active exploitation of the land's riches, once confined to the Northeast and Appalachian regions, had spread across the continent (see map).

The mining frontier advanced rapidly, drawing thousands of people to California, Nevada, Idaho, Montana, and Colorado in the 1850s and 1860s.

Mining and Lumbering

Prospectors tended to be restless optimists, willing to tramp mountains and deserts, searching icy streams for a telltale glint of precious metal. They shot game for food and financed their explorations by convincing merchants to advance credit for equipment in return for a share of the lode yet to be discovered. When their credit ran out, unlucky prospectors took jobs and saved up for another search for riches.

Extracting minerals from the ground involved high expenses for excavation and transportation. Thus individual prospectors who discovered veins of metal usually sold their claims to mining syndicates, lived it up off their new wealth, and then set off on another quest. The mining companies, often financed by eastern investors, had ample capital to bring in engineers, heavy machinery, railroad lines, and work crews. Although discoveries of gold and silver first drew attention to the West and its resources, such companies usually moved into the Rocky Mountain states to exploit less romantic but equally lucrative bonanzas of lead, zinc, tin, quartz, and copper.

Lumber production, unlike mineral extraction, required vast stretches of land. To obtain it, lumber companies exploited a piece of legislation meant to stimulate western settlement, the Timber and Stone Act (1878). This measure, which applied to land in

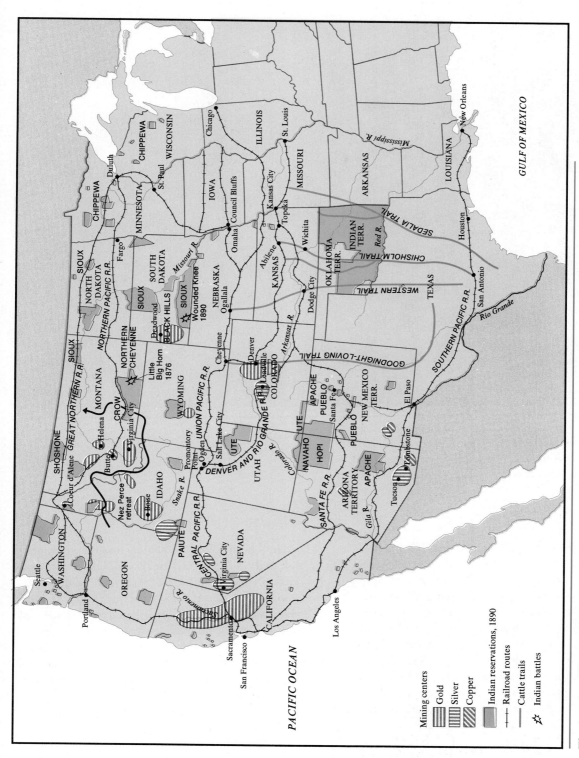

The American West, 1860–1890

Mining centers
- Gold
- Silver
- Copper

Indian reservations, 1890

+ Railroad routes

— Cattle trails

★ Indian battles

PACIFIC OCEAN

GULF OF MEXICO

WASHINGTON
Seattle
Portland
OREGON
IDAHO
MONTANA
Helena
Butte
Coeur d'Alene
Nez Perce retreat
Boise
SHOSHONE
CROW
Virginia City
NORTHERN CHEYENNE
Little Big Horn 1876
BLACK HILLS
Deadwood
NORTH DAKOTA
SIOUX
SOUTH DAKOTA
SIOUX
Wounded Knee 1890
Fargo
NORTHERN PACIFIC R.R.
GREAT NORTHERN R.R.
MINNESOTA
Duluth
St. Paul
CHIPPEWA
WISCONSIN
Chicago
ILLINOIS
St. Louis
MISSOURI
IOWA
Council Bluffs
Omaha
NEBRASKA
Ogallala
Cheyenne
WYOMING
UNION PACIFIC R.R.
Promontory Point
Ogden
Salt Lake City
UTE
UTAH
CENTRAL PACIFIC R.R.
Virginia City
NEVADA
CALIFORNIA
Sacramento
San Francisco
Los Angeles
SANTA FE R.R.
ARIZONA TERRITORY
Tucson
APACHE
Tombstone
NAVAHO
HOPI
PUEBLO
APACHE
NEW MEXICO TERR.
Santa Fe
PUEBLO
El Paso
SOUTHERN PACIFIC R.R.
San Antonio
Rio Grande
TEXAS
Houston
New Orleans
LOUISIANA
ARKANSAS
Mississippi R.
Red R.
INDIAN TERR.
OKLAHOMA TERR.
SEDALIA TRAIL
CHISHOLM TRAIL
WESTERN TRAIL
GOODNIGHT-LOVING TRAIL
Abilene
Wichita
Topeka
Kansas City
KANSAS
Dodge City
Arkansas R.
Denver
Leadville
COLORADO
DENVER AND RIO GRANDE R.R.
Colorado R.
Gila R.
Snake R.
Sacramento R.
Missouri R.
SIOUX
CHIPPEWA
PAIUTE

Two women stand on a hill overlooking Helena, Montana, a typical mining town of the 1870s. In spite of their small numbers, women exerted a settling influence on frontier towns. Montana Historical Society, Helena.

California, Nevada, Oregon, and Washington, allowed private citizens to buy at the low price of $2.50 per acre 160-acre plots "unfit for cultivation" and "valuable chiefly for timber." Taking advantage of the act, lumber companies hired seamen from waterfront boardinghouses to register claims to timberland and turn them over to the companies. By 1900, claimants had bought over 3.5 million acres under Timber and Stone Act provisions, and most of that land belonged to corporations.

While lumbermen were acquiring claims to timberlands in the Northwest, oilmen were beginning to sink wells in the Southwest. In 1900 most of the nation's petroleum still came from fields in the Appalachians and the Midwest, but promising developments were under way in southern California and eastern Texas. The most spectacular strike occurred in 1901 at Spindletop, Texas, where a well shot a stream of oil 160 feet into the air. Although most oil and kerosene were still used for lubrication and lighting, discoveries in the Southwest were to become a vital new source of fuel in the twentieth century.

Much of the natural-resource frontier was a man's world. In 1880, men outnumbered women by more than two to one in Colorado, Nevada, and Arizona,

Frontier Society

yet many western communities had substantial numbers of women. Most women who went to the mining frontier did so for the same reasons men went: to find a fortune. They usually accompanied a husband or father and seldom prospected themselves. Even so, many women realized their own opportunities in the towns, where they provided cooking, laundering, and, in some cases, sexual services for the miners. Some became the family's main breadwinners when their husbands failed to strike it rich. For the most part, women's presence had a settling influence on mining communities. While they pursued new opportunities and freedoms, women also helped to bolster family life and to combat raw materialism and vice by campaigning against drinking, gambling, and whoring.

Many of the mining and lumbering communities were genuinely heterogeneous, containing small numbers of Chinese, Mexicans, Indians, and blacks. Though most Chinese migrated to work on American railroads, some were employed in the camps to do cooking and cleaning. A few blacks also held such jobs. Mexicans and Indians often had been the original settlers of land coveted by whites. Each of these minority groups met with white prejudice, especially when it became evident that the forests and mines would not make everyone rich. California imposed a tax on foreign miners and denied blacks, Indians, and Chinese the right to testify or submit evidence in court. Throughout the West any claims Indians or Mexicans might have had to land sought by white miners were ignored or stolen. Blacks and Chinese who worked in mining camps often suffered abuse and violence. Nonwhites defended themselves as best they could against intimidation, but their most common tactic was to pack up and seek jobs and homes in another town or mining camp.

Inevitably, developers of natural resources were more interested in what the land yielded than in the land itself. To avoid purchase costs, developers used several ploys, some legal and some not. One method was to purchase or rent limited rights to extract resources. Lumbermen would buy permits to fell a cer-

Use of Public Lands

tain number of trees on a given forest tract and share the profits with the landowner. Oilmen and iron miners often leased property from private owners or the government and paid royalties on the minerals extracted. Other practices were corrupt or fraudulent. Some lumbermen simply cut trees on public lands without paying a cent. Even when Congress and the U.S. Land Office tried to prevent fraud by passing tighter legislation and sending out more investigators, many communities resisted in the fear that such crackdowns would slow local economic growth.

Development of new areas brought western territories to the threshold of statehood. In 1889 Republicans seeking to solidify their control of Congress

Admission of New States

pushed through the Omnibus Bill, granting statehood to North Dakota, South Dakota, Washington, and Montana. Wyoming and Idaho were admitted in 1890. Congress denied statehood to Utah until 1896, when the Mormon majority agreed to abandon polygamy.

The mining towns and lumber camps in these states spiced American folk culture and fostered the go-getter optimism that distinguished the American spirit. The lawlessness and hedonism of places like Deadwood, in Dakota Territory, and Tombstone, in Arizona Territory, gave the West notoriety and romance. Characters like Wild Bill Hickok, Poker Alice, and Bedrock Tom became western folk heroes, and fiction writers like Mark Twain and Bret Harte captured for posterity some of the flavor of mining life. But violence and notoriety were far from common. Most miners and lumbermen worked seventy hours a week and had neither time nor money for drinking and gambling, let alone gunfights. Women worked as long or longer as teachers, cooks, laundresses, storekeepers, and housewives; only a very few were gunslingers or dance-hall queens. For most westerners, life was a matter of adapting and surviving.

THE AGE OF RAILROAD EXPANSION

Discovery and development of natural riches provided the base on which the nation's economy expanded. But raw wealth in itself had limited value. In the half-century following the Civil War, the nation's railroads carried these raw materials to the factories, marketplaces, and ports. Indeed, the American economy was refashioned as a web of track spread across the country. This expansion helped to boost the nation's steel industry and spawned a number of other related activities, including coal production, passenger and freight-car manufacture, and depot construction. By the turn of the century, the country's railroad network was virtually complete. Henceforth the goods and raw materials of one section would be available in all other sections of the country.

Railroads both altered American conceptions of time and space and spurred a movement toward standardization. First, by overcoming barriers of distance, railroads transformed space into time. It became easier to measure the separation between places by the amount of time it took to travel from one to the other rather than by the physical distance. Second, railroad scheduling necessitated nationwide agreement on time. Before railroads, each locale had its own time. Community church bells and steeple clocks struck at noon, when the sun was overhead, and people set their own clocks and watches accordingly. But the sun was not overhead at exactly the same moment, so there were variations in time from place to place. To achieve some regularity, railroads set their own time zones, but by 1880 there still were nearly fifty different standards. Finally in 1883 railroads agreed—without consulting Congress, the president, or the courts—to establish four standard time zones for the whole country. Most communities now adjusted their clocks, and railroad time became national time.

Effects of Railroad Construction

Third, railroad construction brought about technological and organizational reforms. By the late 1880s, almost all lines had adopted standard narrow-gauge rails so that their tracks could connect with one another. Such devices as the Westinghouse air brake, an automatic car coupler, and standardized handholds on freight cars made rail transportation safer and more efficient. Organizational advances included systems for coordinating complex passenger and freight schedules and the adoption of uniform freight-classification systems.

Railroads accomplished these feats with the help of some of the largest government subsidies in American history. Railroad executives argued that their activities were benefiting the public interest and that the government should aid them by giving them land from the public domain. Sympathetic governments at the national, state, and local levels responded by providing railroad companies with massive subsidies. Indeed, the federal government gave the railroads over 180 million acres of land. In an age dominated by the doctrine of laissez faire—the belief that government should not interfere in commerce—capitalists argued against government interference in one breath and accepted government aid in the next. Yet without government help, few railroads could have established themselves sufficiently to attract private investment.

Government Subsidy of Railroads

As the nation's rail network expanded, so did competition and duplication. Multiple lines serving individual cities allowed shippers several routes from which to choose. In their quest for new customers, local lines as well as trunk lines cut rates to attract more traffic and outmaneuver competitors. But rate wars soon cut into profits, and wild vacillations in rates angered shippers and farmers. Some kind of stability was clearly desirable.

Competition and Discriminatory Rate Setting

Ironically, while railroad rates generally were falling, complaints about excessively high rates were increasing. Railroads often boosted rates as high as possible on noncompetitive routes in order to compensate for unprofitably low rates on competitive long-distance routes. Thus pricing was not proportionate to distance: rates on short-distance hauls served by only one line could be far higher than those on long-distance hauls served by competing lines.

Railroads also devised other forms of discrimination, such as special contracts with large shippers and free passenger passes for important shippers and politicians. To reduce competition, several railroads made agreements among themselves called *pools,* whose participants shared traffic and earnings and set common rates. Such agreements generally discriminated against small shippers.

These practices upset farmers, retailers, bankers, reform politicians, and even some stockholders. During the 1870s, many of these groups demanded that

Government Regulation of Railroads

government regulate railroads, especially their pricing practices. By 1880, fourteen states had established commissions or other agencies to limit freight and storage rates charged by state-chartered lines. Railroads bitterly fought these laws, but in 1877 the Supreme Court upheld the principle of government regulation of private property in the public interest in *Munn* v. *Illinois.*

Although the principle of regulation had won acceptance, critics charged that state regulatory commissions were either too weak or too subservient to railroads. Moreover, state commissioners had little control over interstate lines and thus could not affect the largest, most powerful railroads. The Supreme Court affirmed this limitation in 1886 by declaring in the *Wabash* case that only Congress and not the states could regulate rates on interstate commerce. Consequently, reformers called for federal regulation.

Congress responded in 1887 by passing the Interstate Commerce Act. The act prohibited pools, rebates, and long-haul–short-haul rate discriminations; and one of its clauses directed that "all charges . . . shall be reasonable and fair." The law also created the Interstate Commerce Commission (ICC) and gave it power to investigate railroads; to issue "cease-and-desist" orders against illegal practices; and to seek court assistance to enforce compliance with the law. But the provisions for enforcement were blurry and left railroads much room for evasion. Moreover, federal judges chipped away at ICC powers. In the *Maximum Freight Rate* case (1897), the Supreme Court ruled that the act did not grant the ICC power to set rates, and in the *Alabama Midlands* case the same year, the Court shattered prohibitions against long-haul–short-haul discriminations.

In spite of such setbacks, the era of railroad reform opened new paths for future generations. The right of the federal government to regulate railroads as a public enterprise did gain court support. Regulation at the state level continued, especially with regard to safety and intrastate rates. Finally, establishment of the ICC gave impetus to the movement to eliminate favoritism in society and the economy.

NATIVE AMERICANS: CASUALTIES OF EXPANSION

Railroad expansion made the vast domain between the Missouri and the Pacific more accessible to settlement. But much of this land was not empty. It was the home of thousands of Native American tribespeople, whose ways of life differed profoundly from those of most white people and whose presence represented a stubborn barrier to whites' exploitation of the land.

As in previous eras, the contact between white and native culture elicited a variety of responses from the Indians. Some tried to adapt to white invaders, by trading with them—usually offering hides in exchange for livestock and guns—and by accepting white alliances as a means of gaining an advantage over rival tribes. Others actively resisted white intru-

A Sioux camp in South Dakota, 1891. The Sioux led a no-madic life, living in harmony with the natural environment; when they packed up and moved on, they left the landscape almost undisturbed. This photograph shows the temporary situation characteristic of their camps. Library of Congress.

sion, using guerrilla tactics to harass settlers, herders, and troops. Still others alternated between alliance and enmity, depending on their leadership, material needs, and relations with other tribes. In the end, however, though they struggled to retain their cul-ture, Indians faced insurmountable odds and an over-whelming migratory invasion.

Although there was great variety of cultures, most native tribes in the West fit into one of two cultural groups. Some were nomadic or seminomadic, subsist-ing on food that they hunted or gathered. These tribes included the Shoshone in the Northwest, the Apache in the Southwest, and the Cheyenne, Da-kota, and Crow in the Plains. Others were more set-tled, depending on farming and gardening. These in-cluded the Zuni, Hopi, and Navajo tribes in the Southwest, plus Pawnee, Mandan, and Hidatsa tribes in the Plains. Tribal organization often was loose, with leadership only vaguely defined, but almost all Indians had highly formalized cultural systems and religions that regarded their relationship with nature as sacred.

Western Indians observed sexual divisions of labor, but their social organization differed greatly from that of white Americans. Generally, men took responsibility for hunting, fishing, and war, and they almost always held the most powerful positions—chief, priest, shaman (medicine man). Women raised children and crops. Often, however, the female side of kinship groups was more influential than the male side, and women had important roles in political, economic, religious, and social affairs. Navajo women controlled most of their families' property, and Apache and Teton Dakota women directed their tribes' most important religious ceremony, the girls' puberty rite.

When white Americans first extensively encountered western Indians in the mid-nineteenth century, they considered Indians as separate peoples with whom they could make treaties. As white settlers began pressing into native territories, the government made treaties with various tribes, ensuring peace and nominally defining boundaries of white and native lands. But the treaties seldom promised the Indians any future land rights; rather, whites assumed that eventually they could settle wherever they wished. Treaties made one week were violated the next, as more settlers streamed into the West.

Between 1850 and 1877, two factors on the Great Plains accelerated the policy of concentrating Indians on reservations: military conquest and destruction of buffalo herds. Native defense of their homelands against white settlers resulted in a series of bloody battles and massacres. The most legendary battle occurred on June 25, 1876, when 2,500 Sioux, led by Chiefs Rain-in-the-Face, Sitting Bull, and Crazy Horse, annihilated white troops led by the rash Colonel George A. Custer near the Little Big Horn River in southern Montana. Though there were other Indian victories as well, shortage of supplies and relentless pursuit by white troops eventually overwhelmed armed Indian resistance and forced the Native Americans onto reservations. At the same time, extermination of the buffalo, which had been so vital to native cultures, was even more decisive than government policy in forcing Indians to change their way of life.

Reservation policy had troublesome consequences. In assigning Indians to specific territory, the United States government promised protection from white encroachment and agreed to provide food, clothing, and other necessities, in effect making Indians dependent on the government. As more reservations were created, it became evident that isolation was impossible. White farmers, miners, and herders continually sought even remote Indian lands. Moreover, Indians continued to be restive. During the 1880s violence between whites and Indians broke out on Apache, Sioux, and other reservations. As a result, whites became more intent on "civilizing" the Native Americans—making them accept whites' values, breaking up their tribal organization, and integrating them into the nation. At the same time, humanitarian concern was heightened by Helen Hunt Jackson's popular book *A Century of Dishonor* (1881), which castigated the government for its unfair treatment of Indians.

In 1887 Congress reversed its reservation policy in the Dawes Severalty Act, which dissolved community-owned tribal lands and granted land allotments to individual families. To prevent Indians from selling these plots to speculators, the government retained ownership of the land for twenty-five years. The act also granted citizenship to all who accepted allotments and authorized the government to sell unallotted land and to set aside the proceeds for the education of Indians.

Dawes Severalty Act

As a result of the Dawes Act, U.S. Indian policy took on three main features. First and foremost, government officials advocated allotting land to individual families because they believed Indians would become civilized by learning how to manage their own property. Ownership would make them more responsible and industrious. Second, bureau officials believed Indians would lose their "barbaric" habits more quickly if their children could be removed and educated in boarding schools away from the old reservations. Third, the bureau tried to suppress traditional religious ceremonies, such as the Sun Dance, and funded white church groups to establish religious schools among the Indians and teach them to become good Christians.

Much of the new Indian policy was ineffective. In the face of efforts by whites to acquire land titles from Indians who were to receive individual plots, the government simply abandoned the program of land allotment. The boarding school program did affect thousands of children, but rarely did they forsake their culture; most returned to their reservations rather than submit to assimilation into white society. Efforts to suppress native religious observances only forced them under cover. And whites did not give up their fears and use of violence. Late in 1890, the Seventh Cavalry massacred two hundred sick and hungry Sioux at a creek in South Dakota called Wounded Knee. Although Native Americans retained some of their culture, the West was won at their expense.

THE RANCHING FRONTIER

Railroad construction and Indian removal set the stage for one of the West's most colorful and romantic industries, cattle ranching. Early in the nineteenth century, huge herds of cattle, originally introduced by the Spanish and developed by Mexican ranchers, roamed southern Texas and bred with cattle brought by American settlers. The resulting longhorn breed multiplied and became valuable by the 1860s, when the East's growing population increased demand for food and railroads made transportation of beef more feasible. By 1870 drovers were herding thousands of Texas cattle northward to railroad connections in Kansas, Missouri, and Wyoming. On these long drives, mounted cowboys (as many as 25

percent of whom were black) supervised the herds, which fed on open grassland along the way.

The long drive gave rise to its own romantic lore, but it was not very efficient. In trekking 1,500 miles, the cattle became sinewy and tough. Herds traveling through Indian lands and farmers' fields were sometimes shot at and later prohibited from such trespass by state laws. The ranchers' only solution was to eliminate long drives by raising herds nearer to railroad routes.

Cattle raisers were like timber cutters: they needed vast stretches of land where their herds could graze and they wanted to incur as little expense as possible to use such land. Thus they

Open-range Ranching

often bought a few acres bordering streams and turned their herds loose on adjacent public domain, which no one would want to own because it lacked water access. By this method, called open-range ranching, a cattle raiser could control thousands of acres by owning only a hundred or so.

By the 1880s the era of the open-range was nearing its end. Ranchers, largely in response to the problem of overgrazing, began to fence in their pastures with barbed wire—even though they had no legal title to the land. Fences destroyed the open range and often provoked disputes between competing ranchers, between cattle raisers and sheep raisers, and between ranchers and farmers who claimed use of the same land. In 1885, President Cleveland ordered removal of illegal fences on public lands and Indian reservations. Although enforcement was slow, the order signaled that free use of public domain was ending.

Open-range ranching made beef a staple of the American diet and created a few fortunes, but its extralegal features could not survive the rush of history. By 1890, well-organized businesses were taking over the cattle industry and applying scientific methods of breeding and feeding. The cowboy became just another corporate wage earner, though the myth of his freedom and individualism grew rather than faded. Most cattle ranchers now owned or leased the land they used, although some illegal fencing of public domain continued.

A family poses in front of their Kansas prairie home. The background shows the flat, treeless environment of the rural frontier. Western History Collection, University of Oklahoma Libraries.

Meanwhile, two new groups were contending with cattle ranchers for supremacy on the Plains. From California and New Mexico, sheepherders moved into land east of the Rockies. More importantly, farmers moved into the West.

FARMING THE PLAINS

Settlement of the Plains and the West involved the greatest migration in American history. Most, though not all, migrants came from the eastern states or Europe. They were lured by offers of cheap land and credit from states and railroads eager to promote settlement. Between 1870 and 1910 the nation's population rose from 40 million to 92 million, and the total urban population swelled by over 400 percent. As a result, demand for farm products grew rapidly. Meanwhile, scientific advances were enabling farmers to use the soil more efficiently. Agricultural experts developed the technique of dry farming, a system of plowing and harrowing that prevented precious moisture from evaporating. Scientists perfected varieties of "hard" wheat whose seeds could withstand northern winters, and millers invented an efficient process for grinding these tougher new wheat kernels into flour. Railroad expansion made remote farming regions more acces-

Migration to the Plains

sible, and grain-elevator construction eased problems of shipping and storage.

Still, life on the Plains was hard. Migrants often encountered scarcities of essentials they had taken for granted back home. Vast stretches of land contained little lumber for housing and fuel.

Hardships of Life on the Plains Pioneer families were forced to build houses of sod and to burn manure for heat. Water was as scarce as timber. Few families were lucky or wealthy enough to buy land near a stream that did not dry up in summer and freeze in winter.

Even more formidable than the terrain of the Plains was its climate. The expanse between the Missouri River and the Rocky Mountains divides climatologically along a line running from Minnesota southwest through Oklahoma, then south through Texas (see map). East of this line, annual rainfall averages about 28 inches, enough for most crops. West of the line, life-giving rain was never certain.

Weather seldom followed predictable cycles on either side of the line. In summer, weeks of torrid heat and parching winds would suddenly give way to violent storms that washed away crops and property. Winter blizzards piled up mountainous snowdrifts that halted all outdoor movement. In March and April, melting snow swelled streams, and flood waters threatened millions of acres. In the fall, a week without rain could turn dry grasslands into tinder, and the slightest spark could ignite a raging prairie fire.

Even when the climate was more moderate, nature could turn vengeful. Weather that was good for crops was also good for insect breeding. Worms and flying pests ravaged corn and wheat. In the 1870s and 1880s grasshopper plagues virtually ate up entire farms. Heralded only by the rising din of buzzing wings, a cloud of insects a mile long would smother the land and devour everything in sight: plants, seeds, tree bark, and clothes. As one farmer lamented, the "hoppers left behind nothing but the mortgage."

Settlers of the Plains also had to contend with social isolation, a factor accentuated by the pattern of settlement. Under the Homestead Act of 1862, for

Social Isolation example, settlers received rectangular-shaped tracts of 160 acres. At most four families could live near each other, but only if they congregated around the same four-corner boundary intersection. In practice, farmers usually lived back from their boundary lines, and at least a half-mile separated farmhouses.

Many observers wrote about the loneliness and monotony of life on the Plains. Men escaped the oppressiveness by working outdoors and taking occasional trips to sell crops or buy supplies. But women were more isolated, confined by domestic chores to the household, where, as one writer remarked, they were "not much better than slaves. It is a weary, monotonous round of cooking and washing and mending and as a result the insane asylum is ⅓d filled with wives of farmers."

Most farm families survived by depending on their inner resolve and by organizing churches and clubs where they could socialize a few times a month. And by the early 1900s, two external de-

Mail-Order Companies and Rural Free Delivery velopments had combined to bring rural settlers into closer contact with modern life. First, starting in the 1870s and 1880s, mail-order houses—Montgomery Ward and Sears, Roebuck—expanded and made products of the industrial society available to almost everyone. Second, during the 1890s, scores of rural communities petitioned Congress for extension of the postal service, and in 1896 the government made Rural Free Delivery (RFD) widely available. Now farmers no longer lacked news and information; they could receive letters, newspapers, advertisements, and catalogues at home nearly every day.

In the years following the Civil War an agricultural revolution was made possible by the expanded use of machinery. When the Civil War drew men away from farms in the upper Mississippi River

Mechanization of Agriculture valley, the women and male laborers who remained behind began using reapers and other implements more extensively to meet demand for grain and to

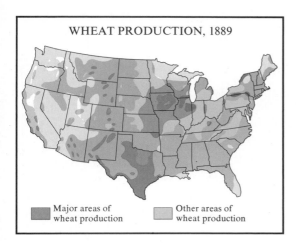

WHEAT PRODUCTION, 1889

■ Major areas of wheat production   ▨ Other areas of wheat production

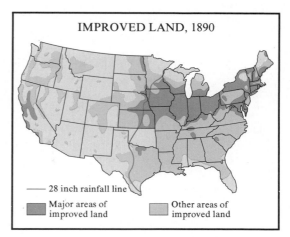

IMPROVED LAND, 1890

— 28 inch rainfall line
■ Major areas of improved land   ▨ Other areas of improved land

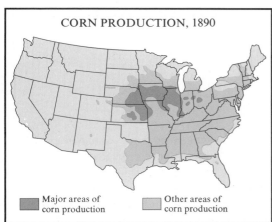

CORN PRODUCTION, 1890

■ Major areas of corn production   ▨ Other areas of corn production

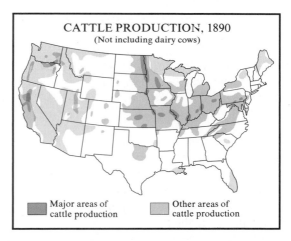

CATTLE PRODUCTION, 1890
(Not including dairy cows)

■ Major areas of cattle production   ▨ Other areas of cattle production

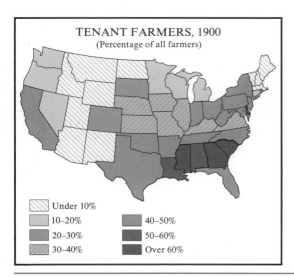

TENANT FARMERS, 1900
(Percentage of all farmers)

▨ Under 10%
▨ 10–20%
▨ 20–30%
▨ 30–40%
▨ 40–50%
▨ 50–60%
▨ Over 60%

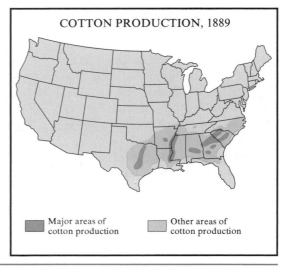

COTTON PRODUCTION, 1889

■ Major areas of cotton production   ▨ Other areas of cotton production

Agricultural Regions, 1889 and 1900   Source:
Charles O. Paullin, *Atlas of the Historical Geography of the United States.*

TIME AND COST OF FARMING AN ACRE OF LAND
BY HAND AND BY MACHINE, 1890

Crop	Hours Required		Labor Cost	
	Hand	Machine	Hand	Machine
Wheat	61	3	$3.65	$ .66
Corn	39	15	$3.62	$1.51
Oats	66	7	$3.73	$1.07
Loose hay	21	4	$1.75	$ .42

Source: Reprinted with permission of Macmillan Publishing Company from *Westward Expansion: A History of the American Frontier,* 2nd ed., by Ray Allan Billington and Martin Ridge, p. 697. © Copyright Macmillan Publishing Company 1960.

take advantage of high prices. After the war, continued demand and high prices encouraged farmers to depend more on machines, and inventors perfected better implements for farm use. Machines dramatically reduced the time and cost of farming a single acre of various crops (see table).

At the same time, Congress and scientists were making efforts to improve existing crops and develop new ones. The 1862 Morrill Land Grant Act gave each state public lands to sell in order to finance agricultural and industrial colleges. And the Hatch Act of 1887 provided for agricultural experiment stations in every state, further encouraging the advancement of farming technology.

Legislative and Scientific Aid to Farmers

Farming received a great boost from science in the late nineteenth century. Californian Luther Burbank developed a wide range of new plants by crossbreeding. And Tuskegee Institute's chemist George Washington Carver created hundreds of new products from peanuts, soybeans, sweet potatoes, and cotton wastes and taught methods of soil improvement. Scientists also developed means of combating plant and animal diseases. Though turbulent times for farmers lay just ahead, development of the agricultural hinterland by settlement, science, and technology made America "the garden of the world."

THE SOUTH AFTER RECONSTRUCTION

In 1880 four times as many farmers lived in the South as on the Plains. Ravaged by a civil war, southern agriculture recovered slowly. High prices for seed and implements, declining prices for crops, taxes, and, most of all, debt trapped many families in perpetual poverty. Attempts to industrialize the South were only marginally successful. Whether interested in an industrialized New South or in agriculture, southerners were generally dependent upon northern money.

During and after Reconstruction, a significant shift in the nature of agricultural labor swept the South. Between 1860 and 1880, the total number of farms in southern states more than doubled, from 450,000 to 1.1 million. But the number of landowners did not increase, and the size of the average farm decreased from 347 to 156 acres. Southern agriculture was now dominated by sharecropping and tenant farming. Over one-third of the farmers counted in 1880 were sharecroppers and tenants, and the proportion increased to two-thirds by 1920.

This system entangled millions of southerners in a web of humiliation. At its center was the crop lien, which worked in the following way. Currency was

Crop-Lien System

scarce, and most farmers were too poor ever to have cash on hand. Forced to borrow in order to buy necessities, they could offer as collateral only what they could grow. Thus a farmer in need of supplies would deal with a nearby "furnishing merchant," who would exchange supplies for a certain portion, or lien, of the farmer's forthcoming crop. The prices charged to credit customers averaged 30 to 40 percent higher than those charged to cash customers. Credit customers also had to pay interest of 33 to 200 percent on the advances they received. After the crop was harvested, farmers frequently found that they lacked sufficient funds to pay the full debt owed to the merchant. Their only choice was to commit the next year's crop and sink deeper into debt.

The lien system caused serious hardship in former plantation areas where black and white tenants and sharecroppers grew cotton for the same markets that had existed before the Civil War. But in the southern backcountry, which in the antebellum era had con-

tained small farms, relatively few slaves, and diversified agriculture, the problems of crop liens were compounded by other economic changes.

New spending habits of backcountry farmers reflected the most important of these changes. In 1884, for example, Jephta Dickson of Jackson County, Georgia, bought $53.37 worth of flour, meal, peas, meat, corn, and syrup from one merchant and $2.53 worth of potatoes, peas, and sugar from another. Such expenditures would have been rare in the upcountry before the Civil War, when most farmers grew almost all the supplies they needed. But after the war yeomen farmers like Dickson shifted from semisubsistence agriculture to more commercialized farming—in the South that meant cotton-raising—because debts incurred during the war and Reconstruction forced them to grow a crop that would bring in more cash and because railroad expansion enabled them to transport cotton to markets more easily than before. As backcountry yeomen put more acres under cotton cultivation, they raised less of what they needed and were forced more frequently into positions where they were at the mercy of merchants.

Poor whites of the rural South also faced a political threat from newly enfranchised blacks. Wealthy white landowners and merchants would not bend to protests over economic distress, but they did agree with poor farmers on the issue of white supremacy and used their power to reinforce the racial order.

The majority of the nation's black people lived in the South and worked in agriculture, where they found that conditions under freedom left them with

Condition of Blacks

the same disadvantages they had borne under slavery. In 1880 some 90 percent of all southern blacks depended for a living on farming or personal and domestic service—the same occupations they had had as slaves.

Pushed into sharecropping and burdened with crop liens, blacks also had to contend with new forms of social and political oppression. With slavery dead, white supremacists had to fashion new means of keeping blacks in a position of inferiority. Southern lead-

In the post-Reconstruction South, black sharecroppers such as these fared little better than under slavery. Tied to crop liens that kept them in perpetual debt, they lived in tiny shacks and struggled against white discrimination.   Brown Brothers.

ers, embittered by northern interference in race relations during Reconstruction and anxious to reassert their authority after the withdrawal of federal troops, instituted racist measures to discourage blacks from voting and legally segregate them from whites.

The overthrow of Reconstruction had not stopped blacks from voting. Although threats and intimidation against them increased, blacks still formed the backbone of the Republican party in the South, and some still won elective offices. White politicians, however, began more actively to seek ways of reducing the so-called Negro vote. Beginning with Georgia in 1877, southern states levied taxes of $1 to $2 on all citizens wishing to vote. Though seemingly trivial, these poll taxes were prohibitive to most black voters,

many of whom were so deeply in debt to furnishing merchants and landlords that they never had cash for any purpose. Other schemes disfranchised black voters who could not read. For example, voters might be required to deposit ballots for different candidates in different ballot boxes. In order to do so correctly, voters had to be able to read instructions; otherwise, their votes were invalidated.

Racial discrimination also stiffened in social affairs. A widespread informal system of separation had governed race relations in the antebellum South. After the Civil War, this system was codified in law. In a series of cases during the 1870s, the Supreme Court opened the door to discrimination by ruling that the Fourteenth Amendment protected citizens' rights only against infringement by state governments. If blacks wanted protection under the law, the Court said, they must seek it from the states. The climax to these rulings came in 1883, when in the *Civil Rights Cases* the Court struck down the 1875 Civil Rights Act, which had prohibited segregation in public facilities such as streetcars, hotels, theaters, and parks. Subsequent lower-court cases in the 1880s established the principle that blacks could be restricted to "separate-but-equal" facilities. The Supreme Court upheld the separate-but-equal doctrine in *Plessy v. Ferguson* (1896) and officially applied it to schools in *Cummins v. County Board of Education* (1899).

Spread of Jim Crow Laws

Thereafter, segregation laws—known as Jim Crow laws—spread rapidly. Discriminatory legislation piled up throughout the South, confronting black people with countless daily reminders of their inferior status. State laws and local ordinances restricted blacks to the rear of streetcars, to separate drinking and toilet facilities, and to separate sections of hospitals, asylums, and cemeteries. Segregation reached such extremes that Atlanta required separate Bibles for black witnesses swearing before court.

In industry, breezes of change were being stimulated by new manufacturing initiatives, but there too a distinctively southern quality prevailed. Two of the South's leading industries in the late nineteenth century relied on the traditional staple crops, cotton and tobacco. In the 1870s, textile mills began to sprout up in the Cotton Belt states. Powered by the region's abundant rivers and streams, manned cheaply by poor whites eager to escape crop liens, and fostered by low taxes, such mills grew rapidly. By 1900 the South had four hundred mills with a total of over 4 million spindles, and twenty years later the region was replacing New England in textile manufacturing supremacy. Proximity to raw materials and cheap labor also aided the tobacco industry, and the invention in 1880 of a cigarette-making machine immensely enhanced the marketability of tobacco.

Industrialization of the South

Cigarettes were manufactured in cities by black and white workers; textile mills were concentrated in small towns and developed their own exploitive labor system. Financed mostly by local investors, mills employed women and children from nearby poor white families and paid them 50 cents a day for twelve or more hours of work. Many companies built squalid villages around their mills and controlled all housing, stores, schools, and churches. Criticism of the company was forbidden, and attempts at union organization were squelched. Mill families soon found that the company store simply replaced the furnishing merchant, and the mill owner replaced the landlord.

Northern and European capitalists sponsored other southern industries. In the Gulf states the lumber in-

IMPORTANT EVENTS

1862	Homestead Act Morrill Land Grant Act
1865–67	War with western Sioux
1876	Custer's Last Stand
1878	Timber and Stone Act
1881	Helen Hunt Jackson, *A Century of Dishonor*
1883	*Civil Rights Cases* Standardization of national time zones
1887	Dawes Severalty Act Interstate Commerce Act Hatch Act
1896	*Plessy v. Ferguson*
1899	*Cummins v. County Board of Education*

dustry became highly significant, and iron and steel production made Birmingham a boom city. Yet in 1900 the South remained as rural as it had been in 1860. The emergence of a New South would have to wait another era.

SUGGESTIONS FOR FURTHER READING

The Western Frontier

Ray A. Billington, *Westward Expansion* (1967); William H. Goetzmann, *Exploration and Empire* (1966); Robert V. Hine, *The American West* (1973); Julie Roy Jeffrey, *Frontier Women* (1979); Frederick Merk, *History of the Westward Movement* (1978); Rodman W. Paul, *The Frontier and the American West* (1971); Henry Nash Smith, *Virgin Land: The American West as Symbol and Myth* (1950); Roberta B. Sollid, *Calamity Jane* (1958); L. Steckmesser, *The Western Hero in History and Legend* (1965).

Railroads

Alfred D. Chandler, ed., *Railroads: The Nation's First Big Business* (1965); Robert W. Fogel, *Railroads and Economic Growth* (1964); Ari Hoogenboom and Olive Hoogenboom, *A History of the ICC* (1970); Gabriel Kolko, *Railroads and Regulation* (1965); Alan Trachtenberg, *The Incorporation of America* (1982); O. O. Winther, *The Transportation Frontier* (1964).

Indians and Ranching

Ralph K. Andrist, *The Long Death: The Last Days of the Plains Indians* (1964); Lewis Atherton, *The Cattle Kings* (1961); Norris Hundley, Jr., ed., *The American Indian* (1974); Francis Paul Prucha, *American Indian Policy in Crisis* (1976); Robert F. Spencer et al., *The Native Americans* (1965); Edward H. Spicer, *Cycles of Conquest: The Impact of Spain, Mexico, and the United States on the Indians of the Southwest* (1962); Robert M. Utley, *The Indian Frontier of the American West, 1846–1890* (1984); Wilcomb E. Washburn, *Red Man's Land/White Man's Law* (1971).

Settlement of the Plains

Allan G. Bogue, *From Prairie to Corn Belt* (1963); Everett Dick, *The Sod-House Frontier* (1937); Gilbert C. Fite, *The Farmer's Frontier* (1966); Fred A. Shannon, *The Farmer's Last Frontier* (1963); Walter Prescott Webb, *The Great Plains* (1931).

The New South

Orville Vernon Burton and Robert C. McMath, Jr., eds., *Toward a New South?: Post–Civil War Southern Communities* (1982); Thomas D. Clark and Albert D. Kirwan, *The South Since Appomattox* (1967); Dewey Grantham, Jr., *The Democratic South* (1963); Steven Hahn, *The Roots of Southern Populism: Yeoman Farmers and the Transformation of the Georgia Upcountry, 1850–1890* (1983); J. Morgan Kousser, *The Shaping of Southern Politics* (1974); Howard N. Rabinowitz, *Race Relations in the Urban South, 1865–1890* (1978); Theodore Saloutos, *Farmer Movements in the South, 1865–1933* (1960); C. Vann Woodward, *The Strange Career of Jim Crow* (1966); C. Van Woodward, *Origins of the New South* (1951).

CHAPTER 17

THE MACHINE AGE

1877–1920

Conrad Carl tried to appear calm, but he was understandably nervous. It was spring 1882, and Carl, who for nearly thirty years had been a tailor in New York City, was appearing before a group of U.S. senators to explain changing work conditions in the tailoring business.

Admitting that his testimony would probably cost him his job, Carl nevertheless answered candidly. When he first began tailoring, Carl explained, he and his wife and children had pieced together garments by hand. The pace of their work was relaxed, yet he was able to save a few dollars each year. Then, said Carl, "in 1854 or 1855, . . . the sewing machine was invented and introduced, and it stitched very nicely, nicer than the tailor could do; and the bosses said: 'We want you to use the sewing machine; you have to buy one.' "

Carl and his fellow tailors used their meager savings to buy machines, hoping they could earn more by producing more. But their employers cut wages instead of raising them. The tailors "found that we

could earn no more than we could without the machine; but the money for the machine was gone now, and we found that the machine was only for the profit of the bosses; that they got their work quicker, and it was done nicer." Moreover, Carl, now old and discouraged, had seen that mechanization had other troubling effects on workers and those around them. "The machine," he said, "makes too much noise and the neighbors want to sleep, and we have to stop sewing earlier, so we have to work faster. We work now in excitement—in a hurry. It is hunting; it is not work at all; it is a hunt."

Conrad Carl's testimony to the Senate committee was one worker's view of the industrialization that was relentlessly overtaking American society. The forces prevailing in the new order were both inspiring and ominous. The factory and the machine broke down manufacturing into minute, routinized tasks and organized work according to dictates of the clock. Corporations merged and amassed frightening power in the quest for productivity and profits. Defenders of the new system devised new social and economic theories to justify it, while critics tried to counteract what they thought were abuses of power. Finally, workers, who had long thought of themselves as valued producers, fought to avoid becoming slaves to the machine.

Industrialization is a process whose complexities defy precise definition. Most simply it is characterized by the production of goods by machine rather than by hand. Factors either related to or resulting from industrialization in America include some of the following:

1. involvement of an increasing proportion of the work force in manufacturing
2. production concentrated in large, intricately organized factories
3. accelerated technological innovation, emphasizing new inventions and applied science
4. expanded markets, no longer merely local and regional in scope
5. growth of a nationwide transportation network based on the railroad, and an accompanying communications network based on the telegraph and telephone
6. increased capital accumulation for investment in expansion of production
7. growth of large enterprises and specialization in all forms of economic activity
8. rapid population increase
9. steady increase in the size and predominance of cities

A few numbers will help illustrate these patterns. In 1860 about a quarter of the American labor force worked in manufacturing and transportation; over half did so in 1920. The number of people gainfully employed rose from 17.4 million in 1880 to 41.6 million in 1920. In 1870 Western Union handled over 9 million telegraph messages on 112,000 miles of wire; by 1900 it processed over 63 million messages on 933,000 miles of wire. And the value of exports increased twelvefold between 1879 and 1920. By the twentieth century, the United States was not only the world's largest producer of raw materials and food, but the most productive industrial nation as well.

Thomas Alva Edison (1847–1931) at work in his laboratory around 1890. Edison developed countless inventions, including the incandescent light bulb, the phonograph, and early forms of motion picture reproduction. He also was a skilled publicist, capable of selling his ideas for commercial purposes. Library of Congress.

TECHNOLOGY AND THE QUEST FOR WEALTH

In 1876, Thomas A. Edison and his associates moved into a long wooden shed in Menlo Park, New Jersey, where Edison intended to turn out "a minor invention every ten days and a big thing every six months or so." He envisioned his Menlo Park laboratory as an invention factory, a place where creative people would pool their ideas and skills to fashion marketable products. Edison, and others like him, helped to make the years between 1865 and 1900 an age of invention. Indeed, the work of inventors was an integral part of American industrialization (see map).

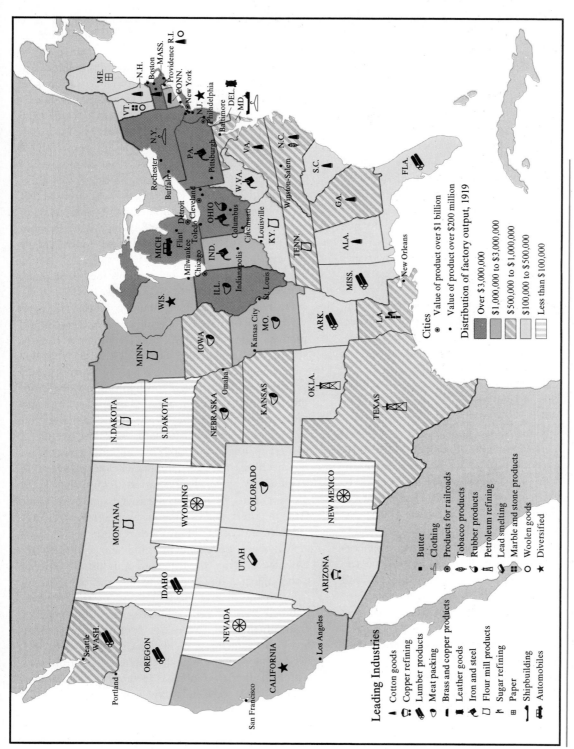

Leading Industries

- ⚓ Cotton goods
- ⚙ Copper refining
- 🪵 Lumber products
- 🐂 Meat packing
- ⚙ Brass and copper products
- 👞 Leather goods
- ⚒ Iron and steel
- ▱ Flour mill products
- ⚒ Lead smelting
- ◰ Paper
- ⛵ Shipbuilding
- 🚗 Automobiles
- Butter
- Clothing
- Products for railroads
- Tobacco products
- Rubber products
- Petroleum refining
- Sugar refining
- Marble and stone products
- Woolen goods
- Diversified

Cities
- ⊙ Value of product over $1 billion
- • Value of product over $200 million

Distribution of factory output, 1919
- Over $3,000,000
- $1,000,000 to $3,000,000
- $500,000 to $1,000,000
- $100,000 to $500,000
- Less than $100,000

Industrial Production, 1919 Source: © American Heritage Publishing Co., Inc., *American Heritage Pictorial Atlas of United States History*; data from U.S. Bureau of the Census, *Fourteenth Census of the United States, 1920.* Vol. IX: *Manufacturing* (Washington: U.S. Government Printing Office, 1921).

Perhaps the biggest of his "big-thing" projects began in 1878 when he formed the Edison Electric Light Company and embarked on a search for a cheap, efficient means of indoor lighting. His major contribution was perfection of an incandescent bulb, which used a filament in a vacuum. At the same time, Edison worked out a *system* of power production and distribution—an improved dynamo and a parallel circuit of wires—that would provide cheap, convenient lighting to a large number of customers. In 1882 Edison built a power plant that would light eighty-five buildings in New York's Wall Street financial district. When this Pearl Street Station began service with great fanfare, a *New York Times* reporter marveled that working in his office at night "seemed almost like writing in daylight."

Birth of the Electrical Industry

Edison's system had a major limitation: it used direct current at low voltage, and could thus send electric power only a mile or two. George Westinghouse, an inventor from Schenectady, New York, solved the problem. Westinghouse used alternating current and transformers to reduce high-voltage power to lower voltage levels, thus making transmission over long distances cheaper.

Once Edison and Westinghouse had made their technological breakthroughs, others helped them distribute their inventions to a wide market. Samuel Insull, Edison's private secretary, deftly attracted investments and organized Edison power plants across the country. In the late 1880s and early 1890s, financiers Henry Villard and J. P. Morgan consolidated patents in electric lighting and merged equipment-manufacturing companies into the General Electric Company. Equally important, General Electric and Westinghouse Electric established research laboratories that paid practical-minded scientists to find new uses for electricity.

Research laboratories did not eliminate individual dreamers. One such optimist was Henry Ford, who in the 1890s worked as an electrical engineer in Detroit's Edison Company and in his spare time experimented with a gasoline-burning internal combustion engine to power a vehicle. Like Edison, Ford had a scheme as well as an invention. In 1909 he declared, "I am going to democratize the automobile." His plan was to produce millions of identical cars in exactly the same fashion. On Ford's assembly lines production was broken down so that each worker had responsibility for only one task, constantly repeated, and there was a continuous flow of these tasks from raw materials to finished product. In 1908, the first year the famous Model T was built, Ford sold 10,000 cars. By 1914, the year after the first moving assembly line was inaugurated, 248,000 Fords were sold. Many of them cost $490 apiece, only about one-fourth of what they would have cost a decade earlier.

Mass Production

Even this price was beyond the means of many workers, who earned at best $2 a day. In 1914, however, Ford tried to boost buying power and spur worker productivity by offering combined wages and profit sharing of $5 a day. "This is neither charity nor wages," he explained, "but profit sharing and efficiency engineering."

Although the timing of mechanization varied from one industry to another, a host of other machines and processes helped to alter the nation's economy and everyday life between 1865 and 1900. The telephone and typewriter revolutionized communications. Sewing machines made mass-produced clothing available to almost everyone. Refrigeration changed American dietary habits by making it easier to preserve food. Cash registers and adding machines revamped accounting and created new clerical jobs.

All these developments and more thrust the United States into the vanguard of industrial nations. Other effects, however, were less positive. Industrial expansion and mechanization destroyed time-honored crafts and subordinated men and women to rigid schedules and repetitive routines. On another level, manufacturers pooled existing patents and tried to monopolize new discoveries by confining research to their own labs. As in farming and mining, bigness and consolidation were engulfing the individual.

The Triumph of Industrialism

In the industrial sector, profits resulted from higher production at lower costs. As railroads and technological innovations made large-scale production more economical, sizable factories began to replace small ones. Only large factories could afford to buy new machines and operate them at full capacity. And large factories could best take advantage of discount rates for shipping products in bulk and for buying raw materials in quantity. Economists call such advantages *economies of scale.*

Machines and large factories made such efficiencies possible, but profitability was as much a matter of organization as of mechanics. Thus by the 1890s, engineers and managers were working intently to increase output economically and efficiently, putting the primary emphasis on time. Of the many people who espoused systems of efficient production, the most influential was Frederick W. Taylor. His experiments involved identifying the "elementary operations of motions" used by specific workers, eliminating "all useless movements," selecting better tools, and devising "a series of motions which can be made quickest and best."

New Emphasis on Efficiency

Taylor's writings helped to make time studies and scientific management national obsessions. Workers' skills became less valued, and managers increasingly controlled the pace and scale of output. Speed rather than quality became the measure of acceptable work, and science rather than tradition determined the right ways of doing things. As integral features of the assembly line, where work was divided into specific time-determined tasks, employees had become another kind of interchangeable part.

At the same time, large manufacturers were adding new marketing techniques to their technological and organizational innovations. Meat processor Gustavus Swift used branch slaughterhouses and refrigeration to enlarge the market for fresh meat. James B. Duke, who organized the American Tobacco Company and made cigarettes a big business, saturated communities with billboards and free samples and offered premium gifts to retailers for selling more cigarettes. Companies like International Harvester and Singer Sewing Machine set up systems for servicing their products and introduced financing schemes to permit customers to buy the machines more easily. In many instances marketing innovations enabled producers to sell directly to retailers, squeezing out wholesalers and eliminating the excess costs wholesaling entailed.

New Marketing Techniques

The Corporate Consolidation Movement

Neither the wonders of industrial production nor the new techniques of market promotion could mask unsettling factors in the American economy. Competition and the resulting race for higher productivity and new markets had costs as well as benefits. New technology demanded that factories operate at near-capacity in order to produce goods most economically. But the more manufacturers produced, the more they had to sell. And in order to sell more, they had to reduce prices. In order to profit more, they expanded production further and often reduced wages. In order to expand, they had to borrow money. In order to repay the money, they had to produce and sell even more. This circular process strangled small firms that could not keep pace and thrust workers into conditions of constant uncertainty. The same cycle affected trade, banking, and transportation as well as manufacturing.

Such conditions encouraged rapid growth, but optimism could dissolve at the hint that debtors were

The corporate consolidation movement resulted in giant trusts, epitomized by John D. Rockefeller's Standard Oil, which was so powerful that critics warned it could enable Rockefeller to convert the Capitol into an oil refinery and hold the White House and Treasury Department in the palm of his hand. Library of Congress.

unable to meet their obligations. In the final third of the nineteenth century, financial panics afflicted the economy at least once a decade, depressing prices, destroying businesses, and putting workers out of jobs. Depressions that began in 1873, 1884, and 1893 each hovered over the nation for several years. Business leaders failed to agree on what caused the declines. In an effort to combat the uncertainty of the business cycle, many businessmen turned to more centralized and cooperative forms of economic power, notably corporations, pools, trusts, and holding companies.

In the nineteenth century, corporations, with their limited liability for stockholders, were the best instruments for raising the capital needed for industrial expansion. But economic disorder and the urge for profits caused corporation managers to seek stability in new and larger forms of economic concentration. At first, however, such efforts were tentative and informal, consisting mainly of cooperative agreements among firms that made the same product or offered the same service. Through these arrangements, called *pools*,

Pools, Trusts, and Holding Companies

competing companies tried to control the market by agreeing how much each should produce and what prices should be charged. Such "gentlemen's agreements" worked during good times when there was enough business for all; but during slow periods, the desire for profits often tempted pool members to evade their commitments by secretly reducing prices or selling more than the agreed quota. The Interstate Commerce Act of 1887 outlawed pools, but by then their usefulness was already fading.

John D. Rockefeller disliked pools, calling them "ropes of sand." In 1879 one of his lawyers adapted an old device called a *trust,* whereby companies in the same industry could be lured or forced into turning over control of their stock to a board of trustees, which then supervised all operations. This device allowed Rockefeller to integrate the management of his original Standard Oil Company of Ohio with that of other companies he controlled, thus strengthening his grip on the highly profitable petroleum industry. Then in 1888 New Jersey adopted new incorporation laws allowing corporations chartered there to own property in other states and to own stock in other corporations (trusts provided for trusteeship but not ownership). This liberalization led to the creation of the *holding company,* which controlled a partial or complete interest in other companies. Holding companies could in turn merge their constituent companies' assets as well as their management. Thus Rockefeller incorporated Standard Oil of New Jersey, merging the assets of forty companies. Holding companies also encouraged the use of *vertical integration,* which allowed companies to take over several levels of production and distribution, including control of raw materials and transportation as well as manufacturing.

Originally designed as an arrangement whereby responsible individuals would manage the financial affairs of people unwilling or unable to handle them alone, the trust became the answer to industry's search for order. Between 1889 and 1903, some three hundred combinations were formed, most of them trusts and holding companies. By far the most spectacular was the U.S. Steel Corporation, financed by J. P. Morgan. This new enterprise, made up of iron-ore properties, freight carriers, wire mills, plate and tubing companies, and other firms, was capitalized at over $1.4 billion.

THE GOSPEL OF WEALTH

Business leaders turned to consolidation under the new forms of corporation both to promote growth and reduce wasteful competition. But the American public believed in open competition. It thus became necessary for the defenders of the monopolistic companies to find a means to justify their size and power. They turned to Social Darwinism, a philosophy that loosely adapted Charles Darwin's theory of the origin of species to the principles of laissez faire. Human society had evolved naturally, the Social Darwinists reasoned, and any interference with existing institutions would only hamper progress and aid the weak. In a free society operating according to the principle of survival of the fittest, power would flow naturally to the most capable. Property holding and acquisition were therefore sacred rights, and wealth was a mark of well-deserved power and responsibility.

Social Darwinism

This philosophy required that people be left free to accumulate and dispose of wealth. In fact, however, the new corporate forms, with their domination of production and finance, prevented most individuals who did not already have wealth from acquiring it. To compensate for this inconsistency, Social Darwinists reasoned that humanitarian elites could provide for the needs of those less fortunate or less capable. Thus the wealthy should endow churches, hospitals, and schools, since such gifts promoted progress by raising the "moral culture" of all classes. Social Darwinists also believed that government should not force the rich, through taxation or regulation, to become more humanitarian.

Paradoxically, business executives who exalted individual initiative and independence also pressed for government assistance. They denounced any

Government Assistance to Business

measures that might aid unions or regulate factory conditions; such legislation, they said, thwarted natural economic laws. At the same time, though, they lobbied forcefully for subsidies, loans, and tax relief that would encourage business growth. Tariffs were by far the largest form of government assistance to industry. By putting high import duties on competing goods from abroad, Congress enabled American producers to keep the prices of their goods relatively high. Industrialists argued that tariff protection encouraged the development of new products and the founding of new enterprises. But tariffs also forced consumers to pay artificially high prices for many products.

DISSENTING VOICES

Writers who attacked trusts argued within the same framework of values as did corporate leaders who defended the new economic system. While defenders insisted that trusts were the natural and efficient outcome of economic development, critics charged that trusts were unnatural because they were created by greed and inefficient because they stifled opportunity. Underlying such charges was a deep-seated fear of monopoly. Those who feared monopoly believed that large corporations could exploit consumers by fixing prices, demean workers by cutting wages, destroy opportunity by eliminating small businesses, and threaten democracy by corrupting politicians.

Many believed there was a better way to achieve progress. By the mid-1880s, a number of young professors began to challenge Social Darwinism and laissez faire. Some, like pioneering sociologist Lester Ward, attacked the application of evolutionary the-

ory to social and economic relations. To Ward, a system that guaranteed survival only to the fittest was wasteful and brutal; instead, he reasoned, cooperative activity, fostered by planning and government intervention, was the best means to unity and happiness. Economists Richard Ely, John R. Commons, and Edward Bemis agreed that natural forces should be harnessed for the public good. Instead of the laissez-faire system, they preferred one of positive assistance by the state.

While academics were recommending intervention into natural economic order, others were proposing more utopian schemes for combating monopolies.

Utopian Economic Schemes

Reformer Henry George, the author of *Progress and Poverty*, declared that inequality stemmed from the ability of a few to profit from rising land values. To restore equality, George proposed to tax the "unearned increment"—the rise in land values caused by increased market demand rather than by owners' improvements—and to eliminate all other taxes. By confiscating undue profits, George insisted, this *single tax* would end monopolistic tendencies and ensure social progress.

Unlike George, who approved of private ownership, novelist Edward Bellamy envisioned a socialist state where government would own and oversee the means of production and distribution and would unite all people under moral laws. Bellamy outlined his vision in the utopian *Looking Backward, 2000–1887*, published in 1886. He warned that catastrophe would result from the extremes of wealth and poverty that characterized American society. The remedy, said Bellamy, was a fully nationalized state free of the greed of bankers, industrialists, lawyers, and politicians.

Meanwhile, public clamor against monopolies and trusts began to prod legislators into action. By the end of the century, fifteen states had constitutional

Antitrust Legislation

provisions outlawing trusts, and twenty-seven had laws forbidding pools. Most of these were states in the agricultural South and West. But problems of definition and enforcement mounted.

State attorneys general lacked the staff and judicial support for a concerted attack on big business, and corporations always found ways to evade restrictions. Consequently, the need for national legislation became more pressing.

In 1890 Congress passed the Sherman Anti-Trust Act. The act made illegal "every contract, combination in the form of trust or otherwise, or conspiracy in the restraint of trade." People found guilty of violating the law faced fines and jail terms, and those wronged by illegal combinations could sue for triple damages. However, the law was vague. It did not define clearly what a restraint of trade was. Moreover, it entrusted interpretation of its provisions to the courts, which at that time were strong allies of business.

The Sherman Anti-Trust Act was intended to encourage free competition by prohibiting unreasonable restraints of trade, but judges—particularly the Supreme Court—blurred distinctions between reasonable and unreasonable. When in 1895 the government prosecuted the so-called Sugar Trust for owning 98 percent of the nation's sugar-refining capacity, eight of nine Supreme Court judges ruled that control of manufacturing did not necessarily mean control of trade (*U.S. v. E. C. Knight Co.*).

This interpretation left the antitrust act with only token power to combat industrial bigness. Ironically, the law did serve government officials as a tool for breaking up labor unions. Courts that did not consider monopolistic production a restraint of trade willingly applied antitrust provisions to union strikes that affected trade.

MECHANIZATION AND THE
CHANGING STATUS OF LABOR

By 1880, the status of labor had shifted dramatically from what it had been a generation earlier.

Most workers could no longer accurately be termed producers—as craftsmen and farmers had traditionally considered themselves. The enlarged working class now consisted mainly of employees—people who worked only when someone else hired them. Whereas producers were paid by consumers according to the quality of what they produced, employees were paid wages based on time spent on the job.

As mass production subdivided manufacturing into minute tasks, workers spent their time repeating one specialized operation. No longer was it up to the worker to decide when to begin and end the workday, when to rest, and what tools and techniques to use. Especially as assembly-line production spread, employees lost their sense of independence. Workers reacted to industrialization by struggling to retain old customs such as having a fellow worker read aloud while they labored. Conversely, employers sought to make workers more docile through temperance and moral reform societies.

As machines and assembly-line production reduced the need for skilled workers, employers cut wage costs by hiring more women and children. Between 1880 and 1900, the numbers of employed women grew from 2.6 million to 8.6 million, and their employment patterns underwent major changes (see figure, page 308). First, the proportion of working women engaged in domestic and personal service jobs (maids, cooks, laundresses), traditionally the most common form of female employment, dropped dramatically as jobs opened in other economic sectors. Some new jobs were in manufacturing—usually menial positions in textile mills and food-processing plants that paid women as little as $1.56 a week for seventy hours of labor.

Employment of Women

Second and more important, a major shift was occurring that set the trend among female workers for much of the twentieth century. The numbers and percentages of women in clerical jobs—clerks, typists, bookkeepers, salespersons—skyrocketed. By 1920 nearly half of all clerical workers were women; in 1880 only 4 percent had been women. Analysts often explain the transformation of the clerical sector

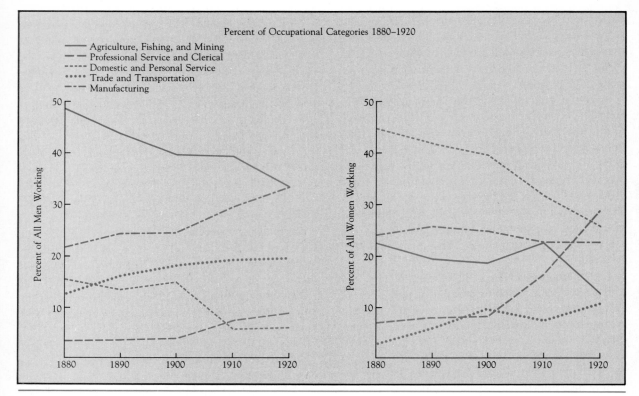

Percent of Occupational Categories 1880–1920

—— Agriculture, Fishing, and Mining
– – Professional Service and Clerical
······ Domestic and Personal Service
•••••• Trade and Transportation
–·– Manufacturing

Percent of Occupational Categories, 1880–1920
Source: U.S. Bureau of the Census, *Census of the United States*, 1880, 1890, 1900, 1910, 1920 (Washington: U.S. Government Printing Office).

by asserting that women would work for lower wages than men would and that women's nimble fingers and toleration of boring work suited them for office and sales-floor labor. A more likely explanation, however, is that machines reduced the skills needed for clerical jobs, and companies were willing to hire large numbers of women streaming into the labor market who needed little training for these jobs.

Although most working children toiled on their parents' farms, the number in nonagricultural occupations tripled between 1870 and 1900. In 1900, 13 percent of all textile workers were below age sixteen. In other industries too, mechanization created a

Employment of Children

number of light unskilled tasks (such as running errands and helping machine operators) that children could handle at a fraction of adult wages. Many parents lied about their children's ages to help them get jobs to supplement the family income. By 1900, child labor laws and further automation had reduced the number of children working in manufacturing, but many more worked in street trades—shining shoes and peddling newspapers—and as helpers in stores.

While working conditions loomed as the major issue laborers had to face, the problem of wages was often the immediate catalyst of worker unrest. Many employers believed in the "iron law of wages," which dictated that employees be paid according to the conditions of supply and demand. In practice the principle meant that employers did not have to raise wages—and could even lower them—as long as there were people who would accept low pay. Employers justified the system with references to old-fashioned individual freedom: if a worker did not like the wages being paid, he or she was free to quit and find a job elsewhere. Wage earners saw things differently. They believed the wage system trapped and exploited them.

Moreover, even steady employment was insecure. Repetitive tasks using high-speed machinery dulled workers' concentration, and the slightest mistake could cause serious injury. The numbers of industrial accidents rose steadily before 1920; these accidents killed or maimed hundreds of thousands of people each year. Even as late as 1913, after factory owners had installed some safety devices, some 25,000 people died in industrial mishaps, and close to 1 million were injured.

Industrial Accidents

Families stricken by such accidents suffered acutely, because disability insurance and pensions were almost nonexistent. Nineteenth-century laissez-faire attitudes prevented protective legislation for workers, and employers would not take responsibility for employees' well-being. As one railroad manager told his workers, "The regular compensation of employees covers all risk or liability to accident. If an employee is disabled . . . , the right to claim compensation is not recognized."

Reformers in several states passed laws to ease working conditions, but the Supreme Court limited their impact by making narrow interpretations of what jobs were dangerous and which workers needed protection. Initially, in *Holden* v. *Hardy* (1896), the Court decided to uphold a law regulating the working hours of miners because their work was so dangerous that overly long

Courts Restrict Labor Reform

hours would increase the threat of injury. In *Lochner* v. *New York* (1905), however, the Court struck down a law limiting bakery workers to a sixty-hour week and a ten-hour day, because baking was not a dangerous enough occupation for the legislature to restrict the right of workers to sell their labor freely. Then, in *Muller* v. *Oregon* (1908), the Court resorted to a different rationale to uphold a law limiting working hours for women to ten a day. Labor legislation for women was necessary, the Court asserted, because a woman's health "becomes an object of public interest and care in order to preserve the strength and vigor of the race." As a result, women were barred from many occupations, such as printing and transportation, which required long or nighttime hours.

Throughout the nineteenth century, tensions rose and fell as workers confronted mechanization. Adjustments were made in different ways as different groups entered the industrial labor force. Some people bent to the demands of the factory, the machine, and the time clock. Others, however, turned to organized resistance.

In many ways, the year 1877 was a historical watershed. In July of that year, a series of strikes broke out among railroad workers who were protesting wage cuts. Violence spread across Pennsylvania and Ohio all the way to Chicago and St. Louis. Venting their anger against corporations rather than against individual employers, rioters attacked railroad property, derailing trains and burning railyards. Militia companies organized by employers broke up picket lines and fired into threatening crowds. In several areas, factory workers, wives, and even local merchants aided the strikers, while railroads enlisted strikebreakers to replace union men.

Strikes of 1877

After more than a month of unprecedented carnage that reached from Maryland to Illinois, Texas, and California, President Rutherford B. Hayes sent federal troops to restore order and end the strikes. His action marked the first significant use of troops to quell labor unrest.

The Haymarket Riot, Chicago, 1886. A bomb explodes among a police brigade trying to break up the labor demonstration. In retaliation, police fired into the crowd of strikers. The caption for the drawing, which appeared in Harper's Weekly, *falsely identified the incident as an "anarchist riot."* Bettmann Archive.

THE UNION MOVEMENT

Anxiety over their loss of independence drove some workers to unionize in protection of their interests. The National Labor Union, which flourished briefly after its founding in 1866, died during the depression of the 1870s. The only broad-based labor organization to survive that depression was the Knights of Labor. Founded in 1869 by Philadelphia garment cutters, the Knights opened their doors to other workers during the 1870s. Under the leadership of Terence V. Powderly, the Knights recruited women and blacks as well as immigrants and unskilled and semiskilled workers, who were excluded from craft unions. Membership mushroomed from 10,000 in 1879 to 730,000 in mid-1886.

Knights of Labor

Strikes presented a dilemma for the Knights. Powderly and other leaders wondered whether the pursuit of immediate goals through this sometimes violent tactic would detract from the union's long-range objective of a Bellamy-type cooperative society. As strikes began to fail in 1886, as Powderly began to denounce radicalism and violence, and as the more militant craft unions broke away, the Knights' membership dwindled. The union survived only in a few small towns, where a brief and vain attempt was made to unite with the Populists in the 1890s. The special interests of craft unions overcame the Knights' general appeal, and dreams of the unity of labor faded.

As the depression of the 1870s subsided and better conditions returned in the early 1880s, a number of labor groups, including the Knights, began to campaign for an eight-hour workday. This effort by workers to regain control of their work gathered most momentum in Chicago, where radical anarchists as well as various craft unions agitated for the cause. On May 1, 1886, the workers' deadline for achieving their goal, city police were mobilized to prevent possible disorder. Two days later a riot broke out at the McCormick reaper factory, where police shot and killed two workers and wounded several others. The next evening, labor groups organized a rally at Haymarket Square, near downtown Chicago, to protest police brutality. As a company of police officers approached the meeting, a bomb exploded near their front ranks, killing seven and injuring sixty-seven. Mass arrests of anarchists and unionists followed. Eventually eight men, all anarchists, were tried for and convicted of the bombing, though there was no evidence of their guilt. Four were executed and one committed suicide in prison. The remaining three were pardoned in 1893 by Illinois governor John P. Altgeld, who believed they had been victims of the "malicious ferocity" of the courts.

Haymarket Riot

The Haymarket bombing drew public attention to labor campaigns for better conditions but also revived middle-class fear of radicalism. In several cities police forces and armories were strengthened. And employer associations designed to counter labor militancy multiplied.

The newly formed American Federation of Labor was the major workers' organization to emerge after the 1886 upheavals. A combination of national craft unions, the AFL initially had about 140,000 members, most of whom were skilled native workers. Led by Samuel Gompers, the pragmatic and opportunistic head of the Cigar Makers' Union, AFL unions avoided the idealistic rhetoric of worker solidarity (they excluded unskilled industrial workers) to press for specific goals, such as higher wages, shorter hours, and the right to bargain collectively. By 1917 the organization included 111 national unions, 27,000 local unions, and 2.5 million members.

American Federation of Labor

The AFL and the labor movement in general staggered in the early 1890s, when once again labor violence evoked public fears. In July 1892, Henry C. Frick, the stubborn president of the Carnegie Steel Company, closed the company plant in Homestead, Pennsylvania, when the AFL-affiliated Amalgamated Association of Iron and Steelworkers refused to accept pay cuts and went on strike. Shortly thereafter, angry workers attacked and routed three hundred Pinkerton guards hired by Frick to protect the plant. State militia were called in, and after five months the strikers gave in.

In 1894, workers at the Pullman Palace Car Company walked out in protest over exploitive policies at the company town near Chicago. The paternalistic company head, George Pullman, owned and controlled all land and buildings, the school, the bank, and the water and gas systems. One laborer grumbled, "We are born in a Pullman house, fed from the Pullman shop, taught in the Pullman school, catechized in the Pullman church, and when we die we shall be buried in the Pullman cemetery and go to the Pullman hell."

Pullman Strike

One thing Pullman would not do was negotiate with workers. When the depression that began in 1893 threatened his business, Pullman managed to maintain profits and pay dividends to stockholders by cutting wages 25 to 40 percent but holding firm on rents and prices in the model town. Workers, squeezed into debt and deprivation, sent a committee to Pullman in May 1894 to protest his policies. Pullman reacted by firing three of the committee. The enraged workers, most of whom had joined the American Railway Union, called a strike. Pullman retaliated by shutting down the plant. When the American Railway Union, led by the charismatic young organizer Eugene V. Debs, voted to aid the strikers by boycotting all Pullman cars, Pullman stood firm and rejected arbitration. The railroad owners' association then enlisted the aid of U.S. Attorney General Richard Olney, who obtained a court injunction to prevent the union from "obstructing the railways and holding up the mails." President Grover Cleveland sent federal troops to Chicago, supposedly to protect the mails but in reality to crush the strike. Within a month the strike was over, and Debs was jailed for six months for contempt of court in defying the injunction.

After the turn of the century, a number of battles occurred between workers and employers in the mining industry. Out of the western struggles emerged the Industrial Workers of the World (IWW), a radical organization that fused the Knights of Labor vision of worker solidarity with the tactics of strikes and sometimes sabotage. Using the rhetoric of class conflict—"The final aim is revolution"—the IWW attracted far greater attention than its small membership warranted.

It must be emphasized that during the half-century following the Civil War, only a small fraction of American workers belonged to unions. Labor organizers took no interest in large segments of the industrial labor force and intentionally excluded others. Many unions, such as those of the AFL, were openly hostile toward women. Of the 6.3 million employed women in 1910, only 125,000 were in unions. Yet female employees could organize and fight employers as bitterly as men could.

Since the early years of industrialization, female workers had organized their own unions; some, such

Women and the Labor Movement

as the Collar Laundry Union of Troy, New York, organized in the 1860s, had been successful in carrying out strikes and achieving higher wages. The first broad-based women's union was the Women's Trade Union League (WTUL), founded in 1903 and patterned after a similar union in England. The WTUL worked for protective legislation for women workers, sponsored educational activities, and joined the cause for women's suffrage. In 1909 it joined with the International Ladies' Garment Workers' Union in support of a massive strike against New York City sweatshops. Although the WTUL had some forceful working-class leaders—notably Agnes Nestor, a glove maker, Rose Schneiderman, a cap maker, and Mary Anderson, a shoe worker—it was dominated by middle-class women who had humane but generally nonmilitant purposes in helping working women. In the early 1920s, the WTUL fought a constitutional amendment guaranteeing equal rights to women, arguing that women needed protection from exploitation more than they needed equality. Such reasoning fitted the assertion of males who argued that women belonged in their own sphere at home, out of the work force and out of unions. As the WTUL gradually backed away from active union organization, it lost the support of working-class women, and by 1930 it had virtually dissolved.

Organized labor also excluded most immigrant and black workers. Some trade unions welcomed skilled immigrants—in fact, foreign-born craftsmen were prominent leaders of several unions—but only the Knights of Labor and the IWW had firm policies of accepting immigrants and blacks. A few AFL unions included blacks, but the vast majority had exclusion policies. Resentments already fueled by long-held prejudices increased when blacks and immigrants worked as strikebreakers. It is likely that few strikebreakers understood the full effects of such employment when they were recruited to fill the jobs of striking workers; but even for those who did, the lure of employment was too great to resist.

For most American workers, then, the machine

Immigrants, Blacks, and the Labor Movement

work. Moreover, as wages rose, living costs increased even faster. The industrial transformation had thrust the United States into international leadership in economic capability. But in factories as well as on farms, some people were beginning to question whether a system based on ever-greater profits was the best way for Americans to create a world of peace and prosperity.

SUGGESTIONS FOR FURTHER READING

General

Daniel J. Boorstin, *The Americans: The Democratic Experience* (1973); Thomas C. Cochran and William Miller, *The Age of Enterprise* (1942); Ray Ginger, *The Age of Excess* (1965); Samuel P. Hays, *The Response to Industrialism* (1975).

Technology and Invention

Roger Burlingame, *Henry Ford* (1957); Sigfried Giedion, *Mechanization Takes Command* (1948); Matthew Josephson, *Edison* (1959); Leo Marx, *The Machine in the Garden: Technology and the Pastoral Ideal* (1964); Elting E. Morison, *Men, Machines, and Modern Times* (1966); Nathan Rosenberg, *Technology and American Economic Growth* (1972); Harold I. Sharlin, *The Making of the Electrical Age* (1963); Peter Temin, *Steel in Nineteenth Century America* (1964).

Industrialism, Industrialists, and Corporate Growth

W. Elliot Brownlee, *Dynamics of Ascent: A History of the American Economy*, 2nd ed. (1979); Stuart Bruchey, *Growth of the Modern Economy* (1973); Alfred D. Chandler, *The Visible Hand: The Managerial Revolution in American Business* (1977); Alfred D. Chandler, *Strategy and Structure:*

age had mixed results. Industrial wages rose between 1877 and 1914, boosting purchasing power and enabling the creation of a mass market for standardized goods. Yet in 1900 most employees worked sixty hours a week at wages that averaged 20 cents an hour for skilled work and 10 cents an hour for unskilled

Chapters in the History of American Industrial Enterprise (1966); Thomas C. Cochran, *Business in American Life* (1972); David F. Hawkes, *John D.: The Founding Father of the Rockefellers* (1980); Matthew Josephson, *The Robber Barons* (1934); Edward C. Kirkland, *Industry Comes of Age* (1961); Harold C. Livesay, *Andrew Carnegie and the Rise of Big Business* (1975); Daniel Nelson, *Managers and Workers: Origins of the New Factory System in the United States, 1880–1920* (1975); Glen Porter, *The Rise of Big Business* (1973).

Attitudes toward Industrialism

Sidney Fine, *Laissez Faire and the General Welfare State* (1956); Louis Galambos and Barbara Barron Spence, *The Public Image of Big Business in America* (1975); Richard Hofstadter, *Social Darwinism in American Thought*, rev. ed. (1955); T. Jackson Lears, *No Place of Grace: Antimodernism and the Transformation of American Culture* (1981); Robert McCloskey, *American Conservatism in the Age of Enterprise* (1951); John L. Thomas, *Alternative America: Henry George, Edward Bellamy, Henry Demarest Lloyd and the Adversary Tradition* (1983).

Work and Labor Organization

Melvyn Dubofsky, *Industrialism and the American Worker* (1975); Melvyn Dubofsky, *We Shall Be All: A History of the Industrial Workers of the World* (1969); Leon Fink, *Workingmen's Democracy: The Knights of Labor and American Politics* (1982); Philip S. Foner, *The Great Labor Uprising of 1877* (1977); Herbert G. Gutman, *Work, Culture and Society in Industrializing America* (1976); Stuart Bruce Kaufman, *Samuel Gompers and the Origins of the American Federation of Labor* (1973); Alice Kessler-Harris, *Out to Work: A History of Wage-Earning Women in the United States* (1982); Harold Livesay, *Samuel Gompers and Organized Labor in America* (1978); Milton Meltzer, *Bread and Roses: The Struggle of American Labor, 1865–1915* (1967); Stephen Meyer III, *The Five Dollar Day: Labor Management and Social Control in the Ford Motor Company, 1908–1921* (1981); David Montgomery, *Workers' Control in America: Studies in the History of Work, Technology, and Labor Struggles* (1979); Barbara Mayer Wertheimer, *We Were There: The Story of Working Women in America* (1977); Irwin Yellowitz, *Industrialization and the American Labor Movement* (1977).

CHAPTER 18

THE CITY AND
EVERYDAY LIFE
1877–1920

For nearly thirty years, Frank Ventrone had successfully pursued his dream, until one night his world literally shattered. In the 1880s Ventrone had emigrated from southern Italy to Providence, Rhode Island. By saving money and buying property, Ventrone became a prominent businessman in the city's fast-growing Italian immigrant community. Ventrone's biggest success was a pasta business that furnished the community's staple food. But this business was also the source of his trouble.

In the summer of 1914, food prices were rising, and Ventrone followed the trend by increasing the price of his pasta. Angered by the threat to their already overburdened incomes, people of Providence's Italian section vented their frustration against Ventrone. On a warm August weekend, they marched through the neighborhood, broke windows in a block of property owned by Ventrone, entered his business establishment, and dumped his stock of macaroni into the

street. When police arrived to quell the disturbance, rioters resisted with catcalls and violence, insisting that the matter was an internal one, to be resolved by the community. The next Monday, Ventrone's agent met with community members and agreed to lower his prices. Ventrone had overstepped the bounds of ethnic loyalty and had suffered as a result.

The Providence "macaroni riot," with its various dimensions—the transfer of immigrant cultures from Old World to New; the mobility of some people from rags to respectability; the continued poverty of others amid economic uncertainty; the eruption of violence—was just one of millions of events that came to characterize life in America. The driving forces behind the changing nature of American society were industrialization and urbanization. They occurred in the half-century between the end of Reconstruction and 1920. From a demographic perspective, the population shifts were dramatic. In the United States of 1880 seven out of every ten people lived on farms or in towns with fewer than 2,500 people. By 1920, a milestone had been reached: a majority of the people—51.4 percent—dwelled in cities.

Operating in tandem with the movement of people into the cities was the tendency of Americans to focus increasingly on consumption rather than production. The nation's farms and industries were producing so much that Americans could afford to reorient their attitudes toward material wants. What had once been accessible to only a few was becoming available to many; what had formerly been dreams were becoming necessities. No trend affected everyday life more decisively than this one. And as Americans tried to adapt to the new values of consumption and its attendant conflicts, they raised questions about themselves that have not been resolved to this day.

The Birth of the Modern City

By 1900, the modern American city was reaching maturity. From Boston to San Francisco, developed areas sprawled outward several miles from the original central core. No longer did walking distance determine a city's size, and no longer did different social groups live physically close together—poor near rich, immigrant near native, black near white. Instead, cities were divided into distinct districts: working-class neighborhoods, black ghettos, a ring of suburbs, business districts.

New Shape of the City

Two forces, mass transportation and economic change, were responsible for this new arrangement. Steam-powered commuter railroads had appeared in a few cities during the 1850s and 1860s, but not until the late 1870s did inventors begin to mechanize municipal mass transit. The first power-driven devices were cable cars—carriages that traveled over tracks by clamping onto a moving underground wire. Cheaper than horse cars, cable cars could also haul passengers up and down steep hills. By the 1890s, however, electric-powered streetcars were replacing the early forms of mass transit. Between 1890 and 1902, total mileage of electrified track in American cities grew from 1,300 to 22,000 miles.

Mechanization of Mass Transportation

In a few cities, trolley companies raised part of their track onto stilts, enabling vehicles to travel through jammed downtown districts without interference from other traffic. And in Boston, New York, and Philadelphia, transit firms dug underground passages for their cars, also to avoid tie-ups and delays. Elevated railroads and subways were extremely expensive to construct. They thus appeared only in the few cities where companies could amass enough capital to build them and where there were enough riders to make for high profits.

Mass transit lines launched millions of urban dwellers into outlying neighborhoods and created a commuting public. Now those who could afford the fare—usually five cents a ride—could live outside the crowded, dirty central city and still return there for work, shopping, and entertainment. Working-class families, whose incomes rarely topped a dollar a day, found the fare too high and could not take advantage of the streetcars. But for the growing middle class, a home in a quiet, tree-lined neighborhood became a real possibility. Real estate development boomed around the periphery of scores of cities. Between 1890 and 1920, for example, developers in the Chicago area opened 800,000 new lots—enough to house at least three times the city's population in 1890. A home several miles from downtown was inconvenient, but the benefits seemed to outweigh the costs.

Beginnings of Urban Sprawl

Urban sprawl was essentially unplanned. Investors

who bought land in anticipation of settlement paid little attention to the need for parks, traffic control, and public services. Moreover, construction of mass transit was guided by the profit motive and thus served the urban public unevenly. Streetcar lines serviced mainly those neighborhoods that promised the most riders—whose fares, in other words, would provide dividends for stockholders.

Public transportation altered commercial as well as residential patterns. As consumers moved outward, businesses followed. Branches of downtown department stores and banks joined groceries, theaters, drugstores, taverns, and specialty shops to create neighborhood shopping centers, the forerunners of today's shopping malls. Meanwhile, the urban core became the work zone, where offices, stores, warehouses, and factories hulked over streets clogged with traffic.

Cities also became the main arenas for industrial growth, generating and attracting concentrations of economic power. As centers of resources, labor, transportation, and communications, cities provided everything factories needed. Capital accumulated by the cities' commercial enterprises fed industrial investment, and urban populations furnished consumers for new products. Thus urban growth and industrialization wound together in a mutually beneficial spiral. The further industrialization advanced, the more opportunities it created for work and investment in cities. Increased opportunity drew more people to cities; as workers and as consumers, they in turn fueled further industrialization.

Urban-Industrial Development

Urban and industrial growth transformed the national economy and freed the United States from dependence on European capital and manufactured goods. Imports and foreign investments still flowed into the country. But by the early 1900s, cities and their factories, stores, and banks were converting the United States from a debtor agricultural nation into a major industrial, financial, and exporting power.

PEOPLING THE CITIES: MIGRANTS AND IMMIGRANTS

The population of a given place can grow in three ways: by extension of its borders to include nearby land and people; by natural increase—an excess of births over deaths; and by migration—an excess of in-migrants over out-migrants. Between the Civil War and the early 1900s, many cities annexed nearby suburbs, thereby increasing their populations. More important, annexation added land where new city dwellers could live. Cities like Chicago, Minneapolis, and Cincinnati incorporated hundreds of undeveloped square miles into their borders in the 1880s, only to see them fill up in succeeding decades. Although annexation did increase urban populations, its major effect was to enlarge the physical size of cities.

How Cities Grew

Natural increase did not account for more than 20 percent of any city's population increase in any given decade. Instead, migration and immigration made by far the greatest contribution to urban population growth. Each year millions of people were on the move, many of them lured by the cities' promise of opportunity. Although many farm families left rural America for the nation's cities, most of the urban newcomers were immigrants from Europe. A great number of immigrants did not intend to stay. They hoped instead to make enough money to return home and live in greater comfort and security. For every hundred foreigners who entered the country, around thirty left. Still, most of the 26 million immigrants who arrived between 1870 and 1920 stayed, and the great majority settled in cities, where they helped to shape modern American culture.

Major Waves of Migration and Immigration

The United States had been the destination of im-

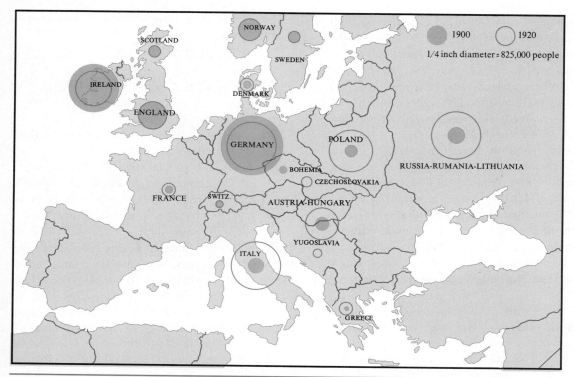

Sources of Foreign-born Population, 1900 and 1920

migrants from northern and western Europe since the 1840s, but after 1880 a second wave of mass immigration began from new sources.

The New Immigration Though northern and western Europeans continued to arrive, the new wave contained mainly people from eastern and southern Europe, plus smaller contingents from Canada, Mexico, and Japan (see map and figure). For example, two-thirds of the immigrants who arrived in the 1880s were from Germany, England, Ireland, and Scandinavia; between 1900 and 1909, however, two-thirds were from Italy, Austria-Hungary, and Russia. By 1910 arrivals from Mexico were beginning to outnumber arrivals from Ireland, and large numbers of Japanese had moved to the West Coast and Hawaii.

Differences between the two waves of immigrants were in many ways more imagined than real. Many Americans feared that the strange customs, non-Protestant religions, illiteracy, and poverty of the "new" immigrants made them less desirable and assimilable than the "old" immigrants, whose languages and beliefs seemed less alien. In reality, however, the old and new immigrants resembled each other more closely than many Americans wished to believe. The majority of both groups were young—between fifteen and forty-four years old—and male. Both groups settled chiefly in cities, and both lived initially in old districts of the central city vacated by residents who had moved to new outlying neighborhoods.

Perhaps most important, all immigrants brought with them memories of their homelands and adjusted to American life in light of those memories. In new surroundings where the language was a struggle, immigrants anchored their lives on what they knew best: their culture. Many immigrant neighborhoods

Chapter 18: The City and Everyday Life, 1877–1920

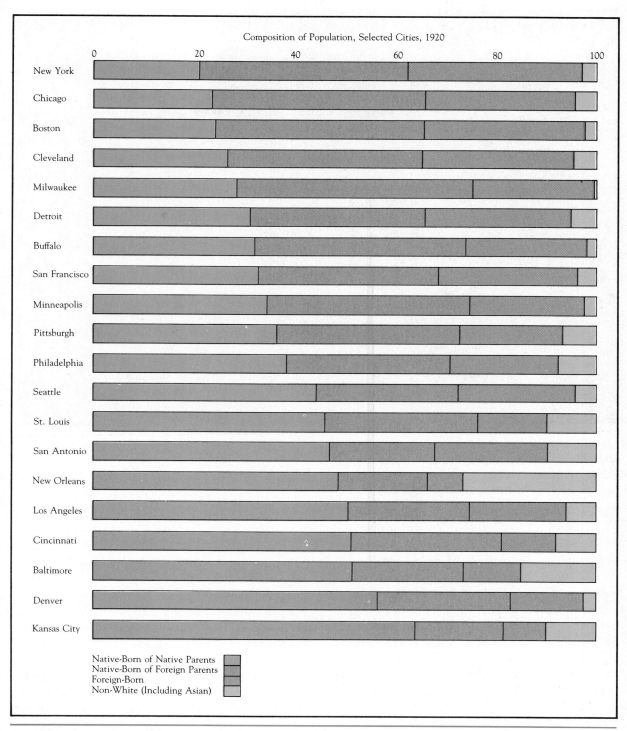

Composition of Population, Selected Cities, 1920

New York
Chicago
Boston
Cleveland
Milwaukee
Detroit
Buffalo
San Francisco
Minneapolis
Pittsburgh
Philadelphia
Seattle
St. Louis
San Antonio
New Orleans
Los Angeles
Cincinnati
Baltimore
Denver
Kansas City

Native-Born of Native Parents
Native-Born of Foreign Parents
Foreign-Born
Non-White (Including Asian)

Composition of Population, Selected Cities, 1920

An immigrant family at home in their tenement. Though immigrant families were often large and their living conditions difficult, the newcomers displayed resilience and persistence in adapting to a strange environment. The people shown here were poor but proud, with a sense of integrity that shows in their faces.   Bettmann Archive.

were made up of enclaves of Italians from the same province, Japanese from the same island district, and Russian Jews from the same *shtetl* (village). In these transplanted communities, Old World customs persisted. People practiced their religions as they always had, held traditional feasts and pageants, married within their group, and pursued old feuds with people from rival villages and provinces.

Immigrant Cultures

Yet the very diversity of American cities forced immigrants to modify their attitudes and habits. Few newcomers could avoid contact with people different from themselves, and few could prevent such contacts from altering their traditional ways of life. Although many foreigners identified themselves by their village or region of birth, and organized their mutual benefit and fraternal societies along these lines, some immigrant institutions, like newspapers and churches, had to appeal to an entire nationalist group in order to survive. Immigrants struggled to maintain their native languages and to pass them down to younger generations, but English was taught in the schools and needed on the job; it soon penetrated nearly every community. And because the goods available in America often differed from those of the homeland, immigrants had to adjust their lifestyles to resemble those of other Americans. They continued to cook ethnic meals using American foods, but many bought the ready-made clothing and mass-produced furniture that were commonplace in the larger society.

The influx of so many immigrants between 1870 and 1920 transformed the United States from a basically Protestant nation into a society of Protestants, Catholics, and Jews. Newcomers from Italy, Hungary, and what would become Czechoslovakia, Yugoslavia, and Poland joined the Irish and Germans to boost the proportion of Catholics in several large cities. German and eastern European immigrants gave New York one of the largest Jewish populations in the world.

In the 1880s, another group of migrants began to move into American cities. Thousands of rural blacks moved northward and westward, fleeing crop liens, violence, and political oppression and seeking better employment.

Black Migration to the Cities

Although numbers of black urban dwellers would grow much larger after 1915, thirty-two cities contained 10,000 or more blacks by 1900, and 79 percent of all blacks outside the South lived in cities. Black migrants resembled foreign immigrants in their peasant backgrounds and economic motivations, but they differed in several important ways. Because few factories would employ blacks, most black workers found jobs in the service sector—cleaning, cooking, carting. Also, because the majority of jobs in domestic and personal service were traditionally female jobs, black women outnumbered black men in most cities.

Together the three major migrant groups that peopled American cities—native whites, foreigners, and native blacks—sowed the seeds of modern American culture, to which each group made important contributions. Cities nurtured a rich cultural variety: American folk music and literature, Italian cuisine, Irish comedy, Yiddish theater, Afro-American jazz and dance, and much more. Like their predecessors, newcomers in the late nineteenth century changed their environment as much as they were changed by it.

LIVING CONDITIONS IN THE INNER CITY

Population growth created intense pressures on the public and private sectors of the city. Masses of people jammed inner-city districts, where they were known less for their cultural contributions than for the problems they bred. American cities seemed to harbor all the afflictions that plague modern society: poverty, disease, crime, decay, and other unpleasant conditions that result when large numbers of people live close together. City dwellers generally adjusted as best they could until technology, science, private enterprise, or public authority could alleviate their problems. Some remarkable successes were achieved. In the late nineteenth century and early twentieth, construction of buildings, homes, streets, sewers, and schools proceeded at a furious pace. American cities set world standards for fire protection and water purification. Yet other ills still awaited solution.

One of the most persistent shortcomings of American cities has been their failure to provide adequate housing to all who need it. The failure has roots in nineteenth-century urban development.

Housing Problems

In spite of massive construction in the 1880s and early 1900s, population growth outpaced housing supplies. This condition especially affected working-class families, who, because of low-paying jobs, had to rent their living quarters. As cities grew, landlords took advantage of shortages in low-cost rental housing by splitting up existing buildings to house more people, constructing multiple-unit tenements, and hiking rents. Low-income families adjusted to high costs and short supply by sharing space and expenses. Thus it became common in many big cities for a one-family apartment to be occupied by two or three families or by one family plus a number of paying boarders.

Inside many buildings, living conditions were intolerable. The largest rooms were barely ten feet wide, and interior rooms either had no windows at all or opened onto narrow shafts that bred vermin and rotten odors. Few buildings had indoor plumbing, and the only source of heat was coal-burning stoves.

In several places housing problems aroused concerned citizens to mount reform campaigns. New York State took the lead in 1867, 1879, and 1901 by legislating light, ventilation, and safety codes for new tenement buildings. A few reformers, such as Jacob Riis and Lawrence Veiller, advocated housing low-income families in model tenements, with more spacious, airier rooms and better facilities. Model tenements, however, required landlords and investors to accept lower profits—a sacrifice few were willing to make. Neither reformers nor public officials would consider government financing of better housing, fearing such a step would undermine private enterprise.

Scientific and technological advances, however, enhanced the quality of urban life. Following the general acceptance of the bacteria theory of disease, cities established more efficient water purification and sewage disposal systems. Public health regulations helped to reduce the death rate for tuberculosis and to control such diseases as cholera, typhoid fever, and diphtheria. Modernized firefighting equipment and streetlighting made the cities safer places in which to live. None of these improvements, however, lightened the burden of poverty borne by large numbers of city dwellers.

Since colonial days, Americans have never agreed on how much responsibility the general public should

Behind the tenements that housed poor working-class families in many cities were even more squalid alley structures such as these in Chicago. In cellars and in these old wooden houses that had been moved back to make room for newer brick buildings lived the poorest of the poor. *Chicago Historical Society ICHi-00800.*

assume for poor relief. In the late nineteenth and early twentieth centuries, many people held to the traditional beliefs that anyone could escape poverty through hard work and clean living and that poverty was inevitable only because some people were weaker than others. Yet close observation of the poor caused some social welfare workers to conclude that people's environments, rather than their personal defects, caused poverty.

This new attitude, which had been gaining ground since the mid-nineteenth century, fueled drives for building codes, factory regulations, and public-health measures. Nevertheless, most middle- and upper-class Americans remained wedded to the belief that in a society of abundance only the unfit were poor, and that relief of poverty should be tolerated but never encouraged. As one charity worker urged, relief

Chapter 18: THE CITY AND EVERYDAY LIFE, 1877–1920

"should be surrounded by circumstances that shall . . . repel every one . . . from accepting it."

Even more than crowding and pauperism, crime and disorder alarmed Americans and nurtured fears that urban growth, especially the growth of slums, was corrupting the nation. The more cities grew, it seemed, the more they shook with violence. Native whites were quick to blame immigrants and blacks for the so-called crime waves that swept the nation. Yet it is possible that as a greater proportion of the population was concentrated in cities, crime merely became more conspicuous and sensational rather than more prevalent. To be sure, urban wealth and the mingling of different kinds of people provided new opportunities for organized thievery, petty larceny, vice, and violent grudge-settling. But how do such activities compare to the lawlessness and brutality of backwoods mining camps and southern plantations? Moreover, in spite of distress over Irish bank-robbery gangs, German pickpockets, and Italian Black Hand murderers, there is little evidence that more immigrants than natives populated the rogues' gallery.

One thing does seem certain; city life in the late nineteenth and early twentieth centuries certainly supported the thesis that there is a tradition of violence in the United States. Cities served as arenas for many of the era's worst riots. Besides the violence that often erupted during strikes or times of depression, there were race riots: in Wilmington, North Carolina, 1898; Atlanta, Georgia, 1906; Springfield, Illinois, 1908. In cities of the Southwest and Pacific Coast, Chinese and Mexican immigrants often felt the sting of native intolerance.

Solving the mounting problems of city life seemed to many Americans to demand greater government action. Thus city governments passed more laws and ordinances that regulated housing, provided poverty relief, and expanded police power. Yet public responsibility always ended at the boundaries of private property. Constrained by laissez faire, local governments could do little to provide a better life for many of their citizens. Eventually some advances in housing construction, sanitation, and medical care did reach slum dwellers. But for most people, the only hope was to look to the next generation or to move elsewhere.

PROMISES OF MOBILITY

Between the Civil War and the First World War, Baptist minister Russell Conwell delivered the same sermon more than six thousand times to untold millions across the United States. Titled "Acres of Diamonds," his immensely popular lecture affirmed the belief that any American could achieve success. People did not have to look very far for riches, Conwell preached; acres of diamonds lay at everyone's feet. Night after night, Conwell declared to his audiences that it was one's "Christian and Godly" duty to attain riches. But how possible was it for people actually to improve their lot and fulfill that duty?

Basically, there were three ways a person could get ahead: occupational advancement (and the higher income that accompanied it); property acquisition (and the potential for greater wealth it represented); and migration to an area of better conditions and greater opportunity. These options were open chiefly to white men. Although many women worked, owned property, and migrated, their social standing was usually defined by the men in their lives—their husbands, fathers, or other kin. Many women did improve their economic status by marrying men with wealth or potential, but other avenues were mostly closed. Men and women who were Afro-American, American Indian, Hispanic-American, or Asian-American had even fewer opportunities for success. Pinned to the bottom of society by prejudice, these groups were expected to accept their inherited station.

To a large number of people, however, the urban and industrial expansion of the late nineteenth century should have offered broad opportunity for occupational mobility. Thousands of small businesses were needed to supply goods and services to burgeoning urban populations. And corporations required a variety of managerial and clerical personnel. Only a few traveled the rags-to-riches path, but considerable movement occurred along the path from rags to moderate success.

Occupational Mobility

Rates of occupational mobility in late-nineteenth- and early-twentieth-century American communities were slow but steady. Some people slipped from a higher to a lower rung of the occupational ladder, but rates of upward movement were almost always double the downward rates. Although patterns were far from consistent, immigrants generally experienced lower rates of upward mobility and higher rates of downward mobility than natives did. Still, regardless of birthplace, the chances for a white male to rise occupationally over the course of his career or to have a higher-status job than his father had were relatively good.

In addition to or instead of advancing occupationally, a person could achieve social mobility by acquiring property. But property was not easy to acquire in turn-of-the-century America. Banks and savings institutions were far stricter in their lending practices than they would become after the 1930s, when the federal government began to insure real estate financing. Mortgage loans carried relatively high interest rates and short repayment periods. Nevertheless, a general rise in wage rates enabled many families to build savings accounts, which could be used as down payments on property. Indeed, the 1900 federal census noted that the United States had the highest home ownership rate among all Western nations except Denmark, Norway, and Sweden.

Acquisition of Property

Finally, each year millions of families tried to improve their living conditions by packing up and moving elsewhere. In general, Americans followed the maxim that movement means improvement. This urge to move affected every region, every city. From Boston to San Francisco, from Minneapolis to San Antonio, no more than half the families residing in a city at any one time could be found there ten years later.

Residential Mobility

In addition to population movement between cities, many people moved from one residence to another within the same city. Today, one in every five American families moves in a given year. A hundred years ago, the proportion was closer to one in four, or even one in three. Population turnover affected almost every neighborhood, every ethnic and occupational group.

Rapid residential flux undermined the stability of even the most homogeneous neighborhoods. Rarely did a single nationality comprise a clear majority in any large area, even when that area was known as Little Italy, Jewtown, Over-the-Rhine, or Greektown. Residential change dispersed immigrants from their original areas of settlement into many different neighborhoods. In New York, Boston, and other eastern ports, ethnically homogeneous districts did exist, and people tended to change residences within those districts rather than move away from them. Elsewhere, however, most immigrant families lived dispersed in ethnically mixed neighborhoods rather than in ghettos.

Ethnic Neighborhoods and Ghettos

If the term *ghetto* is defined as a place of enforced residence from which escape is at best difficult, only nonwhites in this era had a true ghetto experience. Wherever Asians and Mexicans immigrated, they encountered discrimination in housing, occupations, and other areas of public life. Though these groups often preferred to remain separate in Chinatowns and *barrios,* white Americans made every effort to keep them confined.

Prejudice and discrimination not only trapped blacks at the bottom of the occupational ladder but operated in housing markets to limit their residential opportunities. Whites organized protective associations that pledged not to sell homes in white neighborhoods to blacks, and occasionally used violence to scare away black families who did move in. Such efforts seldom worked. Whites who lived on the edge of black neighborhoods often fled, leaving their homes and apartments to be sold and rented to black occupants. By 1920 ten Chicago census tracts were over 75 percent black. In Detroit, Cleveland, Los Angeles, and Washington, D.C., two-thirds or more of the total black population lived in only two or three wards. Within these districts, blacks nurtured distinct cultural institutions that helped them adjust to urban life: storefront churches, business and educational organizations, social clubs, and saloons. But the ghettos also bred frustration, the result of stunted opportunity and racial bigotry. Color, more than any other factor, made the urban experiences of blacks different from those of whites.

All groups, however, including blacks, could and did move—if not from one part of the city to another, then from one city to another. Americans were always seeking greener pastures, and the hope that things might be better somewhere else acted as a kind of safety valve, relieving some of the tensions and frustrations that simmered inside the city. At times these emotions erupted into violence; more often, people simply left to seek a better life elsewhere.

THE RISE OF URBAN BOSS POLITICS

The sudden growth and mounting rivalry among social and economic interest groups that occurred in the late nineteenth century mired cities in a governmental swamp. From suburbs to slums, burgeoning populations, business expansion, and technological change created urgent needs for water, sewers, police and fire protection, schools, parks, and many other services. Such needs strained government institutions beyond their capacities. Further-more, city governments approached these needs in a disorganized fashion.

Power thrives on confusion, and out of this governmental chaos arose the political machine. Unlike political parties, which ideally exist for higher purposes than merely electing their candidates to office, machines were organizations whose main goal was getting and keeping political power. In order to achieve that goal, a machine had to win popular support. Machine politicians routinely used bribery and graft to further their ends. But they could not have succeeded if they had not provided relief, security, and municipal services to large numbers of people. By doing so, machine politicians alleviated many urban problems and accomplished things that other agencies had been unable or unwilling to attempt.

Machines were also beneficiaries of the new urban conditions. As cities grew larger and economically more complex, business leaders either vied to use government to advance their own interests or withdrew from local affairs to pursue their interests in interurban or interregional economic organizations. At the same time, hordes of newcomers, often unskilled and foreign-born, crowded into the cities. Enfranchised by liberal voting qualifications, the men of these groups became a substantial political force. These circumstances bred a new kind of leader: the political boss. Conflicting interest groups needed brokers who could bypass governmental stalemates, and urban newcomers had needs that required government attention. Bosses and machines filled those needs.

The system rested on a popular base and was held together by loyalty and service. City machines were coalitions of smaller machines that derived their power directly from the neighborhoods, particularly inner-city neighborhoods inhabited by the native and immigrant working classes. In return for votes, bosses provided jobs, built parks and bathhouses, distributed food to the needy, and helped when someone ran afoul of the law. Such personalized service cultivated

Political Machines

mass attachment to the boss; never before had government or public leaders assumed such responsibility for people in need.

In order to finance their largesse and support their system, bosses exchanged favors for votes or money. Their power over local government enabled machines to control the letting of contracts, the granting of utility or streetcar franchises, and the distribution of city jobs. Recipients of city business and jobs were expected to repay the machine with money and votes. Bosses called this process gratitude; critics called it graft. Moreover, machines dispensed favors to illegal businesses as well as legitimate ones. Payoffs from gambling, prostitution, and illegal liquor traffic were important sources of machine revenue. In an era when unemployment insurance and welfare were virtually unknown, however, machines were valued despite these shortcomings.

CIVIC REFORM

Machine politics brought some order to city government, met some of the needs of immigrants and other inner-city residents, and lined the pockets of some leaders and their business allies. But the boss system also alarmed the established classes inhabiting the outlying neighborhoods and sensitized many men and women to the problems of urban growth. At the same time when the bosses were consolidating their power, a reform movement was organizing to destroy political machines and improve the quality of urban life. Anxious over the mounting poverty, crowding, and disorder that seemed to accompany population expansion, and convinced that urban services were making taxes too high, civic reformers organized to oust bosses and to install more responsible leaders at the helm of urban administration.

Urban reform derived from the industrial system's emphasis on eliminating waste and inefficiency. Business-minded reformers believed government could be made more efficient by running it like a business. They believed that the only way to prevent civic decay was to elect officials who would hold down expenses and prevent corruption. Thus the major goals of reform leaders were to reduce city budgets, make government employees work longer, and cut taxes.

Structural Reforms in Government

As a means of introducing sound business principles to government, civic reformers supported a number of structural changes, such as city-manager and commission forms of government and nonpartisan, citywide election of officials. Each of these reforms was aimed at removing politics from government. Experts would control decision making at the local level, and the ward and neighborhood power bases of the bosses would be undermined.

A few reformers did move beyond structural changes to a genuine concern for social problems. Mayors like Detroit's Hazen S. Pingree (1889–1896), Toledo's Samuel "Golden Rule" Jones (1897–1904), and Cleveland's Thomas L. Johnson (1901–1909) worked to provide jobs for poor people, to reduce charges by transit and utilities companies, and to establish greater governmental responsibility for the welfare of all citizens. Some supported public ownership of gas, electric, and telephone companies—a quasi-socialistic reform that alienated their business allies. But most civic reformers could not match the bosses' political savvy and soon found themselves out of power.

Social Reform

Nevertheless, the seeds of social reform were beginning to sprout outside politics. Convinced that laissez-faire ideology could no longer work in a complex urban-industrial world and driven by an urge to identify and address urban problems, a number of men and women—mostly young and middle-class—embarked on campaigns for social betterment. These urban social reformers operated within a variety of fields and sought solutions to a variety of problems. Housing reformers wanted local government to pass building codes to ensure safety in tenements.

Protestant reformers influenced by the Social Gospel movement, which emphasized social responsibility as a means to salvation, built churches in slum neighborhoods and urged businesses to be socially responsible. Educational reformers saw public schools as a means of preparing immigrants and their children for citizenship by teaching them American values as well as the English language.

Perhaps the most ambitious and inspiring feature of the urban reform movement was the settlement house. Patterned after London's Toynbee Hall, settlements were efforts by young, educated, middle-class men and women to live in slum neighborhoods and bridge the gulf between classes, in hopes that people could learn from each other. Early settlement founders such as Jane Addams, Florence Kelley, and Graham Taylor wanted to improve the lives of working-class people by helping them to obtain an education, an appreciation of the arts, better jobs, and better housing. They provided a wide array of services, from vocational classes to child care for working mothers. But they also attempted to remake the working class in their own middle-class image.

Urban reformers wanted to save cities, not abolish them. They believed that urban life could be improved by restoring feelings of service and cooperation among all citizens. Reformers often failed to realize, however, that cities were diverse places where different people had different views of what reform actually meant. As a result of such attitudes, the accomplishments of urban reform were mixed: the American reform tradition merged idealism with naiveté and insensitivity.

THE LEGACY OF URBANISM

Urban America seldom functioned smoothly; in fact, there really was no coherent urban community, only a collection of subcommunities. As a result of immigration and urbanization, the United States had become a culturally pluralistic society.

Cultural Pluralism

Literary critic Randolph Bourne dubbed the United States "a cosmopolitan federation of national colonies." This kind of reasoning produced hyphenated identifications: people considered themselves Irish-American, Italo-American, Polish-American, and the like.

Pluralism and its attendant interest-group loyalties made politics an important institution. If America was not a melting pot, then different groups were competing with each other for power, wealth, and status. When lack of skills, education, capital, and influence closed off paths to success, immigrants turned to politics to protect their interests and to open up new opportunities. American cities became arenas in which different groups formed coalitions to achieve their goals. But such coalitions were fragile, and their membership shifted according to the issue in question.

Adherents of different cultural traditions battled over how much control government should exercise over people's lives. The most provocative issue was

Cultural-Political Alignments

about the use of leisure time and celebration of Sunday, the Lord's day. In the Puritan tradition, natives supported "blue laws" designed to prevent the desecration of the Christian Sabbath by prohibiting various commercial and recreational activities. European immigrants, accustomed to feasting and playing after church, fought Sunday closings of saloons and other restrictions on the only day they had free for fun and relaxation. Similar splits developed over public versus parochial schools and prohibition versus the free availability of liquor.

Such efforts at government control generally failed, though, because too many people had a stake in the country's cultural diversity. By 1920, immigrants and their offspring outnumbered natives in many cities, and the national economy depended on the new workers and consumers. They had helped to make the United States an urban nation with a rich and varied culture. And modern American political

Streets clogged with people and vehicles, canyon walls of tall
buildings, a hodgepodge of signs and banners, and a maze of
overhead wires gave the modern American city its image of
growth and bustling activity.   Courtesy of The New-York
Historical Society.

Chapter 18: THE CITY AND EVERYDAY LIFE, 1877–1920

liberalism, with its sensitivity to individual liberty, owes much to them.

STANDARDS OF LIVING

I f the affluence of a society can be measured by how quickly it converts luxuries into commonplace articles of everyday life, the United States was indeed becoming affluent in the years between 1880 and 1920. In 1880, for example, only wealthy women could afford silk stockings, and only residents of Florida, Texas, and California could enjoy the luxury of fresh oranges. In 1921, however, Americans bought 217 million pairs of silk stockings and ate 248 crates of oranges per 1,000 people. How did Americans afford these goods? How did changes in standards of living come about?

What people can afford depends largely on their resources and incomes. Data for the period from 1880 to 1920 are scattered, but there is no doubt that incomes rose. As always, the rich got richer. But incomes also rose among the middle classes. For example, the average pay for clerical workers rose 36 percent between 1890 and 1910 (see table, page 330). In the early 1900s, employees of the federal executive branch were averaging $1,072 a year, and college professors $1,100—not handsome sums, but much more than manual workers received. With these incomes, the middle class could afford relatively comfortable housing. A six- to seven-room house cost around $3,000 to buy or build and $15 to $20 per month to rent.

Wages for industrial workers increased as well, though they varied widely and income figures were deceiving. On the average, the annual wages of industrial workers rose from $486 in 1890 to $630 in 1910. Hourly rates in industries with large female work forces were lower than those in industries with predominantly male work forces. Also, regional variations were wide. Nevertheless, wages for all moved upward (see table). Pay for farm laborers followed the same trend, though wages remained relatively low because generally those workers received room and board along with their pay.

But wage increases mean little if living costs rise as fast as or faster than income. In fact, this is what happened in the United States around the turn of the century. Rarely did the income for a particular occupation rise at the same rate as the cost of living. Thus, particularly for the working class, it was becoming harder, not easier, to pay for life's necessities.

Cost of Living

How then could working-class Americans afford the new goods and services that the industrial age offered? Obviously, many could not. Still, a working-class family could raise its income and partake at least partially in consumer society by sending children and women into the labor market. Thus in a household where the father made $600 a year, the wages of other family members might lift the total to $800 or $900. Many families also rented household space to boarders and lodgers, a practice that could yield up to $200 a year. These means of increasing family income enabled people to spend more and save more.

Supplements to Family Income

Scientific developments eased some of life's struggles, and their impact on living standards increased after 1900. Advances in medical care and better living conditions sharply reduced death rates and extended the life span. Between 1900 and 1920, for example, life expectancy rose six years, and the death rate dropped by 24 percent. During the same period there were spectacular declines in the death rates from typhoid, diphtheria, influenza (except for a harsh epidemic in 1918 and 1919), tuberculosis, and intestinal ailments—diseases that had been the scourge of earlier generations. There were, however, significantly more deaths from cancer, diabetes, and heart disease. Americans also found more

Higher Life Expectancy

AMERICAN LIVING STANDARDS, 1880–1920

	1880	1890	1900	1910	1920
Income and earnings					
Annual income:					
clerical worker		$848		$1,156	
public school teacher		$256		$492	
industrial worker		$486		$630	
farm laborer		$233		$336	
Hourly wage:					
soft-coal miner		$0.18[a]		$0.21	
iron worker		$0.17[a]		$0.23	
shoe worker		$0.14[a]		$0.19	
paper worker		$0.12[a]		$0.17	
Labor statistics					
Number of people in labor force	17.4 million	28.5 million			41.7 million
Average workweek, manufacturing		60 hours		51 hours	47.4 hours
Food costs					
10 pounds potatoes		$0.16		$0.17	
Dozen eggs		$0.21		$0.34	
1 pound bacon		$0.12½		$0.25	
Demographic data					
Life expectancy at birth:					
women			48.3 years		54.6 years
men			46.3 years		53.6 years
Death rate per 1,000 people			172		130
Birthrate per 1,000 people	39.8		32.3		27.7
Other					
Number of students in public high schools		203,000			2.3 million
Advertising expenditures	$20 million		$95 million	$500 million	
Telephones per 100 people		0.3[b]	2.1[c]		12.6[d]

[a]1892 [b]1891 [c]1901 [d]1921

ways to kill: though the suicide rate remained about the same, homicides and automobile deaths increased dramatically between 1900 and 1920.

FAMILY LIFE

Though the overwhelming majority of Americans continued to live their lives within a family, this most basic of social institutions underwent considerable strain during the industrial era. As American society became more affluent and complex, it generated new institutions—schools, social clubs, political organizations, and others—that competed with the family to provide nurture, education, companionship, and security. Yet the family retained its fundamental usefulness as a cushion in a hard, uncertain world.

Throughout modern Western history, most people have lived in two overlapping kinds of basic unit: the household and the family. A *household* is a residential unit, a group of related and/or unrelated people who live in the same abode. A *family* is a group of people related by kinship, some of whom typically live together. The distinction between household and family is important in describing how Americans lived in the late nineteenth and early twentieth centuries.

Family and Household Structures

At the most elementary level, Americans between 1877 and 1920 grouped themselves in traditional ways. As in the past, the vast majority of American households consisted of *nuclear families*—usually a married couple with or without children and including no other relatives. About 15 to 20 percent of households consisted of *extended families,* which might include grandparents, grandchildren, aunts and uncles, in-laws, cousins, or combinations of such relatives. About 5 percent of the population lived alone.

The relative size of nuclear families did change over time, however. In 1880 the birth rate was 39.9 live births per 1,000 people; by 1920 it had dropped to 27.7. The reasons for this decline remain unclear. The pattern seems to have been that women in the settled eastern areas of the country were ending childbearing at an earlier age than were women in western areas. Possibly the greater availability of arable land in the West encouraged larger families; differences in a child's productivity may also have had an effect. On the farms, where children could work at home or in the fields at an early age, a new child contributed a new set of hands to the family work force. But in the wage-based eastern economy, children could not contribute significantly to the family income for many years.

Birth Rates

Though fertility rates among blacks, immigrants, and rural dwellers were consistently higher than those of white native urban dwellers, the birth rates of all groups fell dramatically. As a result, families with six or eight children became less common; three or four children became more common. The size of the nuclear family had declined and had done so over a short time span.

In spite of the predominance of the nuclear family, the household typically expanded and contracted drastically over the lifetime of a given family. First, the size of the family fluctuated as children were born, and later left home. Second, the process of leaving home made for huge numbers of young people— and some older people—who lived as boarders and lodgers, especially in cities. Middle- and working-class families commonly took in boarders to help pay the rent or to occupy unused rooms vacated by grown children.

Boarding

The practice of boarding stirred middle-class concern about health and morality. Some reformers complained of "the lodger evil." Yet for many immigrants and young people who had left home, boarding was a transitional stage of life. For such people a quasi-family environment was provided.

Within both nuclear and extended families kinship had important functions, especially for immigrants and others in need. At a time when welfare and service agencies were rare, the family continued to be the institution to which people could turn. Immigrants, for example, often took in newly arrived relatives. Nearby family members could help each other out with child care, meals, shopping, advice, consolation, and the like. Relatives also obtained jobs for each other.

Kinship Obligations

The obligations of kinship, however, were not always welcome or even helpful. Immigrant families often put pressure on last-born children to stay at home and care for aging parents, a practice that stifled those children's opportunities for education, marriage, and economic independence. Tensions also developed when one relative felt another was not helping out enough. Nevertheless, kinship, for better or worse, provided people a means of coping with the stresses of urban industrial society.

At the turn of the century, family life and its functions were both changing and holding firm. New institutions assumed tasks formerly performed by the family. Schools made education more of a community responsibility. Employment agencies, personnel offices, labor unions, and legislatures began to take responsibility for employee recruitment and job security. In addition, migration and a soaring divorce rate seemed to be splitting families apart: 19,633 divorces were granted in the United States in 1880; by 1920, that number had grown to 167,105. Yet in the face of these changes, the family remained a resilient institution.

THE NEW LEISURE AND MASS CULTURE

On December 2, 1889, as hundreds of workers paraded through Worcester, Massachusetts, in support of shorter working hours, a group of carpenters hoisted a banner that proclaimed, "Eight Hours for Work, Eight Hours for Rest, Eight Hours for What We Will." That last phrase, "for What We Will," was significant, for it marked recognition of a special segment of everyday life that belonged to the individual. Increasingly, leisure activities filled this time segment, among working classes as well as middle and upper classes.

For a nation nurtured on a frontier tradition of hard work and distaste for wasted time, the leisure-time revolution of the late nineteenth century marked a dramatic shift. The revolution was made possible by the invention of labor-saving devices. For both factory workers and white collar employees, the work week was reduced. By the early 1900s, many Americans were enmeshed in the business of play.

Increase in Leisure Time

The vanguard of the trend was sports, of which football and especially baseball were popular among males. In 1845 baseball's rules had been codified, and by 1890 professional games had been played before crowds of more than 51,000 people. And in 1903 the champions of the National League (formed in 1876) played the champions of the American League (formed in 1901) in the first World Series. About the time that baseball was becoming entrenched as the national pastime, the violent sport of football began to attract public attention.

Football had first gained popularity at the intercollegiate level among those who could afford a college education. Soon colleges were employing nonstudents—called "tramp athletes"—to play on their teams. Winning at virtually any cost became important—18 players died and over 150 were seriously injured in 1905. Such violence stirred President Theodore Roosevelt, who convened a White House conference to discuss the game. From this meeting came the Intercollegiate Athletic Association (renamed the National College Athletic Association in 1910), an organization designed to police college sports and to make them less violent.

Sports

Meanwhile women also developed an interest in

By the end of the nineteenth century, recreation of all sorts became a value of, and attainable by, almost all classes for the first time in American history. Note the free-spirited relaxation of these bathers on a Coney Island beach; their poses contrast markedly with the stiff formality of people on city streets and the serious concentration of people at work.   Library of Congress.

sports. At the college level, basketball became a popular game. The sport's rules were modified by Senda Berenson of Smith College. Her changes limited dribbling and running and encouraged passing. By the turn of the century intercollegiate basketball games among women were common.

There were, of course, sports enjoyed by both sexes. Croquet, which swept the nation after the Civil War, was popular among middle- and upper-class people. And bicycling became so popular that the 1900 census declared, "Few articles . . . have created so great a revolution in social conditions as the bicycle." Both croquet and cycling were important in

an era when the removal of work from the home had begun to separate men and women; these two recreational activities created social contact between the sexes.

The "revolution in social conditions" referred to in the 1900 census, however, pertained to clothing styles. The constraints of Victorian fashions gave way to more comfortable and practical styles suitable for cycling, and the freer styles of cycling costumes (divided skirts and simple undergarments) influenced everyday fashion.

The rise of American show business paralleled the rise of sports, and similarly became a mode of leisure created by and for the common people. Circuses had existed in America since the 1820s.

Circuses

But after the Civil War, railroads enabled circuses to reach more of the country, and the popularity of the big show increased enormously. Circuses offered two main attractions: so-called freaks of nature, both human and animal, and the temptation and conquest of death. More important, however, was the sheer astonishment aroused by the trapeze artists, lion tamers, high-wire artists, acrobats, and clowns.

Several branches of American show business matured with the growth of cities. Popular drama, musical comedy, and vaudeville all gave Americans a

Popular Drama and Musical Comedy

chance to escape from the harsh realities of urban-industrial life into melodrama, adventure, and comedy. The plots were simple, the heroes and villains instantly recognizable. For urbanized people increasingly distant from the frontier, popular plays brought to life the mythical Wild West and Old South through stories of Davy Crockett, Buffalo Bill, and Civil War romances. Virtue, honor, and justice always triumphed in melodramas, reinforcing the popular belief that even in an uncertain and disillusioning world, goodness would nevertheless prevail.

Musical comedies raised audiences' spirits with song, humor, and dance. American musical comedy grew out of the lavishly costumed operettas popular in Europe. By introducing American themes (often involving ethnic groups), folksy humor, and catchy tunes and dances, these shows launched the nation's most popular songs and entertainers. George M. Cohan, the master of the American musical comedy after the turn of the century, helped to advance a sense of national superiority with such songs as "Yankee Doodle Dandy" and "You're a Grand Old Flag."

The French term *vaudeville* first referred to light drama with musical interludes, but in the United States vaudeville became a unique entertainment form. It was probably the most popular entertainment in early-twentieth-century America because its variety made it attractive to mass audiences. Shows in-cluded magic and animal acts, juggling, stunts, comedy (especially ethnic humor), and

Vaudeville

song and dance. Around 1900, the number of vaudeville theaters and troupes skyrocketed. The most famous promoter, Florenz Ziegfeld, brilliantly packaged popular entertainment in a stylish format—the Ziegfeld Follies—and gave the nation a new model of femininity, the Ziegfeld Girl, whose graceful dancing and alluring costumes were meant to suggest a haunting sensuality.

Lillian Russell, vaudeville singer and comedienne Fanny Brice, and burlesque queen Eva Tanguay attracted intensely loyal fans, commanded handsome fees, and won respect for their genuine talents. In contrast to the demure Victorian female, they conveyed pluck and creativity. But show business, which provided new economic activities for women, blacks, and immigrants, also indulged in stereotyping and exploitation.

Before the 1890s, the only form of entertainment open to black performers was the minstrel show. By century's end, however, minstrel shows had given

Blacks and Immigrants in Vaudeville

way to more sophisticated musicals, and blacks had begun to break into vaudeville. As stage sets shifted from the plantation to the city, the music shifted from folk tunes to ragtime. Pandering to the prejudice of white audiences, composers and performers of both races ridiculed blacks. Even Burt Williams, a highly paid black comedian and dancer who was one of the era's most talented performers, achieved his tormented success mainly by playing the stereotypical roles of darky and dandy.

Shortly after 1900, live entertainment began to yield to an even more accessible form of amusement: moving pictures. Perfected by Thomas Edison in the

Movies

early 1890s, movies began as slot-machine peepshows in penny arcades and billiard parlors. Eventually images were projected onto a screen so large audiences could view them, and a new medium was born.

Producers soon discovered, however, that a film could tell a story. By 1910 motion pictures had become an art form, thanks to creative directors like D. W. Griffith. Griffith's most famous work, *The Birth of a Nation* (1915), an epic film about the Civil War and Reconstruction, fanned racial prejudice by depicting blacks as threatening white moral values; its exaltation of the Ku Klux Klan also helped to revive the hooded empire. But the film's innovative techniques—close-ups, fade-outs, and battle scenes—gave viewers heightened drama and excitement.

The still camera, modernized by inventor George Eastman, enabled ordinary people to make their own photographic images; and the phonograph, another of Edison's inventions, made possible musical performances at home. The spread of movies, photography, and phonograph records meant that access to live performances no longer limited people's exposure to art and entertainment.

To some extent, the new amusements and pastimes had a homogenizing influence, bringing together disparate ethnic and social groups into a common experience. Parks, ball fields, vaudeville shows, and movies were designed for and appealed to everyone; they were nonsectarian and apolitical. Yet various groups adopted leisure institutions in their own way. For example, in some communities working-class immigrant groups used parks and amusement parks as locations for traditional family and ethnic gatherings. Thus as Americans learned to play, their leisure—like their work and politics—was shaped by pluralistic forces.

THE TRANSFORMATION OF MASS COMMUNICATIONS

With so many new things to do and buy, how did Americans decide what they wanted? Two new types of communication influenced consumer tastes and mass opinion. Modern advertising molded people's needs and consumption patterns; and popular journalism spread mass culture throughout the country.

In the United States, advertising has meant more than just selling. Advertisers aim to *invent* a demand. Indeed, the growth in the late nineteenth century of large companies that mass-produced consumer goods gave advertisers the task of creating "consumption communities"—bodies of consumers loyal to a particular brand name.

The major vehicle for advertising was the newspaper. In 1879 Wanamaker's department store placed the first full-page ad, and at about the same time newspapers began to allow advertisers to print pictures of products. Such attention-getting techniques transformed advertising into news. More than ever before, people read the newspapers to find out what was for sale as well as what was happening.

Just as advertising became news, news became a form of advertising, or at least of publicity. Canny publishers made people crave news. Joseph Pulitzer,

Yellow Journalism
a Hungarian immigrant who bought the *New York World* in 1883, pioneered the development of journalism as a branch of mass culture. Believing that newspapers should be "dedicated to the cause of the people rather than to that of the purse potentates," Pulitzer filled the *World* with stories of disasters, crimes, and scandals. Sensational headlines, set in large bold type like that of advertisements, screamed from every page. Pulitzer's journalists not only reported the news but sought it out—and sometimes even created it. Pulitzer also popularized the comics, and the yellow ink they were printed in gave his emphasis on the sensational the nickname "yellow journalism." The success enjoyed by Pulitzer caused others, most notably William R. Hearst, to adopt his techniques.

By the early twentieth century, the communications media, like the mass consumption of goods, were becoming commonplace. Alongside newspapers, mass-circulation magazines offered human-interest stories, muckraking exposés, titillating fiction, and eye-catching advertisements to a growing mass market. And the total number of books published more than quadrupled between 1880 and 1917, reflecting a growing literacy rate (94 percent in 1920).

Other forms of communication were also expanding. By 1920 the telephone was becoming a commonly used instrument, and increasing numbers of people were sending telegrams and letters. Little wonder, then, that the term *community* took on new dimensions. More than ever before, people in different parts of the country knew about and discussed the same staples of mass culture, whether it was a sensational murder, a sex scandal, or the fortunes of a particular entertainer or athlete.

POPULAR LITERATURE

American culture has long focused one eye on an increasingly complex technological future while casting the other at a sentimentalized, simpler past. When modern wonders like telephones, high-speed printing presses, phonographs, and cameras made information and entertainment more accessible, people demanded diversions that reaffirmed the traditional values of optimism, individualism, and freedom. Thus in 1914, just when they were beginning to appreciate fully automobiles, movies, and electricity, Americans made Edgar Rice Burrough's *Tarzan of the Apes* a best seller.

Popular fiction writers concentrated on the sensational. Since the 1840s, low-priced, paperbound novels had circulated widely among the literate public. After the Civil War such books, called dime novels, became the most widely read variety of American literature, especially among youths. These adventure publications offered three types of stories. The first evoked the Wild West. Intertwining fact and fiction, writers wove adventure stories around fa-

Dime Novels

mous folk heroes like Buffalo Bill Cody, the Lone Star Ranger, and Wild Bill Hickok. During the 1880s, however, many authors, recognizing the lure and growing impact of city life, began to give their tales urban settings and themes. Detective thrillers became the leading type of popular urban fiction. Just before the end of the century, science fiction and superheroes came to the fore.

One popular writer, Horatio Alger, moved beyond the fantasies of dime novels and offered his readers a formula for contending with new social and economic forces. Each of his 130 books tells the success story of an adolescent boy facing the problem of finding a place in an urban industrial world. Through ambition, honesty, luck, courage, and thrift, Alger's heroes overcome some obstacle, as well as poverty, and attain success. Alger believed in a cause-and-effect relationship between virtue and wealth.

Moral Messages of Popular Fiction

Just before Alger's death in 1899, one of America's most popular superheroes, Frank Merriwell, was created by Gilbert Patten (using the pen name of Burt Standish). Frank Merriwell's adventures had a common theme that accorded with the way many Americans liked to think of themselves and their nation: he attempted and accomplished the impossible. Merriwell became one of the first character models in popular fiction. A picture of refinement and valor, he taught by example, not by preaching. Even his name symbolized American virtues: according to Patten, "I took the three qualities I most wanted him to represent—frank and merry in nature, well in body and mind—and made the name Frank Merriwell."

Young women found escape and inspiration in sentimental tales about growing up and about animals. One of the most widely read was Louisa May Alcott's *Little Women*, published in two parts in 1868 and 1869. This novel, which eventually sold over 2 million copies, recreated the domestic delights and moral trials of four girls based on Alcott and her sisters. A generation later, Gene Stratton-Porter's romantic novels about childhood, like *Freckles* (1904) and *Laddie* (1913), became best sellers. Others in the

Frank Merriwell, the fictional hero of hundreds of sports and adventure stories, was a popular character model for young men. In this story, first published in Tip Top Weekly, *an unscrupulous sportsman tries to bribe Frank into teaching him his secret pitch, the "double shoot." Frank not only resists the temptation but teaches a moral lesson in the process. Culver Pictures.*

melodrama set in the Roman Empire, was of particular importance because it heralded a rage for historical fiction that has not yet subsided.

While some popular writers focused on escapism, others were trying to introduce realism into romance. During the 1870s and 1880s, a number of "local color" writers began producing works that depicted the people and environment of a particular region more realistically. Essentially, they used authentic manners, customs, and speech to depict a romantic, rustic past. The movement was largely centered in the South, whose writers felt compelled to rebuild the region's image. But the realist movement permeated other regions as well. Indeed, it began in the Far West and the Midwest.

Local Colorists

One local colorist, Mark Twain (the pen name of Samuel Clemens), moved beyond romance and adventure, and in doing so won recognition from both intellectuals and the masses. He was best known for his books about the American West: *Tom Sawyer* (1876), *Life on the Mississippi* (1883), and *Huckleberry Finn* (1884). These antisentimental novels were realistic portrayals of western life and of human weakness. Twain was sensitive to both the comic and the tragic sides of life, and his writing reflected the dynamic energy and materialism of his era.

Literary Classics

A number of Twain's contemporaries shunned the falseness of escape writing and focused instead on the moral tests life holds. Realists like William Dean Howells, Edith Wharton, and Henry James wrote chiefly about upper-class Americans (James usually wrote about Americans in Europe), but other realists examined the lives of more ordinary folk and in so doing opened new literary vistas. These writers, sometimes called naturalists, often viewed life in terms of the survival of the fittest; they portrayed ruthless struggles for life and power in frank detail. Their descriptions of slum life, sexual immorality, and violence portrayed a side of America that local colorists avoided.

The escapism of popular fiction and the realism of

same vein were Anna Sewell's *Black Beauty* (1890) and Kate Douglas Wiggins's *Rebecca of Sunnybrook Farm* (1903).

Popular literature for adults also oozed with escapism and sentimentality. The best-selling titles of the late nineteenth century included romances about mythical places of chivalry and honor. *Ben Hur* (1880), General Lew Wallace's powerful religious

serious fiction, though seemingly at odds, offered similar commentaries on the American society of the early twentieth century. It was no coincidence that Frank Merriwell replaced Horatio Alger's heroes in popular fiction around 1900: by then Americans knew that it took more than honesty, energy, and a timely rescue to become rich. Naturalist writers, for example, saw that the new demands the industrial age placed on individuals threatened the traditional American values of family, nature, frugality, and moral restraint.

SUGGESTIONS FOR FURTHER READING

Urban Growth

Howard P. Chudacoff, *The Evolution of American Urban Society*, rev. ed. (1981); Arthur M. Schlesinger, *The Rise of the City* (1933); Jon Teaford, *City and Suburb: The Political Fragmentation of Metropolitan America, 1850–1970* (1979); Sam Bass Warner, Jr., *The Urban Wilderness* (1972); Sam Bass Warner, Jr., *Streetcar Suburbs* (1962).

Immigration, Ethnicity, and Religion

Aaron I. Abell, *American Catholicism and Social Action* (1960); Josef J. Barton, *Peasants and Strangers: Italians, Rumanians, and Slovaks in an American City* (1975); John Bodnar *et al.*, *Lives of Their Own: Blacks, Italians, and Poles in Pittsburgh, 1900–1960* (1982); John W. Briggs, *An Italian Passage* (1978); Jack Chen, *The Chinese of America* (1980); John B. Duff, *The Irish in the United States* (1971); Mario T. Garcia, *Desert Immigrants: The Mexicans of El Paso, 1880–1920* (1981); Nathan Glazer and Daniel P. Moynihan, *Beyond the Melting Pot*, rev. ed. (1970); Caroline Golab, *Immigrant Destinations* (1977); Milton Gordon, *Assimilation in American Life* (1964); Victor Greene, *For God and Country: The Rise of Polish and Lithuanian Ethnic Consciousness in America* (1975); Oscar Handlin, *The Uprooted*, 2nd ed. (1973); John Higham, *Strangers in the Land: Patterns of American Nativism* (1955); Harry Kitano, *Japanese Americans: The Evolution of a Subculture* (1969); Matt S. Maier and Feliciano Rivera, *The Chicanos: A History of Mexican Americans* (1972); Humbert S. Nelli, *The Italians of Chicago* (1970); Moses Rischin, *The Promised City: New York's Jews* (1962).

Urban Needs and Services

Robert H. Bremner, *From the Depths: The Discovery of Poverty* (1956); Thomas L. Philpott, *The Slum and the Ghetto* (1978); James F. Richardson, *The New York Police* (1970); Barbara Gutmann Rosencrantz, *Public Health and the State* (1972); Mel Scott, *American City Planning Since 1890* (1969); Christopher Tunnard and Henry Hope Reed, *American Skyline* (1955); David B. Tyack, *The One Best System: A History of American Urban Education* (1974).

Mobility and Race Relations

Howard P. Chudacoff, *Mobile Americans* (1972); Clyde Griffen and Sally Griffen, *Natives and Newcomers* (1977); David M. Katzman, *Before the Ghetto* (1973); Thomas Kessner, *The Golden Door* (1977); Kenneth L. Kusmer, *A Ghetto Takes Shape* (1976); Gilbert Osofsky, *Harlem: The Making of a Ghetto* (1966); Howard N. Rabinowitz, *Race Relations in the Urban South* (1978); Allan H. Spear, *Black Chicago* (1967); Stephan Thernstrom, *The Other Bostonians: Poverty and Progress in the American Metropolis* (1973); Olivier Zunz, *The Changing Face of Inequality: Urbanization, Industrial Development, and Immigrants in Detroit, 1880–1920* (1982).

Boss Politics

John M. Allswang, *Bosses, Machines and Urban Voters* (1977); Alexander B. Callow, Jr., ed., *The City Boss in America* (1976); Bruce M. Stave, ed., *Urban Bosses, Machines, and Progressive Reformers* (1972).

Urban Reform

John D. Buenker, *Urban Liberalism and Progressive Reform* (1973); James B. Crooks, *Politics and Progress* (1968); Melvin Holli, *Reform in Detroit* (1969); C. H. Hopkins, *The Rise of the Social Gospel in American Protestantism* (1940); Roy M. Lubove, *The Progressives and the Slums* (1962); Martin J. Schiesl, *The Politics of Efficiency: Municipal Administration and Reform in America* (1977).

Family and Individual Life Cycles

W. Andrew Achenbaum, *Old Age in the New Land* (1979); Carl N. Degler, *At Odds: Women and the Family in America* (1980); Michael Gordon, ed., *The American Family in Social-Historical Perspective*, 3rd ed. (1983); Carole Haber, *Beyond Sixty-five: Dilemmas of Old Age in America's Past* (1983); Tamara K. Hareven, *Family Time and Industrial Time: The Relationship Between the Family and Work in a New England Industrial Community* (1981); Joseph Kett, *Rites of Passage: Adolescence in America* (1979); David J. Pivar, *Purity Crusade: Sexual Morality and Social Control, 1868–1900* (1973); Virginia Yans-McLaughlin, *Family and Community: Italian Immigrants in Buffalo* (1977).

Mass Entertainment and Leisure

Robert Clyde Allen, *Vaudeville and Film, 1895–1915: A Study in Media Interaction* (1977); Gunther Barth, *City People* (1980); John F. Kasson, *Amusing the Million: Coney Island at the Turn of the Century* (1978); Donald J. Mrozek, *Sport and American Mentality, 1880–1910* (1983); Joseph A. Musselman, *Music in the Cultured Generation: A Social History of Music in America, 1870–1900* (1971); Benjamin G. Rader, *American Sports* (1983); Roy Rosenzweig, *Eight Hours for What We Will! Workers and Leisure in an Industrial City, 1870–1920* (1983); Robert Sklar, *Movie-Made America* (1976); Robert C. Toll, *On with the Show: The First Century of Show Business in America* (1976).

Advertising and Journalism

George Jurgens, *Joseph Pulitzer and the* New York World (1966); Frank L. Mott, *American Journalism*, 3rd ed. (1962); Daniel Pope, *The Making of Modern Advertising* (1983); W. A. Swanberg, *Citizen Hearst* (1961); Bernard A. Weisberger, *The American Newspaperman* (1961).

Popular Literature

John G. Cawelti, *Apostles of Success in America* (1965); John L. Cutler, *Patten and His Merriwell Saga* (1934); Frank L. Mott, *Golden Multitudes: The Story of Best Sellers in the United States* (1947); Moses Rischin, ed., *The American Gospel of Success* (1965); Henry Nash Smith, *Mark Twain* (1962); John W. Tebbell, *From Rags to Riches: Horatio Alger, Jr. and the American Dream* (1963).

CHAPTER 19

GILDED AGE POLITICS
1877–1900

The political platform written by the newly organized People's party that met in Omaha, Nebraska, in July 1892 seethed with discontent. Claiming to speak "in the name and on behalf of the people
of this country," the platform's preamble charged that
the nation had been

> brought to the verge of moral, political, and ma-
> terial ruin. Corruption dominates the ballot-box,
> the legislatures, the Congress, and touches even
> . . . the bench. . . . The fruits of the toil of mil-
> lions are boldly stolen to build up colossal fortunes
> for a few. . . . From the same prolific womb of
> governmental injustice we breed the two great
> classes—tramps and millionaires.

To thousands of Americans in the late nineteenth
century, these words represented a measured sense of
reality.

The transformation of the nation by industrialization, urbanization, and the commercialization of agriculture introduced disruptive forces that threatened
time-honored customs and institutions. Members of
the People's party, called Populists, were mostly farmers who believed that new, large-scale modes of production undermined their rights to equality and freedom. Like other protesters, such as labor unions and
socialists, the Populists concluded that the economic
system created irresponsible concentrations of power
and wealth that would crush small producers and
control government. Therefore they gathered in
Omaha to preserve a civilization of cooperation and
justice against the greed of market competition and
the despotism of big business.

Populists believed that politics and government
had been captured by the forces of monopoly and ir-
responsibility. In some ways they were right. Corruption and greed tugged at the fabric of democracy, and
the venality of the era prompted novelists Mark
Twain and Charles Dudley Warner to dub it the
Gilded Age. Congress, though split by powerful par-

tisan and regional rivalries, did grapple with important issues, such as the tariff and the currency, and passed some legislation initiating needed reforms. But also, many congressional accomplishments were either weak compromises or favors to special interests. Meanwhile, the judiciary became active in determining public policy. By defending vested rights of property against state and federal regulation, the courts supported the emerging power of big business. The presidency was filled by a series of honest, respectable men who seldom took legislative initiatives, and when they did, they often found themselves beaten back by Congress and the courts.

During the 1870s and 1880s, serious problems resulted from social and economic change. The gap between those with political influence and those who were excluded was becoming a chasm, further separating opposing interest groups: farmers versus businesspeople; debtors versus creditors; blacks versus whites; employees versus employers. Then in the 1890s, two developments brought the social and economic turmoil to a boiling point and brought about political change: the climax of rural discontent that accompanied the transformation of the West and South and a deep economic depression that resulted from flaws in the industrial system. In the midst of these crises, a presidential campaign in 1896 compressed all the symbols of the era into a single election. The nation emerged from the turbulent 1890s with new political alignments, just as it had developed new economic configurations. These alignments prepared the way for the new century and for an era of reform.

POLITICAL EQUILIBRIUM AND EMOTIONAL ISSUES

The historian Henry Adams, grandson and great-grandson of presidents, wrote that in American political history, the period between 1870 and 1895

Higher Voter Participation

"was poor in purpose and barren in results." But from the voters' perspective, politics appeared anything but barren. At no other time in the nation's history was public interest in elections higher. Except in the South, where blacks faced growing voting restrictions, 80 to 90 percent of eligible voters cast ballots in local and national elections. (Fewer than 50 percent typically do so today.)

Politics was the prime form of mass entertainment, outdistancing even baseball, vaudeville, and circuses. Though only men could vote, campaigns were community events that excited women and children as well. Voting was only the last stage in a process that included rallies, parades, picnics, and speeches, all of which were as much public amusement as civic responsibility.

Politics was a personal as well as a community activity. People formed strong loyalties to both individual politicians and parties. These allegiances were usually evenly distributed, so that no one party predominated for long. Between 1877 and 1897, Republicans held the presidency for twelve years, Democrats for eight. The same party controlled the presidency and both houses of Congress for only three two-year spans: the Republicans twice, the Democrats once. The balance persisted despite the admission of six territories to statehood during this period.

In some ways, the major parties resembled each other. Both were led by wealthy men, and both tried to appeal to farmers and wage earners as well as merchants and manufacturers. But differences in religious and ethnic values separated voters in the two parties. People who became Republicans were usually *pietistic*: Anglo-Saxon Protestants who believed that salvation was achieved through good works and encouraging others to be moral. They wanted government to legislate moral behavior.

The Democratic party, by contrast, attracted people whose culture was *ritualistic*: Roman Catholics, Jews, and high-church Protestants who believed that a person should accept the world as it is and that the way to salvation involved following the beliefs and rituals of the church. They preferred to leave questions of morality to individual conscience, rather than to government. Thus they opposed government regulation of individual behavior.

These cultural differences—pietism versus ritualism—made for emotional conflicts over social issues, especially on the local level. But at the national level and in Congress, parties split over long-standing political and economic issues, such as sectional controversies, patronage, tariffs, and the currency.

Long after Reconstruction ended, Americans were haunted by the conflicts and disruptions that had followed the Civil War. Republicans capitalized on the war by "waving the bloody shirt" whenever they faced a Democratic challenge. As one Republican orator harangued in 1876, "Every man that tried to destroy this nation was a Democrat. . . ." In the South voters also waved the bloody shirt, calling all Republicans traitors. The use of such emotional appeals persisted well into the 1880s.

Sectional Conflict

Politicians were not the only ones who attempted to profit by keeping the memory of the war alive. In the 1880s and 1890s, the Grand Army of the Republic, an organization of Union Army veterans numbering over 400,000, allied itself with the Republican party and pressured Congress into legislating generous pensions for former soldiers and their widows. Certainly many pensions were well deserved. Union soldiers had been poorly paid, and the war had widowed thousands of women. But for many other veterans, the emotional wake of the great conflict provided an opportunity to profit at the public's expense.

Few politicians could afford to oppose Civil War pensions, but a number of reformers attempted to dismantle the spoils system. The practice of awarding government jobs to party workers, regardless of their qualifications, had blossomed after the Civil War. As building construction, the postal service, the diplomatic corps, and other government activities expanded, so did the number of jobs on the public payroll. Elected officials scrambled to control new appointments as a means of cementing support for themselves and their parties. In return for the relatively short hours and high pay of government jobs, appointees pledged their votes and a portion of their earnings.

Civil Service Reform

A system so susceptible to corruption vexed a growing number of independents, who began advocating appointments and promotions based on merit rather than connections. The movement grew during the 1870s, when scandals in the Grant administration bared the defects of the spoils system. It reached full flower in 1881 with the formation of the National Civil Service Reform League. That same year, Charles Guiteau, a frustrated and demented civil service job-seeker, assassinated President James Garfield, and the murder hastened the drive for civil service reform. Late in 1882 Congress passed the Pendleton Civil Service Act, and President Chester Arthur signed it early in 1883.

The law outlawed political contributions by officeholders and created the Civil Service Commission, which would supervise competitive examinations for government positions. Significantly, however, the act gave the commission jurisdiction over only about 10 percent of federal jobs—although the president could expand the list. Nevertheless the law, and especially the provision outlawing political contributions, signaled a change.

Civil service reform has often been considered one of the major accomplishments of the Gilded Age; yet its actual impact can be debated. Certainly the system of hiring government workers needed improvement. But civil service reformers were not egalitarians who would give all qualified Americans a chance to participate in government. They were conservatives who wanted to restore an era when public servants were chosen from among men whose birth, wealth, and education supposedly fitted them for leadership.

In the 1880s tariffs and money, not government jobs, attracted the most attention in Congress. Through the mid-nineteenth century Congress had raised tariff rates to protect American manufactured goods and some agricultural products from Euro-

Tariff Policy

pean competition. By the 1880s there were separate tariffs on over four thousand items, and the resulting revenues were making for an embarrassing surplus in the federal treasury. Though a few economics professors and farmers argued for free trade, most Americans still believed high tariffs were necessary to support industry and preserve the jobs of wage earners.

The Republican party, claiming responsibility for economic growth, made protective tariffs a core feature of its policies. Democrats complained that tariffs made prices artificially high, benefiting those interests whose products were protected while hurting farmers, whose crops were not protected, and consumers, who had to buy manufactured goods. Although Democrats generally saw a need for some protection of American goods and raw materials, they favored lower tariff rates to encourage foreign trade and to reduce the treasury surplus.

Privileged interests continued to dominate tariff policy in the 1890s. When in 1894 House Democrats supported by President Grover Cleveland passed a bill to reduce tariff rates, Senate Republicans, aided by southern Democrats eager to protect their region's infant industries, added some six hundred amendments restoring most cuts. In 1897 a new tariff bill, the Dingley Act, raised rates even further, though it greatly expanded reciprocity provisions. Introduced in the McKinley Tariff of 1890, reciprocity gave the president authority to remove items from the free list if their countries of origin placed unreasonable tariffs on American goods.

The currency controversy was even more tangled than the tariff issue. In brief, it involved opposing reactions to the fall in prices caused by increased industrial and agricultural production after the Civil War. Farmers, most of whom were debtors, suffered because they had to pay fixed mortgage and interest payments even while their incomes declined because prices for their crops were dropping. Correctly perceiving that an insufficient money supply had made their debts more expensive relative to other prices, farmers favored schemes like the coinage of silver to increase the amount of currency in

Monetary Policy

circulation. Creditors, on the other hand, believed that overproduction had caused the price decline. They favored a more stable, tightly controlled money supply backed only by gold as a means of maintaining the confidence of native and foreign investors in the American economy.

But the issue involved more than economics. The creditor-versus-debtor conflict translated into haves versus have-nots. It also involved a sectional cleavage, the western silver-mining areas and agricultural regions of the South and West against the more conservative industrial Northeast.

Prior to the 1870s, the government had coined both silver and gold dollars; a silver dollar weighed sixteen times more than a gold dollar, meaning that gold was officially worth sixteen times as much as silver. But gold discoveries since 1848 had increased the supply, lowering gold's market price relative to that of silver. Producers of silver, which was now worth more than one-sixteenth the value of gold, preferred to sell their metal on the open market rather than to the government. As a result, silver dollars disappeared from circulation—owners hoarded them rather than spend them—and in 1873 Congress officially stopped coining silver dollars. At about the same time, European nations also stopped buying silver. Thus the United States and many of its trading partners adopted the gold standard, meaning that their currency was backed chiefly by gold.

Within a few years, however, new mines in the American West began to flood the market with silver, and its price dropped. Gold was now worth more than sixteen times what silver was worth. It became profitable to spend silver dollars—and would have been worthwhile to sell silver to the government in return for gold, but the government was no longer buying it. Debtors, who saw silver as a means of expanding the currency supply, now joined with silver producers to denounce the "Crime of '73" and to press for resumption of coinage at the old sixteen-to-one ratio.

Congress, split into silver and gold factions, tried to neutralize the issue with compromise legislation: the Bland-Allison Act of 1878, which required the treasury to buy $2 to $4 million worth of silver each month; and the Sherman Silver Purchase Act of 1890, which fixed the monthly purchase of silver in weight (4.5 million ounces) rather than in dollars. But neither act satisfied the different interest groups. The Sherman Act, passed partially in response to an economic decline in the mid-1880s, failed to expand the money supply. As the price of silver dropped, the government, now required only to buy a certain weight of silver, could spend less to purchase the stipulated number of ounces. Thus the money supply was not increased as substantially as some had hoped.

While debates over tariffs and money raged, Congress and state legislatures began to face the issue of women's suffrage more squarely than ever before. Late

Women's
Suffrage

in 1869 a Missouri couple, Francis and Virginia Minor, drew up a resolution stating that the Constitution and its amendments had already given women the right to vote. According to the recently adopted Fourteenth Amendment, the Constitution granted citizenship to "all persons born or naturalized in the United States," and no state could abridge the "privileges or immunities" of any citizen, including his—or, said the Minors, her—right to vote. Eventually the Minors, with support from the National Woman Suffrage Association (NWSA), sued a St. Louis registrar who had refused to permit Mrs. Minor to vote. In 1874 the Supreme Court ruled that suffrage did not automatically accompany citizenship and that states could legally withhold voting rights from certain classes of citizens, such as criminals, the insane—and women.

Four years later Susan B. Anthony, the indomitable fighter for human rights, convinced Senator A. A. Sargent of California, a strong supporter of women's suffrage, to introduce a constitutional amendment stating that "the right of citizens of the United States to vote shall not be denied or abridged by the United States or by any state on account of sex." The bill was killed by a Senate committee, but supporters reintroduced it several times over the next eighteen years. On the few occasions when the bill reached the Senate floor, it was voted down by sen-

Sheet music for a late-nineteenth-century song about women's suffrage. Women increased their agitation for the vote until in 1878 a constitutional amendment granting them suffrage was introduced in Congress. The Senate killed the measure that year, but women's groups like the National Suffrage Association continued to fight for the cause. *Courtesy, American Antiquarian Society.*

ators who expressed fears that suffrage would interfere with women's family responsibilities and ruin female virtue.

While the NWSA and others fought for the vote on the national level, the American Woman Suffrage Association worked for constitutional amendments at the state level. (The two suffrage groups joined in 1890 to form the National American Woman Suffrage Association.) Between 1870 and 1910, there were seventeen referenda in eleven states (all but three of which were west of the Mississippi River) to legalize women's suffrage. These attempts seldom succeeded, but women attained partial victories. By 1890 nineteen states allowed women to vote on school issues, three granted suffrage on tax and bond issues, and the groundwork was well laid for the next generation's battle for national voting rights.

Thus legislative leaders addressed some of the basic issues of the day, but they failed to agree on clear solutions. Congressmen and their constituents were so divided among factions and interest groups that the only passable legislation was the kind, like the Pendleton Act, that was ideal to no one but acceptable to most. And while complex problems like the tariff demanded careful study, most politicians preferred to devote their energies to party and factional concerns.

THE DECLINE OF THE PRESIDENCY

In the years between 1877 and 1900, American presidents contrasted sharply with more headstrong predecessors like Jackson and Lincoln. Proper, honorable, and honest, Presidents Hayes, Garfield, Arthur, Cleveland, Harrison, and McKinley won public respect but seldom provoked strong emotions. Not one of them was an inspiring personality, nor could any of them dominate the factional chieftains of their parties.

Rutherford B. Hayes (1877 to 1881) personified the belief that the president was a caretaker elected to execute what Congress initiated. Honest and self-controlled, Hayes avoided such controversial issues as the tariff and sectional rivalry. He did, however, take a conservative position on currency, and ordered out troops to quell the 1877 railroad strikes. Hayes also pleased

Hayes, Garfield, and Arthur

civil service advocates by appointing reformer Carl Schurz to the cabinet and battling New York's patronage king, Senator Roscoe Conkling. But Hayes demanded that his own appointees contribute to Republican coffers for the 1878 elections.

When Hayes refused to run for re-election in 1880, Republicans selected another Ohio congressman and Civil War hero, James A. Garfield. After defeating the Democrats' Winfield Scott Hancock, also a Civil War hero, by just 40,000 votes out of over 9 million, Garfield spent most of his brief presidency trying to secure an independent position among party potentates, but his opportunity to make lasting contributions ended with his assassination in 1881.

Garfield's vice president and successor was New York politician Chester A. Arthur, a protégé of the notorious Senator Conkling. Arthur had been nominated for vice president only to help the Republicans carry New York State; his elevation to the presidency made reformers shudder. Yet he became a dignified and temperate executive. Like his two predecessors, Arthur had no taste for his office. Suffering from illness, he made little effort to run in 1884.

In the 1884 presidential campaign the Republicans nominated Senator James G. Blaine of Maine and the Democrats named New York's Governor Grover Cleveland. On election day Cleveland beat Blaine by only 23,000 popular votes; his tiny margin of 1,149 votes in New York gave him that state's 36 electoral votes, enough to squeeze a 219-to-182 victory in the electoral college. Cleveland may have won New York because in the last week of the campaign a local Protestant minister publicly equated Democrats with "rum, Romanism, and rebellion" (drinking, Catholicism, and the Civil War). Democrats eagerly publicized the slur among New York's numerous Irish-Catholic population, urging voters to protest by turning out for Cleveland.

Cleveland, the first Democratic president since Buchanan, exercised more vigorous leadership than had his immediate predecessors. He used the veto extensively against outrageous pension bills, and he extended the scope of civil service. But his most forceful action was his unsuccessful campaign for tariff reform. Worried about the growing treasury surplus, Cleveland urged Congress to cut duties on raw materials and manufactured goods. When advisers warned him that his stand might weaken his chances for re-election, the president retorted, "What is the use of being elected or re-elected, unless you stand for something?" Cleveland's firmness did not prevail, though. The Mills tariff bill of 1888, passed by the House in response to Cleveland's wishes, was killed by the Senate.

Cleveland and Harrison

The Democrats renominated Cleveland in 1888, and the Republicans selected Benjamin Harrison, the grandson of President William Henry Harrison. The campaign was less savage than the 1884 campaign had been, but it was far from clean. Quite helpful to Harrison were the pervasive bribery and multiple voting that helped him to win Indiana by just 2,300 votes and New York by only 14,000. (Democrats also indulged in bribery and vote fraud, but the Republicans were more successful at it.) These crucial states assured Harrison's victory; though Cleveland outpolled Harrison by 90,000 popular votes, Harrison carried the electoral vote by 233 to 168.

Harrison was the first president since 1875 whose party controlled both houses of Congress, but he did little to take advantage of this circumstance. Several aspects of his administration were contradictory. Harrison was a fiscal conservative, but under his administration Congress passed the first peacetime budget to exceed $1 billion. At Harrison's urging the House passed a "force bill" to protect blacks' civil rights by allowing federal courts to investigate irregularities in voter registration and jury selection; but Republican senators filibustered and then tabled the bill. And though Harrison supported protective tariff rates and reciprocity agreements to aid business, he agreed to the Sherman Anti-Trust Act and the Sherman Silver Purchase Act (1890), both of which were considered damaging to business.

Cleveland and Harrison ran against each other again in 1892. This time Cleveland attracted heavy contributions from business and beat Harrison by 380,000 popular votes and by 277 to 145 electoral votes.

In office once more, Cleveland took bolder steps to meet the problems of currency, tariffs, and labor unrest. But his actions reflected a narrow orientation to the interests of business and bespoke political weakness. In order to protect the nation's gold reserve, which was shrinking during the Panic of 1893, Cleveland enlisted aid from bankers, who bailed out the nation on terms highly favorable to themselves. And when 120,000 boycotting railroad workers paralyzed western trade in the 1894 Pullman strike, Cleveland bowed to the requests for federal troops from railroad managers and Attorney General Richard Olney. Throughout Cleveland's second term, events—particularly the economic downturn and the Populist ferment—seemed too much for the president. Cleveland's party abandoned him in 1896.

STIRRINGS OF AGRARIAN
UNREST

While the political system in Washington faltered, inequities in the new agricultural and industrial systems created the first rumblings of a mass democratic movement that was to shake American society in the late nineteenth century. The agrarian revolt was born of the despair brought about by crop liens, furnishing merchants, declining farm prices, rising costs, high interest and railroad rates, weather, insects, and isolation. Once under way, it inspired visions of a truly cooperative, democratic society.

Even before the full impact of these developments was felt, farmers had begun to organize to relieve their mounting distress. With aid from Oliver H. Kelley of the Department of Agriculture, farmers founded a network of local organizations called Granges in almost every state during the late 1860s and early 1870s. By 1875 the Grange had nearly twenty thousand local branches and over 1 million members. Strongest in the Midwest and South, Granges served chiefly as social organizations, sponsoring meetings and educational events to help relieve the loneliness of farm life.

Grange Movement

As membership flourished, Granges moved beyond social functions into economic and political action. At its 1874 national convention, the Grange proposed to avoid high retail prices by forming local cooperatives to buy equipment and supplies directly from manufacturers. Granges also encouraged the formation of sales cooperatives, whereby farmers would pool their grain and dairy products and then divide the profits. In politics, Grangers used their numbers to some advantage, electing sympathetic legislators and pressing for laws to regulate transportation and storage rates.

In spite of their progressive, even radical, efforts, Granges nevertheless declined in the late 1870s. The requirement that cooperatives run on a cash-only basis excluded large numbers of farmers who never had any cash. Efforts to regulate business and transportation withered when corporations won court support against "Granger laws." After a brief assertion of influence, the Grange reverted to an organization of farmers' social clubs. Its short-lived agrarian campaign served, however, as a precedent for future action.

Rural activism then shifted to the Farmers' Alliances, two networks of organizations—one in the Plains and one in the South—that by 1890 constituted a genuine mass movement.

Farmers' Alliances

The first alliances sprang up in Texas, where hard-pressed farmers rallied against crop liens, furnishing merchants, and railroads in particular, and against money power in general. Adopting an effective system of traveling lecturers to recruit members, alliance leaders extended the movement to other southern states. By 1889 the Southern Alliance boasted over 3 million members, including the pow-

Mary E. Lease (1850–1933) was a fiery and controversial speaker for the Farmers' Alliance and the Populist party in Kansas. Tall and intense, she had a deep, almost hypnotic voice that made her an effective publicist for the farmers' cause. She was one of the founders of the Populist party and gave a seconding speech to the nomination of James B. Weaver at the party convention in 1892.   Library of Congress.

erful Colored Farmers' National Alliance, which claimed over 1 million black members. A similar movement flourished in the Plains, where by the late 1880s 2 million members were organized in Kansas, Nebraska, and the Dakotas.

Alliance members not only pushed the Grange concept of cooperation but also proposed a scheme to alleviate the most serious rural problems: lack of cash and credit. The subtreasury plan called for the federal government to construct warehouses in every major agricultural county. At harvest time, farmers could store their crops in these subtreasuries while awaiting higher prices, and the

Subtreasury Plan

government would loan farmers treasury notes amounting to 80 percent of the market price the stored crops would bring. Farmers could use these subtreasury notes as legal tender to pay debts and make purchases. Once the stored crops were sold, farmers would pay back the loans plus small interest and storage fees.

Growing membership and rising confidence drew alliances more deeply into politics. By 1890, farmers had elected a number of officeholders sympathetic to their programs—especially in the South. In the Midwest, alliance candidates often ran on independent third-party tickets, and achieved some success in Kansas, Nebraska, and the Dakotas. During the summer of 1890, the Kansas Alliance held a "convention of the people" and nominated candidates who swept the fall elections. Formation of this People's party, whose members were called Populists, gave a name to the movement that grew out of alliance political activism. Two years later, after overcoming regional differences, the People's party held a convention in Omaha, drafted a platform, and nominated a presidential candidate.

Rise of Populism

The Omaha Platform was one of the most comprehensive reform documents in American history. Most of its planks addressed three central issues: transportation, land, and money. Frustrated with weak state and federal regulation, the Populists demanded government ownership of railroad and telegraph lines. They called on the federal government to reclaim all land owned for speculative purposes by railroads and aliens. The monetary plank called for a flexible currency system based on free and unlimited coinage of silver that would increase the money supply and enable farmers to pay their debts more easily. Other planks advocated a graduated income tax, postal savings banks, the direct election of U.S. senators, and shorter hours for workers. As its presidential candidate, the party nominated James B. Weaver of Iowa, a former Union general.

Although Weaver lost badly in 1892, he garnered over 1 million popular votes (8 percent of the total), winning majorities in four states and 22 electoral votes. Not since 1856 had a third party won so many votes in its first national effort. The party's central dilemma—whether to stand by its ideals at all costs or compromise those ideals in order to gain power—still loomed ahead.

THE DEPRESSION OF THE 1890s

Early in 1893, shortly before Grover Cleveland assumed the presidency for the second time, a seemingly minor but ominous economic event occurred: the Philadelphia and Reading Railroad, once a thriving and profitable line, went bankrupt. Like other railroads, the Philadelphia and Reading had borrowed heavily to lay track and build new stations and bridges. But overexpansion cut into revenues. Profits dwindled, and the company was unable to pay its debts.

The same problem nagged manufacturers. For example, output at the McCormick farm machinery factories was nine times greater in 1893 than it had been in 1879, but revenues had only tripled. To compensate, the company tried to boost profits by automating its plants and squeezing more work out of fewer laborers. But this strategy only enlarged the debt and increased unemployment.

Banks suffered too. As primary lending agents, they found their problems compounded when customers defaulted. The failure of the National Cordage Company in May 1893 set off a chain reaction of business and bank closings. During the first four months of 1893, 28 banks failed. By June the number reached 128. In 1894 one adviser warned President Cleveland, "We are on the eve of a very dark night." He was right; between 1893 and 1897, the nation suffered the worst economic depression it had yet experienced.

As the depression deepened, currency problems reached a critical stage. The Sherman Silver Purchase Act of 1890 had committed the government to

Currency Problems

buy 4.5 million ounces of silver each month. Payment was to be in gold, at the ratio of one ounce of gold for every sixteen ounces of silver. But the western mining boom made silver more plentiful, and its value relative to gold fell. Thus every month the government exchanged gold, whose worth remained fairly constant, for less valuable silver. Fearful that the dollar, which was based on the treasury's holdings in silver and gold, was losing its value, merchants at home and abroad began to exchange paper money and securities for gold. As a result, the nation's gold reserves dwindled, falling below the psychologically significant level of $100 million in April 1893.

President Cleveland, promising to protect the gold reserves, called a special session of Congress to repeal the Sherman Silver Purchase Act. But the run on the treasury continued. By early 1895 gold reserves had fallen to only $41 million. In desperation, Cleveland accepted an offer of 3.5 million ounces of gold in return for $62 million worth of federal bonds from a banking syndicate led by J. P. Morgan. When the bankers resold the bonds to the public, they profited handsomely at the nation's expense. Cleveland claimed that the gold reserves had been saved, but discontented farmers, workers, silver miners, and even some members of Cleveland's own party saw only humiliation in the president's actions.

In the final years of the century, new gold discoveries, good harvests, and saner industrial growth brought better times. But the depression had hastened the crumbling of an old system and the emergence of a new one. The processes of industrial development and technological change had been under way for some time. But the organizational features of the new business system—consolidation and a trend toward bigness—were just beginning to solidify when the depression hit.

Emergence of New Economic Structures

What had happened was that the national economy had reached the point of interdependence, the point at which the fortunes of a business in one part of the country or the world had repercussions elsewhere. By the 1890s railroads were overextended; their reckless investments inevitably crumbled. And when railroads collapsed, they pulled other industries down with them. In the first half of 1893, for example, thirty-two steel companies failed. In all, five hundred banks and sixteen thousand businesses toppled into bankruptcy that same year.

To complicate matters, American farmers had to contend not only with fluctuating transportation rates and falling crop prices at home, but also with Canadian and Russian wheat growers, Argentine cattle ranchers, Indian and Egyptian cotton producers, and Australian wool producers. When farmers fell into debt and lost their purchasing power, their depressed condition in turn affected the economic health of railroads, farm-implements manufacturers, banks, and other businesses. The downward spiral reversed late in 1897, but the depression had left deep scars.

DEPRESSION-ERA PROTESTS

The depression bared a number of problems in the industrial system. For half a century technological and organizational changes had been widening the gap between employers and employees. By the 1890s workers' protests against exploitation threatened economic and political upheaval. In 1894, when the American economy plunged, there were over thirteen hundred strikes and countless riots. Violence reached an alarming pitch, and radical rhetoric escalated. Contrary to the fears of business leaders, all the protesters were not anarchists or communists from Europe eager to sabotage American democracy. The disaffected included thousands of men and women who simply wanted a better chance, regardless of how the government was organized.

Socialism was part of this undercurrent. Led by Daniel DeLeon, the fiery West Indian–born lawyer and lecturer who dominated the Socialist Labor Party, they agreed with Karl Marx, the father of communism, that whoever controlled the means of production held the power to determine how well people lived. Marx predicted that workers throughout the world would become so discontented they would revolt and seize factories, farms, banks, and transportation lines. The governments resulting from this revolution would end exploitation and erase class differences, paving the way for a new order of social justice.

Socialism

American socialism suffered from internal disagreements and lack of strong leadership. DeLeon had an antagonistic personality and could not unite the Socialist Labor Party. But events in 1894 triggered changes within the movement. That year the government's quashing of the Pullman strike and of the newly formed American Railway Union created a new and inspiring socialist leader. Eugene V. Debs, the railway union's president, had become a socialist while serving a six-month prison term for defying an injunction against the strike. Once released, the bald, forceful Indianan became the leading spokesperson for American socialism, combining visionary Marxism with Jeffersonian and Populist antimonopolism. Though never good at organizing, Debs attracted huge audiences and captivated them with passionate eloquence.

In 1894, however, it was not the tall, animated Debs but a short, quiet, frustrated businessman from Massillon, Ohio, who captured public attention. His name was Jacob S. Coxey, and he had a vision. Coxey had become convinced that, to help debtors, the government should issue paper money unbacked by gold—purposeful inflation, in other words. As the depression spread, Coxey recommended a federal job program financed by an issue of $500 million of this "legal tender" paper money to relieve unemployment and revive consumer spending. He planned to publicize his scheme by leading a march from Massillon to Washington, D.C., gathering a "commonweal army" of unemployed workers along the way.

Coxey's Army

Coxey's troops, including women and children, entered the capital on April 30. The next day the citizen army of some five hundred people marched to the Capitol, armed with "war clubs of peace." When Coxey and a few others vaulted the wall surrounding the Capitol grounds, mounted police moved in and routed the crowd. Coxey tried to speak from the Capitol steps, but the police arrested him and dragged him away. As the arrests and clubbings continued, Coxey's dreams of a demonstration of 400,000 jobless workers dissolved. Like the strikes, the people's first march on Washington had yielded to police muscle.

Coxey's march was an expression of frustration by people who were seeking relief from the uncertainties of industrialization. Today, in an age of union contracts, regulation of business, and government-sponsored job relief in times of high unemployment, their goals do not appear radical. Yet the brutal reactions of officials reveal how threatening the dissenters must have seemed.

POPULISTS AND THE SILVER CRUSADE

Populists too were part of the activist current of protest. In 1892 their presidential candidate had received over 1 million votes, and as late as 1894 Populist candidates were making good showings in local and state elections throughout the West and South. Nevertheless, like all third parties, the Populists were underfinanced and underorganized. They had strong and colorful candidates, but not enough of them to wrest control from the two major parties. Moreover, the two major parties fought to destroy Populist voting strength, especially in the South.

By the 1890s, the threat of biracial political dissent posed by the farmers' alliance movement prompted southern white Democrats to take urgent action. During the 1880s southern legislatures had enacted several measures to curtail black voting, including poll taxes and literacy tests. Believing these measures inadequate to thwart a coalition of black and white voters in the Populist party and fearful that northern Republicans might enact federal supervision of elections, southern states in the 1890s tried more directly to prevent all blacks from voting.

Disfranchisement was accomplished in clever and devious ways. In 1876 the Supreme Court had affirmed that the Fifteenth Amendment prohibited states from denying the vote to people "on account of race, color, or previous condition of servitude." But, said the court, Congress had no control over state elections beyond provisions set by the Fifteenth Amendment (*U.S. v. Reese*). Subsequently, state legislatures found ways to exclude black voters without ever mentioning race, color, or previous condition of servitude. In 1890, Mississippi led the way by requiring all voters to prove they could read and interpret the state constitution. Registration officials applied much stiffer standards to blacks than whites. In 1898 Louisiana enacted the first "grandfather clause," which excluded from voting anyone whose ancestors were ineligible to vote before 1867; other southern states soon followed suit. These and other measures proved effective. By the early 1900s, blacks had effectively lost their political rights in every southern state except Tennessee.

To a large extent, white supremacist fears were unjustified, for fundamental factors impeded acceptance of blacks by white Populists. Most white farmers could not put aside their racism. Many came from families that had supported the Ku Klux Klan during Reconstruction, some had once even owned slaves, and they considered blacks to be a permanently inferior people who would never be able to do things for themselves. And poor whites seemed to take comfort in the belief that there would always be people worse off than they were. Thus Populists seldom addressed needs of black farmers and used white supremacist rhetoric in order to avoid charges that they encouraged racial mingling.

On the national level, the Populist crusade against the "money power" settled on the issue of silver.

Though the currency problem was one of the most complex facing American political leaders, many people saw silver as a simple solution to the nation's ills. To them, free silver meant the end of special privilege for the rich and the return of government to the people. William H. Harvey, author of the immensely popular *Coin's Financial School* (1894), preached that by coining silver "you increase the value of all property by adding to the number of money units in the land. You make it possible for the debtor to pay his debts; business to start anew, and revivify all the industries of the country, which must remain paralyzed so long as silver as well as all other property is measured by a gold standard."

Free Silver

Using this kind of reasoning, Populists adopted free coinage of silver as their political battle cry. But as the elections of 1896 approached, they faced the dilemma of what strategy to use in order to translate their few previous electoral victories into much greater success. Would they lose their identity by joining with sympathetic factions of the major parties, or would they remain independent as a third party and settle for at best minor successes?

THE ELECTION OF 1896

The presidential campaign of 1896 brought the nation's political wanderings to a climax. Each party was divided. Republicans, under the direction of Marcus Alonzo Hanna, a prosperous Ohio industrialist, had the fewest problems. Since early in 1895, Hanna had been maneuvering to win the nomination for Ohio's governor, William McKinley. By the time the party convened in St. Louis in 1896, Hanna had corralled enough delegates to succeed. The Republicans' only trauma occurred when the party adopted a moderate platform supporting gold, rejecting a prosilver stance proposed

McKinley and Bryan

William McKinley (1843–1901) ran for president in 1896 on a platform that linked business prosperity with national prestige and economic well-being.   Library of Congress.

by Senator Henry M. Teller of Colorado. Teller, who had been among the party's founders forty years earlier, walked out of the convention in tears, taking a small group of silver Republicans with him.

At the Democratic convention, silver delegates paraded through the Chicago Amphitheatre wearing silver badges and waving silver banners. "All the silverites need is a Moses," remarked a *New York World* reporter. They found one in William Jennings Bryan.

Bryan had arrived at the Democratic national convention in Chicago in July 1896 as a member of a contested Nebraska delegation. The convention, as expected, chose to seat Bryan and his colleagues instead of a competing faction that supported the gold standard. Shortly afterward, as a member of the party's resolutions committee, Bryan helped to write a platform calling for free coinage of silver.

When the platform was presented to the full convention, Bryan rose to speak on its behalf. In the heat and humidity of the Chicago summer, Bryan's now-famous closing words gripped the delegates:

> Having behind us the producing masses of this nation and the world, supported by the commercial interests, the laboring interests, and the toilers everywhere, we will answer their [the wealthy classes'] demand for a gold standard by saying to them: You shall not press down upon the brow of labor this crown of thorns, you shall not crucify mankind upon a cross of gold.

The speech could not have been more timely; indeed, Bryan planned it to be so. Friends who had been pushing Bryan for the presidential nomination now had no trouble enlisting support. The convention flowed to Bryan, and the "great campaign" had begun in earnest.

Bryan's nomination presented the Populist party with a dilemma. Should Populists join Democrats in support of Bryan, or should they nominate their own candidate and preserve their party's independence? Each faction had its supporters. In the end the convention compromised, first naming the Populist Tom Watson of Georgia as its vice-presidential nominee and then nominating Bryan for the presidency.

The election results revealed that the political stand-off had finally ended. McKinley, the symbol of Republican pragmatism and the new economic order, beat Bryan by over 600,000 popular votes and by 271 to 176 in the electoral college. It was the most lopsided presidential election since 1872.

Election Results

Democrats and Populists had done all they could to rally the nation. But the obsession with the silver issue undermined their cause. Silver especially prevented the Populists from building the urban-rural

IMPORTANT EVENTS

1873	Coinage of silver dollar ends		Sherman Silver Purchase Act
1873–78	Depression		Sherman Anti-Trust Act
1876	Hayes elected president	1892	Populist convention in Omaha
	U.S. v. Reese		Cleveland elected president
1878	Bland-Allison Act	1893	Repeal of Sherman Silver Purchase
	Anthony Amendment defeated in		Act
	Congress	1893–97	Depression
1880	Garfield elected president	1894	Wilson-Gorman Tariff
1881	Garfield assassinated; Arthur assumes		Pullman strike; Debs arrested and
	presidency		turns to socialism
1883	Pendleton Civil Service Act		Coxey's march
1884–85	Depression	1895	Cleveland deals with bankers to save
1884	Cleveland elected president		gold reserve
1887	Collapse of farm prices	1896	McKinley elected president
1888	Harrison elected president	1897	Dingley Tariff
1890	McKinley Tariff	1900	Gold Standard Act
			McKinley re-elected

coalition that would have given them political breadth. Urban workers shied away from the silver issue because they feared the high prices that would result. Labor leaders like Samuel Gompers of the AFL, though partly sympathetic, would not join with Populists because they were unconvinced that farmers were employees, like industrial workers. And socialists like Daniel DeLeon denounced the Populists because, unlike socialists, they still believed in free enterprise. Thus the Populist cause fizzled in 1896.

As president, McKinley signed the Gold Standard Act (1900), which required that all paper money be backed by gold, and continued to support high pro-

The McKinley Presidency

tective tariffs. Good times, brought about by an upswing of the business cycle and an increased money supply from new gold discoveries, enabled McKinley to beat Bryan again in 1900. Freed from the care of the economy, McKinley spent most of his time on foreign affairs.

As a result of the 1896 campaign, political parties learned that in future elections they would have to be sensitive to the pluralism of American society. They would have to satisfy a broad spectrum of interests rather than march under the banner of moral perfection. The reform spirit would survive, but its success would depend on cooperation, not on the sermons of righteous evangelists. Ironically, by 1920 many of the Populists' reform goals would be achieved, including regulation of railroads, banks, and utilities; shorter working hours; a variant of the subtreasury system; a graduated income tax; direct election of senators; the secret ballot; and more. These reforms succeeded because a number of groups united behind them. Immigration, urbanization, and industrialization had transformed the United States into a pluralistic society where compromise among interest groups had become a political fact of life. The election of 1896 and the end of the Gilded Age equilibrium confirmed that transformation.

SUGGESTIONS FOR FURTHER READING

General

Sean Denis Cashman, *America in the Gilded Age* (1984); Ray Ginger, *The Age of Excess,* 2nd ed. (1975); H. Wayne Morgan, *From Hayes to McKinley* (1969); Alan Trachtenberg, *The Incorporation of America: Culture and Society in the Gilded Age* (1982); R. Hal Williams, *Years of Decision: American Politics in the 1890s* (1978).

Parties and Political Issues

John H. Dobson, *Politics in the Gilded Age* (1972); Eleanor Flexner, *Century of Struggle: The Women's Rights Movement in the United States* (1959); Elisabeth Griffith, *In Her Own Right: The Life of Elizabeth Cady Stanton* (1984); Ari A. Hoogenboom, *Outlawing the Spoils: The Civil Service Movement* (1961); Morton Keller, *Affairs of State* (1977); Paul Kleppner, *The Third Electoral System, 1853–1892* (1979); Paul Kleppner, *The Cross of Culture* (1970); Walter T. K. Nugent, *Money and American Society* (1968); A. M. Paul, *Conservative Crisis and the Rule of Law: Attitudes of Bar and Bench, 1887–1895* (1969); John G. Sproat, *The Best Men: Liberal Reformers in the Gilded Age* (1968); Tom E. Terrill, *The Tariff, Politics, and American Foreign Policy, 1874–1901* (1973).

Currents of Protest

William M. Dick, *Labor and Socialism in America* (1972); John P. Diggins, *The American Left in the Twentieth Century* (1973); Ray Ginger, *Bending Cross: A Biography of Eugene Victor Debs* (1969); Nick Salvatore, *Eugene V. Debs: Citizen and Socialist* (1982); David Shannon, *The Socialist Party of America* (1955).

Populism and the Election of 1896

Paolo Coletta, *William Jennings Bryan: Political Evangelist* (1964); Paul W. Glad, *McKinley, Bryan, and the People* (1964); Paul W. Glad, *The Trumpet Soundeth: William Jennings Bryan and His Democracy* (1964); Lawrence Goodwyn, *Democratic Promise: The Populist Moment in America* (1976); Sheldon Hackney, *Populism to Progressivism in Alabama* (1969); Steven Hahn, *The Roots of Southern Populism* (1983); John D. Hicks, *The Populist Revolt* (1931); Richard Hofstadter, *The Age of Reform: From Bryan to FDR* (1955); J. Morgan Kousser, *The Shaping of Southern Politics* (1974); Walter T. K. Nugent, *The Tolerant Populists* (1963); Norman Pollack, ed., *The Populist Mind* (1967); Allan Weinstein, *Prelude to Populism: Origins of the Silver Issue* (1970).

CHAPTER 20

THE PROGRESSIVE ERA
1895–1920

Writing to his friend Henry Ford in 1912, Thomas Edison complained that American society needed overhauling:

> In a lot of respects we Americans are the rawest and crudest of all. Our production, our factory laws, our charities, our relations between capital and labor, our distribution—all wrong, out of gear. We've stumbled along for a while, trying to run a new civilization in old ways, but we've got to start to make this world over.

Americans had always been preoccupied with reforming their society, with "making it over," but between the 1890s and the end of the First World War, an intensified rush of reform swept the country. More and more people who felt as Edison did tried to address the problems of their time directly. Their efforts shaped what can be called the Progressive era.

By the 1910s many reformers were calling themselves progressives, and a new political party by that name had formed to embody their principles. Since that time historians have used the term *progressivism* to refer to the reform spirit in general, while disagreeing over the movement's meaning and its membership. It is probably most accurate to consider the era between 1895 and 1920 as characterized by a series of movements, each aimed in one way or another at renovating or restoring American society, its values, and its institutions.

The urge toward reform had many causes. Industrialization had brought unprecedented productivity, awesome technology, and a cornucopia of new consumer goods. But it had also included labor problems, wasteful use of natural resources, and abuse of corporate power. The rapidly growing network of cities facilitated the amassing and distribution of goods, services, and cultural amenities but also magnified the problems of poverty, disease, crime, and political corruption. Massive influxes of immigrants and the rise of a new class of managers and professionals shook the foundations of the old social classes. And the debilitating depression that blanketed the nation from 1893 to 1897 made many leading citizens realize what working people had known for some time: the central promise of American life was not being kept. Equality of opportunity—whether economic, political, or social—was a myth.

Progressives tried to surmount these problems by organizing their ideas and actions around three basic themes. First, they would end abuses of power. Second, progressives aimed to replace corrupt power with the power of reformed social institutions. Third, they wanted to apply principles of science and efficiency on a nationwide scale to all economic, social, and political institutions.

WHO WERE THE PROGRESSIVES?

The Progressive era emerged out of the new political atmosphere that formed after the tumultuous election of 1896 and the issues raised by urban reformers in the previous half-century. As the twentieth century dawned, the loyalty that political parties had once commanded seriously eroded, and voter turnouts declined considerably. Parties and elections, it seemed, were losing their functions of providing Americans with a means of influencing government policies.

Instead, the political system was opening up to entry by various and shifting interest groups, many of which supported reform issues related to their activities. These organizations included professional associations, such as the American Bar Association; women's organizations, such as the National American Woman Suffrage Association; and issue-oriented lobbies, such as the National Consumers' League. Members of these organizations hoped to advance their own interests and to educate others about their goals. They made politics much more fragmented and

issue-focused than in earlier eras. Moreover, the prevailing issues of the Progressive era were urban. The progressive quest for social justice, educational and legal reform, and streamlining of government was actually an extension of the urban-reform goals of the previous half-century.

The formation of the National Municipal League in 1895 and the National Civic Federation in 1900 signaled the beginning of the new reform era. The National Municipal League served as a forum for debate on issues of civic reform, such as bossism versus civil service, revisions of tax laws, nonpartisan elections, and municipal ownership of public utilities. The National Civic Federation broadened discussion of social reforms, such as workers' compensation and arbitration of labor disputes.

Organizations and individuals who accepted the three progressive themes—opposition to abuse of power, reform of social institutions, quest for cooperation and scientific efficiency—could be found in almost all levels of society. The new middle class, consisting of men and women in the professions of law, medicine, social work, religion, teaching, and business, formed the vanguard of the progressives. Repelled by inefficiency and immorality in business, government, and human relations, these people set out to apply scientific techniques they had learned in their professions to problems of the larger society.

Many middle-class progressive reformers were motivated by personal indignation, if not revulsion, at corruption and injustice. This feeling was expressed by journalists whom Theodore Roosevelt dubbed *muckrakers* (alluding to a character in John Bunyan's *Pilgrim's Progress* who rejected a crown for a muckrake). These writers investigated and attacked social, economic, and political wrongs. Their fact-filled articles and books exposed such offenses as the sale of tainted meat, fraudulent insurance schemes, and prostitution. Lincoln Steffens's articles in *McClure's,* later published as *The Shame of the Cities* (1904), ranked among the highlights of muckraker journalism. Other well-known muckraking efforts included Upton Sinclair's novel *The Jungle* (1906), which attacked the meatpacking industry, and David Graham Phillips's *Treason of the Senate* (1906).

Middle-class indignation also revealed itself in opposition to party politics. Reformers had a strong distaste for the bargaining and self-serving they believed permeated boss-ridden parties. They felt, as the journalist William Allen White did, that machines and bosses should "be reduced to mere political scrap iron by the rise of the people." (When reformers referred to "the people," they all too often meant middle-class people like themselves.) To improve the political process, these progressives advocated such reforms as nominating candidates through direct primaries instead of party caucuses and nonpartisan elections, to prevent the corruption and bribery that party loyalties seemed to breed.

Political Reformers

To involve more people and to make legislators more responsible, they advocated three political reform devices: the initiative, which would enable voters to propose new laws on their own; the referendum, which would enable voters to accept or reject a law at the ballot box; and the recall, which would allow voters to remove officials and judges from office before their terms were up. Their goal was to reclaim government by replacing the favoritism of the boss system with rational, accountable management chosen by a responsible electorate.

Progressive reformers, then, had an aversion to party politics, not to government. They turned to government for aid in achieving most of their goals, for they became convinced that only government had the leverage they needed. But political power was only a means toward scientific and bureaucratic ends; to Progressive reformers, especially middle-class professionals, knowledge was the key to progress. Scientific method—system, planning, control, predictability—was central to their values. Just as corporations were applying scientific management to achieve economic efficiency, progressives used expertise and planning to achieve social and political efficiency.

The progressive spirit also stirred some elite business leaders. Successful executives like Alexander Cassatt of the Pennsylvania Railroad supported limited government regulation and political reforms as means of protecting their interests from more radical political elements. Others were humanitarians who worked unselfishly for social justice. Business leaders guided organizations like the Municipal Voters' League and the U.S. Chamber of Commerce, which supported limited political and economic reform. Their aim was to stabilize society by imposing the model of corporate organization on institutions like schools, hospitals, and local government. Women of the elite classes often led reform organizations like the YWCA, which sponsored aid and education for the growing numbers of unmarried working women who had moved away from their families, and the Women's Christian Temperance Union, which was the largest women's organization of its time and which participated in numerous causes besides those linked with drinking.

Upper-Class Reformers

But not all progressive reformers had middle- or upper-class standing. During this era vital elements of what would become modern American liberalism grew out of the working-class urban experience. By the close of the nineteenth century, many urban workers were pressing for government intervention to ensure safety and promote welfare. They wanted improvements in housing and health, safe factories, shorter working hours, workers' compensation, and other reforms. Often these were the very people who supported the political bosses, supposedly the enemies of reform. Workers knew that bosses needed to cultivate support among their constituents and would cater to voters' needs. And in fact bossism was not necessarily at odds with humanitarianism.

Working-Class Reformers

After 1900, voters from inner-city districts populated by migrant and immigrant working-class families elected a number of progressive legislators who had trained in the arena of machine politics. The chief goal of these legislators was to establish government responsibility for alleviating the hardship that had resulted from urban-industrial growth. They opposed such reforms as prohibition, Sunday closing laws, civil service, and nonpartisan elections, all of which conflicted with their constituents' interests.

Some deeply frustrated workers wanted more than progressive reform. They wanted a different society. The majority of socialists united behind Eugene V.

Socialists

Debs. Though Debs was never able to develop a consistent program beyond his opposition to war and bourgeois materialism, he was a spellbinding speaker for the radical cause. On his speaking tours, he touched increasing numbers of disenchanted workers and intellectuals. As candidate for the Socialist party, Debs won 400,000 votes in his 1904 campaign for the presidency, and in 1912, at the pinnacle of his and his party's career, he polled over 900,000.

With their stinging attacks on exploitation and unfair privilege, Debs and other socialists like Milwaukee's Victor Berger and New York's Morris Hilquit made attractive overtures to reform-minded people. Some, such as settlement-house worker and child-labor reformer Florence Kelley, identified with the socialist cause. But most progressives avoided radical attacks on free enterprise. Municipal ownership of public utilities was as far as they would go toward changing the system. Indeed, progressives had too much at stake in the capitalist system to overthrow it.

But it would be a mistake to imagine that the progressive spirit touched all of American society between 1895 and 1920. There were still large numbers of people, heavily represented in Congress, who opposed reform. They disliked government interference in economic affairs—except when it strengthened the tariff—and saw nothing wrong with existing power structures. Outside government, this outlook was represented by business leaders like J. P. Morgan, John D. Rockefeller, and E. H. Harriman. Within government, this ideology was expressed by old-guard Republicans like Senator Nelson W. Aldrich of Rhode Island and House Speaker Joseph Cannon of Illinois.

Progressive reformers operated from the center of the ideological spectrum. Moderate, concerned, sometimes contradictory, they believed on the one hand that the laissez-faire system was obsolete and on the other that radical challenges to the fundamentals of capitalism were dangerous. Like the Jeffersonians, they believed in the conscience and will of the people; like the Hamiltonians, they opted for a strong central government to act in the interest of conscience.

GOVERNMENTAL AND LEGISLATIVE REFORM

By the turn of the century, professionals and intellectuals were accepting the notion that government could and should exert more power to ensure justice and well-being. They were becoming convinced that a simple, inflexible government was ineffective in a complex industrial age, and that public power was needed to counteract corruption and exploitation. But before reformers could use such power in ways they believed to be necessary, they would have to recapture government from the politicians whose greed had soiled the democratic system. Thus an important thrust of progressive activity was the effort to root out corruption in government.

Reformers first attacked this problem in the cities, trying to redirect government through structural reforms such as civil service, nonpartisan elections, and tighter scrutiny of public expenditures. After 1900 the momentum for reform brought into being the city-manager and city-commission forms of government and public ownership of utilities.

The reform movement produced a number of skillful, influential, and often charismatic governors who used executive power to achieve change. Their ranks included Braxton Bragg Comer of Alabama and Hoke Smith of Georgia, who introduced business regulations and other reforms in the South; Albert Cummins of Iowa and Hiram Johnson of California, who battled the railroads that dominated their states; and Woodrow Wilson of New Jersey, whose administrative reforms were copied by other governors. Such men were not always saints, however. Smith supported the disfranchisement of blacks, and Johnson discriminated against Japanese-Americans.

Progressive Governors

Probably the most notable progressive governor was Wisconsin's Robert M. La Follette. A self-made small-town lawyer, La Follette rose through the ranks of the state Republican party to the governorship in 1900. As governor he initiated a multipronged reform program that included direct primaries, more equitable taxes, and regulation of railroad rates. He also established regulatory commissions staffed with experts, whose investigations supplied La Follette with facts and figures that he used in fiery speeches to muster public support for his policies. After three terms as governor, La Follette was elected senator and carried his progressive ideals into national politics. "Battling Bob" had a rare ability to take a tempered, scientific approach to reform while still appealing to the people with moving rhetoric. His goal, he once asserted, "was not to 'smash' corporations, but to drive them out of politics, and then to treat them exactly the same as other people are treated."

Not all state leaders were as successful as La Follette. To be sure, the crusade against party politics and corruption did accomplish some permanent changes. By 1916 all but three states had direct primaries, and many states had adopted the initiative, referendum, and recall. And political reformers achieved a major goal in 1913 when the states ratified the Seventeenth Amendment, which provided for the direct election of U.S. senators (formerly elected by state legislatures, which often were corrupted by private interests). But political reforms did not always bring about the desired results. Party bosses, better organized and more experienced than reformers, were still able to dominate elections. Moreover, political reformers found that entrenched power, aided by the courts, many times could counterattack and defeat progressive campaigns.

New state laws aimed at bettering social welfare had greater impact than most political reforms, especially in factories. Broadly interpreting their powers to protect the health and safety of their citizens, many states enacted factory inspection laws, and by 1916 nearly two-thirds of the states had insurance for victims of industrial accidents. Under pressure from the National Child Labor Committee, nearly every state established a minimum age (varying from twelve to sixteen) for employment, and prohibited employers from working children more than eight or ten hours a day. Such laws, however, were hard to enforce. Several groups also joined forces to limit working hours for women. After the Supreme Court upheld Oregon's ten-hour limit in 1908, many more states passed laws protecting women workers. Finally, efforts of the American Association for Old Age Security began to succeed in 1914, when Arizona established old-age pensions. Though the law was struck down by the courts, the First World War renewed interest in pensions, and in the 1920s many states enacted laws to provide for needy older people.

Progressive Legislation

These and other social reforms were strongly opposed by people who thought them detrimental to their self-interest or a threat to the free enterprise system. The National Association of Manufacturers coordinated the battle against regulation of business and working conditions. And legislators friendly to special interests connived to weaken the new laws by failing to fund their enforcement.

Reformers themselves were not always certain about what was progressive, especially in terms of human behavior. The main problem seemed to be whether or not it was possible to create a desirable moral climate through legislation. Some reformers, such as the members of the Social Gospel movement, believed that only church-based inspiration and humanitarian work, rather than legislation, could transform society. But other people believed state intervention was necessary to achieve purity, especially in drinking habits and sexual behavior.

Moral Reform

The formation of the Anti-Saloon League in 1893 had marked a new turn in the long campaign against drunkenness and its effects on society. This organization of reformers joined with the Women's Christian Temperance Union (founded in 1873) to publicize the connections between alcoholism and health problems, poverty, unemployment, and family breakups. The result was that a large number of states, counties, towns, and city wards restricted the sale and consumption of liquor. In 1918 prohibitionists induced Congress to pass the Eighteenth Amendment, prohibiting the manufacture, sale, and transportation of intoxicating liquors. After ratification by the states, the amendment was implemented in 1920.

Public outrage boiled over after 1900 when muckraking journalists exposed interstate and international rings that kidnapped young women and forced them to become prostitutes, a practice called white slavery. Middle-class moralists, already alarmed by a perceived link between immigration and prostitution, prodded governments to investigate the problem and recommend corrective legislation. By 1915 nearly every state had outlawed brothels and the soliciting of sex. And in 1910 Congress passed the Mann Act, or White Slave Traffic Act, prohibiting interstate and international transportation of women for immoral purposes.

Like prohibition, the Mann Act had reactionary as well as progressive elements. Even so, it reflected growing sentiment that state and national governments could improve human behavior. Reformers believed that the source of evil was not original sin but the social environment. If evil were human-made, then it could be human-destroyed.

ASSAULT ON OLD ASSUMPTIONS IN EDUCATION AND LAW

Reformers had long envisioned education as a means of bettering society. As early as 1883, psychologist G. Stanley Hall, whose ideas strongly influenced John Dewey, had noted that the experiences of modern urban schoolchildren were much different from those of their farm-bred parents and grandparents. In the early nineteenth century, school curricula chiefly taught moralistic pieties. *McGuffey's Readers,* used by primary schools throughout the nation, contained homilies such as "By virtue we secure happiness" and "One deed of shame is succeeded by years of penitence." Hall and Dewey, however, asserted that education had to adjust in order to prepare children for productive citizenship and self-fulfilling lives. Children, not subject matter, should be the focus of school policy, and schools should serve as community centers and instruments of social progress. Above all, said Dewey, education should relate directly to experience. Children should be encouraged to discover things for themselves. Rote memorization and outdated subjects should be replaced by subjects relevant to students' lives. To Dewey, personal growth, not mastery of a given body of knowledge, was the goal of human existence.

Progressive Education

Personal growth also became the driving principle behind college education. The purpose of American colleges and universities had traditionally been to train a select few for the professions of law, medicine, teaching, and religion. But in the late nineteenth century, places of higher education multiplied, spurred by public aid

Growth of Colleges and Universities

and increases in the number of people who could afford tuition. Furthermore, educators sought to make learning meaningful to more students. Harvard University, under Charles W. Eliot, president from 1869 to 1909, pioneered in substituting electives for required courses and in experimenting with new teaching techniques.

As colleges and universities expanded, so did their enrollment of women. Between 1890 and 1910 the number of females enrolled in institutions of higher learning swelled from 56,000 to 140,000. By the latter date, 106,000 women attended coeducational institutions, while 34,000 attended women's colleges. By 1920, women accounted for 47.3 percent of all college students, disproving the notion that women were mentally and physically inferior to men. But discrimination lingered; women were discouraged from taking courses in science and mathematics, and most medical schools refused to accept women.

The law, like education, began to exhibit new emphases on experience and scientific principles. Oliver Wendell Holmes, Jr., associate justice of the

Progressive Legal Thought

Supreme Court between 1902 and 1932, led the attack on the old view of law as universal and unchanging. Holmes's view that law should reflect society's needs challenged the judicial practice of invoking traditional beliefs and precedents in an inflexible way that often obstructed social legislation. Louis D. Brandeis, a brilliant lawyer who later joined Holmes on the Supreme Court, carried legal reform one step farther by insisting that judges' opinions be based on factual, scientifically gathered information about social realities. In the landmark case *Muller* v. *Oregon* (1908), Brandeis mustered extensive scientific evidence to convince the Supreme Court to uphold Oregon's law limiting women's working hours.

The new legal thought, however, met some tough resistance. Judges brought up on laissez-faire economic theory continued to strike down the kind of law progressive lawyers thought necessary for effective reform. Thus in 1905 the Supreme Court over-turned a New York law limiting bakers' working hours (*Lochner* v. *New York*) in spite of Holmes's forceful dissent. As in other cases where it struck down reform, the Court's majority argued that the Fourteenth Amendment protected an individual's right to make contracts without government interference, and that this protection thus superseded reform sentiments. Also, judges weakened federal regulations by invoking the Tenth Amendment, which prohibited the federal government from interfering in matters reserved for state supervision. Thus the judiciary's use of constitutional principles governing freedom of contract and the division of government powers continually impeded reform.

The judiciary during the Progressive era was not entirely negative. Courts did sustain some regulatory measures, particularly those affecting the safety of the general public. A string of decisions, beginning in 1898 with *Holden* v. *Hardy,* in which the Supreme Court upheld Utah's mining regulations, supported use of state police powers to protect the health, safety, and morals of their citizens. The judiciary also recognized federal police powers and Congress's authority in interstate commerce in sustaining such federal legislation as the Pure Food and Drug Act, the Meat Inspection Law, and the Mann Act. In these instances the welfare of citizens took precedence over the Tenth Amendment.

Meanwhile, social scientists joined with doctors and organizations like the National Consumers' League to bring about some of the most far-reaching

National Consumers' League and Public Health Reform

of progressive reforms: those in the area of public health. Founded by Josephine Shaw, a socially prominent Massachusetts widow, the National Consumers' League initially worked to improve wages and conditions of young women employed in department stores. After settlement worker Florence Kelley became the league's general secretary, the organization expanded its activities to include women's suffrage, protection of child laborers, and removal of potential health hazards. Local branches supported such consumer protection measures as the licensing of food vendors and inspection of dairies. They also urged city governments to fund neighborhood clinics that provided health education and medical care to the poor.

Between the end of the nineteenth century and the First World War, a new breed of men and women pressed for institutional change as well as political reform. Largely middle-class in background, trained by new professional standards, confident that new ways of thinking would bring progress, these people helped to broaden government's role in meeting the needs of a mature industrial society.

CHALLENGES TO RACIAL AND SEXUAL DISCRIMINATION

W. E. B. Du Bois, the forceful black scholar and teacher, ended an essay in his book *The Souls of Black Folk* (1903) with a call that heralded the twentieth-century civil rights movement: "By every civilized and peaceful method," he wrote, "we must strive for the right which the world accords to men."

By "men" Du Bois meant all human beings, not just one sex. But his statement and its context suggest the dilemma that vexed the two largest groups of underprivileged Americans in the early 1900s: women and nonwhites. Both lived in a society dominated by white males. Both suffered from disfranchisement, discrimination, and humiliation. And for both groups the progressive challenge to old ideas and customs gave impetus to their struggles for rights, but it posed thorny questions as well. Should women and blacks strive to become just like white men, with white men's values and power as well as their rights? Or was there something unique about racial and sexual identity that should be retained at the risk of sacrificing some gains?

Black leaders differed over how—and whether—to achieve assimilation. In the wake of emancipation, ex-slave Frederick Douglass had urged "ultimate assimilation through self-assertion, and on no other terms." Other blacks, who favored isolation from cruel white society, supported migration back to Africa or establishment of all-black communities in Oklahoma Territory and Kansas. Still others advocated militancy.

Most blacks, however, could neither escape nor conquer white society. They thus had to find other routes to improvement. Self-help, a strategy articulated by educator Booker T. Washington, was one of the most popular alternatives. Born a slave in 1856, Washington worked his way through school and in 1881 founded Tuskegee Institute in Alabama, a vocational school for blacks. There he developed the philosophy that blacks' hopes for assimilation lay in at least temporarily accommodating themselves to whites. Rather than fighting for political rights, he said, blacks should work hard, acquire property, and prove they were worthy of their rights. Washington voiced his views in a widely acclaimed speech at the Atlanta Exposition in 1895. Whites, including progressives, welcomed Washington's policy of accommodation and chose to regard him as representative of all blacks.

Booker T. Washington

Although Washington never argued that blacks were inferior to whites, he seemed, to some black leaders, to favor second-class citizenship. In 1905 a group of "anti-Bookerites" convened near Niagara Falls and pledged a more militant pursuit of such rights as unrestricted voting, equal access to economic opportunity, integration, and equality before the law. Spokesperson for the Niagara movement was W. E. B. Du Bois, a vociferous critic of the Atlanta Compromise. A New Englander with a Ph.D. from Harvard, Du Bois had the background of a typical progressive. He used scientific methods to compile fact-filled sociological studies of black ghetto dwellers, and he wrote poetically for the cause of civil

W. E. B. Du Bois

rights. In his essays and speeches, Du Bois treated Washington politely, but he could not accept Washington's submission to white domination.

Du Bois showed that accommodation was an unrealistic strategy, but his own solution may have been just as fanciful. A blunt elitist, Du Bois believed that an intellectual vanguard of cultivated, highly trained blacks, which he called the Talented Tenth, would save the race by setting an example to whites and uplift other blacks. Inevitably, such sentiments had more attraction for middle-class white liberals than for black sharecroppers. Thus when Du Bois and his allies formed the National Association for the Advancement of Colored People (1909), which aimed to use legal redress in the courts to end racial discrimination, the leadership consisted chiefly of white progressives. (Most white progressives, however, had little concern for the plight of the nation's blacks.)

Whatever strategy they pursued—accommodation or agitation—black Americans faced continued oppression. In fact, those who managed to acquire property and education encountered increased resentment. And the federal government only aggravated conditions. Under the administration of Woodrow Wilson, segregation within the federal government expanded; southern cabinet members supported racial separation in the rest rooms, restaurants, and offices of government buildings and balked at hiring black workers. Commenting on Wilson's racism in 1913, Booker T. Washington wrote, "I have never seen the colored people so discouraged and so bitter as they are at the present time."

During this time too, the progressive challenge to social relations stirred women to seek liberation from the home. Their struggle raised questions of identity that resembled those blacks were facing. What tactics should women use to achieve equality, and what should be their role in society? Could women achieve equality with men and at the same time change male-dominated society?

The Progressive era included a number of efforts by and on behalf of women to extend their influence beyond domestic bounds. Some of these efforts derived from radical impulses.

Women's Clubs Feminist Charlotte Perkins Gilman sounded a clarion call in her book *Women and Economics* (1898), declaring that domesticity and female innocence were obsolete and attacking the male monopoly on economic opportunity. This and Gilman's other writings moved some women, but even more were swept up by the women's club movement, which brought middle-class women together to press politically for the alleviation of social problems.

A number of women joined the birth control movement led by Margaret Sanger. As a visiting nurse in New York's East Side immigrant neighborhoods, Sanger distributed informa-

Birth Control tion about contraception in hopes of preventing unwanted pregnancies and their tragic consequences among poor women. Her crusade, however, captured the attention of middle-class women, who wanted to limit their own families and to control the growth of immigrant masses. It also aroused the opposition of men and women who saw birth control as a threat to family and morality. In 1914 moral purists caused Sanger to be indicted for sending obscene literature (articles on contraception) through the mail, forcing her to flee the country for a year. Sanger persevered and in 1921 formed the American Birth Control League, which enlisted physicians and social workers to convince judges to allow distribution of birth control information. Most states still prohibited the sale of contraceptives, but the issue had entered the realm of public discussion.

Like birth control, the women's suffrage movement, which dated back to the mid-nineteenth century, drew much of its support from the middle class.

Suffragists Suffragists achieved their first successes at the local level; by 1912 nine states, all of them in the West, allowed women to vote. After 1900 women pressed increasingly for the vote on the national level. The suffragists' tactics ranged from the moderate but persistent propaganda campaigns of the National Amer-

TO THE MALE CITIZEN

This cartoon supporting women's rights addressed the illogical attitudes of those who believed women should stay out of public affairs. "No man denies that government is public house-keeping," the caption pointed out. Were women allowed to hold office, the artist's reasoning suggested, they could keep public administration—as well as the streets—clean. The Schlesinger Library, Radcliffe College.

ican Woman Suffrage Association, led by Carrie Chapman Catt, to the active picketing and marching of the National Woman's party, led by Alice Paul. All these activities heightened public awareness of the suffragist cause. More decisive, however, was women's participation on the home front during the First World War as factory laborers, medical volunteers, and municipal workers. Their efforts convinced legislators that women could shoulder public responsibilities and gave final impetus to passage of the Nineteenth Amendment in June 1919.

Although women's clubs and the suffrage movement attracted mostly middle-class women, some efforts were made to encourage feelings of sisterhood among all classes. Since the early nineteenth century, a number of well-to-do women had recognized that all females had common grievances; that feeling gained ground in the early 1900s. Thus Alva Belmont, a wealthy supporter of the shirtwaist workers' strike, said in 1909, "It was my interest in women, in women everywhere and every class that drew my attention and sympathies first to the striking shirtwaist girls." This feeling of sisterhood formed the basis of the feminist movement.

But women's united efforts failed to create an interest group solid enough or powerful enough to dent political, economic, and social systems run by men. Like blacks, women knew that voting rights would mean little until people's attitudes could be changed. As the feminist Crystal Eastman observed in the aftermath of the suffrage crusade,

Men are saying perhaps, "Thank God, this everlasting women's fight is over!" But women, if I know them, are saying, "Now at last we can begin."

THEODORE ROOSEVELT AND THE REVIVAL OF THE PRESIDENCY

The Progressive era's theme of reform—in politics, institutions, and social relations—directed attention to government, especially the federal government, as the ultimate agent of change. At first, however, the federal government seemed incapable of assuming such responsibility. Then suddenly, in September 1901, the climate changed. The assassination of President William McKinley by an anarchist named Leon Czolgosz vaulted Theodore Roosevelt, the young, vigorous vice president, into the White House.

As president, Roosevelt became a Progressive hero. At heart, though, he was a conservative. His impulsive patriotism, admiration for big business, and dislike of anything he considered effeminate recalled the previous era of unbridled expansion, when raw power prevailed in social and economic affairs. Yet Roosevelt came to conclusions similar to those reached by progressives. His sense of history convinced him that the kind of small government Jefferson had hoped for would not suffice in the modern industrial era. Instead, economic development necessitated a Hamiltonian system of government powerful enough to guide national affairs.

Roosevelt's presidency inaugurated the federal regulation of economic affairs that has characterized

President Theodore Roosevelt (1858–1919) giving one of his dynamic speeches. With his broad interests and energetic leadership, Roosevelt revitalized the presidency and gave it much of its twentieth-century character. Library of Congress.

twentieth-century American history. Roosevelt first turned his attention to big business, where the combination movement had produced giant trusts that controlled almost every sector of the economy. Though Roosevelt has a reputation as a trustbuster, he actually believed in consolidation as the most efficient means to achieve material and technological progress. Rather than return to uncontrolled competition, he preferred to distinguish between good and bad trusts, and to prevent the bad ones from manipulating markets. Thus he instructed

Regulation of Trusts

the Justice Department to use antitrust laws to prosecute the railroad, meatpacking, and oil trusts, which he believed had unscrupulously exploited the public. Roosevelt's policy triumphed in 1904 when the Supreme Court ordered the dissolution of the Northern Securities Company, the huge railroad combination created by J. P. Morgan and his powerful business allies. In general, however, Roosevelt preferred cooperation between business and government. And he exerted pressure on business to regulate itself.

Roosevelt also pushed for regulatory legislation, especially after 1904, when he won a resounding electoral victory by garnering the votes of progressives and businesspeople alike. After a year of wrangling with business lobbyists in Congress, he succeeded in 1906 in getting passage of the Hepburn Act, which imposed stricter control over railroads and expanded the powers of the Interstate Commerce Commission. The act gave the ICC more authority to fix railroad rates, though it did allow the courts to overturn rate decisions.

Roosevelt showed a similar willingness to compromise on legislation to ensure pure food and drugs. For decades reformers had been urging government

Pure Food and Drug Laws

regulation of patent medicines and processed meat. The outcry against fraud and adulteration heightened in 1906 with the publication of Upton Sinclair's *Jungle*. On reading Sinclair's novel, Roosevelt ordered an investigation of the meat-packing industry. Finding Sinclair's descriptions accurate, he supported the Pure Food and Drug Act and the Meat Inspection Act, both passed in 1906. Like the Hepburn Act, these laws reinforced the principle of government regulation. But as part of the compromise to obtain their passage, the government had to pay for inspections, and meatpackers could appeal government decisions in court.

Roosevelt's policy on labor issues resembled his stance toward business. When, for example, the United Mine Workers struck against coal-mine owners in 1902, the president intervened by using the progressive tactics of investigation and arbitration. The mine workers, led by feisty John Mitchell,

wanted higher pay and an eight-hour day, but the owners stubbornly refused to recognize the union or arbitrate the grievances. As winter approached and fuel shortages threatened, Roosevelt warned that he would use federal troops to reopen the mines, thereby forcing both sides to accept arbitration of the dispute by a special commission. The commission decided in favor of higher wages and reduced hours, but also declared that the owners did not have to recognize the union. The decision, according to Roosevelt, created a "square deal" for all. The strike settlement illustrated Roosevelt's belief that the president or his agents should have a say in which labor demands were legitimate and which were not.

On the issue of conservation, Roosevelt displayed the same mix of flamboyant executive action and quiet compromise that he applied to other domestic

Conservation

matters. He built a reputation as a determined conservationist, using presidential power to add almost 150 million acres to the national forests and to preserve vast areas of water and coal from private plunder. True to the progressive spirit, Roosevelt wanted a "well-conceived plan" for resource management. But compromises and factors beyond his control weakened his scheme. Timber and mining companies shunned supervision of their wasteful practices, and Congress never authorized enough funds to enforce federal regulations.

During his last year in office, Roosevelt moved farther away from the Republican party's traditional alliance with big business. He lashed out at irresponsible actions of "malefactors of great wealth" and supported stronger regulation of business and heavier taxation of the rich. Having promised in 1904 that he would not seek re-election, Roosevelt backed his friend Secretary of War William Howard Taft for the nomination in 1908. The Democrats nominated William Jennings Bryan for the third time, but the Great Commoner lost again. Aided by Roosevelt, who still had strong popular influence, Taft won by 1.25 million popular votes and a 2 to 1 margin in the electoral college.

Early in 1909 Roosevelt went to Africa to shoot

game, leaving Taft to face the political problems his predecessor had managed to postpone. Foremost among them were tariff rates, which had risen to excessive levels. Honoring Taft's pledge to cut rates, the House passed a bill sponsored by Representative Sereno E. Payne that provided for numerous downward revisions. Senate protectionists prepared to revise the House bill in an upward direction, but progressives, led by La Follette, fought back. In the end the protectionists rewrote the bill, and Taft signed it. To many progressives, Taft had failed the test of filling Roosevelt's shoes.

Taft Administration

The progressive and conservative wings of the Republican party were rapidly drifting apart. Soon after the tariff controversy a group of insurgents in the House, led by George Norris of Nebraska, challenged Speaker "Uncle Joe" Cannon of Illinois, whose power over committee assignments and scheduling of debate could make or break a piece of legislation. Taft first supported and then abandoned the insurgents, who nevertheless managed to liberalize procedures by enlarging the important rules committee and removing its appointments from Cannon's control. Meanwhile, Taft also angered conservationists by allowing Secretary of the Interior Richard A. Ballinger to remove 1 million acres of forest and mineral land from the reserved list and to fire Gifford Pinchot, the government's chief forester, when he protested a questionable sale of coal lands in Alaska.

In reality Taft was as sympathetic to reform as Roosevelt was. He prosecuted more trusts than Roosevelt; expanded the national forest reserves; signed the Mann-Elkins Act of 1910, which bolstered regulatory powers of the ICC; and supported such labor reforms as the eight-hour day and mine safety legislation. The Sixteenth Amendment, which legalized a federal income tax, and the Seventeenth Amendment, which provided for direct election of U.S. senators, were initiated during Taft's presidency. Like Roosevelt, Taft was forced to compromise with big business, but he lacked Roosevelt's ability to maneuver and to publicize the issues he supported.

Thus in 1910, when Roosevelt returned from Africa, he found his party torn and tormented. Anti-Taft reformers formed the National Progressive Republican League and rallied behind Robert La Follette for president in 1912. Another wing of the party stood loyal to Taft. Finally, when La Follette became ill, Roosevelt threw his hat in the ring for the Republican presidential nomination.

Taft's supporters controlled the convention and nominated him for a second term, but Roosevelt forces formed a third party—the Progressive, or Bull Moose, party—and nominated the fifty-three-year-old former president. Meanwhile, the Democrats endured forty-six ballots before selecting as their candidate New Jersey's progressive governor, Woodrow Wilson. The Socialists, by now an organized and growing party, nominated their perennial candidate, Eugene V. Debs. The campaign exposed voters to the most thorough evaluation of the American system in nearly a generation.

WOODROW WILSON AND THE EXTENSION OF REFORM

Wilson won the election with 42 percent of the popular vote—he was a minority president, though he did capture 435 out of 531 electoral votes. Roosevelt received about 27 percent of the popular vote. Taft finished a poor third, polling 23 percent of the popular vote and only 8 electoral votes. Debs won an impressive 900,000 votes, 6 percent of the total. Thus fully three-quarters of the electorate supported some alternative to the restrained approach to government that Taft represented. The results allowed Wilson to interpret the election as a popular mandate to subdue powerful trusts and broaden the federal government's concern for social reform.

The campaign had featured a sharp debate over the fundamentals of progressive government. On one side stood Roosevelt with a system called the New

Looking like a preacher, Woodrow Wilson (1856–1924) delivers a speech at a campaign rally. Wilson's forceful, carefully crafted speeches, which resembled moral lectures more than political pitches, raised citizens' expectations for the fulfillment of his idealistic promises.   Brown Brothers.

The New Nationalism and the New Freedom

Nationalism. Roosevelt foresaw a new era of national unity in which governmental authority would balance and coordinate economic activity. He would not destroy big business, which he saw as an efficient way to organize production. Rather, he would establish regulatory commissions, groups of experts who would protect citizens' interests and ensure the wise use of concentrated economic power.

Wilson offered a more idealistic scheme in his New Freedom. He believed that concentration of economic power threatened individual liberty, that monopolies had to be broken so that the marketplace could again become open. But he did not want to restore laissez faire. Like Roosevelt, Wilson would enhance governmental authority to protect and regulate. But Wilson stopped short of the combination of big business and big government inherent in Roosevelt's New Nationalism.

Roosevelt and Wilson stood closer together than their rhetoric implied. Both men strongly supported equality of opportunity, conservation of natural resources, fair wages for workers, and social betterment for all classes. Perhaps more important, both would expand government activity through strong personal leadership and bureaucratic reform.

As president, Wilson had to blend his New Freedom ideals with New Nationalism precepts, and in so doing he set the direction of federal economic policy for much of the twentieth century.

Wilson's Policy on Business Regulation

The corporate merger movement had proceeded so far that restoration of free competition was impossible. Thus Wilson could only acknowledge economic concentration and try to prevent its abuse by expanding the government's regulatory powers. His administration moved toward that end with passage in 1914 of the Clayton Anti-Trust Act and a bill creating the Federal Trade Commission (FTC). The Clayton Act extended the Sherman Anti-Trust Act of 1890 by outlawing quasi-monopolistic practices such as price wars aimed at destroying competition and interlocking directorates (management of two or more competing companies by the same executives). The FTC, which replaced the Bureau of Corporations, was to investigate corporations and issue cease-and-desist orders against unfair trade practices. As with ICC rulings, accused companies could appeal FTC orders in the courts. Nevertheless, the FTC represented a further step in the protection of consumers.

Wilson increased federal regulation of finance with the Federal Reserve Act of 1913. The law established the nation's first centralized banking system since Andrew Jackson destroyed the Second Bank of the United States. Twelve newly created district banks would hold the reserves of member banks throughout the nation. The district banks would loan money to member banks at a low interest rate, called the *discount rate*. By adjusting this rate (and thus the amount of money a bank could afford to borrow), the district banks could loosen or tighten credit.

Perhaps the only act of Wilson's first administration that promoted free competition was the Underwood Tariff, passed in 1913. For years rising prices had thwarted consumers' desires for the material benefits of the industrial age. Some prices were unnaturally high because government tariffs had discouraged importation of cheap foreign materials and manufactured products. The Underwood Tariff encouraged imports by drastically reducing or eliminating tariff rates. To recover revenues lost due to the reductions, the act levied a graduated income tax on U.S. residents—an option made possible earlier that year when the Sixteenth Amendment was ratified. The income tax was tame by today's standards. Incomes under $4,000 were exempt; thus almost all factory workers and farmers escaped the tax. People and corporations earning $4,000 to $20,000 had to pay a 1 percent tax, and the rate for higher incomes rose gradually to a maximum of 6 percent on earnings over $500,000. Such rates made no holes in the pockets of the rich.

Tariff and Tax Reform

The outbreak of war in Europe and the approaching presidential campaign prompted Wilson to support stronger reforms in 1916. Concerned that food shortages might result if farmers could not borrow money to sustain production, the president backed the Federal Farm Loan Act of 1916. The measure created twelve federally supported banks that would lend money at moderate interest rates to farmers. To stave off railroad strikes that might disrupt transportation at a time of national emergency, Wilson pushed passage of the Adamson Act of 1916, which mandated an eight-hour day and time-and-a-half for overtime for railroad laborers. Finally, Wilson courted the support of social reformers by backing laws that outlawed child labor and provided workers' compensation for federal employees who suffered from injury or illness.

In selecting their candidate to oppose Wilson in 1916, the Republicans snubbed Theodore Roosevelt in favor of Charles Evans Hughes, former reform governor of New York and Supreme Court justice. Wilson ran on a platform of peace, progressivism, and preparedness. Many voters were attracted by the Democratic party's campaign slogan: "He Kept Us Out of War." Wilson received 9.1 million votes to Hughes's 8.5 million, and the president barely won in the electoral college by a 277-to-254 count.

Election of 1916

THE PROGRESSIVE ERA IN PERSPECTIVE

The Progressive era was characterized by a welter of confusing and sometimes contradictory goals. Certainly there was no single progressive movement. On the national level, reform programs ranged from Roosevelt's New Nationalism, with its faith in big government as a coordinator of big business, to Wilson's New Freedom, with its promise to dissolve economic concentrations and legislate open competition. At the state and local levels, reformers pursued causes as varied as neighborhood improvement, government reorganization, public ownership of utilities, betterment of working conditions, and moral revival.

The failure of many progressive initiatives testifies to the strength of opposition to reform as well as ambiguities within the reform movements themselves. By asserting constitutional and liberty-of-contract maxims, the courts struck down some key progressive legislation. In states and cities, adoption of the initiative, referendum, and recall did not encourage greater participation in government; either those mechanisms were seldom used or they became the tools of special interests. On the federal level, new regulatory agencies rarely had the resources for thorough investigations. Thus government remained un-

Important Events

1893	Anti-Saloon League founded	1909	NAACP founded
			Mann-Elkins Act
1895	Booker T. Washington's Atlanta Exposition speech	1910	White Slave Traffic Act
1898	*Holden v. Hardy*	1912	Roosevelt runs for president on Progressive (Bull Moose) ticket
1900	McKinley re-elected		Wilson elected president
1901	McKinley assassinated; Roosevelt assumes presidency	1913	Sixteenth and Seventeenth Amendments ratified
1903	Elkins Act		Underwood Tariff
			Federal Reserve Act
1904	*Northern Securities* case	1914	Federal Trade Commission Act
	Roosevelt elected president		Clayton Anti-Trust Act
			Sanger indicted
1905	Niagara Falls Convention		
1906	Hepburn Act	1916	Wilson re-elected
	Pure Food and Drug Act		Federal Farm Loan Act
			Adamson Act
1907	Economic panic		
1908	Taft elected president	1919	Eighteenth Amendment ratified
	Muller v. Oregon	1920	Nineteenth Amendment ratified

der the influence of business and industry, a condition that many people considered quite satisfactory.

Yet in spite of all their weaknesses, the numerous reform movements that characterized the Progressive era did refashion the nation's future. Industrialists became more conscious of public opinion, and politicians became less dictatorial. Progressive legislation gave government tools with which to protect consumers. But perhaps most important, progressives challenged old institutions and old ways of thinking. They raised questions about the quality of American life that, though they remained unresolved, made the nation more aware of its principles and promises.

SUGGESTIONS FOR FURTHER READING

General

John W. Chambers, *The Tyranny of Change: America in the Progressive Era* (1980); Arthur Ekirch, *Progressivism in America* (1974); Louis Filler, *The Muckrakers*, rev. ed. (1980); Richard Hofstadter, *The Age of Reform* (1955); William R. Hutchinson, *The Modernist Impulse in American*

Protestantism (1976); Gabriel Kolko, *The Triumph of Conservatism* (1963); David W. Noble, *The Progressive Mind*, rev. ed. (1981); Robert Wiebe, *The Search for Order* (1968).

Regional Studies

Dewey Grantham, *Southern Progressivism: The Reconciliation of Progress and Tradition* (1983); Richard L. McCormick, *From Realignment to Reform: Political Change in New York State, 1893–1910* (1981); George E. Mowry, *The California Progressives* (1951); David P. Thelen, *Robert La Follette and the Insurgent Spirit* (1976); C. Vann Woodward, *Origins of the New South* (1951).

Legislative Issues and Reform Groups

Norman H. Clark, *Deliver Us from Evil: An Interpretation of American Prohibition* (1976); Allen F. Davis, *Spearheads for Reform: The Social Settlements and the Progressive Movement, 1890–1914* (1967); Ruth Rosen, *The Lost Sisterhood: Prostitution in America, 1900–1918* (1982); James H. Timberlake, *Prohibition and the Progressive Crusade* (1963); Walter I. Trattner, *Crusade for the Children* (1970). (For works on socialism, see listings at end of Chapter 19.)

Education, Law, and the Social Sciences

Jerold S. Auerbach, *Unequal Justice: Lawyers and Social Change in Modern America* (1976); Lawrence Cremin, *The Transformation of the School: Progressivism in American Education* (1961); David W. Marcell, *Progress and Pragmatism: James, Dewey, Beard, and the American Idea of Progress* (1974); Philippa Strum, *Louis D. Brandeis, Justice for the People* (1984); David Tyack and Elizabeth Hansot, *Managers of Virtue: Public School Leadership in America, 1820–1980* (1982).

Women

Lois Banner, *Women in Modern America: A Brief History*, 2nd ed. (1984); Ruth Borden, *Women and Temperance* (1980); Carl N. Degler, *At Odds: Women and the Family in America* (1980); Linda Gordon, *Woman's Body, Woman's Right: A Social History of Birth Control in America* (1976); Aileen Kraditor, *The Ideas of the Women's Suffrage Movement* (1965); Ellen Condliffe Lagemann, *A Generation of Women: Education in the Lives of Progressive Reformers* (1979); William L. O'Neill, *Everyone Was Brave: The Rise and Fall of Feminism in America* (1969); Rosalind Rosenberg, *Beyond Separate Spheres: Intellectual Roots of Modern Feminism* (1982); Elyce J. Rotella, *From Home to Office: U.S. Women and Work, 1870–1930* (1981); Sheila M. Rothman, *Woman's Proper Place* (1978).

Blacks

John Dittmer, *Black Georgia in the Progressive Era, 1900–1920* (1977); Louis R. Harlan, *Booker T. Washington: The Wizard of Tuskegee, 1901–1915* (1983); Charles F. Kellogg, *NAACP* (1970); James M. McPherson, *The Abolitionist Legacy: From Reconstruction to the NAACP* (1975); August Meier, *Negro Thought in America, 1880–1915* (1963); Elliot M. Rudwick, *W. E. B. Du Bois* (1969).

Roosevelt, Taft, and Wilson

John M. Blum, *Woodrow Wilson and the Politics of Morality* (1956); John M. Blum, *The Republican Roosevelt*, 2nd ed. (1954); Paolo E. Coletta, *The Presidency of William Howard Taft* (1973); John Milton Cooper, Jr., *The Warrior and the Priest: Woodrow Wilson and Theodore Roosevelt* (1983); Arthur S. Link, *Wilson*, 5 vols. (1947–1965); Edmund Morris, *The Rise of Theodore Roosevelt* (1979).

CHAPTER 21

THE QUEST FOR EMPIRE
1865–1914

William H. Seward's travels through scenic Alaska in August 1869 revived his enthusiasm for the huge territory he had, as secretary of state, bought from Russia two years earlier. In a speech at Sitka, Seward told white citizens that Alaska was certain to become a "shipyard for the supply of all nations." Seward's oratory reflected the optimism of those nineteenth-century Americans like himself who saw little but grandeur in the nation's future. Indeed, the nation had long been on an expansionist course. According to the Russian minister to the United States, the American "destiny is always to expand."

But the American desire for more space, more land, more markets, and more resources was tempered in the late nineteenth century. Although most Americans applauded expansionism, some were uneasy with *imperialism:* the imposition of control over other peoples, undermining their sovereignty. Imperialism could take a variety of forms, both formal (annexation, colonialism, or military occupation) and informal (the threat of intervention or economic manipulation). Anti-imperialist critics feared that an overseas American empire would undermine institutions at home, invite perpetual war, and violate honored principles.

This chapter is the story of the roots and sources of American expansionism, the tremendous growth of American activity abroad in the late nineteenth century, the building of an overseas empire, and the momentous 1890s debate between imperialists and anti-imperialists over the fundamental course of American foreign policy. After 1900 it is the story of the opportunities opened and the troubles encountered in managing, protecting, and expanding an empire that stretched from Latin America to Asia and that faced threats from restless nationalists, commercial competitors, and other expansive great nations.

EXPANSIONISM REVIVED

The Civil War had temporarily interrupted the country's expansionist course. Once freed from that conflict, however, Americans North and South scouted new frontiers to conquer. Seward eyed Cuba, President Ulysses Grant coveted Santo Domingo, and others envisioned new outposts in the Pacific Ocean. Religious leaders contemplated the conversion of "natives" and "savages" to Christianity. Businesspeople and farmers talked of untapped overseas markets. Nationalists spoke of exporting America's superior political principles and practices to other peoples. And to ensure the success of these dreams, to protect all these activities, American leaders planned for an enlarged modern navy of the first order.

American Nationalism

After the searing Civil War, American leaders tried to heal sectional wounds with soothing patriotic oratory. The 1876 centennial celebration emphasized national unity; Confederate and Union soldiers met to exchange captured flags; patriotic societies like the Daughters of the American Revolution (1890) were organized. Notions of American exceptionalism and manifest destiny were revived. To the Reverend Josiah Strong, author of the influential book *Our Country* (1885), Americans were a special, God-favored Anglo-Saxon race destined to lead others. To Social Darwinists, Americans were a superior people who would surely overcome all competition and thrive.

Domestic Roots of Foreign Policy

Foreign policy has always sprung from the domestic setting of a nation—its needs, wants, moods, and ideals. The people who guided America's expansionist foreign relations were the same people who kindled the spirit of national growth at home. Most Americans paid scant attention to external issues or to the intense in-

William H. Seward (1801–1872) had a vision of empire matched by few Americans. This ambitious secretary of state added Alaska and Midway Island to the United States domain, but anti-imperialists and political foes thwarted his plans for other territorial acquisitions.   Library of Congress.

ternational rivalry of the post–Civil War era. But America's leaders—in politics, business, labor, agriculture, religion, journalism, education, and the military—were alert to the nation's place in world affairs.

The expansionism so evident at home after the Civil War was deeply intertwined with foreign policy. The national network of railroads, for example, made it possible for Iowa farmers to transport their crops to seaboard cities and then on to foreign markets. Their livelihood was thus tied to international market conditions, to the outcomes of foreign wars, and to the time-honored American principle of freedom of the seas. The tariff too was an issue in both domestic politics and world affairs. Tariff increases designed to protect American industry and agriculture from foreign competition adversely affected those who sold to America, prompting them to enact retaliatory tariffs on American products. And the massive influx of immigrants caused diplomatic problems as well as social upheaval at home. Moreover, notions of racial superiority and Jim Crow practices at home influenced American policies toward Asian and Latin American peoples of color, who were considered inferior. In short, the threads of domestic and foreign policy were densely interwoven.

The spokesmen for expansion and empire belonged to what scholars have labeled the foreign-policy elite or opinion leaders. Better read and better traveled than most Americans, more cosmopolitan than provincial in outlook, and politically active, they influenced the making of foreign policy. Unlike domestic policy, foreign policy is seldom shaped by the people. It was this small group, including Theodore Roosevelt, Henry Cabot Lodge, and Elihu Root, whose opinion counted, and increasingly they urged an imperialist course.

Foreign Policy Elite

With a characteristic mixture of self-interest and idealism, United States leaders believed that imperialism benefited both Americans and those who came under American control. When they intervened in other lands or lectured weaker states, Americans defended their behavior on the grounds that they were extending the blessings of liberty and prosperity to less fortunate people. To critics at home and abroad, however, American paternalism appeared hypocritical. They charged that the use of coercion to compel resistant foreigners to behave and think like Americans violated cherished American principles. The persistent American belief that other people cannot solve their own problems and that only the American model of government will work produced what historian William Appleman Williams has called "the tragedy of American diplomacy."

FACTORY, FARM, AND FOREIGN AFFAIRS

Many business people and farmers were part of the foreign-policy public that savored expansionism. They sought profits from foreign sales, but fear generated foreign trade as well. The nation's farms and factories produced more than Americans could consume. Foreign commerce, it was believed, could be a safety valve to avert or relieve depression.

The tremendous economic growth of the United States after the Civil War stimulated foreign trade. From the 1860s to 1914, in fact, foreign trade grew faster than the national income. By the 1870s the United States began to enjoy a long-term favorable balance of trade (exporting more than it imported). In 1870 United States exports totaled $451 million; by 1914 they had reached $2.5 billion. Although exports of manufactured items increased, agricultural goods accounted for about three-quarters of the total in 1870 and about two-thirds in 1900. Manufactured goods led export sales for the first time in 1913, when the United States ranked third behind only Britain and Germany in the export of manufactures.

Growth of Foreign Trade

America's large businesses looked to foreign markets, especially in the 1890s, when it became clear that the output of industrial products was outdistancing consumption. In the 1870s and 1880s about two-thirds of all American petroleum was exported, and in succeeding decades the figure was about one-half. Fifteen percent of America's iron and steel, 50 percent of its copper, and 16 percent of its agricultural implements were sold abroad by the turn of the century, making many workers in those industries dependent on exports.

Foreign economic expansion was also measured in other ways. Direct American investments abroad

Singer sewing machines were exported throughout the globe in the late nineteenth century. Here the King of Ou (the Caroline Islands, in the Pacific) operates the Great Civilizer. The caption for this company-sponsored photograph read: "The Herald of Civilization—Missionary Work of the Singer Manufacturing Company." But the profitable Singer business was interested in more than improving peoples' standard of living; three-quarters of the sewing machines sold in the world in 1890 were Singers. Courtesy, Robert B. Davies, Peacefully Working to Conquer the World.

reached $3.5 billion by 1914, placing the United States among the top four investor countries. This high ranking convinced some that the financial center of the world was passing from London to New York.

American economic expansion in Latin America was especially impressive and aroused the nation's diplomatic interest in its neighbors to the south.

Economic Expansion in Latin America

United States exports to Latin America, which exceeded $50 million in the 1870s, topped $300 million in 1914. Investments by United States citizens in Latin America amounted to a towering $1.26 billion in 1914. In Central America, the United Fruit Company, owner of more than 1 million acres of land, became a major economic and political force. It developed transportation, cultivated land, and fought to eradicate yellow fever and malaria. As for Mexico, American capitalists came to own its railroads and mines. By 1910, Americans controlled 43 percent of Mexican property and produced more than half that nation's oil.

Economic expansion abroad meant more than pocketbook profits for farmers and businessmen. For nationalists, a vigorous foreign trade was a sign of greatness, a source of pride. Foreign commerce was also a mechanism for exerting political influence. Indeed, by the early twentieth century American economic interests were influencing policies on taxes and natural resources in countries like Cuba and Mexico. American interests were responsible for drawing Hawaii into the American imperial net and for spreading American cultural values abroad. Religious missionaries and Singer executives, for example, joined hands in promoting the "civilizing medium" of the sewing machine. "The world is to be Christianized and civilized," declared Josiah Strong. "And what is the process of civilizing but the creating of more and higher wants. Commerce follows the missionary."

Most Americans championed economic expansion. But some critics, called anti-imperialists, drew the line between expansionism and imperialism: the first should not lead to the second; mutually beneficial commercial intercourse should not yield to the domination of one nation over another. Profitable and fair trade relationships, yes; exploitation, no. And, others advised, American business activity abroad should not draw the United States into unwanted diplomatic crises and wars.

LOOKING OUTWARD,
1860s–1880s

The American empire was built gradually, sometimes haltingly, in the years following the Civil War. One of its chief architects was William H.

William H. Seward

Seward. As secretary of state (1861–1869), he envisioned a large, coordinated American empire encompassing Canada, the Caribbean, Cuba, Central America, Mexico, Hawaii, Iceland, Greenland, and certain Pacific islands. This empire would be built not by war but by a natural process of gravitation toward the attractive republican United States. Commerce would hurry the process, he thought. To ensure the unity of his American empire, Seward appealed for a canal across Central America, a transcontinental American railroad to link up with the markets of Asia, and a telegraph system to speed communications.

Most of Seward's plans for acquiring territory were blocked by a combination of anti-imperialists and political foes. Anti-imperialists like Senator Carl Schurz and E. L. Godkin, editor of the magazine *The Nation*, believed that the country had enough unsettled land, and that creation of a showcase of democracy and prosperity at home was the best way to persuade other peoples to adopt American institutions and principles. Some anti-imperialists, sharing the racism of the times, did not want to annex territory populated by "inferior" dark-skinned people, such as Santo Domingo or slavery-plagued Cuba. And Seward's political antagonists hoped to punish him by denying him his dreams.

Seward did enjoy some successes. When an American naval officer seized the Midway Islands in 1867, Seward laid claim to them for the United States. The same year he paid Russia $7.2 million for the 591,000 square miles of Alaska. The secretary's forceful handling of French interference in Mexico also furthered his reputation. In 1861, Napoleon III had placed Archduke Ferdinand Maximilian of Austria on the throne in Mexico. Preoccupied with the Civil War, Seward could do little to help the Mexicans dislodge the intruding Europeans. But in 1866, citing the Monroe Doctrine, he told the French to get out as American troops headed for the Mexican border. Napoleon, troubled at home and now opposed by both Mexicans and Americans, abandoned his venture.

Seward's dream of a world knit together into a giant communications system was satisfied. In 1866, through the persevering efforts of Cyrus Field, an un-

Impact of the Telegraph

derwater transatlantic cable linked European and American telegraph networks. And Americans strung telegraph lines to Latin America, reaching Chile in 1890. Information about markets, diplomatic crises, and war flowed steadily and quickly to the United States.

Seward's successor, Hamilton Fish (1869–1877), inherited the knotty and emotional problem of the *Alabama* claims. The *Alabama* and other vessels built

Anglo-American Relations

by Great Britain for the Confederacy during the Civil War had marauded Union shipping. Fish patiently took to the bargaining table the question of British compensation for the damage. In 1871 Britain and America signed the Washington Treaty, whereby the British apologized and agreed to the creation of a tribunal, which later awarded the United States $15.5 million. Disputes over fishing rights along the North Atlantic coast and the hunting of seals in the Bering Sea near Alaska also dogged Anglo-American relations and would continue to do so for decades. Yet the two powers, however competitive, were slowly coming to the conclusion that rapprochement rather than confrontation best served their interests.

The convening of the first Pan-American Conference in Washington, D.C., in 1889 bore witness to

Pan-American Conference

growing ties between the United States and Latin America. Sponsored by Secretary of State James G. Blaine, the conference was designed to improve commercial relations. The Latin American conferees toured United States factories and then negotiated several general agreements to promote trade. To improve inter-American cooperation, they founded the Pan-American Union.

As the United States acquired new territories and markets and extended its influence abroad, the call went out for an improved and enlarged navy. Captain Alfred T. Mahan became a major popularizer for the "New Navy." Since foreign trade was vital to the nation's well-being, he argued, the nation required an efficient navy to protect its shipping, and in turn a navy required colonies for bases. Mahan's widely read book *The Influence of Sea Power upon History* (1890) sat on every good expansionist's shelf. Theodore Roosevelt consulted Mahan, sharing his belief in the links between trade, navy, and colonies.

Until its modernization the American navy was in a sorry state. Many of its wooden ships were rotting. But in 1883 Congress authorized construction of the

New Navy

first steel warships. Gradually the navy shifted from sail to steam and from wood to steel. New Navy ships like the *Maine*, the *Oregon*, the *Boston*, and the *Columbia* thrust the United States into naval prominence. Incidentally, many of these steel vessels were named for states and cities in a deliberate campaign to kindle patriotism and local support for naval expansion. The enlarged navy provided the United States with the tools to expand and build a greater empire.

CRISES IN THE 1890s: HAWAII, VENEZUELA, AND CUBA

When the United States became engaged in a number of crises in the 1890s, the New Navy warships were put to the test. For decades the Hawaiian Islands had commanded American attention.

This major Pacific way station was significant for trade with Asia and had long been a site of missionary work. Its undeveloped but strategic port of Pearl Harbor tempted naval expansionists, and the vast sugar plantations of the islands attracted American entrepreneurs. In 1875 the United States signed a treaty granting Hawaiian sugar duty-free entry to the American market; the Hawaiian sugar industry boomed and became dependent on mainland business. When the Congress revised the tariff laws in the early 1890s, however, it eliminated the special protection for Hawaiian sugar and gave American producers a bounty of two cents a pound. American planters in Hawaii were severely hurt. To gain exemption from American tariffs, a group of planters called the Annexation Club plotted a revolution.

In January 1893 the white minority overthrew the native monarch, Queen Liliuokalani. Their success stemmed in part from the support of the chief American diplomat in Honolulu, John L.

Annexation of Hawaii

Stevens, who saw to it that sailors from the warship *Boston* encircled the royal palace. Stevens informed Washington that the "Hawaiian pear is now fully ripe, and this is the golden hour for the United States to pluck it." Against the protests of Japan, whose nationals accounted for about 40 percent of Hawaii's population, President Benjamin Harrison sent a treaty of annexation to the Senate. But incoming President Grover Cleveland, an expansionist who disapproved of forced annexation, withdrew it. Five years later, on July 7, 1898, during the Spanish-American-Cuban-Filipino War, President William McKinley successfully maneuvered annexation through Congress.

The Venezuelan crisis of 1895 also gave the United States an opportunity to express its expansive mood. For decades Venezuela and Great Britain had squabbled over the border between Venezuela and British Guiana. The disputed territory contained rich gold deposits. When Venezuela asked for American help, President Cleveland decided that the "mean and hoggish" British had to be warned away.

Venezuelan Crisis

In July 1895, Secretary of State Richard Olney sent the British a brash 12,000-word message. After reminding them of the Monroe Doctrine, Olney declared: "To-day the United States is practically sovereign on this continent, and its fiat is law upon the subjects to which it confines its interposition."

This statement of United States hegemony did not impress the British, who rejected American interference in what they considered a local issue. But neither London nor Washington wanted war. The British, seeking international friends to counter an intensifying German competition, quietly retreated from the crisis. In 1896 an Anglo-American arbitration board divided the disputed territory. Throughout the deliberations Venezuela was barely consulted. Thus the United States displayed a trait common to imperialists: a disregard for the rights and sensibilities of small nations.

In 1895 another crisis rocked Latin America: the Cuban revolution against Spain. From 1868 to 1878 the Cubans had battled their mother country to no avail. Slavery was abolished but **Cuban Revolution** independence denied. The Cuban rebels waited for another chance. José Martí, one of the heroes of Cuban history, collected money, arms, and men in the United States. As in the case of Hawaii, a change in American tariff policy hastened the revolution. The Wilson-Gorman Tariff (1894) imposed a duty on Cuban sugar, which had been entering the United States duty-free. The Cuban economy, highly dependent on exports, was thrown into turmoil.

From American soil, Martí launched a revolution that became gruesome in its human and material costs. Rebels burned cane fields and razed mills. Under the command of Valeriano **Spanish** Weyler, soon dubbed the Butcher, **Reconcentra-** Spanish officials instituted a policy **tion Policy** of "reconcentration": hundreds of thousands of Cubans were herded into fortified towns and camps to separate them from the insurgents. Camp conditions were ghastly; hunger, starvation, and killer diseases took a heavy toll. As much as one-quarter of the total Cuban popula-

tion perished in these reconcentration centers. Weyler's forces ransacked the countryside, Cuba's economy deteriorated badly, and American investments of $50 million were jeopardized.

As tragic stories of atrocity and destruction reached the United States—and were played up by the American yellow press—people grew angry with the Spanish and sympathetic toward the insurrectionists. In late 1897 a new government came to power in Madrid. The Spanish modified reconcentration and promised that Cuba would be given some autonomy.

When President McKinley came to office he was already an expansionist. And the 1896 Republican platform on which McKinley ran demanded both an enlarged American empire and Cuban independence. In his annual message of December 1897, McKinley surveyed the Cuban crisis, ruling out American intervention while Spain was walking the path of reform. He wanted to avoid war if at all possible.

Events in the first few months of 1898 sabotaged the Spanish reforms and exhausted American patience. Early in January, anti-reform pro-Spanish loyalists and army personnel rioted in **Sinking of** Havana. After the riots, Washington **the Maine** ton officials ordered the battleship *Maine* to Havana harbor to demonstrate United States concern over the violence and to protect American citizens if need be. On February 15 an explosion ripped the *Maine*, killing 260 American officers and crew. Americans were quick to blame Spain for the disaster.

Spain's image in the United States had been undermined a week earlier when William Randolph Hearst's inflammatory *New York Journal* published a stolen private letter from Enrique Dupuy de Lôme, the Spanish minister in Washington. In the letter de Lôme scorned McKinley as "weak and a bidder for the admiration of the crowd" and revealed Spanish determination to fight on in Cuba. In March the irritated president asked for $50 million in defense funds, and Congress complied unanimously. The naval board created to investigate the sinking of the *Maine* then reported that a mine had caused the explosion. (Actually, the explosion was most likely caused by an internal accident.) The panel did not assign responsibility, but restless Americans continued to blame Spain.

McKinley's diplomatic options were greatly reduced by the impact of these events. He decided to send Spain an ultimatum. In late March the United States insisted that Spain accept an armistice, end reconcentration altogether, and designate McKinley as arbiter. The basic American goal was Cuban independence, but the president and his diplomats never so informed Spain. Yet no Spanish government could have given up Cuba and remained in office.

The Spanish did make concessions. They abolished reconcentration and accepted an armistice on the condition that the insurgents agree first. McKinley had wanted more; he began to write a message to Congress. After completing his speech, however, he received the news that Spain had gone one step further and declared a unilateral armistice. The weary McKinley hesitated but chose to go to Congress with a war message nonetheless. He could no longer tolerate the chronic disorder just ninety miles off the American coast. In his address on April 11, the president did not ask for a declaration of war against Spain but rather for an authorization to use force, as "an impartial neutral," to effect "a rational compromise between the contestants."

THE SPANISH-AMERICAN-CUBAN-FILIPINO WAR

Congress debated for over a week and then on April 19 declared Cuba free and independent, directing the president to use force to remove Spanish authority from the island. The legislators also passed the Teller Amendment, which disclaimed any American intention to annex Cuba. McKinley beat back a congressional amendment to recognize the rebel government, for he believed the Cubans were unready for self-government and would first need a period of tutoring by Americans.

The motives of those Americans who favored war were mixed and complex. McKinley's message of April 11 expressed a humanitarian impulse to stop the bloodletting; concern for commerce and property; and the psychological need to end the nightmarish anxiety once and for all. Republican politicians advised McKinley that they would lose the upcoming congressional elections unless the Cuban question was solved. And many businesspeople who had been hesitant before the crisis of early 1898, joined many farmers in the belief that removing Spain from Cuba would open new markets for surplus production—to which the depression of the 1890s had given some urgency.

Inveterate imperialists saw the war as an opportunity to fulfill what Senator Henry Cabot Lodge called the "large policy." Naval enthusiasts could prove the worth of the New Navy. Religious leaders too saw merit in war. Social Gospel advocate Washington Gladden remarked that "in saving others we may save ourselves." Some conservatives, alarmed by violent labor strikes and Populism, welcomed war as a national unifier. Sensationalism also figured in the march to war. Assistant Secretary of the Navy Theodore Roosevelt and others too young to remember the inhumanity of the Civil War looked on war as adventure. The yellow press exaggerated stories of atrocities. But underlying all explanations of American acceptance of war was the spirit and reality of expansionism, which had been moving the nation ever outward in the last half of the nineteenth century.

John Hay called it "a splendid little war," but it was hardly splendid. Over 5,400 Americans died, but only 379 of them in combat. The rest fell to malaria and yellow fever. Disease-carrying mosquitos were unrelenting, food was bad, and medical care was unsophisticated. Soldiers were issued heavy woolen uniforms in a tropical climate, and the stench of body odor was sickening. For black troops there was no relief from racism and Jim Crow.

Before Americans began to fight and die in Cuba, the first news of war came from faraway Asia. It surprised many Americans, who knew little about the steady United States push into the Pacific, the dreams of farmers and businesspeople for a huge market in China, or the foreign-policy elite's knowledge of the Spanish colony of the Philippines. On May 1 Commodore George Dewey's New Navy ship the *Olympia* steamed into Manila Bay, the Philippines, and wrecked the Spanish fleet. Dewey became an instant hero. His sailors had to be handed volumes of the *Encyclopaedia Britannica* to acquaint them with this strange land, but officials in Washington knew that Manila ranked with Pearl Harbor and Pago Pago as a choice harbor.

Commodore Dewey in the Philippines

Facing rebels and Americans in both Cuba and the Philippines, Spanish resistance collapsed rapidly. The Spanish Caribbean fleet, trapped in Santiago harbor, made a desperate attempt to escape but was destroyed by American warships on July 3. Several days later, the island of Puerto Rico fell to the invading Americans. Manila surrendered in August under pressure from Americans and Filipino insurgents led by Emilio Aguinaldo. Undermanned and ill-equipped, Spain sued for peace. The combatants signed an armistice on August 12.

In Paris in December, American and Spanish negotiators agreed on the peace terms: independence for Cuba; cession of the Philippines, Puerto Rico, and Guam to the United States; and American payment of $20 million to Spain for the new territory. Filipino nationalists tried to persuade American officials to set their nation free, but they were rebuffed. The American empire now stretched deep into Asia; and the annexation of Wake Island (1898), Hawaii (1898), and Samoa (1899) gave American traders, missionaries, and naval promoters other stepping-stones to China. Puerto Rico provided in the Caribbean a long-desired base that could help protect an American-built isthmian canal. And the United States would soon acquire another naval base at Guantánamo Bay in Cuba.

Treaty of Paris

TASTE OF EMPIRE: IMPERIALISTS AND ANTI-IMPERIALISTS DEBATE

During the war the *Washington Post* detected "a new appetite, a yearning to show our strength. . . . The taste of empire is in the mouth of the people. . . ." But as the debate over the Treaty of Paris intensified in the United States, it became evident that many Americans found the taste sour. Anti-imperialists like Mark Twain, William Jennings Bryan, William Graham Sumner, Andrew Carnegie, Charles Francis Adams, Jr., and Senator George Hoar argued vigorously against annexation of the Philippines. They were disturbed that a war to free Cuba had led to an empire. Some cited the Declaration of Independence and the Constitution: the conquest of people against their will violated self-determination. Other anti-imperialists disliked the increased power of the president in the checks-and-balances system. Anti-imperialist critics emphasized domestic priorities over foreign ventures and argued that the United States could acquire overseas markets without having to subjugate peoples abroad. The imperialists replied with their familiar arguments of patriotism, destiny, and commerce.

Anti-Imperialist Arguments

The anti-imperialists entered the debate with many handicaps. Possession of the Philippines was an accomplished fact; the anti-imperialists' role was thus a negative one. Then, too, they were internally divided, never able to launch an effective campaign. Although many of them belonged to the Anti-Imperialist League, they differed on so many domestic issues that it was difficult for them to speak with one voice on a foreign question. They were also inconsistent: Carnegie would accept colonies if they were not acquired by force; Hoar voted for the annexation of Hawaii but against that of the Philippines. The imperialists sneered that some of their critics were

"Declined with thanks" read this 1900 Puck magazine cartoon. President McKinley measures Uncle Sam, fattened by a series of territorial meals, as a group of anti-imperialists led by Senator Carl Schurz futilely attempt to administer an antidote. The message was clear: the United States would continue to expand. Library of Congress.

hypocrites, showing more concern for Filipinos than for American Indians, blacks, unskilled workers, or destitute immigrants.

On February 6, 1899, the Senate passed the Treaty of Paris by a 57-to-27 vote. Most Republicans voted with their president; 22 Democrats voted no, but 10 voted for the treaty. The latter group was probably influenced by Bryan, who had served as a colonel during the war; he urged a favorable vote in order to end the war and then push for Philippine independence. An amendment promising independence as soon as the Filipi-

Senate Approval of Treaty of Paris

nos formed a stable government was defeated only by the tie-breaking ballot of the vice president.

TROUBLES IN ASIA

Meanwhile the Germans, Japanese, Russians, British, and French were creating spheres of interest (see map, page 382) in China, the Sick Man of Asia. Within their spheres, the imperial powers

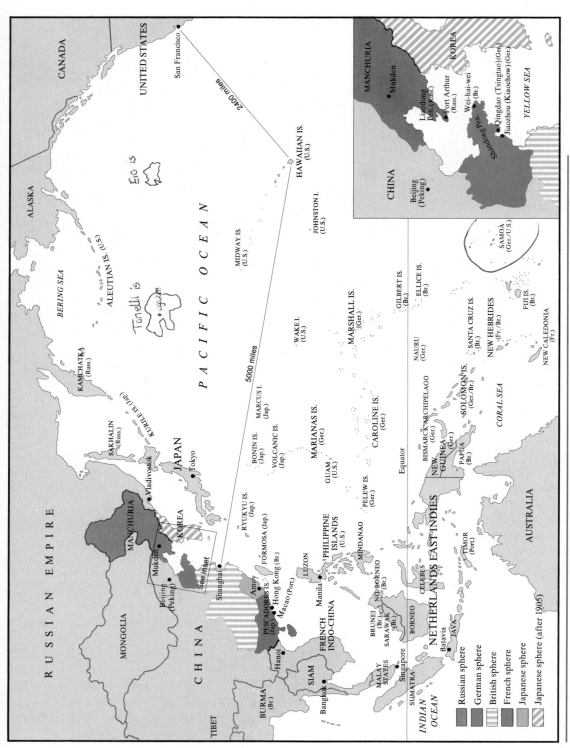

Imperialism in Asia: Turn of the Century

built fortified bases, leased territory, and claimed exclusive economic privileges. American business interests and missionary societies petitioned Washington to halt the dismemberment before they were closed out. What good were the Philippines as stepping-stones to China if there was nothing left to step into? asked some.

Secretary of State John Hay recognized that the United States could not force the imperial powers from China. But he was determined to protect American commerce. In September 1899

Open Door Policy

Hay sent the imperial nations a note asking them to offer assurances that they would respect the principle of equal trade opportunity—an Open Door—for all nations in their spheres. Germany, France, and the others sent evasive replies. Then in 1900, a secret Chinese society called the Boxers revolted against the foreigners in their midst and laid siege to the foreign legations in Beijing (Peking). The United States joined the imperialists in sending troops to Beijing to lift the siege. And Hay, in a note dated July 3, 1900, again asked for "equal and impartial trade." He also instructed the other nations to preserve China's territorial integrity.

Hay's foray into Asian politics settled little, but the Open Door policy thereafter became a central element in United States diplomacy. Actually, the Open Door had long been an American principle, for as a trading nation the United States opposed barriers to international commerce and demanded equal access to markets. After 1900, when the United States began to emerge as the premier world trader, the Open Door policy became an instrument first to pry open markets and then to dominate them. But the Open Door was not just a policy; it also became an ideology. The tenets of this ideology were that America's domestic well-being required exports, that foreign trade would suffer interruption unless the United States intervened abroad to implant American principles and keep markets open, and that any area closed to American products, citizens, or ideas threatened the survival of the United States itself.

In the Philippines, meanwhile, the United States antagonized its new colonials. Emilio Aguinaldo, the Philippine nationalist leader, believed that Dewey had promised independence for his

Philippine Insurrection

country, yet Aguinaldo was ordered out of Manila and isolated from decisions affecting his nation. Racial slurs like *gugu* and *nigger* infuriated the Filipinos, and they felt betrayed by the Treaty of Paris. Americans' paternalistic attitude toward their new charges grated on Filipino nationalist feelings.

In January 1899 Aguinaldo proclaimed an independent Philippine Republic. Soon the Filipinos took up arms. Before the Philippine Insurrection was suppressed in 1901, over 5,000 Americans and over 200,000 Filipinos were dead. The atrocities committed by both sides were abominable. The defeat of the Filipinos was followed by the Americanization of the islands. In 1916 the Jones Act promised Filipino independence, but the promise was not fulfilled until after the Second World War.

Possession of the Philippines meant American participation in the turbulent politics of Asia. The major contender for influence in the area was Japan, and the Open Door policy was no deterrent to its advances. When

Japanese-American Rivalry

competition for Manchuria and Korea led to the Russo-Japanese War (1904–1905), Japan scored quick victories over the stunned Russians. Roosevelt mediated the crisis at the Portsmouth Conference in New Hampshire. The peace settlement, he hoped, would preserve a balance of power in Asia. It did not. In 1905, in the Taft-Katsura Agreement, the United States conceded Japanese hegemony over Korea in return for Japan's pledge not to undermine the American position in the Philippines. To alert Japan to American naval power and to persuade Congress to increase the navy's budget, Roosevelt in 1907 sent the "Great White Fleet" on a world tour, with conspicuous stops in the Pacific. The Japanese were duly impressed.

Troubles with Japan boiled to the surface in 1906 when the San Francisco school board, reflecting the anti-Orientalism of the West Coast, segregated all

Chinese, Koreans, and Japanese in a special school. Japan protested this discrimination against its citizens. Because there was little President Roosevelt could do to budge the insistent Californians, he struck a gentleman's agreement with Tokyo restricting Japanese immigration to the United States.

Despite the Root-Takahira Agreement (1908), in which the United States recognized Japan's interests in Manchuria and Japan again pledged the security of American possessions in the Pacific, Japanese-American relations deteriorated. Japan became alarmed by President Taft's ineffectual attempt at dollar diplomacy, inducing American bankers to join an international consortium to build a Chinese railway. Dollar diplomacy was an effort to use private funds to serve American diplomatic goals and at the same time to garner profits for American financiers. Realizing neither purpose, Taft's venture seemed only to embolden the Japanese to solidify and extend their holdings in China as they would do later during the First World War.

THE FRUITS AND TASKS OF EMPIRE IN LATIN AMERICA

In its own backyard of Latin America, the United States was unfettered, and intervention was the order of the day (see map). The Teller Amendment had outlawed annexation but did not rule out American control of postwar Cuba. American troops remained there until 1902. Marines were there again from 1906 to 1909, in 1912, and from 1917 to 1922. Washington further manifested its hegemony over Cuba by forcing that nation to include the Platt Amendment in its constitution. The Platt Amendment prohibited Cuba from signing a treaty with another nation that might impair Cuba's independence. In short, all treaties had to be approved by the United States. Cuba was also forced to agree that the United States had the right to intervene to preserve the island's independence and to protect "life, property, and individual liberty." Finally, the United States required Cuba to lease a naval base (Guantánamo) to the Americans.

Panama was the site of one of Theodore Roosevelt's boldest expansionist ventures. United States fascination with an isthmian canal in Central America, to link the waters of the Pacific and Atlantic, was long-standing. American business interests lobbied for a canal, citing better access to Asian and Latin American markets. But three obstacles had to be overcome. First, the Clayton-Bulwer Treaty with Britain (1850) provided for joint control of a Central American canal. President Theodore Roosevelt persuaded the British, who were cultivating United States friendship and who knew that their influence in the region was diminishing, to step aside (Hay-Pauncefote Treaty of 1901). Second, Colombia was driving a hard bargain in talks over a canal to be cut through its province of Panama. Roosevelt urged Panamanian rebels to declare independence from Colombia, and he sent American warships to the isthmus to ensure the success of the rebellion. In 1903 the United States signed a treaty with the new nation of Panama: the United States was awarded a canal zone and long-term rights to its control; Panama was guaranteed its independence. Third, the cost of constructing a canal was enormous. Roosevelt, having overcome the British and Colombian problems, successfully pressed an obliging Congress for substantial funds.

The completion of the Panama Canal in 1914 marked a major technological achievement. The special bearings and gears used to operate the locks were manufactured by a Wheeling, West Virginia, firm; some fifty Pittsburgh factories and shops made the various bolts and steel girders; and the General Electric Company produced the electrical apparatus. People greeted the canal's opening the way people in the 1960s hailed the landing on the moon.

As for the rest of the Caribbean, it became an

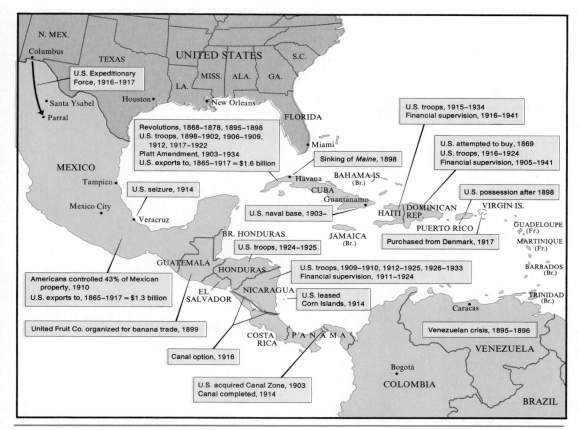

The labels visible on the map:

- N. MEX.
- Columbus
- TEXAS
- **U.S. Expeditionary Force, 1916–1917**
- Santa Ysabel
- Parral
- Houston
- UNITED STATES
- MISS. ALA. GA.
- LA.
- S.C.
- New Orleans
- FLORIDA
- Miami
- **U.S. troops, 1915–1934 / Financial supervision, 1916–1941**
- **Revolutions, 1868–1878, 1895–1898 / U.S. troops, 1898–1902, 1906–1909, 1912, 1917–1922 / Platt Amendment, 1903–1934 / U.S. exports to, 1865–1917 = $1.6 billion**
- **U.S. attempted to buy, 1869 / U.S. troops, 1916–1924 / Financial supervision, 1905–1941**
- MEXICO
- Tampico
- **U.S. seizure, 1914**
- Mexico City
- Veracruz
- **Sinking of _Maine_, 1898**
- Havana
- BAHAMA IS. (Br.)
- CUBA
- Guantánamo
- HAITI
- DOMINICAN REP.
- VIRGIN IS.
- **U.S. possession after 1898**
- **U.S. naval base, 1903–**
- PUERTO RICO
- GUADELOUPE (Fr.)
- MARTINIQUE (Fr.)
- **Purchased from Denmark, 1917**
- BR. HONDURAS
- JAMAICA (Br.)
- **U.S. troops, 1924–1925**
- BARBADOS (Br.)
- GUATEMALA
- HONDURAS
- **U.S. troops, 1909–1910, 1912–1925, 1926–1933 / Financial supervision, 1911–1924**
- **Americans controlled 43% of Mexican property, 1910 / U.S. exports to, 1865–1917 = $1.3 billion**
- EL SALVADOR
- NICARAGUA
- **U.S. leased Corn Islands, 1914**
- TRINIDAD (Br.)
- Caracas
- **United Fruit Co. organized for banana trade, 1899**
- COSTA RICA
- PANAMA
- **Venezuelan crisis, 1895–1896**
- VENEZUELA
- **Canal option, 1916**
- Bogotá
- COLOMBIA
- **U.S. acquired Canal Zone, 1903 / Canal completed, 1914**
- BRAZIL

The United States and Latin America

American lake. "Speak softly and carry a big stick," said Roosevelt. In 1904 the president announced his

Roosevelt Corollary

Roosevelt Corollary to the Monroe Doctrine, warning Latin Americans to stabilize their politics and finances to forestall European meddling in their affairs. "Chronic wrongdoing," he lectured, might require "intervention by some civilized nation, and in the Western Hemisphere the adherence of the United States to the Monroe Doctrine may force the United States, however reluctantly, in flagrant cases of such wrongdoing or impotence, to the exercise of an international police power." Roosevelt and his successors were not bluffing. From 1900

to 1917, American troops intervened in Cuba, Panama, Nicaragua, the Dominican Republic, Mexico, and Haiti. American officials took over customs houses to control tariff revenues and thus governmental budgets; they renegotiated foreign debts with American banks; they trained national guards and ran elections.

The United States set out to police the Caribbean in the name of order. Whether such order was achieved by the landing of marines, the development

The Quest for Order

of a national guard, a managed electoral process, or a manipulated economy, it was deemed necessary to guarantee United States security

IMPORTANT EVENTS

1861–69	Seward is secretary of state		1900	Second Open Door note
1866	Transatlantic cable completed			U.S. exports total $1.5 billion
	France withdraws from Mexico			McKinley re-elected
1867	Alaska and Midway acquired		1901	Theodore Roosevelt becomes

1861–69   Seward is secretary of state

1866   Transatlantic cable completed
France withdraws from Mexico

1867   Alaska and Midway acquired

1871   *Alabama* claims settled

1883   Advent of New Navy

1887   U.S. gains naval rights to Pearl Harbor

1889   First Pan-American Conference

1890   Alfred T. Mahan, *The Influence of Sea Power upon History*

1893   Severe depression begins
Hawaiian revolution begins

1895   Crisis over Venezuela
Cuban revolution begins
Japan defeats China

1896   McKinley elected president

1898   Sinking of the *Maine*
Spanish-American-Cuban-Filipino War
Hawaii and Wake Island annexed
Treaty of Paris

1899   Senate passes Treaty of Paris
United Fruit Company founded
First Open Door note
Outbreak of Philippine Insurrection

1900   Second Open Door note
U.S. exports total $1.5 billion
McKinley re-elected

1901   Theodore Roosevelt becomes president
Aguinaldo captured
Hay-Pauncefote Treaty

1903   Panama breaks from Colombia
U.S. granted canal rights in Panama

1904   Roosevelt Corollary

1905   Taft-Katsura Agreement
Portsmouth Conference
U.S. imposes financial supervision on Dominican Republic

1906   San Francisco segregates Asian schoolchildren
U.S. invades Cuba

1907   Great White Fleet
Gentleman's agreement with Japan

1908   Root-Takahira Agreement

1910   Mexican Revolution begins

1912   U.S. troops enter Cuba again
U.S. troops occupy Nicaragua

1914   U.S. troops invade Mexico
First World War begins
Panama Canal opens

and prosperity. After Roosevelt helped to slice off Panama from Colombia and initiated construction of the Panama Canal, Washington would not tolerate disturbances that might threaten the vital waterway.

Order was believed essential to American commerce and investment too. Finally, order seemed imperative to Americans eager to remake Latin American societies in the image of the United States. "When properly directed there is no people not fitted for self-government," Woodrow Wilson remarked. Furthermore, "every nation needs to be drawn into the tutelage of America."

Roosevelt, Taft, and Wilson gave varying expression to this quest for order. The Rough Rider saw world affairs as a constant struggle for international power. The United States, in its own interest, had to lay claim to as much power as possible. Taft emphasized dollar diplomacy: dollars, not bullets, he predicted, would effect stability and enhance American interests. Wilson was no less a nationalist or pragmatist in desiring to safeguard and expand American prosperity and security. He ordered troops to Haiti, the Dominican Republic, and Mexico, justifying military force by proclaiming it "our peculiar duty" to teach other peoples "order and self-control" and "the drill and habit of law and obedience." Wilson became known for his missionary paternalism, his insistence on liberal capitalism and constitutional government. Whether by means of Roosevelt's big stick, Taft's dollars, or Wilson's sermons—in fact, each president used all three methods—United States behavior toward its southern neighbors was imperialistic, because it denied some of them the freedom to make their own choices and thwarted their national sovereignty. The United States possessed few colonies, but developed an empire nonetheless—an informal one largely marked by economic and political control rather than formal annexation.

One of the assumptions that governed United States policy toward Europe was that European nations should not intervene in Western Hemispheric affairs; the Monroe Doctrine, European officials now knew, had power behind it. Another assumption of American policy toward Europe was that the United States should stand outside continental embroilments. And a third was that America's best interests lay in cooperation with Great Britain—the "great rapprochement."

From the Civil War to the First World War, expansionism and empire were central to American foreign policy. By 1914 Americans held extensive interests in a world made smaller by modern technology. The outward reach of American policy from Seward to Wilson met opposition from domestic critics, but the trend was never seriously diverted. Ideas of racial supremacy, the belief that the nation needed foreign markets to absorb surplus production so the domestic economy could thrive, a mission to uplift the less fortunate, and emotional appeals to national greatness—all fed the appetite for foreign adventure and commitments.

In 1914 Americans braced themselves for the immediate shock of full-scale war in Europe. In the long term, however, their foreign policy would be preoccupied with challenges to United States hegemony from proud and resentful nationalists victimized by American paternalism. And Americans who sincerely believed that they had been helping others to enjoy a better life would feel betrayed and baffled that their foreign clients could be so ungrateful.

SUGGESTIONS FOR FURTHER READING

General

Robert L. Beisner, *From the Old Diplomacy to the New, 1865–1900*, 2nd ed. (1986); Charles S. Campbell, *The Transformation of American Foreign Relations, 1865–1900* (1976); Richard D. Challener, *Admirals, Generals, and American Foreign Policy, 1889–1914* (1973); John A. S. Grenville and George B. Young, *Politics, Strategy, and American Diplomacy* (1967); David Healy, *U.S. Expansionism* (1970); Walter LaFeber, *The New Empire* (1963); Ernest R. May, *American Imperialism* (1968); Milton Plesur, *America's Outward Thrust* (1971); David M. Pletcher, *The Awkward Years* (1962); Emily Rosenberg, *Spreading the American Dream* (1982); Rubin F. Weston, *Racism in United States Imperialism* (1972); William Appleman Williams, *The Tragedy of American Diplomacy*, rev. ed. (1962).

Theodore Roosevelt and Other Expansionists

Howard K. Beale, *Theodore Roosevelt and the Rise of America to World Power* (1956); John M. Blum, *The Republican Roosevelt* (1954); John M. Cooper, Jr., *The Warrior and the Priest: Woodrow Wilson and Theodore Roosevelt* (1983); Lewis L. Gould, *The Presidency of William McKinley* (1981); William H. Harbaugh, *The Life and Times of Theodore Roosevelt* (1975); Frederick Marks III, *Velvet on Iron: The Diplomacy of Theodore Roosevelt* (1979); Edmund Morris, *The Rise of Theodore Roosevelt* (1979); Ernest N. Paolino, *The Foundations of the American Empire* (1973) (on Seward); William C. Widenor, *Henry Cabot Lodge and the Search for an American Foreign Policy* (1980). (For works on Woodrow Wilson, see Chapter 22.)

Economic Expansion and the Navy

See the works by Beisner, Campbell, and LaFeber cited above; Benjamin F. Cooling, *Gray Steel and Blue Water Navy* (1979); Kenneth J. Hagan, ed., *In Peace and War,* 2nd ed. (1984); Kenneth J. Hagan, *American Gunboat Diplomacy and the Old Navy, 1877–1889* (1973); Walter R. Herrick, *The American Naval Revolution* (1966); Peter Karsten, *The Naval Aristocracy* (1972); Robert Seager II, *Alfred Thayer Mahan* (1977); Ronald Spector, *Admiral of the New Empire* (1974) (on Dewey); Mira Wilkins, *The Emergence of the Multinational Enterprise* (1970); William Appleman Williams, *The Roots of the Modern American Empire* (1969).

The Spanish-American-Cuban-Filipino War

Graham A. Cosmas, *An Army for Empire* (1971); Willard B. Gatewood, Jr., *Black Americans and the White Man's Burden, 1898–1903* (1975); Gerald F. Linderman, *The Mirror of War: American Society and the Spanish-American War* (1974); Ernest R. May, *Imperial Democracy* (1961); Julius Pratt, *Expansionists of 1898* (1936); David F. Trask, *The War with Spain in 1898* (1981).

Anti-Imperialism and the Peace Movement

Robert L. Beisner, *Twelve Against Empire* (1968); Kendrick A. Clements, *William Jennings Bryan, Missionary Isolationist* (1983); Charles DeBenedetti, *Peace Reform in American History* (1980); C. Roland Marchand, *The American Peace Movement and Social Reform, 1898–1918* (1973); David S.

Patterson, *Toward a Warless World* (1976); E. Berkeley Tompkins, *Anti-Imperialism in the United States* (1970). (See also works in Chapter 22.)

Relations with Cuba and Latin America

Samuel F. Bemis, *The Latin American Policy of the United States* (1943); David Healy, *The United States in Cuba, 1898–1902* (1963); Walter LaFeber, *Inevitable Revolutions: The United States in Central America* (1983); Walter LaFeber, *The Panama Canal* (1979); Lester D. Langley, *The Banana Wars* (1983); Lester D. Langley, *The United States and the Caribbean, 1900–1970* (1980); Lester D. Langley, *Struggle for the American Mediterranean* (1976); David McCullough, *The Path Between the Seas: The Creation of the Panama Canal, 1870–1914* (1977); Dexter Perkins, *The Monroe Doctrine, 1867–1907* (1937); Ramon Ruiz, *Cuba* (1968); Karl M. Schmitt, *Mexico and the United States, 1821–1973* (1974).

Asia and the Pacific

Charles S. Campbell, *Special Business Interests and the Open Door Policy* (1951); Warren I. Cohen, *America's Response to China*, 2nd ed. (1980); Michael Hunt, *The Making of a Special Relationship: The United States and China to 1914* (1983); Akira Iriye, *Pacific Estrangement: Japanese and American Expansion, 1897–1911* (1972); Akira Iriye, *Across the Pacific* (1967); Jerry Israel, *Progressivism and the Open Door* (1971); Robert McClellan, *The Heathen Chinee: A Study of American Attitudes Toward China, 1890–1905* (1971); Thomas J. McCormick, *China Market* (1967); Charles E. Neu, *The Troubled Encounter* (1975) (on Japan); Merze Tate, *The United States and the Hawaiian Kingdom* (1965); Paul A. Varg, *The Making of a Myth: The United States and China, 1897–1912* (1968); Paul A. Varg, *Missionaries, Chinese, and Diplomats* (1958); Marilyn Blatt Young, *The Rhetoric of Empire* (1968).

The Philippines: Insurrection and Colony

John M. Gates, *Schoolbooks and Krags: The United States Army in the Philippines, 1898–1902* (1973); Glenn A. May, *Social Engineering in the Philippines* (1980); Stuart C. Miller, *"Benevolent Assimilation"* (1982); Julius Pratt, *America's Colonial Experiment* (1950); Daniel B. Schirmer, *Republic or*

Chapter 21: The Quest for Empire, 1865–1914

Empire? (1972); Peter Stanley, *A Nation in the Making: The Philippines and the United States, 1899–1921* (1974); Richard E. Welch, *Response to Imperialism: American Resistance to the Philippine War* (1972).

Britain and Canada

Kenneth Bourne, *Britain and the Balance of Power in North America, 1815–1908* (1967); Charles S. Campbell, *From Revolution to Rapprochement: The United States and Great Britain, 1783–1900* (1974); Adrian Cook, *The Alabama Claims* (1975); Bradford Perkins, *The Great Rapprochement* (1968).

CHAPTER 22

AMERICA AT WAR
1914–1920

"Oh, my God, what am I to do?" murmured Woodrow Wilson. Just moments before he had been holding Ellen Axson Wilson's hand when she died after years of suffering kidney disease. Two days earlier, on August 4, 1914, as he kept vigil at her bedside, the president had drafted a message offering American mediation to end the menacing war the European nations had just begun. Seldom have such painful personal and official burdens fallen on a president. Now, at a time of wrenching bereavement, when the partner who had always helped him in times of crisis was gone, Woodrow Wilson faced momentous decisions about America's place in the First World War.

The Great War in Europe shocked Woodrow Wilson and the American people: it seemed a throwing off of civilization. Americans had, of course, witnessed and participated in the years of international competition for colonies, markets, and weapons supremacy. Sporadic military encounters had disturbed

the peace, but full-scale war was thought to be a barbarity of the past. "The nineteenth-century view of history as progress," the historian Henry F. May has written, "received a shattering blow."

For almost three years President Wilson kept America out of the world war. He sought to protect American interests as a neutral trader and to improve the nation's military posture, all the while lecturing the belligerents to rediscover their humanity and to respect international law. But American neutrality, lives, and property fell victim to British and German naval warfare. In early 1917, with his characteristic crusading zeal, the president asked Congress for a declaration of war. America joined the battle not just to win the war but to reform the world that would emerge from it.

The American people in the era of the First World War, even after over a decade of progressive reform, remained heterogeneous and fractious. In 1914 labor-capital confrontations claimed headlines. Racial an-

tagonisms were evident in Wilson's decision to segregate federal buildings in Washington, D.C., and by
continued lynchings of blacks (fifty-one in 1914).
Nativists protested the fast pace of immigration.
Many women articulated the case for equality among
the sexes and for female suffrage, while most men
restated the case for traditional subordination.
German-Americans were denounced as traitors, and
pacifists were harassed. Moreover, the federal government trampled on civil liberties to silence critics.
Thus the war experience accentuated and intensified
the nation's social divisiveness.

America's participation in the war wrought massive changes and accelerated trends already in motion. Wars are emergencies; the normal way of doing
things surrenders to the extraordinary and exaggerated. This period witnessed greater powers for the
presidency, the military draft, unprecedented centralization and integration of the economy, increased
standardization of products, and unusual cooperation
between government and business. The war experience also helped cause the splintering and fading of
the progressive movement, although reformers did
put wartime effort into a few issues, such as prohibition and women's suffrage. But, Jane Addams remarked sadly, "the spirit of fighting burns away all
those impulses . . . which foster the will to justice."

The United States came out of the war a major
power in a disrupted and economically hobbled
world. Yet Americans who had marched to battle as
if on a crusade grew disillusioned. They recoiled from
the spectacle of the victors squabbling over the spoils
and they chided Wilson for failing to deliver his
promised "peace without victory." The president appealed for American membership in a new international organization, the League of Nations, which he
touted as a vehicle for reforming world politics. But
the Senate killed his diplomatic offspring, fearful that
it might entangle Americans once again in Europe's
problems, impede the growth of the American empire, and compromise the country's traditional unilateralism in international affairs. On many fronts,
then, Americans during the era of the First World
War were at war with themselves.

THE QUESTION OF NEUTRALITY

The war that erupted in August 1914 grew from
tangled roots. Years of imperialist competition
over trade, colonies, allies, and armaments had generated two diplomatic groups. The
Triple Alliance joined together Germany, Austria-Hungary, and Italy.
The Triple Entente combined Britain, France, and Russia. All had
economic and territorial ambitions,
but Germany seemed particularly bold as it rivaled
Britain for world leadership. A series of crises in the
Balkans (southeastern Europe) started a chain of
events that propelled the European nations into
battle.

European Origins of the First World War

Slavic nationalists sought to build a Slavic state by
adding territories to independent Serbia. Bosnia, part
of the Austro-Hungarian Empire, was one of those
coveted territories. In June 1914, at Sarajevo, Bosnia, the heir to the Austro-Hungarian throne was assassinated by a Slavic revolutionary linked to Serbia.
Austria-Hungary consulted Germany, which urged
toughness. Serbia called upon its Slavic friend Russia
for help. Russia looked to its ally France. When Austria-Hungary declared war against Serbia in late July,
Russia began to mobilize its armies. But Germany
struck first, declaring war against Russia on August 1
and against France two days later. The British hesitated, but when Germany slashed into Belgium to get
at France, Britain declared war against Germany on
August 4. Eventually Turkey joined the Central Powers of Germany and Austria-Hungary, and Japan and
Italy joined the Allies of Britain, France, and Russia.
The world was aflame (see map, page 392).

President Wilson at first sought to distance America from the conflagration by issuing a proclamation
of neutrality. He also asked Americans to refrain from
taking sides. The president's appeal for American
neutrality and unity at home, however, collided
with three realities. First, ethnic groups in the

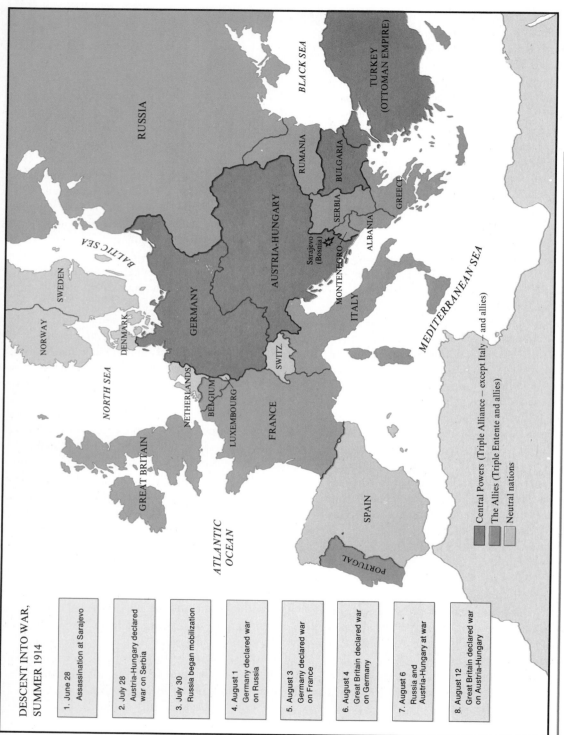

DESCENT INTO WAR, SUMMER 1914

1. June 28
Assassination at Sarajevo

2. July 28
Austria-Hungary declared war on Serbia

3. July 30
Russia began mobilization

4. August 1
Germany declared war on Russia

5. August 3
Germany declared war on France

6. August 4
Great Britain declared war on Germany

7. August 6
Russia and Austria-Hungary at war

8. August 12
Great Britain declared war on Austria-Hungary

Central Powers (Triple Alliance — except Italy — and allies)

The Allies (Triple Entente and allies)

Neutral nations

RUSSIA

SWEDEN

NORWAY

DENMARK

NORTH SEA

BALTIC SEA

GREAT BRITAIN

NETHERLANDS

BELGIUM

LUXEMBOURG

GERMANY

FRANCE

SWITZ.

ATLANTIC OCEAN

SPAIN

PORTUGAL

AUSTRIA-HUNGARY

ITALY

RUMANIA

Sarajevo (Bosnia)

SERBIA

MONTENEGRO

ALBANIA

BULGARIA

GREECE

BLACK SEA

TURKEY (OTTOMAN EMPIRE)

MEDITERRANEAN SEA

Europe Goes to War

United States naturally took sides. Many German-Americans and anti-British Irish-Americans (Ireland was then trying to break free from British rule) cheered for the Central Powers. Americans of British and French ancestry applauded the Allies. Anglo-American traditions and slogans like "Remember Lafayette," as well as the sheer number of Americans with roots in the Allied nations, drew a majority to the Allied cause.

Ethnic Ties to Europe

Second, America's economic links with the Allies also rendered neutrality difficult, if not impossible. England had long been one of the nation's best customers. New war-inspired orders flooded American companies and farms, pulling the economy out of its recession. In 1914 American exports to England and France were $753 million; in 1916 the figured spurted to $2.75 billion. In the same period, however, exports to Germany dropped from $345 million to only $29 million. Much of the American-Allied trade was financed through private American loans, amounting to $2.3 billion during the period of neutrality; in stark contrast, Germany received only $27 million.

Economic Links with the Belligerents

From Germany's perspective, of course, the linkage between the American economy and the Allies meant that the United States had become the quite-unneutral Allied arsenal and bank. Under international law the British—who controlled the seas—could buy contraband (war-related goods) and noncontraband from neutrals at their own risk. It was Germany's responsibility, not America's, to stop the trade in ways that international law prescribed: an effective blockade of the enemy's territory or the seizure of all goods from belligerent (British) ships and contraband from neutral (American) ships.

The third reason why neutrality did not work derived from the pro-Allied sympathies of Wilson administration officials. Wilson believed a German victory would destroy government by law and "free industry and enterprise." The president's chief advisers and diplomats—Colonel Edward House, Secretary of State Robert Lansing, and Ambassador to London Walter Hines Page among them—also shared these sentiments and were often openly pro-Allied in their viewpoints.

Pro-Allied Sympathies

Wilson and his aides also believed that Wilsonian principles stood a better chance of international acceptance if Britain, rather than the Central Powers, sat astride the postwar world. Wilsonianism—the body of ideas Wilson espoused—consisted of traditional American diplomatic principles. His ideal world was to be open in every sense of the word: no barriers to commerce, no impediments to democratic politics, no secret diplomatic deals. Empires were to be opened up in keeping with the principle of self-determination and armaments were to be reduced. Wilson envisioned free-market, nonexploitive capitalism and political constitutionalism for all nations, to ensure the good society and world peace. Wilson also articulated the traditional belief in American exceptionalism. America, he believed, had a mission to reform international relations and other societies. American progressivism was to be projected onto the world. "We created this Nation," he intoned, "not to serve ourselves, but to serve mankind."

Wilsonianism

To say that American neutrality was never a real possibility, given ethnic loyalties, economic ties, and Wilsonian preferences, is not to say that Wilson sought to enter the war. He emphatically wanted to keep the United States out, and in fact did so for two and a half years. But the United States finally did enter the war, because Americans got caught in the Allied–Central Power crossfire. The British, "ruling the waves and waiving the rules," declared a loose, ineffective, and hence illegal blockade; defined a broad list of contraband (including foodstuffs) which was not supposed to be shipped to Germany by neutrals; mined the North Sea; and harassed neutral shipping by seizing cargoes. To counter German submarines, the British flouted international law by arming their merchant ships and

British Naval Policy

flying neutral (sometimes American) flags. Wilson frequently protested British violations of neutral rights, but London often deftly defused American criticism by paying for confiscated cargoes.

Germany was determined to lift the injurious blockade and to end American-Allied commerce. These ambitious tasks were assigned to the submarine. In February 1915 Berlin announced that it was creating a war zone around the British Isles. All enemy ships in the area would be sunk; neutral vessels were warned to stay out so as not to be attacked by mistake; and passengers from neutral nations like the United States were warned to stay off enemy ships. Wilson stiffly informed Germany that the United States was holding it to "strict accountability" for any losses of American life and property.

Wilson interpreted existing international law in the strictest sense. Such law held that an attacker had to warn a passenger or merchant ship before attacking, so that passengers and **The Submarine** crew could disembark into lifeboats **and** for safety. But the submarine, an **International** extremely vulnerable vessel when **Law** surfaced, postdated that rule, and Wilson refused to adjust tradition to this new weapon of war. Berlin frequently complained to Wilson that he was denying the Germans the one weapon they could use to break the British economic stranglehold, disrupt the Allies' substantial connection with American producers and bankers, and win the war.

FROM THE LUSITANIA TO WAR

Over the next few months the U-boats sank ship after ship. Then the sinking of the *Lusitania* forced the submarine issue for Wilson. The swift British passenger liner left New York City on May 1, 1915, with over 1,200 passengers and a cargo of food-stuffs and contraband, including ammunition. Before "*Lucy's*" departure, the newspapers carried an unusual announcement from the German embassy: travelers on British vessels were warned that a war zone existed and that Allied ships in those waters "are liable to destruction." On May 7, off the Irish coast, U-20 unleashed torpedoes at the vessel; the *Lusitania* carried 1,198 people, including 128 Americans, to their deaths.

Even though the ship carried armaments, argued Wilson, the sinking was a brutal assault on innocent people. But he ruled out a military response. Secretary of State William Jennings **Reaction to the** Bryan advised that Americans not **Sinking of the** be permitted to travel on belliger- **Lusitania** ent ships and that passenger vessels not be allowed to carry war goods. Bryan also urged that simultaneous protest notes be sent to London and Berlin. Wilson rejected Bryan's counsel, as well as that of Theodore Roosevelt and others who clamored for war. Instead he sent a note to Berlin insisting on the right of Americans to sail on belligerent ships and demanding that Germany cease its inhumane submarine warfare. When the president refused to ban American travelers from belligerent ships, Bryan resigned in protest.

Germany, seeking to avoid war with America, ordered its U-boat commanders to halt attacks on passenger liners. But in mid-August another British vessel, the *Arabic*, was sunk; two American lives were lost. The Germans hastened to pledge that never again would an unarmed passenger ship be attacked without warning.

In March 1916 an attack on the *Sussex*, a French vessel crossing the English Channel, took the United States a step closer to war. Four Americans on that ship were injured. Stop the marauding submarines, Wilson lectured Berlin, or he would sever diplomatic relations. Again the Germans backed off, pledging not to attack merchant vessels without warning.

Sentiment for peace remained strong, as evidenced by Wilson's victory on a peace platform in the 1916 election. After his triumph, Wilson futilely labored once again to bring the belligerents to the conference table. In early 1917 he advised them to temper their acquisitive war aims, appealing for a "peace without victory."

Then in early February 1917, Germany startled the Wilson administration by launching unrestricted submarine warfare. All vessels, belligerent or neutral, warship or merchant, would be attacked if sighted in the declared war zone. This bold decision represented a calculated risk that submarines could impede the valuable munitions shipments from America to England and thus defeat the Allies before Americans could be mobilized and ferried across the Atlantic to enter the fight. Wilson quickly broke off diplomatic relations with Berlin. Everybody waited for the inevitable collision.

With this German challenge to American neutral rights and economic interests came a German threat to American security. In late February, the British intercepted and handed to the American government a telegram addressed to the German minister in Mexico from Foreign Secretary Arthur Zimmermann. The minister was instructed to tell the Mexican government that if it joined a military alliance against the United States, Germany would help Mexico to recover the territories it was forced to give up to its northern neighbor in 1848. At the time Mexican-American relations were extremely tense. The Mexican government was threatening to nationalize American properties. Wilson had twice ordered American troops onto Mexican soil: in 1914 at Vera Cruz, to avenge a petty slight to the American uniform and flag, and again in 1916 in northern Mexico, where General John J. Pershing tried to capture the elusive Pancho Villa after his raid on an American border town. Lansing and Wilson agreed that Zimmermann's telegram constituted "a conspiracy against this country."

Zimmermann Telegram

Soon after learning of Zimmermann's ploy, Wilson asked Congress for "armed neutrality" to defend American lives and commerce. Specifically he requested the authority to arm American merchant ships, and more generally the power to "employ any other instrumentalities or methods that may be necessary." In the midst of the debate, Wilson released Zimmermann's telegram to the press; the nation was stunned. Still, antiwar Senators Robert M. La Follette and George Norris, among others, saw the armed-ship bill as a blank check for the president to move the country to war and filibustered it to death. Wilson proceeded to arm America's commercial vessels anyway. The action came too late to prevent the sinking of several American ships. War cries echoed across the nation.

On April 2, 1917, the president stepped before a hushed Congress. Solemnly he chided the Germans for "warfare against mankind." Wilson explained American grievances: Germany's violation of the principle of freedom of the seas, disruption of American commerce, attempt to stir up trouble in Mexico, and violation of human rights by killing innocent Americans. Wilson's most famous words rang out: "The world must be made safe for democracy." Congress quickly declared war against Germany, by a vote of 373 to 50 in the House and 82 to 6 in the Senate. The first woman ever to sit in Congress, Montana's Jeannette Rankin, elected in 1916, cast a ringing "no" vote that won her high ranking in the pantheon of American pacifism.

Declaration of War

For principle, for morality, for honor, for commerce, for security—for all these reasons the United States took up arms against Germany. In the most general sense, America went to war to reform world politics, not to destroy Germany. That is, by early 1917 Wilson seemed to believe that America could not claim a seat at the peace conference unless it became a combatant. At such a conference, Wilson intended to put into constitutional form the principles he thought essential to a stable world order, to promote democracy and the Open Door, and to outlaw revolution and aggression. Quite simply, Woodrow Wilson decided for war to gain an American-fashioned peace.

TAKING UP ARMS

Even before the war decision, the United States had been preparing for combat. Encouraged by such groups as the National Security League and the

Antiwar Sentiment

Navy League, and by mounting public outrage against Germany's submarine warfare, the president in 1915 began to plan a substantial military buildup. Meanwhile, antiwar critics vowed to block preparedness. Some pacifist progressives became active in an antiwar coalition, the American Union Against Militarism. Jane Addams and Carrie Chapman Catt founded the Women's Peace party, and both Henry Ford and Andrew Carnegie worked for peace. But the peace movement was splintered, and it could not prevent passage of preparedness measures, such as the National Defense Act (1916).

To raise an army after the declaration of war, Congress in 1917 passed the Selective Service Act, requiring the registration of all males between the

Raising an Army

ages of twenty and thirty (later changed to eighteen and forty-five). National service, proponents believed, would not only prepare the nation for battle but also promote efficiency, order, democracy, personal sacrifice, and nationalism. Critics, on the other hand, feared that "Prussianism," not democratization, would instead be the likely outcome.

On July 5, 1917, over 9.5 million men signed up for the "great national lottery." By war's end, 24 million men had been registered by local draft boards. Over 4.8 million served in the armed forces, 2 million of whom fought in France. The typical soldier was a draftee twenty-one to twenty-three years old, white, single, and poorly educated (most had not attended high school). Perhaps as many as 18 percent were foreign-born, and 400,000 were black. Some women became navy clerks; others served in the U.S. Army Signal Corps and Nurse Corps. On college

Government posters became a popular medium to rally Americans to the armed forces and domestic mobilization. In this poster, artist Howard Chandler Christy uses the traditional theme of war as masculine enterprise to recruit sailors. National Archives.

campuses, 150,000 students entered the Student Army Training Corps or similar navy and marine units.

President Wilson and General Pershing (now head of the American Expeditionary Force) all worried that the young soldiers, once away from their home environments, would turn to vice—especially prostitutes and liquor. They were right. To protect the supposed novices with social armor, the government created the Commission on Training Camp Activities to coordinate the work of the YMCA, the Knights of

Columbus, the Salvation Army, the Red Cross, and the Jewish Welfare Board, among others.

Jim Crow was in the army too. Fearing a black soldiery, many southern politicians opposed the drafting of blacks. But the army needed men, white and black. The NAACP and W. E. B.

Segregation in the Army

Du Bois urged blacks to join the fight for "world liberty," optimistically thinking that a war to make the world safe for democracy would blur the color line at home. They were greatly disappointed. Military leaders segregated facilities, discouraged blacks from becoming officers, and assigned black recruits to menial labor. Ugly racial slurs echoed through the camps. In Houston, Texas, angry black soldiers responded to goading from whites by seizing arms and killing thirteen of them. Official white retaliation was immediate and excessive. After brief "trials," thirteen blacks were executed; another six were hanged after an unsuccessful appeal of their death sentences; others were court-martialed and given long prison terms.

In Europe, Pershing wisely refused to submerge American troops in Allied units (officially the United States declared itself an Associated power). Allied commanders had wedded themselves to unimaginative trench warfare, producing military stalemate and ghastly casualties. Zigzag trenches fronted by barbed wire and mines stretched across France. Beyond the muddy and stinking trenches lay "no man's land." When ordered out, soldiers would charge the German lines, also a maze of trenches. Machine guns mowed them down; chlorine gas, first used by Germany in 1915, poisoned them. And so little was gained. At the Battle of the Somme in 1916 the British and French suffered 600,000 dead or wounded to earn only 125 square miles (the Germans lost 500,000 men). Pershing would not commit his clean, fresh "doughboys" to this death-dealing type of warfare.

Firsthand war, the Americans soon learned, was quite different from the abstract slogans spoken at home to glorify the nation's participation. They came to know the muck and stink of trench warfare and the horrors of poison gas. Fifty-one thousand Ameri-

An American soldier of Company K, 110th Infantry Regiment, receives first aid during fighting at Varennes, France. *National Archives.*

cans lost their lives in battle and another 230,000 were wounded; the mortality toll from disease was greater. Many of the 62,000 soldiers and sailors who died from disease were among the 550,000 Americans who were killed by the influenza epidemic of 1918.

The influx of American men and material decided the outcome of the First World War. The Americans tipped the balance toward the Allies. Actually the inexperienced Americans did not

Americans in Combat in France

engage in much combat until after the lull of the severe winter of 1917 and 1918. Then in the spring, after knocking Russia out of the war and closing the eastern front, the Germans launched a major offensive. Kaiser Wilhelm's forces got within fifty miles of Paris; American troops helped to blunt their advance at Château-Thierry. In September over 1 million Americans joined British and French troops in the Allied offensive that pushed the Germans back. Its submarine warfare a dismal failure, its ground war a shambles, its troops and cities mutinous, abandoned by Turkey and Austria, Germany sued for peace. The armistice was signed on November 11, 1918.

The armistice was Wilsonian. That is, the president insisted that his Fourteen Points, which he had enunciated in January, be made the general terms for peace negotiations. The Allies balked, but Wilson scared them into acceptance by threatening a separate peace with Germany. The Fourteen Points were a summary of Wilsonianism. The first five called for diplomacy in the "public view," freedom of the seas, lower tariffs, reductions in armaments, and the decolonization of empires. Points 6 through 13 appealed for self-determination for national groups in Europe. For Wilson the last point was the most essential, the vehicle for achieving all the others: "a general association of nations" or League of Nations. Having won the war, the resolute Wilson set out to win the peace.

THE HOME FRONT

"It is not an army that we must shape and train for war," declared the president; "it is a nation." The United States was a belligerent for only nineteen months, but the impact of the war on domestic America was conspicuous. In that comparatively short period the national government quickly geared the economy to war needs and marshaled public opinion. As never before, the state intervened in American life. An unprecedented concentration of bureaucratic power developed in Washington, D.C.

The federal government and private business became partners during the war. Dollar-a-year executives flocked to the nation's capital from major companies; they retained their corporate salaries while serving in administrative and consulting capacities. Early in the war, the government relied on several industrial committees for advice on purchases and prices. But evidence of self-interested businesspeople cashing in

Business-Government Cooperation

on the national interest aroused public protest. As a result the committees were disbanded in July 1917 in favor of the War Industries Board (WIB). Business-government cooperation was also stimulated by the suspension of antitrust laws; by cost-plus contracts, which guaranteed companies a healthy profit and a means to pay higher wages to head off labor strikes; by the virtual abandonment of competitive bidding; and by a floor placed under prices to ensure profits.

Hundreds of new government agencies, staffed largely by businesspeople, came into being. Some of the superagencies placed unprecedented controls on the economy. The Food Administration, led by Herbert Hoover, undertook programs to improve production and conserve food through voluntary action; it also set prices and regulated distribution. Americans were urged to grow "victory gardens" in their backyards and to eat meatless and wheatless meals. The Railroad Administration took over the snarled and financially troubled railway industry. When strikes threatened the telephone and telegraph companies, the federal government seized and ran them.

The largest and potentially most powerful of the wartime agencies was the War Industries Board. Designed as a clearinghouse to coordinate the national economy and headed after early 1918 by millionaire financier Bernard Baruch, the WIB faced the enormous task of satisfying both Allied and domestic needs. Although the WIB seemed all-powerful, in reality it had to conciliate competing interest groups and compromise with the businesspeople whose advice it so valued.

The performance of the mobilized economy was mixed, but it delivered enough men and materiel to France to ensure the defeat of the Central Powers. About a quarter of all American production was diverted to war needs. Farmers enjoyed boom years as they put more acreage into production and watched prices go up. Induced to produce more at a faster pace, farmers mechanized as never before. Some industries enjoyed substantial increases because of wartime demand, and the gross national product soared.

Organized labor sought a partnership with government too, but its gains were far less spectacular than those of business. For unions the war seemed to offer opportunities for recognition and better pay. Samuel Gompers, president of the AFL, threw his loyalty to the Wilson administration, promising to deter strikes. He and other moderate labor leaders were rewarded with appointments to high-level wartime government agencies. The National War Labor Board, created to mediate labor disputes, ruled out strikes and lockouts but fostered the eight-hour day and guaranteed workers the right to organize for collective bargaining. Unionization moved at a fast pace; from roughly 2.7 million in 1916, union membership climbed to over 4 million in 1919. The AFL could not curb strikes by the radical Industrial Workers of the World (IWW) or rebellious AFL locals: in the nineteen war months, over six thousand strikes occurred. During these months, many workers gained a forty-eight hour week. Given the high cost of living, however, workers' earnings rose only slightly.

Wartime Labor Relations

As the needs of the military and a decline in immigration affected the traditional sources of laborers, the call went out to women, blacks, and Mexican-Americans. Though the number of women in the work force increased slightly, the real story was that many shifted from one job to another, sometimes into formerly male domains. Some white women left domestic service for factories, moved from clerking in department stores to stenography and typing, and departed textile mills for employment in firearms plants. Twenty percent or more of all workers in the wartime manufacture of electrical machinery, airplanes, and food were women. As white women took advantage of the new opportunities, black women took some of their places in domestic service and in textile factories.

Women in the Work Force

The movement of women into jobs that had been the preserve of males generated controversy. Male workers complained that women destabilized the work environment with their higher productivity; women answer that they were used to seasonal em-

Goggled women workers, hired by the Bethlehem Steel Corporation to replace men gone to war, tend their machines. Courtesy Bethlehem Steel.

ployment and piecework and hence worked at a faster pace. Men protested that women undermined the wage system by working for lower pay; women pointed out that male-dominated companies discriminated against them and unions denied them membership. Finally, male employees resented the spirit of independence evident among women whose labor was now greatly valued.

When the war was over, the gains women had made were largely reversed. The attitude that women's proper sphere was the home changed very little. Some married working women found that their husbands and children resented the disruption of home life. Moreover, reformers complained that working mothers were neglecting their children. Many women lost their jobs to returning veterans.

Wartime mobilization wrought significant changes for the black community. Wartime jobs in the North provided an escape from southern social, political,

Black Migration to the North

and economic oppression. During the war years, southern blacks undertook a great migration to northern cities to work in railroad yards, packing houses, steel mills, shipyards, and coal mines. Between 1910 and 1920, about a half-million black Americans uprooted themselves to move north. Most were young (twenty to twenty-four years old) males seeking economic opportunity.

New jobs and improved opportunities could not erase the fact that blacks, North and South, continued to be a minority in a white society. When the United States entered the First World War, there was not one black judge in the entire country and segregation was social custom. The Ku Klux Klan began to revive and racist films like D. W. Griffith's *Birth of a Nation* (1915) further fed prejudice. Lynching statistics exposed the wide gap between American declarations of humanity in the war and the American practice of inhumanity at home: between 1914 and 1920, 382 blacks were lynched, some of them in military uniform.

Northern whites who resented the "Negro invasion" vented their anger in riots. In East St. Louis, Illinois, in 1917, whites opposed to black employ-

Race Riots

ment in a defense plant rampaged through the streets; forty blacks and nine whites lost their lives. In the bloody "Red Summer" of 1919, race riots rocked two dozen cities and towns. The worst race war occurred in Chicago, where thirty-eight people died in a riot sparked by an incident at a segregated beach.

The war also affected Mexican-Americans, whose numbers increased from 385,000 in 1910 to 740,000 in 1920. They lived largely in the southwestern

Mexican-American Migration

states and California, belonged to the Catholic Church, and worked mostly in agriculture as field laborers. Before the war Mexicans had migrated to the United States to

seek better incomes and to escape the convulsions of the Mexican Revolution. Many entered illegally. But in 1917 the United States passed an immigration act with a head tax and a literacy test that slowed Mexican migration. When the United States entered the First World War, many Mexicans returned home, fearful they would be drafted. Thus, at a time when southwestern growers needed more labor to meet the wartime demand for foodstuffs, their work force was actually shrinking. The growers appealed to Washington for help. Federal officials first assured aliens that they would not be drafted into the armed forces and then exempted agricultural workers from the act of 1917, a waiver that lasted until 1920. As a result, over 100,000 Mexicans migrated to the Southwest. Some filled jobs left vacant by Mexican-Americans who, like blacks, had migrated north to work in industry.

THE ATTACK ON CIVIL LIBERTIES

"Woe be to the man that seeks to stand in our way in this day of high resolution." Woodrow Wilson's passionate words were aimed at dissenters who questioned his war decision, the draft, and his management of wartime affairs. An official and unofficial campaign to silence critics swept the nation. Headed by George Creel, the Committee on Public Information (CPI), in effect a propaganda agency, set out to shape and mobilize public opinion by means of anti-German tracts, speeches, films, and "self-censorship" of the press. The CPI encouraged people to spy on their neighbors and report any suspicious behavior. Exaggeration, fearmongering, distortion, half-truths, and mindless emotionalism were the stuff of the CPI's "mind mobilization."

The Wilson administration also guided through an obliging Congress the Espionage Act (1917) and the

Sedition Act (1918). The first statute forbade "false statements" designed to impede the draft or promote military insubordination and banned from the mails materials considered treasonous. The Sedition Act made it unlawful to obstruct the sale of war bonds and to use "disloyal, profane, scurrilous, or abusive" language against the government, the Constitution, the flag, and the military uniform. These loosely worded laws gave the government wide latitude to crack down on those with whom it differed. Over two thousand people were prosecuted under the acts and many others were intimidated into silence. Among them was Eugene Debs, who received a ten-year sentence for his criticism of the war and defense of free speech.

Espionage and Sedition Acts

State and local governments joined the campaign. Officials banned what they considered "pro-German" books from public schools; the governor of Iowa prohibited the use of any language but English in schools and public places; and Pittsburgh banned Beethoven's music. Everywhere teachers who questioned the war faced dismissal by hostile school boards. And at Columbia University, antiwar Professor J. M. Cattell, a distinguished psychologist, was fired. His colleague Charles Beard, a prowar historian, resigned in protest: "If we have to suppress everything we don't like to hear, this country is resting on a pretty wobbly basis."

The point was just that: Wilson and his officers tried to crush what they did not like to hear. In particular, the administration concentrated on the IWW and the Socialist party. The war emergency and the frank opposition of those two radical organizations gave progressives and conservatives alike an opportunity to throttle their political rivals. Soon after the declaration of war, government agents raided union meetings and arrested IWW leaders. The army was sent into western mining and lumbering regions to put down IWW strikes on the pretense that they were pro-German. Under the immigration acts, alien members of the IWW were deported. Town after town evicted the "Wobblies," and

Persecution of Radicals

by the end of the war most of the union's leaders were in jail. The Socialist party fared little better.

The Supreme Court, itself attuned to the pulse of the times, upheld the Espionage Act. Justice Oliver Wendell Holmes, in *Schenck v. U.S.* (1919), expressed the Court's unanimous opinion that in time of war the First Amendment could be restricted: "Free speech would not protect a man falsely shouting fire in a theater and causing panic." If words "are of such a nature as to create a clear and present danger that they will bring about the substantial evils that Congress has a right to prevent," Holmes went on, free speech could be limited. In another case, *Abrams v. U.S.* (1919), the Court voted 7 to 2 that the Sedition Act was constitutional. This time, Holmes, writing the minority opinion, expressed concern that the "free trade in ideas" was being jeopardized.

THE RED SCARE

In the last few months of the war, guardians of Americanism began to label dissenters not only pro-German, but pro-Bolshevik. After the Bolshevik Revolution in the fall of 1917, American hatred for Kaiser Germany was readily transferred to Communist Russia. When the new Russian government under V. I. Lenin made peace with Germany in early 1918, thereby closing the eastern front, Americans felt betrayed. President Wilson, who refused to recognize the new regime, actually attempted to subvert the Bolshevik Revolution by ordering troops to Russia and participating in a blockade of the country. At home, too, the Wilson administration was moving against radicals and others imprecisely defined as Bolsheviks or Communists. After the war Americans remained edgy: the war had disrupted race relations, the workplace, and the family; it had increased the cost of living; postwar unemployment loomed; and in 1919 the Russian Communists established the Comintern to promote world revolution. Americans found it easy to blame their postwar troubles on new scapegoats.

A rash of labor strikes in 1919 helped spark the Red Scare. All told, over 3,300 strikes involving 4 million laborers occurred that year, including a general strike in Seattle in February. In May, bombs were sent through the mails to prominent Americans; most of the devices were intercepted and dismantled. Police never captured the conspirators. The common and not-unreasonable assumption was that anarchists and others bent on the destruction of the American way of life were responsible. Next came the Boston police strike in September; some thought it part of a Bolshevik conspiracy. The governor of Massachusetts, Calvin Coolidge, gained fame by proclaiming that nobody had the right to strike against the public safety. State guardsmen were brought in to replace the striking police force.

Especially ominous in September was the walkout of 350,000 steel workers. One of the leaders of the steel strike was William Z. Foster, a radical who joined the Communist party after the strike began. His presence in a labor movement seeking legitimate bread-and-butter goals permitted political and business leaders to dismiss the steel strike as a foreign threat orchestrated by American radicals. There was actually no conspiracy, and the strike collapsed in 1920. Indeed, the American left was badly splintered and incapable of mounting a threat to the established order.

Steel Strike

But Attorney General A. Mitchell Palmer believed that the "blaze of revolution" was "burning up the foundations of society." To stamp out the radical fire, Palmer created the Bureau of Investigation and appointed J. Edgar Hoover to run it. Hoover organized a file of thousands of index cards bearing the names of alleged radical individuals and organizations. In 1919 agents jailed IWW members and deported alien radicals like Emma Goldman. Again, state and local governments took their cue from Washington. The New York state legislature expelled five duly elected Socialist members. States passed peacetime sedition acts under which hundreds of people were arrested.

The Red Scare reached a climax in January 1920 when the attorney general staged his Palmer Raids. Using J. Edgar Hoover's information, government agents in thirty-three cities broke into meeting halls, poolrooms, and homes without search warrants. Four thousand people were thrown into overcrowded jails and denied counsel. Of this number, about 550 were deported.

Palmer Raids

Palmer's disregard for elementary civil liberties soon drew criticism. Civil libertarians and lawyers pointed out that Palmer's blatant tactics ignored the Constitution, that many of the arrested "Communists" had committed no crimes, and that some were not even radicals. Palmer's call for a peacetime sedition act alarmed leaders of many political persuasions. His dire prediction that major violence would mar May Day 1920 proved mistaken. Palmer's exaggerations, his scenarios of Bolshevik conspiracy, simply exceeded the truth so far that he lost credibility.

The campaign against free speech in the period from 1917 through 1920 left casualties. Critics, radical or otherwise, were afraid to speak their minds. Debate, so essential to democracy, was curbed. Reform suffered as reformers either joined in the antiradicalism or became victims of it. The radical movement was badly weakened, the IWW becoming virtually extinct and the Socialist party paralyzed. Moreover, the actions of the government had threatened the Bill of Rights and reflected the willingness of some progressives to use authoritarian means to achieve their goal of a reformed society.

THE PEACE CONFERENCE AND LEAGUE FIGHT

As the Red Scare threatened American democracy, Woodrow Wilson struggled to make his Fourteen Points a reality. When the president departed for the Paris peace conference in December 1918, he faced obstacles erected by his political enemies, by the Allies, and by himself. Some observers suggested that the ambitious Wilson, confident of his own abilities and convinced that destiny directed his course, underestimated his task.

In the 1918 congressional elections, Wilson had urged a vote for the Democrats as a sign of support for his peace goals. But the Republicans gained control of both houses, signaling trouble for Wilson in two ways. First, any peace treaty would have to be submitted for approval to a potentially hostile Senate; second, Wilson's stature had been diminished in the eyes of foreign leaders. After this setback, Wilson aggravated his political problems by not naming any senator to the American Peace Commission, refusing to take any prominent Republican with him to the conference, and failing to consult with the Senate Foreign Relations Committee before he sailed for Paris.

Another obstacle in Wilson's way was the Allies' determination to impose a harsh, vengeful peace on the Germans. Georges Clemenceau of France, David Lloyd George of Britain, and Vittorio Orlando of Italy—with Wilson, the Big Four—were formidable adversaries. They had signed secret treaties during the war and expected to enlarge their empires at Germany's expense. They scoffed at the headstrong, self-impressed president who wanted to deny them the spoils of war.

The victors demanded that Germany pay a huge reparations bill. Wilson called for a small indemnity, fearing that a resentful and economically hobbled Germany might turn to Bolshevism or disrupt the postwar community in some other way. Unable to moderate the Allied position, the president reluctantly gave way, agreeing to a clause blaming the war on the Germans and to the creation of a reparations commission to determine a figure (later set at $33 billion).

Paris Conference

As for decolonization (the breaking up of empires) and the principle of self-determination, Wilson only partially overcame the land-grabbing mood of the conference. The conferees placed former German and Turkish colonies under the control of other imperial nations in a League-administered "mandate" system. France and Britain, for example, obtained parts of the Middle East, and Japan gained authority over Germany's colonies in the Pacific. The mandate system was a halfway station between outright imperial domination and independence. In other compromises, Japan was granted influence over China's Shandong Peninsula, and France was permitted occupation rights in Germany's Rhineland. Elsewhere in Europe, however, Wilson's prescriptions fared better. Out of Austria-Hungary and Russia came the new independent states of Austria, Hungary, Yugoslavia, Czechoslovakia, and Poland. Wilson and his colleagues also built a *cordon sanitaire* of new westward-looking nations (Finland, Estonia, Latvia, and Lithuania) around Russia to quarantine the Bolshevik contagion.

Wilson worked especially hard on the charter for the League of Nations. In the long run, he believed, the League would moderate the harshness of the Allied peace terms and temper imperial ambitions. He devised a League that reflected the power of large nations like the United States: an influential council of five permanent members (great powers) and elected delegates from smaller states; an assembly for discussion; and a World Court. The heart of the League covenant, as well as the centerpiece of Wilson's international reform program, was the collective security provision contained in Article 10, in which members agreed to respect and preserve each other's territorial integrity.

League of Nations

Americans vigorously debated the merits of the treaty. Several criticisms were voiced: Wilson had bastardized his own principles; he had conceded Shandong to Japan; he had personally killed a provision affirming the racial equality of all peoples. There was no mention in the treaty of freedom of the seas; there was no reduction in tariffs. Negotiations had been conducted in private, and reparations promised to be punishing. And Article 10

Debate over the Treaty

raised serious questions: Would the United States be obligated to use armed force to ensure collective security?

Wilson pleaded for understanding and lectured his opponents. Did they not realize that compromises were necessary given the awesome, stubborn resistance of the Allies, who had threatened to jettison the conference unless Wilson made concessions? Did they not recognize that the League would rectify wrongs? Could they not see that membership in the League would give the United States "leadership in the world"? Senator Lodge was unimpressed. A Harvard-educated Ph.D. and partisan Republican, Lodge packed the Foreign Relations Committee with critics of the League. He introduced reservations to the treaty: one stated that the nation's immigration acts could not be subject to League decision; another held that Congress had to approve any obligation under Article 10.

In September 1919, Wilson embarked on a speaking tour of the United States. Growing more exhausted every day, he dismissed his critics as "absolute, contemptible quitters." In Colorado, while delivering another passionate speech, the president collapsed. A few days later, in Washington, D.C., he suffered a stroke that paralyzed his left side. Although his mind remained alert, he became grumpy and peevish, fearful of displaying weakness and unable to conduct the heavy business of the presidency. Told by advisers to placate senatorial critics so the treaty would have a chance of passing, Wilson stubbornly refused to compromise. From Democrats in the Senate he demanded loyalty—a vote against all reservations.

The Senate first tested the treaty's strength in November. In two votes, one on the treaty with reservations and one without, the Senate rejected it. A group of sixteen "Irreconcilables," determined to defeat any treaty, voted nay each time. Again, in March 1920, the Senate fell short of the necessary two-thirds vote of approval. Had Wilson permitted Democrats to compromise, he could have achieved his fervent goal

Senate Rejection of the Treaty

of American membership in the infant League of Nations.

Who or what was responsible for the defeat of the treaty? The answer lies in the fact that at the core of the debate was a fundamental issue of American foreign policy: whether the United States would endorse collective security or pursue its traditional path of unilateralism, as articulated in Washington's Farewell Address and the Monroe Doctrine. Wilson lost because he could not overcome the American desire for freedom of choice in international relations and for nonalignment. Woodrow Wilson failed to create a new world order through reform; he promised more than he could deliver.

THE EXPERIENCE OF WAR

America emerged from the war years an unsettled mix of the old and the new. Above all else the war exposed the heterogeneity of the American people and the deep divisions among them: white versus black, nativist versus immigrant, capital versus labor, dry versus wet, men versus women, radical versus progressive or conservative, pacifist versus interventionist, nationalist versus internationalist.

During the war the federal government intervened in the economy and influenced people's everyday lives as never before. In the period 1916 to 1919 annual federal expenditures increased 2,500 percent. Wilsonian wartime policies nourished the continued growth of big business and of oligopoly (the control of a whole industry by a few large companies). The wartime cooperation of business and government also encouraged the growth of trade associations. Standardization of products contributed to the further development of a mass society.

Enlarged Federal Role

America's changed place in world affairs also held significance for later generations. By 1920 the United States was the world's leading economic power, pro-

IMPORTANT EVENTS

1914	American troops invade Mexico First World War begins		Sedition Act Eugene Debs imprisoned U.S. troops at Château-Thierry U.S. troops intervene in Russia Influenza epidemic Republicans win congressional elections Armistice
1915	Germany declares war zone around British Isles German U-boat sinks *Lusitania* Bryan resigns in protest		
1916	U.S. troops invade Mexico again *Sussex* torpedoed National Defense Act Wilson re-elected	1919	Paris Peace Conference at Versailles Eighteenth Amendment ratified May Day bombings American Legion founded Red Summer; Chicago race riot Steel strike U.S. Communist party founded President Wilson suffers stroke Treaty of Paris rejected by Senate *Schenck v. U.S.*
1917	Germany declares unrestricted submarine warfare Zimmermann telegram Russian Revolution U.S. entry into First World War Selective Service Act Espionage Act Race riot in East St. Louis, Illinois War Industries Board created		
1918	Wilson announces Fourteen Points	1920	Red Scare and Palmer Raids Nineteenth Amendment ratified

ducing 40 percent of its coal, 70 percent of its petroleum, and half its pig iron. It rose to first rank in world trade.

The international system born in these years was unstable and fragmented. The process of decolonization was set in motion at this time. Nationalist leaders like Ho Chi Minh of Indochina and Mahatma Gandhi of India, taking to heart the Wilsonian principle of self-determination, vowed to achieve independence for their peoples. Communism became a new and disruptive force in world politics, and the Russians bore a grudge against the Allies, who had futilely tried to thwart their revolution. The new states in Central and Eastern Europe proved weak, dependent on outsiders for security. Germans bitterly

resented the harsh peace settlement. And the war debts and reparations problems would dog international order for years.

The war experience also changed Americans' mood. The war was grimy and ugly, far less glorious than Wilson's lofty rhetoric had it. People recoiled from the photographs of bodies dangling from barbed wire, poison-gas victims, and battle-shocked faces. American soldiers were eager to return home. Apparently tired of idealism and cynical about their ability to right wrongs, they craved the latest baseball scores. Still, for the doughboys the army years were memorable, a turning point in their lives.

Those progressives who had believed entry into the war would deliver the millennium now marveled at their naiveté. Many lost their enthusiasm for crusades, and many others turned away in disgust from the bickering of the victors. Woodrow Wilson himself had remarked soon after taking office in 1913, before the Great War, "There's no chance of progress and reform in an administration in which war plays the principal part." From the vantage point of 1920, looking back on the array of distempers at home and abroad, Wilson would have to agree with his fellow citizens that progress and reform had been dealt blows.

SUGGESTIONS FOR FURTHER READING

General

John W. Chambers, *The Tyranny of Change* (1980); Otis L. Graham, Jr., *The Great Campaigns* (1971); Ellis W. Hawley, *The Great War and the Search for a Modern Order* (1979); Henry F. May, *The End of American Innocence* (1964); Emily S. Rosenberg, *Spreading the American Dream* (1982); Bernadotte Schmitt and Harold E. Vedeler, *The World in the Crucible: 1914–1919* (1984); Ronald Steel, *Walter Lippmann and the American Century* (1980); David P. Thelan, *Robert M. La Follette and the Insurgent Spirit* (1976).

Woodrow Wilson and His Diplomacy

Thomas A. Bailey and Paul B. Ryan, *The Lusitania Disaster* (1975); John W. Coogan, *The End of Neutrality* (1981); John M. Cooper, Jr., *The Warrior and the Priest: Woodrow Wilson and Theodore Roosevelt* (1983); Patrick Devlin, *Too Proud to Fight* (1975); Robert H. Ferrell, *Woodrow Wilson and World War I* (1985); Lloyd C. Gardner, *Safe for Democracy* (1984); Ross Gregory, *The Origins of American Intervention in the First World War* (1971); Manfred Jonas, *The United States and Germany* (1984); N. Gordon Levin, Jr., *Woodrow Wilson and World Politics* (1968); Arthur S. Link, ed., *Woodrow Wilson and a Revolutionary World, 1913–1921* (1982); Arthur S. Link, *Woodrow Wilson: Revolution, War,*

and Peace (1979); Arthur S. Link, *Wilson*, 5 vols. (1947–1965); Ernest R. May, *The World War and American Isolation, 1914–1917* (1959); Jeffrey J. Safford, *Wilsonian Maritime Diplomacy* (1977); Barbara Tuchman, *The Zimmermann Telegram* (1958); Edwin A. Weinstein, *Woodrow Wilson: A Medical and Psychological Biography* (1981).

The American Military and the First World War

Arthur E. Barbeau and Florette Henri, *The Unknown Soldiers: Black American Troops in World War I* (1974); J. Garry Clifford, *The Citizen Soldiers* (1972); Edward M. Coffman, *The War to End All Wars* (1968); Harvey A. DeWeerd, *President Wilson Fights His War* (1968); Marvin E. Fletcher, *The Black Soldier and Officer in the United States Army, 1891–1917* (1974); Thomas C. Leonard, *Above the Battle* (1978); David Trask, *The United States in the Supreme War Council* (1961); Russell F. Weigley, *The American Way of War* (1973).

The Home Front

Valerie Jean Conner, *The National War Labor Board* (1983); Alfred W. Crosby, Jr., *Epidemic and Peace, 1918* (1976); Robert D. Cuff, *The War Industries Board* (1973); Maurine W. Greenwald, *Women, War, and Work* (1980); Michael T. Isenberg, *War on Film* (1981); David M. Kennedy, *Over Here* (1980); Seward W. Livermore, *Politics Is Adjourned* (1966); Barbara J. Steinson, *American Women's Activism in World War I* (1982); Stephen L. Vaughn, *Holding Fast the Inner Lines: Democracy, Nationalism, and the Committee on Public Information* (1979).

Black Americans

Robert V. Haynes, *A Night of Violence: The Houston Riot of 1917* (1976); Florette Henri, *Black Migration* (1975); Elliot M. Rudwick, *Race Riot at East St. Louis, July 2, 1917* (1964); William M. Tuttle, *Race Riot: Chicago in the Red Summer of 1919* (1970).

Wartime Dissent, Civil Liberties, and the Red Scare

David Brody, *Labor in Crisis: The Steel Strike of 1919* (1965); Charles Chatfield, *For Peace and Justice: Pacifism in America, 1914–1941* (1971); Stanley Cohen, *A. Mitchell*

Palmer (1963); Charles DeBenedetti, *Origins of the Modern Peace Movement* (1978); Sondra Herman, *Eleven Against War* (1969); Donald Johnson, *The Challenge to American Freedoms* (1963); C. Roland Marchand, *The American Peace Movement and Social Reform, 1898–1918* (1973); Paul L. Murphy, *World War I and the Origin of Civil Liberties* (1979); Robert K. Murray, *Red Scare* (1955); H. C. Peterson and Gilbert C. Fite, *Opponents of War, 1917–1918* (1968); William Preston, *Aliens and Dissenters* (1966); Harry N. Scheiber, *The Wilson Administration and Civil Liberties, 1917–1921* (1960); James Weinstein, *The Decline of Socialism in America, 1912–1923* (1967).

Hostility Toward Bolshevik Russia

Peter G. Filene, *Americans and the Soviet Experiment, 1917–1933* (1967); John L. Gaddis, *Russia, the Soviet Union, and the United States* (1978); George F. Kennan, *The Decision to Intervene* (1958); George F. Kennan, *Russia Leaves the War* (1956); Betty M. Unterberger, *America's Siberian Expedition, 1918–1920* (1956); William Appleman Williams, *American-Russian Relations, 1781–1947* (1952).

Versailles and the League Fight

Thomas A. Bailey, *Woodrow Wilson and the Great Betrayal* (1945); Thomas A. Bailey, *Woodrow Wilson and the Lost Peace* (1944); Inga Floto, *Colonel House in Paris* (1973); Herbert Hoover, *The Ordeal of Woodrow Wilson* (1958); Warren F. Kuehl, *Seeking World Order* (1969); Arno Mayer, *Politics and Diplomacy of Peacemaking* (1967); Ralph A. Stone, *The Irreconcilables* (1970); William C. Widenor, *Henry Cabot Lodge and the Search for an American Foreign Policy* (1980).

Aftermath

Stanley Cooperman, *World War I and the American Mind* (1970); Malcolm Cowley, *Exile's Return* (1951); Paul Fussell, *The Great War and Modern Memory* (1975); Stuart I. Rochester, *American Liberal Disillusionment in the Wake of World War I* (1977); Stephen R. Ward, ed., *The War Generation: Veterans of the First World War* (1975).

CHAPTER 23

THE NEW ERA OF
THE 1920s

At 9:39 P.M. on August 6, 1926, a young American woman trudged out of the rough sea onto the English coast. Nineteen-year-old Gertrude Ederle had left France that morning in an attempt to swim the English Channel, a feat that only five men and no women had ever accomplished. She not only succeeded but swam the treacherous thirty-mile stretch in 14 hours 31 minutes, the fastest time yet recorded.

Ederle's conquest of the Channel, wrote the *Literary Digest,* "would be hailed as a battle won for feminism" and the "unanswerable refutation of the masculine dogma that woman is, in the sense of physical power and efficiency, inferior to man." Yet the name of Ederle was never as renowned as those of the era's most admired males: Jack Dempsey, "Babe" Ruth, and Charles Lindbergh. And along with adulation, the young woman's feat inspired exploitative swimsuit ads linking physical fitness to sex appeal.

The ads were but another sign of the times. During the 1920s the flower of consumerism reached full bloom. Spurred by advertising and new forms of credit, Americans eagerly bought automobiles, radios, real estate, and stocks. The majority of the population enjoyed an unparalleled standard of living. As in the Gilded Age of the late nineteenth century, government policies supported the interests of business. The most fundamental and perplexing trend of the 1920s was the effect of the new mass consumer culture on individuals and communities. Changes in work habits, family responsibilities, and health care fostered new uses of time and new attitudes about proper behavior.

In many ways the Ederle story illustrates the complexities and ironies of the new era of the 1920s. The decade was a time both of great accomplishments—in economic productivity as well as athletics—and of frivolous commercial stunts, contests, and fads. It was a time of swift social change, of frankness and liberation. But the winds of change also stirred up waves of reaction. The new, more liberal values repelled some groups, such as the Ku Klux Klan, immigration restrictionists, and religious fundamentalists. Such groups reacted by trying to restore a society of simpler values, where people knew their place and deviants were not tolerated. Yet in spite of their efforts, material bounty and increased leisure time enticed Americans into a variety of new mass amusements, including games, sports, and movies. In an impersonal world, Americans had turned to mass culture to personalize their lives.

POSTWAR OPTIMISM

Poor Richard's Almanac would have sold poorly in the 1920s. Few Americans of that era had much interest in the virtues of thrift and sobriety that Benjamin Franklin had preached. They saw more attraction in acquisition, amusement, and salesmanship. Instead of traditional homilies like "waste not, want not," they harkened to the advice of an advertising executive: "Make the public want what you have to sell. Make 'em pant for it." Though poverty and social injustice still infected the country, many people shared the belief, as journalist Joseph Wood Krutch put it, that "the future was bright and the present was good fun at least."

The decade did not begin very brightly. Besides political wrangling over membership in the League of Nations and ratification of the Treaty of Paris and the Red Scare, the nation suffered a frightening economic decline. For two years after the First World War, consumer spending drove prices up. Then in 1920 people stopped buying, and the export trade and industrial production dropped as wartime orders ended. Net farm income plunged. Unemployment, which had hovered around 2 percent in 1919, passed 12 percent in 1921. The railroad and mining industries suffered declining profits, and layoffs spread through New England as textile companies abandoned outdated factories for the raw materials and cheap labor of the South.

Recovery began in 1922 and continued unevenly until 1929. During this period, industrial output nearly doubled. Electric motors were responsible for much of the rise; by 1929 electricity powered 70 percent of American industry. With the use of electricity and assembly lines, factories turned out an increasing variety of products. The expansion of manufacturing and services led to higher profits and wages. And increased incomes, when combined with installment credit plans, fueled a new consumerism.

Postwar Economic Recovery

Behind the prosperity, an economic revolution was climaxing. First, the consolidation movement that had given birth to trusts and holding companies in the late nineteenth century reached a new stage. Although Progressive-era trustbusting had harnessed big business to some extent, it had not halted *oligopoly*—the control of a whole industry by a few large firms. By the 1920s oligopolies dominated not only production but marketing, distribution, and even financing. In businesses as varied as automobile manufacturing, steel production, meatprocessing, and railroads, a few sprawling integrated companies predominated. Oligopolistic firms, like General Electric, General Motors, and U.S. Steel, developed specialized management techniques to maximize profits and minimize market uncertainties.

The organizational movement that had begun around 1900 also matured in the 1920s. Myriad business and professional associations sprang up to protect their members' interests. Retailers and small manufacturers formed trade associations to pool information and coordinate planning. Farm bureaus and cooperative associations promoted scientific agriculture, lobbied for government protection, and tried to stabilize the market. Lawyers, engineers, and social scientists cooperated with business to promote economic growth.

THE BUSINESS OF GOVERNMENT, THE GOVERNMENT OF BUSINESS

In this outburst of expansion, many Americans shed their fear of big business—swayed in part by the testimonials of probusiness propagandists. "Among the nations of the earth today," one writer proclaimed in 1921, "America stands for one idea: *Business. . . .*" All branches of the federal government supported business. In 1921 Congress reduced taxes on corporations and wealthy individuals, and in 1922 it raised tariff rates. Presidents Harding, Coolidge, and Hoover appointed strong cabinet officers who pursued policies favorable to business. Regulatory agencies such as the Federal Trade Commission and the Interstate Commerce Commission cooperated with corporations more than they regulated them. And the Supreme Court upheld big business and struck down reform in cases such as *Bailey v. Drexel Furniture Company* (1922), which voided restrictions on child labor; and *Adkins v. Children's Hospital* (1923), which overturned a minimum wage law for women because it infringed on liberty of contract.

The revival of business prompted political analysts to lament the death of progressivism. Yet many of the Progressive era's achievements were sustained and consolidated in these years.

Extension of Progressive Reforms Although federal trustbusting declined, regulatory commissions and other government agencies still monitored business activities and worked to reduce wasteful practices. In Congress a sizable corps of reformers, led by George Norris of Nebraska and Robert La Follette of Wisconsin, kept progressive causes alive by supporting labor legislation, federal aid to farmers, and government operation of a federally constructed hydroelectric dam at Muscle Shoals, Alabama. Most reform, however, occurred at the state and local levels. Following initiatives begun before the First World War, thirty-four states instituted or expanded workers' compensation laws in the 1920s. At the same time many states established old-age pensions and other welfare programs.

Organized labor, which had gained ground during the Progressive era, suffered setbacks during the 1920s. Public opinion, influenced by prosperity and probusiness rhetoric, turned against workers who disrupted everyday life with strikes. Both the federal government and the Supreme Court frequently stifled union attempts to exercise power during these years. Meanwhile, large corporations worked to counteract the appeal of unions by promising workers pensions, profit-sharing, and company-sponsored social and sporting events—a policy that became known as *welfare capitalism.* In such a climate, union membership fell from 5.1 million in 1920 to 3.6 million in 1929.

Suppression of Labor Unions

A symbol of the decade's goodwill toward business was President Warren G. Harding, a Republican elected in 1920 at a time when the populace wanted to avoid national and international crusades. Harding selected some capable assistants, notably Secretary of State Charles Evans Hughes, Secretary of Commerce Herbert Hoover, Secretary of the Treasury Andrew Mellon, and Secretary of Agriculture Henry A. Wallace. Harding also backed some important reforms. He helped streamline the budget, supported antilynching legislation, approved bills assisting farm cooperatives and liberalizing farm credit, and unlike his predecessor Wilson, was generally tolerant on civil liberties issues.

Harding Administration

Harding's problem was that he appointed some predatory friends to positions from which they infested government with corruption. Charles Forbes of the Veterans' Bureau served time in Leavenworth prison after being convicted of fraud and bribery in connection with government contracts. Attorney General Harry Daugherty was implicated in a scheme of accepting bribes and in other fraudulent acts; he escaped prosecution only by refusing to testify against himself. In the most notorious case of all, Secretary of the Interior Albert Fall accepted bribes to lease government property to private oil companies. For his role in the affair, called the Teapot Dome scandal after a Wyoming oil reserve that had been turned over to the Mammoth Oil Company, Fall was fined $100,000 and spent a year in jail. He was the first cabinet officer to be so disgraced.

In June 1923, few Americans knew how corrupt Harding's administration had become. The president, however, had become disillusioned. Amid rumors of mismanagement and crime, he told journalist William Allen White, "My God, this is a hell of a job. I have no trouble with my enemies. . . . But my friends, my God-damned friends . . . they're the ones that keep me walking the floor nights." On a speaking tour of the West that summer, Harding became ill; he died in San Francisco on August 2. Harding's successor, Vice President Calvin Coolidge, a former governor of Massachusetts, had first attracted national attention by his firm stand against striking Boston policemen in 1919, a policy that won him the vice-presidential nomination in 1920. Usually, however, he was content to let events take their course.

Coolidge had great respect for private enterprise. Fortunately for him, his presidency coincided with extraordinary business prosperity. Aided by Andrew Mellon, whom he retained as secretary of the treasury, and other cabinet officers, his administration balanced the budget, reduced government debt, lowered income-tax rates (especially for the rich), and began construction of a national highway system. The only disruptions arose over farm policy. Responding to farmers' complaints of falling prices, Congress twice passed bills to establish government-backed price supports for staple crops (the McNary-Haugen bills of 1927 and 1928). But Coolidge exercised his executive privilege and vetoed the measure both times.

Coolidge Prosperity

"Coolidge prosperity" was the determining issue in the presidential election of 1924. That year both major parties ran candidates who accepted business supremacy. The Republicans nominated Coolidge with little dissent. At their national convention the Dem-
ocrats endured 103 ballots before settling on John W. Davis, a corporation lawyer from New York. Remnants of the progressive movement, along with various farm, labor, and socialist groups, formed a new Progressive party and nominated Robert M. La Follette, the aging reformer from Wisconsin. Coolidge beat Davis by 15.7 million to 8.4 million popular votes, 382 to 136 electoral votes. La Follette finished third, receiving a respectable but ineffective 4.8 million popular votes and 13 electoral votes.

MATERIALISM UNBOUND

"One day," Henry Ford recalled, "someone brought to us a slogan which read: 'Buy a Ford and Save the Difference.' I crossed out the 'save' and inserted 'spend'—'Buy a Ford and Spend the Difference.' It is the wiser thing to do. Society lives by circulation and not by congestion." Ford's ardent consumerism was a major theme of the 1920s, to which he contributed materially as well as philosophically.

Indeed, between 1919 and 1929 the gross national product—the total value of all goods and services produced in the United States—swelled by 40 percent. Wages and salaries also increased (though not as much), while the cost of living remained relatively stable. The result was that people had more purchasing power. And they spent as Americans had never spent. By 1929 two-thirds of all Americans lived in dwellings that had electricity, one-fourth of all families owned electric vacuum cleaners, and one-fifth had electric toasters. Many could afford these and other items such as radios, washing machines, and movie tickets only because more than one family member worked or because the breadwinner took a second job. Nevertheless, new products and services were available to more than just the rich.

Expansion of the Consumer Society

Of all the era's technological and economic won-

"Everyone owns a car but us"~

You, too, can own an automobile without missing the money, and *now*, is
the time to buy it — through the easiest and simplest method ever devised:

Ford Weekly Purchase Plan

Thousands of families, who thought a car was out of the question
because of limited incomes, found that they could easily, quickly
and surely buy a car of their own under this remarkable plan

You *can* own an automobile, and you *should*. It will mean so much to you. It will add much to the happiness of your family that is worth while. It will bring the most glorious pleasures into your life. It will increase your chances for success. It will give you and your family a social and business prestige that will be invaluable—and which you, and every family, should enjoy. A car is a symbol of success—a mark of achievement, and it brings opportunities to you that you would probably never secure otherwise. You should have a car of your own, and you can.

The Ford Plan makes it possible for anyone to own an automobile. It is so easy, simple and practical that many who could easily pay "spot cash" take advantage of it—and buy their car from weekly earnings. The plan is simply wonderful! Before you realize it, you are driving your own automobile. If you have felt that you did not make enough to buy a car, you must read The Ford Plan Book. Send for it. See how easy it is to get a car of your own, *now*, and pay for it without missing the money. It seems almost too good to be true, doesn't it? *But it is true.* Get the book—at once. Simply mail the coupon. *Mail it today!*

Give your family the advantages which others have. Get a car of your own. The Ford Plan Book tells you "how" you can buy a car and pay for it without missing the money. Get it! Read it!

Mail Coupon Now. This Book Will be Sent by Return Mail.

COUPON

FORD MOTOR COMPANY
Dept. B-5   Detroit, Michigan
Please send me your book, "The Ford Plan," which fully explains your easy plan for owning an automobile.

Name _____

R. F. D. Box or St. & No. _____

Town _____   State _____

Ford Motor Company
Detroit

IT IS EASY TO OWN A CAR BY USING THIS PLAN

By the 1920s, not only was an automobile affordable, especially through installment payments such as the "Ford Weekly Purchase Plan," but also there was strong social pressure on families to own one. As this advertisement so vividly illustrates, Americans were made to feel that they needed an automobile for the pleasure and status it would bring them.   Photo courtesy of Ford Motor Company.

ders, the automobile was the vanguard. During the 1920s automobile registrations soared from 8 million to 23 million. Mass production and competition had brought down prices, making cars affordable even to some working-class families. By 1926 a Ford Model T cost under $300 and a Chevrolet sold for $700—at a time when workers in manufacturing earned around $1,300 a year and clerical workers about $2,300.

Effects of the Automobile

The motor car altered society as much as the railroad had seventy-five years earlier. Public officials were forced to pay more attention to safety regulations and traffic control. The growing choice of models (there were 108 different automobile manufacturers in 1923) and colors allowed automobile owners to suit their personal tastes in a growing mass society. But most important, the car was the ultimate symbol of social equality.

More than ever, Americans' taste for automobiles and other goods and services was whetted by advertising. By 1929 total advertising earnings reached $3.4 billion, more than was spent on all types of formal education.

Advertising

For many, advertising became the language of a new gospel. In his best-selling *The Man Nobody Knows* (1925), advertising executive Bruce Barton called Jesus "the founder of modern business" because he "picked up twelve men from the bottom ranks of business and forged them into an organization that conquered the world."

Although daily newspaper circulation declined during the 1920s, over 10 million families owned radios by the decade's end. A new advertising medium had been discovered. Station KDKA in Pittsburgh pioneered in commercial radio broadcasting beginning in 1920; by 1922 there were 508 such stations. By 1929 the National Broadcasting Company, which had begun to assemble a network of radio stations three years earlier, charged advertisers $10,000 to sponsor an hour-long show. Commercial intermissions at movie houses and highway billboards also reminded viewers to buy.

CITIES, MIGRANTS, AND SUBURBS

The expansion of consumerism bespoke not only an economically mature nation but an urbanized one. By the 1920s, the city had become the locus of the national experience, and urban expansion occurred across the nation. Cities in warm climates, such as Miami, Tampa, and San Diego, underwent the most explosive growth.

Continuing Urbanization

During the 1920s, an estimated 6 million Americans left their farms for nearby or distant cities. Blacks accounted for a sizable portion of the migrants. Crushed by tenant farming and lured by industrial jobs, 1.5 million blacks moved cityward during the 1920s, accelerating a trend begun a decade earlier. The black populations of New York, Chicago, Detroit, and Houston doubled during these years. When overcrowding burst the boundaries of the black ghetto and blacks spilled over into nearby white neighborhoods, racial violence often resulted.

In response partly to their new urban experiences and partly to race riots and threats, thousands of blacks in northern cities joined movements that glorified black independence. The most influential of these black nationalist groups was the Universal Negro Improvement Association (UNIA), headed by Marcus Garvey, a Jamaican immigrant who believed blacks should separate themselves from a corrupt white society. Proclaiming, "I am the equal of any white man," Garvey cultivated race pride and promoted black capitalism. His newspaper, the *Negro World*, refused to publish ads for hair straighteners and skin-lightening cosmetics, and his Black Star shipping line was intended to help blacks emigrate to Africa.

Marcus Garvey

The UNIA declined in the mid-1920s when the Black Star line went bankrupt (unscrupulous dealers had sold the line dilapidated ships) and when antiradical fears prompted government prosecution (ten of the organization's leaders were arrested on charges of anarchism and Garvey was deported for mail fraud). Nevertheless, the organization had attracted a huge following (contemporaries estimated it at 500,000; Garvey claimed 6 million) in New York, Chicago, Detroit, and other cities. And Garvey's speeches had served notice that blacks had their own

aspirations, which they could and would translate into action.

The newest immigrants to American cities came from Mexico and Puerto Rico. As in the nineteenth century, many Mexicans moved north to work as agricultural laborers in the Southwest, but in the 1920s a large number also flowed into growing cities like Denver, San Antonio, Los Angeles, and Tucson. Victims of Anglo discrimination, Mexicans crowded into low-rent, inner-city districts. Yet their communities, called *barrios*, provided an environment in which the immigrants could sustain customs and values of the homeland and develop institutions to help them adapt to American society

Mexican and Puerto Rican Immigrants

The 1920s also saw a great influx of Puerto Ricans to the mainland. A shift in the island's economy from sugar to coffee production had created a surplus population willing to move and attracted by contracts from American employers seeking cheap labor. Most Puerto Rican migrants moved to New York City, where they formed *barrios* in parts of Brooklyn and Manhattan. Puerto Rican communities contained some educated elites—doctors, lawyers, business owners—who served as ethnic leaders.

As urban growth peaked, suburban growth accelerated. Although towns had existed around the edges of urban centers since the nation's earliest years, prosperity and easier transportation—mainly the automobile—made the urban fringe more accessible in the 1920s. Between 1920 and 1930, suburbs of Chicago, Cleveland, and Los Angeles grew five to ten times as fast as the central cities. Most, but not all, of these suburbs were middle- and upper-class bedroom communities.

Growth of the Suburbs

The bulging cities and suburbs fostered the new mass culture that gave the decade its character. Most of the consumers who jammed retail establishments, movie houses, and sporting arenas were city and suburb dwellers. Cities and suburbs were the places where people flouted law and morality by patronizing speakeasies (illegal saloons), wearing outlandish clothes and listening to jazz. And yet the ideal of small-town society survived. While intellectuals carped that small towns stifled personal growth, Americans reminisced about the innocence and simplicity of a world gone by. This was the dilemma of a modern nation: how could one anchor oneself in a world of rampant material and social change?

NEW RHYTHMS
OF EVERYDAY LIFE

Amid all the change, Americans developed new social values and new ways of using time. Increasingly, people were splitting their daily lives into three distinct compartments: work, family, and leisure. Each type of time was altered in the 1920s. For many people, time on the job shrank. Among industrial workers the five-and-one-half-day workweek (half a day on Saturday) became common. Many white-collar employees enjoyed two days off and worked a forty-hour week. Annual vacations were becoming a standard job benefit for white-collar workers, whose numbers grew by 40 percent during the decade.

Family time is harder to measure, but certain figures suggest important changes. As birth control became more widely accepted, birthrates dropped noticeably between 1920 and 1930, decreasing the proportion of families with five or more children. Over the same period the divorce rate rose. In 1920 there was one divorce in every 7.5 marriages; in 1929 the national ratio was 1 in 6, and in many cities it was 2 in 7. Lower birthrates, more divorce, plus longer life expectancy meant that adults devoted a smaller portion of their lives to parental and other family tasks.

At the same time the availability of ready-to-wear clothes, preserved foods, and mass-produced furniture meant that family members spent less time producing household necessities. **Household Management** Wives still spent most of their day cleaning, cooking, mending, and otherwise maintaining the home, but new machines lightened some of their tasks. Instead of being a producer of food and clothing, the wife now became chief consumer, doing the shopping and making sure the family spent its money wisely.

The ready availability of washing machines, hot water, and commercial soap put greater pressure on wives to keep everything clean. Advertisers tried to coax women into buying products by making them feel guilty for not giving enough attention to cleaning the home, caring for the children, and tending to personal hygiene. Thus, while the industrial and service sectors became more specialized as a result of technological advances, housewives retained a wide variety of responsibilities and added new ones as well.

While family time shifted and work time decreased, nonwork, nonfamily activities expanded. High school enrollment quadrupled between 1910 and 1929; by 1929 over a third of all high school graduates went on to college. And as the use of electricity spread, people stayed up later at night to read or listen to the radio. They filled their expanding leisure time with automobile rides, sports events, motion pictures, shopping, and other forms of amusement.

With more people spending time away from work and family, new values were inevitable. Especially among the middle class but among the working class, too, clothes became a means to personal expression and freedom. The **Social Values** line between inappropriate and acceptable behavior blurred as smoking, swearing, and frankness about sex became more common. Thousands who had never read psychoanalyst Sigmund Freud's theories were certain that he prescribed an uninhibited sex life as the key to mental health. Birth-control advocate Margaret Sanger gained a large following in respectable circles. Newspapers, magazines, motion pictures, and popular songs made certain that Americans did not suffer from "sex starvation."

Still other trends contributed to the breakdown of traditional values. Because child-labor laws and compulsory-school-attendance laws kept children in school longer than was common in earlier generations, schools and peer groups now played a greater role in socializing children. Parents tended to rely less on family tradition and more on child-care manuals in raising their children. Old-age homes, public health clinics, and workers' compensation reduced the family's responsibilities even further.

Although the home remained a female domain, women continued to stream into the labor force during the 1920s. By 1930 10.8 million women worked,
Jobs for Women an increase of over 2 million since the war's end. The sex segregation that had long characterized occupations continued; most female workers could be found in jobs where few men worked. More than a million women were teachers and nurses. Some 2.2 million were typists, bookkeepers, and office clerks, a tenfold increase since 1920; another 736,000 were salespeople in stores. Increasingly large numbers of women took jobs as waitresses and hairdressers. Almost 2 million women worked in factories, though their numbers grew very little over the decade.

Women's foray into work outside the home reflected an extension of their family roles. Although they worked for a combination of reasons, the
Married Women in the Labor Force economic needs of their families shaped the job experiences of most women. The consumerism of the 1920s prompted working-class and middle-class families to satisfy their wants either by living beyond their means or by sending women and children into the labor force. In previous eras, most of these extra wage earners were young and single. But in the 1920s, married women joined the group, a trend that has increased down to the present. Many women were forced into the labor market because the pressures of poverty gave them no other choice. The proportion of black women in the work force, for example, was twice that of white women.

Feminists in the 1920s directed their concern to the issue of married women in the labor force. A number of female writers believed that the separation of place of work from place of residence had left women at home to tend household chores that few men would do. Women's earlier functions as economic producers of food and clothes, said feminists, had lapsed into passive roles as child nurturers and homemakers; the result was economic dependency. The way to restore married women's sense of worth in a money-oriented society was for them to have gainful employment. But because feminists tried to separate the notion of career from domestic roles, they had little appeal to women who placed family needs, not individual needs, above all else. The fact that feminist messages reached a rather small audience also limited the impact of the movement. Thus few women took up the call for equal pay and equal opportunity voiced by Alice Paul, leader of the new National Women's party, who in 1922 supported an equal rights amendment to the Constitution. Indeed, after obtaining the vote in 1920, many women seemed to turn their backs on politics.

Whether they worked or not, all types of women were exposed to alternative images of femininity. Short skirts and bobbed hair, regarded as signs of
Alternative Images of Femininity sexual freedom, became common among office workers and store clerks as well as among middle-class college coeds. Several studies claimed that sexual experimentation, including premarital sex, increased among young women during the decade. The most popular models of female behavior were not chaste, sentimental heroines but movie vamps like Clara Bow, the "It Girl," and Gloria Swanson, who specialized in torrid love affairs on and off the screen. And though not everyone was a flapper, as the young independent-minded woman was called, many women clearly asserted their equality with men.

These new social trends represented a sharp break with the more restrained culture of the nineteenth century. But social change, as always, did not proceed smoothly. As the decade wore on, various groups prepared to defend against the threat to older, more familiar values.

LINES OF DEFENSE

In the spring of 1920 the leader of a newly formed organization decided to hire two public-relations experts to recruit members. Using modern advertising techniques, the promoters canvassed cities and towns in the South, Southwest, and Midwest. By 1923 the organization, a revived Ku Klux Klan, claimed 5 million members. Its appeal was based on fear.

The Klan was the most sinister reactionary movement of the 1920s. Founded in 1915 by William J. Simmons, an Atlanta evangelist and insurance sales-

Ku Klux Klan man who wanted to purify southern culture, the new Invisible Empire revived the hoods, intimidating tactics, and mystical terms of its forerunner. But the new Klan was broader in membership and in objectives than the old. Its chapters fanned outward from the deep South and for a time wielded frightening power in all other regions of the country. And unlike the first Klan, which terrorized mostly blacks, the new Klan directed its venom toward a variety of groups.

Assuming the role of moral protector, Klan members meted out vigilante justice to bootleggers, wife beaters, and adulterers; forced schools to adopt Bible readings and stop teaching the theory of evolution; and campaigned against Catholic and Jewish political candidates. By the mid-1920s, however, the Invisible Empire was on the wane, outnumbered by its foreign-stock opponents and rocked by scandal. (In 1925 Indiana Grand Dragon David Stephenson allegedly kidnapped and raped a woman who later died either from taking poison or from an infection caused by

bites on her body; Stephenson was convicted of second-degree murder on the grounds that he was responsible for her suicide.)

The Ku Klux Klan had no monopoly on bigotry. The 1920s bared the pervasiveness of intolerance in American society. Since the 1880s a number of groups had been urging an end to free immigration. Huge influxes of Catholic and Jewish immigrants, these nativists charged, clogged inner-city slums, upset traditional norms with their drinking habits, and stubbornly held to alien religious and political beliefs.

Nativist sentiment was also reflected in continued fear of radicalism. The most notorious outburst of hysteria occurred in 1921, when a court convicted

Sacco and Vanzetti Nicola Sacco and Bartolomeo Vanzetti, two immigrant anarchists, of murdering a guard and paymaster during a robbery in South Braintree, Massachusetts. But Sacco and Vanzetti's main offenses seem to have been their political beliefs and Italian origins, since evidence failed to prove their involvement in the robbery. Judge Webster Thayer nevertheless openly sided with the prosecution, privately calling the defendants "those anarchist bastards." Amid protest, the two were executed in August 1927.

Congress responded to the mounting nativist pressure in 1921, 1924, and 1927 by passing laws that established yearly immigration quotas for each

Immigration Quotas nationality. These quotas favored northern and western Europeans, reflecting the prejudices of natives against newer immigrant groups from southern and eastern Europe. The Emergency Quota, or Johnson, Act of 1921 provided that the annual immigration of any given nationality could not exceed 3 percent of the number of immigrants from that nation residing in the United States in 1910. But this law, meant to be temporary, did not satisfy restrictionists' aims, so Congress replaced it with the National Origins Act of 1924. The new law set the quota at 2 percent of each nationality residing in the United States in 1890. The National Origins

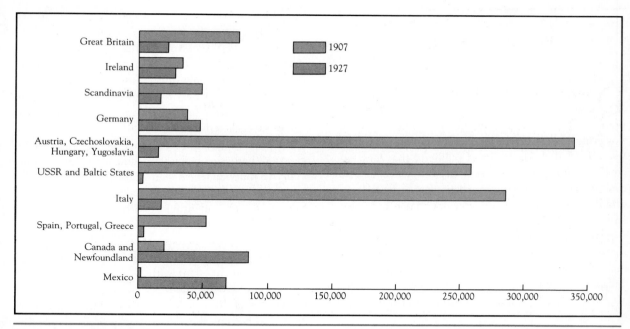

Immigration, 1907 and 1927

Act was amended in 1927, at which time Congress set a limit of 150,000 immigrants a year—including 65,721 from Great Britain and 25,957 from Germany, but only 5,802 from Italy and 2,712 from Russia. These laws virtually excluded Asians, but left the door open to peoples from the Western Hemisphere. Soon Canadians, Mexicans, and Puerto Ricans became the largest groups of newcomers (see figure).

The impulse to insure moral purity stirred religious fundamentalists at this time, too. In 1925 fundamentalist Christianity clashed with new scientific theory in a celebrated case in Dayton, **Scopes Trial** Tennessee. Early that year the Tennessee legislature passed a law forbidding public school instructors to teach the theory that humans had evolved from lower forms of life rather than from Adam and Eve. Shortly thereafter, high school teacher John Thomas Scopes, who had volunteered to serve in a test case, was arrested for violating the law. Scopes's trial that summer became a headline event, with William Jennings Bryan, former secretary of state and three-time presidential candidate, arguing for the prosecution, and a team of civil-liberties lawyers headed by Clarence Darrow arguing for the defense. Although Scopes was convicted—clearly he had broken the law—modernists claimed victory; the testimony, they believed, had shown fundamentalism to be at odds with secular social trends.

The emotional responses Americans made to events during the 1920s were part of a larger attempt to sustain old, local values in a fast-moving, materialistic world. Even as they attempted to hold to the past, however, most Americans adjusted in some way to the new order. They went to movies and sporting events, listened to the radio, and generally tried to find release from societal pressures in a world of leisure.

THE AGE OF PLAY

During the 1920s Americans developed an almost insatiable thirst for recreation, to which entrepreneurs responded quickly. The decade marked the flowering of fads, frivolities, and what contemporaries called ballyhoo, a blitz of publicity that lent exaggerated importance to some person or event. The new games and fancies were particularly attractive to middle-class families with large spendable incomes. In the early 1920s the Chinese tile game of mahjongg was the rage. By the mid-1920s people were turning to crossword puzzles; a few years later they adopted miniature golf as their new craze. Throughout the decade dance fads like the Charleston riveted public attention, aided by radio music and the growing popularity of jazz.

In addition to their active participation in leisure activities, Americans were avid spectators, particularly of movies and sports. In 1922 movies attracted 40 million viewers a week; by 1930 the number had reached 100 million—at a time when total population was just over 120 million. The introduction of sound in *The Jazz Singer* in 1927 and of color a few years later made movies even more attractive and realistic. The most popular films were mass spectacles such as Cecil B. DeMille's *Ten Commandments* (1923), movies with lurid titles such as *A Woman Who Sinned* (1924), and slapstick comedies. Ironically, the comedies, with their often poignant satire of the human condition, carried the most thought-provoking messages.

Movies

Spectator sports also boomed. Each year millions packed stadiums, arenas, and parks to watch athletic events. By the late 1920s gate receipts from college football alone had surpassed $21 million. In an age when technology and mass production had robbed experiences and objects of their uniqueness, sports provided the unpredictability and drama that people craved. Newspapers and radio captured and exaggerated this drama, feeding news to an eager public and often overpromoting events with unrestrained narrative. Baseball attracted a huge following. On discovering that home runs aroused excitement, major league team owners redesigned the ball to make it livelier. Thereafter, attendance at major-league games skyrocketed.

Sports, movies, and the news gave Americans a galaxy of heroes. As society became more anonymous and the individual less significant, people clung to heroic personalities as a means of identifying with the unique. Boxing, football, and baseball produced the biggest sports heroes. Heavyweight champion Jack Dempsey attracted the first of many million-dollar gates in his fight with Georges Carpentier in 1921. Harold "Red" Grange, running back for the University of Illinois football team, thrilled thousands and became the idol of sportswriters. Baseball's major hero was George Herman "Babe" Ruth. Ruth's annual home run totals increased from a record 29 in 1919, to 54 in 1920, 59 in 1924, and 60 in 1927. His exaggerated gestures on the field, defiant lifestyle, and boyish grin endeared him to millions and made him a national legend.

Sports Heroes

If Americans identified with the physical exploits of sports stars, they fulfilled a yearning for romance and adventure through adulation of movie stars. The films and personal lives of Douglas Fairbanks, Gloria Swanson, Charlie Chaplin, and scores of others were discussed in parlors and pool halls across the country. Perhaps the decade's most touted personality was Rudolph Valentino, whose Latin machismo made women swoon and prompted men to copy his pomaded hairdo and slick sideburns.

Movie Stars and Public Heroes

News promoters created their own heroes outside the worlds of athletics and entertainment. Flagpole sitters, marathon dancers, and other record seekers regularly occupied the front pages. The most notable news hero was Charles A. Lindbergh, the pilot whose

Rudolph Valentino in The Sheik, *his most famous movie. With flashing eyes and wanton smile, Valentino carries a swooning woman to his tent. This immensely popular movie earned a million dollars for Paramount Pictures. Museum of Modern Art/Film Stills Archive.*

daring nonstop solo flight across the Atlantic in 1927 was cheered by millions. A modest, independent midwesterner whom writers dubbed the Lone Eagle, Lindbergh accepted fame but did not try to profit from it. Because his quiet personality contrasted so starkly with the ballyhoo that surrounded him, Americans honored him even more fervently.

In part the adulation of Lindbergh may have reflected guilt, for in their quest for fun and individual expression—liberties that Prohibition seemed to deny—Americans became lawbreakers and supporters of crime. The constitutional amendment and federal law that prohibited the

Prohibition

manufacture, sale, and transportation of alcoholic beverages worked very well at first. Per capita consumption of liquor dropped, arrests for drunkenness diminished, and the price of illegal booze rose higher than the average worker could afford. But after about 1925 the noble experiment broke down in the cities, where the desire for personal freedom overwhelmed the weak means of enforcement.

Criminals were quick to recognize the possibilities of the situation. But though Prohibition encouraged organized crime, it did not create it. Gangs or mobs, the most notorious of which belonged to Chicago's Al Capone, had provided illegal goods and services long before the 1920s. As Capone explained it, "Prohibition is business. All I do is supply a demand."

Thus during the 1920s Americans were caught between two value systems. On the one hand, the Puritan tradition of hard work, sobriety, and restraint—"waste not, want not"—still prevailed, especially in rural areas where new diversions were unavailable. On the other hand, a liberating age of play beckoned. At no previous time in American history had so many opportunities for recreation presented themselves.

CULTURAL CURRENTS

This tension between value systems pulled artists and intellectuals in new directions. Rejection of old beliefs energized an experimental movement in literature, art, and music. Fear that

Literature of Alienation

materialism and conformity were being fostered by mass society gave this movement a bitterly critical tinge. Indeed, many of the era's leading literary figures, finding the vulgar materialism of the time hostile to their art, succumbed to disillusionment and became known as the Lost Generation. Some moved to Europe in protest. Although these writers' main goals were to create new forms of expression and portray emotion realistically, they also produced biting social commentary. The dominant themes of their social criticism were middle- and upper-class materialism and the impersonality of modern society. F. Scott Fitzgerald's novels and Eugene O'Neill's plays exposed America's overemphasis on money and success. The powerful antiwar sentiments of John Dos Passos's *Three Soldiers* (1921) and Hemingway's *A Farewell to Arms* (1929) were skillfully interwoven with passionate criticism of the impersonality of modern relationships.

Perhaps the most trenchant social criticism flowed from the pen of H. L. Mencken. A Baltimore newspaperman and founder of the *American Mercury*, Mencken jabbed at prevailing customs with stinging cynicism. No group, no individual was too sacred to escape his satire. He jeered at the inane quest for status of the middle-class "booboisie," labeled Woodrow Wilson a "self-bamboozled presbyterian," and scorned political reformers as "saccharine liberals" and "jitney messiahs."

A spiritual discontent quite different from that of white writers inspired the work of a new generation of young black artists. Largely middle-class and well educated, these writers often re-

Harlem Renaissance

jected the amalgamation of black and white cultures, exalting the militantly assertive "New Negro," proud of his or her African heritage. Most of them lived in Harlem, the black section of upper Manhattan. In this "Negro Mecca" black intellectuals and artists celebrated modern black culture in what became known as the Harlem Renaissance.

Harlem in the 1920s fostered a number of gifted writers, among them Langston Hughes, who wrote forceful and sometimes humorous poems, stories, and essays; Countee Cullen, a poet with moving lyrical skills; and Claude McKay, whose militant verses sounded a clarion call for rebellion against bigotry. Jean Toomer's novels and poems portrayed black life with passionate realism, and Alain Locke's essays gave direction to the artistic renaissance. Much of this group's writing addressed issues of identity. For though black intellectuals took pride in African culture, they also realized that black Americans had to assert themselves and come to terms with themselves as Americans.

Although black authors did not reach many people, black musicians had considerable influence. The Jazz Age, as the decade is sometimes called, owed its

Jazz

name to the music that grew out of black urban culture. With its emotional rhythms and emphasis on improvisation, jazz blurred the distinction between composer and performer and created a new intimacy between performer and audience.

As blacks moved north, they brought jazz with them. By the 1920s dance halls and bars featured jazz. Gifted black performers like trumpeter Louis Armstrong, trombonist Kid Ory, and singer Bessie Smith enjoyed widespread fame. The music recorded by these and other black artists gave black Americans a distinctive place in the new consumer culture. More important, jazz endowed America with its most distinctive art form.

In many ways the 1920s were the most creative years the nation had yet experienced. Influenced by jazz and by experimental writing, painters such as Georgia O'Keeffe and John Marin tried to forge a distinctively American style of painting. And although European composers and performers still dominated classical music, Americans such as Henry Cowell, who pioneered electronic music, and Aaron Copland, who built orchestral and vocal works around native folk motifs, began careers that later won wide acclaim. George Gershwin gave popular music increased respectability by blending jazz, classical, and folk musical forms in his serious compositions, musical dramas, and numerous hit tunes. In architecture, Frank Lloyd Wright's "prairie-style" houses, churches, and schools reflected the magnificence of the American landscape. At the beginning of the decade, essayist Harold Stearns had complained that "the most . . . pathetic fact in the social life of America today is emotional and aesthetic starvation." By 1929 such a contention was hard to support.

THE ELECTION OF 1928

Whatever doubts intellectuals may have had about materialism in the 1920s faded before the confident rhetoric of politics. Herbert Hoover epitomized that confidence in his speech accepting the Republican nomination for president in the summer of 1928. "We in America today," Hoover boasted, "are nearer to the final triumph over poverty than ever before in the history of any land. . . . We have not yet reached the goal, but, given a chance to go forward with the policies of the last eight years, we shall soon, with the help of God, be in sight of the day when poverty will be banished from this nation."

As Hoover's opponent, the Democrats chose Governor Alfred E. Smith of New York, whose career contrasted markedly with that of Hoover. Whereas Hoover had rural, native, Protestant, business roots and had never run for public office, Smith was an urbane, gregarious politician of immigrant stock whose career was rooted in New York City's Tammany Hall. Smith was also the first Roman Catholic to run for president on a major party ticket. As such, he had considerable appeal among urban ethnic groups, who were voting in increasing numbers, but he lost southern and rural votes for the same reason.

Al Smith

Though Smith waged a dynamic campaign, Hoover, who stressed the nation's prosperity, won the popular vote by 21 million to 15 million, the electoral vote by 444 to 87. But Smith's candidacy had important effects on the Democratic party. Smith carried the nation's twelve largest cities, which formerly had given majorities to Republican candidates, and lured millions of foreign-stock voters to the polls for the first time. From 1928 onward, the Democratic party would solidify this urban base, which, when combined with its traditional strength in the South, made the party a formidable force in national elections.

Democrats and Republicans both had reasons to be encouraged in 1928. But a few people had begun to grow uneasy over the nation's economic climate. Just before Hoover stood in front of his party and predicted the conquest of poverty, a banker surveyed the soaring stock market and observed,

Stocks look dangerously high to me. This bull market has been going on for a long time and al-

SUGGESTIONS FOR FURTHER READING

Overviews of the 1920s

Frederick Lewis Allen, *Only Yesterday* (1931); Paul A. Carter, *Another Part of the Twenties* (1977); Ellis Hawley, *The Great War and the Search for a Modern Order* (1979); William E. Leuchtenburg, *The Perils of Prosperity* (1958).

Business and the Economy

Irving L. Bernstein, *The Lean Years: A History of the American Worker, 1920–1933* (1960); James J. Flink, *The Car Culture* (1975); John Rae, *The Road and the Car in American Life* (1971); Robert Zieger, *Republicans and Labor, 1919–1929* (1969).

Politics and Law

David Burner, *The Politics of Provincialism* (1968); Paula Elder, *Governor Alfred E. Smith: The Politician as Reformer* (1983); Allan J. Lichtman, *Prejudice and the Old Politics: The Presidential Election of 1928* (1979); Samuel Lubell, *The Future of American Politics* (1952); Donald R. McCoy, *Calvin Coolidge* (1967); Alpheus Mason, *The Supreme Court from Taft to Warren* (1958); Robert K. Murray, *The Harding Era* (1969); George Tindall, *The Emergence of the New South* (1967); Joan Hoff Wilson, *Herbert Hoover: The Forgotten Progressive* (1975).

Blacks and Hispanics

Rodolfo Acuna, *Occupied America: A History of Chicanos* (1980); E. D. Cronon, *Black Moses: The Story of Marcus Garvey* (1955); Matt S. Meier and Feliciano Rivera, *The Chicanos* (1972); Gilbert Osofsky, *Harlem: The Making of a Ghetto* (1965); Alan Spear, *Black Chicago* (1967); Theodore Vincent, *Black Power and the Garvey Movement* (1971).

Women and the Family

W. Andrew Achenbaum, *Shades of Gray: Old Age, American Values, and Federal Policies Since 1920* (1983); William

though prices have slipped a bit recently, they might easily slip a good deal more. Business is none too good. Of course if you buy the right stock you'll probably be all right in the long run and you may even make a profit. But if I were you I'd wait awhile and see what happens.

Little did the banker know how sound his advice was. In the next several years the era of expansion and frivolity would end, and the economy would have to be rebuilt.

H. Chafe, *The American Woman: Her Changing Social, Economic, and Political Role* (1972); Ruth Schwartz Cowan, *More Work for Mother* (1983); Linda Gordon, *Woman's Body, Woman's Right: A Social History of Birth Control in America* (1976); Lois Scharf, *To Work and to Wed* (1980); Susan Strasser, *Never Done: A History of American Housework* (1982); Winifred D. Wandersee, *Women's Work and Family Values, 1920–1940* (1981).

Lines of Defense

David M. Chalmers, *Hooded Americanism: The History of the Ku Klux Klan* (1965); Norman F. Furnis, *The Fundamentalist Controversy* (1954); John Higham, *Strangers in the Land: Patterns of American Nativism* (1955); G. L. Joughin and E. M. Morgan, *The Legacy of Sacco and Vanzetti* (1948); William G. McLoughlin, *Modern Revivalism* (1959); Andrew Sinclair, *Prohibition: The Age of Excess* (1962).

Mass Culture

Erik Barbouw, *A Tower of Babel: A History of Broadcasting in the United States to 1933* (1966); Robert Creamer, *Babe* (1974); Kenneth S. Davis, *The Hero, Charles A. Lindbergh* (1959); Paula Fass, *The Damned and the Beautiful: American Youth in the 1920s* (1977); Randy Roberts, *Jack Dempsey, The Manassa Mauler* (1979); Robert Sklar, *Movie-made America* (1976).

Literature and Thought

George H. Douglas, *H. L. Mencken* (1978); Robert Elias, *Entangling Alliances with None: An Essay on the Individual in the American Twenties* (1973); Nathan I. Huggins, *Harlem Renaissance* (1971); David L. Lewis, *When Harlem Was in Vogue* (1981); Roderick Nash, *The Nervous Generation: American Thought, 1917–1930* (1969); Kenneth M. Wheller and Virginia L. Lussier, eds., *Women and the Arts and the 1920s in Paris and New York* (1982).

CHAPTER 24

THE GREAT DEPRESSION
AND THE NEW DEAL
1929–1941

"*Anything wrong with* my work for company?" asked an autoworker of Slavic descent who had just been fired by the Ford Motor Company after fourteen years of employment. No, his work had been good, but cars were not selling. "I have no money now . . . lose my home quick, what I do children, what I do doctor?" When two of his daughters went to work to support the family and their sick mother, he cried, "I ain't man now."

People like John Boris were among the three thousand men and women who gathered on March 7, 1932, for a hunger march to Ford's huge River Rouge plant in Dearborn, just outside Detroit, Michigan. Most of the marchers were unemployed Ford workers. Dearborn-Detroit authorities nonetheless blamed the march on the Communist party and met the protesters with a phalanx of police. A battle that erupted took the lives of four marchers.

The fundamental source of this trouble was not the Communist party, not the marchers, not the Dearborn police, not Henry Ford himself, but a nationwide disaster called the Great Depression. It began in 1929 with the stock market crash. Slowly but steadily, cascading tremors moved through the economy, and the nation sank from economic downturn to depression.

Americans tried to puzzle out the many interrelated causes of the depression, but to little avail. Questions of underconsumption and international trade, after all, bedeviled even the experts. Americans found it especially difficult to understand how people could be hungry when farmers' bins were overflowing or how workers could be unemployed when they remained able-bodied and eager and the factories stood in place. Only one thing was certain: too many Americans did not have enough money to buy the goods stocked in their local stores. Stunned by the magnitude of their plight, Americans found their faith in themselves and in their dream of success shaken. But they did not turn to violent revolt or political extremism. Instead, they improvised to survive, and they looked to their governments for help.

Although President Hoover activated the federal government more than any of his predecessors had done in an economic crisis, he opposed direct relief. When he refused to take measures strong enough to relieve their hardship, Americans peacefully resorted to a traditional method of voicing disapproval: they turned Hoover out of office in the election of 1932. They replaced the somber Hoover with smiling Franklin D. Roosevelt, who had promised vigorous action and who projected hope in a time of despair.

THE NEW DAY

In early 1929, when Hoover entered the White House, the byword was optimism. In his inaugural address the president proclaimed a New Day, telling his listeners that the future was "bright with hope." The new president, known popularly as the Great Engineer, was a proven administrator who had gained a reputation for compassion as well as for brilliance as head of food relief for Europe following the First World War. But not everyone in his administration shared his enlightened attitudes. Sitting in the cabinet, composed largely of businessmen, were six millionaires. Andrew Mellon stayed on as secretary of the treasury. These appointees to high office were smug devotees of the existing order, champions of a capitalist utopia. Innovation was not expected from them. In the lower ranks, on the other hand, Hoover brought in the New Patriots, mostly young professionals who agreed with the president that scientific methods could be applied to government to solve its problems.

Before the Great Depression sapped the national

Hoover Administration

Herbert Hoover (1874–1964), wealthy mining engineer and businessman, headed a relief program during the First World War and served as secretary of commerce in the 1920s. His reputation for brilliance and compassion was tarnished when as president he faced the Great Depression.   Library of Congress.

spirit, reverence for what Hoover called "the American system" ran high. The belief that individuals were responsible for their own condition, that unemployment or poverty suggested personal failing, was widespread. Prevailing thought also held that changes in the business cycle were natural and therefore not to be tampered with. Depressions were to be weathered stoically until the economy inevitably wound its way back to prosperity. As for the government, its job was limited: to ensure equal opportunity and to stimulate the economy through judicious advice and public works projects. "The spread of government," concluded Hoover, "destroys initiative and thus destroys character."

Much of this thinking was, of course, shallow, self-serving, or utopian. Self-interested businesspeople had often tinkered with the system. Government had long played favorites or neglected to blow the referee's whistle. Equal opportunity was denied to Americans who were nonwhite or female. Educational programs were segregated and unequal. Both government and business were hostile to labor unions (in 1929 only 10 percent of the nonagricultural work force was unionized). Discriminatory wages for women and minorities, the stretch-out (more work for the same pay), automation, and safety hazards also plagued workers. At least one-third of the nation's farmers were tenants or sharecroppers—dependent, propertyless, and unable even to join the race. Because of these conditions, income and wealth were maldistributed.

Hoover himself knew that not all was well. "The only trouble with capitalism is capitalists," he complained. "They're too damned greedy." Hoover's ideal capitalist was one who tempered his self-interest to advance the general welfare, who cooperated with others to build a progressive, nonexploitive society. He later admitted that most businesspeople did not approach this ideal.

THE GREAT CRASH AND THE GREAT DEPRESSION

Toward the end of the 1920s all seemed well to Wall Street stockbrokers. The bull market attracted millions of buyers, many of whom joined the speculative binge by buying their shares on margin (paying only a portion of the cost in cash and borrowing the rest) or investing their savings. By October 1929 brokers' loans to stock purchasers amounted to a staggering $8.5 billion. One businessman was so enthusiastic about the boom that he proclaimed that "anyone not only can be rich, but ought to be rich" by speculating in the stock market.

The get-rich-quick mentality was jolted in September and early October when stock prices dropped. Analysts attributed the dip to "shaking out the lunatic fringe." But on October 24, Black Thursday, a record number of shares was traded; many stocks sold at low prices, and some could find no takers. At noon, banking leaders met at the headquarters of J. P. Morgan and Company to halt the skid and restore confidence. They put up $20 million, told everybody about it, and ceremoniously began by buying ten thousand shares of United States Steel. The mood changed and some stocks rallied.

Wall Street Crash

But the nation gradually succumbed to panic. News of Black Thursday spread across the country, and trouble ("sell!") ricocheted back to New York via telephone. Another bolt struck on Black Tuesday (October 29) when stock prices plunged again. Hoover assured Americans that the economy was sound. He shared the popular assumption that the stock market's ills could be quarantined from a generally healthy economy. He was wrong.

The crash ultimately helped to unleash a devastating depression. The economic downturn did not come suddenly; it was more like a leak in a punctured tire than a blowout. There were several interrelated causes of the Great Depression. The first was the increasing weakness of the economy in the 1920s. During the decade, the agricultural sector was plagued with overproduction, declining prices for farm products, mounting debts, bankruptcies, and small bank failures. Some industries, like coal, railroads, and textiles, were in distress long before 1929, and two mainstays of economic growth, autos and construction, also declined early. What all these weaknesses meant by 1929 was that major sec-

Economic Weaknesses

tors of the economy were not expanding. Indeed, the opposite was true: unsold inventories stacked up in warehouses, investments dwindled, laborers were sent home, and consumer purchases dropped off.

Second and related, the onset and severity of the depression can be attributed to underconsumption. That is, production (supply) had outstripped con-

Under-consumption

sumption (demand). Wages and mass purchasing power had lagged behind the industrial surge of the 1920s; the workers who produced the new consumer products ultimately could not afford to buy them. Why did purchasing decline? Laborers and farmers constituted the great majority of consumers. Yet, as we have seen, farmers suffered economic distress and had to trim their purchases. And as industries like coalmining, auto manufacture, and construction declined, they laid off men and women who then lacked the money to sustain buying. Other laborers lost their jobs because machines displaced them. There was, in short, a sizable nonconsuming group. Moreover, the nation's unequal distribution of wealth compounded the problem. Because income was concentrated at the top of America's economic ladder—with the rich—much of it was put into luxuries, savings, stock-market speculation, and investments instead of being spent on consumer goods.

Third, the American business system was shaky, for a few large corporations in each industry—oligopolies—unbalanced it. Not only did many of these

Large Corporations

companies speculate dangerously on the stock market; they built pyramid-like businesses based on shady, if legal, manipulation of assets through holding companies. If one part of the edifice collapsed, the entire structure crumbled. Such was the case with Samuel Insull's mighty electrical empire, wherein one company held the stock of another company, which held the stock of another company, and so on. Even Insull admitted that he was not sure how it all worked; his sixty-five chairmanships, eighty-five directorships, and seven presi-

dencies confused him as much as anybody else. His empire collapsed in 1932.

The depression derived, fourth, from pell-mell, largely unregulated, speculation on the stock market. Corporations and banks invested large sums in stocks;

Speculation on the Stock Market

some speculated in their own issues. Brokers sold stocks to buyers who put up little cash, borrowed in order to purchase, and then used the stocks they bought as collateral for their loans. When the stocks came tumbling down, so did brokers, bankers, and companies. From 1930 to 1933 stock-market losses climbed to $85 billion.

International economic troubles constitute a fifth explanation for the coming of the depression. As the world's leading creditor and trader, the United States

International Economic Troubles

was deeply involved with the world economy. Billions of dollars in loans had flowed to Europe during the First World War and then during postwar reconstruction. Yet in the late 1920s American investors were beginning to keep their money at home, to invest it in the more exciting and lucrative stock market. Europeans, unable to borrow more funds and unable to sell their goods easily in the American market because of high tariffs, began to buy less from America and to default on their debts. Pinched at home, they raised their own tariffs, further crippling international commerce, and withdrew their investments from America.

Finally, government policies and practices contributed to the crash and depression. The federal government failed to regulate the wild speculation. It nei-

The Failure of Federal Policies

ther checked corporate power nor raised income taxes to encourage a more equitable distribution of income. Indeed, it lowered taxes, thus promoting the uneven distribution. And the Federal Reserve Board pursued easy-credit policies, even though it knew the easy money was paying for the speculative binge. The "Fed" blundered again in 1931 by tightening the money market at a time when just the opposite was needed: a loosening to spur borrowing and spending.

DESPAIRING AMERICANS

As the economy limped into the 1930s, statistics began to tell the story of a human tragedy. Between 1929 and 1933 a hundred thousand businesses failed; corporate profits fell from $10 billion to $1 billion; and the gross national product was cut in half. What happened to America's banks—and savings—illustrates especially well the cascading nature of the Great Depression. Banks tied into the stock market or foreign investments were badly weakened; some failed. When nervous Americans made runs on banks to salvage their threatened savings, a powerful momentum—panic—took command. In 1929, 659 banks folded; in 1930 the number of failures climbed to 1,350. The next year proved worse, 2,293 banks shutting their doors, and another 1,453 ceased to do business in 1932. By 1933, 9 million savings accounts had been lost.

Americans lost savings—and jobs. Although most people remained employed, day after day thousands of men and women received severance slips. Unemployment increased from 4 million at the beginning of 1930 to 13 million (one-fourth of the work force) in early 1933. And millions more were underemployed. Hoover asked businesspeople not to cut wages. Hourly wages did hold steady for a while, but weekly earnings began to drop off as hours were trimmed back. Then hourly wages were reduced in industry after industry. Overall, labor income dropped by 40 percent during Hoover's presidency.

Blacks and the unskilled lost their jobs first; whites and managerial personnel were let go last. Black women were more likely to lose jobs than white women. Desperate whites proved willing to take menial jobs once held largely by blacks, and because white employers preferred to hire whites, blacks were pushed out of the labor force.

People's diets deteriorated, malnutrition became common, and the undernourished fell victim more easily to disease. Some people quietly lined up at Red Cross and Salvation Army soup kitchens or queued in breadlines. Others ate only potatoes, crackers, or dandelions, stole dog biscuits from the local dog pound, or scratched through garbage cans for bits of food. Millions of Americans were not only hungry and ill; they were cold. Unable to afford fuel, some huddled in unheated tenements and shacks. Families doubled up in crowded apartments, but some who were unable to pay the rent were evicted, furniture and all. Urban jungles, bitterly called Hoovervilles, sprouted up, constructed from packing boxes and other debris.

Deterioration of Health

In the countryside, economic hardship deepened. Between 1929 and 1933 farm income was cut in half. Though farm prices dropped 60 percent, production decreased only 6 percent as individual farmers struggled to make up for lower prices by producing more, thereby creating an excess. And the surplus that so depressed agricultural prices could not be exported, since foreign demand had shrunk. Drought, foreclosure, clouds of hungry grasshoppers, and bank failures further plagued the American farmer. On southern cotton plantations, black sharecroppers barely subsisted on an income of less than $300 a year; whites fared little better with $400.

Plight of the Farmers

Some Americans became transients in search of jobs or food. Desperate tenant farmers—husbands, wives, and children—walked the roads of the South. The California Unemployment Commission reported in 1932 that an "army of homeless" had trooped into the state and moved constantly from place to place, forced by one town after another to move on. Hundreds of thousands jumped aboard freight trains—"rode the rods"—or hitchhiked. Some boys and girls wandered on their own, living in hobo jungles usually populated by adults.

Going West—1933, *painted by Robinson Boardman. This stark rendering of anxious migrants searching for work and a happier life is typical of art produced during the depression era. National Museum of American Art, Smithsonian Institution; Gift of Mr. and Mrs. Alexander Lowenthal and Family.*

Across America economic woe and geographical mobility changed marriage patterns and family life. People postponed marriage, and married couples postponed having children. More-

Marriage and the Family

over, the self-esteem of jobless husbands and fathers was undermined, especially when women took jobs to support their families. Yet in most families the husband remained the dominant partner.

For millions of Americans the movies provided escape from their economic troubles. One studio put it this way: "There's a Paramount Picture probably

Movies as an Escape from Hardship

around the corner. See it and you'll be out of yourself, living someone else's life." The "someone elses" included gangsters, whose lives were success stories in a disordered society, and comedians like the horseplaying Marx brothers, who poked fun at convention. Seductive Mae West demonstrated that woman could be the hunter as well as the hunted. There were also musicals like the popular *Gold Diggers* series and horror films like *Dracula* (1931) and *Frankenstein* (1931). And then there was the giant monster in *King Kong* (1933), who scaled the Empire State Building and smashed his way through New York City. *King Kong,* wrote historian Robert Sklar, "may have given the audiences precisely the proper combination of fear for the survival of their society and pleasure at seeing someone, if only a doomed gorilla, vent his rage at it."

THE TEMPERED PROTEST

Most Americans met the new crisis not with violence, protest, or political extremism, but with bewilderment and an inability to fix the blame. They scorned businesspeople, of course, but often they blamed themselves as well. A psychiatrist describing unemployed miners wrote, "They hung around street corners and in groups. They gave each other solace. They were loath to go home because they were indicted, as if it were their fault for being jobless. A jobless man was a lazy good-for-nothing. . . . They felt despised, they were ashamed of themselves." This was the stuff not of revolution, but of self-hatred and melancholy.

Scattered protests did, however, raise the specter of popular revolt. In Iowa's Cow War of 1931, angry farmers assailed state tuberculin inspectors who condemned diseased cattle but gave farmers little compensation for their losses. In Nebraska, Iowa, and Minnesota, farmers protesting low prices put up barricades, stopped trucks, and dumped milk and vegetables on the road. Some of these demonstrations were organized by the Farmers' Holiday Association. Its leader, Milo Reno, urged farmers to take a holiday—keep their products off the market until they commanded better prices. The Sioux City milk strike of 1932 was the association's most dramatic effort, but like others it failed to alter significantly the terrible economic position of farmers.

Farmers' Holiday Association

The most spectacular confrontation shook Washington, D.C., in summer 1932. Congress was considering a bill authorizing immediate issuance of bonuses of $2.4 billion already allotted to First World War veterans, but not due for payment until 1945. To lobby for the bill, 15,000 unemployed veterans and their families converged on the tense nation's capital, calling themselves the Bonus Expeditionary Force (BEF). They camped in crude shacks on vacant lots and in empty government buildings. Though President Hoover threw his weight against the bonus bill, the House passed it. The showdown came in the Senate, which voted "no" after much debate. Many of the bonus marchers then left Washington, but several thousand stayed on. In July General Douglas MacArthur, assisted by Majors Dwight D. Eisenhower and George S. Patton, met the veterans and their families with cavalry, tanks, and bayonet-bearing soldiers. The BEF hurled back stones and bricks. What followed shocked the nation. Men and women were chased down by horsemen; children were teargassed; shacks were set afire. When presidential hopeful Franklin D. Roosevelt heard about the attack on the Bonus Army, he turned to his friend Felix Frankfurter and said: "Well, Felix, this will elect me."

Bonus Expeditionary Force

With capitalism on its knees, American Communist leaders anticipated large gains for their party. Across the nation they organized "unemployed councils" to arouse class consciousness and to agitate for jobs and food. In March 1930 they conducted urban demonstrations, some of which ended in violent clashes with local police. And with the slogan "Fight—Don't Starve," they led a hunger march on Washington, D.C., in 1931. Their tangles with authority publicized the real human tragedy of the depression. Still, the Communist party gained few followers.

HOOVER HOLDS THE LINE

When daily appeals for government relief for the jobless reached the White House, Hoover at first became defensive, if not hostile. He rejected direct relief—derisively called the dole—because he believed it would undermine character and individualism. Hoover thus appeared to a growing number of Americans to be heartless and inflexible. Rather than deal with the quarter of the work force that was jobless, he emphasized the many who were still on the payrolls.

True to his beliefs, the president urged people to help themselves and their neighbors. He applauded private voluntary relief through charitable agencies. Yet when the need was greatest, donations declined. State and urban officials found their treasuries drying up too. Meanwhile, those calling for federal action got no sympathy from Secretary of the Treasury Mellon, who advised the president to "let the slump liquidate itself. Liquidate labor, liquidate stocks, liquidate the farmers, liquidate real estate. . . . It will purge the rottenness out of the system."

Reliance on Private Relief

But as the depression intensified, Hoover's opposition to federal action diminished. He met with business and labor leaders, winning pledges from them to maintain wages and production and to avoid strikes. He urged state governors to increase their expenditures on public works. And he created the President's Organization on Unemployment Relief (POUR) to generate private contributions for relief of the destitute. Unfortunately, POUR accomplished little.

Hoover's spurring of federal public works projects (including the Boulder, or Hoover, and Grand Coulee dams) did provide some jobs. Help also came from the Federal Farm Board, which supported agricultural prices by lending money to cooperatives to buy products and keep them off the market. To retard the collapse of the international monetary system, Hoover announced a moratorium on the payment of First World War debts and reparations (1931).

The president also reluctantly asked Congress to charter the Reconstruction Finance Corporation (RFC). Created in 1932, the RFC was designed to make loans to banks, insurance **Reconstruction** companies, and railroads and later **Finance** to state and local governments. **Corporation** The theory behind the RFC was that it would lend money to large entities at the top of the economic system, and benefits would trickle down to people at the bottom through a sort of percolation process. It did not work; banks continued to collapse and small companies to go into bankruptcy.

Despite warnings from prominent economists, Hoover also signed the Hawley-Smoot Tariff (1930). A congressional compromise serving special interests, the tariff raised duties by about one-third. Hoover argued that the tariff would help farmers and manufacturers by keeping foreign goods off the market. Actually, the tariff further weakened the economy by making it even more difficult for foreign nations to sell their products and thus earn the money to buy American products.

Like most of his contemporaries, Hoover believed that a balanced budget was sacred, and deficit spending sinful. In 1931 he appealed for a decrease in federal expenditures and an increase in taxes. The following year he supported a sales tax on manufactured goods. The sales tax was defeated, but the Revenue Act of 1932 raised corporate, excise, and personal income taxes. Hoover seemed caught in a contradiction: he urged people to spend to spur recovery, but his tax policies deprived them of spending money.

Although Hoover expanded public works projects and approved loans to some institutions, he vetoed a variety of relief bills presented to him by the Democratic Congress. He also vetoed a multipurpose development project for the Tennessee River, arguing that its cheap electricity would compete with power from private companies. Clinging to his old viewpoints, Hoover stretched government activities as far as he thought he could without violating his cherished principles.

Hoover's traditionalism was well demonstrated by his handling of Prohibition. The law was not and could not be enforced. Yet Hoover resisted the mounting public pressure for repeal. Opponents argued not only that Prohibition encouraged crime, but that its repeal would stimulate economic recovery in Milwaukee and St. Louis, increase demand for grain, and revive the nation's old beer, liquor, and pretzel factories. But the president would not, he said, tamper with the Constitution, and the liquor industry, having no socially redemptive value, was best left depressed. Instead, Hoover pushed for better enforcement of the Eighteenth Amendment. And during the presidential election campaign of 1932, he stood firm against repeal. As on other issues, Hoover held the line.

Tradition in Time of Crisis: The Election of 1932

Herbert Hoover and the Republican party faced dreary prospects in 1932. The tired and sullen president grumbled at reporters, banks continued to close, and memories of the Bonus March persisted. Hoover kept pointing to international causes for the economic crisis, when Americans were less concerned with abstract explanations than with tomorrow's meal. But what soured public opinion most was that Hoover seemed not to lead at a time when innovative generalship was required.

Franklin D. Roosevelt, on the other hand, enjoyed a different reputation. He was born into the upper class of tradition and privilege, the only child of doting parents who heaped on him all sorts of advantages. He graduated from Harvard in 1903, and in fall 1904, he entered the School of Law at Columbia University. A few months later he announced his engagement to his fifth cousin once removed, Anna Eleanor Roosevelt, the niece of President Theodore Roosevelt. The next spring they were married.

Democratic Candidate Franklin D. Roosevelt

Roosevelt began the practice of law, but had other ambitions—political ones. In 1910, he was elected to the New York State Assembly. In 1912 he accepted Woodrow Wilson's offer of the post of assistant secretary of the navy. For eight years Roosevelt helped expand American naval forces, gaining confidence and shedding much of his smugness. And he learned lessons about the emergence of the United States as a world power and the need for decisive presidential leadership in times of crisis.

In 1920, running as the Democratic vice-presidential candidate, Roosevelt was defeated. He suffered his most devastating loss the next year, however, when he was stricken by polio and totally paralyzed in both legs. What should he do next? Should he retire from public life, a rich invalid? His answer and his wife's was no. Throughout the 1920s Franklin and Eleanor contended with his new handicap. In this personal struggle, he grew more patient and more understanding of those who suffer. People who had known him before commented that polio had made him a "twice born man," that his "fight against that dread disease had evidently given him new moral and physical strength."

Re-entering politics, Roosevelt became a spokesperson for progressive Democrats. In 1928 he was elected governor of New York. As governor, he appealed to the American penchant for optimism, undertaking vigorous relief programs and establishing an unemployment commission. He also endorsed and worked for old-age pensions and protective legislation for labor unions. With this record, he became an obvious prospect for the 1932 Democratic presidential nomination. When he accepted that nomination, Roosevelt promised a "new deal for the American people," suggesting his intention of implementing at the national level the types of programs he had started in New York.

The two party platforms differed little, but the Democrats were willing to abandon Prohibition and to launch federal relief. Roosevelt, playing the political game superbly, would agree with Hoover that the budget had to be balanced, then appeal for costly new programs. When Roosevelt spoke of the forgotten man and declared himself ready to provide direct relief to individuals, Hoover boiled. "This campaign is more than a contest between two men," he said. "It is more than a contest between two parties. It is a contest between two philosophies of government."

More people went to the polls in 1932 than in any election since the First World War. In a crisis-ridden moment Americans quietly, calmly, even routinely, followed tradition and peacefully exchanged one government for another. Roosevelt's 22.8 million popular votes far outdistanced Hoover's 15.8 million. Democrats also won overwhelming control of the Senate and the House.

1932 Election Results

To prepare a national political platform, Roosevelt surrounded himself with a "brain trust" of lawyers and university professors. Bigness was unavoidable in the modern American economy, these experts reasoned; thus the cure for the nation's ills was not to go on a rampage of trustbusting, but to place large corporations, monopolies, and oligopolies under effective government regulation. "We are no longer afraid of bigness," declared Columbia professor Rexford G. Tugwell, speaking in the tradition of Theodore Roosevelt's New Nationalism.

Roosevelt's "Brain Trust"

Roosevelt and his brain trust agreed that it was es-

tion. If the demand for a product remained constant
and the supply were cut, they reasoned, the price
would rise. Producers would make higher profits, and
workers would earn more money. This method of
combating a depression had been called the economics of scarcity. Unlike Hoover, Roosevelt also advocated immediate and direct relief to the unemployed.
Finally, Roosevelt and his advisers demanded that
the federal government engage in centralized economic planning and experimentation to bring about
recovery.

On the afternoon of March 2, 1933, President-
elect Roosevelt and his family and friends boarded a
train for Washington, D.C., and the inauguration
ceremony. Roosevelt was carrying with him rough
drafts of two presidential proclamations, one sum-
moning a special session of Congress, the other declaring a national bank holiday, suspending banking
transactions throughout the nation. Thirty-eight
states had closed their banks to prevent a run on
funds by nervous depositors. It was time for Roosevelt
to produce the New Deal he had promised the American people.

RESTORING CONFIDENCE

"First of all," declared the newly inaugurated president, "let me assert my firm belief that the only
thing we have to fear is fear itself—nameless, unrea-
soning, unjustified terror." In his inaugural address

sential for the government to restore purchasing
power to farmers, blue-collar workers, and the middle
classes, and that the way to do so was to cut produc-

Roosevelt scored his first triumph as president, instilling hope and courage in the rank and file. Roosevelt attacked the nation's bankers, accusing them of having "fled from their high seats in the temple of our civilization." He invoked "the analogue of war," asserting that, if need be, "I shall ask the Congress for the one remaining instrument to meet the crisis— broad Executive power to wage a war against the emergency, as great as the power that would be given to me if we were in fact invaded by a foreign foe."

On March 5, Roosevelt declared a four-day national bank holiday and summoned Congress to an emergency session. Congress convened on March 9 to begin what observers would call the Hundred Days. The first measure, the Emergency Banking Relief Bill, was introduced on March 9, passed sight unseen by unanimous House vote, approved 73 to 7 in the Senate, and signed by the president that evening. The act provided for the reopening, under Treasury Department license, of banks that were solvent and the reorganization and management of those that were not. It also prohibited gold hoarding and export. But it was a conservative law that upheld the status quo, leaving the nation's banking system essentially unchanged, with the same people in charge.

Beginning of the Hundred Days

On March 10, another conservative New Deal bill was introduced in Congress; ten days later it became law. Called the Economy Act, its purpose was to balance the federal budget by chopping veterans' benefits and allowances by $400 million and reducing by $100 million the pay of federal employees. Under Roosevelt, the budget balancers had won a battle that could not have been won under Hoover. Despite the deflationary effects of this legislation, the important point was that Roosevelt had acted and had done so boldly.

On Sunday evening, March 12, the president broadcast the first of his fireside chats, and 60 million people heard his comforting voice on their radios. His message: banks were once again safe places for depositors' savings. On Monday

First Fireside Chat

morning the banks opened their doors, but instead of queuing up to withdraw their savings, people waited outside to deposit their money. The bank runs were over; people had regained confidence in their political leadership, their banks, even their economic system.

LAUNCHING THE NEW DEAL

On March 16, the president sent to Congress the Agricultural Adjustment Bill, his plan to restore farmers' purchasing power. If overproduction was the cause of farmers' problems—falling prices and mounting surpluses—then the government had to encourage farmers to grow less food. Under the domestic allotment plan, the government would pay farmers to reduce their acreage or plow under crops already in the fields. Farmers would receive payments based on *parity*, a system of regulated prices for corn, cotton, wheat, rice, hogs, and dairy products that would allow them the same purchasing power they had had during the prosperous period of 1909 through 1914. In effect, the government was making up the difference between the actual market value of farm products and the income farmers needed to make a profit. The funds for the subsidies would come from taxes levied on the processors of agricultural commodities. Against vehement opposition, the Agricultural Adjustment Act (AAA) was passed on May 12, implementing a farm policy based upon the economics of scarcity.

Agricultural Adjustment Act

Meanwhile, other relief measures became law. On March 21 the president requested massive infusions of relief of three kinds: a job corps called the Civilian Conservation Corps (CCC); direct cash grants to the states to provide relief payments for needy citizens; and public

Civilian Conservation Corps (CCC)

works projects. Ten days later Congress approved the CCC, which ultimately put 2.5 million young men between the ages of eighteen and twenty-five to work planting trees, clearing camping areas and beaches, and building bridges, dams, reservoirs, fish ponds, and fire towers. Then on May 12 Congress passed the Federal Emergency Relief Act, which authorized $500 million in aid to state and local governments.

Roosevelt's proposed plan for public works became Title II of the National Industrial Recovery Act (NIRA). Passed on June 16, it established in the Public Works Administration (PWA) a fund of $3.3 billion to build roads, sewage and water systems, public buildings, and a host of other projects, including ships and naval aircraft. The purpose of the PWA was to prime the economic pump to spur economic recovery.

If the AAA was the agricultural cornerstone of the New Deal, the National Industrial Recovery Act was the industrial cornerstone. The NIRA was a testimony to the New Deal belief in national planning as opposed to an individualistic, intensely competitive, laissez-faire economy. It was essential, the planners argued, for businesses to end cutthroat competition and raise prices by limiting production. Like the War Industries Board (WIB) during the First World War, the NIRA exempted businesses from antitrust laws through the National Recovery Administration (NRA), whose symbol, the Blue Eagle, was meant to encourage cooperation. Under the law, competing businesses met with representatives of workers and consumers to draft codes of fair competition, which limited production and established prices.

Economic Planning under the NIRA

With businesses enjoying new concessions, workers wanted a share of the pie too. Congress guaranteed their right to unionize and to bargain collectively in Section 7(a) of the NIRA, which called for industry-wide codes establishing minimum wages and maximum hours.

One of the boldest programs that Congress enacted during this period concerned the badly depressed Tennessee River valley, which ran through Tennessee, North Carolina, Kentucky, Virginia, Mississippi, Georgia, and Alabama. For years progressives led by Senator George Norris of Nebraska had advocated government operation of the Muscle Shoals electric power and nitrogen facilities on the Tennessee River. But Roosevelt's Tennessee Valley Authority (TVA), as finally established in May 1933, was a much broader program than the progressive plan. Its dams would not only serve to control floods, but they could also generate hydroelectric power, reclaim and reforest land, and prevent soil erosion. The TVA also would produce and sell nitrogen fertilizers to private citizens and nitrate explosives to the government; dig a 650-mile navigation channel from Knoxville to Paducah; and construct public power facilities as a yardstick for determining fair rates for privately produced electric power. The goal of the TVA was nothing less than enhancement of the economic well-being of the entire Tennessee River valley.

Congress finally adjourned on June 16, its Hundred Days completed. Roosevelt had delivered fifteen messages to Congress, and fifteen significant laws had been enacted (see table, page 436). Among these laws were the Federal Securities Act, to compel brokers to tell the truth about new securities issues, and the Banking Act of 1933, which set up the Federal Deposit Insurance Corporation for insuring bank deposits. Finally, on April 19 the United States abandoned the gold standard by announcing that it would no longer guarantee the gold value of the dollar abroad. Freed from the gold standard, Roosevelt used his monetary policy as another tool for economic recovery.

End of the Hundred Days

Throughout the remainder of 1933 and the spring and summer of 1934, more New Deal bills became law. Indeed, there seemed to be something for everybody in the New Deal. Here was interest-group democracy at work, with government benefits accruing not only to business but to agriculture and labor; to farm and homeowners; to corporations, railroads, and city governments; and to the jobless. In the midst of this coalition of all interests

Broker State Democracy

NEW DEAL ACHIEVEMENTS

	Labor	Agriculture	Business and Industrial Recovery	Relief	Reform
1933	Section 7A of NIRA	Agricultural Adjustment Act Farm Credit Act	Emergency Banking Act Economy Act Beer and Wine Revenue Act Banking Act of 1933 (guaranteed deposits) National Industrial Recovery Act	Civilian Conservation Corps Federal Emergency Relief Act Home Owners Refinancing Act Public Works Administration Civil Works Administration	TVA Federal Securities Act
1934	National Labor Relations Board				Securities Exchange Act
1935	National Labor Relations (Wagner) Act	Resettlement Administration Rural Electrification Administration		Works Progress Administration and National Youth Administration	Banking Act of 1935 Social Security Act Public Utilities Holding Company Act Revenue Act (wealth tax)
1937		Farm Security Administration			
1938	Fair Labor Standards Act	Agricultural Adjustment Act of 1938			

Source: Adapted by permission from Charles Sellers, Henry May, and Neil R. McMillen, *A Synopsis of American History*, 6th ed., pp. 342–343. Copyright © 1985 by Houghton Mifflin Company.

was President Roosevelt, the artful broker who weighed the claims of competing interest groups. And this broker state appeared to be working. In 1933 almost 13 million people had been jobless. Following New Deal legislation the figure fell steadily to 11.4 million in 1934, 10.6 million in 1935, and 9 million in 1936. Net farm income rose from $2.5 billion in 1932 to just over $3 billion in 1933, almost $3.5 billion in 1934, and $5.85 billion in 1935. And manufacturing salaries and wages also increased, jumping from $6.25 billion in 1933 to over $9.5 billion two years later and almost $13 billion in 1937.

There was no doubt about the popularity of either the New Deal or Roosevelt. In the 1934 congressional elections, the Democrats gained ten seats in the House and ten in the Senate. The New Deal, according to Arthur Krock of the *New York Times,* had won "the most overwhelming victory in the history of American politics." And as for Roosevelt, "he has been all but crowned by the people," wrote William Allen White.

REACTIONS AGAINST
THE NEW DEAL

Yet there was more than one way to read employment and income statistics and election returns. For example, though unemployment had dropped from a high of 13 million (25 percent) in 1933 to 9 million (16.9 percent) in 1936, it had been only 1.5 million (3.2 percent) in 1929. And though manufacturing wages and salaries had reached almost $13 billion in 1937, that figure was almost $1.5 billion less than the total for 1929. In other words, regardless of the New Deal's successes, it had a long way to go before reaching pre-Depression standards.

With the arrival of partial economic recovery, many businesspeople and conservatives became vocal critics of the New Deal. Some charged there was

Conservative Critics of the New Deal

too much taxation and government regulation. Others criticized the deficit financing of relief and public works. According to still others, the New Deal had subverted individual initiative and self-reliance by providing welfare payments.

If businesspeople felt the government was their enemy, others thought the government favored business too much. For a while, government propaganda urging Americans to support the NRA quieted the debate, particularly during 1933. In time, however, the criticism grew. Farmers, labor unions, individual entrepreneurs, and antitrust critics complained that the NRA set prices too high and favored large-scale producers over small businesses. And the federal courts began to scrutinize the constitutionality of the legislation in cases brought by critics.

The AAA came under attack as well because of its encouragement of cutbacks in production. In 1933 farmers had plowed under 10.4 million acres of cotton and slaughtered 220,000 sows and 6 million pigs—at a time when people were ill-clothed and ill-fed. Though for landowning farmers the program was successful, the average person found such waste to be shocking. And what about tenant farmers and sharecroppers? They too were supposed to receive government payments for taking crops out of cultivation, but very few of them, especially if they were black, received what they were entitled to. Furthermore, the AAA's hopes that landlords would keep their tenants on the land even while cutting production were not fulfilled. In the South the number of sharecropper farms dropped from 776,278 in 1930 to 541,291 in 1940. The result was a homeless population, some of whom, known in the folklore of the times as "Okies" and "Arkies," packed up and took off for California.

Demagogic Attacks on the New Deal

As dissatisfaction mounted, so too did the appeal of various demagogues. Father Charles Coughlin, a Roman Catholic priest whose weekly radio sermons offered a curious combination of anti-Communism, anticap-

Senator Huey Long of Louisiana (center) had a mass following in the 1930s, and he had presidential ambitions. But he was assassinated in 1935, the same evening this photograph was taken. Long fell into the arms of James O'Connor (left), a political crony, while Louisiana's Governor O. K. Allen (right) seized a pistol and dashed into a corridor after the murderer, shouting, "If there's shooting, I want to be in on it."   National Archives.

italism, and anti-Semitism, was one of the more famous. According to Coughlin, the worst abuses of capitalism had been inflicted by the Jews. He became increasingly critical of the AAA's plowing under of crops and slaughtering of livestock, and he began to criticize the New Deal for having "out-Hoovered Hoover."

Another challenge to the New Deal came from Dr. Francis E. Townsend, who had conceived what he called an Old Age Revolving Pensions plan. Un-der Townsend's scheme the government would pay monthly pensions of $200 to all citizens over age sixty, on condition that they spent the money in the same month they received it. Townsend claimed his plan would not only aid the aged but cure the depression by pumping enormous purchasing power into the economy. Though the plan was fiscally impossible, it had a powerful emotional appeal, for it addressed the needs of deprived senior citizens.

And then there was Huey Long, "the Kingfish,"

perhaps the most successful demagogue in American history. In 1928 Long was elected governor of Louisiana with the slogan "Every Man a King, But No One Wears a Crown." At first Long supported the New Deal; but he found the Economy Act and the NRA too conservative, and began to believe that Roosevelt had fallen captive to big business and big money. Long countered in 1934 with the Share Our Wealth Society, which advocated the seizure by taxation of all incomes over $1 million and all inheritances over $5 million. With those funds, the government would furnish each family a homestead allowance of $5,000 and an annual income of $2,000. By mid-1935 Long's movement claimed 7 million members, and few doubted that Long aspired to the presidency. Though an assassin's bullet extinguished his ambition in September 1935, the Share Our Wealth movement persisted.

Some politicians of the 1930s, like Floyd Olson, governor of Minnesota, declared themselves socialists. Olson sought a third party that would "preach the gospel of government and collective ownership of the means of production and distribution." In neighboring Wisconsin the left-wing Progressive party re-elected Robert La Follette, Jr., to the Senate in 1934, sent seven of the state's ten representatives to Washington, and placed La Follette's brother Philip in the governorship. And the old muckraker Upton Sinclair almost won the Democratic gubernatorial nomination in California in 1934 on the platform End Poverty in California (EPIC).

Left-Wing Critics of the New Deal

Perhaps the most controversial alternative to the New Deal was the Communist party of the United States of America (CPUSA). In 1932 a number of distinguished writers had endorsed the Communist presidential candidate, William Z. Foster. But membership in the CPUSA remained small until 1935, when the party leadership changed its strategy. Proclaiming "Communism is Twentieth Century Americanism," the CPUSA disclaimed any intention of overthrowing the United States government and began to cooperate with left-wing labor unions, student groups, and writers' organizations. Still, at its high point for the decade in 1938, the CPUSA had only 55,000 members.

In addition to challenges from the right and the left, the New Deal was threatened by the Supreme Court. In January 1935, in *Panama Refining Co.* v. *Ryan,* the Court struck down part of the NIRA. By granting the president power to prohibit interstate and foreign shipment of oil, the Court ruled, Congress had unconstitutionally delegated legislative power to the executive branch. Then on May 27 the Court unanimously struck down the whole NIRA (*Schechter* v. *U.S.*) on the grounds that it gave excessive legislative power to the White House, and that the commerce clause of the Constitution did not give the federal government authority to regulate intrastate business. Roosevelt's industrial recovery program was dead. In January 1936 his farm program met a similar fate when the Court invalidated the AAA (*U.S.* v. *Butler*), deciding that agriculture was a local problem.

Supreme Court Decisions against the New Deal

As Roosevelt looked ahead to the presidential election of 1936, he saw that he was in danger of losing his capacity to lead and to govern. His coalition of all interests was breaking up; radicals and demagogues were offering Americans alternative programs; and the Supreme Court was dismantling the New Deal. In the spring and summer of 1935, Roosevelt took the initiative once more, and the New Deal scored some of its biggest victories. So impressive was the new legislation that some historians have called it the Second New Deal.

THE SECOND NEW DEAL

The first triumph of the Second New Deal was an innocuous-sounding but momentous law called the Emergency Relief Appropriation Act, which

Congress passed and Roosevelt signed in April 1935. The act authorized the president to issue executive orders establishing massive public works programs for the jobless, including the Works Progress Administration (WPA).

Later renamed the Work Projects Administration, the WPA ultimately employed more than 8.5 million people. By the time it was terminated in 1943, the WPA had built over 650,000 miles of highways, streets, and roads, 125,000 public buildings, and 8,000 parks, as well as numerous bridges, airports, and other structures. But WPA did more than lay bricks. Its Federal Theatre Project brought plays, vaudeville shows, and circuses to cities and towns across the country, and WPA artists painted murals in post offices and other public buildings. The Federal Music Project and the WPA Dance Theatre sponsored laboratories for young composers and choreographers. And the Federal Writers' Project hired writers like Conrad Aiken, John Cheever, Claude McKay, John Steinbeck, and Richard Wright to write local guidebooks and regional, ethnic, and folk histories.

Besides the WPA, the Emergency Relief Appropriation Act funded other relief and public works measures. The Resettlement Administration (RA) resettled destitute families and organized rural homestead communities and suburban greenbelt towns for low-income workers. The Rural Electrification Administration (REA) distributed electricity to isolated rural areas. And the National Youth Administration (NYA) sponsored work relief programs for young adults and provided jobs for the part-time employment of students.

As significant as these achievements were, Roosevelt wanted new legislation, some of it aimed at controlling the activities of big business. The Supreme Court had condemned the government-business cooperation that had been the foundation of the First Hundred Days. And businesspeople had become increasingly critical of Roosevelt and the New Deal. Now Roosevelt determined that if big business would not cooperate with government, government should "cut the giants down to size" through antitrust suits and heavy corporate taxes. In June he asked Congress to enact five major bills: a labor bill sponsored by Senator Robert Wagner; a Social Security bill; a banking bill; a measure to regulate public-utilities holding companies; and a "soak-the-rich" tax bill.

These were the Second Hundred Days. On July 5 the National Labor Relations (Wagner) Act granted workers the right to unionize and to bargain collectively. The act empowered the National Labor Relations Board to supervise the election of bargaining units and agents and to issue cease-and-desist injunctions against harassment of union members by employers.

On August 15 Roosevelt signed the Social Security Act, which established a cooperative federal-state system of unemployment compensation and old-age and survivors' insurance. Social Security was a conservative measure: the government did not pay for old-age benefits; workers and their bosses did. The tax was also regressive (the more workers earned, the less they were taxed proportionately) and deflationary (it took money out of people's pockets that it did not repay for years). Finally, many people were ineligible for coverage under the law, including farm workers, domestic servants, and many hospital and restaurant workers. But the act was still a milestone. It acknowledged the government's responsibility to establish a system of insurance for the aged, the dependent, the disabled, and the temporarily unemployed.

In the next two weeks Roosevelt gained the remainder of what he had asked for, including the Banking Act of 1935, the Public Utilities Holding Company (Wheeler-Rayburn) Act, and the Revenue (Wealth Tax) Act of 1935. The Wealth Tax Act, which some critics saw as the president's attempt to "steal Huey's thunder," did not result in a redistribution of income, though it did increase the income taxes paid by the wealthy. It also increased taxes on inheritances, large gifts, and profits from the sale of property.

The Second Hundred Days indicated not only that the president was once again in charge, but that he was set to run for re-election. The campaign was less heated than might have been expected, however. Naturally the Republican nominee, Governor Alf Landon of Kansas, criticized Roosevelt, but he did not advocate a wholesale repeal of the New Deal. When the ballots were counted, Roosevelt had won a landslide victory, polling 27.8 million votes to Landon's 16.7 million. The Democrats carried every state except Maine and Vermont and won huge majorities in the House and Senate.

Election of 1936

The Democratic victory of 1936 stemmed from what observers have called the "New Deal coalition." The growing strength of the party in the cities, the suffering wrought by the Great Depression, and the New Deal response to social distress had converged to make Roosevelt the champion of the urban masses, as well as of farmers and the elderly. Labor, especially the new unions of the Congress of Industrial Organizations (CIO), was an indispensable member of the coalition. And black voters in northern cities, most of whom had been Republicans prior to the 1930s, now cast their lot with the Democratic party. The Democratic party had become the dominant half of the two-party system.

New Deal Coalition

ROOSEVELT'S SECOND TERM: THE UNREALIZED PROMISE

Despite the bold and unprecedented steps of his first term, Roosevelt faced a darkening horizon during his second term. The economy faltered again between 1937 and 1939, bringing renewed unemployment and suffering. And Europe drew closer to war, threatening to drag the United States into the conflict. To gain support for his foreign and military policies, Roosevelt began to court conservative politicians. The eventual result was the demise of the New Deal.

In several instances Roosevelt caused his own defeat. The Supreme Court had invalidated much of the work of the First Hundred Days; now Roosevelt feared it would do the same with the Second Hundred Days. So in February 1937 the president sent to Congress his Judiciary Reorganization Bill. What the federal judiciary needed, he claimed, was a more enlightened and progressive world view. Four of the justices steadfastly opposed the New Deal; three generally approved of it; and two were swing votes.

What Roosevelt requested was the authority to add a federal judge whenever an incumbent who had already served at least ten years failed to retire within six months of reaching age seventy. He wanted the power to name up to fifty additional federal judges, including six to the Supreme Court. Though Roosevelt spoke of understaffed courts and aged and feeble judges, it was obvious that he envisioned using the bill to create a Supreme Court sympathetic to the New Deal.

Roosevelt's Court-packing Plan

Opposition to Roosevelt's attempt to pack the Court was widespread and vocal. Naturally, Republicans and some conservative Democrats opposed the bill, but liberals resisted as well. In the end Roosevelt had to concede defeat. The bill he signed made pensions available to retiring judges, but it denied him the power to increase the number of judges.

This episode had an ironic final twist. During the public debate over court packing, the two swing-vote justices began to vote in favor of liberal, pro–New Deal rulings. In spring 1937, for example, the court upheld a Washington state minimum-wage statute, the Wagner Act (*N.L.R.B.* v. *Jones & Laughlin Steel Corp.*), and the Social Security Act, all by 5-to-4 votes. Moreover, encouraged by pensions, judges past the age of seventy did begin to retire, and the president was able to appoint seven new Supreme Court justices between 1937 and 1941. Roosevelt had lost the legislative battle but won the war for a more progressive judicial outlook.

Another New Deal defeat, the renewed economic recession of 1937 through 1939, had no unexpected payoffs. Roosevelt had never abandoned his commitment to the balanced budget. In 1937, confident that most of the problems of the Depression had been solved, he began to order drastic cutbacks in government spending. At the same time, the Federal Reserve Board, concerned over a 3.6 percent inflation rate, tightened credit. The two actions sent the economy into a tailspin; unemployment soared from 14.3 percent in 1937 to 19.1 percent the next year. In response to the new recession Roosevelt revived deficit financing.

Recession of 1937–1939

Roosevelt's personal campaign against three conservative southern Democrats in the off-year elections of 1938 further revealed his desperation. Senators Walter George of Georgia, "Cotton Ed" Smith of South Carolina, and Millard Tydings of Maryland, all critics of the New Deal, won re-election despite Roosevelt's campaigning against them. As it turned out, Roosevelt would soon need the support of these conservatives for his programs of military rearmament and preparedness.

In spring 1938, with conflict over events in Europe commanding more and more of the nation's attention, the New Deal came to an end. The last significant laws enacted were a new Agricultural Adjustment Act and the Fair Labor Standards Act, which established minimum wages and maximum hours for many but by no means all workers.

THE RISE OF THE CIO

Organized labor benefited as much as farmers and businesspeople did from New Deal legislation. On enactment, Section 7(a) of the NIRA inspired union leaders to organize and recruit new members. "Millions of workers throughout the nation," recalled American Federation of Labor (AFL) President William Green, "stood up for the first time in their lives to receive their charter of industrial freedom." By October 1933 an additional 1.5 million workers had enlisted in unions, bringing total membership to 4 million. With passage of the Wagner Act in mid-1935, labor union recruiting received another big boost; within three years total membership surpassed 7 million.

But these gains did not always come easily. Management put up determined resistance in the 1930s, hiring armed thugs to intimidate workers and break up strikes. Labor confronted yet another obstacle in the AFL craft unions' traditional skepticism and hostility toward industrial unions. Craft unions typically consisted of skilled workers in a particular trade. Industrial unions represented all the workers in a given industry, skilled and unskilled. The organizing gains in the 1930s were far more impressive in industrial unions than in craft unions, with hundreds of thousands of workers joining unions in such industries as autos, garments, rubber, and steel. What resulted was a struggle for control of the labor movement between craft and industrial union leaders.

Rivalry Between Craft and Industrial Unions

Attempts to reconcile the craft and industrial union movements failed, and in late 1935 John L. Lewis of the United Mine Workers resigned as vice-president of the AFL. He and other industrial unionists within the AFL formed the Committee for Industrial Organization (CIO). In 1938 the AFL expelled the CIO unions, and the CIO reorganized itself as the Congress of Industrial Organizations. By that time CIO membership stood at 3.7 million, more than the AFL's 3.4 million.

The CIO, which in the 1930s evolved into a pragmatic, bread-and-butter labor organization, had organized millions of workers who had never before had an opportunity to join a union. One of these unions, the United Auto Workers (UAW), scored a major victory in late 1936. The union demanded recognition from General Motors, Chrysler, and Ford. When GM refused, the UAW launched a new kind of strike: the sit-down. Beginning in the Fisher Body plants in Flint, Michigan, workers refused to leave the plants. To discourage the strikers, GM managers turned off the heat; when that tactic failed, they called the police, who were met by a barrage of missiles—iron bolts, coffee mugs, and pop bottles. When the police resorted to tear gas, the strikers turned the plant's water hoses on them, and the police retreated.

Sit-down Strikes

The strike lasted for weeks. GM obtained a court order to evacuate the plant, but the strikers continued, risking imprisonment and fines. With the support of their families and neighborhoods, the workers stuck to their rigid discipline. Community women organized an "emergency brigade" to picket and deliver food and supplies to the strikers. In 1937 the UAW prevailed: GM agreed to recognize the union. Chrysler signed a similar agreement, but Ford held out for four more years.

In 1937, too, the Steel Workers Organizing Committee (SWOC) signed a contract with the nation's largest steelmaker, U.S. Steel, that guaranteed an eight-hour day and a forty-hour week. Other steel companies refused to go along, however. Confrontations between these so-called little steel companies and the SWOC led to violence. On Memorial Day in Chicago, strikers and their families had joined with sympathizers in a peaceful picket line in front of the Republic Steel plant. Suddenly and without provocation the police opened fire. They continued to shoot into the crowd even as people turned away and began to run.

Memorial Day Massacre

As senseless as the Memorial Day Massacre was—ten had been killed—its occurrence was not surprising. During the 1930s industries had hired private police agents and accumulated large stores of arms and ammunition for use in deterring workers from organizing and joining unions. Republic Steel, for example, was the nation's largest single purchaser of tear and sickening gas. Youngstown Sheet and Tube owned 8 machine guns, 369 rifles, 190 shotguns, 450 revolvers, and thousands of rounds of ammunition.

Through it all, the CIO continued to enroll new members. By the end of the decade the CIO had succeeded in organizing most of the nation's mass-production industries.

MIXED PROGRESS FOR NONWHITES

For black Americans the early depression years were ones of great trial. Like some earlier Republican presidents, Herbert Hoover tried to push blacks out of the party. This "lily-white" GOP effort was designed to entice southern whites into the party. Moreover, Hoover appointed few blacks to federal office, disbanded the Negro division of the Republican National Committee, rejected appeals for an antilynching law, and nominated a southern white supremacist to a position on the Supreme Court.

Scottsboro became a celebrated civil liberties case that symbolized the ugliness of race relations in the depression era. One afternoon in March 1931, a freight train pulled into the yard at Paint Rock, near Scottsboro, Alabama. When the train stopped, armed sheriff's deputies arrested nine young blacks, charging them with roughing up some white hobos and throwing them off the train earlier in the day. When two white women who were removed from the same freight claimed that the blacks had raped them, an angry white mob gathered. Within two weeks eight of the "Scottsboro boys" had been convicted of rape by all-white juries and sentenced to death. The ninth, only twelve years old, was favored by a hung jury. But because court-

Scottsboro Trials

appointed lawyers had offered little defense for the youths, the Supreme Court overturned the convictions (1932) on the grounds that the accused had not been granted adequate legal counsel.

New trials opened in 1933, again with all-white juries. Medical evidence showed that the women had not had intercourse on the train. Nevertheless, the first defendant up for retrial, Haywood Patterson, was once again found guilty. Judge James Horton, who had stated that under American law "we know neither black nor white," was convinced that Patterson was an innocent victim of racial hatred. The courageous Horton overturned the jury's decision.

In 1936 Patterson was retried, found guilty, and given a seventy-five-year sentence. Four of the other youths were sentenced to life imprisonment, and the state dropped charges against the remaining four. Not until 1950 were all five out of jail—four by parole and Patterson by escaping from his work gang. Scottsboro's constitutional implications were important for the future: for the first time the Supreme Court used the Fourteenth Amendment as a vehicle to apply the criminal protection procedures of the Bill of Rights to the states (previously they had been applied only to the federal government).

It was against this background of injustice and insensitivity toward Afro-Americans that blacks first began to appraise Franklin Roosevelt. They soon found the New York Democrat to be the most appealing president since Lincoln. Part of Roosevelt's attraction was the courageous way he bore his physical disability. And when the president received black visitors at the White House and created a Black Cabinet, his actions contrasted favorably with Herbert Hoover's.

The Black Cabinet, or black brain trust, was unique in United States history. Never before had there been so many black advisers at the White House, and never had they been highly trained professionals. There were black lawyers, journalists, and doctors of philosophy; black experts on housing, labor, and social welfare. William H. Hastie and Rob-

Black Cabinet

ert C. Weaver, both of whom held advanced degrees from Harvard, served in the Department of the Interior. Mary McLeod Bethune, a college president, was director of the Division of Negro Affairs of the National Youth Administration. Eugene Kinckle Jones, executive secretary of the National Urban League, and Lawrence A. Oxley, a professional social worker, served in comparable posts in the departments of Commerce and Labor. Black social scientists, among them Ralph Bunche, Abram L. Harris, and Rayford W. Logan, acted as government consultants.

There were also among the New Dealers some whites who had committed themselves to first-class citizenship for Afro-Americans. Foremost among these people was Eleanor Roosevelt. The president himself, however, remained uncommitted to black civil rights. Furthermore, some New Deal programs functioned in ways that were definitely hostile to black Americans. The AAA, rather than benefiting black tenant farmers and sharecroppers, actually forced many of them off the land. The Federal Housing Administration (FHA) refused to guarantee mortgages on houses purchased by blacks in white neighborhoods. The CCC was racially segregated, as was much of the TVA. Finally, waiters, cooks, hospital orderlies, janitors, farm workers, and domestics, many of whom were black, were excluded from Social Security coverage and from the minimum-wage provisions of the Fair Labor Standards Act of 1938.

Antiblack Effects of the New Deal

Confronted with the mixed message of the New Deal, some blacks concluded that ultimately they could depend only on themselves and organized self-help and direct-action movements. Nowhere was the trend toward direct action more evident than in the March on Washington Movement of 1941. In that year billions of federal dollars flowed into American industry as the nation prepared for the possibility of another world war. The government funds generated many

March on Washington Movement

In 1938 Eleanor Roosevelt presented the NAACP's Spingarn Medal to the black opera star Marian Anderson. A year later when the Daughters of the American Revolution refused to let Anderson perform in Washington's Constitution Hall, Roosevelt arranged for her to sing before a much larger crowd at the Lincoln Memorial.   Metropolitan Opera Archives.

thousands of new jobs, but discrimination deprived blacks of their fair share. One executive in the aircraft industry notified black job applicants that "the Negro will be considered only as janitors and in other similar capacities." So in early 1941, A. Philip Randolph, president of the Brotherhood of Sleeping Car Porters, proposed that blacks march on the nation's capital to demand equal access to jobs in defense industries. Fearing the possibility of riots and the possibility of Communist infiltration of the movement, Roosevelt announced that if Randolph would cancel

the march, he would issue an executive order prohibiting discrimination in war industries and in the government. The result was Executive Order No. 8802, issued on June 25, 1941, which established the Fair Employment Practices Committee (FEPC).

Native Americans benefited more directly than blacks from the New Deal. Prior to Roosevelt's inauguration, many Indians had suffered hunger, disease, and even starvation. At the heart of the Indians' suffering was a 1929 ruling by the U.S. comptroller general that landless tribes were ineligible for federal aid. Arguing that these Indians were no longer a national legal responsibility, the Indian Bureau had not requested congressional funds to help them. With the coming of the New Deal, however, federal policy changed. Roosevelt appointed John Collier commissioner of Indian affairs. In the 1920s, as founder of the American Indian Defense Association, Collier had crusaded for Indian landownership; now he championed the Indian Reorganization (Wheeler-Howard) Act of 1934, which ended the allotment policy of the Dawes Severalty Act of 1887. Since passage of that bill, Indian landholdings had dropped from 138 million acres to 48 million acres. The Indian Reorganization Act sought to reverse the process by restoring lands to tribal ownership and forbidding future division of Indian lands into individual parcels. Other provisions of the act enabled tribes to obtain loans for economic development and to establish self-government. Collier also encouraged the perpetuation of Indian religions and cultures.

Mexican-Americans also suffered extreme hardship during the Depression, but no government programs benefited them. Indeed, because of a variety of government discouragements, many Mexican-Americans packed up their belongings and left the United States. According to the federal census, the Mexican-born population dropped from 617,000 in 1930 to 377,000 in 1940. One reason for this sharp decline was that many employers had changed their minds about the desirability of hiring Mexican-

American farm workers. In the 1920s farmers had boasted that Mexican-Americans were a cheap, docile labor supply and would not join unions. But in the 1930s Mexican-Americans belied their image by engaging in prolonged and sometimes bloody strikes.

The New Deal offered little help to these Mexican-Americans. The AAA was created to assist property-owning farmers, not migratory farm workers. The Wagner Act did not cover farm workers' unions, nor did the Social Security Act or the Fair Labor Standards Act cover farm laborers. One New Deal agency, the Farm Security Administration (FSA), was established in 1937 to help farm workers, in part by setting up migratory labor camps. But the FSA came too late to help Mexican-Americans, most of whom had by that time been replaced by dispossessed white farmers.

In just a few years, however, Mexican-Americans would be back. With the onset of the Second World War, the United States would again need Mexican-Americans to work in the fields and on the railroads. In 1942 the United States and Mexico would agree to the *bracero* program, whereby Mexicans would be admitted to the United States on short-term work contracts, with guarantees of minimum wages, inspected housing, and return transportation.

WOMEN, WORK, AND THE DEPRESSION

In *It's Up to the Women* (1933), Eleanor Roosevelt wrote that during economic depressions, wives and mothers often had to bear a heavier responsibility than husbands and fathers. Many women followed the maxim "Use it up, wear it out, make it do, or do without." Women bought day-old bread and cheap cuts of meat; they

Wives and Mothers Face the Depression

relined old coats with blankets and saved string, rags, and broken crockery for possible future use. In short, many families with reduced incomes were able to maintain their standard of living only because of astute women shoppers or because women substituted their own labor in the home for goods and services they used to purchase.

An irony of the 1930s was that women's assistance with family expenses did not improve their status. As the sociologists Robert and Helen Lynd observed at the time: "The men, cut adrift from their usual routine, lost much of their sense of time and dawdled helplessly and dully about the streets; while in the homes the women's world remained largely intact and the round of cooking, housecleaning, and mending became if anything more absorbing." But even while women were making increased contributions to the family, their husbands, including those without jobs, still exercised authority over the family.

What added to this irony was that during the 1930s more women than ever left the home to become paid workers in the labor force. In 1930 over 10.5 million women were paid workers; ten years later, the female labor force topped 13 million. These women obtained and held onto their jobs despite widespread hostility to their working.

Some people in the 1930s argued that male unemployment stemmed directly from women working. Magazine editor Norman Cousins wrote: "Simply fire the women, who shouldn't be working anyway, and hire the men. Presto! No unemployment. No relief rolls. No depression." And when a Gallup poll in 1936 asked whether wives should work if their husbands had jobs, 82 percent of the respondents (including 75 percent of the women) answered no. Severe job discrimination resulted from these attitudes. A 1939 survey showed that most insurance companies, banks, and public utilities had policies against married women working. From 1932 to 1937 federal law prohibited more than one family member from working for the civil service, and because wives usually earned less than their husbands, they were the ones who quit their government jobs.

Still, married women constituted 35 percent of the female work force in 1940, an increase from 29 percent in 1930 and 15 percent in 1900. But how did they find work? One explanation is that the occupations in which women were concentrated, such as clerical and sales positions and nursing, shrank less than those in manufacturing, where men had held most of the jobs. Just as important, the economy had become so segregated into "men's jobs" and "women's jobs" that men rarely competed for work performed by women.

Women were active participants in the New Deal. There was in Washington a "women's network" of government and Democratic party officials who were united by their attitudes toward social reform and the role of women in politics and government. At the center of the network was Eleanor Roosevelt, who was her husband's valued adviser. Frances Perkins, the secretary of labor, was the nation's first woman cabinet officer. Other historic New Deal appointments included the first woman federal appeals judge and the first women ambassadors.

The New Deal did take into account women's needs, but only if reminded forcefully to do so. The maximum-hour and minimum-wage provisions mandated by the NRA, for example, won women's applause. Women workers in the lowest-paying jobs, many of them laboring under sweatshop conditions, had the most to gain from these standards. At the same time, some NRA codes mandated pay differentials based on gender, so that women's minimum wages were lower than those for men. Federal relief agencies, such as the Civil Works Administration and the Federal Emergency Relief Administration, put only one woman to work for every eight to ten men placed in relief jobs. A popular New Deal program, the Civilian Conservation Corps, was limited by law to young men, and women who were low-income workers, especially in agriculture and domestic service, were not protected by the 1935 Social Security Act or the 1938 Fair Labor Standards Act.

The "Women's Network"

THE ELECTION OF 1940 AND THE LEGACY OF THE NEW DEAL

As the presidential election of 1940 approached, many people wondered whether Roosevelt would run for a third term (no president had ever served more than two terms). Roosevelt himself seemed undecided until May 1940, when Hitler's military advances apparently convinced him to stay on. The Republican candidate was Wendell Willkie, a utility executive who had been an anti–New Deal Democrat throughout most of the 1930s.

Willkie campaigned against the New Deal, contending that its meddling in the affairs of business had failed to return the nation to prosperity. He also criticized the government's lack of military preparedness. But Roosevelt pre-empted the defense issue by beefing up military and naval contracts. When Willkie reversed his approach and accused Roosevelt of being a warmonger, the president promised, "Your boys are not going to be sent into any foreign wars."

Willkie never did come up with an effective campaign issue, and when the votes were tallied on election day, Roosevelt had received 27 million votes to Willkie's 22 million. In the electoral college, Roosevelt buried Willkie 449 to 82. Although the New Deal was over, Roosevelt was still riding a wave of public approval.

Any analysis of the New Deal must begin with Franklin Delano Roosevelt. Assessments of his career varied widely during his presidency. Most historians have considered him a truly great president, citing his courage, his buoyant self-confidence, his willingness to experiment, and his capacity to inspire the nation during the most somber days of the depression. But those who have criticized him have charged that he was too pragmatic, that he failed to formulate a bold and coherent strategy of economic recovery and political and economic reform.

IMPORTANT EVENTS

1928	Herbert Hoover elected president
1929	Federal Farm Board created Stock market crash
1930	Hawley-Smoot Tariff
1931	Scottsboro affair Hoover calls for moratorium on World War I debts and reparations Iowa's Cow War

1932	Reconstruction Finance Corporation
	  established
	Ford Hunger March in Dearborn,
	  Michigan
	Sioux City milk strike
	Bonus March on Washington, D.C.
	Franklin D. Roosevelt elected
	  president

1933	13 million Americans unemployed National Bank Holiday Roosevelt's Hundred Days Agricultural Adjustment Act (AAA) Tennessee Valley Authority (TVA) National Industrial Recovery Act (NIRA)

1934	Dr. Francis Townsend's Old Age
	  Revolving Pensions plan
	Huey Long's Share Our Wealth
	  Society established
	Indian Reorganization (Wheeler-
	  Howard) Act
	Major Democratic victories in
	  congressional elections

	Father Charles Coughlin's National Union for Social Justice established
1935	Emergency Relief Appropriation Act Works Progress Administration *Schechter* v. *U.S.* invalidates NIRA National Labor Relations Act Social Security Act Huey Long assassinated Committee for Industrial Organization (CIO) established
1936	*U.S.* v. *Butler* invalidates AAA Roosevelt re-elected

1937	United Auto Workers' sit-down
	  strikes
	Roosevelt introduces his "Court-
	  packing" plan
	N.L.R.B. v. *Jones & Laughlin* upholds
	  the Wagner Act
	Memorial Day Massacre
	Farm Security Administration

1937–39	Business recession
1938	AFL expels the CIO unions Fair Labor Standards Act Roosevelt's unsuccessful "purge" of southern Democratic senators 10.4 million Americans unemployed
1940	Roosevelt re-elected
1941	March on Washington Movement Fair Employment Practices Committee (FEPC) established

Chapter 24: THE GREAT DEPRESSION AND THE NEW DEAL, 1929–1941

Though scholars have debated Roosevelt's performance, they all agree that he transformed the presidency. "Only Washington, who made the office, and

Strengthening of the Presidency

Jackson, who remade it," Clinton Rossiter, a political scientist, observed, "did more than Roosevelt to raise it to its present condition of strength, dignity, and independence." Scholars in a later era would charge that Roosevelt laid the foundations of the "imperial presidency." But whether for good or ill, Roosevelt strengthened not only the presidency but the whole federal government. "For the first time for many Americans," historian William Leuchtenburg has written, "the federal government became an institution that was directly experienced. More than state and local governments, it came to be *the* government."

The New Deal laid the foundation of America's welfare system on which subsequent presidential administrations would build. Roosevelt's was the first administration to use deficit spending as a means of stimulating the economy. The New Deal also brought about limited change in the nation's power structure by forcing business interests to share their political clout with others. Finally, the labor movement gained influence in Washington, and farmers got more of what they wanted from Congress and the White House. But there was no real increase in the power of Afro-Americans and other minorities. And if people wanted their voices to be heard, they had to organize in labor unions, trade associations, or other special-interest lobbies.

The New Deal failed in its fundamental purpose: to put people back to work. As late as 1938, over 10 million men and women were still jobless. That year

New Deal Failure to Solve Unemployment

unemployment was 19.1 percent; over the next two years it fell no lower than 14.6 percent. What plagued the nation throughout the 1930s was underconsumption: people and businesses either could not or would not purchase enough goods to sustain high levels of employment.

In the end it was not the New Deal but massive government spending during the Second World War that put people back to work. In 1941, as a result of mobilization for war, unemployment would drop to 9.9 percent, and in 1944, at the height of the war, only 1.2 percent of the labor force would be jobless.

SUGGESTIONS FOR FURTHER READING

Hoover and His Administration

William W. Barber, *From New Era to New Deal* (1986); David Burner, *Herbert Hoover* (1979); Martin L. Fausold, *The Presidency of Herbert C. Hoover* (1985); Martin L. Fausold and George T. Mazuzan, eds., *The Hoover Presidency* (1974); Ellis W. Hawley, *The Great War and the Search for a Modern Order* (1979); William E. Leuchtenburg, *The Perils of Prosperity, 1914–1932* (1958); James S. Olson, *Herbert Hoover and the Reconstruction Finance Corporation, 1931–1933* (1977); Edgar E. Robinson and Vaughn D. Bornet, *Herbert Hoover* (1975); Albert V. Romasco, *The Poverty of Abundance: Hoover, The Nation, The Depression* (1965); Richard N. Smith, *An Uncommon Man* (1984); Harris G. Warren, *Herbert Hoover and the Great Depression* (1959); Joan Hoff Wilson, *Herbert Hoover: Forgotten Progressive* (1975).

The Great Depression and Its Causes

Lester V. Chandler, *America's Greatest Depression, 1929–1941* (1970); John K. Galbraith, *The Great Crash*, 50th anniv. ed. (1979); Robert L. Heilbroner and Aaron Singer, *The Economic Transformation of America*, 2nd ed. (1984); Susan Kennedy, *The Banking Crisis of 1933* (1973); Charles Kindleberger, *The World in Depression, 1929–1939* (1973); Broadus Mitchell, *Depression Decade* (1947); Jim Potter, *The American Economy Between the Wars* (1974); George Soule, *Prosperity Decade* (1947); Gordon Thomas and Max Morgan-Witts, *The Day the Bubble Burst* (1979).

The New Deal and Hard Times

Caroline Bird, *The Invisible Scar* (1965); Paul K. Conkin, *The New Deal*, 2nd ed. (1975); Otis L. Graham, Jr., *Encore for Reform: The Old Progressives and the New Deal* (1967); Ellis W. Hawley, *The New Deal and the Problem of Monopoly* (1966); William E. Leuchtenburg, *Franklin D. Roosevelt and the New Deal* (1963); Katie Loucheim, ed., *The Making of the New Deal* (1983); Robert S. McElvaine, *The Great Depression* (1984); Albert U. Romasco, *The Politics of Recovery: Roosevelt's New Deal* (1983); Harvard Sitkoff, ed., *Fifty Years Later: The New Deal Evaluated* (1985); Studs Terkel, *Hard Times* (1970); Tom E. Terrill and Jerrold Hirsch, eds., *Such as Us: Southern Voices of the Thirties* (1978); David Tyack et al., *Public Schools in Hard Times* (1984).

Franklin D. Roosevelt

James MacGregor Burns, *Roosevelt: The Lion and the Fox* (1956); Frank Freidel, *Franklin D. Roosevelt*, 4 vols. (1952–1973); Joseph P. Lash, *Eleanor and Franklin* (1971); William E. Leuchtenburg, *In the Shadow of FDR* (1983); Arthur M. Schlesinger, Jr., *The Age of Roosevelt*, 3 vols. (1957–1960).

Alternatives to the New Deal

David H. Bennett, *Demagogues in the Depression* (1969); Alan Brinkley, *Voices of Protest: Huey Long, Father Coughlin & the Great Depression* (1982); Harvey Klehr, *The Heyday of American Communism: The Depression Decade* (1984); Mark Naison, *Communists in Harlem During the Depression* (1983); James T. Patterson, *Congressional Conservatism and the New Deal* (1967); Leo Ribuffo, *The Old Christian Right: The Protestant Far Right from the Great Depression to the Cold War* (1983); Frank A. Warren, *An Alternative Vision: The Socialist Party in the 1930s* (1976); T. Harry Williams, *Huey Long* (1969); George Wolkskill, *The Revolt of the Conservatives: A History of the American Liberty League, 1934–1940* (1962).

Agriculture

David E. Conrad, *The Forgotten Farmers: The Story of Sharecroppers in the New Deal* (1965); R. Douglas Hurt, *The Dust Bowl: An Agricultural and Social History* (1981); Theodore M. Saloutos, *The American Farmer and the New Deal* (1982); Walter J. Stein, *California and the Dust Bowl Migration* (1973); Donald Worster, *Dust Bowl: The Southern Plains in the 1930s* (1979).

Labor

John Barnard, *Walter Reuther and the Rise of the Auto Workers* (1983); Irving Bernstein, *Turbulent Years: A History of the American Worker, 1933–1941* (1969); Cletus E. Daniel, *Bitter Harvest: A History of California Farmworkers, 1870–1941* (1981); Melvin Dubofsky and Warren Van Tine, *John L. Lewis* (1977); Sidney Fine, *Sit-Down: The General Motors Strike of 1936–1937* (1969); August Meier and Elliott Rudwick, *Black Detroit and the Rise of the UAW* (1979); David Milton, *The Politics of U.S. Labor* (1980).

Nonwhites

Dan T. Carter, *Scottsboro*, rev. ed. (1979); Abraham Hoffman, *Unwanted Mexican Americans in the Great Depression: Repatriation Pressures, 1929–1939* (1974); Laurence C. Kelly, *The Assault on Assimilation: John Collier and the Origins of Indian Policy Reform* (1983); John B. Kirby, *Black Americans in the Roosevelt Era: Liberalism and Race* (1980); Carey McWilliams, *North from Mexico* (1949); Donald L. Parman, *The Navajos and the New Deal* (1975); Mark Reisler, *By the Sweat of Their Brow: Mexican Immigrant Labor in the United States, 1900–1940* (1976); Harvard Sitkoff, *A New Deal for Blacks* (1978); Nancy J. Weiss, *Farewell to the Party of Lincoln: Black Politics in the Age of FDR* (1983); Robert L. Zangrando, *The NAACP Crusade Against Lynching* (1980).

Women

Julia Kirk Blackwelder, *Women of the Depression: Caste and Culture in San Antonio, 1929–1939* (1984); Joan Hoff-Wilson and Marjorie Lightman, eds., *Without Precedent: The Life and Career of Eleanor Roosevelt* (1984); Alice Kessler-Harris, *Out to Work* (1982); Lois Scharf, *To Work and to Wed: Female Employment, Feminism, and the Great Depression* (1980); Winifred Wandersee, *Women's Work and Family Values, 1920–1940* (1981); Susan Ware, *Holding Their Own: American Women in the 1930s* (1982); Susan Ware, *Beyond Suffrage: Women in the New Deal* (1981).

Cultural and Intellectual History

Daniel Aaron, *Writers on the Left: Episodes in American Literary Communism* (1961); Andrew Bergman, *We're in the Money: Depression America and Its Films* (1971); Jerre Mangione, *The Dream and the Deal: The Federal Writers' Project, 1935–1943* (1972); Milton Meltzer, *Brother, Can You Spare a Dime?* (1969); Richard H. Pells, *Radical Visions and American Dreams: Culture and Social Thought in the Depression Years* (1973); Robert Sklar, *Movie-made America* (1975); Warren I. Sussman, "The Thirties," in Stanley Coben and Lorman Ratner, eds., *The Development of an American Culture*, 2nd ed. (1983), 215–260.

CHAPTER 25

DIPLOMACY
IN A BROKEN WORLD
1920–1941

On December 24, 1921, prisoner #9653 strode out of Atlanta's federal penitentiary. After a train ride to Washington, D.C., he entered the White House to meet the man who had just pardoned him. "Well," said the good-natured President Warren G. Harding, "I have heard so damned much about you, Mr. Debs, that I am now very glad to meet you personally." They had a good talk, and Eugene V. Debs told reporters that Harding was a "gentleman" who "possesses human impulses." By releasing Debs, the most prominent of the jailed antiwar critics, Harding was telling the people that the United States was liquidating the war and returning to what he called "normalcy."

The president took several other steps in November 1921 that further demonstrated his resolve to put the war behind him. He buried the Unknown Soldier in Arlington Cemetery to initiate, he said, "a new and lasting era of peace." He signed peace treaties with the defeated Central Powers, until then technically still at war with the United States because the Senate had rejected the Treaty of Paris with its offending League provisions. That month, too, he opened an international conference in Washington, where the United States insisted on a major reduction in naval armaments to ensure a stable world order.

Harding's desire to shove the war into the past and his emphasis on avoiding entanglements with Europe should not be interpreted to mean that Americans cut themselves off from international affairs after the First World War. To be sure, Americans were disillusioned with their war experience. But they remained quite active in the world in the 1920s—from gunboats on Chinese rivers to negotiations in the financial centers of Europe to interventions in Latin America. The most useful description of interwar foreign policy is *independent internationalism:* that is, the United States was active on a global scale but retained its independence of action, its traditional unilateralism.

At the same time, many Americans called themselves *isolationists.* By that label they meant that they wanted to isolate themselves from Europe's political squabbles, from military alliances and interventions, and from commitments like the League of Nations that might restrict their freedom of choice. Americans, then, were isolationists in their desire to avoid war, but independent internationalists in their behavior in foreign affairs.

The desire to avoid war led American leaders to search for nonmilitary means to exercise power. In the aftermath of the First World War, Americans had grown disenchanted with military methods of achieving order and protecting American prosperity and security. American diplomats thus put increasing emphasis on conferences, moral lectures and calls for peace, nonrecognition of disapproved regimes, arms control, and economic and financial ties in accord with the principle of the Open Door. They pulled American troops out of Caribbean states, fashioning a Good Neighbor policy that would reduce hostility to United States influence in the region.

American policies and power, however, failed to create a stable world order. The debts and reparations tangle left over from the First World War bedeviled world finance and trade. More than any other event, the Great Depression of the 1930s undercut stability. The global economic cataclysm spawned revolutions in Latin America and political extremism, militarism, and war in Europe and Asia. The peace and disarmament agreements of the 1920s were smashed. In answer especially to the turmoil in Europe sparked by Germany's drive to restore its power, the United States passed the Neutrality Acts.

Yet in the late 1930s, Americans, along with President Franklin D. Roosevelt, changed their minds. Perceiving Germany and Japan as terrible menaces to the national interest, Roosevelt first appealed for preparedness and then begged the nation to abandon its neutrality in order to aid Britain and France. To deter Japanese expansion in the Pacific, Roosevelt cut off supplies of vital American products like oil. But economic warfare intensified antagonisms. Japan's surprise attack on Pearl Harbor finally brought the United States into the Second World War.

THE SEARCH FOR PEACE AND ORDER IN THE 1920s

In the early 1920s Secretary of State Charles Evans Hughes predicted that "there will be no permanent peace unless economic satisfactions are enjoyed." Like the nation's business leaders, Hughes expected American economic expansion to bring about world stability: out of economic prosperity would spring a world free from political extremes, revolution, aggression, and war. The government thus facilitated business activities abroad.

United States economic influence became conspicuous after the First World War. By the late 1920s the United States produced about half the world's industrial goods, ranked first among exporters, and also acted as the financial capital of the world. To many foreigners, this American economic expansionism was imperialistic. Argentine diplomat and critic Manuel Ugarte went so far as to assert that the United States was a new Rome: it annexed wealth rather than territory.

Economic Expansion

Other foreigners, however, were grateful to Americans for a helping hand. Europe lay in shambles at the end of the war. From 1914 to 1921 there were 60 million casualties in Europe from world war, civil war, massacre, epidemic, and famine. Crops, livestock, factories, trains, forests, bridges—little had been spared. The plight of Europeans drew American sympathies and aid in the form of food.

But if Americans won praise from Europeans for their humanitarianism, they earned the nickname

funky

Uncle Shylock for their handling of war debts and

First World War Debts and Reparations

reparations, an issue that dogged international relations for a decade. Twenty-eight nations were tangled in the web of inter-Allied debts, which totaled $26.5 billion, about half of it owed to the United States. Europeans urged Americans to forgive the debts as a magnanimous contribution to the war. But American leaders insisted on repayment.

The debts question was linked to Germany's $33 billion reparations bill. Hobbled by inflation and economic disorder, Germany had begun to default on its payments. Americans grew worried that German economic troubles would spawn radicalism. To keep Germany afloat, American bankers loaned millions of dollars to the floundering nation. A triangular relationship developed: American investors' money flowed to Germany; German reparations payments went to the Allies; the Allies then paid some of their debts to the United States. The American-crafted Dawes Plan of 1924 greased the financial tracks by reducing Germany's annual payments, extending the repayment period, and providing still more loans. And the United States gradually scaled down Allied obligations, cutting the debt by half during the 1920s.

But the triangular arrangement was dependent on continued German borrowing in the United States. In 1928 and 1929, however, American lending abroad declined sharply as investors plowed their money into the more lucrative stock market. The American-negotiated Young Plan of 1929, which reduced the total of Germany's reparations, salvaged little as the international economy sputtered and collapsed. By 1931, when Hoover declared a moratorium on payments, the Allies had paid back only $2.6 billion. Wracked by depression, they defaulted on the rest.

In the end, American economic power had proved unable to sustain a healthy world economy. But many nations shared responsibility for the failure. The selfish and vengeful Europeans might have trimmed Germany's huge indemnity. The Germans might

"Come on in. I'll treat you right. I used to know your daddy."
Clarence D. Batchelor's haunting antiwar cartoon recalling the human tragedy of the First World War. The artist won a Pulitzer Prize for his statement. Copyright 1987 New York News Inc. Reprinted with permission.

have borrowed less from abroad and taxed themselves more. The Bolsheviks might have agreed to pay rather than repudiate Russia's $4 billion indebtedness. And Americans might have tried for a comprehensive, multinational settlement and lowered their tariffs, giving Europeans a market in which to earn the money to pay off their debt.

American influence also failed to curb militarism and prevent war. The nation's efforts began at the Washington Conference (1921–1922). There the United States discussed with eight other nations limits on naval armaments. Britain, the United States, and Japan, the three top naval powers, faced a costly naval arms race, and they welcomed the opportunity to deflect it. In the Five-Power Treaty the delegates set a ten-year moratorium on the construction of large, or capital, ships, and established a total tonnage ratio of 5:5:3:1.75:1.75 among the five top nations (Britain, United States, Japan, France, Italy). The first three nations actually agreed to dismantle some existing vessels to meet the ratio. They also pledged not to build new fortifications in their Pacific possessions (such as the Philippines for the United States).

Several other agreements were reached at the conference. The Nine-Power Treaty reaffirmed the Open Door in China, recognizing Chinese sovereignty. In the Four-Power Treaty, the United States, England, Japan, and France agreed to respect each other's Pacific possessions and to consult in the event of aggression in Asia. In another agreement Japan pledged to pull back from Shandong and Russian Siberia. But although the treaties signed at Washington provided a rare example of mutual disarmament, they did not, critics pointed out, limit submarines, destroyers, or cruisers, and there were no provisions for enforcement of the Open Door declaration.

Peace advocates also placed their hopes in the Kellogg-Briand Pact of 1928, eventually signed by sixty-two nations. The signatories agreed simply to "condemn recourse to war for the solution of international controversies, and renounce it as an instrument of national policy. . . ." The treaty's backers billed it as a first step in a long journey toward international cooperation and the outlawry of war. Lacking provisions for enforcement, however, it proved impotent in the 1930s.

The League of Nations, also looked to as a peacemaker, exhibited a conspicuous feebleness, not only because the United States refused to join, but because members themselves usually chose not to use it to settle disputes. Starting in the mid-1920s, however,

American officials did participate discreetly in League meetings on public health, prostitution, drug trafficking, and other such questions. And individual jurists like Charles Evans Hughes served on the World Court in Geneva, although the United States refused to join that institution also.

SPHERE OF INFLUENCE
IN LATIN AMERICA

In Latin America the interwar themes of independent internationalism, isolationism, nonmilitary means, and the destabilizing impact of the Great Depression were prominent. Before the First World War the United States had thrown an imperial net over much of the region. By the 1920s the supposed benefits of American expansionism—hospitals, schools, roads, telephones, and irrigation systems—were evident in much of Latin America, but United States imperialism meant meddling in the internal affairs of Latin American nations. United States financial advisers supervised government budgets in the Caribbean, and in 1920 American soldiers occupied Cuba, the Dominican Republic, Haiti, Panama, and Nicaragua.

Yet these military expeditions to Latin America were becoming unpopular and counterproductive. Congressional critics complained about the denial of self-determination to Latin Americans and the dispatch of troops abroad without congressional approval. Businesspeople feared the destruction of property by angry Latins. And in 1932 Secretary of State Henry L. Stimson, who was concerned about Japanese incursions in China, worried that similar intervention in Latin America by the United States would render his protests meaningless.

Turning away pragmatically from military intervention, then, the United States sought less controversial methods of maintaining its influence in Latin

Good Neighbor Policy — America: Pan-Americanism; support for strong native leaders; the training of national guards; economic penetration; Export-Import Bank loans; and, when necessary, political subversion. Although the process began before his presidency, Roosevelt gave it a name in 1933: the Good Neighbor policy. It meant that the United States would be less blatant in its domination—less willing to defend exploitive business practices, less eager to send in military expeditions, and less wary of consultation with Latin Americans.

Nevertheless, the training of national guards went hand in hand with support of dictators: many Latin American dictators rose to power through the ranks of a national guard trained by the United States. For example, before **Training of National Guards** the United States withdrew its troops from the Dominican Republic in 1924, American personnel created a constabulary. One of its first officers was Rafael Leónidas Trujillo, who became head of the National Army in 1928. Trujillo became president in 1930 through fraud and intimidation and ruled the Dominican Republic with an iron fist until his assassination in 1961. "He may be an S.O.B.," Roosevelt remarked candidly, "but he is our S.O.B."

In Nicaragua the experience was similar. The United States occupied Nicaragua from 1912 to 1925 and returned in late 1926 during a civil war. The justification for United States involvement was the need to clean up and stabilize Nicaragua's politics. When the marines departed in 1933, they left behind a powerful national guard headed by General Anastasio Somoza. With American backing, the Somoza family ruled Nicaragua from 1936 to 1979 through corruption, political suppression, and torture.

The long Marine Corps occupation of black Haiti from 1915 to 1934 had similar negative results. American officials censored the Haitian press; manipulated elections; wrote the consti- **Occupation of Haiti** tution; jailed or killed thousands of protesters; managed government finances; and created a national

From the leftist magazine New Masses *came this critique of United States intervention in Nicaragua, a nation occupied by American troops, 1912–1925 and 1926–1933. Library of Congress.*

guard. Under American supervision, the National City Bank of New York became the owner of the Haitian Banque Nationale and the United States became Haiti's largest trading partner.

American black leaders were particularly alert to Haitian issues. Just before his death, Booker T. Washington spoke of the "benevolence" of American intentions and relished the prospect of establishing another Tuskegee Institute in the island nation. But W. E. B. Du Bois angrily criticized the "rape" of Haiti. And James Weldon Johnson of the National Association for the Advancement of Colored People reported that Haitians forced to work without pay (the *corvée* system) to build roads "were in the same category with the convicts in the Negro chain gangs" of the American South.

When Haitians resorted to violent protest against American rule in 1929, President Hoover vetoed a further military build-up and began plans to withdraw American soldiers. His investigative commission concluded: "The failure of the Occupation to understand the social problems of Haiti, its brusque attempt to implant democracy by drill and harrow, its determination to set up a middle class . . . explain why, in part, the high hopes of our good works in this land have not been realized."

The Cubans, too, grew restless under American domination. By 1929 American investments in the Caribbean nation totaled $1.5 billion, up from $220 million in 1913. The American military uniform was conspicuous at the naval base at Guantánamo Bay as well. But during the Cuban revolution of 1933, in open defiance of the American warships cruising offshore, rebels made Professor Ramón Grau San Martín president. Grau declared the Platt Amendment, which accorded the United States the right to intervene in Cuban affairs, null and void, seized some American-owned mills, failed to repay American bank loans, and talked of land reform. A startled United States refused to recognize the new government and encouraged a coup by army sergeant Fulgencio Batista in 1934. During the dictatorial Batista era, which lasted until 1959, Cuba protected American investments and granted the United States military sites. In return it received military aid, loans, abrogation of the Platt Amendment, and a favorable sugar tariff.

Domination of Cuba

The pattern was different in Mexico. In 1917 the Mexicans adopted a new constitution specifying that all "land and waters" and all subsoil raw materials (like oil) belonged to the Mexican nation—a clear threat to American landholdings and petroleum interests. Here was a unique case: a weak, undeveloped Latin American nation issuing a direct challenge to the powerful United States.

Confrontation with Mexico

Washington and Mexico City wrangled for years over the rights of American economic interests. Then, in 1938, Mexico boldly expropriated the prop-

erty of all foreign-owned petroleum companies. The United States countered by reducing purchases of Mexican silver and encouraging a business boycott of the upstart nation. But President Roosevelt decided to compromise, because he feared the Mexicans would sell their oil to the aggressors Germany and Japan. In 1941 the United States conceded that Mexico owned its raw materials and could treat them as it saw fit; and Mexico compensated American companies for their lost property. American power had been diminished, setting a precedent to which Latin American nationalists would refer in the future.

Roosevelt's movement toward nonmilitary methods—the Good Neighbor policy—paid off in the Declaration of Panama (1939), wherein Latin American governments drew a security line around the hemisphere and warned aggressors away. In exchange for more trade and foreign aid, Latin American governments also reduced their sales of raw materials to Germany, Japan, and Italy and increased shipments to the United States. On the eve of the war, then, the United States' sphere of influence was virtually intact, ready to back American military and diplomatic policies.

THE GREAT DEPRESSION AND GROWING ISOLATIONISM

Cordell Hull, secretary of state from 1933 to 1944, liked to say that the character of international relations derived from economic conditions. In the 1930s the effect of economics was particularly apparent. The depression wrecked international finance and trade. In the late 1920s, when First World War debts and reparations proved too much for the shattered European economies to bear, international finance collapsed. Banks failed and world trade faltered.

The United States actually added to the burdens

of the world economy with the Hawley-Smoot Tariff (1930), a selfish move that shut off the American market to European nations struggling to earn cash to pay off their war debts. President Hoover's moratorium on debts payments in 1931 came too late. By 1932 about twenty-five nations had retaliated against the American tariff by imposing similar restrictions on American imports. In short, economic nationalism gained momentum.

Cordell Hull was beside himself over the world's conspicuous nose dive into economic nationalism. Calling the protective tariff the "king of evils," Hull successfully pressed Congress to pass the Reciprocal Trade Agreements Act in 1934. The act, which would guide American economic foreign policy thereafter, empowered the president to reduce American tariffs by as much as 50 percent through special agreements with foreign countries. The central feature of the act was the *most-favored-nation principle,* whereby the United States was entitled to the lowest tariff rate set by a nation with which it had an agreement. In 1934 Hull also sponsored the creation of the Export-Import Bank, a government agency that provided loans to foreigners for the purchase of American goods. Hull's ambitious programs stood as rare examples of internationalism in an era of rampant nationalism.

Cordell Hull's Economic Foreign Policy

As depression-induced authoritarianism, racial hatred, and military expansion descended upon Europe and Asia, Americans reasserted their isolationist beliefs. A 1937 Gallup poll found that nearly two-thirds of the people asked about the First World War thought American participation had been a mistake. Conservative isolationists feared higher taxes and increased federal power if the nation went to war again. Liberal isolationists spoke of the need to give domestic problems priority. Other critics feared that by attempting to spread democracy abroad, Americans would lose it at home.

Isolationist Thought

Isolationism was a truly national phenomenon that cut across socioeconomic, ethnic, party, and sectional lines and attracted a majority of the American people. What united isolationists was the opinion that there were alternatives to American involvement in another futile Old World war. Only when events grew uglier and more menacing toward the end of the Depression decade would many, like President Roosevelt, change their minds.

Some liberal isolationists, critical of business practices at home, charged that corporate "merchants of death" were undermining the national interest by assisting the aggressors. From 1934 to 1936 a congressional committee chaired by Senator Gerald P. Nye held hearings on the role of business interests in the American decision to enter the First World War. The hearings did not prove that businesspeople and financiers had dragged reluctant Americans into the war, but they did uncover evidence that corporations had bribed foreign politicians to improve arms sales in the 1920s and 1930s and had lobbied against arms control. And records show that isolationists were correct to suspect American business ties with Nazi Germany and fascist Italy. Twenty-six of the top one hundred American corporations in 1937 had contractual agreements with Germany. And after Italy attacked Ethiopia in 1935, American petroleum, copper, and iron and steel scrap exports to Italy increased substantially, despite Roosevelt's call for a moral embargo on those items.

Business Ties with the Aggressors

EUROPEAN UPHEAVAL AND AMERICAN NEUTRALITY

In depression-wracked Germany, where 6 million workers were unemployed in the early 1930s, Adolf Hitler came to power. Like Benito Mussolini, who had gained control of Italy in 1922, Hitler was a fascist. Fascism (called Nazism, or National Socialism, in Germany) was a collection of ideas and prejudices that included supremacy of the state over the individual; of dictatorship over democracy; of authoritarianism over freedom of speech; and of militarism and war over peace. The Nazis vowed not only to revive German economic and military strength, but to "purify" the German "race" of Jewish influence, for which they blamed Germany's problems.

Hitler's Germany

In 1933, resentful of the punitive terms of the 1919 Treaty of Paris, Hitler pulled Germany out of the League of Nations, ended reparations payments, and began to rearm. Secretly laying plans for the conquest of neighboring states, he watched admiringly as Mussolini's troops invaded the African nation of Ethiopia in 1935. The next year Hitler ordered his goose-stepping troopers into the Rhineland, an area the Treaty of Paris had declared demilitarized. Germany's timid neighbor France did not resist.

Soon the aggressors began to join hands. In the fall of 1936 Italy and Germany formed an alliance called the Rome-Berlin Axis. Shortly thereafter Germany and Japan united against Russia in the Anti-Comintern Pact. To these events Britain and France responded with a policy of appeasement, hoping to curb Hitler's expansionist appetite by permitting him a few nibbles. But the policy eventually proved disastrous; taking advantage of European caution, the German leader continually raised his demands.

In those hair-trigger times, a civil war in Spain turned into an international struggle. From 1936 to 1939 the Loyalist Republicans battled the fascist-backed insurgents under Francisco Franco. Hitler and Mussolini sent military aid to Franco; Russia assisted the Loyalists. France and Britain held to the fiction of a nonintervention pledge that even Italy and Germany had signed. And about three thousand American volunteers known as the Lincoln Battalion joined the fight on the side of the Republicans. When Franco won in 1939, his victory tightened the grip of fascism on the European continent.

Early in 1938 Hitler once again tested the limits of European patience when he sent his soldiers into Austria to annex that nation. In September of the

The Nazi leader Adolf Hitler (1889–1945) in a propagandistic German painting. Hitler is surrounded by the images that came to symbolize hate, genocide, and war: Nazi flags with emblems of the swastika; Iron Cross on the dictator's pocket; saluting Nazi troops. U.S. Army.

same year he seized the Sudeten region of Czechoslovakia. Appeasement reached its peak that month at the Munich Conference when France and Britain, without consulting the helpless Czechs, agreed to allow Hitler this one last territorial bite. British Prime Minister Neville Chamberlain returned home to proclaim "peace in our time," confident he had satiated the dictator. But in March 1939 Hitler swallowed the rest of Czechoslovakia. Poland was next on his list. Scuttling appeasement, London and Paris announced they would stand by their ally. Undaunted, Germany neutralized Russia by signing the Nazi-Soviet Pact and with Russia struck Poland on September 1. Britain and France declared war on Germany two days later. The Second World War had begun.

President Franklin D. Roosevelt witnessed these events with sadness and anxiety. Like his famous older cousin Theodore, Franklin as a young man

Franklin D. Roosevelt

believed that the United States should exert leadership in the world community and flex its military muscle to ensure American security and prosperity. He was an expansionist and interventionist who had imbibed the belief that Americans knew what was best for other societies. Like most Americans during the interwar period, Roosevelt talked less about preparedness and more about disarmament and the horrors of war. When Europe and Asia were torn by economic and political crisis and war in the 1930s, Roosevelt at first declared that the United States should avoid foreign squabbles and he signed the Neutrality Acts.

However much they opposed fascism and disapproved aggression, Roosevelt and his fellow Americans tried to stay clear of the recurrent crises of the 1930s. With each crisis isolationist

Neutrality Acts

sentiment rose. In a series of acts Congress sought to protect the nation by stopping contacts that had compromised American neutrality two decades earlier. The Neutrality Act of 1935 prohibited arms shipments to either side in a war once the president had declared the existence of belligerency. The Neutrality Act of 1936 forbade loans to belligerents. A joint resolution in 1937 declared the United States neutral in the Spanish Civil War; Roosevelt then embargoed arms shipments to both sides. And finally, the Neutrality Act of 1937 introduced the cash-and-carry principle: warring nations wishing to trade with the United States would have to pay cash for their purchases and carry the goods away in their own ships. The act also forbade Americans from traveling on vessels of belligerent nations.

But Roosevelt was deeply troubled by the arrogant behavior of the "three bandit nations," Germany, Italy, and Japan. He was disgusted by Nazi persecution of the Jews and by Japanese slaughter of Chinese civilians. Privately he snarled against the refusal of the British and French to collar Hitler in their own backyards. And he worried that the United States was militarily ill-prepared to confront the aggressors.

The United States had not been neglecting its military. Roosevelt's New Deal public works programs included millions for the construction of new ships. In 1935 the president requested the largest peacetime defense budget in American history; three years later, in the wake of Munich, he asked Congress for funds to build up the air force. The president also began to cast about for ways to encourage the British and French to show more backbone. One result was his agreement in January 1939 to sell bombers to France.

In his annual message early in 1939, the president lashed out at the international lawbreakers. Soon afterward he urged Congress to repeal the arms embargo and permit the sale of muni-

Roosevelt Proposes Repeal of Arms Embargo

tions to belligerents on a cash-and-carry basis. Roosevelt saw repeal as an aid to Britain, which dominated the seas. And although he did not yet have the votes to win repeal, he stepped up his public condemnation of the aggressors.

When Europe fell into the abyss of war in September 1939, Roosevelt declared neutrality. But unlike Woodrow Wilson, he did not ask Americans to be neutral in thought, and he pressed again for repeal of the arms embargo. After much lobbying, debate, and bipartisan consultation, however, Congress revised the neutrality legislation. In November 1939 it lifted the embargo on contraband and approved cash-and-carry exports of arms. Now Roosevelt was ready to aid the Allies—short of war—and to challenge the isolationists more boldly.

Soviet Russia was a special problem in American foreign relations. Following Wilsonian precedent, the Republican administration of the 1920s had not recognized the Soviet government. To

Relations with Russia

Americans the Communists were also godless, radical malcontents bent on destroying the American way of life. Yet American businesses began to enter the Soviet marketplace, offering technology and machinery. By 1930 Russia was the largest buyer of American agricultural and industrial equipment.

In the early 1930s, however, trade began to slump. To stimulate business and help the United States pull out of the depression, some businesspeople began to lobby for diplomatic recognition of Russia. President Roosevelt, believing that it was foolish not to recognize such a major country, agreed that a change in policy was necessary. He also recognized that closer Russian-American ties might deter Japanese aggression in Asia. For these reasons the United States recognized the Soviet Union in 1933.

A New Order in Asia

If United States power was massive in Latin America and limited in Europe, it was minuscule in Asia. Still, there were American interests in that region that official Washington believed it needed to defend: the Philippines and Pacific islands; religious missions; trade and investments; and the Open Door in China. Americans increasingly saw the Japanese as a threat to these interests, and specifically as strong-willed expansionists bent on subjugating China and unhinging the Open Door doctrine of equal trade and investment opportunity.

The highly nationalistic Chinese Revolution of 1911 still rumbled in the 1920s. In the late 1920s Jiang Jieshi (Chiang Kai-shek) emerged as the pre-eminent leader of this convulsed

Rise of Jiang Jieshi in China
nation. Jiang ousted Communists from the Guomindong party, forcing Mao Zedong and his followers to flee to the hills. Americans applauded his anti-Bolshevik measures and his conversion in 1930 to Christianity. Satisfied with Jiang, United States officials signed a treaty in 1928 restoring to the Chinese control of tariffs.

Japanese-American relations had seldom been cordial. As the Japanese intruded farther and farther into China in their drive for raw materials, they collided with America's Open Door

Japanese Seizure of Manchuria
policy. Relations deteriorated after the Japanese military seized Manchuria in September 1931 (see map, page 462). Only nominally a Chinese region, Manchuria was important to the Japanese both as a buffer against the Russians and as a vital source of coal, iron, timber, and food. More than half of Japan's foreign investments were in Manchuria. Lacking the power to force Japanese withdrawal, the United States responded with a moral lecture called the Stimson Doctrine (1932), which declared that the United States would not recognize any impairment of China's sovereignty or of the Open Door policy.

Hardly cowed by protests from Western capitals, Japan continued to harry China. In mid-1937 full-scale Sino-Japanese war erupted. In an effort to help China, Roosevelt refused to declare the existence of war, thus not invoking the Neutrality Acts and thereby allowing the Chinese to buy weapons in the United States. In a stirring speech denouncing the aggressors in October 1937, he called for a "quarantine" to curb the "epidemic of world lawlessness."

Japan's declaration of a "New Order" in Asia "banged, barred, and bolted" the Open Door, as one American official observed. Alarmed, the Roosevelt administration found small ways to assist China and thwart Japan in 1938 and 1939. Military equipment flowed to the Chinese, as did a $25 million loan. Secretary of State Hull declared a moral embargo against the shipment of airplanes to Japan. The navy continued to grow, helped by a billion-dollar congressional appropriation in 1938. And in mid-1939 the United States abrogated the 1911 Japanese-American trade treaty. Yet America continued to ship oil, cotton, and machinery to Japan. The administration hesitated to initiate economic sanctions for fear they would spark an Asian war at a time when the more serious threat was emanating from Berlin. When war broke out in

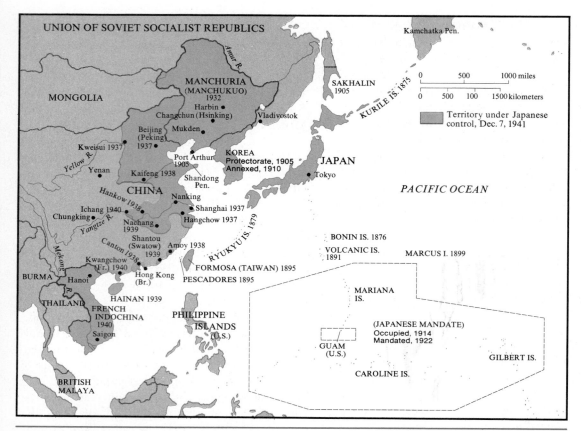

Japanese Expansion Before Pearl Harbor

Europe in 1939, Japanese-American relations were stalemated.

◉N THE BRINK, 1939–1941

Polls showed that Americans strongly favored the Allies, and that most supported aid to Britain and France; but the great majority emphatically wanted the United States to remain at peace. Troubled by this conflicting advice—defeat Hitler, aid the Allies, but stay out of war—the president between

1939 and 1941 gradually moved the United States from neutrality to undeclared war and then to war itself.

During those tense months of inching toward belligerency, isolationist sentiment declined. Alarmed by the swift defeat of one European nation after another, some liberals left the isolationist fold, which became more and more the province of conservatives. Die-hard isolationists organized the America First Committee in fall 1940; interventionists, meanwhile, joined the Committee to Defend America by Aiding the Allies (formed in mid-1940).

Decline of Isolationism

In September 1939 Poland succumbed to German

Chapter 25: DIPLOMACY IN A BROKEN WORLD, 1920–1941

The German Advance, 1939–1942

stormtroopers in two weeks (see map). In November Soviet Russia marched into Finland, prompting Roosevelt to denounce "this dreadful rape"; by March 1940 Finland had been defeated. The following month Germany invaded Denmark and Norway, a month later the Netherlands and Belgium. In July 1940 France collapsed. Would England be next?

In the meantime, Roosevelt began to aid the faltering Allies. In May 1940 he ordered the sale of surplus First World War equipment to Britain and France. In July he cultivated bipartisan support for the war by naming Republicans Henry L. Stimson and Frank Knox, ardent backers of aid to the Allies, secretaries of war and navy respectively. In September he announced that by executive agreement he

was trading fifty old American destroyers for leases to eight British bases, including Newfoundland, Bermuda, and Jamaica. Two weeks later he signed into law the Selective Training and Service Act, the first peacetime military draft in American history.

Through the fall Roosevelt spoke of the need for a huge foreign aid program to save England from the Nazis. The United States, he implored, must become the "great arsenal of democracy." In January 1941 the contro-

Lend-Lease Act

versial Lend-Lease bill was introduced in Congress. The president argued that America had a moral obligation to provide the British with weapons, just as a neighbor lends a garden hose to fight a fire. The bill cleared

Congress in March 1941, and $7 billion was appropriated. By the end of the war $50 billion in Lend-Lease aid had been distributed, mostly to England.

To ensure the safe delivery of Lend-Lease goods, Roosevelt ordered the navy to patrol halfway across the Atlantic and sent American troops to Greenland. Then a stunning turn of events in Europe spurred a new decision. In June 1941 Hitler struck his erstwhile ally Russia. By November Lend-Lease aid was flowing to appreciative Russians.

In August 1941 Churchill and Roosevelt met for four days off Newfoundland. At this conference the two leaders wrote the Atlantic Charter, a set of war

Atlantic Charter

aims reminiscent of Wilsonianism: collective security, disarmament, self-determination, economic co-operation, and freedom of the seas. Later, on January 1, 1942, twenty-six nations signed the Declaration of the United Nations, pledging themselves to fulfill the charter.

In September 1941 the United States moved closer to an open confrontation with Germany. After a German U-boat fired at the destroyer *Greer*, Roosevelt denounced the act of "piracy" and declared that the United States would convoy British merchant ships all the way to Iceland. He failed to mention that the *Greer* had been trailing the submarine, giving its position to British airplanes. The next month another American destroyer, the *Reuben James*, was torpedoed, and over one hundred sailors lost their lives. Congress responded by scrapping the cash-and-carry program and authorizing armed American merchant ships to transport munitions to England.

In retrospect it seems ironic that the Second World War came to the United States via Asia, where Roosevelt so wanted to avoid it in order to concentrate American resources on the defeat

Cutoff of Trade with Japan

of Germany. In September 1940 Americans read the unwelcomed news of the Tripartite Pact, an alliance among Germany, Italy, and Japan. Roosevelt slapped an embargo on shipments of aviation fuel and scrap metal to Japan. The next summer Washington responded to Japanese occupation of French Indo-

china by freezing Japanese assets in the United States. The action virtually ended Japanese trade with the United States, making it impossible for Japan to secure much needed American oil.

Tokyo recommended a high-level meeting between President Roosevelt and the prime minister, Prince Konoye, but the United States rejected the idea. American officials insisted that the Japanese first agree to respect China's sovereignty and territorial integrity, and to honor the Open Door policy—in short, to get out of China. Roosevelt also told the Japanese ambassador that his nation would have to withdraw from the Tripartite Pact.

As the president's advisers tried to string out Japanese-American talks in order to buy time to fortify the Philippines and check the fascists in Europe,

Attack on Pearl Harbor

cryptographers worked on the Japanese code ("Operation Magic"). On breaking the diplomatic code, experts informed Roosevelt that Japan would go to war if the oil embargo was not lifted. Then on December 1 the president was informed that Japanese task forces were being ordered into battle. Secretary Stimson explained later that the United States let Japan fire the first shot so as "to have the full support of the American people" and "so that there should remain no doubt in anyone's mind as to who were the aggressors." Fearing that they could not win a prolonged war, the Japanese plotted a daring raid on Pearl Harbor in Hawaii. A flotilla of Japanese aircraft carriers crossed three thousand miles of ocean, and on the morning of December 7, planes stamped with the Rising Sun swept down on the unsuspecting American naval base, killing more than 2,400 people, sinking several battleships, and smashing aircraft.

But how could Pearl Harbor have happened? Americans asked. Roosevelt did not, as his critics later charged, conspire to leave the fleet vulnerable to attack, so the United States could enter the Second World War through the "back door" of Asia. The base was unready—not on red alert—because a message of warning from Washington had been sent by Western Union telegraph rather than by navy cable

IMPORTANT EVENTS

1921	Washington Conference opens
1922	Mussolini comes to power in Italy
1924	Dawes Plan for German reparations
	U.S. departs Dominican Republic
1926	American troops occupy Nicaragua
1927	Jiang Jieshi attacks Communists in China
1928	Kellogg-Briand Pact
1929	Onset of the Great Depression
	Young Plan for German reparations
1930	Hawley-Smoot Tariff
1931	Japan seizes Manchuria
1932	Stimson Doctrine
1933	Hitler comes to power in Germany
	U.S. recognition of Soviet Russia
	Good Neighbor policy announced
	U.S. subverts Cuban revolution
1934	Reciprocal Trade Agreements Act
	Export-Import Bank founded
1935	Italy invades Ethiopia
	Neutrality Act
1936	U.S. votes for nonintervention at Pan-American Conference
	Outbreak of Spanish Civil War
	Neutrality Act
1937	Neutrality Act
	Roosevelt's quarantine speech
1938	Mexico nationalizes American-owned oil companies
	Munich Conference
1939	Nazi-Soviet pact
	Germany invades Poland
	Second World War begins
	U.S. repeals arms embargo
1940	Soviets invade Finland
	Committee to Defend America by Aiding the Allies formed
	Tripartite Pact
	Destroyer-bases deal
	America First Committee formed
	Selective Service Act
1941	Lend-Lease Act
	Germany attacks Russia
	U.S. freezes Japanese assets
	Atlantic Charter
	Greer incident
	Japan attacks Pearl Harbor

and arrived too late. Base commanders were relaxed, thinking Hawaii, so far from Japan, an unlikely target for all-out attack. They expected the assault to come at British Malaya, Thailand, or the Philippines. Mistakes were made, but there was not a conspiracy.

On December 8, referring to the previous day as a "date which will live in infamy," Roosevelt asked Congress for a declaration of war against Japan. Three days later Germany and Italy declared war against the United States. The war had become a global conflict. As they had so many times before, Americans flocked to the colors. Isolationists now joined the president in spirited calls for victory. "We are going to win the war, and we are going to win the peace that follows," Roosevelt predicted.

SUGGESTIONS FOR FURTHER READING

General and 1920s Foreign Policy

Thomas H. Buckley, *The United States and the Washington Conference, 1921–1922* (1970); Frank Costigliola, *Awkward Dominion: American Political, Economic, and Cultural Relations with Europe, 1919–1933* (1984); Robert H. Ferrell, *American Diplomacy in the Great Depression* (1957); Arnold A. Offner, *The Origins of the Second World War* (1975); Emily S. Rosenberg, *Spreading the American Dream* (1982); Raymond Sontag, *A Broken World, 1919–1939* (1971).

The Peace Movement and Kellogg-Briand Pact

Charles Chatfield, *For Peace and Justice: Pacifism in America, 1914–1941* (1971); Charles DeBenedetti, *The Peace Reform in American History* (1980); Charles DeBenedetti, *Origins of the Modern American Peace Movement, 1915–1929* (1978); Robert H. Ferrell, *Peace in Their Time* (1952); Harold Josephson, *James T. Shotwell and the Rise of Internationalism in America* (1976).

The United States in the World Economy

Frederick Adams, *Economic Diplomacy* (1976); Derek H. Aldcroft, *From Versailles to Wall Street, 1919–1929* (1977); Herbert Feis, *The Diplomacy of the Dollar, 1919–1932* (1950); Lloyd C. Gardner, *Economic Aspects of New Deal Diplomacy* (1964); Michael J. Hogan, *Informal Entente: The Private Structure of Cooperation in Anglo-American Economic Diplomacy, 1918–1928* (1977); Charles Kindleberger, *The World in Depression* (1973); Mira Wilkins, *The Maturing of Multinational Enterprise* (1974); Joan Hoff Wilson, *American Business and Foreign Policy, 1920–1933* (1971).

Latin America

Bruce J. Calder, *The Impact of Intervention* (1984) (on Dominican Republic); Alton Frye, *Nazi Germany and the American Hemisphere, 1933–1941* (1967); Irwin F. Gellman, *Good Neighbor Diplomacy* (1979); David Green, *The Containment of Latin America* (1971); Walter LaFeber, *Inevitable Revolutions: The United States in Central America* (1983); Lester D. Langley, *The United States and the Caribbean, 1900–1970* (1980); Neil Macaulay, *The Sandino Affair* (1967); Stephen G. Rabe, *The Road to OPEC* (1982) (on Venezuela); Robert I. Rotberg, *Haiti* (1971); Ramon Ruiz, *Cuba* (1968); Karl M. Schmitt, *Mexico and the United States, 1821–1973* (1974); Bryce Wood, *The Making of the Good Neighbor Policy* (1961).

Isolationism and Isolationists

Warren I. Cohen, *The American Revisionists* (1967); Wayne S. Cole, *Roosevelt and the Isolationists, 1932–1945* (1983); Wayne S. Cole, *America First* (1953); Manfred Jonas, *Isolationism in America, 1935–1941* (1966); Richard Lowitt, *George W. Norris*, 3 vols. (1963–1978); John Wiltz, *In Search of Peace: The Senate Munitions Inquiry, 1934–1936* (1963).

Franklin D. Roosevelt and Europe

Thomas A. Bailey and Paul B. Ryan, *Hitler vs. Roosevelt* (1979); Edward Bennett, *Recognition of Russia* (1970); James MacGregor Burns, *Roosevelt: The Lion and the Fox* (1956); James V. Compton, *The Swastika and the Eagle* (1967); Robert Dallek, *Franklin D. Roosevelt and American Foreign Policy, 1932–1945* (1979); Robert A. Divine, *The Reluctant Belligerent*, 2nd ed. (1979); Robert A. Divine, *Roosevelt and World War II* (1969); Manfred Jonas, *The United States and Germany* (1984); Warren F. Kimball, *The Most Unsordid Act: Lend-Lease, 1939–1941* (1969); Thomas R. Maddux, *Years of Estrangement: American Relations with the Soviet Union, 1933–1941* (1980); Julius W. Pratt, *Cordell Hull*, 2 vols. (1964); David Reynolds, *The Creation of the Anglo-American Alliance, 1937–1941* (1982); Bruce Russert, *No Clear and Present Danger* (1972).

China, Japan, and the Coming of War in Asia

Dorothy Borg and Shumpei Okomoto, eds., *Pearl Harbor as History* (1973); R. J. C. Butow, *Tojo and the Coming of* the War (1961); Warren I. Cohen, *America's Response to China*, 2nd ed. (1980); Roger Dingman, *Power in the Pacific* (1976); Herbert Feis, *The Road to Pearl Harbor* (1950); Akira Iriye, *Across the Pacific* (1967); Akira Iriye, *After Imperialism: The Search for a New Order in the Far East, 1921–1931* (1965); Charles Neu, *The Troubled Encounter: The United States and Japan* (1975); Paul W. Schroeder, *The Axis Alliance and Japanese-American Relations, 1941* (1958);

Jonathan Utley, *Going to War with Japan, 1937–1941* (1985).

Pearl Harbor

Martin V. Melosi, *The Shadow of Pearl Harbor* (1977); Gordon W. Prange, *At Dawn We Slept* (1981); John Toland, *Infamy* (1982); Roberta Wohlstetter, *Pearl Harbor* (1962).

CHAPTER 26

THE SECOND WORLD WAR
AT HOME AND ABROAD
1941–1945

"*We are going* on a mission to drop a bomb different from any you have ever seen or heard about," Colonel Paul Tibbets informed his crew on the small Pacific island of Tinian. Silent and incredulous, they listened to "Old Bull" describe the strange new weapon, which packed the destructive power of twenty thousand tons of TNT. Resting in the bay of a converted B-29 named the *Enola Gay,* after Tibbets's mother, was "Little Boy"—a ten-thousand-pound uranium bomb on which the airmen had scribbled anti-Japanese graffiti.

On August 6, 1945, the crew put on welder's goggles and made their run on the unsuspecting city of Hiroshima. When the bomb hit target, a flash of dazzling light shot across the sky; then two violent slaps rocked the plane. "My God!" gasped co-pilot Captain Robert Lewis as he watched a huge purplish mushroom cloud boil 40,000 feet into the atmosphere. Dense smoke, swirling fires, and suffocating dust soon engulfed the ground for miles. Much of the city was leveled almost instantly.

Approximately 130,000 people were killed at Hiroshima; tens of thousands more suffered painful burns and nuclear poisoning. As Hiroshima suffered its unique nightmare, Washington, D.C., celebrated its military and scientific triumph. "This is the greatest thing in history," exclaimed President Harry S Truman on hearing of the successful mission.

For forty-five months Americans had fought abroad to subdue aggressors. After military engagements against the fascists in North Africa and Italy, in June 1944 American troops had joined the dramatic crossing of the English Channel on D-Day. The massive invasion forced the Germans to retreat through France to Germany. In the Pacific, Americans drove the Japanese from one island after another before turning to the atomic bombs that demolished Hiroshima and Nagasaki and helped spur a Japanese surrender in August.

Throughout the war the Allies—Britain, Russia, and the United States—were held together by their common goal of defeating Germany. But they squabbled over many issues: when the second, or western, front would be opened; how a new international organization would be structured; how Eastern Europe, liberated from the Germans, would be reconstructed; how Germany itself would be governed after defeat. At the end of the war Allied leaders seemed more intent on keeping and expanding their own nations' spheres of influence than on building a community of mutual interest.

At home Americans united behind the war effort, collecting scrap metal, rubber, and old newspapers and planting victory gardens. The federal government mobilized all traditional sectors of the economy—industry, finance, agriculture, and labor—as well as new ones: higher education and science. For this was a scientific and technological war, supported by the development of new weapons like the atomic bomb.

For millions of Americans the war was a time to relocate in other parts of the country. Not only did 16 million men and women serve in the armed forces between 1941 and 1945, but blacks, Mexican-Americans, and whites migrated to war-production centers in the North and the West. Employers' negative attitudes toward women workers eased during the Second World War, and millions of married middle-class women took jobs in war industries.

In these and other ways the United States and its people underwent profound change during the course of the war. The Second World War was truly a watershed in American history.

WINNING THE SECOND WORLD WAR

"We are now in the midst of a war, not for conquest, not for vengeance, but for a world in which this Nation, and all that this Nation represents, will be safe for our children." President Roo-

sevelt was speaking just two days after the surprise attack on Pearl Harbor. Americans believed with Roosevelt that they were defending their homes and families against aggressive and satanic Nazis and Japanese. Few of them, however, knew much about the principles of the Atlantic Charter or about United States war aims.

In the army's propaganda films and in the popular mind, the Allies were heroic partners in a common effort against evil. Actually, wartime relations among the United States, Great Britain, and the Soviet Union ran hot and cold. Although winning the war claimed top priority, Allied leaders knew that military decisions had political consequences. Thus an undercurrent of suspicion ran beneath the surface of Allied cooperation.

Roosevelt, British Prime Minister Winston Churchill, and Soviet Premier Josef Stalin differed vigorously over the opening of a second, or western,

Second Front Controversy

front. Stalin pressed for a British-American landing on the northern coast of Europe to draw German troops away from the eastern front, but Churchill would not agree. The Russians therefore did most of the fighting and dying on land, while the British and Americans concentrated on getting Lend-Lease supplies across the Atlantic and harassing the Germans from the air.

Roosevelt was particularly sensitive to the Russian burden. And he feared that Russia might be knocked out of the war, leaving Hitler free to send his goose-stepping soldiers into England. In 1942 Roosevelt told the Russians they could expect the Allies to open a second front later that year. The move across the English Channel, later tagged Operation Overlord, was exactly what Stalin sought to take pressure off his wracked country. But Churchill, fearing heavy British losses in a premature invasion, balked; he favored a series of small jabs at the enemy's Mediterranean forces.

Churchill won the debate. Instead of attacking France, the western Allies invaded North Africa in November 1942. "We are striking back," the cheered president declared. News from Russia also buoyed

Roosevelt. In the battle for Stalingrad (September 1942 to January 1943), probably the turning point of the war, the Red Army defeated the Germans, forcing Hitler's divisions to retreat. But in early 1943 Stalin was told once again that the second front would be delayed. He was not mollified by the Allied invasion of Italy in the summer of 1943. When Italy surrendered in September, it capitulated to American and British officers; Russian officials were not invited to participate. Stalin grumbled that the arrangement smacked of a separate peace.

With the Grand Alliance badly strained, Roosevelt sought reconciliation through personal diplomacy. The three Allied leaders met in Teheran, Iran, in December 1943. Stalin dismissed Churchill's repetitious justifications for further delaying the second front. Roosevelt had had enough too; with Stalin he rejected Churchill's proposal for another peripheral attack, this time through the Balkans to Vienna. The three finally agreed to launch Overlord in early 1944.

Like a coiled spring bursting free, the second front opened in the dark morning hours of June 6, 1944: D-Day.

D-Day Two hundred thousand Allied troops under the command of General Eisenhower, scrambled ashore in Normandy, France, in the largest amphibious landing in history. After digging in at now-famous places like Utah and Omaha beaches and gaining reinforcements, Allied forces broke through disorderly German lines and gradually ground inland, reaching Paris in August. That same month another force invaded southern France and threw the stunned Germans back. Allied troops soon spread across the countryside, liberating France and Belgium and entering Germany itself in September. In December German panzer divisions counterattacked in Belgium's Ardennes Forest, hoping to push on to Antwerp to halt the flow of Allied supplies through that major Belgian port. After weeks of heavy fighting in what has come to be called the Battle of the Bulge—because of the noticeable dent in the Allied line—the Allies pushed the enemy back once again. Meanwhile, battle-hardened Russian troops streamed through Poland and cut a path to the German capital, Berlin. American forces crossed the Rhine in March 1945 and captured the heavily industrial Ruhr valley. Some units peeled off to enter Austria and Czechoslovakia, where they met up with Russian soldiers. In bomb-ravaged Berlin, defended largely by teenage boys and old men, Adolf Hitler killed himself in his bunker. On May 8 Germany surrendered.

Allied strategists had devised a "Europe first" formula: knock out Germany first and then concentrate on an isolated Japan. Nevertheless, the Pacific theater claimed headlines throughout the war, for the American people regarded Japan as the United States' chief enemy. By mid-1942 Japan had seized the Philippines, Guam, Wake, Hong Kong, Singapore, Malaya, and the Dutch East Indies. In the Philippines in 1942 Japanese soldiers forced American prisoners, weak from insufficient rations, to walk sixty-five miles, clubbing, shooting, or starving to death about ten thousand of them. The Bataan Death March intensified the American hatred of the Japanese.

In April 1942 Americans began to strike back. They bombed Tokyo, and in May, in the momentous Battle of the Coral Sea, carrier-based U.S. planes halted a Japanese advance toward Australia (see map). The next month American forces defeated the Japanese at Midway, sinking four of the enemy's valuable aircraft carriers. The Battle of Midway broke the Japanese momentum and relieved the threat to Hawaii. Thereafter, Japan was never able to match American manpower, sea power, air power, or economic power.

General Douglas MacArthur's strategy was to "island-hop" toward Japan itself, skipping the most strongly fortified points whenever possible and taking

American Offensive in the Pacific weaker ones. American forces also set out to sink Japan's merchant marine, without which the enemy could neither supply its armies nor obtain vital raw materials. The first American offensive was at Guadalcanal in the Solomons (1942). Over the next few years U.S. troops attacked the Gilberts (1943), the Marianas (1944), and the Philippines (1944). Then in early 1945 both sides took heavy losses at Iwo Jima and Okinawa. In

Chapter 26: THE SECOND WORLD WAR AT HOME AND ABROAD, 1941–1945

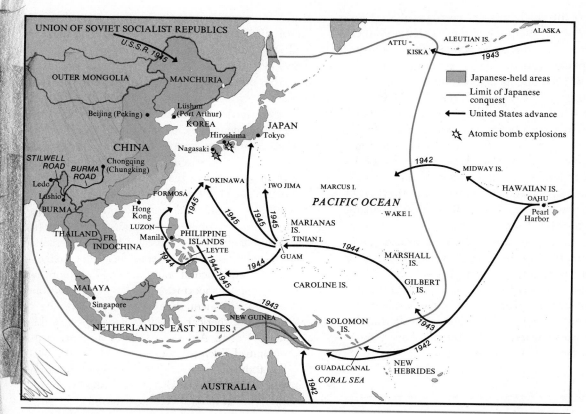

The Pacific War Source: By permission of the publisher, from *American Foreign Policy: A History* by Paterson et al., p. 398. (Lexington, Mass.: D.C. Heath and Company, 1983).

desperation, Japanese pilots began suicide (*kamikaze*) attacks, flying their planes directly into American ships.

Hoping to avoid a humiliating unconditional surrender (and to preserve the emperor's sovereignty), Japanese leaders refused to admit defeat. They hung on while American bombers leveled their cities. In one staggering attack on Tokyo on May 23, 1945, American planes dropped napalm-filled bombs that engulfed the city in a firestorm. Eighty-three thousand people died.

Impatient for victory, American leaders began to plan a fall invasion of the Japanese islands, an expe-

dition that was sure to bring high casualties. But the successful development of an atomic bomb by American scientists provided another route to victory. Shortly after the atomic bombing of Hiroshima and Nagasaki the Japanese surrendered, on the condition that their emperor would remain, at least theoretically, the nation's ruler. Formal ceremonies were held September 2 aboard the battleship *Missouri*. The war was over.

Most Americans agreed with President Truman that the atomic bombing of two Japanese cities had been necessary, to end the war as quickly as possible and to save American lives. Use of the bomb to achieve victory had, in fact, been the primary assumption of the Manhattan Project (the secret atomic bomb project). At the highest governmental levels and among atomic scientists, alternatives had been discussed: detonate the bomb on an unpopulated Pacific island, with international observers as witnesses; blockade and bomb Japan conventionally; pursue the hints that Tokyo was willing to negotiate; encourage a Russian declaration of war. But Truman's aides had rejected these options on the grounds that they would take too long and would not convince the tenacious Japanese they had been beaten.

Why the Atomic Bomb Was Used

Diplomatic considerations also sped the decision to use the bomb. It might serve as a deterrent against aggression; it might intimidate Russia into making concessions in Eastern Europe; it might end the war in the Pacific before Russia could claim a role in the management of Asia. "If it explodes, as I think it will," Truman remarked, "I'll certainly have a hammer on those boys" (the Russians).

ECONOMIC EFFECTS OF THE
WAR AT HOME

The Second World War had been won at great cost not only abroad, but also on the American home front. While the guns boomed in Europe and Asia, the war changed American lives and institutions. One month after Pearl Harbor, President Roosevelt had established the War Production Board (WPB). First on the WPB's list of tasks was the conversion from civilian to military production. Factories that had manufactured silk ribbons began to turn out silk parachutes; automobile companies switched to the production of tanks and airplanes; adding-machine companies converted to make automatic pistols. Factories had to be expanded and new ones

built. Moreover, whole new industries, the best known of which was synthetic rubber, had to be created. The Japanese had captured most of the world's supply of natural rubber. The WPB was so successful that the production of durable goods more than tripled.

To gain the cooperation of business, the WPB and other government agencies met it more than halfway. The government guaranteed profits in the form of cost-plus-fixed-fee contracts, generous tax writeoffs, and exemption from antitrust prosecution. And it allowed prime contractors to distribute subcontracts as they saw fit, including those involving scarce war-related materials.

Government Incentives to Business

From mid-1940 through September 1944 the government awarded contracts totaling $175 billion, no less than two-thirds of which went to the top one hundred corporations. General Motors received 8 percent of the total; big awards also went to other automobile companies, as well as to aircraft, steel, electrical, and chemical companies. Though no one had yet thought to call it the "military-industrial complex," as President Dwight Eisenhower would in 1961, the web of government-business interdependence had begun to be woven.

The big also got bigger in science and higher education. To develop radar and do other research, the Massachusetts Institute of Technology received contracts valued at $117 million. The California Institute of Technology came next, with contracts totaling $83 million, followed by Harvard, Columbia, the University of California, Johns Hopkins, and the University of Chicago. The most spectacular result of a government contract with a university was, of course, the atomic bomb; its testing was run by the University of California at Berkeley.

Big labor also grew bigger during the war. Union membership ballooned from 8.5 million in 1940 to 14.75 million in 1945. In 1942, to minimize labor-management conflict, President Roosevelt created the National War Labor Board (NWLB), sometimes referred to as the Supreme Court for labor disputes. As a result of its Little Steel formula, which limited wage increases to increases in the cost of living, the NWLB was soon confronted with wildcat strikes and other work stoppages that tripled the production time lost in 1943. But the worst labor disruptions of 1943 came in the coal fields, where 450,000 soft-coal miners and 80,000 anthracite miners struck.

To discourage further work stoppages, Congress passed the War Labor Disputes, or Smith-Connally, Act of June 1943. The act conferred on the president the authority to seize and operate any strike-bound plant deemed necessary to the national security, and established a mandatory thirty-day cooling-off period before any new strike could be called. The Smith-Connally Act also gave the NWLB the legal authority to settle labor disputes for the duration of the war.

Agriculture also made an impressive contribution to the war effort, not only through farmers' hard work but through the introduction of labor-saving machinery to replace the men and women who had gone to the front or migrated to war-production centers. Farming was in the midst of a transition from the family-owned and -operated farm to the large-scale, mechanized agribusiness dominated by banks, insurance companies, and farm co-ops. The Second World War accelerated the trend. Like business and labor, agriculture was becoming more consolidated as it contributed to the war effort.

Increased Mechanization of Agriculture

At the head of the burgeoning national economy stood the federal government. The WPB and the NWLB were only two of the host of new agencies that sprang up: others included the Office of Price Administration, the War Manpower Commission, the Office of War Mobilization, the Office of War Information, and the Office of Scientific Research and Development. The national debt jumped from $49 billion in 1941 to $259 billion in 1945.

The federal government was, of course, also responsible for mobilizing the military. By 1945 well over 12 million men and women were serving in the armed forces. The army topped the list with 8.3 million, including 100,000 WACs (members of the Women's Army Corps). Though women were prohib-

The federal government used a variety of methods to exhort home-front Americans to obey wartime regulations. This Office of War Information poster suggested that the gas cheat was betraying his patriotic duty to support American troops. National Archives.

ited from engaging in combat duty, they worked at a variety of noncombat jobs, not only in the WACs but as WAVES in the navy, as pilots in the WAFS (Women's Auxiliary Ferrying Squadron), and as members of the *Semper Paratus* Always Ready Service (SPARS) and the Women's Reserve of the Marine Corps.

Most troops served overseas for an average of about sixteen months. Some, of course, never returned: total deaths exceeded 405,000; total wounded, 670,000. In terms of human life, the cost of the war was second only to that of the Civil War. Still, compared with losses suffered by other nations,

B-17 pilots return from a training flight in their Flying Fortress Pistol Packin' Mama. WAF pilots ferried the planes for the Air Corps.   U.S. Air Force Photo.

U.S. figures were low. Less than 1 percent of the population was killed or wounded in the war; the Soviet Union lost 8 percent of its population—20 million people.

CIVIL LIBERTIES AND THE INTERNMENT OF JAPANESE-AMERICANS

Once the United States entered the war, its leaders had to consider whether enemy agents were operating within its borders. It was clear that not all Americans were enthusiastic supporters of the nation's involvement in the war. Following Pearl Harbor, several thousand "enemy aliens" were arrested and taken into custody, some of them Nazi agents who had accumulated firearms, shortwave radios, and codes in the course of their work. Other people had conscientious objections to the war. During the Second World War conscientious objectors (COs) had to have a religious (as opposed to moral or ethical) reason for refusing military service. About 25,000 qualified COs accepted noncombat service. An additional 12,000 were placed in civilian public-service camps. Some—5,500 in all, three-fourths of whom were Jehovah's Witnesses—refused to participate in any way; they were imprisoned.

The one enormous exception to the nation's gen-

Branded members of an enemy race by the government, more than 100,000 Japanese-Americans were rounded up and shipped to internment camps. Included among the evacuees were children and the elderly. National Archives.

made me feel like murdering those responsible."

The internees were sent to flood-damaged lands at Relocation, Arkansas; to the intermountain terrain of Wyoming and the desert of western Arizona; and to other arid and desolate spots in the West. Although the names were evocative—Topaz, Utah; Rivers, Arizona; Heart Mountain, Wyoming; Manzanar, California—the camps themselves were bleak and demoralizing. Behind barbed wire stood tarpapered wooden barracks where entire families lived in a single room furnished only with cots, blankets, and a bare light bulb. Toilets and dining and bathing facilities were communal; privacy was almost nonexistent. Besides their freedom, these Japanese-Americans lost property valued at $500 million, along with their positions in the truck-garden, floral, and fishing industries. Indeed, their economic competitors were among the most vocal proponents of their relocation.

The Supreme Court upheld the government's policy of internment. In wartime, the Court said in the *Hirabayashi* ruling (1943), "residents having ethnic affiliations with an invading enemy may be a greater source of danger than those of different ancestry." And in the *Korematsu* case (1944), the Court, with three justices dissenting, approved the removal of the Nisei from the West Coast. One dissenter, Justice Frank Murphy, denounced the decision as the "legalization of racism." The most ominous appraisal came from Circuit Court Judge William Denman, who in an earlier ruling wrote that "the identity of this doctrine with that of the Hitler generals . . . justifying the gas chambers of Dachau is unmistakable."

Not until 1983, forty-one years after he had been placed in a government camp, did Fred Korematsu have the satisfaction of hearing a federal judge rule that he—and by implication all the detainees—had been the victim of "unsubstantiated facts, distortions and misrepresentations of at least one military commander whose views were affected by racism." In 1982 the government's special Commission on Wartime Relocation and Internment of Civilians recommended compensating the victims of this policy.

erally creditable wartime civil liberties record was the internment in "relocation centers" of approximately 112,000 Japanese-Americans. Of these people, 70,000 were Nisei, or native-born citizens of the United States. Charges of criminal behavior were never brought against Japanese-Americans; none were ever indicted or tried for espionage, treason, or sedition. Their imprisonment was based not on suspicion or evidence of treason, but on ethnic origin—the fact that they were of Japanese descent.

Internment in "Relocation Centers"

"It was really cruel and harsh," recalled Joseph Y. Kurihara, a citizen and a veteran of the First World War. "To pack and evacuate in forty-eight hours was an impossibility. Seeing mothers completely bewildered with children crying from want and peddlers taking advantage and offering prices next to robbery

JOBS AND RACISM ON THE HOME FRONT

For other nonwhite groups in America, the Second World War would prove to be a mixed blessing, providing both the benefits of employment and the insults of racism. For many black Americans, the war was a watershed, the point at which they determined to make a stand against racial discrimination. Several factors highlighted Afro-American involvement in the war: the presence of nearly 1 million black men and women in the armed services; the mass migration of blacks, particularly from the rural South to the urban North and West, to work in war industries; and the participation of black people in all kinds of wartime activities—buying war bonds, serving as air-raid wardens, and volunteering for the Red Cross.

Though blacks in the service were still segregated, they made some real advances in the direction of racial equality during these years. For the first time the

Black Troops
War Department sanctioned the training of blacks as pilots. After instruction at Tuskegee Institute in Alabama, pilots saw heroic service in such all-black units as the Ninety-ninth Pursuit Squadron, winner of eighty Distinguished Flying Crosses. And some blacks reached positions of leadership. In 1940 Colonel Benjamin O. Davis became the first black brigadier general. Wherever black people were offered opportunities to distinguish themselves, they proved they were just as capable as whites.

Set against these accomplishments, however, were serious failures in race relations. Race riots instigated by whites occurred on military bases, and white civilians assaulted black soldiers and sailors throughout the South. When the War Department issued an order in mid-1944 forbidding racial segregation in military recreation and transportation, the *Montgomery Advertiser* replied, "Army orders, even armies, even bayonets, cannot force impossible and unnatural social relations upon us."

Of course, experiences such as these caused black soldiers and sailors to wonder what, in fact, they were fighting for. Why, they asked, should they help to defend a nation that treated them like second-class citizens? They noted that the Red Cross separated blood taken from whites and blacks, as if there were some difference. But most telling was the charge that American racism was little different from German racism.

At the same time, there were positive reasons for blacks to participate in the war effort. Perhaps this was an opportunity, as the NAACP believed, "to persuade, embarrass, compel and shame our government and our nation . . . into a more enlightened attitude toward a tenth of its people." Proclaiming that in the Second World War they were waging a "Double V" campaign (for victory at home and abroad), blacks were more militant than before, and readier than ever to protest. As a result membership in civil rights organizations soared.

Because of the war, blacks found new opportunities in industry. To secure defense jobs, 1.2 million blacks migrated from the South to the industrial cities of the

Black War Workers
North and West in the 1940s. More than half a million became active members of CIO unions. As their earning power increased, so did their standard of living and political power. Indeed, urban blacks were becoming a swing vote in local, state, and presidential elections.

But along with the benefits of urban life came liabilities. The migrants had to make enormous emotional and cultural adjustments, and white hostility and ignorance made their task particularly difficult. In 1942 more than half of all northern whites believed that blacks should live in segregated neighborhoods and attend segregated schools. Such attitudes caused many to fear that the summer of 1943 would prove to be another Red Summer. And indeed, almost 250 racial conflicts ex-

Race Riots of 1943

ploded in forty-seven cities that year. The worst of the 1943 race riots bloodied the streets of Detroit in June. At the end of thirty hours of rioting, twenty-five blacks and nine whites lay dead.

The federal government did practically nothing to prevent further racial violence. From Roosevelt on down, most federal officials put the war first, domestic reform second. But governmental neglect could not discourage Afro-Americans and their century-old civil rights movement. By war's end they were ready—politically, economically, and emotionally—to wage the struggle for voting rights and for equal access to public accommodations and institutions.

Not all racial violence was directed against blacks. In the 1943 Los Angeles zoot suit riot, the victims were Mexican-Americans. In the eyes of the rioters, most of whom were sailors and soldiers, people of Mexican origin were as despicable as those whose roots were African. In 1942, the United States and Mexico had agreed to the *bracero* program, whereby Mexicans were admitted to the United States on short-term work contracts. Although the newcomers suffered racial discrimination and segregation, they seized the economic opportunities that had become available. In Los Angeles, 17,000 people of Mexican descent found shipyard jobs where before the war there had been none available. Mexican-American teenagers in that city joined street gangs (members were called *pachucos*), adopted ducktail haircuts, and donned "zoot suits": long coats (called "drapes") with wide, padded shoulders, pegged pants, wide-brimmed hats, and long watch chains. Whites' racial hatred boiled over in June, and for four days mobs invaded Mexican-American neighborhoods. Not only did white policemen look the other way, but the city of Los Angeles even passed an ordinance that made it a crime to wear a zoot suit within city limits.

Such experiences made life difficult for people of Mexican descent within the United States. Although the war opened up brief economic opportunities for Mexican-Americans, these years were not the watershed experience that they were for Afro-Americans.

A Milestone for Women

If the Second World War was a turning point for Afro-Americans, it was equally or even more so for the women of America. War temporarily ended the Depression era hostility toward working women. In five years, 6 million women entered the work force and the number of working women increased by 57 percent. Moreover, the typical newcomer was not a young, single woman; she was married and over thirty-five.

But statistics tell only part of the story. There was a change in attitude toward heavy labor for women. Up to the early months of the war employers had insisted that women were not suited for industrial jobs. "Almost overnight," said Mary Anderson, head of the Women's Bureau of the Department of Labor, "women were reclassified by industrialists from a marginal to a basic labor supply for munitions making." Women became riveters, lumberjacks, welders, crane operators, keel benders, toolmakers, shell loaders, cowgirls, blast-furnace cleaners, locomotive greasers, police officers, taxi drivers, and football coaches.

Women in War Production

The new employment opportunities increased women's geographic and occupational mobility. Especially noteworthy were the gains made by black women; over 400,000 quit work as domestic servants to enjoy the better working conditions, higher pay, and union benefits of industrial employment. Over 7 million women moved from their original counties of residence to new locations during the war. Many sought jobs in the rapidly expanding aircraft industry, which increased its employment of women from 4,000 in December 1941 to 310,000 two years later.

Public opinion quickly changed from hostility to support of women's war work. Newspapers and magazines, radio and movies proclaimed Rosie the Riveter a war hero. But very few people asserted that women's war work should bring about a permanent shift in sex roles. This was merely a response to a national emergency.

Though women increased their wages when they acquired better jobs, they still received lower pay than men, even for the same work. In 1945 women in manufacturing earned only 65 percent of what men were paid. And working women, particularly working mothers, suffered in other ways as well. Perhaps the most persistent problem was the near-absence of supportive services such as child-care centers and communal kitchens. Some of the most serious wartime social problems were a direct result of the lack of such services. During the war there were increases in juvenile delinquency, venereal disease, teenage pregnancy, and the incidence of "eight-hour orphans," or "latchkey children," left alone while their mothers worked eight-hour shifts in war plants.

"Women's Work"

At the same time that millions of women and youths were entering the work force, hundreds of thousands of women were getting married. From 1939 to 1942 the marriage rate rose from 73 marriages per 1,000 unmarried women to 93 per 1,000. Some couples scrambled to get married so they could spend time together before the man was sent overseas. Some doubtless married and had children to qualify for military deferments. But the rush to get married was also fueled by prosperity. Along with the rise in the marriage rate was an increase in the number of divorces. In 1939, 25,000 couples secured divorces; in 1945, 485,000.

Increase in Marriage, Divorce, and Birth Rates

Ironically, women's efforts to hold their families together during the war posed problems for returning fathers. Women war workers had brought home the wages; they had taken over the budgeting of expenses and the writing of checks. In countless ways they had proved they could hold the reins in their husbands' absence. Some men had difficulty accepting the idea that their families could survive and even prosper without them.

And what of the women who wanted to remain in the labor market? Many were forced by employers, or by their husbands, to quit. Others chose to leave their jobs for a year or two, but then returned to work. And throughout the rest of the 1940s and 1950s, millions more who had never worked took jobs.

The Decline of Liberalism and the Election of 1944

Another wartime trend was the decline of political liberalism. Even before Pearl Harbor, liberals had suffered major defeats. Some Democrats hoped to revive the reform movement during the war, but Republicans and conservative Democrats were on guard against such a move. Republican Senator Robert Taft and his fellow conservatives successfully blocked reform.

Part of the Democrats' problem was that, unlike the 1930s, the war years were a time of full employment. Once people had acquired jobs and gained some economic security, they began to be more critical of New Deal policies. The New Deal coalition had always had the potential for fragmentation. Southern white farmers had little in common with northern blacks or white factory workers. And in northern cities, blacks and whites who had voted for Roosevelt in 1940 competed for jobs and housing and would soon collide in race riots.

With Republican victories in 1942, the alliance of conservative southern Democrats and Republicans became a formidable threat to New Deal programs. In 1942 and 1943 the conservative coalition actually abolished several New Deal relief and social-welfare agencies, including the Work Projects Administration.

But though enfeebled, liberalism was far from dead. The liberal agenda began with a pledge to se-

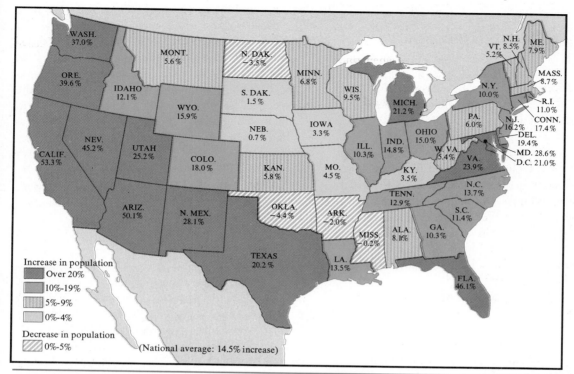

A Nation on the Move, 1940–1950   Source: U.S. Bureau of the Census, *Portfolio of United States Census Maps, 1950* (Washington: U.S. Government Printing Office, 1953), p. 4.

cure full employment. Roosevelt emphasized the concept in his Economic Bill of Rights, delivered as part of his 1944 State of the Union address. Every American had a right, the president declared, to a decent job; sufficient food, shelter, and clothing; and financial security in unemployment, illness, and old age. If to accomplish those goals the government had to operate at a deficit, Roosevelt was willing to do so. But first he had to be re-elected.

In 1944 the Republicans were optimistic about their prospects for regaining the presidency. New York Governor Thomas E. Dewey, a moderate with ability but a dull personality, secured the nomination. Despite rumors of ill health, Roosevelt was elected for a fourth term. His margin of victory (53.4 per-

cent), however, was the narrowest since 1916. It was the urban vote that returned Roosevelt to the White House. Wartime population shifts had much to do with the cities' new political clout. New workers—notably southern whites who had been lifelong Democrats and southern blacks who had never before voted—had migrated to the urban industrial centers (see map). Added to the urban vote was a less obvious factor. Many voters seemed to be exhibiting what has been called "depression psychosis." Fearful that hard times would return once war contracts were terminated, they remembered New Deal relief programs and voted for Roosevelt. Finally, many Americans wanted Roosevelt's experienced hand to guide the nation, and the world, to a lasting peace.

WARTIME DIPLOMACY

The lessons of the post–First World War period weighed heavily on the minds of American diplomats throughout the war. Americans vowed to make a peace that would ensure a postwar world free from depression, totalitarianism, and war. Thus American goals included the Open Door and lower tariffs; self-determination for liberated peoples; avoidance of the debts-reparations tangle that had plagued Europe after the First World War; expansion of the United States sphere of influence; and management of world affairs by what Roosevelt once called the Four Policemen: Russia, China, Great Britain, and the United States.

Although the major Allies concentrated on defeating the aggressors, their suspicions of one another undermined cooperation. For the Allies Eastern European questions proved the most

Allied Disagreement over Eastern Europe

difficult. The Russians sought to fix their boundaries where they had stood before Hitler attacked in 1941. In the case of Poland, this meant that the part of the country the Soviets had invaded and captured in 1939 would become Russian territory. The British and Americans hesitated, preferring to deal with Eastern Europe at the end of the war. Yet in October 1944 Churchill and Stalin, without Roosevelt's participation, struck a bargain: Russia would gain Rumania and Bulgaria as a sphere of influence; Britain would have the upper hand in Greece; and the two would share authority in Yugoslavia and Hungary.

Poland was a special case. In 1943 Moscow had broken off diplomatic relations with the conservative Polish government-in-exile in London. The Poles had angered Moscow when they asked the International Red Cross to investigate German charges that the Russians had massacred thousands of Polish army officers in the Katyn Forest. Then an uprising in War-

saw in July 1944 complicated matters still further. To the dismay of the world community, Soviet armies stood aside as German troops slaughtered 166,000 people and devastated the city. Finally, in late 1944 and early 1945 the Soviets spawned a pro-Communist government in Lublin. Thus near the end of the war Poland had two competing governments, one in London and another in Lublin.

Early in the war the Allies had begun talking about a new international organization. At Teheran in 1943 Roosevelt called for an institution controlled by

Creation of the United Nations Organization

the Four Policemen. The next year, in a Washington, D.C., mansion called Dumbarton Oaks, American, British, Russian, and Chinese representatives conferred on the details. The conferees approved a preliminary charter for a United Nations Organization, providing for a supreme Security Council, dominated by the great powers, and a weak General Assembly. The Security Council would have five permanent members, each with veto power; Britain had insisted that France be one of them. Meanwhile, the Russians, hoping to counter pro-British and pro-American blocs in the General Assembly, sought separate membership for its sixteen Soviet republics. This issue was not resolved, but the meeting proved a success nevertheless.

The diplomatic batting average on another problem, Nazi treatment of the Jews, was considerably lower. Even before the war Nazi officials had targeted

Jewish Refugees from the Holocaust

Jews throughout Europe for extermination. By war's end, about 6 million Jews had been forced into concentration camps and systematically killed by firing squads, unspeakable tortures, and gas chambers. Many others who survived the Holocaust could never forget the terror. During the depression the United States and other nations had refused to relax their immigration restrictions to save Jews fleeing persecution. Bureaucrats applied the rules so strictly—requiring legal documents fleeing Jews could not possibly provide—that

Chapter 26: The Second World War at Home and Abroad, 1941–1945

otherwise qualified refugees were kept out of the country. From 1933 to 1945 less than 40 percent of the German-Austrian quota was filled.

When evidence mounted that Hitler intended to exterminate the Jews, British and American representatives met in Bermuda (1943) but came up with no plans. Secretary Hull made a discouraging report to the president, emphasizing "the unknown cost of moving an undetermined number of persons from an undisclosed place to an unknown destination." Appalled, Secretary of the Treasury Henry Morgenthau, Jr., charged that the State Department's foot-dragging made the United States an accessory to murder. Early in 1944, stirred by Morgenthau's well-documented plea, Roosevelt created the War Refugee Board, which set up refugee camps in Europe and saved thousands from death.

But American officials waited too long to act, and they missed a chance to destroy the gas chambers and ovens at the extermination camp at Auschwitz in occupied Poland. They had aerial photographs and diagrams of the camp, but they argued· that bombing it would detract from the war effort or prompt the Germans to step up the anti-Jewish terror. In 1944 American planes bombed synthetic oil and rubber plants in the industrial sector of Auschwitz, only five miles from the gas chambers and crematoria, but left the camp itself untouched.

The three Allied leaders—Winston Churchill, Franklin D. Roosevelt, and Josef Stalin—met at Yalta in February 1945. Having been president for twelve years, Roosevelt showed signs of age and fatigue. Franklin D. Roosevelt Library.

THE YALTA CONFERENCE

AND A FLAWED PEACE

With the war in Europe nearing an end, Roosevelt urged another summit meeting. The three Allied leaders met at Yalta, on the Russian Crimea, in early February 1945. Controversy has surrounded the conference ever since. Roosevelt was obviously ill, and critics of the Yalta agreements later charged that Roosevelt was too weak to resist the demands of a guileful Stalin. The evidence suggests, however, that Roosevelt was mentally alert.

Each of the Allies entered into the conference with definite goals. Britain sought a place for France in occupied Germany, a curb on Soviet influence in Poland, and protection for the vulnerable British Empire. Russia wanted reparations from Germany, to assist in the massive task of rebuilding at home; possessions in Asia; continued influence in Poland; and a permanently weakened Germany. The United States lobbied for the United Nations Organization, where it believed it could ex-

Allied Goals at Yalta

ercise influence; for a Soviet declaration of war against Japan; for recognition of China as a major power; and for compromise between rival factions in Poland.

Military positions at the time of the conference helped to shape the final agreements. Soviet troops had occupied much of Eastern Europe, including Poland, and the Russians were set against the return of the London government. Under Roosevelt's leadership Stalin and Churchill reached a compromise: a boundary favorable to Russia in the east; postponement of the western boundary issue; and the creation of a "more broadly based" coalition government that would include members of the Polish London government-in-exile. Free elections would be held sometime in the future. The agreement was vague, but given Soviet occupation of Poland, Roosevelt considered it "the best I can do."

As for Germany, the Big Three agreed that it would be divided into four zones, the fourth to go to France. On the question of reparations, the Americans and Russians agreed that an Allied committee would consider the sum of $20 billion as a basis for discussion in the future.

Other issues found trade-offs. Stalin promised to declare war on Japan two or three months after Hitler's defeat. The Soviet premier also consented to sign a treaty of friendship and alliance with Jiang Jieshi (Chiang Kai-shek), America's ally in China, rather than with the Communist Mao Zedong. In return the United States agreed to Russia's taking the southern part of Sakhalin Island and Lüshun (Port Arthur). Regarding the new world organization, Roosevelt and Churchill granted the Soviets three votes in the General Assembly. Finally, the conferees accepted the Declaration of Liberated Europe, pledging to establish order and to rebuild economies by democratic methods.

Yalta marked the high point of the Grand Alliance; each of the Allies came away with something, in the tradition of diplomatic give-and-take. But as the great powers jockeyed for influence at the close of the war, neither the spirit nor the letter of Yalta held

firm. The crumbling of the alliance became evident at the Potsdam Conference, which took place between July 17 and August 2, 1945. Roosevelt had died in April, and Harry S Truman had replaced him. Truman was a novice at international diplomacy and less patient with the Russians.

Potsdam Conference

Despite major differences, the Big Three agreed on general policies toward Germany: complete disarmament; elimination of industry used for military production; and dissolution of Nazi institutions and laws. In a compromise over reparations, they decided that each occupying nation should take reparations from its own zone; but they could not agree on a total figure. To resolve other issues, such as peace treaties with Italy, Finland, and Hungary, the Big Three created the Council of Foreign Ministers.

Hitler once said, "We may be destroyed, but if we are, we shall drag a world with us—a world in flames." True to Hitler's words, modern warfare had made rubble of European and Asian cities. The war also created immense human suffering. Everywhere ghostlike people wandered about searching desperately for food, and mourning those who would never come home. Russia had lost 20 million people; Poland 5.8 million; Germany 4.5 million. In all, about 35 million Europeans died as a result of the war. In Asia untold millions of Chinese and 2 million Japanese died.

Only one major combatant escaped these grisly statistics: the United States. Its cities were not burned and its fields were not trampled. American deaths from the war were few compared with the losses of other nations. In fact, Americans came out of the Second World War more powerful than they had gone in. They alone had the atomic bomb. What is more, only the United States had the capital and economic resources to spur international recovery. America was, gloated Truman, a "giant."

Postwar Supremacy of the United States

Events at home and abroad during the Second World War had transformed the United States. For

IMPORTANT EVENTS

1941	Japan attacks Pearl Harbor; U.S. enters Second World War
1942	National War Labor Board established
	War Production Board established
	Internment of 112,000 Japanese-Americans in "relocation camps"
	War Manpower Commission established
	Bataan Death March
	Battles of Coral Sea and Midway
	Office of War Information established
	Manhattan Project established
	Allied invasion of North Africa
	Republican gains in Congress
	Synthetic-rubber program begins
1943	Russian victory at Stalingrad
	Strikes by soft-coal and anthracite miners
	Office of War Mobilization established
	War Labor Disputes (Smith-Connally) Act
	Race riots in Detroit, Harlem, and 45 other cities
	Allied invasion of Italy
	Teheran Conference
1944	Roosevelt requests Economic Bill of Rights
	War Refugee Board established
	Supreme Court upholds Japanese-American internment
	Normandy landings (D-Day)
	Dumbarton Oaks Conference
	Roosevelt re-elected
	U.S. retakes Philippines
1945	Yalta Conference
	Battles of Iwo Jima and Okinawa
	Roosevelt dies; Truman assumes presidency
	United Nations founded
	Germany surrenders
	Potsdam Conference
	Atomic bombs devastate Hiroshima and Nagasaki
	Japan surrenders

many Americans in 1945, life was fundamentally different from what it had been before Pearl Harbor. The Academy Award–winning film for 1946 was *The Best Years of Our Lives,* the painful story of the postwar readjustments of three veterans and their families and friends. Not only veterans' lives had been changed by the experiences of war; with the advent of the Cold War, millions of younger men would be inducted into the armed forces over the next thirty years. War and the expectation of war would become part of American life.

Though the gains made during the war by blacks and women were overdue, other changes were less welcome. The war had stimulated the trend toward bigness in business, labor, and government. In the next few years, government agencies that had been conceived as temporary would become permanent and would grow in size and influence. And the seeds of the military-industrial complex were sown in these years. For better or worse—and clearly there were elements of both—the Second World War was a turning point in the nation's history.

Suggestions for Further Reading

Fighting the War

Stephen A. Ambrose, *Eisenhower*, vol. 1 (1983); Stephen A. Ambrose, *The Supreme Commander* (1970); Hanson Baldwin, *Battles Lost and Won* (1966); A. Russell Buchanan, *The United States in World War II*, 2 vols. (1964); Peter Calvocoressi and Guy Wint, *Total War* (1972); R. Ernest Dupuy, *World War II* (1969); Kent R. Greenfield, *American Strategy in World War II* (1963); B. H. Liddell Hart, *History of the Second World War* (1970); Max Hastings, *OVERLORD: D-Day and the Battle of Normandy* (1984); Clayton D. James, *The Years of MacArthur, 1941–1945* (1975); Richard M. Leighton and Robert W. Coakley, *Global Logistics and Strategy, 1940–1945*, 2 vols. (1955–1968); Samuel Eliot Morison, *The Two-Ocean War* (1963); Samuel Eliot Morison, *Strategy and Compromise* (1958); Forrest C. Pogue, *George C. Marshall*, 3 vols. (1963–1973); Bradley F. Smith, *The Shadow Warriors: O.S.S. and the Origins of the C.I.A.* (1983); Ronald H. Spector, *Fighting Against the Sun: The American War with Japan* (1984); Russell F. Weigley, *The American Way of War* (1973); Gordon Wright, *The Ordeal of Total War, 1939–1945* (1968).

Diplomatic Issues

Robert Beitzell, *The Uneasy Alliance* (1972); James MacGregor Burns, *Roosevelt: The Soldier of Freedom* (1970); Winston S. Churchill, *The Second World War*, 6 vols. (1948–1953); Diane Clemens, *Yalta* (1970); Robert Dallek, *Franklin D. Roosevelt and American Foreign Policy, 1932–1945* (1979); Robert A. Divine, *Roosevelt and World War II* (1969); Herbert Feis, *Churchill, Roosevelt, and Stalin* (1957); George C. Herring, *Aid to Russia, 1941–1946* (1973); Akira Iriye, *Power and Culture: The Japanese-American War, 1941–1945* (1981); Gabriel Kolko, *The Politics of War* (1968); William R. Louis, *Imperialism at Bay: The United States and the Decolonization of the British Empire* (1978); William H. McNeill, *America, Britain, and Russia* (1953); Vojtech Mastny, *Russia's Road to the Cold War* (1979);

Arthur D. Morse, *While Six Million Died* (1968); Gaddis Smith, *Diplomacy During the Second World War, 1941–1945* 2nd ed. (1985); Michael Stoff, *Oil, War, and American Security* (1980); Mark Stoler, *The Politics of the Second Front* (1977); David S. Wyman, *The Abandonment of the Jews: America and the Holocaust, 1941–1945* (1984).

The Home Front

John Morton Blum, *V Was for Victory: Politics and American Culture During World War II* (1976); Alan Clive, *State of War: Michigan in World War II* (1979); Philip J. Funigiello, *The Challenge to Urban Liberalism: Federal-City Relations During World War II* (1978); Mark Jonathan Harris et al., *The Homefront* (1984); John W. Jeffries, *Testing the Roosevelt Coalition: Connecticut Society and Politics in the Era of World War II* (1979); Richard R. Lingeman, *Don't You Know There's a War On? The American Home Front, 1941–1945* (1970); Geoffrey Perrett, *Days of Sadness, Years of Triumph: The American People 1939–1945* (1973); Richard Polenberg, *War and Society: The United States, 1941–1945* (1972); Studs Terkel, ed., *"The Good War": An Oral History of World War Two* (1984).

Mobilizing for War

Bruce Catton, *The War Lords of Washington* (1948); George Q. Flynn, *The Mess in Washington: Manpower Mobilization in World War II* (1979); Eliot Janeway, *The Struggle for Survival* (1951); Paul A. C. Koistinen, *The Hammer and the Sword: Labor, the Military, and Industrial Mobilization, 1920–1945* (1979); Donald Nelson, *Arsenal of Democracy* (1946); William M. Tuttle, Jr., "The Birth of an Industry: The Synthetic Rubber 'Mess' in World War II," *Technology and Culture*, 22 (1981), 35–67; Gerald T. White, *Billions for Defense: Government Finance by the Defense Plant Corporation During World War II* (1980).

Farmers and Workers, Soldiers and Sailors

Melvyn Dubofsky and Warren H. Van Tine, *John L. Lewis: A Biography* (1977); Nelson Lichtenstein, *Labor's War at Home: The CIO in World War II* (1983); Bill Mauldin, *Up Front* (1968 ed.); Joel Seidman, *American Labor from Defense to Reconversion* (1953); Samuel A. Stouffer et al., *The American Soldier*, 2 vols. (1949); Walter W. Wilcox, *The Farmer in the Second World War* (1947).

Japanese-American Internment

Commission on Wartime Relocation and Internment of Civilians, *Personal Justice Denied* (1982); Roger Daniels, *Concentration Camps U.S.A.* (1971); Bill Hosokawa, *Nisei: The Quiet Americans* (1969); Peter Irons, *Justice at War: The Story of the Japanese American Internment Cases* (1983); Jacobus tenBroek et al., *Prejudice, War and the Constitution: Causes and Consequences of the Evacuation of the Japanese Americans in World War II* (1954); Michi Weglyn, *Years of Infamy: The Untold Story of America's Concentration Camps* (1976).

Science and Education

James Phinney Baxter, *Scientists Against Time* (1946); Isaac Kandel, *The Impact of War upon American Education* (1948); Daniel J. Kevles, *The Physicists* (1977).

Politics

James C. Foster, *The Union Politic: The CIO Political Action Committee* (1975); Donald R. McCoy, "Republican Opposition in Wartime, 1941–1945," *Mid-America*, 49 (1967), 174–189; Roland Young, *Congressional Politics in the Second World War* (1956).

Afro-Americans and Wartime Violence

A. Russell Buchanan, *Black Americans in World War II* (1977); Dominic J. Capeci, Jr., *Race Relations in Wartime Detroit* (1984); Dominic J. Capeci, Jr., *The Harlem Riot of 1943* (1977); Lee Finkle, *Forum for Protest: The Black Press During World War II* (1975); Phillip McGuire, ed., *Taps for a Jim Crow Army: Letters from Black Soldiers in World War II* (1982); Mauricio Mazon, *The Zoot-Suit Riots* (1984); Harvard Sitkoff, "Racial Militancy and Interracial Violence in the Second World War," *Journal of American History*, 58 (1971), 661–681; Neil A. Wynn, *The Afro-American and the Second World War* (1976).

Women

Karen T. Anderson, "Last Hired, First Fired: Black Women Workers During World War II," *Journal of American History*, 69 (1982), 82–97; Karen T. Anderson, *Wartime Women: Sex Roles, Family Relations, and the Status of Women During World War II* (1981); M. Joyce Baker, *Images of Women in Film: The War Years, 1941–1945* (1981); William H. Chafe, *The American Woman: Her Changing Social, Economic, and Political Roles, 1920–1970* (1972); Sherna Berger Gluck, "Interlude or Change: Women and the World War II Work Experience," *International Journal of Oral History*, 3 (1982), 92–113; Chester W. Gregory, *Women in Defense Work During World War II: An Analysis of the Labor Problem and Women's Rights* (1974); Susan M. Hartmann, *The Home Front and Beyond: American Women in the 1940s* (1982); Leila J. Rupp, *Mobilizing Women for War: German and American Propaganda, 1939–1945* (1978).

The Atomic Bomb

Gar Alperovitz, *Atomic Diplomacy* (1965); Barton J. Bernstein, ed., *The Atomic Bomb* (1976); Robert J. C. Butow, *Japan's Decision to Surrender* (1954); Herbert Feis, *The Atomic Bomb and the End of World War II* (1966); Gregg Herken, *The Winning Weapon* (1981); Martin J. Sherwin, *A World Destroyed* (1975).

CHAPTER 27

THE COLD WAR
AND AMERICAN POLITICS
1945–1953

President Harry S Truman was exhausted on March 13, 1947, as his official plane flew him from Washington to his Florida vacation spot in Key West. The day before, in a controversial speech to a joint session of Congress, the president had announced the Truman Doctrine. Without mentioning the Soviet Union by name, he equated its policies with the former "totalitarian regimes" of Germany and Japan. "I believe," he said, "that it must be the policy of the United States to support free peoples who are resisting attempted subjugation by armed minorities or by outside pressures." These words became the backbone of containment, a doctrine that in the coming years would not only lead the United States into armed conflict in Asia, the Middle East, and Latin America but also heighten fears at home that a Communist conspiracy had gained control of the federal government.

The central theme of Truman's presidency was anti-Communism at home and abroad. A week later, on March 21, Truman made another momentous decision. Through an executive order, he announced the Employee Loyalty Program for the executive branch of the government. Henceforth, all agency heads had to ensure that each employee under their jurisdictions was a loyal American. In doubtful cases, the boss had to appoint a loyalty board to hear the evidence and make recommendations. For the first time, government officials had the authority to pass judgment on a job applicant's personal beliefs and past associations. People already on the job who were accused of disloyalty were presumed to be guilty, not innocent.

When Franklin D. Roosevelt died in office in April 1945, Truman had acceded to the presidency. Contrary to his later "Give 'em hell, Harry" image, Truman's initial response to this challenge was a deep feeling of inadequacy." "I'm not big enough for this job," he confided to a friend. Even an experienced, well-respected president would have faced an enormous task in guiding the nation's transition from war to peace. But the new president was little more than an obscure politician. "Who is Harry Truman?" Americans asked themselves when they heard the news of Roosevelt's death.

Although Roosevelt had chosen Truman as his running mate in 1944, he had left the vice president in the dark about crucial foreign and military policies, even including the development of the atomic bomb. With the deterioration of Soviet-American relations, however, the new president got a quick education.

Because Truman perceived the Soviet threat as a global one, he decided to project American power on a worldwide scale. The president and his advisers created in foreign affairs a theme of anti-Communism that revealed itself in policies that protected and expanded American overseas interests, challenged the Soviets, created alliance systems, rebuilt Western Europe and Japan, and favored a military build-up over diplomacy. This globalism, with containment as its guide, brought the United States into crisis after crisis.

As in foreign policy, the new president got a crash course in the intricacies of governing the United States. At home, the nation's reconversion from war to peace was not smooth, and Truman angered liberals, conservatives, farmers, consumers, and union members during his first year as president. In 1946 voters responded to inflation and a wave of strikes by electing a Republican Eightieth Congress. But just two years later, partly because of public approval of his decisive foreign policy, Truman confounded political experts by winning the presidency in his own right.

As Truman's victory indicated, however, Cold War politics were volatile. And the key domestic issues of the period—black civil rights and the anti-Communist witch hunt called McCarthyism—were the most highly charged of all. The outbreak of the Korean War in June 1950 intensified domestic dis-

content. The military sta[...] citizens; inflation began [...] evidence of corruption su[...] Truman's popularity plum[...] cast their presidential vo[...] General Dwight D. Eisen[...]

THE SOURCES OF THE COLD WAR

Unsettled International Environment

After overseeing the defeat of Germany and Japan, President Truman participated in the rapid deterioration of Soviet-American relations— the Cold War. In this new conflict, competitive ideologies, propaganda, reconstruction programs, military alliances, atomic arms development, and spheres of influence condemned the world once again to instability and fear. Some conflict was inevitable after the Second World War, because the international environment was so unsettled. First, the world was in serious economic trouble because the war had reduced much of Europe and Japan to rubble and virtually destroyed national economies. Second, the collapse of Germany and Japan created power vacuums that drew the two major powers into collision as they sought to claim influence in countries where the Axis had once held sway. Third, political turmoil within nations spurred Soviet-American competition. In Greece and China, for example, where civil wars were waged between leftists and conservative regimes, the two powers favored different sides. Fourth, empires were disintegrating. In this process of decolonization, the European imperial nations were forced to withdraw by nationalist rebels and by their own financial constraints. New nations arose in the Middle East and Asia, and America and Russia competed to win them as friends who might provide military bases, resources, and markets.

People and governments in the postwar period faced the awesome job of rebuilding. Berlin, which had been reduced to rubble, was an example. National Archives.

Conflict may have been inevitable because of these international conditions, but the Cold War may not have been. That is, the national policies of the United States and the Soviet Union and their leaders' conduct of diplomacy exacerbated rather than resolved postwar issues. Each country saw the other as the world's bully. If Americans feared "communist aggression," Russians feared "capitalist encirclement." In mirror image, each side saw the other as the obstacle to peace.

"We are in this thing all over the world," Secretary of State James F. Byrnes (1945–1947) told Truman's cabinet. Why were Americans "all over the world"? For one reason, they had determined never to repeat the experience of the 1930s. They vowed no more depressions that would spawn political extremism and in turn produce war; no more Munichs, no more appeasement. It seemed to Americans in the 1940s that Nazi Germany had merely been replaced by Soviet Russia, that communism was simply the flip side of the totalitarian coin. The popular term "Red fascism" captured this sentiment.

American officials also knew that the nation's economic well-being depended on an activist foreign policy. In the postwar years the United States was the largest supplier of goods to world markets. That trade was jeopardized by the postwar economic paralysis of Europe and by discriminatory trade practices that violated the Open Door doctrine. "Any serious failure to maintain this flow," declared an assistant secretary of state, "would put millions of American businessmen, farmers, and workers out of business." Indeed, exports constituted about 10 percent of the gross national product. Both the domestic industrial and agricultural economies depended upon foreign outlets. Finally, the United States needed to export in order to pay for imports such as zinc, tin, and manganese. Economic expansionism, so much a part of pre–Cold

War history, thus remained a central feature of post-war foreign relations.

New strategic theory also propelled the United States toward an activist, expansionist, globalist diplomacy. To be ready for a military challenge in the postwar air age, American strategists believed that the nation's defenses had to begin far beyond its own borders. Thus the United States felt compelled to acquire overseas bases to guard the approaches to the Western Hemisphere. Overseas bases would also permit the United States to launch offensive attacks with might and speed.

American Strategic Thinking

President Truman, who shared these assumptions, had a personality that tended to increase international tensions. Whereas Franklin D. Roosevelt had been ingratiating, patient, and evasive, Truman was brash, impatient, and direct. He seldom displayed the appreciation of subtleties so essential to successful diplomacy. After his first meeting with the Soviet statesman V. M. Molotov, Truman commented: "I gave it to him straight 'one-two to the jaw.' I let him have it straight." This simplistic display of toughness became a trademark of American Cold War diplomacy.

As for the Soviets, they were not easy to get along with either. Dean Acheson, a high-ranking diplomat from 1945 to 1947 and secretary of state from 1949 to 1953, found them rude and abusive. Indeed, Premier Josef Stalin's blunt *nyets* strung American ears. But more than Soviet style bothered Americans. Soviet territorial ambitions—and successes—included a portion of eastern Poland, the Baltic states of Lithuania, Latvia, and Estonia, and parts of Finland and Rumania. In Eastern Europe Russian officials began to suppress non-Communists.

American Anti-Soviet Views

For their part, the Russians remembered how the hostile West had attempted to ostracize them before. Driven by memories of the past, by fear of a revived Germany, by the huge task of reconstruction, and by

living in view of the past

Marxist-Leninist doctrine, the Soviets suspected capitalist nations of plotting once again to extinguish the Communist flame. They protested that the Americans were surrounding them with hostile bases and practicing atomic and dollar diplomacy.

"After World War II," Senator J. William Fulbright remembered, "we were sold on the idea that Stalin was out to dominate the world." This view pitted a generous United States against a selfish Soviet Union. But Fulbright came to believe that the Soviets probably never intended to dominate the world, and they certainly lacked the capability to do so. Russia emerged from the war with a weak military establishment, a hobbled economy, and obsolete technology. Knowing this, American leaders did not expect the Soviets to attack Western Europe or to start a war they obviously could not sustain. The Soviet Union was a regional power in Eastern Europe, but not a global menace.

American officials nonetheless exaggerated the Soviet threat. There are several reasons why. First, President Truman liked things in black and white. Nuances, ambiguities, and counter-evidence were often glossed over to satisfy Truman's penchant for the simple answer. Second, military officers often overplayed the Soviet threat to persuade Congress to pass larger defense budgets. Third, some Americans fixed their attention, as they had since the Bolshevik Revolution of 1917, on the utopian communist goal of world revolution rather than on actual Soviet behavior. Fourth, American leaders feared that the terrible postwar conditions of poverty and social unrest abroad would leave United States strategic and economic interests vulnerable to political disorders that the Soviets might exploit. In other words, Americans feared less a direct Soviet attack and more the Soviets' potential seizing of opportunities to challenge American interests, perhaps through subversion. Last and overall, the United States, flushed with its own strength, took advantage of the postwar power vacuum to expand its overseas interests and shape a peace on American terms.

Question of the Soviet Threat

COLD WAR CRISES AND THE CONTAINMENT DOCTRINE

One of the first Soviet-American clashes concerned Poland. In 1945 the Soviets violated a Yalta agreement by refusing to admit conservative Poles from London to the Communist government in Lublin. The Russians also snuffed out civil liberties in the former Nazi satellite of Rumania. And after allowing free elections in Hungary and Czechoslovakia, they supported Communist coups in both nations. First Hungary (1947) and then Czechoslovakia (1948) succumbed to Communist subversion.

Soviet Domination of Eastern Europe

To justify their actions the Soviets complained that the United States was reviving Russia's traditional enemy, Germany. Russia also charged that the United States was pursuing a double standard in intervening in the affairs of Eastern Europe but expecting Russia to stay out of Latin America and Asia. They pointed to the lack of free elections in United States–backed Latin American dictatorships. Americans insisted that their spheres of influence were far more open, their methods far less repressive than the Russians'.

Another issue that divided America and Russia was the atomic bomb. The Soviets believed that the Americans were practicing "atomic diplomacy"—maintaining a frightening nuclear monopoly and bragging about it to scare the Soviets into diplomatic concessions. At a stormy foreign ministers' conference in 1945, Soviet Commissar of Foreign Affairs V. M. Molotov asked Secretary of State Byrnes if he had an atomic bomb in his side pocket. Byrnes replied that southerners "carry our artillery in our hip pocket. If you don't cut out all this stalling and let us get down to work, I am going to

Atomic Diplomacy

pull an atomic bomb out of my hip pocket and let you have it."

In this atmosphere of suspicion and distrust, the United States and the Soviet Union could not agree on the international control of atomic energy. The American proposal, called the Baruch Plan, provided for America's abandoning its monopoly after the world's fissionable materials had been brought under the authority of an international agency. The Soviets retorted that this plan denied them the right to develop their own bomb while the United States continued its supremacy.

The two adversaries also collided in Iran. By wartime agreement, British, American, and Russian troops occupied Iran. When American petroleum companies asked the Iranian government for an oil concession, Moscow sniffed a capitalist plot on its border. In March 1946, the date agreed on for troop withdrawal, the Russians stayed on in violation of the wartime treaty. Americans angrily accused the U.S.S.R. of intending to take over Iran. Iranian and Soviet diplomats managed to negotiate a settlement in April: Soviet soldiers would depart from Iran in exchange for an oil concession. Americans claimed a Cold War victory, believing their tough words had forced the Soviets to withdraw their troops. In 1947 they turned the tables by persuading the Iranians to go back on their promise of a Russian oil concession. Moscow cried that it had been double-crossed.

Crisis in Iran

Soviets and Americans clashed on every front in 1946. They could not agree on the unification of Germany, so they built up their zones independently. The new World Bank and International Monetary Fund, created at the 1944 Bretton Woods Conference to stabilize trade and finance, also became tangled in the Cold War struggle. The Soviets refused to join because the United States so dominated both institutions. In early 1946 Washington extended a $3.5 billion loan to Great Britain but turned down a similar Soviet request.

When in early February 1946 Stalin gave a pre-election speech depicting a world threatened by capitalist acquisitiveness, the American chargé d'affaires in Moscow, George F. Kennan, concluded that Russian fanaticism made even a temporary understanding impossible. Kennan's pessimistic "long telegram" to Washington fed the growing belief that only toughness would work with the Russians. On March 5, Winston Churchill made his stirring Iron Curtain speech, warning that Eastern European countries were being cut off from the West by Russia.

The Cold War escalated further on March 12, 1947, when in response to a request from the British, who could no longer afford to fund their Greek client government, the president asked **Truman Doctrine** Congress for $400 million in aid to Greece and Turkey. The United States must help "free peoples who are resisting attempted subjugation by armed minorities or by outside pressure," Truman declared; it was time to contain communism. The president's statement became known as the Truman Doctrine. There was no evidence that the Soviets were involved in the Greek civil war. Nevertheless the money was appropriated and the insurgents defeated.

In July 1947 George F. Kennan, director of the State Department's policy planning staff, offered another statement of what became known as the containment doctrine. Writing under the name "Mr. X" in the magazine *Foreign Affairs*, this expert on Soviet affairs advocated a "policy of firm containment, designed to confront the Russians with unalterable counterforce at every point where they show signs of encroaching upon the interests of a peaceful and stable world." Together with the Truman Doctrine, Kennan's article became the chief manifesto of Cold War foreign policy. Critic Walter Lippmann complained that the policy did not distinguish between areas vital and peripheral to American security.

Lippmann was happier with the Marshall Plan. On June 5, 1947, Secretary of State George C. Marshall (1947–1949) announced that the United States would finance a massive European **Marshall Plan** recovery program. Though Marshall did not exclude Eastern Europe or the Soviet Union, few American leaders believed that Russia and its allies would want to join an American-dominated project. And indeed, they did not join. Launched in 1948, the Marshall Plan sent $12.4 billion to Western Europe before the program ended in 1951 (see map, page 492). To stimulate business at home, the legislation said the foreign aid dollars must be spent in the United States. The Marshall Plan was a mixed success. In Europe, it caused inflation, failed to solve a serious balance-of-payments problem, and took only tentative steps toward economic integration. But it also sparked impressive Western European industrial production and investment and started the region toward self-sustaining economic growth. By 1952 the recovery program had given way to military assistance.

To strengthen the nation's defenses, Truman worked with Congress to streamline the government's administrative structure under the National Security Act (July 1947). The act created the Department of Defense, the National Security Council (NSC) to advise the president, and the Central Intelligence Agency (CIA) to conduct spying and information gathering. By the early 1950s the CIA had expanded its functions to include covert (secret) operations aimed at overthrowing unfriendly foreign leaders.

One of the most electric moments in the Cold War came in June 1948, when the Russians cut off Western access to the jointly occupied city of Berlin, located well inside the Soviet zone of **Berlin Blockade and Airlift** Germany. Before the Soviets' bold move, the Americans, French, and British had agreed to fuse their zones into what became known as West Germany. The three allies planned to integrate West Germany, including the three Western sectors of Berlin, into the Western European economy, complete with a reformed German currency. The Soviets, fearing a resurgent Germany tied to the American Cold War camp, may have sparked the Berlin crisis to stimulate negotiations. But if they thought Truman would compromise, they guessed wrong. Instead the president ordered a massive airlift of food, fuel,

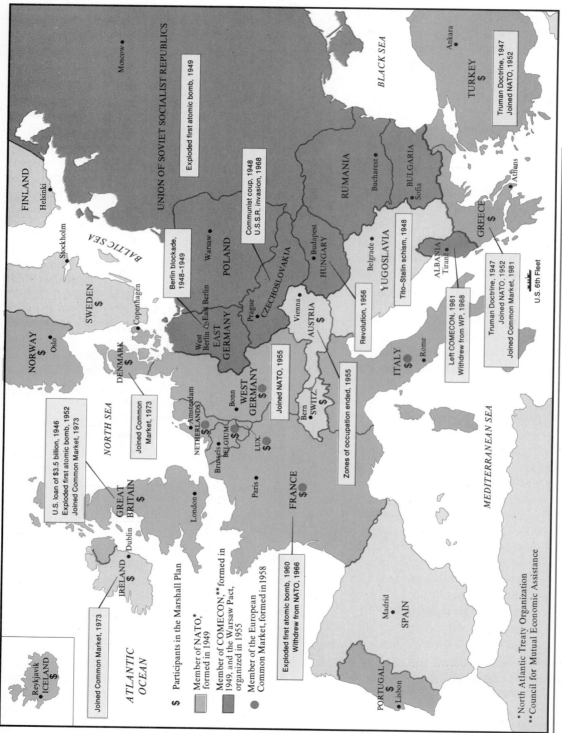

Divided Europe

Map labels and annotations:

ATLANTIC OCEAN

ICELAND $ — Reykjavik
Joined Common Market, 1973

IRELAND $ — Dublin
Joined Common Market, 1973

GREAT BRITAIN $ — London
U.S. loan of $3.5 billion, 1946
Exploded first atomic bomb, 1952
Joined Common Market, 1973

NORTH SEA

FRANCE $ — Paris
Exploded first atomic bomb, 1960
Withdrew from NATO, 1966

SPAIN — Madrid

PORTUGAL — Lisbon

NETHERLANDS $ — Amsterdam
BELGIUM $ — Brussels
LUX. $
Joined Common Market, 1973

WEST GERMANY $ — Bonn
Joined NATO, 1955

SWITZ. — Bern

AUSTRIA $ — Vienna
Zones of occupation ended, 1955

ITALY $ — Rome
Joined COMECON, 1961
Withdrew from WP, 1968

MEDITERRANEAN SEA

NORWAY $ — Oslo
SWEDEN $ — Stockholm
DENMARK $ — Copenhagen
Joined Common Market, 1973

BALTIC SEA

FINLAND — Helsinki

EAST GERMANY — East Berlin, West Berlin
Prague
Berlin blockade, 1948-1949

POLAND — Warsaw

CZECHOSLOVAKIA

HUNGARY — Budapest
Revolution, 1956

RUMANIA — Bucharest

YUGOSLAVIA — Belgrade
Tito-Stalin schism, 1948

ALBANIA — Tiranë

BULGARIA — Sofia

GREECE $ — Athens
Truman Doctrine, 1947
Joined NATO, 1952
Joined Common Market, 1981

UNION OF SOVIET SOCIALIST REPUBLICS — Moscow
Exploded first atomic bomb, 1949
Communist coup, 1948
U.S.S.R. invasion, 1968

BLACK SEA

TURKEY — Ankara
Truman Doctrine, 1947
Joined NATO, 1952

U.S. 6th Fleet

Legend:

$ — Participants in the Marshall Plan

Member of NATO,* formed in 1949

Member of COMECON,** formed in 1949, and the Warsaw Pact, organized in 1955

Member of the European Common Market, formed in 1958

* North Atlantic Treaty Organization
** Council for Mutual Economic Assistance

and other supplies to the isolated city—a plane almost every minute. Finally, in May 1949, their image badly damaged, the Soviets lifted the blockade. They had spurred the very result they feared: the creation of the Federal Republic of Germany (West Germany) that month. In retaliation they founded the German Democratic Republic (East Germany).

On April 4, 1949, believing that a military shield should be added to the economic shelf of the Marshall Plan, the United States, Canada, and much of Western Europe founded the North Atlantic Treaty Organization (NATO). The treaty aroused considerable debate at home, for not since 1778 had the United States entered a formal European military alliance. Critics feared that the treaty would provoke Russia, cause American troops to be stationed in Europe, and allow the president to commit forces to combat without a declaration of war. Truman responded that NATO would give Europeans the will to resist communism. And it would function as a "tripwire," bringing the full military and atomic force of the United States to bear on the Soviet Union if it dared to cross the East-West line. The Senate ratified the treaty, as it did all Truman's major foreign policy requests.

Creation of NATO

The American nuclear monopoly ended in 1949 when the Soviets exploded an atomic bomb. Early in 1950 President Truman had ordered the production of the hydrogen bomb. And in May Congress finally endorsed funds for technical assistance to developing nations, to draw them into the American sphere of influence (a plan called the Point Four Program, after point 4 of Truman's 1949 inaugural address).

A month earlier, the National Security Council had delivered to the president a top-secret document numbered NSC-68. Predicting continued tension with the Communists and describing a "shrinking world of polarized power," the report appealed for an enlarged military budget to counter the Soviet global design American strategists perceived. Administration officials worried about how to sell this strong prescription to the voters and budget-conscious con-

NSC-68

gressional representatives. "We were sweating over it, and then—with regard to NSC-68—thank God Korea came along," recalled one of Dean Acheson's aides.

THE COLD WAR IN ASIA

When the Korean War erupted in mid-1950, it came in the wake of vast changes in Asia. The Second World War had accelerated the process of decolonization begun during the First World War. Occupied with defending themselves and then with rebuilding after the war, imperial countries were no longer able to resist their colonies' demands for independence. Britain gave up India and what are now Pakistan and Bangladesh in 1947, Burma and Ceylon in 1948. The Dutch reluctantly let go of Indonesia in 1949. Only the French fought on in Indochina, finally retiring from that outpost in 1954.

The defeat of Japan brought about the division of its empire among the victors. Korea was divided between the United States and the Soviet Union. The Pacific islands (the Marshalls, Marianas, and Carolines) came under American control. Half of Sakhalin went to Russia as agreed at Yalta, and Formosa (Taiwan) was returned to the Chinese. As for Japan itself, the United States monopolized its reconstruction. General Douglas MacArthur, the director of the American occupation, wrote a democratic constitution for Japan, revitalized its economy, and destroyed the weapons and warships of the Japanese military.

Reconstruction of Japan

Though United States supremacy in Japan was an established fact, the Russians would not recognize it. Thus, after squabbling with Russia for years over a peace treaty with Japan, the United States finally signed a separate peace in 1951. The treaty restored Japan's sovereignty, ended the occupation, granted the United States a military base at Okinawa, and permitted American troops to be stationed in Japan. Tokyo and Washington also initialed a defense pact. The people who had been called beasts after their surprise attack on Pearl Harbor were now American allies.

Meanwhile, America's Chinese ally was faltering. The United States was feeding and fueling Jiang Jie-shi's (Chiang Kai-shek's) Nationalist army in its bat-

Chinese Civil War

tle against Mao Zedong and Zhou Enlai's Communists. Immediately after the Second World War American troops had occupied northern China, flown Nationalist soldiers to Manchuria, and stayed on to advise Generalissimo Jiang. Despite $3 billion in American aid from 1945 to 1949, however, Jiang proved a weak and unreliable friend. His government was both corrupt and out of touch with the peasants, who were attracted by Communist promises of land reform.

Still, American leaders saw Jiang as the only viable alternative to Mao. In the *White Paper* of 1949—a long government report on America's efforts to contain communism through aid to Jiang—Secretary Acheson asserted that the "Communist leaders have . . . publicly announced their subservience to a foreign power." Thus the United States rejected overtures for talks from the Chinese Communists. But Americans overestimated Mao's dependence on Russia. The Soviets had given Mao little support; indeed they preferred a weak China under Jiang to a strong one under Mao. Truman's refusal to allow talks with the Communists, however, left Mao little choice; he leaned toward the Soviets.

In fall 1949, after numerous military setbacks, Jiang fled to the island of Formosa, and Mao proclaimed the People's Republic of China. For several

Nonrecognition of the People's Republic of China

reasons the United States decided not to recognize the new government. First, American officials were alarmed by a new Sino-Soviet treaty of friendship signed in February 1950. Second, Mao's followers had harassed Americans and seized American-owned property in China. Third, Mao was now

openly hostile to the United States. Fourth, Dean Acheson believed that Mao would conquer Formosa, thus eliminating Jiang, and that frictions between Beijing and Moscow would ultimately convince Mao to sever his ties with the Soviets. Finally, a noisy group of Republican critics, called the China lobby, attacked the Truman administration for having "lost" China. The United States would not recognize the People's Republic of China until 1979.

Reaching for some way to offset Jiang's collapse, the National Security Council urged the president to fortify "friendly and independent" states in Asia as a bulwark against Communist expansion. In February 1950 the United States recognized the French puppet regime of Bao Dai in Vietnam, and a few months later decided to extend aid to the beleaguered French there. In April the National Security Council sent the president its alarming report NSC-68. And in May more funds went to Jiang Jieshi in Formosa.

A ROUGH TRANSITION AT HOME

As the Truman administration struggled with the Cold War abroad, it also faced the huge task of economic conversion from war to peace. Even before

Postwar Job Layoffs

the war's end, cutbacks in production had caused layoffs. Workers at the Ford Motor Company's massive Willow Run plant outside Detroit, where nine thousand Liberator bombers had been produced, were let go in spring 1945. Ten days after the victory over Japan, 1.8 million people received pink slips and 640,000 filed for unemployment compensation. The peak of postwar unemployment came in March 1946, when 2.7 million people were seeking work.

Despite these figures, the United States was not teetering on the brink of depression in 1945. People had plenty of savings to spend and suddenly there were new houses and cars for them to buy. Easy credit and new war-inspired industries like synthetic rubber and electronics promoted the buying spree. As a result, though war production began to wind down in 1944, the gross national product continued to rise in 1945. Thus the nation's postwar problem was not depression; it was inflation. Throughout 1945 and 1946 prices skyrocketed; the inflation rate for 1946 was 18.2 percent.

Truman declared his determination not only to combat unemployment and inflation, but also to expand on New Deal programs begun in the 1930s. On

Truman's Reconversion Plan

September 6, 1945, he delivered to Congress a twenty-one-point message urging extension of unemployment compensation, an increase in the minimum wage, adoption of permanent farm-price supports, and new public works projects. Truman revived Roosevelt's Economic Bill of Rights: every able-bodied American had a right to a job. Should the economy fail to provide one, the government should create it. Congress responded to Truman's message with the Employment Act of 1946, which announced that the government would use its resources, including deficit spending if necessary, to achieve "maximum employment, production, and purchasing power." The act established the Council of Economic Advisers to assist the president. But it fell short of Truman's hopes: Congress had deleted a commitment to absolute full employment.

Meanwhile, though prices were spiraling upward, many people were earning less than they had during the war. The wartime Little Steel formula had limited

Upsurge in Labor Strikes

workers to cost-of-living pay increases, and the end of war production had eliminated much of their overtime work. But while wages and salaries had declined slightly in 1946, net profits had reached all-time highs. Indignant that they were not sharing in the increased prosperity, over 4.5 million men and women left their jobs to strike in 1946. Workers forced nationwide shutdowns in the coal, automobile, steel, and electric industries and halted railroad and maritime transportation.

John L. Lewis's [...] the most powerful [...] was the nation's p[...] when soft-coal pro[...] and automobile ou[...] was canceled, thou[...] twenty-two states r[...] conserve coal. Th[...] legitimate—higher [...] a royalty of ten cen[...] ices and welfare and pension funds—a two-week truce in May failed to produce a solution. On May 21, with time running out and the country still desperate for coal, Truman ordered the seizure of the mines. Lewis and the government reached an accord a week later and the miners returned to work. But within six months the agreement had collapsed, and once again the government seized the mines.

There was no doubt in 1946 about the growing unpopularity of labor unions and their leadership. Many Americans believed that the unions were responsible

Truman's Attack on the Unions

for strikes that not only restricted the output of consumer goods and inflated prices, but also threatened the national security. In May, when a nationwide railroad strike was threatened, Truman made a dramatic appearance before a joint session of Congress. If the government seized a strike-bound industry, he said, and the workers in that industry refused to honor a presidential order to return to work, "I [would] request the Congress immediately to authorize the President to draft into the Armed Forces of the United States all workers who are on strike against their government." He also requested authority to strip strikers of seniority benefits, to take legal action against union leaders, and to fine and even imprison them for contempt. Truman's speech alienated not only railroad workers but union members in general. Many dedicated themselves to defeating him in the upcoming presidential election.

Truman fared little better in his direction of the Office of Price Administration. Now that the war was over, powerful interests wanted OPA controls lifted.

sumers were impatient with
shortages and black-market prices,
and manufacturers and farmers
wanted to jack up prices legally. Yet
controls expired in mid-1946 and infla-
se higher, people became angry.
epublicans made the most of public discontent.
Got enough meat?" asked Republican Congressman
John M. Vorys of Ohio. "Got enough houses? Got
enough OPA? . . . Got enough inflation? . . . Got
enough debt? . . . Got enough strikes?" When the
votes were tabulated, the Republicans had won a majority in both houses of the Eightieth Congress and
captured twenty-five of thirty-two nonsouthern governorships. The White House in 1948 seemed within
their grasp.

THE EIGHTIETH CONGRESS AND
THE ELECTION OF 1948

The politicians who ruled the Eightieth Congress,
both Republicans and southern Democrats,
were committed conservatives. Although they supported Truman's foreign policy, they perceived the
Republican landslide as a mandate to reverse the New
Deal, to curb the power of government and of labor.
Truman had had little success with the Seventy-ninth
Congress; he would have even less success with this
one. Ironically, however, it would be the Eightieth
Congress that would help him to win the presidency
in 1948. For if Truman had alienated labor, farmers,
and liberals, the Eightieth Congress made them livid.

One extremely unpopular measure was the Taft-
Hartley Act, which Congress adopted over Truman's
veto in 1947. A revision of the Wagner Act of
1935, the bill prohibited the closed
shop, in which only union members could be hired. Moreover,
the Taft-Hartley Act forbade union

Taft-Hartley
Act

contributions to political funds in federal elections;
required union leaders to sign non-Communist affi-
davits; and mandated an eighty-day cooling-off period in strikes that imperiled the national security.
Truman's veto of the bill vindicated him in the eyes
of organized labor.

Throughout 1947 and into 1948 the Eightieth
Congress offended numerous interest groups, which
in turn swung back to Truman. For example, the
president asked Congress for continued price supports
for farmers; the Eightieth Congress responded with
weakened price supports. The president requested
nationwide health insurance; the Eightieth Congress
refused. It was the same with federal funding of public
housing and aid to public education; with broadened
and increased unemployment compensation, old-age
and survivors' benefits, and the minimum wage;
and with antilynching, anti-poll tax, and fair-
employment legislation. Truman proposed; Congress
rejected or ignored his requests.

But Republicans seemed oblivious to public opinion. Not since 1928 had they been so confident of
capturing the presidency, and most political experts
agreed. "Only a political miracle,"
stated *Time*, "or extraordinary stu-
pidity on the part of the Republicans can save the Democratic party."
At their national convention, Republicans strengthened their position by nominating for president and
vice president the governors of the nation's two most
populous states: Thomas E. Dewey of New York and
Earl Warren of California.

Campaign of
1948

Truman, who received the Democratic nomination, found himself fighting more than just Republicans. Leftist elements of the party, especially those
critical of the Truman Doctrine, started a new Progressive party under the leadership of former vice
president Henry Wallace. Segregationists, angered
over the Democratic party's adoption of a civil rights
plank, formed the States Rights Democratic party
(Dixiecrats) and nominated Governor Strom Thur-
mond of South Carolina. If Wallace's candidacy did
not destroy Truman's chances, experts said, the Dixiecrats certainly would.

So few pollsters predicted that President Harry S Truman (1884–1972) would win in 1948 that the Chicago Tribune *announced his defeat before all the returns were in. Here a victorious Truman pokes fun at the newspaper for the premature headline.   UPI/Bettmann Newsphotos.*

But Truman had ideas of his own. He called the Eightieth Congress into special session and demanded that it enact all the planks in the Republican platform. If Republicans really wanted to transform their ideals into law, said Truman, this was the time to do it. After Congress had met for two weeks and accomplished nothing of significance, Truman took to the road. Traveling more than 30,000 miles by train, he delivered scores of whistle-stop speeches denouncing the "do-nothing" Eightieth Congress.

Still, no amount of furious campaigning on Truman's part seemed likely to change the predicted outcome. Hours before the returns were in, the *Chicago Tribune* had printed a headline announcing "DEWEY DEFEATS TRUMAN."

Yet as the votes were counted early into the morning, it became clear that Truman had confounded the experts. The final tally was 24.1 million popular votes, 304 electoral votes, for Truman; 21.9 million popular votes, 189 electoral votes, for Dewey. Not only had Truman won four more years in the White House, but the Democrats had regained control of Congress—in the House by a majority of ninety-three, in the Senate by twelve.

TRUMAN ON CIVIL RIGHTS

The postwar years were a period of gathering strength for Afro-Americans. Truman and other politicians knew they would have to compete for the growing black vote in urban-industrial states like California, Illinois, Michigan, Ohio, Pennsylvania, and New York. Many Republicans now cultivated the black vote. Thomas Dewey, who as governor of New York had pushed successfully for the establishment of a fair employment practices commission, was particularly popular with blacks. In Harlem, which had gone Democratic by a 4-to-1 margin in 1938, Dewey won by large margins in 1942 and 1946.

Certainly, then, Truman had political reasons for supporting black civil rights. But he also felt a moral obligation to blacks. For one thing, he believed that it was only fair that each American, regardless of race, should enjoy the full rights of citizenship. More than that, Truman was horrified by a report that police in Aiken, South Carolina, had gouged out the eyes of a black sergeant just three hours after he had been discharged from the army. Several weeks later, on December 5, 1946, Truman signed an executive order establishing the President's Committee on Civil Rights.

A year later the committee delivered its report, *To Secure These Rights.* Among the committee's recommendations, which would become the agenda for the

President's Committee on Civil Rights civil rights movement for the next twenty years, were the enactment of federal antilynching, antisegregation, antibrutality, and anti–poll tax laws. *To Secure These Rights* also

called for laws guaranteeing voting rights and equal employment opportunity, and for the establishment of a permanent commission on civil rights and a civil rights division within the Department of Justice. Congress failed to act, but for the first time since Reconstruction, a president acknowledged the federal government's responsibility to protect Afro-Americans.

Truman also used the power of the executive to proclaim a policy of "fair employment throughout the federal establishment." And his Committee on Equality of Treatment and Opportunity in the Armed Services issued a report, *Freedom to Serve,* in 1950 stating that racial desegregation would "make for a better Army, Navy, and Air Force." Though strong, at times even fierce, opposition to desegregation existed within the military, by the outbreak of the Korean War segregated units were being phased out.

Blacks also benefited from a series of Supreme Court decisions. The trend toward judicial support of civil rights had begun in the late 1930s, when

Supreme Court Decisions on Civil Rights the NAACP established its Legal Defense Fund. At the time, the NAACP was trying to destroy the separate-but-equal doctrine by insisting on its literal interpretation. In higher education, the NAACP figured, the cost of racially separate schools was prohibitive. "You can't build a cyclotron for one [black] student," the president of the University of Oklahoma acknowledged. As a result, in the 1940s black students won admission to professional and graduate schools at a number of state universities. The NAACP also scored notable victories in two other cases. In 1944, in *Smith v. Allwright,* the Supreme Court outlawed the whites-only primaries held by the Democratic party in some southern states, branding them a violation of the Fifteenth Amendment. Two years later the Court declared segregation in interstate bus transportation unconstitutional.

A change in social attitudes accompanied these gains in black political and legal power. Books such as Gunnar Myrdal's *American Dilemma* (1944) and

Jackie Robinson cracked the color line in major league baseball when he joined the Brooklyn Dodgers for the 1947 season. Robinson won rookie-of-the-year honors and was later elected to the Baseball Hall of Fame. In this game against the Phila-delphia Phillies, Robinson stole home.   Wide World Photos.

Richard Wright's *Native Son* (1940) and *Black Boy* (1945) had increased white awareness of the social injustice that plagued blacks. A new black middle class had emerged, composed of college-educated activists, veterans, and union workers. Blacks and whites were working together in CIO unions and with service organizations such as the National Council of Churches. And in 1947 a black baseball player, Jackie Robinson, cracked the major-league color barrier and electrified crowds with his spectacular hitting and base running.

Cold War pressures also benefited blacks. As the Soviet Union was quick to point out, the United States could not pose as the leader of the free world, or condemn the denial of human rights behind the Iron Curtain, so long as it condoned racism at home. Nor could it convince new African and Asian nations

of its dedication to human rights if Afro-Americans were subjected to segregation, disfranchisement, and racial violence. To win the support of nonaligned nations, the United States would have to live up to its own ideals.

MCCARTHYISM *lurking against communism (paranoia)*

A common misconception about the postwar era is that anti-Communist hysteria began in 1950 with the furious speeches of Senator Joseph R. McCarthy. Actually, anti-Communism had been part of the American political temper ever since the First

World War and the Red Scare of 1919 and 1920. McCarthy did not create this hysteria; he manipulated it to his own advantage. He was, though, undeniably the most successful and frightening redbaiter the country had ever seen.

To a great extent President Truman initiated the postwar crusade against communism. Truman was concerned over the wartime increase in the nation's Communist party membership (80,000 in 1943–1944) and by the revelation in 1945 that classified government documents had been found in the offices of *Amerasia*, a little-known magazine whose editors sympathized with the Chinese Communists. He was also bothered by a report that Soviet spies were operating in Canada.

Spurred by these revelations, Truman in March 1947 ordered investigations into the loyalty of the more than 3 million employees of the U.S. government. In 1950 the government began discharging people deemed "security risks." Some were purged for homosexuality or alcoholism; others became victims of guilt by association. None were allowed to confront their accusers.

Truman's Loyalty Probe

The wellspring of this fear of communism was the Cold War, and Truman was not alone in peddling fear. Conservatives and liberal Democrats joined him. Republicans used the same technique to attack the Democratic candidates for president in 1948 and 1952; liberal Democrats used it to discredit the far-left, pro-Wallace wing of their party. In many ways, then, the anti-Communist hysteria of the late 1940s was a phenomenon created by professional politicians and promoted by labor union officials, religious leaders, Hollywood moguls, and other influential figures.

Despite the false accusations, there was cause for alarm—especially in 1949. In that year, the Russians exploded their first atomic bomb, and the Chinese Communists, finally victorious in the civil war, proclaimed the People's Republic of China. Furthermore, in 1949, a former State Department official, Alger Hiss, was on trial for denying that he had passed to the Russians "numerous secret, confidential

Hiss Trial

and restricted documents." When Truman and Secretary of State Dean Acheson came to his defense, some people began to suspect that the Democrats had something to hide. In 1950 Hiss was convicted of perjury. That same year the British arrested Klaus Fuchs, a nuclear scientist, for providing Soviet agents with secrets from the atomic-bomb project at Los Alamos, New Mexico.

It was in this atmosphere that Senator Joseph McCarthy mounted a rostrum in Wheeling, West Virginia, and gave the existing state of mind a name: McCarthyism. The State Department, he asserted, was "thoroughly infested with Communists," and the most dangerous person in the State Department was Dean Acheson. Reporters wrote that the senator claimed to have a list of 205 Communists working in the State Department; later McCarthy lowered the figure to "57 card-carrying members," then raised it to 81. No matter the number. What McCarthy needed was a winning campaign issue, and he had found it. Republicans, distraught over losing what had appeared to be a sure victory in 1948, were eager to support his attack.

McCarthy's Attack on the State Department

The widespread support for anti-Communist measures was also apparent in the adoption, over Truman's veto, of the Internal Security, or McCarran, Act of 1950. The act made it unlawful for anyone to "contribute to the establishment . . . of a totalitarian dictatorship," required members of "Communist-front" organizations to register with the government, and prohibited such people from holding defense jobs or traveling abroad. And in a telling decision in 1951 (*Dennis et al.* v. *U.S.*), the Supreme Court upheld the Smith Act, a law passed in 1940 making it illegal to support or belong to an organization advocating the overthrow of the government by force, and ordered the imprisonment of eleven American Communist leaders.

McCarthy and McCarthyism gained momentum throughout 1950. Nothing seemed to slow the senator down, not even attacks by other Republicans. Seven Republican senators broke with their colleagues and publicly condemned McCarthy for his "selfish political exploitation of fear, bigotry, ignorance, and intolerance." A Senate committee reported that his charges against the State Department were "a fraud and a hoax." But McCarthy had much to sustain him, including the arrest for espionage of Julius and Ethel Rosenberg in July and August. In 1951 the Rosenbergs were found guilty of recruiting and supervising a spy at the Los Alamos atomic laboratory and sentenced to death. In spite of protests that the Rosenbergs were victims of anti-Communist hysteria, they were executed in 1953. Perhaps even more helpful to McCarthy, however, was the outbreak of the Korean War in June 1950.

THE KOREAN WAR AND ITS GLOBAL CONSEQUENCES

In the early morning hours of June 25, 1950, thousands of troops under the banner of the Democratic People's Republic of Korea (North Korea) moved across the 38th parallel into the Republic of Korea (South Korea). For years the two Koreas had skirmished along the border the great powers had drawn for them in 1945. Both regimes sought reunification of the divided country, but each on its own terms. Now it appeared that the North Koreans, heavily armed by the Russians, would realize their goal by force. After huddling with his advisers, the president decided to intervene; he ordered MacArthur to send arms to South Korea and to attack North Korean forces from the air. Thinking beyond Korea, he directed the Seventh Fleet to patrol the waters between the Chinese mainland and Jiang's sanctuary, Formosa. Finally, on June 30, Truman ordered American troops into battle. After the Security Council, in the Soviet delegate's absence, voted to assist South Korea, MacArthur became United Nations Commander.

Truman acted decisively for war because he believed, in the Cold War mentality of the time, that the Soviets had masterminded the North Korean attack. Unanswered questions, however, dog the thesis that Russia started the Korean War. When it voted to aid South Korea, the Soviet delegate was absent from the Security Council because he was protesting the United Nations' refusal to seat the People's Republic of China. If the Soviets had fomented the war in Korea, it is surprising that their delegate was not present to veto aid to South Korea. Then, too, why did the Soviets give so little aid to North Korea once the war broke out? Did the war, as some historians have suggested, begin as a Korean civil conflict rather than as part of the Soviet-American confrontation?

Origins of the Korean War

In June 1950 such questions were not being asked. Truman and his aides never doubted that Russia or international Communism was testing their policy of containment; that American prestige was at stake; and that failure to act in Korea would prompt Russian aggression in Iran or Berlin. And, having bragged about toughness against Communism before, Truman could not now refrain from acting against North Korea.

At first the war went badly for American troops, who accounted for about 90 percent of United Nations forces. Pushed into the tiny Pusan perimeter at the base of South Korea, the Eighth Army weathered numerous North Korean assaults. Then on September 15, 1950, MacArthur launched an amphibious landing at Inchon, several hundred miles behind North Korean lines (see map, page 502). The operation was so successful it enabled American leaders to redefine their goals from the containment of North Korea to the reunification of Korea by force.

Inchon

Within several weeks American troops had driven deeply into North Korea. The Chinese watched warily; Mao issued public warnings that China could not permit the continued bombing of its transportation links with Korea or the annihilation of North Korea itself. But MacArthur and officials in Washing-

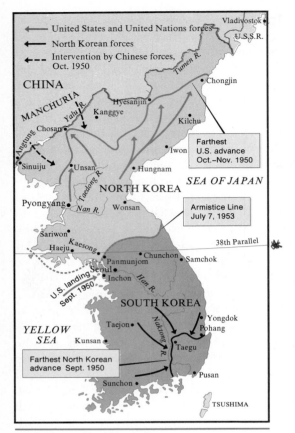

United States and United Nations forces
North Korean forces
Intervention by Chinese forces, Oct. 1950

Vladivostok
U.S.S.R.

CHINA

MANCHURIA

Yalu R.

Tumen R.

Chongjin

Hyesanjin
Kanggye
Kilchu
Chosan
Antung
Sinuiju
Unsan
Iwon
Hungnam

Farthest U.S. advance Oct.–Nov. 1950

NORTH KOREA

Taedong R.

SEA OF JAPAN

Pyongyang
Nan R.
Wonsan

Armistice Line July 7, 1953

Sariwon
Kaesong
Haeju
38th Parallel
Chunchon
Samchok
Panmunjom
Seoul
Inchon
Han R.

U.S. landing Sept. 1950

SOUTH KOREA

Taejon
Naktong R.
Yongdok
Pohang
Taegu

YELLOW SEA

Kunsan

Farthest North Korean advance Sept. 1950

Pusan
Sunchon

TSUSHIMA

The Korean War, 1950–1953   Source: By permission of the publisher, from *American Foreign Policy: A History* by Paterson et al., p. 474. (Lexington, Mass.: D.C. Heath and Company, 1983).

ton shrugged off the statements. In late October Americans tangled with some **Chinese Entry into the Korean War** Chinese soldiers, who pulled back quickly after the encounter. This may have been one of many signals to the United States that American advances to the Chinese border should halt, or China would enter the war. On November 26, tens of thousands of Chinese troops counterattacked, surprising the general's forces and driving them pellmell southward. Embarrassed, MacArthur demanded that Washington order a massive air attack on China. Tru-

man, after reflecting upon the costs of a wider war, rejected MacArthur's advice.

By March 1951 the military lines had stabilized around the 38th parallel. Truman contemplated negotiations, and the Soviets stated publicly that they favored a political settlement. But **Truman Fires MacArthur** MacArthur had other ideas. The general was making reckless public statements, calling for an attack on China or for Jiang's return to the mainland. He also hinted that the president was practicing appeasement, and he denounced the concept of limited war. On April 10 Truman fired the general for insubordination. MacArthur, returned home to a hero's welcome, and Truman's popularity sagged. Truman was backed, however, by the chairman of the Joint Chiefs of Staff, General Omar Bradley. Escalation could bring Russia into battle, Bradley pointed out, and it was unwise to exhaust American resources in Asia when there were allies in Europe to be protected.

Armistice talks began in July 1951, but the fighting and dying went on for two more years. Though the president-elect, Dwight D. Eisenhower, went to **The POW Question** Korea personally in December 1952 to fulfill a campaign pledge, his post-election visit brought no settlement. The sticking point in the negotiations was the fate of the prisoners of war (POWs): thousands of North Korean and Chinese captives did not want to return home. On July 23, 1953, an armistice was finally signed. The combatants agreed to hand the POW question over to a special panel of neutral nations (which later gave prisoners their choice of staying or leaving). The North Korean–South Korean line was set close to the 38th parallel, the prewar boundary. Thus ended a frustrating war—a limited war that Americans, accustomed to victory, had not won. The experience was indeed sobering, as was the casualty list of 54,000 Americans dead and 103,000 wounded. Total killed and wounded for all combatants in the Korean War was 1.9 million.

The Korean War had major political consequences. Bipartisanship in foreign policy eroded fur-

IMPORTANT EVENTS

1945	Yalta Conference		Berlin blockade and airlift
	Roosevelt dies; Truman assumes presidency		Truman elected president
	United Nations founded	1949	North Atlantic Treaty Organization founded
	Germany surrenders		Russia explodes atomic bomb
	Potsdam Conference		Communist victory in China
	Atomic bombs devastate Hiroshima and Nagasaki	1950	Klaus Fuchs arrested as atomic spy
	Japan surrenders		Alger Hiss convicted of perjury
	Truman's 21-point economic message to Congress		Hydrogen bomb project announced
			McCarthy alleges Communists in government
1946	Crisis over Iran		*Freedom to Serve*
	Employment Act of 1946		NSC-68
	Churchill's Iron Curtain speech		Point Four Program launched
	Strikes by coal miners		Korean War begins
	Paris Peace Conference		Julius and Ethel Rosenberg arrested
	Baruch Plan		Inchon
	Inflation reaches 18.2 percent		Internal Security (McCarran) Act
	Republicans win both houses of Congress		U.S. troops cross the 38th parallel
			China enters the Korean War
1947	Truman Doctrine	1951	Armistice talks begin in Korea
	Truman's Employee Loyalty Program		*Dennis et al. v. U.S.*
	Communist takeover in Hungary	1952	Hydrogen bomb exploded
	Taft-Hartley Act		Eisenhower elected president
	Kennan's "Mr. X" article		Republicans win both houses of Congress
	Marshall Plan announced		
	To Secure These Rights	1953	Korean War ends
	National Security Act		
1948	Communist coup in Czechoslovakia		

ther, and the powers of the presidency grew as Congress deferred to Truman time and again. Truman had never gone to Congress for a declaration of war, for he believed that as commander-in-chief he had the authority to

Debate over Globalist Policy

send troops to Korea. The war also set off a great national debate. Conservative critics of globalism suggested that America should reduce its overseas commitments and draw its defense line in the Western Hemisphere. But Republican John Foster Dulles countered that "a defense that accepts encirclement quickly decomposes." The advocates of global defense won the debate. Increased aid flowed to allies around the world, and military budgets remained high.

WARTIME DISCONTENT AND
THE ELECTION OF 1952

As the 1952 presidential election approached, the Democrats foundered. Added to frustration with the war and hysteria over Communism was the revelation of influence-peddling by some of Truman's cronies. Known as "five-percenters," these presidential appointees had offered government contracts in return for 5-percent kickbacks. One employee of the executive branch admitted under oath, "I have only one thing to sell and that is influence." Once again the Democratic party seemed doomed.

What sealed its fate was the Republican candidate, General Dwight D. Eisenhower. "Ike" was a bona fide war hero with a winning smile and a catchy campaign slogan: "I Like Ike." His opponent
The Republican Ticket was Adlai Stevenson, the thoughtful, literate, and witty governor of Illinois. During the campaign, Eisenhower remained silent on the subject of McCarthyism, while his running mate, Senator Richard M. Nixon of California, scored points by referring to Stevenson as "Adlai the appeaser . . . who got a Ph.D. from Dean Acheson's College of Cowardly Communist Containment." The election was never much of a contest; Eisenhower won almost 34 million popular votes and 442 electoral votes to Stevenson's 27 million popular and 89 electoral votes.

Although Truman was highly unpopular when he left office in 1953, historians now rate him among the nation's ten best presidents. He came to office suddenly and with little experience, but in eight years he greatly strengthened the powers of the presidency.

Truman's Presidential Legacy At the onset of the Cold War he had announced policies to contain any presumed threat of Soviet expansion. During his presidency the Central Intelligence Agency, National Security Council, Council of Economic Advisers, and a unified Department of Defense were all created. Truman's main problems stemmed from his overreaction to the alleged threat of Communist subversion in government. Finally, he sent American troops to fight in Korea without a declaration of war from Congress.

At the same time, Truman was still a New Dealer who fought for social welfare programs and legislation for farmers and workers. His Fair Deal, most of which was enacted during subsequent presidential administrations, included first-class citizenship for Afro-Americans. He showed his spunk and courage in 1948, when he pulled the biggest upset in American political history. When he left office in 1953, he had set the United States on a course from which it would not veer in the future and had cast a long shadow across the country's twentieth-century history.

SUGGESTIONS FOR FURTHER
READING

Origins of the Cold War and Policy Toward Europe

Stephen Ambrose, *Rise to Globalism*, 3rd ed. (1983); Richard J. Barnet, *The Alliance* (1983); Seyom Brown, *The Faces of Power* (1983); Leonard Dinnerstein, *America and the Survivors of the Holocaust* (1982); John L. Gaddis, *The United States and the Origins of the Cold War, 1941–1947* (1972); Louis Halle, *The Cold War as History* (1967); Laurence S. Kaplan, *The United States and NATO* (1984); Walter LaFeber, *America, Russia, and the Cold War, 1945–1980,*

4th ed. (1980); Melvyn Leffler, "The American Concept of National Security and the Beginnings of the Cold War, 1945–1948," *American Historical Review,* 89 (1984), 346–381; David McLellan, *Dean Acheson* (1976); Thomas G. Paterson, *On Every Front: The Making of the Cold War* (1979); Thomas G. Paterson, *Soviet-American Confrontation* (1973); Gaddis Smith, *Dean Acheson* (1972); William Taubman, *Stalin's American Policy* (1982); Bernard A. Weisberger, *Cold War, Cold Peace* (1984); Imanuel Wexler, *The Marshall Plan Revisited* (1983); Daniel Yergin, *Shattered Peace* (1977).

Truman Doctrine, Containment, and the Middle East

Thomas H. Etzold and John L. Gaddis, eds., *Containment* (1978); Richard M. Freeland, *The Truman Doctrine and the Origins of McCarthyism* (1972); John L. Gaddis, *Strategies of Containment* (1982); Bruce R. Kuniholm, *The Origins of the Cold War in the Near East* (1980); Walter Lippmann, *The Cold War* (1947); William R. Louis, *The British Empire in the Middle East, 1945–1951* (1984); Aaron D. Miller, *Search for Security* (1980); Thomas G. Paterson, ed., *Containment and the Cold War* (1973); Michael B. Stoff, *Oil, War, and American Security* (1980); Samuel F. Wells, Jr., "Sounding the Tocsin: NSC-68 and the Soviet Threat," *International Security,* 4 (1979), 116–158; Lawrence S. Wittner, *American Intervention in Greece, 1943–1949* (1982).

China and Asia

Robert M. Blum, *Drawing the Line* (1982); Dorothy Borg and Waldo Heinrichs, eds., *Uncertain Years* (1980); Russell Buhite, *Soviet-American Relations in Asia, 1945–1954* (1982); Warren I. Cohen, *America's Response to China,* 2nd ed. (1980); Herbert Feis, *Contest over Japan* (1967); Akira Iriye, *The Cold War in Asia* (1974); E. J. Kahn, Jr., *The China Hands* (1975); Gary May, *China Scapegoat: The Diplomatic Ordeal of John Carter Vincent* (1979); Charles E. Neu, *The Troubled Encounter: The United States and Japan* (1975); Michael Schaller, *The United States and China in the Twentieth Century* (1979); William W. Stueck, Jr., *The Road to Confrontation: American Policy Toward China and Korea, 1947–1950* (1981); Christopher Thorne, *Allies of a Kind* (1978); Tang Tsou, *America's Failure in China, 1941–1950* (1963); Nancy B. Tucker, *Patterns in the Dust:*

Chinese-American Relations and the Recognition Controversy, 1949–1950 (1983).

Politics during the Truman Administration

Barton J. Bernstein, ed., *Politics and Policies of the Truman Administration* (1970); Robert J. Donovan, *Tumultuous Years: The Presidency of Harry S Truman, 1949–1953* (1982); Robert J. Donovan, *Conflict and Crisis: The Presidency of Harry S Truman, 1945–1948* (1977); Robert H. Ferrell, *Harry S Truman and the Modern American Presidency* (1983); Alonzo L. Hamby, *Beyond the New Deal: Harry S Truman and American Liberalism* (1973); V. O. Key, *Southern Politics in State and Nation* (1949); Norman D. Markowitz, *The Rise and Fall of the People's Century: Henry A. Wallace and American Liberalism, 1941–1948* (1973); Donald R. McCoy, *The Presidency of Harry S Truman* (1984); Richard Norton-Smith, *Thomas E. Dewey and His Times* (1982); Allen Yarnell, *Democrats and Progressives: The 1948 Presidential Election as a Test of Postwar Liberalism* (1974).

Truman and the Economy

Jack Stokes Ballard, *The Shock of Peace: Military and Economic Demobilization After World War II* (1983); Richard O. Davies, *Housing Reform During the Truman Administration* (1966); R. Alton Lee, *Truman and Taft-Hartley* (1966); Allen J. Matusow, *Farm Policies and Politics in the Truman Years* (1967); Arthur F. McClure, *The Truman Administration and the Problems of Postwar Labor* (1969).

Civil Rights

William C. Berman, *The Politics of Civil Rights in the Truman Administration* (1970); Richard M. Dalfiume, *Desegregation of the U.S. Armed Forces* (1969); Donald R. McCoy and Richard T. Ruetten, *Quest and Response: Minority Rights and the Truman Administration* (1973); Jules Tygiel, *Baseball's Great Experiment: Jackie Robinson and His Legacy* (1983).

McCarthyism

David Caute, *The Great Fear* (1978); Larry Ceplair and Steven Englund, *The Inquisition in Hollywood* (1983); Robert Griffith, *The Politics of Fear: Joseph R. McCarthy and the Senate* (1970); Stanley I. Kutler, *The American Inquisition: Justice and Injustice in the Cold War* (1982); Mary Sperling

McAuliffe, *Crisis on the Left: Cold War Politics and American Liberals, 1947–1954* (1978); Victor Navasky, *Naming Names* (1980); William L. O'Neill, *A Better World: Stalinism and the American Intellectuals* (1983); David M. Oshinsky, *A Conspiracy So Immense: The World of Joe McCarthy* (1983); Ronald Radosh and Joyce Milton, *The Rosenberg File* (1983); Thomas C. Reeves, *The Life and Times of Joe McCarthy* (1982); Walter and Miriam Schneir, *Invitation to an Inquest* (1983 ed.); Athan Theoharis, *Seeds of Repression: Harry S Truman and the Origins of McCarthyism* (1971); Allen Weinstein, *Perjury: The Hiss-Chambers Case* (1978).

The Korean War and Korean-American Relations

Ronald J. Caridi, *The Korean War and American Politics* (1969); Bruce Cumings, ed., *Child of Conflict* (1983); Bruce Cumings, *The Origins of the Korean War* (1980); Charles Dobbs, *The Unwanted Symbol* (1981); Joseph C. Goulden, *Korea* (1982); Glenn D. Paige, *The Korean Decision* (1968); Robert R. Simmons, *The Strained Alliance* (1975); John W. Spanier, *The Truman-MacArthur Controversy and the Korean War* (1959); Allen Whiting, *China Crosses the Yalu* (1960).

CHAPTER 28

AN AGE OF
FRAGILE CONSENSUS
1953–1961

The signs of patriotism were everywhere. Whether beating Russian athletes at the Olympics or marveling at the nation's powerful military machine, Americans celebrated their country as the best place on earth. And to trumpet that difference, sermonized the Presbyterian minister George M. Docherty on February 7, 1954, religion should be enlisted. "One nation, indivisible, with liberty and justice for all"— American schoolchildren recited those famous words every morning in pledges of allegiance to the flag. With President Dwight D. Eisenhower sitting in his congregation that day, the Reverend Docherty implored political leaders to insert "under God" after "one nation" in the flag pledge. The president agreed, and Congress hastened to make the change.

This small episode conjoining religion, patriotism, and politics befitted the 1950s, an age of consensus. In that decade Americans generally shared a belief in anti-Communism and economic progress. President Eisenhower was active in articulating the two beliefs and devising programs to satisfy them. But he moved cautiously and preferred a hidden-hand style to conspicuous displays of political arm-twisting.

Believing that Communists posed a mortal danger to the American system, the Eisenhower administration expanded Truman's loyalty program, endorsed restrictive legislation, and purged the State Department. The president was reluctant to confront directly Senator Joseph McCarthy, whose anti-Communist tactics proved reckless. McCarthy eventually destroyed himself with his excesses. To maintain economic growth, Eisenhower pursued staunchly Republican goals: a balanced budget, reduced government spending, lower taxes, low inflation, private enterprise, a return of power to the states, and modest federal efforts to stimulate economic development. The Eisenhower officials did not attempt to roll back the New Deal and Fair Deal. In fact, however reluctantly, they expanded the welfare state.

Holding to their consensus thinking, white Americans celebrated their economic system for providing a high standard of living. But recurrent recessions and continued poverty in the midst of plenty raised doubts that economic progress had bestowed its benefits on all. An infant civil rights movement especially challenged the consensus view. Not only were most blacks at the bottom of the economic ladder; they were being denied their constitutional rights. How would blacks be brought into the consensus? The president, Congress, southern whites, black civil rights activists—all gave different answers as they debated the Supreme Court's 1954 *Brown* decision.

In foreign affairs, too, Eisenhower's low-key style and the two features of the consensus were evident. Eisenhower essentially continued Truman's Cold War policies, applying the containment doctrine worldwide. To wage the Cold War, the administration relied on nuclear weapons and interventions, some of them by a major new instrument of foreign policy, the Central Intelligence Agency (CIA). Many of the CIA's covert operations were directed against governments in the Third World, where new states were emerging from colonialism to nationhood. Americans feared that revolutionary nationalism and unrest in Third World countries was being or would be exploited by Communists linked to a Soviet-led international conspiracy. And in Latin America the United States faced several revolutionary challenges to its hegemony. Those challenges often took the form of an economic nationalism that threatened American companies. The United States, then, intervened abroad not just to stop communism, but also to protect American economic overseas interests.

Consensus and the Politics of Eisenhower's First Term

Smiling Ike, with his folksy style, displays of confusion, and frequent escapes from the Oval Office to the golf course, fueled Democratic charges that he failed to lead—"the bland leading the bland." But it was not that simple. Dwight D. Eisenhower was no stranger to hard work. His style was to play down his political role and highlight his role as chief of state. Eisenhower relied considerably upon staff work, delegated authority to departments, and shied away from close involvement in the legislative process. Sometimes this meant that he was not well informed on details, giving the impression that he was out of touch with his own government. He was not, and he remained a very popular president.

During Eisenhower's presidency, with few exceptions, white Americans clung to the status quo. Demand for reform was deemed not only unnecessary but downright unpatriotic. The country was engaged in a moral struggle with Communism, people believed, and during such a crusade one should support, not criticize, the government. Almost everywhere he looked, the historian Henry Steele Commager saw conformity: "the uncritical and unquestioning acceptance of America as it is." A weak minority on the left advocated checks on the political power of corporations and a noisy minority on the right vilified the government for a supposed wishy-washy campaign against Communism, but both liberal Democrats and moderate Republicans avoided extremism of any variety, satisfied to be occupying "the vital center." Along with this attitude of conformity went trust in and respect for established authority. In government, business, labor, the military, religion, and education, Americans let those at the top bargain on their behalf, and they chose to pursue economic goals more than moral ones.

The Consensus Mood

Scholars of the 1950s who subscribed to the consensus proclaimed the "end of ideology" in America. Consensus historians like Daniel Boorstin did not deny the existence of conflict in the American past, but they ascribed it less to flaws in society than to psychologically disturbed personalities. Among the people historians identified as maladjusted were abolitionists, feminists, Populists,

Consensus Historiography

On July 4, 1961, patriotic residents of Chicago neighborhood posed in front of their flag-draped homes. Patriotism was a prominent characteristic of the age of consensus.   National Archives.

and progressive reformers. The consensus interpretation thus shifted the focus away from society's faults—slavery, sexism, or political corruption—and placed it on the critics who demanded reform.

In this age of consensus, President Eisenhower approached his duties with a philosophy of "dynamic conservatism," explaining that he would be "conservative when it comes to money and liberal when it comes to human beings." Eisenhower's was "an Administration representing business and industry," admitted Interior Secretary Douglas McKay. One journalist referred to the cabinet as

"Dynamic Conservatism"

"eight millionaires and a plumber"—an accurate description. In keeping with the philosophy of his appointees, Eisenhower gave top priority to slicing the federal budget and minimizing government regulation of the economy. And he sought, but generally failed, to repeal or chisel away at two New Deal achievements: farm price supports and federally subsidized hydroelectric power.

Eisenhower made better headway with other issues. In 1954 Congress approved the St. Lawrence Seaway project to construct a canal between Montreal and Lake Erie. This inland waterway was intended to spur the economic development of the

Midwest by linking the Great Lakes to the Atlantic Ocean. That year, too, Eisenhower signed into law amendments to the Social Security Act that raised benefits and added 7.5 million workers, largely self-employed farmers, to the program's coverage. In the first of many such measures during the decade, the Housing Act (1954) provided federal funds for the construction of houses for low-income families displaced by urban renewal projects. Congress also obliged the president in 1954 with tax reform that increased deductions and raised business depreciation allowances and the Atomic Energy Act, which granted private companies the right to own reactors and nuclear materials for the production of electric power.

Recovering from a heart attack in 1955, President Dwight D. Eisenhower (1890–1969) registers his famous smile from a hospital wheelchair. He went on to win re-election decisively in 1956. Wide World Photos.

The Eisenhower administration also presided over a dramatic change in the lives of Native Americans. In 1953, Congress adopted *termination*, whose purpose it was to liquidate Indian reservations and end federal services. Eisenhower officials seemed disposed toward the new policy because it would reduce federal costs and serve states' rights by eliminating federal trusteeship, making Indians subject to state laws. Critics—including most Indians—denounced termination as another white attempt to grab Indian lands. Between 1954 and 1960, the federal government withdrew its benefits from sixty-one tribes, and about one in eight Indians abandoned the reservation in return for small relocation payments. Under the new policies many Indians joined the urban poor. By the time termination was halted in the 1960s, so much human tragedy had visited Native Americans that observers compared their modern plight to their distress in the late nineteenth century.

Termination Policy for Native Americans

In the 1954 congressional elections, voters revealed that while they still liked Ike, at heart they remained loyal to the Democratic party. The voters gave the Democrats control of both houses of Congress. Lyndon B. Johnson became the new Senate majority leader. An

Interstate Highway System

energetic, pragmatic politician from Texas, he tried to work with the Republican White House to achieve legislation. A notable accomplishment was the Highway Act of 1956. This law authorized the spending of $31 billion over the next thirteen years to build a 41,000-mile interstate highway system, intended to permit the military to move around the nation more easily and to assist commerce. As the largest public works program in American history, the interstate highways invigorated the tourist industry, further weakened the already ailing railroads, and spurred the growth of the suburbs.

Although Eisenhower suffered a heart attack in September 1955, he regained his strength in months and soon declared his intention to run again. With much relief the Republicans nominated the popular president for a second term. The Democrats ran Adlai E. Stevenson once more. Eisenhower won a landslide victory in 1956: 35.6 million votes and 457 electoral votes to Stevenson's 26 million and 73. Still, his personal victory did not aid the Republicans in Congress, where the Democrats continued to dominate.

Election of 1956

THE DECLINE OF MCCARTHYISM

During Eisenhower's first term, one of the most vexing problems for the administration was the conduct of Senator Joseph R. McCarthy. His no-holds-barred search for subversives in government turned up none, but it did affront political fair play, decency, and civil liberties. The president privately labeled the senator a "pimple on the path of progress," but he avoided directly confronting him. Eisenhower also feared that a showdown would splinter the Republican party. Instead the president spoke against unnamed "demagogues thirsty for personal power," and hoped the media and Congress would bring McCarthy down.

Eisenhower on McCarthy

While Eisenhower tried his quiet strategy to undermine the senator, his administration practiced its own brand of anti-Communism. In 1953 Eisenhower broadened Truman's loyalty program and denied clemency to Julius and Ethel Rosenberg. The two, having received the death penalty for the crime of treason, were then executed. Late that year the president suspended the security clearance of J. Robert Oppenheimer, the celebrated physicist who had directed the atomic bomb project at Los Alamos during the Second World War. Oppenhei-

Oppenheimer Case

mer's "crimes" were not that he was either disloyal to his nation or a risk to its security, but rather that he had apparently later misrepresented a 1943 conversation with a friend on Soviet interest in atomic secrets and that he had opposed the government's crash program to develop the hydrogen bomb. In 1954 the Communist Control Act demonstrated that both liberals and conservatives shared the consensus of anti-Communism. In effect making membership in the Communist party illegal, the measure passed the Senate unanimously and the House 265 to 2.

As for Senator McCarthy, he finally undercut himself by taking on the U.S. Army in front of millions of television viewers. At issue was the senator's wild accusation that the army was shielding and promoting Communists. The Army-McCarthy hearings, held by a Senate subcommittee in 1954, became a showcase for his abusive treatment of witnesses. McCarthy alternately ranted and, appearing drunk, slurred his words. Finally, after he had attacked a young lawyer who was not even involved in the hearings, Joseph Welch, counsel for the army, asked, "Have you no sense of decency, sir?" The gallery erupted in applause. In December 1954 the Senate condemned McCarthy, not for defiling the Bill of Rights but for sullying the dignity of the Senate. He remained a senator, but exhaustion and alcohol took their toll. He died in 1957 at the age of forty-eight.

Senate Condemnation of McCarthy

President Eisenhower's reluctance publicly to discredit McCarthy gave the senator, other right-wing members of Congress, and some private and public institutions enough rein to damage the nation and destroy the careers of many innocent people. Eisenhower's own government-sponsored McCarthyism demoralized and frightened federal workers, some of whom were driven from public service. The anti-Communist campaigns of the 1950s also discouraged people from freely expressing themselves and hence from debating critical issues of the time. Fear and a contempt for the Bill of Rights, then, helped sustain the consensus.

An Awakened Civil Rights Movement

Prosecutor = Marshal

In 1954 the NAACP won a historic victory against segregation. The Supreme Court's decision in *Brown v. Board of Education of Topeka* involved cases

Brown v. Board of Education of Topeka

from Kansas, Delaware, South Carolina, Virginia, and the District of Columbia, which were grouped under one unanimous ruling. Written by Chief Justice Earl Warren, the Court's ruling concluded that "in the field of public education the doctrine of 'separate but equal' has no place. Separate educational facilities are inherently unequal." A year later the Court demanded the desegregation of schools "with all deliberate speed."

Though some border states quietly implemented the order, a majority of southern communities defied the Court, at times violently. Business and professional people formed White Citizens' Councils for the express purpose of resisting the order. Known familiarly as "uptown Ku Klux Klans," the councils used their economic power against black civil rights activists. The Klan itself experienced a resurgence, and new groups surfaced. But the most effective resistance tactic was the enactment of state laws that paid tuition for white children attending private schools. In some cases, desegregated public schools were ordered closed.

Eisenhower, who sympathized with white southerners, hoped to avoid a confrontation on the issue. This desire to sidestep the issue was thwarted in

Little Rock, Arkansas, Crisis

September 1957 when the governor of Arkansas, Orval E. Faubus, intervened to halt a local plan for the gradual desegregation of Little Rock's Central High School. Faubus mobilized troops of the Arkansas National Guard to block the entry of black students. Eisenhower

Martin Luther King, Jr. (1929–1968) helped organize the Montgomery, Alabama, bus boycott that led to the desegregation of public transportation. Here, in 1956, he is surrounded by reporters on the first integrated bus run. Ebony Magazine.

made no effort to stop Faubus's actions. In late September, after bowing to a federal judge's order, Faubus withdrew the guardsmen. Eight black children slipped inside Central High, as hundreds of jeering whites threatened to storm the school. The next day, fearing violence, Eisenhower federalized the Arkansas National Guard and ordered 1,100 paratroopers flown in to ensure the children's safety. Troops patrolled the school for the rest of the year, but Little Rock officials closed all public high schools in 1958 and 1959 rather than desegregate them.

Meanwhile, the civil rights movement was gaining momentum elsewhere. In December 1955 Rosa Parks refused to give up her seat to a white passenger on a public bus in Montgomery, Alabama. Jim Crow practices required that blacks sit at the back of the bus and, when asked, surrender their seats to whites.

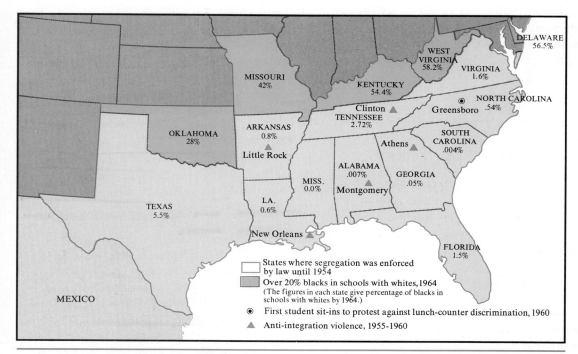

Desegregation in the South, 1954–1964 Source: Redrawn by permission of Macmillan Publishing Company, Inc. by Peter Kingsland. Copyright © 1968 by Martin Gilbert.

Mrs. Parks's arrest ignited a year-long black boycott of the city's bus system. Blacks walked or carpooled. With the bus company near bankruptcy and downtown merchants hurt by declining sales, city officials began harassing tactics to frighten blacks into abandoning the boycott. But the black community's leader, Martin Luther King, Jr., urged them to persevere.

King was an Atlanta-born, twenty-seven-year-old Baptist minister who had recently earned a Ph.D. at Boston University. He insisted on nonviolent peaceful protest in the spirit of India's leader Gandhi. Although he was jailed and a bomb blew the front from his house, King persisted. What King gave to blacks was the "absence of fear," remembered black leader Bayard Rustin. With the aid

Martin Luther King, Jr.

of a 1956 Supreme Court decision that declared Alabama's Jim Crow laws unconstitutional, Montgomery blacks triumphed. They won again in 1957 when Congress passed the Civil Rights Act, which created the U.S. Commission on Civil Rights. That same year the Southern Christian Leadership Conference was organized. Under King's leadership, the organization coordinated civil rights activities.

In early 1960 four black students from North Carolina Agricultural and Technical College in Greensboro sat down at a segregated lunch counter and ordered coffee. Though they were refused service and were physically and verbally abused, they would not budge. Thus began the sit-in movement, which spread from the South to the North, rolling back segregation in many public accommodations

The Sit-ins

(see map, page 513). Inspired by the sit-ins, some participants organized the Student Nonviolent Coordinating Committee (SNCC) in fall 1960. In the face of angry white mobs, SNCC members challenged the status quo.

EISENHOWER-DULLES FOREIGN POLICY AND THE COLD WAR

Dwight D. Eisenhower had had more experience in foreign affairs than domestic affairs before he became president. He had lived and traveled in Europe, Asia, and Latin America. During the Second World War General Eisenhower came to know Europe well, negotiated with world leaders, and made tough decisions of international consequence. After the war he served as Army Chief of Staff and NATO Supreme Commander and learned the essentials of nuclear weapons development and secret intelligence operations. Like most Americans, Eisenhower accepted the Cold War consensus assumptions about the threat of Communism and the need for a global watch by the United States. As president he controlled the making of foreign policy and enjoyed comfortable vote margins in Congress on key resolutions and programs.

For the most part, Eisenhower and Secretary of State John Foster Dulles continued Truman's containment policy, but introduced some memorable phrases to distinguish their administration from Truman's. Thinking containment too defensive a concept, Dulles invented *liberation*. (He did not, however, explain precisely how the countries of Eastern Europe could be freed from Soviet control.) *Massive retaliation* was the administration's phrase for the nuclear obliteration of the Soviet state or its assumed client, the People's Republic of China, if they took aggressive actions. The ability of

Eisenhower-Dulles Policies

the United States to make such a threat was thought to provide *deterrence,* or the prevention of hostile Soviet behavior.

Related to both massive retaliation and deterrence was the *New Look* of the American military. Eisenhower and Dulles emphasized air power and nuclear weaponry and de-emphasized conventional forces. The president's preference for heavy weapons stemmed in part from his desire to trim the federal budget ("more bang for the buck" in the words of the time). With this huge military arsenal, the United States in the 1950s practiced *brinkmanship*: not backing down in a crisis, even if it meant taking the nation to the brink of war. Eisenhower also popularized the *domino theory,* according to which small, weak nations would fall to Communism like a row of dominoes if they were not propped up by the United States. Adopting a globalist perspective on wrenching changes in the Third World, the Eisenhower administration conducted a diplomacy of holding the line—against Soviet Russia, Communist China, neutralism, Communism, socialism, nationalism, and revolution everywhere.

After the death of Stalin in 1953, Eisenhower hoped for a relaxation of Soviet-American relations, but instead witnessed alternating thaws and freezes. The nuclear arms race accelerated as the two superpowers developed new military technology and nuclear delivery systems. In November 1952 the United States detonated the first hydrogen bomb. In March 1954 the biggest bomb the United States had ever tested destroyed the Pacific island of Bikini. This fifteen-megaton H-bomb was 750 times as powerful as the atomic bomb that leveled Hiroshima.

The Soviets, who had tested their first H-bomb in 1953, shocked Americans in October 1957 by propelling the first manmade satellite, *Sputnik*, into outer space. Just two months earlier, Soviet technicians had fired the first intercontinental ballistic missile (ICBM). Americans now felt vulnerable to air attack and inferior to the Russians in rocket technology. But the United States soon tested its own ICBMs. It also en-

Sputnik and the Missile Race

larged its fleet of long-range bombers (the B-52s) and deployed intermediate-range missiles in Europe targeted against the Soviet Union. By the end of 1960 Americans had produced Polaris-missile-bearing submarines as well.

Through flights by the CIA's U-2 spy planes, American officials knew that the Soviets had deployed very few ICBMs. Yet critics charged that Eisenhower had allowed the United States to fall behind in the missile race. The much-publicized "missile gap" was actually a false notion inspired in part by political partisanship. As the 1950s closed, then, the United States enjoyed overwhelming strategic dominance because of its "triad" of long-range bombers, submarine-launched ballistic missiles (SLBMs), and ICBMs.

Still, President Eisenhower was uneasy about the arms race. He feared nuclear war, and the cost of the new weapons made it difficult to balance the budget. He also doubted the need for more and bigger nuclear weapons. How many times, he once asked, "could [you] kill the same man?" Spurred by such thoughts and by neutralist and Soviet appeals, the president cautiously initiated arms control proposals. But because he did not trust the Soviets, arms control talks never became a top priority. To satisfy world opinion about radioactive fallout, however, the two powers unilaterally suspended atmospheric testing from late 1958 to fall 1961, when the Soviets resumed it. The United States began underground testing at the same time.

While the nuclear arms race gained momentum, Russia and the United States waged the Cold War. The year 1955 provided a brief respite from the intensity of the competition. First, the superpowers agreed to end their ten-year joint occupation of Austria, making it an independent neutral state. And, second, Eisenhower and Soviet leader Nikita Khrushchev journeyed to Geneva for high-level talks. This first summit meeting in ten years produced no important resolutions, but the conferees "disagreed so nicely," as one reporter put it.

Events in Eastern Europe soon returned the Cold War to the more familiar fierce acrimony. In 1956 Khrushchev called for "peaceful coexistence" between capitalists and Communists, **Eastern Europe** denounced Stalin, and suggested that Moscow would tolerate different brands of Communism. Soon revolts against Soviet power erupted in Poland and Hungary, testing this new permissiveness. Moscow saw its new military alliance, the Warsaw Pact (1955), endangered and quickly crushed the rebellions. The United States could do little but open its doors to Hungarian immigrants.

In an effort to ease tensions, Khrushchev and Eisenhower planned a summit meeting for Paris in May 1960. But two weeks before the conference, an American U-2 spy plane carrying high-powered cameras crashed 1,200 miles inside the Soviet Union. **U-2 Incident** Moscow announced that it had been shot down. At first Washington denied that its planes flew over Soviet territory, but Russian officials blasted that story by displaying the captured CIA pilot, Francis Gary Powers, his aircraft, and the pictures he had snapped of Soviet military installations. Moscow demanded an apology, Washington refused, and the Russians walked out of the Paris summit.

While West and East sparred over Europe, both kept a wary eye on the People's Republic of China (PRC). Despite growing evidence of a Sino-Soviet split, most American officials continued to think of Communism as a unified world movement. The United States refused to open diplomatic relations with the Chinese government and continued to give aid to Jiang Jieshi on Formosa, which the Chinese claimed as part of the PRC. Washington worried about PRC calls for colonial rebellion and its support for the revolutionaries in Indochina.

In 1954 and 1955 a crisis brought the two nations to the brink of war. Just a few miles off the Chinese coast sat the tiny islands of Quemoy and Matsu. Jiang's forces used them as bases for **Quemoy and Matsu** commando raids against the PRC. In fall 1954 China bombarded the islands. Eisenhower decided to defend the outposts, and he let it be known he was considering the use of nuclear weapons. Massive retaliation over such an insignificant issue? "Let's keep the Reds guessing," advised John Foster Dulles. But what if they guessed wrong? asked critics. Congress passed the Formosa Resolution (1955), which authorized the president to send troops to Formosa and adjoining islands. Two years later the United States installed on Formosa missiles capable of carrying nuclear warheads. In 1958 war again loomed over Quemoy and Matsu. The crisis passed, but defense of the islands became an issue in the election of 1960 at home.

INTERVENTIONS IN THE
THIRD WORLD

If Eisenhower believed that he had contained the Sino-Soviet threat, he was very much less confident about challenges elsewhere in the world. In the 1940s, as a result of changes wrought by the Second World War, a cavalcade of new nations began to alter the international community. In the period from 1943 to 1983 no fewer than ninety countries cast off their colonial bonds (see map).

These profound stirrings arose in what is now known as the Third World, a general term applied to those parts of the global community belonging to neither of the other two "worlds": the United States and its allies in the capitalist "West" and the Soviet Union and its allies in the Communist "East." Third World Nations on the whole are nonwhite, nonindustrialized, and located in the southern half of the globe—Asia, Africa, the Middle East, and Latin America. With Cold War lines drawn fairly tightly in Europe by the early 1950s, Soviet-American rivalry shifted increasingly to the Third World. Much was at stake. Third World nations possessed strategic raw materials such as manganese, oil, and tin. They also attracted foreign investment and provided markets,

especially for American products and technology. Finally, the great powers looked to them for support in the United Nations and for sites to be used as military and intelligence bases.

But many Third World states, like India, Ghana, Egypt, and Indonesia, did not wish to take sides in the contest between the great powers. To the dismay of both Washington and Moscow, they proudly declared themselves neutral, or nonaligned, in the Cold War. Eisenhower and Dulles considered neutralism an immoral stance, a first step along the road to Communism.

Neutralism

If this negative view of neutralism inhibited United States efforts to strengthen relations with the Third World, so did America's domestic race relations. In August 1955, the ambassador from India, G. L. Mehta, walked into a restaurant at the Houston International Airport, sat down, and waited to order. But Texas law required that whites and blacks be served in separate dining facilities. The dark-skinned diplomat, who had seated himself in a white-only area, was told to move. The insult stung deeply and was not soon forgotten.

American Racism as Handicap

Because such embarrassments were not uncommon in the 1950s, Secretary of State Dulles complained that segregationist practices threatened United States efforts to gain the friendship of Third World countries. When the attorney general appealed to the Supreme Court to strike down school segregation, he stated that American racial discrimination "furnished grist for the Communist propaganda mills."

United States hostility toward revolution also obstructed the American quest for influence in the Third World. Despite its own history, the United States has been uncomfortable with significant twentieth-century revolutions. Although Americans paid lip service to the Spirit of '76, they were intolerant of revolutionary disorder—in part because Third World revolutions were directed against their Cold War allies, but also

American Intolerance of Revolution

Chapter 28: AN AGE OF FRAGILE CONSENSUS, 1953–1961

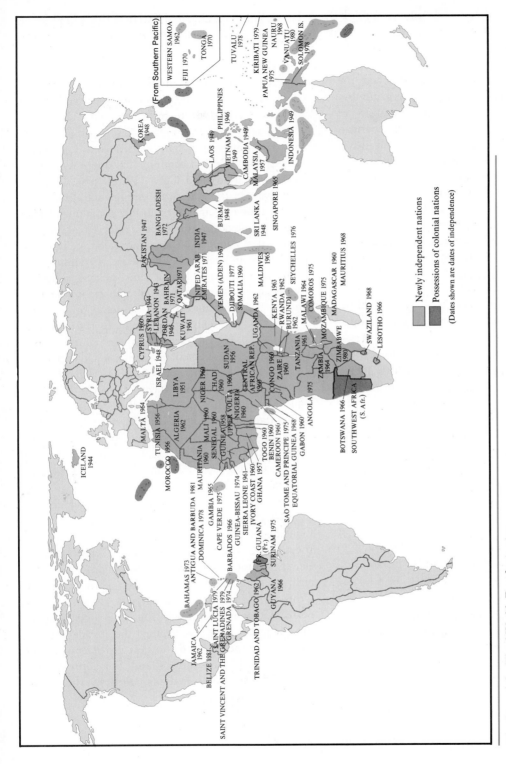

The Rise of the Third World: Decolonization since 1943

Legend:
- Newly independent nations
- Possessions of colonial nations

(Dates shown are dates of independence)

(From Southern Pacific)

WESTERN SAMOA 1962
FIJI 1970
TONGA 1970
TUVALU 1978
KIRIBATI 1979
NAURU 1968
VANUATU 1980
SOLOMON IS. 1978
PAPUA NEW GUINEA 1975

KOREA 1948
PHILIPPINES 1946
LAOS 1949
VIETNAM 1949
CAMBODIA 1949
INDONESIA 1949
MALAYSIA 1957
BURMA 1948
SINGAPORE 1965
SRI LANKA 1948

BANGLADESH 1972
PAKISTAN 1947
INDIA 1947
MALDIVES 1965
SEYCHELLES 1976
MADAGASCAR 1960
MAURITIUS 1968
COMOROS 1975
MOZAMBIQUE 1975

UNITED ARAB EMIRATES 1971
YEMEN (ADEN) 1967
DJIBOUTI 1977
SOMALIA 1960
UGANDA 1962
KENYA 1963
RWANDA 1962
BURUNDI 1962
TANZANIA 1961
MALAWI 1964
ZAMBIA 1964
ZIMBABWE 1980
SWAZILAND 1968
LESOTHO 1966

CYPRUS 1960
SYRIA 1944
LEBANON 1943
JORDAN 1946
BAHRAIN 1971
KUWAIT 1961
QATAR 1971
ISRAEL 1948

SUDAN 1956
CONGO 1960
ZAIRE 1960
CENTRAL AFRICAN REP. 1960
ANGOLA 1975
BOTSWANA 1966
SOUTHWEST AFRICA (S. Afr.)

MALTA 1964
TUNISIA 1956
MOROCCO 1956
LIBYA 1951
ALGERIA 1962
NIGER 1960
CHAD 1960
MALI 1960
SENEGAL 1960
MAURITANIA 1960
UPPER VOLTA 1960
NIGERIA 1960
GUINEA 1958
BENIN 1960
TOGO 1960
CAMEROON 1960
GHANA 1957
GABON 1960
EQUATORIAL GUINEA 1968
SAO TOME AND PRINCIPE 1975
IVORY COAST 1960
SIERRA LEONE 1961
GUINEA-BISSAU 1974
GAMBIA 1965
CAPE VERDE 1975

ICELAND 1944

BAHAMAS 1973
ANTIGUA AND BARBUDA 1981
DOMINICA 1978
SAINT LUCIA 1979
SAINT VINCENT AND THE GRENADINES 1979
GRENADA 1974
BARBADOS 1966
JAMAICA 1962
BELIZE 1981
TRINIDAD AND TOBAGO 1962
FR. GUIANA (Fr.)
GUYANA 1966
SURINAM 1975

because such upheavals threatened American investments, markets, and military bases.

Still another obstacle in America's relations with the rising Third World was the country's great wealth. Foreigners both envied and resented the "people of plenty." American movies offered enticing glimpses of middle-class materialism; American products drew attention at international trade fairs and were coveted items at native marketplaces. And Americans stationed overseas often flaunted their superior standard of living. Finally, many foreign peoples resented the ample profits that American corporations extracted from them. For all these reasons, the United States found itself often not the model but the target of revolution.

America's Wealth as a Problem

The Soviet Union enjoyed only a slight edge, if any, in the race to win friends in the Third World. It was true that Communist ideology encouraged anti-colonialism. But Moscow could not easily explain away its subjugation of Eastern European countries. The Soviet invasion of Hungary in 1956 earned Russia international condemnation. Though Khrushchev toured India and Burma in the mid-1950s, those nations refused to become Soviet clients. They were not about to replace one imperial master with another. Ultimately the Soviets, like the Americans, concluded that Third World nations were playing the two superpowers against each other in order to garner larger amounts of aid and arms.

Obstacles to Soviet Influence

Nonetheless, the United States often interpreted Third World anti-imperialism, political instability, and attacks on foreign-owned property as Soviet-inspired, rather than as expressions of nationalism or internal racial, religious, and ethnic divisiveness. Americans too simply labeled radicals, nationalists, reformers, and neutralists as Communists. To thwart these presumed enemies, the United States resorted to alignments with unrepresentative but friendly regimes.

The United States also utilized the CIA to meet Third World challenges. In the 1950s and later, the CIA bribed foreign politicians, subsidized foreign newspapers, hired mercenaries, conducted sabotage, sponsored labor unions, circulated "disinformation" (false information), plotted the assassination of foreign leaders like Cuba's Fidel Castro, and staged coups. The CIA helped overthrow the governments of Iran (1953) and Guatemala (1954), but failed in attempts to topple regimes in Indonesia (1958) and Cuba (1961). The CIA and other parts of the American intelligence community followed the principle of "plausible deniability." That is, covert operations should be conducted and the decisions that launched them concealed so that the president could deny any knowledge of them.

CIA Covert Operations

In Latin America, long a United States sphere of influence, where poverty, overpopulation, illiteracy, and foreign exploitation fed discontent, anti-American feelings grew. In 1951 the leftist Jacobo Arbenz Guzmán was elected president of Guatemala, a poor country whose largest landowner was the American-owned United Fruit Company. To fulfill his promise of land reform, Arbenz expropriated United Fruit's uncultivated land and offered compensation. United Fruit dismissed the offer. Instead, United Fruit set out to rally Washington by falsely claiming that a Communist threat existed in Guatemala.

CIA in Guatemala

Officials cut aid to Guatemala, and the CIA began Operation el Diablo, a secret attempt to subvert the Guatemalan government. When Arbenz learned that the CIA was working against him, he turned to Russia, thus reinforcing American suspicions. The CIA airlifted arms into Guatemala, dropping them at United Fruit facilities, and in June 1954 CIA-supported Guatemalans struck from Honduras. American planes bombed the capital, the invaders drove Arbenz from power, and the new pro-American regime returned United Fruit's land. But Latin Americans wondered what had happened to the Good Neighbor policy.

In the Middle East the Eisenhower administration

also confronted challenges to United States influence. American stakes there included the survival of the Jewish state of Israel and extensive oil holdings. Oil-rich Iran was a special friend, for the ruling shah had granted American oil companies a 40 percent interest in a new petroleum consortium in return for CIA help in the overthrow of his rival, Mohammed Mosadegh (1953).

The major threat to American interests in the Middle East came from Egypt, where the fervent Arab nationalist Gamal Abdel Nasser rose to power determined to push the British out of the

Suez Crisis

Suez Canal Zone and the Israelis out of Palestine. The United States was caught in a double bind. It did not wish to anger the Arabs, for fear of losing its oil holdings. Nor did it wish to lose its ally Israel. But when Nasser declared neutrality in the Cold War, Dulles lost patience with him. In July 1956 American officials withdrew their offer to help finance the Aswan Dam, a project to provide inexpensive electricity and water for thirsty Egyptian farmlands. Nasser quickly nationalized the British-owned Suez Canal, intending to use its profits to build the dam.

Fearing interruption of the Middle Eastern oil trade, from which Western Europe received 75 percent of its oil, the British and French conspired with Israel "to knock Nasser off his perch." On October 29, 1956, the Israelis invaded the Suez, joined two days later by Britain and France. Eisenhower, who had not been consulted, fumed. He bluntly told London, Paris, and Tel Aviv to pull out. The foreign troops withdrew, Egypt paid $81 million for the canal, and Russia built the Aswan Dam.

In early 1957, in an effort to improve the Western position in the Middle East and protect American interests there, the president proclaimed what became known as the Eisenhower Doctrine.

Eisenhower Doctrine

The United States would intervene in the Middle East, he said, if any government threatened by a Communist takeover asked for help. Fourteen thousand American troops scrambled ashore in Lebanon the next year to quell an internal political dispute. Amer-

ican critics protested that the United States was wrongfully acting as the world's policeman.

The Second Term and the Election of 1960

In part because of the demands of overseas activism, Eisenhower faced rising federal expenditures in his second term. In the first three years of his presidency he had managed to trim the

Deficit Spending

budget, largely by controlling defense spending. But he discovered that he had to tolerate deficit spending to achieve his goals. One reason for the administration's resort to deficit spending was the need to cushion the impact of three recessions—in the years 1953 and 1954, 1957 and 1958, and 1960 and 1961. A sluggish economy and unemployment (it peaked in 1958 at 7.6 percent) also reduced the tax dollars the federal government collected.

In 1958, a year after *Sputnik*, Eisenhower signed the National Defense Education Act. It created a multimillion-dollar loan fund for college students and granted money to the states for upgrading teaching in the sciences and foreign languages. After this legislative success, the administration was rocked by the resignation of the president's chief aide, Sherman Adams, for influence-peddling and by large Republican losses in the 1958 congressional elections. The Democrats, helped by the public outcry against Adams, the economic slump, and discontent among farmers, captured the Senate 64 to 34 and the House 282 to 154.

The election of 1960 was one of the closest and most spirited in the twentieth century. Although Democratic candidate John F. Kennedy shared the tenets of the

John F. Kennedy

consensus, he asserted that he could expand the benefits of economic progress and win foreign disputes through more vigorous leadership. His running mate was Senator Lyndon B. Johnson of Texas, who was added to the ticket to hold white southerners in the Democratic party as the civil rights issue heated up. Republican candidate Richard M. Nixon, the forty-seven-year-old vice president from California, and his running mate, Ambassador Henry Cabot Lodge, Jr., of Massachusetts, expected a rugged campaign.

Kennedy, exploiting the media to great advantage, ran a risky, yet ultimately brilliant, race. Knowing his major liability was his Roman Catholicism, he addressed that issue head-on. He traveled to the Bible Belt to tell a group of Houston ministers that he respected the separation of church and state and would take his orders from the American people, not the Pope. Seeing a major opportunity in the black vote, and calculating that Johnson could keep the white South loyal to the Democrats, Kennedy responded to an appeal to help Martin Luther King, Jr., gain release from a Georgia county jail. A major asset to Kennedy was the unsavory image that Nixon presented in that nation's first televised debate between presidential candidates. Nixon came across as surly and heavy-jowled.

Foreign policy became a major issue. Nixon claimed that because Kennedy lacked experience in foreign affairs he could not stand up to Khrushchev. Kennedy shot back, "I was not the Vice President of the United States who presided over the Communization of Cuba." While Kennedy hit hard on Cuba, Nixon played on the senator's statement that Quemoy and Matsu were not worth defending. Kennedy's most effective theme was that Eisenhower and Nixon had let American prestige and power slip. The Democratic candidate offered Cold War victory instead of stalemate; and he vowed to secure Third World countries as allies.

In an election that saw the highest voter participation (62.8 percent) in half a century, Kennedy defeated Nixon by the razor-slim margin of 118,000 votes. The electoral college margin, 303 to 219, was much closer than the numbers suggest. Slight shifts

in the popular vote in Illinois and Texas would have made Nixon the victor. Electoral fraud in Illinois and Texas may have figured in Kennedy's victory. Although his Catholicism lost him votes, especially in the Midwest, it also gained him about 80 percent of Catholic voters. Religious bigotry, then, did not decide this election, and Kennedy became the first Roman Catholic president.

Assessments of the Eisenhower administration used to emphasize its conservatism, passive style, limited achievements, and hesitancy to confront difficult issues. And they pointed to Eisenhower's reluctance to take strong stands, keep abreast of events, or inspire needed reforms. In recent years scholars have been researching in the now declassified documents of the consensus era, and interpretations are changing. Many have begun to stress Eisenhower's influential style, command of policymaking, sensibly moderate approach to most problems, political savvy, and great popularity. He was, in short, not an aging bystander in the 1950s, but a competent, pragmatic, compassionate leader who gave the American people what they wanted—economic growth and unrelenting anti-Communism. Most historians would agree that the record of the Eisenhower presidency is mixed. At home he failed to deal with the problems that would wrack the country in the next decade: racism, poverty, urban decay. In foreign policy, he found no way to relax Cold War tensions, and in the end he accelerated the nuclear arms race that he so disliked. He unleashed the CIA upon the Third World and failed to adjust American diplomacy to the immense changes there. On the other hand, when compared with his successors, Eisenhower was cautious. He kept military budgets under control and managed crises so that the United States avoided major military ventures abroad.

In Eisenhower's final radio and television address before leaving office in early 1961, he issued a warning. Because of the Cold War, he observed, the United States had been "compelled to create a permanent industry of vast proportions," as well as a standing army of 3.5 million. "Now this conjunction of an immense military establishment and a large arms industry is new in the American experience." In it, he went on, resides the "potential for the disastrous rise of misplaced power." The demands of national security, then, had created a powerful interest group that threatened the very existence of liberty. No doubt he was thinking about the 1960 congressional report, which showed that there were 1,400 retired military officers above the rank of major, including 261 generals and admirals, employed by the one hundred leading defense contractors. Eisenhower urged Americans to guard against the "military-industrial complex." They did not.

Eisenhower's Warning Against "Military-Industrial Complex"

Suggestions for Further Reading

An Age of Consensus

Daniel Bell, *The End of Ideology* (1960); Paul A. Carter, *Another Part of the Fifties* (1983); George Lipsitz, *Class & Culture in Cold War America* (1981); Ronald Lora, *Conservative Minds in America* (1971); George H. Nash, *The Conservative Intellectual Movement in America: Since 1945* (1976); Richard H. Pells, *The Liberal Mind in a Conservative Age* (1985); David M. Potter, *People of Plenty* (1954); David Riesman with Nathan Glazer and Reuel Denney, *The Lonely Crowd* (1950); William H. Whyte, *The Organization Man* (1956).

Dwight D. Eisenhower

Stephen E. Ambrose, *Eisenhower,* 2 vols. (1983–1984); Robert H. Ferrell, ed., *The Eisenhower Diaries* (1981); Peter

Lyon, *Eisenhower* (1974); Herbert Parmet, *Eisenhower and the American Crusades* (1972).

Eisenhower and the Politics of the 1950s

Charles C. Alexander, *Holding the Line* (1975); Larry W. Burt, *Tribalism in Crisis: Federal Indian Policy, 1953–1961* (1982); Barbara B. Clowse, *Brainpower for the Cold War: The Sputnik Crisis and the National Defense Education Act of 1958* (1981); Fred I. Greenstein, *The Hidden-Hand Presidency* (1982); Gary W. Reichard, *The Reaffirmation of Republicanism: Eisenhower and the Eighty-third Congress* (1975); Elmo Richardson, *The Presidency of Dwight D. Eisenhower* (1979); Bernard Schwartz, *Super Chief: Earl Warren and His Supreme Court* (1983).

Civil Rights

Numan V. Bartley, *The Rise of Massive Resistance: Race and Politics in the South During the 1950s* (1969); Robert F. Burk, *The Eisenhower Administration and Black Civil Rights* (1984); William H. Chafe, *Civilities and Civil Rights* (1980) (on Greensboro sit-in); Elizabeth Huckaby, *Crisis at Central High, Little Rock, 1957–1958* (1980); Martin Luther King, Jr., *Stride Toward Freedom: The Montgomery Boycott* (1958); Richard Kluger, *Simple Justice: The History of* Brown *v.* Board of Education *and Black America's Struggle for Equality* (1975); Stephen B. Oates, *Let the Trumpet Sound: The Life of Martin Luther King, Jr.* (1982); Howell Raines, *My Soul Is Rested* (1977); Harvard Sitkoff, *The Struggle for Black Equality, 1954–1980* (1981).

Eisenhower-Dulles Foreign Policy

Blanche W. Cook, *The Declassified Eisenhower* (1981); Robert A. Divine, *Eisenhower and the Cold War* (1981); Michael Guhin, *John Foster Dulles* (1972); Townsend Hoopes, *The Devil and John Foster Dulles* (1973); Burton I. Kaufman, *Trade and Aid: Eisenhower's Foreign Economic Policy* (1982).

Nuclear Arms Race

Paul Boyer, *By the Bomb's Early Light* (1986); Robert A. Divine, *Blowing in the Wind: The Nuclear Test Ban Debate, 1954–1960* (1978); Lawrence Freedman, *The Evolution of Nuclear Strategy* (1981); Gregg Herken, *Counsels of War* (1985); Jerome Kahan, *Security in the Nuclear Age* (1975); Walter A. McDougall, *. . . The Heavens and the Earth: A Political History of the Space Age* (1985); Michael Mandelbaum, *The Nuclear Question* (1979); George Quester, *Nuclear Diplomacy* (1970); Chalmers M. Roberts, *The Nuclear Years: The Arms Race and Arms Control, 1945–1970* (1970).

The United States and the Third World

Stephen E. Ambrose, *Ike's Spies: Eisenhower and the Espionage Establishment* (1981); Richard J. Barnet, *Intervention and Revolution*, rev. ed. (1972); Chester L. Cooper, *The Lion's Last Roar: Suez, 1956* (1978); Richard Immerman, *The CIA in Guatemala* (1982); Donald Neff, *Warriors at Suez* (1981).

CHAPTER 29

AMERICAN SOCIETY DURING THE POSTWAR BOOM 1945–1960s

Five mornings a week through the 1950s and 1960s, the same scene was played out at the bus stop at Pennsylvania Avenue and 12th Street in the District of Columbia. This was the final destination for the Red Line buses traveling from Virginia's northern suburbs to the nation's capital. Eight or nine of every ten people who debarked at that intersection were men dressed in business suits and carrying briefcases. Most were government civil servants. All were white.

The incoming passengers barely noticed the line of people waiting behind a railing to catch the return trip to the suburbs. Practically without exception, every rider on the outbound journey was a black woman from Washington's inner-city neighborhoods. Tidily dressed, many carrying shopping bags with work clothes folded inside, these women were domestic servants in the affluent homes of Washington's lawyers, bankers, politicians, lobbyists, and high-ranking bureaucrats and military officers. Next to the poverty or near-poverty to which these maids, cooks,

and laundresses returned at night, the opulent white world stood in sharp contrast.

The contrast was heightened by the fact that in 1945 the United States had entered a twenty-five-year economic boom, whose cornerstones were the automobile, housing, and defense industries. As the gross national product grew, income levels rose and property ownership spread. Automobiles rolled from assembly lines; houses and schools sprang up throughout the country. More and more Americans, including many unionized blue-collar workers, bought homes in the suburbs and consumed a seemingly endless supply of goods and services. But while three of every four Americans were enjoying the economy of abundance, the fourth American was poor.

With the publication of Michael Harrington's *Other America* in 1962, people became aware of this contradiction in their midst. America's poor, wrote Harrington, "exist within the most powerful and rich society the world has ever known. Their misery has continued while the majority of the nation talked of itself as being 'affluent.'" Crowded into the cities or living in rural isolation, the poor had "dropped out of sight and out of mind," particularly to comfortable residents in the suburbs.

Just as deprivation and pessimism defined the poor, so material comfort and optimism were the hallmarks of the middle class. The most obvious expression of postwar optimism was the baby boom. From 1946 to 1961 births hit record highs. As this age group has grown older, it has had a successive impact on housing, elementary and secondary education, fads and popular music, higher education, and the adult job market.

To many people, it seemed that the American dream had come true. Whatever the nation's faults, it was the world's foremost land of opportunity. Americans boasted that they enjoyed political self-determination through the vote and social mobility through the melting pot. And public education, "the engine of democracy," guaranteed a better life to all who were willing to study and work hard. The exceptions to the dream went unnoticed by most Americans. And the lack of equal opportunities for women was concealed by an emphasis on femininity, piety, and family togetherness.

THE POSTWAR ECONOMIC BOOM

As Americans entered the postwar era, some wondered whether it would resemble another postwar epoch, the get-rich-quick Roaring Twenties. Most Americans expected a replay not of the 1920s, however, but of the 1930s. After all, it was the war that had created jobs and prosperity; surely the end of war would bring a slump.

As it turned out, neither prediction was correct. The United States in 1945 entered one of its longest, steadiest periods of growth and prosperity. The keys to this success were increasing output and increasing

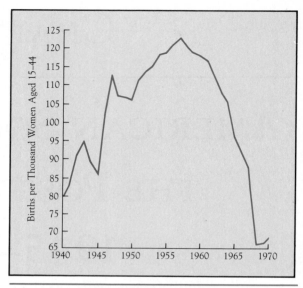

Birth Rate, 1940–1970 Source: Adapted from U.S. Bureau of the Census, *Historical Statistics of the United States, Colonial Times to 1970*, Bicentennial Edition (Washington: U.S. Government Printing Office, 1975), p. 49.

demand. In the twenty-five years after 1945 the American economy grew at an average rate of 3.5 percent per year. Even with occasional recessions the gross national product seldom faltered, rising from just over $200 billion in 1946 to close to $1 trillion in 1970. Indeed, the rate of economic growth during these years was of such magnitude that the real purchasing power of Americans increased by 60 percent.

Crucial to the postwar economic boom was the baby boom, which was both a cause and an effect of prosperity. In 1950, 3.5 million babies were born, a sizable jump from the 2.5 million born in 1940. It was natural for the birthrate to soar immediately following the Second World War. What was confounding was that it continued to do so throughout the late 1940s and 1950s (see figure), reversing the downward trend in birthrates that had prevailed for one hundred

Baby Boom

Babies meant big business for companies that produced baby foods, clothing, toys, and diapers. "In its first year as a consumer," read the caption for this 1958 Life *photo, "baby is a potential market for $800 worth of products."* Yale Joel, Life Magazine © 1958 Time Inc.

fifty years. Between 1946 and 1961, more than 63.5 million babies were born in the United States, making the baby-boom generation the largest by far in the nation's history.

The baby boom spelled business for builders, manufacturers, and school systems. "Take the 3,548,000 babies born in 1950," wrote Sylvia F. Porter in her syndicated newspaper column. "Bundle them into a batch, bounce them all over the bountiful land that is America. What do you get?" Porter's answer:

"Boom. The biggest, boomiest boom ever known in history. Just imagine how much these extra people, these new markets, will absorb—in food, in clothing, in gadgets, in housing, in services. Our factories must expand just to keep pace."

Of the three cornerstones of the postwar economic boom, two were related to the upsurge in births.

Auto Sales

The first was a construction boom to provide houses and schools for all these children. Office buildings, shopping centers, factories, airports, and stadiums also sprang up across the country. Much of this construction took place in the suburbs. But the postwar suburbanization of America would have been impossible without the second cornerstone, automobile manufacturing, for in the sprawling new communities a car was a necessity.

The third cornerstone of the postwar economic boom was military spending. When the Defense Department was finally established in 1949, the nation was spending just over $13 billion a year on defense. By 1951, the Defense Department's budget was over $22 billion. Two years later it was over $50 billion. Except for a short dip from 1954 to 1958, it has been going up ever since.

Military Spending

The invention of the transistor in 1948 inaugurated the computer revolution and stunning advances in electronics. Business and governments were so eager to buy electronic data-processing machines that sales zoomed from $25 million in 1953 to $1 billion in 1960. By the early 1960s thousands of computers had been produced and sold.

The evolution of electronics was a tradeoff for the American people. Computers brought about a rapid rise in productivity through the automation of numerous industries. But in doing so they stimulated technological unemployment. The spread of electronic technology also promoted the concentration of ownership in industry. Sophisticated technology was expensive to develop or purchase. Often only large corporations could afford it; small corporations were shut out of the market. Indeed, large corporations with capital and experience in high technology became so powerful they began to expand into related industries.

But not all expansion was a matter of diversification into related fields. Beginning in the early 1950s a third great merger wave swept American business. Unlike the first two waves, in the 1890s and 1920s, this new wave was distinguished by conglomerate mergers. A *conglomerate* merged companies in totally unrelated fields as a hedge against instability in a particular market or industry. The new wave of mergers resulted in unprecedented concentration of industrial assets.

Conglomerate Mergers

Even the labor movement experienced a merger. In 1955 the American Federation of Labor and the Congress of Industrial Organizations put aside their differences and established the AFL-CIO. Most new jobs, however, were opening up not in the heavy industries but in the union-resistant white-collar service trades. Thus union membership remained fairly constant.

The postwar economic boom was a good time for unionized blue-collar workers, many of whom enjoyed a middle-class lifestyle that heretofore had been the exclusive province of white-collar workers, businesspeople, and professionals. Because most union jobs paid well, these workers could obtain mortgages for suburban homes, especially if their spouses were also working. Many enjoyed job security, paid vacations, and retirement plans. And they were more secure against inflation. In 1948 General Motors and the United Auto Workers Union agreed on automatic cost-of-living adjustments (COLAs) in workers' wages, a practice that spread to other industries.

The trend toward economic consolidation brought changes in agriculture as well as business and labor. While new machines such as mechanical cotton-, tobacco-, and grape-pickers and crop-dusting planes revolutionized farming methods, increased use of fertilizers and pesticides raised the cash value of farm output by 120 percent (in constant dollars) between 1945 and 1970. Meanwhile labor productivity tripled. The resulting improvement in profitability drew large investors into agriculture. By the 1960s it took money—big money—to become a farmer. In many cases only banks, insurance companies, and other large businesses could afford the necessary land, machinery, and fertilizer.

Agricultural Consolidation

By no means did all the effects of economic growth benefit the average American. In agriculture the movement toward consolidation threatened survival of the family farm. From 1945 to 1970 the nation's farm population declined from 24.4 million to just under 10 million. When the harvesting of cotton in the South was mechanized in the 1940s and 1950s, more than 4 million people were displaced. One result was a shift of this poverty to the North and the cities.

The significant changes that postwar growth produced in industry and agriculture were matched by changes in Americans' buying habits and lifestyles. For many Americans the postwar economic boom brought what the economist John Kenneth Galbraith called the affluent society.

THE AFFLUENT SOCIETY

As America's productivity grew by leaps and bounds in the postwar years, so did its appetite for goods and services. In the affluent postwar years middle-class Americans could afford to satisfy desires for a home or a car that they had had to defer during the depression and the war. If they lacked the cash to buy what they wanted, they borrowed the money. Credit to support the nation's shopping spree grew from over $8 billion worth of short- and intermediate-term loans in 1946 to $127 billion in 1970. Here was the economic basis of the consumer culture.

As Americans consumed goods and services, they were using up the world's resources. Consumption of crude petroleum soared 118 percent from 1946 to 1970, but domestic production increased only 97 percent. The extra oil had to be imported. Electricity use jumped too, from 270 billion kilowatt-hours to 1.6 trillion. By the mid-1960s the United States, with only 5 percent of the world's population, produced and consumed over one-third of the world's goods and services.

Advances in public health were a particularly happy effect of postwar prosperity. The average life span increased from 65.9 years in 1945 to 70.9 in 1970. Regular prenatal and pediatric care led to a major reduction in the infant mortality rate. New wonder drugs, streptomycin, for example, cut the number of deaths caused by influenza and postsurgical infection. And the dreaded disease polio was virtually eliminated in 1955 when the Salk vaccine was approved for public use.

Improvements in Public Health

Millions of Americans began their search for the affluent society by migrating to the Sunbelt. This mass migration had started during the Second World War, when GIs and their families were ordered to new duty stations and war workers moved to the shipyards and aircraft factories of San Diego and other cities of the West and South. Soon the Sunbelt encompassed most of America's southern rim, the area running from southern California across the Southwest and South all the way to the Atlantic Coast. The economic bases of the Sunbelt's spectacular growth were easy to identify: agribusiness, the aerospace industry, the oil industry, real estate development, recreation, and, of course, defense spending.

Growth of the Sunbelt

The millions of people who left the chilly industrial cities of the North and East for sunnier climes strengthened the political clout of the Sunbelt. In a book published in 1969, Kevin Phillips, a conservative Republican, predicted an emerging Republican majority based on the votes of the South and West. Richard Nixon's triumph in the presidential election of 1968 seemed to support Phillips's thesis. So did the tendency of political parties to nominate Sunbelt candidates for national office. (Each presidential election from 1964 through 1984 was won by a Sunbelt candidate.)

The economic boom that made for the political pre-eminence of the Sunbelt also brought increased security for whole classes of Americans. And the expanding economy combined with federal welfare leg-

Despite America's postwar economic boom, many people still lived in poverty. In 1945 these black farm workers in Belle-glade, Florida, had little hope for the future. Fifteen years later their plight was unchanged, as the historic television documentary "A Harvest of Shame" made clear in 1960. National Archives/Photo Researchers.

islation to reduce poverty. But even with the reduction in poverty, there was little redistribution of income.

THE OTHER AMERICA

In the postwar age of abundance, most Americans found it especially hard to acknowledge the presence of poverty in their midst. But according to the Bureau of Labor Statistics, in 1962 about 42.5 million Americans (nearly one out of every four people) were poor. These Americans earned less than $4,000 per year for a family of four. Age, race, sex, education, and marital status were all factors in their poverty. One-fourth of the poor were over sixty-five. More than a third of the poor were under eighteen. One-fifth were nonwhite, including almost half the nation's black population and more than half the Native American population. Two-thirds lived in households headed by a person with an eighth-grade education or less, and one-forth lived in households headed by a single woman. For all these people, there was little reason for hope.

In the years after 1945, while millions of Americans, most of them white, were settling in the suburbs, the poor congregated in the inner cities. By 1970 the black population, which had been 48.6 percent urban in 1940, had become 81.4 percent urban. Joining Afro-Americans in the exodus to the cities were poor whites from the southern Appalachians, who moved to Cincinnati, Baltimore, St. Louis, Columbus, Detroit, and Chicago. Latin Americans arrived in growing numbers from Mexico, Puerto Rico, the Dominican Republic, Colombia, Ecuador, and Cuba.

Next to Afro-Americans, the largest group of urban newcomers were the Mexican-Americans, or Chicanos. Millions came during and after the war as farm workers, and increasingly they remained to make their lives in the United States. Despite the initiation in 1953 of Operation Wetback, a program to find and deport illegal aliens, Mexicans continued to enter the country in large numbers, many of them illegally. Many settled in cities.

Native Americans made up the country's poorest group, with an average annual income that was half the amount of the poverty level. Indians moved to the cities in the 1950s and 1960s, particularly after Congress in 1953 adopted the policy of termination. Accustomed to the life of the reservation, many had difficulty adjusting to the city. Indeed, the tragedy of many groups who migrated to cities was that, instead of finding a place to prosper, they found only a dumping ground for the poor.

Not all the poor, however, lived in cities. By 1960, 30 percent lived in small towns and 15 percent on farms. Tenant farmers and sharecroppers, both black and white, suffered economic hardship. Migratory farm workers lived in abject poverty. And elderly people tended to be poor regardless of where they lived.

A large share of the poor were women. Well-paying employment opportunities were limited and there was extensive occupational segregation, with low-paying positions being labeled women's work. Although in 1945 many women had wanted to remain in the factories and shipyards, they were pushed out to make way for returning veterans. And those who tried later to return to industrial work were discouraged. Moreover, many women's jobs were not covered by either the minimum wage or Social Security. Finally, if divorce, desertion, or death did rend a family, it was usually the woman who was left to bear responsibility for the health and welfare of children. Many ex-husbands did not make their child-support payments. And on welfare, or a salary that paid women sixty cents for each dollar a man got, many single mothers and their children slipped into poverty.

One of the least-known effects of economic hardship on the poor has been physical and emotional illness. A study done in the late 1950s in New Haven, Connecticut, found that the rate of treated psychiatric illness was three times as high for the lowest fifth of income earners as it was for the upper-middle and upper classes. Psychiatrists at Cornell University's medical school described the "low social economic status individual" as "rigid, suspicious," and having "a fatalistic outlook on life. . . . They are prone to depression, have feelings of futility, lack of belongingness . . . and a lack of trust in others." During the economic recession of 1960, a social worker from Rochester, New York, bemoaned a sharp rise in "marital discord and desertions of families by the father, increased welfare dependency, increased crime, especially robberies, burglaries and muggings, and alcoholism." Ironically, all of this suffering was occurring in a nation that was being heralded as the affluent society.

THE GROWTH OF SUBURBS

A combination of motives drew people to the suburbs. Many wanted to leave behind the sounds and smells of the city and be closer to nature. They wanted homes with yards so that, as one suburbanite put it, "every kid [would have] an opportunity to grow up with grass stains on his pants." Or they wanted the privacy and quiet that detached

The suburbs promised a haven for the families of the baby boom. In this housing project in Lakewood Park, California, new families moved in at a rate of 25 per day during the last three months of 1950.   National Archives.

homes provided, as well as family rooms, extra closets, and utility rooms. Many were also looking for a community of like-minded people, a place where they could have a measure of political influence. Big-city government was dense and impenetrable. In the suburbs citizens could become involved in government and have an impact, particularly on the education their children received. Indeed, the general welfare of their children seemed to be the major concern of suburbanites.

Government funding and policies helped families settle in the suburbs. Low-interest GI mortgages and Federal Housing Administration mortgage insurance made the difference for people who **Housing Boom** would otherwise have been unable to afford a home. Such easy credit combined with postwar prosperity to produce a construction boom. From 1945 to 1946 housing starts climbed from 326,000 to over 1 million, and in 1950 they approached 2 million. Never before had new starts exceeded 1 million; not until the early 1980s would they dip below that level.

At the same time highway construction opened up rural lands for the development of suburban communities. In 1947 Congress authorized the construction of a 37,000-mile chain of highways, and in 1956 President Eisenhower signed the Highway Act, which launched a 41,000-mile nationwide network. Federal funds spent on highways swelled from $79 million in 1946 to $2.9 billion in 1960, and a huge $4.6 billion in 1970.

Highway Construction

The spurt in highway construction combined with the mushrooming of suburbia to produce the *megalopolis*, a term first used by urban experts in the early 1960s to refer to the almost uninterrupted metropolitan complex stretching along the northeastern seaboard of the United States. Beginning in Boston and extending 600 miles south through New York, Philadelphia, Baltimore, and Washington, "Boswash" encompassed parts of eleven states and a population of 49 million people, all tied together by interstate highways. Other megalopolises that took shape following the Second World War were "Chipitts," a band of heavy industry and dense population stretching from Chicago to Pittsburgh, and "San-San"—San Francisco to San Diego.

Middle-class whites benefited more than other Americans from the government-supported housing and highway boom. For example, the FHA refused to guarantee suburban home loans to the poor, non-whites, Jews, and other "inharmonious racial and ethnic groups." And some federal programs actually worsened conditions for the poor. The National Housing Act of 1949 was passed to provide for urban redevelopment (slum clearance) and the construction of 810,000 units of low-income public housing in four years. But twenty years passed before the housing units were built. Meanwhile, existing housing for the poor was removed and replaced by parking lots, highways, public buildings, and shopping centers.

Socially, the suburban emphasis on family togetherness tended to isolate families. Writing in 1957, sociologist David Riesman criticized "the decentralization of leisure in the suburbs . . . as the home itself, rather than the neighborhood, becomes the chief gathering place for the family— either in the 'family room' with its games, its TV, its informality, or outdoors around the barbecue." The floor plan of the ranch-style home, at whose center was the TV set enthroned on a swivel, was suited to the stay-at-home lifestyle. Even when families traveled, they were isolated in the family car.

Critics of Suburban Life

Riesman was only one of many critics of suburban living. The word *suburbia*, Scott Donaldson wrote in

The Suburban Myth (1969), had "unpleasant overtones, suggesting nothing so much as some kind of scruffy disease." And C. Wright Mills, a sociologist, castigated white-collar suburbanites, who "sell not only their time and energy but their personalities as well. They sell . . . their smiles and their kindly gestures."

When all the pluses and minuses were tallied, however, most residents of suburbia seemed to prefer family togetherness to any other lifestyle of which they were aware. Of the college students interviewed by Riesman in the 1950s, the vast majority looked forward to living in the suburbs.

IDEALS OF MOTHERHOOD AND THE FAMILY

Dr. Spock on Childrearing

Change also occurred within the American family; some of it was due to the publication in 1946 of Dr. Benjamin Spock's *Baby and Child Care*. The book, which quickly became a bible for new parents, answered many common questions about childrearing. But unlike earlier manuals, *Baby and Child Care* urged mothers (but not fathers, because Spock assigned them little formal role in childrearing) to think of their children first. Dr. Spock's predecessors during the previous thirty years had advised mothers to consider their own needs as well as their children's. But women who embraced Spock's philosophy tried to be mother, teacher, psychologist, and buddy to their children all at once. If they failed in any of these prescribed roles, guilt often resulted.

Momism

At the same time Philip Wylie, author of the book *Generation of Vipers*, denounced such selfless behavior as Momism. In the guise of sacrificing for her children, Wylie wrote, Mom was pursuing "love of herself." She smothered her children with affection so they would become emotionally dependent on her and would not want to leave home. Other experts agreed. But women were caught in a double bind, for if they pursued a life outside the home they were accused of being "imitation men" or "neurotic" feminists.

A reason for woman's dilemma was the conflicting roles she was expected to fulfill. On the one hand, the home was premised on a full-time housewife who, with little regard for her own needs, provided her husband and children a haven from the outside world. On the other hand, women continued the wartime trend toward work outside the home. The female labor force rose from 16.8 million in 1946 to 31.6 million in 1970. These women entered the labor force lacking the support of an organized women's movement and without challenging sex-role stereotypes. Many of them, of course, were their families' sole source of income; they had to work. Still others took jobs not to challenge male dominance but to earn additional family income, enjoy adult company, or bolster their self-esteem. Despite the cult of motherhood, most new entrants to the job market were married and had children.

Immediately after the Second World War, many American families moved into Quonset huts on college campuses. Accompanied by wives and babies, former GIs were getting an education. The legislation making it possible was the Servicemen's Readjustment Act of 1944, or GI Bill of Rights. Over 1 million enrolled in 1946—almost one out of every two students. Despite dire predictions to the contrary, the veterans succeeded as students.

GI Bill

These veterans were determined to succeed so they and their families could prosper, so their children could grow up in grassy suburban yards and attend good public schools. Men and women of their generation had been children and adolescents during the economic deprivation of the 1930s. Because they had experienced the separation from friends and family caused by the Second

Family Togetherness

World War, these men and women became exponents of "family togetherness." Such togetherness included family TV-watching, outings to parks and beaches, and Little League games. The destination of many family vacations was Disneyland, which opened in Anaheim, California, in 1955.

Most American families were preoccupied with education. But the Soviet launching of *Sputnik* (1957) made education a matter of national security as well. Congress responded in 1958 with the National Defense Education Act (NDEA), which funded public school programs in mathematics, foreign languages, and science as well as college loans and fellowships. Parents were quick to endorse the new programs. After all, public education was the engine of democracy, a guarantee of both upward social mobility and military superiority.

Education of the Baby Boom Generation

Just as education became intertwined with national security, religion became synonymous with patriotism. As President Eisenhower put it, "recognition of the Supreme Being is the first, the most basic expression of Americanism." In America's Cold War with the "godless" Soviet Union, ministers, priests, and rabbis became foot soldiers in the battle for souls. Religious leaders emphasized family togetherness in their appeals for new converts. "The family that prays together stays together" was a famous slogan used during the 1950s and 1960s. The Bible topped the bestseller lists, and books with religious themes, such as the Reverend Norman Vincent Peale's *Power of Positive Thinking* (1952), sold in the millions. Meanwhile evangelist Billy Graham exhorted television viewers and stadium audiences throughout the country. From 1945 to 1970 church membership nearly doubled.

Although Americans were eager to improve their minds and souls, they were not ready until the 1960s to liberate themselves sexually. When Dr. Alfred Kinsey, director of the Institute for Sex Research at Indiana University, and his colleagues published their pioneering book *Sexual Behavior in the Human Male* (1948), the American public was shocked. On the basis of interviews with numerous men, Kinsey estimated that 95 percent of American men had engaged in masturbation, premarital or extramarital intercourse, or homosexual behavior. Five years later the Kinsey group caused even more of a disturbance with *Sexual Behavior in the Human Female*, which revealed that 62 percent of women masturbated and 50 percent had intercourse before marriage. Sex was nothing new, of course, but its existence was seldom acknowledged in polite conversation or respectable publications—and most Americans preferred that situation.

AMERICA AT PLAY

The prosperity that marked the postwar era was reflected in the materialistic values and pleasures of the period. Having satisfied their basic needs for food, clothing, and shelter, growing numbers of Americans turned their attention to luxury items. Indeed, the quest of middle-class families for the latest conveniences made shopping a form of recreation.

Of the new luxuries, television was the most revolutionary in its effects. One man who grew up in the postwar ear recalled the purchase of the first

TV Enters the American Home

family TV set in 1950. "And so the monumental change began in our lives and those of millions of other Americans. More than a year passed before we again visited a movie theater. Money which previously would have been spent for books was saved for the TV payments. Social evenings with friends became fewer and fewer still because we discovered we did not share the same TV program interests."

Entertainment was TV's number one product. Situation comedies and action series were among the most popular shows. Topping these categories in the 1950s were *I Love Lucy*, starring Lucille Ball, and *Dragnet*, a detective series. Family togetherness was a theme of *Father Knows Best* and *Leave It to Beaver*. As

daily average TV viewing time increased (six hours in 1971), critics worried that TV's distorted presentation of the world would significantly define people's sense of reality.

As television brought the world into their living rooms, Americans began to read newspapers and news magazines a little less carefully, and to listen to radio a lot less frequently. But de-

Paperback Books

spite the lure of the tube, book readership went up. One reason for the increased consumption of literature was the mass marketing of the inexpensive paperbound book. Pocket Books hit the market in 1939; soon westerns, detective stories, and science fiction filled the newsstands, supermarkets, and drugstores. The comic book, which had become popular in 1938 with the introduction of Superman, became another drugstore standard. Reprints of hardcover books and condensed books also did well.

One obvious casualty of the stay-at-home suburban culture was the motion picture. From 1946 to 1948 Americans had attended movies at the rate of nearly 90 million a week. By 1950 the figure had dropped to 60 million a week; by 1960, 40 million. Thus the postwar years saw the steady closing of movie theaters—with the notable exception of the drive-in, which appealed to car-oriented suburban families.

There was one crucial exception to the downturn in moviegoing. By the late 1950s the first children of the postwar baby boom had become adolescents, and

Rise of the Youth Subculture

though their parents preferred to stay home and watch television, they themselves flocked to the theaters. No less than 72 percent of moviegoers during the 1950s were under age thirty. Hollywood responded to this youthful new audience with films portraying young people as sensitive and intelligent, adults as boorish and hostile: *The Wild One, Rebel Without a Cause, Blackboard Jungle*. The cult of youth had been born.

Soon the music industry was catering to teens with cheap 45 rpm records. Bill Haley, the Everly Brothers, and Buddy Holly thrilled teenagers with their music. Elvis Presley horrified their parents with his

The most popular rock-and-roll star of the 1950s was Elvis Presley. Presley's records sold millions of copies, but so freely did he bump and grind that Ed Sullivan, the host of a popular weekly television variety show, pronounced him "unfit for a family audience." Leviton-Atlanta/Black Star.

suggestive gyrations. Although the roots of the new music lay in black rhythm-and-blues, most white stars did not acknowledge the debt. Presley's hit tune "Hound Dog," for example, had originally been performed by the black singer Big Mama Thornton, but Thornton received little credit for her contribution. Among the black rock-and-roll stars of the 1950s were Chuck Berry and Little Richard.

While white performers copied black rhythm-and-blues, serious black jazz artists like Charlie Parker and Dizzy Gillespie experimented with "bebop." In the 1950s jazz became increasingly fused with classical themes, compositions, and instrumentation. Intellectuals began to study this art form, which had once been looked down on as vulgar.

In the arts Martha Graham was lauded in international dance circles, and Jackson Pollock became the pivotal figure of the abstract expressionist movement, which in the 1950s established New York City as a center of the art world. Rather than work with the traditional painter's easel, Pollock spread his canvas on the floor, where he was free to walk around it, "work from the four sides and literally be *in* the painting." In the 1960s artists of the Pop Art movement satirized the consumer society, using commercial techniques to depict everyday objects. Andy Warhol painted Campbell's soup cans; other artists did blow-ups of ice-cream sundaes, hamburgers, and comic-strip panels.

Every era has its fads. Slinky, selling for a dollar, began loping down people's stairs in 1947; Silly Putty was introduced in 1950. The 1950s also had 3-D movies and hula hoops. Although most crazes were short-lived, they created multimillion-dollar industries and effectively promoted dozens of movies and TV shows. Other postwar crazes are still with us— Scrabble, paint-by-number sets, and Barbie dolls, to name just a few. Frisbee-throwing has not only survived but has prevailed over similar outdoor games.

Needless to say, the consensus society of the 1950s and early 1960s was not receptive to social criticism. The filmgoing public preferred noncontroversial doses of Doris Day and Rock Hudson. Readers bought novels and retreated into the criminal underworld, the wild West, or science-fiction fantasy. Even serious artists tended to ignore the country's social problems.

There were exceptions. Ralph Ellison's *Invisible Man* (1952) gave white Americans a glimpse of the psychic costs to black Americans of exclusion from the white American dream. Two films—*Gentleman's Agreement* (1947) and *Home of the Brave* (1949)—examined anti-Semitism and white racism. And in the 1950s, one group of writers repudiated the conventional world of the middle class and the suburbs. Rejecting the same social niceties Kinsey had challenged, the writers of the Beat (for "beatific") Generation flaunted their freewheeling sexuality and consumption of drugs. The Beats produced

Fads

Beat Generation

IMPORTANT EVENTS

1945	Demobilization of 12 million GIs
1946	Beginning of the baby boom Spock, *Baby and Child Care* Over 1 million GIs enroll in colleges
1947	Gross national product ($231.3 billion) begins postwar rise 8,000 families own TVs
1948	Kinsey, *Sexual Behavior in the Human Male*
1949	National Housing Act
1952	Peale, *The Power of Positive Thinking* Ellison, *Invisible Man*
1953	*The Wild One* Kinsey, *Sexual Behavior in the Human Female*
1955	Salk polio vaccine approved for use AFL-CIO merger *Rebel Without a Cause*
1956	Highway Act Ginsberg, *Howl*
1957	Peak of baby boom (4.3 million births) Soviet Union launches *Sputnik I* Kerouac, *On the Road*
1958	National Defense Education Act
1960	Gross national product reaches $503.7 billion
1962	Harrington, *The Other America*
1970	Gross national product reaches $977.1 billion Suburbs surpass central cities in population

some memorable prose and poetry, including Allen Ginsberg's long poem *Howl* (1956) and Jack Kerouac's *On the Road* (1957), and they offered American youth an alternative to their parents' materialism and righteous self-congratulation.

One of the most influential books of postwar years was the best-selling *Affluent Society* (1958), by economist John Kenneth Galbraith. Galbraith's thesis dovetailed with the prevalent belief that economic growth would bring prosperity to everyone. Some would have more than others, of course, but in time everybody would have enough. "Production has eliminated the more acute tensions associated with [economic] inequality," Galbraith wrote. Not until chapter 23 did the author mention poverty; when he did, he dismissed it as not "a universal or massive affliction," but "more nearly an afterthought."

Only in the 1960s would comfortable Americans of the middle class discover that millions of poor people lived in America (see Chapter 31). Politically and culturally, the later 1960s would be vastly different from the consensus years that preceded them. Ironically, it would be the products of suburbia—the children of the baby boom—who formed the vanguard of the assault not only on poverty, but on the whole value system of the American middle class.

SUGGESTIONS FOR FURTHER READING

The Affluent Society

Carl Abbott, *The New America* (1981); Robert H. Bremner and Gary W. Reichard, eds., *Reshaping America: Society and Institutions* (1982); David P. Calleo, *The Imperious Economy* (1982); John Kenneth Galbraith, *The Affluent Society* (1958); John Kenneth Galbraith, *American Capitalism* (1952); Robert Heilbroner, *The Limits of American Capitalism* (1966).

Farmers and Workers

Gilbert C. Fite, *American Farmers* (1981); James R. Green, *The World of the Worker* (1980); Howell John Harris, *The Right to Manage: Industrial Relations in the 1940s* (1982); John L. Shover, *First Majority—Last Minority: The Transforming of Rural Life in America* (1976).

The Baby Boom

Richard A. Easterlin, *Birth and Fortune* (1980); Landon Y. Jones, *Great Expectations: America & The Baby Boom Generation* (1980); Diane Ravitch, *The Troubled Crusade: American Education, 1945–1980* (1983).

The Other America

Joseph H. Cash and Herbert T. Hoover, eds., *To Be an Indian: An Oral History* (1971); Harry M. Caudill, *Night Comes to the Cumberland* (1963); J. Wayne Flynt, *Dixie's Forgotten People: The South's Poor Whites* (1979); Leo Grebler et al., *Mexican-American People* (1970); Michael Harrington, *The Other America* (1981 ed.); Herman P. Miller, *Rich Man, Poor Man* (1971); Dorothy K. Newman et al., *Politics and Prosperity: Black Americans and White Institutions, 1940–75* (1978); James T. Patterson, *America's Struggle Against Poverty, 1900–1985* (1986); David S. Walls and John B. Stephenson, eds., *Appalachia in the Sixties* (1972).

Suburbia

William B. Dobriner, *Class in Suburbia* (1963); Mark I. Gelfand, *A Nation of Cities* (1975); Dolores Hayden, *Redesigning the American Dream* (1984); Kenneth T. Jackson, *Crabgrass Frontier: The Suburbanization of America* (1985); Zane L. Miller, *Suburb* (1982); John B. Rae, *The American Automobile* (1965); Robert C. Wood, *Suburbia* (1959); Gwendolyn Wright, *Building the Dream: A Social History of Housing in America* (1981).

Women, Motherhood, and the Family

William H. Chafe, *The American Woman: Her Changing Social, Economic, and Political Role, 1920–1970* (1972); Ruth Schwartz Cowan, *More Work for Mother* (1983); Carl Degler, *At Odds: Woman and the Family in America from the Revolution to the Present* (1980); Betty Friedan, *The Femi-*

nine Mystique (1963); Susan M. Hartmann, *The Homefront and Beyond: American Women in the 1940s* (1982); Susan Estabrook Kennedy, *If All We Did Was to Weep at Home: A History of White Working-Class Women in America* (1979); Alice Kessler-Harris, *Out to Work: A History of Wage-Earning Women in the United States* (1982); Mirra Komarovsky, *Blue-Collar Marriage* (1962); Susan Strasser, *Never Done: A History of American Housework* (1982).

Popular Culture

John W. Aldridge, *In Search of Heresy: American Literature in an Age of Conformity* (1956); Peter Biskind, *Seeing Is Believing: How Hollywood Taught Us to Stop Worrying and Love the Fifties* (1983); Paul A. Carter, *Another Part of the Fifties* (1983); Kenneth C. Davis, *Two-Bit Culture: The Paperbacking of America* (1984); Andrew Dowdy, *The Films of the Fif-*

ties (1973); Maxwell Geismar, *American Moderns* (1958); Charlie Gillett, *The Sound of the City: The Rise of Rock 'N' Roll,* rev. ed. (1983); Serge Guilbaut, *How New York Stole the Idea of Modern Art* (1983); Jeffrey Hart, *When the Going Was Good: American Life in the Fifties* (1982); Douglas T. Miller and Marion Novak, *The Fifties* (1977); Gerald Nicosia, *Memory Babe: A Critical Biography of Jack Kerouac* (1983).

Television

Erik Barnouw, *Tube of Plenty,* rev. ed. (1982); Leo Bogart, *Age of Television* (1958); George Comstock *et al., Television and Human Behavior* (1978); Frank Mankiewicz and Joel Swerdlow, *Remote Control: Television and the Manipulation of American Life* (1978).

CHAPTER 30

VIETNAM AND THE COLD WAR: AMERICAN FOREIGN POLICY 1961–1981

The Joint Chiefs of Staff (JCS) memorandum lay on the table. Its recommendation: add another 100,000 to the 80,000 American troops already in Vietnam, because the war was not going well. "Is there anyone here of the opinion we should not do what the memorandum says?" asked President Lyndon B. Johnson of his advisers, assembled for a tense meeting on the morning of July 21, 1965. Only Undersecretary of State George W. Ball spoke up: "Mr. President, I can foresee a perilous voyage, very dangerous." Johnson asked, "What other road can I go?" Ball answered directly, "Take our losses, let their government fall apart, negotiate, discuss, knowing full well there will be a probable take-over by the Communists."

The next day Johnson huddled with the military brass. The generals told him that more men, more bombings, and more money were needed to keep America's South Vietnamese ally in power against the North Vietnamese and Vietcong. "But if we put

in 100,000 men won't they put in an equal number, and then where will we be?" Johnson asked. He became excited, asking tough questions. When an admiral claimed that if the United States did not back the faltering South Vietnamese regime, allies around the world would lose faith in America's word, Johnson knew better: "We have few allies really helping us now." And have the bombing raids hurt the enemy? Not really, the generals answered, but if more sites were added to the target list, they would. Johnson grew worried: "Isn't this going off the diving board?"

In late July a troubled President Johnson nonetheless decided to keep that "commitment" by giving the JCS what it wanted. A major decision of the Vietnam War, it meant that the United States was assuming, for the first time, primary responsibility for fighting the war. Fearing a national debate, Johnson muted his decision's importance when he announced it. By the end of 1965 nearly 200,000 American combat troops were at war in Vietnam. Yet Congress had not passed a declaration of war, and the American people remained largely ignorant of the government's massive venture in Southeast Asia. Ball later concluded that Johnson's July decision was "the greatest single error that America had made in its national history."

Vietnam, either because of the searing war experience itself or because of the lessons Americans later drew from that experience, bedeviled the Kennedy, Johnson, Nixon, and Carter presidencies. Other themes crowded the international agenda in the 1960s and 1970s: continued Soviet-American competition for global influence with dramatic swings from conciliation to confrontation in the Cold War, an accelerating nuclear arms race, turmoil in the Third World, eruptions in the Middle East, mean-spirited Cuban-American hostilities, and disorder in the world economy. But Vietnam, where Cold War and Third World issues seemed to merge, dominated American foreign policy. Kennedy enlarged a United States presence in Southeast Asia, Johnson Americanized the war, Nixon spent considerable energy trying to end the war without losing it, and Carter struggled with the postwar consequences of defeat. As he wound down the American combat role in Vietnam, Nixon also inched toward détente with the Soviet Union and China and intervened in Third World disputes to protect American interests he thought threatened. Carter sought to reverse the deterioration of American influence in the Third World and to continue détente, but the Iranian hostage crisis and a flare-up in Soviet-American relations dashed most of his hopes and returned the world to frigid Cold War.

Throughout the 1960s and 1970s Americans became uneasy not only about the troubled position of the United States in world affairs, but also about the disorder wrought at home by foreign entanglements. Foreign policy and domestic developments had been traditionally interconnected, and foreign policy had always sprung from the domestic setting of the nation—its needs, wants, moods, and ideals. Yet the experience of the Vietnam War called those needs, wants, moods, and ideals into question, because a majority of Americans came to see the effects of the war as a threat to their economic well-being, social stability, and political system.

KENNEDY AND THE QUEST FOR COLD WAR VICTORY

John F. Kennedy's diplomacy owed much to the past. He remembered the tragedy of appeasement in the 1930s as well as the triumph of containment in the 1940s. Just as Nazism had been turned back and Communism contained, now in the 1960s Communism would be routed. That there would be no halfway measures was apparent in Kennedy's inaugural address: "Let every nation know that we shall pay any price, bear any burden, meet any hardship, support any friend, oppose any foe to assure the survival and the success of liberty."

Kennedy as Cold War Activist

Khrushchev matched Kennedy's rhetoric with an endorsement of "wars of national liberation" in the Third World. The Soviet leader also bragged about Russian ICBMs, raising American anxiety over Soviet capabilities. Intelligence data soon proved the premier's claim false. Kennedy nonetheless sought to fulfill his campaign commitment to a military buildup based on the principle of *flexible response*. Junking Eisenhower's concept of massive retaliation, which emphasized nuclear weapons, Kennedy sought ways to meet any kind of warfare, from guerrilla combat in the jungles to a nuclear showdown. In this way, he reasoned, he could contain both the Soviet Union and Third World revolutionary movements. Kennedy's actions only helped to goad Russia into an accelerated arms race.

During this time Berlin continued to claim headlines. The Russians again demanded negotiations to end the Western occupation of Berlin. But Kennedy

Berlin Wall saw the historic city as "the great testing place of Western courage and will." Instead of negotiating, he asked Congress in 1961 for an additional $3.2 billion for defense and the authority to call up reservists. Events took an ugly turn in August 1961 when the Soviets erected the Berlin Wall, a concrete-and-barbed-wire barricade designed to halt the exodus of East Germans into West Berlin. Yet another example of Soviet repression, the wall inspired protests all over the non-Communist world. When Kennedy visited the wall in 1963 he stirred a mass rally of West Berliners with the words "Ich bin ein Berliner" ("I am a Berliner").

But it was over Cuba, a nation whose allegiance the United States had taken for granted since the turn of the century, that Kennedy had his most serious confrontation with the Soviet Union (see map). Cuba became an obsession of American policymakers in 1959, when Fidel Castro ousted America's long-time ally Fulgencio Batista. President Eisenhower had made a last-minute attempt to install a friendly military regime there and to deny Castro his hard-fought revolutionary triumph. From the start Castro determined to break the influence of American business. The Cuban leader nationalized some American-owned property, suspended promised elections, indulged in a barrage of anti-American rhetoric, and in early 1960 signed a trade treaty with Russia. In mid-1960 Eisenhower sharply reduced American purchases of Cuban sugar, and Castro responded by seizing American-owned companies.

In March 1960, Eisenhower had ordered the CIA to train Cuban exiles for an invasion of their homeland. Just before he left office Eisenhower broke diplomatic relations with Castro and **Bay of Pigs** advised Kennedy to advance plans for the invasion. Kennedy, who preferred victory over compromise, never attempted to negotiate Cuban-American troubles with Castro. Instead, he listened to the CIA. The picture sketched by the CIA appealed to Kennedy: Cuban exiles would land at the Bay of Pigs and secure a beachhead; the Cuban people would rise up against Castro; a Revo-

lutionary Council organized in the United States would enter Havana in triumph. But when the Bay of Pigs attack began in April 1961, the Cuban people did not rise up in sympathy with the invaders, and within two days the poorly planned and executed invasion collapsed.

Kennedy did not suffer defeat easily. Soon he and his advisers set about finding other means to unseat Castro. As part of a plan called Operation Mongoose, government agents moved to disrupt the Cuban economy and to oust the nation from the Organization of American States. The CIA continued to aid anti-Castro groups in Miami and plotted with organized crime leaders to assassinate Castro.

Cuba soon became the site of one of the scariest crises of the Cold War. Had there been no Bay of Pigs and no Operation Mongoose, Fidel Castro has said, there would have been no missile crisis. For Castro, American hostility represented a real threat to Cuba's independence. And for the Russians, American actions were a challenge to the only pro-Communist regime in Latin America. In an attempt to counter American intervention, Castro and Khrushchev devised a daring plan: installation of Soviet missiles and nuclear bombers in Cuba.

Although the Kennedy administration was aware of a Soviet military buildup on the island, it was not until October 14, 1962, that a U-2 plane photographed medium-range missile **Cuban Missile Crisis** sites. The president ordered a special advisory executive committee to find a way to remove the missiles from Cuba. Some members advised a surprise air strike, likely to kill both Russian technicians and Cubans. But Attorney General Robert Kennedy scotched that idea; he wanted no Pearl Harbors on his brother's record. The JCS recommended a full-scale military invasion. But that approach risked a prolonged war with Cuba, a Soviet attack against Berlin, or even nuclear holocaust. Soviet expert Charles Bohlen unsuccessfully urged quiet, direct negotiations with Soviet officials. It was Secretary of Defense Robert S. McNamara who proposed the most acceptable formula: a naval quarantine of Cuba.

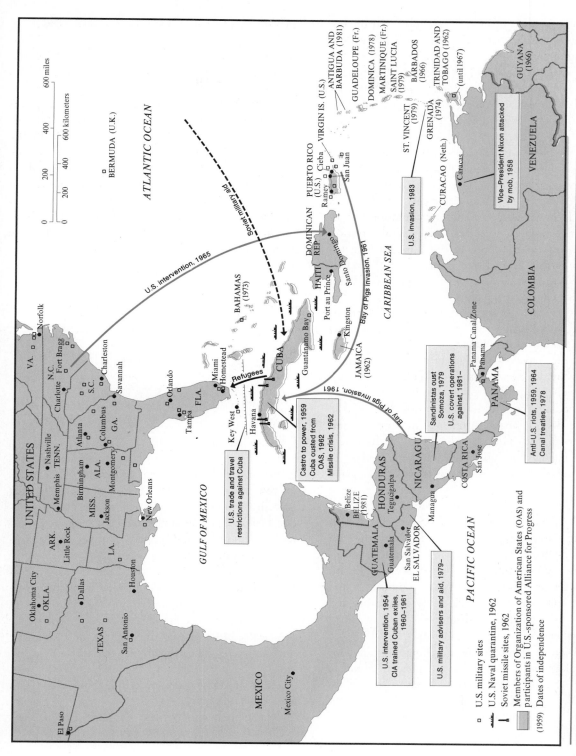

The United States in the Caribbean and Central America

Map labels and features:

600 miles
600 kilometers
0 200 400 600

ATLANTIC OCEAN

BERMUDA (U.K.)

Soviet military aid

U.S. intervention, 1965

VA.
Norfolk
N.C.
Fort Bragg
Charleston
S.C.
Charlotte
Savannah
GA.
Atlanta
Columbus
ALA.
Montgomery
Birmingham
MISS.
Jackson
New Orleans
LA.
TENN.
Nashville
Memphis
ARK.
Little Rock
OKLA.
Oklahoma City
Dallas
TEXAS
San Antonio
El Paso

UNITED STATES

Orlando
FLA.
Tampa
Miami
Homestead
Key West
Havana
Refugees

GULF OF MEXICO

U.S. trade and travel restrictions against Cuba

Castro to power, 1959
Cuba ousted from OAS, 1962
Missile crisis, 1962

CUBA

BAHAMAS (1973)

Guantánamo Bay

HAITI
Port au Prince
DOMINICAN REP.
Santo Domingo

JAMAICA (1962)
Kingston

Bay of Pigs invasion, 1961

PUERTO RICO (U.S.)
Ramey
Cieba
San Juan
VIRGIN IS. (U.S.)

ANTIGUA AND BARBUDA (1981)
GUADELOUPE (Fr.)
DOMINICA (1978)
MARTINIQUE (Fr.)
SAINT LUCIA (1979)
BARBADOS (1966)
TRINIDAD AND TOBAGO (1962)
(until 1967)
GUYANA (1966)

ST. VINCENT (1979)
GRENADA (1974)
U.S. Invasion, 1983

CURACAO (Neth.)
Caracas

Vice-President Nixon attacked by mob, 1958

VENEZUELA

COLOMBIA

CARIBBEAN SEA

MEXICO
Mexico City

PACIFIC OCEAN

GUATEMALA
Guatemala
BELIZE (1981)
Belize
HONDURAS
Tegucigalpa
EL SALVADOR
San Salvador
NICARAGUA
Managua
COSTA RICA
San José
PANAMA
Panama
Panama Canal Zone

U.S. intervention, 1954
CIA trained Cuban exiles, 1960–1961

U.S. military advisers and aid, 1979–

Sandinistas oust Somoza, 1979
U.S. covert operations against, 1981–

Anti-U.S. riots, 1959, 1964
Canal treaties, 1978

Bay of Pigs Invasion, 1961

Legend:

□ U.S. military sites
⊣ U.S. Naval quarantine, 1962
⊥ Soviet missile sites, 1962
Members of Organization of American States (OAS) and participants in U.S.-sponsored Alliance for Progress
(1959) Dates of independence

The United States in the Caribbean and Central America

This halfway response gave the administration the flexibility to escalate or negotiate, depending on the Russian response.

Over national television on October 22, Kennedy informed the Soviets of American policy and demanded their retreat. American warships headed for the Caribbean, B-52s loaded with nuclear bombs took to the skies, and American military forces around the globe went on alert. Khrushchev first replied that the missiles would be withdrawn if Washington pledged never to attack Cuba again. Then he demanded the removal of American missiles from Turkey. Kennedy accepted the first condition but rejected the second. (Privately the administration made an informal promise to the Russians to withdraw the missiles from Turkey in the future.) On October 28 Khrushchev accepted the American pledge to respect Cuban sovereignty and promised to ship the missiles back to the Soviet Union. Americans breathed a collective sigh of relief; this was, said many, Kennedy's finest hour.

But critics have asked whether the crisis was necessary. Why did Kennedy resort to public brinkmanship rather than private talks? Was he motivated by the forthcoming congressional elections? Did he need to prove his toughness? After all, the strategic balance of power was not seriously altered by the placement of missiles in Cuba. Kennedy went to the nuclear brink when he didn't need to, his critics have said.

The Cuban missile crisis humiliated the Soviets. Exposed as nuclear inferiors, the Soviets vowed to catch up—and they managed to do so by the late 1960s. The crisis did produce some relaxation in Soviet-American relations. The superpower leaders installed a teletype "hot line" between Washington and Moscow staffed round the clock by translators and technicians, signed a test-ban treaty, and refrained from further confrontation in Berlin.

Elsewhere in the Third World, Kennedy called for "peaceful revolution" based on the concept of *nation building*. The idea was to bring Third World countries into the American orbit by helping them through the

Nation
Building

infant stages of nationhood. Programs like the Peace Corps and the Alliance for Progress (for Latin America) focused on improving agriculture, transportation, health care, and communications.

Besides such special programs, Kennedy relied on *counterinsurgency*: the training of native police forces by American military and technical advisers. The assumption was that American soldiers—especially the Special Forces units, or Green Berets—would provide a protective shield against insurgents while American civilian personnel worked on economic projects. But as presidential adviser Arthur M. Schlesinger, Jr., later wrote, counterinsurgency proved "a ghastly illusion. Its primary consequence was to keep alive the American belief in their capacity and right to intervene in foreign lands."

DESCENT INTO THE LONGEST WAR: VIETNAM

The belief in the right to influence the internal affairs of other countries led to disaster in Southeast Asia. How Vietnam became the site of America's longest war (1950 to 1975); how the world's most powerful nation spent itself in a futile attempt to subdue a peasant people; how those people suffered enormous losses of life and property and yet persisted, is one of the tragic stories of modern history.

The story begins with the French takeover of Vietnam during the late nineteenth century (see Vietnam Chronology). For decades

History of
Imperialism in
Vietnam

the French exploited the colony for its rice, rubber, tin, and tungsten, beating back peasant rebellions. Not until the Second World War, when the Japanese moved into Indochina, did French authority collapse.

Seizing their chance, the Vietminh, an anti-im-

VIETNAM CHRONOLOGY, 1861–1961

1861–87	French consolidate colonial rule in Indochina
1890	Ho Chi Minh born
1920	Ho Chi Minh joins Communist party
1940	Japan occupies Indochina
1941	Vietminh organized
	OSS cooperates with Vietminh
1945	Ho declares independence
1946	Anticolonial war against France begins
1950	U.S. recognizes governments of Bao Dai
	U.S. sends military aid to French for war in Vietnam
1954	Dienbienphu crisis
	Geneva conference and accords
	Temporary partition of Vietnam
	U.S. backs government of Diem
1955	Diem, with U.S. support, rejects Geneva accords
1956	Diem begins crackdown on opponents
1957	Anti-Diem insurgents begin terrorist attacks
1959	North Vietnam begins sending aid to Communists in the South
1960	National Liberation Front (Vietcong) organized in the South
1961	President Kennedy decides to increase U.S. military role in Vietnam

Note: For Vietnam events after 1961, see Important Events, page 556.

perialist coalition led by Communists, began guerrilla warfare against the Japanese. Led by the nationalist Ho Chi Minh, they collaborated with American Office of Strategic Services (OSS) agents to harass the Japanese. OSS officers who worked with Ho in Vietnam were impressed by his determination to free his country of outsiders, and by his frequent references to the United States as a revolutionary model. When Ho declared Vietnam's independence in September 1945, he wrote to the Truman administration requesting political support and economic assistance for his new government. His letters were never an-

swered. The United States did not recognize Vietnamese independence, preferring to support its Cold War ally, France, against a Communist who had lived for a time in Russia.

Because of France's attempt to restore colonial rule, Vietnam was initially seen as a French problem. But when Jiang Jieshi went down to defeat in China, the United States was aroused to action. The Truman administration made two crucial decisions in early 1950. First, it recognized the French puppet government of Bao Dai. Thus in Vietnamese eyes the United States became in essence a colonial power, an ally of the hated French. Second, the administration agreed to send weapons, and ultimately military advisers, to the French. By 1954 the United States had invested over $2 billion in the war and was bearing 78 percent of its cost.

Despite American aid, the French lost steadily to the Vietminh. Finally, in 1954 Ho's forces surrounded the French fortress at Dienbienphu. What would the United States do? Eisenhower was cautious. If American forces became directly involved in the war—as distinct from merely advising the French—he might not be able to limit the nation's involvement. As one high-level doubter remarked, "One cannot go over Niagara Falls in a barrel only slightly."

Nevertheless, Eisenhower worried aloud at the prospect of a Communist victory, comparing the weak nations of the world to a row of dominoes, all of which would topple if just one fell. He asked the British to help, but they would make no commitment. At home, members of Congress refused to support military action unless the British went along.

To add to the administration's problems, the French wanted out. They agreed to peace talks at Geneva, where France, the United States, Russia, Britain, China, Laos, and Cambodia joined the two competing Vietnamese regimes. The 1954 Geneva accords, signed by France and Ho's Democratic Republic of Vietnam, temporarily divided Vietnam at the 17th parallel, with Ho's government confined to the North. National elections would be held in 1956, and the country would thereupon be unified. Neither North nor South was to join a military alliance or permit foreign military bases on its soil.

Certain that the Geneva agreements would ultimately mean Communist victory, the United States refused to sign and set about to sabotage them. Thus American CIA personnel began secret operations against the North, and in the South support flowed to the anti-French leader Ngo Dinh Diem. A Catholic in a Buddhist nation, Diem lacked popular sup-

port. But with American aid and a rigged election, he beat back his opponents. When Ho called for national elections in keeping with the Geneva agreements, Diem and Eisenhower refused, fearing the charismatic Vietminh leader would win. In September 1954 the United States joined Britain, France, Australia, New Zealand, the Philippines, Thailand, and Pakistan in an anti-Communist pact called the Southeast Asia Treaty Organization (SEATO). In a special protocol SEATO extended protection to South Vietnam.

Meanwhile, Diem became bent on dictatorial leadership. He abolished village elections, appointed people beholden to him to public office, threw dissenters into jail, and shut down newspapers that criticized his regime. Communists and non-Communists alike struck back. The Vietminh assassinated hundreds of Diem's village officials. With the support of peasants who had been victimized by Diem's regime, in late 1960 they organized the National Liberation Front, or Vietcong. Civil war had erupted in South Vietnam.

In the United States, the newly elected President Kennedy decided to stand firm against the Vietcong. He had suffered the humiliations of the Bay of Pigs and the Berlin Wall; he feared further criticism should the United States back down in Asia. But more important, he sought a Cold War victory. By late 1963, 16,700 American "advisers" were stationed in Vietnam, 489 of whom died that year. The same year an American project called the strategic hamlet program, which aimed to separate peasants from the Vietcong by uprooting them, backfired. Meanwhile, when Diem's troops attacked Buddhist protesters, monks poured gasoline over their robes and ignited themselves in the streets of Saigon.

Diem, American officials decided, had to go. Through the CIA, the United States quietly encouraged South Vietnamese generals to stage a coup. With the ill-concealed backing of Ambassador Henry Cabot Lodge, the generals

Geneva Conference

Civil War in South Vietnam

Removal of Diem

struck in early November 1963. Diem was captured and murdered—only a few weeks before Kennedy himself met death by an assassin's bullet.

With new governments in Saigon and Washington, some analysts thought it an appropriate time for reassessment. The Vietcong, United Nations General Secretary U Thant, France, and others called for a coalition government in South Vietnam. But the new American president, Lyndon B. Johnson, would have none of it; he sought only victory.

JOHNSON AND THE WAR WITHOUT VICTORY

Johnson saw the world in simple terms—them against us—and privately disparaged both his allies and his enemies. Vietnam was a "raggedy-ass fourth-rate country," his critics at home "rattlebrains." Johnson sometimes lied or exaggerated, creating what reporters referred to as a credibility gap. His greatest liability, however, was that he held firmly to fixed ideas about American superiority, the menace of communism, and the necessity of global intervention.

By early 1964 the Vietcong controlled nearly half of South Vietnam. Because the new Saigon government was shaky and seemed to be leaning toward neutralism, United States officials cooperated in a second coup. In neighboring Laos, American bombers hit supply routes connecting the Vietcong with the North Vietnamese. Laos, where the CIA had manipulated politics for years and where in 1962 non-Communists and Communists agreed to a neutralist government, was increasingly drawn into a wider Southeast Asian war. The bombings were kept secret from the American Congress and people.

An incident in the Gulf of Tonkin, off the coast of North Vietnam, accelerated American warmaking (see map, page 546). In August 1964, the U.S.S.

Tonkin Gulf Incident

Maddox, while monitoring South Vietnamese commando raids against North Vietnam, came under attack from northern patrol boats, which suffered heavy damage. The unharmed *Maddox* sailed away. On August 4, now joined by another destroyer, the *Maddox* moved again toward the North Vietnamese shore. During bad weather, sonar technicians reported what they thought were enemy torpedoes; the two destroyers began firing ferociously. Yet when the captain of the *Maddox* asked his crew members what had happened, not one had seen or heard hostile gunfire.

Johnson, however, seized the chance to go on national television and announce retaliatory air strikes above the 17th parallel. He also secured from Congress the Tonkin Gulf resolution, which authorized the president to "take all necessary measures to repel any armed attack against the forces of the United States and to prevent further aggression." The vote was 466 to 0 in the House and 88 to 2 in the Senate. Over time the Tonkin Gulf resolution would come to serve as the declaration of war Congress never voted on. Only in 1970 would senators repeal it.

Tonkin Gulf Resolution

His popularity buoyed by his forceful response to the Tonkin Gulf incident, Johnson won the presidency in his own right in the fall of 1964. At his direction the military mapped plans for stepped-up bombing of North Vietnam and Laos. Following an enemy attack at Pleiku in February 1965, Johnson initiated Operation Rolling Thunder, a sustained bombing program above the 17th parallel. Before the war's end, the United States would drop more bomb tonnage on Vietnam than it had in all of the Second World War. The president also sent more troops to the South; by 1969, 543,400 American troops were stationed there.

The "Americanization" of the war in Vietnam under Johnson bothered growing numbers of Americans, especially as increased television coverage brought the ugliness of combat into their homes

C H I N A

BURMA

Black R.

Red R.

• Dienbienphu

Hanoi

Haiphong

Harbor mined, 1972

Communist–Pathet Lao victory, 1975

Gulf of Tonkin

PLAIN OF JARS

⊙ **Maddox incident, 1964**

NORTH VIETNAM

HAINAN

L A O S

Vientiane

• Vinh

Mu Gia Pass

Ca R.

U.S. Seventh Fleet operations during the war

Udon Thani ■   ■ Nakhon Phanom

Demilitarized Zone

Khe Sanh   Quang Tri

Sépone •   A Chau

Lang Vei   • Hue

Demarcation Line, July 1954

SOUTH CHINA SEA

■ *Khon Kaen*

Kham Duc

Da Nang

T H A I L A N D

Mekong R.

• My Lai

Chu Lai

• Ta Khli

Ubon Ratchathani ■

Dak To

Quang Ngai

■ *Rachasima*

Kontum

Pleiku ■

An Khe

■ *Don Muang*

• Duc Co ■

■ *Qui Nhon*

• Bangkok

K A M P U C H E A
(CAMBODIA)

CENTRAL HIGHLANDS

• Tuy Hoa

Ban Me Thuot

Sattahip

Nha Trang

U.S. invasion, 1970

• *Dalat*

■ *Can Ranh Bay*

Communist–Khmer Rouge victory, 1975

Phnom Penh •

Bu Dop

Vietnamese invasion, 1978

SOUTH VIETNAM

Chau Duc

Cholon   Bien Hoa

Tan Son Nhut ■   *Long Binh*

Saigon

Vung Tau

Vietcong and North Vietnamese victory and U.S. withdrawal, 1975

Gulf of Siam

My Tho

Vinh Long

Can Tho ■   Ben Tre

⊙

Mekong Delta

Mayaguez incident, 1975

Ca Mau

CA MAU PENINSULA

0   100   200 miles

0   100   200   300 kilometers

→ Ho Chi Minh Trail

⇨ Boat-People Refugees after 1975

☆ Major battles of the Tet Offensive, January 1968

■ Major U.S. bases during the war

Southeast Asia and the Vietnam War

An American marine tries to revive a wounded GI in the inhospitable terrain of Khe Sanh Valley, near the Demilitarized Zone in South Vietnam in 1967. The fallen marine soon died, as did over 57,000 other Americans in their nation's longest war. Wide World Photos.

every night. The pictures and stories were not pretty. Innocent civilians were caught in the line of fire; refugees flooded "pacification" camps; villages considered friendly to the enemy were burned to the ground. To destroy Vietcong hiding places, pilots sprayed chemical defoliants like Agent Orange over the landscape. Stories of atrocities made their way home. Most gruesome was the My Lai massacre in March 1968 (not made public until twenty months later because of a military cover-up). An American unit, frustrated by its inability to pin down an elusive enemy and eager to revenge the loss of some buddies, shot to death scores of unarmed women and children.

Although many incidents of the deliberate shooting of civilians, torturing and killing of prisoners, taking of Vietnamese ears as trophies, and burning of villages have been recorded, most

American
Troops in
Vietnam

American soldiers were not committing atrocities. They were trying instead to save their young lives (their average age was only nineteen) and serve the United States mission by killing enemy troops, whom they usually called "gooks." Many of these Americans made up the rear-echelon forces that supported the "grunts" or "boonierats" in the field. Wherever they were, soliders met an inhospitable environment, for no place in Vietnam was secure.

As the war ground on to no discernible conclusion, the army grew troubled, and morale sagged. Racial tensions intensified as "black power" militants tangled with whites muttering racial slurs. Drug abuse became serious. "Fragging," the murder of an officer by soldiers using hand grenades or other weapons, also increased. "Grenades leave no fingerprints. Nobody's going to jail," recalled a helicopter pilot.

By 1968 Johnson faced criticism both inside and outside the government. Secretary of Defense Mc-Namara and Undersecretary of State George Ball resigned in protest. Senator J. William Fulbright, chairman of the Foreign Relations Committee, began to conduct hearings on whether the national interest was being served by pursuing the war. And Senator Eugene McCarthy decided to challenge Johnson for the Democratic presidential nomination.

Johnson dug in, snapping at his critics and vowing to continue the battle, cheered by opinion polls that showed Americans actually favoring escalation over withdrawal. At times he halted the bombing to encourage Ho Chi Minh to negotiate. Such pauses, however, were often accompanied by increases in American troop strength. American terms were unacceptable to the Communists: nonrecognition of the Vietcong; withdrawal of northern soliders from the South; and an end to North Vietnamese military aid to the Vietcong.

THE PAINFUL WITHDRAWAL

FROM VIETNAM

In January 1968 a shocking event forced Johnson to reappraise his position. During Tet, the Vietnamese lunar new year, Vietcong and North Vietnamese forces struck all across South Vietnam, hitting and capturing provincial capitals. In Sai-

gon raiders actually occupied the American embassy for several hours. American and

Tet Offensive   South Vietnamese units eventually regained much lost ground, inflicting heavy casualties on the enemy. But the Tet offensive jolted Americans. If all of America's firepower and dollars and half a million troops couldn't defeat the Vietcong, could anything?

The Tet offensive and its impact on public opinion hit the White House like a thunderclap. The new secretary of defense, Clark Clifford, told Johnson the war could not be won, even if the 206,000 more soldiers requested by the army were sent to Vietnam. Strained by exhausting sessions with advisers, realizing that further escalation would not bring victory, and faced with serious opposition within his own party, Johnson changed course. In an appearance on television (March 31) he announced that he had stopped the bombing of most of North Vietnam, asked Hanoi to begin negotiations, and surprised the nation by dropping out of the presidential race. The United States, knowing it could not win, would at least try not to lose.

Richard M. Nixon, Johnson's successor, decided to pursue "peace with honor" through "Vietnamization" of the war—building up South Vietnamese forces to replace American troops. And he announced the Nixon Doctrine: that the United States would help those Asian nations that helped themselves. Slowly he began to withdraw American troops from Vietnam, decreasing their number to 139,000 by the end of 1971. But he also increased the bombing in the North, hoping to pound Hanoi into making concessions. Nixon's national security adviser, Henry A. Kissinger, called it jugular diplomacy.

In April 1970 American and South Vietnamese troops invaded Cambodia in search of arms depots and enemy forces that used it as a sanctuary. The escalation sparked renewed protest at

Invasion of   home. Demonstrations swept col-
Cambodia   lege campuses; the Senate forbade the expenditure of funds on the new war. But Nixon and Kissinger were unmoved. They continued to escalate the war, ordering "pro-

In July 1968 a war-weary President Lyndon B. Johnson (1908–1977). Just months before, stunned by the Tet offensive, Johnson had decided to drop out of politics and initiate peace talks. Lyndon Baines Johnson Library.

tective reaction strikes" against the North; acceleration of the CIA's Operation Phoenix (the assassination of thousands of enemy civilians in the South); the secret bombing of Cambodia; the mining of Haiphong harbor; and in December 1972, a massive air strike called the Christmas bombing.

Meanwhile the peace talks seemed to be going nowhere. But Kissinger was meeting privately with Le Duc Tho, the chief delegate from North Vietnam.

Cease-Fire Agreement

Finally on January 27, 1973, Kissinger and Le signed a cease-fire agreement. The United States promised to withdraw its remaining troops within sixty days. Other troops would stay in place, and a coalition government that included the Vietcong would eventually be formed in the South. Pleased that a peace had been made, critics nonetheless noted that the terms of the agreement could have

been accepted in 1969, and over twenty thousand American lives could have been spared.

Leaving behind some advisers, the United States pulled its troops out of Vietnam and reduced its aid program. Both North and South soon violated the cease-fire, and full-scale war erupted once more. As many had predicted, the feeble South Vietnamese government could not hold out. On April 29, 1975, South Vietnam collapsed.

The overall costs of the war were immense. Over 57,000 Americans and hundreds of thousands of Asians died in the struggle. In monetary terms the war cost the United States more than $150 billion, and as was inevitable, billions more would be paid in future veterans' benefits. At home the war brought inflation, political schism, attacks on civil liberties, and retrenchment from reform programs. The war also had negative consequences internationally: delay in moving toward better relations with the Soviet Union and the People's Republic of China, friction with allies, and the alienation of Third World nations.

Meanwhile, in South Vietnam, Cambodia, and Laos, Communists assumed power and instituted repressive governments. Acute hunger afflicted the people of those devastated lands. Soon refugees were crowding aboard unsafe vessels in an attempt to escape their battered homelands. Many of these "boat people" immigrated to the United States, where Americans, reluctant to be reminded of their defeat in Asia, received them with mixed feelings. But thoughtful Americans realized that the United States, which had relentlessly bombed, burned, and defoliated once-rich agricultural lands, bore more than a slight responsibility for the plight of the Southeast Asian peoples.

NIXON, KISSINGER, AND DÉTENTE

With the war over, Nixon and Kissinger pursued a foreign policy designed to promote a global balance of power, or equilibrium, and to curb revolution and radicalism in the Third World. The popular word for the new posture toward the Soviets was *détente*, meaning limited cooperation through negotiations, within a general environment of rivalry. But détente was essentially the old policy of containment refurbished. Its purpose was to check Soviet expansion and limit the Soviet arms buildup.

Détente

Nixon and Kissinger pursued détente with extraordinary energy. They expanded trade relations with Russia; a 1972 deal sent $1 billion worth of American grain to the Soviets at bargain prices. To slow the costly arms race, the Nixon administration initiated Strategic Arms Limitations Talks (SALT) with the

SALT Talks

Soviets. In 1972 the talks produced a SALT treaty that limited antiballistic missile (ABM) systems. ABM systems were defensive systems that made offensive missiles less vulnerable to attack and hence encouraged the other side to build more missiles to overcome ABM protection. Limiting ABMs was thus a step toward halting a spiraling arms race. A second agreement placed a five-year freeze on the number of offensive nuclear missiles each side could have. At the time of the agreement the Soviets held an advantage in total missiles, but the United States had more warheads per missile. American MIRVs (multiple independently targeted reentry vehicles) could fire several warheads at different targets in midflight. In short, the United States had a 2-to-1 advantage in deliverable warheads. Because SALT did not restrict MIRVs, the nuclear arms buildup continued.

Nixon and Kissinger also cultivated détente with the People's Republic of China, ending almost three decades of Sino-American hostility. In February 1972 the president made a historic trip to what he used to call "Red" China. The Chinese Communists welcomed him because they sought to improve trade and they hoped friendlier Chinese-American relations would make the Soviets—the new Chinese enemy—more cautious. Nixon reasoned the same way. In the end, the conferees agreed to disagree on a number of issues, except one: Russia should not be permitted to make gains in Asia. Official diplomatic recognition and exchange of ambassadors was effected in 1979.

Opening to China

Tortuous events in the Middle East, however, revealed how fragile the Nixon-Kissinger grand strategy was. When Nixon took office in 1969 the Middle East was, in the president's words, a "powder keg." In the Six-Day War (1967) Israel had seized the West Bank and the ancient city of Jerusalem from Jordan, the Golan Heights from Syria, and the Sinai Peninsula from Egypt (see map). To further complicate matters, Palestinian Arabs, many of them expelled from their homeland in 1948 when the nation of Israel was created, had organized the

Arab-Israeli Hostilities

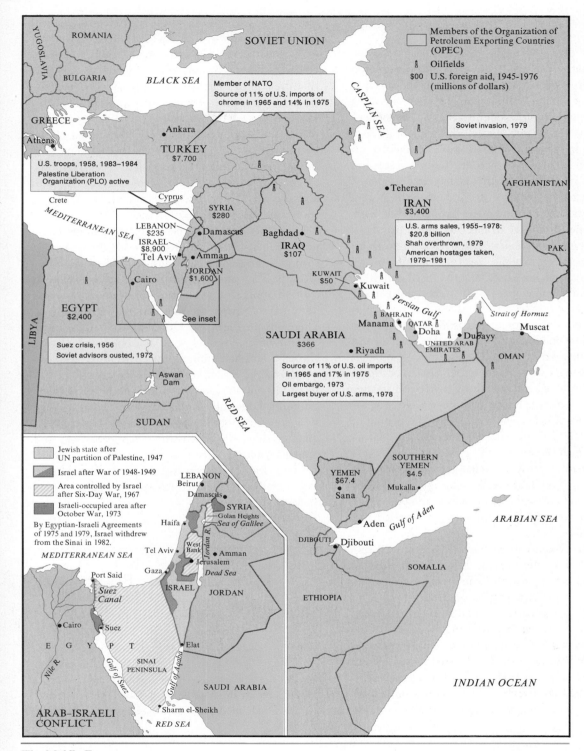

The Middle East

Palestine Liberation Organization (PLO) and pledged to destroy Israel.

On October 6, 1973, Egypt and Syria attacked Israel. In spite of détente, Moscow and Washington headed for a confrontation; both superpowers put their armed forces—including nuclear—on alert. At the same time, in an attempt to pressure Americans into taking a pro-Arab stance, the Organization of Petroleum Exporting Countries (OPEC) imposed an embargo on shipments of oil to the United States and a dramatic increase in oil prices occurred.

Faced with an energy crisis at home, the Nixon administration had to find a way to end Middle Eastern hostilities. Kissinger arranged a cease-fire and undertook "shuttle diplomacy," flying back and forth repeatedly between Middle Eastern capitals in an exhausting search for a settlement. In March 1974 OPEC lifted the oil embargo. The next year Kissinger persuaded Egypt and Israel to accept a United Nations peace-keeping force in the Sinai. But other problems remained: the homeless Palestinian Arabs; Israeli occupation of Jerusalem and the West Bank; Israel's insistence on building settlements in occupied lands; and Arab threats to destroy the Jewish state.

In Latin America, Nixon continued Cold War interventionist policies. In 1970, when the people of Chile elected the Marxist Salvadore Allende president, Nixon suspended foreign aid to Chile. The CIA moved to disrupt the Chilean economy, fuel anti-Allende criticism, and encourage a military coup. In 1973 a military junta ousted and killed Allende.

Intervention in Latin America

In Africa, Nixon-Kissinger maneuvers proved less successful. During the 1960s and early 1970s the CIA channeled funds to some of the groups fighting for the liberation of Angola from Portuguese colonial rule—at the same time that Washington publicly supported Portugal. After Angola won its independence in 1975, civil war erupted. The United States, which stepped up covert aid, and South Africa, which sent troops, backed one faction while the Soviets helped another. When Congress learned about the secret

Angola

aid, it voted to cut all funds. Kissinger complained that the Soviets would gain a foothold in Africa. But many members of Congress argued that Americans could not decide the outcome of an African civil war; that the United States should not be aligned with the white racist regime of South Africa; and that diplomacy should have been tried. After a leftist government came to power in Angola, Washington took a keener interest in the rest of Africa, building economic ties, sending arms to friendly black nations, and putting more distance between the United States and the white minority governments in Rhodesia (now Zimbabwe) and South Africa.

Like other Americans before him, Kissinger clung to the belief that the United States had the answers to most international problems. In his view the Third World was a mere sideshow to the Soviet-American confrontation; and the United States had to defend its interests there against nationalist challenges. Therefore, in the mid-1970s about 686,000 American military personnel were stationed abroad; the United States had military links with ninety-two nations; and American arms sales overseas climbed to about $10 billion. These so-called commitments were maintained not only to impress Moscow, but to serve as a counterrevolutionary force against nationalist stirrings that threatened American economic and strategic interests. Nixon and Kissinger stood, then, in a long line of leaders who counterpoised American power against foreign peoples determined to decide their own fate.

RICH NATIONS, POOR NATIONS: THE NORTH-SOUTH DIALOGUE

If disputes in the Middle East, Latin America, and Africa bedeviled the Nixon-Kissinger grand design for world order, global economic issues also heightened political disorder. Kissinger explained that "international political stability requires international economic stability." But in the 1970s there was little economic stability. Indeed, national economies were affected by a global recession, high oil prices, inflation, and increased tariff rates. And many Third World nations had built up huge international debts. Third World countries (the "South") insisted that the wealthier, industrial "North" share economic resources and the power to exploit them.

The United States could not escape these problems because it was a major participant in the world economy. Although America's economic standing had declined since the olympian days of the 1940s and 1950s, Americans remained the richest people in the world. The United States produced about one-third of the world's goods and services. Moreover, American investments abroad totaled over $133 billion by the mid-1970s. These investments explain in part why the United States was an interventionist power.

Multinational corporations became a symbol and a target of the conspicuous American economic position overseas. American-based multinationals like

Multinational Corporations Exxon and General Motors actually enjoyed budgets and incomes larger than those of most countries. These giant firms brought home profits and exported American culture. But they aroused criticism. American workers protested that these global oligopolies stole their jobs by moving their plants abroad in search of cheaper labor. People of the "South" also complained that multinationals exploited poor countries, robbing them of their natural resources; that they corrupted politics; that they sometimes provided "cover" for CIA agents; and that they evaded taxes by clever manipulations of their books.

Multinational officers and government officials defended these enterprises, pointing out that they invested in risky ventures that brought economic progress, including the transfer of technology. Multinationals, they insisted, helped rationalize a chaotic world economy. Nonetheless, many countries passed laws requiring a certain percentage of native ownership. Other states simply nationalized multinational properties.

Another question that pitted North against South was the Law of the Sea treaty, patiently composed in the 1970s through extended negotiations. Developing nations argued that the rich

Law of the Sea seabed resources of petroleum and minerals should be shared among all nations as a "common heritage of mankind." The industrial states tended to prefer private enterprise or national exploitation, reaping the profits and raw materials for themselves. In the early 1980s the global community hammered out a compromise between international and national controls and rights, but the United States rejected the treaty in 1983. Angry Third World nations railed against what they perceived as selfish economic imperialism, whereas many American allies who supported the compromise predicted a chaotic future of competing claims of ownership, territorial disputes, and threats to freedom of navigation similar to the colonial powers' scramble for advantage in Africa and Asia in the late nineteenth century. Like other international economic issues, this one promised a future of political instability—and perhaps war.

CARTER AND A REINVIGORATED COLD WAR

President Jimmy Carter was "deeply troubled by the lies our people had been told" during the Vietnam War, and he asked Americans to put their "inordinate fear of Communism" behind them. His secretary of state, Cyrus R. Vance, said that he had learned from the Vietnam War that the United States could not "prop up a series of regimes that lacked popular support" and that "there can be no going back to a time when we thought there could be American solutions to every problem."

Hawkish leaders who debated the meaning of the war, however, claimed that America's ignoble failure in Vietnam undermined the nation's credibility and tempted enemies to exploit opportunities at the expense of United States interests. They pointed to a Vietnam syndrome—a mood suspicious of foreign entanglements. They advised that next time the military should be permitted to do its job, free from the constraints of whimsical public opinion and timid politicians. America lost in Vietnam, they asserted, because the American people lost their guts and will at home. They urged Carter to stop at no expense to expand the military and face down America's many adversaries.

Lessons of Vietnam

Others drew different lessons. Some people blamed the war on strong-willed presidents like Johnson and pusillanimous Congresses that had conceded too much power to the executive branch. Trim the powers of the imperial presidency, they counseled, and America would become less interventionist. Others took a more hard-headed, even fatalistic, view: as long as the United States remained an industrial giant, with strong ideological, strategic, economic, and political needs that could only be satisfied through activism abroad, then the nation would continue to be expansionist and interventionist. Still others found fault with the containment doctrine: it failed to make distinctions between areas peripheral and areas vital to the national security and relied too heavily upon military means. Many of these critics thus advised Carter: not more, but less, bluster; not more, but less, military; not more, but less, interventionism.

During Carter's presidency public discussion of the Vietnam War intensified. Some of the war's 2.8 million veterans called for better benefits, especially asking for help to deal with "post-traumatic stress disorder." This illness of nightmares and extreme nervousness was different from the shell shock of the First World War or the battle fatigue of the Second. Doctors reported that the disorder stemmed largely from the fact that soldiers saw so many women, children, and elderly persons killed in Vietnam. Many returning veterans were also stung by the unsympathetic glances of Americans who did not want to be reminded of the unpleasant war or who blamed them for losing a war that could not be won.

In this environment of conflicting answers and lessons Carter vowed to chart a new course. When he took office in 1977 he pledged to give as much attention to North-South as to East-West issues, to reduce the American military presence overseas, to cut back arms sales, and to slow the nuclear arms race. "The soul of our foreign policy," he intoned, would be the championing of individual human rights abroad. A deeply religious man, Carter intended to infuse international relations with moral force.

Carter's Goals

From the start Carter's statements were inconsistent, and administration officials squabbled among themselves. One source of the problem was Zbigniew Brzezinski, a Polish-born national security adviser. The stern-faced Brzezinski was an old-fashioned Cold Warrior, a critic of détente who tended to view foreign crises in globalistic terms: that is, he blamed them on the Soviet Union. More and more Carter listened to Brzezinski; Vance resigned in April 1980, deploring the American drift toward military power as a substitute for diplomacy.

Despite Carter's goals, détente deteriorated and the Cold War revived. The president first angered the Soviets by calling on them to respect their citizens' human rights and tolerate dissent. Moscow told him to mind his own business. Then American officials denounced Russia for sponsoring Cuban troops in Africa. And as Sino-American relations improved following the Nixon visit, Soviet leaders worried that the United States was playing its "China card"— building up their rival in order to threaten them.

A thaw came in 1979 when negotiations produced a new treaty, SALT-II, that acknowledged Soviet-American nuclear parity. The agreement placed a ceiling of 2,250 delivery vehicles (long-range bombers, ICBMs, and submarine-based missiles) on each side and imposed limits on the number of warheads and the development of new kinds of nuclear weapons. Critics from the right charged that the treaty favored the Soviets; critics from the left protested that it did not go far enough toward quelling the arms race. As if to prove both sides correct, Carter soon announced that the United States would construct an expensive new MX missile system that would shuttle ICBMs back and forth along a vast maze of underground tunnels designed to confuse attackers.

SALT-II

Meanwhile, events in Afghanistan led to a Soviet-American confrontation. In December 1979 the Red Army bludgeoned its way into the Soviets' southern neighbor to shore up the faltering Communist government, under siege by Moslem rebels. But the rebels persisted, with some aid from the CIA, and analysts predicted that the Soviet Union had sunk into its own Vietnam. Determined to make the U.S.S.R. "pay a concrete price for their aggression," an embittered Carter shelved SALT-II, suspended shipments of grain and high-technology equipment to Russia, and launched an international boycott of the 1980 Summer Olympics in Moscow. The president also announced what was quickly dubbed the Carter Doctrine: the United States would intervene, unilaterally and militarily if necessary, against further Soviet aggression in the petroleum-rich Persian Gulf. But all his efforts failed to dislodge the Soviets from Afghanistan.

Carter met his toughest test in Iran, where in early 1979 the shah was toppled from his throne by revolutionaries under the leadership of the Ayatollah Ruhollah Khomeini, a wrathfully anti-American Moslem cleric. In November, after the exiled shah was admitted to the United States for medical treatment, mobs stormed the American embassy in Teheran and took American personnel as hostages, demanding the return of the shah for trial, along with his wealth. Although the Iranians eventually released a few of the prisoners, fifty-two others languished over a year under Iranian guard.

Hostage Crisis in Iran

Carter would not return the shah to Iran or apol-

Egypt's President Anwar al-Sadat (1918–1981), President Jimmy Carter (1924–   ), and Israeli Prime Minister Menachem Begin (1913–   ), left to right, clasp hands to celebrate the historic signing, on March 26, 1979, of the Egyptian-Israeli Peace Treaty. A triumph of American diplomacy by the president in intense negotiations with the two Mideast leaders at Camp David, Maryland, the document provided only a brief respite from the violent politics of the region. National Archives, Carter Project.

ogize for past instances of American involvement there (such as the CIA's 1953 intervention that restored the shah to his throne). Unable to gain the hostages' freedom through public appeals, foreign emissaries, or United Nations delegations, the president took steps to isolate Iran economically. He froze Iranian assets in the United States and appealed to American allies, largely unsuccessfully, to reduce trade with the Moslem state. In April 1980 Carter broke diplomatic relations with Iran and ordered a daring rescue mission that miscarried after an equipment failure in the sandy Iranian desert. The hostages were not freed until January 1981, 444 days after their capture. In the agreement that led to their release, the United States released Iranian assets and promised not to intervene again in Iran's internal affairs.

Elsewhere in the Middle East, Carter enjoyed some

IMPORTANT EVENTS

1960	Kennedy elected president		SALT-I treaty
			Nixon re-elected
1961	Peace Corps founded		
	Alliance for Progress	1973	Vietnam cease-fire agreement
	Bay of Pigs invasion		Allende ousted in Chile
	Berlín crisis		Arab-Israeli War
	U.S. military buildup		Arab oil embargo
1962	Cuban missile crisis	1974	Nixon resigns; Ford becomes president
1963	Test-ban treaty		New International Economic Order
	Diem assassinated in Vietnam		
	Kennedy assassinated; Johnson assumes presidency	1975	Egyptian-Israeli peace agreement
			Communists take power in South Vietnam
1964	Tonkin Gulf incident and resolution		Civil war in Angola
	Johnson elected president	1976	Carter elected president
1965	U.S. invasion of Dominican Republic	1977	Human rights policy launched
	Johnson Americanizes Vietnam War	1978	Panama Canal treaties
1967	Six-Day War in the Middle East	1979	Egyptian-Israeli peace accord (Camp David)
1968	Tet offensive in Vietnam		Hostages taken in Iran
	My Lai massacre		SALT-II treaty
	Vietnam peace talks open in Paris		Soviets invade Afghanistan
	Nixon elected president		Grain embargo and boycott of Olympic Games against Soviets
1969	543,400 U.S. troops in Vietnam	1980	Secretary Vance resigns
	Nixon begins withdrawal		Reagan elected president
	Détente policy announced	1981	American hostages in Iran released
1970	Invasion of Cambodia		
1971	*Pentagon Papers* released		
1972	Nixon visits China		

success. Through his tenacious personal diplomacy at a Camp David meeting in 1979, the president persuaded Egypt and Israel to agree to Israel's phased withdrawal from the Sinai, which had been occupied since 1967. Other Arab states denounced the agreement for not requiring Israel to relinquish other occupied territories. But the treaty at least ended warfare along one boundary in this troubled area of the world.

Carter also had some success elsewhere in the

Chapter 30: VIETNAM AND THE COLD WAR: AMERICAN FOREIGN POLICY, 1961–1981

Third World. His appointment of Andrew Young, a black civil rights activist and member of Congress, as ambassador to the United Nations earned goodwill among developing nations. Young believed that the United States should stay out of local disputes, even if Communists were involved. Third World leaders were shocked, however, when Young was forced to resign in 1979 after meeting privately with representatives of the Palestine Liberation Organization, which the United States had refused to recognize as a legitimate group.

In Latin America, Carter concluded two treaties with Panama that provided for gradual return of the Canal Zone to that Central American country.

Carter and Latin America And he initially compromised with nationalist forces in Nicaragua, a nation that had been ruled for decades by the dictatorial Somoza family. When leftist rebels, known as Sandinistas, overthrew Anastasio Somoza in 1979, Carter at first tried to tame their radicalism, but failing, then recognized the revolutionary government. In early 1981, however, he shut off aid to Nicaragua to demonstrate disapproval of the Sandinistas' curbing of civil liberties, growing ties with Castro's Cuba, and alleged assistance to rebels in El Salvador, where another regime friendly to the United States was threatened by internal upheaval.

Carter's diplomatic record never met his aspirations. More American military personnel were stationed overseas in 1980 (489,000) than in 1976 (460,000); the

Debate on Carter's Record defense budget climbed; foreign arms sales grew from $8.3 billion in 1977 to $15.3 billion in 1980; and the United States and NATO agreed to install cruise and Pershing-II missiles in Western Europe. Carter's human rights policy also proved inconsistent. That is, he applied the human rights test to some nations (the Soviet Union, Argentina, and Chile), but not to American allies (South Korea, the shah's Iran, and the Philippines). Carter's successes in the Middle East, Latin America, and Africa became overshadowed by the shrillness of an invigorated Cold War.

Carter's performance did not satisfy Americans who wanted superiority in foreign affairs—a reinstatement of the considerable military edge the United States had had in the early days of the Cold War. Critics chided the administration for a post-Vietnam "loss of will." An Oklahoma couple urged Carter to take up once again Teddy Roosevelt's big stick. "And club the hell out of them if you need to," grumbled the husband.

This nostalgia for old-fashioned American militancy found a ringing voice in President Ronald Reagan, elected in 1980 after a campaign in which he charged that the United States was falling behind the Soviets in the arms race and retreating under fire from the Third World. Reagan promised to abandon détente and SALT-II, dramatically increase the military budget, and support right-wing governments that stood by American foreign policy. The United States, it appeared, had come full circle—back to 1961 when John F. Kennedy had decided to win the Vietnam War.

SUGGESTIONS FOR FURTHER READING

General and Soviet-American Relations

Stephen Ambrose, *Rise to Globalism*, 3rd ed. (1983); Richard J. Barnet, *The Alliance* (1983); John L. Gaddis, *Strategies of Containment* (1982); John L. Gaddis, *Russia, the Soviet Union, and the United States* (1978): Alexander L. George and Richard Smoke, *Deterrence in American Foreign Policy* (1974); Raymond L. Garthoff, *Détente and Confrontation: American Soviet Relations from Nixon to Reagan* (1985); Robert C. Johansen, *The National Interest and the Human Interest* (1980); Walter LaFeber, *America, Russia, and the Cold War, 1945–1985*, 5th ed. (1985); Alvin Z. Rubenstein and Donald E. Smith, eds., *Anti-Americanism in the Third World* (1985); Adam B. Ulam, *Dangerous Relations* (1983).

Kennedy and Johnson Diplomacy

George W. Ball, *The Past Has Another Pattern* (1982); Warren I. Cohen, *Dean Rusk* (1980); David Halberstam, *The Best and the Brightest* (1972); Jim Heath, *Decade of Disillusionment* (1975); Lyndon B. Johnson, *The Vantage Point* (1971); Madeleine G. Kalb, *The Congo Cables* (1982); Doris Kearns, *Lyndon Johnson and the American Dream* (1976); Richard D. Mahoney, *JFK: Ordeal in Africa* (1983); Herbert S. Parmet, *JFK* (1983); Arthur M. Schlesinger, Jr., *Robert Kennedy and His Times* (1978); Arthur M. Schlesinger, Jr., *A Thousand Days* (1965); Richard Walton, *Cold War and Counterrevolution* (1972).

Latin America and Cuba

Graham Allison, *Essence of Decision: Explaining the Cuban Missile Crisis* (1971); Samuel Baily, *The United States and the Development of South America, 1945–1975* (1977); Cole Blasier, *Hovering Giant* (1974); Herbert Dinerstein, *The Making of a Missile Crisis* (1976); Walter LaFeber, *Inevitable Revolutions: The United States in Central America* (1983); Walter LaFeber, *The Panama Canal* (1979); Stephen G. Rabe, *The Road to OPEC: United States Relations with Venezuela* (1982); Peter Wyden, *Bay of Pigs* (1979).

Middle East

George Lenczowski, *The Middle East in World Affairs*, 4th ed. (1980); William B. Quandt, *Decade of Decision: American Policy Toward the Arab-Israeli Conflict, 1967–1976* (1977); Barry Rubin, *Paved with Good Intentions: The American Experience and Iran* (1980); Robert W. Stookey, *America and the Arab States* (1975).

The Vietnam War and Southeast Asia

Larry Berman, *Planning a Tragedy* (1982); Frances Fitz-Gerald, *Fire in the Lake* (1972); Leslie H. Gelb and Richard K. Betts, *The Irony of Vietnam* (1979); William C. Gibbons, *The U.S. Government and the Vietnam War* (1986); George C. Herring, *America's Longest War*, 2nd ed. (1986); Arnold R. Isaacs, *Without Honor: Defeat in Vietnam and Cambodia* (1983); George McT. Kahin, *Intervention* (1986); Stanley Karnow, *Vietnam* (1983); Gabriel Kolko, *Anatomy of a War* (1986); Kathryn Marshall, *In the Combat Zone: An Oral History of Women in Vietnam, 1966–1975* (1987); Al Santoli, *Everything We Had* (1981); William Shawcross, *Sideshow: Kissinger, Nixon, and the Destruction of Cambodia* (1979); Ronald H. Spector, *United States Army in Vietnam* (1983); Wallace Terry, *Bloods: An Oral History of the Vietnam War by Black Veterans* (1984); Nancy Zaroulis and Gerald Sullivan, *Who Spoke Up? American Protest Against the War in Vietnam, 1963–1975* (1984).

The Lessons of Vietnam

Walter H. Capps, *The Unfinished War* (1982); Herbert Hendin and Ann P. Haas, *Wounds of War: The Psychological Aftermath of Combat in Vietnam* (1984); Myra MacPherson, *Long Time Passing: Vietnam and the Haunted Generation* (1984); Norman Podhoretz, *Why We Were in Vietnam* (1982); Harrison E. Salisbury, eds., *Vietnam Reconsidered* (1984); Harry G. Summers, Jr., *On Strategy: A Critical Analysis of the Vietnam War* (1982).

Nixon, Kissinger, and Détente

Richard J. Barnet, *The Giants* (1977); Seymour M. Hersh, *The Price of Power* (1983); Stanley Hoffmann, *Primacy or World Order* (1978); Stanley Hoffmann, "The Case of Dr. Kissinger," *New York Review of Books*, 26 (December 6, 1979), 14ff.; Bernard Kalb and Marvin Kalb, *Kissinger* (1974); Henry Kissinger, *Years of Upheaval* (1982); Roger Morris, *Uncertain Greatness: Henry Kissinger and American Foreign Policy* (1977); Andrew J. Pierre, *The Global Politics of Arms Sales* (1982); Tad Szulc, *The Illusion of Peace* (1978).

Carter's Foreign Policy

Zbigniew Brzezinski, *Power and Principle* (1983); Jimmy Carter, *Keeping Faith* (1982); Warren Christopher et al., *American Hostages in Iran* (1985); James Fallows, *National Defense* (1981); Gaddis Smith, *Morality, Reason, and Power* (1986); Cyrus Vance, *Hard Choices* (1983); Sandy Vogelgesang, *American Dream, Global Nightmare* (1980).

The CIA and Counterinsurgency

Philip Agee, *Inside the Company* (1975); Douglas S. Blaufarb, *The Counterinsurgency Era* (1977); Victor Marchetti and John D. Marks, *The CIA and the Cult of Intelligence* (1974); Thomas Powers, *The Man Who Kept the Secrets* (1979); John Stockwell, *In Search of Enemies* (1978); David Wise, *The American Police State* (1976).

Nuclear Arms Race and SALT

Desmond Ball, *Politics and Force Levels: The Strategic Missile Program of the Kennedy Administration* (1980); Glenn T. Seaborg, *Kennedy, Khruschchev, and the Test Ban* (1981); David N. Schwartz, *NATO's Nuclear Dilemmas* (1983); Stanford Arms Control Group, *International Arms Control*, 2nd ed. (1984).

The World Economy and North-South Issues

Richard J. Barnet, *The Lean Years* (1980); Richard J. Barnet and Ronald Müller, *The Global Reach: The Power of the Multinational Corporations* (1974); David P. Calleo, *The Imperious Economy* (1982); Alfred E. Eckes, *The U.S. and the Global Struggle for Minerals* (1979); Charles A. Jones, *The North-South Dialogue* (1983); Robert K. Olson, *U.S. Foreign Policy and the New International Economic Order* (1981); William Paddock and Paul Paddock, *Time of Famines* (1976); Joan E. Spero, *The Politics of International Economic Relations*, 2nd ed. (1981).

CHAPTER 31

REFORM, RADICALISM, AND DISAPPOINTED EXPECTATIONS
1961–1973

The first dreadful flash from Dallas clattered over newsroom teletype machines across the country at 1:34 P.M., Eastern Standard Time. People still remember precisely where they were and what they were doing on November 22, 1963, when they heard that President John F. Kennedy had been shot and killed. For them, time stopped at that moment in what psychologists call flashbulb memory, the freeze-framing of an exceptionally emotional event down to the most incidental detail.

For four days in late November 1963, Americans wept, prayed, and stared at their television sets, numbed by the unbelievable. Throughout the afternoon and night before the funeral, 250,000 people trod silently past the coffin in the Capitol Rotunda. Jacqueline Kennedy and her daughter, Caroline, paid a last visit to kneel and kiss the coffin. On the fourth day, a million people lined the streets of Washington and millions more watched on television as the pres-

ident's body was borne by horse-drawn caisson from the Capitol to St. Matthew's Cathedral to Arlington Cemetery.

"In retrospect," the British journalist Godfrey Hodgson has written, "people looked back to Friday, November 22, 1963, as the end of a time of hope, the beginning of a time of troubles." What was ironic about America's outpouring of grief was that the Kennedy administration had failed in many of its goals. Few successes distinguished his legislative record, and there was already opposition to America's deepening involvement in Vietnam. But John Kennedy's assassination was a national tragedy. In their grief Americans remembered how he had inspired their hopes for peace, prosperity, and social justice.

In the early 1960s, hope had run high among millions of Americans, including the nation's poor. Kennedy's call for a New Frontier had inspired liberal Democrats and young idealists to work to eliminate poverty, segregation, and voting rights abuses. Americans also supported Kennedy's desire to court the Third World and prevail in the Cold War. Lyndon B. Johnson, Kennedy's successor in the White House, presided over the Great Society, and Congress responded to his urgings with a flood of legislation. The 1960s saw more economic, political, and social reform than any period since the New Deal. But even during these years of liberal triumphs, anger occasionally flared into violence. Beginning with the assassination in 1963, ten years of events ensued—including bloody race riots, the murder of other political and civil rights leaders, and the war in Vietnam—that shattered the Kennedy and Johnson optimism.

In the cities, many Afro-Americans were angry that they still lived in poverty and segregation despite the civil rights movement and the passage of landmark civil rights laws. Their discontent exploded during the 1960s. In July 1967, for example, twenty-six people were killed in Newark, New Jersey, in warfare between blacks, the police, and army troops. This event was followed a week later by the Detroit race riot, which led to the deaths of forty-three persons. The next year the National Advisory Commission on Civil Disorders, chaired by Governor Otto Kerner of Illinois, released its report on the causes of race riots. "The nation is rapidly moving toward two increasingly separate Americas . . . a white society principally located in suburbs, in smaller central cities, and in peripheral parts of large central cities; and a Negro society largely concentrated within large central cities."

This social turbulence along with the growing movement opposing the Vietnam War brought down the presidency of Lyndon Johnson and gave rise to Black Power, the radical politics of the New Left, and a revived women's movement. But Johnson's departure from office did not produce calm. Richard Nixon, who was elected president in 1968, polarized the nation still further. Nixon's two immediate predecessors had been destroyed in office: both Dallas and Vietnam evoked those tragedies. A third place,

Caroline Kennedy kisses her father as her mother watches. President John F. Kennedy (1917–1963) and his wife, Jacqueline, seemed to symbolize youthful energy and idealism. Kennedy's New Frontier gave hope to nonwhites and the poor. National Archives.

Watergate, was to signify Richard Nixon's downfall. Battered by these events, by 1973 many Americans had ceased to believe in the American dream.

KENNEDY AND THE NEW FRONTIER

He was, as Norman Mailer wrote of President John F. Kennedy, "our leading man." The handsome, vigorous new chief executive was young, the first president born in the twentieth century. Perceived by the public as an intellectual, he had a genuinely inquiring mind, and as a patron of the arts, he brought wit and sophistication to the White House.

In a departure from the Eisenhower administration's staid, conservative image, the new president surrounded himself with young men of intellectual verve, who proclaimed that they had fresh ideas for invigorating the nation. Yet Kennedy appointed no women to significant posts. The writer David Halberstam called these men "the best and the brightest." Secretary of Defense Robert McNamara, forty-four, had been an assistant professor at Harvard at age twenty-four and later the whiz-kid president of the Ford Motor Company. Kennedy's special assistant for national security affairs, McGeorge Bundy, forty-one, had become a dean at Harvard at age thirty-four with only a bachelor's degree. Kennedy himself was only forty-three, and his brother Robert, the attorney general, was thirty-five.

"The Best and the Brightest"

Kennedy's program, the New Frontier, was immensely ambitious, promising no less than civil rights for blacks; federal aid to farmers and to education; medical care for all; and the abolition of poverty. But Kennedy promised far more than he could deliver. By August 1961, eight months into his first term, it was evident that Kennedy lacked the ability to move Congress.

Despite his rhetoric, Kennedy pursued civil rights with a lack of vigor. Black activists thus had to continue their struggle without strong overt support from the White House. The tactic most commonly used was nonviolent civil disobedience. Volunteers organized by the Southern Christian Leadership Conference (SCLC), headed by Martin Luther King, Jr., deliberately violated segregation laws by sitting in at whites-only lunch counters, libraries, and bus stations throughout the South. When arrested they went to jail as an act of conscience. In May 1961 "Freedom Riders" with the racially integrated Congress of Racial Equality (CORE) boarded buses and braved attacks by southern white mobs for daring to desegregate interstate transporta-

Civil Rights Movement

tion. Meanwhile black students in the South joined the Student Non-Violent Coordinating Committee (SNCC). More than any other volunteers, it was these field workers who walked the dusty back roads of Mississippi and Georgia, encouraging blacks to resist segregation and register to vote.

As the civil rights movement gained momentum in the early 1960s, President Kennedy gradually made a commitment to first-class citizenship for blacks. In September 1962 he ordered U.S. marshals to protect and assist James Meredith, the first black student to attend the University of Mississippi. Finally in June 1963 Kennedy requested legislation to outlaw segregation in places of public accommodation. When more than 250,000 people gathered at the Lincoln Memorial during the March on Washington that August, they did so with the knowledge that President Kennedy was at last on their side.

Meanwhile, television news programs brought civil rights struggles into Americans' homes. The story was sometimes grisly. In 1963 Medgar Evers, director of the NAACP in Mississippi, was murdered in his own driveway. That same year Birmingham, Alabama, police attacked civil rights demonstrators with snarling dogs, firehoses, and cattle prods.

Then, while Kennedy's public accommodations bill was being held up by a Senate filibuster, two horrifying events helped to convince reluctant politicians that action on civil rights was long overdue. In September white terrorists exploded a bomb during Sunday-morning services at Birmingham's Sixteenth Street Baptist Church. Sunday school was in session, and four black girls were killed. A little more than two months later, John Kennedy was assassinated in Dallas.

Historians have wondered what John Kennedy would have accomplished had he lived. Although his legislative achievements were meager, he inspired idealism in Americans. Kennedy had created a sense of national purpose through his support of the space program. And thousands of Americans joined the Peace Corps, volunteering to spend two years of their lives in this Kennedy-created

Kennedy in Retrospect

program. In recent years, however, some writers have described not Kennedy's idealism, but his recklessness in world events, such as authorizing CIA assassination attempts on the life of Cuba's Premier Fidel Castro. To counteract that assessment, it is clear that Kennedy had begun to grow as president during his last few months in office. He made a moving appeal for racial equality, and he called for reductions in Cold War tensions. Then there was the Kennedy aura. James Reston of the *New York Times* called Kennedy "a story-book President," handsome, graceful, "with poetry on his tongue and a radiant young woman at his side."

JOHNSON AND THE GREAT SOCIETY

The new president, Lyndon Johnson, made civil rights his top legislative priority. "No memorial oration or eulogy," he told a joint session of Congress five days after the assassination, "could more eloquently honor President Kennedy's memory than the earliest passage of the civil rights bill." It was a happy coincidence for the civil rights movement that Johnson, a southerner, had become president. Within months Johnson had signed into law the Civil Rights Act of 1964, which outlawed discrimination not only in public accommodations but also in employment on the basis of race, color, religion, sex, or national origin. The act also authorized the government to withhold funds from public agencies that discriminated on the basis of race, and it gave the attorney general powers to guarantee voting rights and end school segregation.

Civil Rights Act of 1964

Johnson enunciated another priority in January 1964, in his first State of the Union address: "The administration today, here and now, declares unconditional war on poverty." Eight months later, he signed into law the Economic Opportunity Act of 1964, which allocated almost $1 billion to fight poverty. The act became the opening salvo in Johnson's War on Poverty. Finally, Johnson secured the $13.5 billion tax cut for which Kennedy had labored unsuccessfully.

In the year following Kennedy's death, Johnson sought to govern by consensus, appealing to the shared values and aspirations of the majority of the nation. Judging by his lopsided victory over his Republican opponent in 1964, Senator Barry Goldwater of Arizona, he succeeded. Johnson garnered 61 percent of the popular vote and the electoral votes of all but six states.

Election of 1964

Riding on Johnson's coattails, the Democrats won staggering majorities in both the House (295 to 140) and the Senate (68 to 32). Johnson knew that the moment for further reform had arrived. "Hurry, boys, hurry," Johnson told his staff just after the election. "Get that legislation up to the Hill and out. Eighteen months from now ol' Landslide Lyndon will be Lame-Duck Lyndon." Congress responded in 1965 and 1966 with the most sweeping reform legislation since 1935.

Three bills enacted in 1965 were legislative milestones. The Medicare program insured the elderly against medical and hospital bills. The Elementary and Secondary Education Act became the first general program of federal aid to education. And the Voting Rights Act of 1965 empowered the attorney general to supervise voter registration in areas where fewer than half the minority residents of voting age were registered. When Johnson became president, only one-fourth of the South's black population was registered to vote; when he left office in 1969 the proportion was approaching two-thirds. Even in the most resistant states, that trend has continued. Only 6.7 percent of Mississippi's black citizens were registered to vote in 1964; in 1981 the figure was 70 percent.

Other accomplishments during Johnson's presidency included establishment of the Department of Housing and Urban Development; water and air quality improvement acts; the Teacher Corps to work

Shortly after the assassination of President Kennedy, Vice President Johnson was sworn in as the thirty-sixth president of the United States. The ceremony took place on the presidential plane as it returned to Washington from Dallas. Standing on Johnson's right is his wife, Lady Bird; on his left, a stunned Jacqueline Kennedy.   AP/Wide World Photos.

in impoverished school districts; college scholarships and loans; and appropriations for the most ambitious federal housing program since 1949. And in 1968 Johnson signed his third civil rights act, banning racial and religious discrimination in the sale and rental of housing. Another provision of this legislation, known as the Indian Bill of Rights, extended those constitutional protections to reservation Indians living under tribal self-government.

Even more ambitious was Johnson's War on Poverty. Because the gross national product had in-

War on Poverty

creased, Johnson and his advisers reasoned that the government could expect a "fiscal dividend" of several billion dollars in additional tax revenues. They decided to spend the extra money to wipe out poverty through education and job training programs. As the War on Poverty evolved in 1965 and 1966, it included the Job Corps and Neighborhood Youth Corps, to provide marketable skills, work experience, remedial education, and counseling for young people; the Work-Experience Program for unemployed fathers and mothers; Project Head Start, to prepare low-income preschoolers for grade school; and Upward Bound, for high school students from low-income families who aspired to a college education. Other antipoverty programs were Legal Services for the Poor; Volunteers in Service to America (VISTA); and the Model Cities program, which directed federal funds toward upgrading employment, housing, education, and health in targeted neighborhoods.

The War on Poverty, in tandem with a rising gross national product, substantially alleviated hunger and suffering in the United States. Especially significant

Successes in Reducing Poverty

was the doubling of federal spending for Social Security, health, welfare, and education that occurred between 1965 and 1970. During the same years, the GNP leapt from $685 billion to $977 billion The result was a startling reduction in the number of poor people, from 25 percent of the population in 1962 to 11 percent in 1973.

Johnson had the good fortune to preside at the same time as a liberal Supreme Court. In 1962, led by Chief Justice Earl Warren, the Court began handing down a series of liberal decisions. In *Baker* v. *Carr* (1962) and subsequent rulings, it declared that the principle of "one person, one vote" must prevail at both state and national levels, thus forcing reapportionment of state legislatures. And it outlawed required Bible readings and prayers in public schools, explaining that such practices placed an "indirect coercive pressure upon religious minorities."

The Court also attacked the constitutional basis of McCarthyism, ruling in 1965 that a person need not register with the government as a member of a sub-

Civil Rights Rulings

versive organization, for to do so would violate constitutional safeguards against self-incrimination. It also ruled on birth control, holding in *Griswold* v. *Connecticut* (1964) that a state law prohibiting the use of contraceptives by married persons violated "a marital right of privacy" and was unconstitutional. The Court upheld the Civil Rights Act of 1964 and the Voting Rights Act of 1965, and it broadened the interpretation of the Fourteenth Amendment by outlawing segregation in private businesses. And in other rulings that particularly upset conservatives, the Court decreed that books, magazines, and films could not be banned as obscene unless they were "found to be utterly without redeeming social value."

Perhaps most controversial was the Court's transformation of the criminal justice system. Beginning with *Gideon* v. *Wainwright* (1963), the Court ruled that a poor person charged with a felony had the right to a state-appointed lawyer. In *Escobedo* v. *Illinois* (1964), it decreed that the accused had the right to counsel during interrogation and could remain silent. And in *Miranda* v. *Arizona* (1966), it added that police had to inform criminal suspects that they could see a lawyer and remain silent and that any statements they made could be used against them.

The period of liberal ascendancy was short-lived. Disillusioned with America's deepening involvement in Vietnam, many of Johnson's allies rejected both him and his liberal consensus. At the same time, black civil rights activists questioned the benefits of a racially integrated society and proclaimed the rise of Black Power.

RACE RIOTS AND THE MOVEMENT TOWARD BLACK POWER

Even as the civil rights movement registered legal and constitutional victories, some activists began to grumble that the federal government was not to be trusted. During the Mississippi Summer Project of 1964, hundreds of college-age volunteers from the North had joined SNCC and CORE field workers to establish "freedom schools" for black children. Many of these volunteers believed that the Federal Bureau of Investigation was hostile to the civil rights movement. They alleged that FBI Director J. Edgar Hoover was a racist, and they were disturbed by rumors, later confirmed, that Hoover had wiretapped and bugged Martin Luther King, Jr.'s rooms and planted stories in the newspapers about his sexual improprieties. Why, activists asked themselves, had Johnson allowed Hoover to remain in office?

Indeed, some FBI informants had not only joined the Ku Klux Klan; they had reportedly become leaders of the terrorist group. One of them had organized

Violent Attacks on Civil Rights Workers

several atrocities, including the bombing of Birmingham's Sixteenth Street Baptist Church in 1963. Small wonder that during summer 1964 there was an upsurge in racist violence in the South, particularly in Mississippi. White vigilantes bombed and burned two dozen black churches there between June and October, and three civil rights workers were murdered in Philadelphia, Mississippi, by a group including sheriff's deputies. Instead of protecting the civil rights workers, southern police had assaulted and arrested them.

Meanwhile, northern blacks began to consider their situation. They knew their circumstances were deteriorating. Their neighborhoods were more segregated than ever, for whites had responded to the black migration from the South by fleeing to the suburbs. Their median income was little more than half that of whites, and black unemployment in the mid-1960s was twice that of whites. For black males between eighteen and twenty-five it was five times as high. Many black families, particularly those headed solely by women, lived in perpetual poverty. Such were the conditions in 1964 that caused the first of the "long hot summers" of race riots in northern cities. In Harlem and Rochester, New York, and in several cities in New Jersey black anger boiled over.

If 1964 was fiery and violent, 1965 was even more so. In August blacks gutted the Los Angeles neighborhood of Watts; thirty-four people were killed (see

Watts Race Riot

map). Other cities exploded in rioting between 1966 and 1968. Unlike the race riots of 1919 and 1943, white mobs did not provoke the violence; instead, blacks exploded in fury over their joblessness and lack of opportunity, looting white-owned stores, setting fires, and throwing rocks. Still, as indicated several years later by the Kerner Commission, "white society is deeply implicated in the ghetto. White institutions created it, white institutions maintain it, and white society condones it."

It was obvious that many blacks, especially in the North, had begun to question whether the nonviolent civil rights movement had ever addressed their needs. In 1963 Martin Luther King, Jr., had appealed to whites' humanitarian instincts in his "I have a dream" speech. But another voice was beginning to be heard, one that urged blacks to seize their freedom "by any means necessary." It was the voice of Malcolm X, a one-time pimp and street hustler, who, while in prison, had converted to the Nation of Islam religion, commonly known as the Black Muslims.

The Black Muslims, a small sect that espoused separatism from white society, condemned the "white devil" as the chief source of evil in the world. They

Malcolm X

attempted to dissociate themselves from white society and exhorted blacks to lead sober lives and practice thrift. Unlike Martin Luther King, Jr., they advocated violence in self-defense. By the early 1960s Malcolm X had become their chief spokesperson, and his advice was straightforward: "If someone puts a hand on you, send him to the cemetery."

Malcolm X was murdered in a hail of bullets in February 1965; his assassins were Black Muslims who believed he had betrayed their cause. It was true that he had modified some of his ideas just before his death. He had met whites who were not devils, he said, and he had expressed cautious support for the nonviolent civil rights movement. Still, for both blacks and whites, Malcolm X symbolized black defiance and self-respect.

Within a year of Malcolm X's death, Stokely Carmichael, chairman of SNCC, called on blacks to as-

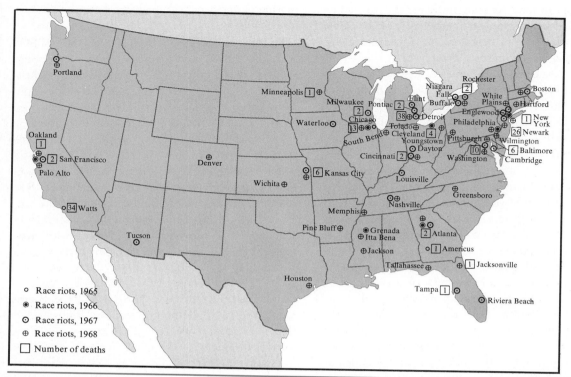

Race Riots, 1965–1968

sert Black Power. Carmichael believed that in order to be truly free from white oppression, blacks had to control their own institutions—businesses, politics, schools. Soon organizations that had been committed to racial integration and nonviolence began to embrace Black Power. SNCC and CORE purged white members and repudiated integration, arguing that black people needed power, not white friendship.

Black Power

The wellspring of this new militance was black nationalism, the concept that black peoples everywhere in the world shared a unique history and cultural heritage that set them apart from whites. College students pressed for black studies programs, and blacks began to call themselves black or Afro-American rather than Negro. At the same time a sense of urgency developed among reform-minded whites, especially college students. On college campuses across the nation, a vocal minority of the baby boom generation set out to "change the system."

THE NEW LEFT AND THE COUNTERCULTURE

In the fall of 1964 Mario Savio returned to Berkeley from Mississippi, where he had been working in a SNCC summer project. There Savio had become convinced that the same power structure that dominated black lives in the South also controlled students' lives in the university. "Last summer I went to

Mississippi to join the struggle there for civil rights. This fall, I am engaged in another part of the same struggle, this time in Berkeley. . . . The same rights are at stake in both places," Savio wrote.

What was wrong with Berkeley? In 1964 the University of California was in many ways a model university, with a worldwide reputation for excellence. Its chancellor, the economist Clark Kerr, had written *The Uses of the University,* in which he likened the university to a big business. But that was what bothered some students. Berkeley, a "multiversity" with tens of thousands of students, had become hopelessly impersonal. "I am a student," rang one lament of the Free Speech Movement (FSM). "Do not fold, spindle, or mutilate."

Free Speech Movement

The struggle began in September 1964, when the university administration banned political recruitment in Sproul Plaza, the students' traditional gathering place. Savio and other students defied Kerr's ban; the administration suspended them or had them arrested. On October 1 several thousand students surrounded a police car in which a militant was being held, immobilizing it for thirty-two hours. Then in December the FSM seized and occupied the main administration building. Governor Pat Brown dispatched state police to Berkeley, and over eight hundred people were arrested. Angry students shut down classes for several days in protest. By the end of the decade, the activism born at Berkeley would spread to hundreds of other campuses.

Over two years before the confrontation in Berkeley, another group of students had met in Port Huron, Michigan, to form Students for a Democratic Society (SDS). Like their leaders, Tom Hayden and Al Haber, most SDS members were white college students, the children of middle-class Americans. In their platform, the Port Huron Statement, they condemned racism, poverty amidst plenty, powerful corporations, and the Cold War. Above all, SDS called upon America to practice its democratic ideals, not just pay them lip service. SDS sought nothing less than the revital-

Students for a Democratic Society (SDS)

ization of democracy through the return of power to the people.

Inspired by the Free Speech Movement and SDS, a minority of students joined the New Left. Some were Marxists, others black nationalists, anarchists, or pacifists. Some believed in pursuing social change through negotiation; others were revolutionaries who thought compromise impossible. All were united in their hatred of racism and the war in Vietnam.

New Left

In the wake of the New Left appeared a phenomenon that observers called the counterculture. Revolutionary figures like Mao Zedong and Fidel Castro became campus idols. Millions of students experimented with marijuana, amphetamines, and hallucinogenic drugs. But it was music more than anything else that reflected the new attitudes. Long before the Beatles sang, "You say you want a revolution," it was evident that their music had inspired one. Soon music was the chief vehicle for the countercultural assault on the status quo. Barry McGuire warned of nuclear holocaust in "Eve of Destruction," and Bob Dylan promised revolutionary answers "blowing in the wind." Young people cheered Jimi Hendrix, who sang of life in a drug-induced "purple haze"; Janis Joplin, who brought black blues to white Americans; and the Buffalo Springfield, who urged youth to stop and "look what's goin' down."

Counter-cultural Revolution

Rock festivals became cultural happenings, the most famous of which was Woodstock (1969), an upstate New York festival that attracted 400,000 people. The huge crowd endured several days of rain and mud together, without shelter and without violence. Some among them began to dream of a peaceful "Woodstock nation" based on love, drugs, and rock music. Beatle John Lennon expressed it best: "All we are saying is give peace a chance."

While some youths sought alternative experiences simply through drugs and music, others tried to construct alternative ways of life. Among the most conspicuous were the hippies. In the Haight-Ashbury section of San Francisco, "flower children" created an urban subculture as distinctive as that of any China-town or Little Italy. "Hashbury" inspired numerous other communal living experiments.

Just as the New Left attracted a minority of students, so the counterculture represented only a small proportion of American youth. But to discon-

Drugs and Sex

certed middle-class parents, hippies seemed to be everywhere. Parents carped about long hair, love beads, and patched jeans. They complained that "acid rock" was loud, discordant, even savage. And they feared their children would suffer lifelong damage from drugs. Perhaps most disturbing were the casual sexual mores their children adopted, partly as a result of the availability of birth-control pills. For many young people, living together no longer equaled living in sin. And as attitudes toward premarital sex changed, so did notions about pornography, homosexuality, sex roles, and familial relationships.

For both cultural and political reasons, the slogan "Make Love, Not War" became popular at mid-decade. As the war in Vietnam escalated, the New Left and the counterculture discovered a common cause. Students held teach-ins on the war—open forums for discussion among students, professors, and guest speakers.

Thousands of young men also expressed their opposition to the war by fleeing the draft. By the end of 1972 more than 30,000 draft resisters were living in Canada, an additional 10,000 had fled to Sweden, Mexico, and other countries, and 10,000 more were living under false identities in the United States. During the war half a million men committed draft violations, including an estimated quarter-million who never registered and another 110,000 who burned their draft cards in protest.

Marches and demonstrations against the war became a popular protest tactic. In April 1965, 25,000 people marched on the White House, and that fall

Antiwar Protests

the National Committee to End the War in Vietnam mobilized over 80,000 in demonstrations across the country. In October 1967, the March on the Pentagon of 100,000 people confirmed government officials' fears that the convergence of student activists, the New Left, and the counterculture threatened the nation's warmaking powers.

1968: A YEAR OF PROTEST, VIOLENCE, AND LOSS

As stormy and violent as the years from 1963 through 1967 had been, many Americans still tried to downplay the nation's distress in hopes it would go away. But in 1968 a series of quakes hit them even harder. The first shock came in January when the U.S.S. *Pueblo*, a navy intelligence ship, was captured by the North Koreans near the port of Wonsan. A week later came the Tet offensive. For the first time many Americans believed they might lose the war. Meanwhile, American casualties increased. In a two-week period in May more than eleven hundred U.S. soldiers died.

Controversy over the war deepened. Within the Democratic party, two men rose to challenge Johnson for the 1968 presidential nomination. One of them, the war hawk Governor George C. Wallace of Alabama, exhorted Americans to "stand up for America." The other, Senator Eugene McCarthy of Minnesota, entered the New Hampshire primary solely to contest Johnson's war policies. On March 12 McCarthy won 42 percent of the popular vote and 20 of 24 convention delegates. Yet another Democrat, Senator Robert F. Kennedy of New York, would soon enter the fray.

On March 31, President Johnson went on national television and announced a scaling-down of the bombing in North Vietnam. Then he hurled a political thunderbolt—he would not be a candidate for re-election.

Less than a week later a white assassin named James Earl Ray shot and killed Martin Luther King,

Americans mourned when Robert F. Kennedy was assassinated. Earlier in 1968, Kennedy had joined César Chávez as the Mexican-American leader of the United Farm Workers ended a fast.   UPI/Bettmann Newsphotos.

Jr., in Memphis. Ray's crime aroused instant rage in the nation's ghettos. Blacks rioted in 168 cities and towns, looting and burning white businesses and property. Thirty-four blacks and five whites died in the violence. In Chicago, Mayor Richard Daley ordered police to shoot to kill arsonists. Across the nation hatred mounted on both sides.

Assassination of Martin Luther King, Jr.

Student protests multiplied that spring not only in the United States but in Paris, Mexico City, and elsewhere in the world. Between January and June 1968 over two hundred demonstrations rocked colleges and universities across the country. Students protested university involvement in the military-industrial complex. In New York students at Columbia University occupied the president's office and other buildings for ten days. On April 30, at the request of Columbia's president, one thousand club-swinging city policemen stormed the occupied buildings, injuring 150 protesters and onlookers.

In April and May Gallup polls reported Robert Kennedy the front-running presidential candidate among Democrats. Kennedy had lost to McCarthy in the Oregon primary but won in California that June. While Kennedy was celebrating his victory in

Los Angeles's Ambassador Hotel, a young Arab nationalist, Sirhan Sirhan, stepped

Assassination of Robert Kennedy

forward with a .22-caliber revolver and fired repeatedly at Kennedy. The assassin despised Kennedy for his unwavering support of Israel.

Violence erupted again in August at the Democratic national convention in Chicago. The Democrats were divided among supporters of Vice President Hubert Humphrey (Lyndon Johnson's candidate), peace candidate Eugene McCarthy, and Senator George McGovern of South Dakota, who had inherited some of Kennedy's support. Adding to the dissension were several mule-drawn wagons driven by blacks from the Poor People's Campaign; thousands of antiwar protesters; and the Youth International Party, or Yippies, who had traveled to Chicago for a Festival of Life, which they contrasted pointedly with "Lyndon and Hubert's celebration of death."

The Chicago police force was still in the psychological grip of Mayor Daley's shoot-to-kill directive. Twelve thousand police were assigned to twelve-

Violence at the Democratic Convention

hour shifts and another twelve thousand army troops and National Guardsmen were on call with rifles, bazookas, and flamethrowers. On Michigan Avenue, in front of the Conrad Hilton Hotel, they at-

tacked, wading into ranks of demonstrators, reporters, and TV camera operators. Throughout the nation viewers watched as club-swinging police beat protesters to the ground. When onlookers rushed to shield the injured, they too were clubbed.

The Democratic convention nominated Humphrey for president and Senator Edmund Muskie of Maine for vice president. Like Johnson, Humphrey was a political descendant of the New Deal and an unstinting supporter of the war. Opposing Humphrey in the 1968 election were Richard M. Nixon, the Republican nominee, and Governor George Wallace of Alabama, who ran as the nominee of the American Independent party.

When the votes were tabulated, Nixon emerged the winner. Just four years after the Goldwater de-

bacle, the Republicans had captured the White House, though by the slimmest of margins. Wallace collected almost 10 million votes, or 13.5 percent of the total, the best performance by a third party since 1924. His strong showing made Nixon a minority president, elected with only 43 percent of the popular vote.

THE REBIRTH OF FEMINISM

During the turbulence of the 1960s, another liberation movement gained momentum, at first quietly and then on the picket line. Following the adoption of the Nineteenth Amend-

The Feminine Mystique

ment in 1920, the women's rights movement had languished. But in the 1960s feminism was reborn. In

The Feminine Mystique (1963), Betty Friedan wrote that the American home had become a "comfortable concentration camp." TV advertisers, magazine writers, beauticians, and psychiatrists had conspired to create the image of a woman "gaily content in a world of bedroom, kitchen, sex, babies and home." Any woman who was dissatisfied with such surroundings was considered neurotic. But as Friedan pointed out, the woman who spent her life in a world of children sacrificed her adult frame of reference and sometimes her very identity.

Friedan's book inspired the founding in 1966 of the National Organization for Women (NOW). A reform organization, NOW battled for "equal rights in partnership with men" by lobbying for

Radical Feminism

legislation and testing laws in the courts. Not long after NOW's formation, a new generation of radical

feminists emerged—once again, the baby boom was making an impact on American life. Most were white and well educated; many were the daughters of working mothers. Most had been raised in the era of sexual liberation, in which birth-control pills and

This healthy, normal baby has a handicap.
She was born female.

When she grows up, her job opportunities will be limited, and her pay low. As a sales clerk, for instance, she'll earn half of what a man does. If she goes to college, she'll still earn less than many men with a 9th grade education. Maybe you don't care—but it's a fact—job discrimination based on sex is against the law. And it's a waste. Think about your own daughter—she's handicapped too.

Womanpower. It's much too good to waste.

The National Organization for Women (NOW), founded in 1966, went from 1,000 members in 1967 to 40,000 members in 1974. This advertisement—developed by the NOW Legal Defense and Education Fund—made a simple and pointed statement about sexual inequality.   NOW Legal Defense and Education Fund, Inc.

other contraceptives were taken for granted. The intellectual ferment of their movement produced a new literature in which feminists challenged everything from women's economic, political, and legal inequality to sexual double standards and sex-role stereotypes.

Unlike the members of NOW, the radical feminists practiced direct action, as when they picketed the 1968 Miss America contest in Atlantic City. One woman auctioned off an effigy of Miss America: "Gentlemen, I offer you the 1969 model. . . . She walks. She talks. She smiles on cue. *And* she does the housework." Into the "freedom trash can" the pickets dumped false eyelashes, curlers, girdles, and *Playboy*. These feminists protested the view of women as servants and sex objects who were pressured to conform to male-imposed "beauty standards."

Radical feminists joined in consciousness-raising groups where they discussed sensitive issues such as homosexuality. In 1969 and 1970 NOW had forced lesbians to resign from membership and offices in the organization. This rift was healed in 1971, largely because homosexuals had begun to fight back. Examples of militancy—by blacks, radical feminists, and antiwar protesters—helped inspire the gay rights movement. Throughout the 1950s and most of the 1960s, many homosexuals had feared that disclosing their sexual preference would cause them to lose their jobs, friends, and families. But in June 1969 that began to change. In New York City's Greenwich Village, a riot erupted between police and the patrons of the Stonewall Inn, a gay bar. Police who raided the bar were not prepared for the volley of beer bottles that greeted them. Rioting continued well into the night. As John D'Emilio has written: "Stonewall thus marked a critical divide in the politics and consciousness of homosexuals and lesbians. A small, thinly spread reform effort suddenly grew into a large, grass-roots movement for liberation. The quality of gay life in America was permanently altered as a furtive subculture moved aggressively into the open."

Gay Rights Movement

For working women in the 1960s, the problems were sex discrimination in employment, lack of professional opportunities, unequal pay for equal work, lack of adequate day care for children, and prohibitions against abortion. Another harsh reality women encountered was "occupational segregation," which became even more pronounced as women flooded entry-level jobs in female-dominated fields like secretarial and clerical work. Women complained of occupational ghettos in which work was broken down into men's jobs and

Occupational Segregation

women's jobs and where women were concentrated in the lower-paying positions. Many women with college educations earned less than men with eighth-grade educations. It was natural that two feminist goals of the 1960s were equal job opportunity and equal pay for equal work.

Despite significant opposition, women made impressive gains. They entered professional schools in record numbers: from 1969 to 1973, the numbers of

Educational and Legal Advances for Women

women law students almost quadrupled and of women medical students more than doubled. Under Title IX of the Educational Amendments of 1972, female college athletes gained the right to the same financial support as male athletes. In the same year Congress approved the Equal Rights Amendment (ERA) and sent it to the states for ratification. (The Equal Rights Amendment states, "Equality of rights under the law shall not be denied or abridged by the United States or by any State on account of sex.") In two 1973 cases (*Roe v. Wade* and *Doe v. Bolton*), the Supreme Court struck down state laws that made abortion a crime. As a result of these victories the women's movement gained new confidence. "If the 1960s belonged to the blacks, the next ten years are ours," remarked one feminist.

NIXON AND THE PERSISTENCE OF CHAOS

Richard Nixon's presidency was born in chaos. In 1969 a hundred black students armed with rifles and shotguns seized the student union at Cornell University and occupied the building for thirty-six hours. Bloody confrontations occurred at Berkeley, San Francisco State, Wisconsin, and scores of other colleges and universities. And in October 1969, three hundred Weathermen, members of an SDS splinter group, raced through Chicago's downtown district, smashing windows and attacking police officers in an attempt to incite armed class struggle. A month later half a million people assembled peacefully at the Washington Monument on Moratorium Day to call for an end to the Vietnam War.

One bright spot for Nixon in 1969 was the flight of *Apollo 11,* a manned spaceship, to the moon. After separating in space from the *Apollo* craft, the lunar

Moon Landing

module reached its destination in mid-July, and on July 21 astronaut Neil Armstrong made history by taking the first step onto the moon's surface. After taking rock and soil samples, Armstrong and his flightmate, Edwin Aldrin, successfully rendezvoused with the *Apollo* command ship, docked, and returned to earth.

But this was a momentary respite. On April 30, 1970, President Nixon appeared on television to announce that the United States had launched an "incursion" into Cambodia. The war

Deaths at Kent State University

at home escalated in response. On May 4, Ohio National Guardsmen fired into a group of protesting students at Kent State University, killing four and wounding eleven. Enraged students elsewhere went on strike, shutting down 250 campuses and pouring into the nation's capital to lobby against the war. Nixon referred to the protesters contemptuously as "these bums, you know, blowing up the campuses."

While police and soldiers waged official violence in 1970, revolutionaries conducted an unofficial campaign of terror. They bombed the New York offices of Mobil Oil, IBM, General Telephone and Electronics, and various banks. And there were scores of politically motivated skyjackings.

Worst of all, as far as many Americans were concerned, was street crime. Sales of pistols, burglar alarms, and bullet-proof vests

Fear of Crime

soared, as did the demand for private guards and special police. Conservatives accused liberals of causing the crime wave by coddling criminals.

In the wake of this new wave of riots and violent crime, Nixon became convinced that the nation was plunging into anarchy. And he worried, as had Lyndon Johnson before him, that the antiwar movement was Communist-inspired. In June 1970 he ordered the FBI, the CIA, the National Security Agency, and the Defense Intelligence Agency to formulate a coordinated attack on "internal threats." "Everything is valid," a Nixon aide told the group, "everything is possible." Had it not been for FBI Director J. Edgar Hoover's refusal to cooperate in the illegal plot, the group would have had free rein to open mail, tap telephones, and break into citizens' homes and offices.

The administration also worked to put the Democratic party on the defensive. Vice President Spiro Agnew took to the road in September to warn the country of threats to its internal security and exhort people to vote Republican in the upcoming congressional elections. The campaign strategy was to portray Democrats as a radical fringe. But Republican attempts to discredit the Democrats failed.

Politics of Divisiveness

Nixon's fortunes declined further in 1971. On June 13 the *New York Times* began to publish the Pentagon Papers, a top-secret study of the Vietnam War ordered in 1967 by then Secretary of Defense McNamara. The *Times* had obtained the papers from Daniel Ellsberg, a disillusioned defense analyst with the RAND Corporation, a think tank for analyzing national defense policies. The study revealed that the government had consistently lied to the American people about the war.

Pentagon Papers

In 1971 Nixon also had to contend with inflation, a problem not entirely of his making. Rather, it was Lyndon Johnson's policy of guns and butter—massive deficit financing to support both the Vietnam War and the Great Society—that had fueled inflation. By January 1971 the United States suffered from a 5.3-percent inflation rate and a 6-percent unemployment rate. Soon the word *stagfla-*

Skyrocketing Inflation

tion would be coined to describe this coexistence of economic recession (stagnation) and inflation.

THE SOUTHERN STRATEGY AND THE ELECTION OF 1972

Political observers believed that Nixon would have a hard time running for re-election on his first-term record. Having urged Americans to use "cool" words and "lower our voices," he had ordered Vice President Agnew to denounce the press and student protesters. Having espoused unity, he had practiced the politics of polarization. Having campaigned as a fiscal conservative, he had authorized near-record budget deficits. And having promised peace, he had widened the war in Southeast Asia.

Moreover, congressional accomplishments had been made more in spite of Nixon than because of him. Eighteen-year-olds gained the vote, Social Security payments and food-stamp funding were increased, and the Occupational Safety and Health Administration was established. Congress responded to the growing environmental movement by passing the Clean Air Act, the Water Quality Improvement Act, and the Resource Recovery Act. (Nixon opposed most of these social welfare, environmental, and voting rights bills.)

Democratic Legislative Victories

In his campaign for re-election, Nixon was less interested in running on his record than in employing a "southern strategy" of political conservatism. A product of the Sunbelt himself, Nixon was attuned to the growing political power of that conservative region. Thus he appealed to "the silent majority," the white suburbanites, blue-collar workers, Catholics, and ethnic

Nixon's Southern Strategy

President Richard M. Nixon (1913–   ) and Vice President Spiro T. Agnew (1918–   ) celebrate their re-election in 1972. Both resigned in disgrace before completing the second term.   National Archives, Nixon Project.

groups of "middle America." As in the 1970 congressional elections, Nixon equated the Republican party with law and order and the Democratic party with permissiveness, crime, drugs, pornography, the hippie lifestyle, student radicalism, black militancy, feminism, homosexuality, and the dissolution of the family.

To a great extent the campaign waged by Nixon's Democratic opponent, Senator George McGovern of South Dakota, handed victory to the president. In the California primary McGovern suggested that the federal government bestow $1,000 on all Americans "from the poorest migrant workers to the Rockefellers." A fiscally irresponsible idea—and a frightening one to the middle classes, who surmised they would

have to pay for it—McGovern's pledge provided deadly ammunition to the Republicans in the general election. When McGovern committed himself to a $30-billion cut in the defense budget, people began to fear he was a neo-isolationist who would reduce the United States to a second-rate power. McGovern's proposals split the Democrats between his supporters—blacks, feminists, antiwar activists, young militants—and old-guard urban bosses, labor and ethnic leaders, and southerners.

Nixon's victory in November was overwhelming. He polled 47 million votes, 60.7 percent of the votes cast. McGovern received only 29 million and won in just one state, Massachusetts, and in the District of Columbia. Nixon's southern strategy was supremely

IMPORTANT EVENTS

1960	Kennedy elected president
1961	Freedom Ride
1962	John Glenn orbits globe
	SDS's Port Huron Statement
1963	Friedan, *The Feminine Mystique*
	March on Washington
	Birmingham, Alabama, Baptist church bombed
	Kennedy assassinated; Johnson assumes the presidency
1964	Economic Opportunity Act
	Civil Rights Act of 1964
	First of the "long hot summers"
	Free Speech Movement
	Johnson elected president
1965	Malcolm X assassinated
	Antiwar demonstrations
	Voting Rights Act of 1965
	Watts race riot
1966	National Organization for Women (NOW) established
1967	Race riots in Newark, Detroit, and other cities

	March on the Pentagon
1968	U.S.S. *Pueblo* captured by North Korea
	Martin Luther King, Jr., assassinated
	Race riots in 168 cities and towns
	Civil Rights Act of 1968
	Antiwar protests escalate
	Robert F. Kennedy assassinated
	Violence at Democratic convention
	Nixon elected president
1969	Stonewall riot
	Apollo II moon landing
	Woodstock festival
1970	U.S. invades Cambodia
	Students killed at Kent State University and Jackson State University
1971	Pentagon Papers
	Nixon's New Economic Policy
1972	Equal Rights Amendment (ERA) approved by Congress
	Nixon re-elected

successful: he carried all of the Deep South, which had once been solidly Democratic.

Nixon's Landslide Victory

He also gained a majority of the urban vote, winning over such long-time Democrats as blue-collar workers, Catholics, and ethnics. Only blacks, Jews, and low-income voters stuck by the Democrats. Remarkably, the Democrats retained control of both houses of Congress and won two additional seats in the Senate.

When John F. Kennedy delivered his inaugural address in 1961, he had challenged Americans to "pay any price, bear any burden, meet any hardship" to defend freedom and inspire the world. Twelve years later, Richard M. Nixon echoed that rhetoric: "Let us pledge to make these four years the best four years in America's history. . . ." Largely because of the president's own actions, however, the next four years would be among the most dismal in the nation's history.

Suggestions for Further Reading

General

Godfrey Hodgson, *America in Our Time* (1976); Peter Joseph, *Good Times: An Oral History of America in the Nineteen Sixties* (1973); Allen J. Matusow, *The Unraveling of America: A History of Liberalism in the 1960's* (1984); Charles R. Morris, *A Time of Passion: America 1960–1980* (1984); William O'Neill, *Coming Apart: An Informal History of America in the 1960s* (1971); Milton Viorst, *Fire in the Streets: America in the 1960s* (1979).

The Kennedy Administration

David Halberstam, *The Best and the Brightest* (1972); Jim F. Heath, *Decade of Disillusionment: The Kennedy-Johnson Years* (1975); Ralph G. Martin, *A Hero for Our Time* (1983); Herbert S. Parmet, *J.F.K.—The Presidency of John F. Kennedy* (1983); Arthur M. Schlesinger, Jr., *A Thousand Days: John F. Kennedy in the White House* (1965); Theodore C. Sorenson, *Kennedy* (1965); Theodore H. White, *The Making of the President* (1961); Garry Wills, *The Kennedy Imprisonment* (1982).

The Johnson Administration

Carl M. Brauer, "Kennedy, Johnson, and the War on Poverty," *Journal of American History*, 69 (1982), 98–119; Robert A. Divine, ed., *Exploring the Johnson Years* (1981); Ronnie Dugger, *The Politician* (1982); Hugh Davis Graham, *The Uncertain Triumph: Federal Education Policy in the Kennedy and Johnson Years* (1984); Lyndon B. Johnson, *The Vantage Point* (1971); Doris Kearns, *Lyndon Johnson and the American Dream* (1976); Sar A. Levitan and Robert Taggart, *The Promise of Greatness* (1976); Charles Murray, *Losing Ground: American Social Policy 1950–1980* (1983); Frances Fox Piven and Richard A. Cloward, *Regulating the Poor* (1971); Carl Solberg, *Hubert Humphrey* (1984); Theodore H. White, *The Making of the President 1964* (1965).

Civil Rights and Black Power

Carl M. Brauer, *John F. Kennedy and the Second Reconstruction* (1977); Clayborne Carson, *In Struggle: SNCC and the Black Awakening of the 1960s* (1981); William H. Chafe, *Civilities and Civil Rights: Greensboro, North Carolina, and the Black Struggle for Freedom* (1980); David J. Garrow, *Bearing the Cross: Martin Luther King, Jr., and the Southern Christian Leadership Conference* (1986); August Meier and Elliott Rudwick, *CORE* (1973); Malcolm X and Alex Haley, *The Autobiography of Malcolm X* (1965); Stephen B. Oates, *Let the Trumpet Sound: The Life of Martin Luther King, Jr.* (1982).

Warren Court

William O. Douglas, *The Court Years 1939–1975* (1980); Anthony Lewis, *Gideon's Trumpet* (1964); Charles Morgan, Jr., *One Man, One Voice* (1979); Bernard Schwartz, *Super Chief: Earl Warren and His Supreme Court* (1983); Earl Warren, *The Memoirs of Earl Warren* (1977).

The New Left and the Antiwar Movement

Wini Breines, *Community and Organization in the New Left* (1983); Todd Gitlin, *The Whole World Is Watching: Mass Media in the Making and Unmaking of the New Left* (1980); James Miller, *"Democracy Is in the Streets": From Port Huron to the Siege of Chicago* (1987); Thomas Powers, *Vietnam, the War at Home* (1984); Kirkpatrick Sale, *SDS* (1973); Sohnya Sayres et al., eds., *The 60s, Without Apology* (1984); Jon Wiener, *Come Together: John Lennon in His Time* (1984); Nancy Zaroulis and Gerald Sullivan, *Who Spoke Up? American Protest Against the War in Vietnam 1963–1975* (1984).

The Counterculture

Stanley Booth, *Dance with the Devil: The Rolling Stones and Their Times* (1984); Morris Dickstein, *Gates of Eden: American Culture in the Sixties* (1977); Philip Norman, *Shout! The Beatles in Their Generation* (1981); Theodore Roszak, *The Making of a Counter Culture* (1968); Philip Slater, *The Pursuit of Loneliness*, rev. ed. (1976).

The Nixon Administration

John Ehrlichman, *Witness to Power* (1982); Richard M. Nixon, *RN: The Memoirs of Richard Nixon* (1978); Leon E. Panetta and Peter Gall, *Bring Us Together: The Nixon Team and the Civil Rights Retreat* (1971); Raymond Price, *With Nixon* (1977); Jonathan Schell, *The Time of Illusion* (1975); Leonard Silk, *Nixonomics* (1972); Theodore H. White, *The Making of the President 1972* (1973); Theodore H. White, *The Making of the President 1968* (1969); Garry Wills, *Nixon Agonistes* (1970).

The Rebirth of Feminism

William H. Chafe, *The American Woman: Her Changing Social, Economic, and Political Role, 1920–1970* (1972); Sara Evans, *Personal Politics* (1978); Betty Friedan, *The Feminine Mystique* (1963); Judith Hole and Ellen Levine, *Rebirth of Feminism* (1971); Alice Kessler-Harris, *Out to Work: A History of Wage-Earning Women in the United States* (1982); Kate Millett, *Sexual Politics* (1970); Robin Morgan, ed., *Sisterhood Is Powerful* (1970); Sheila M. Rothman, *Women's Proper Place* (1978); Gayle Graham Yates, *What Women Want: The Ideas of the Movement* (1975).

CHAPTER 32

DISILLUSIONMENT AND ECONOMIC UNCERTAINTY 1973–1981

*N*ight *watchman Frank* Wills was making his rounds at the Watergate apartment-office complex in Washington, D.C., on June 17, 1972, when he noticed that two doors connecting the building to an underground garage had been taped to keep them from locking. Wills removed the tape, but when he returned thirty minutes later he found it had been replaced. He promptly telephoned the police to report the illegal entry. At 2:30 A.M., police arrested five men who were attaching listening devices to telephones in the sixth-floor offices of the Democratic National Committee.

One of the men arrested was James W. McCord, a former CIA employee who had become security coordinator of the Committee to Re-elect the President (CREEP). The other four were anti-Castro Cubans from Miami. Unknown to the police, two other men had been in the Watergate building illegally at the time of the break-in. One was E. Howard Hunt, a one-time CIA agent who had become CREEP's security chief. The other was G. Gordon Liddy, a for-

mer FBI agent serving on the staff of the White House Domestic Council. What were these men trying to find in the Democrats' offices? What did they hope to overhear on the telephones? Most important, who had ordered the break-in?

In the next twenty-two months the American people would learn the answers to some but not all of these questions. What had at first appeared to be a third-rate burglary would turn out to be part of an official plot to destroy a free presidential election. As the shoddy story of Watergate unfolded, Americans' disillusion grew. Most had grown up believing their country was the most powerful, the most righteous, the most democratic, and the most bountiful in the history of humankind. By the early 1980s, far fewer Americans clung to such beliefs, and many wondered why they had not shed their innocence earlier.

And while the American people worried about morality in government, the nation's economic troubles deepened. The Arab oil embargo of 1973 led to the realization that the United States was not a fortress that could stand alone; it was dependent for its survival on imported oil. Long gasoline lines, the declining value of the dollar, and persistent stagflation dogged Americans; the postwar economic boom was over.

Politicians seemed unable to cope with the struggling economy. President Gerald Ford's weak WIN program to Whip Inflation Now did not impress voters, who turned him out of office in 1976. Jimmy Carter, who defeated Ford, fared just as badly. Under Carter inflation reached new heights and unemployment remained high.

Women and nonwhites were particularly hard hit by inflation and unemployment, for they were usually the last hired and the first to be laid off. Minorities did achieve some victories in the 1970s, though. Women made educational gains and won legislative seats in Washington and in various state houses. Many Afro-Americans attended college and joined the middle class or were elected to political office. But opposition to the aspirations of both groups mounted steadily.

Some Americans decided that if they could not reform society, they could at least develop their own individual potential. For them, the 1970s were the Me Decade. Millions of people took to jogging; others meditated, ate health food, or developed their assertiveness skills. But some observers thought they detected an undercurrent of desperation. By 1980 public opinion polls disclosed that most Americans found the present worse than the past and believed the future would be worse yet.

As the 1980 presidential election approached, Americans looked back on a decade of economic difficulties. With the purchasing power of their paychecks eroded by inflation, many people had raided their savings. They saw once-proud automobile and steel plants age and close. As a result of "deindustrialization," many jobs were jeopardized and some disappeared forever.

It was in this context that Ronald Reagan rode a wave of conservatism into office, promising a return to old-fashioned morality and a balanced budget. But Reagan soon found those goals were easier to talk of than to achieve.

NIXON AND THE WATERGATE SCANDAL

Watergate actually began in 1971, when the White House established not only CREEP but the overlapping Special Investigations Unit, known familiarly as the Plumbers, to stop the leaking of confidential information to the press. Following publication of the Pentagon Papers, the Plumbers burglarized the office of Daniel Ellsberg's psychiatrist in an attempt to find information to discredit Ellsberg. It was the Plumbers who broke into the Democratic National Committee's headquarters to photograph documents and install wiretaps. And it was CREEP that raised money to pay the Plumbers' expenses both before and after the break-in.

The arrest of the Watergate burglars generated furious activity in the White House. Incriminating documents were shredded, E. Howard Hunt's name was expunged from the White House **White House** telephone directory, and Nixon **Cover-up** ordered his chief of staff, H. R. Haldeman, to discourage the FBI's investigation into the burglary on the pretext that it might compromise national security. Nixon also authorized CREEP payments in excess of $460,000 to keep Hunt and others from implicating the White House in the crime.

Thanks to White House efforts to cover up the scandal, the break-in went practically unnoticed by the electorate. Had it not been **Watergate** for the diligent efforts of report- **Hearings and** ers, government special prosecu- **Investigations** tors, federal judges, and congressional representatives, Nixon might

AUTH

7/18/73

During testimony before a Senate committee investigating Watergate, a White House aide revealed that President Nixon had had tape recorders installed in the White House. This cartoon, which needs no caption, suggests the public's reaction to the electronic surveillance. © *1974, Washington Post Writers Group, reprinted with permission.*

have succeeded in disguising his involvement in Watergate. Slowly, however, the ball of lies and distortions began to unravel. In early 1973, U.S. District Court Judge John Sirica tried the burglars, one of whom, James McCord, implicated his superiors in CREEP and at the White House. From May until November, the Senate Select Committee on Campaign Practices, chaired by Senator Sam Ervin, heard testimony from White House aides. John Dean acknowledged not only that there had been a cover-up, but that the president had directed it. Another aide, Alexander Butterfield, shocked the committee and the nation by disclosing that Nixon had had a taping system installed in the White House, and that conversations about Watergate had been recorded.

Nixon feigned innocence, but on April 30, 1973, he announced the resignations of his two chief White House aides, John Erlichman and H. R. Haldeman.

And he appointed Archibald Cox, a Harvard law professor, as special Watergate prosecutor. But when Cox sought nine White House tapes by means of a court order, Nixon decided to fire him. Both Attorney General Elliot Richardson and his deputy, William Ruckelshaus, resigned rather than carry out the president's order to dismiss Cox. Finally the special prosecutor was fired by the next-ranking official in the Department of Justice. The public outcry provoked by the so-called Saturday Night Massacre (October 20, 1973) compelled the president to agree to the appointment of a new special prosecutor, Leon Jaworski. When Nixon still refused to surrender the tapes, Jaworski took him to court.

Saturday Night Massacre

Throughout 1973 and 1974, enterprising reporters uncovered details of the break-in, the hush money, and the various people from Nixon on down who had taken part in the cover-up. White House aides and CREEP subordinates began to go on trial, with Nixon cited as their "unindicted co-conspirator." *Washington Post* reporters Carl Bernstein and Bob Woodward found an informant known as Deep Throat, who provided damning evidence against Nixon and his aides. As Nixon's story became less credible, his hold on the tapes became more tenuous. In late April 1974 the president finally released an edited version of the tapes.

The tapes, however, were replete with gaps. They swayed neither the public nor the House Judiciary Committee, which had begun to draft articles of impeachment against the president. Nixon was still trying to hang onto the tapes when on July 24 the Supreme Court, in *U.S.* v. *Nixon,* unanimously ordered him to surrender the recordings to Judge Sirica. At about the same time, the Judiciary Committee began to conduct nationally televised hearings. After several days of testimony the committee voted for impeachment on three of five counts: obstruction of justice through the payment of hush money to witnesses, lying, and withholding of evidence; defiance of a congressional subpoena of the tapes; and the use of the CIA, the FBI, and the Internal Revenue Service to deprive Americans of their constitutional rights of privacy and free speech.

On August 5 the president finally handed over the complete tapes, which he knew would condemn him. Four days later he resigned, the first president to do so.

Nixon's successor was the new vice president, Gerald R. Ford. Vice President Spiro Agnew had resigned in October 1973 after pleading no contest to charges of income-tax evasion and acceptance of bribes. Under the provisions of the Twenty-fifth Amendment, Nixon had nominated Ford, minority leader of the House, to replace Agnew. Ford's colleagues hailed the new president as a "decent" and "good" man, but Ford's first substantive act provoked a cry of public indignation: he pardoned Nixon.

The Watergate scandal prompted the reform of abuses of presidential power, some of which dated from the Roosevelt administration. In 1973 Congress passed the War Powers Act, which mandated that "in every possible instance" the president must consult with Congress before sending American troops into foreign wars. And in 1974 Congress produced the Congressional Budget and Impoundment Control Act, which prohibited the impoundment of federal money—a tactic Nixon had used to thwart congressional legislation. In actions directly related to Watergate, Congress attacked campaign fund-raising abuses and the misuse of government agencies. The Federal Election Campaign Act of 1972 had restricted campaign spending to no more than ten cents per constituent, and required candidates to report individual contributions of more than $100. In 1974 Congress enacted additional legislation that set ceilings on campaign contributions and expenditures for House, Senate, and presidential elections. Finally, to aid citizens who were victims of dirty-tricks campaigns, Congress strengthened the Freedom of Information Act. The new legislation permitted access to "reasonably" described government documents and provided penalties if the government "arbitrarily or capriciously" withheld such information.

Post-Watergate Restrictions on Executive Power

Chapter 32: Disillusionment and Economic Uncertainty, 1973–1981

The Energy Crisis and the End of the Postwar Economic Boom

The fallout from Watergate was not the only problem confronting the nation in the early 1970s. More disruptive in the long run was the Arab oil embargo of 1973. The American people had grown up on cheap, abundant energy and made no effort to conserve it. By fall 1973 the country was consuming so much energy that it had to import one-third of its oil supplies.

Price increases ordered by the Organization of Petroleum Exporting Countries (OPEC) struck the United States another blow. From January 1973 to January 1974 oil prices rose 350 percent. In March 1974 the majority of OPEC members lifted the five-month-old embargo, but prices remained high. As people grappled with the price hikes, multinational oil companies prospered. Profits jumped 70 percent in 1973. Public resentment of oil companies mounted; many citizens suspected company officers were in league with the Arabs.

OPEC Price Increases and Rising Inflation

The boost in the price of imported oil reverberated through the entire economy. Inflation jumped from 3.3 percent in 1972 to a frightening 11 percent in 1974. At the same time recession hit the auto industry. In Detroit General Motors laid off thirty-eight thousand workers—6 percent of its domestic work force—indefinitely and put another forty-eight thousand on leave for up to ten days at a time. The reason was obvious: sales of gas-guzzling American autos had plummeted as consumers rushed to purchase energy-efficient foreign subcompacts. Moreover, the ailing American auto companies that were not selling cars were not buying steel, glass, rubber, or tool-and-die products either. Soon the recession in the auto industry spread to other manufacturers, who not only quit hiring new workers but also began laying off experienced employees with seniority.

Unlike earlier postwar recessions, this one did not fade away in a year or two. Part of the reason was the coexistence of inflation. In the earlier recessions, Democrats, as well as many Republicans, had held to a policy of neo-Keynesianism. That is, they had manipulated federal policies to minimize the swings in the business cycle—both fiscal policies, covering taxes and government spending, and monetary policies, including interest rates and the money supply. Thus they hoped to keep employment up and inflation down. The federal government could heat up, or stimulate, the economy by increasing spending, cutting taxes, increasing the money supply, and decreasing the interest rates charged to banks that borrowed from the Federal Reserve System. And it could lower the flame by reversing these policies. Beginning in the 1970s, however, joblessness and prices both began to rise sharply. Policies to correct one problem seemed only to exacerbate the other.

Even in the best of times, the economy would have been hard pressed to produce jobs for the millions of baby boomers who would join the labor market in the 1970s. As it was, economic activity created 26.5 million additional jobs during the decade, a remarkable increase of 32.3 percent. But because of deindustrialization, there was a shift in the occupational structure. As heavy industries collapsed, laid-off workers took jobs in fast-food restaurants, all-night gas stations, and convenience stores, but at half their former wages.

The Shifting Occupational Structure

There were other problems, too. One was a slowing of growth in productivity, or the average output of goods per hour of labor. Between 1947 and 1965 American industrial productivity had increased an average of 3.3 percent a year, raising manufacturers' profits and decreasing the cost of products to consumers. But from 1966 to 1970 the annual productivity increase averaged only 1.5 percent; it fell further to 1.4 percent between 1971 and

Decreased Productivity

1975 and to a mere 0.2 percent between 1976 and 1980. Meanwhile, Japan's productivity had been growing at about four times the 1970s rate because of heavy automation. The resulting cost savings to Japanese manufacturers made their products more competitive in the American market, and cut into American manufacturers' sales.

The lag in productivity was not matched by a decrease in workers' expectations. Wage increases regularly exceeded production increases, and some economists blamed the raises for inflation. Indeed, wages and prices that went up seldom came down again, regardless of market conditions. Managers of the nation's basic industries—steel, autos, rubber—complained that the automatic cost-of-living adjustments in their labor contracts left them little margin to restrain price hikes.

Another spur to inflation was easy credit, particularly between 1975 and 1979. Fearing an era of scarcity, many people went on a buying spree. Household and business borrowing more than tripled (from $94 billion to $328 billion). More people had credit cards. This credit explosion helped bid up the price of everything, from houses to gold. But some people, especially farmers, borrowed more than they could afford. The nation's farm debt in 1971 was $54.5 billion; by 1980 it had reached $165.8 billion. Overburdened with debts, many farmers would face bankruptcy in the 1980s.

Easy Credit and Inflation

Every expert had a scapegoat to blame for the nation's economic doldrums. Labor leaders cited foreign competition and called for tariffs to protect American goods. Some businesspeople and economists said the cost of obeying federal health and safety laws and pollution controls added to the price of goods. Critics urged officials to abolish the Environmental Protection Agency and the Occupational Safety and Health Administration, and pressed for deregulation of the oil, airline, and trucking industries on the theory that competition would bring prices down.

Above all, critics attacked the federal government's massive spending programs; the mounting national debt, they said, was the sad result. Since the New Deal, both Republican and Democratic administrations had resorted to pump priming to cure recessions. But the Johnson administration's attempt to finance both the War on Poverty and the Vietnam War evidently had backfired. Critics of neo-Keynesian pump priming pointed to the resulting stagflation as evidence of the failure of New Deal and Great Society economics.

Inflation was certainly getting out of hand. It had begun to climb in 1966 and 1967; when it reached 5.9 percent in 1970, President Nixon had reacted by trying to restrain federal spending, and the Federal Reserve Board had tightened credit. By the time Gerald Ford became president in 1974, OPEC price increases had pushed the rate to 11 percent. Appalled, Ford created WIN, a voluntary program that encouraged businesses, consumers, and workers to save energy and form grassroots anti-inflation organizations.

Government Response to the Economic Crisis

WIN was much too weak to be effective. Ford's ultimate response to inflation, like Nixon's, was to curb federal spending and encourage the Federal Reserve Board to tighten credit. As before, these actions prompted a recession—only this time it was the worst recession in forty years. While the economy stagnated, tax revenues plummeted. As a result the federal deficit for the fiscal year 1976 to 1977 hit $60 billion, and unemployment jumped to 8.5 percent in 1975.

Neither Nixon nor Ford devised lasting solutions to the energy crisis. Nixon did outline a six-point energy program. But when OPEC ended the embargo (March 1974), the crisis seemed to pass, and with it the incentive to prevent future shortages.

The energy crisis intensified public debate over nuclear power. For the sake of energy independence, advocates asserted, the United States had to rely more on nuclear energy. Environmental activists countered that the risk of nuclear accident was too great and there was no safe way to store nuclear waste. Accidents in the nuclear plants at Brown's Ferry, Alabama (1975), and Three Mile Island, Pennsylvania

Nuclear Power

(1979), gave credence to the activists' claims. By 1979, however, ninety-six reactors were under construction, and thirty more were on order.

Meanwhile, the combined effects of the energy crisis, stagflation, and the flight of industry and the middle class to the suburbs and the South were producing fiscal disaster in the nation's cities. Not since 1933, when Detroit defaulted on its debts, had an American city gone bankrupt. But in November 1975 New York City was near financial collapse, unable to meet its payroll and make payments on bonds. Ford vowed "to veto any bill that has as its purpose a federal bail-out of New York City," but after the Senate and House Banking Committees approved loan guarantees, he relented, and the city was saved. New York was not alone in its financial problems; other Frostbelt cities in the North and East were in trouble, saddled with growing welfare rolls, deindustrialization, and a declining tax base. In December 1978 Cleveland became the first American city to default since the Great Depression.

Throughout Ford's term Congress enjoyed new power. Though Ford almost routinely vetoed its bills, Congress in most cases overrode his vetoes. Watergate and the new criticism of the imperial presidency accounted for Congress's new self-confidence. There was also the fact that, for the first time in the nation's history, both the president and the vice president lacked the popular mandate of having been elected to office; one of Ford's first acts as president had been to select former Governor Nelson Rockefeller of New York to be his vice president.

On inauguration day President Carter and his wife, Rosalynn, caught the public's fancy by walking from the Capitol to the White House. Despite this symbolic beginning, Carter became increasingly isolated both from the American people and from Congress. National Archives, Carter Project.

THE FAILED PROMISE OF THE CARTER PRESIDENCY

While Ford struggled with a Democratic Congress, the Democratic party prepared for the presidential election of 1976. Against the background

Election of 1976

of Watergate secrecy and corruption, one candidate in particular promised honesty and openness. "I will never lie to you," pledged Jimmy Carter, an obscure one-term former governor of Georgia. When this born-again Christian promised voters efficiency and decency in government, they believed him. Carter secured the Democratic nomination and chose Senator Walter Mondale, a liberal from Minnesota, as his running mate.

Neither Carter nor President Ford, the Republican candidate, inspired much interest. On election day only 53.5 percent of the electorate voted. Nevertheless, an analysis of the turnout was instructive. One political commentator concluded that the vote was "fractured to a marked degree along the fault line separating the haves and the have-nots." Carter gained almost 90 percent of the black and Mexican-American vote and squeaked to victory by a slim 1.7 million votes out of 80 million. Ford's appeal was strongest among middle- and upper-middle-class voters.

Carter's major domestic accomplishments were in energy, transportation, and conservation policy. To encourage domestic production of oil he instituted phased decontrol of oil prices. To
Carter
Administration
moderate the social effects of the energy crisis he called for a windfall-profits tax on excessive profits resulting from decontrol, and grants to the poor and elderly for the purchase of heating fuel. He supported deregulation of the airline, trucking, and railroad industries and persuaded Congress to ease federal control of banks. His administration established a $1.6 billion "superfund" to clean up abandoned chemical-waste sites. And finally, he placed over 100 million acres of Alaskan land under the federal government's protection as national parks, national forests, and wildlife refuges.

Despite his accomplishments, Carter soon alienated party members. Elected as an outsider, he remained one, failing to develop working relationships with congressional leaders. Moreover, his support of deregulation and his opposition to wage and price controls and gasoline rationing ran counter to the liberal Democratic position. Seeing inflation as more of a threat to the nation's economic health than either recession or unemployment, Carter announced that his top priority would be to cut federal spending, even though doing so would add to the jobless rolls.

By 1980 the economy was a shambles. Inflation had jumped in 1979 to 13.4 percent, and buyers

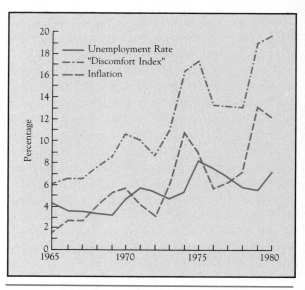

Discomfort Index (Unemployment plus Inflation), 1965–1980 Source: *Economic Report of the President: 1980* (Washington: U.S. Government Printing Office, 1981), pp. 238, 263.

around the world had lost confidence in the dollar, causing unprecedented increases in
Economic
Discomfort
in 1980
the price of gold. To steady the dollar and curb inflation, the Federal Reserve Board had taken drastic measures in late 1979: it had raised the rates at which it loaned money to banks. As a result auto loans became more difficult to obtain, mortgage interest rates leaped beyond 15 percent, and the prime lending rate (the rate charged to businesses) hit an all-time high of 20 percent. Worse still, by 1980 the nation was in a full-fledged recession, with an unemployment rate of 7.5 percent. And the combined high inflation and high unemployment rates had produced a staggeringly high discomfort index of just under 20 percent (see figure). Moreover, the Iranian hostage crisis made Carter and the United States appear ineffectual. In 1980 many Americans blamed their incumbent president for the problems that beset the country.

Chapter 32: DISILLUSIONMENT AND ECONOMIC UNCERTAINTY, 1973–1981

NONWHITES AND NEW IMMIGRANTS

Carter and his predecessors in the 1970s, Nixon and Ford, presided over a nation in which many nonwhites saw their economic fortunes decline. Joblessness plagued blacks, Native Americans, and Hispanics, as well as the new immigrants who arrived during the decade. As a result of the sluggish economy, poverty was still a national problem in 1980, and blacks made up a disproportionate share of the poor.

The weight of poverty fell heavily on black children. A 1981 Children's Defense Fund survey reported that black children in the United States were four times more likely than whites to be born in poverty, twice as likely to drop out of school before twelfth grade, five times as likely as white teenagers to be murdered, and three times as likely to be unemployed. Indeed, in 1980 the unemployment rate for black male teenagers in the inner cities hovered around 50 percent.

Tied to the high unemployment rate was the increase in the number of young black families headed by single women. Between 1960 and 1975 the number of fatherless black families rose 130 percent. Many of these families were headed by unmarried teenagers who were forced to rely on welfare to support their children. Like young black males, welfare mothers suffered from a sense of futility. Many were children of the welfare system; it was the only life they knew.

Some whites and even other blacks grumbled that poor blacks were responsible for their own poverty. Their own forebears had seized the opportunities at hand and raised themselves up by their bootstraps, whites insisted; why couldn't today's blacks do the same? But the job market was far different in the 1970s from what it

Declining Job Opportunities for Blacks

had been twenty-five, fifty, or seventy-five years before. Most jobs required skills the poor and undereducated did not have.

But even as the plight of the black poor worsened, the black middle class expanded. Black college students increased from 282,000 in 1966 to over 1 million in 1976. During this period an estimated 30 percent of the urban black population joined the middle class, and many moved to the suburbs or to better housing in the cities. By 1980 about one-third of all black high school graduates were going on to college, the same proportion as among white youths. At least at the upper levels of black society, the dream of equality was being realized.

Black Middle Class

In his provocative book *The Declining Significance of Race* (1978), William Julius Wilson, a University of Chicago sociologist, spoke of the emergence of two black Americas, one very poor, the other affluent. Blacks living in inner cities and possessed of few job skills found themselves "locked in the low-wage sector . . . where there is little opportunity for advancement and rates of job turnover are high." Meanwhile middle-class blacks, better educated than poor blacks, were able to obtain jobs in government and business. Wilson concluded that "the life chances of blacks" were "based far more on their present economic class position than on their status as black Americans."

As middle-class blacks were making gains, resentful whites complained that they were being victimized by "reverse discrimination." To meet federal affirmative-action requirements, some schools and companies had established quotas for minorities and women. In some cases the requirements for quota groups were lower than those for whites. In a 5-to-4 ruling in 1978 the Supreme Court outlawed quotas but upheld the principle of affirmative action (*Bakke* v. *University of California*).

White Backlash

Anger over a special standard for blacks combined with the effects of stagflation and opposition to busing to produce an upsurge in racism in the 1970s. In Boston, where busing caused numerous riots, a group

In Boston in 1976, antibusing protesters tried to impale a
black man with a flagstaff. This photograph of the ugly incident
won a Pulitzer Prize.   Stanley Forman/Boston Herald-
American.

of white students protesting busing attacked a black
passer-by outside City Hall, running at him with the
sharp end of a flagstaff flying an American flag. Tension rose not only in Boston, but across the nation.
Membership in the Ku Klux Klan grew from about
five thousand in 1978 to ten thousand just two years
later.

Blacks were tense, too, and they showed it more
openly than in the past. "After 350 years of fearing whites," Charles Silberman wrote in *Criminal
Violence, Criminal Justice* (1978),
Black Anger   "black Americans have discovered
that fear runs the other way, that
whites are intimidated by their very presence. . . .

The taboo against expression of anti-white anger is
breaking down, and 350 years of festering hatred has
come spilling out." That hatred erupted several times
in summer 1980, most notably in Miami and Chattanooga, after all-white juries acquitted whites of the
murder of blacks. (In Miami the defendants were
white policemen; in Chattanooga, Ku Klux Klansmen.) Miami's three days of rioting left eighteen
dead, four hundred injured, and $100 million worth
of property damage.

Every bit as angry as blacks were American Indians. Their new militancy had burst into the headlines
in November 1969, when a small group of Indians
seized Alcatraz Island in San Francisco Bay. Arguing

Chapter 32: Disillusionment and Economic Uncertainty, 1973–1981

that an 1868 Sioux treaty entitled them to possession of unused federal lands, the Indians occupied the island until summer 1971. Two years later, members of the American Indian Movement (AIM) seized eleven hostages and a trading post on the Pine Ridge Reservation at Wounded Knee, South Dakota, the place where troops of the 7th Cavalry had massacred the Sioux in 1890. Their seventy-one-day confrontation with federal marshals ended with a government agreement to examine the treaty rights of the Oglala Sioux.

Indian Militancy

Like many blacks, Indians were trapped in poverty. In the late 1970s the unemployment rate among Indians was 40 percent. Nine out of ten Indians lived in substandard housing, and the high school dropout rate averaged 53 percent. Being an Indian was also unhealthy: Native Americans suffered the highest incidence of alcoholism, tuberculosis, and suicide of any ethnic group in the United States.

Since 1924 Indians have had dual legal status as United States citizens and as members of tribal nations subject to special treaty agreements with the United States. But their dual status has proved a curse, in large part because the government has not honored its treaty commitments—especially when Indian lands contained valuable minerals. In 1946 Congress established the Indian Claims Commission to compensate Indians for lands stolen from them. Under the legislation lawyers for the Native American Rights Fund and other groups scored notable victories in the 1970s. The Chippewa in the upper Midwest, Indians in the Puget Sound area of Washington, and the Cheyenne-Arapaho tribes in Oklahoma won protection of their hunting and fishing rights and restitution of their land and water. In 1971 President Nixon signed a bill returning to the Taos Pueblo their sacred forest of Blue Lake in New Mexico. And in 1980 the Supreme Court ordered the government to pay $117 million plus interest to the Sioux Indian Nation for the Black Hills of South Dakota, stolen from them when gold was discovered there in the 1870s.

Indian Suits for Lost Lands

As Indians fought to regain old rights, Hispanics struggled to make a place for themselves in the United States. An influx of immigrants unequaled since the turn of the century coupled with a high birthrate had made Hispanic peoples America's fastest-growing minority by the 1970s. Of the more than 20 million Hispanics living in the United States in the 1970s, 8 million were Mexican-Americans concentrated in Arizona, California, Colorado, New Mexico, and Texas. Several million Puerto Ricans and perhaps 1 million Cubans clustered principally on the East Coast.

Hispanic-Americans

Besides these officially acknowledged Hispanics, between 8 million and 12 million more undocumented workers, or illegal aliens, lived in the United States. Beginning in the mid-1960s, large numbers of poverty-stricken Mexicans began to cross the poorly guarded 2,000-mile border between Mexico and the United States. The movement north continued in the 1970s and 1980s. (Legislation adopted in 1986 made it possible for many of these aliens to become citizens of the United States.) By 1980, one out of every four Texans and one out of every five Californians was Mexican-American. As David Lizarraga, director of the East Los Angeles Community Union, explained: "If I were in Mexico now, I'd be running across that wire as fast as I could. This is the land of opportunity."

But poverty awaited these new immigrants, as it had previous groups of newcomers. The median family income for Mexican-Americans in 1979 was $11,421, as compared with $16,284 for non-Hispanic families. Nineteen percent of Mexican-Americans lived below the poverty line. Puerto Ricans were worse off, with a median family income of about $8,300, and 30 percent of their number living in poverty. Though the problems with which Hispanics contended were similar to those confronting other nonwhites, they also faced a language barrier.

Most Hispanics preferred their family-centered culture to Anglo culture, and for that reason they resisted assimilation. "What we are saying," explained Daniel Villanueva, a TV executive, "is that we want to be here, but without losing our language and our culture. They are a richness, a treasure that we don't care to lose." A Puerto Rican woman in New York added, "We have been trying to become American for too long, and we are forgetting our roots, culture and the values of our nationality."

Hispanic Cultural Pride

Instead, like other minorities, Hispanics wanted power—"brown power." César Chávez's United Farm Workers had been the first Hispanic interest group to gain national attention. Another group, the militant Brown Berets, attracted notice for their efforts to provide meals to preschoolers and courses in Chicano studies and consciousness-raising to older students. And throughout the 1970s a Mexican-American political party, La Raza Unida, was a potent force in the Southwest and East Los Angeles. Still, for a group soon to become the nation's largest minority, Hispanics exercised a disproportionately small share of political power.

New Influx of Immigrants

During the late 1970s and early 1980s, still other new immigrants joined America's population. Between 1970 and 1980 the United States absorbed more new nonwhite residents than in any one decade in American history. Refugees of the Vietnam War arrived from Indochina, and other immigrants came from the Philippines, Korea, Taiwan, India, the Dominican Republic, and Jamaica. In 1980, 160,000 boat people poured in from the islands of Cuba and Haiti. Although well-wishers were on hand to greet these people, the history of the nation's treatment of nonwhites did not augur well for them.

WOMEN'S STRUGGLES

In the 1970s, while civil rights struggles engaged the energies of various racial and ethnic groups, increasing numbers of women committed themselves to the struggle for equality with men. Feminists had scored some impressive legislative victories. In 1974 Congress passed the Equal Credit Opportunity Act, which enabled women to get bank loans and obtain credit cards on the same terms as men. Even more significant were the gains women made, along with blacks and other minorities, as a result of affirmative action in hiring. As mandated by the Civil Rights Act of 1964 and the establishment of the Equal Employment Opportunity Commission, women and minorities had to receive the same consideration as white males when applying for a job. In the field of criminal law, many states revised their statutes on rape, prohibiting lawyers from stressing the previous sexual experience of rape victims.

Antifeminist Movement

Still, women continued to encounter barriers in their quest for equality. One of the most formidable was the antifeminist, or "profamily," movement, which contended that men should lead and women should follow, particularly within the family. The backlash against feminism became an increasingly powerful political force in the 1970s. In defense of the family, antifeminists campaigned against the Equal Rights Amendment (ERA), the gay rights movement, and abortion on demand. Anita Bryant and Phyllis Schlafly gained fame by arguing that all these issues were interrelated and that they endangered traditional American values.

Equal Rights Amendment

Antifeminists blocked ratification of the Equal Rights Amendment, which whizzed through thirty-five state legislatures in the late 1970s and then faltered three votes short of the required three-fourths. Schlafly's STOP ERA campaign had falsely claimed that the ERA would abolish alimony, force women to fight in combat, and prohibit separate-sex restrooms. Shortly after the deadline for ratification (June 1982) the ERA was reintroduced in Congress, and the long process of amendment adoption began again.

Many antifeminists also participated in the antiabortion, or "prolife," movement, which sprang up almost overnight in the wake of the Supreme Court's

1973 decisions in *Roe v. Wade* and *Doe v. Bolton.* Along with Catholics, Mormons, and other religious opponents of abortion, the prolife movement gave support to the successful legislative efforts of Representative Henry Hyde of Illinois in 1976 to cut off most Medicaid funds for abortions. In summer 1980 the Supreme Court upheld the Hyde amendment, deciding that the government had no obligation to make even medically necessary abortions available to the poor (*Harris* v. *McRae*).

As activists in the women's struggle looked to the future, they had to acknowledge certain harsh realities. One was the impact of the economic recessions of the 1970s and early 1980s.

Effects of a Glutted Job Market
In a tight job market, it was difficult for most outsiders—women and nonwhites—to become insiders. Though affirmative action had certainly helped women to gain employment and receive promotions, jobs had to be available in the first place for women to benefit. Added to job scarcity was the continuing problem of occupational segregation, in which women were concentrated in lower-paying positions while most men enjoyed much higher incomes. By the end of the 1970s, female workers still took home only 59 cents to every male worker's dollar.

Perhaps the most disturbing trend was what *Newsweek* called "the Superwoman Squeeze." According to a report by the Worldwatch Institute in 1980, most working wives and mothers, even those with full-time jobs, "retained an unwilling monopoly on unpaid labor at home." Husbands were generally less than eager to do household tasks.

Increased Burdens on Women

It appeared, too, that the feminist ferment of the 1970s had dwindled by the early 1980s. Some women seemed to take for granted the gains of that decade, believing that equality of opportunity had been secured for all time. Others concentrated on planning their lives so they could have both a career and a family without shortchanging either—or themselves—in the process.

THE ME DECADE

At the beginning of 1980, the editors of *Time* magazine observed that the 1970s had been "erected upon the smoldering wreckage of the '60s." In the 1970s the nation had turned apathetic, and perhaps nowhere was this new attitude more evident than among youth. In the 1960s American youths had worked for change in the nation's social, political, and cultural life. But in the 1970s their younger brothers and sisters rejected revolutionary idealism. Older Americans took refuge, too, from a lost war, political scandal, and economic distress. As a theologian put it, Americans "have a beleaguered sense in their bones that the old order is dying. Very few want a radical alternative, but few also are working to develop a rationale for the system we've got."

Instead, in the 1970s, a period the social commentator Tom Wolfe called the Me Decade, Americans turned inward, concentrating on self-expression and personal improvement. Transactional Analysis (TA), a form of psychotherapy emphasizing interpersonal relationships, was popularized in Eric Berne's *Games People Play* (1969) and Thomas Harris's *I'm OK—You're OK* (1969). Transcendental Meditation (TM), a yogic discipline, drew 350,000 adherents and spawned over two hundred teaching centers. In addition to these fads, other new therapies and exotic religions flourished, as did such eastern religions and practices of long-standing as Zen and yoga.

Human Potential Movement

As millions of Americans sought to fill spiritual and emotional voids through esoteric movements, millions more were drawn to traditional Christian beliefs. According to a 1977 survey, about 70 million Americans defined themselves as born-again Christians, and 10 million claimed to have had the experience since 1975. Religious revivals and evangelical sects were not new, of course,

Spiritual Revival

but by the mid-1970s they were a growth industry. In the latter years of the decade evangelicals grossed $200 million annually in sales of religious books, and the Virginia-based Christian Broadcast Network earned nearly $60 million from its four stations and 130 affiliates.

Besides the relatively harmless human potential movements and the traditional religious enthusiasms, a dark undercurrent of cultlike adherence to charismatic leaders ran through the 1970s. In 1973 and 1974, the Reverend Sun Myung Moon, Korean founder of the Unification Church, converted young Americans to his religion, a curious blend of Christianity, anti-Communism, and worship of Moon as a messiah. "Moonies" disposed of their possessions, moved into communes, and raised funds for the church by selling ginseng tea, candles, flowers, and peanuts. Critics charged that Moon and his disciples had brainwashed their converts. Soon worried parents were attempting to kidnap their children from the Unification Church and its influence.

Messianic Cults

Yet another facet of "me-ness" was the phenomenon called "Roots." The 1977 television series, based on a best-selling book by Alex Haley, dramatized the author's family history beginning with his ancestor, Kunta Kinte, a Gambian boy sold into slavery. "Roots" spawned an interest in family trees that touched all races and ethnic groups. More important, the sheer numbers of Americans exposed to the book and television series (130 million watched the eight-part series) helped to sensitize the public to the agonies of slavery and racism.

When middle-class Americans went running to libraries to research their family trees during the 1970s, they usually did so in an expensive pair of Nikes, Pumas, or Adidas, for this was the decade of the jogger. James Fixx's *Complete Book of Running* (1977) enjoyed tremendous popularity, and literature on running, physical fitness, diet, and health jammed bookshelves and magazine racks. Perhaps America was no longer the best nation

Physical Fitness Craze

it could be, but Americans were determined to make themselves the healthiest individuals they could be.

As the decade drew to a close, Christopher Lasch, a history professor at the University of Rochester, condemned the nation's behavior as self-indulgent and apolitical. In *The Culture of Narcissism* (1979), Lasch branded Americans an emotionally shallow, anxiety-ridden people desperately trying to ignore the waning of their nation's power. He cited advertising and the human potential movement as causes of the nation's malaise. But there was little evidence that the trend was changing. In a decade of exhausted public passions, private passions reigned supreme.

RONALD REAGAN AND THE ELECTION OF 1980

By 1980 the nation's mood had turned conservative. In 1978 California voters had approved a tax-cutting referendum called Proposition 13, which had reduced property taxes and put stringent limits on state spending for social programs. On the national level conservatives lobbied for a constitutional amendment to prohibit federal budget deficits and organized for the 1980 elections. One conservative campaign group, the National Conservative Political Action Committee (NCPAC), targeted a number of liberal senators for defeat. And a number of evangelical Christians joined with the conservatives, hoping to use the body politic in their fight against abortion, gay rights, sex in movies, and the ERA.

Resurgence of Conservatism

From the beginning, the front-runner for the Republican presidential nomination was conservative Ronald Reagan, a former movie actor and two-term governor of California. Reagan appealed to both traditional political conservatives and the new breed

Election of 1980

of social-issue conservatives. In the Democratic party, President Carter easily beat back Senator Edward Kennedy's challenge for the nomination. As the incumbent, Carter had to accept political responsibility not only for high inflation and unemployment but for the Americans being held hostage in Iran. When the votes were counted, Reagan had won 51 percent of the popular vote and all but forty-nine electoral votes. Carter carried only six states. John Anderson, a Republican who ran as an independent, garnered 7 percent of the popular vote.

More startling than Reagan's sweep was the capture of eleven Senate seats by Republican candidates, a victory that gave the party a majority in that house. Conservative advertising campaigns had succeeded in defeating most of the targeted liberals, including Senators George McGovern and Frank Church. Republicans also gained thirty-three seats in the house and four state governorships. It seemed clear that Democrats would be running scared in the 1980s.

On January 20, 1981, Ronald Reagan was inaugurated as president. He pledged to work for "an era of national renewal," for "a healthy, vigorous, growing economy that provides equal opportunities for all Americans." On the same day, after 444 days in captivity, the American hostages boarded an airplane that flew them from Teheran to freedom. Yellow ribbons welcomed the freed Americans, and the nation rejoiced. Seldom had a new administration had a more auspicious beginning.

SUGGESTIONS FOR FURTHER READING

Watergate

John W. Dean, *Blind Ambition* (1976); Seymour M. Hersh, "The Pardon: Nixon, Ford, Haig, and the Transfer of Power," *Atlantic Monthly*, 252 (1983), 55–78; Jim Hougan, *Secret Agenda* (1984); Leon Jaworski, *The Right and the Power* (1976); J. Anthony Lukas, *Nightmare: The Underside of the Nixon Years* (1976); John J. Sirica, *To Set the Record Straight* (1979); Theodore White, *Breach of Faith* (1975); Bob Woodward and Carl Bernstein, *The Final Days* (1976); Bob Woodward and Carl Bernstein, *All the President's Men* (1974).

Energy Shortages, Economic Woes

Richard J. Barnet, *The Lean Years: Politics in the Age of Scarcity* (1980); Daniel Bell, *The Coming of the Post-Industrial Society* (1973); John M. Blair, *The Control of Oil* (1976); Barry Bluestone and Bennett Harrison, *The Deindustrialization of America* (1982); David P. Calleo, *The Imperious Economy* (1982); Barry Commoner, *The Politics of Energy* (1979); Robert L. Heilbroner, *An Inquiry into the Human Prospect* (1974); Harry Mauer, *Not Working: An Oral History of the Unemployed* (1979); John E. Schwarz, *America's Hidden Success* (1983); Robert Sherrill, *The Oil Follies of 1970–1980* (1983); Robert Stobaugh and Daniel Yergin, eds., *Energy Future* (1979); Lester C. Thurow, *The Zero-Sum Society* (1980).

The Ford Administration

Gerald R. Ford, *A Time to Heal* (1979); Robert T. Hartmann, *Palace Politics* (1980); Ron Nessen, *It Sure Looks Different from the Inside* (1978); A. James Reichley, *Conservatives in an Age of Change: The Nixon and Ford Administrations* (1981); James L. Sundquist, *The Decline and Resurgence of Congress* (1981).

The Carter Administration

Griffin Bell, *Taking Care of the Law* (1982); Joseph A. Califano, *Governing America* (1981); Jimmy Carter, *Keeping Faith* (1982); Rosalynn Carter, *First Lady from Plains* (1984); Betty Glad, *Jimmy Carter: From Plains to the White House* (1980); Haynes Johnson, *In the Absence of Power* (1980); Hamilton Jordan, *Crisis* (1982); Jody Powell, *The Other Side of the Story* (1984); Laurence H. Shoup, *The Carter Presidency & Beyond* (1980).

Women and the Family

Susan Brownmiller, *Against Our Will: Men, Women and Rape* (1975); Andrea Dworkin, *Right-Wing Women* (1983); Barbara Ehrenreich, *The Hearts of Men: American Dreams and the Flight from Commitment* (1983); Kenneth Keniston, *All Our Children: The American Family Under Pressure* (1977); Christopher Lasch, *Haven in a Heartless World: The Family Besieged* (1977); Kristin Luker, *Abortion and the Politics of Motherhood* (1984); Maggie Scarf, *Unfinished Business: Pressure Points in the Lives of Women* (1980).

Nonwhites and New Immigrants

Thomas J. Archdeacon, *Becoming American* (1983); John Crewden, *The Tarnished Door: The New Immigrants and the Transformation of America* (1983); Vine Deloria, *Behind the Trail of Broken Treaties* (1974); Dorothy K. Newman *et al.*, *Protests, Politics, and Prosperity: Black Americans and White Institutions, 1940–1974* (1978); Carol B. Stack, *All Our Kin: Strategies for Survival in a Black Community* (1975); Arnulfo D. Trejo, ed., *The Chicanos: As We See Ourselves* (1979); William Julius Wilson, *The Declining Significance of Race: Blacks and Changing American Institutions*, 2nd ed. (1980).

The Me Decade

Peter Clecak, *America's Quest for the Ideal Self: Dissent and Fulfillment in the Sixties and Seventies* (1983); Jim Hougan, *Decadence: Radical Nostalgia, Narcissism, and Decline in the Seventies* (1975); Christopher Lasch, *The Culture of Narcissism* (1978); Edwin Schur, *The Awareness Trap: Self-Absorption Instead of Social Change* (1976); Gail Sheehy, *Passages: Predictable Crises in Adult Life* (1976); Tom Wolfe, "The 'Me' Decade and the Third Great Awakening," *New York*, 9 (1976), 26–40; Daniel Yankelovich, *New Rules: Searching for Self-Fulfillment in a World Turned Upside Down* (1981).

The New Conservatism and the Election of Ronald Reagan

Peter N. Carroll, *It Seemed Like Nothing Happened: The Tragedy and Promise of America in the 1970s* (1982); Alan Crawford, *Thunder on the Right* (1980); Elizabeth Drew, *Portrait of an Election* (1981); Jack W. Germond and Jules Witcover, *Blue Smoke and Mirrors: How Reagan Won and Why Carter Lost the Election of 1980* (1981); Jeff Greenfield, *The Real Campaign* (1982); David W. Reinhard, *The Republican Right Since 1945* (1983); Kirkpatrick Sale, *Power Shift: The Rise of the Southern Rim and Its Challenge to the Eastern Establishment* (1975); Peter Steinfels, *The Neoconservatives* (1979); F. Clifton White, *Why Reagan Won* (1981).

Chapter 33

A Turn to the Right: America Since 1981

Ronald Reagan and Franklin D. Roosevelt were alike in a number of ways. Both men were skillful performers; both projected warm images that inspired confidence. Reagan openly admired Roosevelt's style. The writer David McCullough, after interviewing Reagan in the White House, concluded that the president "sees Roosevelt as his 'kind of guy'—confident, cheerful, theatrical, larger than life." The irony, of course, was that Reagan's goal was to repeal Roosevelt's New Deal, not to champion it. Indeed, when Reagan began his second term in 1985, he announced that his "new American Emancipation" would "tear down economic barriers and liberate the spirit of enterprise" by eradicating the excesses of fifty years of Democratic liberalism.

President Reagan's policies met with varying degrees of popularity during his two terms. But public support for the man himself was usually strong, a testament to the vibrant appeal of the image he projected. Hugh Heclo, a professor of government at Harvard, believed that Reagan was popular because "he actually seems like a normal human being. He's knowable, he's likable. He's not *weird*. You think of Johnson and Nixon and Carter. And then there's Reagan. He's someone you'd be happy to have in your living room."

The split between Reagan's personal popularity and the support given his policies was so complete that even controversies within his administration and problems in his domestic and foreign policies had little effect on the regard Americans had for the man. Representative Patricia Schroeder, a Colorado Democrat, gave this phenomenon a memorable label when she said that Reagan was "perfecting the Teflon-coated presidency. . . . He sees to it that nothing sticks to him."

Reagan was adept at reflecting the nation's mood. A proponent of prayer in the public schools and an opponent of abortion, the president urged a return to the standards of morality that had dominated American culture before the 1960s. His foreign policies were widely applauded by those who were proud their country would "stand up to" the Soviet Union again. After Vietnam and the humiliation of the Iranian hostage situation, Reagan made Americans feel good about being American.

The pursuit of conservative goals characterized Reagan's agenda. His economic policies were highlighted by two major tax bills, the Gramm-Rudman bill, which called for a balanced federal budget, and attacks on the welfare system as well as on federal health, safety, and environmental regulations.

Reagan's conservatism in foreign policy was shaped by a belief that previous administrations had shown weakness toward the Soviet Union, Cuba, Third World countries, and terrorists. The president set out to swell the American military arsenal, denounce and intimidate the Soviets, unseat leftist governments through military intervention or covert operations, and settle civil wars in the Middle East and Central America.

The president's popularity probably peaked during the time of his 1984 re-election, when he carried forty-nine states. Then, in 1986, a series of setbacks scratched his Teflon coating. Congressional elections held that year resulted in the Republicans' losing control of the Senate and the Democrats' increasing their majority in the House. Twelve of the sixteen Republican senators for whom Reagan had personally campaigned were defeated. And a major scandal surfaced: it was discovered that the administration had secretly sold arms to Iran and had diverted profits from the sale to the *contras* in Nicaragua. The president's job approval rating dropped from 64 percent in October 1986 to 40 percent in March 1987. In the spring of 1987, joint Senate-House hearings on the Iran-*contra* affair began. The president faced serious problems during his last two years in office.

Ronald Reagan (1911–   ) assumed the presidency confident that his policies and leadership would restore both prosperity and national pride. In the manner of Franklin D. Roosevelt fifty years earlier, Reagan's confidence was infectious.   Bill Pierce/Time Magazine.

"REAGANOMICS"

When he took office in 1981, President Reagan wasted little time in announcing his plans for "a new beginning." In February he launched an attack on economic problems. First, he asked Congress for spending cuts in domestic programs, including urban aid, Medicare and Medicaid, food stamps, welfare subsidies for the working poor, and school meals. In July Congress met most of Reagan's demands by paring $35.2 billion from social and cultural programs. Reagan initiated another round of budget cuts totaling $13 billion in September, resulting, among other things, in the removal of 1 million food-stamp recipients from government rolls.

Major changes in the tax system constituted the second part of Reagan's economic plan. Reagan was a fervent believer in supply-side economics, which

Tax Reform called for reductions in the income taxes of the affluent and of corporations in order to stimulate savings and investments. New capital would be invested, the argument went, and would produce new plants, new jobs, and new products, and as prosperity returned, the profits at the top would trickle down through the middle classes to the poor at the bottom. Economic growth and expanding opportunities would again be the hallmarks of American society. Reagan thus proposed slashing income taxes by 30 percent over three years. Congress responded in August with a five-year, $750-billion tax cut, the largest ever in American history. The act's major feature was a 25-percent reduction in personal income taxes over the next three years. Other provisions increased business investment tax credits and depreciation allowances and lowered the maximum tax on all income from 70 to 50 percent. Wealthy people gained the most from these tax cuts.

But Americans still complained about the federal tax code. The existing law included fifteen tax rates on personal income, as well as numerous special breaks that benefitted middle- and, in particular, upper-income families. Some individuals with incomes in excess of $1 million paid no federal income taxes whatsoever. Even some major corporations avoided paying taxes.

Congress responded to the mounting criticism by enacting a sweeping tax reform bill in 1986. Under the new law, which became fully operational in 1988, personal income would be taxed at just two rates, 15 and 28 percent. Approximately 6 million people with incomes at or below the poverty level would be exempt from federal income taxes. An estimated $120 billion of the tax burden was shifted from individuals to businesses. The law preserved some special breaks (deductions for mortgage interest and state income taxes, for example), but many others (like deductions for state sales taxes) were eliminated.

A third item occupied Reagan's agenda: a vigorous assault on federal environmental, health, and safety regulations that, Reagan believed, unnecessarily and excessively reduced business profits and discouraged economic growth. A lightning rod for this effort was Secretary of the Interior James Watt, who said that his objective was to "mine more, drill more, cut more timber, to use our resources rather than simply keep them locked up." Even the business-oriented *Wall Street Journal* observed that the president was "naming regulators who by virtue of attitude or inexperience are more likely to be nonregulators." Opponents of the administration's environmental policies maintained their resistance and in early 1987 won a major victory when both the Senate and the House overrode a veto of the Clean Water Act.

Reagan's attack on economic problems scored two notable successes during his first two years in office: the inflation rate plummeted, as did the cost of borrowing money. The prime rate for bank loans, which had reached a record high of 21.5 percent in early 1981, dropped to 10.5 percent by early 1983. Inflation fell from 12.4 percent in 1980 to less than 7 percent in 1982. Oil led the way in price declines. In 1981 the United States was awash in oil, as world production exceeded demand by 2 million barrels a day.

But there was also a sobering explanation for the decline in inflation. By mid-1981 the nation was mired in a recession that not only persisted, but deepened. During the last three months of the year, the gross national product fell, and there was a sharp drop in sales of cars and houses; housing starts were down more than half from 1978. With declining economic activity, unemployment went up, soaring in October to 8 percent, the highest level in almost six years.

A year later, in October 1982, unemployment had reached 10.1 percent. In addition to those people who were out of work, a record number of Americans were forced to work part-time because they could not find full-time jobs. Most of the jobless were adult men, particularly black men who suffered an unemployment rate of 19.8 percent. Many of the unemployed were blue-collar workers in such ailing "smokestack industries" as autos, steel, and rubber. Unemployment reached a post-1940 high in April 1983, peaking at 10.2 percent.

The business of agriculture in the 1980s was also faltering and near collapse. Farmers suffered not only from floods and droughts, but also from burdensome debts they had incurred at high interest rates. Many lost their property through mortgage foreclosures and farm auctions. Others filed for bankruptcy.

By 1984, however, the economy began to heat up and did so without causing inflation to boil. The gross national product rose 6.8 percent in 1984, the sharpest increase since 1951, and mid-year unemployment fell to a four-year low of 7.1 percent. In 1985 unemployment was 7.2 percent; the inflation rate was 3.6 percent.

Poverty became a serious problem once again in the 1980s. The number of Americans living in poverty increased from 26.1 million (11.7 percent) in 1979 to 33.1 million (14 percent) in 1985, when a family of four was classified as poor if its annual cash income was less than $10,989. The poverty rate among whites was 11.4 percent, 31.3 percent among blacks, and 29 percent among Hispanics in 1985. With one exception, poverty had returned to the levels that existed before the enactment of President Lyndon B. Johnson's Great Society. That exception was the elderly. The poverty rate among Americans over sixty-five was lower than that for the population at large, revealing that politicians had been paying attention to the needs of this rapidly growing group.

Poverty Levels

REAGAN AND THE VOTER

When the political parties began mounting their 1984 presidential campaigns, it quickly became evident that Reagan could defeat any Democratic nominee. The list of Reagan's re-election credentials included the recent rebound in the economy. A second factor in Reagan's favor was people's perception of him as a strong and attractive leader in foreign and national affairs. In contrast, the Democratic candidate, Walter Mondale, former Minnesota senator, and vice president under Jimmy Carter, had to struggle to prove that he was not a "wimp," that he too would stand up to the Soviet Union and to terrorists. Third, Reagan was the enthusiastic choice of the political right as well as of social, cultural, and religious conservatives across the country. And he won the approval of millions of other Americans who agreed with his television ads emphasizing patriotism after two decades of turmoil and self-doubt. Finally, the Democrats did not pose a convincing alternative. The party was in disarray, its policies seemed time-worn, and its presidential candidate aroused little excitement.

Reagan's Re-election Assets

What enthusiasm there was for the Democratic ticket arose from Mondale's historic selection of Congresswoman Geraldine Ferraro as the first female vice-presidential candidate of a major party. Ferraro showed herself to be an intelligent, indefatigable campaigner.

But the Democratic party was out of step with the nation's social and cultural conservatism. Reagan's personality, on the other hand, seemed to fit the public mood. In 1980 the pollster Daniel Yankelovich had reported that the United States had gone "almost overnight from a nation of optimists to a nation of pessimists." Four years later Yankelovich's polls told him that "the defeatism is gone." The cycle had turned sharply to the right once again, as it had in the 1920s and 1950s.

Several important groups did oppose Ronald Reagan's re-election, however. His most vocal critics were women, nonwhites, and labor leaders. In late 1983 the *New York Times* reported a "gender gap" between men's and women's opinions of Reagan's performance: far fewer women (38 percent) than men (53 percent) believed Reagan deserved re-election. Reagan's opposition to the Equal Rights Amendment, abortion on demand, and the concept of "equal pay for jobs of comparable worth" won him the enmity of many feminists. But the biggest cause of the gender gap was Reagan's social wel-

Reagan's Opposition

fare, health, and education cuts. Critics accused him of accelerating the "feminization of poverty."

Black civil rights leaders also opposed Reagan's re-election; they joined feminists in assailing the president's appointments. Whereas 12 percent of President Carter's high-level jobholders were black and 12.1 percent women, Reagan's comparable totals were 4.1 percent black and 8 percent women. Reagan had appointed three women to his cabinet, and he had made history by appointing Sandra Day O'Connor the first female associate justice of the Supreme Court, but blacks could find little to applaud in Reagan's performance. The Reagan administration fought against renewing intact the Voting Rights Act of 1965, expressed opposition to busing and affirmative action, and was criticized for lax enforcement of fair-housing laws and laws banning sexual and racial discrimination in federally funded education programs.

Hispanic and Native Americans joined Afro-Americans in blasting the administration's policies. The League of United Latin American Citizens censured Reagan for his "very, very dismal record" in dealing with their problems, and the National Tribal Chairman's Association charged that within two years of Reagan's election, "the delivery of services by federal agencies to Indians was in a shambles."

Joining women and nonwhites in the anti-Reagan camp was the AFL-CIO. Even without Reagan in the White House, hard times would have hit the labor unions. Faced with the recession and unemployment, union negotiators had to settle for contracts that offered their members far less than in the recent past, including substantial pay cuts and reductions in benefits. Unions also suffered large membership losses as unemployment hit the smokestack industries, and their efforts to unionize the high-growth electronics and service sectors of the economy were failing. And in 1984 the Supreme Court ruled that companies declaring bankruptcy could unilaterally cancel union contracts to which they had agreed earlier, without even having a hearing.

Reagan made the unions' hard times worse. He pre-sided over the government's busting of the Professional Air Traffic Controllers Organization (PATCO) during the union's 1981 strike. His appointees to the National Labor Relations Board consistently voted against labor and for management. Although it seemed that Reagan was clearly labor's enemy, union leaders could not rally their members to oppose his re-election. An estimated 44 percent of union families had voted for Reagan in 1980; many still responded positively to his genial personality, his espousal of old-fashioned values, and his anti-communism.

Reagan's opponents during the 1984 campaign decried the "country club ethics" of his appointees, several of whom resigned after accusations that they had behaved illegally or improperly. The number-two administrators in both the CIA and the Department of Defense left office after newspaper reports that they had taken part in questionable stock transactions. Richard Allen, the national security adviser, resigned after the disclosure that he had accepted gifts, including money and watches, from Japanese journalists for arranging interviews with Nancy Reagan, the president's wife. And in 1984, when Reagan nominated his close friend Edwin Meese to be attorney general of the United States, allegations arose that Meese had accepted "sweetheart loans" from individuals who were later appointed to positions in the Reagan administration.

In ordinary political times, the issue of corruption in government ("the sleaze factor") should have bolstered the Democrats in 1984. But voters did not seem to hold the president personally responsible for his administration's failings.

During the campaign Mondale attempted to debate what he defined as the issues, but Reagan preferred to invoke the theme of leadership and communicate traditional values to his audience. Rather than discuss the federal deficit, tax policy, and the nuclear arms race, Reagan relied on slogans like the title of his unofficial campaign song, "I'm Proud to Be an American." Mondale chastised

The 1984 Campaign

Reagan for the federal deficit; but when Mondale announced that he would raise taxes to cut the deficit, he lost voter support.

Religion became an unexpectedly hot issue. Mondale predicted that if Reagan were re-elected, he would nominate only conservative, prolife justices to the Supreme Court and thus overturn the Warren Court's liberal legacy. Reagan responded that "religion and politics are necessarily related" and called opponents of school prayer "intolerant of religion." Millions of religious conservatives saw a vote for Reagan as an extension of their moral commitments. (In 1986, following Warren Burger's decision to leave the Court, Reagan nominated William Rehnquist for chief justice and appointed Antonin Scalia to fill Rehnquist's seat. When another vacancy occurred in 1987, he nominated federal judge Robert Bork for the position. Bork was ultimately defeated. All three men were considered strong voices of conservatism.)

Mondale also attacked Reagan's foreign policy, but to little avail. The Democratic candidate favored a mutual freeze in nuclear testing, arms control talks, an end to the covert war against Nicaragua, and negotiations over Central America. Reagan dismissed Mondale's suggestions as "policies of weakness." Despite Reagan's minimal success in world affairs, Mondale was unable to make political gains on foreign policy issues largely because Reagan had generated a flag-waving patriotism that supported the president's military buildup and sharp anti-Soviet utterances.

Reagan's victory in 1984 was never in doubt, but his forty-nine-state total led observers to conclude that he had transformed American politics. Columnists and scholars wrote that he had forged a new right coalition that could dominate national politics for years to come. Some compared this election to Franklin D. Roosevelt's comparable sweep in 1936 (he took forty-six of forty-eight states) that had put the final stamp on the New Deal coalition.

Two years later the notion that Reagan's new conservative coalition would control the national agenda was dispelled. In the 1986 congressional elections the president actively campaigned in sixteen states,

The 1986 Elections

urging the American people to continue the "Reagan Revolution" by voting Republican. The voters rejected Reagan's plea. The Democrats regained control of the Senate and increased their majority in the House. The president was still a popular figure, but a majority of voters seemed to have reservations about the administration's domestic and foreign policies.

REAGAN'S FOREIGN POLICY: THE SOVIETS AND THE NUCLEAR ARMS RACE

Ronald Reagan's foreign policy was driven by five beliefs rooted in America's past. "His is a kind of 1952 world," remarked one of Reagan's former aides. First, Reagan and the conservatives he selected to advise him believed that a malevolent Soviet Union was the source of the world's troubles. Reagan charged that the Soviets were prepared "to commit any crime, to lie, to cheat" to achieve a communist world. He attributed Third World disorders to Soviet intrigue, rejecting analyses that argued, for example, that the civil wars in Central America derived not from Soviet meddling, but from deep-seated local sources of economic instability, poverty, and class oppression.

Reagan's Foreign Policy Views

Second, the Reagan administration believed that a major American military buildup would thwart the Soviet threat and intimidate the Soviets into negotiating on terms favorable to the United States. Reagan launched an eight-year, $2.3-trillion defense budget, most of which Congress approved. He pushed plans for the B-1 bomber, a much enlarged navy, production of poison gas, beefed-up special forces units for counterinsurgency, the MX missile, and an anti-missile defense system in space (titled the Strategic Defense Initiative, or SDI, but quickly dubbed "Star Wars"). In 1985 the Pentagon spent an average of $28 million an hour, twenty-four hours a day, seven days a week.

Third, Reagan and his advisers believed that nations must embrace private capitalism and reject managed economies. They frequently lectured Third World countries on the virtues of private enterprise. Overall, the Reagan administration silenced the North-South dialogue.

Fourth, the administration decided to provide open support to anti-communist forces that were fighting the Soviets or Soviet-backed governments. Known as the Reagan Doctrine, the policy clearly violated the sovereignty of such nations as Afghanistan, Kampuchea, Angola, and Nicaragua. In most cases Congress approved of funneling aid through the CIA to forces the president called "freedom fighters." Ironically, the Reagan Doctrine often presented leftist governments in the Third World with little choice but to establish closer ties with the Soviet Union.

Fifth, Ronald Reagan believed Americans must abandon their post-Vietnam "self-doubt" and renew their mission of converting foreign peoples to the American model. Most Americans shared Reagan's feelings that the United States had been ignobly retreating from global power and leadership. Besides talking tough and enlarging the military to reverse this trend, Reagan revitalized the CIA and expanded its covert operations abroad. "America is back, standing tall," bragged the president in 1984 during a revival of passionate American patriotism.

Reagan's expansion of the military, his coolness toward arms control, his utterances about winning a limited nuclear war, his quest for nuclear supremacy, and his insistence on placing new

Nuclear Arms Race cruise and Pershing-II missiles in Western Europe stimulated a lively international debate. Talks on limiting intermediate-range nuclear forces (INF) based in Europe—such as the Soviet SS-20 missiles targeted against Western Europe and the American cruise and

Pershing missiles aimed at Russia—did get under way in late November 1981. The American proposal was called the zero option: the United States would not deploy its missiles in Western Europe if the Soviet Union would dismantle all of its SS-20s. Moscow replied that the plan did not take into account that, already, American long-range bombers and submarine-based missiles could reach the Soviet Union. Moreover, the Soviets said, Reagan's scheme did not count British and French nuclear forces aimed at the Soviet Union. Critics believed that Reagan's plan was more a propaganda ploy to quiet a worried public than a serious step toward arms control. The INF talks collapsed in November 1983 after the first American cruise and Pershing-II missiles were installed in Western Europe.

Reagan's substitute for the SALT talks, the Strategic Arms Reduction Talks (START), began in June 1982. But in December of the next year they too faltered. These difficult negotiations attracted intense American public interest. In the largest peaceful protest in American history, in June 1982, 1 million people marched through New York City to support a nuclear arms freeze. And the House of Representatives, over the opposition of the White House, passed a freeze resolution in 1983. Because of such public opinion, pressure from NATO allies, worry that a more expensive and more dangerous nuclear arms race loomed, and the belief that reinvigorated American military power gave the United States a strong bargaining position, Reagan officials resumed discussions on arms control with the Soviets in early 1985.

In October 1986, Soviet leader Mikhail Gorbachev met with President Reagan at Reykjavik, Iceland. The initial purpose of the meeting was to lay the foundation for a full summit. Gorbachev, however, surprised Reagan with a broad set of proposals dealing with virtually every facet of the nuclear arms question. His approach was designed to appeal to Western European public opinion, but it also represented a desire to curb the expensive arms race. Gorbachev conditioned his proposals on America's willingness to confine the Strategic Defense Initiative to the laboratory; Reagan refused to place such restrictions on the project. The meeting ended with the two powers deadlocked.

Several months later the Soviets proposed the removal of all intermediate-range missiles from Europe. This time Gorbachev dropped his demands regarding SDI. The initial Western reaction to the plan was favorable, but within a matter of weeks some European leaders were worrying about the implications of removing the nuclear umbrella from the continent; in a conventional war, the Warsaw Pact nations had a decided advantage over the NATO powers.

INTERVENTIONS IN THE THIRD WORLD AND FOREBODING FORECASTS

Reagan believed that the Soviets and their clients the Cubans were fomenting disorder in the Third World, especially in Central America. The region of Guatemala, Honduras, El Salvador, Nicaragua, and Costa Rica was a traditional sphere of influence for the United States. To Reagan officials, El Salvador appeared to be a textbook case of communist aggression. In that very poor country, revolutionaries challenged the government, which was dominated by the military and a small, landed elite. The regime used (or could not control) right-wing "death squads" that killed thousands of dissidents and other citizens, as well as some American missionaries who worked with landless peasants. Believing that the war against the rebels could be successfully concluded in a short time, Reagan eschewed negotiations and increased military assistance to the Salvadoran regime.

The controversial intervention in the Salvadoran civil war sparked a debate that sounded much like that which had erupted over the war in Vietnam. Those who urged negotiations thought Reagan was wrong to interpret the conflict as an East-West con-

test. Oppression and poverty, not communist plots, caused people to pick up guns to fight the regime, they argued. Resurrecting the discredited domino theory, Reagan warned that if the "Communists" were not stopped in El Salvador they would soon be at the Mexican-American border. When that exaggerated argument convinced few, Reagan turned to a strategic case. Central America, he said, hugs the Caribbean Sea—"our lifeline to the outside world." In time of war, the Soviets could cripple American shipping from Caribbean bases. All of this assumed, of course, that the Soviets were in fact trying to take over El Salvador; critics rejected that assumption.

Although Congress voted funds for the American involvement in El Salvador, it stipulated that the United States government would have to certify every six months that the Salvadoran government was making improvements in human rights or the funds would be cut off. To keep the aid flowing, American officials made strained yet positive statements twice a year that left many human rights observers incredulous. The Reagan administration's case was helped somewhat in May 1984 when a United States–influenced election produced a government under the popular José Napoleon Duarte. Still, the guerrillas fought on and grew in numbers, showing no signs of being deterred by the continued infusion of substantial American arms, economic assistance, and CIA operatives.

Elsewhere in Central America the Reagan administration intervened, threatening a regional war. Nicaragua was ruled by a leftist government, the Sandinistas. To succeed with their plans for improvements in health and education, they had invited several thousand Cubans into their hospitals and schools. Cuban military advisers helped them reorganize their army, and Soviet arms were ordered. Early on, Reagan denounced the government, charging that it was becoming a Soviet puppet and was sending arms to the rebels in El Salvador. The Reagan administration soon strove to topple the Nicaraguan government. The United States conducted military maneuvers off the coast

Actions Against Nicaragua

The Russians (bear) and Americans (Uncle Sam) often explained their meddling in the affairs of other nations by claiming that they had to intervene in order to halt the expansion of the other. To the unhappy people whose sovereignty was violated, however, such an explanation was not convincing because it ignored the conspicuous, self-interested drive of the two great powers for control of small countries. By Auth for the Philadelphia Inquirer.

and staged war games in neighboring Honduras, where major American bases were built. The CIA also began, in 1982, to train, arm, and direct over ten thousand counterrevolutionaries, called *contras*. From Honduras the *contras* killed Nicaraguan officials and civilians, and destroyed oil refineries, transportation facilities, medical clinics, and day-care centers.

In the spring of 1984 it became known that the CIA had mined the harbors of Nicaragua, causing merchant ships to be blown up. Negative international and American opinion cascaded down on Washington. The harbors were cleared of explosives; the World Court ruled that Nicaragua had the right

to sue the United States for damages. Both houses of Congress passed a nonbinding resolution to halt the mining operations. In mid-1984 Congress voted to stop American aid to the *contras*. But the undeclared war against well-armed Nicaragua continued, prompting critics to assert that the United States was forcing Nicaragua into the communist camp. Moreover, they protested, the United States was bypassing opportunities to negotiate. The Nicaraguans, for example, accepted the objectives of the Contadora group (Mexico, Venezuela, Colombia, and Panama), which included the reduction of foreign military bases and advisers in Central America. But the Reagan administration refused to endorse the Contadora peace plan; as in El Salvador, it preferred a military solution.

The United States also opted for a military solution in Grenada. This tiny Caribbean island, troubled by political strife, was ruled by a leftist government friendly with Cuba. Using the pretense that several hundred Americans studying medicine in Grenada had to be protected, and that the Soviets intended to spread subversion from the island, the president in October 1983 ordered the marines to invade the nation. As a result of the invasion, the Cubans on the island were deported and a new government was implanted. The United Nations passed a resolution condemning this example of gunboat diplomacy. Most Americans, however, cheered Reagan's actions.

Reagan tried to use military solutions in the Middle East, too. As a result of attacks from Palestine Liberation Organization (PLO) camps in Lebanon,

Crisis in Lebanon
Israeli troops invaded that civil war–torn country in June 1982, cutting their way to the capital, Beirut, and inflicting massive damage. The beleaguered PLO and various Lebanese factions called upon Syria to contain the Israelis. Civilian deaths rose to at least ten thousand, and a million people became refugees. In August, as part of a peacekeeping force, U.S. Marines entered Lebanon and eventually dug in around Beirut. Their mission ill-defined, the American troops soon became allied with the faction that controlled the Lebanese government and exchanged fire with other factions and with Syrians. In October 1983, terrorist bombs demolished a marine barracks, killing 240 American servicemen. In February of the next year, with Lebanon reeling from civil war and Syrian and Israeli occupation, Reagan recognized failure and pulled the marines out. In the wake of the Lebanese tragedy, American leaders grew wary of Mideast ventures. Still, the United States had commitments (the defense of Israel), political friends (Saudi Arabia), enemies (Iran and Libya), and oil supplies that would continue to draw it into the area.

In the mid-1980s Libya attracted the attention of the United States. For many years the leader of Libya, Moammar Gadhafi, had been identified by the United States as a sponsor of terrorist acts. His support of terrorism and Libya's insistence that its boundary extended 200 miles into the Gulf of Sidra (the United States said 12 miles) created tension between the two nations.

In April 1986, a terrorist bomb killed an American serviceman in a Berlin disco. A little more than a week later, American aircraft conducted early morning raids on Libya. The air strikes

The Libyan Strike
focused on targets in or near Tripoli and Benghazi. Beyond being designed to demonstrate America's refusal to tolerate terrorism (Reagan claimed to have proof that Gadhafi was responsible for the Berlin bombing), the air strikes were apparently intended to kill Gadhafi. Five F-111s attacked the military barracks at Bab al Azizia, the site of Gadhafi's residence. The Libyan leader was not injured, but his adopted infant daughter died in the attack. Americans largely supported the action; Europeans generally opposed it. Many observers wondered what the attacks accomplished. They neither killed nor discredited Gadhafi, and they did not deter terrorists or the nations that supported them.

The euphoria that Americans felt after the invasion of Grenada and the bombing of Libya was short-lived, for the United States faced bewildering international problems that seemed immune to military solutions. First, global economic issues threatened world order and American prosperity. Third World nations were sinking more and more deeply into debt, less able to repay loans or to purchase goods. In 1986 America's trade deficit (the result of more imports than exports) stood at a staggering $169.8 billion. Second, famine took a ghastly human toll and contributed to political instability. In the early 1980s population experts estimated that hunger-related deaths numbered between 13 and 18 million people annually. Drought-ravaged Africa was hardest hit.

A third major, long-term international problem was the deterioration of the global environment. Soil erosion hurt food production at a time when the world's population was growing rapidly. Toxic wastes, acid rain, shortages of clean water, and the over-cutting of forests escalated environmental decline, which, in turn, burdened governments that seemed unable to respond. Fourth, international drug traffic was causing health problems for millions, enriching criminals who sometimes gained political influence (as in Bolivia and Colombia), and financing the activities of terrorists (as in Peru). Fifth, America was facing a future of uneasy relations with allies. NATO was splintering, and once-valuable allies were rocked by political unrest, imperiling American military bases and intelligence-gathering stations. Sixth, religious and racial tensions undermined stability and spawned war. Sikhs and Hindus fought one another in India; Christians and Moslems battled in Lebanon; the Shiite Moslems governing Iran were at war with the Sunni Moslems of Iraq; Roman Catholics and Protestants bloodied each other in Northern Ireland.

Finally, South Africa represented a special problem. There a blatantly racist white minority ruled a predominantly nonwhite people (85 percent) through the segregationist policy South Africa of *apartheid* and political repression. The Reagan administration refrained from criticizing South Africa, preferring instead what it called "constructive engagement." But there was a vocal, widespread movement against *apartheid* in the United States, and American public opinion triggered some official responses. Many major American corporations with holdings in South Africa ceased doing business in that country. Some states adopted divestment laws; that is, they withdrew dollars from American companies active in South Africa. In 1986 Congress imposed some economic sanctions against South Africa. Many analysts predicted that revolution was inevitable there.

The Philippine Islands seemed to be the one bright spot in a troubled Third World. Popular support for Corazon Aquino, the widow of a slain opposition leader, forced an end to the government of Ferdinand Marcos. As *Time* Philippine magazine noted, "Marcos had effectively moved his country backward, Revolution

from prosperity to poverty, from general peace to communist insurgency." As he had become more authoritarian, the White House had pressured him to become more democratic. In a move designed to appease Washington, Marcos ordered elections for February 1986.

In full view of the world's press, Marcos conducted a massively corrupt election. The U.S. Senate objected to the fraud, and both the Philippine defense minister and the chief of the armed forces declared Aquino the victor. Marcos had himself inaugurated but under mounting pressure left the country the next day for America. The United States openly supported President Aquino. In May 1987 a majority of the Philippine electorate gave Aquino's backers control of the nation's legislature.

AN ADMINISTRATION
UNDER FIRE

As Reagan began his last two years in office, his administration was in trouble. One item of mounting concern to the American public was the size of the national debt. Although Republicans blamed the deficit on the Democrats, almost half of the national debt accrued from fiscal 1982 through fiscal 1986, a time when Reagan sat in the White House and the Republicans controlled the Senate. During this five-year period, tax reductions and high defense budgets helped add $954 billion to the total debt.

Concern for the budget led in late 1985 to the enactment of the Gramm-Rudman bill, which called for a balanced federal budget by fiscal 1991 through a gradual reduction of the annual deficit. While few politicians argued over the need for a balanced budget, heated debates over which expenditures to cut divided conservatives from liberals and the White

House from the Congress. The president's proposed budget for fiscal 1988, a record-setting $1.024 trillion, recommended less spending for food stamps, housing grants for the elderly, student aid, mass transit, and the farm program. On the other hand, the president requested an additional $22.3 billion for defense. Reagan contended that both a balanced budget and his budgetary requests could be met without increasing taxes.

Democrats in Congress saw things differently. They preferred to hold the line on military spending and increase the money going to the various human services. The Democrats also favored a moderate tax increase. As the time drew near for the enactment of the fiscal 1988 budget, neither side seemed willing to bend.

The annual trade deficit presented another economic problem. Between the end of 1984 and the end of 1986, the annual trade deficit increased from $102 billion to $169.8 billion. Each increase in the trade deficit seemed to add converts to the protectionist camp, which favored charging tariffs on and limiting numbers of foreign goods sold in the United States. The protectionists were especially angry with Japan, a nation whose trade surplus with the United States amounted to $56.8 billion in 1986. President Reagan argued against protectionism but decided to take action against Japan.

For many years Americans complained that Japanese trade practices made it difficult for American goods to compete on the Japanese market. At the same time, Japanese products ranging from automobiles to microcomputers were widely accepted in the United States. In 1985 Japan responded to pressure from the United States by placing quotas on the numbers of automobiles that Japanese manufacturers could export to the United States and by promising to open Japanese markets to certain goods. This, however, did not satisfy Washington.

In early 1987 President Reagan, in an attempt to protect the American microchip industry, ordered trade sanctions against Japan. Specifically, he levied $300 million in tariffs on Japanese electronic products. Because the total volume of trade between the two nations in 1986 exceeded $112 billion, these tariffs were largely symbolic. The United States was sending a message to Japan—open your markets and engage in fair trade practices or face the possibility of additional duties. In Japan some referred to the aftermath of Reagan's actions as *Kaisen zen-ya* ("the eve of war"). Neither side wanted a trade war, but a meeting between Prime Minister Yasuhiro Nakasone and President Reagan in April 1987 failed to resolve the issue. Two months later, however, the president ordered a partial lifting of the sanctions.

"The Eve of War"

Reagan's troubles with Japan coincided with a major problem at home. It was revealed that in 1985 and 1986, a time when Reagan was publicly stating that he would never negotiate with terrorists, the United States was secretly selling arms to Iran. In exchange for the arms the administration was hoping to improve relations with moderate factions in Iran and secure the release of American hostages held in Lebanon. After U.S. arms were shipped to Iran through Israel in September 1985, hostage Benjamin Weir was released; the release of two more hostages followed additional shipments of arms in 1986. In the meantime, militants took three other Americans hostage.

The November 1986 revelation that the administration had sold arms to Iran damaged Reagan's credibility and raised questions of illegality. A few weeks later, Attorney General Edwin Meese announced that funds from the sale of these weapons had been diverted to the *contras* in Nicaragua. This action seemed to be in direct violation of the 1984 Boland amendments, prohibiting government agencies from aiding the *contras*. Reagan appointed a commission headed by former senator John Tower of Texas to investigate these events. The Tower commission held hearings and reported that the Iran policy was amateurish and counterproductive, that the president had been "poorly advised and poorly served," and that Reagan seemed to be an uninvolved and forgetful leader who "clearly didn't understand what was going on."

When Congress convened in January 1987, both

Midway through Reagan's presidency, Congress passed legislation that denied further military aid to the Nicaraguan contras. Reagan signed these bills, but as the Iran-contra hearings revealed, such assistance was sent anyway—through a secret network organized by members of the National Security Council. Here several rebels try on new fatigues. J.B. Pictures.

houses created committees to investigate what became known as the Iran-*contra* affair. By that time the national security adviser, John Poindexter, had resigned, and Marine Lt. Col. Oliver North, a National Security Council official, had been fired. Both exercised their rights under the Fifth Amendment and refused to answer questions before congressional committees.

Beginning in May 1987, the House and the Senate conducted joint televised hearings on the Iran-*contra* affair. Robert McFarlane, a former national security adviser, was one of the first to testify. McFarlane

Iran-*contra* Hearings

suggested that North had operated under the direction of the former head of the CIA, William Casey (who died shortly before McFarlane appeared before the committee). In his testimony before the joint committee, North asserted that he believed the president had been fully aware of the scheme to divert profits from the Iranian arms sales to the *contras*. Poindexter testified, however, that he had personally authorized the diversion and had withheld information from the president to protect him from political embarrassment. The revelations

AIDS has become a devastating epidemic and a controversial political and social issue. During a Washington, D.C., demonstration calling for an increase in funds for research into the fatal illness, this protester—himself an AIDS victim—was arrested by police officers who wore gloves to protect themselves from infection. *James Colburn/Photoreporters.*

promised to continue, as would the questions about who was in control of the administration's foreign policy decisions.

Finally, a major health threat was confronting society. In 1981 a disease called acquired immune deficiency syndrome (AIDS) was first observed in the

AIDS

United States. AIDS was caused by a virus that attacked cells in the immune system, making its victims susceptible to deadly infections and cancers. AIDS was initially linked to the sexual behavior of homosexuals, but the disease rapidly moved into the het-

IMPORTANT EVENTS

1981	Prime interest rate at 21.5 percent
	Congress approves Reagan's budget cuts
	Largest tax cut in U.S. history
	U.S. steps up role in El Salvador
	AIDS first observed
	Unemployment at 8 percent
1982	Prime interest rate falls to 14 percent
	START negotiations begin
	U.S. troops ordered to Lebanon
1983	Prime interest rate at 10.5 percent
	Terrorists kill U.S. Marines in Lebanon
	Invasion of Grenada
	U.S. missiles deployed in Western Europe
	Unemployment climbs to 10.2 percent
1984	U.S. troops leave Lebanon
	Congress passes amendments halting aid to *contras*
	Ferraro becomes first woman vice-presidential candidate of a major party
	Reagan re-elected
	Inflation falls to 4 percent
	Unemployment drops to 7.1 percent
1985	Reagan inaugurated
	Gramm-Rudman bill passed
	Inflation at 3.6 percent
	Poverty level at 14 percent
1986	Sweeping tax-reform bill passed
	U.S. bombs Libya
	Iran-*contra* affair revealed
	Democrats regain control of Senate, increase majority in House
1987	U.S. trade sanctions leveled against Japan
	Joint Iran-*contra* hearings begin in Congress

erosexual community. The virus was most often transmitted through infected body fluids exchanged during sexual contact and the multiple use of intravenous needles by drug users. Between 1981 and late 1986, 15,850 Americans died from the disease; officials estimated that AIDS would reach epidemic proportions by the 1990s. There were early indications that AIDS was having an effect on the sexual behavior of Americans. And in the government there was disagreement over the kind of education needed to combat the spread of the disease as well as speculation about the impact the disease would have on American health-care systems.

And so the Reagan administration faced some boiling issues during its last two years in office. In his first six years as president, Reagan had scored impressive political successes and an overwhelming re-election victory. Observers compared him favorably to Franklin Roosevelt and argued that, like Roosevelt, he had transformed American politics. But by mid-1987 many supporters had developed doubts about the wisdom and even the legality of certain White House operations. Special prosecutors were investigating not only Lt. Col. North and other figures in the Iran-*contra* affair, but also Attorney General Meese and two former White House aides for alleged illegal lobbying activities. Although Reagan continued to enjoy personal popularity, Americans increasingly wondered whether he had a sure grasp of his office. The main challenge of his last two years in office was to reassert his leadership and avoid becoming a lame duck president. President Reagan's ability to meet this challenge would help to determine not only his political legacy but also his appraisal by historians.

SUGGESTIONS FOR FURTHER READING

The Conservative Politics of Ronald Reagan

Ronald Brownstein and Nina Easton, *Reagan's Ruling Class* (1983); Lou Cannon, *Reagan* (1982); Joan Claybrook, *Retreat from Safety: Reagan's Attack on America's Health* (1984); Robert Dallek, *Ronald Reagan: The Politics of Symbolism* (1984); Ronnie Dugger, *On Reagan* (1983); Fred Greenstein, ed., *The Reagan Presidency* (1983); Jonathan Lash, *A Season of Spoils: The Story of the Reagan Administration's Attack on the Environment* (1984); John L. Palmer and Isabel V. Sawhill, eds., *The Reagan Experiment* (1982); Gillian Peele, *Revival and Reaction: The Right in Contemporary America* (1984); Kevin Phillips, *Post-Conservative America* (1982); Garry Wills, *Reagan's America* (1986).

Reaganomics

Frank Ackerman, *Reaganomics* (1982); Michael Harrington, *The New American Poverty* (1984); Robert Lekachman, *Greed Is Not Enough* (1983); Frances Fox Piven and Richard Cloward, *The New Class War* (1982); David Stockman, *The Triumph of Politics* (1986); Sidney Weintraub and Marvin Goodstein, eds., *Reaganomics in the Stagflation Economy* (1983).

Reagan's Foreign Policy and the Nuclear Arms Race

Ruth Adams and Susan Cullen, eds., *The Final Epidemic: Physicians and Scientists on Nuclear War* (1981); William M. Arkin and Richard Fieldhouse, *Nuclear Battlefields* (1985); Richard J. Barnet, *The Alliance: America, Europe, Japan* (1983); Alexander Haig, *Caveat: Realism, Reagan, and Foreign Policy* (1984); Harvard Nuclear Study Group, *Living with Nuclear Weapons* (1983); Ole R. Holsti and James R. Rosenau, *American Leadership in World Affairs: Vietnam and the Breakdown of Consensus* (1984); George F. Kennan, *The Nuclear Delusion* (1982); National Academy of Sciences, *Nuclear Arms Control* (1985); Kenneth A. Oye, *et al.*, eds., *Eagle Defiant* (1983); Strobe Talbott, *Deadly Gambits: The Reagan Administration and the Stalemate in Nuclear Arms Control* (1984); Strobe Talbott, *The Russians and Reagan* (1984). (Also see the *America and the World* series published by *Foreign Affairs* magazine and the *Great Decisions* series published by the Foreign Policy Association.)

Central America

Raymond Bonner, *Weakness and Deceit: U.S. Policy and El Salvador* (1984); Tom Buckley, *Violent Neighbors* (1984); Charles Clements, *Witness to War* (1984); Kenneth M. Coleman and George C. Herring, eds., *The Central America Crisis* (1985); Martin Diskin, ed., *Trouble in Our Backyard* (1984); Walter LaFeber, *Inevitable Revolutions*, rev. ed. (1984); Robert S. Leiken, ed., *Central America* (1984); Richard A. White, *The Morass* (1984).

APPENDIX

HISTORICAL REFERENCE

BOOKS BY SUBJECT

Encyclopedias, Dictionaries, Atlases, Chronologies, and Statistics

General

Geoffrey Barraclough, ed., *The Times Atlas of World History* (1979); *Concise Dictionary of American Biography* (1980); *Concise Dictionary of American History* (1983); *Dictionary of American Biography* (1928–   ); *Dictionary of American History* (1976–1978); Robert H. Ferrell and John S. Bowman, eds., *The Twentieth Century: An Almanac* (1984); Edward W. Fox, *Atlas of American History* (1964); George H. Gallup, *The Gallup Poll: Public Opinion, 1935–1971* (1972) and *1972–1977* (1978); John A. Garraty, ed., *Encyclopedia of American Biography* (1974); Bernard Grun, *The Timetables of History* (1975); Stanley Hochman, *Yesterday and Today* (1979); *International Encyclopedia of the Social Sciences* (1968–   ); Kenneth T. Jackson and James T. Adams, *Atlas of American History* (1978); R. Alton Lee, ed., *Encyclopedia USA* (1983–   ); Michael Martin and Leonard Gelber, *Dictionary of American History* (1981); Richard B. Morris, *Encyclopedia of American History* (1982); *National Cyclopedia of American Biography* (1898–   ); Arthur M.

Schlesinger, Jr., ed., *The Almanac of American History* (1983); *Scribner Desk Dictionary of American History* (1984); U.S. Bureau of the Census, *Historical Statistics of the United States* (1975); U.S. Department of the Interior, *National Atlas of the United States* (1970).

The American Revolution

Mark M. Boatner, III, *Encyclopedia of the American Revolution* (1974); Lester J. Cappon, ed., *Atlas of Early American History: The Revolutionary Era, 1760–1790* (1976); Douglas W. Marshall and Howard H. Peckham, *Campaigns of the American Revolution* (1976); Gregory Palmer, ed., *Biographical Sketches of Loyalists of the American Revolution* (1984); *Rand-McNally Atlas of the American Revolution* (1974).

Architecture

William D. Hunt, Jr., ed., *Encyclopedia of American Architecture* (1980).

Blacks

Peter M. Bergman, *The Chronological History of the Negro in America* (1969); Rayford W. Logan and Michael R. Winston, eds., *The Dictionary of American Negro Biography* (1983); W. A. Low and Virgil A. Clift, eds., *Encyclopedia of Black America* (1981); Harry A. Ploski and James Williams, eds., *The Negro Almanac* (1983); Erwin A. Salk, ed., *A Layman's Guide to Negro History* (1967); Mabel M. Smythe, ed., *The Black American Reference Book* (1976); Edgar A. Toppin, *A Biographical History of Blacks in America* (1971).

Cities and Towns

Charles Abrams, *The Language of Cities: A Glossary of Terms* (1971); John L. Androit, ed., *Township Atlas of the United States* (1979); Ory M. Nergal, ed., *The Encyclopedia of American Cities* (1980). *See also* "Politics and Government."

The Civil War

Mark M. Boatner, III, *The Civil War Dictionary* (1959); *The Civil War Almanac* (1983); E. B. Long, *The Civil War Day by Day* (1971); Mark E. Neely, Jr., *The Abraham Lincoln Encyclopedia* (1982); Craig L. Symonds, *A Battlefield Atlas of the Civil War* (1983); U.S. War Department, *The Official Atlas of the Civil War* (1958); Jon L. Wakelyn, ed., *Biographical Dictionary of the Confederacy* (1977); Ezra J. Warner and W. Buck Yearns, *Biographical Register of the Confederate Congress* (1975). *See also* "The South."

Conservation

Forest History Society, *Encyclopedia of American Forest and Conservation History* (1983).

The Constitution and Supreme Court

Congressional Quarterly, *Guide to the Supreme Court* (1979); Leon Friedman and Fred I. Israel, eds., *The Justices of the United States Supreme Court, 1789–1978* (1980); *Judges of the United States* (1980).

Crime

Sanford H. Kadish, ed., *Encyclopedia of Crime and Justice* (1983); Carl Sifakis, *The Encyclopedia of American Crime* (1982).

Culture and Folklore

M. Thomas Inge, ed., *Handbook of American Popular Culture* (1979–1981); Marjorie Tallman, *Dictionary of American Folklore* (1959); Justin Wintle, ed., *Makers of Nineteenth Century Culture, 1800–1914* (1982). *See also* "Entertainment," "Music," and "Sports."

The Economy and Business

Christine Ammer and Dean S. Ammer, *Dictionary of Business and Economics* (1983); Douglas Auld and Graham Bannock, *The American Dictionary of Economics* (1983); Douglas Greenwald, *Encyclopedia of Economics* (1982); John N. Ingham, *Biographical Dictionary of American Business Leaders* (1983); Glenn G. Munn, *Encyclopedia of Banking and Finance* (1973); David W. Pearce, *Dictionary of Modern Economics* (1983); Glenn Porter, *Encyclopedia of American Economic History* (1980).

Education

Lee C. Deighton, ed., *The Encyclopedia of Education* (1971); Joseph C. Kiger, ed., *Research Institutions and Learned Societies* (1982); John F. Ohles, ed., *Biographical Dictionary of American Educators* (1978).

Entertainment

Tim Brooks and Earle Marsh, *The Complete Directory to Prime Time Network TV Shows, 1946–present* (1979); Barbara N. Cohen-Stratyner, *Biographical Dictionary of Dance* (1982); John Dunning, *Tune in Yesterday* [radio] (1967); Stanley Green, *Encyclopedia of the Musical Film* (1981); *Notable Names in the American Theater* (1976); *New York Times Encyclopedia of Television* (1977); Andrew Sarris, *The American Cinema: Directors and Directions, 1929–1968* (1968); Evelyn M. Truitt, *Who Was Who on Screen* (1977). *See also* "Culture and Folklore," "Music," and "Sports."

Foreign Policy

Alexander DeConde, ed., *Encyclopedia of American Foreign Policy* (1978); John E. Findling, *Dictionary of American Diplomatic History* (1980); *International Geographic Encyclopedia and Atlas* (1979); Warren F. Kuehl, ed., *Biographical Dictionary of Internationalists* (1983); George T. Kurian, *Encyclopedia of the Third World* (1981); Richard B. Morris and Graham W. Irwin, eds., *Harper Encyclopedia of the Modern World* (1970); Jack C. Plano, ed., *The International Relations Dictionary* (1982); Jack E. Vincent, *A Handbook of International Relations* (1969).

Immigration and Ethnic Groups

American Jewish Biographies (1982); Stephanie Bernardo, *The Ethnic Almanac* (1981); Matt S. Meier and Feliciano Rivera, *Dictionary of Mexican American History* (1981); Stephan Thernstrom, ed., *Harvard Encyclopedia of American Ethnic Groups* (1980).

Indians

Frederick J. Dockstader, *Great North American Indians* (1977); *Handbook of North American Indians* (1978–); Barry Klein, ed., *Reference Encyclopedia of the American Indian* (1978).

Labor

Gary M. Fink, ed., *Biographical Dictionary of American Labor Leaders* (1974); Gary M. Fink, ed., *Labor Unions* (1977); Philip S. Foner, *First Facts of American Labor* (1984).

Literature

James T. Callow and Robert J. Reilly, *Guide to American Literature* (1976–1977); *Dictionary of Literary Biography* (1978–); Eugene Ehrlich and Gorton Carruth, *The Oxford Illustrated Literary Guide to the United States* (1982); Jon Tuska and Vicki Piekarski, *Encyclopedia of Frontier and Western Fiction* (1983). *See also* "Culture and Folklore," "The South," and "Women."

Medicine

Martin Kaufman, *et al.*, eds., *Dictionary of American Medical Biography* (1984).

Music

John Chilton, *Who's Who of Jazz* (1972); Edward Jablonski, *The Encyclopedia of American Music* (1981); Roger Lax and Frederick Smith, *The Great Song Thesaurus* (1984). *See also* "Culture and Folklore" and "Entertainment."

Politics and Government: General and Elections

Congressional Quarterly, *Congress and the Nation, 1945–1976* (1965–1977); Congressional Quarterly, *Guide to U.S. Elections* (1975); Jack P. Greene, ed., *Encyclopedia of American Political History* (1984); Kenneth C. Martis, *The Historical Atlas of United States Congressional Districts, 1789–1983* (1982); Edwin V. Mitchell, *An Encylopedia of American Politics* (1968); Svend Peterson, *A Statistical History of the American Presidential Elections* (1963); William Safire,

Safire's Political Dictionary (1978); Richard M. Scammon, ed., *America at the Polls* (1965); Edward L. and Frederick H. Schapsmeier, eds., *Political Parties and Civic Action Groups* (1981); Arthur M. Schlesinger, Jr., and Fred I. Israel, eds., *History of American Presidential Elections, 1789–1968* (1971); Robert Scruton, *A Dictionary of Political Thought* (1982); Hans Sperber and Travis Trittschuh, *American Political Terms* (1962). *See also* "The Constitution and Supreme Court," "States and the West," and the following section.

Politics and Government: Leaders

Roy R. Glashan, comp., *American Governors and Gubernatorial Elections, 1775–1978* (1979); Otis L. Graham, Jr., and Meghan R. Wander, eds., *Franklin D. Roosevelt: His Life and Times* (1985); Melvin G. Holli and Peter d'A. Jones, eds., *Biographical Dictionary of American Mayors, 1820–1980: Big City Mayors* (1981); Joseph E. Kallenbach and Jessamine S. Kallenbach, *American State Governors, 1776–1976* (1977); Thomas A. McMullin and David Walker, *Biographical Directory of American Territorial Governors* (1984); *Political Profiles, Truman Years to . . .* (1978); John W. Raimo, ed., *Biographical Directory of American Colonial and Revolutionary Governors, 1607–1789* (1980); John W. Raimo, ed., *Biographical Directory of the Governors of the United States, 1789–1978* (1978); John W. Raimo, ed., *Biographical Directory of the Governors of the United States, 1978–1983* (1984); Robert Sobel, ed., *Biographical Directory of the United States Executive Branch, 1774–1977* (1977); U.S. Congress, Senate, *Biographical Directory of the American Congress, 1774–1971* (1971); Robert Vexler, *The Vice-Presidents and Cabinet Members* (1975). *See also* the previous section.

Religion

Henry Bowden, *Dictionary of American Religious Biography* (1977); John T. Ellis and Robert Trisco, *A Guide to American Catholic History* (1982); Edwin S. Gaustad, *Historical Atlas of Religion in America* (1976); Samuel S. Hill, Jr., ed., *Encyclopedia of Religion in the South* (1984); J. Gordon Melton, *The Encyclopedia of American Religions* (1978); Mark A. Noll and Nathan O. Hatch, eds., *Eerdmans Handbook to Christianity in America* (1983); Arthur C. Piepkorn, *Profiles in Brief: The Religious Bodies of the United States and Canada* (1977–1979).

Science

Charles C. Gillispie, ed., *Dictionary of Scientific Biography* (1970–   ); National Academy of Sciences, *Biographical Memoirs* (1877–   ).

Social Issues

Louis Filler, *A Dictionary of American Social Reform* (1963); Louis Filler, *Dictionary of American Social Change* (1982); Robert S. Fogarty, *Dictionary of American Communal and Utopian History* (1980); Mark E. Lender, *Dictionary of American Temperance Biography* (1984); Alvin J. Schmidt, *Fraternal Organizations* (1980). *See also* "Crime."

The South

Robert Bain, *et al.*, eds., *Southern Writers: A Biographical Dictionary* (1979); Kenneth Coleman and Charles S. Gurr, eds., *Dictionary of Georgia Biography* (1983); William C. Ferris and Charles R. Wilson, eds., *Encyclopedia of Southern Culture* (1986); David C. Roller and Robert W. Twyman, eds., *The Encyclopedia of Southern History* (1979); Walter P. Webb, *et al.*, eds., *The Handbook of Texas* (1952, 1976). *See also* "Politics and Government" and "States and the West."

Sports

Ralph Hickok, *New Encyclopedia of Sports* (1977); Ralph Hickok, *Who Was Who in American Sports* (1971); Zander Hollander, *The NBA's Official Encyclopedia of Pro Basketball* (1981); Frank G. Menke and Suzanne Treat, *The Encyclopedia of Sports* (1977); *The NFL's Official Encyclopedic History of Professional Football* (1977); Paul Soderberg, *et al.*, *The Big Book of Halls of Fame in the United States and Canada* (1977). *See also* "Culture and Folklore."

States and the West

John Clayton, ed., *The Illinois Fact Book and Historical Almanac, 1673–1968* (1970); Doris O. Dawdy, *Artists of the American West* (1974–1984); Howard R. Lamar, ed., *The Reader's Encyclopedia of the American West* (1977); Mose Y. Sachs, ed., *The Worldmark Encyclopedia of the States* (1981). *See also* "Politics and Government" and "The South."

Wars and the Military

R. Ernest Dupuy and Trevor N. Dupuy, *The Encyclopedia of Military History* (1977); Holger H. Herwig and Neil M. Heyman, *Biographical Dictionary of World War I* (1982); Michael Kidrow and Dan Smith, *The War Atlas: Armed Conflict, Armed Peace* (1983); Roger J. Spiller and Joseph G. Dawson, III, eds., *Dictionary of American Military Biography* (1984); U.S. Military Academy, *The West Point Atlas of American Wars, 1689–1953* (1959); *Webster's American Military Biographies* (1978). *See also* "The American Revolution," "The Civil War," and "World War II."

Women

Edward T. James, *et al.*, *Notable American Women, 1607–1950* (1971); Lina Mainiero, ed., *American Women Writers* (1979–1982); Barbara Sicherman and Carol H. Green, eds., *Notable American Women, The Modern Period* (1980).

World War II

Marcel Baudot, *et al.*, eds., *The Historical Encyclopedia of World War II* (1980); Simon Goodenough, *War Maps: Great Land Battles of World War II* (1983); Robert Goralski, *World War II Almanac, 1931–1945* (1981); John Keegan, ed., *The Rand-McNally Encyclopedia of World War II* (1977); Thomas Parrish, ed., *The Simon and Schuster Encyclopedia of World War II* (1978); Louis L. Snyder, *Louis L. Snyder's Historical Guide to World War II* (1982); U.S. Military Academy, *Campaign Atlas to the Second World War: Europe and the Mediterranean* (1980); Peter Young, ed., *The World Almanac Book of World War II* (1981). *See also* "Wars and the Military."

DECLARATION OF INDEPENDENCE IN CONGRESS, JULY 4, 1776

The unanimous declaration of the thirteen United States of America

When, in the course of human events, it becomes necessary for one people to dissolve the political bonds which have connected them with another, and to assume, among the powers of the earth, the separate and equal station to which the laws of nature and of nature's God entitle them, a decent respect to the opinions of mankind requires that they should declare the causes which impel them to the separation.

We hold these truths to be self-evident: That all men are created equal; that they are endowed by their Creator with certain unalienable rights; that among these are life, liberty, and the pursuit of happiness; that, to secure these rights, governments are instituted among men, deriving their just powers from the consent of the governed; that whenever any form of government becomes destructive of these ends, it is the right of the people to alter or to abolish it, and to institute new government, laying its foundation on such principles, and organizing its powers in such form, as to them shall seem most likely to effect their safety and happiness. Prudence, indeed, will dictate that governments long established should not be changed for light and transient causes; and accordingly all experience hath shown that mankind are more disposed to suffer, while evils are sufferable, than to right themselves by abolishing the forms to which they are accustomed. But when a long train of abuses and usurpations, pursuing invariably the same object, evinces a design to reduce them under absolute despotism, it is their right, it is their duty, to throw off such government, and to provide new guards for their future security. Such has been the patient sufferance of these colonies; and such is now the necessity which constrains them to alter their former systems of government. The history of the present King of Great Britain is a history of repeated injuries and usurpations, all having in direct object the establishment of an absolute tyranny over these states. To prove this, let facts be submitted to a candid world.

He has refused his assent to laws, the most wholesome and necessary for the public good.

He has forbidden his governors to pass laws of immediate and pressing importance, unless suspended in their operation till his assent should be obtained; and, when so suspended, he has utterly neglected to attend to them.

He has refused to pass other laws for the accommodation of large districts of people, unless those people would relinquish the right of representation in the legislature, a right inestimable to them, and formidable to tyrants only.

He has called together legislative bodies at places unusual, uncomfortable, and distant from the depository of their public records, for the sole purpose of fatiguing them into compliance with his measures.

He has dissolved representative houses repeatedly, for opposing, with manly firmness, his invasions on the rights of the people.

He has refused for a long time, after such dissolutions, to cause others to be elected; whereby the legislative powers, incapable of annihilation, have returned to the people at large for their exercise; the state remaining, in the mean time, exposed to all the dangers of invasions from without and convulsions within.

He has endeavored to prevent the population of these states; for that purpose obstructing the laws for naturalization of foreigners; refusing to pass others to encourage their migration hither, and raising the conditions of new appropriations of lands.

He has obstructed the administration of justice, by refusing his assent to laws for establishing judiciary powers.

He has made judges dependent on his will alone, for the tenure of their offices, and the amount and payment of their salaries.

He has erected a multitude of new offices, and sent hither swarms of officers to harass our people and eat out their substance.

He has kept among us, in times of peace, standing armies, without the consent of our legislatures.

He has affected to render the military independent of, and superior to, the civil power.

He has combined with others to subject us to a jurisdiction foreign to our constitution, and unacknowledged by our laws, giving his assent to their acts of pretended legislation:

For quartering large bodies of armed troops among us;

For protecting them, by a mock trial, from punishment for any murders which they should commit on the inhabitants of these states;

For cutting off our trade with all parts of the world;

For imposing taxes on us without our consent;

For depriving us, in many cases, of the benefits of trial by jury;

For transporting us beyond seas, to be tried for pretended offenses;

For abolishing the free system of English laws in a neighboring province, establishing therein an arbitrary government, and enlarging its boundaries, so as to render it at once an example and fit instrument for introducing the same absolute rule into these colonies;

For taking away our charters, abolishing our most valuable laws, and altering fundamentally the forms of our governments;

For suspending our own legislatures, and declaring themselves invested with power to legislate for us in all cases whatsoever.

He has abdicated government here, by declaring us out of his protection and waging war against us.

He has plundered our seas, ravaged our coasts, burned our towns, and destroyed the lives of our people.

He is at this time transporting large armies of foreign mercenaries to complete the works of death, desolation, and tyranny already begun with circumstances of cruelty and perfidy scarcely paralleled in the most barbarous ages, and totally unworthy the head of a civilized nation.

He has constrained our fellow-citizens, taken captive on the high seas, to bear arms against their country, to become the executioners of their friends and brethren, or to fall themselves by their hands.

He has excited domestic insurrection among us, and has endeavored to bring on the inhabitants of our frontiers the merciless Indian savages, whose known rule of warfare is an undistinguished destruction of all ages, sexes, and conditions.

In every stage of these oppressions we have petitioned for redress in the most humble terms; our repeated petitions have been answered only by repeated injury. A prince, whose character is thus marked by every act which may define a tyrant, is unfit to be the ruler of a free people.

Nor have we been wanting in our attentions to our British brethren. We have warned them, from time to time, of attempts by their legislature to extend an unwarrantable jurisdiction over us. We have reminded them of the circumstances of our emigration and settlement here. We have appealed to their native justice and magnanimity; and we have conjured them, by the ties of our common kindred, to disavow these usurpations, which would inevitably interrupt our connections and correspondence. They, too, have been deaf to the voice of justice and of consanguinity. We must, therefore, acquiesce in the necessity which denounces our separation, and hold them, as we hold the rest of mankind, enemies in war, in peace friends.

We, therefore, the representatives of the United States of America, in General Congress assembled, appealing to the Supreme Judge of the world for the rectitude of our intentions, do, in the name and by the authority of the good people of these colonies, solemnly publish and declare, that these United Colonies are, and of right ought to be, FREE AND INDEPENDENT STATES; that they are absolved from all allegiance to the British crown, and that all political connection between them and the state of Great Britain is, and ought to be, totally dissolved; and that, as free and independent states, they have full power to levy war, conclude peace, contract alliances, establish commerce, and do all other acts and things which independent states may of right do. And for the support of this declaration, with a firm reliance on the protection of Divine Providence, we mutually pledge to each other our lives, our fortunes, and our sacred honor.

JOHN HANCOCK
and fifty-five others

CONSTITUTION OF THE UNITED STATES OF AMERICA AND AMENDMENTS

Preamble

We the people of the United States, in order to form a more perfect union, establish justice, insure domestic tranquillity, provide for the common defense, promote the general welfare, and secure the blessings of liberty to ourselves and our posterity, do ordain and establish this Constitution for the United States of America.

Article I

Section 1 All legislative powers herein granted shall be vested in a Congress of the United States, which shall consist of a Senate and a House of Representatives.

Section 2 The House of Representatives shall be composed of members chosen every second year by the people of the several States, and the electors in each State shall have the qualifications requisite for electors of the most numerous branch of the State Legislature.

No person shall be a Representative who shall not have attained to the age of twenty-five years, and been seven years a citizen of the United States, and who shall not, when elected, be an inhabitant of that State in which he shall be chosen.

Representatives and direct taxes shall be apportioned among the several States which may be included within this Union, according to their respective numbers, *which shall be determined by adding to the whole number of free persons, including those bound to service for a term of years and excluding Indians not taxed, three-fifths of all other persons.* The actual enumeration shall be made within three years after the first meeting of the Congress of the United States, and within every subsequent term of ten years, in such manner as they shall by law direct. The number of Representatives shall not exceed one for every thirty thousand, but each State shall have at least one Representative; *and until such enumeration shall be made, the State of New Hampshire shall be entitled to choose three, Massachusetts eight, Rhode Island and Providence Plantations one, Connecticut five, New York six, New Jersey four, Pennsylvania eight, Delaware one, Maryland six, Virginia ten, North Carolina five, South Carolina five, and Georgia three.*

When vacancies happen in the representation from any State, the Executive authority thereof shall issue writs of election to fill such vacancies.

The House of Representatives shall choose their Speaker and other officers; and shall have the sole power of impeachment.

Section 3 The Senate of the United States shall be composed of two Senators from each State, *chosen by the legislature thereof,* for six years; and each Senator shall have one vote.

Immediately after they shall be assembled in consequence of the first election, they shall be divided as equally as may be into three classes. The seats of the Senators of the first class shall be vacated at the expiration of the second year, of the second class at the expiration of the fourth year, and of the third class at the expiration of the sixth year, so that one-third may be chosen every second year; and if vacancies happen by resignation or otherwise, during the recess of the legislature of any State, the Executive thereof may make temporary appointments until the next meeting of the legislature, which shall then fill such vacancies.

No person shall be a Senator who shall not have attained to the age of thirty years, and been nine years a citizen of the United States, and who shall not, when elected, be an inhabitant of that State for which he shall be chosen.

The Vice-President of the United States shall be President of the Senate, but shall have no vote, unless they be equally divided.

The Senate shall choose their other officers, and also a President *pro tempore,* in the absence of the Vice-President, or when he shall exercise the office of President of the United States.

The Senate shall have the sole power to try all impeachments. When sitting for that purpose, they shall be on oath or affirmation. When the President of the United States is tried, the Chief Justice shall preside: and no person shall be convicted without the concurrence of two-thirds of the members present.

Judgment in cases of impeachment shall not extend fur-

Passages no longer in effect are printed in italic type.

ther than to removal from the office, and disqualification to hold and enjoy any office of honor, trust or profit under the United States: but the party convicted shall nevertheless be liable and subject to indictment, trial, judgment and punishment, according to law.

Section 4 The times, places and manner of holding elections for Senators and Representatives shall be prescribed in each State by the legislature thereof; but the Congress may at any time by law make or alter such regulations, except as to the places of choosing Senators.

The Congress shall assemble at least once in every year, and such meeting *shall be on the first Monday in December, unless they shall by law appoint a different day.*

Section 5 Each house shall be the judge of the elections, returns and qualifications of its own members, and a majority of each shall constitute a quorum to do business; but a smaller number may adjourn from day to day, and may be authorized to compel the attendance of absent members, in such manner, and under such penalties, as each house may provide.

Each house may determine the rules of its proceedings, punish its members for disorderly behavior, and with the concurrence of two-thirds, expel a member.

Each house shall keep a journal of its proceedings, and from time to time publish the same, excepting such parts as may in their judgment require secrecy; and the yeas and nays of the members of either house on any question shall, at the desire of one-fifth of those present, be entered on the journal.

Neither house, during the session of Congress, shall, without the consent of the other, adjourn for more than three days, nor to any other place than that in which the two houses shall be sitting.

Section 6 The Senators and Representatives shall receive a compensation for their services, to be ascertained by law and paid out of the treasury of the United States. They shall in all cases except treason, felony and breach of the peace, be privileged from arrest during their attendance at the session of their respective houses, and in going to and returning from the same; and for any speech or debate in either house, they shall not be questioned in any other place.

No Senator or Representative shall, during the time for which he was elected, be appointed to any civil office under the authority of the United States, which shall have been created, or the emoluments whereof shall have been increased, during such time; and no person holding any office under the United States shall be a member of either house during his continuance in office.

Section 7 All bills for raising revenue shall originate in the House of Representatives; but the Senate may propose or concur with amendments as on other bills.

Every bill which shall have passed the House of Representatives and the Senate, shall, before it become a law, be presented to the President of the United States; if he approve he shall sign it, but if not he shall return it with objections to that house in which it originated, who shall enter the objections at large on their journal, and proceed to reconsider it. If after such reconsideration two-thirds of that house shall agree to pass the bill, it shall be sent, together with the objections, to the other house, by which it shall likewise be reconsidered, and, if approved by two-thirds of that house, it shall become a law. But in all such cases the votes of both houses shall be determined by yeas and nays, and the names of the persons voting for and against the bill shall be entered on the journal of each house respectively. If any bill shall not be returned by the President within ten days (Sundays excepted) after it shall have been presented to him, the same shall be a law, in like manner as if he had signed it, unless the Congress by their adjournment prevent its return, in which case it shall not be a law.

Every order, resolution, or vote to which the concurrence of the Senate and House of Representatives may be necessary (except on a question of adjournment) shall be presented to the President of the United States; and before the same shall take effect, shall be approved by him or being disapproved by him, shall be repassed by two-thirds of the Senate and House of Representatives, according to the rules and limitations prescribed in the case of a bill.

Section 8 The Congress shall have power

To lay and collect taxes, duties, imposts, and excises, to pay the debts and provide for the common defense and general welfare of the United States; but all duties, imposts and excises shall be uniform throughout the United States;

To borrow money on the credit of the United States;

To regulate commerce with foreign nations, and among the several States, and with the Indian tribes;

To establish an uniform rule of naturalization, and uniform laws on the subject of bankruptcies throughout the United States;

To coin money, regulate the value thereof, and of foreign coin, and fix the standard of weights and measures;

To provide for the punishment of counterfeiting the securities and current coin of the United States;

To establish post offices and post roads;

To promote the progress of science and useful arts by securing for limited times to authors and inventors the exclusive right to their respective writings and discoveries;

To constitute tribunals inferior to the Supreme Court;

To define and punish piracies and felonies committed on the high seas and offenses against the law of nations;

To declare war, grant letters of marque and reprisal, and make rules concerning captures on land and water;

To raise and support armies, but no appropriation of money to that use shall be for a longer term than two years;

To provide and maintain a navy;

To make rules for the government and regulation of the land and naval forces;

To provide for calling forth the militia to execute the laws of the Union, suppress insurrections, and repel invasions;

To provide for organizing, arming, and disciplining the militia, and for governing such part of them as may be employed in the service of the United States, reserving to the States respectively the appointment of the officers, and the authority of training the militia according to the discipline prescribed by Congress;

To exercise exclusive legislation in all cases whatsoever, over such district (not exceeding ten miles square) as may, by cession of particular States, and the acceptance of Congress, become the seat of government of the United States, and to exercise like authority over all places purchased by the consent of the legislature of the State, in which the same shall be, for erection of forts, magazines, arsenals, dock-yards, and other needful buildings;—and

To make all laws which shall be necessary and proper for carrying into execution the foregoing powers, and all other powers vested by this Constitution in the government of the United States, or in any department or officer thereof.

Section 9 The migration or importation of such persons as any of the States now existing shall think proper to admit shall not be prohibited by the Congress prior to the year 1808; but a tax or duty may be imposed on such importation, not exceeding $10 for each person.

The privilege of the writ of habeas corpus shall not be suspended, unless when in cases of rebellion or invasion the public safety may require it.

No bill of attainder or ex post facto law shall be passed.

No capitation, or other direct, tax shall be laid, unless in proportion to the census or enumeration herein before directed to be taken.

No tax or duty shall be laid on articles exported from any State.

No preference shall be given by any regulation of commerce or revenue to the ports of one State over those of another; nor shall vessels bound to, or from, one State, be obliged to enter, clear, or pay duties in another.

No money shall be drawn from the treasury, but in consequence of appropriations made by law; and a regular statement and account of the receipts and expenditures of all public money shall be published from time to time.

No title of nobility shall be granted by the United States: and no person holding any office of profit or trust under them, shall, without the consent of the Congress, accept of any present, emolument, office, or title, of any kind whatever, from any king, prince, or foreign state.

Section 10 No State shall enter into any treaty, alliance, or confederation; grant letters of marque and reprisal; coin money; emit bills of credit; make anything but gold and silver coin a tender in payment of debts; pass any bill of attainder, ex post facto law, or law impairing the obligation of contracts, or grant any title of nobility.

No State shall, without the consent of Congress, lay any imposts or duties on imports or exports, except what may be absolutely necessary for executing its inspection laws: and the net produce of all duties and imposts, laid by any State on imports or exports, shall be for the use of the treasury of the United States; and all such laws shall be subject to the revision and control of the Congress.

No State shall, without the consent of Congress, lay any duty of tonnage, keep troops or ships of war in time of peace, enter into any agreement or compact with another State, or with a foreign power, or engage in war, unless actually invaded, or in such imminent danger as will not admit of delay.

Article II

Section 1 The executive power shall be vested in a President of the United States of America. He shall hold his office during the term of four years, and, together with the Vice-President, chosen for the same term, be elected as follows:

Each State shall appoint, in such manner as the legislature thereof may direct, a number of electors, equal to the whole number of Senators and Representatives to which the State may be entitled in the Congress; but no Senator or Representative, or person holding an office of trust or profit under the United States, shall be appointed an elector.

The electors shall meet in their respective States, and vote by ballot for two persons, of whom one at least shall not be an inhabitant of the same State with themselves. And they shall make a list of all the persons voted for, and of the number of votes for each; which list they shall sign and certify, and transmit sealed to the seat of government of the United States, directed to the President of the Senate. The President of the Senate shall, in the presence of the Senate and House of Representatives, open all the certificates, and the votes shall then be counted. The person having the greatest number of votes shall be the President, if such number be a majority of the whole number of electors appointed; and if there be more than one who have such majority, and have an equal number of votes, then the House of Representatives shall immediately choose by ballot one of them for President; and if no person have a majority, then from the five highest on the list said house shall in like manner choose the President. But in choosing the President the votes shall be taken by States, the representation from each State having one vote; a quorum for this purpose shall consist of a member or members from two-thirds of the States, and a majority of all the States shall be necessary to a choice. In every case, after the choice of the President, the person having the greatest number of votes of the electors shall be the Vice-President. But if there should remain two or more who have equal votes, the Senate shall choose from them by ballot the Vice-President.

The Congress may determine the time of choosing the electors and the day on which they shall give their votes; which day shall be the same throughout the United States.

No person except a natural-born citizen, *or a citizen of the United States at the time of the adoption of this Constitution,* shall be eligible to the office of President; neither shall any person be eligible to that office who shall not have attained to the age of thirty-five years, and been fourteen years a resident within the United States.

In case of the removal of the President from office or of his death, resignation, or inability to discharge the powers and duties of the said office, the same shall devolve on the Vice-President, and the Congress may by law provide for the case of removal, death, resignation, or inability, both of the President and Vice-President, declaring what officer shall then act as President, and such officer shall act accordingly, until the disability be removed, or a President shall be elected.

The President shall, at stated times, receive for his services a compensation, which shall neither be increased nor diminished during the period for which he shall have been elected, and he shall not receive within that period any other emolument from the United States, or any of them.

Before he enter on the execution of his office, he shall take the following oath or affirmation:—"I do solemnly swear (or affirm) that I will faithfully execute the office of the President of the United States, and will to the best of my ability preserve, protect and defend the Constitution of the United States."

Section 2 The President shall be commander in chief of the army and navy of the United States, and of the militia of the several States, when called into the actual service of the United States; he may require the opinion, in writing, of the principal officer in each of the executive departments, upon any subject relating to the duties of their respective offices, and he shall have power to grant reprieves and pardons for offenses against the United States, except in cases of impeachment.

He shall have power, by and with the advice and consent of the Senate, to make treaties, provided two-thirds of the Senators present concur; and he shall nominate, and by and with the advice and consent of the Senate, shall appoint ambassadors, other public ministers and consuls, judges of the Supreme Court, and all other officers of the United States, whose appointments are not herein otherwise provided for, and which shall be established by law: but Congress may by law vest the appointment of such inferior officers, as they think proper, in the President alone, in the courts of law, or in the heads of departments.

The President shall have power to fill up all vacancies that may happen during the recess of the Senate, by granting commissions which shall expire at the end of their next session.

Section 3 He shall from time to time give to the Congress information of the state of the Union, and recommend to their consideration such measures as he shall judge necessary and expedient; he may, on extraordinary occasions, convene both houses, or either of them, and in case of disagreement between them, with respect to the time of adjournment, he may adjourn them to such time as he shall think proper; he shall receive ambassadors and other public ministers; he shall take care that the laws be faithfully executed, and shall commission all the officers of the United States.

Section 4 The President, Vice-President and all civil officers of the United States shall be removed from office on impeachment for, and on conviction of, treason, bribery, or other high crimes and misdemeanors.

Article III

Section 1 The judicial power of the United States shall be vested in one Supreme Court, and in such inferior courts as the Congress may from time to time ordain and establish. The judges, both of the Supreme and inferior courts, shall hold their offices during good behavior, and shall, at stated times, receive for their services a compensation which shall not be diminished during their continuance in office.

Section 2 The judicial power shall extend to all cases, in law and equity, arising under this Constitution, the laws of the United States, and treaties made, or which shall be made, under their authority;—to all cases affecting ambassadors, other public ministers and consuls;—to all cases of admiralty and maritime jurisdiction;—to controversies to which the United States shall be a party;—to controversies between two or more States;—*between a State and citizens of another State*;—between citizens of different States;—between citizens of the same State claiming lands under grants of different States, and between a State, or the citizens thereof, and foreign states, citizens or subjects.

In all cases affecting ambassadors, other public ministers and consuls, and those in which a State shall be party, the Supreme Court shall have original jurisdiction. In all the other cases before mentioned, the Supreme Court shall have appellate jurisdiction, both as to law and fact, with such exceptions, and under such regulations, as the Congress shall make.

The trial of all crimes, except in cases of impeachment, shall be by jury; and such trial shall be held in the State where said crimes shall have been committed; but when not committed within any State, the trial shall be at such place or places as the Congress may by law have directed.

Section 3 Treason against the United States shall consist only in levying war against them, or in adhering to their enemies, giving them aid and comfort. No person shall be convicted of treason unless on the testimony of two witnesses to the same overt act, or on confession in open court.

The Congress shall have power to declare the punishment of treason, but no attainder of treason shall work corruption of blood, or forfeiture except during the life of the person attainted.

Article IV

Section 1 Full faith and credit shall be given in each State to the public acts, records, and judicial proceedings of every other State. And the Congress may by general laws prescribe the manner in which such acts, records, and proceedings shall be proved, and the effect thereof.

Section 2 The citizens of each State shall be entitled to all privileges and immunities of citizens in the several States.

A person charged in any State with treason, felony, or other crime, who shall flee from justice, and be found in another State, shall on demand of the executive authority of the State from which he fled, be delivered up, to be removed to the State having jurisdiction of the crime.

No person held to service or labor in one State, under the laws thereof, escaping into another, shall, in consequence of any law or regulation therein, be discharged from such service or labor, but shall be delivered up on claim of the party to whom such service or labor may be due.

Section 3 New States may be admitted by the Congress into this Union; but no new State shall be formed or erected within the jurisdiction of any other State; nor any State be formed by the junction of two or more States, or parts of States, without the consent of the legislatures of the States concerned as well as of the Congress.

The Congress shall have power to dispose of and make all needful rules and regulations respecting the territory or other property belonging to the United States; and nothing in this Constitution shall be so construed as to prejudice any claims of the United States, or of any particular State.

Section 4 The United States shall guarantee to every State in this Union a republican form of government, and shall protect each of them against invasion; and on application of the legislature, or of the executive (when the legislature cannot be convened), against domestic violence.

Article V

The Congress, whenever two-thirds of both houses shall deem it necessary, shall propose amendments to this Constitution, or, on the application of the legislatures of two-thirds of the several States, shall call a convention for proposing amendments, which, in either case, shall be valid to all intents and purposes, as part of this Constitution, when ratified by the legislatures of three-fourths of the several States, or by conventions in three-fourths thereof, as the one or the other mode of ratification may be proposed by the Congress; provided *that no amendments which may be made prior to the year one thousand eight hundred and eight shall in any manner affect the first and fourth clauses in the ninth section of the first article*; and that no State, without its consent, shall be deprived of its equal suffrage in the Senate.

Article VI

All debts contracted and engagements entered into, before the adoption of this Constitution, shall be as valid against the United States under this Constitution, as under the Confederation.

This Constitution, and the laws of the United States which shall be made in pursuance thereof; and all treaties made, or which shall be made, under the authority of the United States, shall be the supreme law of the land; and the judges in every State shall be bound thereby, anything in the Constitution or laws of any State to the contrary notwithstanding.

The Senators and Representatives before mentioned, and the members of the several State legislatures, and all executive and judicial officers, both of the United States and of the several States, shall be bound by oath or affirmation to support this Constitution; but no religious test shall ever be required as a qualification to any office or public trust under the United States.

Article VII

The ratification of the conventions of nine States shall be sufficient for the establishment of this Constitution between the States so ratifying the same.

Done in Convention by the unanimous consent of the States present, the seventeenth day of September in the year of our Lord one thousand seven hundred and eighty-seven and of the Independence of the United States of America the twelfth. In witness whereof we have hereunto subscribed our names.

GEORGE WASHINGTON
and thirty-seven others

Amendments to the Constitution*

Amendment I

Congress shall make no law respecting an establishment of religion, or prohibiting the free exercise thereof; or abridging the freedom of speech, or of the press; or the right of the people peaceably to assemble, and to petition the government for a redress of grievances.

Amendment II

A well-regulated militia being necessary to the security of a free State, the right of the people to keep and bear arms shall not be infringed.

Amendment III

No soldier shall, in time of peace, be quartered in any house without the consent of the owner, nor in time of war, but in a manner to be prescribed by law.

Amendment IV

The right of the people to be secure in their persons, houses, papers, and effects, against unreasonable searches and seizures, shall not be violated, and no warrants shall issue but upon probable cause, supported by oath or affirmation, and particularly describing the place to be searched, and the persons or things to be seized.

Amendment V

No person shall be held to answer for a capital, or otherwise infamous crime, unless on a presentment or indictment of

---

*The first ten Amendments (the Bill of Rights) were adopted in 1791.

a grand jury, except in cases arising in the land or naval forces, or in the militia, when in actual service in time of war or public danger; nor shall any person be subject for the same offense to be twice put in jeopardy of life or limb; nor shall be compelled in any criminal case to be a witness against himself, nor be deprived of life, liberty, or property, without due process of law; nor shall private property be taken for public use without just compensation.

Amendment VI

In all criminal prosecutions, the accused shall enjoy the right to a speedy and public trial, by an impartial jury of the State and district wherein the crime shall have been committed, which district shall have been previously ascertained by law, and to be informed of the nature and cause of the accusation; to be confronted with the witnesses against him; to have compulsory process for obtaining witnesses in his favor, and to have the assistance of counsel for his defense.

Amendment VII

In suits at common law, where the value in controversy shall exceed twenty dollars, the right of trial by jury shall be preserved, and no fact tried by a jury shall be otherwise reexamined in any court of the United States, than according to the rules of the common law.

Amendment VIII

Excessive bail shall not be required, nor excessive fines imposed, nor cruel and unusual punishments inflicted.

Amendment IX

The enumeration in the Constitution, of certain rights, shall not be construed to deny or disparage others retained by the people.

Amendment X

The powers not delegated to the United States by the Constitution, nor prohibited by it to the States, are reserved to the States respectively, or to the people.

Amendment XI
[Adopted 1798]

The judicial power of the United States shall not be construed to extend to any suit in law or equity, commenced or prosecuted against one of the United States by citizens of another State, or by citizens or subjects of any foreign state.

Amendment XII
[Adopted 1804]

The electors shall meet in their respective States, and vote by ballot for President and Vice-President, one of whom, at least, shall not be an inhabitant of the same State with themselves; they shall name in their ballots the person voted for as President, and in distinct ballots the person voted for as Vice-President, and they shall make distinct lists of all persons voted for as President, and of all persons voted for as Vice-President, and of the number of votes for each, which lists they shall sign and certify, and transmit sealed to the seat of government of the United States, directed to the President of the Senate;—the President of the Senate shall, in the presence of the Senate and House of Representatives, open all the certificates and the votes shall then be counted;—the person having the greatest number of votes for President shall be the President, if such number be a majority of the whole number of electors appointed; and if no person have such majority, then from the persons having the highest numbers not exceeding three on the list of those voted for as President, the House of Representatives shall choose immediately, by ballot, the President. But in choosing the President, the votes shall be taken by States, the representation from each State having one vote; a quorum for this purpose shall consist of a member or members from two-thirds of the States, and a majority of all the States shall be necessary to a choice. And if the House of Representatives shall not choose a President whenever the right of choice shall devolve upon them, before *the fourth day of March* next following, then the Vice-President shall act as President, as in the case of the death or other constitutional disability of the President.

The person having the greatest number of votes as Vice-President shall be the Vice-President, if such number be a majority of the whole number of electors appointed; and if no person have a majority, then from the two highest numbers on the list the State shall choose the Vice-President; a quorum for the purpose shall consist of two-thirds of the whole number of Senators, and a majority of the whole number shall be necessary to a choice. But no person constitutionally ineligible to the office of President shall be eligible to that of Vice-President of the United States.

Amendment XIII
[Adopted 1865]

Section 1 Neither slavery nor involuntary servitude, except as a punishment for crime whereof the party shall have been duly convicted, shall exist within the United States, or any place subject to their jurisdiction.

Section 2 Congress shall have power to enforce this article by appropriate legislation.

Amendment XIV
[Adopted 1868]

Section 1 All persons born or naturalized in the United States, and subject to the jurisdiction thereof, are citizens of the United States and of the State wherein they reside. No State shall make or enforce any law which shall abridge the privileges or immunities of citizens of the United States; nor shall any State deprive any person of life, liberty, or property, without due process of law; nor deny to any person within its jurisdiction the equal protection of the laws.

Section 2 Representatives shall be apportioned among the several States according to their respective numbers, counting the whole number of persons in each State, excluding Indians not taxed. But when the right to vote at any election for the choice of Electors for President and Vice-President of the United States, Representatives in Congress, the executive and judicial officers of a State, or the members of the legislature thereof, is denied to any of the male inhabitants of such State, being twenty-one years of age and citizens of the United States, or in any way abridged, except for participation in rebellion, or other crime, the basis of representation therein shall be reduced in the proportion which the number of such male citizens shall bear to the whole number of male citizens twenty-one years of age in such State.

Section 3 No person shall be a Senator or Representative in Congress, or Elector of President and Vice-President, or hold any office, civil or military, under the United States,

or under any State, who, having previously taken an oath, as a member of Congress, or as an officer of the United States, or as a member of any State legislature, or as an executive or judicial officer of any State, to support the Constitution of the United States, shall have engaged in insurrection or rebellion against the same, or given aid or comfort to the enemies thereof. Congress may, by a vote of two-thirds of each house, remove such disability.

Section 4 The validity of the public debt of the United States, authorized by law, including debts incurred for payment of pensions and bounties for services in suppressing insurrection or rebellion, shall not be questioned. But neither the United States nor any State shall assume or pay any debt or obligation incurred in aid of insurrection or rebellion against the United States, or any claim for the loss of emancipation of any slave; but all such debts, obligations, and claims shall be held illegal and void.

Section 5 The Congress shall have power to enforce, by appropriate legislation, the provisions of this article.

Amendment XV
[Adopted 1870]

Section 1 The right of citizens of the United States to vote shall not be denied or abridged by the United States or by any State on account of race, color, or previous condition of servitude.

Section 2 The Congress shall have power to enforce this article by appropriate legislation.

Amendment XVI
[Adopted 1913]

The Congress shall have power to lay and collect taxes on incomes, from whatever source derived, without apportionment among the several States, and without regard to any census or enumeration.

Amendment XVII
[Adopted 1913]

Section 1 The Senate of the United States shall be composed of two Senators from each State, elected by the people thereof, for six years; and each Senator shall have one vote. The electors in each State shall have the qualifications requisite for electors of [voters for] the most numerous branch of the State legislatures.

Section 2   When vacancies happen in the representation of any State in the Senate, the executive authority of such State shall issue writs of election to fill such vacancies: Provided, that the Legislature of any State may empower the executive thereof to make temporary appointments until the people fill the vacancies by election as the Legislature may direct.

Section 3   This amendment shall not be so construed as to affect the election or term of any Senator chosen before it becomes valid as part of the Constitution.

Amendment XVIII
[Adopted 1919; Repealed 1933]

Section 1   After one year from the ratification of this article the manufacture, sale, or transportation of intoxicating liquors within, the importation thereof into, or the exportation thereof from the United States and all territory subject to the jurisdiction thereof, for beverage purposes, is hereby prohibited.

Section 2   The Congress and the several States shall have concurrent power to enforce this article by appropriate legislation.

Section 3   This article shall be inoperative unless it shall have been ratified as an amendment to the Constitution by the legislatures of the several States, as provided by the Constitution, within seven years from the date of the submission thereof to the States by the Congress.

Amendment XIX
[Adopted 1920]

Section 1   The right of citizens of the United States to vote shall not be denied or abridged by the United States or by any State on account of sex.

Section 2   The Congress shall have power to enforce this article by appropriate legislation.

Amendment XX
[Adopted 1933]

Section 1   The terms of the President and Vice-President shall end at noon on the 20th day of January, and the terms of Senators and Representatives at noon on the 3d day of January, of the years in which such terms would have ended if this article had not been ratified; and the terms of their successors shall then begin.

Section 2   The Congress shall assemble at least once in every year, and such meeting shall begin at noon on the 3d day of January, unless they shall by law appoint a different day.

Section 3   If, at the time fixed for the beginning of the term of the President, the President-elect shall have died, the Vice-President-elect shall become President. If a President shall not have been chosen before the time fixed for the beginning of his term, or if the President-elect shall have failed to qualify, then the Vice-President-elect shall act as President until a President shall have qualified; and the Congress may by law provide for the case wherein neither a President-elect nor a Vice-President-elect shall have qualified, declaring who shall then act as President, or the manner in which one who is to act shall be selected, and such persons shall act accordingly until a President or Vice-President shall have qualified.

Section 4   The Congress may by law provide for the case of the death of any of the persons from whom the House of Representatives may choose a President whenever the right of choice shall have devolved upon them, and for the case of the death of any of the persons from whom the Senate may choose a Vice-President whenever the right of choice shall have devolved upon them.

Section 5   Sections 1 and 2 shall take effect on the 15th day of October following the ratification of this article.

Section 6   This article shall be inoperative unless it shall have been ratified as an amendment to the Constitution by the Legislatures of three-fourths of the several States within seven years from the date of its submission.

Amendment XXI
[Adopted 1933]

Section 1   The eighteenth article of amendment to the Constitution of the United States is hereby repealed.

Section 2   The transportation or importation into any State, Territory, or Possession of the United States for delivery or use therein of intoxicating liquors, in violation of the laws thereof, is hereby prohibited.

Section 3   This article shall be inoperative unless it shall have been ratified as an amendment to the Constitution by conventions in the several States, as provided in the Constitution, within seven years from the date of submissions thereof to the States by the Congress.

Amendment XXII
[Adopted 1951]

Section 1   No person shall be elected to the office of President more than twice, and no person who has held the office of President, or acted as President, for more than two years of a term to which some other person was elected President shall be elected to the office of President more than once. But this article shall not apply to any person holding the office of President when this article was proposed by the Congress, and shall not prevent any person who may be holding the office of President, or acting as President, during the term within which this article becomes operative from holding the office of President or acting as President during the remainder of such term.

Section 2   This article shall be inoperative unless it shall have been ratified as an amendment to the Constitution by the legislatures of three-fourths of the several States within seven years from the date of its submission to the States by the Congress.

Amendment XXIII
[Adopted 1961]

Section 1   The District constituting the seat of Government of the United States shall appoint in such manner as the Congress may direct:

A number of electors of President and Vice-President equal to the whole number of Senators and Representatives in Congress to which the District would be entitled if it were a State, but in no event more than the least populous State; they shall be in addition to those appointed by the States, but they shall be considered for the purposes of the election of President and Vice-President, to be electors appointed by a State; and they shall meet in the District and perform such duties as provided by the twelfth article of amendment.

Section 2   The Congress shall have the power to enforce this article by appropriate legislation.

Amendment XXIV
[Adopted 1964]

Section 1   The right of citizens of the United States to vote in any primary or other election for President or Vice-President, for electors for President or Vice-President, or for Senator or Representative in Congress, shall not be denied or abridged by the United States or any State by reason of failure to pay any poll tax or other tax.

Section 2   The Congress shall have the power to enforce this article by appropriate legislation.

Amendment XXV
[Adopted 1967]

Section 1   In case of the removal of the President from office or of his death or resignation, the Vice President shall become President.

Section 2   Whenever there is a vacancy in the office of the Vice President, the President shall nominate a Vice President who shall take office upon confirmation by a majority vote of both Houses of Congress.

Section 3   Whenever the President transmits to the President pro tempore of the Senate and the Speaker of the House of Representatives his written declaration that he is unable to discharge the powers and duties of his office, and until he transmits to them a written declaration to the contrary, such powers and duties shall be discharged by the Vice President as Acting President.

Section 4   Whenever the Vice President and a majority of either the principal officers of the executive departments or of such other body as Congress may by law provide, transmit to the President pro tempore of the Senate and the Speaker of the House of Representatives their written declaration that the President is unable to discharge the powers and duties of his office, the Vice President shall immediately assume the powers and duties of the office as Acting President.

Thereafter, when the President transmits to the President pro tempore of the Senate and the Speaker of the House of Representatives his written declaration that no inability exists, he shall resume the powers and duties of his office unless the Vice President and a majority of either the principal officers of the executive department[s] or of such other body as Congress may by law provide, transmit within four days to the President pro tempore of the Senate and the Speaker of the House of Representatives their written declaration that the President is unable to discharge the powers and duties of his office. Thereupon Congress shall decide the issue, assembling within forty-eight hours for that purpose if not in session. If the Congress, within twenty-one days after receipt of the latter written declaration, or, if Congress is not in session, within twenty-one days after Congress is required to assemble, determines by two-thirds vote of both Houses that the President is unable to discharge the powers and duties of his office, the Vice President shall continue to discharge the same as Acting President; otherwise, the President shall resume the powers and duties of his office.

Amendment XXVI
[Adopted 1971]

Section 1 The right of citizens of the United States, who are eighteen years of age or older, to vote shall not be denied or abridged by the United States or by any States on account of age.

Section 2 The Congress shall have power to enforce this article by appropriate legislation.

Population of the United States

Year	Number of States	Population	Percent Increase	Population Per Square Mile	Percent Urban/ Rural	Percent Male/ Female	Percent White/ Nonwhite	Persons Per Household	Median Age
1790	13	3,929,214		4.5	5.1/94.9	NA/NA	80.7/19.3	5.79	NA
1800	16	5,308,483	35.1	6.1	6.1/93.9	NA/NA	81.1/18.9	NA	NA
1810	17	7,239,881	36.4	4.3	7.3/92.7	NA/NA	81.0/19.0	NA	NA
1820	23	9,638,453	33.1	5.5	7.2/92.8	50.8/49.2	81.6/18.4	NA	16.7
1830	24	12,866,020	33.5	7.4	8.8/91.2	50.8/49.2	81.9/18.1	NA	17.2
1840	26	17,069,453	32.7	9.8	10.8/89.2	50.9/49.1	83.2/16.8	NA	17.8
1850	31	23,191,876	35.9	7.9	15.3/84.7	51.0/49.0	84.3/15.7	5.55	18.9
1860	33	31,443,321	35.6	10.6	19.8/80.2	51.2/48.8	85.6/14.4	5.28	19.4
1870	37	39,818,449	26.6	13.4	25.7/74.3	50.6/49.4	86.2/13.8	5.09	20.2
1880	38	50,155,783	26.0	16.9	28.2/71.8	50.9/49.1	86.5/13.5	5.04	20.9
1890	44	62,947,714	25.5	21.2	35.1/64.9	51.2/48.8	87.5/12.5	4.93	22.0
1900	45	75,994,575	20.7	25.6	39.6/60.4	51.1/48.9	87.9/12.1	4.76	22.9
1910	46	91,972,266	21.0	31.0	45.6/54.4	51.5/48.5	88.9/11.1	4.54	24.1
1920	48	105,710,620	14.9	35.6	51.2/48.8	51.0/49.0	89.7/10.3	4.34	25.3
1930	48	122,775,046	16.1	41.2	56.1/43.9	50.6/49.4	89.8/10.2	4.11	26.4
1940	48	131,669,275	7.2	44.2	56.5/43.5	50.2/49.8	89.8/10.2	3.67	29.0
1950	48	150,697,361	14.5	50.7	64.0/36.0	49.7/50.3	89.5/10.5	3.37	30.2
1960	50	179,323,175	18.5	50.6	69.9/30.1	49.3/50.7	88.6/11.4	3.33	29.5
1970	50	203,302,031	13.4	57.4	73.5/26.5	48.7/51.3	87.6/12.4	3.14	28.0
1980	50	226,545,805	11.4	64.0	73.7/26.3	48.6/51.4	86.0/14.0	2.76	30.0
1985	50	238,740,000	5.4	64.0	NA/NA	48.7/51.3	84.9/15.1	2.73	31.5

NA = Not available.

Immigrants to the United States

Immigration Totals by Decade

Years	Number	Years	Number
1820–1830	151,824	1911–1920	5,735,811
1831–1840	599,125	1921–1930	4,107,209
1841–1850	1,713,251	1931–1940	528,431
1851–1860	2,598,214	1941–1950	1,035,039
1861–1870	2,314,824	1951–1960	2,515,479
1871–1880	2,812,191	1961–1970	3,321,677
1881–1890	5,246,613	1971–1980	4,493,000
1891–1900	3,687,546	1981–1985	2,864,400
1901–1910	8,795,386	Total	52,520,020

Source: U.S. Bureau of the Census, *Historical Statistics of the United States, Colonial Times to 1970* (1975), Part I, pp. 105–106; U.S. Bureau of the Census, *Statistical Abstract of the United States, 1987* (1986), p. 11.

Regional Origins of Immigrants (in percentages)

Period	Total Europe	Europe North and West[a]	Europe East and Central[b]	Europe South and Other[c]	Western Hemisphere	Asia	All Other
1821–1830	69.2	67.1	—	2.1	8.4	—	22.4
1831–1840	82.8	81.8	—	1.0	5.5	—	11.7
1841–1850	93.3	92.9	0.1	0.3	3.6	—	3.1
1851–1860	94.4	93.6	0.1	0.8	2.9	1.6	1.1
1861–1870	89.2	87.8	0.5	0.9	7.2	2.8	0.8
1871–1880	80.8	73.6	4.5	2.7	14.4	4.4	0.4
1881–1890	90.3	72.0	11.9	6.3	8.1	1.3	0.3
1891–1900	96.5	44.5	32.8	19.1	1.1	1.9	0.5
1901–1910	92.5	21.7	44.5	26.3	4.1	2.8	0.6
1911–1920	76.3	17.4	33.4	25.5	19.9	3.4	0.4
1921–1930	60.3	31.7	14.4	14.3	36.9	2.4	0.4
1931–1940	65.9	38.8	11.0	16.1	30.3	2.8	0.9
1941–1950	60.1	47.5	4.6	7.9	34.3	3.1	2.5

continued

Regional Origins of Immigrants (in percentages), continued

Period	Total Europe	Europe North and West[a]	Europe East and Central[b]	Europe South and Other[c]	Western Hemisphere	Asia	All Other
1951–1960	52.8	17.7	24.3	10.8	39.6	6.0	1.6
1961–1970	33.8	11.7	9.4	12.9	51.7	12.9	1.7
1971–1980	17.8	4.3	5.4	7.9	42.9	36.4	2.9
1981–1985	11.2	3.8	5.1	2.2	37.3	48.0	3.5

Note: dash indicates less than 0.1 percent.

[a]Great Britain, Ireland, Norway, Sweden, Denmark, Iceland, Netherlands, Belgium, Luxembourg, Switzerland, France.

[b]Germany (Austria included, 1938–1945), Poland, Czechoslovakia (since 1920), Yugoslavia (since 1920), Hungary (since 1861), Austria (since 1861, except 1938–1945), U.S.S.R. (excludes Asian U.S.S.R. between 1931 and 1963), Latvia, Estonia, Lithuania, Finland, Romania, Bulgaria, Turkey (in Europe).

[c]Italy, Spain, Portugal, Greece, and other European countries not classified elsewhere.

Source: Stephan Thernstrom, ed., *Harvard Encyclopedia of American Ethnic Groups* (1980), p. 480; and U.S. Bureau of the Census, *Statistical Abstract of the United States, 1987* (1986), p. 11. Reprinted by permission of Harvard University Press.

Major Sources of Immigrants by Country (in thousands)

Period	Germany	Italy	Britain	Ireland	Austria-Hungary	Russia[a]	Canada	Denmark, Norway, Sweden[b]	Mexico	West Indies
1820–1830	8	—	27	54	—	—	2	—	5	4
1831–1840	152	2	76	207	—	—	14	2	7	12
1841–1850	435	2	267	781	—	—	42	14	3	14
1851–1860	952	9	424	914	—	—	59	25	3	11
1861–1870	787	12	607	436	8	3	154	126	2	9
1871–1880	718	56	548	437	73	39	384	243	5	14
1881–1890	1,453	307	807	655	354	213	393	656	2[c]	29
1891–1900	505	652	272	388	593	505	3	372	—	—[d]
1901–1910	341	2,046	526	339	2,145	1,597	179	505	50	108
1911–1920	144	1,110	341	146	896	922	742	203	219	123
1921–1930	412	455	330	221	64	89	925	198	459	75
1931–1940	114	68	29	13	11	7	109	11	22	16
1941–1950	227	58	132	28	28	4	172	27	61	50
1951–1960	478	185	192	57	104	6	378	57	300	123
1961–1970	191	214	206	40	26	7	413	43	454	470
1971–1979	68	124	122	11	15	31	156	13	584	668
Total	6,985	5,300	4,906	4,727	4,317	3,423	4,125	2,495	2,176	1,726

Notes: Numbers are rounded. Dash indicates less than one thousand.

[a]Includes Finland, Latvia, Estonia, and Lithuania.

[b]Includes Iceland.

[c]Figure for 1881–1885 only.

[d]Figure for 1894–1900 only.

Source: U.S. Bureau of the Census, *Historical Statistics of the United States: Colonial Times to 1970* (1975), Part I, pp. 105–108; U.S. Bureau of the Census, *Statistical Abstract of the United States, 1984* (1983), p. 91.

Year	Farm Population (in thousands)	Percent of Total Population	Number of Farms (in thousands)	Total Acres (in thousands)	Average Acreage Per Farm	Corn Production (millions of bushels)	Wheat Production (millions of bushels)
1850	NA	NA	1,449	293,561	203	592[a]	100[a]
1860	NA	NA	2,044	407,213	199	839[b]	173[b]
1870	NA	NA	2,660	407,735	153	1,125	254
1880	21,973	43.8	4,009	536,082	134	1,707	502
1890	24,771	42.3	4,565	623,219	137	1,650	449
1900	29,875	41.9	5,740	841,202	147	2,662	599
1910	32,077	34.9	6,366	881,431	139	2,853	625
1920	31,974	30.1	6,454	958,677	149	3,071	843
1930	30,529	24.9	6,295	990,112	157	2,080	887
1940	30,547	23.2	6,102	1,065,114	175	2,457	815
1950	23,048	15.3	5,388	1,161,420	216	3,075	1,019
1960	15,635	8.7	3,962	1,176,946	297	4,314	1,355
1970	9,712	4.8	2,949	1,102,769	374	4,200	1,370
1980	6,051	2.7	2,428	1,042,000	427	6,600	2,400
1983	5,787	2.5	2,370	1,024,000	432	4,200	2,400

[a]Figure for 1849.
[b]Figure for 1859.
NA = Not available.

The American Worker

Year	Total Number of Workers	Males as Percent of Total Workers	Females as Percent of Total Workers	Married Women as Percent of Female Workers	Female Workers as Percent of Female Population	Percent of Labor Force Unemployed	Percent of Workers in Labor Unions
1870	12,506,000	85	15	NA	NA	NA	NA
1880	17,392,000	85	15	NA	NA	NA	NA
1890	23,318,000	83	17	13.9	18.9	4 (1894 = 18%)	NA
1900	29,073,000	82	18	15.4	20.6	5	3
1910	38,167,000	79	21	24.7	25.4	6	6
1920	41,614,000	79	21	23.0	23.7	5 (1921 = 12%)	12
1930	48,830,000	78	22	28.9	24.8	9 (1933 = 25%)	7
1940	53,011,000	76	24	36.4	27.4	15 (1944 = 1%)	27
1950	59,643,000	72	28	52.1	31.4	5	25
1960	68,877,000	68	32	59.9	37.7	5.4	26
1970	82,049,000	63	37	63.4	43.3	4.8	25
1980	108,544,000	58	42	59.7	51.5	7.0	23
1983	113,226,000	57	43	58.9	52.9	9.5	19[a]

[a]1984 figure.
NA = Not available.

TERRITORIAL EXPANSION OF THE UNITED STATES

Territory	Date Acquired	Square Miles	How Acquired
Original states and territories	1783	888,685	Treaty with Great Britain
Louisiana Purchase	1803	827,192	Purchase from France
Florida	1819	72,003	Treaty with Spain
Texas	1845	390,143	Annexation of independent nation
Oregon	1846	285,580	Treaty with Great Britain
Mexican Cession	1848	529,017	Conquest from Mexico
Gadsden Purchase	1853	29,640	Purchase from Mexico
Alaska	1867	589,757	Purchase from Russia
Hawaii	1898	6,450	Annexation of independent nation
The Philippines	1899	115,600	Conquest from Spain (granted independence in 1946)
Puerto Rico	1899	3,435	Conquest from Spain
Guam	1899	212	Conquest from Spain
American Samoa	1900	76	Treaty with Germany and Great Britain
Panama Canal Zone	1904	553	Treaty with Panama (returned to Panama by treaty in 1978)
Corn Islands	1914	4	Treaty with Nicaragua (returned to Nicaragua by treaty in 1971)
Virgin Islands	1917	133	Purchase from Denmark
Pacific Islands Trust (Micronesia)	1947	8,489	Trusteeship under United Nations (some granted independence)
All others (Midway, Wake, and other islands)		42	

ADMISSION OF STATES INTO THE UNION

State	Date of Admission	State	Date of Admission
1. Delaware	December 7, 1787	26. Michigan	January 26, 1837
2. Pennsylvania	December 12, 1787	27. Florida	March 3, 1845
3. New Jersey	December 18, 1787	28. Texas	December 29, 1845
4. Georgia	January 2, 1788	29. Iowa	December 28, 1846
5. Connecticut	January 9, 1788	30. Wisconsin	May 29, 1848
6. Massachusetts	February 6, 1788	31. California	September 9, 1850
7. Maryland	April 28, 1788	32. Minnesota	May 11, 1858
8. South Carolina	May 23, 1788	33. Oregon	February 14, 1859
9. New Hampshire	June 21, 1788	34. Kansas	January 29, 1861
10. Virginia	June 25, 1788	35. West Virginia	June 20, 1863
11. New York	July 26, 1788	36. Nevada	October 31, 1864
12. North Carolina	November 21, 1789	37. Nebraska	March 1, 1867
13. Rhode Island	May 29, 1790	38. Colorado	August 1, 1876
14. Vermont	March 4, 1791	39. North Dakota	November 2, 1889
15. Kentucky	June 1, 1792	40. South Dakota	November 2, 1889
16. Tennessee	June 1, 1796	41. Montana	November 8, 1889
17. Ohio	March 1, 1803	42. Washington	November 11, 1889
18. Louisiana	April 30, 1812	43. Idaho	July 3, 1890
19. Indiana	December 11, 1816	44. Wyoming	July 10, 1890
20. Mississippi	December 10, 1817	45. Utah	January 4, 1896
21. Illinois	December 3, 1818	46. Oklahoma	November 16, 1907
22. Alabama	December 14, 1819	47. New Mexico	January 6, 1912
23. Maine	March 15, 1820	48. Arizona	February 14, 1912
24. Missouri	August 10, 1821	49. Alaska	January 3, 1959
25. Arkansas	June 15, 1836	50. Hawaii	August 21, 1959

Year	Number of States	Candidates	Parties	Popular Vote	% of Popular Vote	Electoral Vote	% Voter Participation[b]
1789	11	**George Washington**	No party designations			69	
		John Adams				34	
		Other candidates				35	
1792	15	**George Washington**	No party designations			132	
		John Adams				77	
		George Clinton				50	
		Other candidates				5	
1796	16	**John Adams**	Federalist			71	
		Thomas Jefferson	Democratic-Republican			68	
		Thomas Pinckney	Federalist			59	
		Aaron Burr	Democratic-Republican			30	
		Other candidates				48	
1800	16	**Thomas Jefferson**	Democratic-Republican			73	
		Aaron Burr	Democratic-Republican			73	
		John Adams	Federalist			65	
		Charles C. Pinckney	Federalist			64	
		John Jay	Federalist			1	
1804	17	**Thomas Jefferson**	Democratic-Republican			162	
		Charles C. Pinckney	Federalist			14	
1808	17	**James Madison**	Democratic-Republican			122	
		Charles C. Pinckney	Federalist			47	
		George Clinton	Democratic-Republican			6	
1812	18	**James Madison**	Democratic-Republican			128	
		DeWitt Clinton	Federalist			89	
1816	19	**James Monroe**	Democratic-Republican			183	
		Rufus King	Federalist			34	
1820	24	**James Monroe**	Democratic-Republican			231	
		John Quincy Adams	Independent Republican			1	
1824	24	**John Quincy Adams**	Democratic-Republican	108,740	30.5	84	26.9
		Andrew Jackson	Democratic-Republican	153,544	43.1	99	
		Henry Clay	Democratic-Republican	47,136	13.2	37	
		William H. Crawford	Democratic-Republican	46,618	13.1	41	
1828	24	**Andrew Jackson**	Democratic	647,286	56.0	178	57.6
		John Quincy Adams	National Republican	508,064	44.0	83	
1832	24	**Andrew Jackson**	Democratic	688,242	54.5	219	55.4
		Henry Clay	National Republican	473,462	37.5	49	
		William Wirt	Anti-Masonic	101,051	8.0	7	
		John Floyd	Democratic			11	

Year	Number of States	Candidates	Parties	Popular Vote	% of Popular Vote	Electoral Vote	% Voter Participation[b]
1836	26	**Martin Van Buren**	Democratic	765,483	50.9	170	57.8
		William H. Harrison	Whig			73	
		Hugh L. White	Whig	739,795	49.1	26	
		Daniel Webster	Whig			14	
		W. P. Mangum	Whig			11	
1840	26	**William H. Harrison**	Whig	1,274,624	53.1	234	80.2
		Martin Van Buren	Democratic	1,127,781	46.9	60	
1844	26	**James K. Polk**	Democratic	1,338,464	49.6	170	78.9
		Henry Clay	Whig	1,300,097	48.1	105	
		James G. Birney	Liberty	62,300	2.3		
1848	30	**Zachary Taylor**	Whig	1,360,967	47.4	163	72.7
		Lewis Cass	Democratic	1,222,342	42.5	127	
		Martin Van Buren	Free Soil	291,263	10.1		
1852	31	**Franklin Pierce**	Democratic	1,601,117	50.9	254	69.6
		Winfield Scott	Whig	1,385,453	44.1	42	
		John P. Hale	Free Soil	155,825	5.0		
1856	31	**James Buchanan**	Democratic	1,832,955	45.3	174	78.9
		John C. Frémont	Republican	1,339,932	33.1	114	
		Millard Fillmore	American	871,731	21.6	8	
1860	33	**Abraham Lincoln**	Republican	1,865,593	39.8	180	81.2
		Stephen A. Douglas	Democratic	1,382,713	29.5	12	
		John C. Breckinridge	Democratic	848,356	18.1	72	
		John Bell	Constitutional Union	592,906	12.6	39	
1864	36	**Abraham Lincoln**	Republican	2,206,938	55.0	212	73.8
		George B. McClellan	Democratic	1,803,787	45.0	21	
1868	37	**Ulysses S. Grant**	Republican	3,013,421	52.7	214	78.1
		Horatio Seymour	Democratic	2,706,829	47.3	80	
1872	37	**Ulysses S. Grant**	Republican	3,596,745	55.6	286	71.3
		Horace Greeley	Democratic	2,843,446	43.9	[a]	
1876	38	**Rutherford B. Hayes**	Republican	4,036,572	48.0	185	81.8
		Samuel J. Tilden	Democratic	4,284,020	51.0	184	
1880	38	**James A. Garfield**	Republican	4,453,295	48.5	214	79.4
		Winfield S. Hancock	Democratic	4,414,082	48.1	155	
		James B. Weaver	Greenback-Labor	308,578	3.4		
1884	38	**Grover Cleveland**	Democratic	4,879,507	48.5	219	77.5
		James G. Blaine	Republican	4,850,293	48.2	182	
		Benjamin F. Butler	Greenback-Labor	175,370	1.8		
		John P. St. John	Prohibition	150,369	1.5		

Year	Number of States	Candidates	Parties	Popular Vote	% of Popular Vote	Electoral Vote	% Voter Participation[b]
1888	38	**Benjamin Harrison**	Republican	5,477,129	47.9	233	79.3
		Grover Cleveland	Democratic	5,537,857	48.6	168	
		Clinton B. Fisk	Prohibition	249,506	2.2		
		Anson J. Streeter	Union Labor	146,935	1.3		
1892	44	**Grover Cleveland**	Democratic	5,555,426	46.1	277	74.7
		Benjamin Harrison	Republican	5,182,690	43.0	145	
		James B. Weaver	People's	1,029,846	8.5	22	
		John Bidwell	Prohibition	264,133	2.2		
1896	45	**William McKinley**	Republican	7,102,246	51.1	271	79.3
		William J. Bryan	Democratic	6,492,559	47.7	176	
1900	45	**William McKinley**	Republican	7,218,491	51.7	292	73.2
		William J. Bryan	Democratic; Populist	6,356,734	45.5	155	
		John C. Wooley	Prohibition	208,914	1.5		
1904	45	**Theodore Roosevelt**	Republican	7,628,461	57.4	336	65.2
		Alton B. Parker	Democratic	5,084,223	37.6	140	
		Eugene V. Debs	Socialist	402,283	3.0		
		Silas C. Swallow	Prohibition	258,536	1.9		
1908	46	**William H. Taft**	Republican	7,675,320	51.6	321	65.4
		William J. Bryan	Democratic	6,412,294	43.1	162	
		Eugene V. Debs	Socialist	420,793	2.8		
		Eugene W. Chafin	Prohibition	253,840	1.7		
1912	48	**Woodrow Wilson**	Democratic	6,296,547	41.9	435	58.8
		Theodore Roosevelt	Progressive	4,118,571	27.4	88	
		William H. Taft	Republican	3,486,720	23.2	8	
		Eugene V. Debs	Socialist	900,672	6.0		
		Eugene W. Chafin	Prohibition	206,275	1.4		
1916	48	**Woodrow Wilson**	Democratic	9,127,695	49.4	277	61.6
		Charles E. Hughes	Republican	8,533,507	46.2	254	
		A. L. Benson	Socialist	585,113	3.2		
		J. Frank Hanly	Prohibition	220,506	1.2		
1920		**Warren G. Harding**	Republican	16,143,407	60.4	404	49.2
		James M. Cox	Democratic	9,130,328	34.2	127	
		Eugene V. Debs	Socialist	919,799	3.4		
		P. P. Christensen	Farmer-Labor	265,411	1.0		
1924	48	**Calvin Coolidge**	Republican	15,718,211	54.0	382	48.9
		John W. Davis	Democratic	8,385,283	28.8	136	
		Robert M. La Follette	Progressive	4,831,289	16.6	13	
1928	48	**Herbert C. Hoover**	Republican	21,391,993	58.2	444	56.9
		Alfred E. Smith	Democratic	15,016,169	40.9	87	
1932	48	**Franklin D. Roosevelt**	Democratic	22,809,638	57.4	472	56.9
		Herbert C. Hoover	Republican	15,758,901	39.7	59	
		Norman Thomas	Socialist	881,951	2.2		

Year	Number of States	Candidates	Parties	Popular Vote	% of Popular Vote	Electoral Vote	% Voter Participation[b]
1936	48	Franklin D. Roosevelt	Democratic	27,752,869	60.8	523	61.0
		Alfred M. Landon	Republican	16,674,665	36.5	8	
		William Lemke	Union	882,479	1.9		
1940	48	Franklin D. Roosevelt	Democratic	27,307,819	54.8	449	62.5
		Wendell L. Wilkie	Republican	22,321,018	44.8	82	
1944	48	Franklin D. Roosevelt	Democratic	25,606,585	53.5	432	55.9
		Thomas E. Dewey	Republican	22,014,745	46.0	99	
1948	48	Harry S Truman	Democratic	24,179,345	49.6	303	53.0
		Thomas E. Dewey	Republican	21,991,291	45.1	189	
		J. Strom Thurmond	States' Rights	1,176,125	2.4	39	
		Henry A. Wallace	Progressive	1,157,326	2.4		
1952	48	Dwight D. Eisenhower	Republican	33,936,234	55.1	442	63.3
		Adlai E. Stevenson	Democratic	27,314,992	44.4	89	
1956	48	Dwight D. Eisenhower	Republican	35,590,472	57.6	457	60.6
		Adlai E. Stevenson	Democratic	26,022,752	42.1	73	
1960	50	John F. Kennedy	Democratic	34,226,731	49.7	303	62.8
		Richard M. Nixon	Republican	34,108,157	49.5	219	
1964	50	Lyndon B. Johnson	Democratic	43,129,566	61.1	486	61.7
		Barry M. Goldwater	Republican	27,178,188	38.5	52	
1968	50	Richard M. Nixon	Republican	31,785,480	43.4	301	60.6
		Hubert H. Humphrey	Democratic	31,275,166	42.7	191	
		George C. Wallace	American Independent	9,906,473	13.5	46	
1972	50	Richard M. Nixon	Republican	47,169,911	60.7	520	55.2
		George S. McGovern	Democratic	29,170,383	37.5	17	
		John G. Schmitz	American	1,099,482	1.4		
1976	50	Jimmy Carter	Democratic	40,830,763	50.1	297	53.5
		Gerald R. Ford	Republican	39,147,793	48.0	240	
1980	50	Ronald Reagan	Republican	43,899,248	50.8	489	52.6
		Jimmy Carter	Democratic	35,481,432	41.0	49	
		John B. Anderson	Independent	5,719,437	6.6	0	
		Ed Clark	Libertarian	920,859	1.1	0	
1984	50	Ronald Reagan	Republican	54,451,521	58.8	525	53.3
		Walter Mondale	Democratic	37,565,334	40.5	13	

Candidates receiving less than 1 percent of the popular vote have been omitted. Thus the percentage of popular vote given for any election year may not total 100 percent.

Before the passage of the Twelfth Amendment in 1804, the Electoral College voted for two presidential candidates; the runner-up became vice president.

Before 1824, most presidential electors were chosen by state legislatures, not by popular vote.

[a]Greeley died shortly after the election; the electors supporting him then divided their votes among minor candidates.

[b]Percent of voting-age population casting ballots.

1. President	**George Washington**	1789–1797	
Vice President	John Adams	1789–1797	
2. President	**John Adams**	1797–1801	
Vice President	Thomas Jefferson	1797–1801	
3. President	**Thomas Jefferson**	1801–1809	
Vice President	Aaron Burr	1801–1805	
Vice President	George Clinton	1805–1809	
4. President	**James Madison**	1809–1817	
Vice President	George Clinton	1809–1813	
Vice President	Elbridge Gerry	1813–1817	
5. President	**James Monroe**	1817–1825	
Vice President	Daniel Tompkins	1817–1825	
6. President	**John Quincy Adams**	1825–1829	
Vice President	John C. Calhoun	1825–1829	
7. President	**Andrew Jackson**	1829–1837	
Vice President	John C. Calhoun	1829–1833	
Vice President	Martin Van Buren	1833–1837	
8. President	**Martin Van Buren**	1837–1841	
Vice President	Richard M. Johnson	1837–1841	
9. President	**William H. Harrison**	1841	
Vice President	John Tyler	1841	
10. President	**John Tyler**	1841–1845	
Vice President	none		
11. President	**James K. Polk**	1845–1849	
Vice President	George M. Dallas	1845–1849	
12. President	**Zachary Taylor**	1849–1850	
Vice President	Millard Fillmore	1849–1850	
13. President	**Millard Fillmore**	1850–1853	
Vice President	none		
14. President	**Franklin Pierce**	1853–1857	
Vice President	William R. King	1853–1857	
15. President	**James Buchanan**	1857–1861	
Vice President	John C. Breckinridge	1857–1861	
16. President	**Abraham Lincoln**	1861–1865	
Vice President	Hannibal Hamlin	1861–1865	
Vice President	Andrew Johnson	1865	
17. President	**Andrew Johnson**	1865–1869	
Vice President	none		
18. President	**Ulysses S. Grant**	1869–1877	
Vice President	Schuyler Colfax	1869–1873	
Vice President	Henry Wilson	1873–1877	
19. President	**Rutherford B. Hayes**	1877–1881	
Vice President	William A. Wheeler	1877–1881	
20. President	**James A. Garfield**	1881	
Vice President	Chester A. Arthur	1881	

21. President	**Chester A. Arthur**	1881–1885	
Vice President	none		
22. President	**Grover Cleveland**	1885–1889	
Vice President	Thomas A. Hendricks	1885–1889	
23. President	**Benjamin Harrison**	1889–1893	
Vice President	Levi P. Morton	1889–1893	
24. President	**Grover Cleveland**	1893–1897	
Vice President	Adlai E. Stevenson	1893–1897	
25. President	**William McKinley**	1897–1901	
Vice President	Garret A. Hobart	1897–1901	
	Theodore Roosevelt	1901	
26. President	**Theodore Roosevelt**	1901–1909	
Vice President	Charles Fairbanks	1905–1909	
27. President	**William H. Taft**	1909–1913	
Vice President	James S. Sherman	1909–1913	
28. President	**Woodrow Wilson**	1913–1921	
Vice President	Thomas R. Marshall	1913–1921	
29. President	**Warren G. Harding**	1921–1923	
Vice President	Calvin Coolidge	1921–1923	
30. President	**Calvin Coolidge**	1923–1929	
Vice President	Charles G. Dawes	1925–1929	
31. President	**Herbert C. Hoover**	1929–1933	
Vice President	Charles Curtis	1929–1933	
32. President	**Franklin D. Roosevelt**	1933–1945	
Vice President	John N. Garner	1933–1941	
	Henry A. Wallace	1941–1945	
	Harry S Truman	1945	
33. President	**Harry S Truman**	1945–1953	
Vice President	Alben W. Barkley	1949–1953	
34. President	**Dwight D. Eisenhower**	1953–1961	
Vice President	Richard M. Nixon	1953–1961	
35. President	**John F. Kennedy**	1961–1963	
Vice President	Lyndon B. Johnson	1961–1963	
36. President	**Lyndon B. Johnson**	1963–1969	
Vice President	Hubert H. Humphrey	1965–1969	
37. President	**Richard M. Nixon**	1969–1974	
Vice President	Spiro T. Agnew	1969–1973	
	Gerald R. Ford	1973–1974	
38. President	**Gerald R. Ford**	1974–1977	
Vice President	Nelson A. Rockefeller	1974–1977	
39. President	**Jimmy Carter**	1977–1981	
Vice President	Walter F. Mondale	1977–1981	
40. President	**Ronald Reagan**	1981–	
Vice President	George Bush	1981–	

	Term of Service	Years of Service	Life Span		Term of Service	Years of Service	Life Span
John Jay	1789–1795	5	1745–1829	John McLean	1829–1861	32	1785–1861
John Rutledge	1789–1791	1	1739–1800	Henry Baldwin	1830–1844	14	1780–1844
William Cushing	1789–1810	20	1732–1810	James M. Wayne	1835–1867	32	1790–1867
James Wilson	1789–1798	8	1742–1798	Roger B. Taney	1836–1864	28	1777–1864
John Blair	1789–1796	6	1732–1800	Philip P. Barbour	1836–1841	4	1783–1841
Robert H. Harrison	1789–1790	—	1745–1790	John Catron	1837–1865	28	1786–1865
James Iredell	1790–1799	9	1751–1799	John McKinley	1837–1852	15	1780–1852
Thomas Johnson	1791–1793	1	1732–1819	Peter V. Daniel	1841–1860	19	1784–1860
William Paterson	1793–1806	13	1745–1806	Samuel Nelson	1845–1872	27	1792–1873
John Rutledge*	1795	—	1739–1800	Levi Woodbury	1845–1851	5	1789–1851
Samuel Chase	1796–1811	15	1741–1811	Robert C. Grier	1846–1870	23	1794–1870
Oliver Ellsworth	1796–1800	4	1745–1807	Benjamin R. Curtis	1851–1857	6	1809–1874
Bushrod Washington	1798–1829	31	1762–1829	John A. Campbell	1853–1861	8	1811–1889
Henry B. Brown	1890–1906	16	1836–1913	Nathan Clifford	1858–1881	23	1803–1881
George Shiras, Jr.	1892–1903	10	1832–1924	Noah H. Swayne	1862–1881	18	1804–1884
Howell E. Jackson	1893–1895	2	1832–1895	Samuel F. Miller	1862–1890	28	1816–1890
Edward D. White	1894–1910	16	1845–1921	David Davis	1862–1877	14	1815–1886
Rufus W. Peckham	1895–1909	14	1838–1909	Stephen J. Field	1863–1897	34	1816–1899
Joseph McKenna	1898–1925	26	1843–1926	Salmon P. Chase	1864–1873	8	1808–1873
Oliver W. Holmes	1902–1932	30	1841–1935	William Strong	1870–1880	10	1808–1895
William R. Day	1903–1922	19	1849–1923	Joseph P. Bradley	1807–1892	22	1813–1892
William H. Moody	1906–1910	3	1853–1917	Ward Hunt	1873–1882	9	1810–1886
Horace H. Lurton	1910–1914	4	1844–1914	Morrison R. Waite	1874–1888	14	1816–1888
Charles E. Hughes	1910–1916	5	1862–1948	John M. Harlan	1877–1911	34	1833–1911
Willis Van Devanter	1911–1937	26	1859–1941	William B. Woods	1880–1887	7	1824–1887
Joseph R. Lamar	1911–1916	5	1857–1916	Stanley Matthews	1881–1889	7	1824–1889
Alfred Moore	1799–1804	4	1755–1810	Horace Gray	1882–1902	20	1828–1902
John Marshall	1801–1835	34	1755–1835	Samuel Blatchford	1882–1893	11	1820–1893
William Johnson	1804–1834	30	1771–1834	Lucius Q. C. Lamar	1888–1893	5	1825–1893
H. Brockholst Livingston	1806–1823	16	1757–1823	Melville W. Fuller	1888–1910	21	1833–1910
Thomas Todd	1807–1826	18	1765–1826	David J. Brewer	1890–1910	20	1837–1910
Joseph Story	1811–1845	33	1779–1845	Edward D. White	1910–1921	11	1845–1921
Gabriel Duval	1811–1835	24	1752–1844	Mahlon Pitney	1912–1922	10	1858–1924
Smith Thompson	1823–1843	20	1768–1843	James C. McReynolds	1914–1941	26	1862–1946
Robert Trimble	1826–1828	2	1777–1828	Louis D. Brandeis	1916–1939	22	1856–1941

continued

	Term of Service	Years of Service	Life Span		Term of Service	Years of Service	Life Span
John H. Clarke	1916–1922	6	1857–1945	Fred M. Vinson	1946–1953	7	1890–1953*
William H. Taft	1921–1930	8	1857–1930	Tom C. Clark	1949–1967	18	1899–1977
George Sutherland	1922–1938	15	1862–1942	Sherman Minton	1949–1956	7	1890–1965
Pierce Butler	1922–1939	16	1866–1939	Earl Warren	1953–1969	16	1891–1974
Edward T. Sanford	1923–1930	7	1865–1930	John Marshall Harlan	1955–1971	16	1899–1971
Harlan F. Stone	1925–1941	16	1872–1946	William J. Brennan, Jr.	1956–	—	1906–
Charles E. Hughes	1930–1941	11	1862–1948	Charles E. Whittaker	1957–1962	5	1901–1973
Owen J. Roberts	1930–1945	15	1875–1955	Potter Stewart	1958–1981	23	1915–
Benjamin N. Cardozo	1932–1938	6	1870–1938	Byron R. White	1962–	—	1917–
Hugo L. Black	1937–1971	34	1886–1971	Arthur J. Goldberg	1962–1965	3	1908–
Stanley F. Reed	1938–1957	19	1884–1980	Abe Fortas	1965–1969	4	1910–
Felix Frankfurter	1939–1962	23	1882–1965	Thurgood Marshall	1967–	—	1908–
William O. Douglas	1939–1975	36	1898–1980	Warren C. Burger	1969–1986	17	1907–
Frank Murphy	1940–1949	9	1890–1949	Harry A. Blackmun	1970–	—	1908–
Harlan F. Stone	1941–1946	5	1872–1946	Lewis F. Powell, Jr.	1971–	—	1907–
James F. Byrnes	1941–1942	1	1879–1972	William H. Rehnquist	1971–	—	1924–
Robert H. Jackson	1941–1954	13	1892–1954	John P. Stevens, III	1975–	—	1920–
Wiley B. Rutledge	1943–1949	6	1894–1949	Sandra Day O'Connor	1981–	—	1930–
Harold H. Burton	1945–1958	13	1888–1964	Antonin Scalia	1986–	—	1936–

*Appointed and served one term, but not confirmed by the Senate.

Note: Chief justices are in italics.

INDEX

Brandywine Creek, battle of, 93
Brant, Joseph, 93, 93 (illus.)
Brant, Mary, 93
Breckenridge, John C., 239
Breed's Hill (Bunker Hill), battle of, 87–88
Breevoort, Henry Jr., and Laura Carson, 174
Bretton Woods Conference, 490
Brice, Fanny, 334
Brinkmanship, 514
Britain: colonization by, 1–2, 12–16 (*see also* Colonies, English); social disruption in (post–1530), 13; ethnocentrism of, 14–15, 29; and decreased migration to colonies, 30; Jacobite rebellions in, 46–47; tax policies of, 64, 69, 70–75; and French and Indian War, 67–68; Americans see as corrupt, 100; U.S. trade with, 110; and Napoleonic Wars, 141, 143; as Monroe Doctrine protector, 149; and southern cotton growing, 191; and Civil War, 259; rapprochement with, 376, 378, 387; and decolonization, 403, 493 (*see also* Decolonization); in World War II, 468, 469, 480, 481–482; and Suez crisis, 519; and Indochina, 544
Broker state democracy, 435, 437
Brook Farm, 209
Brooks, Preston, 237
Brown, John, 187, 237, 239
Brown, Noah, 143
Brown, Pat (Edmund), 568
Brown, William Hill, 101
Brown Berets, 590
Brown v. Board of Education of Topeka, 508, 512
"Brown power," 590
Brown's Ferry, Alabama, 584–585
Bruce, Blanche K., 276
Bryan, William Jennings, 352, 366, 380, 381, 394, 417
Bryant, Anita, 590
Brzezinski, Zbigniew, 554
Buchanan, James, 235, 237, 238
Budget, federal: under Harrison, 346; Hoover for balancing of, 431; and deficit spending, 431, 442, 479, 495, 519, 584; and Roosevelt's policies, 432, 434, 442, 479; Eisenhower's approach to, 509; and nuclear weapons, 514; and neo-Keynesian policies, 583
Buffalo, destruction of, 281, 289
"Buffalo Bill" (William F. Cody), 281, 334, 336
Buffalo Springfield, 568
Bull Moose party, 367
Bull Run, battle of, 246
Bunche, Ralph, 444

Bundy, McGeorge, 562
Bunker Hill, battle of, 87–88
Burbank, Luther, 294
Burger, Warren, 601
Burgesses, House of, *see* House of Burgesses
Burgoyne, Gen. ("Gentleman Johnny"), 92, 93, 94
"Burned-over" district, 207
Burnside, Ambrose, 248
Burr, Aaron, 125, 128, 140–141
Burroughs, Edgar Rice, 336
Bushy Run, battle of, 68
Business: Supreme Court protection of, 147; specialization in, 161, 171, 173; and limited liability, 162; during Civil War (North), 251, 252; mail-order companies, 292; marketing innovations in, 303; corporate consolidation in, 304–305; and Gospel of Wealth, 305–306; and antitrust legislation, 306–307, 365–366, 435, 472; government run as, 326; in World War I, 398, 404; *1920s* thriving of, 410; advertising in (1920s), 412; organized crime as, 420; Great Depression causes in, 426–427; and New Deal, 435, 437, 440, 449; and arms sales, 458; in World War II, 472–473; post-WWII prosperity, 494–495; and fads, 535; multiversity as, 568; and South Africa, 606. *See also* Corporations; Industry; Market economy
Business cycles, 155, 303–304, 425, 583
Butler, Andrew P., 237
Butler, Benjamin, 272
Butler, Pierce, 190
Butterfield, Alexander, 581
Byrnes, James F., 488, 490

Cabinet: establishment of, 119; and Tenure of Office Act, 271
Cabot, John, 9
Calhoun, John C., 143, 147, 214, 217, 223, 239
California: as frontier, 167; U.S. gains, 228; admission of, 230–231; oil fields in, 284; migration to (1930s), 437
California Gold Rush, 166–167
Calvert, Cecilius (Lord Baltimore), and Calvert family, 16
Calvin, John, and Calvinism, 12, 13, 18, 60
Cambodia, 544, 550; invasion of, 548–549, 573
Camden, South Carolina, battle of, 94
Cameron, Paul Carrington, 195
Campaigns, political, *see* Political campaigns
Campbell, John A., 277
Camp David meeting, 555 (illus.), 556

Canada: French trading posts in, 11; in French and Indian War, 67; Revolutionary War campaign in, 88; in War of *1812*, 143–145; border agreements with, 148; border dispute with, 220–221; immigrants from, 318, 417; draft resisters to, 569
Canals, 153, 157, 158
Canary Islands, trade with, 36
Cannon, Joseph ("Uncle Joe"), 358, 367
Capital, and industrialization, 300
Capitalism: Civil War flourishing of, 253; Marx's critique of, 350; and progressives, 358; welfare, 410; Hoover on, 426; Communist attacks on, 430; Reagan's pushing on Third World, 602. *See also* Business; Corporations; Laissez faire
Capone, Al, 420
Caribbean, 541 (map); slave trade to, 31; New England trade with, 36; slave population in, 46; expansion into, 384–386; U.S. troops out of, 453. See also *individual countries*
Carl, Conrad, 299
Carmichael, Stokely, 566–567
Carnegie, Andrew, 380, 396
Carpetbaggers, 274
Carter, Jimmy, 553–557, 555 (illus.), 585–586; human-rights policy of, 554, 557; and inflation, 580; and *1980* election, 593
Carter, Rosalynn, 585 (illus.)
Carter Doctrine, 555
Carteret, George, 28
Cartier, Jacques, 9
Carver, George Washington, 294
Casey, William, 608
Cass, Lewis, 226, 229, 230
Cassatt, Alexander, 357
Castle Garden immigrant center, 178
Castro, Fidel, 518, 540, 563, 568
Catawba Indians, 65
Catherine of Aragon, 12
Catholic church: and women, 8; and English Reformation, 12, 16; and JFK as president, 520. *See also* Anti-Catholicism
Catt, Carrie Chapman, 364, 396
Cattell, J. M., 401
Caucus system, 214
Cayuga Indians, 34, 93
Cemetery Ridge, charge on, 258
Central America, 541 (map), 603. See also *individual countries*
Central Intelligence Agency (CIA), 504, 508; against Third World, 518, 520; and Bay of Pigs, 540; and Laos, 545; in Chile, 552; in Angola, 552; in Iran, 518, 519, 555; and Castro, 518, 519, 563; in Afghanistan, 555;

Central Intelligence Agency (*cont.*) against antiwar movement, 574; under Reagan, 602; in El Salvador, 603; in Nicaragua, 604

Central Pacific Railroad, 252

Century of Dishonor, A (Jackson), 289

Chamber of Commerce, U.S., 357

Chamberlain, Neville, 459

Champlain, Lake, campaign on, 145

Chancellorsville, battle of, 256–257

Chaplin, Charlie, 418

Charity: in Social Darwinist view, 305; during Great Depression, 430

Charles I, king of England, 13, 19, 26

Charles II, king of England, 26, 28, 39

Charles VII, king of France, 8

Charles River Bridge v. *Warren Bridge*, 156

Charleston, South Carolina, 94, 186, 195, 200, 226, 242

Chase, Samuel, 136, 265

Chattanooga, battle of, 260

Chattanooga, race riots in, 588

Chávez, César, 570, 590

Checks and balances, 107, 113, 114

Cheever, John, 440

Chenango Canal, 153

Cherokee Indians, 33, 68, 86, 87, 110, 129, 183–185

Cherokee Nation v. *Georgia*, 183

Chesapeake Affair, 142

Chesapeake colonies: founding of, 13–14, 16; indentured servants in, 16; family life in, 17; politics in, 17–18; slavery in, 29–30, 31; government in, 39; slave population in, 46; economic development of, 49; black population of, 52; plantation life in, 53, 54; civic rituals in, 56; migration from, 129. *See also* Maryland; Virginia

Chesnut, Mary Boykin, 196

Cheyenne Indians, 288, 589

Chicago, 171, 400, 413, 529

Chicanos, *see* Mexican-Americans

Chickasaw Indians, 110, 183, 184

Child labor, 308, 329; on farms, 308, 331; and Progressive era, 359, 369; Supreme Court decision on, 410

Children: in 18th-century family, 52; *1920s* rearing of, 415; and WWII working mothers, 478; and suburbanization, 530; and Dr. Spock, 531; and Momism, 531–532

Chile: independence gained by, 149; Allende overthrown in, 552; and human rights policy, 557

China: trade with, 110; and Open Door policy, 381–383; Japan in, 384, 403, 455; Jiang Jieshi's leadership in, 461; U.S. aid to (1938–39), 461; and United Nations, 480; civil war in, 487, 494

China, People's Republic of, 494, 500, 515; and United Nations, 501; in Korean War, 501–502; and Indochina conference, 544; and Vietnam War, 550; opening to, 550

"China card," 554

China lobby, 494

Chinese immigrants, 285, 323, 383–384

"Chipitts," 531

Chippewa Indians, 68, 110, 145, 589

Chisholm v. *Georgia*, 119

Choctaw Indians, 110, 183

Christian Broadcast Network, 592

Christianity: and European exploration, 9; and Indians, 14, 20, 290; slavery allowed by, 29; evangelical, 129, 207, 219, 591–592, 592; slaves' adoption of, 199; and overseas expansionism, 373; fundamentalist, 417; born-again, 591

Christmas bombing, 549

Church, Frank, 593

Churches and sects: evangelical, 129; disestablishment of, 130; and slavery, 204; Reconstruction efforts of, 276; black, 276

Churchill, Winston, 469, 470, 480, 482, 491

Church-state relations: in New England colonies, 21–22; and JFK as Catholic, 520; and school prayers, 565; and Reagan on school prayer, 601

CIA, *see* Central Intelligence Agency

Cigarettes and cigars, southern manufacture of, 193, 297

Cincinnati, Ohio, 161, 171, 185, 186, 529

Circuses, 334

Cities and city life: in eighteenth century, 52; growth of (1800–60), 171, 172 (map); life in (1800–60), 173, 174, 208; of Old South, 191, 193; in Confederate states, 249; and industrialization, 300; geographic development of, 316–317; migrants and immigrants in, 317–321; inner-city living conditions, 321–323; ghettoes in, 324–325; machine politics in, 325–326; urban reform in, 326–327; *barrios* in, 324, 413; cultural pluralism in, 327; suburbanization of, 413, 529–531 (*see also* Suburbs); poverty in, 529; megalopolis produced by, 531; financial difficulties of, 585

Civic reform, 326–327

Civic rituals: in colonial Chesapeake, 56; anti-British protests as, 74; Constitution parades as, 118

Civilian Conservation Corps (CCC), 434–435, 444, 447

Civil religion, 130; and pledge of allegiance, 507

Civil Rights Act (1875), 278, 297

Civil Rights Act (1957), 513

Civil Rights Act (1964), 563, 590

Civil rights and liberties: in Pennsylvania, 28; in Northwest Ordinance, 111; free blacks for, 187; and Abolitionists, 212; and Slave Power, 228; during Civil War, 249, 251, 253; and black codes, 268, 269; and southern Reconstruction governments, 274; as Reconstruction goal, 277, 278; and "force bill," 346; and Du Bois, 362; WWI attack on, 400–401; Palmer Raids against, 402; Harding on, 410; and Scottsboro Trials, 443; and WWII internment of Japanese, 474–475; Truman's support of, 498–499; and McCarthyism, 511; Nixon program against, 574

Civil Rights Cases, 297

Civil rights movement, 508, 512–514, 562; agenda for, 498; violence against, 562, 566; and FBI, 565–566; and black power, 566–567; Reagan opposed by, 600

Civil service reform, 342

Civil War, 246–262; and secession, 240–242; beginning of, 242, 242 (illus.); motives for fighting, 245, 254; impact of, 245–246, 263; northern blockade in, 246, 249, 259–260; casualties in, 246, 253, 261, 262, 473; and Emancipation Proclamation, 254–256; and northern diplomacy, 259; costs of, 263; emotional aftermath of, 342, 373

Civil Works Administration, 447

Clark, William, 138

Class conflict and class interest: and yeomen in South, 242; of southern blacks and yeomen whites, 274, 275; and IWW, 312; and Communist Party on Depression, 430. *See also* Social class

Clausewitz, Karl von, 260

Clay, Henry: as War Hawk, 143; American System of, 147, 217; and Missouri Compromise, 151; in *1824* election, 214; and Second Bank of United States, 218; and *1844* election, 223–224; as slavery-issue leader, 226, 240; and Compromise of *1850*, 230–231; death of, 233

Clayton Anti-Trust Act (1914), 368

Clayton-Bulwer Treaty (1850), 384

Clean Air Act, 574

Clean Water Act, 598

Clemenceau, Georges, 403

Clemens, Samuel (Mark Twain), 285, 337

Dawes Severalty Act (1887), 289, 445
Dean, John, 581
Death and death rates: in Chesapeake, 17; in slave passage, 31; for southern children (1860), 196; from industrial accidents, 309; as lowered by public health programs, 322; decrease in (1900–20), 329–331. *See also* Life expectancy
Debs, Eugene V., 312, 350, 358, 367, 401, 452
Debt, national: Hamilton's plan for, 120–121; Republican reduction of, 136; from Civil War, 263, 269; under Reagan, 606
Declaration of Independence, 89–90; and women and blacks, 132; and *Wealth of Nations*, 155; and Seneca Falls convention, 178; and slavery, 212; as anti-imperialist, 380
Declaration of Liberated Europe, 482
Declaration of Panama, 457
Declaration of Rights and Grievances, 82–83
Declaratory Act, 72–73
Declining Significance of Race, The (Wilson), 587
Decolonization, 403, 405, 487, 493, 517 (fig.). *See also* Third World
Deere, John, 165
Defense Intelligence Agency, 574
Deficit financing, 431, 442, 479, 495, 519, 584
Deindustrialization, 580, 583, 585
Delany, Martin, 187
Delaware, 26, 104, 186, 242
Delaware and Hudson Canal, 153
Delaware Indians, 28, 65, 68, 69, 111
DeLeon, Daniel, 349–350, 353
D'Emilio, John, 572
DeMille, Cecil B., 418
Democracy: and republican viewpoint, 100; interest-group, 435, 437; and SDS Platform, 568. *See also* Representative government
Democratic party, 215, 216; vs. Whigs, 219; *1860* convention of, 226; in *1848* election, 230; and slavery issue, 230; and Kansas-Nebraska Bill, 233; Southern, 235–237, 238–239; and *1860* election, 239; opposing Civil War in North, 258–259; and *1896* election, 352; realignment of (1928), 421; dominance of (1936), 441; *1968* convention of, 571; McGovern's splitting of, 575
Democratic-Republican party, 216. *See also* Democratic party; Republican party (vs. Federalists)
Democratic-Republican societies, 123, 124
Demographic factors, *see* Birth rates;

Death and death rates; Divorce; Life expectancy; Population
Dempsey, Jack, 408, 418
Deniability, plausible, 518
Denman, William, 475
Dennis et al. v. U.S., 500
Denver, 413
Department of Defense, 504
Deposit Act (1836), 218
Depression, Great, 424–425, 428–429; causes of, 424; protest against, 429–430; Hoover's response to, 430–432; and New Deal, 433–437, 449 (*see also* New Deal); and women, 446–447; international/German aspects of, 453, 454, 455; voters' memories of, 479
Depressions and panics: in *1764*, 70, 74; after Revolution, 111–112; of *1807*, 142; of *1819* (1819–23), 149, 167, 215, 218; of *1837*, 162, 220; of *1839–43*, 155, 163, 220; of *1857*, 155, 164; of *1870s* (1873), 278, 304, 311; of *1884*, 304; of *1893–97*, 304, 341, 346, 348–349, 356. *See also* Business cycles; Recessions
Detective novels, 336
Détente, 539, 550, 554, 557
Deterrence theory, 514
Detroit, Michigan, 68, 171, 413, 477, 529, 561
Developing nations, *see* Third World
Dewey, Comm. George, 380, 383
Dewey, John, 360
Dewey, Thomas E., 479, 496, 497, 498
Dias, Bartholomew, 9
Dickinson, John, 73, 74, 83, 100, 113
Diem, Ngo Dinh, 544–545
Diet and nutrition: of slaves, 197, 198; in colonies, 17, 48; in Great Depression, 428; for physical fitness, 592
Dime novels, 336
Dingley Act (1897), 343
Disability insurance, 309, 359
Disarmament: Rush-Bagot Treaty on, 148; and Washington Conference, 454–455; Kellogg-Briand Pact on, 455
Discomfort index, 586, 586 (fig)
Discrimination: against free blacks, 104–105, 185–186; against blacks in housing, 324–325; in women's education, 361; against women workers, 399; against Mexicans, 413; against blacks in employment, 445; against women in jobs, 446; by FHA, 531. *See also* Racism; Segregation
Disease: among Indians, 1, 11, 18; in Chesapeake, 17; in 18th-century cities, 52; in Civil War, 253; bacteria theory of, 322; decline in threat from, 329; in Cuban cam-

paign, 379; new drugs and vaccines against, 527; and poverty, 529; AIDS, 609–610
Disneyland, 532
District of Columbia, 134, 212, 230, 231
Divorce: and republican view of marriage, 103; increase in (1880–1920), 332; in 1920s, 414; during World War II, 478; and child support, 529
Dixiecrats, 496
Docherty, George M., 507
Doe v. Bolton, 573, 590
Doeg Indians, 35
Dollar diplomacy, 384, 387, 489
Domesticity, ideal of, 177, 178, 208, 363. *See also* Family life
Dominican Republic: U.S. intervention in, 385, 387, 455, 456; immigrants from, 529, 590
Dominion of New England, 39–40
Domino theory, 514, 544
Donaldson, Scott, 531
Dos Passos, John, 420
Douglas, Stephen A., 226, 230–231, 233, 238–239, 239
Douglass, Frederick, 185, 186, 211, 212, 362
Draft: by Confederate government, 248, 249–251, 256; by Union government, 254, 258, 259; in World War I, 396, 400; for World War II, 463, 474; as threat for strikers, 495; Vietnam-War protests against, 569
Draft resisters, 569
Dragging Canoe, 86
Dred Scott decision, 237–239, 277
Drug use and traffic: among Vietnam troops, 548; and counterculture, 568, 569; as international problem, 606; and AIDS, 610
Duane, James, 82
Duarte, José Napoleon, 603
Du Bois, W. E. B., 362, 362–363, 397, 456
Duel, code of, 202
Duke, James B., 303
Duke of York, *see* James II
Dulles, John Foster, 503, 514, 516, 519
Dumbarton Oaks Conference, 480
Duniway, Abigail Scott, 167
Dunmore, Lord, 85 (illus.), 86
Dutch immigrants, 28, 59, 179
Dylan, Bob, 568
Dynamic conservatism, 509

East India Company, 77
Eastman, Crystal, 365
Eastman, George, 335
East St. Louis, 400
Economic Bill of Rights, 479, 495

Madison, James (*cont.*)
    Alien and Sedition Acts, 127; and *Marbury v. Madison*, 137; as president, 142, 146–147
Mahan, Alfred T., 377
Mail, *see* Post Office, U.S.
Mailer, Norman, 561
Mail–order companies, 292
Maine, 13, 35–36, 185. *See also* New England
Maine, sinking of, 378–379
Malcolm X, 566
Mali, empire of, 7
Mandan Indians, 288
Mandate system, 403
Manhattan Project, 472
Manifest destiny, 156, 166, 221, 228, 373. *See also* Westward expansion
Mann, Horace, 210–211
Mann Act (1910), 360
Mann–Elkins Act (1910), 367
Manufacturing: War of 1812 as spur to, 146, 152, 161; depression in (1818), 149; American system of, 159–160; growth of (1800–50), 161; southern use of slaves in, 201; mass production in, 302, 303, 307, 309. *See also* Business; Industry
Manumission, 104, 186. *See also* Emancipation
Mao Zedong, 461, 482, 494, 501, 568
Marbury v. Madison, 137
March on the Pentagon, 569
March on Washington (1963), 562
March on Washington Movement (1941), 444
Marcos, Ferdinand, 606
Marietta, Ohio, 111
Marin, John, 421
Market economy, 154–155; farming in, 154–155, 162, 165, 235, 295; Thoreau's attitude toward, 206; and utopian communities, 208. *See also* Business; Laissez faire
Marriage: women's status in (18th-century), 52; and Judith Sargent Murray, 102; men's vs. women's role in, 103, 176–177; republican view of, 103, 177; and southern women, 196; in Great Depression, 429, 446; in World War II, 478; and working wives, 591. *See also* Family life; Sexual division of labor
Married Women's Property Act (1839), 196–197
Marshall, George C., 491
Marshall, James, 166
Marshall, John, 126, 137, 147, 156, 183–184
Marshall Plan, 491
Martí, José, 378
Marx, Karl, 350
Marx Brothers, 429

Maryland: English colony in, 16–18; and English Civil War, 26; as proprietorship, 26; Protestant Association revolt in, 40; slavery conditions in, 54; and emancipation of slaves, 104; and Articles of Confederation, 108; and Civil War, 242, 253. *See also* Chesapeake colonies
Mason, George, 114
Massachusettensis (Daniel Leonard), 84
Massachusetts: slavery in, 29; as royal colony, 39, 41; public education for girls in, 101; slavery abolished in, 104; as industrialized, 162; blacks as voting in, 185; population density in (1860), 191; and public-schooling, 210; public accommodations law in, 267. *See also* New England
Massachusetts Bay Company and Colony, 19, 39
Massachusettts Government Act (1774), 78
Massasoit, 35
Mass communications, 335–336
Mass culture: and leisure, 332; sports, 332–333; show business, 334; movies, 334–335; communications media, 335–336; in literature, 336–338; of 1920s, 409, 413–414; paperback books, 533; music industry, 533–534
Massive retaliation, 514, 516, 539
Mass production, 302, 303
Mass transportation, 316–317
Materialism, *see* Consumerism
Mather, Cotton, 36, 57
Mather, Increase, 37–38
Maximilian, Archduke Ferdinand, emperor of Mexico, 376
Maximum Freight Rate case, 287
May, Henry F., 390
Maya, 5, 10
Mayflower, 18
Mayflower Compact, 18
Maysville Road bill, 216
Measles, among Indians, 11
Meat Inspection Act (1906), 366
Mechanization: of agriculture, 165, 252, 292, 294, 294t, 473; of mass transportation, 316; of cotton harvesting, 527
Mechanization of industry, 302, 303
Me Decade, 580, 591–592
Media, mass, 335–336. *See also* Muckrakers; Newspapers; Radio broadcasting; Television
Medicare program, 563, 597
Medicine: Enlightenment's impact on, 57; in Civil War, 248, 253, 254; advances in, 329, 527; in Cuban campaign, 379
Meese, Edwin, 600, 607, 610

Megalopolis, 531
Mehta, G. L., 516
Mein, John, 63, 64 (illus.)
Mellon, Andrew, 410, 411, 425, 430
Melville, Herman, 209
Memorial Day Massacre, 443
Mencken, H. L., 420
Menéndez de Avilés, Pedro, 32
Mercantilism, 38, 155
Merchants: in 17th-century New England, 36–38; in eighteenth century, 48, 49; and nonimportation, 72; and Townshend Acts, 74–75; as loyalists or patriots, 84; navy needed by (early 1800s), 139; in clothing trade, 160; of Old South, 193; in crop-lien system, 295. *See also* Business; Trade
Meredith, James, 562
Merriwell, Frank, 336, 338
Messianic cults, 592
Metacomet (King Philip), 35
Methodists, 61, 129
Mexican-Americans, 318, 529, 589; on frontier, 285; intolerance toward, 323; ghetto experience of, 324; in World War I, 400; in 1920s, 413; during Great Depression, 445–446; in WWII riots, 477; and 1976 election, 586; citizenship allowed for, 589
Mexican War, 227–228
Mexico: Aztecs in, 1, 5, 9–10, 11; independence gained by, 149; and Texas, 221, 224; economic expansion into, 375; French intervention in, 376; U.S. intervention in, 385, 387, 395; Zimmermann Telegram to, 395; oil expropriation by, 457; in Contadora group, 604
Miami, Florida, 588
Miami confederacy, 111, 117, 129
Miami Indians, 111
Miantonomi, 20
Michaux, André, 138
Middle Atlantic states: economic dominance of, 158; farming in, 165
Middle class: expansion of (19th-century), 174; among progressives, 356–357; among blacks, 499, 587; prosperity of (1950s/1960s), 524; blue-collar workers as, 526
Middle colonies, economic development in, 49
Middle East: and Eisenhower administration, 518–519; Nixon-Kissinger strategy for, 550–552; Carter's efforts in, 555 (illus.), 555–557; Reagan policy in, 605
Middle Passage, 31
"Midnight appointments," by Adams, 136
Midway, battle of, 470

Philippines (cont.)
immigrants from, 590; Marcos
ousted in, 606
Philipse family, 59–60
Phillips, David Graham, 357
Phillips, Kevin, 527
Phonograph, 335
Photography, 335
Physical fitness, 592
Pickering, John, 136
Pickering, Timothy, 140
Pierce, Franklin, 232–233, 235
Pietism, and Gilded Age political par-
ties, 341–342
Pike, Zebulon, 138–139
Pinchot, Gifford, 367
Pinckney, Charles Cotesworth, 126,
139, 142
Pinckney, Thomas, 124–125, 125–126
Pinckney, William, 141
Pinckney's Treaty, 124–125, 137
Pingree, Hazen S., 326
Pitt, William, 67, 73
Pittsburgh, Pennsylvania, 171
Pizarro, Francisco, 10, 11
Plains: Indians of, 281, 288–289; farm-
ing of, 291–294
Plan of Union (Albany Congress), 65
Plantation economy, 191
Plantation life, 53–54, 195–197
Platt Amendment, 384, 457
Plausible deniability, 518
Plessy v. Ferguson, 297
"Plumbers" unit, 580
Pluralism: cultural, 327, 335; and 1896
election, 353–354
Plymouth, founding of, 18
Pocahontas, 14
Pocket veto, 218
Poindexter, John, 608
Point Four Program, 493
Pokanoket, 18
Poker Alice, 285
Poland: in World War II, 459, 462–
463; Soviet-American disputes
over, 480, 490; anti-Soviet revolts
in, 515
Police, 173
Police brutality, and Haymarket Riot,
311
Police strike, Boston, 402, 411
Political campaigns: Republicans'/
Federalists' direct appeals, 139–140;
by Whigs, 219; of Truman, 497
Political parties, see Parties, political
Politics: in Chesapeake, 17–18;
Winthrop's communal vision of, 19,
20, 58; deference vs. equality in,
58, 61; ideal vs. reality in, 59; and
slaveholders vs. nonslaveholders,
203, 242; and Antimasonry, 213–
214; end of caucus system, 214; of
urban machines, 325–326; and cul-

tural pluralism, 327; high interest
in (1870–95), 341; Progressives'
reforms in, 356, 357, 359, 369; and
Catholicism of presidential can-
didates, 421, 520; in age of consen-
sus, 508–509; SDS view of, 568
Politics, partisan, 117; colonial "court
parties" vs. "country" interests, 42;
vs. expectation of consensus, 117;
beginning of, 123; and Democratic–
Republican societies, 123, 124; of
Emancipation Proclamation, 255;
and Wilson at WWI peace con-
ference, 403; Agnew's divisiveness
in, 574
Polk, James K., 223–224, 226, 227–229
Poll taxes, 296
Pollock, Jackson, 535
Polo, Marco, 8
Pontiac, 68
Pontiac's Uprising, 68
Pools, 304–305; railroad, 287
Poor People's Campaign, 571
Poor Richard's Almanac, 409
Pop Art, 535
Popé, 33
Popular literature, 336–337
"Popular sovereignty" for territories,
229–230, 230, 231, 238
Population: Indian, 5; doubling of in
England, 13; native- vs. foreign-
born, 17, 42, 58; of New England
(1700), 35; growth of (18th-cen-
tury), 45–46; of blacks (in col-
onies), 16, 27, 30–31, 46, 49, 52;
growth of (1800–60), 153–154,
167, 171; of blacks (1800–60), 186,
187t; distribution of in South, 191;
of West (1870–90), 282; growth of
(1870–1910), 291; and industrialization, 300; farm-city shift in (1800–
1920), 316; growth of in cities
(1877–1920), 317–318, 319 (map)
Populism and Populist party, 348, 350,
351; and Knights of Labor, 311; and
Free Silver, 351, 352–353; and 1896
election, 352–353; fear of, 379; vs.
"end of ideology," 508–509
Porter, Sylvia F., 525
Port Huron Statement, 568
Portsmouth Conference, 383
Portuguese: explorations by, 9; and
slavery, 29
Post Office, U.S., 156, 167, 292
Potawatomi Indians, 68, 110, 143, 182,
183
Potsdam Conference, 482
Poverty: in 18th-century cities, 48; of
women, 48, 208, 415, 528, 529; in
early 19th-century cities, 174, 208;
in Confederacy, 249; debates on
responsibility for, 322–323, 587;
Hoover sees end of, 421; as per-

sonal shortcoming, 425; and Eisenhower, 520; in affluent society
(1950s and 1960s), 523–524, 528–
529; geographical shift of, 527; and
urban renewal, 531; in Galbraith's
analysis, 536; 1960s assault on, 536,
562; War on, 563, 564–565; and
black discontent, 566; of young
blacks (1970s), 587; of Indians,
589; of Hispanic immigrants, 589;
in 1980s, 599; feminization of, 600
Powderly, Terence V., 310
Power of Sympathy (Brown), 101
Powers, Francis Gary, 515
Powhatan, 14
Powhatan Confederacy, 14, 15–16
Pre-emption Act (1841), 167
Prejudice, see Discrimination; Racism;
Segregation
Presbyterians, 129
Prescott, Samuel, 87
Presidency: constitutional decisions
on, 114; and veto power, 119, 216,
218–219, 345; Civil War powers of,
253; decline of, 345–346; and
Theodore Roosevelt, 365–366;
FDR's strengthening of, 449; under
Truman, 503, 504; and plausible
deniability, 518; and lessons of Viet-
nam, 554; and Watergate, 582, 585;
Teflon-coated (Reagan), 596, 600
President's Committee on Civil Rights,
498
President's Organization on Unemploy-
ment Relief (POUR), 431
Presley, Elvis, 533–534
Princeton, battle of, 92
Privateering, 108
Proclamation of 1763, 68
"Profamily" movement, 590
Professional Air Traffic Controllers Organization (PATCO), 600
Profit sharing, by Ford, 302
Progress and Poverty (George), 306
Progressive era and movement, 355–
358, 362, 369–370; themes of, 356;
opposition to, 358, 359; govern-
ment as concern of, 357, 358; legislation enacted in, 359–360; and
education, 360–361; and legal
thought, 361; and National
Consumers' League, 361–362; and
women, 362, 363–365; and blacks,
362–363; and Theodore Roosevelt
presidency, 365–366; and Taft
presidency, 367; and Wilson
presidency, 367–369; and World
War I, 391, 405–406; in Red Scare,
402; in 1920s, 410
Progressive (Bull Moose) party,
367
Progressive party (1924), 411
Progressive party (1948), 496

Yellow journalism, 335
Yeomen farmers, 193–194, 202–203; in
  Georgia, 34; as Democrats, 236;
  class interests of, 242; Civil War suffering of, 249; in Johnson's plans,
  268; commercialized farming by,
  295

Yorktown, battle of, 95
Young, Andrew, 557
Young, Brigham, 210
Young Plan (1929), 454
Youth subculture, 533–534
Youth International Party (Yippies),
  571

Zero option, 602
Zhou Enlai, 494
Ziegfeld, Florenz, 334
Zimmermann telegram, 395
Zoot suit riot, 477
Zuni Indians, 288